W9-AQQ-181

TYPES OF DRAMA

Plays and Essays

Third Edition

SYLVAN BARNET
Tufts University

MORTON BERMAN
Boston University

WILLIAM BURTO
University of Lowell

Little, Brown and Company
Boston   Toronto

COPYRIGHT © 1981 BY SYLVAN BARNET, MORTON BERMAN, AND
WILLIAM BURTO
COPYRIGHT © 1977, 1972 BY LITTLE, BROWN AND COMPANY (INC.)

ALL RIGHTS RESERVED. NO PART OF THIS BOOK MAY BE REPRODUCED
IN ANY FORM OR BY ANY ELECTRONIC OR MECHANICAL MEANS
INCLUDING INFORMATION STORAGE AND RETRIEVAL SYSTEMS WITHOUT
PERMISSION IN WRITING FROM THE PUBLISHER, EXCEPT BY A RE-
VIEWER WHO MAY QUOTE BRIEF PASSAGES IN A REVIEW.

LIBRARY OF CONGRESS CATALOG CARD NO. 80-82552

ISBN 0-316-08208-2

9 8 7 6 5

MV

Published simultaneously in Canada
by Little, Brown & Company (Canada) Limited

PRINTED IN THE UNITED STATES OF AMERICA

NOTE: *The last section of verse on page 8 is reprinted with permis-*
sion of Macmillan Publishing Co., Inc. and Macmillan London
Limited from Collected Poems *by William Butler Yeats. Copyright*
1940 by Georgie Yeats, renewed 1968 by Bertha Georgie Yeats,
Michael Butler Yeats and Anne Yeats.

PREFACE

In this edition of *Types of Drama* we have added eight plays: Marlowe's *Doctor Faustus*, Ibsen's *A Doll's House*, Strindberg's *The Ghost Sonata*, Synge's *Riders to the Sea*, O'Neill's *Desire Under the Elms*, Wilder's *The Matchmaker*, Beckett's *Happy Days*, and Pinter's *The Dumb Waiter*. We have also added short essays by Louis Kronenberger and Martin Esslin. From the previous edition we have retained those plays and essays that instructors valued most highly, and we have also retained our commentaries on the plays, Peter Arnott's "The Script and the Stage" (which gives the reader an idea of how a director turns a script into a performance), and an essay of our own, "Writing about Drama," which — with the other editorial apparatus — helps students to write their own essays in courses.

The PLAYS, apart from the first (*A Doll's House*, used to introduce students to "The Language of Drama"), are arranged chronologically within the categories of tragedy, comedy, and tragicomedy. They cover a range of years and types, but in no case were they chosen only to represent a period or a type. All were chosen because of their dramatic value. Those not written in English are represented in the best modern translations.

The COMMENTARIES are relatively short. They are not attempts to explicate the plays, but we think they contain some useful and relevant points that will also be helpful with other plays. For example, the commentary on *A Midsummer Night's Dream* includes comments on two traditions of comedy, "critical" comedy and "romantic" comedy, but most of this material is relevant to other plays in the book. Similarly, the discussion of pathos in the commentary on *Death of a Salesman* goes beyond the play in question. But even those of the commentaries that are sharply focused on a given play do not seek to utter the last word. On the contrary, they seek to provide material that will stimulate discussion in class or that may be the topic of a writing assignment. For example, the commentary on *Doctor Faustus* offers a mini-anthology of conflicting interpretations; that on *Desire Under the Elms* offers several of O'Neill's own remarks (students might be invited to analyze the play in terms of one of them); and that on *Happy Days* is chiefly a series of questions. We also include, at the beginning of the book, a general introduction to basic concepts and critical terminology, and a brief analysis of the dramaturgy of the first play, *A Doll's House*.

The ESSAYS are not analyses of particular plays, though of course they do include some specific discussions; they are fairly general, and therefore any of the essays on tragedy, for example, can be profitably read in conjunction with any of the tragedies.

The GLOSSARY, drawn in part from the more detailed glossary in our *Aspects of Drama*, is a dictionary of two hundred basic critical and historical terms that are likely to come up in an introductory course. Some of these terms are discussed at length in the commentaries, but they are given again in the glossary itself.

Our ideas about drama have been shaped by many playwrights and many critics. Doubtless we are not aware of all of the influences upon us, but we know we are much indebted to Gerald Else, Northrop Frye, Helen Gardner, Richmond Lattimore, Konrad Lorenz, Maynard Mack, D. H. Monro, Reinhold Niebuhr, and L. J. Potts. If other critics find they have contributed to this book, we hope that they will be as charitable as lovers in a comedy, and will accept our apologies and our thanks.

We have been fortunate in getting permission to print important modern plays and distinguished modern translations of older plays, and we are grateful to the authors, translators, and publishers who have cooperated. Many teachers have given advice that helped us prepare this new edition: Franz Blaha, Dorothy H. Brown, Franklin Case, Leonard Casper, S. Alan Chesler, Carol Cloos, David G. Collins, Rosemary K. Curb, Jim Dyer, Jack Garrison, Arthur L. Goerdt, Bruce Golden, Wilfred L. Guerin, Tinsley Helton, Roy R. Hudson, Rosan A. Jordan, Naomi Liebler, Allena Longfellow, Norman McMillan, Russell J. Meyer, Michael Neuman, Richard L. Newby, Oyekan Owomoyela, Leslie Phillips, Richard Reed, Dennis K. Renner, Loren Reser, Dolores J. Sarafinshi, David K. Sauer, Stephen B. Scott, J. G. Severns, Hassell B. Sledd, Carleen M. Spano, Charles Stanford, Mark Stavig, George E. Tylutki, Sidney Vance, Bruno von Lutz, Joseph H. Wessling, Helen M. Whall, and Harvey S. Woll.

We are especially indebted to Jeanne Newlin of the Harvard Theatre Collection, Athan Anagostopoulos, Arthur Friedman, and Seymour Simches for assistance in finding photographs. Oscar Brockett and Harry Ritchie generously answered queries, and Marcia Stubbs provided many helpful suggestions. Our thanks also go to Charles Christensen, Jane Aaron, Martha Clasquin, Joan Feinberg, David Giele, Ellen Silver, Lynn Lloyd, and Dana Norton of Little, Brown, who never let us get away with anything.

S.B.

M.B.

W.B.

TABLE OF CONTENTS

THE NATURE OF DRAMA 1

THE LANGUAGE OF DRAMA 21

TRAGEDY 67

vi

COMEDY 437

TRAGICOMEDY 633

THE SCRIPT AND THE STAGE Peter Arnott 781

The Author. The Actors. The Director. The Designers. The Mechanics of Production.

WRITING ABOUT DRAMA 795

Why Write? Analysis. A Sample Analysis. Writing a Comparison. Communicating Judgments. Asking Questions to Get Answers. Review: How to Write an Effective Essay. Remarks about Manuscript Form.

A GLOSSARY OF DRAMATIC TERMS 815

THE NATURE OF DRAMA

1. Tragedy and Comedy

Whimsical assertions that all men are Platonists or Aristotelians, or liberals or conservatives ("Nature wisely does contrive / That every boy and every gal / That's born into the world alive / Is either a little Liberal / Or else a little Conservative") reveal a tendency to divide things into two. Two is about right: peace and war, man and woman, day and night, life and death. There may be middle cases; there is the cold war, and Edmund Burke suggested that no man can point to the precise moment that divides day from night — but Burke also suggested that everyone can make the useful distinction between day and night. The distinction between comedy and tragedy may not always be easy to make, but until the twentieth century it was usually clear enough. *Hamlet*, which in Horatio's words is concerned with "woe or wonder," is a tragedy; *A Midsummer Night's Dream*, which in Puck's words is concerned with things that pleasingly "befall preposterously," is a comedy. The best plays of our century, however, are another thing, and discussion of these plays — somewhat desperately called tragicomedy — will be postponed until the end of this introduction.

What befalls — preposterous or not — is the *action of the play*. The gestures on the stage are, of course, "actions," but they are not the action of the play in the sense of Aristotle's use of *praxis* or "action" in *The Poetics*, a fragmentary treatise of the fourth century B.C. that remains the starting point for most discussions of drama. For Aristotle, drama is the imitation (i.e., representation, re-presentation, re-creation) by impersonators, of an action. In tragedy the action is serious and important, something that matters, done by people who count (e.g., King Oedipus' discovery that he has killed his father and married his mother); in comedy (for Aristotle), the action is done by unimportant laughable people who make mistakes that do not cause us pain. Commonly the tragic action is a man's perception of a great mistake he has made; he suffers intensely and perhaps dies, having exhausted all the possibilities of his life. The comic action often is the exposure of folly and the renewal rather than the exhaustion of human nature. Crabby parents, for example, find that they cannot keep young lovers apart, and so they join in the marriage festivities. Byron jocosely put the matter thus:

IMITATION
OF AN
ACTION

> All tragedies are finished by a death,
> All comedies are ended by a marriage.

All tragedies and all comedies do not in fact end thus, but the idea is right; tragedy has the solemnity, seriousness, and finality we often associate with death,* and comedy has the joy and fertility and suggestion of a new life we

---

* Shakespeare's tragedies all end with the death of the tragic hero, but a good many Greek tragedies do not. In *Oedipus the King* the hero remains alive, but he is blind and banished and seems to have exhausted the possibilities of his life. Some other Greek tragedies have what can reasonably be called a happy ending, i.e., some sort of joyful reconciliation. For ex-

often associate with marriage. This concept of *an action* (i.e., an underlying motif, not merely gestures) in tragedy and in comedy makes clear that comedy is not a mere matter of jokes or funny bits of business. It also makes clear what the Greek comic playwright Menander meant when he told a friend that he had composed a play, and now had only to write the dialogue: he had worked out the happenings that would embody the action, and there remained only the slighter task of providing the spirited words. The same idea is implicit in Ibsen's comment that the drafts of his plays differed "very much from each other in characterization, not in action." The action or happening dramatized in a tragedy or a comedy may be conceived of as a single course or train of events manifested on the stage by a diversity of activities. Think of such expressions as "the closing of the frontier," or "the revival of learning"; each might be said to denote an action, though such action is seen only in its innumerable manifestations. The *Iliad* announces its action in the first line: "Sing, goddess, of the wrath of Achilles." The "action" is not, of course, always explicitly announced in a literary work. Among Ibsen's preliminary notes as he worked toward *Hedda Gabler* we find such entries as "They [i.e., women] all have a leaning towards sensuality, but are afraid of the scandal," "Men and women don't belong to the same century," and "The play is to be about 'the insuperable' — the longing and striving to defy convention, to defy what people accept (including Hedda)." Clearly, Ibsen was trying to get hold of his central point and then develop a plot that would reveal it.

HAPPENINGS AND HAPPENINGS

A tragic playwright takes some happening, from history (for example, the assassination of Julius Caesar), or from fiction (Shakespeare derived *Othello* from an Italian short story), or from his own imagination, and he makes or shapes or arranges episodes that clarify the action. He makes (in common terminology) a *plot* that embodies the action or spiritual content. (Even when the playwright draws on history, he makes his own plot because he selects and rearranges the available historical facts.) A glance at a very different kind of drama, recently popular, helps to clarify the distinction between a plot that embodies an action or a happening, and mere unconnected activities, happenings, events. In the early 1960's there was a good deal of interest in "Events" or "Happenings" (the latter term was derived from a performance in 1959 of something called *18 Happenings in 6 Parts*), performances in which activities were not connected so as to form a coherent plot that manifested an underlying action. Sample: a girl alternately washes her feet, puts tape over her mouth, dances with a board, sprays paint from a can onto a wall, and finally disrobes. Such a performance may display wit, agility, and other virtues and skills, but it is not a play in the traditional sense, despite its playfulness. Neither would a re-enactment of everything that Julius Caesar did during his last

---

ample, in Sophocles' *Philoctetes*, the weapon which has been taken from the sick Philoctetes is returned to him, and Heracles, a messenger from Zeus, announces that Philoctetes will be healed. But these tragedies with happy endings, like those with unhappy endings, deal with "important" people, and they are about "serious" things. If there is finally joy, it is a solemn joy.

days or hours be a play with an action, for drama is not so much concerned with what in fact *happened* as with some sort of typical and coherent or unified thing that *happens*, a significant action. Sometimes, of course, history provides substantial material for drama, but even Shakespeare's *Julius Caesar* takes frequent liberties with the facts as Shakespeare knew them, and Shakespeare's source, the biographer Plutarch, doubtless had already assimilated the facts to a literary form. At most we can say that history provided Shakespeare with a man whose life lent itself well to an established literary form. Not every life does lend itself thus. We are told that Aeschylus, the earliest tragic playwright who has left us any complete plays, was killed when an eagle mistook his bald head for a rock and dropped a turtle on it to break the shell. Aeschylus' death was a great loss, but it did not have the unified significant action required of tragedy. By chance an eagle that had captured a turtle was near to Aeschylus, and Aeschylus by chance (or rather by his chemistry) was bald. There is no relation between these two circumstances; Aeschylus' death (allegedly) happened this way, and we can account for it, but the event has no intelligible unity. (A sentence from Vladimir Nabokov's *Pale Fire* comes to mind: if one is contemplating suicide, "jumping from a high bridge is not recommended even if you cannot swim, for wind and water abound in weird contingencies, and tragedy ought not to culminate in a record dive or a policeman's promotion.") In tragedy things cohere. The hero normally does some deed and suffers as a consequence. Actions have consequences in the moral world no less than in the materialistic world of the laboratory. The tragic playwright's solemn presentation of "the remorseless working of things," Alfred North Whitehead pointed out (in his *Science and the Modern World*, 1925), is "the vision possessed by science," and it cannot be accidental that the two great periods of tragic drama, fifth-century B.C. Athens and England around 1600, are periods of scientific inquiry. UNITY

This emphasis on causality means that the episodes are related, connected, and not merely contiguous. Generally the formula is to show the tragic hero moving toward committing some deed that will cause great unintended suffering, committing it, and then, by seeing the consequences, learning the true nature of his deed. The plot, that is, involves a credible character whose doings are related to his nature. For Aristotle, in the best sort of tragedy the tragic hero is an important person, almost pre-eminently virtuous, who makes some sort of great mistake that entails great suffering. Calamity does not descend upon him from above, does not happen *to* him, nor does he consciously will a destructive act; he merely makes a great mistake. The mistake is Aristotle's *hamartia*, sometimes translated as "error," sometimes as "flaw." Probably Aristotle did not mean by hamartia a trait, such as rashness or ambition, which the translation "flaw" implies, but simply meant an action based on a mental error, a sort of false step. Oedipus, erroneously thinking that Polybus and Meropê are his parents, flees from them when he hears that he will kill his father and sleep with his mother. His action is commendable, but it happens to be a great mistake because it brings him to his real parents. Nevertheless, despite the THE TRAGIC HERO HAMARTIA scholarly elucidations of Aristotle, we can sometimes feel that the erring action proceeds from a particular kind of character, that a person with different traits would not have acted in the same way. The Oedipus that we see in the play, for example, is a self-assured quick-tempered man — almost a rash man, we might say — who might well have neglected to check the facts before he fled from Corinth. There are at least times, even when reading *Oedipus the King,* when one feels with George Meredith (1828–1909) that

> in tragic life, God wot,
> No villain need be! Passions spin the plot:
> We are betrayed by what is false within.

HYBRIS From this it is only a short step to identifying hamartia with a flaw, and the flaw most often attributed to the tragic hero is *hybris,* a word that for the Greeks meant something like "bullying," "abuse of power," but in dramatic criticism usually is translated as "overweening pride." The tragic hero forgets that (in Montaigne's words) "on the loftiest throne in the world we are still sitting only on our own rear," and he believes his actions are infallible. King Lear, for example, banishes his daughter Cordelia with "Better thou / Hadst not been born than not t' have pleased me better." Macbeth, told that he will be king of Scotland, chooses to make the prophecy come true by murdering his guest, King Duncan; Brutus decides that Rome can be saved from tyranny only by killing Caesar, and he deludes himself into thinking he is not murdering Caesar but sacrificing Caesar for the welfare of Rome.

PERIPETEIA We have talked of hamartia and hybris in tragedy; two more Greek words, *peripeteia* and *anagnorisis,* also common in discussions of tragedy, ought to be mentioned. A peripeteia (sometimes anglicized to "peripety" or translated as "reversal") occurs when the action takes a course not intended by the doer. Aristotle gives two examples: (1) the Messenger comes to cheer up Oedipus by freeing him from fears but the message heightens Oedipus' fears; (2) Danaus (in a lost play) prosecutes a man but is himself killed. The second example, by the way, reminds one of *The Merchant of Venice,* in which Shylock, calling upon the law, in effect demands Antonio's death and finds that his own life may be lawfully taken. A few other examples may be useful: Oedipus fled from Corinth to avoid contact with his parents, but his flight brought him to them; Macbeth kills Duncan to gain the crown but his deed brings him fearful nights instead of joyful days; Lear, seeking a peaceful old age, puts himself in the hands of two daughters who maltreat him, and banishes the one daughter who later will comfort him. The Bible — especially the Old Testament — is filled with such peripeties or ironic actions. For example, the Philistines brought Samson before them to entertain them, and he performed his most spectacular feat by destroying his audience. But the archetypal tragic story is that of Adam and Eve: aiming to be like gods, they lost their immortality and the earthly paradise, and brought death to themselves.

ANAGNORISIS The other Greek word, anagnorisis, translated as "recognition" or "discovery" or "disclosure," seems to have meant for Aristotle a clearing up of some misunderstanding, for example, the proper identification of someone or the revelation of some previously unknown fact. But later critics have given it a richer meaning and used it to describe the hero's perception of his true nature or his true plight. In the narrow sense, it is an anagnorisis or "recognition" when King Lear learns that Regan and Goneril are ungrateful and cruel. In the wider sense, the anagnorisis is in his speech in III.IV when he confesses his former ignorance and neglect:

> Poor naked wretches, wheresoe'er you are,
> That bide the pelting of this pitiless storm,
> How shall your houseless heads and unfed sides,
> Your looped and windowed raggedness, defend you
> From seasons such as these? O, I have ta'en
> Too little care of this! Take physic, pomp;
> Expose thyself to feel what wretches feel,
> That thou mayst shake the superflux to them,
> And show the heavens more just.

Similarly Hamlet's "There is special providence in the fall of a sparrow," and Othello's "one that loved not wisely, but too well," may be called recognition scenes. Here is Macbeth's recognition that his purpose has been frustrated, that his deed has been ironic:

> My way of life
> Is fall'n into the sear, the yellow leaf,
> And that which should accompany old age,
> As honor, love, obedience, troops of friends,
> I must not look to have.

"Troops of friends" abound in comedy. Where tragedy is primarily the dramatization of the single life that ripens and then can only rot, that reaches its fullest and then is destroyed, comedy is primarily the dramatization of the renewing of the self and of social relationships. The tragic figure is isolated from society, partly by his different nature, and partly by his tragic act; comedy suggests that selfhood is found not in assertion of individuality, but in joining in the fun, in becoming part of the flow of common humanity. Where tragedy suggests an incompatibility between the energy or surge of life and the laws of life or the norms of society, comedy suggests that norms are valid and necessary. The tragic hero does what he feels compelled to do; he asserts himself, and is intensely aware that he is a special person and not a member of the crowd. But that his mistake always reveals that he is hybristic is not at all certain. The Greek tragic hero is commonly set against a chorus of ordinary mortals who caution him, wring their hands, and lament his boldness, but these ordinary mortals are always aware that if they are law-abiding men, they are also less fully men than the hero. That they obey society's laws is not due to superior virtue, to the triumph of reason over will, to self-discipline; rather, their obedience is due to a lower vision, or to timidity, and indeed sometimes to a fear of what resides in their own breasts. The tragic hero is, of course, in one way inferior to those about him; his mistake costs him great suffering, and he is thus immobilized as the others are not. But his greatness remains indisputable; the anguish that at times paralyzes Hamlet also makes him greater

THE SOCIAL
WORLD OF
COMEDY

TRAGIC
ISOLATION

than, say, Horatio and Laertes. In fact the tragic hero is circumscribed, certainly after the deed, when he is necessarily subject to the consequences (Brutus kills Caesar and finds that he brings to Rome a turmoil that makes him flee from Rome, and ultimately makes him take his own life); even before doing the tragic deed the hero is circumscribed because his action proceeds from something, either from his personality or his circumstances. Still, his action seems to him to be freely his, and indeed we feel that it is an action that a lesser man could not perform. Which is almost a way of saying that it can be argued that a tragic hero may err not so much from weakness as from strength. Why can Iago so easily deceive Othello? Not because Othello is an unthinking savage, or an unsophisticated foreigner, but because (as Iago admits) Othello is of a "loving noble nature," and, again,

TRAGIC VIRTUE

> The Moor is of *a free and open nature*
> *That thinks men honest* that but seem to be so;
> And will as tenderly be led by th' nose
> As asses are.

Why can Claudius see to it that Laertes murders Hamlet during a fencing match? Not because Hamlet is a poor fencer, or a coward, but because Hamlet,

> *Most generous, and free from all contriving,*
> Will not peruse the foils.

TRAGIC JOY

This is not to say that the tragic hero is faultless, or that he is quite happy with himself and with his action; but he does experience a kind of exultation even in his perception that disaster is upon him. If he grieves over his deed, we sense a glory in his grief, for he finds, like Captain Ahab, that in his topmost grief lies his topmost greatness. At last he sees everything and knows that nothing more can be experienced. He has lived his life to its limits. Othello puts it thus:

> Here is my journey's end, here is my butt,
> And very seamark of my utmost sail.

(In a comedy Shakespeare tells us that "journeys end in lovers meeting," that is, the end is a new beginning.) In "Under Ben Bulben" William Butler Yeats (1865–1939) suggests the sense of completeness that the tragic hero experiences when, under the influence of a great passion, he exhausts his nature and seems to be not a man among men but a partner (rather than a subject) of fate:

> Know that when all words are said
> And a man is fighting mad,
> Something drops from eyes long blind,
> He completes his partial mind,
> For an instant stands at ease,
> Laughs aloud, his heart at peace.
> Even the wisest man grows tense
> With some sort of violence
> Before he can accomplish fate,
> Know his work or choose his mate.

Elsewhere Yeats put his distinction between the tragic hero and the world he is up against thus: "Some Frenchman* has said that farce is the struggle against a ridiculous object, comedy against a movable object, tragedy against an immovable; and because the will, or energy, is greatest in tragedy, tragedy is the more noble; but I add that 'will or energy is eternal delight,' and when its limit is reached it may become a pure, aimless joy, though the man, the shade, still mourns his lost object." And one more passage by Yeats, this one from a play, again calling attention to the revelation of life — joyful to behold — apparent when an impassioned man expresses his fullest nature:

> I would have all know that when all falls
> In ruin, poetry calls out in joy,
> Being the scattering hand, the bursting pod,
> The victim's joy among the holy flame,
> God's laughter at the shattering of the world.

All this is to say splendidly that we sometimes feel admiration for the passionate man, for the man determined to do and to be, and we sense his superiority (as he himself senses it) to the law-abiding men who surround him, perhaps no more so than when his nobility undoes him, i.e., when we see the incompatibility between passionate self-assertion and the laws of life.

But there are contexts and times when we find passionate self-assertion funny (there are contexts and times, too, when we find it vicious, but that is another matter). Much depends on what is being asserted, and what or who the antagonist is. Recall Brunetière's opinion, or rather Yeats' version of it, that tragedy dramatizes a struggle against an immovable object, comedy a struggle against a movable one. King Lear against his tigerish daughters is a tragic figure, but a pedant against a dull schoolboy may be a comic one. The lament of the tragic hero is proportionate to the event, but the effort extended by the comic figure is absurdly disproportionate. Furthermore, as Henri Bergson (1859–1941) pointed out, the comic figure usually is a sort of mechanism, repeating his actions and catch phrases with clocklike regularity in contexts where they are inappropriate. He quotes Latin on every occasion, or he never travels without his pills, or he always wants to know how much something costs, or he is forever spying on his wife. Bergson, who suggested that the comic is "the mechanical encrusted on the living," illustrated his point by telling of the customs officers who bravely rescue the crew of a sinking vessel, and then ask, the moment the shore is reached, "Have you anything to declare?" The mechanical question, inappropriate in the situation, reveals that the officers value trivial regulations as much as they value life itself. In *The Circus* Charlie Chaplin is dusting things off; he comes upon the magician's bowl of goldfish, takes the fish out and wipes them, and then returns them to the bowl. Real life, too, affords examples of this sort of comic behavior. Emerson mentions that the biologist Camper, who had spent six months studying hairless water mammals, said he almost began to see people as narwhales, por-

COMIC ASSERTION

* Yeats is rather freely summarizing Ferdinand Brunetière's *La Loi du théâtre*. A translation of Brunetière's treatise is available in *European Theories of the Drama*, ed. Barrett H. Clark.

poises, and marsouins. This is whimsy, of course, but Emerson goes on to tell of a visit to a dying friend. On his way to the friend, Emerson met the physician, who had just left the patient. The physician, Emerson says, "accosted me in great spirits, with joy sparkling in his eyes. 'And how is my friend, the reverend Doctor?' I inquired. 'O, I saw him this morning; it is the most correct apoplexy I have ever seen: face and hands livid, breathing stertorous, all the symptoms perfect.' And he rubbed his hands with delight."

COMIC JOY   Emerson's doctor, valuing symptoms rather than life, nicely fulfills Bergson's formula. And in his high spirits — ludicrously out of place in the context — he inadvertently illustrates another aspect of comedy, its prevailing high spirits. The comic world is a world of delight in variety; even its hardships are not lasting. In *As You Like It* when Rosalind, daughter of a banished duke, complains of the frustrations of life, "O, how full of briers is this working-day world," Celia gives the right reply: "They are but burrs, cousin, thrown upon thee in holiday foolery." (But if Celia were to give this answer too often she would become laughable herself.) The comic world seems to be presided over by a genial tolerant deity who enjoys the variety that crosses the stage. The sketchbooks of the Japanese artist Hokusai (1760–1849) wonderfully reveal this comic delight in humanity. There are pages of fat men, pages of thin men (no less engagingly drawn), pages of men making funny faces, and there is a delightful drawing of a man holding a magnifying glass in front of his face so that his nose seems enormous. The comic playwright gives us something of this range of types and grotesques, and he gives us also variety in language (e.g., puns, inverted clichés, malapropisms) and variety in episodes (much hiding behind screens, dressing in disguise). The character, then, who insists on being himself, who mechanically holds to a formula of language or of behavior, is laughably out of place in the world of varied people who live and let

COMIC ISOLATION   live. What comedy does not tolerate is intolerance; it regularly suggests that the intolerant — for example the pedant and the ascetic — are fools and probably hypocrites. Here is the self-righteous Alceste, in Molière's *The Misanthrope*:

> Some men I hate for being rogues: the others
> I hate because they treat the rogues like brothers,
> And, lacking a virtuous scorn for what is vile,
> Receive the villain with a complaisant smile.
> Notice how tolerant people choose to be
> Toward that bold rascal who's at law with me.

Philinte genially replies, "Let's have an end of rantings and of railings, / And show some leniency toward human failings. / This world requires a pliant rectitude; / Too stern a virtue makes one stiff and rude." Here is the puritanical Malvolio in *Twelfth Night*, trying to quiet down some tipsy but genial revelers:

> My masters, are you mad? Or what are you? Have you no wit, manners nor honesty, but to gabble like tinkers at this time of night? Do ye make an alehouse of my lady's house? ... Is there not respect of place, persons, nor time in you?

He is aptly answered: "Art any more than a steward? Dost thou think, because thou art virtuous, there shall be no more cakes and ale?" This suspicion of a "virtue" that is opposed to cakes and ale runs through the history of comedy. In Shakespeare's *Love's Labor's Lost*, the young noblemen who vow to devote themselves to study, and to forgo the company of women, are laughed at until they accept their bodies and admit interest in those of the ladies. The celebration of the human body, or at least the good-natured acceptance of it which is present in comedy is well-put by the General in Anouilh's *The Waltz of the Toreadors*. (The life-buoy he refers to is "the ideal.")

> You're in the ocean, splashing about, doing your damndest not to drown, in spite of whirlpools and cross currents. The main thing is to do the regulation breast-stroke and if you're not a clod, never to let the life-buoy out of sight. No one expects any more than that out of you. Now if you relieve yourself in the water now and then, that's your affair. The sea is big, and if the top half of your body still looks as though it's doing the breast-stroke, nobody will say a word.

One way of distinguishing between comedy and tragedy is summarized in Horace Walpole's aphorism, "This world is a comedy to those that think, a tragedy to those that feel." Life seen thoughtfully, with considerable detachment, viewed from above, as it were, is an amusing pageant, and the comic writer gives us something of this view. With Puck we look at the antics in the forest, smile tolerantly, and say with a godlike perspective, "Lord, what fools these mortals be!" But in tragedy we are to a greater degree engaged; the tragic dramatist manages to make us in large measure identify ourselves with the hero, feel his plight as if it were our own, and value his feelings as he values them, so that with Othello we may say "The pity of it."* Yeats noticed this when he said that "character is continuously present in comedy alone," and that "tragedy must always be a drowning and breaking of the dykes that separate man from man.... It is upon these dykes comedy keeps house." And Yeats again: "Nor when the tragic reverie is at its height do we say, 'How well that man is realised, I should know him were I to meet him in the street,' for it is always ourselves that we see upon the [tragic] stage."

One consequence of this distinction between tragedy and comedy, between looking-at and feeling-with, is that the comic plot is usually more intricate than the tragic plot, and less plausible. The comic plot continues to trip up its characters, bringing them into numerous situations that allow them to display their folly over and again. The complex comic plot is often arbitrary, full of the workings of Fortune or Chance, and we delight at each new unexpected or unlikely happening. In tragedy, Fate (sometimes in the form that "character is destiny") or Necessity rules, there is the consistency and inevitability, the "remorseless working of things," that has already been mentioned. If Macbeth were struck dead by a falling roof tile while he dozed in the palace

DETACHMENT AND ENGAGEMENT

TRAGIC FATE AND COMIC FORTUNE IN PLOTS

---

* Bergson's theory that a human being — an organism — is comical when it behaves mechanically requires, as Bergson said, a modification: feelings must be suppressed. A crippled man is not comic despite his mechanical limp, because we feel for him. Comedy requires, Bergson said, an "anesthesia of the heart."

after a good meal, instead of dying on Macduff's sword, or if Brutus were to die by slipping in his bath, instead of dying on the very sword with which he killed Caesar, we would have arbitrary happenings that violate the spirit of everything that precedes. But the unexpected letters and the long-lost relatives that often turn up at the close of a comedy are thoroughly in the spirit of the comic vision, which devalues not only rigidly consistent character but rigidity of every sort, even of plot. Tragedy usually follows a straight course, comedy a delightfully twisted one.

COMIC BEGINNINGS AND ENDINGS

The rigid behavior of some of comedy's laughably serious characters (e.g., misers, jealous husbands, stern fathers) is paralleled in the rigid circumstances that often are sketched at the beginning of a comedy. In *As You Like It*, the rightful duke has been banished by his usurping brother, and (a sort of parallel) an attractive young nobleman has been confined "rustically at home" by *his* brother. Gilbert and Sullivan, to draw on familiar material, afford plenty of examples of comedy's fondness for a cantankerous beginning: *The Mikado* opens with a chorus of Japanese noblemen whose code of etiquette makes them appear to be "worked by strings"; they live in a town where a law ordered that "all who flirted, leered or winked / Should forthwith be beheaded." (Comedy often begins with a society dominated by some harsh law.) Although this law has been suspended, another harsh decree is in effect: the pretty Yum-Yum is betrothed to her old guardian, Ko-Ko. We learn, too, that her appropriate wooer, Nanki-Poo, is a prince who has had to disguise himself as a humble wandering minstrel to escape his father's decree that he marry Katisha, an old and ugly lady of the court. After various doings in a comedy, a new — presumably natural, prosperous, fertile, and free — society is formed, usually centered around lovers who are going to be married. Yum-Yum and Nanki-Poo finally contrive to get married, evading Katisha and Ko-Ko, who make the best of things by marrying each other. The whole business is satisfactorily explained to the Mikado, who affably accepts, and ruffled tempers are soothed:

> The threatened cloud has passed away,
> And brightly shines the dawning day;
> What though the night may come too soon,
> We've years and years of afternoon!
>
> Then let the throng
> Our joy advance,
> With laughing song
> And merry dance,
> With joyous shout and ringing cheer,
> Inaugurate our new career!

The first four lines are sung by the young lovers, the remaining six are sung by "All," the new, or renewed, society, free from unnatural law. *H.M.S. Pinafore* begins with lovers who cannot marry because of disparity in rank, but ends with appropriate shifts in rank so that there can be "three loving pairs on the same day united."

In comedy there is often not only an improbable turn in events but an improbable (but agreeable) change in character — or at least in rank; trouble-some persons become enlightened, find their own better nature, and join in the fun, commonly a marriage-feast. Finding one's own nature is common in tragedy, too, but there self-knowledge is co-terminous with death or some death-like condition, such as blindness. *Oedipus the King* ends with a note of finality, even though Oedipus is alive at the end; the fact that twenty-five years later Sophocles decided to write a play showing Oedipus' apotheosis does not allow us to see the earlier play as less than complete. The chorus in *Oedipus the King* has the last word:

SELF-
KNOWLEDGE

> This man was Oedipus.
> That mighty King, who knew the riddle's mystery,
> Whom all the city envied, Fortune's favorite.
> Behold, in the event, the storm of his calamities,
> And, being mortal, think on that last day of death,
> Which all must see, and speak of no man's happiness
> Till, without sorrow, he hath passed the goal of life.

Or consider the irreparable loss at the end of Shakespeare's tragedies: "This was the noblest Roman of them all"; "We that are young / Shall never see so much, nor live so long"; "The rest is silence." But comedy ends with a new beginning, a newly formed society, usually a wedding party; the tragic figure commonly awakens to the fact that he has made a big mistake and his life is over, but the comic figure commonly awakens to his better nature. He usually sheds his aberration and is restored to himself and to a renewed society. In *As You Like It,* for example, Oliver is for much of the play a "most unnatural brother," but he is at last converted by his brother's natural goodness and he gains a lovely wife. Alceste's refusal to change, at the end of *The Misanthrope,* helps to push that comedy toward the borderline between comedy and tragedy. Oedipus learns that his parents were not those whom he had supposed, and he learns that even the mighty Oedipus can be humbled. Othello comes to see himself as a man "that loved not wisely but too well," and, having reached his journey's end, he executes justice upon himself by killing himself. That is, at the end of the play he finds himself, but this finding of the self separates him forever from those around him, whereas the comic figure who finds himself usually does so by putting aside in some measure his individuality and by submitting himself to a partner or to the group.

Thomas Hardy, whose view of life was bleak (it has been said that in Hardy fornication always produces offspring), said:

> Tragedy is true guise,
> Comedy lies.

But the visions of comedy and tragedy are equally true and do not conflict; rather, they are different visions and represent different psychological states. And they are equally useful. The tragic vision may have more prestige, but it is no small thing to make men laugh, to call attention amusingly to the follies and joys of life, and to help develop the sense of humor — and humility — that may be indispensable to survival in a world continually threatened by aggressive ideals that demand uncritical acceptance. Infants smile easily, and children laugh often, but growing up is often attended by a frightening seriousness. True, hostile laughter, the scarcely veiled aggressiveness that manifests itself in derision, remains an adult possession, but the laughter evoked by the best comedy is good-natured while it is critical, and it is in part directed at ourselves. We look at bumbling humanity and we recall Puck's words, "Lord, what fools these mortals be." This is not to say that the comic vision is cynical; rather, it attributes to folly what less generous visions attribute to ill-will or to hopeless corruption, and when it laughs it forgives. Analyses of laughter are sometimes funny but more often they are tedious; still, they at least pay the comic spirit the compliment of recognizing it as worthy of man's best efforts.

2. Tragicomedy

TRAGICOMEDY
BEFORE 1900

The word "tragicomedy" is much newer than the words "tragedy" and "comedy"; it first appears about 186 B.C., when Plautus spoke of *tragicocomoedia* in his *Amphitryon*, a Roman comedy in which gods assume mortal shapes in order to dupe a husband and seduce his wife. Mercury, in a joking prologue to the play, explains the author's dilemma:

> I'll make it a mixture, a tragicomedy. It wouldn't be right for me to make
> it all a comedy since kings and gods appear. Well, then, since there's a
> slave part too, I'll do as I said and make it a tragicomedy.

But the play is a traditional comedy, unalloyed with the solemnity, terror, and pity of tragedy. It shows laughable activities that finally turn out all right. It should be mentioned again, however, that although tragedy and comedy were clearly separated in the ancient world, not all ancient tragedies ended with death, or even ended unhappily. Aeschylus' trilogy, *The Oresteia*, ends with reconciliation and solemn joy (but it has been bought at the price of great suffering), and Sophocles' *Philoctetes* and Euripides' *Iphigeneia at Taurus* end with catastrophes averted. They were tragic for the Greeks because momentous issues were treated seriously, though we might say that the plots have a comic structure because they end happily. In the Renaissance there was much fussing over the meanings of tragedy, comedy, and tragicomedy, but most theoreticians inclined to the view that tragedy dealt with noble figures engaged in serious actions, was written in a lofty style, and ended unhappily; comedy dealt with humbler figures engaged in trivial actions, was written in relatively common diction, and ended happily. Tragicomedy, whether defined as some mixture (e.g., high people in trivial actions) or as a play in which, to quote Sir Philip Sidney, the writer "thrust in the clown by head and shoulders to play a part in majestical matters," was for the most part scorned by academic critics as a mongrel. It was merely additive, bits of comedy added to a tragedy. At best the advocates for tragicomedy could argue that a play without the terror of tragedy and the absurdity of comedy can cover a good deal of life and can please a good many tastes. But this sort of play, unlike modern tragicomedy, is not so much a union of tragedy and comedy as an exclusion of both, lacking, for example, the awe we associate with tragedy and the fun we associate with comedy.

In the twentieth century the word and the form have become thoroughly respectable; indeed, it is now evident that most of the best plays of our century are best described not as tragedies or as comedies but as tragicomedies — distinctive fusions (not mere aggregations) of tragedy and comedy. For a start we can take William Hazlitt's statement that "man is the only animal that laughs and weeps; for he is the only animal that is struck with the difference between what things are, and what they ought to be." This implication that the subjects of tragedy and of comedy are one rather than two has recently been amplified by Cyrus Hoy, who suggests that a single principle underlies tragedy and comedy (pp. 642–648): man has an ideal of human conduct, but circumstances and his own limitations make his belief that he can fulfill this ideal illusory. Still man persists, appearing "nobly enduring, stubbornly unyielding . . . foolishly blind," or (as in most tragicomedy) some indissoluble combination of these. Most of the best playwrights of the twentieth century have adopted the more complicated mixed view. Comedy had customarily invoked a considerable degree of detachment; in Bergson's formula (1900), already quoted, comedy requires an anesthesia of the spectator's heart as he watches folly on the stage. Tragedy, on the other hand, customarily invoked a considerable degree of involvement or sympathy; in Walpole's formula, also already quoted, "The world is a comedy to those that think, a tragedy to those that feel." But tragicomedy shows us comic characters for whom we feel deep sympathy. Pirandello in his essay *Umorismo* (1908) gives an interesting example of the phenomenon. Suppose, he says, we see an elderly woman with dyed hair and much too much make-up. We find her funny; but if we realize that she is trying to hold the attention of her husband, our sympathy is aroused. Our sense of her absurdity is not totally dissipated, but we feel for her and so our laughter is combined with pity. There are moments like this in earlier comedies, the most famous probably is Shylock's "Hath not a Jew eyes . . .? If you poison us do we not die?" in which we suddenly see Shylock not unsympathetically from the outside, as a funny-looking man with odd dietary habits but sympathetically as a man who shares our feelings. Despite such a moment, *The Merchant of Venice* is clearly a comedy, a festive play with a happy ending, and on the whole Shylock is a figure for unsympathetic laughter.

Changes in our ethical conceptions, however, have caused us to see him with increased sympathy, just as we now see madness, or the sufferings of animals, with greater sympathy than our ancestors did. Our attitudes since, say,

DETACHMENT
AND
ENGAGEMENT
AGAIN

the middle of the eighteenth century have shifted a good deal, giving us a new sense of the nature of man, and we ought briefly to look at this new sense and its background.

First, a disclaimer. There are still many different attitudes and many kinds of plays. But the theater that is vital today is not the Broadway musical, the earnest problem-play, or the well-made drawing-room comedy (though these

THEATER
OF THE
ABSURD

continue to be written) but a fairly unified body of drama called the absurd, whose major writers are Beckett, Genet, and Ionesco. Their theme is man's anguish, but their techniques are those of comedy: improbable situations and unheroic characters who say funny things. These writers differ, of course, and differ from play to play, but they are all preoccupied with the loneliness of man in a world without the certainties afforded by God or by optimistic rationalism. This loneliness is heightened by a sense of impotence derived partly from an awareness of man's inability to communicate in a society that has made language meaningless, and partly from an awareness of the precariousness of man's existence in an atomic age. Behind this vision are some two hundred years of thinking that have conspired to make it difficult to think of any man as a hero who confronts a mysterious cosmic order. Man, Ionesco says in *Notes and Counter Notes*, is "cut off from his religious and metaphysical roots."* One of the milestones in Western man's journey toward contemporary nihilism is the bourgeois drama of the middle of the eighteenth century, which sought to show the dignity of the common man but which, negatively put, undermined the concept of a tragic *hero*. Instead of showing a heroic yet universal man, it showed man in relation to his society, thus paving the way for Arthur Miller's Willy Loman, who apparently would have been okay, as we all would be, if our economic system allowed for early retirement. Miller's play makes no claim for Willy's grandeur or for the glory of life; it claims only that he is an ordinary man at the end of his rope in a deficient society and that he is entitled to a fair deal.

Other landmarks on the road to man's awareness of his littleness are, like bourgeois drama, developments in thinking that were thought by their builders

DIMINUTION
OF MAN

to be landmarks on the road to man's progressive conquest of fear. Among these we can name Darwin's *The Origin of Species* (1859), which, in the popular phrase, seemed to record man's progress "up from apes," but which, more closely read, reduced man to the product of "accidental variations" and left God out of the picture, substituting for a cosmic order a barbaric struggle for existence. (In the second edition, 1860, Darwin spoke of life as "breathed by the creator," but the creator was not Darwin's concern and he later abandoned all religious beliefs. Probably he retained his belief that the process of "natural selection works solely by and for the good of each being," but by 1889 his disciple Huxley saw it differently. Huxley said he knew of no study "so

* From *Notes and Counter Notes: Writings on the Theatre* by Eugène Ionesco, p. 257. Translated from the French by Donald Watson. Copyright © 1964 by Grove Press, Inc. Reprinted by permission of the publisher, Grove Press, Inc.

unutterably saddening as that of the evolution of humanity.") Karl Marx, studying the evolution of societies at about the same time, was attributing man's
sense of alienation to economic forces, thereby implying that man had no
identity he could properly call his own. Moreover, Marxist thinking, like
Darwinian thinking, suggested that a man could not do anything of really
great importance, nor could he be blamed for his misfortunes. At the end of
the nineteenth century, and in the early twentieth century, Freud, also seeking to free man from tyranny, turned to the forces within man's mind. Ironically, the effort to chart man's unconscious drives and anarchic impulses in
order to help man to know himself induced a profound distrust of the self:
we can scarcely be confident of our behavior, for we know that apparently
heroic behavior has unconscious unheroic motives rooted in the experiences
of infancy. Tragic heroes are men with complexes, and religious codes are
only wishful thinking.

The result of such developments in thought seems to be that, a "tragic
sense" in the twentieth century commonly means a despairing or deeply uncertain view, something very different from what it meant in Greece and·in
Elizabethan England. This uncertainty is not merely about the cosmos but
even about character or identity. In 1888, in the Preface to *Miss Julie*, Strindberg called attention to the new sense of the instability of character:

DISSOLUTION
OF
CHARACTER
AND PLOT

> I have made the people in my play fairly "characterless." The middle-class
> conception of a fixed character was transferred to the stage, where the
> middle class has always ruled. A character there came to mean an actor
> who was always one and the same, always drunk, always comic or always
> melancholy, and who needed to be characterized only by some physical
> defect such as a club foot, a wooden leg, or a red nose, or by the repetition
> of some such phrase such as, "That's capital," or "Barkis is willin'."
> . . . Since the persons in my play are modern characters, living in a transi-
> tional era more hurried and hysterical than the previous one at least, I
> have depicted them as more unstable, as torn and divided, a mixture of
> the old and the new.

In 1902, in his preface to *A Dream Play*, he is more explicit: "Anything may
happen, anything seems possible and probable. . . . The characters split, double, multiply, vanish, solidify, blur, clarify." Strindberg's view of the fluidity of
character — the characterlessness of character, one might say — has continued
and is apparent in O'Neill's *The Emperor Jones*, in almost all of Pirandello's
work, in the underground film, and in much of the Theater of the Absurd.
Ionesco, in *Fragments of a Journal*, says "I often find it quite impossible to
hold an opinion about a fact, a thing or a person. Since it's all a matter of
interpretation, one has to choose a particular interpretation."* (One thinks too

---

* From *Fragments of a Journal* by Eugène Ionesco, p. 131. Translated by Jean Stewart.
Copyright © by Faber and Faber Ltd. Reprinted by permission of the publishers, Grove
Press, Inc., and Faber and Faber Ltd.

of Dr. Borg in Bergman's *Wild Strawberries* who in effect withdrew from society because a man cannot really know his fellows.) In *Notes and Counter Notes* Ionesco said, "chance formed us," and that we would be different if we had different experiences; characteristically a few years later he said that he was no longer sure that he believed in chance.

Along with the sense of characterlessness, or at least of the mystery of character, there developed in the drama (and in the underground film and the novel) a sense of plotlessness, or fundamental untruthfulness of the traditional plot that moved by cause and effect. "Plots," Ionesco has said in *Conversations*, "are never interesting," and again he has said that a play should be able to stop at any point; it ends only because "the audience has to go home to bed. . . . It's true for real life. Why should it be different for art?"* Ionesco has treated his own plots very casually, allowing directors to make "all the cuts needed" and suggesting that endings other than those he wrote are possibilities. After all, in a meaningless world one can hardly take a dramatic plot seriously. In Ionesco's *Victims of Duty* a character defends a new kind of irrational, anti-Aristotelian drama: "The theater of my dreams would be irrationalist. . . . The contemporary theater doesn't reflect the cultural tone of our period, it's not in harmony with the general drift of the other manifestations of the modern spirit. . . . We'll get rid of the principle of identity and unity of character. . . . Personality doesn't exist." A policeman-psychologist (a materialist who demands law and order) offers an old-fashioned view: "I don't believe in the absurd, everything hangs together, everything can be comprehended . . . thanks to the achievements of human thought and science," but he is murdered by the anti-Aristotelian.†

Thus, Beckett's *Waiting for Godot* ends — as the first act ended — without anything ending:

> VLADIMIR: Well? Shall we go?
> ESTRAGON: Yes, let's go.
>
> *They do not move.*
> *Curtain.*‡

To bring an action to a completion, as drama traditionally did, is to imply an orderly world of cause and effect, of beginnings and endings, but for the dram-

---

* From *Conversations with Eugène Ionesco* by Claude Bonnefoy. Translated by Jan Dawson. Copyright © 1966 by Editions Pierre Belfond. Copyright © 1970 by Faber and Faber Limited. Reprinted by permission of Holt, Rinehart and Winston and Faber and Faber Limited, Publishers.

† From *Three Plays* by Eugène Ionesco, pp. 157–159. Translated by Donald Watson. Copyright © 1958 by John Calder (Publishers) Limited. Reprinted by permission of the publisher, Grove Press, Inc.

‡ Translated from the French by the author. Copyright © 1954 by Grove Press. Reprinted by permission of the publisher, Grove Press, Inc.

atists of the absurd, there is no such pattern. At best it is *Hamlet* as Tom Stoppard's Rosencrantz and Guildenstern see it: they are supposed to do a job they don't understand, and instead of a pattern or "order" they encounter only "Incidents! Incidents! Dear God, is it too much to expect a little sustained action?" Well, yes; it is too much to expect.

There can be no tragedy, because, as Ionesco explains in *Notes*, tragedy admits the existence of fate or destiny, which is to say it admits the existence of objective (however incomprehensible) laws ruling the universe, whereas the new comic perception of incongruity is that existence itself is absurd because there is no objective law. The new comic vision is far darker than the old tragic vision; it has nothing in it of what Yeats called "tragic joy." But what is our reaction to this joyless comedy? Let Ionesco, whose plays sometimes include meaningless babble, have the last word:

THE TRAGEDY
OF COMEDY

> The fact of being astonishes us, in a world that now seems all illusion and pretense, in which all human behavior tells of absurdity and all history of absolute futility; all reality and all language appear to lose their articulation, to disintegrate and collapse, so what possible reaction is there left, when everything has ceased to matter, but laugh at it all.*

* From *Notes and Counter Notes: Writings on the Theatre* by Eugène Ionesco, p. 163. Translated from the French by Donald Watson. Copyright © 1964 by Grove Press, Inc. Reprinted by permission of the publisher, Grove Press, Inc.

THE LANGUAGE OF DRAMA

ISBN 11 688 451

Although a play usually tells a story, "the medium of drama," as Ezra Pound observed, "is not words, but persons moving about on a stage using words." Take Ibsen's *A Doll's House* as an example. The gist of the story is this: Nora, without her husband knowing it, forged a document so that she and her husband could spend a year in Italy; this trip to a warm climate was necessary to preserve her husband's life. When Torvald, the husband, learns the truth and is in danger of being exposed as the husband of a forger, instead of either taking the blame or at least standing by Nora, to Nora's amazement he savagely turns on her. When the forged document is returned, so that it can be destroyed rather than made public, he exclaims, "I'm saved," at which point Nora asks, "And I?" Torvald forgives Nora, but Nora now understands that Torvald has never loved her but has only played with her, treating her like a doll and keeping her from making something of her life. Finding that she no longer loves him and that therefore she cannot continue to live with him, at the end of the play she leaves the house for no specified destination. The last thing we hear is the sound of the door closing behind her.

This is moderately interesting, and it has some roots in fact. Ibsen actually knew a woman who had forged a check to pay for a trip that her husband's health required. When the husband learned the truth, he turned on her and had her committed to an asylum, though later, for the sake of their children, he allowed her to return to their home. Ibsen, of course, added a good deal and changed the ending; but even if he had not made these changes, a play about this family would — if it were any good — be very different from an account in *Time* or *People*, because, as Pound says, a play is made not out of words but out of "persons moving about on a stage using words."

Let's begin with the stage and its setting. When the curtain goes up on a performance of *A Doll's House*, the audience sees "a pleasant living room, tastefully but not expensively furnished." Additional details, such as "etchings on the walls," and "a small bookcase with deluxe editions," tell us much about the kind of people who live here. We shall learn more about these people when we see the clothes that they wear and hear the words that they speak, but even now — from seeing their living room — we know that they are people who hold the conventional middle-class values. The "deluxe editions" in the bookcase, for example, are more for show than for reading.

In some plays there are several sets — sometimes in sharp contrast — but in *A Doll's House* there is only one set, and perhaps we come to feel that this omnipresent room is a sort of prison that stifles its inhabitants or, as the title of the play implies, that this room keeps its inhabitants at a distance from the realities of life. At the end of the play, Nora escapes from this box and enters the real world. We might look, too, at the ways in which some of the furniture and the properties work in the play. Very early, when Torvald begins to lecture Nora about incurring debts, she "walks over toward the stove." It is scarcely too subtle to conclude that she is seeking a place of warmth or security when confronted by Torvald's chilling words. We may not *consciously* come to this conclusion, but that doesn't matter. Indeed, later in this

A Doll's House: setting as a revelation of values. (Photograph: University Theatre.)

act, Torvald, sitting near the stove, says quite naturally, "Ah, it's nice and warm in here." Or consider the use Ibsen makes of the Christmas tree. In Act I, when Nora's world is still relatively undisturbed, the tree, adorned with candles and flowers, is in the center of the stage. By the end of this act Nora is terrified, and when the curtain goes up for the second act, we see the tree thrust into a corner, "stripped, shabby-looking, with burnt-down candles." Again, we may not consciously conclude that Ibsen, through the tree, is telling us something about Nora, but surely the tree — at first gay, then forlorn — somehow has an impact on us.

LIGHTING   Speaking of candles, or of lighting, in the second act a stage direction tells us, as Nora's terror grows, "Darkness begins to fall during the following scene." Later in the scene, when Dr. Rank confesses he loves Nora and thereby adds to her confusion, Nora seeks to regain her composure by ordering the maid to bring in a lamp — a natural desire, given her sense that she is threatened sexually, but also a symbol of illumination, for now the secret is out in the open. Finally, in the last act, when Nora forcefully explains to

Torvald that she now sees things clearly, they are sitting on opposite sides of a table with a lighted lamp on it.

The setting of even a realistic play, then, including the furniture and the lighting, is a means by which a playwright communicates. Another realistic play, *The Cherry Orchard*, juxtaposes the orchard (the dying aristocratic way of life) with telephone poles and a town (the new industrial way of life). In *Death of a Salesman*, Willy Loman's "fragile-seeming home" is surrounded by "a solid vault of apartment houses," Miller thereby conveying the vulnerability of the individual. A bare stage, too (much used in contemporary drama; for example, in the plays of Beckett), by virtue of its barrenness says something about the human being's isolation or alienation. Although one frequently hears that the Elizabethan stage was bare and that Shakespeare's plays are most effective on a bare stage, in fact the Elizabethan stage was an elaborate piece of architecture, suggestive of a completely ordered universe, and when appropriate the stage was decorated with banners. But it could be bleak when bleakness was required. At the end of the second act of *King Lear*, Gloucester tells us what we are to imagine: "Alack, the night comes on, and the high winds / Do sorely ruffle. For many miles about / There's scarce a bush." Again, this locale says something about the impoverished people who move in it.

In returning to *A Doll's House*, and to Ezra Pound's comment on the nature of drama, let us continue for a moment to talk about the ways in which drama even without dialogue says something. Costumes tell us a good COSTUME deal, on the stage as in life. They do not necessarily tell the truth about their wearers, but they tell us what the wearers want us to believe. If, on the street, we see someone who is wearing workman's clothes, we conclude that he may be a workman — or that for some reason (say, political or sexual) he wants us to think that he is a workman; in any case the clothes make a statement, conscious or not. In the first act, Nora wears ordinary clothing, but in the middle of the second act she puts on "a long, many-colored shawl" when she frantically rehearses her tarantella. The shawl, of course, is supposed to be appropriate to the Italian dance, but surely its multitude of colors also helps to express Nora's conflicting emotions, her near hysteria, expressed too in the fact that "her hair comes loose and falls down over her shoulders," but "She doesn't notice." The shawl and her disheveled hair, then, *speak* to us as clearly as the dialogue does. In the middle of the third act, after the party and just before the showdown, Nora appears in her "Italian costume," and Helmer wears "evening dress" under an open black cloak. She is dressed for a masquerade (her whole life has been a masquerade, it turns out), and Torvald's formal suit and black cloak help to express the stiffness and the blight that have forced her to present a false front throughout their years of marriage. A little later, after Nora sees that she has never really known her husband for the selfish creature he is, she leaves the stage, and when she returns she is "in an everyday dress." The pretense is over. She is no longer Torvald's "doll." When she finally leaves the stage — leaving the house —

she "Wraps her shawl around her." This is not the "many-colored shawl" she used in rehearsing the dance, but the "big, black shawl" she wears when she returns from the dance. The blackness of this shawl helps to express the death of her old way of life; Nora is now aware that life is not child's play.

Ibsen did not, of course, invent the use of costumes as dramatic language; it goes back to the beginnings of drama, and one has only to think of Hamlet's "inky cloak," or of Lear tearing off his clothing, or of the fresh clothing in which Lear is garbed after his madness in order to see how eloquently costumes can speak. To this can be added the matter of disguises — for example, Edgar's disguise in *King Lear* — which are removed near the end of plays, when the truth is finally revealed and the characters can be fully themselves. In short, the removal of disguises *says* something.

GESTURES   Gestures, too, are a part of the language of drama. Helmer "playfully pulls [Nora's] ear," showing his affection; Nora claps her hands; Mrs. Linde (an old friend of Nora's) "tries to read but seems unable to concentrate," and so forth. All such gestures clearly and naturally convey states of mind. One of the most delightful and revealing gestures in the play occurs when, in the third act, Helmer demonstrates to Mrs. Linde the ugliness of knitting ("Look here: arms pressed close to the sides") and the elegance of embroidering ("... with your right [hand] you move the needle — like this — in an easy, elongated arc"). None of his absurd remarks throughout the play is quite so revealing of his absurdity as is this silly demonstration.

Some gestures, or stage directions that imply gestures, are a bit more complex. For example, when Nora "walks cautiously over to the door to the study and listens," this direction conveys Nora's fear that her husband may detect her foibles — or even her crime. We read this stage direction almost at the start of the play, when we do not yet know who is who or what is what, but we do know, from this gesture alone, that Nora is not at ease even in her own home. And when Mrs. Linde sees her former lover, Krogstad, she "starts, looks, turns away toward the window," a natural enough reaction but one that indicates her desire to escape from this confining box-set. Similarly, when Nora "wildly" dances during her rehearsal in the second act, the action of course indicates the terrible agitation in her mind. One other, quieter example: in Act III, when the dying Dr. Rank for the last time visits Nora in order to gain comfort, she lights his cigar, and a moment later Rank replies — these are his last words — "And thanks for the light." Thus we not only hear words about a cigar, but we *see* an act of friendship, a flash of light in this oppressive household.

SOUND   Like the setting, the costumes, and the gestures, the sound effects in a
EFFECTS   play are important. Footsteps on stairs, or the swish and slight thud of a letter dropping into a mailbox on the door, can have an electrifying effect. In *A Doll's House* the music of the tarantella communicates Nora's frenzy, but the most famous sound effect is reserved for the very end of the play, when Nora walks out on Helmer: "From downstairs comes the sound of a

A Doll's House: a symbolic gesture. (Photograph: Harvard Theatre Collection.)

heavy door slamming shut." Nothing could better "say" anything about Nora's decision to choose a new life.

Simply to widen the canvas, we can add an example from Shakespeare: the sound of the storm in *King Lear* is a reflection of Lear's disordered kingdom, disordered family, and disordered mind. Similarly, the "scream" of the subway in LeRoi Jones's *Dutchman*, the sound of the axes cutting down the trees in *The Cherry Orchard*, and the flute ("telling of grass and trees and the horizon") in *Death of a Salesman* are not merely realism.

But, of course, dialogue is the most persistent sound in a play. A good playwright gives us not a transcript of our chaotic fragmentary sentences but   DIALOGUE language that continually reveals character and that furthers plot. (As one critic has said, "Dialogue is what the characters *do* to each other.") Look at the first few lines that Nora and her husband exchange:

HELMER (*in his study*): Is that my little lark twittering out there?
NORA (*opening some of the packages*): That's right.
HELMER: My squirrel bustling about?
NORA: Yes.
HELMER: When did squirrel come home?

Helmer's "Is that my little lark twittering out there?" and his "My squirrel bustling about?" are affectionate but horribly condescending; and Nora's brief responses, "That's right" and "Yes," indicate — though probably even she does not know it — her aversion to such oppressive affection. If we contrast her perfunctory words here with her long speeches to Helmer at the end of the play, when she has seen the light, we realize how fully the lark-squirrel has turned into an articulate human being.

PLOT AND CHARACTER

The point need not be labored; there is scarcely a line in the play that does not reveal the speaker's character and at the same time add a twist to the plot. We can briefly examine one episode. When Nora and Helmer, in the first act, discuss Krogstad's forgery, we are getting not only *exposition* (a setting forth of information that the audience must know), and preparation for later events (Helmer will discharge Krogstad from the bank); we are also getting a revelation of Helmer's character (the lecture on dishonesty). But, even more important, we are getting a development in Nora's character, for, unknown to Helmer, Nora sees a resemblance between herself and Krogstad, and Nora is coming to the realization that her supposedly loving husband may judge her (if he learns the truth) as harshly as he judges Krogstad.

THEME

What does the play add up to? What is the underlying theme or meaning of the play? Some critics, arguing that the concept of theme is meaningless, hold that any play gives us only an extremely detailed history of some imaginary people. But surely this view is desperate. Ibsen himself began work on *A Doll's House* by jotting down some "Notes for a Modern Tragedy":

There are two kinds of moral laws, two kinds of conscience, one for men and one, quite different, for women. They don't understand each other; but in practical life, woman is judged by masculine law, as though she weren't a woman but a man.

The wife in the play ends by having no idea what is right and what is wrong; natural feelings on the one hand and belief in authority on the other lead her to utter distraction.

Of course, Ibsen probably began by thinking about the real woman who forged a check to pay for the trip to save her sick husband, but the passage just quoted is the earliest writing relevant to the play. As Ibsen worked on the play, he (not surprisingly) produced characters and a plot that have a life of their own; but even if they depart from his preliminary note, these characters and this plot add up to something. (A plot is what happens; a theme is what the happenings add up to.) Some readers see in *A Doll's*

House a play about a woman's place in a man's world, or a play about women's rights, but Ibsen himself (years after writing the play) said he had a larger theme: "I am not even sure what women's rights really are. To me it has been a question of human rights." Certainly the play deals, as Ibsen implies, with the enslavement of one person by another. At last Torvald dimly seems to recognize that Nora is a human being, not a doll; and Nora perceives that such a recognition could lead to "a true marriage." To the reply that themes such as "marriage must be based on mutual respect" and "self-knowledge is acquired only painfully" are mere truisms, we can counter: Yes, but the truisms are presented in such a way that they take on life and become a part of us, whereas mere truisms are something of which we say, "I've heard it said, and I guess it's so." And surely we are in no danger of equating the play with the theme that we sense underlies it. We never believe that our statement of the theme is really the equivalent of the play itself. The play, we recognize, presents the theme with such detail that our statement of the theme is only a wedge that helps us to enter the play so we may more fully (in Henry James's word) "appropriate" it.

A DOLL'S HOUSE

Henrik Ibsen

Translated by Otto Reinert

Henrik Ibsen (1828–1906) was born in Skien, Norway, of wealthy parents who soon after his birth lost their money. Ibsen worked as a pharmacist's apprentice, but at the age of twenty-two he had written his first play, a promising melodrama entitled *Cataline*. He engaged in theater work in Norway, and then in Denmark and Germany. By 1865 his plays had won him a state pension that enabled him to settle in Rome. After writing romantic, historic, and poetic plays, he turned to realistic drama with *The League of Youth* (1869). Among the major realistic "problem plays" are *A Doll's House* (1879), *Ghosts* (1881), and *An Enemy of the People* (1882). In *The Wild Duck* (1884) he moved toward a more symbolic tragic comedy, and his last plays, written in the nineties, are highly symbolic. *Hedda Gabler* (1890) looks backward to the plays of the eighties rather than forward to the plays of the nineties.

CHARACTERS

TORVALD HELMER, *a lawyer*
NORA, *his wife*
DR. RANK
MRS. LINDE
KROGSTAD

THE HELMERS' THREE SMALL CHILDREN
The children's NURSE, *Anne-Marie*
A HOUSEMAID
A PORTER

Sam Waterston as Helmer and Liv Ullmann as Nora in the 1975 production directed by Tormod Skagestad. (Photograph: Joseph Abeles Studio.)

The Scene: The Helmers' living room

ACT I

A pleasant living room, tastefully but not expensively furnished. A door on the rear wall, right, leads to the front hall; another door, left, to HELMER'S *study. Between the two doors a piano. A third door in the middle of the left wall; further front a window. Near the window a round table with easy chairs and a small couch. Toward the rear of the right wall a fourth door; further front ·a tile stove with a rocking chair and a couple of armchairs in front of it. Between the stove and the side door a small table. Copperplate etchings on the walls. A whatnot with porcelain figurines and other small objects. A small bookcase with deluxe editions. A rug on the floor; fire in the stove. Winter day.*

The doorbell rings, then the sound of the front door opening. NORA, *dressed for outdoors, enters, humming cheerfully. She carries several packages, which she puts down on the table, right. She leaves the door to the front hall open; there a* PORTER *is seen holding a Christmas tree and a basket. He gives them to the* MAID, *who has let them in.*

NORA: Be sure to hide the Christmas tree, Helene. The children mustn't see it till after we've trimmed it tonight. (*Opens her purse; to the* PORTER.) How much?

PORTER: Fifty øre.

NORA: Here's a crown. No, keep the change. (*The* PORTER *thanks her, leaves.* NORA *closes the door. She keeps laughing quietly to herself as she takes off her coat, etc. She takes a bag of macaroons from her pocket and eats a couple. She walks cautiously over to the door to the study and listens.*) Yes, he's home. (*Resumes her humming, walks over to the table, right.*)

HELMER (*in his study*): Is that my little lark twittering out there?

NORA (*opening some of the packages*): That's right.

A Doll's House by Henrik Ibsen, translated by Otto Reinert. Copyright © 1977 by Otto Reinert. Reprinted by permission of Little, Brown and Company.

HELMER: My squirrel bustling about?

NORA: Yes.

HELMER: When did squirrel come home?

NORA: Just now. (*Puts the bag of macaroons back in her pocket, wipes her mouth.*) Come out here, Torvald. I want to show you what I've bought.

HELMER: I'm busy right now! (*After a little while he opens the door and looks in, pen in hand.*) Bought, eh? All that? So little wastrel has been throwing money around again?

NORA: Oh, but Torvald, this Christmas we can be a little extravagant, can't we? It's the first Christmas we haven't had to watch every penny.

HELMER: I don't know about that. We certainly don't have money to throw away.

NORA: Yes, Torvald, we do. A little, anyway. Just a tiny little bit? Now that you're going to get that big salary and all and make lots and lots of money.

HELMER: Starting at New Year's, yes. But payday isn't till the end of the quarter.

NORA: That doesn't matter. We can always borrow.

HELMER: Nora! (*Goes over to her and playfully pulls her ear.*) There you go being irresponsible again. Suppose I borrowed a thousand crowns today and you spent it all for Christmas and on New Year's Eve a tile from the roof laid me out cold?

NORA (*putting her hand over his mouth*): I won't have you say such horrid things.

HELMER: But suppose it happened. Then what?

NORA: If it did, I wouldn't care whether we owed money or not.

HELMER: But what about the people I had borrowed from?

NORA: Who cares about them! They are strangers!

HELMER: Nora, Nora, you *are* a woman. No, really! You know how I feel about that. No debts! A home in debt isn't a free home, and if it isn't free it isn't beautiful. We've managed nicely so far, you and I, and that's the way we'll go on. It won't be for much longer.

NORA (*walks over toward the stove*): All right, Torvald. Whatever you say.

HELMER (*follows her*): Come, come, my little songbird mustn't droop her wings. What's this? Can't have a pouty squirrel in the house, you know. (*Takes out his wallet.*) Nora, what do you think I have here?

NORA (*turns around quickly*): Money!

HELMER: Here. (*Gives her some bills.*) Don't you think I know Christmas is expensive?

NORA (*counting*): Ten — twenty — thirty — forty. Thank you, thank you, Torvald. This helps a lot.

HELMER: I certainly hope so.

NORA: It does, it does! But I want to show you what I got. It was cheap, too. Look. New clothes for Ivar. And a sword. And a horse and a trumpet for Bob. And a doll and a little bed for Emmy. It isn't any good, but it wouldn't last, anyway. And here's some dress material and scarves for the maids. I feel bad about old Anne-Marie, though. She really should be getting much more.

HELMER: And what's in here?

NORA (*cries*): Not till tonight!

HELMER: I see. But now what does my little spendthrift have in mind for herself?

NORA: Oh, nothing. I really don't care.

HELMER: Of course you do. Tell me what you'd like. Within reason.

NORA: Oh, I don't know. Really, I don't. The only thing —

HELMER: Well?

NORA (*fiddling with his buttons, without looking at him*): If you really want to give me something, you might — you could —

HELMER: All right, let's have it.

NORA (*quickly*): Some money, Torvald. Just as much as you think you can spare. Then I'll buy myself something one of these days.

HELMER: No, really, Nora —

NORA: Oh yes, please, Torvald. Please? I'll wrap the money in pretty gold paper and hang it on the tree. Won't that be nice?

HELMER: What's the name for little birds that are always spending money?

NORA: Wastrels, I know. But please let's do it my way, Torvald. Then I'll have time to decide what I need most. Now that's sensible, isn't it?

HELMER (*smiling*): Oh, very sensible. That is, if you really bought yourself something you could use. But it all disappears in the household expenses or you buy things you don't need. And then you come back to me for more.

NORA: Oh, but Torvald —

HELMER: That's the truth, dear little Nora, and you know it. (*Puts his arm around her.*) My wastrel is a little sweetheart, but she *does* go through an awful lot of money awfully fast. You've no idea how expensive it is for a man to keep a wastrel.

NORA: That's not fair, Torvald. I really save all I can.

HELMER (*laughs*): Oh, I believe that. All you can. Meaning, exactly nothing!

NORA (*hums, smiles mysteriously*): You don't know all the things we songbirds and squirrels need money for, Torvald.

HELMER: You know, you're funny. Just like your father. You're always looking for ways to get money, but as soon as you do, it runs through your fingers and you can never say what you spent it for. Well, I guess I'll just have to take you the way you are. It's in your blood. Yes, that sort of thing is hereditary, Nora.

NORA: In that case, I wish I had inherited many of Daddy's qualities.

HELMER: And I don't want you any different from just what you are — my own sweet little songbird. Hey! — I think I just noticed something. Aren't you looking — what's the word? — a little — sly — ?

NORA: I am?

HELMER: You definitely are. Look at me.

NORA (*looks at him*): Well?

HELMER (*wagging a finger*): Little sweettooth hasn't by any chance been on a rampage today, has she?

NORA: Of course not. Whatever makes you think that?

HELMER: A little detour by the pastryshop maybe?

NORA: No, I assure you, Torvald —

HELMER: Nibbled a little jam?

NORA: Certainly not!

HELMER: Munched a macaroon or two?

NORA: No, really, Torvald, honestly —

HELMER: All right. Of course I was only joking.

NORA (*walks toward the table, right*): You know I wouldn't do anything to displease you.

HELMER: I know. And I have your promise. (*Over to her.*) All right, keep your little Christmas secrets to yourself, Nora darling. They'll all come out tonight, I suppose, when we light the tree.

NORA: Did you remember to invite Rank?

HELMER: No, but there's no need to. He knows he'll have dinner with us. Anyway, I'll see him later this morning. I'll ask him then. I did order some good wine. Oh Nora, you've no idea how much I'm looking forward to tonight!

NORA: Me too! And the children, Torvald! They'll have such a good time!

HELMER: You know, it *is* nice to have a good, safe job and a comfortable income. Feels good just thinking about it. Don't you agree?

NORA: Oh, it's wonderful!

HELMER: Remember last Christmas? For three whole weeks you shut yourself up every evening till long after midnight, making ornaments for the Christmas tree and I don't know what else. Some big surprise for all of us, anyway. I'll be damned if I've ever been so bored in my whole life!

NORA: I wasn't bored at all.

HELMER (*smiling*): But you've got to admit you didn't have much to show for it in the end.

NORA: Oh, don't tease me again about that! Could I help it that the cat got in and tore up everything?

HELMER: Of course you couldn't, my poor little Nora. You just wanted to please the rest of us, and that's the important thing. But I *am* glad the hard times are behind us. Aren't you?

NORA: Oh yes. I think it's just wonderful.

HELMER: This year I won't be bored and lonely. And you won't have to strain your dear eyes and your delicate little hands —

NORA (*claps her hands*): No I won't, will I, Torvald? Oh, how wonderful, how lovely, to hear you say that! (*Puts her arm under his.*) Let me tell you how I think we should arrange things, Torvald. Soon as Christmas is over — (*The doorbell rings.*) Someone's at the door. (*Straightens things up a bit.*) A caller, I suppose. Bother!

HELMER: Remember, I'm not home.

MAID (*in the door to the front hall*): Ma'am, there's a lady here —

NORA: All right. Ask her to come in.

MAID (*to* HELMER): And the Doctor just arrived.

HELMER: Is he in the study?

MAID: Yes, sir.

(HELMER *exits into his study. The* MAID *shows* MRS. LINDE *in and closes the door behind her as she leaves.* MRS. LINDE *is in travel dress.*)

MRS. LINDE (*timid and a little hesitant*): Good morning, Nora.

NORA (*uncertainly*): Good morning.

MRS. LINDE: I don't believe you know who I am.

NORA: No — I'm not sure — Though I know I should — Of course! Kristine! It's you!

MRS. LINDE: Yes, it's me.

NORA: And I didn't even recognize you! I had no idea! (*In a lower voice.*) You've changed, Kristine.

MRS. LINDE: I'm sure I have. It's been nine or ten long years.

NORA: Has it really been that long? Yes, you're right. I've been so happy these last eight years. And now you're here. Such a long trip in the middle of winter. How brave!

MRS. LINDE: I got in on the steamer this morning.

NORA: To have some fun over the holidays, of course. That's lovely. For we *are* going to have fun. But take off your coat! You aren't cold, are you? (*Helps her.*) There, now! Let's sit down here by the fire and just relax and talk. No, you sit there. I want the rocking chair. (*Takes her hands.*) And now you've got your old face back. It was just for a minute, right at first — Though you are a little more pale, Kristine. And maybe a little thinner.

MRS. LINDE: And much, much older, Nora.

NORA: Maybe a little older. Just a teeny-weeny bit, not much. (*Interrupts herself, serious.*) Oh, but how thoughtless of me, chatting away like this! Sweet, good Kristine, can you forgive me?

MRS. LINDE: Forgive you what, Nora?

NORA (*in a low voice*): You poor dear, you lost your husband, didn't you?

MRS. LINDE: Three years ago, yes.

NORA: I know. I saw it in the paper. Oh please believe me, Kristine. I really meant to write you, but I never got around to it. Something was always coming up.

MRS. LINDE: Of course, Nora. I understand.

NORA: No, that wasn't very nice of me. You poor thing, all you must have been through. And he didn't leave you much, either, did he?

MRS. LINDE: No.

NORA: And no children?

MRS. LINDE: No.

NORA: Nothing at all, in other words?

MRS. LINDE: Not so much as a sense of loss — a grief to live on —

NORA (*incredulous*): But Kristine, how can that *be*?

MRS. LINDE (*with a sad smile, strokes* NORA's *hair*): That's the way it sometimes is, Nora.

NORA: All alone. How awful for you. I have three darling children. You can't see them right now, though; they're out with their nurse. But now you must tell me everything —

MRS. LINDE: No, no; I'd rather listen to you.

NORA: No, you begin. Today I won't be self-ish. Today I'll think only of you. Except there's one thing I've just got to tell you first. Something marvelous that's happened to us just these last few days. You haven't heard, have you?

MRS. LINDE: No; tell me.

NORA: Just think. My husband's been made manager of the Mutual Bank.

MRS. LINDE: Your husband — ! Oh, I'm so glad!

NORA: Yes, isn't that great? You see, private law practice is so uncertain, especially when you won't have anything to do with cases that aren't — you know — quite nice. And of course Torvald won't do that, and I quite agree with him. Oh, you've no idea how delighted we are! He takes over at New Year's, and he'll be get-ting a big salary and all sorts of extras. From now on we'll be able to live in quite a different way — exactly as we like. Oh, Kristine! I feel so carefree and happy! It's lovely to have lots and lots of money and not have to worry about a thing! Don't you agree?

MRS. LINDE: It would be nice to have enough, at any rate.

NORA: No, I don't mean just enough. I mean lots and lots!

MRS. LINDE (*smiles*): Nora, Nora, when are you going to be sensible? In school you spent a great deal of money.

NORA (*quietly laughing*): Yes, and Torvald says I still do. (*Raises her finger at* MRS. LINDE.) But "Nora, Nora" isn't so crazy as you all think. Believe me, we've had nothing to be ex-travagant with. We've both had to work.

MRS. LINDE: You too?

NORA: Yes. Oh, It's been little things mostly — sewing, crocheting, embroidery — that sort of thing. (*Casually.*) And other things too. You know, of course, that Torvald left government service when we got married? There was no chance of promotion in his department, and of course he had to make more money than he had been making. So for the first few years he worked altogether too hard. He took jobs on the side and worked day and night. It turned out to be too much for him. He became seri-ously ill. The doctors told him he needed to go south.

MRS. LINDE: That's right; you spent a year in Italy, didn't you?

NORA: Yes, we did. But you won't believe how hard it was to get away. Ivar had just been born. But of course we had to go. Oh, it was a wonderful trip. And it saved Torvald's life. But it took a lot of money, Kristine.

MRS. LINDE: I'm sure it did.

NORA: Twelve hundred dollars of the old money.[1] Four thousand eight hundred crowns. That's a lot.

MRS. LINDE: Yes. So it's lucky you have it when something like that happens.

NORA: Well, actually we got the money from Daddy.

MRS. LINDE: I see. That was about the time your father died, I believe.

NORA: Yes, just about then. And I couldn't even go and take care of him. I was expecting little Ivar any day. And I had poor Torvald to look after, desperately sick and all. My dear, good Daddy! I never saw him again, Kristine. That's the saddest thing that's happened to me since I got married.

MRS. LINDE: I know you were very fond of him. But then you went to Italy?

NORA: Yes, for now we had the money, and the doctors urged us to go. So we left about a month later.

MRS. LINDE: And when you came back your husband was well again?

NORA: Healthy as a horse!

MRS. LINDE: But — the doctor?

NORA: What do you mean?

MRS. LINDE: I thought the maid said it was the doctor, that gentleman who came the same time I did.

NORA: Oh, that's Doctor Rank. He doesn't come as a doctor. He's our closest friend. He looks in at least once every day. No, Torvald hasn't been sick once since then. And the chil-dren are strong and healthy, too, and so am I. (*Jumps up and claps her hands.*) Oh god, Kris-tine! Isn't it wonderful to be alive and happy! Isn't it just lovely! — But now I'm being mean again, talking only about myself and my things.

[1] In 1875 Norway joined the international mone-tary union based on the gold standard. The monetary unit changed from the old silver specie dollar (*Daler*) to the crown (*Krone*), redeemable in gold. As Nora's remark implies, there were four crowns to a dollar.

(*Sits down on a footstool close to* MRS. LINDE *and puts her arms on her lap.*) Please, don't be angry with me! Tell me, is it really true that you didn't care for your husband? Then why did you marry him?

MRS. LINDE: Mother was still alive, but she was bedridden and helpless. And I had my two younger brothers to look after. I didn't think I had the right to turn him down.

NORA: No, I suppose. So he had money then?

MRS. LINDE: He was quite well off, I think. But it was an uncertain business, Nora. When he died, the whole thing collapsed and there was nothing left.

NORA: And then — ?

MRS. LINDE: Well, I had to manage as best I could. With a little store and a little school and anything else I could think of. The last three years have been one long work day for me, Nora, without any rest. But now it's over. My poor mother doesn't need me any more. She passed away. And the boys are on their own too. They've both got jobs and support themselves.

NORA: What a relief for you —

MRS. LINDE: No, not relief. Just a great emptiness. Nobody to live for any more. (*Gets up, restlessly.*) That's why I couldn't stand it any longer in that little hole. It's got to be easier to find something to keep me busy and occupy my thoughts here in town. With a little luck I should be able to find a good, steady job — something in an office —

NORA: Oh but Kristine, that's exhausting work, and you look worn out already. It would be much better if you went to a resort.

MRS. LINDE (*Walks over to the window*): I don't have a Daddy who can give me the money, Nora.

NORA (*getting up*): Oh, don't be angry with me.

MRS. LINDE (*over to her*): Dear Nora, don't *you* be angry with *me*. That's the worst thing about my kind of situation: you become so bitter. You've nobody to work for, and yet you have to look out for yourself, somehow. You got to keep on living, and so you become selfish. Do you know — when you told me about your husband's new position I was delighted not so much for your sake as for my own.

NORA: Why was that? Oh, I see. You think maybe Torvald can give you a job?

MRS. LINDE: That's what I had in mind.

NORA: And he will too, Kristine. Just leave it to me. I'll be ever so subtle about it. I'll think of something nice to tell him, something he'll like. I so much want to help you.

MRS. LINDE: That's very good of you, Nora — making an effort like that for me. Especially since you've known so little trouble and hardship in your own life.

NORA: I — have known so little — ?

MRS. LINDE (*smiling*): Oh well, some sewing or whatever it was. You're still a child, Nora.

NORA (*with a toss of her head, walks away*): You shouldn't sound so superior.

MRS. LINDE: I shouldn't?

NORA: You're just like all the others. None of you think I'm good for anything really serious.

MRS. LINDE: Well, now —

NORA: That I've never been through anything difficult.

MRS. LINDE: But Nora! You just told me all your troubles!

NORA: That's nothing! (*Lowers her voice.*) I haven't told you about *it*.

MRS. LINDE: It? What's that? What do you mean?

NORA: You patronize me, Kristine, and that's not fair. You're proud that you worked so long and so hard for your mother.

MRS. LINDE: I don't think I patronize anyone. But it *is* true that I'm both proud and happy that I could make mother's last years comparatively easy.

NORA: And you're proud of all you did for your brothers.

MRS. LINDE: I think I have the right to be.

NORA: And so do I. But now I want to tell you something, Kristine. I have something to be proud and happy about too.

MRS. LINDE: I don't doubt that for a moment. But what exactly do you mean?

NORA: Not so loud! Torvald mustn't hear — not for anything in the world. Nobody must know about this, Kristine. Nobody but you.

MRS. LINDE: But what is it?

NORA: Come here. (*Pulls her down on the couch beside her.*) You see, I *do* have something to be proud and happy about. I've saved Torvald's life.

MRS. LINDE: Saved — ? How do you mean — "saved"?

NORA: I told you about our trip to Italy. Torvald would have died if he hadn't gone.

MRS. LINDE: I understand that. And so your father gave you the money you needed.

NORA (*smiles*): Yes, that's what Torvald and all the others think. But —

MRS. LINDE: But what?

NORA: Daddy didn't give us a penny. *I* raised that money.

MRS. LINDE: *You* did? That whole big amount?

NORA: Twelve hundred dollars. Four thousand eight hundred crowns. *Now* what do you say?

MRS. LINDE: But Nora, how could you? Did you win the state lottery?

NORA (*contemptuously*): State lottery! (*Snorts.*) What would be so great about that?

MRS. LINDE: Where did it come from then?

NORA (*humming and smiling, enjoying her secret*): Hmmm. Tra-la-la-la-la!

MRS. LINDE: You certainly couldn't have borrowed it.

NORA: Oh? And why not?

MRS. LINDE: A wife can't borrow money without her husband's consent.

NORA (*with a toss of her head*): Oh, I don't know — take a wife with a little bit of a head for business — a wife who knows how to manage things —

MRS. LINDE: But Nora, I don't understand at all —

NORA: You don't have to. I didn't say I borrowed the money, did I? I could have gotten it some other way. (*Leans back.*) An admirer may have given it to me. When you're as tolerably goodlooking as I am —

MRS. LINDE: Oh, you're crazy.

NORA: I think you're dying from curiosity, Kristine.

MRS. LINDE: I'm beginning to think you've done something very foolish, Nora.

NORA (*sits up*): Is it foolish to save your husband's life?

MRS. LINDE: I say it's foolish to act behind his back.

NORA: But don't you see: he couldn't be told! You're missing the whole point, Kristine. We couldn't even let him know how seriously ill he was. The doctors came to *me* and told me his life was in danger, that nothing could save him but a stay in the south. Don't you think I tried to work on him? I told him how lovely it would be if I could go abroad like other young wives. I cried and I begged. I said he'd better remember what condition I was in, that he had to be nice to me and do what I wanted. I even hinted he could borrow the money. But that almost made him angry with me. He told me I was being irresponsible and that it was his duty as my husband not to give in to my whims and moods — I think that's what he called it. All right, I said to myself, you've got to be saved somehow, and so I found a way —

MRS. LINDE: And your husband never learned from your father that the money didn't come from him?

NORA: Never. Daddy died that same week. I thought of telling him all about it and asking him not to say anything. But since he was so sick — It turned out I didn't have to —

MRS. LINDE: And you've never told your husband?

NORA: Of course not! Good heavens, how could I? He, with his strict principles! Besides, you know how men are. Torvald would find it embarrassing and humiliating to learn that he owed me anything. It would upset our whole relationship. Our happy, beautiful home would no longer be what it is.

MRS. LINDE: Aren't you ever going to tell him?

NORA (*reflectively, half smiling*): Yes — one day, maybe. Many, many years from now, when I'm no longer young and pretty. Don't laugh! I mean when Torvald no longer feels about me the way he does now, when he no longer thinks it's fun when I dance for him and put on costumes and recite for him. Then it will be good to have something in reserve — (*Interrupts herself.*) Oh, I'm just being silly! That day will never come. — Well, now, Kristine, what do you say about my great secret? Don't you think I'm good for something too? — By the way, you wouldn't believe all the worry I've had because of it. It's been very hard to meet my obligations on schedule. You see, in business there's something called quarterly interest and something called installments on the principal, and those things are terribly hard to come up with. I've had to save a little here and a little there, whenever I could. I couldn't use much of the housekeeping money, for Torvald has to eat well. And I couldn't use what I got for clothes for the children. They have to look nice, and I didn't think it would be right to spend less than I got — the sweet little things!

MRS. LINDE: Poor Nora! So you had to take it from your own allowance?

NORA: Yes, of course. After all, it was my affair. Every time Torvald gave me money for a new dress or what have you, I never used more than half of it. I always bought the cheapest, simplest things for myself. Thank god, everything looks good on me, so Torvald never noticed. But it was hard many times, Kristine, for it's fun to have pretty clothes. Don't you think?

MRS. LINDE: Certainly.

NORA: Anyway, I had other ways of making money too. Last winter I was lucky enough to get some copying work. So I locked the door and sat up writing every night till quite late. God! I often got so tired — ! But it was great fun, too, working and making money. It was almost like being a man.

MRS. LINDE: But how much have you been able to pay off this way?

NORA: I couldn't tell you exactly. You see, it's very difficult to keep track of that kind of business. All I know is I have been paying off as much as I've been able to scrape together. Many times I just didn't know what to do. (*Smiles.*) Then I used to imagine a rich old gentleman had fallen in love with me —

MRS. LINDE: What! What old gentleman?

NORA: Phooey! And now he was dead and they were reading his will, and there it said in big letters, "All my money is to be paid in cash immediately to the charming Mrs. Nora Helmer."

MRS. LINDE: But dearest Nora — who *was* this old gentleman?

NORA: For heaven's sake, Kristine, don't you see! There *was* no old gentleman. He was just somebody I made up when I couldn't think of any way to raise the money. But never mind him. The old bore can be anyone he likes to for all I care. I have no use for him or his last will, for now I don't have a single worry in the world. (*Jumps up.*) Dear god, what a lovely thought that is! To be able to play and have fun with the children, to have everything nice and pretty in the house, just the way Torvald likes it! Not a care! And soon spring will be here, and the air will be blue and high. Maybe we can travel again. Maybe I'll see the ocean again! Oh, yes, yes! — it's wonderful to be alive and happy!

(*The doorbell rings.*)

MRS. LINDE (*getting up*): There's the doorbell. Maybe I better be going.

NORA: No, please stay. I'm sure it's just someone for Torvald —

MAID (*in the hall door*): Excuse me, ma'am.

There's a gentleman here who'd like to see Mr. Helmer.

NORA: You mean the Bank Manager.

MAID: Sorry, ma'am; the Bank Manager. But I didn't know — since the Doctor is with him —

NORA: Who is the gentleman?

KROGSTAD (*appearing in the door*): It's just me, Mrs. Helmer.

(MRS. LINDE *starts, looks, turns away toward the window.*)

NORA (*takes a step toward him, tense, in a low voice*): You? What do you want? What do you want with my husband?

KROGSTAD: Bank business — in a way. I have a small job in the Mutual, and I understand your husband is going to be our new manager —

NORA: So it's just — ?

KROGSTAD: Just routine business, ma'am. Nothing else.

NORA: All right. In that case, why don't you go through the door to the office. (*Dismisses him casually as she closes the door. Walks over to the stove and tends the fire.*)

MRS. LINDE: Nora — who was that man?

NORA: His name's Krogstad. He's a lawyer.

MRS. LINDE: So it *was* him.

NORA: Do you know him?

MRS. LINDE: I used to — many years ago. For a while he worked as a clerk in our part of the country.

NORA: Right. He did.

MRS. LINDE: He has changed a great deal.

NORA: I believe he had a very unhappy marriage.

MRS. LINDE: And now he's a widower, isn't he?

NORA: With many children. There now; it's burning nicely again. (*Closes the stove and moves the rocking chair a little to the side.*)

MRS. LINDE: They say he's into all sorts of business.

NORA: Really? Maybe so. I wouldn't know. But let's not talk about business. It's such a bore.

RANK (*appears in the door to* HELMER'S *study*): No, I don't want to be in the way. I'd rather talk to your wife a bit. (*Closes the door and notices* MRS. LINDE.) Oh, I beg your pardon. I believe I'm in the way here too.

NORA: No, not at all. (*Introduces them.*) Doctor Rank. Mrs. Linde.

RANK: Aha. A name often heard in this house. I believe I passed you on the stairs coming up.

MRS. LINDE: Yes. I'm afraid I climb stairs very slowly. They aren't good for me.

RANK: I see. A slight case of inner decay, perhaps?

MRS. LINDE: Overwork, rather.

RANK: Oh, is that all? And now you've come to town to relax at all the parties?

MRS. LINDE: I have come to look for a job.

RANK: A proven cure for overwork, I take it?

MRS. LINDE: One has to live, Doctor.

RANK: Yes, that seems to be the general opinion.

NORA: Come on, Doctor Rank — you want to live just as much as the rest of us.

RANK: Of course I do. Miserable as I am, I prefer to go on being tortured as long as possible. All my patients feel the same way. And that's true of the moral invalids too. Helmer is talking with a specimen right this minute.

MRS. LINDE (*in a low voice*): Ah!

NORA: What do you mean?

RANK: Oh, this lawyer, Krogstad. You don't know him. The roots of his character are decayed. But even he began by saying something about having *to live* — as if it were a matter of the highest importance.

NORA: Oh? What did he want with Torvald?

RANK: I don't really know. All I heard was something about the bank.

NORA: I didn't know that Krog — that this Krogstad had anything to do with the Mutual Bank.

RANK: Yes, he seems to have some kind of job there. (*To* MRS. LINDE.) I don't know if you are familiar in your part of the country with the kind of person who is always running around trying to sniff out cases of moral decrepitude and as soon as he finds one puts the individual under observation in some excellent position or other. All the healthy ones are left out in the cold.

MRS. LINDE: I should think it's the sick who need looking after the most.

RANK (*shrugs his shoulders*): There we are. That's the attitude that turns society into a hospital.

(NORA, *absorbed in her own thoughts suddenly starts giggling and clapping her hands.*)

RANK: What's so funny about that? Do you even know what society is?

NORA: What do I care about your stupid society! I laughed at something entirely different — something terribly amusing. Tell me, Doctor Rank — all the employees in the Mutual Bank, from now on they'll all be dependent on Torvald, right?

RANK: Is that what you find so enormously amusing?

NORA (*smiles and hums*): That's my business, that's my business! (*Walks around.*) Yes, I do think it's fun that we — that Torvald is going to have so much influence on so many people's lives. (*Brings out the bag of macaroons.*) Have a macaroon, Doctor Rank.

RANK: Well, well — macaroons. I thought they were banned around here.

NORA: Yes, but these were some that Kristine gave me.

MRS. LINDE: What! I?

NORA: That's all right. Don't look so scared. You couldn't know that Torvald won't let me have macaroons. He's afraid they'll ruin my teeth. But who cares! Just once in a while — ! Right, Doctor Rank? Have one! (*Puts a macaroon into his mouth.*) You too, Kristine. And one for me. A very small one. Or at most two. (*Walks around again.*) Yes, I really feel very, very happy. Now there's just one thing I'm dying to do.

RANK: Oh? And what's that?

NORA: Something I want to say so Torvald could hear.

RANK: And why can't you?

NORA: I don't dare to, for it's not nice.

MRS. LINDE: Not nice?

RANK: In that case, I guess you'd better not. But surely to the two of us — ? What is it you'd like to say to Helmer?

NORA: I want to say, "goddammit!"

RANK: Are you out of your mind!

MRS. LINDE: For heaven's sake, Nora!

RANK: Say it. Here he comes.

NORA (*hiding the macaroons*): Shhh!

(HELMER *enters from his study, carrying his hat and overcoat.*)

NORA (*going to him*): Well, dear, did you get rid of him?

HELMER: Yes, he just left.

NORA: Torvald, I want you to meet Kristine. She's just come to town.

HELMER: Kristine — ? I'm sorry; I don't think —

NORA: Mrs. Linde, Torvald dear. Mrs. Kristine Linde.

HELMER: Ah, yes. A childhood friend of my wife's, I suppose.

MRS. LINDE: Yes, we've known each other for a long time.

NORA: Just think; she has come all this way just to see you.

HELMER: I'm not sure I understand —

MRS. LINDE: Well, not really —

NORA: You see, Kristine is an absolutely fantastic secretary, and she would so much like to work for a competent executive and learn more than she knows already —

HELMER: Very sensible, I'm sure, Mrs. Linde.

NORA: So when she heard about your appointment — they got a wire about it — she came here as fast as she could. How about it, Torvald? Couldn't you do something for Kristine? For my sake? Please?

HELMER: Quite possibly. I take it you're a widow, Mrs. Linde?

MRS. LINDE: Yes.

HELMER: And you've had office experience?

MRS. LINDE: Some — yes.

HELMER: In that case I think it's quite likely that I'll be able to find you a position.

NORA (claps her hands): I knew it! I knew it!

HELMER: You've arrived at a most opportune time, Mrs. Linde.

MRS. LINDE: Oh, how can I ever thank you —

HELMER: Not at all, not at all. (Puts his coat on.) But today you'll have to excuse me —

RANK: Wait a minute; I'll come with you. (Gets his fur coat from the front hall, warms it by the stove.)

NORA: Don't be long, Torvald.

HELMER: An hour or so, no more.

NORA: Are you leaving, too, Kristine?

MRS. LINDE (putting on her things): Yes, I better go and find a place to stay.

HELMER: Good. Then we'll be going the same way.

NORA (helping her): I'm sorry this place is so small, but I don't think we very well could —

MRS. LINDE: Of course! Don't be silly, Nora. Goodbye, and thank you for everything.

NORA: Goodbye. We'll see you soon. You'll be back this evening, of course. And you too, Doctor Rank; right? If you feel well enough? Of course you will. Just wrap yourself up.

(General small talk as all exit into the hall. Children's voices are heard on the stairs.)

NORA: There they are! There they are! (She runs and opens the door. THE NURSE ANNE-MARIE enters with the children.) Come in! Come in! (Bends over and kisses them.) Oh, you sweet, sweet darlings! Look at them, Kristine! Aren't they beautiful?

RANK: No standing around in the draft!

HELMER: Come along, Mrs. Linde. This place isn't fit for anyone but mothers right now.

(DOCTOR RANK, HELMER, and MRS. LINDE go down the stairs. The NURSE enters the living room with the CHILDREN. NORA follows, closing the door behind her.)

NORA: My, how nice you all look! Such red cheeks! Like apples and roses. (The children all talk at the same time.) You've had so much fun? I bet you have. Oh, isn't that nice! You pulled both Emmy and Bob on your sleigh? Both at the same time? That's very good, Ivar. Oh, let me hold her for a minute, Anne-Marie. My sweet little doll baby! (Takes the smallest of the children from the NURSE and dances with her.) Yes, yes, of course; Mama'll dance with you too, Bob. What? You threw snowballs? Oh, I wish I'd been there! No, no; I want to take their clothes off, Anne-Marie. Please let me; I think it's so much fun. You go on in. You look frozen. There's hot coffee on the stove.

(The NURSE exits into the room to the left. NORA takes the children's wraps off and throws them all around. They all keep telling her things at the same time.)

NORA: Oh, really? A big dog ran after you? But it didn't bite you? Of course not. Dogs don't bite sweet little doll babies. Don't peek at the packages, Ivar! What's in them? Wouldn't you like to know! No, no; that's something terrible! Play? You want to play? What do you want to play? Okay, let's play hide-and-seek. Bob hides first. You want me to? All right. I'll go first.

(Laughing and shouting, NORA and the children play in the living room and in the adjacent room, right. Finally, NORA hides herself under the table; the children rush in, look for her, can't find her. They hear her *low giggle, run to the table, lift the rug that covers it, see her. General hilarity. She crawls out, pretends to scare them. New delight. In the meantime there has been a knock on the door between the living room and the front hall, but nobody has noticed. Now the door is opened halfway;* KROGSTAD *appears. He waits a little. The playing goes on.*)

KROGSTAD: Pardon me, Mrs. Helmer —

NORA (*with a muted cry turns around, jumps up*): Ah! What do you want?

KROGSTAD: I'm sorry. The front door was open. Somebody must have forgotten to close it —

NORA (*standing up*): My husband isn't here, Mr. Krogstad.

KROGSTAD: I know.

NORA: So what do you want?

KROGSTAD: I'd like a word with you.

NORA: With — ! (*To the children in a low voice.*) Go in to Anne-Marie. What? No, the strange man won't do anything bad to mama. When he's gone we'll play some more. (*She takes the children into the room to the left and closes the door.*)

NORA (*tense, troubled*): You want to speak with me?

KROGSTAD: Yes I do.

NORA: Today — ? It isn't the first of the month yet.

KROGSTAD: No, it's Christmas Eve. It's up to you what kind of holiday you'll have.

NORA: What do you want? I can't possibly —

KROGSTAD: Let's not talk about that just yet. There's something else. You do have a few minutes, don't you?

NORA: Yes. Yes, of course. That is —

KROGSTAD: Good. I was sitting in Olsen's restaurant when I saw your husband go by.

NORA: Yes — ?

KROGSTAD: — with a lady.

NORA: What of it?

KROGSTAD: May I be so free as to ask: wasn't that lady Mrs. Linde?

NORA: Yes.

KROGSTAD: Just arrived in town?

NORA: Yes, today.

KROGSTAD: She's a good friend of yours, I understand?

NORA: Yes, she is. But I fail to see —

KROGSTAD: I used to know her myself.

NORA: I know that.

KROGSTAD: So you know that. I thought as

much. In that case, let me ask you a simple question. Is Mrs. Linde going to be employed in the bank?

NORA: What makes you think you have the right to cross examine me like this, Mr. Krogstad — you, one of my husband's employees? But since you ask, I'll tell you. Yes, Mrs. Linde is going to be working in the bank. And it was I who recommended her, Mr. Krogstad. Now you know.

KROGSTAD: So I was right.

NORA (*walks up and down*): After all, one does have a little influence, you know. Just because you're a woman, it doesn't mean that — Really, Mr. Krogstad, people in a subordinate position should be careful not to offend someone who — oh well —

KROGSTAD: — has influence?

NORA: Exactly.

KROGSTAD (*changing his tone*): Mrs. Helmer, I must ask you to be good enough to use your influence on my behalf.

NORA: Oh? What do you mean?

KROGSTAD: I want you to make sure that I am going to keep my subordinate position in the bank.

NORA: I don't understand. Who is going to take your position away from you?

KROGSTAD: There's no point in playing ignorant with me, Mrs. Helmer. I can very well appreciate that your friend would find it unpleasant to run into me. So now I know who I can thank for my dismissal.

NORA: But I assure you —

KROGSTAD: Never mind. I just want to say you still have time. I advise you to use your influence to prevent it.

NORA: But Mr. Krogstad, I don't have any influence — none at all.

KROGSTAD: No? I thought you just said —

NORA: Of course I didn't mean it that way. I! Whatever makes you think that I have any influence of that kind on my husband?

KROGSTAD: I went to law school with your husband. I have no reason to think that the Bank Manager is less susceptible than other husbands.

NORA: If you're going to insult my husband, I'll have to ask you to leave.

KROGSTAD: You're brave, Mrs. Helmer.

NORA: I'm not afraid of you any more. After New Year's I'll be out of this thing with you.

KROGSTAD (*more controlled*): Listen, Mrs.

Helmer. If necessary, I'll fight as for my life to keep my little job in the bank.

NORA: So it seems.

KROGSTAD: It isn't just the money; that's really the smallest part of it. There is something else — Well, I guess I might as well tell you. It's like this. I'm sure you know, like everybody else, that some years ago I committed — an impropriety.

NORA: I believe I've heard it mentioned.

KROGSTAD: The case never came to trial, but from that moment all doors were closed to me. So I took up the kind of business you know about. I had to do something, and I think I can say about myself that I have not been among the worst. But now I want to get out of all that. My sons are growing up. For their sake I must get back as much of my good name as I can. This job in the bank was like the first rung on the ladder. And now your husband wants to kick me down and leave me back in the mud again.

NORA: But I swear to you, Mr. Krogstad; it's not at all in my power to help you.

KROGSTAD: That's because you don't want to. But I have the means to force you.

NORA: You don't mean you're going to tell my husband I owe you money?

KROGSTAD: And if I did?

NORA: That would be a mean thing to do. (*Almost crying.*) That secret, which is my joy and my pride — for him to learn about it in such a coarse and ugly way — to learn it from *you* — ! It would be terribly unpleasant for me.

KROGSTAD: Just unpleasant?

NORA (*heatedly*): But go ahead! Do it! It will be worse for you than for me. When my husband realizes what a bad person you are, you're certainly going to lose your job.

KROGSTAD: I asked you if it was just domestic unpleasantness you were afraid of?

NORA: When my husband finds out, of course he'll pay off the loan, and then we won't have anything more to do with you.

KROGSTAD (*stepping closer*): Listen, Mrs. Helmer — either you have a very bad memory, or you don't know much about business. I think I had better straighten you out on a few things.

NORA: What do you mean?

KROGSTAD: When your husband was ill, you came to me to borrow twelve hundred dollars.

NORA: I knew nobody else.

KROGSTAD: I promised to get you the money —

NORA: And you did.

KROGSTAD: — I promised to get you the money on certain conditions. At the time you were so anxious about your husband's health and so set on getting him away that I doubt very much that you paid much attention to the details of our transaction. That's why I remind you of them now. Anyway, I promised to get you the money if you would sign an I.O.U., which I drafted.

NORA: And which I signed.

KROGSTAD: Good. But below your signature I added a few lines, making your father security for the loan. Your father was supposed to put his signature to those lines.

NORA: Supposed to — ? He did.

KROGSTAD: I had left the date blank. That is, your father was to date his own signature. You recall that, don't you, Mrs. Helmer?

NORA: I guess so —

KROGSTAD: I gave the note to you. You were to mail it to your father. Am I correct?

NORA: Yes.

KROGSTAD: And of course you did so right away, for no more than five or six days later you brought the paper back to me, signed by your father. Then I paid you the money.

NORA: Well? And haven't I been keeping up with the payments?

KROGSTAD: Fairly well, yes. But to get back to what we were talking about — those were difficult days for you, weren't they, Mrs. Helmer?

NORA: Yes, they were.

KROGSTAD: Your father was quite ill, I believe.

NORA: He was dying.

KROGSTAD: And died shortly afterwards?

NORA: That's right.

KROGSTAD: Tell me, Mrs. Helmer; do you happen to remember the date of your father's death? I mean the exact day of the month?

NORA: Daddy died on September 29.

KROGSTAD: Quite correct. I have ascertained that fact. That's why there is something peculiar about this (*takes out a piece of paper*), which I can't account for.

NORA: Peculiar? How? I don't understand —

KROGSTAD: It seems very peculiar, Mrs. Helmer, that your father signed this promissory note three days after his death.

NORA: How so? I don't see what —

KROGSTAD: Your father died on September 29. Now look. He has dated his signature October 2. Isn't that odd?

(NORA *remains silent*)

KROGSTAD: Can you explain it?

(NORA *still silent*)

KROGSTAD: I also find it striking that the date and the month and the year are not in your father's handwriting but in a hand I think I recognize. Well, that might be explained. Your father may have forgotten to date his signature and somebody else may have done it here, guessing at the date before he had learned of your father's death. That's all right. It's only the signature itself that matters. And that is genuine, isn't it, Mrs. Helmer? Your father *did* put his name to this note?

NORA (*after a brief silence tosses her head back and looks defiantly at him*): No, he didn't. I wrote Daddy's name.

KROGSTAD: Mrs. Helmer — do you realize what a dangerous admission you just made?

NORA: Why? You'll get your money soon.

KROGSTAD: Let me ask you something. Why didn't you mail this note to your father?

NORA: Because it was impossible. Daddy was sick — you know that. If I had asked him for his signature I would have had to tell him what the money was for. But I couldn't tell him, as sick as he was, that my husband's life was in danger. That was impossible. Surely you can see that.

KROGSTAD: Then it would have been better for you if you had given up your trip abroad.

NORA: No, that was impossible! That trip was to save my husband's life. I couldn't give it up.

KROGSTAD: But didn't you realize that what you did amounted to fraud against me?

NORA: I couldn't let that make any difference. I didn't care about you at all. I hated the way you made all those difficulties for me, even though you knew the danger my husband was in. I thought you were cold and unfeeling.

KROGSTAD: Mrs. Helmer, obviously you have no clear idea of what you have done. Let me tell you that what I did that time was no more and no worse. And it ruined my name and reputation.

NORA: You! Are you trying to tell me that you did something brave once in order to save your wife's life?

KROGSTAD: The law doesn't ask about motives.

NORA: Then it's a bad law.

KROGSTAD: Bad or not — if I produce this note in court you'll be judged according to the law.

NORA: I refuse to believe you. A daughter shouldn't have the right to spare her dying old father worry and anxiety? A wife shouldn't have the right to save her husband's life? I don't know the laws very well, but I'm sure that somewhere they make allowance for cases like that. And you, a lawyer, don't know that? I think you must be a bad lawyer, Mr. Krogstad.

KROGSTAD: That may be. But business — the kind of business you and I have with one another — don't you think I know something about that? Very well. Do what you like. But let me tell you this: if I'm going to be kicked out again, you'll keep me company. (*He bows and exits through the front hall.*)

NORA (*pauses thoughtfully; then, with a defiant toss of her head*): Oh, nonsense! Trying to scare me like that! I'm not all that silly. (*Starts picking up the children's clothes; soon stops.*) But — ? No! That's impossible! I did it for love!

THE CHILDREN (*in the door to the left*): Mama, the strange man just left. We saw him.

NORA: Yes, yes; I know. But don't tell anybody about the strange man. Do you hear? Not even Daddy.

THE CHILDREN: We won't. But now you'll play with us again, won't you, mama?

NORA: No, not right now.

THE CHILDREN: Oh, but mama — you promised.

NORA: I know, but I can't just now. Go to your own room. I've so much to do. Be nice now, my little darlings. Do as I say. (*She nudges them gently into the other room and closes the door. She sits down on the couch, picks up a piece of embroidery, makes a few stitches, then stops.*) No! (*Throws the embroidery down, goes to the hall door and calls out:*) Helene! Bring the Christmas tree in here, please! (*Goes to the table, left, opens the drawer, halts.*) No — that's impossible!

MAID (*with the Christmas tree*): Where do you want it, ma'am?

NORA: There. The middle of the floor.

MAID: You want anything else?

NORA: No, thanks. I have everything I need. (*The* MAID *goes out.* NORA *starts trimming the tree.*) I want candles — and flowers — That awful man! Oh, nonsense! There's nothing wrong. This will be a lovely tree. I'll do everything you want me to, Torvald. I'll sing for you — dance for you —

(HELMER, *a bundle of papers under his arm, enters from outside.*)

NORA: Ah — you're back already?

HELMER: Yes. Has anybody been here?

NORA: Here? No.

HELMER: That's funny. I saw Krogstad leaving just now.

NORA: Oh? Oh yes, that's right. Krogstad was here for just a moment.

HELMER: I can tell from your face that he came to ask you to put in a word for him.

NORA: Yes.

HELMER: And it was supposed to be your own idea, wasn't it? You were not to tell me he'd been here. He asked you that too, didn't he?

NORA: Yes, Torvald, but —

HELMER: Nora, Nora, how could you! Talking to a man like that and making him promises! And lying to me about it afterwards — !

NORA: Lying — ?

HELMER: Didn't you say nobody had been here? (*Shakes his finger at her.*) My little songbird must never do that again. Songbirds are supposed to have clean beaks to chirp with — no false notes. (*Puts his arm around her waist.*) Isn't that so? Of course it is. (*Lets her go.*) And that's enough about that. (*Sits down in front of the fireplace.*) Ah, it's nice and warm in here. (*Begins to leaf through his papers.*)

NORA (*busy with the tree. After a brief pause*): Torvald.

HELMER: Yes.

NORA: I'm looking forward so much to the Stenborgs' costume party day after tomorrow.

HELMER: And I can't wait to find out what you're going to surprise me with.

NORA: Oh, that silly idea!

HELMER: Oh?

NORA: I can't think of anything. It all seems so foolish and pointless.

HELMER: Ah, my little Nora admits that?

NORA (*behind his chair, her arms on the back of the chair*): Are you very busy, Torvald?

HELMER: Well —

NORA: What are all those papers?

HELMER: Bank business.

NORA: Already?

HELMER: I've asked the board to give me the authority to make certain changes in organization and personnel. That's what I'll be doing over the holidays. I want it all settled before New Year's.

NORA: So that's why this poor Krogstad —

HELMER: Hm.

NORA (*leisurely playing with the hair on his neck*): If you weren't so busy, Torvald, I'd ask you for a great, big favor.

HELMER: Let's hear it, anyway.

NORA: I don't know anyone with better taste than you, and I want so much to look nice at the party. Couldn't you sort of take charge of me, Torvald, and decide what I'll wear — help me with my costume?

HELMER: Aha! Little Lady Obstinate is looking for someone to rescue her?

NORA: Yes, Torvald. I won't get anywhere without your help.

HELMER: All right. I'll think about it. We'll come up with something.

NORA: Oh, you *are* nice! (*Goes back to the Christmas tree. A pause.*) Those red flowers look so pretty. — Tell me, was it really all that bad what this Krogstad fellow did?

HELMER: He forged signatures. Do you have any idea what that means?

NORA: Couldn't it have been because he felt he had to?

HELMER: Yes, or like so many others he may simply have been thoughtless. I'm not so heartless as to condemn a man absolutely because of a single imprudent act.

NORA: Of course not, Torvald!

HELMER: People like him can redeem themselves morally by openly confessing their crime and taking their punishment.

NORA: Punishment — ?

HELMER: But that was not the way Krogstad chose. He got out of it with tricks and evasions. That's what has corrupted him.

NORA: So you think that if — ?

HELMER: Can't you imagine how a guilty person like that has to lie and fake and dissemble wherever he goes — putting on a mask before everybody he's close to, even his own wife and children? It's this thing with the children that's the worst part of it, Nora.

NORA: Why is that?

HELMER: Because when a man lives inside such a circle of stinking lies he brings infection into his own home and contaminates his whole family. With every breath of air his children inhale the germs of something ugly.

NORA (*moving closer behind him*): Are you so sure of that?

HELMER: Of course I am. I have seen enough examples of that in my work. Nearly all young criminals have had mothers who lied.

NORA: Why mothers — particularly?

HELMER: Most often mothers. But of course fathers tend to have the same influence. Every lawyer knows that. And yet, for years this Krogstad has been poisoning his own children in an atmosphere of lies and deceit. That's why I call him a lost soul morally. (*Reaches out for her hands.*) And that's why my sweet little Nora must promise me never to take his side again. Let's shake on that. — What? What's this? Give me your hand! There! Now that's settled. I assure you, I would find it impossible to work in the same room with that man. I feel literally sick when I'm around people like that.

NORA (*withdraws her hand and goes to the other side of the Christmas tree*): It's so hot in here. And I have so much to do.

HELMER (*gets up and collects his papers*): Yes, and I really should try to get some of this reading done before dinner. I must think about your costume too. And maybe just possibly I'll have something to wrap in gilt paper and hang on the Christmas tree. (*Puts his hand on her head.*) Oh my adorable little songbird! (*Enters his study and closes the door.*)

NORA (*after a pause, in a low voice*): It's all a lot of nonsense. It's not that way at all. It's impossible. It has to be impossible.

NURSE (*in the door, left*): The little ones are asking ever so nicely if they can't come in and be with their mama.

NORA: No, no, no! Don't let them in here! You stay with them, Anne-Marie.

NURSE: If you say so, ma'am. (*Closes the door.*)

NORA (*pale with terror*): Corrupt my little children — ! Poison my home — ? (*Brief pause; she lifts her head.*) That's not true. Never. Never in a million years.

ACT II

The same room. The Christmas tree is in the corner by the piano, stripped, shabby-looking, with burnt-down candles. NORA's *outdoor clothes are on the couch.* NORA *is alone. She walks around restlessly. She stops by the couch and picks up her coat.*

NORA (*drops the coat again*): There's somebody now! (*Goes to the door, listens.*) No. Nobody. Of course not — not on Christmas. And not tomorrow either.[1] — But perhaps — (*Opens the door and looks.*) No, nothing in the mailbox. All empty. (*Comes forward.*) How silly I am! Of course he isn't serious. Nothing like that could happen. After all, I have three small children.

(*The* NURSE *enters from the room, left, carrying a big carton.*)

NURSE: Well, at last I found it — the box with your costume.

NORA: Thanks. Just put it on the table.

NURSE (*does so*): But it's all a big mess, I'm afraid.

NORA: Oh, I wish I could tear the whole thing to little pieces!

NURSE: Heavens! It's not as bad as all that. It can be fixed all right. All it takes is a little patience.

NORA: I'll go over and get Mrs. Linde to help me.

NURSE: Going out again? In this awful weather? You'll catch a cold.

NORA: That might not be such a bad thing. How are the children?

NURSE: The poor little dears are playing with their presents, but —

NORA: Do they keep asking for me?

NURSE: Well, you know, they're used to being with their mama.

NORA: I know. But Anne-Marie, from now on I can't be with them as much as before.

NURSE: Oh well. Little children get used to everything.

NORA: You think so? Do you think they'll forget their mama if I were gone altogether?

NURSE: Goodness me — gone altogether?

NORA: Listen, Anne-Marie; something I've often wondered about. How could you bring yourself to leave your child with strangers?

NURSE: But I had to, if I were to nurse you.

NORA: Yes, but how could you *want* to?

---

[1] In Norway both December 25 and 26 are legal holidays.

NURSE: When I could get such a nice place? When something like that happens to a poor young girl, she'd better be grateful for whatever she gets. For *he* didn't do a thing for me — the louse!

NORA: But your daughter has forgotten all about you, hasn't she?

NURSE: Oh no! Not at all! She wrote to me both when she was confirmed and when she got married.

NORA (*putting her arms around her neck*): You dear old thing — you were a good mother to me when I was little.

NURSE: Poor little Nora had no one else, you know.

NORA: And if my little ones didn't, I know you'd — oh, I'm being silly! (*Opens the carton.*) Go in to them, please. I really should — . Tomorrow you'll see how pretty I'll be.

NURSE: I know. There won't be anybody at that party half as pretty as you, ma'am. (*Goes out, left.*)

NORA (*begins to take clothes out of the carton. In a moment she throws it all down.*) If only I dared to go out. If only I knew nobody would come — that nothing would happen while I was gone. — How silly! Nobody'll come. Just don't think about it. Brush the muff. Beautiful gloves. Beautiful gloves. Forget it. Forget it. One, two, three, four, five, six — (*Cries out.*) There they are! (*Moves toward the door, stops irresolutely.*)

(MRS. LINDE *enters from the hall. She has already taken off her coat.*)

NORA: Oh, it's you, Kristine. There's no one else out there, is there? I'm so glad you're here.

MRS. LINDE: They told me you'd asked for me.

NORA: I just happened to walk by. I need your help with something — badly. Let's sit here on the couch. Look. Torvald and I are going to a costume party tomorrow night — at Consul Stenborg's upstairs — and Torvald wants me to go as a Neapolitan fisher girl and dance the Tarantella. I learned it when we were on Capri, don't you know.

MRS. LINDE: Well, well! So you'll be putting on a whole show?

NORA: Yes. Torvald thinks I should. Look, here's the costume. Torvald had it made for me while we were there. But it's all so torn and everything. I just don't know —

MRS. LINDE: Oh that can be fixed. It's not that much. The trimmings have come loose in a few places. Do you have needle and thread? Ah, here we are. All set.

NORA: I really appreciate it, Kristine.

MRS. LINDE (*sewing*): So you'll be in disguise tomorrow night, eh? You know — I may come by for just a moment, just to look at you. — Oh dear, I haven't even thanked you for the nice evening last night.

NORA (*gets up, moves around*): Oh I don't know. I don't think last night was as nice as it usually is. — You should have come to town a little earlier, Kristine. — Yes, Torvald knows how to make it nice and pretty around here.

MRS. LINDE: You too, I should think. After all, you're your father's daughter. By the way, is Dr. Rank always as depressed as he was last night?

NORA: No, last night was unusual. He's a very sick man, you know — very sick. Poor Rank, his spine is rotting away or something. Tuberculosis, I think. You see, his father was a nasty old man with mistresses and all that sort of thing. Rank has been sickly ever since he was a little boy.

MRS. LINDE (*dropping her sewing to her lap*): But dearest Nora, where have you learned about things like that?

NORA (*still walking about*): Oh, you know — with three children you sometimes get to talk with — other wives. Some of them know quite a bit about medicine. So you pick up a few things.

MRS. LINDE (*resumes her sewing. After a brief pause*): Does Dr. Rank come here every day?

NORA: Every single day. He's Torvald's oldest and best friend, after all. And my friend too, for that matter. He's part of the family, almost.

MRS. LINDE: But tell me, is he quite sincere? I mean, isn't he the kind of man who likes to say nice things to people?

NORA: No, not at all. Rather the opposite, in fact. What makes you say that?

MRS. LINDE: When you introduced us yesterday, he told me he'd often heard my name mentioned in this house. But later on it was quite obvious that your husband really had no idea who I was. So how could Dr. Rank — ?

NORA: You're right, Kristine, but I can explain that. You see, Torvald loves me so very much that he wants me all to himself. That's what he says. When we were first married he got jealous, almost, when I as much as mentioned anybody from back home that I was fond of. So of course I soon stopped doing that. But with Dr. Rank I often talk about home. You see, he likes to listen to me.

MRS. LINDE: Look here, Nora. In many ways you're still a child. After all, I'm quite a bit older than you and have had more experience. I want to give you a piece of advice. I think you should get out of this thing with Dr. Rank.

NORA: Get out of what thing?

MRS. LINDE: Several things in fact, if you want my opinion. Yesterday you said something about a rich admirer who was going to give you money —

NORA: One who doesn't exist, unfortunately. What of it?

MRS. LINDE: Does Dr. Rank have money?

NORA: Yes he does.

MRS. LINDE: And no dependents?

NORA: No. But — ?

MRS. LINDE: And he comes here every day?

NORA: Yes, I told you that already.

MRS. LINDE: But how can that sensitive man be so tactless?

NORA: I haven't the slightest idea what you're talking about.

MRS. LINDE: Don't play games with me, Nora. Don't you think I know who you borrowed the twelve hundred dollars from?

NORA: Are you out of your mind! The very idea — ! A friend of both of us who sees us every day — ! What a dreadfully uncomfortable position that would be!

MRS. LINDE: So it really isn't Dr. Rank?

NORA: Most certainly not! I would never have dreamed of asking him — not for a moment. Anyway, he didn't have any money then. He inherited it afterwards.

MRS. LINDE: Well, I still think that may have been lucky for you, Nora dear.

NORA: The idea! It would never have occurred to me to ask Dr. Rank — . Though I'm sure that if I did ask him —

MRS. LINDE: But of course you won't.

NORA: Of course not. I can't imagine that would ever be necessary. But I am quite sure that if I told Dr. Rank —

MRS. LINDE: Behind your husband's back?

NORA: I must get out of — this other thing. That's also behind his back. I *must* get out of it.

MRS. LINDE: That's what I told you yesterday. But —

NORA (*walking up and down*): A man man-

ages these things so much better than a woman —

MRS. LINDE: One's husband, yes.

NORA: Silly, silly! (*Stops.*) When you've paid off all you owe, you get your I.O.U. back; right?

MRS. LINDE: Yes, of course.

NORA: And you can tear it into a hundred thousand little pieces and burn it — that dirty, filthy paper!

MRS. LINDE (*looks hard at her, puts down her sewing, rises slowly*): Nora — you're hiding something from me.

NORA: Can you tell?

MRS. LINDE: Something's happened to you, Nora, since yesterday morning. What is it?

NORA (*going to her*): Kristine! (*Listens.*) Shhh. Torvald just came back. Listen. Why don't you go in to the children for a while. Torvald can't stand having sewing around. Get Anne-Marie to help you.

MRS. LINDE (*gathers some of the sewing things together*): All right, but I'm not leaving here till you and I have talked.

(*She goes out left, just as* HELMER *enters from the front hall.*)

NORA (*towards him*): I have been waiting and waiting for you, Torvald.

HELMER: Was that the dressmaker?

NORA: No, it was Kristine. She's helping me with my costume. Oh Torvald, just wait till you see how nice I'll look!

HELMER: I told you. Pretty good idea I had, wasn't it?

NORA: Lovely! Marvelous! And wasn't it nice of me to go along with it?

HELMER (*his hand under her chin*): Nice? To do what your husband tells you? All right, you little rascal; I know you didn't mean it that way. But don't let me interrupt you. I suppose you want to try it on.

NORA: And you'll be working?

HELMER: Yes. (*Shows her a pile of papers.*) Look. I've been down to the bank. (*Is about to enter his study.*)

NORA: Torvald.

HELMER (*halts*): Yes?

NORA: What if your little squirrel asked you ever so nicely —

HELMER: For what?

NORA: Would you do it?

HELMER: Depends on what it is.

NORA: Squirrel would run around and do all

sorts of fun tricks if you'd be nice and agreeable.

HELMER: All right. What is it?

NORA: Lark would chirp and twitter in all the rooms, up and down —

HELMER: So what? Lark does that anyway.

NORA: I'll be your elfmaid and dance for you in the moonlight, Torvald.

HELMER: Nora, don't tell me it's the same thing you mentioned this morning?

NORA (*closer to him*): Yes, Torvald. I beg you!

HELMER: You really have the nerve to bring that up again?

NORA: Yes. You've just got to do as I say. You *must* let Krogstad keep his job.

HELMER: My dear Nora. It's his job I intend to give to Mrs. Linde.

NORA: I know. And that's ever so nice of you. But can't you just fire somebody else?

HELMER: This is incredible! You just don't give up, do you? Because *you* make some foolish promise, *I* am supposed to — !

NORA: That's not the reason, Torvald. It's for your own sake. That man writes for the worst newspapers. You've said so yourself. There's no telling what he may do to you. I'm scared to death of him.

HELMER: Ah, I understand. You're afraid because of what happened before.

NORA: What do you mean?

HELMER: You're thinking of your father, of course.

NORA: Yes. Yes, you're right. Remember the awful things they wrote about Daddy in the newspapers? I really think they might have forced him to resign if the ministry hadn't sent you to look into the charges and if you hadn't been so helpful and understanding.

HELMER: My dear little Nora, there is a world of difference between your father and me. Your father's official conduct was not above reproach. Mine is, and I intend it to stay that way as long as I hold my position.

NORA: Oh, but you don't know what vicious people like him may think of. Oh, Torvald! Now all of us could be so happy together here in our own home, peaceful and carefree. Such a good life, Torvald, for you and me and the children! That's why I implore you —

HELMER: And it's exactly because you plead for him that you make it impossible for me to keep him. It's already common knowledge in the bank that I intend to let Krogstad go. If it gets out that the new manager has changed his mind because of his wife —

NORA: Yes? What then?

HELMER: No, of course, that wouldn't matter at all as long as little Mrs. Pighead here got her way! Do you want me to make myself look ridiculous before my whole staff — make people think I can be pushed around by just anybody — by outsiders? Believe me, I'd soon find out what the consequences would be! Besides, there's another thing that makes it absolutely impossible for Krogstad to stay on in the bank now that I'm in charge.

NORA: What's that?

HELMER: I suppose in a pinch I could overlook his moral shortcomings —

NORA: Yes, you could; couldn't you, Torvald?

HELMER: And I understand he's quite a good worker, too. But we've known each other for a long time. It's one of those imprudent relationships you get into when you're young that embarrass you for the rest of your life. I guess I might as well be frank with you: he and I are on a first name basis. And that tactless fellow never hides the fact even when other people are around. Rather, he seems to think it entitles him to be familiar with me. Every chance he gets he comes out with his damn "Torvald, Torvald." I'm telling you, I find it most awkward. He would make my position in the bank intolerable.

NORA: You don't really mean any of this, Torvald.

HELMER: Oh? I don't? And why not?

NORA: No, for it's all so petty.

HELMER: What! Petty? You think I'm being petty!

NORA: No, I *don't* think you are petty, Torvald dear. That's exactly why I —

HELMER: Never mind. You think my reasons are petty, so it follows that I must be petty too. Petty! Indeed! By god, I'll put an end to this right now! (*Opens the door to the front hall and calls out.*) Helene!

NORA: What are you doing?

HELMER (*searching among his papers*): Making a decision. (*The* MAID *enters.*) Here. Take this letter. Go out with it right away. Find somebody to deliver it. But quick. The address is on the envelope. Wait. Here's money.

MAID: Very good, sir. (*She takes the letter and goes out.*)

HELMER (*collecting his papers*): There now, little Mrs. Obstinate!

NORA (*breathless*): Torvald — what was that letter?

HELMER: Krogstad's dismissal.

NORA: Call it back, Torvald! There's still time! Oh Torvald, please — call it back! For my sake, for your own sake, for the sake of the children! Listen to me, Torvald! Do it! You don't know what you're doing to all of us!

HELMER: Too late.

NORA: Yes. Too late.

HELMER: Dear Nora, I forgive you this fear you're in, although it really is an insult to me. Yes, it is! It's an insult to think that I am scared of a shabby scrivener's revenge. But I forgive you, for it's such a beautiful proof how much you love me. (*Takes her in his arms.*) And that's the way it should be, my sweet darling. Whatever happens, you'll see that when things get really rough I have both strength and courage. You'll find out that I am man enough to shoulder the whole burden.

NORA (*terrified*): What do you mean by that?

HELMER: All of it, I tell you —

NORA (*composed*): You'll never have to do that.

HELMER: Good. Then we'll share the burden, Nora — like husband and wife, the way it ought to be. (*Caresses her.*) Now are you satisfied? There, there, there. Not that look in your eyes — like a frightened little dove. It's all your own foolish imagination. — Why don't you practice the Tarantella — and your tambourine, too. I'll be in the inner office. When I close both doors I won't hear a thing. You may make as much noise as you like. (*Turning in the doorway.*) And when Rank comes, why don't you tell him where to find me. (*He nods to her, enters his study carrying his papers, and closes the door.*)

NORA (*transfixed by terror, whispers*): He would do it. He'll do it. He'll do it in spite of the whole world. — No, this mustn't happen. Anything rather than that! There must be a way — ! (*The doorbell rings.*) Doctor Rank! Anything rather than that! Anything — anything at all!

(*She passes her hand over her face, pulls herself together, and opens the door to the hall. DR. RANK is out there, hanging up his coat. Darkness begins to fall during the following scene.*)

NORA: Hello there, Dr. Rank. I recognized your ringing. Don't go in to Torvald yet. I think he's busy.

RANK: And you?

NORA (*as he enters and she closes the door behind him*): You know I always have time for you.

RANK: Thanks. I'll make use of that as long as I can.

NORA: What do you mean by that? "As long as you can"?

RANK: Does that frighten you?

NORA: Well, it's a funny expression. As if something was going to happen.

RANK: Something is going to happen that I've long been expecting. But I admit I hadn't thought it would come quite so soon.

NORA (*seizes his arm*): What is it you've found out? Dr. Rank — tell me!

RANK (*sits down by the stove*): I'm going downhill fast. There's nothing to be done about that.

NORA (*with audible relief*): So it's *you* —

RANK: Who else? No point in lying to myself. I'm in worse shape than any of my other patients, Mrs. Helmer. These last few days I've been conducting an audit on my inner condition. Bankrupt. Chances are that within a month I'll be rotting up in the cemetery.

NORA: Shame on you! Talking that horrid way!

RANK: The thing itself is horrid — damn horrid. The worst of it, though, is all that other horror that comes first. There is only one more test I need to make. After that I'll have a pretty good idea when I'll start coming apart. There is something I want to say to you. Helmer's refined nature can't stand anything hideous. I don't want him in my sick room.

NORA: Oh but Dr. Rank —

RANK: I don't want him there. Under no circumstance. I'll close my door to him. As soon as I have full certainty that the worst is about to begin I'll give you my card with a black cross on it. Then you'll know the last, horrible destruction has started.

NORA: Today you're really quite impossible. And I had hoped you'd be in a particularly good mood.

RANK: With death on my hands? Paying for someone else's sins? Is there justice in that? And yet there isn't a single family that isn't ruled by that same law of ruthless retribution, in one way or another.

NORA (*puts her hands over her ears*): Poppycock! Be fun! Be fun!

RANK: Well, yes. You may just as well laugh

at the whole thing. My poor, innocent spine is suffering for my father's frolics when he was a young lieutenant.

NORA (*over by the table, left*): Right. He was addicted to asparagus and goose liver paté, wasn't he?

RANK: And truffles.

NORA: Of course. Truffles. And oysters too, I think.

RANK: And oysters. Obviously.

NORA: And all the port and champagne that go with it. It's really too bad that goodies like that ruin your backbone.

RANK: Particularly an unfortunate backbone that never enjoyed any of it.

NORA: Ah yes, that's the saddest part of it all.

RANK (*looks searchingly at her*): Hm —

NORA (*after a brief pause*): Why did you smile just then?

RANK: I didn't. It was you who laughed.

NORA: No, it was you who smiled, Dr. Rank!

RANK (*gets up*): I see you're more of a mischief-maker than I thought.

NORA: I feel like mischief today.

RANK: So it seems.

NORA (*with both her hands on his shoulders*): Dear, dear Dr. Rank, don't you go and die and leave Torvald and me.

RANK: Oh, you won't miss me for very long. Those who go away are soon forgotten.

NORA (*with an anxious look*): Do you believe that?

RANK: You'll make new friends, and then —

NORA: Who'll make new friends?

RANK: Both you and Helmer, once I'm gone. You yourself seem to have made a good start already. What was this Mrs. Linde doing here last night?

NORA: Aha — Don't tell me you're jealous of poor Kristine?

RANK: Yes I am. She'll be my successor in this house. As soon as I have made my excuses, that woman is likely to —

NORA: Shh — not so loud. She's in there.

RANK: Today too? There you are!

NORA: She's mending my costume. My god, you really *are* unreasonable. (*Sits down on the couch.*) Now be nice, Dr. Rank. Tomorrow you'll see how beautifully I'll dance, and then you are to pretend I'm dancing just for you — and for Torvald too, of course. (*Takes several items out of the carton.*) Sit down, Dr. Rank; I want to show you something.

RANK (*sitting down*): What?

NORA: Look.

RANK: Silk stockings.

NORA: Flesh-colored. Aren't they lovely? Now it's getting dark in here, but tomorrow — No, no. You only get to see the foot. Oh well, you might as well see all of it.

RANK: Hm.

NORA: Why do you look so critical? Don't you think they'll fit?

RANK: That's something I can't possibly have a reasoned opinion about.

NORA (*looks at him for a moment*): Shame on you. (*Slaps his ear lightly with the stocking.*) That's what you get. (*Puts the things back in the carton.*)

RANK: And what other treasures are you going to show me?

NORA: Nothing at all, because you're naughty. (*She hums a little and rummages in the carton.*)

RANK (*after a brief silence*): When I sit here like this, talking confidently with you, I can't imagine — I can't possibly imagine what would have become of me if I hadn't had you and Helmer.

NORA (*smiles*): Well, yes — I do believe you like being with us.

RANK (*in a lower voice, lost in thought*): And then to have to go away from it all —

NORA: Nonsense. You're not going anywhere.

RANK (*as before*): — and not leave behind as much as a poor little token of gratitude, hardly a brief memory of someone missed, nothing but a vacant place that anyone can fill.

NORA: And what if I were to ask you — ? No —

RANK: Ask me what?

NORA: For a great proof of your friendship —

RANK: Yes, yes — ?

NORA: No, I mean — for an enormous favor —

RANK: Would you really for once make me as happy as all that?

NORA: But you don't even know what it is.

RANK: Well, then; tell me.

NORA: Oh, but I can't, Dr. Rank. It's altogether too much to ask — It's advice and help and a favor —

RANK: So much the better. I can't even begin to guess what it is you have in mind. So for heaven's sake tell me! Don't you trust me?

NORA: Yes, I trust you more than anybody I know. You are my best and most faithful friend. I know that. So I will tell you. All right, Dr.

Rank. There is something you can help me prevent. You know how much Torvald loves me — beyond all words. Never for a moment would he hesitate to give his life for me.

RANK (*leaning over her*): Nora — do you really think he's the only one — ?

NORA (*with a slight start*): Who — ?

RANK: — who'd gladly give his life for you.

NORA (*heavily*): I see.

RANK: I have sworn an oath to myself to tell you before I go. I'll never find a better occasion. — All right, Nora; now you know. And now you also know that you can confide in me, more than in anyone else.

NORA (*gets up. In a calm, steady voice*): Let me get by.

RANK (*makes room for her but remains seated*): Nora —

NORA (*in the door to the front hall*): Helene, bring the lamp in here, please. (*Walks over to the stove.*) Oh, dear Dr. Rank. That really wasn't very nice of you.

RANK (*gets up*): That I have loved you as much as anybody — was that not nice?

NORA: No, not that. But that you told me. There was no need for that.

RANK: What do you mean? Have you known — ?

(*The* MAID *enters with the lamp, puts it on the table, and goes out.*)

RANK. Nora — Mrs. Helmer — I'm asking you: did you know?

NORA: Oh, how can I tell what I knew and didn't know! I really can't say — But that you could be so awkward, Dr. Rank! Just when everything was so comfortable.

RANK: Well, anyway, now you know that I'm at your service with my life and soul. And now you must speak.

NORA (*looks at him*): After what just happened?

RANK: I beg you — let me know what it is.

NORA: There is nothing I can tell you now.

RANK: Yes, yes. You mustn't punish me this way. Please let me do for you whatever anyone *can* do.

NORA: Now there is nothing you can do. Besides, I don't think I really need any help, anyway. It's probably just my imagination. Of course that's all it is. I'm sure of it! (*Sits down in the rocking chair, looks at him, smiles.*) Well, well, well, Dr. Rank! What a fine gentle-

man you turned out to be! Aren't you ashamed of yourself, now that we have light?

RANK: No, not really. But perhaps I ought to leave — and not come back?

NORA: Don't be silly; of course not! You'll come here exactly as you have been doing. You know perfectly well that Torvald can't do without you.

RANK: Yes, but what about you?

NORA: Oh, I always think it's perfectly delightful when you come.

RANK: That's the very thing that misled me. You are a riddle to me. It has often seemed to me that you'd just as soon be with me as with Helmer.

NORA: Well, you see, there are people you love, and then there are other people you'd almost rather be with.

RANK: Yes, there is something in that.

NORA: When I lived home with Daddy, of course I loved him most. But I always thought it was so much fun to sneak off down to the maids' room, for they never gave me good advice and they always talked about such fun things.

RANK: Aha! So it's *their* place I have taken.

NORA (*jumps up and goes over to him*): Oh dear, kind Dr. Rank, you know very well I didn't mean it that way. Can't you see that with Torvald it is the way it used to be with Daddy?

(*The* MAID *enters from the front hall.*)

MAID: Ma'am! (*Whispers to her and gives her a caller's card.*)

NORA (*glances at the card*): Ah! (*Puts it in her pocket.*)

RANK: Anything wrong?

NORA: No, no; not at all. It's nothing — just my new costume —

RANK: But your costume is lying right there!

NORA: Oh yes, that one. But this is another one. I ordered it. Torvald mustn't know —

RANK: Aha. So that's the great secret.

NORA: That's it. Why don't you go in to him, please. He's in the inner office. And keep him there for a while —

RANK: Don't worry. He won't get away. (*Enters* HELMER's *study.*)

NORA (*to the* MAID): You say he's waiting in the kitchen?

MAID: Yes. He came up the back stairs.

NORA: But didn't you tell him there was somebody with me?

MAID: Yes, but he wouldn't listen.

NORA: He won't leave?

MAID: No, not till he's had a word with you, ma'am.

NORA: All right. But try not to make any noise. And, Helene — don't tell anyone he's here. It's supposed to be a surprise for my husband.

MAID: I understand, ma'am — (*She leaves.*)

NORA: The terrible is happening. It's happening, after all. No, no, no. It can't happen. It won't happen. (*She bolts the study door.*)

(*The* MAID *opens the front hall door for* KROGSTAD *and closes the door behind him. He wears a fur coat for traveling, boots, and a fur hat.*)

NORA (*toward him*): Keep your voice down. My husband's home.

KROGSTAD: That's all right.

NORA: What do you want?

KROGSTAD: To find out something.

NORA: Then hurry. What?

KROGSTAD: I expect you know I've been fired.

NORA: I couldn't prevent it, Mr. Krogstad. I fought for you as long and as hard as I could, but it didn't do any good.

KROGSTAD: Your husband doesn't love you any more than that? He knows what I can do to you, and yet he runs the risk —

NORA: Surely you didn't think I'd tell him?

KROGSTAD: No, I really didn't. It wouldn't be like Torvald Helmer to show that kind of guts —

NORA: Mr. Krogstad, I insist that you show respect for my husband.

KROGSTAD: By all means. All due respect. But since you're so anxious to keep this a secret, may I assume that you are a little better informed than yesterday about exactly what you have done?

NORA: Better than *you* could ever teach me.

KROGSTAD: Of course. Such a bad lawyer as I am —

NORA: What do you want of me?

KROGSTAD: I just wanted to see how you were, Mrs. Helmer. I've been thinking about you all day. You see, even a bill collector, a pen pusher, a — anyway, someone like me — even he has a little of what they call a heart.

NORA: Then show it. Think of my little children.

KROGSTAD: Have you and your husband thought of mine? Never mind. All I want to tell you is that you don't need to take this business too seriously. I have no intention of bringing charges right away.

NORA: Oh no, you wouldn't; would you? I knew you wouldn't.

KROGSTAD: The whole thing can be settled quite amicably. Nobody else needs to know anything. It will be between the three of us.

NORA: My husband must never find out about this.

KROGSTAD: How are you going to prevent it? Maybe you can pay me the balance on the loan?

NORA: No, not right now.

KROGSTAD: Or do you have some way of raising the money in the next few days?

NORA: None I intend to make use of.

KROGSTAD: It wouldn't do you any good, anyway. Even if you had the cash in your hand right this minute, I wouldn't give you your note back. It wouldn't make any difference *how* much money you offered me.

NORA: Then you'll have to tell me what you plan to use the note *for.*

KROGSTAD: Just keep it; that's all. Have it on hand, so to speak. I won't say a word to anybody else. So if you've been thinking about doing something desperate —

NORA: I have.

KROGSTAD: — like leaving house and home —

NORA: I have!

KROGSTAD: — or even something worse —

NORA: How did you know?

KROGSTAD: — then: don't.

NORA: How did you know I was thinking of *that?*

KROGSTAD: Most of us do, right at first. I did, too, but when it came down to it I didn't have the courage —

NORA (*tonelessly*): Nor do I.

KROGSTAD (*relieved*): See what I mean? I thought so. You don't either.

NORA: I don't. I don't.

KROGSTAD: Besides, it would be very silly of you. Once that first domestic blow-up is behind you — . Here in my pocket is a letter for your husband.

NORA: Telling him everything?

KROGSTAD: As delicately as possible.

NORA (*quickly*): He mustn't get that letter. Tear it up. I'll get you the money somehow.

KROGSTAD: Excuse me, Mrs. Helmer. I thought I just told you —

NORA: I'm not talking about the money I owe you. Just let me know how much money you want from my husband, and I'll get it for you.

KROGSTAD: I want no money from your husband.

NORA: Then, what *do* you want?

KROGSTAD: I'll tell you, Mrs. Helmer. I want to rehabilitate myself; I want to get up in the world; and your husband is going to help me. For a year and a half I haven't done anything disreputable. All that time I have been struggling with the most miserable circumstances. I was content to work my way up step by step. Now I've been kicked out, and I'm no longer satisfied just getting my old job back. I want more than that; I want to get to the top. I'm quite serious. I want the bank to take me back but in a higher position. I want your husband to create a new job for me —

NORA: He'll never do that!

KROGSTAD: He will. I know him. He won't dare not to. And once I'm back inside and he and I are working together, you'll see! Within a year I'll be the manager's right hand. It will be Nils Krogstad and not Torvald Helmer who'll be running the Mutual Bank!

NORA: You'll never see that happen!

KROGSTAD: Are you thinking of — ?

NORA: Now I *do* have the courage.

KROGSTAD: You can't scare me. A fine, spoiled lady like you —

NORA: You'll see, you'll see!

KROGSTAD: Under the ice, perhaps? Down in that cold, black water? Then spring comes, and you float up again — hideous, ugly, unrecognizable, hair all gone —

NORA: You don't frighten me.

KROGSTAD: Nor you me. One doesn't do that sort of thing, Mrs. Helmer. Besides, what good would it do? He'd still be in my power.

NORA: Afterwards? When I'm no longer — ?

KROGSTAD: Aren't you forgetting that your reputation would be in my hands?

(NORA *stares at him, speechless.*)

KROGSTAD: All right; now I've told you what to expect. So don't do anything foolish. When Helmer gets my letter I expect to hear from him. And don't you forget that it's your husband himself who forces me to use such means again. That I'll never forgive him. Goodbye, Mrs. Helmer. (*Goes out through the hall.*)

NORA (*at the door, opens it a little, listens*): He's going. And no letter. Of course not! That would be impossible! (*Opens the door more.*) What's he doing? He's still there. Doesn't go down. Having second thoughts — ? Will he — ?

(*The sound of a letter dropping into the mailbox. Then* KROGSTAD's *steps are heard going down the stairs, gradually dying away.*)

NORA (*with a muted cry runs forward to the table by the couch. Brief pause*): In the mailbox. (*Tiptoes back to the door to the front hall.*) There it is. Torvald, Torvald — now we're lost!

MRS. LINDE (*enters from the left, carrying* NORA's *Capri costume*): There now. I think it's all fixed. Why don't we try it on you —

NORA (*in a low, hoarse voice*): Kristine, come here.

MRS. LINDE: What's wrong with you? You look quite beside yourself.

NORA: Come over here. Do you see that letter? There, look — through the glass in the mailbox.

MRS. LINDE: Yes, yes; I see it.

NORA: That letter is from Krogstad.

MRS. LINDE: Nora — it was Krogstad who lent you the money!

NORA: Yes, and now Torvald will find out about it.

MRS. LINDE: Oh believe me, Nora. That's the best thing for both of you.

NORA: There's more to it than you know. I forged a signature —

MRS. LINDE: Oh my god — !

NORA: I just want to tell you this, Kristine, that you must be my witness.

MRS. LINDE: Witness? How? Witness to what?

NORA: If I lose my mind — and that could very well happen —

MRS. LINDE: Nora!

NORA: — or if something were to happen to me — something that made it impossible for me to be here —

MRS. LINDE: Nora, Nora! You're not yourself!

NORA: — and if someone were to take all the blame, assume the whole responsibility — Do you understand — ?

MRS. LINDE: Yes, yes; but how can you think — !

NORA: — then you are to witness that that's

not so, Kristine. I am not beside myself. I am perfectly rational, and what I'm telling you is that nobody else has known about this. I've done it all by myself, the whole thing. Just remember that.

MRS. LINDE: I will. But I don't understand any of it.

NORA: Oh, how could you! For it's the wonderful that's about to happen.

MRS. LINDE: The wonderful?

NORA: Yes, the wonderful. But it's so terrible, Kristine. It mustn't happen for anything in the whole world!

MRS. LINDE: I'm going over to talk to Krogstad right now.

NORA: No, don't. Don't go to him. He'll do something bad to you.

MRS. LINDE: There was a time when he would have done anything for me.

NORA: He!

MRS. LINDE: Where does he live?

NORA: Oh, I don't know — Yes, wait a minute (*reaches into her pocket*) — here's his card. — But the letter, the letter — !

HELMER (*in his study, knocks on the door*): Nora!

NORA (*cries out in fear*): Oh, what is it? What do you want?

HELMER: That's all right. Nothing to be so scared about. We're not coming in. For one thing, we can't. You've bolted the door, you know. Are you trying on your costume?

NORA: Yes — yes, I am. I'm going to be so pretty, Torvald.

MRS. LINDE (*looking at the card*): He lives just around the corner.

NORA: I know, but it's no use. Nothing can save us now. The letter is in the mailbox.

MRS. LINDE: And your husband has the key?

NORA: Yes. He always keeps it with him.

MRS. LINDE: Krogstad must ask for his letter back, unread. He's got to think up some pretext or other —

NORA: But this is just the time of day when Torvald —

MRS. LINDE: Delay him. Go in to him. I'll be back as soon as I can. (*She hurries out through the hall door.*)

NORA (*walks over to* HELMER's *door, opens it, and peeks in*): Torvald!

HELMER (*still offstage*): Well, well! So now one's allowed in one's own living room again. Come on, Rank. Now we'll see — (*In the doorway.*) But what's this?

NORA: What, Torvald dear?

HELMER: Rank prepared me for a splendid metamorphosis.

RANK (*in the doorway*): That's how I understood it. Evidently I was mistaken.

NORA: Nobody gets to admire me in my costume before tomorrow.

HELMER: But, dearest Nora — you look all done in. Have you been practicing too hard?

NORA: No, I haven't practiced at all.

HELMER: But you'll have to, you know.

NORA: I know it, Torvald. I simply must. But I can't do a thing unless you help me. I have forgotten everything.

HELMER: Oh it will all come back. We'll work on it.

NORA: Oh yes, please, Torvald. You just have to help me. Promise? I am so nervous. That big party —. You mustn't do anything else tonight. Not a bit of business. Don't even touch a pen. Will you promise, Torvald?

HELMER: I promise. Tonight I'll be entirely at your service — you helpless little thing. — Just a moment, though. First I want to — (*Goes to the door to the front hall.*)

NORA: What are you doing out there?

HELMER: Just looking to see if there's any mail.

NORA: No, no! Don't, Torvald!

HELMER: Why not?

NORA: Torvald, I beg you. There is no mail.

HELMER: Let me just look, anyway. (*Is about to go out.*)

(NORA *by the piano, plays the first bars of the Tarantella dance.*)

HELMER (*halts at the door*): Aha!

NORA: I won't be able to dance tomorrow if I don't get to practice with you.

HELMER (*goes to her*): Are you really all that scared, Nora dear?

NORA: Yes, so terribly scared. Let's try it right now. There's still time before we eat. Oh please, sit down and play for me, Torvald. Teach me, coach me, the way you always do.

HELMER: Of course I will, my darling, if that's what you want. (*Sits down at the piano.*)

NORA (*takes the tambourine out of the carton, as well as a long, many-colored shawl. She quickly drapes the shawl around herself. She leaps into the middle of the floor and cries*): Play for me! I want to dance!

(HELMER *plays and* NORA *dances.* DR. RANK *stands by the piano behind* HELMER *and watches.*)

HELMER (*playing*): Slow down, slow down!
NORA: Can't!
HELMER: Not so violent, Nora!
NORA: It has to be this way.
HELMER (*stops playing*): No, no. This won't do at all.
NORA (*laughing, swinging her tambourine*): What did I tell you?
RANK: Why don't you let me play.
HELMER (*getting up*): Good idea. Then I can direct her better.

(RANK *sits down at the piano and starts playing.* NORA *dances more and more wildly.* HELMER *stands by the stove, repeatedly correcting her. She doesn't seem to hear. Her hair comes loose and falls down over her shoulders. She doesn't notice but keeps on dancing.* MRS. LINDE *enters.*)

MRS. LINDE (*stops by the door, dumbfounded*): Ah — !
NORA (*dancing*): We're having such fun, Kristine!
HELMER: My dearest Nora, you're dancing as if it were a matter of life and death!
NORA: It is! It is!
HELMER: Rank, stop. This is sheer madness. Stop it, I say!

(RANK *stops playing;* NORA *suddenly stops dancing.*)

HELMER (*goes over to her*): If I hadn't seen it I wouldn't have believed it. You've forgotten every single thing I ever taught you.
NORA (*tosses away the tambourine*): See? I told you.
HELMER: Well! You certainly need coaching.
NORA: Didn't I tell you I did? Now you've seen for yourself. I'll need your help till the very minute we're leaving for the party. Will you promise, Torvald?
HELMER: You can count on it.
NORA: You're not to think of anything except me — not tonight and not tomorrow. You're not to read any letters — not to look in the mailbox —
HELMER: Ah, I see. You're still afraid of that man.

NORA: Yes — yes, that too.
HELMER: Nora, I can tell from looking at you. There's a letter from him out there.
NORA: I don't know. I think so. But you're not to read it now. I don't want anything ugly to come between us before it's all over.
RANK (*to* HELMER *in a low voice*): Better not argue with her.
HELMER (*throws his arm around her*): The child shall have her way. But tomorrow night, when you've done your dance —
NORA: Then you'll be free.
MAID (*in the door, right*): Dinner can be served any time, ma'am.
NORA: We want champagne, Helene.
MAID: Very good, ma'am. (*Goes out.*)
HELMER: Aha! Having a party, eh?
NORA: Champagne from now till sunrise! (*Calls out.*) And some macaroons, Helene. Lots! — just this once.
HELMER (*taking her hands*): There, there — I don't like this wild — frenzy — Be my own sweet little lark again, the way you always are.
NORA: Oh, I will. But you go on in. You too, Dr. Rank. Kristine, please help me put up my hair.
RANK (*in a low voice to* HELMER *as they go out*): You don't think she is — you know — expecting — ?
HELMER: Oh no. Nothing like that. It's just this childish fear I was telling you about. (*They go out, right.*)
NORA: Well?
MRS. LINDE: Left town.
NORA: I saw it in your face.
MRS. LINDE: He'll be back tomorrow night. I left him a note.
NORA: You shouldn't have. I don't want you to try to stop anything. You see, it's a kind of ecstasy, too, this waiting for the wonderful.
MRS. LINDE: But what is it you're waiting for?
NORA: You wouldn't understand. Why don't you go in to the others. I'll be there in a minute.

(MRS. LINDE *enters the dining room, right.*)

NORA (*stands still for a little while, as if collecting herself. She looks at her watch*): Five o'clock. Seven hours till midnight. Twenty-four more hours till next midnight. Then the Tarantella is over. Twenty-four plus seven — thirty-one more hours to live.

HELMER (*in the door, right*): What's happening to my little lark?

NORA (*to him, with open arms*): Here's your lark!

ACT III

The same room. The table by the couch and the chairs around it have been moved to the middle of the floor. A lighted lamp is on the table. The door to the front hall is open. Dance music is heard from upstairs. MRS. LINDE *is seated by the table, idly leafing through the pages of a book. She tries to read but seems unable to concentrate. Once or twice she turns her head in the direction of the door, anxiously listening.*

MRS. LINDE (*looks at her watch*): Not yet. It's almost too late. If only he hasn't — (*Listens again.*) Ah! There he is. (*She goes to the hall and opens the front door carefully. Quiet footsteps on the stairs. She whispers.*) Come in. There's nobody here.

KROGSTAD (*in the door*): I found your note when I got home. What's this all about?

MRS. LINDE: I've got to talk to you.

KROGSTAD: Oh? And it has to be here?

MRS. LINDE: It couldn't be at my place. My room doesn't have a separate entrance. Come in. We're all alone. The maid is asleep and the Helmers are at a party upstairs.

KROGSTAD (*entering*): Really? The Helmers are dancing tonight, are they?

MRS. LINDE: And why not?

KROGSTAD: You're right. Why not, indeed.

MRS. LINDE: All right, Krogstad. Let's talk, you and I.

KROGSTAD: I didn't know we had anything to talk about.

MRS. LINDE: We have much to talk about.

KROGSTAD: I didn't think so.

MRS. LINDE: No, because you've never really understood me.

KROGSTAD: What was there to understand? What happened was perfectly commonplace. A heartless woman jilts a man when she gets a more attractive offer.

MRS. LINDE: Do you think I'm all that heartless? And do you think it was easy for me to break with you?

KROGSTAD: No?

MRS. LINDE: You really thought it was?

KROGSTAD: If it wasn't, why did you write the way you did that time?

MRS. LINDE: What else could I do? If I had to make a break, I also had the duty to destroy whatever feelings you had for me.

KROGSTAD (*clenching his hands*): So that's the way it was. And you did — *that* — just for money!

MRS. LINDE: Don't forget I had a helpless mother and two small brothers. We couldn't wait for you, Krogstad. You know yourself how uncertain your prospects were then.

KROGSTAD: All right. But you still didn't have the right to throw me over for somebody else.

MRS. LINDE: I don't know. I have asked myself that question many times. Did I have that right?

KROGSTAD (*in a lower voice*): When I lost you I lost my footing. Look at me now. A shipwrecked man on a raft.

MRS. LINDE: Rescue may be near.

KROGSTAD: It *was* near. Then you came.

MRS. LINDE: I didn't know that, Krogstad. Only today did I find out it's your job I'm taking over in the bank.

KROGSTAD: I believe you when you say so. But now that you *do* know, aren't you going to step aside?

MRS. LINDE: No, for it wouldn't do you any good.

KROGSTAD: Whether it would or not — *I* would do it.

MRS. LINDE: I have learned common sense. Life and hard necessity have taught me that.

KROGSTAD: And life has taught me not to believe in pretty speeches.

MRS. LINDE: Then life has taught you a very sensible thing. But you do believe in actions, don't you?

KROGSTAD: How do you mean?

MRS. LINDE: You referred to yourself just now as a shipwrecked man.

KROGSTAD: It seems to me I had every reason to do so.

MRS. LINDE: And I am a shipwrecked woman. No one to grieve for, no one to care for.

KROGSTAD: You made your choice.

MRS. LINDE: I had no other choice that time.

KROGSTAD: Let's say you didn't. What then?

MRS. LINDE: Krogstad, how would it be if we two shipwrecked people got together?

KROGSTAD: What's this!

MRS. LINDE: Two on one wreck are better off than each on his own.

KROGSTAD: Kristine!

MRS. LINDE: Why do you think I came to town?

KROGSTAD: Surely not because of me?

MRS. LINDE: If I'm going to live at all I must work. All my life, for as long as I can remember, I have worked. That's been my one and only pleasure. But now that I'm all alone in the world I feel only this terrible emptiness and desolation. There is no joy in working just for yourself. Krogstad — give me someone and something to work for.

KROGSTAD: I don't believe in this. I think you're just another hysterical female being noble and sacrificing yourself.

MRS. LINDE: Did you ever know me to be hysterical?

KROGSTAD: You really could do this? Listen — do you know about my past? All of it?

MRS. LINDE: Yes.

KROGSTAD: Do you also know what people think of me around here?

MRS. LINDE: A little while ago you sounded as if you thought that together with me you might have become a different person.

KROGSTAD: I'm sure of it.

MRS. LINDE: Couldn't that still be?

KROGSTAD: Kristine — do you know what you are doing? Yes, I see you do. And you really think you have the courage — ?

MRS. LINDE: I need someone to be a mother to, and your children need a mother. You and I need one another. Nils, I believe in you — in the real you. Together with you I dare to do anything.

KROGSTAD (seizes her hands): Thanks, thanks, Kristine — now I know I'll raise myself in the eyes of others. — Ah, but I forget — !

MRS. LINDE (listening): Shh! — There's the Tarantella. You must go; hurry!

KROGSTAD: Why? What is it?

MRS. LINDE: Do you hear what they're playing up there? When that dance is over they'll be down.

KROGSTAD: All right. I'm leaving. The whole thing is pointless, anyway. Of course you don't know what I'm doing to the Helmers.

MRS. LINDE: Yes, Krogstad; I do know.

KROGSTAD: Still, you're brave enough — ?

MRS. LINDE: I very well understand to what extremes despair can drive a man like you.

KROGSTAD: If only it could be undone!

MRS. LINDE: It could, for your letter is still out there in the mailbox.

KROGSTAD: Are you sure?

MRS. LINDE: Quite sure. But —

KROGSTAD (looks searchingly at her): Maybe I'm beginning to understand. You want to save your friend at any cost. Be honest with me. That's it, isn't it?

MRS. LINDE: Krogstad, you may sell yourself for somebody else's sake, but you don't do it twice.

KROGSTAD: I'll ask for my letter back.

MRS. LINDE: No, no.

KROGSTAD: Yes, of course. I'll wait here till Helmer comes down. Then I'll ask him for my letter. I'll tell him it's just about my dismissal — that he shouldn't read it.

MRS. LINDE: No, Krogstad. You are not to do that.

KROGSTAD: But tell me — wasn't that the real reason you wanted to meet me here?

MRS. LINDE: At first it was, because I was so frightened. But that was yesterday. Since then I have seen the most incredible things going on in this house. Helmer must learn the whole truth. This miserable secret must come out in the open; those two must come to a full understanding. They simply can't continue with all this concealment and evasion.

KROGSTAD: All right; if you want to take that chance. But there is one thing I can do, and I'll do it right now.

MRS. LINDE (listening): But hurry! Go! The dance is over. We aren't safe another minute.

KROGSTAD: I'll be waiting for you downstairs.

MRS. LINDE: Yes, do. You must see me home.

KROGSTAD: I've never been so happy in my whole life. (He leaves through the front door. The door between the living room and the front hall remains open.)

MRS. LINDE (straightens up the room a little and gets her things ready): What a change! Oh yes! — what a change! People to work for — to live for — a home to bring happiness to. I can't wait to get to work — ! If only they'd come soon — (Listens.) Ah, there they are. Get my coat on — (Puts on her coat and hat.)

(HELMER's and NORA's voices are heard outside. A key is turned in the lock, and HELMER almost forces NORA into the hall. She is dressed in her Italian costume, with a big, black shawl over her shoulders. He is in evening dress under an open, black domino.)

NORA (*in the door, still resisting*): No, no, no! I don't want to! I want to go back upstairs. I don't want to leave so early.

HELMER: But dearest Nora —

NORA: Oh please, Torvald — please! I'm asking you as nicely as I can — just another hour!

HELMER: Not another minute, sweet. You know we agreed. There now. Get inside. You'll catch a cold out here. (*She still resists, but he guides her gently into the room.*)

MRS. LINDE: Good evening.

NORA: Kristine!

HELMER: Ah, Mrs. Linde. Still here?

MRS. LINDE: I know. I really should apologize, but I so much wanted to see Nora in her costume.

NORA: You've been waiting up for me?

MRS. LINDE: Yes, unfortunately I didn't get here in time. You were already upstairs, but I just didn't feel like leaving till I had seen you.

HELMER (*removing* NORA's *shawl*): Yes, do take a good look at her, Mrs. Linde. I think I may say she's worth looking at. Isn't she lovely?

MRS. LINDE: She certainly is —

HELMER: Isn't she a miracle of loveliness, though? That was the general opinion at the party, too. But dreadfully obstinate — that she is, the sweet little thing. What can we do about that? Will you believe it — I practically had to use force to get her away.

NORA: Oh Torvald, you're going to be sorry you didn't give me even half an hour more.

HELMER: See what I mean, Mrs. Linde? She dances the Tarantella — she is a tremendous success — quite deservedly so, though perhaps her performance was a little too natural — I mean, more than could be reconciled with the rules of art. But all right! The point is: she's a success, a tremendous success. So should I let her stay after that? Spoil the effect? Of course not. So I take my lovely little Capri girl — I might say, my capricious little Capri girl — under my arm — a quick turn around the room — a graceful bow in all directions, and — as they say in the novels — the beautiful apparition is gone. A finale should always be done for effect, Mrs. Linde, but there doesn't seem to be any way of getting that into Nora's head. Poooh — ! It's hot in here. (*Throws his cape down on a chair and opens the door to his study.*) Why, it's dark! Oh yes — of course. Excuse me — (*Goes inside and lights a couple of candles.*)

NORA (*in a hurried, breathless whisper*): Well?

MRS. LINDE (*in a low voice*): I have talked to him.

NORA: And — ?

MRS. LINDE: Nora — you've got to tell your husband everything.

NORA (*no expression in her voice*): I knew it.

MRS. LINDE: You have nothing to fear from Krogstad. But you must speak.

NORA: I'll say nothing.

MRS. LINDE: Then the letter will.

NORA: Thank you, Kristine. Now I know what I have to do. Shh!

HELMER (*returning*): Well, Mrs. Linde, have you looked your fill?

MRS. LINDE: Yes. And now I'll say goodnight.

HELMER: So soon? Is that your knitting?

MRS. LINDE (*takes it*): Yes, thank you. I almost forgot.

HELMER: So you knit, do you?

MRS. LINDE: Oh yes.

HELMER: You know — you ought to take up embroidery instead.

MRS. LINDE: Oh? Why?

HELMER: Because it's so much more beautiful. Look. You hold the embroidery so — in your left hand. Then with your right you move the needle — like this — in an easy, elongated arc — you see?

MRS. LINDE: Maybe you're right —

HELMER: Knitting, on the other hand, can never be anything but ugly. Look here: arms pressed close to the sides — the needles going up and down — there's something Chinese about it somehow —. That really was an excellent champagne they served us tonight.

MRS. LINDE: Well; goodnight, Nora. And don't be obstinate any more.

HELMER: Well said, Mrs. Linde!

MRS. LINDE: Goodnight, sir.

HELMER (*sees her to the front door*): Goodnight, goodnight. I hope you'll get home all right? I'd be very glad to — but of course you don't have far to walk, do you? Goodnight, goodnight. (*She leaves. He closes the door behind her and returns to the living room.*) There! At last we got rid of her. She really is an incredible bore, that woman.

NORA: Aren't you very tired, Torvald?

HELMER: No, not in the least.

NORA: Not sleepy either?

HELMER: Not at all. Quite the opposite. I

feel enormously — animated. How about you?
Yes, you do look tired and sleepy.

NORA: Yes, I am very tired. Soon I'll be
asleep.

HELMER: What did I tell you? I was right,
wasn't I? Good thing I didn't let you stay any
longer.

NORA: Everything you do is right.

HELMER (*kissing her forehead*): Now my
little lark is talking like a human being. But
did you notice what splendid spirits Rank was
in tonight?

NORA: Was he? I didn't notice. I didn't get
to talk with him.

HELMER: Nor did I — hardly. But I haven't
seen him in such a good mood for a long time.
(*Looks at her, comes closer to her.*) Ah! It
does feel good to be back in our own home
again, to be quite alone with you — Oh, how
lovely you are! — my exciting young woman!

NORA: Don't look at me like that, Torvald!

HELMER: Am I not to look at my most
precious possession? All that loveliness that is
mine, nobody's but mine, all of it mine!

NORA (*walks to the other side of the table*):
I won't have you talk to me like that tonight.

HELMER (*follows her*): The Tarantella is
still in your blood. I can tell. That only makes
you all the more alluring. Listen! The guests
are beginning to leave. (*Softly.*) Nora — darling — soon the whole house will be quiet.

NORA: I hope so.

HELMER: Yes, don't you, my darling? Do you
know — when I'm at a party with you, like
tonight — do you know why I hardly ever
talk to you, why I keep away from you, only
look at you once in a while — a few stolen
glances — do you know why I do that? It's
because I pretend that you are my secret love,
my young, secret bride-to-be, and nobody has
the slightest suspicion that there is anything
between us.

NORA: Yes, I know. All your thoughts are
with me.

HELMER: Then when we're leaving and I
lay your shawl around your delicate young
shoulders — around that wonderful curve of
your neck — then I imagine you're my young
bride, that we're coming away from the wedding, that I am taking you to my home for
the first time — that I am alone with you for
the first time — quite alone with you, you
young, trembling beauty! I have desired you
all evening — all my longing has only been for

you. When you were dancing the Tarantella,
chasing, inviting — my blood was on fire; I
couldn't stand it any longer — that's why I
brought you down so early —

NORA: Leave me now, Torvald. Please! I don't
want all this.

HELMER: What do you mean? You're only
playing your little teasing bird game with me;
aren't you, Nora? Don't want to? I'm your
husband, aren't I?

(*There is a knock on the front door.*)

NORA (*with a start*): Did you hear that — ?

HELMER (*on his way to the hall*): Who is it?

RANK (*outside*): It's me. May I come in for
a moment?

HELMER (*in a low voice, annoyed*): Oh,
what does he want now? (*Aloud.*) Just a
minute. (*Opens the door.*) Well! How good
of you not to pass by our door.

RANK: I thought I heard your voice, so I
felt like saying hello. (*Looks around.*) Ah yes
— this dear, familiar room. What a cozy, comfortable place you have here, you two.

HELMER: Looked to me as if you were quite
comfortable upstairs too.

RANK: I certainly was. And why not? Why
not enjoy all you can in this world? As much
as you can and for as long as you can, anyway.
Excellent wine.

HELMER: The champagne, particularly.

RANK: You noticed that too? Incredible how
much I managed to put away.

NORA: Torvald drank a lot of champagne tonight, too.

RANK: Did he?

NORA: Yes, he did, and then he's always so
much fun afterwards.

RANK: Well, why not have some fun in the
evening after a well spent day?

HELMER: Well spent? I'm afraid I can't claim
that.

RANK (*slapping him lightly on the shoulder*):
But you see, I can!

NORA: Dr. Rank, I believe you have been
conducting a scientific test today.

RANK: Exactly.

HELMER: What do you know — little Nora
talking about scientific experiments!

NORA: May I congratulate you on the result?

RANK: You may indeed.

NORA: It was a good one?

RANK: The best possible for both doctor and
patient — certainty.

NORA (*a quick query*): Certainty?

RANK: Absolute certainty. So why shouldn't I have myself an enjoyable evening afterwards?

NORA: I quite agree with you, Dr. Rank. You should.

HELMER: And so do I. If only you don't pay for it tomorrow.

RANK: Oh well — you get nothing for nothing in this world.

NORA: Dr. Rank — you are fond of costume parties, aren't you?

RANK: Yes, particularly when there is a reasonable number of amusing disguises.

NORA: Listen — what are the two of us going to be the next time?

HELMER: You frivolous little thing! Already thinking about the next party!

RANK: You and I? That's easy. You'll be Fortune's Child.

HELMER: Yes, but what is a fitting costume for that?

RANK: Let your wife appear just the way she always is.

HELMER: Beautiful. Very good indeed. But how about yourself? Don't you know what you'll go as?

RANK: Yes, my friend. I know precisely what I'll be.

HELMER: Yes?

RANK: At the next masquerade I'll be invisible.

HELMER: That's a funny idea.

RANK: There's a certain big, black hat — you've heard about the hat that makes you invisible, haven't you? You put that on, and nobody can see you.

HELMER (*suppressing a smile*): I guess that's right.

RANK: But I'm forgetting what I came for. Helmer, give me a cigar — one of your dark Havanas.

HELMER: With the greatest pleasure. (*Offers him his case.*)

RANK (*takes one and cuts off the tip*): Thanks.

NORA (*striking a match*): Let me give you a light.

RANK: Thanks. (*She holds the match; he lights his cigar.*) And now goodbye!

HELMER: Goodbye, goodbye, my friend.

NORA: Sleep well, Dr. Rank.

RANK: I thank you.

NORA: Wish me the same.

RANK: You? Well, if you really want me to —. Sleep well. And thanks for the light. (*He nods to both of them and goes out.*)

HELMER (*in a low voice*): He had had quite a bit to drink.

NORA (*absently*): Maybe so.

(HELMER *takes out his keys and goes out into the hall.*)

NORA: Torvald — what are you doing out there?

HELMER: Got to empty the mailbox. It is quite full. There wouldn't be room for the newspapers in the morning —

NORA: Are you going to work tonight?

HELMER: You know very well I won't. — Say! What's this? Somebody's been at the lock.

NORA: The lock — ?

HELMER: Sure. Why, I wonder. I hate to think that any of the maids — . Here's a broken hairpin. It's one of yours, Nora.

NORA (*quickly*): Then it must be one of the children.

HELMER: You better make damn sure they stop that. Hm, hm. — There! I got it open, finally. (*Gathers up the mail, calls out to the kitchen:*) Helene? — Oh Helene — turn out the light here in the hall, will you? (*He comes back into the living room and closes the door.*) Look how it's been piling up. (*Shows her the bundle of letters. Starts leafing through it.*) What's this?

NORA (*by the window*): The letter! Oh no, no, Torvald!

HELMER: Two calling cards — from Rank.

NORA: From Dr. Rank?

HELMER (*looking at them*): "Doctor of Medicine Rank!" They were on top. He must have put them there when he left just now.

NORA: Anything written on them?

HELMER: A black cross above the name. Look. What a macabre idea. Like announcing his own death.

NORA: That's what it is.

HELMER: Hm? You know about this? Has he said anything to you?

NORA: That card means he's saying goodbye to us. He'll lock himself up to die.

HELMER: My poor friend. I knew of course he wouldn't be with me very long. But so soon —. And this hiding himself away like a wounded animal —

NORA: When it has to be, it's better it happens without words. Don't you think so, Torvald?

HELMER (*walking up and down*): He'd grown so close to us. I find it hard to think of him as gone. With his suffering and loneliness he was like a clouded background for our happy sunshine. Well, it may be better this way. For him, at any rate. (*Stops.*) And perhaps for us, too, Nora. For now we have nobody but each other. (*Embraces her.*) Oh you — my beloved wife! I feel I just can't hold you close enough. Do you know, Nora — many times I have wished some great danger threatened you, so I could risk my life and blood and everything — everything, for your sake.

NORA (*frees herself and says in a strong and firm voice*): I think you should go and read your letters now, Torvald.

HELMER: No, no — not tonight. I want to be with you, my darling.

NORA: With the thought of your dying friend — ?

HELMER: You are right. This has shaken both of us. Something not beautiful has come between us. Thoughts of death and dissolution. We must try to get over it — out of it. Till then — we'll each go to our own room.

NORA (*her arms around his neck*): Torvald — goodnight! Goodnight!

HELMER (*kisses her forehead*): Goodnight, my little songbird. Sleep well, Nora. Now I'll read my letters. (*He goes into his room, carrying the mail. Closes the door.*)

NORA (*her eyes desperate, her hands groping, finds* HELMER's *domino and throws it around her; she whispers, quickly, brokenly, hoarsely*): Never see him again. Never. Never. Never. (*Puts her shawl over her head.*) And never see the children again, either. Never; never. — The black, icy water — fathomless — this — ! If only it was all over. — Now he has it. Now he's reading it. No, no; not yet. Torvald — goodbye — you — the children —

(*She is about to hurry through the hall, when* HELMER *flings open the door to his room and stands there with an open letter in his hand.*)

HELMER: Nora!

NORA (*cries out*): Ah — !

HELMER: What is it? You know what's in this letter?

NORA: Yes, I do! Let me go! Let me out!

HELMER (*holds her back*): Where do you think you're going?

NORA (*trying to tear herself loose from him*): I won't let you save me, Torvald!

HELMER (*tumbles back*): True! Is it true what he writes? Oh my god! No, no — this can't possibly be true.

NORA: It is true. I have loved you more than anything else in the whole world.

HELMER: Oh, don't give me any silly excuses.

NORA (*taking a step towards him*): Torvald — !

HELMER: You wretch! What have you done!

NORA: Let me go. You are not to sacrifice yourself for me. You are not to take the blame.

HELMER: No more playacting. (*Locks the door to the front hall.*) You'll stay here and answer me. Do you understand what you have done? Answer me! Do you understand?

NORA (*gazes steadily at him with an increasingly frozen expression*): Yes. Now I'm beginning to understand.

HELMER (*walking up and down*): What a dreadful awakening. All these years — all these eight years — she, my pride and my joy — a hypocrite, a liar — oh worse! worse! — a criminal! Oh, the bottomless ugliness in all this! Damn! Damn! Damn!

(NORA *silent, keeps gazing at him.*)

HELMER (*stops in front of her*): I ought to have guessed that something like this would happen. I should have expected it. All your father's loose principles — Silence! You have inherited every one of your father's loose principles. No religion, no morals, no sense of duty —. Now I am being punished for my leniency with him. I did it for your sake, and this is how you pay me back.

NORA: Yes. This is how.

HELMER: You have ruined all my happiness. My whole future — you've thrown it away. Oh, it's terrible to think about. I am at the mercy of an unscrupulous man. He can do with me whatever he likes, demand anything of me, command me and dispose of me just as he pleases — I dare not say a word! To go down so miserably, to be destroyed — all because of an irresponsible woman!

NORA: When I am gone from the world, you'll be free.

HELMER: No noble gestures, please. Your father was always full of such phrases too. What good would it do me if you were gone from the world, as you put it? Not the slightest bit of good at all. He could still make the whole thing public, and if he did I wouldn't be surprised if people thought I'd put you up to it. They might even think it was my idea — that it was I who urged you to do it! And for all this I have you to thank — you, whom I've borne on my hands through all the years of our marriage. *Now* do you understand what you've done to me?

NORA (*with cold calm*): Yes.

HELMER: I just can't get it into my head that this is happening; it's all so incredible. But we have to come to terms with it somehow. Take your shawl off. Take it off, I say! I have to satisfy him one way or another. The whole affair must be kept quiet at whatever cost. — And as far as you and I are concerned, nothing must seem to have changed. I'm talking about appearances, of course. You'll go on living here; that goes without saying. But I won't let you bring up the children; I dare not trust you with them. — Oh! Having to say this to one I have loved so much, and whom I still — ! But all that has to be past. It's not a question of happiness any more but of hanging on to what can be salvaged — pieces, appearances — (*The doorbell rings.* HELMER *jumps.*) What's that? So late. Is the worst — ? Has he — ! Hide, Nora! Say you're sick.

(NORA *doesn't move.* HELMER *opens the door to the hall.*)

MAID (*half dressed, out in the hall*): A letter for your wife, sir.

HELMER: Give it to me. (*Takes the letter and closes the door.*) Yes, it's from him. But I won't let you have it. I'll read it myself.

NORA: Yes — you read it.

HELMER (*by the lamp*): I hardly dare. Perhaps we're lost, both you and I. No; I've got to know. (*Tears the letter open, glances through it, looks at an enclosure, a cry of joy.*) Nora!

(NORA *looks at him with a question in her eyes.*)

HELMER: Nora! — No, I must read it again. — Yes, yes; it is so! I'm saved! Nora, I'm saved!

NORA: And I?

HELMER: You too, of course; we're both saved, both you and I. Look! He's returning your note. He writes that he's sorry, he regrets, a happy turn in his life — oh, it doesn't matter what he writes. We're saved, Nora! Nobody can do anything to you now. Oh Nora, Nora —. No, I want to get rid of this disgusting thing first.

Let me see — (*Looks at the signature.*) No, I don't want to see it. I don't want it to be more than a bad dream, the whole thing. (*Tears up the note and both letters, throws the pieces in the stove, and watches them burn.*) There! Now it's gone. — He wrote that ever since Christmas Eve —. Good god, Nora, these must have been three terrible days for you.

NORA: I have fought a hard fight these last three days.

HELMER: And been in agony and seen no other way out than —. No, we won't think of all that ugliness. We'll just rejoice and tell ourselves it's over, it's all over! Oh, listen to me, Nora. You don't seem to understand. It's over. What *is* it? Why do you look like that — that frozen expression on your face? Oh my poor little Nora, don't you think I know what it is? You can't make yourself believe that I have forgiven you. But I have, Nora; I swear to you, I have forgiven you for everything. Of course I know that what you did was for love of me.

NORA: That is true.

HELMER: You have loved me the way a wife ought to love her husband. You just didn't have the wisdom to judge the means. But do you think I love you any less because you don't know how to act on your own? Of course not. Just lean on me. I'll advise you; I'll guide you. I wouldn't be a man if I didn't find you twice as attractive because of your womanly helplessness. You mustn't pay any attention to the hard words I said to you right at first. It was just that first shock when I thought everything was collapsing all around me. I have forgiven you, Nora. I swear to you — I really have forgiven you.

NORA: I thank you for your forgiveness. (*She goes out through the door, right.*)

HELMER: No, stay — (*Looks into the room she entered.*) What are you doing in there?

NORA (*within*): Getting out of my costume.

HELMER (*by the open door*): Good, good. Try to calm down and compose yourself, my poor little frightened songbird. Rest safely; I have broad wings to cover you with. (*Walks around near the door.*) What a nice and cozy home we have, Nora. Here's shelter for you. Here I'll keep you safe like a hunted dove I have rescued from the hawk's talons. Believe me: I'll know how to quiet your beating heart. It will happen by and by, Nora; you'll see. Why, tomorrow you'll look at all this in quite a different light. And soon everything will be just the way it was before. I won't need to keep reassuring you that I have forgiven you; you'll feel it yourself. Did you really think I could have abandoned you, or even reproached you? Oh, you don't know a real man's heart, Nora. There is something unspeakably sweet and satisfactory for a man to know deep in himself that he has forgiven his wife — forgiven her in all the fullness of his honest heart. You see, that way she becomes his very own all over again — in a double sense, you might say. He has, so to speak, given her a second birth; it is as if she had become his wife and his child, both. From now on that's what you'll be to me, you lost and helpless creature. Don't worry about a thing, Nora. Only be frank with me, and I'll be your will and your conscience. — What's this? You're not in bed? You've changed your dress — !

NORA (*in an everyday dress*): Yes, Torvald. I have changed my dress.

HELMER: But why — now — this late — ?

NORA: I'm not going to sleep tonight.

HELMER: But my dear Nora —

NORA (*looks at her watch*): It isn't all that late. Sit down here with me, Torvald. You and I have much to talk about. (*Sits down at the table.*)

HELMER: Nora — what is this all about? That rigid face —

NORA: Sit down. This will take a while. I have much to say to you.

HELMER (*sits down, facing her across the table*): You worry me, Nora. I don't understand you.

NORA: No, that's just it. You don't understand me. And I have never understood you — not till tonight. No, don't interrupt me. Just listen to what I have to say. — This is a settling of accounts, Torvald.

HELMER: What do you mean by that?

NORA (*after a brief silence*): Doesn't one thing strike you, now that we are sitting together like this?

HELMER: What would that be?

NORA: We have been married for eight years. Doesn't it occur to you that this is the first time that you and I, husband and wife, are having a serious talk?

HELMER: Well — serious —. What do you mean by that?

NORA: For eight whole years — longer, in fact — ever since we first met, we have never talked seriously to each other about a single serious thing.

HELMER: You mean I should forever have been telling you about worries you couldn't have helped me with anyway?

NORA: I am not talking about worries. I'm saying we have never tried seriously to get to the bottom of anything together.

HELMER: But dearest Nora, I hardly think that would have been something *you* —

NORA: That's the whole point. You have never understood me. Great wrong has been done to me, Torvald. First by Daddy and then by you.

HELMER: What! by us two? We who have loved you more than anyone else?

NORA (*shakes her head*): You never loved me — neither Daddy nor you. You only thought it was fun to be in love with me.

HELMER: But, Nora — what an expression to use!

NORA: That's the way it has been, Torvald. When I was home with Daddy, he told me all his opinions, and so they became my opinions too. If I disagreed with him I kept it to myself, for he wouldn't have liked that. He called me his little doll baby, and he played with me the way I played with my dolls. Then I came to your house —

HELMER: What a way to talk about our marriage!

NORA (*imperturbably*): I mean that I passed from Daddy's hands into yours. You arranged everything according to your taste, and so I came to share it — or I pretended to; I'm not sure which. I think it was a little of both, now one and now the other. When I look back on it now, it seems to me I've been living here like a pauper — just a hand-to-mouth kind of existence. I have earned my keep by doing tricks for you, Torvald. But that's the way you wanted it. You have great sins against me to answer for, Daddy and you. It's your fault that nothing has become of me.

HELMER: Nora, you're being both unreasonable and ungrateful. Haven't you been happy here?

NORA: No, never. I thought I was, but I wasn't.

HELMER: Not — not happy!

NORA: No; just having fun. And you have always been very good to me. But our home has never been more than a playroom. I have been your doll wife here, just the way I used to be

Daddy's doll child. And the children have been my dolls. I thought it was fun when you played with me, just as they thought it was fun when I played with them. That's been our marriage, Torvald.

HELMER: There is something in what you are saying — exaggerated and hysterical though it is. But from now on things will be different. Playtime is over; it's time for growing up.

NORA: Whose growing up — mine or the children's?

HELMER: Both yours and the children's, Nora darling.

NORA: Oh Torvald, you're not the man to bring me up to be the right kind of wife for you.

HELMER: How can you say that?

NORA: And I — ? What qualifications do I have for bringing up the children?

HELMER: Nora!

NORA: You said so yourself a minute ago — that you didn't dare to trust me with them.

HELMER: In the first flush of anger, yes. Surely, you're not going to count that.

NORA: But you were quite right. I am *not* qualified. Something else has to come first. Somehow I have to grow up myself. And you are not the man to help me do that. That's a job I have to do by myself. And that's why I'm leaving you.

HELMER (*jumps up*): What did you say!

NORA: I have to be by myself if I am to find out about myself and about all those other things too. So I can't stay here any longer.

HELMER: Nora, Nora!

NORA: I'm leaving now. I'm sure Kristine will put me up for tonight.

HELMER: You're out of your mind! I won't let you! I forbid you!

NORA: You can't forbid me anything any more; it won't do any good. I'm taking my own things with me. I won't accept anything from you, either now or later.

HELMER: But this is madness!

NORA: Tomorrow I'm going home — I mean back to my old home town. It will be easier for me to find some kind of job there.

HELMER: Oh, you blinded, inexperienced creature — !

NORA: I must see to it that I get experience, Torvald.

HELMER: Leaving your home, your husband, your children! Not a thought of what people will say!

NORA: I can't worry about that. All I know is that I have to leave.

HELMER: Oh, this is shocking! Betraying your most sacred duties like this!

NORA: And what do you consider my most sacred duties?

HELMER: Do I need to tell you that? They are your duties to your husband and your children.

NORA: I have other duties equally sacred.

HELMER: You do not. What duties would they be?

NORA: My duties to myself.

HELMER: You are a wife and a mother before you are anything else.

NORA: I don't believe that any more. I believe I am first of all a human being, just as much as you — or at any rate that I must try to become one. Oh, I know very well that most people agree with you, Torvald, and that it says something like that in all the books. But what people say and what the books say is no longer enough for me. I have to think about these things myself and see if I can't find the answers.

HELMER: You mean to tell me you don't know what your proper place in your own home is? Don't you have a reliable guide in such matters? Don't you have religion?

NORA: Oh but Torvald — I don't really know what religion is.

HELMER: What's this?

NORA: All I know is what the Reverend Hansen told me when he prepared me for confirmation. He said that religion was *this* and it was *that*. When I get by myself, away from here, I'll have to look into that, too. I have to decide if what the Reverend Hansen said was right, or anyway if it is right for *me*.

HELMER: Oh, this is unheard of in a young woman! If religion can't guide you, let me appeal to your conscience. For surely you have moral feelings? Or — answer me — maybe you don't?

NORA: Well, you see, Torvald, I don't really know what to say. I just don't know. I am confused about these things. All I know is that my ideas are quite different from yours. I have just found out that the laws are different from what I thought they were, but in no way can I get it into my head that those laws are right. A woman shouldn't have the right to spare her dying old father or save her husband's life! I just can't believe that.

HELMER: You speak like a child. You don't understand the society you live in.

NORA: No, I don't. But I want to find out about it. I have to make up my mind who is right, society or I.

HELMER: You are sick, Nora; you have a fever. I really don't think you are in your right mind.

NORA: I have never felt so clearheaded and sure of myself as I do tonight.

HELMER: And clearheaded and sure of yourself you're leaving your husband and your children?

NORA: Yes.

HELMER: Then there is only one possible explanation.

NORA: What?

HELMER: You don't love me any more.

NORA: No; that's just it.

HELMER: Nora! How can you say that!

NORA: I am sorry, Torvald, for you have always been so good to me. But I can't help it. I don't love you any more.

HELMER (*with forced composure*): And this too is a clear and sure conviction?

NORA: Completely clear and sure. That's why I don't want to stay here any more.

HELMER: And are you ready to explain to me how I came to forfeit your love?

NORA: Certainly, I am. It was tonight, when the wonderful didn't happen. That was when I realized you were not the man I thought you were.

HELMER: You have to explain. I don't understand.

NORA: I have waited patiently for eight years, for I wasn't such a fool that I thought the wonderful is something that happens any old day. Then this — thing — came crashing in on me, and then there wasn't a doubt in my mind that now — now comes the wonderful. When Krogstad's letter was in that mailbox, never for a moment did it even occur to me that you would submit to his conditions. I was so absolutely certain that you would say to him: make the whole thing public — tell everybody. And when that had happened —

HELMER: Yes, then what? When I had surrendered my own wife to shame and disgrace — !

NORA: When that had happened, I was absolutely certain that you would stand up and take the blame and say, "I am the guilty one."

HELMER: Nora!

NORA: You mean I never would have accepted such a sacrifice from you? Of course not. But what would my protests have counted against yours? *That* was the wonderful I was waiting for in hope and terror. And to prevent that I was going to kill myself.

HELMER: I'd gladly work nights and days for you, Nora — endure sorrow and want for your sake. But nobody sacrifices his *honor* for his love.

NORA: A hundred thousand women have done so.

HELMER: Oh, you think and talk like a silly child.

NORA: All right. But you don't think and talk like the man I can live with. When you had gotten over your fright — not because of what threatened *me* but because of the risk to *you* — and the whole danger was past, then you acted as if nothing at all had happened. Once again I was your little songbird, your doll, just as before, only now you had to handle her even more carefully, because she was so frail and weak. (*Rises.*) Torvald — that moment I realized that I had been living here for eight years with a stranger and had borne him three children — Oh, I can't stand thinking about it! I feel like tearing myself to pieces!

HELMER (*heavily*): I see it, I see it. An abyss has opened up between us. — Oh but Nora — surely it can be filled?

NORA: The way I am now I am no wife for you.

HELMER: I have it in me to change.

NORA: Perhaps — if your doll is taken from you.

HELMER: To part — to part from you! No, no, Nora! I can't grasp that thought!

NORA (*goes out, right*): All the more reason why it has to be. (*She returns with her street clothes and a small bag, which she sets down on the chair by the table.*)

HELMER: Nora, Nora! Not now! Wait till tomorrow.

NORA (*putting on her coat*): I can't spend the night in a stranger's rooms.

HELMER: But couldn't we live here together like brother and sister — ?

NORA (*tying on her hat*): You know very well that wouldn't last long —. (*Wraps her shawl around her.*) Goodbye, Torvald. I don't want to see the children. I know I leave them in better hands than mine. The way I am now I can't be anything to them.

HELMER: But some day, Nora — some day — ?

NORA: How can I tell? I have no idea what's going to become of me.

HELMER: But you're still my wife, both as you are now and as you will be.

NORA: Listen, Torvald — when a wife leaves her husband's house, the way I am doing now, I have heard he has no further legal responsibilities for her. At any rate, I now release you from all responsibility. You are not to feel yourself obliged to me for anything, and I have no obligations to you. There has to be full freedom on both sides. Here is your ring back. Now give me mine.

HELMER: Even this?

NORA: Even this.

HELMER: Here it is.

NORA: There. So now it's over. I'm putting the keys here. The maids know everything about the house — better than I. Tomorrow, after I'm gone, Kristine will come over and pack my things from home. I want them sent after me.

HELMER: Over! It's all over! Nora, will you never think of me?

NORA: I'm sure I'll often think of you and the children and this house.

HELMER: May I write to you, Nora?

NORA: No — never. I won't have that.

HELMER: But send you things — ? You must let me —

NORA: Nothing, nothing —

HELMER: — help you, when you need help —

NORA: I told you, no; I won't have it. I'll accept nothing from strangers.

HELMER: Nora — can I never again be more to you than a stranger?

NORA (*picks up her bag*): Oh Torvald — then the most wonderful of all would have to happen —

HELMER: Tell me what that would be — !

NORA: For that to happen, both you and I would have to change so that — Oh Torvald, I no longer believe in the wonderful.

HELMER: But I *will* believe. Tell me! Change, so that — ?

NORA: So that our living together would become a true marriage. Goodbye. (*She goes out through the hall.*)

HELMER (*sinks down on a chair near the door and covers his face with his hands*): Nora! Nora! (*Looks around him and gets up.*) All empty. She's gone. (*With sudden hope.*) The most wonderful — ? !

(*From downstairs comes the sound of a heavy door slamming shut.*)

TRAGEDY

OEDIPUS THE KING

Sophocles

Translated into English verse by H. D. F. Kitto

Sophocles (c. 495 B.C.–406 B.C.), the son of a wealthy Athenian, is one of the three Greek tragic writers whose work survives. (The other two are Aeschylus and Euripides.) Of Sophocles' more than one hundred and twenty plays, we have seven. The exact date that *Oedipus the King* was written is not known, but 430 B.C. is a reasonable guess. Some twenty-five years later, when he was almost ninety, Sophocles wrote *Oedipus at Colonus*, dramatizing Oedipus' last deeds.

DRAMATIS PERSONAE

OEDIPUS, *King of Thebes*
PRIEST OF ZEUS
CREON, *brother of Iocasta*
TEIRESIAS, *a Seer*
IOCASTA, *Queen of Thebes*
A CORINTHIAN SHEPHERD
A THEBAN SHEPHERD
A MESSENGER
CHORUS *of Theban citizens*
PRIESTS, ATTENDANTS, *etc.*

Scene: Thebes, before the royal palace.

Giant puppets of Iocasta and Oedipus, made by Remo Buffano, for a Philadelphia production of *Oedipus the King*, designed in 1931 by Robert Edmond Jones. (Photograph: Will Rapport, Harvard Theatre Collection.)

OEDIPUS:

My children, latest brood of ancient Cadmus,
What purpose brings you here, a multitude
Bearing the boughs that mark the suppliant?
Why is our air so full of frankincense,
5 So full of hymns and prayers and lamenta-
 tions?
This, children, was no matter to entrust
To others: therefore I myself am come
Whose fame is known to all — I, Oedipus.
— You, Sir, are pointed out by length of years
10 To be the spokesman: tell me, what is in
Your hearts? What fear? What sorrow? Count
 on all
That I can do, for I am not so hard
As not to pity such a supplication.

PRIEST:

Great King of Thebes, and sovereign Oedipus,
15 Look on us, who now stand before the altars —
Some young, still weak of wing; some bowed
 with age —
The priests, as I, of Zeus; and these, the best
Of our young men; and in the market-place,
And by Athena's temples and the shrine
20 Of fiery divination, there is kneeling,
Each with his suppliant branch, the rest of
 Thebes.
The city, as you see yourself, is now
Storm-tossed, and can no longer raise its head
Above the waves and angry surge of death.
25 The fruitful blossoms of the land are barren,
The herds upon our pastures, and our wives
In childbirth, barren. Last, and worst of all,
The withering god of fever swoops on us
To empty Cadmus' city and enrich
30 Dark Hades with our groans and lamentations.
No god we count you, that we bring our
 prayers,
I and these children, to your palace-door,
But wise above all other men to read
Life's riddles, and the hidden ways of Heaven;
35 For it was you who came and set us free
From the blood-tribute that the cruel Sphinx
Had laid upon our city; without our aid
Or our instruction, but, as we believe,
With god as ally, you gave us back our life.
40 So now, most dear, most mighty Oedipus,
We all entreat you on our bended knees,

From *Sophocles: Three Tragedies. Antigone, Oedipus the King, Electra*, translated by H. D. F. Kitto. Copyright © 1962 by Oxford University Press. Reprinted by permission.

Come to our rescue, whether from the gods
Or from some man you can find means to
 save.
For I have noted, *that* man's counsel is
Of best effect, who has been tried in action. 45
Come, noble Oedipus! Come, save our city.
Be well advised; for that past service given
This city calls you Savior; of your kingship
Let not the record be that first we rose
From ruin, then to ruin fell again. 50
No, save our city, let it stand secure.
You brought us gladness and deliverance
Before; now do no less. You rule this land;
Better to rule it full of living men
Than rule a desert; citadel or ship 55
Without its company of men is nothing.

OEDIPUS:

My children, what you long for, that I know
Indeed, and pity you. I know how cruelly
You suffer; yet, though sick, not one of you
Suffers a sickness half as great as mine. 60
Yours is a single pain; each man of you
Feels but his own. My heart is heavy with
The city's pain, my own, and yours together.
You come to me not as to one asleep
And needing to be wakened; many a tear 65
I have been shedding, every path of thought
Have I been pacing; and what remedy,
What single hope my anxious thought has
 found
That I have tried. Creon, Menoeceus' son,
My own wife's brother, I have sent to Delphi 70
To ask in Phoebus' house what act of mine,
What word of mine, may bring deliverance.
Now, as I count the days, it troubles me
What he is doing; his absence is prolonged
Beyond the proper time. But when he comes 75
Then write me down a villain, if I do
Not each particular that the god discloses.

PRIEST:

You give us hope. — And here is more, for
 they
Are signaling that Creon has returned.

OEDIPUS:

O Lord Apollo, even as Creon smiles, 80
Smile now on us, and let it be deliverance!

PRIEST:

The news is good; or he would not be wearing
That ample wreath of richly-berried laurel.

OEDIPUS:

We soon shall know; my voice will reach so
 far:

85 Creon my lord, my kinsman, what response
Do you bring with you from the god of Delphi?

[*Enter* CREON.]

CREON:
Good news! Our sufferings, if they are guided right,
Can even yet turn to a happy issue.
OEDIPUS:
This only leaves my fear and confidence
90 In equal balance: what did Phoebus say?
CREON:
Is it your wish to hear it now, in public,
Or in the palace? I am at your service.
OEDIPUS:
Let them all hear! Their sufferings distress
Me more than if my own life were at stake.
CREON:
95 Then I will tell you what Apollo said —
And it was very clear. There is pollution
Here in our midst, long-standing. This must we
Expel, nor let it grow past remedy.
OEDIPUS:
What has defiled us? and how are we to purge it?
CREON:
100 By banishing or killing one who murdered,
And so called down this pestilence upon us.
OEDIPUS:
Who is the man whose death the god denounces?
CREON:
Before the city passed into your care,
My lord, we had a king called Laius.
OEDIPUS:
105 So I have often heard. — I never saw him.
CREON:
His death, Apollo clearly charges us,
We must avenge upon his murderers.
OEDIPUS:
Where are they now? And where shall we disclose
The unseen traces of that ancient crime?
CREON:
The god said, Here. — A man who hunts with care
110 May often find what other men will miss.
OEDIPUS:
Where was he murdered? In the palace here?
Or in the country? Or was he abroad?
CREON:
He made a journey to consult the god,
115 He said — and never came back home again.

OEDIPUS:
But was there no report? no fellow traveler
Whose knowledge might have helped you in your search?
CREON:
All died, except one terror-stricken man,
And he could tell us nothing — next to nothing.
OEDIPUS:
And what was that? One thing might lead to much, 120
If only we could find one ray of light.
CREON:
He said they met with brigands — not with one,
But a whole company; they killed Laius.
OEDIPUS:
A brigand would not *dare* — unless perhaps
Conspirators in Thebes had bribed the man. 125
CREON:
There *was* conjecture; but disaster came
And we were leaderless, without our king.
OEDIPUS:
Disaster? With a king cut down like that
You did not seek the cause? Where was the hindrance?
CREON:
The Sphinx. *Her* riddle pressed us harder still; 130
For Laius — out of sight was out of mind.
OEDIPUS:
I will begin again; *I'll* find the truth.
The dead man's cause has found a true defender
In Phoebus, and in you. And I will join you
In seeking vengeance on behalf of Thebes 135
And Phoebus too; indeed, I must: if I
Remove this taint, it is not for a stranger,
But for myself: the man who murdered him
Might make the same attempt on me; and so,
Avenging him, I shall protect myself. — 140
Now you, my sons, without delay, arise,
Take up your suppliant branches. — Someone, go
And call the people here, for I will do
What can be done; and either, by the grace
Of God we shall be saved — or we shall fall. 145
PRIEST:
My children, we will go; the King has promised
All that we came to ask. — O Phoebus, thou
Hast given us an answer: give us too
Protection! grant remission of the plague!

[*Exeunt* CREON, PRIESTS, *etc.*
OEDIPUS *remains.*]

[*Enter the* CHORUS *representing the citizens of Thebes.*]

STROPHE 1

CHORUS:
Sweet is the voice of the god, that
[*mainly dactyls:* $\frac{4}{4}$]¹   sounds in the
Golden shrine of Delphi.
What message has it sent to Thebes? My
    trembling
Heart is torn with anguish.
5 Thou god of Healing, Phoebus Apollo,
How do I fear! What hast thou in mind
To bring upon us now? what is to be fulfilled
From days of old?
Tell me this, O Voice divine,
10 Thou child of golden Hope.

ANTISTROPHE 1

First on the Daughter of Zeus I call for
Help, divine Athene;
And Artemis, whose throne is all the earth,
    whose
Shrine is in our city;
5 Apollo too, who shoots from afar:
Trinity of Powers, come to our defence!
If ever in the past, when ruin threatened us,
You stayed its course
And turned aside the flood of Death,
10 O then, protect us now!

STROPHE 2

[*agitated:* $\frac{3}{8}$] Past counting are the woes we
    suffer;
Affliction bears on all the city, and
Nowhere is any defence against destruction.

¹ Taking a hint from the French translators for the
Budé series I have here and there added to the lyrical
portions a quasi-musical indication of tempo or mood,
on no authority except that of common sense. These
may at least serve to remind the reader, if he needs
reminding, that the lyrics were not recited; they were
a fusion of intense poetry, music, and dancing. Of the
music we know nothing; of the dance we can at least
infer that its range extended from grave processional
movements to the expression of great excitement,
whether of joy or despair. [Kitto.]

The holy soil can bring no increase,
Our women suffer and cry in childbirth   5
But do not bring forth living children.
The souls of those who perish, one by one,
Unceasingly, swift as raging fire,
Rise and take their flight to the dark realms of
    the dead.

ANTISTROPHE 2

Past counting, those of us who perish:
They lie upon the ground, unpitied,
Unburied, infecting the air with deadly pollu-
    tion.
Young wives, and grey-haired mothers with
    them,
From every quarter approach the altars   5
And cry aloud in supplication.
The prayer for healing, the loud wail of
    lament,
Together are heard in dissonance:
O thou golden Daughter of Zeus, grant thy
    aid!

STROPHE 3

[*mainly iambic:* $\frac{3}{8}$] The fierce god of War has
    laid aside
His spear; but yet his terrible cry
Rings in our ears; he spreads death and
    destruction.
Ye gods, drive him back to his distant home!
    For what the light of day has spared,   5
    That the darkness of night destroys.
    Zeus our father! All power is thine:
The lightning-flash is thine: hurl upon him
Thy thunderbolt, and quell this god of War!

ANTISTROPHE 3

We pray, Lord Apollo: draw thy bow
In our defense. Thy quiver is full of
Arrows unerring: shoot! slay the destroyer!
And thou, radiant Artemis, lend thy aid!
    Thou whose hair is bound in gold,   5
Bacchus, lord of the sacred dance,
    Theban Bacchus! Come, show thyself!
Display thy blazing torch; drive from our
    midst

The savage god, abhorred by other gods!
OEDIPUS:
Would you have answer to these prayers?
10   Then hear
My words; give heed; your help may bring
Deliverance, and the end of all our troubles.
Here do I stand before you all, a stranger
Both to the deed and to the story. — What
15 Could I have done alone, without a clue?
But I was yet a foreigner; it was later
That I became a Theban among Thebans.
So now do I proclaim to all the city:
If any Theban knows by what man's hand
20 He perished, Laius, son of Labdacus,
Him I command to tell me all he can;
And if he is afraid, let him annul
Himself the charge he fears; no punishment
Shall fall on him, save only to depart
Unharmed from Thebes. Further, if any
25   knows
The slayer to be a stranger from abroad,
Let him speak out; I will reward him, and
Besides, he will have all my gratitude.
But if you still keep silent, if any man
30 Fearing for self or friend shall disobey me,
This will I do — and listen to my words:
Whoever he may be, I do forbid
All in this realm, of which I am the King
And high authority, to shelter in their houses
35 Or speak to him, or let him be their partner
In prayers or sacrifices to the gods, or give
Him lustral water; I command you all
To drive him from your doors; for he it is
That brings this plague upon us, as the god
40 Of Delphi has but now declared to me. —
So stern an ally do I make myself
Both of the god and of our murdered king. —
And for the man that slew him, whether he
Slew him alone, or with a band of helpers,
45 I lay this curse upon him, that the wretch
In wretchedness and misery may live.
And more: if with my knowledge he be found
To share my hearth and home, then upon me
Descend that doom that I invoke on him.
50 This charge I lay upon you, to observe
All my commands: to aid myself, the god,
And this our land, so spurned of Heaven, so
     ravaged.
For such a taint we should not leave un-
     purged —
The death of such a man, and he your king —
55 Even if Heaven had not commanded us,
But we should search it out. Now, since 'tis I
That wear the crown that he had worn before
     me,

And have his Queen to wife, and common
     children
Were born to us, but that his own did perish,
And sudden death has carried him away —   60
Because of this, I will defend his cause
As if it were my father's; nothing I
Will leave undone to find the man who killed
The son of Labdacus, and offspring of
Polydorus, Cadmus, and of old Agênor.   65
On those that disobey, this is my curse:
May never field of theirs give increase, nor
Their wives have children; may our present
     plagues,
And worse, be ever theirs, for their destruction.
But for the others, all with whom my words   70
Find favour, this I pray: Justice and all
The gods be ever at your side to help you.
CHORUS-LEADER:
Your curse constrains me; therefore will I
     speak.
I did not kill him, neither can I tell
Who did. It is for Phoebus, since he laid   75
The task upon us, to declare the man.
OEDIPUS:
True; but to force the gods against their will —
That is a thing beyond all human power.
CHORUS-LEADER:
All I could say is but a second best.
OEDIPUS:
Though it were third best, do not hold it back.   80
CHORUS-LEADER:
I know of none that reads Apollo's mind
So surely as the lord Teiresias;
Consulting him you best might learn the truth.
OEDIPUS:
Not even this have I neglected: Creon
Advised me, and already I have sent   85
Two messengers. — Strange he has not come.
CHORUS-LEADER:
There's nothing else but old and idle gossip.
OEDIPUS:
And what was that? I clutch at any straw.
CHORUS-LEADER:
They said that he was killed by travelers.
OEDIPUS:
So I have heard; but no one knows a witness.   90
CHORUS-LEADER:
But if he is not proof against *all* fear
He'll not keep silent when he hears your curse.
OEDIPUS:
And will they fear a curse, who dared to kill?
CHORUS-LEADER:
Here is the one to find him, for at last
They bring the prophet here. He is inspired,   95
The only man whose heart is filled with truth.

[*Enter* TEIRESIAS, *led by a boy*.]

OEDIPUS:

Teiresias, by your art you read the signs
And secrets of the earth and of the sky;
Therefore you know, although you cannot see,
100 The plague that is besetting us; from this
No other man but you, my lord, can save us.
Phoebus has said — you may have heard already —
In answer to our question, that this plague
Will never cease unless we can discover
105 What men they were who murdered Laius,
And punish them with death or banishment.
Therefore give freely all that you have learned
From birds or other form of divination;
Save us; save me, the city, and yourself,
110 From the pollution that his bloodshed causes.
No finer task, than to give all one has
In helping others; we are in your hands.

TEIRESIAS:

Ah! what a burden knowledge is, when knowledge
Can be of no avail! I knew this well,
115 And yet forgot, or I should not have come.

OEDIPUS:

Why, what is this? Why are you so despondent?

TEIRESIAS:

Let me go home! It will be best for you,
And best for me, if you will let me go.

OEDIPUS:

But to withhold your knowledge! This is wrong,
120 Disloyal to the city of your birth.

TEIRESIAS:

I know that what you say will lead you on
To ruin; therefore, lest the same befall me
too . . .

OEDIPUS:

No, by the gods! Say all you know, for we
Go down upon our knees, your suppliants.

TEIRESIAS:

125 Because *you* do *not* know! I never shall
Reveal my burden — I will not say *yours*.

OEDIPUS:

You know, and will not tell us? Do you wish
To ruin Thebes and to destroy us all?

TEIRESIAS:

My pain, and yours, will not be caused by me.
Why these vain questions? — for I will not
130   speak.

OEDIPUS:

You villain! — for you would provoke a stone

To anger: you'll not speak, but show yourself
So hard of heart and so inflexible?

TEIRESIAS:

You heap the blame on me; but what is yours
You do not know — therefore *I* am the villain! 135

OEDIPUS:

And who would not be angry, finding that
You treat our people with such cold disdain?

TEIRESIAS:

The truth will come to light, without *my* help.

OEDIPUS:

If it is bound to come, you ought to speak it.

TEIRESIAS:

I'll say no more, and you, if so you choose, 140
May rage and bluster on without restraint.

OEDIPUS:

Restraint? Then I'll show none! I'll tell you all
That I can see in you: I do believe
This crime was planned and carried out by
    you,
All but the killing; and were you not blind 145
I'd say your hand alone had done the murder.

TEIRESIAS:

So? Then I tell you this: submit yourself
To that decree that you have made; from now
Address no word to these men nor to me:
You are the man whose crimes pollute our
    city. 150

OEDIPUS:

What, does your impudence extend thus far?
And do you hope that it will go scot-free?

TEIRESIAS:

It will. I have a champion — the truth.

OEDIPUS:

Who taught you that? For it was not your art.

TEIRESIAS:

No; you! You made me speak, against my will. 155

OEDIPUS:

Speak what? Say it again, and say it clearly.

TEIRESIAS:

Was I not clear? Or are you tempting me?

OEDIPUS:

Not clear enough for me. Say it again.

TEIRESIAS:

You are yourself the murderer you seek.

OEDIPUS:

You'll not affront me twice and go unpunished! 160

TEIRESIAS:

Then shall I give you still more cause for rage?

OEDIPUS:

Say what you will; you'll say it to no purpose.

TEIRESIAS:

I know, *you* do not know, the hideous life

Of shame you lead with those most near to
    you.
OEDIPUS:
165 You'll pay most dearly for this insolence!
TEIRESIAS:
No, not if Truth is strong, and can prevail.
OEDIPUS:
It is — except in you; for you are blind
In eyes and ears and brains and everything.
TEIRESIAS:
You'll not forget these insults that you throw
170 At me, when all men throw the same at you.
OEDIPUS:
You live in darkness; you can do no harm
To me or any man who has his eyes.
TEIRESIAS:
No; I am not to bring you down, because
Apollo is enough; he'll see to it.
OEDIPUS:
175 Creon, or you? Which of you made this plot?
TEIRESIAS:
Creon's no enemy of yours; you are your own.
OEDIPUS:
O Wealth! O Royalty! whose commanding art
Outstrips all other arts in life's contentions!
How great a store of envy lies upon you,
180 If for this scepter, that the city gave
Freely to me, unasked — if now my friend,
The trusty Creon, burns to drive me hence
And steal it from me! So he has suborned
This crafty schemer here, this mountebank,
185 Whose purse alone has eyes, whose art is
    blind. —
Come, prophet, show your title! When the
    Sphinx
Chanted her music here, why did not *you*
Speak out and save the city? Yet such a
    question
Was one for augury, not for mother wit.
You were no prophet then; your birds, your
190   voice
From Heaven, were dumb. But I, who came
    by chance,
I, knowing nothing, put the Sphinx to flight,
Thanks to my wit — no thanks to divination!
And now you try to drive me out; you hope
195 When Creon's king to bask in Creon's favor.
You'll expiate the curse? Ay, and repent it,
Both you and your accomplice. But that you
Seem old, I'd teach you what you gain by
    treason!
CHORUS-LEADER:
My lord, he spoke in anger; so I think,
200 Did you. What help in angry speeches? Come,

This is the task, how we can best discharge
The duty that the god has laid on us.
TEIRESIAS:
King though you are, I claim the privilege
Of equal answer. No, I have the right;
I am no slave of yours— I serve Apollo, 205
And therefore am not listed *Creon's* man.
Listen — since you have taunted me with
    blindness!
You have your sight, and yet you cannot see
Where, nor with whom, you live, nor in what
    horror.
Your parents — do you know them? or that you 210
Are enemy to your kin, alive or dead?
And that a father's and a mother's curse
Shall join to drive you headlong out of Thebes
And change the light that now you see to
    darkness?
Your cries of agony, where will they not reach? 215
Where on Cithaeron will they not re-echo?
Where you have learned what meant the
    marriage-song
Which bore you to an evil haven here
After so fair a voyage? And you are blind
To other horrors, which shall make you one 220
With your own children. Therefore, heap your
    scorn
On Creon and on me, for no man living
Will meet a doom more terrible than yours.
OEDIPUS:
What? Am I to suffer words like this from
    him?
Ruin, damnation seize you! Off at once 225
Out of our sight! Go! Get you whence you
    came!
TEIRESIAS:
Had you not called me, I should not be here.
OEDIPUS:
And had I known that you would talk such
    folly,
I'd not have called you to a house of mine.
TEIRESIAS:
To you I seem a fool, but to your parents, 230
To those who did beget you, I was wise.
OEDIPUS:
Stop! Who were they? Who *were* my parents?
    Tell me!
TEIRESIAS:
This day will show your birth and your destruc-
    tion.
OEDIPUS:
You are too fond of dark obscurities.
TEIRESIAS:
But do you not excel in reading riddles? 235

OEDIPUS:
I scorn your taunts; my skill has brought me
    glory.
TEIRESIAS:
And this success brought you to ruin too.
OEDIPUS:
I am content, if so I saved this city.
TEIRESIAS:
Then I will leave you. Come, boy, take my
    hand.
OEDIPUS:
240 Yes, let him take it. You are nothing but
Vexation here. Begone, and give me peace!
TEIRESIAS:
When I have had my say. No frown of yours
Shall frighten *me*; you cannot injure me.
Here is my message: that man whom you seek
245 With threats and proclamations for the death
Of Laius, he is living here; he's thought
To be a foreigner, but shall be found
Theban by birth — and little joy will this
Bring *him*; when, with his eyesight turned to
    blindness,
250 His wealth to beggary, on foreign soil
With staff in hand he'll tap his way along,
His children with him; and he will be known
Himself to be their father and their brother,
The husband of the mother who gave him
    birth,
255 Supplanter of his father, and his slayer.
— There! Go, and think on this; and if you
    find
That I'm deceived, say then — and not be-
    fore —
That I am ignorant in divination.
    [*Exeunt severally* TEIRESIAS *and* OEDIPUS.]

STROPHE 1

CHORUS:
The voice of god rang out in the holy cavern,
Denouncing one who has killed a King — the
    crime of crimes.
    Who is the man? Let him begone in
    Headlong flight, swift as a horse!
[*anapaests*] For the terrible god, like a warrior
5   armed,
Stands ready to strike with a lightning-flash:
    The Furies who punish crime, and never
    fail,
    Are hot in their pursuit.

ANTISTROPHE 1

The snow is white on the cliffs of high
    Parnassus.
It has flashed a message: Let every Theban
    join the hunt!
    Lurking in caves among the mountains,
    Deep in the woods — where is the man?
[*anapaests*] In wearisome flight, unresting,
    alone,   5
An outlaw, he shuns Apollo's shrine;
    But ever the living menace of the god
    Hovers around his head.

STROPHE 2

[*choriambics*] Strange, disturbing, what the
    wise
Prophet has said. What can he mean?
Neither can I believe, nor can I disbelieve;
I do not know what to say.
I look here, and there; nothing can I find —   5
No strife, either now or in the past,
Between the kings of Thebes and Corinth.
A hand unknown struck down the King;
Though I would learn who it was dealt the
    blow,
That *he* is guilty whom all revere —   10
How can I believe this with no proof?

ANTISTROPHE 2

Zeus, Apollo — they have knowledge;
They understand the ways of life.
Prophets are men, like me; that they can
    understand
More than is revealed to me —
Of that, I can find nowhere certain proof,   5
Though one man is wise, another foolish.
Until the charge is manifest
I will not credit his accusers.
I saw myself how the Sphinx challenged him:
He proved his wisdom; he saved our city;   10
Therefore how can I now condemn him?

    [*Enter* CREON]

CREON:
They tell me, Sirs, that Oedipus the King
Has made against me such an accusation

That I will not endure. For if he thinks
15 That in this present trouble I have done
Or said a single thing to do him harm,
Then let me die, and not drag out my days
With such a name as that. For it is not
One injury this accusation does me;
20 It touches my whole life, if you, my friends,
And all the city are to call me traitor.

CHORUS-LEADER:
The accusation may perhaps have come
From heat of temper, not from sober judg-
ment.

CREON:
What was it made him think contrivances
25 Of mine suborned the seer to tell his lies?

CHORUS-LEADER:
Those were his words; I do not know his
reasons.

CREON:
Was he in earnest, master of himself,
When he attacked me with this accusation?

CHORUS-LEADER:
I do not closely scan what kings are doing. —
30 But here he comes in person from the palace.

[*Enter* OEDIPUS.]

OEDIPUS:
What, *you*? You dare come here? How can
you find
The impudence to show yourself before
My house, when you are clearly proven
To have sought my life and tried to steal my
crown?
35 Why, do you think me then a coward, or
A fool, that you should try to lay this plot?
Or that I should not see what you were
scheming,
And so fall unresisting, blindly, to you?
But you were mad, so to attempt the throne,
40 Poor and unaided; this is not encompassed
Without the strong support of friends and
money!

CREON:
This you must do: now you have had your say
Hear my reply; then yourself shall judge.

OEDIPUS:
A ready tongue! But I am bad at listening —
To you. For I have found how much you hate
45 me.

CREON:
One thing: first listen to what I have to say.

OEDIPUS:
One thing: do not pretend you're not a villain.

CREON:
If you believe it is a thing worth having,
Insensate stubbornness, then you are wrong.

OEDIPUS:
If you believe that one can harm a kinsman 50
Without retaliation, you are wrong.

CREON:
With this I have no quarrel; but explain
What injury you say that I have done you.

OEDIPUS:
Did you advise, or did you not, that I
Should send a man for that most reverend
prophet? 55

CREON:
I did, and I am still of that advice.

OEDIPUS:
How long a time is it since Laius . . .

CREON:
Since Laius did *what*? How can I say?

OEDIPUS:
Was seen no more, but met a violent death?

CREON:
It would be many years now past and gone. 60

OEDIPUS:
And had this prophet learned his art already?

CREON:
Yes, his repute was great — as it is now.

OEDIPUS:
Did he make any mention then of me?

CREON:
He never spoke of you within my hearing.

OEDIPUS:
Touching the murder: did you make no
search? 65

CREON:
No search? Of course we did; but we found
nothing.

OEDIPUS:
And why did this wise prophet not speak *then*?

CREON:
Who knows? Where I know nothing I say
nothing.

OEDIPUS:
This much you know — and you'll do well to
answer:

CREON:
What is it? If I know, I'll tell you freely. 70

OEDIPUS:
That if he had not joined with you, he'd not
Have said that I was Laius' murderer.

CREON:
If he said this, I did not know. — But I
May rightly question you, as you have me.

OEDIPUS:
Ask what you will. You'll never prove *I* killed
75   him.
CREON:
Why then: are you not married to my sister?
OEDIPUS:
I am indeed; it cannot be denied.
CREON:
You share with her the sovereignty of Thebes?
OEDIPUS:
She need but ask, and anything is hers.
CREON:
80   And am I not myself conjoined with you?
OEDIPUS:
You are; not rebel therefore, but a traitor!
CREON:
Not so, if you will reason with yourself,
As I with you. This first: would any man,
To gain no increase of authority,
Choose kingship, with its fears and sleepless
85   nights?
Not I. What I desire, what every man
Desires, if he has wisdom, is to take
The substance, not the show, of royalty.
For now, through you, I have both power and
ease,
90   But were I king, I'd be oppressed with cares.
Not so: while I have ample sovereignty
And rule in peace, why should I want the
crown?
I am not yet so mad as to give up
All that which brings me honor and advantage.
95   Now, every man greets me, and I greet him;
Those who have need of you make much of
me,
Since I can make or mar them. Why should I
Surrender this to load myself with that?
A man of sense was never yet a traitor;
100   I have no taste for that, nor could I force
Myself to aid another's treachery.
    But you can test me: go to Delphi; ask
If I reported rightly what was said.
And further: if you find that I had dealings
105   With that diviner, you may take and kill me
Not with your single vote, but yours and mine,
But not on bare suspicion, unsupported.
How wrong it is, to use a random judgment
And think the false man true, the true man
false!
110   To spurn a loyal friend, that is no better
Than to destroy the life to which we cling.
This you will learn in time, for Time alone
Reveals the upright man; a single day
Suffices to unmask the treacherous.

CHORUS-LEADER:
My lord, he speaks with caution, to avoid   115
Grave error. Hasty judgment is not sure.
OEDIPUS:
But when an enemy is quick to plot
And strike, I must be quick in answer too.
If I am slow, and wait, then I shall find
That he has gained his end, and I am lost.   120
CREON:
What do you wish? To drive me into exile?
OEDIPUS:
No, more than exile: I will have your life.[2]
CREON:
<When will it cease, this monstrous rage of
    yours?>
OEDIPUS:
When your example shows what comes of
envy.
CREON:
Must you be stubborn? Cannot you believe
me?   125
OEDIPUS:
<You speak to me as if I were a fool!>
CREON:
Because I know you're wrong.
OEDIPUS: Right, for myself!
CREON:
It is not right for me!
OEDIPUS: But you're a traitor.
CREON:
What if your charge is false?
OEDIPUS: I have to govern.
CREON:
Not govern badly!

[2] The next two verses, as they stand in the mss., are
impossible. Editors are agreed on this, though no
single remedy has found general acceptance. The mss.
attribute v. 624 [Oedipus' next speech] to Creon, and
v. 625 [Creon's next speech] to Oedipus. I can make
no real sense of this: the only φθόνος, "envy," that is
in question is the envy of his royal power that
Oedipus is attributing to Creon; and the words
ὑπείξων, "yield," "not to be stubborn," and πιστεύσων,
"believe," must surely be used by Creon of Oedipus,
not by Oedipus of Creon. Since a translator who
hopes to be acted must give the actors something to
say, preferably good sense, and cannot fob them off
with a row of dots, I have reconstructed the passage
by guesswork, putting my guesses within brackets. I
have assumed that two verses were lost, one after v.
623 and one after v. 625, and that the wrong attribu-
tion of vv. 624 and 625 followed almost inevitably.
[Kitto.]

130   OEDIPUS: Listen to him, Thebes!
       CREON:
You're not the city! I am Theban too.
       CHORUS-LEADER:
My lords, no more! Here comes the Queen, and not
Too soon, to join you. With her help, you must
Compose the bitter strife that now divides you.

[*Enter* IOCASTA.]

       IOCASTA:
135   You frantic men! What has aroused this wild
Dispute? Have you no shame, when such a plague
Afflicts us, to indulge in private quarrels?
Creon, go home, I pray. You, Oedipus,
Come in; do not make much of what is nothing.
       CREON:
140   My sister: Oedipus, your husband here,
Has thought it right to punish me with one
Of two most awful dooms: exile, or death.
       OEDIPUS:
I have: I have convicted him, Iocasta,
Of plotting secretly against my life.
       CREON:
145   If I am guilty in a single point
Of such a crime, then may I die accursed.
       IOCASTA:
O, by the gods, believe him, Oedipus!
Respect the oath that he has sworn, and have
Regard for me, and for these citizens.

[*In what follows, the parts given to the chorus are sung, the rest, presumably, spoken. The rhythm of the music and dance is either dochmiac, 5-time, or a combination of 3- and 5-time.*]

STROPHE

       CHORUS:
My lord, I pray, give consent.
Yield to us; ponder well.
       OEDIPUS:
What is it you would have me yield?
       CHORUS:
Respect a man ripe in years,
5   Bound by this mighty oath he has sworn.
       OEDIPUS:
Your wish is clear?

       CHORUS: It is.
       OEDIPUS: Then tell it me.
       CHORUS:
Not to repel, and drive out of our midst a friend,
Scorning a solemn curse, for uncertain cause.
       OEDIPUS:
I tell you this: your prayer will mean for me
My banishment from Thebes, or else my death.   10
       CHORUS:
No, no! by the Sun, the chief of gods,
Ruin and desolation and all evil come upon me
If I harbor thoughts such as these!
No; our land racked with plague breaks my heart.
Do not now deal a new wound on Thebes to crown the old!   15
       OEDIPUS:
Then let him be, though I must die twice over,
Or be dishonored, spurned and driven out.
It's your entreaty, and not his, that moves
My pity; he shall have my lasting hatred.
       CREON:
You yield ungenerously; but when your wrath   20
Has cooled, how it will prick you! Natures such
As yours give most vexation to themselves.
       OEDIPUS:
O, let me be! Get from my sight.
       CREON: I go,
Misjudged by you — but these will judge me better [*indicating* CHORUS].

[*Exit* CREON.]

ANTISTROPHE

       CHORUS:
My lady, why now delay?
Let the King go in with you.
       IOCASTA:
When you have told me what has passed.
       CHORUS:
Suspicion came. — Random words, undeserved,
Will provoke men to wrath.   5
       IOCASTA:
It was from both?
       CHORUS: It was.
       IOCASTA: And what was said?

CHORUS:
It is enough for me, more than enough, when I
Think of our ills, that this should rest where it
    lies.
OEDIPUS:
You and your wise advice, blunting my wrath,
Frustrated me — and it has come to this!
CHORUS:
This, O my King, I said, and say again:
    I should be mad, distraught,
    I should be a fool, and worse,
    If I sought to drive you away.
    Thebes was near sinking; you brought her safe
Through the storm. Now again we pray that
    you may save us.
IOCASTA:
In Heaven's name, my lord, I too must know
What was the reason for this blazing anger.
OEDIPUS:
There's none to whom I more defer; and so,
I'll tell you: Creon and his vile plot against me.
IOCASTA:
What has he done, that you are so incensed?
OEDIPUS:
He says that I am Laius' murderer.
IOCASTA:
From his own knowledge? Or has someone
    told him?
OEDIPUS:
No; that suspicion should not fall upon
Himself, he used a tool — a crafty prophet.
IOCASTA:
Why, have no fear of *that*. Listen to me,
And you will learn that the prophetic art
Touches our human fortunes not at all.
I soon can give you proof. — An oracle
Once came to Laius — from the god himself
I do not say, but from his ministers:
His fate it was, that should he have a son
By me, that son would take his father's life.
But he was killed — or so they said — by
    strangers,
By brigands, at a place where three ways meet.
As for the child, it was not three days old
When Laius fastened both its feet together
And had it cast over a precipice.
Therefore Apollo failed; for neither did
His son kill Laius, nor did Laius meet
The awful end he feared, killed by his son.
    So much for what prophetic voices uttered.
Have no regard for them. The god will bring
To light himself whatever thing he chooses.
OEDIPUS:
Iocasta, terror seizes me, and shakes
My very soul, at one thing you have said.

IOCASTA:
Why so? What have I said to frighten you?
OEDIPUS:
I think I heard you say that Laius
Was murdered at a place where three ways
    meet?
IOCASTA:
So it was said — indeed, they say it still.
OEDIPUS:
Where is the place where this encounter
    happened?
IOCASTA:
They call the country Phokis, and a road
From Delphi joins a road from Daulia.
OEDIPUS:
Since that was done, how many years have
    passed?
IOCASTA:
It was proclaimed in Thebes a little time
Before the city offered you the crown.
OEDIPUS:
O Zeus, what fate hast thou ordained for me?
IOCASTA:
What is the fear that so oppresses you?
OEDIPUS:
One moment yet: tell me of Laius.
What age was he? and what was his appear-
    ance?
IOCASTA:
A tall man, and his hair was touched with
    white;
In figure he was not unlike yourself.
OEDIPUS:
O God! Did I, then, in my ignorance,
Proclaim that awful curse against myself?
IOCASTA:
What are you saying? How you frighten me!
OEDIPUS:
I greatly fear that prophet was not blind.
But yet one question; that will show me more.
IOCASTA:
For all my fear, I'll tell you what I can.
OEDIPUS:
Was he alone, or did he have with him
A royal bodyguard of men-at-arms?
IOCASTA:
The company in all were five; the King
Rode in a carriage, and there was a Herald.
OEDIPUS:
Ah God! How clear the picture is! . . . But who,
Iocasta, brought report of this to Thebes?
IOCASTA:
A slave, the only man that was not killed.
OEDIPUS:
And is he round about the palace now?

IOCASTA:

No, he is not. When he returned, and saw
You ruling in the place of the dead King,
He begged me, on his bended knees, to send
him
80 Into the hills as shepherd, out of sight,
As far as could be from the city here.
I sent him, for he was a loyal slave;
He well deserved this favor — and much more.

OEDIPUS:

Could he be brought back here — at once — to
see me?

IOCASTA:

85 He could; but why do you desire his coming?

OEDIPUS:

I fear I have already said, Iocasta,
More than enough; and therefore I will see
him.

IOCASTA:

Then he shall come. But, as your wife, I ask
you,
What is the terror that possesses you?

OEDIPUS:

And you shall know it, since my fears have
90 grown
So great; for who is more to me than you,
That I should speak to *him* at such a moment?
My father, then, was Polybus of Corinth;
My mother, Meropê. My station there
95 Was high as any man's — until a thing
Befell me that was strange indeed, though not
Deserving of the thought I gave to it.
A man said at a banquet — he was full
Of wine — that I was not my father's son.
100 It angered me; but I restrained myself
That day. The next I went and questioned
both
My parents. They were much incensed with
him
Who had let fall the insult. So, from them,
I had assurance. Yet the slander spread
105 And always chafed me. Therefore secretly,
My mother and my father unaware,
I went to Delphi. Phoebus would return
No answer to my question, but declared
A thing most horrible: he foretold that I
110 Should mate with my own mother, and beget
A brood that men would shudder to behold,
And that I was to be the murderer
Of my own father.
                    Therefore, back to Corinth
I never went — the stars alone have told me
115 Where Corinth lies — that I might never see
Cruel fulfillment of that oracle.
So journeying, I came to that same spot

Where, as you say, this King was killed. And
now,
This is the truth, Iocasta: when I reached
The place where three ways meet, I met a
herald,   120
And in a carriage drawn by colts was such
A man as you describe. By violence
The herald and the older man attempted
To push me off the road, I, in my rage,
Struck at the driver, who was hustling me.   125
The old man, when he saw me level with him,
Taking a double-goad, aimed at my head
A murderous blow. He paid for that, full
measure.
Swiftly I hit him with my staff; he rolled
Out of his carriage, flat upon his back.   130
I killed them all. — But if, between this
stranger
And Laius there was any bond of kinship,
Who could be in more desperate plight than I?
Who more accursèd in the eyes of Heaven?
For neither citizen nor stranger may   135
Receive me in his house, nor speak to me,
But he must bar the door. And it was none
But I invoked this curse on my own head!
And I pollute the bed of him I slew
With my own hands! Say, am I vile? Am I   140
Not all impure? Seeing I must be exiled,
And even in my exile must not go
And see my parents, nor set foot upon
My native land; or, if I do, I must
Marry my mother, and kill Polybus   145
My father, who engendered me and reared me.
If one should say it was a cruel god
Brought this upon me, would he not speak
right?
No, no, you holy powers above! Let me
Not see that day! but rather let me pass   150
Beyond the sight of men, before I see
The stain of such pollution come upon me!

CHORUS-LEADER:

My lord, this frightens me. But you must
hope,
Until we hear the tale from him that saw it.

OEDIPUS:

That is the only hope that's left to me;   155
We must await the coming of the shepherd.

IOCASTA:

What do you hope from him, when he is
here?

OEDIPUS:

I'll tell you: if his story shall be found
The same as yours, then I am free of guilt.

IOCASTA:

But what have *I* said of especial note?   160

OEDIPUS:

You said that he reported it was brigands
Who killed the King. If he still speaks of
      "men,"
It was not I; a single man, and "men,"
Are not the same. But if he says it was
165 A traveler journeying alone, why then,
The burden of the guilt must fall on me.

IOCASTA:

But that *is* what he said, I do assure you!
He cannot take it back again! Not I
Alone, but the whole city heard him say it!
170 But even if he should revoke the tale
He told before, not even so, my lord,
Will he establish that the King was slain
According to the prophecy. For that was clear:
His son, and mine, should slay him. — He,
      poor thing,
175 Was killed himself, and never killed his father.
Therefore, so far as divination goes,
Or prophecy, I'll take no notice of it.

OEDIPUS:

And that is wise. — But send a man to bring
The shepherd; I would not have that ne-
      glected.

IOCASTA:

180 I'll send at once. — But come with me; for I
Would not do anything that could displease
      you.

      [*Exeunt* OEDIPUS *and* IOCASTA.]

STROPHE 1

CHORUS:

I pray that I may pass my life
[*in a steady rhythm*] In reverent holiness of
      word and deed.
For there are laws enthroned above;
Heaven created them,
5 Olympus was their father,
And mortal men had no part in their birth;
Nor ever shall their power pass from sight
In dull forgetfulness;
A god moves in them; he grows not old.

ANTISTROPHE 1

Pride makes the tyrant — pride of wealth
And power, too great for wisdom and restraint;
For Pride will climb the topmost height;
Then is the man cast down
5 To uttermost destruction.

There he finds no escape, no resource.
But high contention for the city's good
May the gods preserve.
For me — may the gods be my defense!

STROPHE 2

If there is one who walks in pride
Of word or deed, and has no fear of Justice,
No reverence for holy shrines —
May utter ruin fall on him!
So may his ill-starred pride be given its reward. 5
Those who seek dishonorable advantage
And lay violent hands on holy things
And do not shun impiety —
Who among these will secure himself from the
      wrath of God?
If deeds like these are honored, 10
Why should I join in the sacred dance?

ANTISTROPHE 2

No longer shall Apollo's shrine,
The holy center of the Earth, receive my
      worship;
No, nor his seat at Abae, nor
The temple of Olympian Zeus,
If what the god foretold does not come to
      pass. 5
Mighty Zeus — if so I should address Thee —
O great Ruler of all things, look on this!
Now are thy oracles falling into contempt, and
      men
Deny Apollo's power.
Worship of the gods is passing away. 10

      [*Enter* IOCASTA, *attended by a girl carrying a
      wreath and incense.*]

IOCASTA:

My lords of Thebes, I have bethought myself
To approach the altars of the gods, and lay
These wreaths on them, and burn this frankin-
      cense.
For every kind of terror has laid hold
On Oedipus; his judgment is distracted. 15
He will not read the future by the past
But yields himself to any who speaks fear.
Since then no words of mine suffice to calm
      him
I turn to Thee Apollo — Thou art nearest —
Thy suppliant, with these votive offerings. 20
Grant us deliverance and peace, for now

Fear is on all, when we see Oedipus,
The helmsman of the ship, so terrified.

[A *reverent silence, while* IOCASTA *lays the
wreath at the altar and sets fire to the
incense. The wreath will remain and the
incense smoke during the rest of the play.*]
[*Enter a* SHEPHERD *from Corinth.*]

CORINTHIAN:
Might I inquire of you where I may find
25 The royal palace of King Oedipus?
Or, better, where himself is to be found?
CHORUS-LEADER:
There is the palace; himself, Sir, is within,
But here his wife and mother of his children.
CORINTHIAN:
Ever may happiness attend on her,
30 And hers, the wedded wife of such a man.
IOCASTA:
May you enjoy the same; your gentle words
Deserve no less. — Now, Sir, declare your pur-
pose;
With what request, what message have you
come?
CORINTHIAN:
With good news for your husband and his
house.
IOCASTA:
What news is this? And who has sent you
35 here?
CORINTHIAN:
I come from Corinth, and the news I bring
Will give you joy, though joy be crossed with
grief.
IOCASTA:
What is this, with its two-fold influence?
CORINTHIAN:
The common talk in Corinth is that they
40 Will call on Oedipus to be their king.
IOCASTA:
What? Does old Polybus no longer reign?
CORINTHIAN:
Not now, for Death has laid him in his grave.
IOCASTA:
Go quickly to your master, girl; give him
The news. — You oracles, where are you now?
45 This is the man whom Oedipus so long
Has shunned, fearing to kill him; now he's
dead,
And killed by Fortune, not by Oedipus.

[*Enter* OEDIPUS, *very nervous.*]

OEDIPUS:
My dear Iocasta, tell me, my dear wife,

Why have you sent to fetch me from the
palace?
IOCASTA:
Listen to *him*, and as you hear, reflect   50
What has become of all those oracles.
OEDIPUS:
Who is this man? — What has he to tell me?
IOCASTA:
He is from Corinth, and he brings you news
About your father. Polybus is dead.
OEDIPUS:
What say you, sir? Tell me the news yourself.   55
CORINTHIAN:
If you would have me first report on this,
I tell you; death has carried him away.
OEDIPUS:
By treachery? Or did sickness come to him?
CORINTHIAN:
A small mischance will lay an old man low.
OEDIPUS:
Poor Polybus! He died, then, of a sickness?   60
CORINTHIAN:
That, and the measure of his many years.
OEDIPUS:
Ah me! Why then, Iocasta, should a man
Regard the Pythian house of oracles,
Or screaming birds, on whose authority
I was to slay my father? But he is dead;   65
The earth has covered him; and here am I,
My sword undrawn — unless perchance *my* loss
Has killed him; so might I be called his slayer.
But for those oracles about my father,
Those he has taken with him to the grave   70
Wherein he lies, and they are come to noth-
ing.
IOCASTA:
Did I not say long since it would be so?
OEDIPUS:
You did; but I was led astray by fear.
IOCASTA:
So none of this deserves another thought.
OEDIPUS:
Yet how can I not fear my mother's bed?   75
IOCASTA:
Why should we fear, seeing that man is ruled
By chance, and there is room for no clear
forethought?
No; live at random, live as best one can.
So do not fear this marriage with your mother;
Many a man has suffered this before —   80
But only in his dreams. Whoever thinks
The least of this, he lives most comfortably.
OEDIPUS:
Your every word I do accept, if she

That bore me did not live; but as she does —
85 Despite your wisdom, how can I but tremble?

IOCASTA:
Yet there is comfort in your father's death.

OEDIPUS:
Great comfort, but still fear of her who lives.

CORINTHIAN:
And who is this who makes you so afraid?

OEDIPUS:
Meropê, my man, the wife of Polybus.

CORINTHIAN:
90 And what in *her* gives cause of fear in *you*?

OEDIPUS:
There was an awful warning from the gods.

CORINTHIAN:
Can it be told, or must it be kept secret?

OEDIPUS:
No secret. Once Apollo said that I
Was doomed to lie with my own mother, and
95 Defile my own hands with my father's blood.
Wherefore has Corinth been, these many years,
My home no more. My fortunes have been
fair. —
But it is good to see a parent's face.

CORINTHIAN:
It was for fear of *this* you fled the city?

OEDIPUS:
100 This, and the shedding of my father's blood.

CORINTHIAN:
Why then, my lord, since I am come in
friendship,
I'll rid you here and now of that misgiving.

OEDIPUS:
Be sure, your recompense would be in keeping.

CORINTHIAN:
It was the chief cause of my coming here
That your return might bring me some advan-
105   tage.

OEDIPUS:
Back to my parents I will never go.

CORINTHIAN:
My son, it is clear, you know not what you
do. . . .

OEDIPUS:
Not know? What is this? Tell me what you
mean.

CORINTHIAN:
If for this reason you avoid your home.

OEDIPUS:
110 Fearing Apollo's oracle may come true.

CORINTHIAN:
And you incur pollution from your parents?

OEDIPUS:
That is the thought that makes me live in
terror.

CORINTHIAN:
I tell you then, this fear of yours is idle.

OEDIPUS:
How? Am I not their child, and they my
parents?

CORINTHIAN:
Because there's none of Polybus in you.   115

OEDIPUS:
How can you say so? Was he not my father?

CORINTHIAN:
I am your father just as much as he!

OEDIPUS:
A stranger equal to the father? How?

CORINTHIAN:
Neither did he beget you, nor did I.

OEDIPUS:
Then for what reason did he call me son?   120

CORINTHIAN:
He had you as a gift — from my own hands.

OEDIPUS:
And showed such love to me? Me, not his
own?

CORINTHIAN:
Yes, his own childlessness so worked on him.

OEDIPUS:
You, when you gave me: had you bought, or
found me?

CORINTHIAN:
I found you in the woods upon Cithaeron.   125

OEDIPUS:
Why were you traveling in that neighborhood?

CORINTHIAN:
I tended flocks of sheep upon the mountain.

OEDIPUS:
You were a shepherd, then, wandering for hire?

CORINTHIAN:
I was, my son; but that day, your preserver.

OEDIPUS:
How so? What ailed me when you took me
up?   130

CORINTHIAN:
For that, your ankles might give evidence.

OEDIPUS:
Alas! why speak of this, my life-long trouble?

CORINTHIAN:
I loosed the fetters clamped upon your feet.

OEDIPUS:
A pretty gift to carry from the cradle!

CORINTHIAN:
It was for this they named you Oedipus.   135

OEDIPUS:
Who did, my father or my mother? Tell me.

CORINTHIAN:
I cannot; he knows more, from whom I had
you.

OEDIPUS:
It was another, not yourself, that found me?
CORINTHIAN:
Yes, you were given me by another shepherd.
OEDIPUS:
Who? Do you know him? Can you name the
140   man?
CORINTHIAN:
They said that he belonged to Laius.
OEDIPUS:
What — him who once was ruler here in
   Thebes?
CORINTHIAN:
Yes, he it was for whom this man was
   shepherd.
OEDIPUS:
And is he still alive, that I can see him?
CORINTHIAN [*turning to the* CHORUS]:
145 You that are native here would know that best.
OEDIPUS:
Has any man of you now present here
Acquaintance with this shepherd, him he
   speaks of?
Has any seen him, here, or in the fields?
Speak; on this moment hangs discovery.
CHORUS-LEADER:
150 It is, I think, the man that you have sent for,
The slave now in the country. But who should
   know
The truth of this more than Iocasta here?
OEDIPUS:
The man he speaks of: do you think, Iocasta,
He is the one I have already summoned?
IOCASTA:
155 What matters who he is? Pay no regard. —
The tale is idle; it is best forgotten.
OEDIPUS:
It cannot be that I should have this clue
And then not find the secret of my birth.
IOCASTA:
In God's name stop, if you have any thought
160 For your own life! My ruin is enough.
OEDIPUS:
Be not dismayed; nothing can prove you base,
Not though I find my mother thrice a slave.
IOCASTA:
O, I beseech you, do not! Seek no more!
OEDIPUS:
You cannot move me. I *will* know the truth.
IOCASTA:
165 I know that what I say is for the best.
OEDIPUS:
This "best" of yours! I have no patience with it.
IOCASTA:
O may you never learn what man you are!

OEDIPUS:
Go, someone, bring the herdsman here to me,
And leave her to enjoy her pride of birth.
IOCASTA:
O man of doom! For by no other name   170
Can I address you now or evermore.
                  [*Exit* IOCASTA.]
CHORUS-LEADER:
The Queen has fled, my lord, as if before
Some driving storm of grief. I fear that from
Her silence may break forth some great disas-
   ter.
OEDIPUS:
Break forth what will! My birth, however
   humble,   175
I am resolved to find. But she, perhaps,
Is proud, as women will be; is ashamed
Of my low birth. But I do rate myself
The child of Fortune, giver of all good,
And I shall not be put to shame, for I   180
Am born of Her; the Years who are my
   kinsmen
Distinguished my estate, now high, now low;
So born, I could not make me someone else
And not do all to find my parentage.

STROPHE 1

CHORUS:
If I have power of prophecy,
[*animated rhythm*] If I have judgment wise
   and sure, Cithaeron
(I swear by Olympus),
Thou shalt be honored when the moon
Next is full, as mother and foster-nurse   5
And birth-place of Oedipus, with festival and
   dancing,
For thou hast given great blessings to our
   King.
To Thee, Apollo, now we raise our cry:
O grant our prayer find favor in thy sight!

ANTISTROPHE

Who is thy mother, O my son?
Is she an ageless nymph among the mountains,
That bore thee to Pan?
Or did Apollo father thee?
For dear to him are the pastures in the hills.   5
Or Hermes, who ruleth from the summit of
   Kyllene?

Or Dionysus on the mountain-tops,
Did he receive thee from thy mother's arms,
A nymph who follows him on Helicon?
OEDIPUS:
10 If I, who never yet have met the man,
May risk conjecture, I think I see the herds-
  man
Whom we have long been seeking. In his age
He well accords; and more, I recognize
Those who are with him as of my own
  household.
15 But as for knowing, you will have advantage
Of me, if you have seen the man before.
  CHORUS-LEADER:
'Tis he, for certain — one of Laius' men,
One of the shepherds whom he trusted most.

[*Enter the* THEBAN SHEPHERD.]

OEDIPUS:
You first I ask, you who have come from
  Corinth:
Is that the man you mean?
20 CORINTHIAN: That very man.
OEDIPUS:
Come here, my man; look at me; answer me
My questions. Were you ever Laius' man?
  THEBAN:
I was; his slave — born in the house, not
  bought.
  OEDIPUS:
What was your charge, or what your way of
  life?
  THEBAN:
25 Tending the sheep, the most part of my life.
  OEDIPUS:
And to what regions did you most resort?
  THEBAN:
Now it was Cithaeron, now the country round.
  OEDIPUS:
And was this man of your acquaintance there?
  THEBAN:
In what employment? Which is the man you
  mean?
  OEDIPUS:
30 Him yonder. Had you any dealings with him?
  THEBAN:
Not such that I can quickly call to mind.
  CORINTHIAN:
No wonder, Sir, but though he has forgotten
I can remind him. I am very sure,
He knows the time when, round about Cithae-
  ron,
35 He with a double flock, and I with one,
We spent together three whole summer sea-
  sons,

From spring until the rising of Arcturus.
Then, with the coming on of winter, I
Drove my flocks home, he his, to Laius' folds.
Is this the truth? or am I telling lies?   40
  THEBAN:
It is true, although it happened long ago.
  CORINTHIAN:
Then tell me: do you recollect a baby
You gave me once to bring up for my own?
  THEBAN:
Why this? Why are you asking me this
  question?
  CORINTHIAN:
My friend, *here* is the man who was that baby! 45
  THEBAN:
O, devil take you! Cannot you keep silent?
  OEDIPUS:
Here, Sir! This man needs no reproof from you.
Your tongue needs chastisement much more
  than his.
  THEBAN:
O best of masters, how am I offending?
  OEDIPUS:
Not telling of the child of whom he speaks.   50
  THEBAN:
He? He knows nothing. He is wasting time.
  OEDIPUS [*threatening*]:
If you'll not speak from pleasure, speak from
  pain.
  THEBAN:
No, no, I pray! Not torture an old man!
  OEDIPUS:
Here, someone quickly! Twist this fellow's
  arms!
  THEBAN:
Why, wretched man? What would you know
  besides?   55
  OEDIPUS:
That child: you gave it him, the one he speaks
  of?
  THEBAN:
I did. Ah God, would I have died instead!
  OEDIPUS:
And die you shall, unless you speak the truth.
  THEBAN:
And if I do, then death is still more certain.
  OEDIPUS:
This man, I think, is trying to delay me.   60
  THEBAN:
Not I! I said I gave the child — just now.
  OEDIPUS:
And got it — where? Your own? or someone
  else's?
  THEBAN:
No, not my own. Someone had given it me.

OEDIPUS:
Who? Which of these our citizens? From
    what house?
THEBAN:
65 No, I implore you, master! Do not ask!
OEDIPUS:
You die if I must question you again.
THEBAN:
Then, 'twas a child of one in Laius' house.
OEDIPUS:
You mean a slave? Or someone of his kin?
THEBAN:
God! I am on the verge of saying it.
OEDIPUS:
70 And I of hearing it, but hear I must.
THEBAN:
His own, or so they said. But she within
Could tell you best — your wife — the truth of
    it.
OEDIPUS:
What, did she give you it?
THEBAN: She did, my lord.
OEDIPUS:
With what intention?
THEBAN: That I should destroy it.
OEDIPUS:
Her own? — How could she?
75 THEBAN: Frightened by oracles.
OEDIPUS:
What oracles?
THEBAN: That it would kill its parents.
OEDIPUS:
Why did you let it go to this man here?
THEBAN:
I pitied it, my lord. I thought to send
The child abroad, whence this man came. And
    he
80 Saved it, for utter doom. For if you are
The man he says, then you were born for ruin.
OEDIPUS:
Ah God! Ah God! This is the truth, at last!
O Sun, let me behold thee this once more,
I who am proved accursed in my conception,
85 And in my marriage, and in him I slew.
        [*Exeunt severally* OEDIPUS,
            CORINTHIAN, THEBAN.]

STROPHE 1

CHORUS:
Alas! you generations of men!
[*glyconics*] Even while you live you are next to
    nothing!
Has any man won for himself

More than the shadow of happiness,
A shadow that swiftly fades away?   5
Oedipus, now as I look on you,
See your ruin, how can I say that
Mortal man can be happy?

ANTISTROPHE 1

For who won greater prosperity?
Sovereignty and wealth beyond all desiring?
The crooked-clawed, riddling Sphinx,
Maiden and bird, you overcame;
You stood like a tower of strength to Thebes.   5
So you received our crown, received the
Highest honors that we could give —
King in our mighty city.

STROPHE 2

Who more wretched, more afflicted now,
With cruel misery, with fell disaster,
Your life in dust and ashes?
    O noble Oedipus!
    How could it be? to come again   5
A bridegroom of her who gave you birth!
How could such a monstrous thing
Endure so long, unknown?

ANTISTROPHE 2

Time sees all, and Time, in your despite,
Disclosed and punished your unnatural mar-
    riage —
A child, and then a husband.
    O son of Laius,
    Would I had never looked on you!   5
I mourn you as one who mourns the dead.
First you gave me back my life,
And now, that life is death.

    [*Enter, from the palace, a* MESSENGER.]

MESSENGER:
My Lords, most honored citizens of Thebes,
What deeds am I to tell of, you to see!   10
What heavy grief to bear, if still remains
Your native loyalty to our line of kings.
For not the Ister, no, nor Phasis' flood,
Could purify this house, such things it hides,
Such others will it soon display to all,   15

Evils self-sought. Of all our sufferings
Those hurt the most that we ourselves inflict.
CHORUS-LEADER:
Sorrow enough — too much — in what was
    known
Already. What new sorrow do you bring?
MESSENGER:
20 Quickest for me to say and you to hear:
It is the Queen, Iocasta — she is dead.
CHORUS-LEADER:
Iocasta, dead? But how? What was the cause?
MESSENGER:
By her own hand. Of what has passed, the
    worst
Cannot be yours: that was, to see it.
25 But you shall hear, so far as memory serves,
The cruel story. — In her agony
She ran across the courtyard, snatching at
Her hair with both her hands. She made her
    way
Straight to her chamber; she barred fast the
    doors
30 And called on Laius, these long years dead,
Remembering their by-gone procreation.
"Through this did you meet death yourself,
    and leave
To me, the mother, child-bearing accursed
To my own child." She cried aloud upon
35 The bed where she had borne a double brood,
Husband from husband, children from a child.
And thereupon she died, I know not how;
For, groaning, Oedipus burst in, and we,
For watching him, saw not *her* agony
And how it ended. He, ranging through the
40   palace,
Came up to each man calling for a sword,
Calling for her whom he had called his wife,
Asking where was she who had borne them all,
Himself and his own children. So he raved.
45 And then some deity showed him the way,
For it was none of us that stood around;
He cried aloud, as if to someone who
Was leading him; he leapt upon the doors,
Burst from their sockets the yielding bars, and
    fell
50 Into the room; and there, hanged by the neck,
We saw his wife, held in a swinging cord.
He, when he saw it, groaned in misery
And loosed her body from the rope. When
    now
She lay upon the ground, awful to see
Was that which followed: from her dress he
    tore
55 The golden brooches that she had been wearing,

Raised them, and with their points struck his
    own eyes,
Crying aloud that they should never see
What he had suffered and what he had done,
But in the dark henceforth they should behold   60
Those whom they ought not; nor should
    recognize
Those whom he longed to see. To such refrain
He smote his eyeballs with the pins, not once,
Nor twice; and as he smote them, blood ran
    down
His face, not dripping slowly, but there fell   65
Showers of black rain and blood-red hail
    together.
    Not on his head alone, but on them both,
Husband and wife, this common storm has
    broken.
Their ancient happiness of early days
Was happiness indeed; but now, today,   70
Death, ruin, lamentation, shame — of all
The ills there are, not one is wanting here.
CHORUS-LEADER:
Now is there intermission in his agony?
MESSENGER:
He shouts for someone to unbar the gates,
And to display to Thebes the parricide,   75
His mother's — no, I cannot speak the words;
For, by the doom he uttered, he will cast
Himself beyond our borders, not remain
To be a curse at home. But he needs strength,
And one to guide him; for these wounds are
    greater   80
Than he can bear — as you shall see; for look!
They draw the bolts. A sight you will behold
To move the pity even of an enemy.

[*The doors open.* OEDIPUS *slowly advances.*]

CHORUS:
O horrible, dreadful sight. More dreadful far

[*These verses sung or chanted in a slow
march-time.*]

Than any I have yet seen. What cruel frenzy   85
Came over you? What spirit with superhuman
    leap
Came to assist your grim destiny?
Ah, most unhappy man!
But no! I cannot bear even to look at you,
Though there is much that I would ask and
    see and hear.   90
But I shudder at the very sight of you.
OEDIPUS [*sings in the dochmiac rhythm*]:
Alas! alas! and woe for my misery!
Where are my steps taking me?

My random voice is lost in the air.
95 O God! how hast thou crushed me!
  CHORUS-LEADER [spoken]:
 Too terribly for us to hear or see.
  OEDIPUS [sings]:
 O cloud of darkness abominable,
 My enemy unspeakable,
 In cruel onset insuperable.
100 Alas! alas! Assailed at once by pain
 Of pin-points and of memory of crimes.
  CHORUS-LEADER:
 In such tormenting pains you well may cry
 A double grief and feel a double woe.
  OEDIPUS [sings]:
 Ah, my friend!
105 Still at my side? Still steadfast?
 Still can you endure me?
 Still care for me, a blind man?
 [Speaks.] For it is you, my friend; I know 'tis
  you;
 Though all is darkness, yet I know your voice.
  CHORUS-LEADER:
110 O, to destroy your sight! How could you bring
 Yourself to do it? What god incited you?
  OEDIPUS [sings]:
 It was Apollo, friends, Apollo.
 He decreed that I should suffer what I suffer;
 But the hand that struck, alas! was my own,
115 And not another's.
 For why should I have sight.
 When sight of nothing could give me plea-
  sure?
  CHORUS:
 It was even as you say.
  OEDIPUS:
 What have I left, my friends, to see,
120 To cherish, whom to speak with, or
 To listen to, with joy?
 Lead me away at once, far from Thebes;
 Lead me away, my friends!
 I have destroyed; I am accursed, and, what is
  more,
125 Hateful to Heaven, as no other.
  CHORUS-LEADER [speaks]:
 Unhappy your intention, and unhappy
 Your fate. O would that I had never known
  you!
  OEDIPUS [sings]:
 Curses on him, whoever he was,
 Who took the savage fetters from my feet,
130 Snatched me from death, and saved me.
 No thanks I owe him,
 For had I died that day
 Less ruin had I brought on me and mine.

  CHORUS:
 That wish is my wish too.
  OEDIPUS:
 I had not then come and slain my father. 135
 Nor then would men have called me
 Husband of her that bore me.
 Now am I God's enemy, child of the guilty,
 And she that bore me has borne too my
  children;
 And if there is evil surpassing evil, 140
 That has come to Oedipus.
  CHORUS-LEADER:
 How can I say that you have counseled well?
 Far better to be dead than to be blind.
  OEDIPUS:
 That what is done was not done for the best
 Seek not to teach me: counsel me no more. 145
 I know not how I could have gone to Hades
 And with these eyes have looked upon my
  father
 Or on my mother; such things have I done
 To them, death is no worthy punishment.
 Or could I look for pleasure in the sight 150
 Of my own children, born as they were born?
 Never! No pleasure there, for eyes of mine,
 Nor in this city, nor its battlements
 Nor sacred images. From these — ah, misera-
  ble! —
 I, the most nobly born of any Theban 155
 Am banned for ever by my own decree
 That the defiler should be driven forth,
 The man accursed of Heaven and Laius' house.
 Was I to find such taint in me, and then
 With level eyes to look *them* in the face? 160
 Nay more: if for my ears I could have built
 Some dam to stay the flood of sound, that I
 Might lose both sight and hearing, and seal up
 My wretched body — that I would have done.
 How good to dwell beyond the reach of pain! 165
 Cithaeron! Why did you accept me? Why
 Did you not take and kill me? Never then
 Should I have come to dwell among the
  Thebans.
 O Polybus! Corinth! and that ancient home
 I thought my father's — what a thing you
  nurtured! 170
 How fair, how foul beneath! For I am found
 Foul in myself and in my parentage.
 O you three ways, that in a hidden glen
 Do meet: you narrow branching roads within
 The forest — you, through my own hands, did
  drink 175
 My father's blood, that was my own. — Ah! do
  you

Remember what you saw me do? And what
I did again in Thebes? You marriages!
You did beget me: then, having begotten,
180 Bore the same crop again, and brought to light
Commingled blood of fathers, brothers, sons,
Brides, mothers, wives; all that there can be
Among the human kind most horrible!
    But that which it is foul to do, it is
185 Not fair to speak of. Quick as you can, I beg,
Banish me, hide me, slay me! Throw me forth
Into the sea, where I may sink from view.
I pray you, deign to touch one so afflicted,
And do not fear: there is no man alive
190 Can bear this load of evil but myself.

CHORUS-LEADER:
To listen to your prayers, Creon is here,
For act or guidance opportune; for he,
In your defection, is our champion.

[*Enter* CREON.]

OEDIPUS:
Alas! alas! How can I speak to him?
195 What word of credit find? In all my commerce
With him aforetime I am proven false.

CREON:
No exultation, Oedipus, and no reproach
Of injuries inflicted brings me here;
But if the face of men moves not your shame,
200 Then reverence show to that all-nurturing fire,
The holy Sun, that he be not polluted
By such accursèd sight, which neither Earth
Nor rain from Heaven nor sunlight can en-
    dure.
    Take him within, and quickly: it is right
205 His kinsmen only should behold and hear
Evils that chiefly on his kinsmen fall.

OEDIPUS:
In Heaven's name — since you cheat my expec-
    tation,
So noble towards my baseness — grant me this:
It is for you I ask it, not myself.

CREON:
210 What is this supplication that you make?

OEDIPUS:
Drive me at once beyond your bounds, where I
Shall be alone, and no one speak to me.

CREON:
I would have done it; but I first desired
To ask the God what he would have me do.

OEDIPUS:
215 No, his command was given in full, to slay
Me, the polluter and the parricide.

CREON:
Those were his words; but in our present need
It would be wise to ask what we should do.

OEDIPUS:
You will inquire for such a wretch as I?

CREON:
I will; for now you may believe the god.   220

OEDIPUS:
Yes; and on you I lay this charge and duty:
Give burial, as you will, to her who lies
Within — for she is yours, and this is proper;
And, while I live, let not my father's city
Endure to have me as a citizen.   225
My home must be the mountains — on Cithae-
    ron,
Which, while they lived, my parents chose to
    be
My tomb: they wished to slay me; now they
    shall.
For this I know: sickness can never kill me,
Nor any other evil; I was not saved   230
That day from death, except for some strange
    doom.
My fate must take the course it will. — Now,
    for my sons,
Be not concerned for them: they can, being
    men,
Fend for themselves, wherever they may be:
But my unhappy daughters, my two girls,   235
Whose chairs were always set beside my own
At table — they who shared in every dish
That was prepared for me — oh Creon! these
Do I commend to you. And grant me this:
To take them in my arms, and weep for them.   240
My lord! most noble Creon! could I now
But hold them in my arms, then I should
    think
I had them as I had when I could see them.
Ah! what is this?
Ah Heaven! do I not hear my dear ones,
    sobbing?   245
Has Creon, in his pity, sent to me
My darling children? Has he? Is it true?

CREON:
It is; they have been always your delight;
So, knowing this, I had them brought to you.

OEDIPUS:
Then Heaven reward you, and for this kind
    service   250
Protect you better than it protected me!
    Where are you, children? Where? O come
    to me!
Come, let me clasp you with a brother's arms,
These hands, which helped your father's eyes,
    once bright,
To look upon you as they see you now —   255
Your father who, not seeing, nor inquiring,
Gave you for mother her who bore himself.

See you I cannot; but I weep for you,
For the unhappiness that must be yours,
260 And for the bitter life that you must lead.
What gathering of the citizens, what festivals,
Will you have part in? Your high celebrations
Will be to go back home, and sit in tears.
And when the time for marriage comes, what
man
265 Will stake upon the ruin and the shame
That *I* am to my parents and to you?
Nothing is wanting there: your father slew
His father, married her who gave him birth,
And then, from that same source whence he
himself
Had sprung, got you. — With these things
270 they will taunt you;
And who will take you then in marriage? —
Nobody;
But you must waste, unwedded and unfruitful.
Ah, Creon! Since they have no parent now
But you — for both of us who gave them life
275 Have perished — suffer them not to be cast out
Homeless and beggars; for they are your kin.
Have pity on them, for they are so young,
So desolate, except for you alone.
Say "Yes," good Creon! Let your hand confirm
it.
280 And now, my children, for my exhortation
You are too young; but you can pray that I
May live henceforward — where I should; and
you
More happily than the father who begot you.
CREON:
Now make an end of tears, and go within.
OEDIPUS:
285 Then I must go — against my will.
CREON:
There is a time for everything.
OEDIPUS:
You know what I would have you do?
CREON:
If you will tell me, I shall know.

OEDIPUS:
Send me away, away from Thebes.
CREON:
The God, not I, must grant you this. 290
OEDIPUS:
The gods hate no man more than me!
CREON:
Then what you ask they soon will give.
OEDIPUS:
You promise this?
CREON: Ah no! When I
Am ignorant, I do not speak.
OEDIPUS:
Then lead me in; I say no more. 295
CREON:
Release the children then, and come.
OEDIPUS:
What? Take these children from me? No!
CREON:
Seek not to have your way in all things:
Where you had your way before,
Your mastery broke before the end. 300

[*There was no doubt a short concluding
utterance from the* CHORUS. *What stands in
the mss. appears to be spurious.*][3]

[3] Few other scholars share Professor Kitto's sus-
picion that the concluding lines in the manuscript are
spurious. The passage is translated thus by J. T.
Sheppard:
CHORUS:
Look, ye who dwell in Thebes. This man was
Oedipus.
That mighty King, who knew the riddle's mystery,
Whom all the city envied, Fortune's favorite.
Behold, in the event, the storm of his calamities,
And, being mortal, think on that last day of death,
Which all must see, and speak of no man's
happiness
Till, without sorrow, he hath passed the goal of life.
[Eds.]

Classroom discussions of *Oedipus the King*, like discussions in books, are
often mostly devoted to the problem of fate and free will. Students (who
ought to be filled with youthful confidence in the freedom of the will) generally argue that Oedipus is fated; instructors (who ought to be old enough to
know that the inexplicable and unwilled often comes about) generally argue
that Oedipus is free and of his own accord performed the actions that fulfilled
the prophecy. Prophecy or prediction or foreknowledge, instructors patiently

explain, is not the same as foreordination. The physician who says that the newborn babe will never develop mentally beyond the age of six is predicting, but he is not ordaining or willing. So, the argument usually runs, the oracle who predicted that Oedipus would kill his father and marry his mother was not *causing* Oedipus to do these things but was simply, in his deep knowledge, announcing what a man like Oedipus would do. But that may be too sophisticated a reading, and a reading that derives from the much later European view of man as a creature who can shape his destiny. It is hard for us — especially if the tragedy we know best is Shakespeare's — to recognize the possibility of another sort of tragic drama which does not relate the individual's suffering to his own actions but which postulates some sort of Necessity that works within him.

Whatever the merits of these views, the spectators or readers undeniably know, when they set out to see or read the play, that Oedipus must end wretchedly. The story is known to us, fixed in Sophocles' text, and Oedipus cannot extricate himself from it. Something along these lines was suggested in the middle of the fourth century B.C. when a Greek comic dramatist complained that the comic writer's task was harder than the tragic writer's: "Tragedy has the best of it since the stories are known beforehand to the spectators even before anyone speaks; so the poet only has to remind them. For if I merely say the name Oedipus, they all know the rest — his father Laius, mother Iocasta, daughters, who his sons are, what will happen to him, what he did." In fact, it should be mentioned, the tragic writer's task was not quite so easy. First of all, we have Aristotle's statement that "even the known legends are known to only a few," and, second, we have evidence that the tragic writer could vary the details. In Homer's *Iliad* we read that Oedipus continued to rule even after his dreadful history was known, but Sophocles exiles him. And a fragment of Euripides indicates that Euripides' Oedipus was blinded by Laius' followers, but Sophocles' Oedipus blinds himself. These are details, but they are rather important ones. Probably the ancient Greeks knew the legends in a rough sort of way, as most of us know the Bible or some nuggets of Roman history. Robert Frost and Archibald MacLeish have both drawn from the Book of Job, but their works are enormously different. A writer who uses Job can scarcely omit Job's great suffering, and he can assume that his audience will know that Job had a wife and some comforters, but he is free to go on from there. Similarly, Brutus must stab Julius Caesar, but that leaves lots of room for other material in a play about Caesar. Shakespeare, by the way, could even assume that the audience that saw his *Julius Caesar* would accept a different version of the facts in his *Antony and Cleopatra*. In *Julius Caesar*, Brutus kills himself, but in *Antony and Cleopatra* Antony says (and presumably he is speaking the truth — the truth, that is, for *that* play) that Brutus died at Antony's hands.

Still, the main outline of Oedipus' life must have been fixed, and for us even the details are forever fixed in Sophocles' version. (We know that the Greeks wrote a dozen plays about Oedipus' discovery of his terrible actions, but only Sophocles' survives.) This means that as we read or watch it, each speech has for us a meaning somewhat different from the meaning it has for the speaker and the audience on the stage. Oedipus says he will hunt out the polluted man; we know, as he and the Thebans do not, that *he* is the hunted as well as the hunter. Oedipus says the killer of King Laius may well try to strike at him; we know that Oedipus will find himself out and will strike out his own eyes. A messenger from Corinth tries to allay Oedipus' fears, but he sets them going. What we are talking about, of course, is tragic irony, or Sophoclean irony, in which words and deeds have a larger meaning for the spectator than for the dramatis personae. And surely it is in part because Sophocles so persistently uses this device of giving speeches a second, awesome significance that we feel the plot is a masterpiece of construction in which Oedipus is caught. If ever a man had confidence in his will, it was Oedipus, but if ever a man moved toward a predicted point, it was Oedipus. He had solved the riddle of the sphinx (by himself, without the aid of birds, he somewhat hybristically boasts), but he did not yet know himself. That knowledge was to come later, when he commendably pursued the quest for Laius' slayer and inevitably found himself. The thing is as inevitable as the history described in the sphinx's riddle, which in J. T. Sheppard's version goes thus:

> A thing there is whose voice is one;
> Whose feet are four and two and three.
> So mutable a thing is none
> That moves in earth or sky or sea.
> When on most feet this thing doth go,
> Its strength is weakest and its pace most slow.

This is the history of man, willy-nilly. In Sophocles' time men grew from crawling infancy, through erect manhood, to bent old age supported by a stick, and so they do in our time, as the child's rhyme still claims:

> Walks on four feet,
> On two feet, on three,
> The more feet it walks on,
> The weaker it be.

There was scarcely an infant weaker than the maimed Oedipus; there was scarcely a man stronger than King Oedipus at his height; and there was scarcely a man more in need of a staff than the blind exile. However free each of his actions — and we can only feel that the man whom we see on the stage is acting freely when he abuses Teiresias and Creon — Oedipus was by fate a man, and thus the largest pattern of his life could be predicted easily enough.

DOCTOR FAUSTUS

Christopher Marlowe

Edited by Sylvan Barnet

Christopher Marlowe (1564–93) was born in Canterbury, England, in the year of Shakespeare's birth. Like Shakespeare, he was of a prosperous middle-class family (his father was a shoemaker), but unlike Shakespeare he went to a university, Corpus Christi College, Cambridge, where he received his B.A. degree in 1584 and his M.A. in 1587. The terms of his scholarship implied that he was preparing for the clergy, but he did not become a clergyman. Shortly before he received his M.A., the university seems to have wished to withhold it, apparently suspecting him of conversion to Roman Catholicism, but the queen's Privy Council intervened on his behalf, stating that he "had done her majesty good service" and had been employed "in matters touching the benefit of his country." His precise service is unknown. Marlowe's first play, *Tamburlaine the Great* (c. 1587), in blank verse (unrhymed iambic pentameter) inaugurated the great age of Elizabethan drama with its "mighty" line. While continuing his career as dramatist, he apparently lived a turbulent life in London: in 1589, involved in a brawl in which a man was killed, Marlowe was jailed (though later released); in 1593 he was again arrested, this time accused of atheism. He was not imprisoned, but before his case could be decided, he was dead, only six years after having left Cambridge, stabbed in a tavern fight while quarreling over the bill. Marlowe wrote seven plays — the dates are uncertain — the most important of which, besides *Doctor Faustus* (c. 1593), were *The Jew of Malta* (c. 1588) and *Edward II* (c. 1591). He did a verse translation of Ovid's *Amores* and left unfinished at the time of his death the long poem *Hero and Leander*.

SPEAKING CHARACTERS

CHORUS
DOCTOR FAUSTUS
WAGNER, *his student and servant*
GOOD ANGEL
BAD ANGEL
VALDES ⎱
CORNELIUS ⎰ *magicians*
Three SCHOLARS
LUCIFER, *prince of devils*
MEPHOSTOPHILIS, *a devil*
ROBIN, *a clown*
BELZEBUB, *a devil*
DICK, *a clown*
POPE ADRIAN

PRIDE ⎱
COVETOUSNESS ⎟
ENVY ⎟
WRATH ⎬ *the Seven Deadly Sins*
GLUTTONY ⎟
SLOTH ⎟
LECHERY ⎰
RAYMOND, *King of Hungary*
BRUNO, *rival Pope appointed by the Emperor*
Two CARDINALS
ARCHBISHOP OF RHEIMS
FRIARS
VINTNER
The German Emperor, CHARLES THE FIFTH

Mark Lamos as Doctor Faustus and Michael Gross as Mephostophilis in the Guthrie Theater production directed by Ken Ruta, Minneapolis, 1976. (Photograph courtesy of the Guthrie Theater.)

MARTINO ⎫
FREDERICK ⎬ *gentlemen at the Emperor's court*
BENVOLIO ⎭
DUKE OF SAXONY
Two SOLDIERS
HORSE-COURSER, *a clown*

CARTER, *a clown*
HOSTESS *of a Tavern*
DUKE OF VANHOLT
DUCHESS OF VANHOLT
SERVANT
OLD MAN

MUTE CHARACTERS

DARIUS OF PERSIA
ALEXANDER THE GREAT
ALEXANDER'S PARAMOUR
HELEN OF TROY
DEVILS
PIPER
CARDINALS

MONKS
FRIARS
ATTENDANTS
SOLDIERS
SERVANTS
Two CUPIDS

[Prologue°] (*Enter* CHORUS.°)

Not marching in the fields of Trasimene°
Where Mars did mate° the warlike Cartha-
    gens,
Nor sporting in the dalliance of love
In courts of kings where state° is overturned,
5 Nor in the pomp of proud audacious deeds
Intends our muse° to vaunt° his heavenly
    verse.
Only this, gentles — We must now perform
The form of Faustus' fortunes, good or bad:
And now to patient judgments we appeal
10 And speak for Faustus in his infancy.
Now is he born of parents base of stock
In Germany within a town called Rhode;°
At riper years to Wittenberg he went
Whereas° his kinsmen chiefly brought him up.
15 So much he profits in divinity
That shortly he was graced° with doctor's name,

Excelling all, and sweetly can dispute
In th' heavenly matters of theology;
Till swoll'n with cunning, of a self-conceit,°
His waxen wings° did mount above his reach   20
And melting, heavens conspired his overthrow!
For falling to a devilish exercise
And glutted now with learning's golden gifts
He surfeits upon cursèd necromancy:°
Nothing so sweet as magic is to him   25
Which he prefers before his chiefest bliss° —
And this the man that in his study sits.

                   (*Exit.*)

[I.i] (FAUSTUS *in his study.*°)

FAUSTUS:
Settle thy studies Faustus, and begin
To sound the depth of that thou wilt profess.°
Having commenced,° be a divine in show —
Yet level° at the end of every art
And live and die in Aristotle's works.   5
Sweet *Analytics,*° 'tis thou hast ravished me.

From *Doctor Faustus* by Christopher Marlowe, edited by Sylvan Barnet. Copyright © 1969 by Sylvan
Barnet. Reprinted by arrangement with The New
American Library, Inc., New York, New York.
Prologue (All material in square brackets has been
added by the editor.) Prologue s.d. **Chorus** a
single actor (here, perhaps, Wagner, Faustus'
servant-student)   1 **Trasimene** Lake Trasimene, site
of one of Hannibal's victories over the Romans, 217
B.C. (Marlowe is not known to have written on
this subject, though lines 3–4 may refer to his
Edward II, and line 5 to his *Tamburlaine*)   2 **Mars
did mate** i.e., the Roman army encountered   4
state government   6 **muse** poet   6 **vaunt** proudly
display   12 **Rhode** Roda   14 **Whereas** where   16
graced (alluding to the official "grace" permitting
the student to take his degree)

19 **cunning, of a self-conceit** ingenuity born of arrogance   20 **waxen wings** (alluding to Icarus, who flew
by means of wings made of feathers waxed to a framework; despite the warning of his father, Icarus soared
too near the sun, the wax melted, and he plunged to
his death)   24 **necromancy** (literally divination by
means of the spirits of the dead, but here probably
equivalent to black magic)   26 **prefers before his
chiefest bliss** sets above his hope of salvation   I.i.s.d.
Faustus in his study (probably at his last line the
Chorus drew back a curtain at the rear of the stage,
disclosing Faustus)   I.i.2 **profess** study and teach   3
commenced taken a degree   4 **level** aim   6 **Analytics** title of two treatises by Aristotle on logic

Bene disserere est finis logices.°
Is to dispute well logic's chiefest end?
Affords this art no greater miracle?

10 Then read no more, thou hast attained that end.
A greater subject fitteth Faustus' wit:°
Bid *on kai me on*° farewell, and Galen° come:
Be a physician Faustus, heap up gold,
And be eternized for some wondrous cure.

15 *Summum bonum medicinae sanitas,*°
The end of physic° is our body's health.
Why Faustus hast thou not attained that end?
Are not thy bills° hung up as monuments
Whereby whole cities have escaped the plague

20 And thousand desperate maladies been cured?
Yet art thou still but Faustus and a man.
Could'st thou make men to live eternally
Or being dead raise them to life again,
Then this profession were to be esteemed.

25 Physic farewell! Where is Justinian?°
Si una eademque res legatur duobus, alter rem,
    alter valorem rei, et cetera.°
A petty case of paltry legacies.
Exhereditare filium non potest pater, nisi° —

30 Such is the subject of the *Institute*
And universal body of the law!
This study fits a mercenary drudge
Who aims at nothing but external trash,
Too servile and illiberal for me.

35 When all is done, divinity is best.
Jerome's Bible,° Faustus, view it well.
Stipendium peccati mors est.° Ha! *Stipendium
    et cetera.* The reward of sin is death?

That's hard: *Si peccasse negamus, fallimur,
et nulla est in nobis veritas.*° If we say   40
that we have no sin, we deceive ourselves,
and there is no truth in us. Why, then be-
like, we must sin, and so consequently die.
Ay, we must die an everlasting death.
What doctrine call you this? *Che serà, serà:*°   45
What will be, shall be! Divinity, adieu!
These metaphysics° of magicians
And negromantic° books are heavenly;
Lines, circles, letters, characters —
Ay, these are those that Faustus most desires.   50
O, what a world of profit and delight,
Of power, of honor, and omnipotence
Is promised to the studious artisan!°
All things that move between the quiet° poles
Shall be at my command: emperors and kings   55
Are but obeyed in their several provinces
But his dominion that exceeds in this°
Stretcheth as far as doth the mind of man:
A sound magician is a demi-god!
Here tire my brains to get° a deity!   60

(*Enter* WAGNER.)

Wagner, commend me to my dearest friends,
The German Valdes and Cornelius.
Request them earnestly to visit me.

WAGNER: I will, sir.   (*Exit.*)

FAUSTUS:
Their conference° will be a greater help to me   65
Than all my labors, plod I ne'er so fast.

(*Enter the* [GOOD] ANGEL *and the* [EVIL]
SPIRIT.°)

GOOD ANGEL:
O Faustus, lay that damnèd book aside
And gaze not on it lest it tempt thy soul
And heap God's heavy wrath upon thy head!

7 **Bene . . . logices** the end (i.e., purpose) of logic is to argue well (Latin)   11 **wit** intelligence   12 **on kai me on** being and not being (Greek)   12 **Galen** Greek authority on medicine, 2nd century A.D.   15 **Summum . . . sanitas** health is the greatest good of medicine (Latin, translated from Aristotle's *Nichomachean Ethics*)   16 **physic** medicine   18 **bills** prescriptions   25 **Justinian** Roman emperor and authority on law (483–565) who ordered the compilation of the *Institutes* (see line 30)   26–27 **Si . . . et cetera** if one thing is willed to two persons, one of them shall have the thing itself, the other the value of the thing, and so forth (Latin)   29 **Exhereditare . . . nisi** a father cannot disinherit his son unless (Latin)   36 **Jerome's Bible** the Latin translation made by St. Jerome (c. 340–420)   37 **Stipendium . . . est** the wages of sin is death (Romans 6:23; if Faustus had gone on to read the rest of the verse, he would have found that "the gift of God is eternal life through Jesus Christ our Lord")

39–40 **Si . . . veritas** from I John 1:8, translated in the next two lines; Faustus neglects the following verse: "If we confess our sins, He is faithful and just to forgive us our sins, and to cleanse us from all unrighteousness"   45 **Che serà, serà** (Italian, translated in the first half of the next line)   47 **metaphysics** subjects lying beyond (or studied after) physics   48 **negromantic** black magical (though probably here also associated with "necromantic," i.e., concerned with raising the spirits of the dead)   53 **artisan** i.e., expert   54 **quiet** motionless   57 **this** i.e., magic   60 **get** beget   65 **conference** conversation   66s.d. **Spirit** Bad Angel, devil (the two angels probably enter the stage from separate doors)

70 Read, read the Scriptures — that° is blasphemy!

BAD ANGEL:

Go forward Faustus, in that famous art
Wherein all nature's treasure is contained.
Be thou on earth as Jove is in the sky,
Lord and commander of these elements!

(*Exeunt* ANGELS.)

FAUSTUS:

75 How am I glutted with conceit of this!°
Shall I make spirits fetch me what I please?
Resolve me of° all ambiguities?
Perform what desperate enterprise I will?
I'll have them fly to India° for gold,
80 Ransack the ocean for orient° pearl,
And search all corners of the new-found world
For pleasant fruits and princely delicates;
I'll have them read me strange philosophy
And tell the secrets of all foreign kings;
85 I'll have them wall all Germany with brass
And make swift Rhine circle fair Wittenberg;
I'll have them fill the public schools° with silk
Wherewith the students shall be bravely° clad.
I'll levy soldiers with the coin they bring
90 And chase the Prince of Parma° from our land
And reign sole king of all the provinces!
Yea, stranger engines for the brunt° of war
Than was the fiery keel° at Antwerp bridge
I'll make my servile spirits to invent.

(*Enter* VALDES *and* CORNELIUS.)

95 Come German Valdes and Cornelius
And make me blest with your sage conference.
Valdes, sweet Valdes, and Cornelius,
Know that your words have won me at the last
To practice magic and concealèd arts.
100 Philosophy is odious and obscure,
Both law and physic are for petty wits,
Divinity is basest of the three —
Unpleasant, harsh, contemptible, and vile.
'Tis magic, magic, that hath ravished me!
105 Then, gentle friends, aid me in this attempt
And I, that have with subtle syllogisms

Graveled° the pastors of the German church
And made the flow'ring pride of Wittenberg
Swarm to my problems° as th' infernal spirits
On sweet Musaeus° when he came to hell, 110
Will be as cunning as Agrippa° was,
Whose shadows made all Europe honor him.

VALDES:

Faustus, these books, thy wit, and our experience
Shall make all nations to canonize us.
As Indian Moors° obey their Spanish lords, 115
So shall the spirits of every element
Be always serviceable to us three:
Like lions shall they guard us when we please,
Like Almain rutters° with their horsemen's staves
Or Lapland giants trotting by our sides; 120
Sometimes like women or unwedded maids
Shadowing° more beauty in their airy brows
Than has the white breasts of the queen of love;
From Venice shall they drag huge argosies
And from America the golden fleece 125
That yearly stuffs old Philip's° treasury,
If learnèd Faustus will be resolute.

FAUSTUS:

Valdes, as resolute am I in this
As thou to live; therefore object it not.

CORNELIUS:

The miracles that magic will perform 130
Will make thee vow to study nothing else.
He that is grounded in astrology,
Enriched with tongues, well seen° in minerals,
Hath all the principles magic doth require.
Then doubt not Faustus but to be renowned 135
And more frequented for this mystery°
Than heretofore the Delphian oracle.°
The spirits tell me they can dry the sea
And fetch the treasure of all foreign wracks,
Yea, all the wealth that our forefathers hid 140
Within the massy° entrails of the earth.

---

70 **that** i.e., the book of magic   75 **conceit of this** i.e., the conception of being a magician   77 **Resolve me of** explain to me   79 **India** either the West Indies (America) or the East Indies   80 **orient** lustrous and precious   87 **public schools** universities   88 **bravely** splendidly   90 **Prince of Parma** Spanish governor-general of the Low Countries during 1579–92   92 **brunt** assault   93 **fiery keel** burning ship sent by the Netherlanders in 1585 against a bridge erected by Parma to blockade Antwerp (Antwerp here is an adjective, not genitive)

107 **Graveled** confounded   109 **problems** questions proposed for disputation   110 **Musaeus** legendary Greek poet   111 **Agrippa** Cornelius Agrippa of Nettesheim (1486–1535), German author of *De occulta philosophia*, a survey of Renaissance magic; Agrippa was believed to have raised spirits ("shadows") from the dead   115 **Indian Moors** American Indians   119 **Almain rutters** German cavalrymen   122 **Shadowing** sheltering   126 **Philip** King Philip II of Spain (1527–98)   133 **well seen** skilled   136 **frequented for this mystery** resorted to for this art   137 **Delphian oracle** oracle of Apollo at Delphi   141 **massy** massive

Then tell me Faustus, what shall we three
    want?°

FAUSTUS:
Nothing, Cornelius. O, this cheers my soul!
Come, show me some demonstrations magical
145 That I may conjure° in some bushy grove
And have these joys in full possession.

VALDES:
Then haste thee to some solitary grove,
And bear wise Bacon's° and Albanus'° works,
The Hebrew Psalter, and New Testament;
150 And whatsoever else is requisite
We will inform thee ere our conference cease.

CORNELIUS:
Valdes, first let him know the words of art,
And then, all other ceremonies learned,
Faustus may try his cunning by himself.

VALDES:
155 First I'll instruct thee in the rudiments,
And then wilt thou be perfecter than I.

FAUSTUS:
Then come and dine with me, and after meat
We'll canvass every quiddity° thereof,
For ere I sleep I'll try what I can do:
160 This night I'll conjure though I die therefor!
                              (Exeunt omnes.°)

[I.ii] (Enter two SCHOLARS.)

I SCHOLAR: I wonder what's become of Faustus that was wont to make our schools ring with
sic probo.°

(Enter WAGNER.)

II SCHOLAR: That shall we presently° know.
5 Here comes his boy.°
I SCHOLAR: How now sirrah,° where's thy
master?
WAGNER: God in heaven knows.
I SCHOLAR: Why, dost not thou know then?
10 WAGNER: Yes, I know, but that follows not.
I SCHOLAR: Go to° sirrah, leave your jesting
and tell us where he is.
WAGNER: That follows not by force of argument, which you, being licentiates,° should

stand upon;° therefore acknowledge your error 15
and be attentive.
    II SCHOLAR: Then you will not tell us?
    WAGNER: You are deceived, for I will tell
you. Yet if you were not dunces,° you would
never ask me such a question. For is he not 20
corpus naturale? And is not that mobile?° Then
wherefore should you ask me such a question?
But that I am by nature phlegmatic,° slow to
wrath, and prone to lechery — to love, I
would say — it were not for you to come 25
within forty foot of the place of execution° —
although I do not doubt but to see you both
hanged the next sessions.° Thus, having triumphed over you, I will set my countenance
like a precisian° and begin to speak thus: 30
Truly, my dear brethren, my master is within
at dinner, with Valdes and Cornelius, as this
wine, if it could speak, would inform your worships; and so, the Lord bless you, preserve you,
and keep you, my dear brethren.   (Exit.) 35
    I SCHOLAR:
O Faustus, then I fear that which I have long
    suspected,
That thou art fall'n into that damnèd art
For which they two are infamous through the
    world.   40
    II SCHOLAR:
Were he a stranger, not allied to me,
The danger of his soul would make me mourn.
But come, let us go and inform the rector.°
It may be his grave counsel may reclaim him.
    I SCHOLAR:
I fear me nothing will reclaim him now.   45
    II SCHOLAR:
Yet let us see what we can do.   (Exeunt.)

[I.iii] (Thunder. Enter LUCIFER and four
DEVILS.° FAUSTUS to them with this
speech.)

FAUSTUS:
Now that the gloomy shadow of the night,

142 **want** lack   145 **conjure** raise spirits   148 **Bacon**
Roger Bacon, medieval friar and scientist   148 **Albanus** perhaps Pietro d'Abano, medieval writer on medicine and philosophy   158 **canvass every quiddity** discuss every essential detail   160s.d. **omnes** all (Latin)
I.ii.3 **sic probo** thus I prove it (Latin)   4 **presently** at
once   5 **boy** servant (an impoverished student)   6
sirrah (term of address used to an inferior)   11 **Go to**
(exclamation of impatience)   14 **licentiates** posses-
sors of a degree preceding the master's degree
15 **stand upon** make much of   19 **dunces** (1) fools
(2) hairsplitters   21 **corpus naturale . . . mobile** natural matter . . . movable (Latin, scholastic definition
of the subject-matter of physics)   23 **phlegmatic**
sluggish   26 **the place of execution** the place of action, i.e., the dining room (with quibble on gallows)
28 **sessions** sittings of a court   30 **precisian** Puritan
(Wagner goes on to parody the style of the Puritans)
43 **rector** head of the university   I.iii.s.d. **Enter . . .
Devils** (they are invisible to Faustus; perhaps they
enter through a trapdoor and climb to the upper
playing area, as implied in V.ii.s.d.)

Longing to view Orion's° drizzling look,
Leaps from th' antarctic world unto the sky
And dims the welkin° with her pitchy breath,
5 Faustus, begin thine incantations
And try if devils will obey thy hest,
Seeing thou hast prayed and sacrificed to them.
Within this circle° is Jehovah's name
Forward and backward anagrammatized,
10 Th' abbreviated names of holy saints,
Figures of every adjunct to° the heavens,
And characters of signs and erring stars,°
By which the spirits are enforced to rise:
Then fear not, Faustus, to be resolute
15 And try the utmost magic can perform.
                                        (*Thunder.*)
Sint mihi dei Acherontis propitii! Valeat numen triplex Iehovae! Ignei, aerii, aquatici, spiritus, salvete! Orientis princeps, Belzebub inferni ardentis monarcha, et Demogorgon, propitiamus vos ut appareat et surgat Mephostophilis! Quid tu moraris? Per Iehovam, Gehennam, et consecratam aquam quam nunc spargo, signumque crucis quod nunc facio, et per vota nostra, ipse nunc surgat nobis dicatus Mephostophilis!°

    (*Enter a* DEVIL.°)

I charge thee to return and change thy shape,
Thou art too ugly to attend on me.
Go, and return an old Franciscan friar:
That holy shape becomes a devil best.
                                        (*Exit* DEVIL.)
30 I see there's virtue in my heavenly words.

2 **Orion** constellation appearing at the beginning of winter, associated with rain   4 **welkin** sky   8 **circle** circle the conjuror draws around him on the ground, to call the spirits and to protect himself from them   11 **adjunct to** heavenly body fixed to   12 **signs and erring stars** signs of the Zodiac and planets   16–25 **Sint ... Mephostophilis** may the gods of the lower region be favorable to me. Away with the trinity of Jehovah. Hail, spirits of fire, air, water. Prince of the east, Belzebub monarch of burning hell, and Demogorgon, we pray to you that Mephostophilis may appear and rise. Why do you delay? By Jehovah, Gehenna, and the holy water which now I sprinkle, and the sign of the cross which now I make, and by our vows, may Mephostophilis himself now rise to serve us (Latin)   25s.d. **Devil** (the word "dragon" oddly appears, after "surgat Mephostophilis," in the preceding conjuration. It makes no sense in the sentence, and it has therefore been omitted from the present text, but perhaps it indicates that a dragon briefly appears at that point, or perhaps the devil referred to in the present stage direction is disguised as a dragon)

Who would not be proficient in this art?
How pliant is this Mephostophilis,
Full of obedience and humility,
Such is the force of magic and my spells.

    (*Enter* MEPHOSTOPHILIS.)

MEPHOSTOPHILIS:
Now Faustus, what wouldst thou have me do?   35
    FAUSTUS:
I charge thee wait upon me whilst I live
To do whatever Faustus shall command,
Be it to make the moon drop from her sphere
Or the ocean to overwhelm the world.
    MEPHOSTOPHILIS:
I am a servant to great Lucifer   40
And may not follow thee without his leave.
No more than he commands must we perform.
    FAUSTUS:
Did not he charge thee to appear to me?
    MEPHOSTOPHILIS:
No, I came now hither of mine own accord.
    FAUSTUS:
Did not my conjuring raise thee? Speak.   45
    MEPHOSTOPHILIS:
That was the cause, but yet *per accidens:*°
For when we hear one rack° the name of God,
Abjure the Scriptures and his savior Christ,
We fly in hope to get his glorious° soul.
Nor will we come unless he use such means   50
Whereby he is in danger to be damned.
Therefore the shortest cut for conjuring
Is stoutly to abjure the Trinity
And pray devoutly to the prince of hell.
    FAUSTUS:
So Faustus hath already done, and holds this
    principle,   55
There is no chief but only Belzebub:
To whom Faustus doth dedicate himself.
This word "damnation" terrifies not me
For I confound hell in Elysium:°
My ghost° be with the old° philosophers!   60
But leaving these vain trifles of men's souls,
Tell me, what is that Lucifer thy lord?
    MEPHOSTOPHILIS:
Arch-regent and commander of all spirits.°
    FAUSTUS:
Was not that Lucifer an angel once?
    MEPHOSTOPHILIS:
Yes Faustus, and most dearly loved of God.   65

46 **per accidens** the immediate (but not ultimate) cause (Latin)   47 **rack** torture   49 **glorious** (1) splendid (2) presumptuous   59 **confound hell in Elysium** do not distinguish between hell and Elysium   60 **ghost** spirit   60 **old** pre-Christian   63 **spirits** devils

FAUSTUS:
How comes it then that he is prince of devils?
MEPHOSTOPHILIS:
O, by aspiring pride and insolence,
For which God threw him from the face of
    heaven.
FAUSTUS:
And what are you that live with Lucifer?
MEPHOSTOPHILIS:
70 Unhappy spirits that fell with Lucifer,
Conspired against our God with Lucifer,
And are forever damned with Lucifer.
FAUSTUS:
Where are you damned?
MEPHOSTOPHILIS:
In hell.
FAUSTUS:
75 How comes it then that thou art out of hell?
MEPHOSTOPHILIS:
Why this is hell, nor am I out of it.
Think'st thou that I who saw the face of God
And tasted the eternal joys of heaven
Am not tormented with ten thousand hells
80 In being deprived of everlasting bliss?
O Faustus, leave these frivolous demands
Which strikes° a terror to my fainting soul!
FAUSTUS:
What, is great Mephostophilis so passionate°
For being deprivèd of the joys of heaven?
85 Learn thou of Faustus manly fortitude
And scorn those joys thou never shalt possess.
Go bear these tidings to great Lucifer:
Seeing Faustus hath incurred eternal death
By desperate thoughts against Jove's deity,
90 Say he surrenders up to him his soul
So he will spare him four and twenty years,
Letting him live in all voluptuousness,
Having thee ever to attend on me,
To give me whatsoever I shall ask,
95 To tell me whatsoever I demand,
To slay mine enemies and to aid my friends
And always be obedient to my will.
Go and return to mighty Lucifer
And meet me in my study at midnight,
100 And then resolve° me of thy master's mind.
MEPHOSTOPHILIS:
I will, Faustus.
FAUSTUS:
Had I as many souls as there be stars

I'd give them all for Mephostophilis.
By him I'll be great emperor of the world,
And make a bridge through° the moving air   105
To pass the ocean with a band of men;
I'll join the hills that bind the Afric shore
And make that country continent to° Spain,
And both contributary to my crown;
The Emperor shall not live but by my leave,   110
Nor any potentate of Germany.
Now that I have obtained what I desired
I'll live in speculation° of this art
Till Mephostophilis return again.   (Exit.)
        [Exeunt LUCIFER and DEVILS.]

[I.iv] (Enter WAGNER and [ROBIN] the Clown.°)

WAGNER: Come hither, sirrah boy.
ROBIN: Boy! O, disgrace to my person!
Zounds,° boy in your face! You have seen many
boys with such pickadevants,° I am sure.
WAGNER: Sirrah, hast thou no comings in?°   5
ROBIN: Yes, and goings out too, you may see
sir.
WAGNER: Alas, poor slave! See how poverty
jests in his nakedness. I know the villain's out
of service, and so hungry that I know he would   10
give his soul to the devil for a shoulder of mutton, though it were blood-raw.
ROBIN: Not so, neither! I had need to have it
well roasted, and good sauce to it, if I pay so
dear, I can tell you.   15
WAGNER: Sirrah, wilt thou be my man and
wait on me? And I will make thee go like Qui
mihi discipulus.°
ROBIN: What, in verse?
WAGNER: No, slave, in beaten° silk and staves- 20
acre.°

105 **through** (pronounced "thorough") 108 **continent to** continuous with 113 **speculation** contemplation I.iv.s.d. **Clown** buffoon 3 **Zounds** by God's wounds 4 **pickadevants** pointed beards 5 **comings in** income (the Clown then quibbles on "goings out," i.e., expenses and also holes in his clothes through which his body pokes) 17–18 **Qui mihi discipulus** one who is my disciple, i.e., like the servant of a learned man (the Latin is the beginning of a poem, familiar to Renaissance schoolboys, on proper behavior) 20 **beaten** embroidered (leading to the quibble on the sense "hit") 21 **stavesacre** preparation from seeds of delphinium, used to kill vermin

82 **strikes** (it is not unusual to have a plural subject — especially when it has a collective force — take a verb ending in –s) 83 **passionate** emotional 100 **resolve** inform

ROBIN: Stavesacre? That's good to kill vermin! Then, belike, if I serve you I shall be lousy.

25 WAGNER: Why, so thou shalt be, whether thou dost it or no; for sirrah, if thou dost not presently bind thyself to me for seven years, I'll turn all the lice about thee into familiars° and make them tear thee in pieces.

30 ROBIN: Nay sir, you may save yourself a labor, for they are as familiar with me as if they paid for their meat and drink, I can tell you.

WAGNER: Well sirrah, leave your jesting and take these guilders.°

35 ROBIN: Yes marry° sir, and I thank you too.

WAGNER: So, now thou art to be at an hour's warning whensoever and wheresoever the devil shall fetch thee.

ROBIN: Here, take your guilders, I'll none of

40 'em!

WAGNER: Not I, thou art pressed.° Prepare thyself, for I will presently raise up two devils to carry thee away. Banio! Belcher!

ROBIN: Belcher! And° Belcher come here I'll

45 belch him. I am not afraid of a devil!

(*Enter two* DEVILS.)

WAGNER: How now sir, will you serve me now?

ROBIN: Ay, good Wagner, take away the devil then.

50 WAGNER: Spirits, away! [*Exeunt* DEVILS.] Now sirrah, follow me.

ROBIN: I will sir! But hark you master, will you teach me this conjuring occupation?

WAGNER: Ay sirrah, I'll teach thee to turn

55 thyself to a dog or a cat or a mouse or a rat or anything.

ROBIN: A dog or a cat or a mouse or a rat? O brave° Wagner!

WAGNER: Villain, call me Master Wagner.

60 And see that you walk attentively, and let your right eye be always diametrally° fixed upon my left heel, that thou mayst *quasi vestigiis nostris insistere.*°

ROBIN: Well sir, I warrant you.   (*Exeunt.*)

28 **familiars** attendant demons   34 **guilders** Dutch coins   35 **marry** indeed (a mild oath, from "by the Virgin Mary")   41 **pressed** enlisted into service 44 **And** if   58 **brave** splendid   61 **diametrally** directly   62–63 **quasi vestigiis nostris insistere** as if to step in our footsteps

[II.i] (*Enter* FAUSTUS *in his study.*)

FAUSTUS:
Now, Faustus, must thou needs be damned;
Canst thou not be saved!
What boots° it then to think on God or heaven?
Away with such vain fancies, and despair —
Despair in God and trust in Belzebub!   5
Now go not backward. Faustus, be resolute!
Why waver'st thou? O something soundeth in mine ear,
"Abjure this magic, turn to God again."
Ay, and Faustus will turn to God again.
To God? He loves thee not;   10
The god thou serv'st is thine own appetite
Wherein is fixed the love of Belzebub!
To him I'll build an altar and a church
And offer lukewarm blood of newborn babes!

(*Enter the two* ANGELS.)

BAD ANGEL:
Go forward, Faustus, in that famous art.   15
GOOD ANGEL:
Sweet Faustus, leave that execrable art.
FAUSTUS:
Contrition, prayer, repentance, what of these?
GOOD ANGEL:
O, they are means to bring thee unto heaven.
BAD ANGEL:
Rather illusions, fruits of lunacy,
That make men foolish that do use them most.   20
GOOD ANGEL:
Sweet Faustus, think of heaven and heavenly things.
BAD ANGEL:
No Faustus, think of honor and of wealth.
                          (*Exeunt* ANGELS.)
FAUSTUS:
Wealth!
Why, the signory of Emden° shall be mine!
When Mephostophilis shall stand by me   25
What power can hurt me? Faustus, thou art safe.
Cast no more doubts! Mephostophilis, come,
And bring glad tidings from great Lucifer.
Is't not midnight? Come Mephostophilis,
Veni, veni, Mephostophile!°   30

II.i.3 **boots** avails   24 **signory of Emden** lordship of the rich German port at the mouth of the Ems 30 **Veni, veni, Mephostophile** come, come, Mephostophilis (Latin)

(*Enter* MEPHOSTOPHILIS.)

Now tell me, what saith Lucifer thy lord?
MEPHOSTOPHILIS:
That I shall wait on Faustus whilst he lives,
So he will buy my service with his soul.
FAUSTUS:
Already Faustus hath hazarded that for thee.
MEPHOSTOPHILIS:
35 But now thou must bequeath it solemnly
And write a deed of gift with thine own blood,
For that security craves Lucifer.
If thou deny it I must back to hell.
FAUSTUS:
Stay Mephostophilis and tell me
40 What good will my soul do thy lord?
MEPHOSTOPHILIS:
Enlarge his kingdom.
FAUSTUS:
Is that the reason why he tempts us thus?
MEPHOSTOPHILIS:
Solamen miseris socios habuisse doloris.°
FAUSTUS:
Why, have you any pain that torture other?°
MEPHOSTOPHILIS:
45 As great as have the human souls of men.
But tell me, Faustus, shall I have thy soul —
And I will be thy slave and wait on thee
And give thee more than thou hast wit to ask?
FAUSTUS:
Ay Mephostophilis, I'll give it him.°
MEPHOSTOPHILIS:
50 Then, Faustus, stab thy arm courageously
And bind thy soul that at some certain day
Great Lucifer may claim it as his own.
And then be thou as great as Lucifer!
FAUSTUS:
Lo, Mephostophilis, for love of thee
Faustus hath cut his arm and with his proper°
55   blood
Assures° his soul to be great Lucifer's,
Chief lord and regent of perpetual night.
View here this blood that trickles from mine
    arm
And let it be propitious for my wish.
MEPHOSTOPHILIS:
60 But Faustus,
Write it in manner of a deed of gift.
FAUSTUS:
Ay so I do — But Mephostophilis,

My blood congeals and I can write no more.
MEPHOSTOPHILIS:
I'll fetch thee fire to dissolve it straight.
                                                        (*Exit.*)
FAUSTUS:
What might the staying of my blood portend?   65
Is it unwilling I should write this bill?°
Why streams it not that I may write afresh:
"Faustus gives to thee his soul"? O there it
    stayed.
Why shouldst thou not? Is not thy soul thine
    own?
Then write again: "Faustus gives to thee his
    soul."   70

(*Enter* MEPHOSTOPHILIS *with the chafer*° *of
fire.*)

MEPHOSTOPHILIS:
See Faustus, here is fire. Set it° on.
FAUSTUS:
So, now the blood begins to clear again.
Now will I make an end immediately.
MEPHOSTOPHILIS [*aside*]:
What will not I do to obtain his soul!
FAUSTUS:
Consummatum est!° This bill is ended: 75
And Faustus hath bequeathed his soul to Luci-
    fer.
— But what is this inscription on mine arm?
Homo fuge!° Whither should I fly?
If unto God, He'll throw me down to hell.
My senses are deceived, here's nothing writ.   80
O yes, I see it plain! Even here is writ
Homo fuge! Yet shall not Faustus fly!
MEPHOSTOPHILIS [*aside*]:
I'll fetch him somewhat to delight his mind.
                                                        (*Exit.*)

(*Enter* DEVILS *giving crowns and rich apparel to* FAUSTUS. *They dance and then depart.*)

(*Enter* MEPHOSTOPHILIS.)

FAUSTUS:
What means this show? Speak, Mephostophilis.
MEPHOSTOPHILIS:
Nothing Faustus, but to delight thy mind   85
And let thee see what magic can perform.

43 Solamen . . . doloris misery loves company (Latin)
44 other others   49 him i.e., to Lucifer   55 proper
own   56 Assures conveys by contract

66 bill contract   70s.d. chafer portable grate   71
it i.e., the receptacle containing the congealed blood
75 Consummatum est it is finished (Latin; a blas-
phemous repetition of Christ's words on the Cross;
see John 19:30)   78 Homo fuge fly, man (Latin)

FAUSTUS:
But may I raise such spirits when I please?
MEPHOSTOPHILIS:
Ay Faustus, and do greater things than these.
FAUSTUS:
Then, Mephostophilis, receive this scroll,
90 A deed of gift of body and of soul:
But yet conditionally that thou perform
All covenants and articles between us both.
MEPHOSTOPHILIS:
Faustus, I swear by hell and Lucifer
To effect all promises between us both.
FAUSTUS:
95 Then hear me read it, Mephostophilis:
"On these conditions following:
First, that Faustus may be a spirit° in form and
    substance.
Secondly, that Mephostophilis shall be his ser-
100   vant and be by him commanded.
Thirdly, that Mephostophilis shall do for him
    and bring him whatsoever.
Fourthly, that he shall be in his chamber or
    house invisible.
105 Lastly, that he shall appear to the said John
    Faustus at all times in what form or shape
    soever he please:
I, John Faustus of Wittenberg, Doctor, by these
    presents, do give both body and soul to
110   Lucifer, prince of the east, and his minister
    Mephostophilis, and furthermore grant
    unto them that, four and twenty years be-
    ing expired, and these articles above writ-
    ten being inviolate,° full power to fetch or
115   carry the said John Faustus, body and soul,
    flesh, blood, or goods, into their habitation
    wheresoever.
                            By me John Faustus.
MEPHOSTOPHILIS: Speak Faustus, do you deliver this as your deed?
FAUSTUS: Ay, take it, and the devil give thee
120 good of it!
MEPHOSTOPHILIS: So now Faustus, ask me
what thou wilt.
FAUSTUS: First will I question with thee about
hell. Tell me, where is the place that men call
hell?
125 MEPHOSTOPHILIS: Under the heavens.

FAUSTUS:
Ay, so are all things else, but whereabouts?
MEPHOSTOPHILIS:
Within the bowels of these elements
Where we are tortured and remain forever.
Hell hath no limits nor is circumscribed
In one self place, but where we are is hell,   130
And where hell is there must we ever be.
And to be short, when all the world dissolves
And every creature shall be purified
All places shall be hell that is not heaven!
FAUSTUS:
I think hell's a fable.   135
MEPHOSTOPHILIS:
Ay, think so still — till experience change thy
    mind!
FAUSTUS:
Why, dost thou think that Faustus shall be
    damned?
MEPHOSTOPHILIS:
Ay, of necessity, for here's the scroll
In which thou hast given thy soul to Lucifer.
FAUSTUS:
Ay, and body too; but what of that?   140
Think'st thou that Faustus is so fond° to imag-
    ine
That after this life there is any pain?
No, these are trifles and mere old wives' tales.
MEPHOSTOPHILIS:
But I am an instance to prove the contrary,
For I tell thee I am damned and now in hell!   145
FAUSTUS:
Nay, and this be hell, I'll willingly be damned —
What, sleeping, eating, walking, and disputing?
But leaving this, let me have a wife, the fairest
    maid in Germany, for I am wanton and
    lascivious and cannot live without a wife.   150
MEPHOSTOPHILIS:
Well Faustus, thou shalt have a wife.
    (He fetches in a woman DEVIL [with fire-
    works].)
FAUSTUS:
What sight is this?
MEPHOSTOPHILIS:
Now Faustus, wilt thou have a wife?
FAUSTUS:
Here's a hot whore indeed! No, I'll no wife.
MEPHOSTOPHILIS:
Marriage is but a ceremonial toy,°   155
                            [Exit SHE-DEVIL.]
And if thou lovest me, think no more of it.

97 **spirit** evil spirit, devil (but to see Faustus as
transformed now into a devil deprived of freedom
to repent is to deprive the remainder of the play of
much of its meaning)   114 **inviolate** unviolated

141 **fond** foolish   155 **toy** trifle

I'll cull thee out° the fairest courtesans
And bring them every morning to thy bed.
She whom thine eye shall like thy heart shall
     have,
160   Were she as chaste as was Penelope,°
As wise as Saba,° or as beautiful
As was bright Lucifer before his fall.
Here, take this book and peruse it well.
The iterating° of these lines brings gold;
165   The framing° of this circle on the ground
Brings thunder, whirlwinds, storm, and light-
     ning;
Pronounce this thrice devoutly to thyself,
And men in harness° shall appear to thee,
Ready to execute what thou command'st.
    FAUSTUS:
170   Thanks Mephostophilis for this sweet book.
This will I keep as chary as my life.
                           (*Exeunt.*°)

[II.ii] (*Enter* FAUSTUS *in his study and* MEPHOSTOPHILIS.)

    FAUSTUS:
When I behold the heavens, then I repent
And curse thee, wicked Mephostophilis,
Because thou has deprived me of those joys.
    MEPHOSTOPHILIS:
'Twas thine own seeking Faustus, thank thyself.
But think'st thou heaven is such a glorious
5   thing?
I tell thee, Faustus, it is not half so fair
As thou or any man that breathe on earth.
    FAUSTUS:
How prov'st thou that?
    MEPHOSTOPHILIS:
'Twas made for man; then he's more excellent.
    FAUSTUS:
If heaven was made for man, 'twas made for
10   me!
I will renounce this magic and repent.

(*Enter the two* ANGELS.)

    GOOD ANGEL:
Faustus, repent: yet° God will pity thee!
    BAD ANGEL:
Thou art a spirit: God cannot pity thee!
    FAUSTUS:
Who buzzeth in mine ears I am a spirit?
Be I a devil, yet God may pity me —   15
Yea, God will pity me if I repent.
    BAD ANGEL:
Ay, but Faustus never shall repent.
                      (*Exit* ANGELS.)
    FAUSTUS:
My heart is hardened, I cannot repent.
Scarce can I name salvation, faith, or heaven,
Swords, poison, halters, and envenomed steel   20
Are laid before me to dispatch myself.
And long ere this I should have done the deed
Had not sweet pleasure conquered deep despair.
Have not I made blind Homer sing to me
Of Alexander's love and Oenon's° death?   25
And hath not he° that built the walls of Thebes
With ravishing sound of his melodious harp
Made music with my Mephostophilis?
Why should I die then or basely despair?
I am resolved, Faustus shall not repent!   30
Come Mephostophilis, let us dispute again
And reason of divine astrology.
Speak, are there many spheres above the moon?
Are all celestial bodies but one globe
As is the substance of this centric° earth?   35
    MEPHOSTOPHILIS:
As are the elements, such° are the heavens,
Even from the moon unto the empyreal orb
Mutually folded in each others' spheres,
And jointly move upon one axle-tree,
Whose terminè° is termed the world's wide
     pole.   40
Nor are the names of Saturn, Mars, or Jupiter
Feigned but are erring stars.°
    FAUSTUS:
But have they all one motion,

II.ii.12 **yet** still, even now   25 **Alexander ... Oenone**
Paris, also called Alexander, was Oenone's lover, but
he later deserted her for Helen of Troy, causing the
Trojan War, the subject of Homer's *Iliad*   26 **he**
Amphion, whose music charmed stones to form the
walls of Thebes   35 **centric** central   36 **such** i.e.,
separate but combined; the idea is that the heavenly
bodies are separate but their spheres are concentric
("folded"), and all — from the nearest (the moon)
to the farthest ("the empyreal orb" or empyrean)
— move on one axletree   40 **terminè** end, extremity
42 **erring stars** planets

---

157 **cull thee out** select for you   160 **Penelope** wife
of Ulysses, famed for her fidelity   161 **Saba** the
Queen of Sheba   164 **iterating** repetition   165
framing drawing   168 **harness** armor   171s.d. **Exeunt** (a scene following this stage direction has probably been lost. Earlier Wagner hired the Clown;
later the Clown is an ostler possessed of one of
Faustus' conjuring books. Possibly, then, the lost
scene was a comic one, showing the Clown stealing
a book and departing)

Both *situ et tempore?*°

45 MEPHOSTOPHILIS: All move from east to west in four and twenty hours upon the poles of the world but differ in their motions upon the poles of the zodiac.

FAUSTUS: These slender questions Wagner can decide.

50 Hath Mephostophilis no greater skill?
Who knows not the double motion of the planets?
That the first is finished in a natural day.°
The second thus: Saturn in thirty years;
Jupiter in twelve; Mars in four; the sun, Venus,
55 and Mercury in a year; the moon in twenty-eight days. These are freshmen's suppositions.° But tell me, hath every sphere a dominion or *intelligentia?*°

MEPHOSTOPHILIS: Ay.

FAUSTUS:
60 How many heavens or spheres are there?

MEPHOSTOPHILIS: Nine: the seven planets, the firmament, and the empyreal heaven.

FAUSTUS: But is there not *coelum igneum et crystallinum?*°

65 MEPHOSTOPHILIS: No Faustus, they be but fables.

FAUSTUS: Resolve me then in this one question. Why are not conjunctions, oppositions, aspects, eclipses all at one time,° but in some
70 years we have more, in some less?

MEPHOSTOPHILIS: *Per inaqualem motum respectu totius.*°

FAUSTUS: Well, I am answered. Now tell me, who made the world?

75 MEPHOSTOPHILIS: I will not.

FAUSTUS: Sweet Mephostophilis, tell me.

MEPHOSTOPHILIS: Move° me not, Faustus!

FAUSTUS: Villain, have not I bound thee to tell me anything?

MEPHOSTOPHILIS:
80 Ay, that is not against our kingdom.
This is. Thou art damned. Think thou of hell!

FAUSTUS:
Think, Faustus, upon God, that made the world.

---

44 **situ et tempore** in place and in time   52 **natural day** twenty-four hours   57 **suppositions** premises 58 **dominion or intelligentia** governing angel or intelligence (believed to impart motion to the sphere) 63–64 **coelum igneum et crystallinum** a heaven of fire and a crystalline sphere (Latin)   69 **at one time** i.e., at regular intervals   71–72 **Per . . . totius** because of unequal speed within the system (Latin) 77 **Move** anger

MEPHOSTOPHILIS:
Remember this!   (*Exit.*)

FAUSTUS:
Ay, go accursèd spirit to ugly hell!
'Tis thou hast damned distressèd Faustus'
    soul. —   85
Is't not too late?

(*Enter the two* ANGELS.)

BAD ANGEL:
Too late.

GOOD ANGEL:
Never too late, if Faustus will repent.

BAD ANGEL:
If thou repent, devils will tear thee in pieces.

GOOD ANGEL:
Repent, and they shall never raze° thy skin.   90
                        (*Exeunt* ANGELS.)

FAUSTUS:
O Christ, my savior, my savior!
Help to save distressèd Faustus' soul.

(*Enter* LUCIFER, BELZEBUB, *and* MEPHO-STOPHILIS.)

LUCIFER:
Christ cannot save thy soul, for He is just.
There's none but I have interest in° the same.

FAUSTUS:
O, what art thou that look'st so terribly?   95

LUCIFER:
I am Lucifer
And this is my companion prince in hell.

FAUSTUS:
O Faustus, they are come to fetch thy soul!

BELZEBUB:
We are come to tell thee thou dost injure us.

LUCIFER:
Thou call'st on Christ contrary to thy promise.   100

BELZEBUB:
Thou should'st not think on God.

LUCIFER:
                        Think on the Devil.

BELZEBUB:
And his dam° too.

FAUSTUS:
Nor will Faustus henceforth. Pardon him for
    this,
And Faustus vows never to look to heaven!
Never to name God or to pray to Him,   105

---

90 **raze** scratch   94 **interest in** legal claim on   102 **dam** mother

To burn His Scriptures, slay His ministers,
And make my spirits pull His churches down.
    LUCIFER:
So shalt thou show thyself an obedient servant,
And we will highly gratify thee for it.
110   BELZEBUB: Faustus, we are come from hell in person to show thee some pastime. Sit down and thou shalt behold the Seven Deadly Sins° appear to thee in their own proper shapes and likeness.
115   FAUSTUS: That sight will be as pleasant to me as Paradise was to Adam the first day of his creation.
    LUCIFER: Talk not of Paradise or creation but mark the show. Go Mephostophilis, fetch them
120 in.

(*Enter the* SEVEN DEADLY SINS [*led by a* PIPER].)

BELZEBUB: Now Faustus, question them of their names and dispositions.
    FAUSTUS: That shall I soon. What art thou, the first?
125   PRIDE: I am Pride. I disdain to have any parents. I am like to Ovid's flea,° I can creep into every corner of a wench: sometimes, like a periwig I sit upon her brow; next, like a necklace I hang about her neck; then, like a fan of feathers
130 I kiss her; and then, turning myself to a wrought smock,° do what I list — But fie, what a smell is here! I'll not speak a word more for a king's ransom unless the ground be perfumed and covered with cloth of arras.°
135   FAUSTUS: Thou art a proud knave indeed. What art thou, the second?
    COVETOUSNESS: I am Covetousness, begotten of an old churl in a leather bag;° and might I now obtain my wish, this house, you and all,
140 should turn to gold that I might lock you safe into my chest. O my sweet gold!
    FAUSTUS: And what art thou, the third?
    ENVY: I am Envy, begotten of a chimney-sweeper and an oyster-wife.° I cannot read and
145 therefore wish all books burned. I am lean with

seeing others eat. O, that there would come a famine over all the world that all might die and I live alone! Then thou shouldst see how fat I'd be. But must thou sit and I stand? Come down, with a vengeance!
150   FAUSTUS: Out, envious wretch! But what art thou, the fourth?
    WRATH: I am Wrath. I had neither father nor mother. I leapt out of a lion's mouth when I was scarce an hour old and ever since have
155 run up and down the world with these case° of rapiers, wounding myself when I could get none to fight withal. I was born in hell! And look to it, for some of you shall be my father.
    FAUSTUS: And what art thou, the fifth?
160   GLUTTONY: I am Gluttony. My parents are all dead, and the devil a penny they have left me, but a small pension: and that buys me thirty meals a day and ten bevers,° a small trifle to suffice nature. I come of a royal pedigree. My
165 father was a gammon° of bacon, and my mother was a hogshead of claret wine. My godfathers were these: Peter Pickled-herring and Martin Martlemas-beef.° But my godmother, O, she was an ancient gentlewoman: her name was
170 Margery March-beer.° Now Faustus, thou hast heard all my progeny,° wilt thou bid me to supper?
    FAUSTUS: Not I.
    GLUTTONY: Then the devil choke thee!
175   FAUSTUS: Choke thyself, glutton! What art thou, the sixth?
    SLOTH: Heigh-ho!° I am Sloth. I was begotten on a sunny bank. Heigh-ho, I'll not speak a word more for a king's ransom.
180   FAUSTUS: And what are you, Mistress Minx, the seventh and last?
    LECHERY: Who, I, sir? I am one that loves an inch of raw mutton° better than an ell of fried stockfish,° and the first letter of my name
185 begins with Lechery.
    LUCIFER: Away to hell, away! On, piper!
    (*Exeunt the* SEVEN SINS.)

112 **Seven Deadly Sins** (so called because they cause spiritual death; they are Pride, Covetousness, Envy, Wrath, Gluttony, Sloth, Lechery) 126 **Ovid's flea** flea in *Carmen de pulce*, a lewd poem mistakenly attributed to Ovid 130–131 **wrought smock** decorated petticoat 134 **cloth of arras** Flemish cloth used for tapestries 138 **leather bag** moneybag (?) 143–44 **chimney-sweeper ... oyster-wife** i.e., dirty and smelly

156 **these case** this pair 164 **bevers** snacks (literally drinks) 166 **gammon** haunch 169 **Martlemas-beef** cattle slaughtered at Martinmas (11 November) and salted for winter consumption 171 **March-beer** strong beer brewed in March 172 **progeny** ancestry 178 **Heigh-ho** (a yawn or tired greeting) 184 **inch of raw mutton** i.e., penis ("mutton" in a bawdy sense commonly alludes to a prostitute, but since here the speaker is a woman, the allusion must be to a male) 184–85 **an ell of ... stockfish** forty-five inches of dried cod

FAUSTUS:
O, how this sight doth delight my soul!

LUCIFER:
But Faustus, in hell is all manner of delight.

FAUSTUS:
190 O, might I see hell and return again safe,
  how happy were I then!

LUCIFER:
Faustus, thou shalt. At midnight I will send
  for thee.
Meanwhile peruse this book and view it thoroughly,
And thou shalt turn thyself into what shape
  thou wilt.

FAUSTUS:
195 Thanks mighty Lucifer.
This will I keep as chary° as my life.

LUCIFER:
Now Faustus, farewell.

FAUSTUS:
Farewell great Lucifer. Come Mephostophilis.
  (*Exeunt omnes several° ways.*)

[II.iii] (*Enter* [ROBIN] *the Clown.*)

ROBIN: What, Dick, look to the horses there
till I come again! I have gotten one of Doctor
Faustus' conjuring books, and now we'll have
such knavery as't passes.

(*Enter* DICK.)

5   DICK: What, Robin, you must come away and
walk the horses.
ROBIN: I walk the horses? I scorn't, 'faith. I
have other matters in hand. Let the horses walk
themselves an° they will. [*Reading*] A *per se°*
10 — a; t, h, e — the; o *per se* — o; deny orgon —
gorgon.° Keep further from me, O thou illiterate and unlearned hostler!
DICK: 'Snails,° what hast thou got there, a
book? Why, thou canst not tell ne'er a word
15 on't.
ROBIN: That thou shalt see presently. Keep
out of the circle, I say, lest I send you into the
hostry° with a vengeance.
DICK: That's like, 'faith! You had best leave

your foolery, for an my master come, he'll con- 20
jure you, 'faith.
ROBIN: My master conjure me? I'll tell thee
what. An my master come here, I'll clap as fair
a pair of horns° on's head as e'er thou sawest in
thy life.   25
DICK: Thou need'st not do that, for my mistress hath done it.
ROBIN: Ay, there be of us here that have
waded as deep into matters as other men — if
they were disposed to talk.   30
DICK: A plague take you! I thought you did
not sneak up and down after her for nothing.
But I prithee tell me in good sadness° Robin,
is that a conjuring book?
ROBIN: Do but speak what thou't have me to 35
do, and I'll do't. If thou't dance naked, put off
thy clothes, and I'll conjure thee about presently. Or if thou't go but to the tavern with me,
I'll give thee white wine, red wine, claret wine,
sack,° muscadine, malmsey, and whippincrust° 40
— hold-belly-hold. And we'll not pay one penny
for it.
DICK: O brave! Prithee let's to it presently,
for I am as dry as a dog.
ROBIN: Come then, let's away.   (*Exeunt.*) 45

[III] (*Enter the* CHORUS.)

Learnèd Faustus,
To find the secrets of astronomy
Graven in the book of Jove's high firmament,
Did mount him up to scale Olympus' top:
Where, sitting in a chariot burning bright   5
Drawn by the strength of yokèd dragons' necks,
He views the clouds, the planets, and the stars,
The tropics, zones,° and quarters of the sky,
From the bright circle° of the hornèd moon
Even to the height of *primum mobile:*°   10
And whirling round with this circumference
Within the concave compass of the pole,
From east to west his dragons swiftly glide
And in eight days did bring him home again.
Not long he stayed within his quiet house   15
To rest his bones after his weary toil

---

196 **chary** carefully 198s.d. **several** various II.iii.
9 **an** if 9 **per se** by itself (Latin; the idea is, "A
by itself spells A") 10–11 **deny orgon — gorgon**
(Robin is trying to read the name "Demogorgon")
13 **'Snails** by God's nails 18 **hostry** hostelry, inn

24 **horns** (as the next speech indicates, horns were
said to adorn the head of a man whose wife was unfaithful) 33 **in good sadness** seriously 40 **sack**
sherry 40 **whippincrust** illiterate pronunciation of
"hippocras," a spiced wine III **Chorus** 8 **zones**
segments of the sky 9 **circle** orbit 10 **primum
mobile** the outermost sphere, the empyrean

But new exploits do hale him out again.
And mounted then upon a dragon's back,
That with his wings did part the subtle air,
20 He now is gone to prove cosmography,°
That measures coasts and kingdoms of the earth,
And as I guess will first arrive at Rome
To see the Pope and manner of his court
And take some part of holy Peter's feast,
25 The which this day is highly solemnized.

(*Exit.*)

[III.i] (*Enter* FAUSTUS *and*
MEPHOSTOPHILIS.)

FAUSTUS:
Having now, my good Mephostophilis,
Passed with delight the stately town of Trier,°
Environed round with airy mountain tops,
With walls of flint, and deep-entrenchèd lakes,°
5 Not to be won by any conquering prince:
From Paris next, coasting the realm of France,
We saw the river Main fall into Rhine,
Whose banks are set with groves of fruitful
     vines:
Then up to Naples, rich Campania,
10 Whose buildings fair and gorgeous to the eye,
The streets straight forth and paved with finest
     brick,
Quarters the town in four equivalents.
There saw we learnèd Maro's° golden tomb,
The way he cut an English mile in length
15 Through° a rock of stone in one night's space.
From thence to Venice, Padua, and the rest,
In one of which a sumptuous temple stands
That threats the stars with her aspiring top,
Whose frame is paved with sundry colored
     stones
20 And roofed aloft with curious work in gold.
Thus hitherto hath Faustus spent his time.
But tell me now, what resting-place is this?
Hast thou, as erst I did command,
Conducted me within the walls of Rome?
MEPHOSTOPHILIS:
25 I have, my Faustus, and for proof thereof
This is the goodly palace of the Pope,
And 'cause we are no common guests

I choose his privy chamber for our use.
     FAUSTUS:
I hope his Holiness will bid us welcome.
     MEPHOSTOPHILIS:
All's one, for we'll be bold with his venison.   30
But now my Faustus, that thou may'st perceive
What Rome contains for to delight thine eyes,
Know that this city stands upon seven hills
That underprop the groundwork of the same:
Just through the midst runs flowing Tiber's
     stream   35
With winding banks that cut it in two parts,
Over the which four stately bridges lean°
That make safe passage to each part of Rome.
Upon the bridge called Ponte Angelo
Erected is a castle passing strong   40
Where thou shalt see such store of ordinance
As that the double cannons forged of brass
Do match the number of the days contained
Within the compass of one complete year,
Beside the gates and high pyramides°   45
That Julius Caesar brought from Africa.
     FAUSTUS:
Now, by the kingdoms of infernal rule,
Of Styx, of Acheron, and the fiery lake
Of ever-burning Phlegethon,° I swear
That I do long to see the monuments   50
And situation of bright-splendent Rome.
Come therefore, let's away.
     MEPHOSTOPHILIS:
Nay stay my Faustus. I know you'd see the Pope
And take some part of holy Peter's feast,
The which this day with high solemnity,   55
This day, is held through Rome and Italy
In honor of the Pope's triumphant victory.
     FAUSTUS:
Sweet Mephostophilis, thou pleasest me.
Whilst I am here on earth let me be cloyed
With all things that delight the heart of man.   60
My four and twenty years of liberty
I'll spend in pleasure and in dalliance,
That Faustus' name, whilst this bright frame
     doth stand,
May be admirèd through the furthest land.
     MEPHOSTOPHILIS:
'Tis well said, Faustus, come then, stand by me 65
And thou shalt see them come immediately.
     FAUSTUS:
Nay stay my Faustus. I know you'd see the Pope
And grant me my request, and then I go.

---

20 **prove cosmography** test maps, i.e., explore the
universe   III.i.2 **Trier** German city on the Moselle,
also known as Trèves   4 **deep-entrenchèd lakes**
moats   13 **Maro** Vergil (Publius Vergilius Maro,
70–19 B.C.)   15 **Through** (pronounced "thorough")

37 **lean** bend   45 **pyramides** obelisk (pronounced
py·ràm·i·des)   48–49 **Styx, Acheron, Phlegethon**
rivers of the underworld

Thou know'st, within the compass of eight
days
We viewed the face of heaven, of earth, and
70   hell.
So high our dragons soared into the air
That looking down the earth appeared to me
No bigger than my hand in quantity —
There did we view the kingdoms of the world,
75   And what might please mine eye I there beheld.
Then in this show let me an actor be
That this proud Pope may Faustus' cunning see!
MEPHOSTOPHILIS:
Let it be so, my Faustus, but first stay
And view their triumphs° as they pass this way.
80   And then devise what best contents thy mind
By cunning in thine art to cross the Pope
Or dash the pride of this solemnity —
To make his monks and abbots stand like apes
And point like antics° at his triple crown,
85   To beat the beads about the friars' pates,
Or clap huge horns upon the cardinals' heads,
Or any villainy thou canst devise —
And I'll perform it, Faustus. Hark, they come!
This day shall make thee be admired° in Rome!

(Enter the CARDINALS and BISHOPS, some
bearing crosiers, some the pillars; MONKS and
FRIARS singing their procession; then the
POPE and RAYMOND King of Hungary, with
BRUNO° led in chains.)

POPE:
90   Cast down our footstool.
RAYMOND:
                            Saxon Bruno, stoop,
Whilst on thy back his Holiness ascends
Saint Peter's chair and state° pontifical.
BRUNO:
Proud Lucifer, that state belongs to me —
95   But thus I fall to Peter, not to thee.
POPE:
To me and Peter shalt thou grov'lling lie
And crouch before the papal dignity!
Sound trumpets then, for thus Saint Peter's
heir
From Bruno's back ascends Saint Peter's chair!

(A flourish° while he ascends.)

Thus as the gods creep on with feet of wool   100
Long ere with iron hands they punish men,
So shall our sleeping vengeance now arise
And smite with death thy hated enterprise.
Lord Cardinals of France and Padua,
Go forthwith to our holy consistory°   105
And read amongst the statutes decretal°
What by the holy council held at Trent°
The sacred synod° hath decreed for him
That doth assume the papal government
Without election and a true consent.   110
Away, and bring us word with speed!
I CARDINAL:
We go my lord.   (Exeunt [two] CARDINALS.)
POPE:
Lord Raymond —   [Talks to him apart.]
FAUSTUS:
Go haste thee, gentle Mephostophilis,
Follow the cardinals to the consistory   115
And as they turn their superstitious books
Strike them with sloth and drowsy idleness
And make them sleep so sound that in their
shapes
Thyself and I may parley with this Pope,
This proud confronter of the Emperor!   120
— And in despite of all his holiness
Restore this Bruno to his liberty
And bear him to the states of Germany!
MEPHOSTOPHILIS:
Faustus, I go.
FAUSTUS:
Dispatch it soon.   125
The Pope shall curse that Faustus came to
Rome.
            (Exit FAUSTUS and MEPHOSTOPHILIS.)
BRUNO:
Pope Adrian, let me have some right of law:
I was elected by the Emperor.
POPE:
We will depose the Emperor for that deed
And curse the people that submit to him.   130
Both he and thou shalt stand excommunicate
And interdict from church's privilege
And all society of holy men.
He grows too proud in his authority,
Lifting his lofty head above the clouds,   135
And like a steeple overpeers the church.
But we'll pull down his haughty insolence.

79 **triumphs** spectacular displays   84 **antics** grotesque
figures, buffoons   89 **admired** wondered at   89s.d.
Raymond King of Hungary ... Bruno (unhistorical
figures; Bruno is the emperor's nominee for the papal
throne)   92 **state** throne   99s.d. **flourish** trumpet
fanfare

105 **consistory** i.e., meeting-place of the papal consistory or senate   106 **statutes decretal** i.e., ecclesiastical laws   107 **council held at Trent** (intermittently from 1545 to 1563)   108 **synod** council

And as Pope Alexander,° our progenitor,°
Trod on the neck of German Frederick,
140 Adding this golden sentence to our praise:
"That Peter's heirs should tread on emperors
And walk upon the dreadful adder's back,
Treading the lion and the dragon down,
And fearless spurn the killing basilisk"° —
145 So will we quell that haughty schismatic
And by authority apostolical
Depose him from his regal government.

BRUNO:
Pope Julius swore to princely Sigismond,
For him and the succeeding Popes of Rome,
150 To hold the emperors their lawful lords.

POPE:
Pope Julius did abuse the church's rites
And therefore none of his decrees can stand.
Is not all power on earth bestowed on us?
And therefore though we would, we cannot err.
155 Behold this silver belt whereto is fixed
Seven golden keys fast sealed with seven seals
In token of our sevenfold power from heaven
To bind or loose, lock fast, condemn, or judge,
Resign° or seal, or whatso pleaseth us.
160 Then he and thou and all the world shall
    stoop —
Or be assurèd of our dreadful curse
To light as heavy as the pains of hell.

(Enter FAUSTUS and MEPHOSTOPHILIS like the
cardinals.)

MEPHOSTOPHILIS [aside]:
Now tell me Faustus, are we not fitted well?

FAUSTUS [aside]:
Yes Mephostophilis, and two such cardinals
165 Ne'er served a holy Pope as we shall do.
But whilst they sleep within the consistory
Let us salute his reverend Fatherhood.

RAYMOND:
Behold my lord, the cardinals are returned.

POPE:
Welcome grave fathers, answer presently,°
170 What have our holy council there decreed
Concerning Bruno and the Emperor
In quittance of° their late conspiracy
Against our state and papal dignity?

FAUSTUS:
Most sacred patron of the church of Rome,
By full consent of all the synod   175
Of priests and prelates it is thus decreed:
That Bruno and the German Emperor
Be held as lollards° and bold schismatics
And proud disturbers of the church's peace.
And if that Bruno by his own assent,   180
Without enforcement of the German peers,
Did seek to wear the triple diadem
And by your death to climb Saint Peter's chair,
The statutes decretal have thus decreed:
He shall be straight condemned of heresy   185
And on a pile of fagots burnt to death.

POPE:
It is enough. Here, take him to your charge
And bear him straight to Ponte Angelo
And in the strongest tower enclose him fast.
Tomorrow, sitting in our consistory   190
With all our college of grave cardinals
We will determine of his life or death.
Here, take his triple crown along with you
And leave it in the church's treasury.
Make haste again,° my good lord cardinals,   195
And take our blessing apostolical.

MEPHOSTOPHILIS [aside]:
So, so! Was never devil thus blessed before.

FAUSTUS [aside]:
Away sweet Mephostophilis, be gone!
The cardinals will be plagued for this anon.
(Exeunt FAUSTUS and MEPHOSTOPHILIS [with
BRUNO].)

POPE:
Go presently and bring a banquet forth,   200
That we may solemnize Saint Peter's feast
And with Lord Raymond, King of Hungary,
Drink to our late and happy victory.

                                        (Exeunt.)

[III.ii] (A sennet° while the banquet is
brought in, and then enter FAUSTUS and
MEPHOSTOPHILIS in their own shapes.)

MEPHOSTOPHILIS:
Now Faustus, come prepare thyself for mirth.
The sleepy cardinals are hard at hand
To censure Bruno, that is posted hence,
And on a proud-paced steed as swift as thought

138 **Pope Alexander** Pope Alexander III (d. 1181)
compelled the emperor Frederick Barbarossa to kneel
before him   138 **progenitor** predecessor   144 **basilisk**
fabulous monster said to kill with a glance   159 **Resign** unseal   169 **presently** immediately   172 **quittance of** requital for

178 **lollards** heretics   195 **again** i.e., to return
III.ii.s.d. **sennet** set of notes played on a trumpet
signaling an approach or a departure

5 Flies o'er the Alps to fruitful Germany,
There to salute the woeful Emperor.

FAUSTUS:
The Pope will curse them for their sloth today
That slept both Bruno and his crown away.
But now, that Faustus may delight his mind
10 And by their folly make some merriment,
Sweet Mephostophilis, so charm me here
That I may walk invisible to all
And do whate'er I please unseen of any.

MEPHOSTOPHILIS:
Faustus, thou shalt. Then kneel down presently,
15   Whilst on thy head I lay my hand
        And charm thee with this magic wand.
        First wear this girdle, then appear
        Invisible to all are here:
        The planets seven, the gloomy air,
20   Hell, and the Furies' forkèd hair,°
        Pluto's blue fire, and Hecat's° tree
        With magic spells so compass thee
        That no eye may thy body see.
So Faustus, now for all their holiness,
25 Do what thou wilt, thou shalt not be discerned.

FAUSTUS:
Thanks Mephostophilis. Now friars, take heed
Lest Faustus make your shaven crowns to bleed.

MEPHOSTOPHILIS:
Faustus, no more. See where the cardinals come.

(Enter POPE [and FRIARS] and all the LORDS
[with KING RAYMOND and the ARCHBISHOP
OF RHEIMS]. Enter the [two] CARDINALS with
a book.)

POPE:
Welcome lord cardinals. Come, sit down.
30 Lord Raymond, take your seat. Friars, attend,
And see that all things be in readiness
As best beseems this solemn festival.

I CARDINAL:
First may it please your sacred Holiness
To view the sentence of the reverend synod
35 Concerning Bruno and the Emperor.

POPE:
What needs this question? Did I not tell you
Tomorrow we would sit i' th' consistory
And there determine of his punishment?
You brought us word, even now, it was decreed

That Bruno and the cursèd Emperor   40
Were by the holy council both condemned
For loathèd lollards and base schismatics.
Then wherefore would you have me view that
    book?

I CARDINAL:
Your Grace mistakes. You gave us no such
    charge.

RAYMOND:
Deny it not; we all are witnesses   45
That Bruno here was late delivered you
With his rich triple crown to be reserved
And put into the church's treasury.

BOTH CARDINALS:
By holy Paul we saw them not.

POPE:
By Peter you shall die   50
Unless you bring them forth immediately.
Hale them to prison, lade their limbs with
    gyves.°
False prelates, for this hateful treachery
Cursed be your souls to hellish misery.
        [Exeunt ATTENDANTS with two CARDINALS.]

FAUSTUS:
So, they are safe. Now Faustus, to the feast.   55
The Pope had never such a frolic guest.

POPE:
Lord Archbishop of Rheims, sit down with us.

ARCHBISHOP:
I thank your Holiness.

FAUSTUS:
Fall to,° the devil choke you an you spare!

POPE:
Who's that spoke? Friars, look about.   60
Lord Raymond, pray fall to. I am beholding
To the Bishop of Milan for this so rare a
    present.

FAUSTUS [aside]:
I thank you, sir!   [Snatches the dish.]

POPE:
How now! Who snatched the meat from me?
Villains, why speak you not?   65
My good Lord Archbishop, here's a most dainty
    dish
Was sent me from a cardinal in France.

FAUSTUS [aside]:
I'll have that too!   [Snatches the dish.]

POPE:
What lollards do attend our Holiness
That we receive such great indignity!   70
Fetch me some wine.

---

20 **Furies' forked hair** (the hair of the Furies consisted of snakes, whose forked tongues may be implied here) 21 **Hecat** Hecate, goddess of magic (possibly her "tree" is the gallows-tree, but possibly "tree" is a slip for "three," Hecate being the triple goddess of heaven, earth, and hell)

52 **gyves** fetters 59 **Fall to** set to work (here, as commonly, "start eating")

FAUSTUS [aside]:
Ay, pray do, for Faustus is adry.
   POPE:
Lord Raymond, I drink unto your Grace.
   FAUSTUS [aside]:
I pledge your Grace.   [Snatches the goblet.]
   POPE:
75 My wine gone too? Ye lubbers, look about
And find the man that doth this villainy,
Or by our sanctitude you all shall die.
I pray, my lords, have patience at this trouble-
    some banquet.
   ARCHBISHOP:
Please it your Holiness, I think it be some
80   ghost crept out of purgatory, and now is
    come unto your Holiness for his pardon.
   POPE:
It may be so:
Go then, command our priests to sing a dirge
To lay the fury of this same troublesome ghost.
                [Exit Attendant.]

[The POPE crosses himself before eating.]

   FAUSTUS:
How now! Must every bit be spicèd with a
85   cross?
Nay then, take that!   [Strikes the POPE.]
   POPE:
O, I am slain! Help me my lords!
O come and help to bear my body hence.
Damned be this soul forever for this deed.
       (Exeunt the POPE and his train.)
   MEPHOSTOPHILIS:
90 Now Faustus, what will you do now?
For I can tell you, you'll be cursed with bell,
    book, and candle.°
   FAUSTUS:
Bell, book, and candle. Candle, book, and bell.
Forward and backward, to curse Faustus to
    hell!

(Enter the FRIARS, with bell, book, and candle for the dirge.)

   I FRIAR:
Come brethren, let's about our business with
    good devotion.
Cursèd be he that stole his Holiness' meat from
95   the table.

Maledicat Dominus!°
Cursèd be he that struck his Holiness a blow
    on the face.
Maledicat Dominus!
             [FAUSTUS strikes a FRIAR.]
Cursèd be he that took Friar Sandelo a blow
    on the pate.
Maledicat Dominus!   100
Cursèd be he that disturbeth our holy dirge.
Maledicat Dominus!
Cursèd be he that took away his Holiness' wine.
Maledicat Dominus!

([FAUSTUS and MEPHOSTOPHILIS] beat the
FRIARS, fling fireworks among them and
exeunt.)

[III.iii] (Enter [ROBIN the] Clown and
DICK with a cup.)

DICK: Sirrah Robin, we were best look that
your devil can answer the stealing of this same
cup, for the vintner's boy follows us at the
hard heels.°
ROBIN: 'Tis no matter, let him come! An he 5
follow us I'll so conjure him as he was never
conjured in his life, I warrant him. Let me see
the cup.

(Enter VINTNER.)

DICK: Here 'tis. Yonder he comes. Now
Robin, now or never show thy cunning.   10
VINTNER: O, are you here? I am glad I have
found you. You are a couple of fine com-
panions!° Pray, where's the cup you stole from
the tavern?
ROBIN: How, how! We steal a cup? Take 15
heed what you say. We look not like cup-
stealers, I can tell you.
VINTNER: Never deny't, for I know you have
it, and I'll search you.
ROBIN: Search me? Ay, and spare not!   20
[Aside.] Hold the cup, Dick. — Come, come.
Search me, search me.
          [VINTNER searches him.]
VINTNER: Come on sirrah, let me search you
now.
DICK: Ay ay, do do. [Aside.] Hold the cup, 25
Robin. — I fear not your searching. We scorn
to steal your cups, I can tell you.
          [VINTNER searches him.]

91 **bell, book, and candle** implements used in ex-
communicating (the bell was tolled, the book closed,
the candle extinguished)

96 **Maledicat Dominus** may the Lord curse him
(Latin) III.iii.3–4 **at the hard heels** hard at heel,
closely   13 **companions** fellows (contemptuous)

VINTNER: Never outface me for the matter, for sure the cup is between you two.

30 ROBIN: Nay, there you lie! 'Tis beyond us both.°

VINTNER: A plague take you. I thought 'twas your knavery to take it away. Come, give it me again.

35 ROBIN: Ay, much! When, can you tell?° [*Aside.*] Dick, make me a circle and stand close at my back and stir not for thy life. Vintner, you shall have your cup anon. [*Aside.*] Say nothing, Dick! O *per se*, o; Demogorgon,
40 Belcher, and Mephostophilis!

(*Enter* MEPHOSTOPHILIS. [*Exit* VINTNER.])

MEPHOSTOPHILIS:
You princely legions of infernal rule,
How am I vexèd by these villains' charms!
From Constantinople have they brought me now
Only for pleasure of these damnèd slaves.

45 ROBIN: By lady sir, you have had a shrewd° journey of it. Will it please you to take a shoulder of mutton to supper and a tester° in your purse and go back again?

DICK: Ay, I pray you heartily, sir. For we
50 called you but in jest, I promise you.

MEPHOSTOPHILIS:
To purge the rashness of this cursèd deed,
First be thou turnèd to this ugly shape,
For apish° deeds transformèd to an ape.

ROBIN: O brave! An ape! I pray sir, let me
55 have the carrying of him about to show some tricks.

MEPHOSTOPHILIS: And so thou shalt. Be thou transformed to a dog and carry him upon thy back. Away, be gone!

60 ROBIN: A dog! That's excellent. Let the maids look well to their porridge-pots, for I'll into the kitchen presently. Come Dick, come.
(*Exeunt the two* CLOWNS.)

MEPHOSTOPHILIS:
Now with the flames of ever-burning fire
I'll wing myself and forthwith fly amain
65 Unto my Faustus, to the Great Turk's court.
(*Exit.*)

[IV] (*Enter* CHORUS.)

When Faustus had with pleasure ta'en the view
Of rarest things and royal courts of kings,
He stayed his course and so returnèd home,
Where such as bare his absence but with grief,
I mean his friends and nearest companions,   5
Did gratulate° his safety with kind words.
And in their conference° of what befell
Touching his journey through the world and air
They put forth questions of astrology
Which Faustus answered with such learnèd skill   10
As they admired and wondered at his wit.
Now is his fame spread forth in every land.
Amongst the rest the Emperor is one,
Carolus the Fifth,° at whose palace now
Faustus is feasted 'mongst his noblemen.   15
What there he did in trial of his art
I leave untold, your eyes shall see performed.
(*Exit.*)

[IV.i] (*Enter* MARTINO *and* FREDERICK
at several° *doors.*)

MARTINO:
What ho, officers, gentlemen!
Hie to the presence° to attend the Emperor.
Good Frederick, see the rooms be voided straight,°
His Majesty is coming to the hall.
Go back and see the state° in readiness.   5

FREDERICK:
But where is Bruno, our elected Pope,
That on a fury's back came post from Rome?
Will not his Grace consort° the Emperor?

MARTINO:
O yes, and with him comes the German conjurer,
The learnèd Faustus, fame of Wittenberg,   10
The wonder of the world for magic art:
And he intends to show great Carolus
The race of all his stout progenitors
And bring in presence of his Majesty

30–31 **beyond us both** (apparently Robin has managed to place the cup at some distance from where he now stands)   35 **When, can you tell** (a scornful reply)   45 **shrewd** bad   47 **tester** sixpence   53 **apish** (1) foolish (2) imitative

IV Chorus   6 **gratulate** express joy in   7 **conference** discussion   14 **Carolus the Fifth** Charles V (1500–58), Holy Roman Emperor   IV.i.s.d. **several** separate   2 **presence** presence-chamber   3 **voided straight** emptied immediately   5 **state** chair of state, throne   8 **consort** attend

15 The royal shapes and warlike semblances
Of Alexander and his beauteous paramour.°
FREDERICK:
Where is Benvolio?
MARTINO:
         Fast asleep, I warrant you.
He took his rouse with stoups° of Rhenish wine
So kindly yesternight to Bruno's health
20 That all this day the sluggard keeps his bed.
FREDERICK:
See, see, his window's ope. We'll call to him.
MARTINO:
What ho, Benvolio!

(*Enter* BENVOLIO *above at a window, in his nightcap, buttoning.*)

BENVOLIO:
What a devil ail you two?
MARTINO:
Speak softly sir, lest the devil hear you,
25 For Faustus at the court is late arrived
And at his heels a thousand furies wait
To accomplish whatsoever the doctor please.
BENVOLIO:
What of this?
MARTINO:
Come, leave thy chamber first, and thou shalt see
30 This conjurer perform such rare exploits
Before the Pope° and royal Emperor
As never yet was seen in Germany.
BENVOLIO:
Has not the Pope enough of conjuring yet?
He was upon the devil's back late enough!
35 And if he be so far in love with him
I would he would post with him to Rome again.
FREDERICK:
Speak, wilt thou come and see this sport?
BENVOLIO:
         Not I.
MARTINO:
Wilt thou stand in thy window and see it then?
BENVOLIO:
Ay, and I fall not asleep i' th' meantime.
MARTINO:
40 The Emperor is at hand, who comes to see
What wonders by black spells may compassed be.
BENVOLIO: Well, go you attend the Emperor. I am content for this once to thrust my

head out at a window, for they say if a man be drunk overnight the devil cannot hurt him 45 in the morning. If that be true, I have a charm in my head shall control him as well as the conjurer, I warrant you.
(*Exit* [MARTINO *with* FREDERICK. BENVOLIO *remains at window*].°)

[IV.ii] (*A sennet.*° CHARLES *the German Emperor,* BRUNO, [*Duke of*] *Saxony,* FAUSTUS, MEPHOSTOPHILIS, FREDERICK, MARTINO, *and* ATTENDANTS.)

EMPEROR:
Wonder of men, renownèd magician,
Thrice-learnèd Faustus, welcome to our court.
This deed of thine in setting Bruno free
From his and our professèd enemy,
Shall add more excellence unto thine art   5
Than if by powerful necromantic spells
Thou could'st command the world's obedience.
For ever be beloved of Carolus!
And if this Bruno thou hast late redeemed°
In peace possess the triple diadem   10
And sit in Peter's chair despite of chance,
Thou shalt be famous through all Italy
And honored of the German Emperor.
FAUSTUS:
These gracious words, most royal Carolus,
Shall make poor Faustus to his utmost power   15
Both love and serve the German Emperor
And lay his life at holy Bruno's feet.
For proof whereof, if so your Grace be pleased,
The doctor stands prepared by power of art
To cast his magic charms that shall pierce through   20
The ebon gates of ever-burning hell,
And hale the stubborn furies from their caves
To compass whatsoe'er your Grace commands.
BENVOLIO: Blood! He speaks terribly. But for all that I do not greatly believe him. He   25

16 **Alexander and his beauteous paramour** Alexander the Great and his mistress Thaïs   18 **took his rouse with stoups** had drinking bouts with full goblets   31 **the Pope** i.e., Bruno

48s.d. **Benvolio remains at window** (because Benvolio does not leave the stage, this scene cannot properly be said to be ended. But the present edition, following its predecessors for convenience of reference, begins a new scene)   IV.ii.s.d. **sennet** trumpet fanfare (the absence of a verb in the rest of the stage direction perhaps indicates that the Emperor and his party do not enter but rather are "discovered," as Faustus may have been discovered at the beginning of I.i, if the Chorus drew back a curtain)   9 **redeemed** freed

looks as like a conjurer as the Pope to a costermonger.°

EMPEROR:
Then Faustus, as thou late didst promise us,
We would behold that famous conqueror
30 Great Alexander and his paramour
In their true shapes and state majestical,
That we may wonder at their excellence.

FAUSTUS:
Your Majesty shall see them presently. —
Mephostophilis away,
35 And with a solemn noise of trumpets' sound
Present before this royal Emperor
Great Alexander and his beauteous paramour.

MEPHOSTOPHILIS:
Faustus, I will.   [Exit.]

BENVOLIO: Well master doctor, an your dev-
40 ils come not away quickly, you shall have me
asleep presently. Zounds,° I could eat myself
for anger to think I have been such an ass all
this while to stand gaping after the devils'
governor and can see nothing.

FAUSTUS:
I'll make you feel something anon if my art
45   fail me not!
My lord, I must forewarn your Majesty
That when my spirits present the royal shapes
Of Alexander and his paramour,
Your Grace demand no questions of the King
50 But in dumb silence let them come and go.

EMPEROR:
Be it as Faustus please; we are content.

BENVOLIO: Ay ay, and I am content too.
And thou bring Alexander and his paramour
before the Emperor, I'll be Actaeon° and turn
55 myself to a stag.

FAUSTUS [aside]: And I'll play Diana and
send you the horns presently.

(Sennet. Enter at one [door] the EMPEROR
ALEXANDER, at the other DARIUS.° They
meet. DARIUS is thrown down. ALEXANDER
kills him, takes off his crown, and offering
to go out, his PARAMOUR meets him. He em-
braceth her and sets DARIUS' crown upon her
head, and coming back both salute the Emperor; who leaving his state offers to em-

brace them, which FAUSTUS seeing suddenly
stays him. Then trumpets cease and music
sounds.)
My gracious lord, you do forget yourself.
These are but shadows, not substantial.

EMPEROR:
O pardon me, my thoughts are so ravished   60
With sight of this renownèd Emperor,
That in mine arms I would have compassed°
    him.
But Faustus, since I may not speak to them,
To satisfy my longing thoughts at full,
Let me this tell thee: I have heard it said   65
That this fair lady whilst she lived on earth,
Had on her neck a little wart or mole.
How may I prove that saying to be true?

FAUSTUS:
Your Majesty may boldly go and see.

EMPEROR:
Faustus, I see it plain!   70
And in this sight thou better pleasest me
Than if I gained another monarchy.

FAUSTUS:
Away, be gone!   (Exit show.)
See, see, my gracious lord, what strange beast
    is yon that thrusts his head out at the
    window!

EMPEROR:
O wondrous sight! See, Duke of Saxony,   75
Two spreading horns most strangely fastened
Upon the head of young Benvolio.

SAXONY:
What, is he asleep or dead?

FAUSTUS:
He sleeps my lord, but dreams not of his horns.

EMPEROR:
This sport is excellent. We'll call and wake   80
    him.
What ho, Benvolio!

BENVOLIO: A plague upon you! Let me sleep
awhile.

EMPEROR: I blame thee not to sleep much,   85
having such a head of thine own.

SAXONY: Look up Benvolio! 'Tis the Emperor calls.

BENVOLIO: The Emperor! Where? O zounds,
my head!   90

EMPEROR: Nay, and thy horns hold, 'tis no
matter for thy head, for that's armed sufficiently.

27 **costermonger** fruit-seller 41 **Zounds** by God's
wounds 54 **Actaeon** legendary hunter who saw the
naked goddess Diana bathing. She transformed him
into a stag, and he was torn to pieces by his own
hounds 57s.d. **Darius** King of Persia, defeated by
Alexander in 334 B.C.

62 **compassed** encompassed, embraced

FAUSTUS: Why, how now Sir Knight? What,
95 hanged by the horns?° This is most horrible!
Fie fie, pull in your head for shame! Let not
all the world wonder at you.
BENVOLIO: Zounds doctor, is this your vil-
lainy?
FAUSTUS:
100 Oh, say not so sir: The doctor has no skill,
No art, no cunning to present these lords
Or bring before this royal Emperor
The mighty monarch, warlike Alexander.
If Faustus do it, you are straight resolved
105 In bold Actaeon's shape to turn a stag.
And therefore my lord, so please your Majesty,
I'll raise a kennel of hounds shall hunt him so
As all his footmanship shall scarce prevail
To keep his carcass from their bloody fangs.
110 Ho, Belimote, Argiron, Asterote!
BENVOLIO: Hold, hold! Zounds, he'll raise
up a kennel of devils I think, anon. Good my
lord, entreat for me. 'Sblood,° I am never able
to endure these torments.
EMPEROR:
115 Then good master doctor,
Let me entreat you to remove his horns.
He has done penance now sufficiently.
FAUSTUS: My gracious lord, not so much for
injury done to me, as to delight your Majesty
120 with some mirth, hath Faustus justly requited
this injurious° knight; which being all I desire,
I am content to remove his horns. Mephostophilis, transform him. And hereafter sir, look
you speak well of scholars.
125 BENVOLIO [aside]: Speak well of ye! 'Sblood,
and scholars be such cuckold-makers to clap
horns of honest men's heads o' this order, I'll
ne'er trust smooth faces and small ruffs° more.
But an I be not revenged for this, would I
130 might be turned to a gaping oyster and drink
nothing but salt water.   [Exit.]
EMPEROR:
Come Faustus, while the Emperor lives,
In recompense of this thy high desert,
Thou shalt command the state of Germany
135 And live beloved of mighty Carolus.
                          (Exeunt omnes.)

[IV.iii] (Enter BENVOLIO, MARTINO,
FREDERICK, and SOLDIERS.)

MARTINO:
Nay, sweet Benvolio, let us sway thy thoughts
From this attempt against the conjurer.
BENVOLIO:
Away! You love me not to urge me thus.
Shall I let slip° so great an injury
When every servile groom jests at my wrongs   5
And in their rustic gambols proudly say,
"Benvolio's head was graced with horns today"?
O, may these eyelids never close again
Till with my sword I have that conjurer slain!
If you will aid me in this enterprise,   10
Then draw your weapons and be resolute;
If not, depart. Here will Benvolio die
But° Faustus' death shall quit° my infamy.
FREDERICK:
Nay, we will stay with thee, betide what may,
And kill that doctor if he come this way.   15
BENVOLIO:
Then, gentle Frederick, hie thee to the grove
And place our servants and our followers
Close in an ambush there behind the trees.
By this, I know, the conjurer is near.
I saw him kneel and kiss the Emperor's hand   20
And take his leave laden with rich rewards.
Then soldiers, boldly fight. If Faustus die,
Take you the wealth, leave us the victory.
FREDERICK:
Come soldiers, follow me unto the grove.
Who kills him shall have gold and endless love.   25
            (Exit FREDERICK with the SOLDIERS.)
BENVOLIO:
My head is lighter than it was by th' horns —
But yet my heart more ponderous than my
            head,
And pants until I see that conjurer dead.
MARTINO:
Where shall we place ourselves, Benvolio?
BENVOLIO:
Here will we stay to bide the first assault.   30
O, were that damnèd hell-hound but in place
Thou soon should'st see me quit my foul dis-
            grace.

(Enter FREDERICK.)

FREDERICK:
Close, close! The conjurer is at hand
And all alone comes walking in his gown.

---

95 **hanged by the horns** (the spreading horns prevent Benvolio from pulling his head inside the
window)   113 **'Sblood** by God's blood   121 **injurious** insulting   128 **small ruffs** (worn by scholars, in
contrast to the large ruffs worn by courtiers)

IV.iii.4 **let slip** ignore   13 **But** unless   13 **quit** avenge

35 Be ready then and strike the peasant° down!
BENVOLIO:
Mine be that honor then! Now sword, strike
    home!
For horns he gave I'll have his head anon.

(*Enter* FAUSTUS *with the false head.*)

MARTINO:
See see, he comes.
BENVOLIO:
                    No words. This blow ends all!
                                  [*Strikes* FAUSTUS.]
Hell take his soul, his body thus must fall.
FAUSTUS:
40 O!
FREDERICK:
Groan you, master doctor?
BENVOLIO:
Break may his heart with groans! Dear Fred-
    erick, see,
Thus will I end his griefs immediately.

[*Cuts off* FAUSTUS' *false head.*]

MARTINO:
Strike with a willing hand! His head is off.
BENVOLIO:
45 The devil's dead, the furies now may laugh.
FREDERICK:
Was this that stern aspect, that awful frown,
Made the grim monarch of infernal spirits
Tremble and quake at his commanding charms?
MARTINO:
Was this that damnèd head whose heart con-
    spired
50 Benvolio's shame before the Emperor?
BENVOLIO:
Ay, that's the head, and here the body lies
Justly rewarded for his villainies.
FREDERICK:
Come let's devise how we may add more shame
To the black scandal of his hated name.
BENVOLIO:
55 First, on his head in quittance of my wrongs
I'll nail huge forkèd horns and let them hang
Within the window where he yoked me first
That all the world may see my just revenge.
MARTINO: What use shall we put his beard
60 to?
BENVOLIO: We'll sell it to a chimney-sweeper.
It will wear out ten birchen brooms, I warrant
you.

FREDERICK: What shall eyes do?
BENVOLIO: We'll put out his eyes, and they   65
shall serve for buttons to his lips to keep his
tongue from catching cold.
MARTINO: An excellent policy! And now sirs,
having divided him, what shall the body do?
                              [FAUSTUS *rises.*]
BENVOLIO: Zounds, the devil's alive again!   70
FREDERICK: Give him his head for God's sake!
FAUSTUS:
Nay keep it. Faustus will have heads and hands,
Ay, all your hearts, to recompense this deed.
Knew you not, traitors, I was limited
For four and twenty years to breathe on earth?   75
And had you cut my body with your swords
Or hewed this flesh and bones as small as sand,
Yet in a minute had my spirit returned
And I had breathed a man made free from harm.
But wherefore do I dally my revenge?   80
Asteroth, Belimoth, Mephostophilis!

(*Enter* MEPHOSTOPHILIS *and other* DEVILS.)

Go horse these traitors on your fiery backs
And mount aloft with them as high as heaven,
Thence pitch them headlong to the lowest hell.
Yet stay, the world shall see their misery,   85
And hell shall after plague their treachery.
Go Belimoth, and take this caitiff° hence
And hurl him in some lake of mud and dirt:
Take thou this other, drag him through the
    woods
Amongst the pricking thorns and sharpest briars: 90
Whilst with my gentle Mephostophilis
This traitor flies unto some steepy rock
That rolling down may break the villain's bones
As he intended to dismember me.
Fly hence, dispatch my charge immediately!   95
FREDERICK:
Pity us, gentle Faustus, save our lives!
FAUSTUS:
Away!
FREDERICK:
      He must needs go that the devil drives.
              (*Exeunt* SPIRITS *with the* KNIGHTS.)

(*Enter the ambushed* SOLDIERS.)

I SOLDIER:
Come sirs, prepare yourselves in readiness.
Make haste to help these noble gentlemen.
I heard them parley with the conjurer.   100

35 **peasant** low fellow   87 **caitiff** wretch

II SOLDIER:
See where he comes, dispatch, and kill the slave!
FAUSTUS:
What's here, an ambush to betray my life?
Then Faustus, try thy skill. Base peasants, stand!
For lo, these trees remove° at my command
105 And stand as bulwarks 'twixt yourselves and me
To shield me from your hated treachery!
Yet to encounter this your weak attempt
Behold an army comes incontinent.°

(FAUSTUS strikes the door, and enter a DEVIL
playing on a drum, after him another bearing
an ensign, and divers with weapons: MEPH-
OSTOPHILIS with fireworks: they set upon the
SOLDIERS and drive them out.)
                                        [Exeunt all.]

[IV.iv] (Enter at several doors BENVOLIO,
FREDERICK, and MARTINO, their heads and
faces bloody and besmeared with mud
and dirt, all having horns on their
heads.)

MARTINO:
What ho, Benvolio!
BENVOLIO: Here! What, Frederick, ho!
FREDERICK:
O, help me gentle friend. Where is Martino?
MARTINO:
Dear Frederick, here,
Half smothered in a lake of mud and dirt,
Through which the furies dragged me by the
5   heels.
FREDERICK:
Martino, see, Benvolio's horns again.
MARTINO:
O misery! How now Benvolio?
BENVOLIO:
Defend me, heaven! Small I be haunted° still?
MARTINO:
Nay fear not man, we have no power to kill.
BENVOLIO:
10 My friends transformèd thus! O hellish spite,
Your heads are all set with horns.
FREDERICK:
                            You hit it right:

It is your own you mean. Feel on your head.
BENVOLIO:
Zounds, horns again!
MARTINO:
              Nay chafe° not man, we all are sped.°
BENVOLIO:
What devil attends this damned magician,
That spite of spite our wrongs are doubled?   15
FREDERICK:
What may we do that we may hide our shames?
BENVOLIO:
If we should follow him to work revenge
He'd join long asses' ears to these huge horns
And make us laughing-stocks to all the world.
MARTINO:
What shall we then do, dear Benvolio?   20
BENVOLIO:
I have a castle joining near these woods,
And thither we'll repair and live obscure
Till time shall alter this our brutish shapes.
Sith° black disgrace hath thus eclipsed our fame,
We'll rather die with grief than live with shame. 25
                            (Exeunt omnes.)

[IV.v] (Enter FAUSTUS and the
HORSE-COURSER.°)

HORSE-COURSER: I beseech your worship, accept of these forty dollars.°
FAUSTUS: Friend, thou canst not buy so good
a horse for so small a price. I have no great
need to sell him, but if thou likest him for ten   5
dollars more, take him, because I see thou hast
a good mind to him.
HORSE-COURSER: I beseech you sir, accept of
this. I am a very poor man and have lost very
much of late by horse-flesh,° and this bargain   10
will set me up again.
FAUSTUS: Well, I will not stand° with thee.
Give me the money. Now sirrah, I must tell you
that you may ride him o'er hedge and ditch and
spare him not. But, do you hear, in any case   15
ride him not into the water.
HORSE-COURSER: How sir, not into the water!
Why, will he not drink of all waters?°

13 **chafe** fret 13 **sped** done for, ruined (because of
the horns) 24 **Sith** since IV.v.s.d. **Horse-courser**
horse trader 2 **dollars** German coins 10 **horse-flesh**
(the possibility of a quibble on "whores' flesh" is
increased by "set me up" and "stand" in the ensuing dialogue) 12 **stand** haggle 18 **drink of all
waters** i.e., go anywhere

104 **remove** move 108 **incontinent** immediately
IV.iv.8 **haunted** (the following line suggests that
there is a quibble on "hunted," Benvolio now resembling a stag)

FAUSTUS: Yes, he will drink of all waters, but
ride him not into the water: o'er hedge and
ditch or where thou wilt, but not into the water. Go bid the hostler deliver him unto you,
and remember what I say.

HORSE-COURSER: I warrant you sir. O joyful
day! Now am I a made man forever.   (Exit.)

FAUSTUS:
What art thou, Faustus, but a man condemned
to die?
Thy fatal time° draws to a final end;
Despair doth drive distrust into my thoughts.
Confound these passions with a quiet sleep.
Tush, Christ did call the thief upon the cross!°
Then rest thee Faustus, quiet in conceit.°
                                   (He sits to sleep.)

(Enter the HORSE-COURSER wet.)

HORSE-COURSER: O what a cozening° doctor
was this! I riding my horse into the water, thinking some hidden mystery had been in the horse,
I had nothing under me but a little straw and
had much ado to escape drowning. Well, I'll go
rouse him and make him give me my forty dollars again. Ho, sirrah doctor, you cozening scab!
Master doctor, awake and rise, and give me my
money again, for your horse is turned to a bot-
tle° of hay. Master doctor!
                                   (He pulls off his leg.)
Alas, I am undone! What shall I do? I have
pulled off his leg.

FAUSTUS: O help, help! The villain hath murdered me!

HORSE-COURSER: Murder or not murder, now
he has but one leg I'll outrun him, and cast this
leg into some ditch or other.   [Exit.]

FAUSTUS: Stop him, stop him, stop him! —
Ha, ha, ha! Faustus hath his leg again, and the
horse-courser a bundle of hay for his forty dollars.

(Enter WAGNER.)

How now, Wagner? What news with thee?

WAGNER: If it please you, the Duke of Vanholt doth earnestly entreat your company, and
hath sent some of his men to attend you with
provision fit for your journey.

FAUSTUS: The Duke of Vanholt's an honorable gentleman, and one to whom I must be no
niggard of my cunning. Come, away!
                                   (Exeunt.)

[IV.vi] (Enter [ROBIN the] Clown, DICK, HORSE-COURSER, and a CARTER.)

CARTER: Come my masters, I'll bring you to
the best beer in Europe. What ho, hostess!
Where be these whores?

(Enter HOSTESS.)

HOSTESS: How now? What lack you? What,
my old guests, welcome.

ROBIN [aside]: Sirrah Dick, dost thou know
why I stand so mute?

DICK [aside]: No Robin, why is't?

ROBIN [aside]: I am eighteen pence on the
score.° But say nothing. See if she have forgotten me.

HOSTESS: Who's this that stands so solemnly
by himself? What, my old guest!

ROBIN: O, hostess, how do you? I hope my
score stands still.

HOSTESS: Ay, there's no doubt of that, for
methinks you make no haste to wipe it out.

DICK: Why hostess, I say, fetch us some beer!

HOSTESS: You shall, presently. — Look up into
th' hall there, ho!   (Exit.)

DICK: Come sirs, what shall we do now till
mine hostess comes?

CARTER: Marry sir, I'll tell you the bravest
tale how a conjurer served me. You know Doctor Fauster?

HORSE-COURSER: Ay, a plague take him! Here's
some on's have cause to know him. Did he conjure thee too?

CARTER: I'll tell you how he served me. As I
was going to Wittenberg t'other day with a load
of hay, he met me and asked me what he should
give me for as much hay as he could eat. Now
sir, I thinking that a little would serve his turn,
bad him take as much as he would for three
farthings. So he presently gave me my money
and fell to eating; and as I am a cursen° man,
he never left eating till he had eat up all my
load of hay.

ALL: O monstrous, eat a whole load of hay!

27 **fatal time** life span   30 **Christ ... cross** (in Luke 23:39–43 Christ promised one of the thieves that he would be with Christ in paradise)   31 **quiet in conceit** with a quiet mind   32 **cozening** deceiving   41 **bottle** bundle

IV.vi.9–10 **on the score** in debt   36 **cursen** i.e., Christian (dialect form)

40 ROBIN: Yes yes, that may be, for I have heard of one that has eat a load of logs.°

HORSE-COURSER: Now sirs, you shall hear how villainously he served me. I went to him yester- 45 day to buy a horse of him, and he would by no means sell him under forty dollars. So sir, be- cause I knew him to be such a horse as would run over hedge and ditch and never tire, I gave him his money. So, when I had my horse, Doc- 50 tor Fauster bade me ride him night and day and spare him no time. "But," quoth he, "in any case ride him not into the water." Now sir, I thinking the horse had had some quality that he would not have me know of, what did I but rid him into a great river — and when I came 55 just in the midst, my horse vanished away and I sate straddling upon a bottle of hay.

ALL: O brave doctor!

HORSE-COURSER: But you shall hear how bravely I served him for it. I went me home to 60 his house, and there I found him asleep. I kept ahallowing and whooping in his ears, but all could not wake him. I seeing that, took him by the leg and never rested pulling till I had pulled me his leg quite off, and now 'tis at home in 65 mine hostry.°

DICK: And has the doctor but one leg then? That's excellent, for one of his devils turned me into the likeness of an ape's face.

CARTER: Some more drink, hostess!

70 ROBIN: Hark you, we'll into another room and drink awhile, and then we'll go seek out the doctor.   (*Exeunt omnes.*)

[IV.vii] (*Enter the* DUKE OF VANHOLT, *his* [SERVANTS,] DUCHESS, FAUSTUS, *and* MEPHOSTOPHILIS.)

DUKE: Thanks master doctor, for these pleas- ant sights. Nor know I how sufficiently to rec- ompense your great deserts in erecting that en- chanted castle in the air, the sight whereof so 5 delighted me, As nothing in the world could please me more.

FAUSTUS: I do think myself, my good lord, highly recompensed in that it pleaseth your Grace to think but well of that which Faustus 10 hath performed. — But gracious lady, it may be that you have taken no pleasure in those sights.

Therefore I pray you tell me what is the thing you most desire to have: be it in the world it shall be yours. I have heard that great-bellied° women do long for things are rare and dainty. 15

DUCHESS: True master doctor, and since I find you so kind, I will make known unto you what my heart desires to have: and were it now sum- mer, as it is January, a dead time of the winter, I would request no better meat° than a dish of 20 ripe grapes.

FAUSTUS: This is but a small matter. Go Mephostophilis, away!   (*Exit* MEPHOSTOPHILIS.) Madam, I will do more than this for your con- tent.

(*Enter* MEPHOSTOPHILIS *again with the grapes.*)

Here, now taste ye these. They should be good, For they come from a far country, I can tell you.   25

DUKE: This makes me wonder more than all the rest, that at this time of the year when every tree is barren of his fruit, from whence you had these ripe grapes.

FAUSTUS: Please it your Grace, the year is di- 30 vided into two circles° over the whole world, so that when it is winter with us, in the contrary circle it is likewise summer with them, as in India, Saba,° and such countries that lie far east, where they have fruit twice a year. From 35 whence, by means of a swift spirit that I have, I had these grapes brought as you see.

DUCHESS: And trust me, they are the sweetest grapes that e'er I tasted.

(*The Clowns* [ROBIN, DICK, CARTER, *and* HORSE-COURSER] *bounce*° *at the gate within.*)

DUKE: What rude disturbers have we at the gate?   40 Go pacify their fury, set it ope, And then demand of them what they would have.

(*They knock again and call out to talk with* FAUSTUS.)

IV.vii.14 **great-bellied** i.e., pregnant   20 **meat** food 31 **two circles** i.e., the northern and the southern hemispheres (though later in the speech he talks of east and west rather than of north and south)   34 **Saba** Sheba   39s.d. **bounce** knock

41 **eat a load of logs** been drunk   65 **hostry** inn

SERVANT:
Why, how now masters, what a coil° is there!
What is the reason° you disturb the Duke?

45   DICK: We have no reason for it, therefore a
fig for him!
SERVANT:
Why saucy varlets, dare you be so bold!
HORSE-COURSER: I hope sir, we have wit
enough to be more bold than welcome.
SERVANT:
50   It appears so. Pray be bold elsewhere
And trouble not the Duke.
DUKE: What would they have?
SERVANT:
They all cry out to speak with Doctor Faustus.
CARTER: Ay, and we will speak with him.
55   DUKE: Will you sir? Commit° the rascals.
DICK: Commit with us! He were as good com-
mit with his father as commit with us!
FAUSTUS:
I do beseech your Grace, let them come in.
They are good subject for a merriment.
DUKE:
60   Do as thou wilt, Faustus, I give thee leave.
FAUSTUS:
I thank your Grace.

(Enter [ROBIN] the Clown, DICK, CARTER,
and HORSE-COURSER.)

Why, how now my good friends?
'Faith, you are too outrageous; but come near,
I have procured your pardons. Welcome all.
ROBIN: Nay sir, we will be welcome for our
65   money, and we will pay for what we take. What
ho, give's half a dozen of beer here, and be
hanged!
FAUSTUS:
Nay, hark you, can you tell me where you are?
CARTER: Ay, marry can I, we are under
70   heaven.
SERVANT:
Ay, but Sir Sauce-box, know you in what place?
HORSE-COURSER: Ay ay, the house is good
enough to drink in. Zounds, fill us some beer,

or we'll break all the barrels in the house and
dash out all your brains with your bottles.   75
FAUSTUS:
Be not so furious. Come, you shall have beer.
My lord, beseech you give me leave awhile;
I'll gage° my credit 'twill content your Grace.
DUKE:
With all my heart, kind doctor, please thyself.
Our servants and our court's at thy command.   80
FAUSTUS:
I humbly thank your Grace. — Then fetch some
     beer.
HORSE-COURSER: Ay marry, there spake a doc-
tor indeed! And 'faith, I'll drink a health to thy
wooden leg for that word.
FAUSTUS:
My wooden leg? What dost thou mean by that? 85
CARTER: Ha, ha, ha, dost hear him Dick? He
has forgot his leg.
HORSE-COURSER: Ay ay, he does not stand
much upon° that.
FAUSTUS:
No, 'faith, not much upon a wooden leg.   90
CARTER: Good lord, that flesh and blood
should be so frail with your worship! Do not
you remember a horse-courser you sold a horse
to?
FAUSTUS: Yes, I remember I sold one a horse. 95
CARTER: And do you remember you bid he
should not ride into the water?
FAUSTUS: Yes, I do very well remember that.
CARTER: And do you remember nothing of
your leg?   100
FAUSTUS: No, in good sooth.
CARTER: Then I pray remember your curtsy.°
FAUSTUS: I thank you sir.
CARTER: 'Tis not so much worth. I pray you
tell me one thing.   105
FAUSTUS: What's that?
CARTER: Be both your legs bedfellows every
night together?
FAUSTUS: Would'st thou make a colossus° of
me that thou askest me such questions?   110
CARTER: No, truly sir, I would make nothing
of you, but I would fain know that.

(Enter HOSTESS with drink.)

43 coil turmoil   44 reason (pronounced like "raisin,"
leading to the quibble on "fig"; a "fig" here is an
obscene contemptuous gesture in which the hand is
clenched and the thumb is thrust between the first
and second fingers, making the thumb resemble the
stem of a fig, or a penis)   55 Commit imprison
(Dick proceeds to quibble on the idea of committing
adultery)

78 gage pledge   88–89 stand much upon (quibble
on "attach much importance to")   102 curtsy (also
called "a leg," hence there is a quibble on the Carter's previous speech)   109 colossus huge statue in
the harbor at Rhodes, between whose legs ships
were said to have sailed

FAUSTUS: Then I assure thee certainly they are.

115 CARTER: I thank you, I am fully satisfied.

FAUSTUS: But wherefore dost thou ask?

CARTER: For nothing, sir, but methinks you should have a wooden bedfellow of one of 'em.

HORSE-COURSER: Why, do you hear sir, did
120 not I pull off one of your legs when you were asleep?

FAUSTUS: But I have it again now I am awake. Look you here sir.

ALL: O horrible! Had the doctor three legs?

125 CARTER: Do you remember sir, how you cozened me and eat up my load of —
(FAUSTUS *charms him dumb.*)

DICK: Do you remember how you made me wear an ape's — [FAUSTUS *charms him.*]

HORSE-COURSER: You whoreson conjuring
130 scab! Do you remember how you cozened me with a ho — [FAUSTUS *charms him.*]

ROBIN: Ha' you forgotten me? You think to carry it away with your "hey-pass" and "re-pass"?° Do you remember the dog's fa —
([FAUSTUS *charms him.*] *Exeunt* CLOWNS.)

135 HOSTESS: Who pays for the ale? Hear you master doctor, now you have sent away my guests, I pray who shall pay me for my a —
([FAUSTUS *charms her.*] *Exit* HOSTESS.)

DUCHESS:
My lord,
We are much beholding to this learnèd man.

DUKE:
140 So are we madam, which we will recompense
With all the love and kindness that we may:
His artful sport drives all sad thoughts away.
(*Exeunt.*)

[V.i] (*Thunder and lightning. Enter* DEVILS *with covered dishes*: MEPHOS-TOPHILIS *leads them into* FAUSTUS' *study. Then enter* WAGNER.)

WAGNER: I think my master means to die shortly. He has made his will and given me his wealth: his house, his goods, and store of golden plate — besides two thousand ducats ready
5 coined. I wonder what he means. If death were nigh, he would not frolic thus. He's now at supper with the scholars, where there's such belly-cheer as Wagner in his life ne'er saw the

like! And see where they come. Belike° the feast is done.° (*Exit.*) 10

(*Enter* FAUSTUS, MEPHOSTOPHILIS, *and two or three* SCHOLARS.)

I SCHOLAR: Master Doctor Faustus, since our conference about fair ladies, which was the beautifulest in all the world, we have determined with ourselves that Helen of Greece was the admirablest lady that ever lived. Therefore 15 master doctor, if you will do us so much favor as to let us see that peerless dame of Greece, whom all the world admires for majesty, we should think ourselves much beholding unto you. 20

FAUSTUS:
Gentlemen,
For that I know your friendship is unfeigned,
It is not Faustus' custom to deny
The just request of those that wish him well:
You shall behold that peerless dame of Greece 25
No otherwise for pomp or majesty
Than when Sir Paris crossed the seas with her
And brought the spoils° to rich Dardania.°
Be silent then, for danger is in words.

(*Music sounds.* MEPHOSTOPHILIS *brings in* HELEN: *she passeth over the stage.*)

II SCHOLAR:
Was this fair Helen, whose admired worth 30
Made Greece with ten years' wars afflict poor Troy?

III SCHOLAR:
Too simple is my wit to tell her worth,
Whom all the world admires for majesty.

I SCHOLAR:
Now we have seen the pride of nature's work,
We'll take our leaves, and for this blessèd sight 35
Happy and blest be Faustus evermore.

FAUSTUS:
Gentlemen, farewell, the same wish I to you.
(*Exeunt* SCHOLARS.)

(*Enter an* OLD MAN.)

OLD MAN:
O gentle Faustus, leave this damnèd art,
This magic that will charm thy soul to hell

133–34 **hey-pass, re-pass** conjuring expressions

V.i.9 **Belike** most likely   1–10 **I think...done** (though printed as prose in the quarto, as here, perhaps this speech should be verse, the lines ending *shortly, wealth, plate, coined, nigh, supper, belly-cheer, like, done*)   28 **spoils** booty (including Helen)   28 **Dardania** Troy

40 And quite bereave° thee of salvation.
Though thou hast now offended like a man,
Do not persever° in it like a devil.
Yet, yet, thou hast an amiable soul°
If sin by custom grow not into nature.
45 Then, Faustus, will repentance come too late!
Then, thou art banished from the sight of
heaven!
No mortal can express the pains of hell!
It may be this my exhortation
Seems harsh and all unpleasant. Let it not.
50 For gentle son, I speak it not in wrath
Or envy of thee but in tender love
And pity of thy future misery:
And so have hope that this my kind rebuke,
Checking° thy body, may amend thy soul.
    FAUSTUS:
Where art thou, Faustus? Wretch, what hast
55   thou done!
        (MEPHOSTOPHILIS *gives him a dagger.*)
Hell claims his right and with a roaring voice
Says "Faustus, come, thine hour is almost
come!"
And Faustus now will come to do thee right!
    OLD MAN:
O stay, good Faustus, stay thy desperate steps!
60 I see an angel hover o'er thy head,
And with a vial full of precious grace
Offers to pour the same into thy soul:
Then call for mercy and avoid despair.
    FAUSTUS:
O friend,
65 I feel thy words to comfort my distressèd soul:
Leave me awhile to ponder on my sins.
    OLD MAN:
Faustus, I leave thee, but with grief of heart,
Fearing the enemy of thy hapless soul.
                            (*Exit.*)
    FAUSTUS:
Accursèd Faustus! Wretch, what hast thou
    done!
70 I do repent, and yet I do despair:
Hell strives with grace for conquest in my breast!
What shall I do to shun the snares of death?
    MEPHOSTOPHILIS:
Thou traitor Faustus, I arrest thy soul
For disobedience to my sovereign lord.
75 Revolt,° or I'll in piecemeal tear thy flesh.

    FAUSTUS:
I do repent I e'er offended him.
Sweet Mephostophilis, entreat thy lord
To pardon my unjust presumption,
And with my blood again I will confirm
The former vow I made to Lucifer.   80
    MEPHOSTOPHILIS:
Do it then, Faustus, with unfeignèd heart
Lest greater dangers do attend thy drift.
    FAUSTUS:
Torment, sweet friend, that base and agèd man
That durst dissuade me from thy Lucifer,
With greatest torment that our hell affords.   85
    MEPHOSTOPHILIS:
His faith is great. I cannot touch his soul.
But what I may afflict his body with
I will attempt, which is but little worth.
    FAUSTUS:
One thing, good servant, let me crave of thee
To glut the longing of my heart's desire: 90
That I may have unto my paramour
That heavenly Helen which I saw of late,
Whose sweet embraces may extinguish clear
Those thoughts that do dissuade me from my
vow,
And keep mine oath I made to Lucifer.   95
    MEPHOSTOPHILIS:
This or what else my Faustus shall desire
Shall be performed in twinkling of an eye.

    (*Enter* HELEN *again, passing over between
    two* CUPIDS.)

    FAUSTUS:
Was this the face that launched a thousand
ships
And burnt the topless° towers of Ilium?°
Sweet Helen, make me immortal with a kiss.   100
Her lips suck forth my soul. See where it flies!
Come Helen, come, give me my soul again.
Here will I dwell, for heaven is in these lips
And all is dross that is not Helena.
I will be Paris, and for love of thee   105
Instead of Troy shall Wittenberg be sacked;
And I will combat with weak Menelaus°
And wear thy colors on my plumèd crest.
Yea, I will wound Achilles° in the heel
And then return to Helen for a kiss.   110
O, thou art fairer than the evening's air

40 **bereave** deprive   42 **persever** (accent on second
syllable)   43 **an amiable soul** a soul worthy of love
54 **Checking** rebuking   75 **Revolt** return (to your
allegiance)

99 **topless** i.e., so tall their tops are beyond sight
99 **Ilium** Troy   107 **Menelaus** Greek king, deserted
by Helen for Paris   109 **Achilles** greatest of the
Greek warriors

Clad in the beauty of a thousand stars,
Brighter art thou than flaming Jupiter
When he appeared to hapless Semele,°
115 More lovely than the monarch of the sky
In wanton Arethusa's° azure arms,
And none but thou shalt be my paramour.
                                    (*Exeunt.*)

[V.ii] (*Thunder. Enter* LUCIFER, BELZE-BUB, *and* MEPHOSTOPHILIS.°)

LUCIFER:
Thus from infernal Dis° do we ascend
To view the subjects of our monarchy,
Those souls which sin seals the black sons of
    hell.
'Mong which as chief, Faustus, we come to thee,
5 Bringing with us lasting damnation
To wait upon thy soul. The time is come
Which makes it forfeit.
MEPHOSTOPHILIS:
                        And this gloomy night
Here in this room will wretched Faustus be.
BELZEBUB:
And here we'll stay
10 To mark him how he doth demean himself.
MEPHOSTOPHILIS:
How should he but in desperate lunacy?
Fond° worldling, now his heart blood dries with
    grief,
His conscience kills it, and his laboring brain
Begets a world of idle fantasies
15 To overreach the devil; but all in vain:
His store of pleasures must be sauced with pain!
He and his servant Wagner are at hand.
Both come from drawing Faustus' latest will.
See where they come.

(*Enter* FAUSTUS *and* WAGNER.)

FAUSTUS:
20 Say Wagner, thou hast perused my will;
How dost thou like it?

WAGNER:
                       Sir, so wondrous well
As in all humble duty I do yield
My life and lasting service for your love.

(*Enter the* SCHOLARS.)

FAUSTUS:
Gramercies,° Wagner. — Welcome gentlemen.
                     [*Exit* WAGNER.]
I SCHOLAR: Now worthy Faustus, methinks 25
your looks are changed.
FAUSTUS:
O gentlemen!
II SCHOLAR:
What ails Faustus?
FAUSTUS: Ah my sweet chamber-fellow, had
I lived with thee, then had I lived still! — But 30
now must die eternally. Look sirs, comes he
not, comes he not?
I SCHOLAR: O my dear Faustus, what imports
this fear?
II SCHOLAR: Is all our pleasure turned to 35
melancholy?
III SCHOLAR: He is not well with being over-
solitary.
II SCHOLAR: If it be so, we'll have physicians
and Faustus shall be cured. 40
III SCHOLAR: 'Tis but a surfeit° sir, fear
nothing.
FAUSTUS: A surfeit of deadly sin that hath
damned both body and soul!
II SCHOLAR: Yet Faustus, look up to heaven 45
and remember mercy is infinite.
FAUSTUS: But Faustus' offense can ne'er be
pardoned. The serpent that tempted Eve may
be saved, but not Faustus! O gentlemen, hear
with patience and tremble not at my speeches. 50
Though my heart pant and quiver to remember that I have been a student here these thirty
years, O, would I had never seen Wittenberg,
never read book. — And what wonders I have
done all Germany can witness, yea all the 55
world, for which Faustus hath lost both Germany and the world, yea heaven itself —
heaven, the seat of God, the throne of the
blessèd, the kingdom of joy — and must remain in hell forever! hell, O hell forever! Sweet 60
friends, what shall become of Faustus being in
hell forever?
II SCHOLAR: Yet Faustus, call on God.
FAUSTUS: On God, whom Faustus hath

---

114 **Semele** beloved by Jupiter, who promised to do
whatever she wished; she asked to see him in his
full splendor, and the sight incinerated her   116
Arethusa a nymph, here apparently loved by Jupiter,
"the monarch of the sky"   V.ii.s.d. **Enter Lucifer,
Belzebub, and Mephostophilis** (probably they rise
out of a trapdoor and ascend to the upper stage,
Mephostophilis descending to the main stage at line
108)   1 **infernal Dis** the underworld (named for its
ruler)   12 **Fond** foolish

24 **Gramercies** thank you   41 **a surfeit** indigestion

65 abjured? On God, whom Faustus hath blasphemed? O my God, I would weep, but the
devil draws in my tears! Gush forth blood instead of tears, yea life and soul! O, he stays my
tongue! I would lift up my hands, but see, they
70 hold 'em, they hold 'em!
    ALL: Who, Faustus?
    FAUSTUS: Why, Lucifer and Mephostophilis.
O gentlemen, I gave them my soul for my
cunning.
75   ALL: O, God forbid!
    FAUSTUS: God forbade it indeed, but Faustus
hath done it. For the vain pleasure of four and
twenty years hath Faustus lost eternal joy and
felicity. I writ them a bill with mine own
80 blood. The date is expired. This is the time.
And he will fetch me.
    I SCHOLAR: Why did not Faustus tell us of
this before, that divines might have prayed for
thee?
85   FAUSTUS: Oft have I thought to have done
so, but the devil threatened to tear me in
pieces if I named God — to fetch me body and
soul if I once gave ear to divinity; and now
'tis too late! Gentlemen, away, lest you perish
90 with me.
    II SCHOLAR: O, what may we do to save
Faustus?
    FAUSTUS: Talk not of me but save yourselves
and depart.
95   III SCHOLAR: God will strengthen me. I will
stay with Faustus.
    I SCHOLAR: Tempt not God, sweet friend,
but let us into the next room and pray for him.
    FAUSTUS: Ay, pray for me, pray for me. And
100 what noise soever you hear, come not unto
me, for nothing can rescue me.
    II SCHOLAR: Pray thou, and we will pray
that God may have mercy upon thee.
    FAUSTUS: Gentlemen, farewell! If I live till
105 morning, I'll visit you. If not, Faustus is gone
to hell.
    ALL: Faustus, farewell.   (*Exeunt* SCHOLARS.)
    MEPHOSTOPHILIS:
Ay, Faustus, now thou hast no hope of heaven.
Therefore, despair! Think only upon hell,
110 For that must be thy mansion, there to dwell.
    FAUSTUS:
O thou bewitching fiend, 'twas thy temptation
Hath robbed me of eternal happiness.
    MEPHOSTOPHILIS:
I do confess it Faustus, and rejoice.
'Twas I, that when thou wert i' the way to
heaven

Dammed up thy passage. When thou took'st
the book 115
To view the Scriptures, then I turned the leaves
And led thine eye.
What, weep'st thou? 'Tis too late, despair,
farewell!
Fools that will laugh on earth, most weep in
hell.   (*Exit.*)

(*Enter the* GOOD ANGEL *and the* BAD ANGEL
at several doors.)

GOOD ANGEL:
O Faustus, if thou hadst given ear to me 120
Innumerable joys had followèd thee.
But thou did'st love the world.
    BAD ANGEL:
                Gave ear to me,
And now must taste hell's pains perpetually.
    GOOD ANGEL:
O, what will all thy riches, pleasures, pomps
Avail thee now?
    BAD ANGEL:
                Nothing but vex thee more, 125
To want in hell, that had on earth such store.

(*Music while the throne*° *descends.*)

GOOD ANGEL:
O, thou hast lost celestial happiness,
Pleasures unspeakable, bliss without end.
Had'st thou affected° sweet divinity,
Hell or the devil had had no power on thee. 130
Had'st thou kept on that way, Faustus behold
In what resplendent glory thou had'st sat
In yonder throne, like those bright shining
saints,
And triumphed over hell! That hast thou lost.
                [*Throne ascends.*]
And now, poor soul, must thy good angel leave
thee, 135
The jaws of hell are open to receive thee.
                (*Exit.*)

(*Hell is discovered.*)

BAD ANGEL:
Now Faustus, let thine eyes with horror stare
Into that vast perpetual torture-house.
There are the furies, tossing damnèd souls
On burning forks. Their bodies boil in lead. 140
There are live quarters° broiling on the coals,
That ne'er can die: this ever-burning chair

126s.d. **throne** (symbolic of heaven)   129 **affected**
preferred   141 **quarters** bodies

Is for o'er-tortured souls to rest them in.
These that are fed with sops of flaming fire
145 Were gluttons and loved only delicates
And laughed to see the poor starve at their gates.
But yet all these are nothing. Thou shalt see
Ten thousand tortures that more horrid be.
FAUSTUS:
O, I have seen enough to torture me.
BAD ANGEL:
Nay, thou must feel them, taste the smart of
150 all:
He that loves pleasure must for pleasure fall.
And so I leave thee Faustus, till anon:
Then wilt thou tumble in confusion.°   (*Exit.*)

(*The clock strikes eleven.*)

FAUSTUS:
O Faustus!
155 Now hast thou but one bare hour to live
And then thou must be damned perpetually.
Stand still, you ever-moving spheres of Heaven
That time may cease and midnight never come:
Fair nature's eye, rise, rise again and make
160 Perpetual day, or let this hour be but a year,
A month, a week, a natural day —
That Faustus may repent and save his soul.
O *lente lente currite noctis equi!*°
The stars move still, time runs, the clock will strike:
The devil will come, and Faustus must be
165 damned!
O, I'll leap up to my God! Who pulls me down?
See, see where Christ's blood streams in the firmament!
One drop of blood will save me. O my Christ! —
Rend not my heart for naming of my Christ!
170 Yet will I call on Him! O spare me, Lucifer! —
Where is it now? 'Tis gone: and see where God
Stretcheth out His arm and bends His ireful brows!
Mountains and hills, come, come and fall on me
And hide me from the heavy wrath of God!
175 No?
Then will I headlong run into the earth.

Gape earth! O no, it will not harbor me.
You stars that reigned at my nativity,
Whose influence hath allotted death and hell,
Now draw up Faustus like a foggy mist   180
Into the entrails of yon laboring cloud
That when you vomit forth into the air,
My limbs may issue from your smoky mouths —
But let my soul mount and ascend to heaven!

(*The watch strikes.*)

O half the hour is passed! 'Twill all be passed anon!   185
O God,
If thou wilt not have mercy on my soul,
Yet for Christ's sake, whose blood hath ransomed me,
Impose some end to my incessant pain!
Let Faustus live in hell a thousand years,   190
A hundred thousand, and at last be saved!
No end is limited to° damnèd souls!
Why wert thou not a creature wanting soul?
Or why is this immortal that thou hast?
O, Pythagoras' metempsychosis,° were that true   195
This soul should fly from me and I be changed
Into some brutish beast.
All beasts are happy, for when they die
Their souls are soon dissolved in elements.
But mine must live still° to be plagued in hell!   200
Cursed be the parents that engendered me!
No Faustus, curse thyself, curse Lucifer
That hath deprived thee of the joys of heaven.

(*The clock strikes twelve.*)

It strikes, it strikes! Now body, turn to air,
Or Lucifer will bear thee quick° to hell!   205
O soul, be changed into small water-drops
And fall into the ocean, ne'er be found.

(*Thunder, and enter the* DEVILS.)

My God, my God! Look not so fierce on me!
Adders and serpents, let me breathe awhile!
Ugly Hell, gape not! Come not Lucifer!   210
I'll burn my books! — O Mephostophilis!
(*Exeunt* [DEVILS *with* FAUSTUS.]°)

192 **limited to** set for   195 **metempsychosis** trans-
migration of souls (a doctrine held by Pythagoras,
philosopher of the sixth century B.C.)   200 **still**
always   205 **quick** alive   211s.d. **Exeunt [Devils
with Faustus]** (possibly the devils drag Faustus into
the "hell" that was "discovered" at V.ii.136, and
then toss his limbs onto the stage, or possibly the
limbs are revealed in V.iii.6 by withdrawing a curtain at the rear of the stage)

153 **confusion** destruction   163 **O . . . equi** slowly,
slowly run, O horses of the night (Latin, adapted
from Ovid's *Amores*, I.xiii.40, where a lover regret-
fully thinks of the coming of the dawn)

[V.iii] (*Enter the* SCHOLARS.)

I SCHOLAR:
Come gentlemen, let us go visit Faustus,
For such a dreadful night was never seen
Since first the world's creation did begin!
Such fearful shrieks and cries were never heard!
Pray heaven, the doctor have escaped the dan-
5   ger.

II SCHOLAR:
O, help us heaven, see, here are Faustus' limbs
All torn asunder by the hand of death!

III SCHOLAR:
The devils whom Faustus served have torn him
    thus:
For 'twixt the hours of twelve and one, me-
    thought
10 I heard him shriek and call aloud for help,
At which self° time the house seemed all on
    fire
With dreadful horror of these damnèd fiends.

II SCHOLAR:
Well gentlemen, though Faustus' end be such
As every Christian heart laments to think on,
15 Yet for he was a scholar once admired
For wondrous knowledge in our German
    schools,

V.iii.11 **self** same

We'll give his mangled limbs due burial;
And all the students, clothed in mourning black,
Shall wait upon° his heavy° funeral.
(*Exeunt.*)

(*Enter* CHORUS.)

Cut is the branch that might have grown full
    straight   20
And burnèd is Apollo's laurel bough°
That sometime grew within this learnèd man.
Faustus is gone: regard his hellish fall,
Whose fiendful fortune may exhort the wise
Only to wonder at° unlawful things,   25
Whose deepness doth entice such forward wits
To practice more than heavenly power permits.
[*Exit.*]

Terminat hora diem; terminat Author opus.°

FINIS

19 **wait upon** attend 19 **heavy** sad 21 **laurel
bough** symbol of wisdom, here associated with
Apollo, god of divination 25 **Only to wonder at**
i.e., merely to observe at a distance, with awe 28
Terminat . . . opus the hour ends the day; the author
ends his work (this Latin tag probably is not Marlowe's but the printer's, though it is engaging to
believe Marlowe wrote it, ending his play at midnight, the hour of Faustus' death)

      The exact date of *Doctor Faustus* is unknown, but it was probably writ-
ten not long before Marlowe was stabbed to death in 1593. It is universally
acknowledged as the first great English tragedy (Shakespeare had barely got
started), but behind it stands the tradition of the morality play, a form that
originated in the late fourteenth century and survived until the latter part of
the sixteenth. The morality play used allegorical figures to dramatize a representative person's struggle in a world of deceitful appearances. In *The Castle
of Perseverance* (early fifteenth century), for example, a character called Mankind is guided by such figures as Good Angel and Conscience in a struggle
against the World, the Flesh, the Devil, the Seven Deadly Sins, and so forth.
Mankind yields to sin, repents, then relapses; Death enters, but dying Mankind calls for God's mercy, and (as we are told in an epilogue) he is
forgiven and allowed to go to heaven. Similarly, *Everyman* (late fifteenth century) shows a figure called Everyman who has put his trust in Goods, Kindred, Fellowship, and so forth, but who learns — when faced with Death —
that these are false friends who will abandon him; he rightly turns to Good

Deeds, who assists him to achieve eternal felicity after death. Despite its happy ending, then, the morality play dramatizes guilt, suffering, and sometimes even death, and thus it approaches tragedy.

In a morality play, good and evil are sharply delineated and the spectator never doubts which is which. In tragedy, however, the issues may be more complicated; the hero may say, with King Lear, "I am a man more sinned against than sinning," and the audience may feel the truth of his assertion. Or the tragic hero may act in defiance of the conventional good, and the spectator may not find it in his heart to condemn the action, partly because the conventional good may seem severely limited, and the defiant act may seem, at least in some degree, noble. In the remainder of this Afterword we present extracts from differing interpretations of *Doctor Faustus*. They may serve as a stimulus while you reflect on the play or study it in the classroom, or as topics for essays. With the exception of the passage by Sylvan Barnet, which is from his edition of the play (published by New American Library in 1969), all are from essays that are conveniently reprinted in *Twentieth Century Interpretations of Doctor Faustus*, ed. Willard Farnham (Englewood Cliffs, N.J.: Prentice-Hall, 1969).

VIEWS OF FAUSTUS AS A TRAGIC HERO

Faustus is still damned, but he is transformed into the sort of personage that Aristotle approves of for the hero of tragedy, essentially human and noble, but led astray by some excusable vice or error. Marlowe's public would see in Doctor Faustus a man and a Christian like themselves, carried a bit too far by ambition and the love of pleasure. He is no radical unbeliever, no natural mate for the devil, conscienceless and heathen, like the typical villain of the Renaissance. On the contrary, he has become a good Protestant, and holds manfully to all those parts of the creed which express his spontaneous affections. A good angel is often overheard whispering in his ear; and if the bad angel finally prevails, it is in spite of continual remorse and hesitation on the Doctor's part. This excellent Faustus is damned by accident or by predestination; he is browbeaten by the devil and forbidden to repent when he has really repented. The terror of the conclusion is thereby heightened; we see an essentially good man, because in a moment of infatuation he had signed away his soul, driven against his will to despair and damnation. The alternative of a happy solution lies almost at hand; and it is only a lingering taste for the lurid and the horrible, ingrained in this sort of melodrama, that sends him shrieking to hell.

GEORGE SANTAYANA

Even "the Serpent that tempted *Eue* may be sau'd." Then why not Faustus? Having become a spirit in form and substance, has he ceased to be a man? Why, when the Old Man all but converts him, should Faustus accept the dagger of Mephostophilis? Why, when he calls upon Christ, is it Lucifer who emerges? George Santayana, acting as devil's advocate, and felicitously stating the case for Faustus as a martyr to the ideals of the Renaissance, would argue that he "is damned by accident or by predestination; he is browbeaten by the devil and forbidden to repent when he has really repented." The pedestrian counterargument would be based on the *Faustbook's* account of Faustus, "neuer falling to repentance truly" but "in all his opinions doubtfull, without faith or hope." Luther, followed by such English theologians as Richard Hooker, in his revolt against Catholicism had made contrition so difficult that at times it seemed virtually unattainable. What was worse for Faustus, he was no ordinary sinner; he was, like Marlowe himself, that impenitent and willful miscreant whom Elizabethan preachers termed a scorner. Far from denying sin or its wages, death, his course of action was premised on their inevitability: *Che serà, serà.* This led him, not to fatalism, but to an extreme act of the will — namely, the commission of an unpardonable sin, a sin against the Holy Ghost. Casuistry could have found theological loopholes, had a penitent Faustus been conceivable. But that would have presupposed an orthodox Marlowe.

HARRY LEVIN

We can say that Faustus makes a choice, and that he is responsible for his choice, but there is in the play a suggestion — sometimes explicit, sometimes only very dimly implicit — that Faustus comes to destruction not merely through his own actions but through the actions of a hostile cosmos that entraps him. In this sense, too, there is something of everyman in Faustus. The story of Adam, for instance, insists on Adam's culpability; Adam, like Faustus, made himself, rather than God, the center of his existence. And yet, despite the traditional expositions, one cannot entirely suppress the common-sense response that if the Creator knew Adam would fall, the Creator rather than Adam is responsible for the fall; Adam ought to have been created of better stuff. To what degree is Faustus, or any tragic hero, victimized? Lear sees himself "more sinned against than sinning," Othello sees himself as one "ensnared" by a "demi-devil," and there are similar statements in almost all of the major tragedies, from Aeschylus' *Prometheus Bound* onward. It can be argued, of course, that the devils cannot control Faustus; they can only come to him when he has laid himself open to them. Mephostophilis says something to this effect when he explains that he has come to Faustus not because Faustus' invocation is compelling, but because Faustus has made himself vulnerable to attack:

> . . . when we hear one rack the name of God,
> Abjure the Scriptures and his savior Christ,
> We fly in hope to get his glorious soul.
> Nor will we come unless he use such means
> Whereby he is in danger to be damned.
> Therefore the shortest cut for conjuring
> Is stoutly to abjure the Trinity
> And pray devoutly to the prince of hell.

This suggests that the devils are not so much independent external creatures as they are aspects of Faustus himself, symbols perhaps of his pride. On the other hand, one can argue that given Faustus' character — his extraordinary abilities that can find no satisfaction in the trivial pursuits of ordinary men — he is not entirely responsible for his actions. He clearly is of a nature different from that of his fellow scholars, whose attainments are far beneath his, and it is not at all evident that such a nature could find satisfaction and fulfill itself in the allowed activities. Faustus' initial speech, in which he masters and tires of four branches of learning, each of which would normally require a lifetime — the liberal arts, medicine, law, and divinity — suggests that he is the victim of the intellectual abilities that were given to him by his Creator.*

SYLVAN BARNET

... along with this incapacity for change to a better state, or repentance, go two other closely related ideas. The initial act is an act against nature, it is a primal sin, in that it contradicts the "essential fact of things," and its author knows that it does so. It is not an act committed by mistake; it is not an error of judgment, it is an error of will. The act is unnatural and so are its results; it deforms the nature which performs it. The second idea is the irony of retributive justice. The act is performed for an imagined good, which appears so infinitely desirable that the conditions for its supposed satisfaction are accepted; but a rigorous necessity reigns and sees to it that though the conditions are exacted literally, the desire is only granted ironically, and this is inevitable, since the desire is for something forbidden by the very nature of man.

HELEN GARDNER

W. H. Auden observed that at the end of a Greek tragedy we say, "What a pity it had to be this way"; at the end of a Christian tragedy, "What a pity it had to be this way when it might have been otherwise." If there is more freedom in Greek tragedy and more of a sense of fate in Christian tragedy than this statement suggests, still it points to the true tragic locus and tone of Marlowe's Doctor Faustus, the first major Elizabethan tragedy and the first to explore the tragic possibilities of the head-on clash of the Renaissance compulsions with the Hebraic-Christian tradition. . . .

Pressing on in spite of the echoes and the doubts, he reaches levels of perception never gained by the less venturous. Like Job, he was not content with having "heard by the hearing of the ear"; he must see with his own eyes. He has frivolous moments (some of them surely not of Marlowe's conceiving), when he boxes the Pope's ears and gets grapes in January. But the random wishes of his early days of conjuring take a more salutary direction. He does not want so much what power will bring — he never takes the [Signory] of Emden, never walls Germany with brass, never clothes the schoolboys in silk. He wants what all men, good and bad, have wanted; to conquer time, space, and ignorance. Above all he wants knowledge: what is hell? where is it? who made the world — "the plants, the herbs, the trees that grow upon the earth"? He cruises hither and yon in the world and above it, exploring all climes and the secrets of the heavens. He delves into the past, makes "blind Homer sing," Amphion play the harp, and Helen appear for a dazzling moment. What Marlowe dramatizes is not only the terror of the black

* From the Introduction by Sylvan Barnet from Doctor Faustus by Christopher Marlowe, edited by Sylvan Barnet. Copyright © 1969 by Sylvan Barnet. Reprinted by arrangement with The New American Library, Inc., New York, New York.

art as the old story told about it and as we see it reflected (in the play) in the eyes of the lesser characters, The Old Man, Wagner, and The Scholars, but the wonder of it — the wonder of the man who dared use it and the wonder of the mysteries it unfolds. . . .

The Devils lead him off, amidst thunder. If he is more sinning than sinned against, he yet has shown great capacities for good as well as evil, and we cannot feel that perfect justice has been done.*

RICHARD B. SEWALL

THE COMEDY IN *Doctor Faustus*

Doctor Faustus is thus the tragedy of a man who in striving boundlessly misdirects great gifts of mind and spirit and hence progressively loses his soul by disintegration as well as by capture. Progressive disintegration in Faustus brings low comedy into the tragedy, to echo clownishly what he is doing to himself or even to draw him into its clownishness. Much of this is far from having the verve and the dramatic import characteristic of Shakespearean low comedy. It has often been held, and not only because of a desire to protect the reputation of Marlowe, that some at least of the comic scenes are not his work. When Faustus himself turns comedian, one may have the thought that Marlowe is making low comedy show the tragic failure of his hero to live up to his high hopes of benefit from magic — a failure that brings him to playing jejune tricks on the world instead of taking imperial control of it or even transforming it.

WILLARD FARNHAM

. . . few even of the play's warmest admirers claim that it lives in the imagination as an entirely satisfying and consistent whole. Interest flags and is fitfully revived. And although the scenes in which Faustus' power is exhibited in such imbecile ways may be defended as presenting the gross stupidity of sin, this always feels to me, in the reading, as an explanation that has been thought up. With one or two exceptions, Faustus' capers represent an escape from seriousness and full realization — not simply on Faustus' part but on Marlowe's: and what they pad out is a crucial gap in the play's imaginative structure. For where, we may ask, are the contrasting positives against which Faustus' misdirection of his energies could be measured?

L. C. KNIGHTS

* From Richard B. Sewall, *The Vision of Tragedy*, published by Yale University Press. Copyright © 1959 by Yale University Press.

THE TRAGEDY OF KING LEAR

William Shakespeare

Edited by Russell Fraser

William Shakespeare (1564–1616) was born in Stratford, England, of middle-class parents. Nothing of interest is known about his early years, but by 1590 he was acting and writing plays in London. He early worked in all three Elizabethan dramatic genres — tragedy, comedy, and history. *Romeo and Juliet,* for example, was written about 1595, the year of *Richard II,* and in the following year he wrote *A Midsummer Night's Dream. Julius Caesar* (1599) probably preceded *As You Like It* by one year, and *Hamlet* probably followed *As You Like It* by less than a year. Among the plays that followed *King Lear* (1605–1606) were *Macbeth* (1605–1606) and several "romances" — plays that have happy endings but that seem more meditative and closer to tragedy than such comedies as *A Midsummer Night's Dream, As You Like It,* and *Twelfth Night.*

[*DRAMATIS PERSONAE*

LEAR, *King of Britain*
KING OF FRANCE
DUKE OF BURGUNDY
DUKE OF CORNWALL, *husband to Regan*
DUKE OF ALBANY, *husband to Goneril*
EARL OF KENT
EARL OF GLOUCESTER
EDGAR, *son to Gloucester*
EDMUND, *bastard son to Gloucester*
CURAN, *a courtier*
OSWALD, *steward to Goneril*
OLD MAN, *tenant to Gloucester*

DOCTOR
LEAR'S FOOL
A CAPTAIN *subordinate to Edmund*
GENTLEMEN *attending on Cordelia*
A HERALD
SERVANTS *to Cornwall*
GONERIL
REGAN } *daughters to Lear*
CORDELIA
KNIGHTS *attending on Lear*, OFFICERS,
    MESSENGERS, SOLDIERS, ATTENDANTS

Scene: Britain]

Charles Laughton as King Lear and Ian Holm as the Fool in the Shakespeare Memorial Theatre production directed by Glen Byam Shaw at Stratford-upon-Avon, England, 1959. (Photograph: Angus McBean. Harvard Theatre Collection.)

ACT I

SCENE I. [*King* LEAR's *palace.*]

Enter KENT, GLOUCESTER, *and* EDMUND.

KENT: I thought the king had more affected°1 the Duke of Albany° than Cornwall.

GLOUCESTER: It did always seem so to us; but now, in the division of the kingdom, it appears not which of the dukes he values most, for equalities are so weighed that curiosity in neither can make choice of either's moiety.°

KENT: Is not this your son, my lord?

GLOUCESTER: His breeding,° sir, hath been at my charge. I have so often blushed to acknowledge him that now I am brazed° to't.

KENT: I cannot conceive° you.

GLOUCESTER: Sir, this young fellow's mother could; whereupon she grew round-wombed, and had indeed, sir, a son for her cradle ere she had a husband for her bed. Do you smell a fault?

KENT: I cannot wish the fault undone, the issue° of it being so proper.°

GLOUCESTER: But I have a son, sir, by order of law, some year elder than this, who yet is no dearer in my account:° though this knave° came something saucily° to the world before he was sent for, yet was his mother fair, there was good sport at his making, and the whoreson° must be acknowledged. Do you know this noble gentleman, Edmund?

EDMUND: No, my lord.

GLOUCESTER: My Lord of Kent. Remember him hereafter as my honorable friend.

EDMUND: My services to your lordship.

KENT: I must love you, and sue° to know you better.

EDMUND: Sir, I shall study deserving.

GLOUCESTER: He hath been out° nine years, and away he shall again. The king is coming.

(*Sound a sennet.° Enter one bearing a coronet,° then King* LEAR, *then the Dukes of* CORNWALL *and* ALBANY, *next* GONERIL, REGAN, CORDELIA, *and* ATTENDANTS.)

LEAR:
Attend the lords of France and Burgundy, Gloucester.

GLOUCESTER:
I shall, my lord.   (*Exit,* [*with* EDMUND].)

LEAR:
Meantime we shall express our darker purpose.°
Give me the map there. Know that we have divided
In three our kingdom; and 'tis our fast° intent
To shake all cares and business from our age,
Conferring them on younger strengths, while we
Unburthened crawl toward death. Our son of Cornwall,
And you our no less loving son of Albany,
We have this hour a constant will to publish°
Our daughters' several° dowers, that future strife
May be prevented° now. The princes, France and Burgundy,
Great rivals in our youngest daughter's love,
Long in our court have made their amorous sojourn,
And here are to be answered. Tell me, my daughters
(Since now we will divest us both of rule,

From *King Lear* by William Shakespeare, edited by Russell Fraser. Copyright © Russell Fraser 1963. Copyright © 1963 Sylvan Barnet. Reprinted by arrangement with The New American Library, Inc., New York, N.Y.

1The degree sign (°) indicates a footnote, which is keyed to the text by the line number. Text references are printed in **boldface** type; the annotation follows in lightface type. The notes are Russell Fraser's. [Eds.]
I.I.2 **affected** loved   2 **Albany** Albanacte, whose domain extended "from the river Humber to the point of Caithness" (Holinshed)   6–7 **equalities . . . moiety** shares are so balanced against one another that careful examination by neither can make him wish the other's portion   9 **breeding** upbringing   11 **brazed** made brazen, hardened   12 **conceive** understand (pun follows)   19 **issue** result (child)   19 **proper** handsome   22 **account** estimation; **knave** fellow (without disapproval)   23 **saucily** (1) insolently (2) lasciviously   25 **whoreson** fellow (literally, son of a whore)

32 **sue** entreat   35 **out** away, abroad   36 s.d. **sennet** set of notes played on a trumpet, signaling the entrance or departure of a procession; **coronet** small crown, intended for Cordelia   39 **darker purpose** hidden intention   41 **fast** fixed   46 **constant . . . publish** fixed intention to proclaim   47 **several** separate   48 **prevented** forestalled

Interest° of territory, cares of state),
Which of you shall we say doth love us most,
55 That we our largest bounty may extend
Where nature doth with merit challenge.°
    Goneril,
Our eldest-born, speak first.
    GONERIL:
Sir, I love you more than word can wield° the
    matter;
Dearer than eyesight, space,° and liberty;
Beyond what can be valued, rich or rare;
No less than life, with grace, health, beauty,
    honor;
As much as child e'er loved, or father found;
A love that makes breath° poor, and speech
    unable:°
Beyond all manner of so much° I love you.
    CORDELIA [aside]:
What shall Cordelia speak? Love, and be
5   silent.
    LEAR:
Of all these 'bounds, even from this line to
    this,
With shadowy forests, and with champains
    riched,°
With plenteous rivers, and wide-skirted
    meads,°
We make thee lady. To thine and Albany's
    issues°
Be this perpetual.° What says our second
'0   daughter,
Our dearest Regan, wife of Cornwall? Speak.
    REGAN:
I am made of that self mettle° as my sister,
And prize me at her worth.° In my true heart
I find she names my very deed of love;°
75 Only she comes too short, that° I profess
Myself an enemy to all other joys
Which the most precious square of sense
    professes,°
And find I am alone felicitate°
In your dear highness' love.

CORDELIA [aside]:   Then poor Cordelia!
And yet not so, since I am sure my love's   80
More ponderous° than my tongue.
    LEAR:
To thee and thine hereditary ever
Remain this ample third of our fair kingdom,
No less in space, validity,° and pleasure
Than that conferred on Goneril. Now, our joy, 85
Although our last and least;° to whose young
    love
The vines of France and milk° of Burgundy
Strive to be interest;° what can you say to draw
A third more opulent than your sisters? Speak.
    CORDELIA:
Nothing, my lord.   90
    LEAR: Nothing?
    CORDELIA: Nothing.
    LEAR:
Nothing will come of nothing. Speak again.
    CORDELIA:
Unhappy that I am, I cannot heave
My heart into my mouth. I love your majesty   95
According to my bond,° no more nor less.
    LEAR:
How, how, Cordelia? Mend your speech a
    little,
Lest you may mar your fortunes.
    CORDELIA: Good my lord,
You have begot me, bred me, loved me. I
Return those duties back as are right fit,°   100
Obey you, love you, and most honor you.
Why have my sisters husbands, if they say
They love you all? Haply,° when I shall wed,
That lord whose hand must take my plight°
    shall carry
Half my love with him, half my care and duty. 105
Sure I shall never marry like my sisters,
To love my father all.
    LEAR:
But goes thy heart with this?
    CORDELIA: Ay, my good lord.
    LEAR:
So young, and so untender?
    CORDELIA:
So young, my lord, and true.   110
    LEAR:
Let it be so, thy truth then be thy dower!

---

53 **Interest** legal right   56 **nature ... challenge** natural affection contends with desert for (or lays claim
to) bounty   58 **wield** handle   59 **space** scope   63
breath language; **unable** impotent   64 **Beyond ...
much** beyond all these comparisons   67 **champains
riched** enriched plains   68 **wide-skirted meads** extensive grasslands   69 **issues** descendants   70 **perpetual** in perpetuity   72 **self mettle** same material or
temperament   73 **prize ... worth** value me the same
(imperative)   74 **my ... love** what my love really is
(a legalism)   75 **that** in that   77 **Which ... pro-
fesses** which the choicest estimate of sense avows
78 **felicitate** made happy

81 **ponderous** weighty   84 **validity** value   86 **least**
youngest, smallest   87 **milk** i.e., pastures   88 **interest** closely connected, as interested parties   96 **bond**
filial obligation   100 **Return ... fit** i.e., am corre-
spondingly dutiful   103 **Haply** perhaps   104 **plight**
troth plight

For, by the sacred radiance of the sun,
The mysteries of Hecate° and the night,
By all the operation of the orbs°
115 From whom we do exist and cease to be,
Here I disclaim all my paternal care,
Propinquity and property of blood,°
And as a stranger to my heart and me
Hold thee from this for ever. The barbarous
    Scythian,°
120 Or he that makes his generation messes°
To gorge his appetite, shall to my bosom
Be as well neighbored, pitied, and relieved,
As thou my sometime° daughter.
    KENT: Good my liege —
    LEAR:
Peace, Kent!
125 Come not between the dragon° and his wrath.
I loved her most, and thought to set my rest°
On her kind nursery.° Hence and avoid my
    sight!
So be my grave my peace, as here I give
Her father's heart from her! Call France. Who
    stirs?
130 Call Burgundy. Cornwall and Albany,
With my two daughters' dowers digest° the
    third;
Let pride, which she calls plainness, marry
    her.°
I do invest you jointly with my power,
Preeminence, and all the large effects
That troop with majesty.° Ourself,° by monthly
135 course,
With reservation° of an hundred knights,
By you to be sustained, shall our abode
Make with you by due turn. Only we shall
    retain
The name, and all th' addition° to a king. The
    sway,

Revenue, execution of the rest,   140
Belovèd sons, be yours; which to confirm,
This coronet° part between you.
    KENT: Royal Lear,
Whom I have ever honored as my king,
Loved as my father, as my master followed,
As my great patron thought on in my
    prayers —   145
    LEAR:
The bow is bent and drawn; make from the
    shaft.°
    KENT:
Let it fall° rather, though the fork° invade
The region of my heart. Be Kent unmannerly
When Lear is mad. What wouldst thou do,
    old man?
Thinkst thou that duty shall have dread to
    speak   150
When power to flattery bows? To plainness
    honor's bound
When majesty falls to folly. Reserve thy state,°
And in thy best consideration° check
This hideous rashness. Answer my life my
    judgment,°
Thy youngest daughter does not love thee
    least,   155
Nor are those empty-hearted whose low sounds
Reverb° no hollowness.°
    LEAR: Kent, on thy life, no more!
    KENT:
My life I never held but as a pawn°
To wage° against thine enemies; nor fear to
    lose it,
Thy safety being motive.°
    LEAR: Out of my sight!   160
    KENT:
See better, Lear, and let me still° remain
The true blank° of thine eye.
    LEAR:
Now by Apollo —
    KENT: Now by Apollo, king,
Thou swear'st thy gods in vain.

---

113 **mysteries of Hecate** secret rites of Hecate (goddess of the infernal world, and of witchcraft)   114 **operation . . . orbs** astrological influence   117 **Propinquity . . . blood** relationship and common blood   119 **Scythian** type of the savage   120 **makes . . . messes** eats his own offspring   123 **sometime** former   125 **dragon** (1) heraldic device of Britain (2) emblem of ferocity   126 **set my rest** (1) stake my all (a term from the card game of primero) (2) find my rest   127 **nursery** care, nursing   131 **digest** absorb   132 **Let . . . her** Let her pride be her dowry and gain her a husband   134–135 **effects . . . majesty** accompaniments that go with kingship   135 **Ourself** the royal "we"   136 **reservation** the action of reserving a privilege (a legalism)   139 **addition** titles and honors

142 **coronet** the crown that was to have been Cordelia's   146 **make . . . shaft** avoid the arrow   147 **fall** strike; **fork** forked head of the arrow   152 **Reserve thy state** retain your kingly authority   153 **best consideration** most careful reflection   154 **Answer . . . judgment** I will stake my life on my opinion   157 **Reverb** reverberate; **hollowness** (1) emptiness (2) insincerity   158 **pawn** stake in a wager   159 **wage** (1) wager (2) carry on war   160 **motive** moving cause   161 **still** always   162 **blank** the white spot in the center of the target (at which Lear should aim)

LEAR: O vassal! Miscreant!°

[*Laying his hand on his sword.*]

165   ALBANY, CORNWALL: Dear sir, forbear!
      KENT:
      Kill thy physician, and the fee bestow
      Upon the foul disease. Revoke thy gift,
      Or, whilst I can vent clamor° from my throat,
      I'll tell thee thou dost evil.
      LEAR: Hear me, recreant!°
170   On thine allegiance,° hear me!
      That thou hast sought to make us break our
          vows,
      Which we durst never yet, and with strained°
          pride
      To come betwixt our sentence° and our power,
      Which nor our nature nor our place can bear,
175   Our potency made good,° take thy reward.
      Five days we do allot thee for provision°
      To shield thee from diseases° of the world,
      And on the sixth to turn thy hated back
      Upon our kingdom. If, on the tenth day
          following,
      Thy banished trunk° be found in our
180   dominions,
      The moment is thy death. Away! By Jupiter,
      This shall not be revoked.
      KENT:
      Fare thee well, king. Sith° thus thou wilt
          appear,
      Freedom lives hence, and banishment is here.

      [*To* CORDELIA.]

185   The gods to their dear shelter take thee, maid,
      That justly think'st, and hast most rightly said.

      [*To* REGAN *and* GONERIL.]

      And your large speeches may your deeds
          approve,°
      That good effects° may spring from words of
          love.
      Thus Kent, O princes, bids you all adieu;
190   He'll shape his old course° in a country new.
                                        (*Exit.*)

(*Flourish.° Enter* GLOUCESTER, *with* FRANCE
and BURGUNDY; ATTENDANTS.)

GLOUCESTER:
Here's France and Burgundy, my noble lord.
LEAR:
My Lord of Burgundy,
We first address toward you, who with this
    king
Hath rivaled for our daughter. What in the
    least
Will you require in present° dower with her,   195
Or cease your quest of love?
BURGUNDY: Most royal majesty,
I crave no more than hath your highness
    offered,
Nor will you tender° less.
LEAR: Right noble Burgundy,
When she was dear° to us, we did hold her so;
But now her price is fallen. Sir, there she
    stands.   200
If aught within that little seeming substance,°
Or all of it, with our displeasure pieced,°
And nothing more, may fitly like° your grace,
She's there, and she is yours.
BURGUNDY: I know no answer.
LEAR:
Will you, with those infirmities she owes,°   205
Unfriended, new adopted to our hate,
Dow'red with our curse, and strangered° with
    our oath,
Take her, or leave her?
BURGUNDY: Pardon me, royal sir.
Election makes not up° on such conditions.
LEAR:
Then leave her, sir; for, by the pow'r that
    made me,   210
I tell you all her wealth. [*To* FRANCE.] For
    you, great king,
I would not from your love make such a stray
To° match you where I hate; therefore
    beseech° you
T' avert your liking a more worthier way°

164 **vassal! Miscreant!** base wretch! Misbeliever   168
vent clamor utter a cry   169 **recreant** traitor   170 **On
thine allegiance** to forswear, which is to commit high
treason   172 **strained** forced (and so excessive)
173 **sentence** judgment, decree   175 **Our . . . good**
my royal authority being now asserted   176 **for provision** for making preparation   177 **diseases** troubles
180 **trunk** body   183 **Sith** since   187 **approve** prove
true   188 **effects** results   190 **shape . . . course** pursue his customary way

190 s.d. **Flourish** trumpet fanfare   195 **present** immediate   198 **tender** offer   199 **dear** (1) beloved
(2) valued at a high price   201 **little seeming substance** person who is (1) inconsiderable (2) outspoken   202 **pieced** added to it   203 **fitly like** please
by its fitness   205 **owes** possesses   207 **strangered**
made a stranger   209 **Election . . . up** no one can
choose   212–213 **make . . . To** stray so far as to   213
beseech I beseech   214 **avert . . . way** turn your
affections from her and bestow them on a better
person

215 Than on a wretch whom nature is ashamed
Almost t' acknowledge hers.
    FRANCE: This is most strange,
That she whom even but now was your best
    object,°
The argument° of your praise, balm of your
    age,
The best, the dearest, should in this trice of
    time
220 Commit a thing so monstrous to dismantle°
So many folds of favor. Sure her offense
Must be of such unnatural degree
That monsters it,° or your fore-vouched°
    affection
Fall into taint;° which to believe of her
225 Must be a faith that reason without miracle
Should never plant in me.°
    CORDELIA: I yet beseech your majesty,
If for° I want that glib and oily art
To speak and purpose not,° since what I well
    intend
I'll do't before I speak, that you make known
230 It is no vicious blot, murder, or foulness,
No unchaste action or dishonored step,
That hath deprived me of your grace and
    favor;
But even for want of that for which I am
    richer,
A still-soliciting° eye, and such a tongue
That I am glad I have not, though not to have
235   it
Hath lost° me in your liking.
    LEAR: Better thou
Hadst not been born than not t' have pleased
    me better.
    FRANCE:
Is it but this? A tardiness in nature°
Which often leaves the history unspoke°
240 That it intends to do. My Lord of Burgundy,
What say you° to the lady? Love's not love

When it is mingled with regards° that stands
Aloof from th' entire point.° Will you have her?
She is herself a dowry.
    BURGUNDY: Royal king,
Give but that portion which yourself proposed,   245
And here I take Cordelia by the hand,
Duchess of Burgundy.
    LEAR:
Nothing. I have sworn. I am firm.
    BURGUNDY:
I am sorry then you have so lost a father
That you must lose a husband.
    CORDELIA: Peace be with Burgundy.   250
Since that respects of fortune° are his love,
I shall not be his wife.
    FRANCE:
Fairest Cordelia, that art most rich being poor,
Most choice forsaken, and most loved despised,
Thee and thy virtues here I seize upon.   255
Be it lawful I take up what's cast away.
Gods, gods! 'Tis strange that from their
    cold'st neglect
My love should kindle to inflamed respect.°
Thy dow'rless daughter, king, thrown to my
    chance,°
Is queen of us, of ours, and our fair France.   260
Not all the dukes of wat'rish° Burgundy
Can buy this unprized precious° maid of me.
Bid them farewell, Cordelia, though unkind.
Thou losest here,° a better where° to find.
    LEAR:
Thou hast her, France; let her be thine, for we   265
Have no such daughter, nor shall ever see
That face of hers again. Therefore be gone,
Without our grace, our love, our benison.°
Come, noble Burgundy.
         (*Flourish. Exeunt* [LEAR, BURGUNDY,
           CORNWALL, ALBANY, GLOUCESTER,
                  and ATTENDANTS].)
    FRANCE:
Bid farewell to your sisters.   270
    CORDELIA:
The jewels of our father,° with washed° eyes

---

217 **your best object** the one you loved most 218
argument subject 220 **dismantle** strip off 223
That monsters it as makes it monstrous, unnatural;
fore-vouched previously sworn 224 **Fall into taint**
must be taken as having been unjustified all along;
i.e., Cordelia was unworthy of your love from the first
225–226 **reason . . . me** my reason would have to be
supported by a miracle to make me believe 227 **for**
because 228 **purpose not** mean to do what I
promise 234 **still-soliciting** always begging 236
lost ruined 238 **tardiness in nature** natural reticence 239 **leaves . . . unspoke** does not announce
the action 241 **What say you** i.e., will you have

242 **regards** considerations (the dowry) 242–243
stands . . . point have nothing to do with the essential
question (love) 251 **respects of fortune** mercenary
considerations 258 **inflamed respect** more ardent
affection 259 **chance** lot 261 **wat'rish** (1) with
many rivers (2) weak, diluted 262 **unprized precious** unappreciated by others, and yet precious 264
here in this place; **where** other place 268 **benison**
blessing 271 **The jewels . . . father** you creatures
prized by our father; **washed** (1) weeping (2)
clearsighted

Cordelia leaves you. I know you what you are,
And, like a sister,° am most loath to call
Your faults as they are named.° Love well our
    father.
275 To your professèd° bosoms I commit him.
But yet, alas, stood I within his grace,
I would prefer° him to a better place.
So farewell to you both.
REGAN:
Prescribe not us our duty.
GONERIL: Let your study
Be to content your lord, who hath received
280 you
At Fortune's alms.° You have obedience
    scanted,°
And well are worth the want that you have
    wanted.°
CORDELIA:
Time shall unfold what plighted° cunning
    hides,
Who covers faults, at last shame them de-
    rides.°
Well may you prosper.
285 FRANCE: Come, my fair Cordelia.
            (Exit FRANCE and CORDELIA.)
GONERIL: Sister, it is not little I have to say
of what most nearly appertains to us both. I
think our father will hence tonight.
REGAN: That's most certain, and with you;
290 next month with us.
GONERIL: You see how full of changes his
age is. The observation we have made of it
hath not been little. He always loved our sister
most, and with what poor judgment he hath
295 now cast her off appears too grossly.°
REGAN: 'Tis the infirmity of his age; yet he
hath ever but slenderly known himself.
GONERIL: The best and soundest of his time°
hath been but rash; then must we look from
300 his age to receive not alone the imperfections

of long-ingrafted° condition,° but therewithal°
the unruly waywardness that infirm and choleric years bring with them.
REGAN: Such unconstant starts° are we like
to have from him as this of Kent's banish-   305
ment.
GONERIL: There is further compliment° of
leave-taking between France and him. Pray
you, let's hit° together; if our father carry
authority with such disposition as he bears,°   310
this last surrender° of his will but offend° us.
REGAN: We shall further think of it.
GONERIL: We must do something, and i' th'
heat.°

                                (Exeunt.)

SCENE II. [The Earl of GLOUCESTER's
            castle.]

Enter EDMUND [with a letter].

EDMUND:
Thou, Nature,° art my goddess; to thy law
My services are bound. Wherefore should I
Stand in the plague of custom,° and permit
The curiosity° of nations to deprive me,
For that° I am some twelve or fourteen moon-
    shines°   5
Lag of° a brother? Why bastard? Wherefore
    base?
When my dimensions are as well compact,°
My mind as generous,° and my shape as true,
As honest° madam's issue? Why brand they us
With base? With baseness? Bastardy? Base?
    Base?   10
Who, in the lusty stealth of nature, take
More composition° and fierce° quality
Than doth, within a dull, stale, tired bed,
Go to th' creating a whole tribe of fops°

273 **like a sister** because I am a sister, i.e., loyal, affectionate   274 **as...named** by their right and ugly names   275 **professèd** pretending to love   277 **prefer** recommend   281 **At Fortune's alms** as a charitable bequest from Fortune (and so, by extension, as one beggared or cast down by Fortune); **scanted** stinted   282 **worth...wanted** deserve to be denied, even as you have denied   283 **plighted** pleated, enfolded   284 **Who...derides** Those who hide their evil are finally exposed and shamed ("He that hideth his sins, shall not prosper")   295 **grossly** obviously   298 **of his time** period of his life up to now

301 **long-ingrafted** implanted for a long time; **condition** disposition; **therewithal** with them   304 **unconstant starts** impulsive whims   307 **compliment** formal courtesy   309 **hit** agree   309–310 **carry...bears** continues, and in such frame of mind, to wield the sovereign power   311 **last surrender** recent abdication; **offend** vex   313–314 **i' th' heat** while the iron is hot
I.ii.1 **Nature** Edmund's conception of Nature accords with our description of a bastard as a natural child   3 **Stand...custom** respect hateful convention   4 **curiosity** nice distinctions   5 **For that** because; **moonshines** months   6 **Lag of** short of being (in age)   7 **compact** framed   8 **generous** gallant   9 **honest** chaste   12 **composition** completeness; **fierce** energetic   14 **fops** fools

15 Got° 'tween asleep and wake? Well then,
Legitimate Edgar, I must have your land.
Our father's love is to the bastard Edmund
As to th' legitimate. Fine word, "legitimate."
Well, my legitimate, if this letter speed,°
20 And my invention° thrive, Edmund the base
Shall top th' legitimate. I grow, I prosper.
Now, gods, stand up for bastards.

(*Enter* GLOUCESTER.)

GLOUCESTER:
Kent banished thus? and France in choler
   parted?
And the king gone tonight? prescribed° his
   pow'r?
25 Confined to exhibition?° All this done
Upon the gad?° Edmund, how now? What
   news?
EDMUND:
So please your lordship, none.
GLOUCESTER:
Why so earnestly seek you to put up° that
   letter?
EDMUND:
I know no news, my lord.
GLOUCESTER:
30 What paper were you reading?
EDMUND: Nothing, my lord.
GLOUCESTER: No? What needed then that
terrible dispatch° of it into your pocket? The
quality of nothing hath not such need to hide
35 itself. Let's see. Come, if it be nothing, I shall
not need spectacles.
EDMUND: I beseech you, sir, pardon me. It is
a letter from my brother that I have not all
o'er-read; and for so much as I have perused, I
40 find it not fit for your o'erlooking.°
GLOUCESTER: Give me the letter, sir.
EDMUND: I shall offend, either to detain or
give it. The contents, as in part I understand
them, are to blame.°
45 GLOUCESTER: Let's see, let's see.
EDMUND: I hope, for my brother's justification, he wrote this but as an essay or taste° of
my virtue.
GLOUCESTER (*reads*): "This policy and rev-

erence° of age makes the world bitter to the 50
best of our times;° keeps our fortunes from us
till our oldness cannot relish° them. I begin to
find an idle and fond° bondage in the oppres-
sion of aged tyranny, who sways, not as it hath
power, but as it is suffered.° Come to me, that 55
of this I may speak more. If our father would
sleep till I waked him, you should enjoy half his
revenue° for ever, and live the beloved of your
brother,
                Edgar." 60
Hum! Conspiracy? "Sleep till I waked him,
you should enjoy half his revenue." My son
Edgar! Had he a hand to write this? A heart
and brain to breed it in? When came you to
this? Who brought it? 65
EDMUND: It was not brought me, my lord;
there's the cunning of it. I found it thrown in
at the casement of my closet.°
GLOUCESTER: You know the character° to be
your brother's? 70
EDMUND: If the matter were good, my lord,
I durst swear it were his; but in respect of
that,° I would fain° think it were not.
GLOUCESTER: It is his.
EDMUND: It is his hand, my lord; but I hope 75
his heart is not in the contents.
GLOUCESTER: Has he never before sounded°
you in this business?
EDMUND: Never, my lord. But I have heard
him oft maintain it to be fit that, sons at 80
perfect° age, and fathers declined, the father
should be as ward to the son, and the son
manage his revenue.
GLOUCESTER: O villain, villain! His very
opinion in the letter. Abhorred villain, unnatu- 85
ral, detested,° brutish villain; worse than
brutish! Go, sirrah,° seek him. I'll apprehend
him. Abominable villain! Where is he?
EDMUND: I do not well know, my lord. If it
shall please you to suspend your indignation 90
against my brother till you can derive from
him better testimony of his intent, you should

---

15 **Got** begot 19 **speed** prosper 20 **invention** plan
24 **prescribed** limited 25 **exhibition** an allowance
or pension 26 **Upon the gad** on the spur of the
moment (as if pricked by a gad or goad) 28 **put up**
put away, conceal 33 **terrible dispatch** hasty putting
away 40 **o'erlooking** inspection 44 **to blame**
blameworthy 47 **essay or taste** test

49–50 **policy and reverence** policy of reverencing
(hendiadys) 51 **best...times** best years of our lives
(i.e., our youth) 52 **relish** enjoy 53 **idle and fond**
foolish 54–55 **who...suffered** which rules, not
from its own strength, but from our allowance 58
revenue income 68 **casement...closet** window of
my room 69 **character** handwriting 72–73 **in...
that** in view of what it is 73 **fain** prefer to 77
sounded sounded you out 81 **perfect** mature 86
detested detestable 87 **sirrah** sir (familiar form of
address)

run a certain course;° where, if you violently proceed against him, mistaking his purpose, it
95 would make a great gap° in your own honor and shake in pieces the heart of his obedience. I dare pawn down° my life for him that he hath writ this to feel° my affection to your honor, and to no other pretense of danger.°

100 GLOUCESTER: Think you so?

EDMUND: If your honor judge it meet,° I will place you where you shall hear us confer of this, and by an auricular assurance° have your satisfaction, and that without any further delay
105 than this very evening.

GLOUCESTER: He cannot be such a monster.

EDMUND: Nor is not, sure.

GLOUCESTER: To his father, that so tenderly and entirely loves him. Heaven and earth!
110 Edmund, seek him out; wind me into him,° I pray you; frame° the business after your own wisdom. I would unstate myself to be in a due resolution.°

EDMUND: I will seek him, sir, presently;°
115 convey° the business as I shall find means, and acquaint you withal.°

GLOUCESTER: These late° eclipses in the sun and moon portend no good to us. Though the wisdom of nature° can reason° it thus and thus,
120 yet nature finds itself scourged by the sequent effects.° Love cools, friendship falls off,° brothers divide. In cities, mutinies;° in countries, discord; in palaces, treason; and the bond cracked 'twixt son and father. This villain of
125 mine comes under the prediction,° there's son against father; the king falls from bias of nature,° there's father against child. We have seen the best of our time.° Machinations,

hollowness,° treachery, and all ruinous disorders follow us disquietly° to our graves. Find 130 out this villain, Edmund; it shall lose thee nothing.° Do it carefully. And the noble and true-hearted Kent banished; his offense, honesty. 'Tis strange. (Exit.)

EDMUND: This is the excellent foppery° of 135 the world, that when we are sick in fortune, often the surfeits of our own behavior,° we make guilty of our disasters the sun, the moon, and stars; as if we were villains on° necessity; fools by heavenly compulsion; knaves, thieves, 140 and treachers by spherical predominance;° drunkards, liars, and adulterers by an enforced obedience of planetary influence;° and all that we are evil in, by a divine thrusting on.° An admirable evasion of whoremaster° man, to lay 145 his goatish° disposition on the charge of a star. My father compounded° with my mother under the Dragon's Tail,° and my nativity° was under Ursa Major,° so that it follows I am rough and lecherous. Fut!° I should have been 150 that° I am, had the maidenliest star in the firmament twinkled on my bastardizing. Edgar —

(Enter EDGAR.)

and pat he comes, like the catastrophe° of the old comedy. My cue is villainous melancholy, 155 with a sigh like Tom o' Bedlam.° — O, these eclipses do portend these divisions. Fa, sol, la, mi.°

EDGAR: How now, brother Edmund; what serious contemplation are you in? 160

EDMUND: I am thinking, brother, of a pre-

93 run . . . course proceed safely, know where you are going 95 gap breach 97 pawn down stake 98 feel test 99 pretense of danger dangerous purpose 101 meet fit 103 auricular assurance proof heard with your own ears 110 wind . . . him insinuate yourself into his confidence for me 111 frame manage 112–113 unstate . . . resolution forfeit my earldom to know the truth 114 presently at once 115 convey manage 116 withal with it 117 late recent 119 wisdom of nature scientific learning; reason explain 120–121 yet . . . effects nonetheless our world is punished with subsequent disasters 121 falls off revolts 122 mutinies riots 124–125 This . . . prediction my son's villainous behavior is included in these portents, and bears them out 126–127 bias of nature natural inclination (the metaphor is from the game of bowls) 128 best . . . time our best days 129 hollowness insincerity 130 disquietly unquietly 131–132 it . . . nothing you will not lose by it 135 foppery folly 137 often . . . behavior often caused by our own excesses 139 on of 141 treachers . . . predominance traitors because of the ascendancy of a particular star at our birth 142–143 by . . . influence because we had to submit to the influence of our star 144 divine thrusting on supernatural compulsion 145 whoremaster lecherous 146 goatish lascivious 147 compounded (1) made terms (2) formed (a child) 148 Dragon's Tail the constellation Draco; nativity birthday 149 Ursa Major the Great Bear 150 Fut 'S foot (an impatient oath) 151 that what 154 catastrophe conclusion 155–156 My . . . Bedlam I must be doleful, like a lunatic beggar out of Bethlehem (Bedlam) Hospital, the London madhouse 157–158 Fa, sol, la, mi Edmund's humming of the musical notes is perhaps prompted by his use of the word division, which describes a musical variation

diction I read this other day, what should follow these eclipses.

EDGAR: Do you busy yourself with that?

165 EDMUND: I promise you, the effects he writes of succeed° unhappily: as of unnaturalness° between the child and the parent, death, dearth, dissolutions of ancient amities,° divisions in state, menaces and maledictions

170 against king and nobles, needless diffidences,° banishment of friends, dissipation of cohorts,° nuptial breaches, and I know not what.

EDGAR: How long have you been a sectary astronomical?°

175 EDMUND: Come, come, when saw you my father last?

EDGAR: Why, the night gone by.

EDMUND: Spake you with him?

EDGAR: Ay, two hours together.

180 EDMUND: Parted you in good terms? Found you no displeasure in him by word nor countenance?°

EDGAR: None at all.

EDMUND: Bethink yourself wherein you may

185 have offended him; and at my entreaty forbear his presence° until some little time hath qualified° the heat of his displeasure, which at this instant so rageth in him that with the mischief of your person it would scarcely allay.°

190 EDGAR: Some villain hath done me wrong.

EDMUND: That's my fear, brother. I pray you have a continent forbearance° till the speed of his rage goes slower; and, as I say, retire with me to my lodging, from whence I will fitly°

195 bring you to hear my lord speak. Pray ye, go; there's my key. If you do stir abroad, go armed.

EDGAR: Armed, brother?

EDMUND: Brother, I advise you to the best.

200 Go armed. I am no honest man if there be any good meaning toward you. I have told you what I have seen and heard; but faintly, nothing like the image and horror° of it. Pray you, away.

EDGAR: Shall I hear from you anon?° 205

EDMUND: I do serve you in this business.

(*Exit* EDGAR.)

A credulous father, and a brother noble,
Whose nature is so far from doing harms
That he suspects none; on whose foolish honesty
My practices° ride easy. I see the business. 210
Let me, if not by birth, have lands by wit.
All with me's meet° that I can fashion fit.°

(*Exit.*)

SCENE III. [*The Duke of* ALBANY'*s palace*.]

Enter GONERIL, *and* [OSWALD, *her*] *steward.*

GONERIL: Did my father strike my gentleman for chiding of his Fool?°

OSWALD: Ay, madam.

GONERIL:
By day and night he wrongs me. Every hour
He flashes into one gross crime° or other 5
That sets us all at odds. I'll not endure it.
His knights grow riotous,° and himself upbraids us
On every trifle. When he returns from hunting,
I will not speak with him. Say I am sick.
If you come slack of former services,° 10
You shall do well; the fault of it I'll answer.°

[*Horns within.*]

OSWALD: He's coming, madam; I hear him.

GONERIL:
Put on what weary negligence you please,
You and your fellows. I'd have it come to question.°
If he distaste° it, let him to my sister, 15
Whose mind and mine I know in that are one,
Not to be overruled. Idle° old man,
That still would manage those authorities
That he hath given away. Now, by my life,
Old fools are babes again, and must be used 20
With checks as flatteries, when they are seen abused.°
Remember what I have said.

---

166 **succeed** follow   166–167 **unnaturalness** unkindness   168 **amities** friendships   170 **diffidences** distrusts   171 **dissipation of cohorts** falling away of supporters   173–174 **sectary astronomical** believer in astrology   181–182 **countenance** expression   185–186 **forbear his presence** keep away from him   186–187 **qualified** lessened   188–189 **with . . . allay** even an injury to you would not appease his anger   192 **have . . . forbearance** be restrained and keep yourself withdrawn   194 **fitly** at a fit time   203 **image and horror** true horrible picture

205 **anon** in a little while   210 **practices** plots   212 **meet** proper; **fashion fit** shape to my purpose   I.iii.2 **Fool** court jester   5 **crime** offense   7 **riotous** dissolute   10 **come . . . services** are less serviceable to him than formerly   11 **answer** answer for   14 **come to question** be discussed openly   15 **distaste** dislike   17 **Idle** foolish   21 **With . . . abused** with restraints as well as soothing words when they are misguided

OSWALD: Well, madam.

GONERIL:

And let his knights have colder looks among
  you.
What grows of it, no matter; advise your
  fellows so.
I would breed from hence occasions, and I
25 shall,
That I may speak.° I'll write straight° to my
  sister
To hold my course. Go, prepare for dinner.
                                    (*Exeunt.*)

SCENE IV. [*A hall in the same.*]

Enter KENT [*disguised*].

KENT:

If but as well I other accents borrow
That can my speech defuse,° my good intent
May carry through itself to that full issue°
For which I razed my likeness.° Now, banished
  Kent,
5 If thou canst serve where thou dost stand
  condemned,
So may it come,° thy master whom thou lov'st
Shall find thee full of labors.

(*Horns within.*° *Enter* LEAR, [KNIGHTS,] *and*
ATTENDANTS.)

LEAR: Let me not stay° a jot for dinner; go,
get it ready. [*Exit an* ATTENDANT.] How now,
10 what art thou?

KENT: A man, sir.

LEAR: What dost thou profess?° What
wouldst thou with us?

KENT: I do profess° to be no less than I
15 seem, to serve him truly that will put me in
trust, to love him that is honest, to converse
with him that is wise and says little, to fear
judgment,° to fight when I cannot choose, and
to eat no fish.°

25 LEAR: What art thou?

KENT: A very honest-hearted fellow and as
poor as the king.

LEAR: If thou be'st as poor for a subject as
he's for a king, thou art poor enough. What
wouldst thou?   25

KENT: Service.

LEAR: Who wouldst thou serve?

KENT: You.

LEAR: Dost thou know me, fellow?

KENT: No, sir, but you have that in your   30
countenance° which I would fain° call master.

LEAR: What's that?

KENT: Authority.

LEAR: What services canst thou do?

KENT: I can keep honest counsel,° ride, run, 35
mar a curious tale in telling it,° and deliver a
plain message bluntly. That which ordinary
men are fit for, I am qualified in, and the best
of me is diligence.

LEAR: How old art thou?   40

KENT: Not so young, sir, to love a woman
for singing, nor so old to dote on her for
anything. I have years on my back forty-eight.

LEAR: Follow me; thou shalt serve me. If I
like thee no worse after dinner, I will not part 45
from thee yet. Dinner, ho, dinner! Where's
my knave?° my Fool? Go you and call my Fool
hither.   [*Exit an* ATTENDANT.]

(*Enter* OSWALD.)

You, you, sirrah, where's my daughter?

OSWALD: So please you —   (*Exit.*)   50

LEAR: What says the fellow there? Call the
clotpoll° back. [*Exit a* KNIGHT.] Where's my
Fool? Ho, I think the world's asleep.

[*Reenter* KNIGHT.]

How now? Where's that mongrel?

KNIGHT: He says, my lord, your daughter is   55
not well.

LEAR: Why came not the slave back to me
when I called him?

KNIGHT: Sir, he answered me in the round-
est° manner, he would not.   60

LEAR: He would not?

KNIGHT: My lord, I know not what the
matter is; but to my judgment your highness is
not entertained° with that ceremonious affection as you were wont. There's a great abate-   65
ment of kindness appears as well in the general

25–26 **breed . . . speak** find in this opportunities for
speaking out   26 **straight** at once
I.iv.2 **defuse** disguise   3 **full issue** perfect result   4
razed my likeness shaved off, disguised my natural
appearance   6 **So . . . come** so may it fall out   7 s.d.
within offstage   8 **stay** wait   12 **What . . . profess**
What do you do?   14 **profess** claim   18 **judgment**
by a heavenly or earthly judge   19 **eat no fish** i.e., (1)
I am no Catholic, but a loyal Protestant (2) I am no
weakling (3) I use no prostitutes

31 **countenance** bearing; **fain** like to   35 **honest
counsel** honorable secrets   36 **mar . . . it** i.e., I
cannot speak like an affected courtier ("curious" =
elaborate, as against plain)   47 **knave** boy   52 **clot-
poll** clodpoll, blockhead   59–60 **roundest** rudest
64 **entertained** treated

dependants° as in the duke himself also and your daughter.

LEAR: Ha? Say'st thou so?

70 KNIGHT: I beseech you pardon me, my lord, if I be mistaken; for my duty cannot be silent when I think your highness wronged.

LEAR: Thou but rememb'rest° me of mine own conception.° I have perceived a most faint

75 neglect° of late, which I have rather blamed as mine own jealous curiosity° than as a very pretense° and purpose of unkindness. I will look further into't. But where's my Fool? I have not seen him this two days.

80 KNIGHT: Since my young lady's going into France, sir, the Fool hath much pined away.

LEAR: No more of that; I have noted it well. Go you and tell my daughter I would speak with her. Go you, call hither my Fool.

[*Exit an* ATTENDANT.]

(*Enter* OSWALD.)

85 O, you, sir, you! Come you hither, sir. Who am I, sir?

OSWALD: My lady's father.

LEAR: "My lady's father"? My lord's knave, you whoreson dog, you slave, you cur!

90 OSWALD: I am none of these, my lord; I beseech your pardon.

LEAR: Do you bandy° looks with me, you rascal?

[*Striking him.*]

OSWALD: I'll not be strucken,° my lord.

95 KENT: Nor tripped neither, you base football° player.

[*Tripping up his heels.*]

LEAR: I thank thee, fellow. Thou serv'st me, and I'll love thee.

KENT: Come, sir, arise, away. I'll teach you
100 differences.° Away, away. If you will measure your lubber's° length again, tarry; but away. Go to!° Have you wisdom?° So.°

[*Pushes* OSWALD *out.*]

LEAR: Now, my friendly knave, I thank thee. There's earnest° of thy service. [*Giving* KENT *money.*]

(*Enter* FOOL.)

FOOL: Let me hire him too. Here's my 105
coxcomb.°

[*Offering* KENT *his cap.*]

LEAR: How now, my pretty knave? How dost thou?

FOOL: Sirrah, you were best° take my cox-
comb.   110

KENT: Why, Fool?

FOOL: Why? For taking one's part that's out of favor. Nay, an° thou canst not smile as the wind sits,° thou'lt catch cold shortly. There, take my coxcomb. Why, this fellow has ban- 115
ished° two on's daughters, and did the third a blessing against his will. If thou follow him, thou must needs wear my coxcomb. — How now, nuncle?° Would I had two coxcombs and two daughters.   120

LEAR: Why, my boy?

FOOL: If I gave them all my living,° I'd keep my coxcombs myself. There's mine; beg another of thy daughters.

LEAR: Take heed, sirrah — the whip.   125

FOOL: Truth's a dog must to kennel; he must be whipped out, when Lady the Brach° may stand by th' fire and stink.

LEAR: A pestilent gall° to me.

FOOL: Sirrah, I'll teach thee a speech.   130

LEAR: Do.

FOOL: Mark it, nuncle.

Have more than thou showest,
Speak less than thou knowest,
Lend less than thou owest,°   135
Ride more than thou goest,°
Learn more than thou trowest,°
Set less than thou throwest;°
Leave thy drink and thy whore,
And keep in-a-door,   140

67 **dependants** servants   73 **rememb'rest** remindest
74 **conception** idea   74–75 **faint neglect** i.e., "weary negligence" (I.III.13)   76 **mine . . . curiosity** suspicious concern for my own dignity   76–77 **very pretense** actual intention   92 **bandy** exchange insolently (metaphor from tennis)   94 **strucken** struck   95–96 **football** a low game played by idle boys, to the scandal of sensible men   100 **differences** of rank   101 **lubber's** lout's   102 **Go to** expression of derisive incredulity; **Have you wisdom** i.e., Do you know what's good for you?; **So** good

104 **earnest** money for services rendered   106 **coxcomb** professional fool's cap, shaped like a coxcomb   109 **you were best** you had better   113 **an if**   113–114 **smile . . . sits** ingratiate yourself with those in power   115–116 **banished** alienated (by making them independent)   119 **nuncle** contraction of "mine uncle"   122 **living** property   127 **Brach** bitch   129 **gall** sore   135 **owest** ownest   136 **goest** walkest   137 **trowest** knowest   138 **Set . . . throwest** bet less than you play for (get odds from your opponent)

And thou shalt have more
Than two tens to a score.°

KENT: This is nothing, Fool.

FOOL: Then 'tis like the breath of an
145 unfee'd° lawyer — you gave me nothing for't.
Can you make no use of nothing, nuncle?

LEAR: Why, no, boy. Nothing can be made
out of nothing.

FOOL [to KENT]: Prithee tell him, so much
150 the rent of his land comes to; he will not
believe a fool.

LEAR: A bitter° fool.

FOOL: Dost thou know the difference, my
boy, between a bitter fool and a sweet one?

155 LEAR: No, lad; teach me.

FOOL:

That lord that counseled thee
    To give away thy land,
Come place him here by me,
    Do thou for him stand.
160 The sweet and bitter fool
    Will presently appear;
The one in motley° here,
    The other found out° there.°

LEAR: Dost thou call me fool, boy?

165 FOOL: All thy other titles thou hast given
away; that thou wast born with.

KENT: This is not altogether fool, my lord.

FOOL: No, faith; lords and great men will
not let me.° If I had a monopoly° out, they
170 would have part on't. And ladies too, they will
not let me have all the fool to myself; they'll
be snatching. Nuncle, give me an egg, and I'll
give thee two crowns.

LEAR: What two crowns shall they be?

175 FOOL: Why, after I have cut the egg i' th'
middle and eat up the meat, the two crowns of
the egg. When thou clovest thy crown i' th'
middle and gav'st away both parts, thou bor'st
thine ass on thy back o'er the dirt.° Thou hadst
180 little wit in thy bald crown when thou gav'st

thy golden one away. If I speak like myself° in
this, let him be whipped° that first finds it so.
[Singing.]

Fools had ne'er less grace in a year,
    For wise men are grown foppish,
And know not how their wits to wear,   185
    Their manners are so apish.°

LEAR: When were you wont to be so full of
songs, sirrah?

FOOL: I have used° it, nuncle, e'er since
thou mad'st thy daughters thy mothers; for   190
when thou gav'st them the rod, and put'st
down thine own breeches, [Singing.]

Then they for sudden joy did weep,
    And I for sorrow sung,
That such a king should play bo-peep°   195
    And go the fools among.

Prithee, nuncle, keep a schoolmaster that can
teach thy Fool to lie. I would fain learn to
lie.

LEAR: And° you lie, sirrah, we'll have you
whipped.   200

FOOL: I marvel what kin thou and thy
daughters are. They'll have me whipped for
speaking true; thou'lt have me whipped for
lying; and sometimes I am whipped for holding my peace. I had rather be any kind o'   205
thing than a fool, and yet I would not be thee,
nuncle: thou hast pared thy wit o' both sides
and left nothing i' th' middle. Here comes one
o' the parings.

(Enter GONERIL.)

LEAR: How now, daughter? What makes   210
that frontlet° on? Methinks you are too much
of late i' th' frown.

FOOL: Thou wast a pretty fellow when thou
hadst no need to care for her frowning. Now
thou art an O without a figure.° I am better   215
than thou art now: I am a fool, thou art
nothing. [To GONERIL.] Yes, forsooth, I will

141–142 have . . . score i.e., come away with more
than you had (two tens, or twenty shillings, make a
score, or one pound)   145 unfee'd unpaid for   152
bitter satirical   162 motley the drab costume of the
professional jester   163 found out revealed; there
the Fool points at Lear, as a fool in the grain   169
let me i.e., let me have all the folly to myself; monop-
oly James I gave great scandal by granting to his
"snatching" courtiers royal patents to deal exclusively
in some commodity   178–179 bor'st . . . dirt like the
foolish and unnatural countryman in Aesop's fable

181 like myself like a fool   182 let . . . whipped
i.e., let the man be whipped for a fool who thinks my
true saying to be foolish   183–186 Fools . . . apish
i.e., fools were never in less favor than now, and the
reason is that wise men, turning foolish, and not
knowing how to use their intelligence, imitate the
professional fools and so make them unnecessary
189 used practiced   195 play bo-peep (1) act like
a child (2) blind himself   199 And if   211 frontlet
frown (literally, ornamental band)   215 figure digit,
to give value to the cipher (Lear is a nought)

hold my tongue. So your face bids me, though
you say nothing. Mum, mum,

220   He that keeps nor crust nor crum,°
    Weary of all, shall want° some.

[*Pointing to* LEAR.]

That's a shealed peascod.°
  GONERIL:
Not only, sir, this your all-licensed° Fool,
But other° of your insolent retinue
225 Do hourly carp and quarrel, breaking forth
In rank° and not-to-be-endurèd riots. Sir,
I had thought by making this well known unto
    you
To have found a safe° redress, but now grow
    fearful,
By what yourself too late° have spoke and
    done,
230 That you protect this course, and put it on
By your allowance;° which if you should, the
    fault
Would not 'scape censure, nor the redresses
    sleep,°
Which, in the tender of° a wholesome weal,°
Might in their working do you that offense,
235 Which else were shame, that then necessity
Will call discreet proceeding.°
  FOOL: For you know, nuncle,

    The hedge-sparrow fed the cuckoo° so long
    That it had it head bit off by it° young.

240 So out went the candle, and we were left
darkling.°
  LEAR: Are you our daughter?
  GONERIL:
Come, sir,
I would you would make use of your good
    wisdom
Whereof I know you are fraught° and put
245   away

These dispositions° which of late transport you
From what you rightly are.
  FOOL: May not an ass know when the cart
draws the horse? Whoop, Jug,° I love thee!
  LEAR:
Does any here know me? This is not Lear.   250
Does Lear walk thus? Speak thus? Where are
    his eyes?
Either his notion° weakens, or his discernings°
Are lethargied° — Ha! Waking? 'Tis not so.
Who is it that can tell me who I am?
  FOOL: Lear's shadow.   255
  LEAR: I would learn that; for, by the marks
of sovereignty,° knowledge, and reason, I
should be false° persuaded I had daughters.
  FOOL: Which° they will make an obedient
father.   260
  LEAR: Your name, fair gentlewoman?
  GONERIL:
This admiration,° sir, is much o' th' savor°
Of other your° new pranks. I do beseech you
To understand my purposes aright.
As you are old and reverend, should be wise.   265
Here do you keep a hundred knights and
    squires,
Men so disordered, so deboshed,° and bold,
That this our court, infected with their man-
    ners,
Shows° like a riotous inn. Epicurism° and lust
Makes it more like a tavern or a brothel   270
Than a graced° palace. The shame itself doth
    speak
For instant remedy. Be then desired°
By her, that else will take the thing she begs,
A little to disquantity your train,°
And the remainders° that shall still depend,°   275
To be such men as may besort° your age,
Which know themselves, and you.
  LEAR: Darkness and devils!
Saddle my horses; call my train together.

---

220 **crum** soft bread inside the loaf   221 **want** lack
222 **shealed peascod** empty pea pod   223 **all-licensed** privileged to take any liberties   224 **other** others   226 **rank** gross   228 **safe** sure   229 **too late** lately   230–231 **put . . . allowance** promote it by your approval   232 **redresses sleep** correction fail to follow   233 **tender of** desire for; **weal** state   234–236 **Might . . . proceeding** as I apply it, the correction might humiliate you; but the need to take action cancels what would otherwise be unfilial conduct in me   238 **cuckoo** which lays its eggs in the nests of other birds   239 **it** its   241 **darkling** in the dark   245 **fraught** endowed

246 **dispositions** moods   249 **Jug** Joan (a quotation from a popular song?)   252 **notion** understanding; **discernings** faculties   253 **lethargied** paralyzed 256–257 **marks of sovereignty** i.e., tokens that Lear is king, and hence father to his daughters   258 **false** falsely   259 **Which** whom (Lear)   262 **admiration** (affected) wonderment; **is . . . savor** smacks much   263 **other your** others of your   267 **deboshed** debauched   269 **Shows** appears; **Epicurism** riotous living   271 **graced** dignified   272 **desired** requested   274 **disquantity your train** reduce the number of your dependents   275 **remainders** those who remain; **depend** attend on you   276 **besort** befit

Degenerate° bastard, I'll not trouble thee:
280 Yet have I left a daughter.

GONERIL:
You strike my people, and your disordered rabble
Make servants of their betters.

(*Enter* ALBANY.)

LEAR:
Woe, that too late repents. O, sir, are you come?
Is it your will? Speak, sir. Prepare my horses.
285 Ingratitude! thou marble-hearted fiend,
More hideous when thou show'st thee in a child
Than the sea-monster.

ALBANY: Pray, sir, be patient.

LEAR:
Detested kite,° thou liest.
My train are men of choice and rarest parts,°
290 That all particulars of duty know,
And, in the most exact regard,° support
The worships° of their name. O most small fault,
How ugly didst thou in Cordelia show!
Which, like an engine,° wrenched my frame of nature
From the fixed place;° drew from my heart all
295 love,
And added to the gall.° O Lear, Lear, Lear!
Beat at this gate that let thy folly in

[*Striking his head.*]

And thy dear judgment out. Go, go, my people.

ALBANY:
My lord, I am guiltless, as I am ignorant
Of what hath moved you.

300 LEAR: It may be so, my lord.
Hear, Nature, hear; dear goddess, hear:
Suspend thy purpose if thou didst intend
To make this creature fruitful.
Into her womb convey sterility,
305 Dry up in her the organs of increase,°
And from her derogate° body never spring
A babe to honor her. If she must teem,°

Create her child of spleen,° that it may live
And be a thwart disnatured° torment to her.
Let it stamp wrinkles in her brow of youth,   310
With cadent° tears fret° channels in her cheeks,
Turn all her mother's pains and benefits°
To laughter and contempt, that she may feel
How sharper than a serpent's tooth it is
To have a thankless child. Away, away!   315

(*Exit.*)

ALBANY:
Now, gods that we adore, whereof comes this?

GONERIL:
Never afflict yourself to know the cause,
But let his disposition° have that scope
As° dotage gives it.

(*Enter* LEAR.)

LEAR:
What, fifty of my followers at a clap?°   320
Within a fortnight?

ALBANY: What's the matter, sir?

LEAR:
I'll tell thee. [*To* GONERIL.] Life and death, I am ashamed
That thou hast power to shake my manhood° thus!
That these hot tears, which break from me perforce,°
Should make thee worth them. Blasts and fogs upon thee!   325
Th' untented woundings° of a father's curse
Pierce every sense about thee! Old fond° eyes,
Beweep° this cause again, I'll pluck ye out
And cast you, with the waters that you loose,°
To temper° clay. Yea, is it come to this?   330
Ha! Let it be so. I have another daughter,
Who I am sure is kind and comfortable.°
When she shall hear this of thee, with her nails
She'll flay thy wolvish visage. Thou shalt find

---

279 **Degenerate** unnatural   288 **kite** scavenging bird of prey   289 **parts** accomplishments   291 **exact regard** strict attention to detail   292 **worships** honor   294 **engine** destructive contrivance   294–295 **wrenched...place** i.e., disorders my natural self   296 **gall** bitterness   305 **increase** childbearing   306 **derogate** degraded   307 **teem** conceive

308 **spleen** ill humor   309 **thwart disnatured** perverse unnatural   311 **cadent** falling; **fret** wear   312 **benefits** the mother's beneficent care of her child   318 **disposition** mood   319 **As** that   320 **at a clap** at one stroke   323 **shake my manhood** i.e., with tears   324 **perforce** involuntarily, against my will   326 **untented woundings** wounds too deep to be probed with a tent (a roll of lint)   327 **fond** foolish   328 **Beweep** if you weep over   329 **loose** (1) let loose (2) lose, as of no avail   330 **temper** mix with and soften   332 **comfortable** ready to comfort

That I'll resume the shape° which thou dost
335　think
I have cast off for ever.

　　　　　　　(*Exit* [LEAR, *with* KENT
　　　　　　　and ATTENDANTS].)

GONERIL:　　　　　Do you mark that?
ALBANY:
I cannot be so partial, Goneril,
To the great love I bear you° —
GONERIL:
Pray you, content. What, Oswald, ho!

[*To the* FOOL].

You, sir, more knave than fool, after your
340　master!
　　　FOOL: Nuncle Lear, nuncle Lear, tarry. Take
the Fool° with thee.

　　　A fox, when one has caught her,
　　　And such a daughter,
345　　Should sure to the slaughter,
　　　If my cap would buy a halter.°
　　　So the Fool follows after.°　　(*Exit.*)

GONERIL:
This man hath had good counsel. A hundred
　knights!
'Tis politic° and safe to let him keep
At point° a hundred knights: yes, that on every
350　dream,
Each buzz,° each fancy, each complaint, dis-
　like,
He may enguard° his dotage with their pow'rs
And hold our lives in mercy.° Oswald, I say!
ALBANY:
Well, you may fear too far.
GONERIL:　　　　　Safer than trust too far.
355　Let me still take away the harms I fear,
Not fear still to be taken.° I know his heart.
What he hath uttered I have writ my sister.
If she sustain him and his hundred knights,
When I have showed th' unfitness —

　　　(*Enter* OSWALD.)

　　　　　　　　　How now, Oswald?
360　What, have you writ that letter to my sister?
　　　OSWALD: Ay, madam.

335 **shape** i.e., kingly role　337–338 **I cannot . . .
you** i.e., even though my love inclines me to you,
I must protest　342 **Fool** (1) the Fool himself (2)
the epithet or character of "fool"　346–347 **halter,
after** pronounced "hauter," "auter"　349 **politic**
good policy　350 **At point** armed　351 **buzz**
rumor　352 **enguard** protect　353 **in mercy** at his
mercy　356 **Not . . . taken** rather than remain fearful of being overtaken by them

GONERIL:
Take you some company,° and away to horse.
Inform her full of my particular° fear,
And thereto add such reasons of your own
As may compact° it more. Get you gone,　365
And hasten your return. [*Exit* OSWALD.] No,
　no, my lord,
This milky gentleness and course° of yours,
Though I condemn not,° yet under pardon,
You are much more attasked° for want of
　wisdom
Than praised for harmful mildness.°　370
ALBANY:
How far your eyes may pierce I cannot tell;
Striving to better, oft we mar what's well.
GONERIL: Nay then —
ALBANY: Well, well, th' event.°　(*Exeunt.*)

SCENE V. [*Court before the same.*]

Enter LEAR, KENT, *and* FOOL.

　　LEAR: Go you before to Gloucester with
these letters. Acquaint my daughter no further
with anything you know than comes from her
demand out of the letter.° If your diligence be
not speedy, I shall be there afore you.　5
　　KENT: I will not sleep, my lord, till I have
delivered your letter.　　　　　(*Exit.*)
　　FOOL: If a man's brains were in's heels,
were't° not in danger of kibes?°
　　LEAR: Ay, boy.　10
　　FOOL: Then I prithee be merry. Thy wit
shall not go slipshod.°
　　LEAR: Ha, ha, ha.
　　FOOL: Shalt° see thy other daughter will use
thee kindly;° for though she's as like this as a　15
crab's° like an apple, yet I can tell what I can
tell.
　　LEAR: Why, what canst thou tell, my boy?
　　FOOL: She will taste as like this as a crab

362 **company** escort　363 **particular** own　365 **compact** strengthen　367 **milky . . . course** mild and gentle way (hendiadys)　368 **condemn not** condemn it
not　369 **attasked** taken to task, blamed　370 **harmful mildness** dangerous indulgence　374 **th' event**
i.e., we'll see what happens
I.v.3–4 **than . . . letter** than her reading of the letter
brings her to ask　9 **were't** i.e., the brains; **kibes** chilblains　11–12 **Thy . . . slipshod** Your brains shall
not go in slippers (because you have no brains to be
protected from chilblains)　14 **Shalt** thou shalt　15
kindly (1) affectionately (2) after her kind or nature　16 **crab** crab apple

20 does to a crab. Thou canst tell why one's nose
stands i' th' middle on's° face?

LEAR: No.

FOOL: Why, to keep one's eyes of° either
side's nose, that what a man cannot smell out,
25 he may spy into.

LEAR: I did her wrong.

FOOL: Canst tell how an oyster makes his
shell?

LEAR: No.

30 FOOL: Nor I neither; but I can tell why a
snail has a house.

LEAR: Why?

FOOL: Why, to put's head in; not to give it
away to his daughters, and leave his horns°
35 without a case.

LEAR: I will forget my nature.° So kind a
father! Be my horses ready?

FOOL: Thy asses are gone about 'em. The
reason why the seven stars° are no moe° than
40 seven is a pretty° reason.

LEAR: Because they are not eight.

FOOL: Yes indeed. Thou wouldst make a
good fool.

LEAR: To take't again perforce!° Monster
45 ingratitude!

FOOL: If thou wert my fool, nuncle, I'd have
thee beaten for being old before thy time.

LEAR: How's that?

FOOL: Thou shouldst not have been old till
50 thou hadst been wise.

LEAR:
O, let me not be mad, not mad, sweet heaven!
Keep me in temper;° I would not be mad!

[*Enter* GENTLEMAN.]

How now, are the horses ready?

GENTLEMAN: Ready, my lord.

55 LEAR: Come, boy.

FOOL:
She that's a maid now, and laughs at my
     departure,
Shall not be a maid long, unless things be cut
     shorter.°

                   (*Exeunt.*)

ACT II

SCENE I. [*The Earl of* GLOUCESTER's castle.]

Enter EDMUND *and* CURAN, *severally.*°

EDMUND: Save° thee, Curan.

CURAN: And you, sir. I have been with your
father, and given him notice that the Duke of
Cornwall and Regan his duchess will be here
with him this night.   5

EDMUND: How comes that?

CURAN: Nay, I know not. You have heard of
the news abroad? I mean the whispered ones,
for they are yet but ear-kissing arguments.°

EDMUND: Not I. Pray you, what are they?   10

CURAN: Have you heard of no likely° wars
toward,° 'twixt the Dukes of Cornwall and
Albany?

EDMUND: Not a word.

CURAN: You may do, then, in time. Fare you   15
well, sir.   (*Exit.*)

EDMUND:
The duke be here tonight? The better!° best!
This weaves itself perforce° into my business.
My father hath set guard to take my brother,
And I have one thing of a queasy question°   20
Which I must act. Briefness° and Fortune,
     work!
Brother, a word; descend. Brother, I say!

(*Enter* EDGAR.)

My father watches. O sir, fly this place.
Intelligence° is given where you are hid.
You have now the good advantage of the
     night.   25
Have you not spoken 'gainst the Duke of
     Cornwall?
He's coming hither, now i' th' night, i' th'
     haste,°
And Regan with him. Have you nothing said

---

21 **on's** of his   23 **of** on   34 **horns** (1) snail's horns
(2) cuckold's horns   36 **nature** paternal instincts
39 **seven stars** the Pleiades; **moe** more   40 **pretty**
apt   44 **To ... perforce** (1) of Goneril, who has
forcibly taken away Lear's privileges; or (2) of Lear,
who meditates a forcible resumption of authority
52 **in temper** sane   56–57 **She ... shorter** The
maid who laughs, missing the tragic implications of
this quarrel, will not have sense enough to preserve
her virginity ("things" = penises)

II.1.s.d. **severally** separately (from different entrances
onstage)   1 **Save** God save   9 **ear-kissing arguments** subjects whispered in the ear   11 **likely** probable   12 **toward** impending   17 **The better** So
much the better   18 **perforce** necessarily   20 **of ...
question** that requires delicate handling (to be
"queasy" is to be on the point of vomiting)   21
Briefness speed   24 **Intelligence** information   27 **i'
th' haste** in great haste

Upon his party° 'gainst the Duke of Albany?
Advise yourself.°
30   EDGAR: I am sure on't,° not a word.
EDMUND:
I hear my father coming. Pardon me:
In cunning° I must draw my sword upon you.
Draw, seem to defend yourself; now quit you°
    well.
Yield! Come before my father! Light ho,
    here!
35 Fly, brother. Torches, torches! — So farewell.
                (*Exit* EDGAR.)
Some blood drawn on me would beget opin-
    ion°

[*Wounds his arm.*]

Of my more fierce endeavor. I have seen
    drunkards
Do more than this in sport. Father, father!
Stop, stop! No help?

    (*Enter* GLOUCESTER, *and* SERVANTS *with
    torches.*)

GLOUCESTER:
40 Now, Edmund, where's the villain?
EDMUND:
Here stood he in the dark, his sharp sword
    out,
Mumbling of wicked charms, conjuring the
    moon
To stand auspicious mistress.
GLOUCESTER: But where is he?
EDMUND:
Look, sir, I bleed.
45 GLOUCESTER: Where is the villain, Edmund?
EDMUND:
Fled this way, sir, when by no means he
    could —
GLOUCESTER:
Pursue him, ho! Go after. [*Exeunt some
SERVANTS.*] By no means what?
EDMUND:
Persuade me to the murder of your lordship;
But that I told him the revenging gods
50 'Gainst parricides did all the thunder bend;°
Spoke with how manifold and strong a bond
The child was bound to th' father. Sir, in fine,°
Seeing how loathly opposite° I stood

To his unnatural purpose, in fell° motion°
With his preparèd sword he charges home   55
My unprovided° body, latched° mine arm;
But when he saw my best alarumed° spirits
Bold in the quarrel's right,° roused to th'
    encounter,
Or whether gasted° by the noise I made,
Full suddenly he fled.
GLOUCESTER: Let him fly far.   60
Not in this land shall he remain uncaught;
And found — dispatch.° The noble duke my
    master,
My worthy arch° and patron, comes tonight.
By his authority I will proclaim it,
That he which finds him shall deserve our
    thanks,   65
Bringing the murderous coward to the stake.
He that conceals him, death.°
EDMUND:
When I dissuaded him from his intent,
And found him pight° to do it, with curst°
    speech
I threatened to discover° him. He replied,   70
"Thou unpossessing° bastard, dost thou think,
If I would stand against thee, would the
    reposal°
Of any trust, virtue, or worth in thee
Make thy words faithed?° No. What I should
    deny —
As this I would, ay, though thou didst produce   75
My very character° — I'd turn it all
To thy suggestion,° plot, and damnèd prac-
    tice.°
And thou must make a dullard of the world,°
If they not thought° the profits of my death
Were very pregnant° and potential spirits°   80
To make thee seek it."
GLOUCESTER: O strange and fastened° villain!
Would he deny his letter, said he? I never got°
    him.

54 **fell** deadly; **motion** thrust (a term from fenc-ing)   56 **unprovided** unprotected; **latched** wounded (lanced)   57 **best alarumed** wholly aroused   58 **Bold . . . right** confident in the rightness of my cause   59 **gasted** struck aghast   62 **dispatch** i.e., he will be killed   63 **arch** chief   67 **death** the same ellipti-cal form that characterizes "dispatch," line 62   69 **pight** determined; **curst** angry   70 **discover** expose   71 **unpossessing** beggarly (landless)   72 **reposal** placing   74 **faithed** believed   76 **character** hand-writing   77 **suggestion** instigation; **practice** device   78 **make . . . world** think everyone stupid   79 **not thought** did not think   80 **pregnant** teeming with incitement; **potential spirits** powerful evil spirits   81 **fastened** hardened   82 **got** begot

29 **Upon his party** censuring his enmity   30 **Ad-vise yourself** Reflect; **on't** of it   32 **In cunning** as a pretense   33 **quit you** acquaint yourself   36 **beget opinion** create the impression   50 **bend** aim   52 **in fine** finally   53 **loathly opposite** bitterly opposed

(*Tucket*° *within.*)

Hark, the duke's trumpets. I know not why he
 comes.
All ports° I'll bar; the villain shall not 'scape;
The duke must grant me that. Besides, his
85 picture
I will send far and near, that all the kingdom
May have due note of him; and of my land,
Loyal and natural° boy, I'll work the means
To make thee capable.°

(*Enter* CORNWALL, REGAN, *and* ATTEN-
DANTS.)

CORNWALL:
How now, my noble friend! Since I came
90 hither,
Which I can call but now, I have heard
 strange news.
 REGAN:
If it be true, all vengeance comes too short
Which can pursue th' offender. How dost, my
 lord?
 GLOUCESTER:
O madam, my old heart is cracked, it's
 cracked.
 REGAN:
95 What, did my father's godson seek your life?
He whom my father named, your Edgar?
 GLOUCESTER:
O lady, lady, shame would have it hid.
 REGAN:
Was he not companion with the riotous
 knights
That tended upon my father?
 GLOUCESTER:
100 I know not, madam. 'Tis too bad, too bad.
 EDMUND:
Yes, madam, he was of that consort.°
 REGAN:
No marvel then, though he were ill affected.°
'Tis they have put° him on the old man's
 death,
To have th' expense and waste° of his reve-
 nues.
105 I have this present evening from my sister
Been well informed of them, and with such
 cautions

That, if they come to sojourn at my house,
I'll not be there.
 CORNWALL: Nor I, assure thee, Regan.
Edmund, I hear that you have shown your
 father
A childlike° office.
 EDMUND: It was my duty, sir. 110
 GLOUCESTER:
He did bewray his practice,° and received
This hurt you see, striving to apprehend him.
 CORNWALL:
Is he pursued?
 GLOUCESTER:
     Ay, my good lord.
 CORNWALL:
If he be taken, he shall never more
Be feared of doing° harm. Make your own
 purpose, 115
How in my strength you please.° For you,
 Edmund,
Whose virtue and obedience° doth this instant
So much commend itself, you shall be ours.
Natures of such deep trust we shall much
 need;
You we first seize on.
 EDMUND: I shall serve you, sir, 120
Truly, however else.
 GLOUCESTER: For him I thank your grace.
 CORNWALL:
You know not why we came to visit you?
 REGAN:
Thus out of season, threading dark eyed night.
Occasions, noble Gloucester, of some prize,°
Wherein we must have use of your advice. 125
Our father he hath writ, so hath our sister,
Of differences,° which° I best thought it fit
To answer from° our home. The several mes-
 sengers
From hence attend dispatch.° Our good old
 friend,
Lay comforts to your bosom,° and bestow 130
Your needful° counsel to our businesses,
Which craves the instant use.°

82 s.d. **Tucket** Cornwall's special trumpet call 84
ports exits, of whatever sort 88 **natural** (1) kind
(filial) (2) illegitimate 89 **capable** able to inherit
101 **consort** company 102 **ill affected** disposed to
evil 103 **put** set 104 **expense and waste** squander-
ing

110 **childlike** filial 111 **bewray his practice** disclose his plot 115 **of doing** because he might do
115–116 **Make ... please** Use my power freely, in
carrying out your plans for his capture 117 **virtue
and obedience** virtuous obedience 124 **prize** importance 127 **differences** quarrels; **which** referring
not to "differences," but to the letter Lear has written
128 **from** away from 129 **attend dispatch** are
waiting to be sent off 130 **Lay ... bosom** console
yourself (about Edgar's supposed treason) 131
needful needed 132 **craves ... use** demands immediate transaction

GLOUCESTER: I serve you, madam.
Your graces are right welcome.
                              (*Exeunt. Flourish.*)

SCENE II. [*Before* GLOUCESTER'*s castle.*]

Enter KENT *and* OSWALD, *severally.*

OSWALD: Good dawning° to thee, friend. Art
of this house?°
KENT: Ay.
OSWALD: Where may we set our horses?
5 KENT: I' th' mire.
OSWALD: Prithee, if thou lov'st me, tell me.
KENT: I love thee not.
OSWALD: Why then, I care not for thee.
KENT: If I had thee in Lipsbury Pinfold,° I
10 would make thee care for me.
OSWALD: Why dost thou use me thus? I
know thee not.
KENT: Fellow, I know thee.
OSWALD: What dost thou know me for?
15 KENT: A knave, a rascal, an eater of broken
meats;° a base, proud, shallow, beggarly, three-
suited,° hundred-pound,° filthy worsted-stock-
ing° knave; a lily-livered, action-taking,° whoreson, glass-gazing,° superserviceable,° finical°
20 rogue; one-trunk-inheriting° slave; one that
wouldst be a bawd in way of good service,° and
art nothing but the composition° of a knave,
beggar, coward, pander, and the son and heir
of a mongrel bitch; one whom I will beat into
25 clamorous whining if thou deniest the least
syllable of thy addition.°
OSWALD: Why, what a monstrous fellow art
thou, thus to rail on one that is neither known
of thee nor knows thee!
30 KENT: What a brazen-faced varlet art thou

to deny thou knowest me! Is it two days since
I tripped up thy heels and beat thee before the
king? [*Drawing his sword.*] Draw, you rogue,
for though it be night, yet the moon shines.
I'll make a sop o' th' moonshine° of you. You 35
whoreson cullionly barbermonger,° draw!
OSWALD: Away, I have nothing to do with
thee.
KENT: Draw, you rascal. You come with
letters against the king, and take Vanity the 40
puppet's° part against the royalty of her father.
Draw, you rogue, or I'll so carbonado° your
shanks. Draw, you rascal. Come your ways!°
OSWALD: Help, ho! Murder! Help!
KENT: Strike, you slave! Stand, rogue! 45
Stand, you neat° slave! Strike!

[*Beating him.*]

OSWALD: Help, ho! Murder, murder!

(*Enter* EDMUND, *with his rapier drawn,*
CORNWALL, REGAN, GLOUCESTER, SERVANTS.)

EDMUND: How now? What's the matter?
Part!
KENT: With you,° goodman boy,° if you 50
please! Come, I'll flesh° ye, come on, young
master.
GLOUCESTER: Weapons? Arms? What's the
matter here?
CORNWALL: Keep peace, upon your lives. He 55
dies that strikes again. What is the matter?
REGAN: The messengers from our sister and
the king.
CORNWALL: What is your difference?° Speak.
OSWALD: I am scarce in breath, my lord. 60
KENT: No marvel, you have so bestirred°
your valor. You cowardly rascal, nature dis-
claims in thee.° A tailor made thee.°

II.ii.1 **dawning** dawn is impending, but not yet arrived   1–2 **Art . . . house** Do you live here?   9 **Lipsbury Pinfold** a pound or pen in which strayed animals
are enclosed ("Lipsbury" may denote a particular
place, or may be slang for "between my teeth")   15–
16 **broken meats** scraps of food   16–17 **three-suited**
the wardrobe permitted to a servant or "knave"   17
hundred-pound the extent of Oswald's wealth, and
thus a sneer at his aspiring to gentility   17–18
worsted-stocking worn by servants   18 **action-taking**
one who refuses a fight and goes to law instead   19
glass-gazing conceited   19 **superserviceable** syco-
phantic, serving without principle; **finical** overfastid-
ious   20 **one-trunk-inheriting** possessing only a
trunkful of goods   21 **bawd . . . service** pimp, to
please his master   22 **composition** compound   26
addition titles

35 **sop . . . moonshine** i.e., Oswald will admit the
moonlight, and so sop it up, through the open wounds
Kent is preparing to give him   36 **cullionly barbermonger** base patron of hairdressers (effeminate man)
40–41 **Vanity the puppet's** Goneril, here identified
with one of the personified characters in the morality
plays, which were sometimes put on as puppet shows
42 **carbonado** cut across, like a piece of meat before
cooking   43 **Come your ways** Get along!   46 **neat**
(1) foppish (2) unmixed, as in "neat wine"   50
With you i.e., the quarrel is with you; **goodman boy**
young man (peasants are "goodmen"; "boy" is a
term of contempt)   51 **flesh** introduce to blood
(term from hunting)   59 **difference** quarrel   61
bestirred exercised   62–63 **nature . . . thee** nature
renounces any part in you   63 **A tailor made thee**
from the proverb "The tailor makes the man"

CORNWALL: Thou art a strange fellow. A
65 tailor make a man?
KENT: A tailor, sir. A stonecutter or a
painter could not have made him so ill, though
they had been but two years o' th' trade.
CORNWALL:
Speak yet, how grew your quarrel?
70 OSWALD: This ancient ruffian, sir, whose life
I have spared at suit of° his gray beard —
KENT: Thou whoreson zed,° thou unnecessary letter! My lord, if you will give me leave,
I will tread this unbolted° villain into mortar
75 and daub the wall of a jakes° with him. Spare
my gray beard, you wagtail!°
CORNWALL: Peace, sirrah!
You beastly° knave, know you no reverence?
KENT:
Yes, sir, but anger hath a privilege.
CORNWALL:
80 Why art thou angry?
KENT:
That such a slave as this should wear a sword,
Who wears no honesty. Such smiling rogues as
these,
Like rats, oft bite the holy cords° atwain
Which are too intrince° t' unloose; smooth°
every passion
85 That in the natures of their lords rebel,
Being oil to fire, snow to the colder moods;
Renege,° affirm, and turn their halcyon beaks°
With every gale and vary° of their masters,
Knowing naught, like dogs, but following.
90 A plague upon your epileptic° visage!
Smile you° my speeches, as I were a fool?
Goose, if I had you upon Sarum Plain,°
I'd drive ye cackling home to Camelot.°

CORNWALL:
What, art thou mad, old fellow?
GLOUCESTER:
How fell you out? Say that.   95
KENT:
No contraries° hold more antipathy
Than I and such a knave.
CORNWALL:
Why dost thou call him knave? What is his
fault?
KENT:
His countenance likes° me not.
CORNWALL:
No more perchance does mine, nor his, nor
hers.   100
KENT:
Sir, 'tis my occupation to be plain:
I have seen better faces in my time
Than stands on any shoulder that I see
Before me at this instant.
CORNWALL: This is some fellow
Who, having been praised for bluntness, doth
affect   105
A saucy roughness, and constrains the garb
Quite from his nature.° He cannot flatter, he;
An honest mind and plain, he must speak
truth.
And° they will take it, so; if not, he's plain.
These kind of knaves I know, which in this
plainness   110
Harbor more craft and more corrupter ends
Than twenty silly ducking observants°
That stretch their duties nicely.°
KENT:
Sir, in good faith, in sincere verity,
Under th' allowance° of your great aspect,°   115
Whose influence,° like the wreath of radiant
fire
On flick'ring Phoebus' front° —
CORNWALL: What mean'st by this?
KENT: To go out of my dialect,° which you
discommend so much. I know, sir, I am no
flatterer. He° that beguiled you in a plain   120

---

71 **at suit of** out of pity for   72 **zed** the letter Z,
generally omitted in contemporary dictionaries   74
unbolted unsifted, i.e., altogether a villain   75 **jakes**
privy   76 **wagtail** a bird that bobs its tail up and
down, and thus suggests obsequiousness   78 **beastly**
irrational   83 **holy cords** sacred bonds of affection
(as between husbands and wives, parents and children)   84 **intrince** entangled, intricate; **smooth** appease   87 **Renege** deny; **halcyon beaks** the halcyon
or kingfisher serves here as a type of the opportunist
because, when hung up by the tail or neck, it was
supposed to turn with the wind, like a weathervane
88 **gale and vary** varying gale (hendiadys)   90 **epileptic** distorted by grinning   91 **Smile you** do you
smile at   92 **Sarum Plain** Salisbury Plain   93 **Camelot** the residence of King Arthur (presumably a particular point, now lost, is intended here)

96 **contraries** opposites   99 **likes** pleases   106–107
constrains . . . nature forces the manner of candid speech to be a cloak, not for candor but for
craft   109 **And** if   112 **silly-ducking observants**
ridiculously obsequious attendants   113 **nicely** punctiliously   115 **allowance** approval; **aspect** (1) appearance (2) position of the heavenly bodies   116
influence astrological power   117 **Phoebus' front**
forehead of the sun   118 **dialect** customary manner
of speaking   120 **He** i.e., the sort of candid-crafty
man Cornwall has been describing

accent was a plain knave, which, for my part, I
will not be, though I should win your displea-
sure to entreat me to't.°
CORNWALL:
What was th' offense you gave him?
OSWALD:
125 I never gave him any.
It pleased the king his master very late°
To strike at me, upon his misconstruction;°
When he, compact,° and flattering his displea-
sure,
Tripped me behind; being down, insulted,
railed,
130 And put upon him such a deal of man°
That worthied him,° got praises of the king
For him attempting who was self-subdued;°
And, in the fleshment° of this dread exploit,
Drew on me here again.
    KENT: None of these rogues and cowards
But Ajax is their fool.°
135 CORNWALL: Fetch forth the stocks!
You stubborn° ancient knave, you reverent°
braggart,
We'll teach you.
    KENT: Sir, I am too old to learn.
Call not your stocks for me, I serve the king,
On whose employment I was sent to you.
You shall do small respect, show too bold
140 malice
Against the grace and person° of my master,
Stocking his messenger.
CORNWALL:
Fetch forth the stocks. As I have life and
honor,
There shall he sit till noon.
    REGAN:
Till noon? Till night, my lord, and all night
145 too.

KENT:
Why, madam, if I were your father's dog,
You should not use me so.
    REGAN: Sir, being his knave, I will.
CORNWALL:
This is a fellow of the selfsame color°
Our sister speaks of. Come, bring away° the
stocks.

(*Stocks brought out.*)

GLOUCESTER:
Let me beseech your grace not to do so.   150
His fault is much, and the good king his
master
Will check° him for't. Your purposed° low
correction
Is such as basest and contemnèd'st° wretches
For pilf'rings and most common trespasses
Are punished with.   155
The king his master needs must take it ill
That he, so slightly valued in° his messenger,
Should have him thus restrained.
    CORNWALL: I'll answer° that.
    REGAN:
My sister may receive it much more worse,
To have her gentleman abused, assaulted,   160
For following her affairs. Put in his legs.

[KENT *is put in the stocks.*]

Come, my good lord, away!
    [*Exeunt all but* GLOUCESTER *and* KENT.]
GLOUCESTER:
I am sorry for thee, friend. 'Tis the duke's
pleasure,
Whose disposition° all the world well knows
Will not be rubbed° nor stopped. I'll entreat
for thee.   165
    KENT:
Pray do not, sir. I have watched° and traveled
hard.
Some time I shall sleep out, the rest I'll whistle.
A good man's fortune may grow out at heels.°
Give° you good morrow.
GLOUCESTER:
The duke's to blame in this. 'Twill be ill
taken.°   (*Exit.*)   170

122–123 **though . . . to't** even if I were to succeed in
bringing your graceless person ("displeasure" personified, and in lieu of the expected form, "your grace")
to beg me to be a plain knave   126 **very late** recently   127 **misconstruction** misunderstanding   128
compact in league with the king   130 **put . . . man**
pretended such manly behavior   131 **worthied him**
made him seem heroic   132 **For . . . self-subdued**
for attacking a man (Oswald) who offered no resistance   133 **fleshment** the bloodthirstiness excited
by his first success or "fleshing"   134–135 **None . . .
fool** i.e., cowardly rogues like Oswald always impose
on fools like Cornwall (who is likened to Ajax: [1]
the braggart Greek-warrior [2] a jakes or privy)   136
stubborn rude; **reverent** old   141 **grace and person**
i.e., Lear as sovereign and in his personal character

148 **color** kind   149 **away** out   152 **check** correct;
purposed intended   153 **contemnèd'st** most despised
157 **slightly valued in** little honored in the person of
158 **answer** answer for   164 **disposition** inclination
165 **rubbed** diverted (metaphor from the game of
bowls)   166 **watched** gone without sleep   168 **A
. . . heels** Even a good man may have bad fortune
169 **Give** God give   170 **taken** received

KENT:
Good king, that must approve° the common
     saw,°
Thou out of heaven's benediction com'st
To the warm sun.°
Approach, thou beacon to this under globe,°
175 That by thy comfortable° beams I may
Peruse this letter. Nothing almost sees miracles
But misery.° I know 'tis from Cordelia,
Who hath most fortunately been informed
Of my obscurèd° course. And shall find time
180 From this enormous state, seeking to give
Losses their remedies.° All weary and o'er-
     watched,
Take vantage,° heavy eyes, not to behold
This shameful lodging. Fortune, good night;
Smile once more, turn thy wheel.°

     (Sleeps.)

          [SCENE III. A wood.]

Enter EDGAR.

EDGAR:
I heard myself proclaimed,
And by the happy° hollow of a tree
Escaped the hunt. No port is free, no place
That guard and most unusual vigilance
Does not attend my taking.° Whiles I may
5   'scape,
I will preserve myself; and am bethought°
To take the basest and most poorest shape
That ever penury, in contempt of man,
Brought near to beast;° my face I'll grime with
     filth,
10 Blanket° my loins, elf° all my hairs in knots,
And with presented° nakedness outface°

171 **approve** confirm; **saw** proverb   172–173 **Thou
. . . sun** i.e., Lear goes from better to worse, from
heaven's blessing or shelter to lack of shelter   174
beacon . . . globe i.e., the sun, whose rising Kent anticipates   175 **comfortable** comforting   176–177
Nothing . . . misery i.e., True perception belongs only
to the wretched   179 **obscurèd** disguised   179–181
shall . . . remedies a possible reading: Cordelia, away
from this monstrous state of things, will find occasion
to right the wrongs we suffer   182 **vantage** advantage
(of sleep)   184 **turn thy wheel** i.e., so that Kent,
who is at the bottom, may climb upward
II.III.2 **happy** lucky   5 **attend my taking** watch to
capture me   6 **am bethought** have decided   8–9
penury . . . beast poverty, to show how contemptible
man is, reduced to the level of a beast   10 **Blanket**
cover only with a blanket; **elf** tangle (into "elflocks,"
supposed to be caused by elves)   11 **presented** the
show of; **outface** brave

The winds and persecutions of the sky.
The country gives me proof° and precedent
Of Bedlam° beggars, who, with roaring voices,
Strike° in their numbed and mortified° bare
     arms   15
Pins, wooden pricks,° nails, sprigs of rosemary;
And with this horrible object° from low° farms,
Poor pelting° villages, sheepcotes, and mills,
Sometimes with lunatic bans,° sometime with
     prayers,
Enforce their charity. Poor Turlygod, Poor
     Tom,°   20
That's something yet: Edgar I nothing am.°
                                            (Exit.)

[SCENE IV. Before GLOUCESTER's castle. KENT
               in the stocks.]

Enter LEAR, FOOL, and GENTLEMAN.

LEAR:
'Tis strange that they should so depart from
     home,
And not send back my messenger.
     GENTLEMAN: As I learned,
The night before there was no purpose° in
     them
Of this remove.°
     KENT: Hail to thee, noble master.
     LEAR: Ha!   5
Mak'st thou this shame thy pastime?°
     KENT: No, my lord.
FOOL: Ha, ha, he wears cruel° garters. Horses
are tied by the heads, dogs and bears by th'
neck, monkeys by th' loins, and men by th'
legs. When a man's overlusty at legs,° then   10
he wears wooden netherstocks.°
     LEAR:
What's he that hath so much thy place
     mistook
To set thee here?
     KENT: It is both he and she,
Your son and daughter.

13 **proof** example   14 **Bedlam** see I.II.155–156   15
Strike stick; **mortified** not alive to pain   16 **pricks**
skewers   17 **object** spectacle; **low** humble   18 **pelting** paltry   19 **bans** curses   20 **Poor . . . Tom** Edgar
recites the names a Bedlam beggar gives himself   21
That's . . . am There's a chance for me in that I am
no longer known for myself
II.IV.3 **purpose** intention   4 **remove** removal   6
Mak'st . . . pastime Are you doing this to amuse yourself?   7 **cruel** (1) painful (2) "crewel," a worsted yarn
used in garters   10 **overlusty at legs** (1) a vagabond
(2) sexually promiscuous (?)   11 **netherstocks** stockings (as opposed to knee breeches, or upperstocks)

15   LEAR: No.
      KENT: Yes.
      LEAR: No, I say.
      KENT: I say yea.
      LEAR: No, no, they would not.
20   KENT: Yes, they have.
      LEAR:
      By Jupiter, I swear no!
      KENT:
      By Juno, I swear ay!
          LEAR: They durst not do't;
      They could not, would not do't. 'Tis worse
          than murder
      To do upon respect° such violent outrage.
25   Resolve° me with all modest° haste which way
      Thou mightst deserve or they impose this
          usage,
      Coming from us.
          KENT: My lord, when at their home
      I did commend° your highness' letters to them,
      Ere I was risen from the place that showed
30   My duty kneeling, came there a reeking post,°
      Stewed° in his haste, half breathless, panting
          forth
      From Goneril his mistress salutations,
      Delivered letters, spite of intermission,°
      Which presently° they read; on° whose con-
          tents
      They summoned up their meiny,° straight took
35   horse,
      Commanded me to follow and attend
      The leisure of their answer, gave me cold
          looks,
      And meeting here the other messenger,
      Whose welcome I perceived had poisoned
          mine,
40   Being the very fellow which of late
      Displayed° so saucily against your highness,
      Having more man than wit° about me, drew;
      He raised° the house, with loud and coward
          cries.
      Your son and daughter found this trespass
          worth°
45   The shame which here it suffers.

---

24 **upon respect** (1) on the respect due to the king
(2) deliberately   25 **Resolve** inform; **modest** becoming   28 **commend** deliver   30 **reeking post** sweating
messenger   31 **stewed** steaming   33 **spite of intermission** in spite of the interrupting of my business
34 **presently** at once; **on** on the strength of   35
meiny retinue   41 **Displayed** showed off   42 **more
... wit** more manhood than sense   43 **raised** aroused
44 **worth** deserving

      FOOL: Winter's not gone yet, if the wild
      geese fly that way.°

          Fathers that wear rags
              Do make their children blind,°
          But fathers that bear bags°   50
              Shall see their children kind.
          Fortune, that arrant whore,
              Ne'er turns the key° to th' poor.

      But for all this, thou shalt have as many
      dolors° for thy daughters as thou canst tell° in   55
      a year.
          LEAR:
      O, how this mother swells up toward my
          heart!
      Hysterica passio,° down, thou climbing sorrow,
      Thy element's° below. Where is this daughter?
          KENT:
      With the earl, sir, here within.
          LEAR: Follow me not;   60
      Stay here.   (*Exit.*)
          GENTLEMAN:
      Made you no more offense but what you speak
          of?
          KENT: None.
      How chance° the king comes with so small a
          number?
      FOOL: And° thou hadst been set i' th' stocks   65
      for that question, thou'dst well deserved it.
          KENT: Why, Fool?
      FOOL: We'll set thee to school to an ant, to
      teach thee there's no laboring i' th' winter.° All
      that follow their noses are led by their eyes but   70
      blind men, and there's not a nose among
      twenty but can smell him that's stinking.° Let
      go thy hold when a great wheel runs down a
      hill, lest it break thy neck with following. But

46–47 **Winter's ... way** More trouble is to come,
since Cornwall and Regan act so ("geese" is used
contemptuously, as in Kent's quarrel with Oswald,
II.ii.92–93)   49 **blind** i.e., indifferent   50 **bags**
moneybags   53 **turns the key** i.e., opens the door   55
dolors (1) sorrows (2) dollars (English name for Spanish and German coins); **tell** (1) about (2) count   57–
58 **mother ... Hysterica passio** hysteria, causing suffocation or choking   59 **element** proper place   64
How chance how does it happen that   65 **And** if
68–69 **We'll ... winter** in the popular fable the ant,
unlike the improvident grasshopper, anticipates the
winter when none can labor by laying up provisions in
the summer; Lear, trusting foolishly to summer days,
finds himself unprovided for, and unable to provide,
now that "winter" has come   69–72 **All ... stinking**
i.e., all can smell out the decay of Lear's fortunes

75 the great one that goes upward, let him draw
thee after. When a wise man gives thee better
counsel, give me mine again. I would have
none but knaves follow it since a fool gives it.

> That sir, which serves and seeks for gain,
80   And follows but for form,°
> Will pack,° when it begins to rain,
>   And leave thee in the storm.
> But I will tarry; the Fool will stay,
>   And let the wise man fly.
85 The knave turns Fool that runs away,
>   The Fool no knave,° perdy.°

KENT: Where learned you this, Fool?
FOOL: Not i' th' stocks, fool.

(*Enter* LEAR *and* GLOUCESTER.)

LEAR:
Deny° to speak with me? They are sick, they
are weary,
90 They have traveled all the night? Mere fetches,°
The images° of revolt and flying off!°
Fetch me a better answer.
GLOUCESTER: My dear lord,
You know the fiery quality° of the duke,
How unremovable and fixed he is
In his own course.
95 LEAR: Vengeance, plague, death, confusion!
Fiery? What quality? Why, Gloucester,
Gloucester,
I'd speak with the Duke of Cornwall and his
wife.
GLOUCESTER:
Well, my good lord, I have informed them so.
LEAR:
Informed them? Dost thou understand me,
man?
GLOUCESTER:
100 Ay, my good lord.
LEAR:
The king would speak with Cornwall. The
dear father
Would with his daughter speak, commands —
tends° — service.

80 **form** show   81 **pack** be off   85–86 **The . . .
knave** i.e., the faithless man is the true fool, for wisdom requires fidelity; Lear's Fool, who remains faithful, is at least no knave   86 **perdy** by God (French
par Dieu)   89 **Deny** refuse   90 **fetches** subterfuges,
acts of tacking (nautical metaphor)   91 **images** exact likenesses; **flying off** desertion   93 **quality** temperament   102 **tends** attends (i.e., awaits); with,
possibly, an ironic second meaning, "tenders," or
"offers"

Are they informed of this? My breath and
blood!
Fiery? The fiery duke, tell the hot duke that —
No, but not yet. May be he is not well.   105
Infirmity doth still neglect all office
Whereto our health is bound.° We are not
ourselves
When nature, being oppressed, commands the
mind
To suffer with the body. I'll forbear;
And am fallen out° with my more headier will°   110
To take the indisposed and sickly fit
For the sound man. [*Looking on* KENT.] Death
on my state!° Wherefore
Should he sit here? This act persuades me
That this remotion° of the duke and her
Is practice° only. Give me my servant forth.°   115
Go tell the duke and's wife I'd speak with them!
Now, presently!° Bid them come forth and
hear me,
Or at their chamber door I'll beat the drum
Till it cry sleep to death.°
GLOUCESTER:
I would have all well betwixt you.   (*Exit.*)   120
LEAR:
O me, my heart, my rising heart! But down!
FOOL: Cry to it, nuncle, as the cockney° did
to the eels when she put 'em i' th' paste° alive.
She knapped° 'em o' th' coxcombs° with a
stick and cried, "Down, wantons,° down!"   125
'Twas her brother that, in pure kindness to his
horse, buttered his hay.°

(*Enter* CORNWALL, REGAN, GLOUCESTER, SER-
VANTS.)

LEAR:
Good morrow to you both.
CORNWALL: Hail to your grace.

(KENT *here set at liberty.*)

107 **Whereto . . . bound** duties which we are required
to perform, when in health   110 **fallen out** angry;
headier will headlong inclination   112 **state** royal
condition   114 **remotion** (1) removal (2) remaining
aloof   115 **practice** pretense; **forth** i.e., out of the
stocks   117 **presently** at once   119 **cry . . . death**
follow sleep, like a cry or pack of hounds, until it kills
it   122 **cockney** Londoner (ignorant city dweller)
123 **paste** pastry pie   124 **knapped** rapped; **coxcombs** heads   125 **wantons** i.e., playful things (with
a sexual implication)   127 **buttered his hay** i.e., the
city dweller does from ignorance what the dishonest
ostler does from craft: greases the hay the traveler has
paid for, so that the horse will not eat

REGAN:
I am glad to see your highness.
     LEAR:
130 Regan, I think you are. I know what reason
     I have to think so. If thou shouldst not be
          glad,
     I would divorce me from thy mother's tomb,
     Sepulchring an adultress.° [To KENT.] O, are
          you free?
     Some other time for that. Beloved Regan,
135 Thy sister's naught.° O Regan, she hath tied
     Sharp-toothed unkindness, like a vulture, here.

     [Points to his heart.]

     I can scarce speak to thee. Thou'lt not believe
     With how depraved a quality° — O Regan!
          REGAN:
     I pray you, sir, take patience. I have hope
140 You less know how to value her desert
     Than she to scant her duty.°
          LEAR: Say? how is that?
          REGAN:
     I cannot think my sister in the least
     Would fail her obligation. If, sir, perchance
     She have restrained the riots of your followers,
     'Tis on such ground, and to such wholesome
145   end,
     As clears her from all blame.
          LEAR:
     My curses on her!
          REGAN: O, sir, you are old,
     Nature in you stands on the very verge
     Of his confine.° You should be ruled, and led
150 By some discretion that discerns your state
     Better than you yourself.° Therefore I pray you
     That to our sister you do make return,
     Say you have wronged her.
          LEAR: Ask her forgiveness?
     Do you but mark how this becomes the
          house:°
155 "Dear daughter, I confess that I am old.

     [Kneeling.]

Age is unnecessary. On my knees I beg
That you'll vouchsafe me raiment, bed, and
     food."
     REGAN:
Good sir, no more. These are unsightly tricks.
Return you to my sister.
     LEAR [rising]:   Never, Regan.
She hath abated° me of half my train,   160
Looked black upon me, struck me with her
     tongue,
Most serpentlike, upon the very heart.
All the stored vengeances of heaven fall
On her ingrateful top!° Strike her young
     bones,°
You taking° airs, with lameness.
     CORNWALL: Fie, sir, fie!   165
     LEAR:
You nimble lightnings, dart your blinding
     flames
Into her scornful eyes! Infect her beauty,
You fen-sucked° fogs, drawn by the pow'rful
     sun,
To fall and blister° her pride.
     REGAN: O the blest gods!
So will you wish on me when the rash mood is
     on.   170
     LEAR:
No, Regan, thou shalt never have my curse.
Thy tender-hefted° nature shall not give
Thee o'er to harshness. Her eyes are fierce, but
     thine
Do comfort, and not burn. 'Tis not in thee
To grudge my pleasures, to cut off my train,   175
To bandy° hasty words, to scant my sizes,°
And, in conclusion, to oppose the bolt°
Against my coming in. Thou better know'st
The offices of nature, bond of childhood,°
Effects° of courtesy, dues of gratitude.   180
Thy half o' th' kingdom hast thou not forgot,
Wherein I thee endowed.
     REGAN: Good sir, to th' purpose.°

(Tucket within.)

132–133 **divorce . . . adultress** i.e., repudiate your dead mother as having conceived you by another man 135 **naught** wicked 138 **quality** nature 139–141 **I have . . . duty** despite the double negative, the passage means, "I believe that you fail to give Goneril her due, rather than that she fails to fulfill her duty" 148–149 **Nature . . . confine** i.e., you are nearing the end of your life 150–151 **some . . . yourself** some discreet person who understands your condition more than you do 154 **becomes the house** suits my royal and paternal position

160 **abated** curtailed 164 **top** head; **young bones** the reference may be to unborn children, rather than to Goneril herself 165 **taking** infecting 168 **fensucked** drawn up from swamps by the sun 169 **fall and blister** fall upon and raise blisters 172 **tenderhefted** gently framed 176 **bandy** volley (metaphor from tennis); **scant my sizes** reduce my allowances 177 **oppose the bolt** bar the door 179 **offices . . . childhood** natural duties, a child's duty to its parent 180 **Effects** manifestations 182 **to th' purpose** come to the point

LEAR:
Who put my man i' th' stocks?
CORNWALL: What trumpet's that?
REGAN:
I know't — my sister's. This approves° her letter,
That she would soon be here.

(*Enter* OSWALD.)

185   Is your lady come?
LEAR:
This is a slave, whose easy borrowed° pride
Dwells in the fickle grace° of her he follows.
Out, varlet,° from my sight.
CORNWALL: What means your grace?
LEAR:
Who stocked my servant? Regan, I have good hope
Thou didst not know on't.

(*Enter* GONERIL.)

190   Who comes here? O heavens!
If you do love old men, if your sweet sway
Allow° obedience, if you yourselves are old,
Make it° your cause. Send down, and take my part.

[*To* GONERIL.]

Art not ashamed to look upon this beard?
195 O Regan, will you take her by the hand?
GONERIL:
Why not by th' hand, sir? How have I offended?
All's not offense that indiscretion finds°
And dotage terms so.
LEAR: O sides,° you are too tough!
Will you yet hold? How came my man i' th' stocks?
CORNWALL:
200 I set him there, sir; but his own disorders°
Deserved much less advancement.°
LEAR: You? Did you?
REGAN:
I pray you, father, being weak, seem so.°
If till the expiration of your month
You will return and sojourn with my sister,

Dismissing half your train, come then to me. 205
I am now from home, and out of that provision
Which shall be needful for your entertainment.°
LEAR:
Return to her, and fifty men dismissed?
No, rather I abjure all roofs, and choose
To wage° against the enmity o' th' air, 210
To be a comrade with the wolf and owl,
Necessity's sharp pinch.° Return with her?
Why, the hot-blooded° France, that dowerless took
Our youngest born, I could as well be brought
To knee° his throne, and, squirelike,° pension beg 215
To keep base life afoot. Return with her?
Persuade me rather to be slave and sumpter°
To this detested groom. [*Pointing at* OSWALD.]
GONERIL: At your choice, sir.
LEAR:
I prithee, daughter, do not make me mad.
I will not trouble thee, my child; farewell. 220
We'll no more meet, no more see one another.
But yet thou art my flesh, my blood, my daughter,
Or rather a disease that's in my flesh,
Which I must needs call mine. Thou art a boil,
A plague-sore, or embossèd carbuncle° 225
In my corrupted blood. But I'll not chide thee.
Let shame come when it will, I do not call it.
I do not bid the Thunder-bearer° shoot,
Nor tell tales of thee to high-judging° Jove.
Mend when thou canst, be better at thy leisure, 230
I can be patient, I can stay with Regan,
I and my hundred knights.
REGAN: Not altogether so.
I looked not for you yet, nor am provided
For your fit welcome. Give ear, sir, to my sister,
For those that mingle reason with your passion° 235

184 **approves** confirms 186 **easy borrowed** (1) facile and taken from another (2) acquired without anything to back it up (like money borrowed without security) 187 **grace** favor 188 **varlet** base fellow 192 **Allow** approve of 193 **it** my cause 197 **finds** judges 198 **sides** breast 200 **disorders** misconduct 201 **advancement** promotion 202 **seem so** act weak

207 **entertainment** maintenance 210 **wage** fight 212 **Necessity's sharp pinch** a summing up of the hard choice he has just announced 213 **hot-blooded** passionate 215 **knee** kneel before; **squirelike** like a retainer 217 **sumpter** pack horse 225 **embossèd carbuncle** swollen boil 228 **Thunder-bearer** Jupiter 229 **high-judging** (1) supreme (2) judging from heaven 235 **mingle...passion** i.e., consider your turbulent behavior coolly and reasonably

Must be content to think you old, and so —
But she knows what she does.
LEAR: Is this well spoken?
REGAN:
I dare avouch° it, sir. What, fifty followers?
Is it not well? What should you need of
    more?
Yea, or so many, sith that° both charge° and
240   danger
Speak 'gainst so great a number? How in one
    house
Should many people, under two commands,
Hold° amity? 'Tis hard, almost impossible.
GONERIL:
Why might not you, my lord, receive atten-
    dance
From those that she calls servants, or from
245   mine?
REGAN:
Why not, my lord? If then they chanced to
    slack° ye,
We could control them. If you will come to
    me
(For now I spy a danger), I entreat you
To bring but five-and-twenty. To no more
250 Will I give place or notice.°
LEAR:
I gave you all.
REGAN: And in good time you gave it.
LEAR:
Made you my guardians, my depositaries,°
But kept a reservation° to be followed
With such a number. What, must I come to
    you
255 With five-and-twenty? Regan, said you so?
REGAN:
And speak't again, my lord. No more with
    me.
LEAR:
Those wicked creatures yet do look well-
    favored°
When others are more wicked; not being the
    worst
Stands in some rank of praise.° [To GONERIL.]
    I'll go with thee.

Thy fifty yet doth double five-and-twenty,   260
And thou art twice her love.°
GONERIL: Hear me, my lord.
What need you five-and-twenty? ten? or five?
To follow° in a house where twice so many
Have a command to tend you?
REGAN: What need one?
LEAR:
O reason° not the need! Our basest beggars   265
Are in the poorest thing superfluous.°
Allow not nature more than nature needs,°
Man's life is cheap as beast's. Thou art a lady:
If only to go warm were gorgeous,
Why, nature needs not what thou gorgeous   270
    wear'st,
Which scarcely keeps thee warm.° But, for true
    need —
You heavens, give me that patience, patience I
    need.
You see me here, you gods, a poor old man,
As full of grief as age, wretched in both.
If it be you that stirs these daughters' hearts   275
Against their father, fool° me not so much
To bear° it tamely; touch me with noble
    anger,
And let not women's weapons, water drops,
Stain my man's cheeks. No, you unnatural
    hags!
I will have such revenges on you both   280
That all the world shall — I will do such
    things —
What they are, yet I know not; but they shall
    be
The terrors of the earth. You think I'll weep.
No, I'll not weep.

(*Storm and tempest.*)

I have full cause of weeping, but this heart   285
Shall break into a hundred thousand flaws°
Or ere° I'll weep. O Fool, I shall go mad!
                    (*Exeunt* LEAR, GLOUCESTER,
                        KENT, and FOOL.)

238 **avouch** swear by   240 **sith that** since; **charge** expense   243 **Hold** preserve   246 **slack** neglect   250 **notice** recognition   252 **depositaries** trustees   253 **reservation** condition   257 **well-favored** handsome   258–259 **not . . . praise** i.e., that Goneril is not so bad as Regan is one thing in her favor

261 **her love** i.e., as loving as she   263 **follow** attend on you   265 **reason** scrutinize   266 **Are . . . superfluous** have some trifle not absolutely necessary   267 **needs** i.e., to sustain life   269–271 **If . . . warm** If to satisfy the need for warmth were to be gorgeous, you would not need the clothing you wear, which is worn more for beauty than warmth   276 **fool** humiliate   277 **To bear** as to make me bear   286 **flaws** (1) pieces (2) cracks (3) gusts of passion   287 **Or ere** before

CORNWALL:
Let us withdraw, 'twill be a storm.
REGAN:
This house is little; the old man and's people
290 Cannot be well bestowed.°
GONERIL:
'Tis his own blame; hath° put himself from
rest°
And must needs taste his folly.
REGAN:
For his particular,° I'll receive him gladly,
But not one follower.
GONERIL: So am I purposed.°
295 Where is my Lord of Gloucester?
CORNWALL:
Followed the old man forth.

(*Enter* GLOUCESTER.)

                         He is returned.
GLOUCESTER:
The king is in high rage.
CORNWALL: Whither is he going?
GLOUCESTER:
He calls to horse, but will I know not whither.
CORNWALL:
'Tis best to give him way, he leads himself.°
GONERIL:
300 My lord, entreat him by no means to stay.
GLOUCESTER:
Alack, the night comes on, and the high winds
Do sorely ruffle.° For many miles about
There's scarce a bush.
REGAN: O, sir, to willful men
The injuries that they themselves procure
Must be their schoolmasters. Shut up your
305   doors.
He is attended with a desperate train,
And what they may incense° him to, being apt
To have his ear abused,° wisdom bids fear.
CORNWALL:
Shut up your doors, my lord; 'tis a wild night.
My Regan counsels well. Come out o' th'
310   storm.
                         (*Exeunt.*)

290 **bestowed** lodged   291 **hath** he hath; **rest** (1) place of residence (2) repose of mind   293 **his particular** himself personally   294 **purposed** determined   299 **give . . . himself** let him go; he insists on his own way   302 **ruffle** rage   307 **incense** incite   307–308 **being . . . abused** he being inclined to harken to bad counsel

ACT III

SCENE I. [A *heath*.]

Storm still.° Enter KENT *and a* GENTLEMAN *severally.*

KENT:
Who's there besides foul weather?
GENTLEMAN:
One minded like the weather most unquietly.°
KENT:
I know you. Where's the king?
GENTLEMAN:
Contending with the fretful elements;
Bids the wind blow the earth into the sea,   5
Or swell the curlèd waters 'bove the main,°
That things might change° or cease; tears his
white hair,
Which the impetuous blasts, with eyeless°
rage,
Catch in their fury, and make nothing of;
Strives in his little world of man° to outscorn   10
The to-and-fro-conflicting wind and rain.
This night, wherein the cub-drawn° bear would
couch,
The lion, and the belly-pinchèd° wolf
Keep their fur dry, unbonneted° he runs,
And bids what will take all.°
KENT: But who is with him?   15
GENTLEMAN:
None but the Fool, who labors to outjest
His heart-struck injuries.
KENT: Sir, I do know you,
And dare upon the warrant of my note°
Commend a dear thing° to you. There is
division,

III.i.s.d. **still** continually   2 **minded . . . unquietly** disturbed in mind, like the weather   6 **main** land   7 **change** (1) be destroyed (2) be exchanged (i.e., turned upside down) (3) change for the better   8 **eyeless** (1) blind (2) invisible   10 **little . . . man** the microcosm, as opposed to the universe or macrocosm, which it copies in little   12 **cub-drawn** sucked dry by her cubs, and so ravenously hungry; **couch** take shelter in its lair   13 **belly-pinched** starved   14 **unbonneted** hatless   15 **take all** like the reckless gambler, staking all he has left   18 **warrant . . . note** strength of what I have taken note (of you)   19 **Commend . . . thing** entrust important business

20   Although as yet the face of it is covered
With mutual cunning, 'twixt Albany and
    Cornwall;
Who have — as who have not, that° their great
    stars
Throned° and set high? — servants, who seem
    no less,°
Which are to France the spies and specula-
    tions
25   Intelligent° of our state. What hath been seen,
Either in snuffs and packings° of the dukes,
Or the hard rein which both of them hath
    borne°
Against the old kind king, or something
    deeper,
Whereof, perchance, these are but furnish-
    ings° —
But, true it is, from France there comes a
30   power°
Into this scattered° kingdom, who already,
Wise in our negligence, have secret feet
In some of our best ports, and are at point°
To show their open banner. Now to you:
35   If on my credit you dare build° so far
To° make your speed to Dover, you shall find
Some that will thank you, making° just° report
Of how unnatural and bemadding° sorrow
The king hath cause to plain.°
40   I am a gentleman of blood and breeding,°
And from some knowledge and assurance° offer
This office° to you.
     GENTLEMAN:
I will talk further with you.
     KENT: No, do not.
For confirmation that I am much more
45   Than my out-wall,° open this purse and take
What it contains. If you shall see Cordelia,
As fear not but you shall, show her this ring,
And she will tell you who that fellow° is

That yet you do not know. Fie on this storm!
I will go seek the king.   50
     GENTLEMAN:
Give me your hand. Have you no more to say?
     KENT:
Few words, but, to effect,° more than all yet:
That when we have found the king — in which
    your pain°
That way, I'll this — he that first lights on
    him,
Holla the other.   (*Exeunt* [*severally*].)   55

SCENE II. [*Another part of the heath.*]

Storm still. Enter LEAR *and* FOOL.

     LEAR:
Blow, winds, and crack your cheeks. Rage,
    blow!
You cataracts and hurricanoes,° spout
Till you have drenched our steeples, drowned
    the cocks.°
You sulph'rous and thought-executing° fires,
Vaunt-couriers° of oak-cleaving thunderbolts,   5
Singe my white head. And thou, all-shaking
    thunder,
Strike flat the thick rotundity° o' th' world,
Crack Nature's molds,° all germains spill° at
    once,
That makes ingrateful° man.
     FOOL: O nuncle, court holy-water° in a dry   10
house is better than this rain water out o'
door. Good nuncle, in; ask thy daughters
blessing. Here's a night pities neither wise man
nor fools.
     LEAR:
Rumble thy bellyful. Spit, fire. Spout, rain!   15
Nor rain, wind, thunder, fire are my daughters.
I tax° not you, you elements, with unkindness.
I never gave you kingdom, called you children,
You owe me no subscription.° Then let fall

---

22 **that** whom   22–23 **stars Throned** destinies have throned   23 **seem no less** seem to be so   24–25 **speculations Intelligent** giving intelligence   26 **snuffs and packings** quarrels and plots   27 **hard . . . borne** close and cruel control they have exercised   29 **furnishings** excuses   30 **power** army   31 **scattered** disunited   33 **at point** ready   35 **If . . . build** if you can trust me, proceed   36 **To** as to   37 **making** for making; **just** accurate   38 **bemadding** maddening   39 **plain** complain of   40 **blood and breeding** noble family   41 **knowledge and assurance** sure and trustworthy information   42 **office** service (i.e., the trip to Dover)   45 **out-wall** superficial appearance   48 **fellow** companion

52 **to effect** in their importance   53 **pain** labor   III.II.2 **hurricanoes** waterspouts   3 **cocks** weathercocks   4 **thought-executing** (1) doing execution as quick as thought (2) executing or carrying out the thought of him who hurls the lightning   5 **Vauntcouriers** heralds, scouts who range before the main body of the army   7 **rotundity** i.e., not only the sphere of the globe, but the roundness of gestation (Delius)   8 **Nature's molds** the molds or forms in which men are made; **all germains spill** destroy the basic seeds of life   9 **ingrateful** ungrateful   10 **court holy-water** flattery   17 **tax** accuse   19 **subscription** allegiance, submission

20 Your horrible pleasure.° Here I stand your
slave,
A poor, infirm, weak, and despised old man.
But yet I call you servile ministers,°
That will with two pernicious daughters join
Your high-engendered battles° 'gainst a head
25 So old and white as this. O, ho! 'tis foul.
    FOOL: He that has a house to put's head in
has a good headpiece.°

         The codpiece° that will house
            Before the head as any,
30   The head and he° shall louse:
            So beggars marry many.°
         The man that makes his toe
            What he his heart should make
         Shall of a corn cry woe,
35   And turn his sleep to wake.°

For there was never yet fair woman but she
made mouths in a glass.°

(*Enter* KENT.)

    LEAR:
No, I will be the pattern of all patience,
I will say nothing.
40 KENT: Who's there?
    FOOL: Marry,° here's grace and a codpiece;
that's a wise man and a fool.°
    KENT:
Alas, sir, are you here? Things that love night
Love not such nights as these. The wrathful
skies
45 Gallow° the very wanderers of the dark
And make them keep° their caves. Since I was
man,

Such sheets of fire, such bursts of horrid°
thunder,
Such groans of roaring wind and rain, I never
Remember to have heard. Man's nature cannot
carry°
Th' affliction nor the fear.
    LEAR: Let the great gods   50
That keep this dreadful pudder° o'er our heads
Find out their enemies now.° Tremble, thou
wretch,
That hast within thee undivulgèd crimes
Unwhipped of justice. Hide thee, thou bloody
hand,
Thou perjured,° and thou simular° of virtue   55
That art incestuous. Caitiff,° to pieces shake,
That under covert and convenient seeming°
Has practiced on° man's life. Close° pent-up
guilts,
Rive° your concealing continents° and cry
These dreadful summoners grace.° I am a man   60
More sinned against than sinning.
    KENT: Alack, bareheaded?
Gracious my lord,° hard by here is a hovel;
Some friendship will it lend you 'gainst the
tempest.
Repose you there, while I to this hard house
(More harder than the stones whereof 'tis
raised,   65
Which even but now, demanding after° you,
Denied me to come in) return, and force
Their scanted° courtesy.
    LEAR: My wits begin to turn.
Come on, my boy. How dost, my boy? Art cold?
I am cold myself. Where is this straw, my
fellow?   70
The art° of our necessities is strange,
That can make vile things precious. Come,
your hovel.
Poor Fool and knave, I have one part in my
heart
That's sorry yet for thee.

---

20 **pleasure** will 22 **ministers** agents 24 **high-engendered battles** armies formed in the heavens 27 **headpiece** (1) helmet (2) brain 28 **codpiece** penis (literally, padding worn at the crotch of a man's hose) 30 **he** it 31 **many** i.e., lice 28–31 **The...many** The man who gratifies his sexual appetites before he has a roof over his head will end up a lousy beggar 32–35 **The...wake** The man who, ignoring the fit order of things, elevates what is base above what is noble, will suffer for it as Lear has, in banishing Cordelia and enriching her sisters 37 **made...glass** posed before a mirror (irrelevant nonsense, except that it calls to mind the general theme of vanity and folly) 41 **Marry** a mild oath, from "By the Virgin Mary" 41–42 **here's...fool** Kent's question is answered: the king ("grace") is here, and the Fool — who customarily wears an exaggerated codpiece; but which is left ambiguous, since Lear has previously been called a codpiece 45 **Gallow** frighten 46 **keep** remain inside

47 **horrid** horrible 49 **carry** endure 51 **pudder** turmoil 52 **Find...now** i.e., discover sinners by the terror they reveal 55 **perjured** perjurer; **simular** counterfeiter 56 **Caitiff** wretch 57 **seeming** hypocrisy 58 **practiced on** plotted against; **Close** hidden 59 **Rive** split open; **continents** containers 59–60 **cry...grace** beg mercy from the vengeful gods (here figured as officers who summoned a man charged with immorality before the ecclesiastical court) 62 **Gracious my lord** my gracious lord 66 **demanding after** asking for 68 **scanted** stinted 71 **art** magic powers of the alchemists, who sought to transmute base metals into precious

FOOL [*Singing*.]

75   He that has and a little tiny wit,
     With heigh-ho, the wind and the rain,
     Must make content with his fortunes fit,°
     Though the rain it raineth every day.

LEAR: True, my good boy. Come, bring us
80 to this hovel.   (*Exit, [with* KENT].)
FOOL: This is a brave° night to cool a
courtesan. I'll speak a prophecy ere I go:

   When priests are more in word than matter;
   When brewers mar their malt with water;
85   When nobles are their tailors' tutors,
   No heretics burned, but wenches' suitors;°
   When every case in law is right,
   No squire in debt nor no poor knight;
   When slanders do not live in tongues;
90   Nor cutpurses come not to throngs;
   When usurers tell their gold i' th' field,°
   And bawds and whores do churches build,°
   Then shall the realm of Albion°
   Come to great confusion.
95   Then comes the time, who lives to see't,
   That going shall be used with feet.°

This prophecy Merlin⌣ shall make, for I live
before his time.   (*Exit*.)

SCENE III. [GLOUCESTER's *castle*.]

Enter GLOUCESTER *and* EDMUND.

GLOUCESTER: Alack, alack, Edmund, I like
not this unnatural dealing. When I desired
their leave that I might pity° him, they took
from me the use of mine own house, charged
5 me on pain of perpetual displeasure neither to
speak of him, entreat for him, or any way
sustain° him.
EDMUND: Most savage and unnatural.
GLOUCESTER: Go to; say you nothing. There
is division° between the dukes, and a worse° 10
matter than that. I have received a letter this
night — 'tis dangerous to be spoken° — I have
locked the letter in my closet.° These injuries
the king now bears will be revenged home;°
there is part of a power° already footed;° we 15
must incline to° the king. I will look° him and
privily° relieve him. Go you and maintain talk
with the duke, that my charity be not of° him
perceived. If he ask for me, I am ill and gone
to bed. If I die for it, as no less is threatened 20
me, the king my old master must be relieved.
There is strange things toward,° Edmund;
pray you be careful.   (*Exit*.)
EDMUND:
This courtesy forbid° thee shall the duke
Instantly know, and of that letter too.   25
This seems a fair deserving,° and must draw
me
That which my father loses — no less than all.
The younger rises when the old doth fall.
     (*Exit*.)

SCENE IV. [*The heath. Before a hovel*.]

Enter LEAR, KENT, *and* FOOL.

KENT:
Here is the place, my lord. Good my lord,
  enter.
The tyranny of the open night's too rough
For nature to endure.

(*Storm still*.)

LEAR: Let me alone.
KENT:
Good my lord, enter here.
LEAR: Wilt break my heart?°
KENT:
I had rather break mine own. Good my lord,
  enter.   5

---

77 **Must . . . fit** must be satisfied with a fortune as tiny
as his wit   81 **brave** fine   83–86 **When . . . suitors**
the first four prophecies are fulfilled already, and
hence "confusion" has come to England: the priest
does not suit his action to his words; the brewer
adulterates his beer; the nobleman is subservient to
his tailor (i.e., cares only for fashion); religious heretics escape, and only those burn (i.e., suffer) who are
afflicted with venereal disease   91 **tell . . . field** count
their money in the open   87–92 **When . . . build** the
last six prophecies, as they are Utopian, are meant
ironically; they will never be fulfilled   93 **Albion**
England   96 **going . . . feet** people will walk on their
feet   97 **Merlin** King Arthur's great magician who,
according to Holinshed's *Chronicles*, lived later than
Lear
III.III.3 **pity** show pity to

7 **sustain** care for   10 **division** falling out; **worse**
more serious (i.e., the French invasion)   12 **spoken**
spoken of   13 **closet** room   14 **home** to the utmost
15 **power** army; **footed** landed   16 **incline to** take
the side of; **look** search for   17 **privily** secretly   18
of by   22 **toward** impending   24 **courtesy forbid**
kindness forbidden (i.e., to Lear)   26 **fair deserving**
an action deserving reward
III.IV.4 **break my heart** i.e., by shutting out the
storm which distracts me from thinking

LEAR:
Thou think'st 'tis much that this contentious storm
Invades us to the skin: so 'tis to thee;
But where the greater malady is fixed,°
The lesser is scarce felt. Thou'dst shun a bear;
10 But if thy flight lay toward the roaring sea,
Thou'dst meet the bear i' th' mouth.° When the mind's free,°
The body's delicate. The tempest in my mind
Doth from my senses take all feeling else,
Save what beats there. Filial ingratitude,
15 Is it not as° this mouth should tear this hand
For lifting food to't? But I will punish home.°
No, I will weep no more. In such a night
To shut me out! Pour on, I will endure.
In such a night as this! O Regan, Goneril,
Your old kind father, whose frank° heart gave
20 all —
O, that way madness lies; let me shun that.
No more of that.
KENT: Good my lord, enter here.
LEAR:
Prithee go in thyself; seek thine own ease.
This tempest will not give me leave to ponder
25 On things would hurt me more, but I'll go in.

[To the FOOL.]

In, boy; go first. You houseless poverty° —
Nay, get thee in. I'll pray, and then I'll sleep.
                              (Exit [FOOL].)
Poor naked wretches, wheresoe'er you are,
That bide° the pelting of this pitiless storm,
30 How shall your houseless heads and unfed sides,
Your looped and windowed° raggedness, defend you
From seasons such as these? O, I have ta'en
Too little care of this! Take physic, pomp;°
Expose thyself to feel what wretches feel,
35 That thou mayst shake the superflux° to them,
And show the heavens more just.
EDGAR [within]: Fathom and half, fathom and half!° Poor Tom!

(Enter FOOL.)

FOOL: Come not in here, nuncle, here's a spirit. Help me, help me!   40
KENT:
Give me thy hand. Who's there?
FOOL: A spirit, a spirit. He says his name's Poor Tom.
KENT:
What art thou that dost grumble there i' th' straw?
Come forth.   45

(Enter EDGAR [disguised as a madman].)

EDGAR: Away! the foul fiend follows me. Through the sharp hawthorn blows the cold wind.° Humh! Go to thy cold bed, and warm thee.°
LEAR: Didst thou give all to thy daughters?   50
And art thou come to this?
EDGAR: Who gives anything to Poor Tom? Whom the foul fiend hath led through fire and through flame, through ford and whirlpool, o'er bog and quagmire; that hath laid   55
knives under his pillow and halters in his pew,° set ratsbane° by his porridge,° made him proud of heart, to ride on a bay trotting horse over four-inched bridges,° to course° his own shadow for° a traitor. Bless thy five wits,°   60
Tom's a-cold. O, do, de, do, de, do, de. Bless thee from whirlwinds, star-blasting,° and taking.° Do Poor Tom some charity, whom the foul fiend vexes. There could I have him now — and there — and there again — and   65
there.

(Storm still.)

LEAR:
What, has his daughters brought him to this pass?°
Couldst thou save nothing? Wouldst thou give 'em all?

47–48 **Through . . . wind** a line from the ballad of "The Friar of Orders Gray"   48–49 **Go . . . thee** a reminiscence of *The Taming of the Shrew*, Induction, line 10, which itself is an echo of a line in Thomas Kyd's *The Spanish Tragedy*   56–57 **knives . . . halters . . . ratsbane** the fiend tempts Poor Tom to suicide   56 **pew** gallery or balcony outside a window   57 **porridge** broth   58–59 **ride . . . bridges** i.e., risk his life   59 **course** chase   60 **for** as; **five wits** common wit, imagination, fantasy, estimation, memory   62 **starblasting** the evil caused by malignant stars   62–63 **taking** pernicious influences   67 **pass** wretched condition

8 **fixed** lodged (in the mind)   11 **i' th' mouth** in the teeth; **free** i.e., from care   15 **as** as if   16 **home** to the utmost   20 **frank** liberal (magnanimous)   26 **houseless poverty** the unsheltered poor, abstracted   29 **bide** endure   31 **looped and windowed** full of holes   33 **Take physic, pomp** Take medicine to cure yourselves, you great men   35 **superflux** superfluity   37–38 **Fathom and half** Edgar, because of the downpour, pretends to take soundings

FOOL: Nay, he reserved a blanket,° else we
70 had been all shamed.

LEAR:
Now all the plagues that in the pendulous° air
Hang fated o'er° men's faults light on thy
    daughters!

KENT:
He hath no daughters, sir.

LEAR:
Death, traitor; nothing could have subdued°
    nature
75 To such a lowness but his unkind daughters.
Is it the fashion that discarded fathers
Should have thus little mercy on° their flesh?
Judicious punishment — 'twas this flesh begot
Those pelican° daughters.

80 EDGAR: Pillicock sat on Pillicock Hill.° Alow,
alow, loo, loo!°

FOOL: This cold night will turn us all to
fools and madmen.

EDGAR: Take heed o' th' foul fiend; obey thy
85 parents; keep thy word's justice;° swear not;
commit not° with man's sworn spouse; set not
thy sweet heart on proud array. Tom's a-cold.

LEAR: What hast thou been?

EDGAR: A servingman, proud in heart and
90 mind; that curled my hair, wore gloves in my
cap;° served the lust of my mistress' heart, and
did the act of darkness with her; swore as
many oaths as I spake words, and broke them
in the sweet face of heaven. One that slept in
95 the contriving of lust, and waked to do it.
Wine loved I deeply, dice dearly; and in
woman out-paramoured the Turk.° False of
heart, light of ear,° bloody of hand; hog in
sloth, fox in stealth, wolf in greediness, dog in
100 madness, lion in prey.° Let not the creaking° of
shoes nor the rustling of silks betray thy poor
heart to woman. Keep thy foot out of brothels,
thy hand out of plackets,° thy pen from

lenders' books,° and defy the foul fiend. Still
through the hawthorn blows the cold wind;   105
says suum, mun, nonny.° Dolphin° my boy,
boy, sessa!° let him trot by.

(*Storm still.*)

LEAR: Thou wert better in a grave than to
answer° with thy uncovered body this extrem-
ity° of the skies. Is man no more than this?   110
Consider him well. Thou ow'st° the worm no
silk, the beast no hide, the sheep no wool, the
cat° no perfume. Ha! here's three on's° are
sophisticated.° Thou art the thing itself; unac-
commodated° man is no more but such a poor,   115
bare, forked° animal as thou art. Off, off, you
lendings!° Come, unbutton here.

[*Tearing off his clothes.*]

FOOL: Prithee, nuncle, be contented, 'tis a
naughty° night to swim in. Now a little fire in
a wild° field were like an old lecher's heart — a   120
small spark, all the rest on's° body, cold. Look,
here comes a walking fire.

(*Enter* GLOUCESTER *with a torch.*)

EDGAR: This is the foul fiend Flibbertigibbet.° He begins at curfew,° and walks till the
first cock.° He gives the web and the pin,°   125
squints° the eye, and makes the harelip; mil-
dews the white° wheat, and hurts the poor
creature of earth.

Swithold footed thrice the old;°
He met the nightmare,° and her nine fold;°   130
    Bid her alight°
And her troth plight,°
And aroint° thee, witch, aroint thee!

103–104 **pen . . . books** i.e., do not enter your name
in the moneylender's account book   106 **suum, mun,
nonny** the noise of the wind   106 **Dolphin** the
French dauphin (identified by the English with the
devil; Poor Tom is presumably quoting from a ballad)
107 **sessa** an interjection: "Go on!"   109 **answer**
confront, bear the brunt of   109–110 **extremity** extreme severity   111 **ow'st** have taken from   113 **cat**
civet cat, whose glands yield perfume; **on's** of us
114 **sophisticated** adulterated, made artificial   114–
115 **unaccommodated** uncivilized   116 **forked** i.e.,
two-legged   117 **lendings** borrowed garments   119
naughty wicked   120 **wild** barren   121 **on's** of his
123–124 **Flibbertigibbet** a figure from Elizabethan
demonology   124 **curfew** 9 P.M.   125 **first cock**
midnight; **web . . . pin** cataract   126 **squints** crosses
127 **white** ripening   129 **Swithold . . . old** Withold
(an Anglo-Saxon saint who subdued demons)
walked three times across the open country   130
nightmare demon; **fold** offspring   131 **alight** i.e.,
from the horse she had possessed   132 **her troth
plight** pledge her word   133 **aroint** be gone

69 **blanket** i.e., to cover his nakedness   71 **pendu-
lous** overhanging   72 **fated o'er** destined to punish
74 **subdued** reduced   77 **on** i.e., shown to   79
pelican supposed to feed on its parent's blood   80
Pillicock . . . Hill probably quoted from a nursery
rhyme, and suggested by "pelican"; "pillicock" is a
term of endearment and the phallus   80–81 **Alow
. . . loo** a hunting call, or the refrain of the song (?)
85 **keep . . . justice** i.e., do not break thy word   86
commit not i.e., adultery   90–91 **gloves . . . cap** i.e.,
as a pledge from his mistress   97 **out-paramoured
the Turk** had more concubines than the sultan   98
light of ear ready to hear flattery and slander   100
prey preying; **creaking** deliberately cultivated, as
fashionable   103 **plackets** opening in skirts

KENT:

How fares your grace?

135   LEAR: What's he?

KENT:

Who's there? What is't you seek?

GLOUCESTER:

What are you there? Your names?

EDGAR: Poor Tom, that eats the swimming
frog, the toad, the todpole, the wall-newt and
140 the water;° that in the fury of his heart, when
the foul fiend rages, eats cow-dung for sallets,°
swallows the old rat and the ditch-dog,° drinks
the green mantle° of the standing° pool; who is
whipped from tithing° to tithing, and stocked,
145 punished, and imprisoned; who hath had three
suits to his back, six shirts to his body,

    Horse to ride, and weapon to wear,
    But mice and rats, and such small deer,°
    Have been Tom's food for seven long year.°

150 Beware my follower!° Peace, Smulkin,° peace,
thou fiend!

GLOUCESTER:

What, hath your grace no better company?

EDGAR:

The Prince of Darkness is a gentleman.
Modo° he's called, and Mahu.°

GLOUCESTER:

155 Our flesh and blood, my lord, is grown so vile
That it doth hate what gets° it.

EDGAR: Poor Tom's a-cold.

GLOUCESTER:

Go in with me. My duty cannot suffer°
T' obey in all your daughters' hard commands.
160 Though their injunction be to bar my doors
And let this tyrannous night take hold upon
    you,
Yet have I ventured to come seek you out
And bring you where both fire and food is
    ready.

LEAR:

First let me talk with this philosopher.
165 What is the cause of thunder?

KENT:

Good my lord, take his offer; go into th'
    house.

LEAR:

I'll talk a word with this same learnèd The-
    ban.°
What is your study?°

EDGAR:

How to prevent° the fiend, and to kill vermin.

LEAR:

Let me ask you one word in private.   170

KENT:

Importune him once more to go, my lord.
His wits begin t' unsettle.

GLOUCESTER: Canst thou blame him?

(*Storm still.*)

His daughters seek his death. Ah, that good
    Kent,
He said it would be thus, poor banished
    man!
Thou say'st the king grows mad — I'll tell thee,
    friend,   175
I am almost mad myself. I had a son,
Now outlawed from my blood;° he sought my
    life
But lately, very late.° I loved him, friend,
No father his son dearer. True to tell thee,
The grief hath crazed my wits. What a night's
    this!   180
I do beseech your grace —

LEAR: O, cry you mercy,° sir.
Noble philosopher, your company.

EDGAR: Tom's a-cold.

GLOUCESTER:

In, fellow, there, into th' hovel; keep thee
    warm.

LEAR:

Come, let's in all.

KENT: This way, my lord.

LEAR: With him!   185
I will keep still with my philosopher.

KENT:

Good my lord, soothe° him; let him take the
    fellow.

GLOUCESTER:

Take him you on.°

KENT:

Sirrah, come on; go along with us.

LEAR:

Come, good Athenian.°   190

139–140 **todpole ... water** tadpole, wall lizard, water
newt   141 **sallets** salads   142 **ditch-dog** dead dog in
a ditch   143 **mantle** scum; **standing** stagnant   144
tithing a district comprising ten families   148–149
But ... year adapted from a popular romance, "Bevis
of Hampton"   148 **deer** game   150 **follower** familiar   150–154 **Smulkin ... Modo ... Mahu** Elizabethan devils, from Samuel Harsnett's *Declaration*
of 1603   156 **gets** begets   158 **suffer** permit me

167 **Theban** i.e., Greek philosopher   168 **study**
particular scientific study   169 **prevent** balk   177
outlawed ... blood disowned and tainted, like a
carbuncle in the corrupted blood   178 **late** recently
181 **cry you mercy** I beg your pardon   187 **soothe**
humor   188 **you on** with you   190 **Athenian** i.e.,
philosopher (like "Theban")

GLOUCESTER:
No words, no words! Hush.
EDGAR:
Child Rowland to the dark tower came;°
His word was still,° "Fie, foh, and fum,
I smell the blood of a British man."°
(*Exeunt.*)

SCENE V. [GLOUCESTER's *castle.*]

Enter CORNWALL *and* EDMUND.

CORNWALL: I will have my revenge ere I
depart his house.
EDMUND: How, my lord, I may be censured,°
that nature thus gives way to loyalty, some-
5 thing fears° me to think of.
CORNWALL: I now perceive it was not altogether your brother's evil disposition made him
seek his death; but a provoking merit, set
a-work by a reprovable badness in himself.°
10 EDMUND: How malicious is my fortune that
I must repent to be just! This is the letter
which he spoke of, which approves° him an
intelligent party° to the advantages° of France.
O heavens, that his treason were not! or not I
15 the detector!
CORNWALL: Go with me to the duchess.
EDMUND: If the matter of this paper be
certain, you have mighty business in hand.
CORNWALL: True or false, it hath made thee
20 Earl of Gloucester. Seek out where thy father
is, that he may be ready for our apprehension.°
EDMUND [*aside*]: If I find him comforting°
the king, it will stuff his suspicion more
fully. — I will persever° in my course of loyalty,
25 though the conflict be sore between that and
my blood.°
CORNWALL: I will lay trust upon° thee, and
thou shalt find a dearer father in my love.
(*Exeunt.*)

SCENE VI. [*A chamber in a farmhouse
adjoining the castle.*]

Enter KENT *and* GLOUCESTER.

GLOUCESTER: Here is better than the open
air; take it thankfully. I will piece out the
comfort with what addition I can. I will not
be long from you.
KENT: All the power of his wits have given   5
way to his impatience.° The gods reward your
kindness.   (*Exit* [GLOUCESTER].)

(*Enter* LEAR, EDGAR, *and* FOOL.)

EDGAR: Frateretto° calls me, and tells me
Nero° is an angler in the lake of darkness.
Pray, innocent,° and beware the foul fiend.   10
FOOL: Prithee, nuncle, tell me whether a
madman be a gentleman or a yeoman.°
LEAR:
A king, a king.
FOOL: No, he's a yeoman that has a gentle-
man to his son; for he's a mad yeoman that   15
sees his son a gentleman before him.
LEAR:
To have a thousand with red burning spits
Come hizzing° in upon 'em —
EDGAR: The foul fiend bites my back.
FOOL: He's mad that trusts in the tameness   20
of a wolf, a horse's health, a boy's love, or a
whore's oath.
LEAR:
It shall be done; I will arraign° them straight.°

[*To* EDGAR.]

Come, sit thou here, most learned justice.°

[*To the* FOOL.]

Thou, sapient° sir, sit here. Now, you she-
foxes —   25
EDGAR: Look, where he° stands and glares.
Want'st thou eyes at trial, madam?°
Come o'er the bourn,° Bessy, to me.

192 **Child . . . came** from a lost ballad (?); "child" =
a candidate for knighthood; "Rowland" was Charle-
magne's nephew, the hero of *The Song of Roland*
193 **His . . . still** his motto was always   193–194 **Fie
. . . man** a deliberately absurd linking of the chivalric
hero with the nursery tale of Jack the Giant-Killer
III.v.3 **censured** judged   4–5 **something fears** somewhat frightens   8–9 **a provoking . . . himself** a stimulating goodness in Edgar, brought into play by a
blamable badness in Gloucester   12 **approves** proves
13 **intelligent party** (1) spy (2) well-informed person; **to the advantages** on behalf of   21 **apprehension** arrest   22 **comforting** supporting (a legalism)
24 **persever** persevere   26 **blood** natural feelings
27 **lay trust upon** (1) trust (2) advance

III.vi.6 **impatience** raging   8 **Fraterretto** Elizabethan
devil, from Harsnett's *Declaration*   9 **Nero** who is
mentioned by Harsnett, and whose angling is reported
by Chaucer in "The Monk's Tale"   10 **innocent** fool
12 **yeoman** farmer (just below a gentleman in rank;
the Fool asks what class of man has most indulged
his children, and thus been driven mad)   18 **hizzing**
hissing   23 **arraign** bring to trial; **straight** straightaway   24 **justice** justicer, judge   25 **sapient** wise
26 **he** i.e., a fiend   27 **Want'st . . . madam** (to
Goneril) i.e., Do you want eyes to look at you during
your trial? The fiend serves that purpose   28 **bourn**
brook (Edgar quotes from a popular ballad)

FOOL:
Her boat hath a leak,
30   And she must not speak
Why she dares not come over to thee.°
    EDGAR: The foul fiend haunts Poor Tom in
the voice of a nightingale.° Hoppedance° cries
35 in Tom's belly for two white herring.° Croak°
not, black angel; I have no food for thee.
    KENT:
How do you, sir? Stand you not so amazed.°
Will you lie down and rest upon the cushions?
    LEAR:
I'll see their trial first. Bring in their evidence.°

[To EDGAR.]

Thou, robèd man of justice, take thy place.

[To the FOOL.]

40 And thou, his yokefellow of equity,°
Bench° by his side. [To KENT.] You are o' th'
    commission;°
Sit you too.
    EDGAR: Let us deal justly.

Sleepest or wakest thou, jolly shepherd?
45   Thy sheep be in the corn;°
And for one blast of thy minikin° mouth
    Thy sheep shall take no harm.°

Purr, the cat is gray.°
    LEAR: Arraign her first. 'Tis Goneril, I here
50 take my oath before this honorable assembly,
she kicked the poor king her father.
    FOOL: Come hither, mistress. Is your name
Goneril?
    LEAR: She cannot deny it.
55   FOOL: Cry you mercy, I took you for a joint
stool.°

LEAR:
And here's another, whose warped looks pro-
    claim
What store° her heart is made on. Stop her
    there!
Arms, arms, sword, fire! Corruption in the
    place!°
False justicer, why hast thou let her 'scape?   60
    EDGAR: Bless thy five wits!
    KENT:
O pity! Sir, where is the patience now
That you so oft have boasted to retain?
    EDGAR [aside]:
My tears begin to take his part so much
They mar my counterfeiting.°   65
    LEAR:
The little dogs and all,
Tray, Blanch, and Sweetheart — see, they bark
    at me.
    EDGAR: Tom will throw his head at them.
Avaunt, you curs.

Be thy mouth or black or° white,   70
Tooth that poisons if it bite;
Mastiff, greyhound, mongrel grim,
Hound or spaniel, brach° or lym,°
Or bobtail tike, or trundle-tail° —
Tom will make him weep and wail;   75
For, with throwing° thus my head,
Dogs leaped the hatch,° and all are fled.

Do, de, de, de. Sessa!° Come, march to wakes°
and fairs and market towns. Poor Tom, thy
horn° is dry.   80
    LEAR: Then let them anatomize Regan. See
what breeds about her heart.° Is there any
cause in nature that make° these hard hearts?
[To EDGAR.] You, sir, I entertain° for one of
my hundred;° only I do not like the fashion of 85

29–31 Her . . . thee the Fool parodies the ballad 33
nightingale i.e., the Fool's singing; Hoppedance Ho-
berdidance (another devil from Harsnett's *Declaration*) 34 white herring unsmoked (as against the
black and sulfurous devil?); Croak rumble (because
his belly is empty) 36 amazed astonished 38 evidence the evidence of witnesses against them 40
yokefellow of equity partner in justice 41 Bench sit
on the bench; commission those commissioned as
king's justices 44–47 Sleepest . . . harm probably
quoted or adapted from an Elizabethan song 45
corn wheat 46 minikin shrill 48 gray devils were
thought to assume the shape of a gray cat 55–56
Cry . . . stool proverbial and deliberately impudent
apology for overlooking a person; a joint stool was a
low stool made by a joiner, perhaps here a stage property to represent Goneril and, in line 57, Regan; "joint
stool" can also suggest the judicial bench; hence
Goneril may be identified by the Fool, ironically,
with those in power, who judge

58 store stuff 59 Corruption . . . place bribery in the
court 65 counterfeiting i.e., feigned madness 70
or . . . or either . . . or 73 brach bitch; lym blood-
hound (from the liam or leash with which he was led)
74 bobtail . . . trundle-tail short-tailed or long-tailed
cur 76 throwing jerking (as a hound lifts its head
from the ground, the scent having been lost) 77
leaped the hatch leaped over the lower half of a
divided door (i.e., left in a hurry) 78 Sessa Be off!;
wakes feasts attending the dedication of a church 80
horn horn bottle which the Bedlam used in begging a
drink (Edgar is suggesting that he is unable to play
his role any longer) 81–82 Then . . . heart i.e., If
the Bedlam's horn is dry, let Regan, whose heart has
become as hard as horn, be dissected 83 make sub-
junctive 84 entertain engage 85 hundred i.e.,
Lear's hundred knights

your garments. You will say they are Persian;°
but let them be changed.

KENT:
Now, good my lord, lie here and rest awhile.

LEAR:
Make no noise, make no noise; draw the
   curtains.°
90 So, so. We'll go to supper i' th' morning.

FOOL: And I'll go to bed at noon.°

(*Enter* GLOUCESTER.)

GLOUCESTER:
Come hither, friend. Where is the king my
   master?

KENT:
Here, sir, but trouble him not; his wits are
   gone.

GLOUCESTER:
Good friend, I prithee take him in thy arms.
95 I have o'erheard a plot of death upon him.
There is a litter ready; lay him in't
And drive toward Dover, friend, where thou
   shalt meet
Both welcome and protection. Take up thy
   master.
If thou shouldst dally half an hour, his life,
100 With thine and all that offer to defend him,
Stand in assurèd loss. Take up, take up,
And follow me, that will to some provision°
Give thee quick conduct.°

KENT: Oppressèd nature sleeps.
This rest might yet have balmed thy broken
   sinews,°
105 Which, if convenience° will not allow,
Stand in hard cure.° [*To the* FOOL.] Come,
   help to bear thy master.
Thou must not stay behind.

GLOUCESTER: Come, come, away!

(*Exeunt* [*all but* EDGAR].)

EDGAR:
When we our betters see bearing our woes,
We scarcely think our miseries our foes.°
110 Who alone suffers suffers most i' th' mind,
Leaving free° things and happy shows° behind;
But then the mind much sufferance° doth
   o'erskip

When grief hath mates, and bearing fellow-
   ship.°
How light and portable° my pain seems now,
When that which makes me bend makes the
   king bow.   115
He childed as I fathered. Tom, away.
Mark the high noises,° and thyself bewray°
When false opinion, whose wrong thoughts°
   defile thee,
In thy just proof repeals and reconciles thee.°
What will hap more° tonight, safe 'scape the
   king!   120
Lurk,° lurk.   [*Exit.*]

SCENE VII. [GLOUCESTER'*s castle.*]

Enter CORNWALL, REGAN, GONERIL, EDMUND,
and SERVANTS.

CORNWALL [*to* GONERIL]: Post speedily to
my lord your husband; show him this letter.
The army of France is landed. [*To* SERVANTS.]
Seek out the traitor Gloucester.
        [*Exeunt some of the* SERVANTS.]

REGAN: Hang him instantly.   5

GONERIL: Pluck out his eyes.

CORNWALL: Leave him to my displeasure.
Edmund, keep you our sister company. The
revenges we are bound° to take upon your
traitorous father are not fit for your beholding. 10
Advise the duke where you are going, to a
most festinate° preparation. We are bound to
the like. Our posts° shall be swift and intelli-
gent° betwixt us. Farewell, dear sister; farewell,
my Lord of Gloucester.°   15

(*Enter* OSWALD.)

How now? Where's the king?

OSWALD:
My Lord of Gloucester hath conveyed him
   hence.
Some five or six and thirty of his knights,
Hot questrists° after him, met him at gate;

---

86 **Persian** gorgeous (ironically of Edgar's rags) 89
curtains Lear imagines himself in bed 91 **And . . .
noon** the Fool's last words 102 **provision** maintenance 103 **conduct** direction 104 **balmed . . . sinews** soothed thy racked nerves 105 **convenience**
fortunate occasion 106 **Stand . . . cure** will be hard
to cure 109 **our foes** enemies peculiar to ourselves
111 **free** carefree, **shows** scenes 112 **sufferance**
suffering

113 **bearing fellowship** suffering has company 114
portable able to be supported or endured 117 **Mark
. . . noises** observe the rumors of strife among those in
power; **bewray** reveal 118 **wrong thoughts** misconceptions 119 **In . . . thee** on the manifesting of your
innocence recalls you from outlawry and restores
amity between you and your father 120 **What . . .
more** whatever else happens 121 **Lurk** hide
III.vii.9 **bound** (1) forced (2) purposing to 12
festinate speedy 13 **posts** messengers 13–14 **intelligent** full of information 15 **Lord of Gloucester**
Edmund, now elevated to the title 19 **questrists**
searchers

20 Who, with some other of the lords depen-
         dants,°
    Are gone with him toward Dover, where they
         boast
    To have well-armèd friends.
    CORNWALL: Get horses for your mistress.
                              [*Exit* OSWALD.]
       GONERIL:
    Farewell, sweet lord, and sister.
       CORNWALL:
    Edmund, farewell.
                    [*Exeunt* GONERIL *and* EDMUND.]
                    Go seek the traitor Gloucester,
25 Pinion him like a thief, bring him before us.
                    [*Exeunt other* SERVANTS.]
    Though well we may not pass upon° his life
    Without the form of justice, yet our power
    Shall do a court'sy to° our wrath, which men
    May blame, but not control.

    (*Enter* GLOUCESTER, *brought in by two or
    three.*)

                    Who's there, the traitor?
       REGAN:
30 Ingrateful fox, 'tis he.
       CORNWALL:
    Bind fast his corky° arms.
       GLOUCESTER:
    What means your graces? Good my friends,
         consider
    You are my guests. Do me no foul play,
         friends.
       CORNWALL:
    Bind him, I say. [SERVANTS *bind him.*]
       REGAN: Hard, hard! O filthy traitor.
       GLOUCESTER:
35 Unmerciful lady as you are, I'm none.
       CORNWALL:
    To this chair bind him. Villain, thou shalt
         find —

    [REGAN *plucks his beard.*°]

       GLOUCESTER:
    By the kind gods, 'tis most ignobly done
    To pluck me by the beard.
       REGAN:
    So white, and such a traitor?
       GLOUCESTER: Naughty° lady,

    These hairs which thou dost ravish from my
         chin   40
    Will quicken° and accuse thee. I am your
         host.
    With robber's hands my hospitable favors°
    You should not ruffle° thus. What will you do?
       CORNWALL:
    Come, sir, what letters had you late° from
         France?
       REGAN:
    Be simple-answered,° for we know the truth.   45
       CORNWALL:
    And what confederacy have you with the
         traitors
    Late footed in the kingdom?
       REGAN:
    To whose hands you have sent the lunatic
         king:
    Speak.
       GLOUCESTER:
    I have a letter guessingly° set down,   50
    Which came from one that's of a neutral
         heart,
    And not from one opposed.
       CORNWALL: Cunning.
       REGAN: And false.
       CORNWALL:
    Where hast thou sent the king?
       GLOUCESTER:
    To Dover.
       REGAN:
    Wherefore to Dover? Wast thou not charged
         at peril° —   55
       CORNWALL:
    Wherefore to Dover? Let him answer that.
       GLOUCESTER:
    I am tied to th' stake, and I must stand the
         course.°
       REGAN:
    Wherefore to Dover?
       GLOUCESTER:
    Because I would not see thy cruel nails
    Pluck out his poor old eyes; nor thy fierce
         sister   60
    In his anointed° flesh rash° boarish fangs.

---

20 **lords dependants** attendant lords (members of
Lear's retinue)   26 **pass upon** pass judgment on   28
do . . . to indulge   31 **corky** sapless (because old)
36 s.d. **plucks his beard** a deadly insult   39 **Naughty**
wicked

41 **quicken** come to life   42 **hospitable favors** face
of your host   43 **ruffle** tear at violently   44 **late** recently   45 **simple-answered** straight forward in answering   50 **guessingly** without certain knowledge
55 **charged at peril** ordered under penalty   57
course coursing (in which a relay of dogs baits a bull
or bear tied in the pit)   61 **anointed** holy (because
king); **rash** strike with the tusk, like a boar

The sea, with such a storm as his bare head
In hell-black night endured, would have
      buoyed° up
And quenched the stellèd° fires.
Yet, poor old heart, he holp° the heavens to
65   rain.
If wolves had at thy gate howled that dearn°
      time,
Thou shouldst have said, "Good porter, turn
      the key."°
All cruels else subscribe.° But I shall see
The wingèd° vengeance overtake such children.
      CORNWALL:
70   See't shalt thou never. Fellows, hold the chair.
Upon these eyes of thine I'll set my foot.
      GLOUCESTER:
He that will think° to live till he be old,
Give me some help. — O cruel! O you gods!
      REGAN:
One side will mock° another. Th' other too.
      CORNWALL:
If you see vengeance —
75   FIRST SERVANT: Hold your hand, my lord!
I have served you ever since I was a child;
But better service have I never done you
Than now to bid you hold.
      REGAN: How now, you dog?
      FIRST SERVANT:
If you did wear a beard upon your chin,
I'd shake it° on this quarrel. What do you
80   mean!°
      CORNWALL: My villain!°

(*Draw and fight.*)

      FIRST SERVANT:
Nay, then, come on, and take the chance of
      anger.
      REGAN:
Give me thy sword. A peasant stand up thus?

(*She takes a sword and runs at him behind,
kills him.*)

FIRST SERVANT:
O, I am slain! my lord, you have one eye left
To see some mischief° on him. O!   85
      CORNWALL:
Lest it see more, prevent it. Out, vile jelly.
Where is thy luster now?
      GLOUCESTER:
All dark and comfortless. Where's my son
      Edmund?
Edmund, enkindle all the sparks of nature°
To quit° this horrid act.
      REGAN: Out, treacherous villain,   90
Thou call'st on him that hates thee. It was he
That made the overture° of thy treasons to us;
Who is too good to pity thee.
      GLOUCESTER:
O my follies! Then Edgar was abused.°
Kind gods, forgive me that, and prosper him.   95
      REGAN:
Go thrust him out at gates, and let him smell
His way to Dover.
                  (*Exit [one], with* GLOUCESTER.)
                  How is't, my lord? How look you?°
      CORNWALL:
I have received a hurt. Follow me, lady.
Turn out that eyeless villain. Throw this slave
Upon the dunghill. Regan, I bleed apace.   100
Untimely comes this hurt. Give me your arm.
                                                (*Exeunt.*)
      SECOND SERVANT:
I'll never care what wickedness I do,
If this man come to good.
      THIRD SERVANT: If she live long,
And in the end meet the old course of death,°
Women will all turn monsters.   105
      SECOND SERVANT:
Let's follow the old earl, and get the Bedlam
To lead him where he would. His roguish
      madness
Allows itself to anything.°
      THIRD SERVANT:
Go thou. I'll fetch some flax and whites of
      eggs
To apply to his bleeding face. Now heaven
      help him.

                                          [*Exeunt severally.*]

---

63 **buoyed** risen   64 **stellèd** (1) fixed (as opposed to the planets or wandering stars) (2) starry   65 **holp** helped   66 **dearn** dread   67 **turn the key** i.e., unlock the gate   68 **All . . . subscribe** All cruel creatures but man are compassionate   69 **wingèd** (1) heavenly (2) swift   72 **will think** expects   74 **mock** make ridiculous (because of the contrast)   80 **shake it** an insult comparable to Regan's plucking of Gloucester's beard; **What . . . mean** i.e., What terrible thing are you doing?   81 **villain** serf (with a suggestion of the modern meaning)

85 **mischief** injury   89 **enkindle . . . nature** fan your natural feeling into flame   90 **quit** requite   92 **overture** disclosure   93 **abused** wronged   97 **How look you** How are you?   104 **meet . . . death** die the customary death of old age   107–108 **His . . . anything** his lack of all self-control leaves him open to any suggestion

ACT IV

SCENE I. [*The heath.*]

Enter EDGAR.

EDGAR:
Yet better thus, and known to be contemned,°
Than still contemned and flattered. To be
　　worst,
The lowest and most dejected° thing of for-
　　tune,
Stands still in esperance,° lives not in fear:
5　The lamentable change is from the best,
The worst returns to laughter.° Welcome then,
Thou unsubstantial air that I embrace!
The wretch that thou hast blown unto the
　　worst
Owes° nothing to thy blasts.

(*Enter* GLOUCESTER, *led by an* OLD MAN.)

　　　　　　　　　　　　But who comes here?
My father, poorly led?° World, world, O
10　　world!
But that thy strange mutations make us hate
　　thee,
Life would not yield to age.°
OLD MAN:　　　　　　　O, my good lord,
I have been your tenant, and your father's
　　tenant,
These fourscore years.
GLOUCESTER:
15　Away, get thee away; good friend, be gone:
Thy comforts° can do me no good at all,
Thee they may hurt.°
OLD MAN:　　　　　You cannot see your way.
GLOUCESTER:
I have no way and therefore want° no eyes;
I stumbled when I saw. Full oft 'tis seen,
20　Our means secure us, and our mere defects
Prove our commodities.° Oh, dear son Edgar,

The food° of thy abusèd° father's wrath!
Might I but live to see thee in° my touch,
I'd say I had eyes again!
OLD MAN:　　　　　How now! Who's there?
EDGAR [*aside*]:
O gods! Who is't can say, "I am at the worst"?　25
I am worse than e'er I was.
OLD MAN:　　　　　　　'Tis poor mad Tom.
EDGAR [*aside*]:
And worse I may be yet: the worst is not
So long as we can say, "This is the worst."°
OLD MAN:
Fellow, where goest?
GLOUCESTER:　　Is it a beggar-man?
OLD MAN:
Madman and beggar too.　　　　　　　　　30
GLOUCESTER:
He has some reason,° else he could not beg.
I' th' last night's storm I such a fellow saw,
Which made me think a man a worm. My son
Came then into my mind, and yet my mind
Was then scarce friends with him. I have
　　heard more since.　　　　　　　　　　35
As flies to wanton° boys, are we to th' gods,
They kill us for their sport.
EDGAR [*aside*]:　　　　How should this be?°
Bad is the trade that must play fool to sorrow,
Ang'ring° itself and others. Bless thee, master!
GLOUCESTER:
Is that the naked fellow?
OLD MAN:　　　　　　Ay, my lord.　　　40
GLOUCESTER:
Then, prithee, get thee gone: if for my sake
Thou wilt o'ertake us hence a mile or twain
I' th' way toward Dover, do it for ancient°
　　love,
And bring some covering for this naked soul,
Which I'll entreat to lead me.
OLD MAN:　　　　　Alack, sir, he is mad.　45
GLOUCESTER:
'Tis the time's plague,° when madmen lead the
　　blind.

IV.i.1 **known ... contemned** conscious of being despised　3 **dejected** abased　4 **esperance** hope　6 **returns to laughter** changes for the better　9 **Owes** is in debt for　10 **poorly led** (1) led like a poor man, with only one attendant (2) led by a poor man　11–12 **But ... age** We should not agree to grow old and hence die, except for the hateful mutability of life　16 **comforts** ministrations　17 **hurt** injure　18 **want** require　20–21 **Our ... commodities** Our resources make us overconfident, while our afflictions make for our advantage

22 **food** i.e., the object on which Gloucester's anger fed; **abusèd** deceived　23 **in** i.e., with, by means of　27–28 **the ... worst** so long as a man continues to suffer (i.e., is still alive), even greater suffering may await him　31 **reason** faculty of reasoning　36 **wanton** (1) playful (2) reckless　37 **How ... be** i.e., How can this horror be?　39 **Ang'ring** offending　43 **ancient** (1) the love the Old Man feels, by virtue of his long tenancy (2) the love that formerly obtained between master and man　46 **time's plague** characteristic disorder of this time

Do as I bid thee, or rather do thy pleasure;°
Above the rest,° be gone.

OLD MAN:
I'll bring him the best 'parel° that I have,
50 Come on't what will.   (*Exit.*)

GLOUCESTER:
Sirrah, naked fellow —

EDGAR:
Poor Tom's a-cold. [*Aside.*] I cannot daub it°
further.

GLOUCESTER:
Come hither, fellow.

EDGAR [*aside*]:
And yet I must. — Bless thy sweet eyes, they
bleed.

GLOUCESTER:
55 Know'st thou the way to Dover?

EDGAR:
Both stile and gate, horse-way and footpath.
Poor Tom hath been scared out of his good
wits.
Bless thee, good man's son, from the foul
fiend!
Five fiends have been in Poor Tom at once; of
60 lust, as Obidicut;° Hobbididence, prince of
dumbness;° Mahu, of stealing; Modo, of murder; Flibbertigibbet, of mopping and mowing;°
who since possesses chambermaids and wait-
ing-women. So, bless thee, master!

GLOUCESTER:
Here, take this purse, thou whom the heavens'
65 plagues
Have humbled to all strokes:° that I am
wretched
Makes thee the happier. Heavens, deal so still!
Let the superfluous° and lust-dieted° man,
That slaves° your ordinance,° that will not see
Because he does not feel, feel your pow'r
70 quickly;
So distribution should undo excess,°

47 **thy pleasure** as you like it   48 **the rest** all   49
'parel apparel   52 **daub it** lay it on (figure from
plastering mortar)   60 **Obidicut** Hoberdicut, a devil
(like the four that follow, from Harsnett's *Declaration*)   61 **dumbness** muteness (like the crimes and
afflictions in the next lines, the result of diabolic
possession)   62 **mopping and mowing** grimacing and
making faces   66 **humbled ... strokes** brought so
low as to bear anything humbly   68 **superfluous**
possessed of superfluities; **lust-dieted** whose lust is
gratified (like Gloucester's)   69 **slaves** (1) tramples,
spurns like a slave (2) tears, rends (Old English
slaefan) (?); **ordinance** law   71 **So ... excess** Then
the man with too much wealth would distribute it
among those with too little

And each man have enough. Dost thou know
Dover?

EDGAR: Ay, master.

GLOUCESTER:
There is a cliff whose high and bending° head
Looks fearfully° in the confinèd deep:°   75
Bring me but to the very brim of it,
And I'll repair the misery thou dost bear
With something rich about me: from that
place
I shall no leading need.

EDGAR: Give me thy arm:
Poor Tom shall lead thee.   (*Exeunt.*)   80

SCENE II. [*Before the Duke of* ALBANY's
palace.]

Enter GONERIL *and* EDMUND.

GONERIL:
Welcome, my lord: I marvel our mild husband
Not met° us on the way.

(*Enter* OSWALD.)

                         Now, where's your master?

OSWALD:
Madam, within; but never man so changed.
I told him of the army that was landed:
He smiled at it. I told him you were coming;   5
His answer was, "The worse." Of Gloucester's
treachery,
And of the loyal service of his son
When I informed him, then he called me sot,°
And told me I had turned the wrong side out:
What most he should dislike seems pleasant to
him;   10
What like,° offensive.

GONERIL [*to* EDMUND]:
Then shall you go no further.
It is the cowish° terror of his spirit,
That dares not undertake:° he'll not feel
wrongs,
Which tie him to an answer.° Our wishes on
the way   15
May prove effects.° Back, Edmund, to my
brother;

74 **bending** overhanging   75 **fearfully** occasioning
fear; **confinèd deep** the sea, hemmed in below
IV.ii.2 **Not met** did not meet   8 **sot** fool   11 **What
like** what he should like   13 **cowish** cowardly   14
undertake venture   15 **tie ... answer** oblige him to
retaliate   15–16 **Our ... effects** Our desires (that
you might be my husband), as we journeyed here,
may be fulfilled

Hasten his musters° and conduct his pow'rs.°
I must change names° at home and give the distaff°
Into my husband's hands. This trusty servant
Shall pass between us: ere long you are like to
20 hear,
If you dare venture in your own behalf,
A mistress's° command. Wear this; spare speech;

[*Giving a favor.*]

Decline your head.° This kiss, if it durst speak,
Would stretch thy spirits up into the air:
25 Conceive,° and fare thee well.
    EDMUND:
Yours in the ranks of death.
    GONERIL: My most dear Gloucester!
                     (*Exit* [EDMUND].)
O, the difference of man and man!
To thee a woman's services are due:
My fool usurps my body.°
    OSWALD: Madam, here comes my lord.
                     (*Exit.*)

(*Enter* ALBANY.)

    GONERIL:
I have been worth the whistle.°
30   ALBANY: O Goneril!
You are not worth the dust which the rude wind
Blows in your face. I fear your disposition:°
That nature which contemns° its origin
Cannot be bordered certain in itself;°
35 She that herself will sliver and disbranch°
From her material sap,° perforce must wither
And come to deadly use.°

    GONERIL:
No more; the text° is foolish.
    ALBANY:
Wisdom and goodness to the vile seem vile:
Filths savor but themselves.° What have you done? 40
Tigers, not daughters, what have you performed?
A father, and a gracious agèd man,
Whose reverence even the head-lugged bear° would lick,
Most barbarous, most degenerate, have you madded.°
Could my good brother suffer you to do it? 45
A man, a prince, by him so benefited!
If that the heavens do not their visible spirits°
Send quickly down to tame these vile offenses,
It will come,
Humanity must perforce prey on itself, 50
Like monsters of the deep.
    GONERIL: Milk-livered° man!
That bear'st a cheek for blows, a head for wrongs;
Who hast not in thy brows an eye discerning
Thine honor from thy suffering;° that not know'st
Fools do those villains pity who are punished 55
Ere they have done their mischief.° Where's thy drum?
France spreads his banners in our noiseless° land,
With plumèd helm° thy state begins to threat,°
Whilst thou, a moral° fool, sits still and cries,
"Alack, why does he so?"
    ALBANY: See thyself, devil! 60
Proper° deformity seems not in the fiend
So horrid as in woman.

17 **musters** collecting of troops; **conduct his pow'rs** lead his army   18 **change names** i.e., exchange the name of "mistress" for that of "master"; **distaff** spinning stick (wifely symbol)   22 **mistress's** lover's (and also, Albany having been disposed of, lady's or wife's)   23 **Decline your head** i.e., that Goneril may kiss him   25 **Conceive** understand (with a sexual implication, that includes "stretch thy spirits," line 24; and "death," line 26: "to die," meaning "to experience sexual intercourse")   29 **My . . . body** My husband wrongfully enjoys me   30 **I . . . whistle** i.e., Once you valued me (the proverb is implied, "It is a poor dog that is not worth the whistling") 32 **disposition** nature   33 **contemns** despises   34 **bordered . . . itself** kept within its normal bounds   35 **sliver and disbranch** cut off   36 **material sap** essential and life-giving sustenance   37 **come . . . use** i.e., be as a dead branch for the burning

38 **text** i.e., on which your sermon is based   40 **Filths . . . themselves** the filthy relish only the taste of filth   43 **head-lugged bear** bear-baited by the dogs, and hence enraged   44 **madded** made mad   47 **visible spirits** avenging spirits in material form   51 **Milk-livered** lily-livered (hence cowardly, the liver being regarded as the seat of courage)   53–54 **discerning . . . suffering** able to distinguish between insults that ought to be resented and ordinary pain that is to be borne   55–56 **Fools . . . mischief** Only fools are sorry for criminals whose intended criminality is prevented by punishment   57 **noiseless** i.e., the drum, signifying preparation for war, is silent   58 **helm** helmet; **thy . . . threat** France begins to threaten Albany's realm   59 **moral** moralizing; but also with the implication that morality and folly are one   61 **Proper** (1) natural (to a fiend) (2) fair-appearing

GONERIL: O vain fool!

ALBANY:
Thou changèd and self-covered° thing, for shame,
Be-monster not thy feature.° Were't my fitness°
65 To let these hands obey my blood,°
They are apt enough to dislocate and tear
Thy flesh and bones: howe'er° thou art a fiend,
A woman's shape doth shield thee.

GONERIL:
Marry, your manhood mew° —

(*Enter a* MESSENGER.)

70 ALBANY: What news?

MESSENGER:
O, my good lord, the Duke of Cornwall's dead,
Slain by his servant, going to° put out
The other eye of Gloucester.

ALBANY: Gloucester's eyes!

MESSENGER:
A servant that he bred,° thrilled with remorse,°
75 Opposed against the act, bending his sword
To his great master, who thereat enraged
Flew on him, and amongst them felled° him dead,
But not without that harmful stroke which since
Hath plucked him after.°

ALBANY: This shows you are above,
80 You justicers,° that these our nether° crimes
So speedily can venge.° But, O poor Gloucester!
Lost he his other eye?

MESSENGER: Both, both, my lord.
This letter, madam, craves° a speedy answer;
'Tis from your sister.

GONERIL [*aside*]:   One way I like this well;
85 But being widow, and my Gloucester with her,

May all the building in my fancy pluck
Upon my hateful life.° Another way,°
The news is not so tart.° — I'll read, and answer.   (*Exit.*)

ALBANY:
Where was his son when they did take his eyes?

MESSENGER:
Come with my lady hither.

ALBANY: He is not here.   90

MESSENGER:
No, my good lord; I met him back° again.

ALBANY:
Knows he the wickedness?

MESSENGER:
Ay, my good lord; 'twas he informed against him,
And quit the house on purpose, that their punishment
Might have the freer course.

ALBANY: Gloucester, I live   95
To thank thee for the love thou showed'st the king,
And to revenge thine eyes. Come hither, friend:
Tell me what more thou know'st.   (*Exeunt.*)

[SCENE III. *The French camp near Dover.*]

Enter KENT *and a* GENTLEMAN.

KENT: Why the King of France is so suddenly gone back, know you no reason?

GENTLEMAN: Something he left imperfect in the state,° which since his coming forth is thought of, which imports° to the kingdom so   5 much fear and danger that his personal return was most required and necessary.

KENT:
Who hath he left behind him general?

GENTLEMAN: The Marshal of France, Monsieur La Far.   10

KENT: Did your letters pierce° the queen to any demonstration of grief?

GENTLEMAN:
Ay, sir; she took them, read them in my presence,

---

63 **changèd and self-covered** i.e., transformed, by the contorting of her woman's face, on which appears the fiendish behavior she has allowed herself (Goneril has disguised nature by wickedness)   64 **Be-monster ... feature** do not change your appearance into a fiend's; **my fitness** appropriate for me   65 **blood** passion   67 **howe'er** but even if   69 **your manhood mew** (1) coop up or confine (pretended) manhood (2) molt or shed it, if that is what is supposed to "shield" me from you   72 **going to** as he was about to   74 **bred** reared; **thrilled with remorse** pierced by compassion   77 **amongst them felled** others assisting, they felled   79 **plucked him after** i.e., brought Cornwall to death with his servant   80 **justicers** judges; **nether** committed below (on earth)   81 **venge** avenge   83 **craves** demands

86–87 **May ... life** These things (line 85) may send my future hopes, my castles in air, crashing down upon the hateful (married) life I lead now   87 **Another way** looked at another way   88 **tart** sour   91 **back** going back
IV.III.3–4 **imperfect ... state** unsettled in his own kingdom   5 **imports** portends   11 **pierce** impel

And now and then an ample tear trilled° down
15 Her delicate cheek: it seemed she was a queen
Over her passion, who most rebel-like
Sought to be king o'er her.
KENT: O, then it moved her.
GENTLEMAN:
Not to a rage: patience and sorrow strove
Who should express her goodliest.° You have seen
20 Sunshine and rain at once: her smiles and tears
Were like a better way:° those happy smilets°
That played on her ripe lip seemed not to know
What guests were in her eyes, which parted thence
As pearls from diamonds dropped. In brief,
25 Sorrow would be a rarity most belovèd,
If all could so become it.°
KENT: Made she no verbal question?
GENTLEMAN:
Faith, once or twice she heaved° the name of "father"
Pantingly forth, as if it pressed her heart;
Cried, "Sisters! Sisters! Shame of ladies! Sisters!
Kent! Father! Sisters! What, i' th' storm? i'
30 th' night?
Let pity not be believed!"° There she shook
The holy water from her heavenly eyes,
And clamor moistened:° then away she started
To deal with grief alone.
KENT: It is the stars,
35 The stars above us, govern our conditions;°
Else one self mate and make could not beget
Such different issues.° You spoke not with her since?
GENTLEMAN: No.
KENT:
Was this before the king returned?
GENTLEMAN: No, since.

KENT:
Well, sir, the poor distressèd Lear's i' th' town; 40
Who sometime in his better tune° remembers
What we are come about, and by no means
Will yield to see his daughter.
GENTLEMAN: Why, good sir?
KENT:
A sovereign° shame so elbows° him: his own unkindness
That stripped her from his benediction, turned her 45
To foreign casualties,° gave her dear rights
To his dog-hearted daughters: these things sting
His mind so venomously that burning shame
Detains him from Cordelia.
GENTLEMAN: Alack, poor gentleman!
KENT:
Of Albany's and Cornwall's powers you heard not? 50
GENTLEMAN:
'Tis so;° they are afoot.
KENT:
Well, sir, I'll bring you to our master Lear,
And leave you to attend him: some dear cause°
Will in concealment wrap me up awhile;
When I am known aright, you shall not grieve 55
Lending me this acquaintance. I pray you, go
Along with me.   [Exeunt.]

[SCENE IV. The same. A tent.]

Enter, with drum and colors, CORDELIA,
DOCTOR, and SOLDIERS.

CORDELIA:
Alack, 'tis he: why, he was met even now
As mad as the vexed sea; singing aloud;
Crowned with rank femiter and furrow-weeds,
With hardocks, hemlock, nettles, cuckoo-flow'rs,
Darnel,° and all the idle weeds that grow 5

14 **trilled** trickled 19 **Who ... goodliest** which should give her the most becoming expression 21 **Were ... way** i.e., improved on that spectacle; **smilets** little smiles 25–26 **Sorrow ... it** sorrow would be a coveted jewel if it became others as it does her 27 **heaved** expressed with difficulty 31 **Let ... believed** Let it not be believed for pity 33 **clamor moistened** moistened clamor, i.e., mixed (and perhaps assuaged) her outcries with tears 35 **govern our conditions** determine what we are 36–37 **Else ... issues** otherwise the same husband and wife could not produce such different children

41 **better tune** composed, less jangled intervals 44 **sovereign** overpowering; **elbows** jogs his elbow (i.e., reminds him) 46 **casualties** chances 51 **'Tis so** i.e., I have heard of them 53 **dear cause** important reason
IV.iv.3–5 **femiter ... Darnel:** femiter fumitory, whose leaves and juice are bitter; furrow-weeds weeds that grow in the furrow, or plowed land; hardocks hoar or white docks (?), burdocks, harlocks; hemlock a poison; nettles plants that sting and burn; cuckoo flow'rs identified with a plant employed to remedy diseases of the brain; Darnel tares, noisome weeds

In our sustaining corn.° A century° send forth;
Search every acre in the high-grown field,
And bring him to our eye. [*Exit an* OFFICER.]
    What can man's wisdom°
In the restoring his bereavèd° sense?
10 He that helps him take all my outward° worth.
    DOCTOR:
There is means, madam:
Our foster-nurse° of nature is repose,
The which he lacks: that to provoke° in him,
Are many simples operative,° whose power
Will close the eye of anguish.
15   CORDELIA: All blest secrets,
All you unpublished virtues° of the earth,
Spring with my tears! be aidant and remedi-
    ate°
In the good man's distress! Seek, seek for him,
Lest his ungoverned rage dissolve the life
That wants the means to lead it.°
    (*Enter* MESSENGER.)
20   MESSENGER: News, madam;
The British pow'rs are marching hitherward.
    CORDELIA:
'Tis known before. Our preparation stands
In expectation of them. O dear father,
It is thy business that I go about;
25 Therefore° great France
My mourning and importuned° tears hath
    pitied.
No blown° ambition doth our arms incite,
But love, dear love, and our aged father's
    right:
Soon may I hear and see him!   (*Exeunt.*)

[SCENE V. GLOUCESTER'*s castle.*]

Enter REGAN *and* OSWALD.

    REGAN:
But are my brother's pow'rs set forth?
    OSWALD: Ay, madam.
Himself in person there?
    OSWALD: Madam, with much ado:°
Your sister is the better soldier.

    REGAN:
Lord Edmund spake not with your lord at
    home?
    OSWALD:
No, madam.   5
    REGAN:
What might import° my sister's letter to him?
    OSWALD:
I know not, lady.
    REGAN:
Faith, he is posted° hence on serious matter.
It was great ignorance,° Gloucester's eyes being
    out,
To let him live. Where he arrives he moves 10
All hearts against us: Edmund, I think, is
    gone,
In pity of his misery, to dispatch
His nighted° life; moreover, to descry
The strength o' th' enemy.
    OSWALD:
I must needs after him, madam, with my
    letter.   15
    REGAN:
Our troops set forth tomorrow: stay with us;
The ways are dangerous.
    OSWALD: I may not, madam:
My lady charged my duty° in this business.
    REGAN:
Why should she write to Edmund? Might not
    you
Transport her purposes° by word? Belike,° 20
Some things I know not what. I'll love thee
    much,
Let me unseal the letter.
    OSWALD: Madam, I had rather —
    REGAN:
I know your lady does not love her husband;
I am sure of that: and at her late° being here
She gave strange eliads° and most speaking looks 25
To noble Edmund. I know you are of her
    bosom.°
    OSWALD: I, madam?
    REGAN:
I speak in understanding: y' are; I know't:
Therefore I do advise you, take this note:°

6 **sustaining corn** life-maintaining wheat; **century** sentry (?); troop of a hundred soldiers 8 **What ... wisdom** what can science accomplish 9 **bereavèd** impaired 10 **outward** material 12 **foster-nurse** fostering nurse 13 **provoke** induce 14 **simples operative** efficacious medicinal herbs 16 **unpublished virtues** i.e., secret remedial herbs 17 **remediate** remedial 20 **wants ... it** i.e., lacks the reason to control the rage 25 **Therefore** because of that 26 **importuned** importunate 27 **blown** puffed up IV.v.2 **ado** bother and persuasion

6 **import** purport, carry as its message 8 **is posted** has ridden speedily 9 **ignorance** folly 13 **nighted** (1) darkened, because blinded (2) benighted 18 **charged my duty** ordered me as a solemn duty 20 **Transport her purposes** convey her intentions; **Belike** probably 24 **late** recently 25 **eliads** amorous looks 26 **of her bosom** in her confidence 29 **take this note** take note of this

30 My lord is dead; Edmund and I have talked;
And more convenient° is he for my hand
Than for your lady's: you may gather more.°
If you do find him, pray you, give him this;°
And when your mistress hears thus much from
you,
35 I pray, desire her call° her wisdom to her.
So, fare you well.
If you do chance to hear of that blind traitor,
Preferment° falls on him that cuts him off.
OSWALD:
Would I could meet him, madam! I should
show
What party I do follow.
40 REGAN: Fare thee well. (*Exeunt.*)

[SCENE VI. *Fields near Dover.*]

Enter GLOUCESTER *and* EDGAR.

GLOUCESTER:
When shall I come to th' top of that same
hill?
EDGAR:
You do climb up it now. Look, how we labor.
GLOUCESTER:
Methinks the ground is even.
EDGAR: Horrible steep.
Hark, do you hear the sea?
GLOUCESTER: No, truly.
EDGAR:
5 Why then your other senses grow imperfect
By your eyes' anguish.°
GLOUCESTER: So may it be indeed.
Methinks thy voice is altered, and thou
speak'st
In better phrase and matter than thou didst.
EDGAR:
Y' are much deceived: in nothing am I changed
But in my garments.
10 GLOUCESTER: Methinks y' are better spoken.
EDGAR:
Come on, sir; here's the place: stand still. How
fearful
And dizzy 'tis to cast one's eyes so low!
The crows and choughs° that wing the midway
air°
Show scarce so gross° as beetles. Half way
down

31 **convenient** fitting   32 **gather more** surmise more
yourself   33 **this** this advice   35 **call** recall   38
Preferment promotion
IV.VI.6 **anguish** pain   13 **choughs** a kind of crow;
midway air i.e., halfway down the cliff   14 **gross**
large

Hangs one that gathers sampire,° dreadful
trade!   15
Methinks he seems no bigger than his head.
The fishermen that walk upon the beach
Appear like mice; and yond tall anchoring°
bark
Diminished to her cock;° her cock, a buoy
Almost too small for sight. The murmuring
surge   20
That on th' unnumb'red idle pebble° chafes
Cannot be heard so high. I'll look no more,
Lest my brain turn and the deficient sight
Topple° down headlong.
GLOUCESTER: Set me where you stand.
EDGAR:
Give me your hand: you are now within a foot   25
Of th' extreme verge: for all beneath the moon
Would I not leap upright.°
GLOUCESTER: Let go my hand.
Here, friend, 's another purse; in it a jewel
Well worth a poor man's taking. Fairies° and
gods
Prosper it with thee! Go thou further off;   30
Bid me farewell, and let me hear thee going.
EDGAR:
Now fare ye well, good sir.
GLOUCESTER: With all my heart.
EDGAR [*aside*]:
Why I do trifle thus with his despair
Is done to cure it.°
GLOUCESTER: O you mighty gods!

(*He kneels.*)

This world I do renounce, and in your sights   35
Shake patiently my great affliction off:
If I could bear it longer and not fall
To quarrel with° your great opposeless° wills,
My snuff° and loathèd part of nature should
Burn itself out. If Edgar live, O bless him!   40
Now, fellow, fare thee well. (*He falls.*)
EDGAR: Gone, sir, farewell.

15 **sampire** samphire, an aromatic herb associated
with Dover Cliffs   18 **anchoring** anchored   19 **cock**
cockboat, a small boat usually towed behind the ship
21 **unnumb'red idle pebble** innumerable pebbles,
moved to and fro by the waves to no purpose 23–
24 **the ... Topple** my failing sight topple me   27
upright i.e., even up in the air, to say nothing of
forward, over the cliff   29 **Fairies** who are supposed
to guard and multiply hidden treasure   33–34 **Why
... it** I play on his despair in order to cure it   37–38
fall ... with rebel against   38 **opposeless** not to be,
and not capable of being, opposed   39 **snuff** the
guttering (and stinking) wick of a burnt-out candle

And yet I know not how° conceit° may rob
The treasury of life, when life itself
Yields to° the theft. Had he been where he
    thought,
45 By this had thought been past. Alive or dead?
Ho, you sir! friend! Hear you, sir! speak!
Thus might he pass° indeed: yet he revives.
What are you, sir?
    GLOUCESTER: Away, and let me die.
    EDGAR:
Hadst thou been aught but gossamer, feathers,
    air,
50 So many fathom down precipitating,°
Thou'dst shivered like an egg: but thou dost
    breathe;
Hast heavy substance; bleed'st not; speak'st; art
    sound.
Ten masts at each° make not the altitude
Which thou hast perpendicularly fell:
55 Thy life's° a miracle. Speak yet again.
    GLOUCESTER:
But have I fall'n, or no?
    EDGAR:
From the dread summit of this chalky bourn.°
Look up a-height;° the shrill-gorged° lark so far
Cannot be seen or heard: do but look up.
    GLOUCESTER:
60 Alack, I have no eyes.
Is wretchedness deprived that benefit,
To end itself by death? 'Twas yet some
    comfort,
When misery could beguile° the tyrant's rage
And frustrate his proud will.
    EDGAR: Give me your arm.
Up, so. How is't? Feel you° your legs? You
65   stand.
    GLOUCESTER:
Too well, too well.
    EDGAR: This is above all strangeness.
Upon the crown o' th' cliff, what thing was
    that
Which parted from you?
    GLOUCESTER: A poor unfortunate beggar.
    EDGAR:
As I stood here below, methought his eyes
Were two full moons; he had a thousand
70   noses,

Horns whelked° and waved like the enridgèd°
    sea:
It was some fiend; therefore, thou happy
    father,°
Think that the clearest° gods, who make them
    honors
Of men's impossibilities,° have preserved thee.
    GLOUCESTER:
I do remember now: henceforth I'll bear   75
Affliction till it do cry out itself,
"Enough, enough," and die. That thing you
    speak of,
I took it for a man; often 'twould say,
"The fiend, the fiend" — he led me to that
    place.
    EDGAR:
Bear free° and patient thoughts.

(*Enter* LEAR [*fantastically dressed with wild
flowers*].)

                    But who comes here?   80
The safer° sense will ne'er accommodate°
His master thus.
    LEAR: No, they cannot touch me for
coining;° I am the king himself.
    EDGAR:
O thou side-piercing sight!   85
    LEAR: Nature's above art in that respect.°
There's your press-money.° That fellow handles
his bow like a crow-keeper;° draw me a
clothier's yard.° Look, look, a mouse! Peace,
peace; this piece of toasted cheese will do't.   90
There's my gauntlet;° I'll prove it on° a giant.

---

71 **whelked** twisted; **enridgèd** i.e., furrowed into
waves 72 **happy father** fortunate old man 73
clearest purest 73–74 **who ... impossibilities** who
cause themselves to be honored and revered by performing miracles of which men are incapable 80
free i.e., emancipated from grief and despair, which
fetter the soul 81 **safer** sounder, saner; **accommodate** dress, adorn 83–84 **touch ... coining** arrest
me for minting coins (the king's prerogative) 86
Nature's ... respect i.e., a born king is superior to
legal (and hence artificial) inhibition; there is also a
glance here at the popular Renaissance debate concerning the relative importance of nature (inspiration) and art (training) 87 **press-money** paid to
conscripted soldiers 88 **crow-keeper** a farmer scar-
ing away crows 89 **clothier's yard** the standard
English arrow was a cloth-yard long; here the injunction is to draw the arrow back, like a powerful archer,
a full yard to the ear 91 **gauntlet** armored glove,
thrown down as a challenge; **prove it on** maintain
my challenge even against

---

42 **how** but what; **conceit** imagination 44 **Yields
to** allows 47 **pass** die 50 **precipitating** falling 53
at each one on top of the other 55 **life's** survival
57 **bourn** boundary 58 **a-height** on high; **gorged**
throated, voiced 63 **beguile** cheat (i.e., by suicide)
65 **Feel you** have you any feeling in

Bring up the brown bills.° O, well flown,°
bird! i' th' clout, i' th' clout:° hewgh!° Give
the word.°
95   EDGAR: Sweet marjoram.°
      LEAR: Pass.
      GLOUCESTER:
I know that voice.
      LEAR: Ha! Goneril, with a white beard!
They flattered me like a dog,° and told me I
100   had white hairs in my beard ere the black ones
were there.° To say "ay" and "no" to
everything that I said! "Ay" and "no" too was
no good divinity.° When the rain came to wet
me once and the wind to make me chatter;
105   when the thunder would not peace at my
bidding; there I found 'em, there I smelt 'em
out. Go to, they are not men o' their words:
they told me I was everything; 'tis a lie, I am
not ague-proof.°
      GLOUCESTER:
110   The trick° of that voice I do well remember:
Is't not the king?
      LEAR: Ay, every inch a king.
When I do stare, see how the subject quakes.
I pardon that man's life. What was thy cause?°
Adultery?
115   Thou shalt not die: die for adultery! No:
The wren goes to't, and the small gilded fly
Does lecher° in my sight.
Let copulation thrive; for Gloucester's bastard
      son
Was kinder to his father than my daughters
120   Got° 'tween the lawful sheets.
To't, luxury,° pell-mell! for I lack soldiers.°
Behold yond simp'ring dame,

92 **brown bills** halberds varnished to prevent rust
(here the reference is to the soldiers who carry them);
well flown falconer's cry; and perhaps a reference to
the flight of the arrow   93 **clout** the target shot at;
hewgh imitating the whizzing of the arrow (?)   94
word password   95 **Sweet marjoram** herb, used as a
remedy for brain disease   99 **like a dog** as a dog
flatters   99–101 **I . . . there** I was wise before I had
even grown a beard   103 **no good divinity** bad theology, because contrary to the biblical saying (II
Corinthians 1:18), "Our word toward you was not
yea and nay"; see also James 5:12, "But let your yea
be yea, and your nay, nay; lest ye fall into condemnation"; and Matthew 5:36–37   109 **ague-proof** secure against fever   110 **trick** intonation   113 **cause**
offense   117 **lecher** copulate   120 **Got** begot   121
luxury lechery; **for . . . soldiers** i.e., (1) whom copulation will supply (?) (2) and am therefore power-
less (?)

Whose face between her forks presages snow,°
That minces° virtue and does shake the head
To hear of pleasure's name.°   125
The fitchew,° nor the soilèd° horse, goes to't
With a more riotous appetite.
Down from the waist they are Centaurs,°
Though women all above:
But to the girdle° do the gods inherit,°   130
Beneath is all the fiend's.
There's hell, there's darkness, there is the
sulphurous pit, burning, scalding, stench,
consumption; fie, fie, fie! pah, pah! Give me
an ounce of civet;° good apothecary, sweeten   135
my imagination: there's money for thee.
      GLOUCESTER:
O, let me kiss that hand!
      LEAR:
Let me wipe it first; it smells of mortality.°
      GLOUCESTER:
O ruined piece of nature! This great world
Shall so wear out to nought.° Dost thou know
      me?   140
      LEAR: I remember thine eyes well enough.
Dost thou squiny° at me? No, do thy worst,
blind Cupid;° I'll not love. Read thou this
challenge;° mark but the penning of it.
      GLOUCESTER:
Were all thy letters suns, I could not see.   145
      EDGAR:
I would not take° this from report: it is,
And my heart breaks at it.
      LEAR: Read.
      GLOUCESTER:
What, with the case° of eyes?
      LEAR: O, ho, are you there with me?° No   150
eyes in your head, nor no money in your
purse? Your eyes are in a heavy case,° your

123 **Whose . . . snow** whose cold demeanor seems
to promise chaste behavior ("forks" = legs)   124
minces squeamishly pretends to   125 **pleasure's
name** the very name of sexual pleasure   126 **fitchew**
polecat (and slang for prostitute); **soilèd** put to pasture, and hence wanton with feeding   128 **Centaurs**
lustful creatures, half man and half horse   130 **girdle**
waist; **inherit** possess   135 **civet** perfume   138 **mortality** (1) death (2) existence   139–140 **This . . .
nought** i.e., The universe (macrocosm) will decay to
nothing in the same way as the little world of man
(microcosm)   142 **squiny** squint, look sideways, like
a prostitute   143 **blind Cupid** the sign hung before a
brothel   144 **challenge** a reminiscence of lines 90–
91   146 **take** believe   149 **case** empty sockets   150
are . . . me is that what you tell me   152 **heavy case**
sad plight (pun on line 149)

purse in a light,° yet you see how this world goes.

GLOUCESTER:

155 I see it feelingly.°

LEAR: What, art mad? A man may see how this world goes with no eyes. Look with thine ears: see how yond justice rails upon yond simple° thief. Hark, in thine ear: change

160 places, and, handy-dandy,° which is the justice, which is the thief? Thou hast seen a farmer's dog bark at a beggar?

GLOUCESTER: Ay, sir.

LEAR: And the creature run from the cur?

165 There thou mightst behold the great image of authority:° a dog's obeyed in office.°

Thou rascal beadle,° hold thy bloody hand!

Why dost thou lash that whore? Strip thy own back;

Thou hotly lusts to use her in that kind°

For which thou whip'st her. The usurer hangs

170 the cozener.°

Through tattered clothes small vices do appear;

Robes and furred gowns° hide all. Plate sin with gold,

And the strong lance of justice hurtless° breaks;

Arm it in rags, a pygmy's straw does pierce it.

None does offend, none, I say, none; I'll able° 'em:

175 Take that° of me, my friend, who have the power

To seal th' accuser's lips. Get thee glass eyes,°

And, like a scurvy politician,° seem

To see the things thou dost not. Now, now, now, now.

180 Pull off my boots: harder, harder: so.

EDGAR:

O, matter and impertinency° mixed!

Reason in madness!

LEAR:

If thou wilt weep my fortunes, take my eyes.

I know thee well enough; thy name is Gloucester:

Thou must be patient; we came crying hither: 185

Thou know'st, the first time that we smell the air

We wawl and cry. I will preach to thee: mark.

GLOUCESTER:

Alack, alack the day!

LEAR:

When we are born, we cry that we are come

To this great stage of fools. This'° a good block.° 190

It were a delicate° stratagem, to shoe

A troop of horse with felt: I'll put't in proof;°

And when I have stol'n upon these son-in-laws,

Then, kill, kill, kill, kill, kill, kill!

(*Enter a* GENTLEMAN, [*with* ATTENDANTS].)

GENTLEMAN:

O, here he is: lay hand upon him. Sir, 195

Your most dear daughter —

LEAR:

No rescue? What, a prisoner? I am even

The natural fool° of fortune. Use me well;

You shall have ransom. Let me have surgeons;

I am cut° to th' brains.

GENTLEMAN: You shall have anything. 200

LEAR:

No seconds?° all myself?

Why, this would make a man a man of salt,°

153 **light** i.e., empty 155 **feelingly** (1) by touch (2) by feeling pain (3) with emotion 159 **simple** common, of low estate 160 **handy-dandy** i.e., choose, guess (after the children's game — "Handy-dandy, prickly prandy" — of choosing the correct hand) 165–166 **image of authority** symbol revealing the true meaning of authority 166 **a dog's . . . office** i.e., whoever has power is obeyed 167 **beadle** parish constable 169 **kind** i.e., sexual act 170 **The usurer . . . cozener** i.e., The powerful money-lender, in his role as judge, puts to death the petty cheat 172 **Robes . . . gowns** worn by a judge 173 **hurtless** i.e., without hurting the sinner 175 **able** vouch for 176 **that** the immunity just conferred (line 175) 177 **glass eyes** spectacles 178 **scurvy politician** vile politic man

181 **matter and impertinency** sense and nonsense 190 **This** this is; **block** various meanings have been suggested, for example, the stump of a tree, on which Lear is supposed to climb; a mounting-block, which suggests "horse" (line 192); a hat (which Lear or another must be made to wear), from the block on which a felt hat is molded, and which would suggest a "felt" (line 192); the proposal here is that "block" be taken to denote the quintain, whose function is to bear blows, "a mere lifeless block" (*As You Like It,* I.ii.247), an object shaped like a man and used for tilting practice; see also *Much Ado About Nothing,* II.i.231–32, "She misused me past the endurance of a block!" and, in the same passage, the associated reference, "I stood like a man at a mark [target]" (lines 237–38) 191 **delicate** subtle 192 **put't in proof** test it 198 **natural fool** born sport (with pun on "natural" = imbecile) 200 **cut** wounded 201 **seconds** supporters 202 **man of salt** i.e., all (salt) tears

To use his eyes for garden water-pots,
Ay, and laying autumn's dust.

GENTLEMAN:
205   Good sir —

LEAR:
I will die bravely,° like a smug° bridegroom.°
      What!
I will be jovial: come, come; I am a king;
Masters, know you that?

GENTLEMAN:
You are a royal one, and we obey you.

210   LEAR: Then there's life in't.° Come, and you
get it, you shall get it by running. Sa, sa, sa,
sa.°

            (*Exit* [*running;* ATTENDANTS *follow*].)

GENTLEMAN:
A sight most pitiful in the meanest wretch,
Past speaking of in a king! Thou hast one
      daughter
215   Who redeems Nature from the general curse
Which twain have brought her to.°

EDGAR:
Hail, gentle° sir.

GENTLEMAN:
                  Sir, speed° you: what's your will?

EDGAR:
Do you hear aught, sir, of a battle toward?°

GENTLEMAN:
Most sure and vulgar:° every one hears that,
Which can distinguish sound.

220   EDGAR: But, by your favor,
How near's the other army?

GENTLEMAN:
Near and on speedy foot; the main descry
Stands on the hourly thought.°

EDGAR: I thank you, sir: that's all.

GENTLEMAN:
Though that the queen on special cause is
      here,
Her army is moved on.

225   EDGAR: I thank you, sir.
            (*Exit* [GENTLEMAN].)

GLOUCESTER:
You ever-gentle gods, take my breath from me;
Let not my worser spirit° tempt me again
To die before you please.

EDGAR: Well pray you, father.

GLOUCESTER:
Now, good sir, what are you?

EDGAR:
A most poor man, made tame° to fortune's
      blows;   230
Who, by the art of known and feeling
      sorrows,°
Am pregnant° to good pity. Give me your
      hand,
I'll lead you to some biding.°

GLOUCESTER: Hearty thanks;
The bounty and the benison° of heaven
To boot, and boot.°

            (*Enter* OSWALD.)

OSWALD:
                  A proclaimed prize!° Most happy!°   235
That eyeless head of thine was first framed°
      flesh
To raise my fortunes. Thou old unhappy
      traitor,
Briefly thyself remember:° the sword is out
That must destroy thee.

GLOUCESTER: Now let thy friendly° hand
Put strength enough to't. [EDGAR *interposes*.]

OSWALD: Wherefore, bold peasant,   240
Dar'st thou support a published° traitor?
      Hence!
Lest that th' infection of his fortune take
Like hold on thee. Let go his arm.

EDGAR:
Chill° not let go, zir, without vurther 'casion.°

OSWALD:
Let go, slave, or thou diest!   245

EDGAR: Good gentleman, go your gait,° and

---

227 **worser spirit** bad angel, evil side of my nature   230 **tame** submissive   231 **art . . . sorrows** instruction of sorrows painfully experienced   232 **pregnant** disposed   233 **biding** place of refuge   234 **benison** blessing   235 **To . . . boot** also, and in the highest degree; **proclaimed prize** i.e., one with a price on his head; **happy** fortunate (for Oswald)   236 **framed** created   238 **thyself remember** i.e., pray, think of your sins   239 **friendly** i.e., because it offers the death Gloucester covets   241 **published** proclaimed   244 **Chill** I will (Edgar speaks in rustic dialect); **vurther 'casion** further occasion   246 **gait** way

206 **bravely** (1) smartly attired (2) courageously; **smug** spick and span; **bridegroom** whose "brave" sexual feats are picked up in the pun on "die"   210 **there's life in't** there's still hope   211–212 **Sa . . . sa** hunting and rallying cry; also an interjection of defiance   215–216 **general . . . to** (1) universal condemnation which Goneril and Regan have made for (2) damnation incurred by the original sin of Adam and Eve   217 **gentle** noble; **speed** God speed   218 **toward** impending   219 **vulgar** common knowledge   222–223 **the main . . . thought** we expect to see the main body of the army any hour

let poor volk° pass. And chud ha' bin
zwaggered° out of my life, 'twould not ha' bin
zo long as 'tis by a vortnight. Nay, come not
250 near th' old man; keep out, che vor' ye,° or
I'se° try whether your costard° or my ballow°
be the harder: chill be plain with you.

OSWALD: Out, dunghill!

(*They fight.*)

EDGAR: Chill pick your teeth,° zir: come; no
255 matter vor your foins.°

[OSWALD *falls.*]

OSWALD:
Slave, thou hast slain me. Villain, take my
     purse:
If ever thou wilt thrive, bury my body,
And give the letters which thou find'st about°
     me
To Edmund Earl of Gloucester; seek him out
260 Upon the English party.° O, untimely death!
Death!   (*He dies.*)

EDGAR:
I know thee well. A serviceable° villain,
As duteous° to the vices of thy mistress
As badness would desire.

GLOUCESTER: What, is he dead?

EDGAR:
265 Sit you down, father; rest you.
Let's see these pockets: the letters that he
     speaks of
May be my friends. He's dead; I am only sorry
He had no other deathsman.° Let us see:
Leave,° gentle wax;° and, manners, blame us
     not:
To know our enemies' minds, we rip their
270   hearts;
Their papers° is more lawful.

(*Reads the letter.*)

"Let our reciprocal vows be remembered. You
have many opportunities to cut him off: if
your will want not,° time and place will be

fruitfully offered. There is nothing done, if he 275
return the conqueror: then am I the prisoner,
and his bed my jail; from the loathed warmth
whereof deliver me, and supply the place for
your labor.
"Your—wife, so I would° say—affectionate 280
servant, and for you her own for venture,°
                                   Goneril."

O indistinguished space of woman's will!°
A plot upon her virtuous husband's life;
And the exchange° my brother! Here in the
     sands   285
Thee I'll rake up,° the post unsanctified°
Of murderous lechers; and in the mature°
     time,
With this ungracious paper° strike° the sight
Of the death-practiced° duke: for him 'tis well
That of thy death and business I can tell.   290

GLOUCESTER:
The king is mad: how stiff° is my vile sense,°
That I stand up, and have ingenious° feeling
Of my huge sorrows! Better I were distract:°
So should my thoughts be severed from my
     griefs,
And woes by wrong imaginations° lose   295
The knowledge of themselves.

                         (*Drum afar off.*)

EDGAR: Give me your hand:
Far off, methinks, I hear the beaten drum.
Come, father, I'll bestow° you with a friend.

                                   (*Exeunt.*)

SCENE VII. [*A tent in the French camp.*]

Enter CORDELIA, KENT, DOCTOR, *and* GENTLE-
MAN.

CORDELIA:
O thou good Kent, how shall I live and work,
To match thy goodness? My life will be too
     short,
And every measure fail me.

280 **would** would like to   281 **and . . . venture** i.e.,
and one who holds you her own for venturing (Edmund had earlier been promised union by Goneril,
"If you dare venture in your own behalf," IV.II.21)
283 **indistinguished . . . will** unlimited range of woman's lust   285 **exchange** substitute   286 **rake up**
cover up, bury; **post unsanctified** unholy messenger
287 **mature** ripe   288 **ungracious paper** wicked letter; **strike** blast   289 **death-practiced** whose death
is plotted   291 **stiff** unbending; **vile sense** hateful
capacity for feeling   292 **ingenious** conscious   293
distract distracted, mad   295 **wrong imaginations**
delusions   298 **bestow** lodge

247 **volk** folk   247–248 **And . . . zwaggered** if I
could have been swaggered   250 **che vor' ye** I warrant you   251 **I'se** I shall; **costard** head (literally,
"apple"); **ballow** cudgel   254 **Chill . . . teeth** I will
knock your teeth out   255 **foins** thrusts   258 **about**
upon   260 **party** side   262 **serviceable** ready to be
used   263 **duteous** obedient   268 **deathsman** exe-
cutioner   269 **Leave** by your leave; **wax** with which
the letter is sealed   271 **Their papers** i.e., to rip their
papers   273–274 **if . . . not** if your desire (and lust)
be not lacking

KENT:
To be acknowledged, madam, is o'erpaid.
5 All my reports go° with the modest truth,
Nor more nor clipped,° but so.
     CORDELIA: Be better suited:°
These weeds° are memories° of those worser
     hours:
I prithee, put them off.
     KENT: Pardon, dear madam;
Yet to be known shortens my made intent:°
10 My boon I make it,° that you know me not
Till time and I think meet.°
     CORDELIA:
Then be't so, my good lord. [*To the* DOCTOR.]
     How does the king?
     DOCTOR:
Madam, sleeps still.
     CORDELIA:
O you kind gods!
15 Cure this great breach in his abusèd° nature.
Th' untuned and jarring senses, O, wind up°
Of this child-changèd° father.
     DOCTOR: So please your majesty
That we may wake the king: he hath slept
     long.
     CORDELIA:
Be governed by your knowledge, and proceed
20 I' th' sway of° your own will. Is he arrayed?

(*Enter* LEAR *in a chair carried by*
SERVANTS.)

     GENTLEMAN:
Ay, madam; in the heaviness of sleep
We put fresh garments on him.
     DOCTOR:
Be by good madam, when we do awake
     him;
I doubt not of his temperance.°
     CORDELIA: Very well.
     DOCTOR:
Please you, draw near. Louder the music
25   there!
     CORDELIA:
O my dear father, restoration hang
Thy medicine on my lips, and let this kiss

Repair those violent harms that my two sisters
Have in thy reverence° made.
     KENT: Kind and dear princess.
     CORDELIA:
Had you not been their father, these white
     flakes°   30
Did challenge° pity of them. Was this a face
To be opposed against the warring winds?
To stand against the deep dread-bolted°
     thunder?
In the most terrible and nimble stroke
Of quick, cross° lightning to watch — poor
     perdu!° —   35
With this thin helm?° Mine enemy's dog,
Though he had bit me, should have stood that
     night
Against my fire; and wast thou fain,° poor
     father,
To hovel thee with swine and rogues° forlorn,
In short° and musty straw?° Alack, alack!   40
'Tis wonder that thy life and wits at once
Had not concluded all.° He wakes; speak to
     him.
     DOCTOR:
Madam, do you; 'tis fittest.
     CORDELIA:
How does my royal lord? How fares your
     majesty?
     LEAR:
You do me wrong to take me out o' th' grave: 45
Thou art a soul in bliss; but I am bound
Upon a wheel of fire,° that mine own tears
Do scald like molten lead.
     CORDELIA: Sir, do you know me?
     LEAR:
You are a spirit, I know. Where did you die?
     CORDELIA:
Still, still, far wide.°   50

29 **reverence** revered person   30 **flakes** hairs (in long
strands)   31 **challenge** claim   33 **deep dread-
bolted** deep-voiced and furnished with the dreadful
thunderbolt   35 **cross** zigzag; **perdu** (1) sentry in a
forlorn position (1) lost one   36 **helm** helmet (his
scanty hair)   38 **fain** pleased   39 **rogues** vagabonds
40 **short** when straw is freshly cut, it is long, and
suitable for bedding, given its flexibility and crisp-
ness; as it is used, it becomes musty, shreds into
pieces, is "short"; in contemporary Maine usage,
"short manure" refers to dung mixed with straw that
has been broken up, "long manure" to dung mixed
with coarse new straw   42 **concluded all** come to a
complete end   47 **wheel of fire** torment associated
by the Middle Ages with hell, where Lear thinks he is
50 **wide** i.e., of the mark (of sanity)

IV.VII.5 **go** conform   6 **clipped** curtailed; **suited**
attired   7 **weeds** clothes; **memories** reminders   9
Yet ... intent to reveal myself just yet interferes with
the plan I have made   10 **My ... it** I ask this reward
11 **meet** fitting   15 **abusèd** disturbed   16 **wind up**
tune   17 **child-changèd** changed, deranged (and
also, reduced to a child) by the cruelty of his children
20 **I' ... of** according to   24 **temperance** sanity

DOCTOR:
He's scarce awake: let him alone awhile.

LEAR:
Where have I been? Where am I? Fair
daylight?
I am mightily abused.° I should ev'n die with
pity,
To see another thus. I know not what to say.
55 I will not swear these are my hands: let's see;
I feel this pin prick. Would I were assured
Of my condition.

CORDELIA: O, look upon me, sir,
And hold your hand in benediction o'er me.
You must not kneel.

LEAR: Pray, do not mock me:
60 I am a very foolish fond° old man,
Fourscore and upward, not an hour more nor
less;
And, to deal plainly,
I fear I am not in my perfect mind.
Methinks I should know you and know this
man,
65 Yet I am doubtful; for I am mainly° ignorant
What place this is, and all the skill I have
Remembers not these garments, nor I know
not
Where I did lodge last night. Do not laugh at
me,
For, as I am a man, I think this lady
To be my child Cordelia.
70 CORDELIA: And so I am, I am.

LEAR:
Be your tears wet? Yes, faith. I pray, weep not.
If you have poison for me, I will drink it.
I know you do not love me; for your sisters
Have, as I do remember, done me wrong.
You have some cause, they have not.
75 CORDELIA: No cause, no cause.

LEAR:
Am I in France?

KENT: In your own kingdom, sir.

LEAR:
Do not abuse° me.

DOCTOR:
Be comforted, good madam: the great rage,°
You see, is killed in him: and yet it is danger
80 To make him even o'er° the time he has lost.
Desire him to go in; trouble him no more
Till further settling.°

CORDELIA:
Will't please your highness walk?°

LEAR: You must bear with me.
Pray you now, forget and forgive. I am old and
foolish.

(Exeunt. Mane[n]t° KENT
and GENTLEMAN.)

GENTLEMAN: Holds it true, sir, that the 85
Duke of Cornwall was so slain?

KENT: Most certain, sir.

GENTLEMAN: Who is conductor of his
people?

KENT: As 'tis said, the bastard son of 90
Gloucester.

GENTLEMAN: They say Edgar, his banished
son, is with the Earl of Kent in Germany.

KENT: Report is changeable.° 'Tis time to 95
look about; the powers° of the kingdom
approach apace.

GENTLEMAN: The arbitrement° is like to be
bloody. Fare you well, sir.   [Exit.]

KENT:
My point and period will be throughly
wrought,°
Or well or ill, as this day's battle's fought. 100
(Exit.)

ACT V

SCENE I. [The British camp near Dover.]

Enter, with drum and colors, EDMUND,
REGAN, GENTLEMEN, and SOLDIERS.

EDMUND:
Know° of the duke if his last purpose hold,°
Or whether since he is advised° by aught
To change the course: he's full of alteration
And self-reproving: bring his constant plea-
sure.°
[To a GENTLEMAN, who goes out.]

REGAN:
Our sister's man is certainly miscarried.° 5

---

83 **walk** perhaps in the sense of "withdraw"   84 s.d.
Mane[n]t remain   95 **Report is changeable** rumors
are unreliable   96 **powers** armies   98 **arbitrement**
deciding encounter   99 **My . . . wrought** the aim and
end, the close of my life, will be completely worked
out
V.I.1 **Know** learn; **last purpose hold** most recent
intention (to fight) be maintained   2 **advised** induced   4 **constant pleasure** fixed (final) decision
5 **miscarried** come to grief

53 **abused** deluded   60 **fond** in dotage   65 **mainly**
entirely   77 **abuse** deceive   78 **rage** frenzy   80
even o'er smooth over by filling in; and hence, "recollect"   82 **settling** calming

EDMUND:
'Tis to be doubted,° madam.
REGAN: Now, sweet lord,
You know the goodness I intend upon you:
Tell me, but truly, but then speak the truth,
Do you not love my sister?
EDMUND: In honored° love.
REGAN:
10   But have you never found my brother's way
To the forfended° place?
EDMUND: That thought abuses° you.
REGAN:
I am doubtful that you have been conjunct
And bosomed with her, as far as we call hers.°
EDMUND:
No, by mine honor, madam.
REGAN:
15   I shall never endure her: dear my lord,
Be not familiar with her.
EDMUND: Fear° me not. —
She and the duke her husband!

(*Enter, with drum and colors,* ALBANY,
GONERIL, [*and*] SOLDIERS.)

GONERIL [*aside*]:
I had rather lose the battle than that sister
Should loosen° him and me.
ALBANY:
20   Our very loving sister, well be-met.°
Sir, this I heard, the king is come to his
daughter,
With others whom the rigor of our state°
Forced to cry out. Where I could not be
honest,°
I never yet was valiant: for this business,
25   It touches us, as° France invades our land,
Not bolds the king, with others, whom, I fear,
Most just and heavy causes make oppose.°
EDMUND:
Sir, you speak nobly.
REGAN: Why is this reasoned?°
GONERIL:
Combine together 'gainst the enemy;

---

6 **doubted** feared   9 **honored** honorable   11 **for-
fended** forbidden; **abuses** (1) deceives (2) demeans,
is unworthy of   12–13 **I . . . hers** I fear that you have
united with her intimately, in the fullest possible way
16 **Fear** distrust   19 **loosen** separate   20 **be-met**
met   22 **rigor . . . state** tyranny of our government
23 **honest** honorable   25 **touches us, as** concerns me,
only in that   26–27 **Not . . . oppose** and not in that
France emboldens the king and others, who have
been led, by real and serious grievances, to take up
arms against us   28 **reasoned** argued

For these domestic and particular broils°   30
Are not the question° here.
ALBANY: Let's then determine
With th' ancient of war° on our proceeding.
EDMUND:
I shall attend you presently at your tent.
REGAN:
Sister, you'll go with us?°
GONERIL: No.   35
REGAN:
'Tis most convenient;° pray you, go with us.
GONERIL [*aside*]:
O, ho, I know the riddle.° — I will go.
(*Exeunt both the* ARMIES.)

(*Enter* EDGAR [*disguised*].)

EDGAR:
If e'er your grace had speech with man so
poor,
Hear me one word.
ALBANY [*to those going out*]:
I'll overtake you. [*To* EDGAR.] Speak.
(*Exeunt* [*all but* ALBANY *and* EDGAR].)
EDGAR:
Before you fight the battle, ope this letter.   40
If you have victory, let the trumpet sound
For° him that brought it: wretched though I
seem,
I can produce a champion that will prove°
What is avouchèd° there. If you miscarry,
Your business of° the world hath so an end,   45
And machination° ceases. Fortune love you.
ALBANY:
Stay till I have read the letter.
EDGAR: I was forbid it.
When time shall serve, let but the herald cry,
And I'll appear again.
ALBANY:
Why, fare thee well: I will o'erlook° thy paper. 50
(*Exit* [EDGAR].)

(*Enter* EDMUND.)

EDMUND:
The enemy's in view: draw up your powers.
Here is the guess° of their true strength and
forces

---

30 **particular broils** private quarrels   31 **question**
issue   32 **th' ancient of war** experienced comman-
ders   34 **us** me (rather than Edmund)   36 **convenient** fitting, desirable   37 **riddle** real reason (for
Regan's curious request)   41–42 **sound For** summon   43 **prove** i.e., by trial of combat   44 **avouchèd**
maintained   45 **of** in   46 **machination** plotting   50
o'erlook read over   52 **guess** estimate

By diligent discovery;° but your haste
Is now urged on you.
    ALBANY: We will greet° the time. (*Exit.*)
    EDMUND:
55 To both these sisters have I sworn my love;
Each jealous° of the other, as the stung
Are of the adder. Which of them shall I take?
Both? One? Or neither? Neither can be
    enjoyed,
If both remain alive: to take the widow
60 Exasperates, makes mad her sister Goneril;
And hardly° shall I carry out my side,°
Her husband being alive. Now then, we'll use
His countenance° for the battle; which being
    done,
Let her who would be rid of him devise
65 His speedy taking off. As for the mercy
Which he intends to Lear and to Cordelia,
The battle done, and they within our power,
Shall never see his pardon; for my state
Stands on me to defend, not to debate.°
                       (*Exit.*)

SCENE II. [*A field between the two camps.*]

Alarum° within. Enter, with drum and colors, LEAR, CORDELIA, *and* SOLDIERS, *over the stage; and exeunt.*
    Enter EDGAR *and* GLOUCESTER.

    EDGAR:
Here, father,° take the shadow of this tree
For your good host; pray that the right may
    thrive.
If ever I return to you again,
I'll bring you comfort.
    GLOUCESTER: Grace go with you, sir.
                (*Exit* [EDGAR].)

(*Alarum and retreat° within.* [*Re*]*enter* EDGAR.)

    EDGAR:
5 Away, old man; give me thy hand; away!

King Lear hath lost, he and his daughter ta'en:°
Give me thy hand; come on.
    GLOUCESTER:
No further, sir; a man may rot even here.
    EDGAR:
What, in ill thoughts again? Men must endure
Their going hence, even as their coming
    hither: 10
Ripeness° is all. Come on.
    GLOUCESTER: And that's true too.
                    (*Exeunt.*)

SCENE III. [*The British camp near Dover.*]

Enter, in conquest, with drum and colors, EDMUND; LEAR *and* CORDELIA, *as prisoners;* SOLDIERS, CAPTAIN.

    EDMUND:
Some officers take them away: good guard,°
Until their greater pleasures° first be known
That are to censure° them.
    CORDELIA: We are not the first
Who with best meaning° have incurred the
    worst.
For thee, oppressèd king, I am cast down;   5
Myself could else out-frown false Fortune's
    frown.
Shall we not see these daughters and these
    sisters?
    LEAR:
No, no, no, no! Come, let's away to prison:
We two alone will sing like birds i' th' cage:
When thou dost ask me blessing, I'll kneel
    down   10
And ask of thee forgiveness: so we'll live,
And pray, and sing, and tell old tales, and
    laugh
At gilded butterflies,° and hear poor rogues
Talk of court news; and we'll talk with them
    too,
Who loses and who wins, who's in, who's out; 15
And take upon's the mystery of things,
As if we were God's spies:° and we'll wear
    out,°

---

53 **By diligent discovery** obtained by careful reconnoitering 54 **greet** i.e., meet the demands of 56 **jealous** suspicious 61 **hardly** with difficulty; **carry . . . side** (1) satisfy my ambition (2) fulfill my bargain (with Goneril) 63 **countenance** authority 68–69 **for . . . debate** my position requires me to act, not to reason about right and wrong
V.II.s.d. **Alarum** a trumpet call to battle 1 **father** i.e., venerable old man (Edgar has not yet revealed his identity) 4 s.d. **retreat** signaled by a trumpet

6 **ta'en** captured 11 **Ripeness** maturity, as of fruit that is ready to fall
V.III.1 **good guard** let them be well guarded 2 **their greater pleasures** the will of those in command, the great ones 3 **censure** pass judgment on 4 **meaning** intentions 13 **gilded butterflies** i.e., gorgeously attired courtiers, fluttering after nothing 16–17 **take . . . spies** profess to read the riddle of existence, as if endowed with divine omniscience 17 **wear out** outlast

In a walled prison, packs and sects of great
 ones
That ebb and flow by th' moon.°
  EDMUND: Take them away.
  LEAR:
20 Upon such sacrifices, my Cordelia,
The gods themselves throw incense.° Have I
 caught thee?
He that parts us shall bring a brand from heaven,
And fire us hence like foxes.° Wipe thine eyes;
The good years° shall devour them,° flesh and
 fell,°
Ere they shall make us weep. We'll see 'em
25 starved first.
Come. [*Exeunt* LEAR *and* CORDELIA, *guarded.*]
  EDMUND:
Come hither, captain; hark.
Take thou this note: go follow them to prison:
One step I have advanced thee; if thou dost
30 As this instructs thee, thou dost make thy way
To noble fortunes: know thou this, that men
Are as the time is:° to be tender-minded
Does not become a sword:° thy great em-
 ployment
Will not bear question;° either say thou'lt do't,
Or thrive by other means.
35   CAPTAIN: I'll do't, my lord.
  EDMUND:
About it; and write happy° when th' hast done.
Mark; I say, instantly, and carry it so°
As I have set it down.
  CAPTAIN:
I cannot draw a cart, nor eat dried oats;
40 If it be man's work, I'll do't. (*Exit* CAPTAIN.)

(*Flourish. Enter* ALBANY, GONERIL, REGAN
[*another* CAPTAIN, *and*] SOLDIERS.)

18–19 **packs . . . moon** intriguing and partisan cliques
of those in high station, whose fortunes change every
month 20–21 **Upon . . . incense** i.e., the gods approve our renunciation of the world 22–23 **He . . .
foxes** No human agency can separate us, but only
divine interposition, as of a heavenly torch parting us
like foxes that are driven from their place of refuge
by fire and smoke 24 **good years** plague and pestilence ("undefined malefic power or agency," *Oxford
English Dictionary*); **them** the enemies of Lear and
Cordelia; **fell** skin 32 **as . . . is** i.e., absolutely determined by the exigencies of the moment 33 **become a sword** befit a soldier 34 **bear question**
admit of discussion 36 **write happy** style yourself
fortunate 37 **carry it so** manage the affair in exactly that manner (as if Cordelia had taken her own
life)

  ALBANY:
Sir, you have showed today your valiant strain,°
And fortune led you well: you have the
 captives
Who were the opposites of° this day's strife:
I do require them of you, so to use them
As we shall find their merits° and our safety 45
May equally determine.
  EDMUND: Sir, I thought it fit
To send the old and miserable king
To some retention and appointed guard;°
Whose° age had charms in it, whose title
 more,
To pluck the common bosom on his side,° 50
And turn our impressed lances in our eyes°
Which do command them. With him I sent
 the queen:
My reason all the same; and they are ready
Tomorrow, or at further space,° t'appear
Where you shall hold your session.° At this
 time 55
We sweat and bleed: the friend hath lost his
 friend;
And the best quarrels, in the heat, are cursed
By those that feel their sharpness.°
The question of Cordelia and her father
Requires a fitter place.
  ALBANY: Sir, by your patience, 60
I hold you but a subject of° this war,
Not as a brother.
  REGAN: That's as we list to grace° him.
Methinks our pleasure might have been de-
 manded,
Ere you had spoke so far. He led our powers,
Bore the commission of my place and person; 65
The which immediacy may well stand up
And call itself your brother.°
  GONERIL: Not so hot:

41 **strain** (1) stock (2) character 43 **opposites of**
opponents in 45 **merits** deserts 48 **retention . . .
guard** confinement under duly appointed guard 49
Whose i.e., Lear's 50 **pluck . . . side** win the sympathy of the people to himself 51 **turn . . . eyes** turn
our conscripted lancers against us 54 **further space**
a later time 55 **session** trial 57–58 **best . . . sharpness** worthiest causes may be judged badly by those
who have been affected painfully by them, and whose
passion has not yet cooled 61 **subject of** subordinate
in 62 **list to grace** wish to honor 65–67 **Bore . . .
brother** was authorized, as my deputy, to take command; his present status, as my immediate representative, entitles him to be considered **your equal**

In his own grace he doth exalt himself
More than in your addition.°
REGAN: In my rights,
70 By me invested, he compeers° the best.
GONERIL:
That were the most,° if he should husband
    you.°
REGAN:
Jesters do oft prove prophets.
GONERIL: Holla, holla!
That eye that told you so looked but a-squint.°
REGAN:
Lady, I am not well; else I should answer
75 From a full-flowing stomach.° General,
Take thou my soldiers, prisoners, patrimony;°
Dispose of them, of me; the walls is thine:°
Witness the world, that I create thee here
My lord, and master.
GONERIL: Mean you to enjoy him?
ALBANY:
80 The let-alone° lies not in your good will.
EDMUND:
Nor in thine, lord.
ALBANY: Half-blooded° fellow, yes.
REGAN [to EDMUND]:
Let the drum strike, and prove my title thine.°
ALBANY:
Stay yet; hear reason. Edmund, I arrest thee
On capital treason; and in thy attaint°
This gilded serpent [pointing to GONERIL]. For
85   your claim, fair sister,
I bar it in the interest of my wife.
'Tis she is subcontracted° to this lord,
And I, her husband, contradict your banes.°
If you will marry, make your loves° to me;
My lady is bespoke.°
90 GONERIL: An interlude!°

69 **your addition** honors you have bestowed on him
70 **compeers** equals   71 **most** most complete invest-
ing in your rights; **husband you** become your husband   73 **a-squint** cross-eyed   75 **From . . . stomach**
angrily   76 **patrimony** inheritance   77 **walls is
thine** i.e., Regan's person, which Edmund has
stormed and won   80 **let-alone** power to prevent
81 **Half-blooded** bastard, and so only half noble   82
prove . . . thine prove by combat your entitlement to
my rights   84 **in thy attaint** as a sharer in the treason
for which you are impeached   87 **subcontracted**
pledged by a contract which is called into question
by the existence of a previous contract (Goneril's
marriage)   88 **contradict your banes** forbid your
announced intention to marry (by citing the pre-
contract)   89 **loves** love-suits   90 **bespoke** already
pledged; **interlude** play

ALBANY:
Thou art armed, Gloucester: let the trumpet
    sound:
If none appear to prove upon thy person
Thy heinous, manifest, and many treasons,
There is my pledge° [throwing down a glove]:
    I'll make° it on thy heart,
Ere I taste bread, thou art in nothing less   95
Than I have here proclaimed thee.
REGAN: Sick, O, sick!
GONERIL [aside]:
If not, I'll ne'er trust medicine.°
EDMUND [throwing down a glove]:
There's my exchange:° what in the world he is
That names me traitor, villainlike he lies:°
Call by the trumpet:° he that dares approach,   100
On him, on you — who not? — I will maintain
My truth and honor firmly.
ALBANY:
A herald, ho!
EDMUND: A herald, ho, a herald!
ALBANY:
Trust to thy single virtue;° for thy soldiers,
All levied in my name, have in my name   105
Took their discharge.
REGAN: My sickness grows upon me.
ALBANY:
She is not well; convey her to my tent.
                    [Exit REGAN, led.]

(Enter a HERALD.)

Come hither, herald. Let the trumpet sound —
And read out this.
CAPTAIN: Sound, trumpet!   110

(A trumpet sounds.)

HERALD (reads): "If any man of quality or
degree° within the lists° of the army will
maintain upon Edmund, supposed Earl of
Gloucester, that he is a manifold traitor, let
him appear by the third sound of the trumpet: 115
he is bold in his defense."
EDMUND: Sound!

(First trumpet.)

HERALD: Again!

(Second trumpet.)

94 **pledge** gage; **make** prove   97 **medicine** poison
98 **exchange** technical term, denoting the glove Edmund throws down   99 **villainlike he lies** the lie
direct, a challenge to mortal combat   100 **trumpet**
trumpeter   104 **single virtue** unaided valor   111–
112 **quality or degree** rank or position   112 **lists**
rolls

HERALD: Again!

(*Third trumpet.*

Trumpet answers within. Enter EDGAR, *at the third sound, armed, a trumpet before him.°*)

ALBANY:

120 Ask him his purposes, why he appears
Upon this call o' th' trumpet.

HERALD: What are you?
Your name, your quality,° and why you answer
This present summons?

EDGAR: Know, my name is lost;
By treason's tooth bare-gnawn and canker-
bit:°

125 Yet am I noble as the adversary
I come to cope.°

ALBANY: Which is that adversary?

EDGAR:
What's he that speaks for Edmund, Earl of
Gloucester?

EDMUND:
Himself: what say'st thou to him?

EDGAR: Draw thy sword,
That if my speech offend a noble heart,

130 Thy arm do thee justice: here is mine.
Behold it is my privilege,
The privilege of mine honors,
My oath, and my profession.° I protest,
Maugre° thy strength, place, youth, and emi-
nence,

135 Despite thy victor sword and fire-new° fortune,
Thy valor and thy heart,° thou art a traitor,
False to thy gods, thy brother, and thy father,
Conspirant° 'gainst this high illustrious prince,
And from th' extremest upward° of thy head

140 To the descent and dust below thy foot,°
A most toad-spotted traitor.° Say thou "No,"
This sword, this arm and my best spirits are
bent°

To prove upon thy heart, whereto I speak,°
Thou liest.

EDMUND:
In wisdom° I should ask thy name,
But since thy outside looks so fair and warlike, 145
And that thy tongue some say° of breeding
breathes,
What safe and nicely° I might well delay°
By rule of knighthood, I disdain and spurn:
Back do I toss these treasons° to thy head;
With the hell-hated° lie o'erwhelm thy heart; 150
Which for they yet glance by and scarcely
bruise,
This sword of mine shall give them instant
way,
Where they shall rest for ever.° Trumpets,
speak!

(*Alarums. [They] fight. [EDMUND falls.]*)

ALBANY:
Save° him, save him!

GONERIL: This is practice,° Gloucester:
By th' law of war thou wast not bound to
answer   155
An unknown opposite;° thou art not vanquished,
But cozened and beguiled.

ALBANY: Shut your mouth, dame,
Or with this paper shall I stop it. Hold, sir;°
Thou° worse than any name, read thine own
evil.
No tearing, lady; I perceive you know it.   160

GONERIL:
Say, if I do, the laws are mine, not thine:
Who can arraign me for't?

ALBANY: Most monstrous! O!
Know'st thou this paper?

GONERIL: Ask me not what I know.
(*Exit.*)

ALBANY:
Go after her; she's desperate; govern° her.

---

119 s.d. **trumpet before him** trumpeter preceding him   122 **quality** rank   124 **canker-bit** eaten by the caterpillar   126 **cope** encounter   131–133 **it ... profession** my knighthood entitles me to challenge you, and to have my challenge accepted   134 **Maugre** despite   135 **fire-new** fresh from the forge or mint   136 **heart** courage   138 **Conspirant** conspiring, a conspirator   139 **extremest upward** the very top   140 **the ... foot** your lowest part (sole) and the dust beneath it   141 **toad-spotted traitor** spotted with treason (and hence venomous, as the toad is allegedly marked with spots that exude venom)   142 **bent** directed

143 **whereto I speak** Edgar speaks from the heart, and speaks to the heart of Edmund   144 **wisdom** prudence (since he is not obliged to fight with one of lesser rank)   146 **say** assay (i.e., touch, sign)   147 **safe and nicely** cautiously and punctiliously; **delay** i.e., avoid   149 **treasons** accusations of treason   150 **hell-hated** hated like hell   151–153 **Which ... ever** which accusations of treason, since as yet they do no harm, even though I have hurled them back, I now thrust upon you still more forcibly, with my sword, so that they may remain with you permanently   154 **Save** spare; **practice** trickery   156 **opposite** opponent   158 **Hold, sir** to Edmund: "Just a moment!"   159 **Thou** probably Goneril   164 **govern** control

EDMUND:
What you have charged me with, that have I
165   done;
And more, much more; the time will bring it
       out.
'Tis past, and so am I. But what art thou
That hast this fortune on° me? If thou'rt
       noble,
I do forgive thee.
       EDGAR: Let's exchange charity.°
170   I am no less in blood° than thou art, Edmund;
If more,° the more th' hast wronged me.
My name is Edgar, and thy father's son.
The gods are just, and of our pleasant° vices
Make instruments to plague us:
175   The dark and vicious place° where thee he got°
Cost him his eyes.
       EDMUND: Th' hast spoken right, 'tis true;
The wheel is come full circle; I am here.°
       ALBANY:
Methought thy very gait did prophesy°
A royal nobleness: I must embrace thee:
180   Let sorrow split my heart, if ever I
Did hate thee or thy father!
       EDGAR: Worthy° prince, I know't.
       ALBANY:
Where have you hid yourself?
How have you known the miseries of your
       father?
       EDGAR:
By nursing them, my lord. List a brief tale;
And when 'tis told, O, that my heart would
185   burst!
The bloody proclamation to escape°
That followed me so near — O, our lives'
       sweetness,
That we the pain of death would hourly die
Rather than die at once!° — taught me to shift
190   Into a madman's rags, t' assume a semblance
That very dogs disdained: and in this habit°

168 **fortune on** victory over   169 **charity** forgiveness
and love   170 **blood** lineage   171 **If more** if I am
more noble (since legitimate)   173 **of our pleasant**
out of our pleasurable   175 **place** i.e., the adulterous
bed; **got** begot   177 **wheel . . . here** i.e., Fortune's
wheel, on which Edmund ascended, has now, in its
downward turning, deposited him at the bottom,
whence he began   178 **gait did prophesy** carriage
did promise   181 **Worthy** honorable   186 **to escape** (my wish) to escape the sentence of death
187–189 **O . . . once** How sweet is life, that we
choose to suffer death every hour rather than make
an end at once   191 **habit** attire

Met I my father with his bleeding rings,°
Their precious stones new lost; became his
       guide,
Led him, begged for him, saved him from
       despair;
Never — O fault! — revealed myself unto him,   195
Until some half-hour past, when I was armed,
Not sure, though hoping, of this good success,
I asked his blessing, and from first to last
Told him our pilgrimage.° But his flawed°
       heart —
Alack, too weak the conflict to support —   200
'Twixt two extremes of passion, joy and grief,
Burst smilingly.
       EDMUND:
                This speech of yours hath moved me,
And shall perchance do good: but speak you
       on;
You look as you had something more to say.
       ALBANY:
If there be more, more woeful, hold it in;   205
For I am almost ready to dissolve,°
Hearing of this.
       EDGAR: This would have seemed a period°
To such as love not sorrow; but another,
To amplify too much, would make much
       more,
And top extremity.°   210
Whilst I was big in clamor,° came there in a
       man,
Who, having seen me in my worst estate,°
Shunned my abhorred° society; but then,
       finding
Who 'twas that so endured, with his strong
       arms
He fastened on my neck, and bellowed out   215
As he'd burst heaven; threw him on my father;
Told the most piteous tale of Lear and him
That ever ear received: which in recounting
His grief grew puissant,° and the strings of life
Began to crack: twice then the trumpets
       sounded,   220
And there I left him tranced.°
       ALBANY: But who was this?

192 **rings** sockets   199 **our pilgrimage** of our (purga-
torial) journey; **flawed** cracked   206 **dissolve** i.e.,
into tears   207 **period** limit   208–210 **but . . . extremity** just one woe more, described too fully, would
go beyond the extreme limit   211 **big in clamor**
loud in lamentation   212 **estate** condition   213
abhorred abhorrent   219 **puissant** overmastering
221 **tranced** insensible

EDGAR:
Kent, sir, the banished Kent; who in disguise
Followed his enemy° king, and did him service
Improper for a slave.

(*Enter a* GENTLEMAN, *with a bloody knife.*)

GENTLEMAN:
Help, help, O, help!
EDGAR: What kind of help?
225   ALBANY: Speak, man.
EDGAR:
What means this bloody knife?
GENTLEMAN: 'Tis hot, it smokes;°
It came even from the heart of — O, she's
    dead!
ALBANY:
Who dead? Speak, man.
GENTLEMAN:
Your lady, sir, your lady: and her sister
230   By her is poisoned; she confesses it.
EDMUND:
I was contracted° to them both: all three
Now marry° in an instant.
EDGAR: Here comes Kent.
ALBANY:
Produce the bodies, be they alive or dead.
                        [*Exit* GENTLEMAN.]
This judgment of the heavens, that makes us
    tremble,
Touches us not with pity.

(*Enter* KENT.)

235   O, is this he?
The time will not allow the compliment°
Which very manners° urges.
KENT.   I am come
To bid my king and master aye° good night:
Is he not here?
ALBANY: Great thing of° us forgot!
Speak, Edmund, where's the king? and where's
240   Cordelia?
See'st thou this object,° Kent?

(*The bodies of Goneril and Regan are
brought in.*)

KENT:
Alack, why thus?

EDMUND: Yet° Edmund was beloved:
The one the other poisoned for my sake,
And after slew herself.
ALBANY:
Even so. Cover their faces.   245
EDMUND:
I pant for life:° some good I mean to do,
Despite of mine own nature. Quickly send,
Be brief in it, to th' castle; for my writ°
Is on the life of Lear and on Cordelia:
Nay, send in time.
ALBANY: Run, run, O, run!   250
EDGAR:
To who, my lord? Who has the office?° Send
Thy token of reprieve.°
EDMUND:
Well thought on: take my sword,
Give it the captain.
EDGAR: Haste thee, for thy life.
                        [*Exit* MESSENGER.]
EDMUND:
He hath commission from thy wife and me   255
To hang Cordelia in the prison, and
To lay the blame upon her own despair,
That she fordid° herself.
ALBANY:
The gods defend her! Bear him hence awhile.
                [EDMUND *is borne off.*]

(*Enter* LEAR, *with* CORDELIA *in his arms,*
[GENTLEMAN, *and others following*].)

LEAR:
Howl, howl, howl, howl! O, you are men of
    stones: 260
Had I your tongues and eyes, I'd use them so
That heaven's vault should crack. She's gone
    for ever.
I know when one is dead and when one lives;
She's dead as earth. Lend me a looking-glass;
If that her breath will mist or stain the stone,°   265
Why, then she lives.
KENT: Is this the promised end?°
EDGAR:
Or image° of that horror?
ALBANY: Fall and cease.°

---

223 **enemy** hostile   226 **smokes** steams   231 **contracted** betrothed   232 **marry** i.e., unite in death
236 **compliment** ceremony   237 **very manners** ordinary civility   238 **aye** forever   239 **thing of** matter
by   241 **object** sight (the bodies of Goneril and
Regan)

242 **Yet** in spite of all   246 **pant for life** gasp for
breath   248 **writ** command (ordering the execution)
251 **office** commission   252 **token of reprieve** sign
that they are reprieved   258 **fordid** destroyed   265
stone i.e., the surface of the crystal looking-glass
266 **promised end** doomsday   267 **image** exact likeness; **Fall and cease** i.e., Let the heavens fall, and
all things finish

LEAR:
This feather stirs; she lives. If it be so,
It is a chance which does redeem° all sorrows
That ever I have felt.
270   KENT: O my good master.
LEAR:
Prithee, away.
EDGAR: 'Tis noble Kent, your friend.
LEAR:
A plague upon you, murderers, traitors all!
I might have saved her; now she's gone for
        ever.
Cordelia, Cordelia, stay a little. Ha,
What is't thou say'st? Her voice was ever
275   soft,
Gentle and low, an excellent thing in woman.
I killed the slave that was a-hanging thee.
GENTLEMAN:
'Tis true, my lords, he did.
LEAR: Did I not, fellow?
I have seen the day, with my good biting
        falchion°
280   I would have made them skip: I am old now,
And these same crosses° spoil me.° Who are
        you?
Mine eyes are not o' th' best: I'll tell you
        straight.°
KENT:
If Fortune brag of two° she loved and hated,
One of them we behold.
LEAR:
This is a dull sight.° Are you not Kent?
285   KENT: The same,
Your servant Kent. Where is your servant
        Caius?°
LEAR:
He's a good fellow, I can tell you that;
He'll strike, and quickly too: he's dead and
        rotten.
KENT:
No, my good lord; I am the very man.
290   LEAR:
I'll see that straight.°

KENT:
That from your first of difference and decay°
Have followed your sad steps.
LEAR: You are welcome hither.
KENT:
Nor no man else:° all's cheerless, dark and
        deadly.
Your eldest daughters have fordone° themselves,
And desperately° are dead.
LEAR: Ay, so I think.   295
ALBANY:
He knows not what he says, and vain is it
That we present us to him.
EDGAR: Very bootless.°

(Enter a MESSENGER.)

MESSENGER:
Edmund is dead, my lord.
ALBANY: That's but a trifle here.
You lords and noble friends, know our intent.
What comfort to this great decay may come°   300
Shall be applied. For us, we° will resign,
During the life of this old majesty,
To him our absolute power: [to EDGAR and
        KENT] you, to your rights;
With boot,° and such addition° as your honors
Have more than merited. All friends shall taste   305
The wages of their virtue, and all foes
The cup of their deservings. O, see, see!
LEAR:
And my poor fool° is hanged: no, no, no life?
Why should a dog, a horse, a rat, have life,
And thou no breath at all? Thou'lt come no
        more,   310
Never, never, never, never, never.
Pray you, undo this button.° Thank you, sir.
Do you see this? Look on her. Look, her
        lips,
Look there, look there. (He dies.)
EDGAR: He faints. My lord, my lord!
KENT:
Break, heart; I prithee, break.

269 **redeem** make good   279 **falchion** small curved
sword   281 **crosses** troubles; **spoil me** i.e., my prow-
ess as a swordsman   282 **tell you straight** recognize
you straightaway   283 **two** i.e., Lear, and some hypo-
thetical second, who is also a prime example of Fortune's inconstancy ("loved and hated")   285 **dull
sight** (1) melancholy spectacle (2) faulty eyesight
(Lear's own, clouded by weeping)   286 **Caius** Kent's
name, in disguise   290 **see that straight** attend to
that in a moment

291 **your . . . decay** beginning of your decline in
fortune   293 **Nor . . . else** no, I am not welcome, nor
is anyone else   294 **fordone** destroyed   295 **desperately** in despair   297 **bootless** fruitless   300
What . . . come whatever aid may present itself to
this great ruined man   301 **us, we** the royal "we"
304 **boot** good measure; **addition** additional titles and
rights   308 **fool** Cordelia ("fool" being a term of
endearment; but it is perfectly possible to take the
word as referring also to the Fool)   312 **undo this
button** i.e., to ease the suffocation Lear feels

315   EDGAR: Look up, my lord!
       KENT:
Vex not his ghost:° O, let him pass! He hates
       him
That would upon the rack° of this tough world
Stretch him out longer.°
       EDGAR: He is gone indeed.
       KENT:
The wonder is he hath endured so long:
320 He but usurped° his life.

316 **Vex . . . ghost** do not trouble his departing spirit
317 **rack** instrument of torture, stretching the victim's
joints to dislocation   318 **longer** (1) in time (2) in
bodily length   320 **usurped** possessed beyond the
allotted term

ALBANY:
Bear them from hence. Our present business
Is general woe. [*To* KENT *and* EDGAR.] Friends
       of my soul, you twain,
Rule in this realm and the gored state sustain.
       KENT:
I have a journey, sir, shortly to go;
My master calls me, I must not say no.   325
       EDGAR:
The weight of this sad time we must obey,°
Speak what we feel, not what we ought to say.
The oldest hath borne most: we that are
       young
Shall never see so much, nor live so long.
                    (*Exeunt, with a dead march.*)

326 **obey** submit to

The best way to understand Shakespeare's tragic vision is, of course, to see and read the tragedies very intelligently, but some help may be gained from a brief consideration of two speeches in *Hamlet*. In the final scene, when Fortinbras and others enter the stage looking for Claudius, they find to their amazement the corpses of Claudius, Gertrude, Laertes, and Hamlet. Horatio, Hamlet's friend, endeavors to bring the visitors up to date:

> What is it you would see?
> If aught of woe or wonder, cease your search.

Fortinbras and his associates are indeed struck with woe and wonder:

> FORTINBRAS: O proud Death,
> What feast is toward in thine eternal cell
> That thou so many princes at a shot
> So bloodily hast struck?
> AMBASSADOR: The sight is dismal.

Horatio seeks to explain: the visitors will hear

> Of carnal, bloody, and unnatural acts,
> Of accidental judgments, casual slaughters,
> Of deaths put on by cunning and forced cause,
> And, in this upshot, purposes mistook
> Fall'n on th'inventors' heads.

The spectators of the play itself have indeed seen "unnatural acts," "deaths put on by cunning," etc., and presumably these spectators have experienced the "woe" and "wonder" that the new arrivals will experience as Horatio sets forth the details.

Let us now look at a second passage from *Hamlet*. The speaker is the despicable Rosencrantz, and there is some flattery of King Claudius in his speech, but the gist of his argument about the death of a king rings true, makes sense:

> The cess of majesty
> Dies not alone, but like a gulf doth draw
> What's near it with it; or it is a massy wheel
> Fixed on the summit of the highest mount,
> To whose huge spokes ten thousand lesser things
> Are mortised and adjoined, which when it falls,
> Each small annexment, petty consequence,
> Attends the boist'rous ruin. Never alone
> Did the King sigh, but with a general groan.

Surely it is understandable that the deaths of, say, Lincoln and Kennedy had a vastly greater effect upon America than the deaths of any number of men in private life. Put crudely, they mattered more.

The speeches together afford some justification of the Elizabethan view that tragedy is concerned with violence done to and by people of high rank. The fall of a man in high position evokes deeper woe and wonder than the snuffing out of a nonentity. The latter may evoke pity, but scarcely awe at the terrifying power of destructiveness or at the weakness that is at the heart of power.

Shakespeare does not merely slap the label of king or prince or general on a character and then assume that greatness has been established. His characters speak great language and perform great deeds. (And, no less important, they have the capacity to suffer greatly.) Lear, in the first scene, gives away — almost seems to create — fertile kingdoms:

> Of all these bounds, even from this line to this,
> With shadowy forests, and with champains riched,
> With plenteous rivers, and wide-skirted meads,
> We make thee lady.

Even in injustice, when he banishes his daughter, Cordelia, for speaking the truth as she sees it, he has a kind of terrible grandeur:

> Let it be so, thy truth then be thy dower!
> For, by the sacred radiance of the sun,
> The mysteries of Hecate and the night,
> By all the operation of the orbs
> From whom we do exist and cease to be,
> Here I disclaim all my paternal care,
> Propinquity and property of blood,
> And as a stranger to my heart and me
> Hold thee from this for ever.

Finally, even in his madness — "a sight most pitiful in the meanest wretch, / Past speaking of in a king" — he has grandeur. To Gloucester's "Is't not the king?" he replies:

> Ay, every inch a king.
> When I do stare, see how the subject quakes.
> I pardon that man's life. What was thy cause?
> Adultery?
> Thou shalt not die: die for adultery! No:
> The wren goes to 't, and the small gilded fly
> Does lecher in my sight.
> Let copulation thrive. . . .

We might contrast Lear's noble voice with Edmund's materialistic comment on the way of the world:

> This is the excellent foppery of the world, that when we are sick in fortune, often the surfeits of our own behavior, we make guilty of our disasters the sun, the moon, and stars; as if we were villains on necessity; fools by heavenly compulsion; knaves, thieves, and treachers by spherical predominance; drunkards, liars, and adulterers by an enforced obedience of planetary influence; and all that we are evil in, by a divine thrusting on. An admirable evasion of whoremaster man, to lay his goatish disposition on the charge of a star. . . . Fut! I should have been that I am, had the maidenliest star in the firmament twinkled on my bastardizing.

Lear seems to be displacing *Hamlet* as the play that speaks to our time. *Hamlet* was especially popular with nineteenth-century audiences, who often found in the uncertain prince an image of their own doubts in a world in which belief in a benevolent divine order was collapsing under the influence of scientific materialism and bourgeois aggressiveness. Many audiences in our age find in *Lear* — where "for many miles about / There's scarce a bush" — a play thoroughly in the spirit of Beckett's *Waiting for Godot,* where the scenery consists of a single tree. Moreover, Lear denounces the hypocrisy of the power structure and exposes the powerlessness of the disenfranchised: "Robes and furred gowns hide all. Plate sin with gold, / And the strong lance of justice hurtless breaks; / Arm it in rags, a pygmy's straw does pierce it." And what of the gods? There are several comments about their nature, but perhaps the most memorable reference to the gods is not a mere comment but one followed by an action: learning that Cordelia is in danger, Albany cries out, "The gods defend her!" and immediately his words are mocked by Lear's entrance on the stage, with the dead Cordelia in his arms.

But the interpretation of *King Lear* as a revelation of the emptiness of life fails to consider at least two things. First, there is an affirmation in those passages in which Lear comes, through heart-rending anguish, to see that he was not what he thought he was. Second, this anagnorisis or recognition is several times associated with love or charity, as when (III.iv) Lear invites the Fool to enter the hovel first and then confesses his guilt in having cared too little for humanity. And this care for humanity is seen in Cordelia, who comes — though ineffectually in the long run — to the aid of her father. It is seen, too, in the nameless servant who at the end of III.vii promises to apply medicine to Gloucester's eyeless sockets; it is seen even in the villainous Edmund, who in dying repents and says, "Some good I mean to do, / Despite mine own nature" (V.iii), and who thereupon tries, unsuccessfully, to save Cordelia. No one would say that these actions turn *King Lear* into a happy vision, but it is perverse to ignore them and to refuse to see that in this play love humanizes as surely as egoism dehumanizes. If the play dramatizes man's desolation, it also dramatizes the love that, while providing no protection against pain or death, makes man's life different from the life of "a dog, a horse, a rat."

HEDDA GABLER

Henrik Ibsen

Translated by Otto Reinert

Henrik Ibsen (1828–1906) was born in Skien, Norway, of wealthy parents who soon after his birth lost their money. Ibsen worked as a pharmacist's apprentice, but at the age of twenty-two he had written his first play, a promising melodrama entitled *Cataline*. He engaged in theater work in Norway, and then in Denmark and Germany. By 1865 his plays had won him a state pension that enabled him to settle in Rome. After writing romantic, historic, and poetic plays, he turned to realistic drama with *The League of Youth* (1869). Among the major realistic "problem plays" are *A Doll's House* (1879), *Ghosts* (1881), and *An Enemy of the People* (1882). In *The Wild Duck* (1884) he moved toward a more symbolic tragic comedy, and his last plays, written in the nineties, are highly symbolic. *Hedda Gabler* (1890) looks backward to the plays of the eighties rather than forward to the plays of the nineties.

CHARACTERS

JØRGEN TESMAN, *University Research Fellow in the History of Civilization*
HEDDA, *his wife*
MISS JULIANE TESMAN, *his aunt*

MRS. ELVSTED
JUDGE BRACK
EILERT LØVBORG
BERTE, *the Tesmans' maid*

Scene: The TESMANS' *villa in a fashionable residential section of the town.*

A note on pronunciation

The approximate Norwegian pronunciation of names likely to be difficult to a speaker of English is suggested below (the syllable in capitals is accented; the unaccented *e* is close to English *e* in *quiet*).

JØRGEN YUR-gen (*g* as in *bargain*)
EILERT LØVBORG AY-lert LUV-borg[1]

JULLE YOOL-le (short *oo*)
BERTE BAIR-te

[1] *Løvborg* means, literally, "leaf-castle" — a fact of possible bearing on the play's symbolism. [Reinert.]

Maggie Smith as Hedda Gabler in the National Theatre Company production directed by Ingmar Bergman, London, 1970. (Photograph: Dominic.)

ACT I

A spacious, handsome, tastefully furnished room. Dark décor. In the rear, a wide doorway with open portieres. Beyond is a smaller room, furnished in the same style as the front room. A door, right, leads to the front hall. Left, French doors, with portieres drawn aside, through which can be seen a part of a roofed verandah and trees with autumn foliage. Front center, an oval table covered with a cloth. Chairs around it. Front right, a wide, dark, porcelain stove, a high-backed easy chair, a footstool with a pillow, and two ottomans. In the corner far right, a sofa and a small, round table. Front left, a sofa, set out from the wall. Far left, beyond the French doors, an upright piano. On both sides of the doorway, rear center, whatnots with knickknacks. Against the rear wall of the inner room, a sofa, and in front of it a table and two chairs. Above the sofa, a portrait of a handsome, elderly man in general's uniform. Over the table hangs a lamp with milky, white glass. There are several bouquets of flowers, in vases and glasses, in various places in the front room. Others are lying on the tables. Thick carpets on the floors of both rooms. The morning sun is shining through the French doors.

MISS JULIANE TESMAN, with hat and parasol, enters right, followed by BERTE, *who carries a bouquet of flowers wrapped in paper.* MISS TESMAN *is a nice-looking woman of 65, of pleasant mien, neatly but not expensively dressed in a gray suit.* BERTE *is a middle-aged servant girl, of rather plain and countrified appearance.*

MISS TESMAN (*stops inside the door, listens, says in a low voice*): On my word — I don't think they are even up yet!

BERTE (*also softly*): That's what I told you, miss. When you think how late the steamer

Hedda Gabler by Henrik Ibsen, translated by Otto Reinert (Chandler Publishing Company). Copyright © 1962 by Harper & Row, Publishers, Inc. Reprinted by permission of the publisher. *Caution:* The holder of copyright in this version of *Hedda Gabler* reserves the exclusive right to perform or represent this work publicly; to make or procure the making of any transcription or record thereof by or from which, in whole or in part, it may in any manner or by any method be exhibited, performed, represented, produced, or reproduced; and to exhibit, perform, represent, produce, or reproduce it in any manner or by any method whatsoever. Application for permission to make any such use of this version should be made to Harper & Row, Publishers, Inc., 10 East 53rd Street, New York, N.Y. 10022.

got in last night. And afterwards! — Goodness! — all the stuff she wanted unpacked before she turned in.

MISS TESMAN: Well — just let them sleep. But fresh morning air — *that* we can give them when they come in here. (*Goes and opens the French doors wide.*)

BERTE (*by the table, lost, still holding the flowers*): Please, miss — I just don't see a bit of space anywhere! I think I'd better put these over here. (*Puts the flowers down on the piano.*)

MISS TESMAN: Well, well, my dear Berte. So you've got yourself a new mistress now. The good Lord knows it was hard for me to let you go.

BERTE (*near tears*): What about me, then, miss! What shall *I* say? I who have served you and Miss Rina all these blessed years.

MISS TESMAN: We shall just have to make the best of it, Berte. That's all. Jørgen can't do without you, you know. He just can't. You've looked after him ever since he was a little boy.

BERTE: Yes, but miss — I'm ever so worried about leaving Miss Rina. The poor dear lying there all helpless. With that new girl and all! She'll never learn how to make things nice and comfortable for an invalid.

MISS TESMAN: Oh yes, you'll see. I'll teach her. And of course, you know, I'll do most of it myself. So don't you worry yourself about my poor sister, Berte.

BERTE: Yes, but there's another thing, too, miss. I'm scared I won't be able to suit young Mrs. Tesman.

MISS TESMAN: Oh, well. Good heavens. So there is a thing or two — Right at first —

BERTE: For I believe she's ever so particular.

MISS TESMAN: Can you wonder? General Gabler's daughter? Just think of the kind of life she was used to when the General was alive. Do you remember when she rode by with her father? That long black riding habit she wore? And the feather in her hat?

BERTE: Oh, I remember, all right. But I'll be blessed if I ever thought she and the young master would make a pair of it.

MISS TESMAN: Nor did I. By the way, while I think of it, Berte. Jørgen has a new title now. From now on you should call him "the Doctor."

BERTE: Yes, the young mistress said something about that, too, last night. Soon as they were inside the door. Then it's really so, miss?

MISS TESMAN: It certainly is. Just think, Berte — they have made him a doctor abroad. During the trip, you know. I hadn't heard a thing about it till last night on the pier.

BERTE: Well, I daresay he could be anything he put his mind to, *he* could — smart as *he* is. But I must say I'd never thought he'd turn to doctoring people, too.

MISS TESMAN: Oh, that's not the kind of doctor he is. (*Nods significantly.*) And as far as that is concerned, there is no telling but pretty soon you may have to call him something grander yet.

BERTE: You don't say! What might that be, miss?

MISS TESMAN (*smiles*): Wouldn't you like to know! (*Moved.*) Ah yes, indeed — ! If only dear Jochum could see from his grave what has become of his little boy! (*Looking around.*) But look, Berte — what's this for? Why have you taken off all the slip covers?

BERTE: She told me to. Said she can't stand slip covers on chairs.

MISS TESMAN: Do you think they mean to make this their everyday living room, then?

BERTE: It sure sounded that way. Mrs. Tesman did, I mean. For he — the doctor — he didn't say anything.

(*JØRGEN TESMAN enters from the right side of the inner room. He is humming to himself. He carries an open, empty suitcase. He is of medium height, youthful-looking, thirty-three years old; somewhat stoutish. Round, open, cheerful face. Blond hair and beard. He wears glasses and is dressed in a comfortable, rather casual suit.*)

MISS TESMAN: Good morning, good morning, Jørgen!

TESMAN (*in the doorway*): Auntie! Dearest Aunt Julle! (*Comes forward and shakes her hand.*) All the way out here — as early as this! Hm?

MISS TESMAN: Well — I just had to drop in for a moment. To see how you are getting along, you know.

TESMAN: Even though you haven't had a good night's sleep.

MISS TESMAN: Oh, that doesn't matter at all.

TESMAN: But you did get home from the pier all right, I hope. Hm?

MISS TESMAN: Oh yes, I certainly did, thank you. The Judge was kind enough to see me all the way to my door.

TESMAN: We were so sorry we couldn't give you a ride in our carriage. But you saw for yourself — all the boxes Hedda had.

MISS TESMAN: Yes, she certainly brought quite a collection.

BERTE (*to TESMAN*): Should I go and ask Mrs. Tesman if there's anything I can help her with?

TESMAN: No, thank you, Berte — you'd better not. She said she'll ring if she wants you.

BERTE (*going right*): Well, all right.

TESMAN: But, look — you might take this suitcase with you.

BERTE (*takes it*): I'll put it in the attic. (*Exits right.*)

TESMAN: Just think, Auntie — that whole suitcase was brimful of copies of old documents. You wouldn't believe me if I told you all the things I have collected from libraries and archives all over. Quaint old items nobody has known anything about.

MISS TESMAN: Well, no, Jørgen. I'm sure you haven't wasted your time on your honeymoon.

TESMAN: No, I think I may say I have not. But take your hat off, Auntie — for goodness' sake. Here! Let me untie the ribbon for you. Hm?

MISS TESMAN (*while he does so*): Ah, God forgive me, if this isn't just as if you were still at home with us!

TESMAN (*inspecting the hat*): My, what a fine-looking hat you've got yourself!

MISS TESMAN: I bought it for Hedda's sake.

TESMAN: For Hedda's sake? Hm?

MISS TESMAN: So she won't need to feel ashamed of me if we ever go out together.

TESMAN (*patting her cheek*): If you don't think of everything, Auntie! (*Puts the hat down on a chair by the table.*) And now — over here to the sofa — we'll just sit and chat for a while till Hedda comes.

(*They seat themselves. She places her parasol in the corner by the sofa.*)

MISS TESMAN (*takes both his hands in hers and gazes at him*): What a blessing it is to have you back again, Jørgen, big as life! You — Jochum's little boy!

TESMAN: For me, too, Aunt Julle. Seeing

you again. For you have been both father and mother to me.

MISS TESMAN: Ah, yes — don't you think I know you'll always keep a spot in your heart for these two old aunts of yours!

TESMAN: So Aunt Rina isn't any better, hm?

MISS TESMAN: Oh no. We mustn't look for improvement in her case, poor dear. She is lying there just as she has been all these years. Just the same, may the good Lord keep her for me a long time yet! For else I just wouldn't know what to do with myself, Jørgen. Especially now, when I don't have you to look after any more.

TESMAN (*pats her back*): There, there, now!

MISS TESMAN (*changing tone*): And to think that you are a married man, Jørgen! And that you were the one to walk off with Hedda Gabler. The lovely Hedda Gabler. Just think! As many admirers as she had!

TESMAN (*hums a little, smiles complacently*): Yes, I daresay I have quite a few good friends here in town who'd gladly be in my shoes, hm?

MISS TESMAN: And such a long and lovely honeymoon you had! More than five — almost six months!

TESMAN: Well, you know — for me it has been a kind of study tour as well. All the collections I had to go through. And the books I had to read!

MISS TESMAN: Yes, I suppose. (*More confidentially, her voice lowered a little.*) But listen, Jørgen — haven't you got something — something special to tell me?

TESMAN: About the trip?

MISS TESMAN: Yes.

TESMAN: No — I don't know of anything besides what I wrote in my letters. They gave me a doctor's degree down there — but I told you that last night; I'm sure I did.

MISS TESMAN: Well, yes, that sort of thing — What I mean is — don't you have certain — certain — expectations?

TESMAN: Expectations?

MISS TESMAN: Ah for goodness' sake, Jørgen! I am your old Auntie, after all!

TESMAN: Certainly I have expectations.

MISS TESMAN: Well!!

TESMAN: I fully expect to be made a professor one of these days.

MISS TESMAN: Professor — oh yes —

TESMAN: I may even say I am quite certain of it. But dear Aunt Julle — you know this just as well as I do!

MISS TESMAN (*laughing a little*): Of course I do. You're quite right. (*Changing topic.*) But about the trip. It must have cost a great deal of money — hm, Jørgen?

TESMAN: Well, now; you know that large stipend went quite a long way.

MISS TESMAN: I just don't see how you made it do for both of you, though.

TESMAN: No, I suppose that's not so easy to understand, hm?

MISS TESMAN: Particularly with a lady along. For I have always heard that is ever so much more expensive.

TESMAN: Well, yes, naturally. That *is* rather more expensive. But Hedda had to have this trip, Auntie! She really had to. Nothing less would do.

MISS TESMAN: No, I daresay. For a wedding journey is quite the thing these days. But now tell me — have you had a chance to look around here yet?

TESMAN: I certainly have. I have been up and about ever since dawn.

MISS TESMAN: And what do you think of it all?

TESMAN: Delightful! Perfectly delightful! The only thing is I don't see what we are going to do with the two empty rooms between the second sitting room in there and Hedda's bedroom.

MISS TESMAN (*with a chuckle*): Oh my dear Jørgen — you may find them useful enough — when the time comes!

TESMAN: Of course, you're right, Auntie! As my library expands, hm?

MISS TESMAN: Quite so, my dear boy. It was your library I was thinking of.

TESMAN: But I'm really most happy on Hedda's behalf. For you know, before we were engaged she used to say she wouldn't care to live anywhere but in Secretary Falk's house.

MISS TESMAN: Yes, just think — wasn't that a lucky coincidence, that it was up for sale right after you had left?

TESMAN: Yes, Aunt Julle. We've certainly been lucky. Hm?

MISS TESMAN: But it will be expensive, my dear Jørgen. Terribly expensive — all this.

TESMAN (*looks at her, a bit crestfallen*): Yes, I daresay it will, Auntie.

MISS TESMAN: Heavens, yes!

TESMAN: How much, do you think? Roughly. Hm?

MISS TESMAN: No, I couldn't possibly say till all the bills arrive.

TESMAN: Well, anyway, Judge Brack managed to get very reasonable terms for us. He said so himself in a letter to Hedda.

MISS TESMAN: Yes, and I won't have you uneasy on that account, Jørgen. Besides, I have given security for the furniture and the carpets.

TESMAN: Security? You? But dear Aunt Julle — what kind of security could you give?

MISS TESMAN: The annuity.

TESMAN (*jumps up*): What! Your and Aunt Rina's annuity?

MISS TESMAN: Yes. I didn't know what else to do, you see.

TESMAN (*standing before her*): But are you clear out of your mind, Auntie! That annuity — that's all the two of you have to live on!

MISS TESMAN: Oh well, there's nothing to get so excited about, I'm sure. It's all just a matter of form, you know. That's what the Judge said, too. For he was kind enough to arrange the whole thing for me. Just a matter of form — those were his words.

TESMAN: That's all very well. Still —

MISS TESMAN: For now you'll have your own salary, you know. And, goodness — what if we do have a few expenses — Help out a bit right at first — ? That would only be a joy for us —

TESMAN: Oh, Auntie! When will you ever stop making sacrifices for my sake!

MISS TESMAN (*gets up, puts her hands on his shoulders*): But what other happiness do I have in this world than being able to smooth your way a little, my own dear boy? Orphan as you were, with no one to lean on but us? And now the goal is in sight, Jørgen. Things may have looked black at times. But heaven be praised; now you've arrived!

TESMAN: Yes, it's really quite remarkable the way things have worked out.

MISS TESMAN: Yes — and those who were against you — who tried to block your way — now they are tasting defeat. They are down, Jørgen! He, the most dangerous of them all, his fall was the greatest! He made his bed, and now he is lying in it — poor, lost wretch that he is!

TESMAN: Have you had any news about Eilert? Since I went away, I mean?

MISS TESMAN: Just that he is supposed to have published a new book.

TESMAN: What? Eilert Løvborg? Recently? Hm?

MISS TESMAN: That's what they say. But I wonder if there can be much to it. What do you think? Ah — but when *your* new book comes, that will be something quite different, Jørgen! What is it going to be about?

TESMAN: It deals with the domestic industries of Brabant during the Middle Ages.

MISS TESMAN: Just think — being able to write about something like that!

TESMAN: But as far as that is concerned, it may be quite some time before it is ready. I have all these collections to put in order first, you see.

MISS TESMAN: Yes, collecting and putting things in order — you certainly know how to do that. In that you are your father's own son.

TESMAN: Well, I must say I am looking forward to getting started. Particularly now, that I've got my own delightful home to work in.

MISS TESMAN: And most of all now that you have the one your heart desired, dear Jørgen.

TESMAN (*embracing her*): Oh yes, yes, Aunt Jule! Hedda — she is the most wonderful part of it all! (*Looks toward the doorway.*) There — I think she is coming now, hm?

(HEDDA *enters from the left side of the inner room. She is twenty-nine years old. Both features and figure are noble and elegant. Pale, ivory complexion. Steel-gray eyes, expressive of cold, clear calm. Beautiful brown hair, though not particularly ample. She is dressed in a tasteful, rather loose-fitting morning costume.*)

MISS TESMAN (*going toward her*): Good morning, my dear Hedda! A very happy morning to you!

HEDDA (*giving her hand*): Good morning, dear Miss Tesman! So early a call? That is most kind.

MISS TESMAN (*seems slightly embarrassed*): And — has the little lady of the house slept well the first night in her new home?

HEDDA: Passably, thank you.

TESMAN (*laughs*): Passably! You are a good one, Hedda! You were sleeping like a log when I got up.

HEDDA: Fortunately. And then, of course, Miss Tesman, it always takes time to get used to new surroundings. That has to come gradually. (*Looks left.*) Oh dear. The maid has left the verandah doors wide open. There's a veritable flood of sunlight in here.

MISS TESMAN (*toward the doors*): Well, then, we'll just close them.

HEDDA: No, no, not that. Tesman, dear, please pull the curtains. That will give a softer light.

TESMAN (*over by the French doors*): Yes, dear. There, now! Now you have both shade and fresh air, Hedda.

HEDDA: We certainly can use some air in here. Such loads of flowers — but, Miss Tesman, please — won't you be seated?

MISS TESMAN: No thanks. I just wanted to see if everything was all right — and so it is, thank goodness. I had better get back to Rina. I know she is waiting for me, poor thing.

TESMAN: Be sure to give her my love, Auntie. And tell her I'll be around to see her later today.

MISS TESMAN: I'll certainly do that! — Oh my! I almost forgot! (*Searches the pocket of her dress.*) I have something for you, Jørgen. Here.

TESMAN: What's that, Auntie? Hm?

MISS TESMAN (*pulls out a flat parcel wrapped in newspaper and gives it to him*): Here you are, dear.

TESMAN (*opens the parcel*): Well, well, well! So you took care of them for me, Aunt Julle! Hedda! Now, isn't that sweet, hm?

HEDDA (*by the whatnot, right*): If you'd tell me what it is —

TESMAN: My old slippers! You know!

HEDDA: Oh really? I remember you often talked about them on the trip.

TESMAN: Yes, for I missed them so. (*Walks over to her.*) Here — now you can see what they're like, Hedda.

HEDDA (*crosses toward stove*): Thanks. I don't know that I really care.

TESMAN (*following*): Just think — Aunt Rina embroidered these slippers for me. Ill as she was. You can't imagine how many memories they hold for me!

HEDDA (*by the table*): Hardly for me.

MISS TESMAN: That's true, you know, Jørgen.

TESMAN: Yes, but — I just thought that now that she's one of the family —

HEDDA (*interrupting*): I don't think we'll get on with that maid, Tesman.

MISS TESMAN: Not get on with Berte?

TESMAN: Whatever makes you say that, dear? Hm?

HEDDA (*points*): Look — she has left her old hat on the chair over there.

TESMAN (*appalled, drops the slippers*): But Hedda — !

HEDDA: What if somebody were to come and see it!

TESMAN: No, no, Hedda — that's Aunt Julle's hat!

HEDDA: Oh?

MISS TESMAN (*picking up the hat*): Yes, indeed it is. And it isn't old either, my dear young lady.

HEDDA: I really didn't look that closely —

MISS TESMAN (*tying the ribbons*): I want you to know that this is the first time I have had it on my head. On my word it is!

TESMAN: And very handsome it is, too. Really a splendid-looking hat!

MISS TESMAN: Oh, I don't know that it is anything so special, Jørgen. (*Looks around.*) My parasol — ? Ah, here it is. (*Picks it up.*) For that is mine, too. (*Mutters.*) Not Berte's.

TESMAN: New hat and new parasol! What do you think of that, Hedda!

HEDDA: Very nice indeed.

TESMAN: Yes, don't you think so? Hm? But, Auntie, take a good look at Hedda before you leave. See how pretty and blooming she looks.

MISS TESMAN: Dear me, Jørgen; that's nothing new. Hedda has been lovely all her days. (*She nods and walks right.*)

TESMAN (*following*): Yes, but have you noticed how full-figured and healthy she looks after the trip? How she has filled out?

HEDDA (*crossing*): Oh — stop it!

MISS TESMAN (*halts, turns around*): Filled out?

TESMAN: Yes, Aunt Julle. You can't see it so well now when she wears that dress. But I, who have the opportunity —

HEDDA (*by the French doors, impatiently*): Oh, you haven't any opportunities at all!

TESMAN: It must be the mountain air in Tyrol.

HEDDA (*curtly interrupting*): I am just as I was when I left.

TESMAN: Yes, so you say. I just don't think you're right. What do you think, Auntie?

MISS TESMAN (*has folded her hands, gazes at HEDDA*): Lovely — lovely — lovely; that is what Hedda is. (*Goes over to her, inclines her head forward with both her hands, and kisses her hair.*) God bless and keep Hedda Tesman. For Jørgen's sake.

HEDDA (*gently freeing herself*): There, there. Now let me go.

MISS TESMAN (*in quiet emotion*): Every single day I'll be over and see you two.

TESMAN: Yes, please do, Auntie. Hm?

MISS TESMAN: Goodbye, goodbye!

(*She leaves through door, right.* TESMAN *sees her out. The door remains ajar.* TESMAN *is heard repeating his greetings for Aunt Rina and his thanks for the slippers. In the meantime,* HEDDA *paces up and down, raises her arms, clenching her fists, as in quiet rage. Opens the curtains by the French doors and stands looking out. In a few moments,* TESMAN *re-enters and closes the door behind him.*)

TESMAN (*picking up the slippers*): What are you looking at, Hedda?

HEDDA (*once again calm and controlled*): Just the leaves. They are so yellow. And withered.

TESMAN (*wrapping the slippers in their paper, putting the parcel down on the table*): Well, you know — we're in September now.

HEDDA (*again restless*): Yes — just think. It's already — September.

TESMAN: Don't you think Aunt Julle acted strange, Hedda? Almost solemn. I wonder why. Hm?

HEDDA: I hardly know her, you see. Isn't she often like that?

TESMAN: Not the way she was today.

HEDDA (*turning away from the French doors*): Do you think she minded that business with the hat?

TESMAN: Oh, I don't think so. Not much. Perhaps a little bit right at the moment —

HEDDA: Well, I'm sorry, but I must say it strikes me as very odd — putting her hat down here in the living room. One just doesn't do that.

TESMAN: Well, you may be sure Aunt Julle won't ever do it again.

HEDDA: Anyway, I'll make it up to her, somehow.

TESMAN: Oh yes, Hedda; if only you would!

HEDDA: When you go over there today, why don't you ask her over for tonight?

TESMAN: I'll certainly do that. And then there is one other thing you could do that she'd appreciate ever so much.

HEDDA: What?

TESMAN: If you could just bring yourself to call her Auntie. For my sake, Hedda, hm?

HEDDA: No, Tesman, no. You really mustn't ask me to do that. I have already told you I can't. I'll try to call her Aunt Juliane. That will have to do.

TESMAN: All right, if you say so. I just thought that now that you're in the family —

HEDDA: Hmmm — I don't know about that — (*She walks toward the doorway.*)

TESMAN (*after a brief pause*): Anything the matter, Hedda? Hm?

HEDDA: I'm just looking at my old piano. It doesn't quite go with the other furniture in here.

TESMAN: As soon as I get my first pay check we'll have it traded in.

HEDDA: No — I don't want to do that. I want to keep it. But let's put it in this inner room and get another one for out here. Whenever it's convenient. I mean.

TESMAN (*a little taken back*): Well — yes — we could do that —

HEDDA (*picks up the bouquet from the piano*): These flowers weren't here last night.

TESMAN: I suppose Aunt Julle brought them for you.

HEDDA (*looking at the flowers*): There's a card here. (*Takes it out and reads.*) "Will be back later." Can you guess who it's from?

TESMAN: No. Who? Hm?

HEDDA: Thea Elvsted.

TESMAN: No, really? Mrs. Elvsted! Miss Rysing that was.

HEDDA: That's right. The one with that irritating head of hair she used to show off with. An old flame of yours, I understand.

TESMAN (*laughs*): Well, now — that didn't last long! Anyway, that was before I knew you, Hedda. Just think — her being in town.

HEDDA: Strange, that she'd call on us. I have hardly seen her since we went to school together.

TESMAN: As far as that goes, I haven't seen her either for — God knows how long. I don't see how she can stand living in that out-of-the-way place. Hm?

HEDDA (*suddenly struck by a thought*): Listen, Tesman — isn't it some place near there that he lives — what's his name — Eilert Løvborg?

TESMAN: Yes, that's right. He is up there, too.

(BERTE *enters right.*)

BERTE: Ma'am, she's here again, that lady who brought those flowers a while back. (*Pointing.*) The flowers you're holding in your hand, ma'am.

HEDDA: Ah, she is? Well, show her in, please.

(BERTE *opens the door for* MRS. ELVSTED *and exits.* MRS. ELVSTED *is of slight build, with a pretty, soft face. Her eyes are light blue, large, round, rather prominent, of a timid and querying expression. Her hair is strikingly light in color, almost whitish, and unusually rich and wavy. She is a couple of years younger than* HEDDA. *She is dressed in a dark visiting dress, tasteful, but not quite in the most recent fashion.*)

HEDDA (*walks toward her. Friendly*): Good morning, my dear Mrs. Elvsted. How very nice to see you again.

MRS. ELVSTED (*nervous, trying not to show it*): Well, yes, it is quite some time since we met.

TESMAN (*shaking hands*): And we, too. Hm?

HEDDA: Thank you for your lovely flowers —

MRS. ELVSTED: Please, don't — I would have come here yesterday afternoon. But I was told you were still traveling —

TESMAN: You've just arrived in town, hm?

MRS. ELVSTED: I got here yesterday, at noon. Oh, I was quite desperate when I learned you weren't home.

HEDDA: Desperate? But why?

TESMAN: But my dear Mrs. Rysing — I mean Mrs. Elvsted —

HEDDA: There is nothing wrong, I hope?

MRS. ELVSTED: Yes there is. And I don't know a single soul other than you that I can turn to here.

HEDDA (*putting the flowers down on the table*): Come — let's sit down here on the sofa.

MRS. ELVSTED: Oh, I'm in no mood to sit!

HEDDA: Of course you are. Come on. (*She pulls* MRS. ELVSTED *over to the sofa and sits down next to her.*)

TESMAN: Well, now, Mrs. — ? Exactly what — ?

HEDDA: Has something — special happened at home?

MRS. ELVSTED: Well, yes — and no. Oh, but I am so afraid you won't understand!

HEDDA: In that case, it seems to me you ought to tell us exactly what has happened, Mrs. Elvsted.

TESMAN: After all, that's why you are here. Hm?

MRS. ELVSTED: Yes, yes, of course. Well, then, maybe you already know — Eilert Løvborg is in town.

HEDDA: Is Løvborg — !

TESMAN: No! You don't say! Just think, Hedda — Løvborg's back!

HEDDA: All right. I can hear.

MRS. ELVSTED: He has been here a week already. Imagine — a whole week! In this dangerous place. Alone! With all that bad company around.

HEDDA: But my dear Mrs. Elvsted — why is he a concern of yours?

MRS. ELVSTED (*with an apprehensive look at her, says quickly*): He tutored the children.

HEDDA: Your children?

MRS. ELVSTED: My husband's. I don't have any.

HEDDA: In other words, your stepchildren.

MRS. ELVSTED: Yes.

TESMAN (*with some hesitation*): But was he — I don't quite know how to put this — was he sufficiently — regular — in his way of life to be thus employed? Hm?

MRS. ELVSTED: For the last two years, there hasn't been a thing to object to in his conduct.

TESMAN: No, really? Just think, Hedda!

HEDDA: I hear.

MRS. ELVSTED: Not the least little bit, I assure you! Not in any respect. And yet — knowing he's here — in the big city — And with all that money, too! I'm scared to death!

TESMAN: But in that case, why didn't he remain with you and your husband? Hm?

MRS. ELVSTED: After his book came out, he was too restless to stay.

TESMAN: Ah yes, that's right. Aunt Julle said he has published a new book.

MRS. ELVSTED: Yes, a big new book, about the course of civilization in general. It came out about two weeks ago. And since it has had such big sales and been discussed so much and made such a big splash —

TESMAN: It has, has it? I suppose this is something he has had lying around from better days?

MRS. ELVSTED: You mean from earlier?

TESMAN: Yes.

MRS. ELVSTED: No; it's all been written since he came to stay with us. During this last year.

TESMAN: Well, now! That's very good news, Hedda! Just think!

MRS. ELVSTED: Yes, if it only would last!

HEDDA: Have you seen him since you came to town?

MRS. ELVSTED: No, not yet. I had a great deal of trouble finding his address. But this morning I finally tracked him down.

HEDDA (*looks searchingly at her*): Isn't it rather odd that your husband — hm —

MRS. ELVSTED (*with a nervous start*): My husband! What about him?

HEDDA: That he sends you to town on such an errand? That he doesn't go and look after his friend himself?

MRS. ELVSTED: Oh, no, no — my husband doesn't have time for things like that. Besides, I have some — some shopping to do, anyway.

HEDDA (*with a slight smile*): Well, in that case, of course —

MRS. ELVSTED (*getting up, restlessly*): And now I beg of you, Mr. Tesman — won't you please receive Eilert Løvborg nicely if he calls on you? And I am sure he will. After all — Such good friends as you two used to be. And then you both do the same kind of work — the same field of study, as far as I know.

TESMAN: We used to, at any rate.

MRS. ELVSTED: Yes. And that's why I implore you to please, please, try to keep an eye on him — you too. You'll do that, Mr. Tesman, won't you? Promise?

TESMAN: With the greatest pleasure, Mrs. Rysing.

HEDDA: Elvsted.

TESMAN: I'll gladly do as much for Eilert as I possibly can. You may certainly count on that.

MRS. ELVSTED: Oh, how good and kind you are! (*Clasps his hands.*) Thank you, thank you, thank you! (*Nervously.*) You see, my husband is so very fond of him.

HEDDA (*getting up*): You ought to write him a note, Tesman. Maybe he won't come without an invitation.

TESMAN: Yes, I suppose that would be the right thing to do, Hedda. Hm?

HEDDA: The sooner the better. Right away, I think.

MRS. ELVSTED (*pleadingly*): If only you would!

TESMAN: I'll write this minute. Do you have his address, Mrs. — Mrs. Elvsted?

MRS. ELVSTED: Yes. (*Pulls a slip of paper from her bag and gives it to him.*) Here it is.

TESMAN: Very good. Well, then, if you'll excuse me — (*Looks around.*) By the way — the slippers? Ah, here we are. (*Leaving with the parcel.*)

HEDDA: Be sure you write a nice, warm, friendly letter, Tesman. And a long one, too.

TESMAN: Certainly, certainly.

MRS. ELVSTED: But not a word that it is I who — !

TESMAN: No, that goes without saying, I should think. Hm? (*Goes out right through inner room.*)

HEDDA (*goes over to* MRS. ELVSTED, *smiles, says in a low voice*): There! We just killed two birds with one stone.

MRS. ELVSTED: What do you mean?

HEDDA: Didn't you see I wanted him out of the room?

MRS. ELVSTED: Yes, to write that letter —

HEDDA: And to speak to you alone.

MRS. ELVSTED (*flustered*): About this same thing?

HEDDA: Exactly.

MRS. ELVSTED (*anxious*): But there *is* nothing more, Mrs. Tesman! Really, there isn't!

HEDDA: Oh yes, there is. There is considerably more. I can see that much. Over here — We are going to have a real, nice, confidential talk, you and I. (*She forces* MRS. ELVSTED *down in the easy chair and seats herself on one of the ottomans.*)

MRS. ELVSTED (*worried, looks at her watch*): But my dear Mrs. Tesman — I had really thought I would be on my way now.

HEDDA: Oh I am sure there is no rush. Now, then. Tell me about yourself. How are things at home?

MRS. ELVSTED: That is just what I don't want to talk about.

HEDDA: But to me — ! After all, we are old schoolmates.

MRS. ELVSTED: But you were a year ahead of me. And I used to be so scared of you!

HEDDA: Scared of me?

MRS. ELVSTED: Terribly. For when we met on the stairs, you always ruffled my hair.

HEDDA: Did I really?

MRS. ELVSTED: Yes. And once you said you were going to burn it off.

HEDDA: Oh, but you know — I wasn't serious!

MRS. ELVSTED: No, but I was such a silly, then. Anyway, afterwards we drifted far apart. Our circles are so very different, you know.

HEDDA: All the more reason for getting close again. Listen. In school we called each other by our first names.

MRS. ELVSTED: Oh I'm sure you're wrong —

HEDDA: I'm sure I'm not! I remember it quite clearly. And now we want to be open with one another, just the way we used to. (*Moves the ottoman closer.*) There, now! (*Kisses her cheek.*) You call me Hedda.

MRS. ELVSTED (*seizes her hands*): Oh you are so good and kind! I'm not used to that.

HEDDA: There, there! And I'll call you my dear Thora, just as in the old days.

MRS. ELVSTED: My name is Thea.

HEDDA: So it is. Of course. I meant Thea. (*Looks at her with compassion.*) So you're not much used to goodness and kindness, Thea? Not in your own home?

MRS. ELVSTED: If I even had a home! But I don't. I never have had one.

HEDDA (*looks at her for a moment*): I thought there might be something like this.

MRS. ELVSTED (*helplessly, looking straight ahead*): Yes — yes — yes —

HEDDA: I ' am not sure if I quite remember — Didn't you first come to your husband as his housekeeper?

MRS. ELVSTED: I was really hired as governess. But his wife — his first wife — was ailing already then and practically bedridden. So I had to take charge of the household as well.

HEDDA: But in the end you became his wife.

MRS. ELVSTED (*dully*): So I did.

HEDDA: Let's see. How long ago is that?

MRS. ELVSTED: Since my marriage?

HEDDA: Yes.

MRS. ELVSTED: About five years.

HEDDA: Right. It must be that long.

MRS. ELVSTED: Oh, those five years! Or mostly the last two or three! Oh, Mrs. Tesman — if you could just imagine!

HEDDA (*slaps her hand lightly*): Mrs. Tesman? Shame on you!

MRS. ELVSTED: Oh yes; all right, I'll try. Yes — if you could just — conceive — understand —

HEDDA (*casually*): And Eilert Løvborg has been living near you for some three years or so, hasn't he?

MRS. ELVSTED (*looks at her uncertainly*): Eilert Løvborg? Yes — he has.

HEDDA: Did you know him before? Here in town?

MRS. ELVSTED: Hardly at all. That is, of course I did in a way. I mean, I knew *of* him.

HEDDA: But up there — You saw a good deal of him; did you?

MRS. ELVSTED: Yes, he came over to us every day. He was supposed to tutor the children, you see. For I just couldn't do it all by myself.

HEDDA: Of course not. And your husband — ? I suppose he travels quite a bit.

MRS. ELVSTED: Well, yes, Mrs. Tes — Hedda — as a public magistrate, you know, he very often has to travel all over his district.

HEDDA (*leaning against the armrest on the easy chair*): Thea — poor, sweet Thea — now you have to tell me everything — just as it is.

MRS. ELVSTED: You'd better ask me, then.

HEDDA: How *is* your husband, Thea? I mean — you know — *really*? To be with. What kind of person is he? Is he good to you?

MRS. ELVSTED (*evasively*): I believe he thinks he does everything for the best.

HEDDA: But isn't he altogether too old for you? He is more than twenty years older, isn't he?

MRS. ELVSTED (*with irritation*): Yes, there is that, too. But there isn't just one thing. Every single little thing about him repels me! We don't have a thought in common, he and I. Not a thing in the world!

HEDDA: But isn't he fond of you all the same? I mean in his own way?

MRS. ELVSTED: I don't know. I think I am just useful to him. And I don't use much money. I am inexpensive.

HEDDA: That is foolish of you.

MRS. ELVSTED (*shakes her head*): Can't be changed. Not with him. I don't think he cares for anybody much except himself. Perhaps the children a little.

HEDDA: And Eilert Løvborg, Thea.

MRS. ELVSTED (*looks at her*): Eilert Løvborg? What makes you think that?

HEDDA: Well, it seems to me that when he sends you all the way to town to look after him. (*With an almost imperceptible smile.*) Besides, you said so yourself. To Tesman.

MRS. ELVSTED (*with a nervous twitch*): Did I? I suppose I did. (*With a muted outburst.*) No! I might as well tell you now as later. For it's bound to come out, anyway.

HEDDA: But my dear Thea — ?

MRS. ELVSTED: All right. My husband doesn't know I've gone!

HEDDA: What! He doesn't know?

MRS. ELVSTED: He wasn't even home. He's away again. Oh, I just couldn't take it any longer, Hedda! It had become utterly impossible. All alone as I was.

HEDDA: So what did you do?

MRS. ELVSTED: I packed some of my things. Just the most necessary. Without telling anybody. And left.

HEDDA: Just like that?

MRS. ELVSTED: Yes. And took the next train to town.

HEDDA: But dearest Thea — how did you dare to do a thing like that!

MRS. ELVSTED (*rises, walks*): What else could I do?

HEDDA: But what do you think your husband will say when you go back?

MRS. ELVSTED (*by the table; looks at her*): Go back to him?

HEDDA: Yes!

MRS. ELVSTED: I'll never go back.

HEDDA (*rises, approaches her slowly*): So you have really, seriously — left everything?

MRS. ELVSTED: Yes. It seemed to me there was nothing else I could do.

HEDDA: And quite openly, too.

MRS. ELVSTED: You can't keep a thing like that secret, anyway.

HEDDA: But what do you think people will say, Thea?

MRS. ELVSTED: In God's name, let them say whatever they like. (*Sits down on the sofa, dully, tired.*) For I have only done what I had to do.

HEDDA (*after a brief silence*): And what do you plan to do with yourself? What sort of work will you do?

MRS. ELVSTED: I don't know yet. I only know I have to live where Eilert Løvborg is. If I am to live at all.

HEDDA (*moves a chair from the table closer to* MRS. ELVSTED, *sits down, strokes her hands*): Thea — tell me. How did this — this friendship between you and Eilert — how did it begin?

MRS. ELVSTED: Oh, it grew little by little. I got some sort of power over him.

HEDDA: Oh?

MRS. ELVSTED: He dropped his old ways. Not because I asked him to. I never dared to do that. But I think he must have noticed how I felt about that kind of life. So he changed.

HEDDA (*quickly suppresses a cynical smile*): So you have — rehabilitated him, as they say. Haven't you, Thea?

MRS. ELVSTED: At least, that's what *he* says. On the other hand, he has turned me into a real human being. Taught me to think — and understand — all sorts of things.

HEDDA: Maybe he tutored you, too?

MRS. ELVSTED: No, not tutored exactly. But he talked to me. About so many, many things. And then came that lovely, lovely time when I could share his work with him. He let me help him!

HEDDA: He did?

MRS. ELVSTED: Yes! Whatever he wrote, he wanted us to be together about it.

HEDDA: Just like two good comrades.

MRS: ELVSTED (*with animation*): Comrades! — that's it! Imagine, Hedda — that's just what he called it, too, Oh, I really ought to feel so happy. But I can't. For you see, I don't know if it will last.

HEDDA: You don't trust him any more than that?

MRS. ELVSTED (*heavily*): The shadow of a woman stands between Eilert Løvborg and me.

HEDDA (*tensely, looks at her*): Who?

MRS. ELVSTED: I don't know. Somebody or other from — his past. I don't think he has ever really forgotten her.

HEDDA: What has he told you about it?

MRS. ELVSTED: He has mentioned it only once — just casually.

HEDDA: And what did he say?

MRS. ELVSTED: He said that when they parted she was going to kill him with a gun.

HEDDA (*cold, controlled*): Oh, nonsense. People don't do that sort of thing here.

MRS. ELVSTED: No, I know. And that is why I think it must be that red-headed singer he used to —

HEDDA: Yes, I suppose so.

MRS. ELVSTED: For I remember people said she carried a loaded gun.

HEDDA: Well, then I'm sure it's she.

MRS. ELVSTED (*wringing her hands*): Yes, but just think, Hedda — now I hear that she — that singer — that she's here in town again, too! Oh, I'm just desperate — !

HEDDA (*with a glance toward the inner room*): Shhh! Here's Tesman. (*Rises and whispers.*) Not a word about all this to anybody, Thea!

MRS. ELVSTED (*jumps up*): No, no. For God's sake — !

(TESMAN, *carrying a letter, enters from the right side of the inner room.*)

TESMAN: There now — here's the missive, all ready to go!

HEDDA: Good. But I believe Mrs. Elvsted wants to be on her way. Wait a moment. I'll see you to the garden gate.

TESMAN: Say, Hedda — do you think Berte could take care of this?

HEDDA (*takes the letter*): I'll tell her.

(BERTE *enters right.*)

BERTE: Judge Brack is here and wants to know if you're receiving.

HEDDA: Yes, ask the Judge please to come in. And — here — drop this in a mailbox, will you?

BERTE (*takes the letter*): Yes, ma'am.

(*She opens the door for* JUDGE BRACK *and exits. The* JUDGE *is forty-five years of age. Rather thickset, but well-built and with brisk athletic movements. Roundish face, aristocratic profile. His hair is short, still almost completely black, very neatly dressed. Lively, sparkling eyes. Thick eyebrows and mustache with cut-off points. He is dressed in an elegant suit, a trifle youthful for his age. He wears pince-nez glasses, attached to a string, and lets them drop from time to time.*)

JUDGE BRACK (*hat in hand, salutes*): May one pay one's respects as early as this?

HEDDA: One certainly may.

TESMAN (*shaking his hand*): You are always welcome. (*Introducing.*) Judge Brack — Miss Rysing —

(HEDDA *groans.*)

BRACK (*bowing*): Delighted!

HEDDA (*looks at him, laughs*): How nice it is to see you in daylight, Judge!

BRACK: You find me changed, perhaps?

HEDDA: A bit younger, I think.

BRACK: Much obliged.

TESMAN: But what do you think of Hedda? Hm? Did you ever see her in such bloom? She positively —

HEDDA: Will you please leave me out of this? You had better thank the Judge for all the trouble he has taken.

BRACK: Oh, nonsense. It's been a pleasure.

HEDDA: Yes, you are indeed a faithful soul. But my friend here is dying to be off. Don't leave, Judge. I'll be back in a minute.

(*Mutual goodbyes.* MRS. ELVSTED *and* HEDDA *exit, right.*)

BRACK: Well, now — your wife — is she tolerably satisfied?

TESMAN: Yes, indeed, and we really can't thank you enough. That is, I understand there will have to be some slight changes made here and there. And there are still a few things — just a few trifles — we'll have to get.

BRACK: Oh? Really?

TESMAN: But we certainly don't want to bother you with that. Hedda said she's going to take care of it herself. But do sit down, hm?

BRACK: Thanks. Maybe just for a moment — (*Sits down by the table.*) There's one thing I'd like to talk to you about, my dear Tesman.

TESMAN: Oh? Ah, I see! (*Sits down.*) I suppose it's the serious part of the festivities that's beginning now. Hm?

BRACK: Oh — there's no great rush as far as the money is concerned. Though I must say I wish we could have established ourselves a trifle more economically.

TESMAN: Out of the question, my dear fellow! Remember, it's all for Hedda! You, who know her so well — ! After all, I couldn't put her up like any little middle-class housewife —

BRACK: No, I suppose — That's just it.

TESMAN: Besides — fortunately — it can't be long now before I receive my appointment.

BRACK: Well, you know — things like that have a way of hanging fire.

TESMAN: Perhaps you have heard something? Something definite? Hm?

BRACK: No, nothing certain — (*Interrupting himself.*) But that reminds me. I have some news for you.

TESMAN: Oh?

BRACK: Your old friend Eilert Løvborg is back in town.

TESMAN: I know that already.

BRACK: So? Who told you?

TESMAN: The lady who just left.

BRACK: I see. What did you say her name was again? I didn't quite catch —

TESMAN: Mrs. Elvsted.

BRACK: Ah yes — the Commissioner's wife. Yes, it's up in her part of the country that Løvborg has been staying, too.

TESMAN: And just think. I am so glad to hear it. He is quite respectable again.

BRACK: Yes, so they say.

TESMAN: And he has published a new book, hm?

BRACK: Oh yes.

TESMAN: Which is making quite a stir.

BRACK: Quite an unusual stir.

TESMAN: Just think! Isn't that just wonderful! He — with his remarkable gifts. And I was so sure he'd gone under for good.

BRACK: That seems to have been the general opinion.

TESMAN: What I don't understand, though, is what he is going to do with himself. What sort of living can he make? Hm?

(*During the last remark* HEDDA *re-enters, right.*)

HEDDA (*to* BRACK, *with a scornful little laugh*): Tesman is forever worrying about how people are going to make a living.

TESMAN: Well, you see, we are talking about poor Eilert Løvborg, Hedda.

HEDDA (*with a quick look at him*): You are? (*Sits down in the easy chair by the stove and asks casually.*) What is the matter with him?

TESMAN: Well, you see, I believe he's run through his inheritance a long time ago. And I don't suppose he can write a new book every year. Hm? So I really must ask how he is going to make out.

BRACK: Maybe I could help you answer that.

TESMAN: Yes?

BRACK: Remember, he has relatives with considerable influence.

TESMAN: Ah — unfortunately, those relatives have washed their hands of him long ago.

BRACK: Just the same, they used to call him the hope of the family.

TESMAN: Yes, before! But he has ruined all that.

HEDDA: Who knows? (*With a little smile.*) I hear the Elvsteds have rehabilitated him.

BRACK: And then this book —

TESMAN: Well, I certainly hope they will help him to find something or other. I just wrote him a letter. Hedda, dear, I asked him to come out here tonight.

BRACK: Oh dear, I am sorry. Don't you remember — you're supposed to come to my little stag dinner tonight? You accepted last night on the pier, you know.

HEDDA: Had you forgotten, Tesman?

TESMAN: So I had.

BRACK: Oh well. I'm sure he won't come, so it doesn't really make any difference.

TESMAN: Why is that? Hm?

BRACK (*gets up somewhat hesitantly, rests his hands on the back of the chair*): Dear Tesman — and you, too, Mrs. Tesman — I cannot in good conscience let you remain in ignorance of something, which — which —

TESMAN: Something to do with Eilert?

BRACK: With both you and him.

TESMAN: But my dear Judge, do speak!

BRACK: You must be prepared to find that your appointment will not come through as soon as you hope and expect.

TESMAN (*jumps up, nervously*): Something's happened? Hm?

BRACK: It may conceivably be made contingent upon the result of a competition.

TESMAN: Competition! Just think, Hedda!

HEDDA (*leaning farther back in her chair*): Ah — I see, I see — !

TESMAN: But with whom? Don't tell me with — ?

BRACK: Precisely. With Eilert Løvborg.

TESMAN (*claps his hands together*): No, no! This can't be! It is unthinkable! Quite impossible! Hm?

BRACK: All the same, that's the way it may turn out.

TESMAN: No, but Judge, this would amount to the most incredible callousness toward me! (*Waving his arms.*) For just think — I'm a married man! We married on the strength of these prospects, Hedda and I. Got ourselves deep in debt. Borrowed money from Aunt Julle, too. After all, I had practically been promised the post, you know. Hm?

BRACK: Well, well. I daresay you'll get it in the end. If only after a competition.

HEDDA (*motionless in her chair*): Just think, Tesman. It will be like a kind of contest.

TESMAN: But dearest Hedda, how can you be so unconcerned!

HEDDA (*still without moving*): I'm not at all unconcerned. I'm dying to see who wins.

BRACK: In any case, Mrs. Tesman, I'm glad you know the situation as it is. I mean — before you proceed to make the little additional purchases I understand you threaten us with.

HEDDA: This makes no difference as far as that is concerned.

BRACK: Really? Well, in that case, of course — Goodbye! (*To* TESMAN.) I'll pick you up on my afternoon walk.

TESMAN: What? Oh yes, yes, of course. I'm sorry; I'm just all flustered.

HEDDA (*without getting up, gives her hand*): Goodbye, Judge. Come back soon.

BRACK: Thanks. Goodbye, goodbye.

TESMAN (*sees him to the door*): Goodbye, my dear Judge. You really must excuse me —

(JUDGE BRACK *exits, right.*)

TESMAN (*pacing the floor*): Oh, Hedda, Hedda! One should never venture into fairyland. Hm?

HEDDA (*looks at him, smiles*): Do *you* do that?

TESMAN: Well, yes — it can't be denied — it was most venturesome of me to rush into marriage and set up a home on the strength of mere prospects.

HEDDA: Well, maybe you're right.

TESMAN: Anyway — we do have our own nice, comfortable home, now. Just think, Hedda — the very home both of us dreamed about. Set our hearts on, I may almost say. Hm?

HEDDA (*rises, slowly, tired*): The agreement was that we were to maintain a certain position — entertain —

TESMAN: Don't I know it! Dearest Hedda — I have been so looking forward to seeing you as hostess in a select circle! Hm? Well, well, well! In the meantime, we'll just have to be content with one another. See Aunt Julle once in a while. Nothing more. And you were meant for such a different kind of life, altogether!

HEDDA: I suppose a footman is completely out of the question.

TESMAN: I'm afraid so. Under the circumstances, you see — we couldn't possibly —

HEDDA: And as for getting my own riding horse —

TESMAN (*aghast*): Riding horse!

HEDDA: I suppose I mustn't even think of that.

TESMAN: Good heavens, no! That goes without saying, I hope!

HEDDA (*walking*): Well — at least I have one thing to amuse myself with in the meantime.

TESMAN (*overjoyed*): Oh thank goodness for that! And what *is* that, Hedda, hm?

HEDDA (*in the doorway, looks at him with suppressed scorn*): My guns — Jørgen!

TESMAN (*in fear*): Your guns!

HEDDA (*with cold eyes*): General Gabler's guns. (*She exits left, through the inner room.*)

TESMAN (*runs up to the doorway, calls after her*): But Hedda! Good gracious! Hedda, dear! Please don't touch those dangerous things! For my sake, Hedda! Hm?

ACT II

The same room at the TESMANS'. *The piano has been moved out and replaced by an elegant little writing desk. A small table has been placed near the sofa, left. Most of the flowers have been removed.* MRS. ELVSTED'S *bouquet is on the big table front center. Afternoon.*

HEDDA, *dressed to receive callers, is alone. She is standing near the open French doors, loading a revolver. Its mate is lying in an open case on the desk.*

HEDDA (*looking down into the garden, calls*): Hello there, Judge! Welcome back!

JUDGE BRACK (*off stage*): Thanks, Mrs. Tesman!

HEDDA (*raises the gun, sights*): I am going to shoot you, Judge Brack!

BRACK (*calls off stage*): No — no — no! Don't point the gun at me like that!

HEDDA: That's what you get for sneaking in the back door! (*Fires.*)

BRACK (*closer*): Are you out of your mind — !

HEDDA: Oh dear — did I hit you?

BRACK (*still off stage*): Stop that nonsense!

HEDDA: Come on in, then.

(JUDGE BRACK, *dressed for dinner, enters, left. He carries a light overcoat over his arm.*)

BRACK: Dammit! Do you still fool around with that thing? What are you shooting at, anyway?

HEDDA: Oh — just firing off into blue air.

BRACK (*gently but firmly taking the gun away from her*): With your permission, Mrs. Tesman. (*Looks at it.*) Ah yes, I remember this gun very well. (*Looks around.*) Where is the case? Ah, here we are. (*Puts the gun in the case and closes it.*) That's enough of that silliness for today.

HEDDA: But in the name of heaven, what do you expect me to do with myself?

BRACK: No callers?

HEDDA (*closing the French doors*): Not a soul. All my close friends are still out of town, it seems.

BRACK: And Tesman is out, too, perhaps?

HEDDA (*by the desk, puts the gun case in a drawer*): Yes. He took off for the aunts' right after lunch. He didn't expect you so early.

BRACK: I should have thought of that. That was stupid of me.

HEDDA (*turns her head, looks at him*): Why stupid?

BRACK: I would have come a little — sooner.

HEDDA (*crossing*): If you had, you wouldn't have found anybody home. For I have been in my room ever since lunch, changing my clothes.

BRACK: And isn't there the tiniest little opening in the door for negotiations?

HEDDA: You forgot to provide one.

BRACK: Another stupidity.

HEDDA: So we'll have to stay in here. And wait. For I don't think Tesman will be back for some time.

BRACK: By all means. I'll be very patient.

(HEDDA *sits on the sofa in the corner.* BRACK *puts his overcoat over the back of the nearest chair and sits down, keeping his hat in his hand. Brief silence. They look at one another.*)

HEDDA: Well?

BRACK (*in the same tone*): Well?

HEDDA: I said it first.

BRACK (*leans forward a little*): All right. Let's have a nice little chat, Mrs. Tesman.

HEDDA (*leans back*): Don't you think it's an eternity since last time we talked! I don't count last night and this morning. That was nothing.

BRACK: You mean — just the two of us?

HEDDA: Mmm. If you like.

BRACK: There hasn't been a day I haven't wished you were back again.

HEDDA: My feelings, exactly.

BRACK: Yours? Really, Mrs. Tesman? And I have been assuming you were having such a wonderful time.

HEDDA: I'd say!

BRACK: All Tesman's letters said so.

HEDDA: Oh yes, he! He's happy just poking through old collections of books. And copying old parchments — or whatever they are.

BRACK (*with a touch of malice*): Well, that's his calling, you know. Partly, anyway.

HEDDA: Yes, so it is. And in that case I suppose — But I! Oh, Judge! You've no idea how bored I've been.

BRACK (*with sympathy*): Really? You're serious?

HEDDA: Surely you can understand that? For a whole half year never to see anyone who knows even a little bit about our circle? And talks our language?

BRACK: Yes, I think I would find that trying, too.

HEDDA: And then the most unbearable thing of all —

BRACK: Well?

HEDDA: — everlastingly to be in the company of the same person —

BRACK (*nods in agreement*): Both early and late — yes. I can imagine — at all possible times —

HEDDA: I said everlastingly.

BRACK: All right. Still, it seems to me that with as excellent a person as our Tesman, it ought to be possible —

HEDDA: My dear Judge — Tesman is a specialist.

BRACK: Granted.

HEDDA: And specialists are not at all entertaining travel companions. Not in the long run, at any rate.

BRACK: Not even — the specialist — one happens to love?

HEDDA: Bah! That nauseating word!

BRACK (*puzzled*): Really, now, Mrs. Tesman — ?

HEDDA (*half laughing, half annoyed*): You ought to try it some time! Listening to talk about the history of civilization, early and late —

BRACK: Everlastingly —

HEDDA: All right. And then this business about the domestic industry in the Middle Ages — ! That's the ghastliest part of it all!

BRACK (*looking searchingly at her*): But in that case — tell me — how am I to explain — ?

HEDDA: That Jørgen Tesman and I made a pair of it, you mean?

BRACK: If you want to put it that way — yes.

HEDDA: Come now. Do you really find that so strange?

BRACK: Both yes and no — Mrs. Tesman.

HEDDA: I had danced myself tired, my dear

Judge. My season was over — (*Gives a slight start.*) No, no — I don't really mean that. Won't think it, either!

BRACK: Nor do you have the slightest reason to, I am sure.

HEDDA: Oh — as far as reasons are concerned — (*Looks at him as if trying to read his mind.*) And, after all, Jørgen Tesman must be said to be a most proper young man in all respects.

BRACK: Both proper and substantial. Most certainly.

HEDDA: And one can't say there is anything exactly comical about him. Do you think there is?

BRACK: Comical? No — o. I wouldn't say that —

HEDDA: All right, then. And he is a most assiduous collector. Nobody can deny that. I think it is perfectly possible he may go quite far, after all.

BRACK (*looks at her rather uncertainly*): I assumed that you, like everybody else, thought he'll in time become an exceptionally eminent man?

HEDDA (*with a weary expression*): Yes, I did. And then, you see — there he was, wanting so desperately to be allowed to provide for me — I don't know why I shouldn't have accepted?

BRACK: No, certainly. From that point of view —

HEDDA: For you know, Judge, that was considerably more than my other admirers were willing to do.

BRACK (*laughs*): Well! Of course I can't answer for all the others. But as far as I am concerned, I have always had a certain degree of — respect for the bonds of matrimony. You know — as a general proposition, Mrs. Tesman.

HEDDA (*lightly*): Well, I never really counted very heavily on *you* —

BRACK: All I want is a nice, confidential circle, in which I can be of service, both in deed and in counsel. Be allowed to come and go like a true and trusted friend —

HEDDA: You mean, of the master of the house — ?

BRACK (*with a slight bow*): To be perfectly frank — rather of the mistress. But by all means — the master, too, of course. Do you know, that kind of — shall I say, triangular? — relationship can really be a great comfort to all parties involved.

HEDDA: Yes, many were the times I missed a second travel companion. To be twosome in the compartment — brrr!

BRACK: Fortunately, the wedding trip is over.

HEDDA (*shakes her head*): There's a long journey ahead. I've just arrived at a station on the way.

BRACK: Well, at the station one gets out and moves around a bit, Mrs. Tesman.

HEDDA: I never get out.

BRACK: Really?

HEDDA: No. For there's always someone around, who —

BRACK (*laughs*): — looks at one's legs; is that it?

HEDDA: Exactly.

BRACK: Oh well, really, now —

HEDDA (*with a silencing gesture*): I won't have it! Rather stay in my seat — once I'm seated. Twosome and all.

BRACK: I see. But what if a third party were to join the couple?

HEDDA: Well, now — *that* would be something altogether different!

BRACK: A proven, understanding friend —

HEDDA: — entertaining in all sorts of lively ways —

BRACK: — and not at all a specialist!

HEDDA (*with audible breath*): Yes, that would indeed be a comfort.

BRACK (*hearing the front door open, looking at her*): The triangle is complete.

HEDDA (*half aloud*): And the train goes on.

(TESMAN, *in gray walking suit and soft hat, enters, right. He carries a pile of paperbound books under his arm. Others are stuffed in his pockets.*)

TESMAN (*as he walks up to the table in front of the corner sofa*): Puuhh — ! Quite some load to carry, all this — and in this heat, too. (*Puts the books down.*) I am positively perspiring, Hedda. Well, well. So you're here already, my dear Judge. Hm? And Berte didn't tell me.

BRACK (*rises*): I came through the garden.

HEDDA: What are all those books?

TESMAN (*leafing through some of them*): Just some new publications in my special field.

HEDDA: Special field, hm?

BRACK: Ah yes — professional publications, Mrs. Tesman.

(BRACK *and* HEDDA *exchange knowing smiles.*)

HEDDA: Do you still need more books?

TESMAN: Yes, my dear. There is no such thing as having too many books in one's special field. One has to keep up with what is being written and published, you know.

HEDDA: I suppose.

TESMAN (*searching among the books*): And look. Here is Eilert Løvborg's new book, too. (*Offers it to her.*) Want to take a look at it, Hedda? Hm?

HEDDA: No — thanks just the same. Or perhaps later.

TESMAN: I glanced at it on my way home.

BRACK: And what do you think of it? As a specialist yourself?

TESMAN: It is remarkable for its sobriety. He never wrote like that before. (*Gathers up all the books.*) I just want to take these into my study. I am so much looking forward to cutting them open! And then I'll change. (*To* BRACK.) I assume there's no rush to be off, is there?

BRACK: Not at all. We have plenty of time.

TESMAN: In that case, I think I'll indulge myself a little. (*On his way out with the books he halts in the doorway and turns.*) By the way, Hedda — Aunt Julle won't be out to see you tonight, after all.

HEDDA: No? Is it that business with the hat, do you think?

TESMAN: Oh, no — not at all. How can you believe a thing like that about Aunt Julle! Just think! No, it's Aunt Rina. She's feeling very poorly.

HEDDA: Isn't she always?

TESMAN: Yes, but it's especially bad today, poor thing.

HEDDA: Well, in that case I suppose she ought to stay home. I shall have to put up with it; that's all.

TESMAN: And you have no idea how perfectly delighted Aunt Julle was, even so. Because of how splendid you look after the trip, Hedda!

HEDDA (*half aloud, rising*): Oh, these everlasting aunts!

TESMAN: Hm?

HEDDA (*walks over to the French doors*): Nothing.

TESMAN: No? All right. Well, excuse me. (*Exits right, through inner room.*)

BRACK: What is this about a hat?

HEDDA: Oh, something with Miss Tesman this morning. She had put her hat down on the chair over there. (*Looks at him, smiles.*) So I pretended to think it was the maid's.

BRACK (*shakes his head*): But my dear Mrs. Tesman — how could you do a thing like that! And to that excellent old lady, too!

HEDDA (*nervously pacing the floor*): Well, you see — something just takes hold of me at times. And then I can't help myself — (*Throws herself down in the easy chair near the stove.*) Oh I can't explain it even to myself.

BRACK (*behind her chair*): You aren't really happy — that's the trouble.

HEDDA (*staring into space*): I don't know any reason why I should be. Do you?

BRACK: Well, yes — partly because you've got the home you've always wanted.

HEDDA (*looks up at him and laughs*): So you too believe that story about my great wish?

BRACK: You mean, there is nothing to it?

HEDDA: Well, yes; there is *something* to it.

BRACK: Well?

HEDDA: There is this much to it, that last summer I used Tesman to see me home from evening parties.

BRACK: Unfortunately — my route was in quite a different direction.

HEDDA: True. You walked on other roads last summer.

BRACK (*laughs*): Shame on you, Mrs. Tesman! So, all right — you and Tesman — ?

HEDDA: One evening we passed by here. And Tesman, poor thing, was practically turning himself into knots trying to find something to talk about. So I felt sorry for all that erudition —

BRACK (*with a doubting smile*): You did? Hm —

HEDDA: I really did. So, just to help him out of his misery, I happened to say that I'd like to live in this house.

BRACK: Just that?

HEDDA: That was all — *that* evening.

BRACK: But afterwards — ?

HEDDA: Yes, my frivolity had consequences, Judge.

BRACK: Unfortunately — that's often the way with frivolities. It happens to all of us, Mrs. Tesman.

HEDDA: Thanks! So in our common enthusiasm for Mr. Secretary Falk's villa Tesman and I found each other, you see! The result was engagement and wedding and honeymoon abroad and all the rest of it. Well, yes, my dear Judge — I've made my bed — I almost said.

BRACK: But this is priceless! And you didn't really care for the house at all?

HEDDA: Certainly not.

BRACK: Not even now? After all, we've set up quite a comfortable home for you here, haven't we?

HEDDA: Oh — it seems to me I smell lavender and rose sachets in all the rooms. But maybe that's a smell Aunt Julle brought with her.

BRACK (*laughs*): My guess is rather the late lamented Secretary's wife.

HEDDA: It smells of mortality, whoever it is. Like corsages — the next day. (*Clasps her hands behind her neck, leans back, looks at him.*) Judge, you have no idea how dreadfully bored I'll be — out here.

BRACK: But don't you think life may hold some task for you, too, Mrs. Tesman?

HEDDA: A task? With any kind of appeal?

BRACK: Preferably that, of course.

HEDDA: Heaven knows what kind of task that might be. There are times when I wonder if — (*Interrupts herself.*) No; I'm sure that wouldn't work, either.

BRACK: Who knows? Tell me.

HEDDA: It has occurred to me that maybe I could get Tesman to enter politics.

BRACK (*laughs*): Tesman! No, really — I must confess that — politics doesn't strike me as being exactly Tesman's line.

HEDDA: I agree. But suppose I were to prevail on him, all the same?

BRACK: What satisfaction could you possibly find in that? If he can't succeed — why do you want him even to try?

HEDDA: Because I am bored, I tell you! (*After a brief pause.*) So you think it's quite out of the question that Tesman could ever become prime minister?

BRACK: Well, you see, Mrs. Tesman — to do that he'd first of all have to be a fairly wealthy man.

HEDDA (*getting up, impatiently*): Yes! There we are! These shabby circumstances I've married into! (*Crosses the floor.*) That's what makes life so mean. So — so — ridiculous! For that's what it is, you know.

BRACK: Personally I believe something else is to blame.

HEDDA: What?

BRACK: You've never been through anything that's really stirred you.

HEDDA: Something serious, you mean?

BRACK: If you like. But maybe it's coming now.

HEDDA (*with a toss of her head*): You are thinking of that silly old professorship! That's Tesman's business. I refuse to give it a thought.

BRACK: As you wish. But now — to put it in the grand style — now when a solemn challenge of responsibility is being posed? Demands made on you? (*Smiles.*) New demands, Mrs. Tesman.

HEDDA (*angry*): Quiet! You'll never see anything of the kind.

BRACK (*cautiously*): We'll talk about this a year from now — on the outside.

HEDDA (*curtly*): I'm not made for that sort of thing, Judge! No demands for me!

BRACK: But surely you, like most women, are made for a duty, which —

HEDDA (*over by the French doors*): Oh, do be quiet! Often it seems to me there's only one thing in the world that I am made for.

BRACK (*coming close*): And may I ask what that is?

HEDDA (*looking out*): To be bored to death. Now you know. (*Turns, looks toward the inner room, laughs.*) Just as I thought. Here comes the professor.

BRACK (*warningly, in a low voice*): Steady, now, Mrs. Tesman!

(TESMAN, *dressed for a party, carrying his hat and gloves, enters from the right side of the inner room.*)

TESMAN: Hedda, any word yet from Eilert Løvborg that he isn't coming, hm?

HEDDA: No.

TESMAN: In that case, I wouldn't be a bit surprised if we have him here in a few minutes.

BRACK: You really think he'll come?

TESMAN: I am almost certain he will. For I'm sure it's only idle gossip that you told me this morning.

BRACK: Oh?

TESMAN: Anyway, that's what Aunt Julle said. She doesn't for a moment believe he'll stand in my way. Just think!

BRACK: I'm very glad to hear that.

TESMAN (*puts his hat and his gloves down

on a chair, right): But you must let me wait for him as long as possible.

BRACK: By all means. We have plenty of time. Nobody will arrive at my place before seven — seven-thirty, or so.

TESMAN: And in the meantime we can keep Hedda company. Take our time. Hm?

HEDDA (*carrying* BRACK's *hat and coat over to the sofa in the corner*): And if worst comes to worst, Mr. Løvborg can stay here with me.

BRACK (*trying to take the things away from her*): Let me, Mrs. Tesman — What do you mean — "if worst comes to worst"?

HEDDA: If he doesn't want to go with you and Tesman.

TESMAN (*looks dubiously at her*): But, dearest Hedda — do you think that will quite do? He staying here with you? Hm? Remember, Aunt Julle won't be here.

HEDDA: No, but Mrs. Elvsted will. The three of us will have a cup of tea together.

TESMAN: Oh yes; *that* will be perfectly all right!

BRACK (*with a smile*): And perhaps the wiser course of action for him.

HEDDA: What do you mean?

BRACK: Begging your pardon, Mrs. Tesman — you've often enough looked askance at my little stag dinners. It's been your opinion that only men of the firmest principles ought to attend.

HEDDA: I should think Mr. Løvborg is firm-principled enough now. A reformed sinner —

(BERTE *appears in door, right*.)

BERTE: Ma'am — there's a gentleman here who asks if —

HEDDA: Show him in, please.

TESMAN (*softly*): I'm sure it's he! Just think!

(EILERT LØVBORG *enters, right. He is slim, gaunt. Of* TESMAN's *age, but he looks older and somewhat dissipated. Brown hair and beard. Pale, longish face, reddish spots on the cheekbones. Dressed for visiting in elegant, black, brand-new suit. He carries a silk hat and dark gloves in his hand. He remains near the door, makes a quick bow. He appears a little embarrassed.*)

TESMAN (*goes over to him, shakes his hand*): My dear Eilert — at last we meet again!

EILERT LØVBORG (*subdued voice*): Thanks

for your note, Jørgen! (*Approaching* HEDDA.) Am I allowed to shake your hand, too, Mrs. Tesman?

HEDDA (*accepting his proffered hand*): I am very glad to see you, Mr. Løvborg. (*With a gesture.*) I don't know if you two gentlemen —

LØVBORG (*with a slight bow*): Judge Brack, I believe.

BRACK (*also bowing lightly*): Certainly. Some years ago —

TESMAN (*to* LØVBORG, *both hands on his shoulders*): And now I want you to feel quite at home here, Eilert! Isn't that right, Hedda? For you plan to stay here in town, I understand. Hm?

LØVBORG: Yes, I do.

TESMAN: Perfectly reasonable. Listen — I just got hold of your new book, but I haven't had a chance to read it yet.

LØVBORG: You may save yourself the trouble.

TESMAN: Why do you say that?

LØVBORG: There's not much to it.

TESMAN: Just think — you saying that!

BRACK: Nevertheless, people seem to have very good things to say about it.

LØVBORG: That's exactly why I wrote it — so everybody would like it.

BRACK: Very wise of you.

TESMAN: Yes, but Eilert — !

LØVBORG: For I am trying to rebuild my position. Start all over again.

TESMAN (*with some embarrassment*): Yes, I suppose you are, aren't you? Hm?

LØVBORG (*smiles, puts his hat down, pulls a parcel out of his pocket*): When *this* appears — Jørgen Tesman — this you must read. For this is the real thing. This is me.

TESMAN: Oh really? And what is it?

LØVBORG: The continuation.

TESMAN: Continuation? Of what?

LØVBORG: Of the book.

TESMAN: Of the new book?

LØVBORG: Of course.

TESMAN: But Eilert — you've carried the story all the way up to the present!

LØVBORG: So I have. And this is about the future.

TESMAN: The future! But, heavens — we don't know a thing about the future!

LØVBORG: No, we don't. But there are a couple of things to be said about it all the same. (*Unwraps the parcel.*) Here, let me show you —

TESMAN: But that's not your handwriting.

LØVBORG: I have dictated it. (*Leafs through portions of the manuscript.*) It's in two parts. The first is about the forces that will shape the civilization of the future. And the second (*riffling through more pages*) — about the course which that future civilization will take.

TESMAN: How remarkable! It would never occur to me to write anything like that.

HEDDA (*over by the French doors, her fingers drumming the pane*): Hmm — I dare say —

LØVBORG (*replacing the manuscript in its wrappings and putting it down on the table*): I brought it along, for I thought maybe I'd read parts of it aloud to you this evening.

TESMAN: That's very good of you, Eilert. But this evening — ? (*Looks at* BRACK.) I'm not quite sure how to arrange that —

LØVBORG: Some other time, then. There's no hurry.

BRACK: You see, Mr. Løvborg, there's a little get-together over at my house tonight. Mainly for Tesman, you know —

LØVBORG (*looking for his hat*): In that case, I certainly won't —

BRACK: No, listen. Won't you do me the pleasure to join us?

LØVBORG (*firmly*): No, I won't. But thanks all the same.

BRACK: Oh come on! Why don't you do that? We'll be a small, select circle. And I think I can promise you a fairly lively evening, as Hed — as Mrs. Tesman would say.

LØVBORG: I don't doubt that. Nevertheless —

BRACK: And you may bring your manuscript along and read aloud to Tesman over at my house. I have plenty of room.

TESMAN: Just think, Eilert! Wouldn't that be nice, hm?

HEDDA (*intervening*): But can't you see that Mr. Løvborg doesn't want to? I'm sure he would rather stay here and have supper with me.

LØVBORG (*looks at her*): With you, Mrs. Tesman?

HEDDA: And with Mrs. Elvsted.

LØVBORG: Ah — ! (*Casually.*) I ran into her at noon today.

HEDDA: Oh? Well, she'll be here tonight. So you see your presence is really required, Mr. Løvborg. Otherwise she won't have anybody to see her home.

LØVBORG: True. All right, then, Mrs. Tesman — I'll stay, thank you.

HEDDA: Good. I'll just tell the maid. (*She rings for* BERTE *over by the door, right.*)

(BERTE *appears just off stage.* HEDDA *talks with her in a low voice, points toward the inner room.* BERTE *nods and exits.*)

TESMAN (*while* HEDDA *and* BERTE *are talking, to* LØVBORG): Tell me, Eilert — is it this new subject — about the future — is that what you plan to lecture on?

LØVBORG: Yes.

TESMAN: For the bookseller told me you have announced a lecture series for this fall.

LØVBORG: Yes, I have. I hope you won't mind too much.

TESMAN: Of course not! But —

LØVBORG: For of course I realize it is rather awkward for you.

TESMAN (*unhappily*): Oh well — I certainly can't expect — that just for my sake —

LØVBORG: But I will wait till you receive your appointment.

TESMAN: Wait? But — but — but — you mean you aren't going to compete with me? Hm?

LØVBORG: No. Just triumph over you. In people's opinion.

TESMAN: Oh, for goodness' sake! Then Aunt Julle was right, after all! I knew it all the time. Hedda! Do you hear that! Just think — Eilert Løvborg isn't going to stand in our way after all.

HEDDA (*tersely*): Our? I have nothing to do with this.

(HEDDA *walks into the inner room, where* BERTE *is bringing in a tray with decanters and glasses.* HEDDA *nods her approval and comes forward again.*)

TESMAN (*during the foregoing business*): How about that, Judge? What do you say to this? Hm?

BRACK: I say that moral victory and all that — hm — may be glorious enough and beautiful enough —

TESMAN: Oh, I agree. All the same —

HEDDA (*looks at* TESMAN *with a cold smile*): You look thunderstruck.

TESMAN: Well, I am — pretty much — I really believe —

BRACK: After all, Mrs. Tesman, that was quite a thunderstorm that just passed over.

HEDDA (*points to the inner room*): How about a glass of cold punch, gentlemen?

BRACK (*looks at his watch*): A stirrup cup. Not a bad idea.

TESMAN: Splendid, Hedda. Perfectly splendid. In such a lighthearted mood as I am now —

HEDDA: Please. You, too, Mr. Løvborg.

LØVBORG (*with a gesture of refusal*): No, thanks. Really. Nothing for me.

BRACK: Good heavens, man! Cold punch isn't poison, you know!

LØVBORG: Perhaps not for everybody.

HEDDA: I'll keep Mr. Løvborg company in the meantime.

TESMAN: All right, Hedda. You do that.

(*He and* BRACK *go into the inner room, sit down, drink punch, smoke cigarettes, and engage in lively conversation during the next scene.* EILERT LØVBORG *remains standing near the stove.* HEDDA *walks over to the desk.*)

HEDDA (*her voice a little louder than usual*): I'll show you some pictures, if you like. You see — Tesman and I, we took a trip through Tyrol on our way back.

(*She brings an album over to the table by the sofa. She sits down in the far corner of the sofa.* LØVBORG *approaches, stops, looks at her. He takes a chair and sits down at her left, his back toward the inner room.*)

HEDDA (*opens the album*): Do you see these mountains, Mr. Løvborg? They are the Ortler group. Tesman has written their name below. Here it is: "The Ortler group near Meran."

LØVBORG (*has looked steadily at her all this time. Says slowly*): Hedda — Gabler!

HEDDA (*with a quick glance sideways*): Not that! Shhh!

LØVBORG (*again*): Hedda Gabler!

HEDDA (*looking at the album*): Yes, that used to be my name. When— when we two knew each other.

LØVBORG: And so from now on — for the whole rest of my life — I must get used to never again saying Hedda Gabler.

HEDDA (*still occupied with the album*): Yes, you must. And you might as well start right now. The sooner the better, I think.

LØVBORG (*with indignation*): Hedda Gabler married? And married to — Jørgen Tesman!

HEDDA: Yes — that's the way it goes.

LØVBORG: Oh, Hedda, Hedda — how could you throw yourself away like that!

HEDDA (*with a fierce glance at him*): What's this? I won't have any of that!

LØVBORG: What do you mean?

(TESMAN *enters from the inner room.*)

HEDDA (*hears him coming and remarks casually*): And this here, Mr. Løvborg, this is from somewhere in the Ampezzo valley. Just look at those peaks over there. (*With a kindly look at* TESMAN.) What did you say those peaks were called, dear?

TESMAN: Let me see. Oh, they — they are the Dolomites.

HEDDA: Right. Those are the Dolomites, Mr. Løvborg.

TESMAN: Hedda, I thought I'd just ask you if you don't want me to bring you some punch, after all? For you, anyway? Hm?

HEDDA: Well, yes; thanks. And a couple of cookies, maybe.

TESMAN: No cigarettes?

HEDDA: No.

TESMAN: All right.

(*He returns to the inner room, then turns right.* BRACK *is in there, keeping an eye on* HEDDA *and* LØVBORG *from time to time.*)

LØVBORG (*still in a low voice*): Answer me, Hedda. How could you do a thing like that?

HEDDA (*apparently engrossed in the album*): If you keep on using my first name I won't talk to you.

LØVBORG: Not even when we're alone?

HEDDA: No. You may think it, but you must not say it.

LØVBORG: I see. It offends your love for — Jørgen Tesman.

HEDDA (*glances at him, smiles*): Love? That's a good one!

LØVBORG: Not love, then.

HEDDA: But no infidelities, either! I won't have it.

LØVBORG: Hedda — answer me just one thing —

HEDDA: Shhh!

(TESMAN *enters with a tray from the inner room.*)

TESMAN: Here! Here are the goodies. (*Puts the tray down.*)

HEDDA: Why don't you get Berte to do it?

TESMAN (*pouring punch*): Because I think it's so much fun waiting on you, Hedda.

HEDDA: But you've filled both glasses. And Mr. Løvborg didn't want any —

TESMAN: I know, but Mrs. Elvsted will soon be here, won't she?

HEDDA: That's right. So she will.

TESMAN: Had you forgotten about her? Hm?

HEDDA: We've been so busy looking at this. (*Shows him a picture.*) Remember that little village?

TESMAN: That's the one just below the Brenner Pass, isn't it? We spent the night there —

HEDDA: — and ran into that lively crowd of summer guests.

TESMAN: Right! Just think — if we only could have had you with us, Eilert! Oh well.

(*Returns to the inner room, sits down, and resumes his conversation with* BRACK.)

LØVBORG: Just tell me this, Hedda —

HEDDA: What?

LØVBORG: Wasn't there love in your feelings for me, either? Not a touch — not a shimmer of love? Wasn't there?

HEDDA: I wonder. To me, we seemed to be simply two good comrades. Two close friends. (*Smiles.*) You, particularly, were very frank.

LØVBORG: You wanted it that way.

HEDDA: And yet — when I look back upon it now, there was something beautiful, something thrilling, something brave, I think, about the secret frankness — that comradeship that not a single soul so much as suspected.

LØVBORG: Yes, wasn't there, Hedda? Wasn't there? When I called on your father in the afternoons — And the General sat by the window with his newspapers — his back turned —

HEDDA: And we two in the sofa in the corner —

LØVBORG: — always with the same illustrated magazine —

HEDDA: — for want of an album, yes —

LØVBORG: Yes, Hedda — and then when I confessed to you — ! Told you all about myself, things the others didn't know. Sat and told you about my orgies by day and night. Dissipation day in and day out! Oh, Hedda — what sort of power in you was it that forced me to tell you things like that?

HEDDA: You think there was some power in me?

LØVBORG: How else can I explain it? And all those veiled questions you asked —

HEDDA: — which you understood so perfectly well —

LØVBORG: That you could ask such questions! With such complete frankness!

HEDDA: *Veiled*, if you please.

LØVBORG: But frankly all the same. All about — that!

HEDDA: And to think that you answered, Mr. Løvborg!

LØVBORG: Yes, that's just what I can't understand — now, afterwards. But tell me, Hedda; wasn't love at the bottom of our whole relationship? Didn't you feel some kind of urge to — purify me — when I came to you in confession? Wasn't that it?

HEDDA: No, not quite.

LØVBORG: Then what made you do it?

HEDDA: Do you find it so very strange that a young girl — when she can do so, without anyone knowing —

LØVBORG: Yes — ?

HEDDA: — that she wants to take a peek into a world which —

LØVBORG: — which — ?

HEDDA: — she is not supposed to know anything about?

LØVBORG: So that was it!

HEDDA: That, too. That, too — I think —

LØVBORG: Companionship in the lust for life. But why couldn't *that* at least have continued?

HEDDA: That was your own fault.

LØVBORG: You were the one who broke off.

HEDDA: Yes, when reality threatened to enter our relationship. Shame on you, Eilert Løvborg! How could you want to do a thing like that to your frank and trusting comrade!

LØVBORG (*clenching his hands*): Oh, why didn't you do it! Why didn't you shoot me down, as you said you would!

HEDDA: Because I'm scared of scandal.

LØVBORG: Yes, Hedda. You are really a coward.

HEDDA: A terrible coward. (*Changing her tone.*) But that was your good luck, wasn't it? And now the Elvsteds have healed your broken heart very nicely.

LØVBORG: I know what Thea has told you.

HEDDA: Perhaps you have told her about us?

LØVBORG: Not a word. She is too stupid to understand.

HEDDA: Stupid?

LØVBORG: In things like that.

HEDDA: And I'm a coward. (*Leans forward, without looking in his eyes, whispers.*) But now I am going to confess something to you.

LØVBORG (*tense*): What?

HEDDA: That I didn't dare to shoot —

LØVBORG: Yes — ?

HEDDA: — that was not the worst of my cowardice that night.

LØVBORG (*looks at her a moment, understands, whispers passionately*): Oh, Hedda! Hedda Gabler! Now I begin to see what was behind the companionship! You and I! So it *was* your lust for life — !

HEDDA (*in a low voice, with an angry glance*): Take care! Don't you believe it!

(*Darkness is falling. The door, right, is opened, and* BERTE *enters.*)

HEDDA (*closing the album, calls out, smiling*): At last! So there you are, dearest Thea! Come in!

(MRS. ELVSTED *enters. She is dressed for a party.* BERTE *exits, closing the door behind her.*)

HEDDA (*on the sofa, reaching out for* MRS. ELVSTED): Sweetest Thea, you have no idea how I've waited for you.

(*In passing,* MRS. ELVSTED *exchanges quick greetings with* TESMAN *and* BRACK *in the inner room. She walks up to the table and shakes* HEDDA'S *hand.* EILERT LØVBORG *rises. He and* MRS. ELVSTED *greet one another with a silent nod.*)

MRS. ELVSTED: Shouldn't I go in and say hello to your husband?

HEDDA: No, never mind that. Leave them alone. They're soon leaving, anyway.

MRS. ELVSTED: Leaving?

HEDDA: They're going out to drink.

MRS. ELVSTED (*quickly, to* LØVBORG): Not you?

LØVBORG: No.

HEDDA: Mr. Løvborg stays here with us.

MRS. ELVSTED (*pulls up a chair, is about to sit down next to* LØVBORG): Oh, how wonderful it is to be here!

HEDDA: Oh no, little Thea. Not that. Not there. Over here by me, please. *I* want to be in the middle.

MRS. ELVSTED: Just as you like. (*She walks in front of the table and seats herself on the*

sofa, on HEDDA's *right.* LØVBORG *sits down again on his chair.*)

LØVBORG (*after a brief pause, to* HEDDA): Isn't she lovely to look at?

HEDDA (*gently stroking her hair*): Just to look at?

LØVBORG: Yes. For you see — she and I — we are real comrades. We have absolute faith in one another. And we can talk together in full freedom.

HEDDA: Unveiled, Mr. Løvborg?

LØVBORG: Well —

MRS. ELVSTED (*in a low voice, clinging to* HEDDA): Oh, I am so happy, Hedda! For just think — he also says I have inspired him!

HEDDA (*looks at her with a smile*): No, really! He says that?

LØVBORG: And she has such courage, Mrs. Tesman! Such courage of action.

MRS. ELVSTED: Oh, my God—courage—! I! I!

LØVBORG: Infinite courage — when it concerns the comrade.

HEDDA: Yes, courage — if one only had that.

LØVBORG: What then?

HEDDA: Then maybe life would be tolerable, after all. (*Changing her tone.*) But now, dearest Thea, you want a glass of nice, cold punch.

MRS. ELVSTED: No, thanks. I never drink things like that.

HEDDA: Then what about you, Mr. Løvborg?

LØVBORG: Thanks. Nothing for me, either.

MRS. ELVSTED: No, nothing for him, either.

HEDDA (*looks firmly at him*): If I say so?

LØVBORG: Makes no difference.

HEDDA (*laughs*): Oh dear! So I have no power over you at all. Is that it?

LØVBORG: Not in that respect.

HEDDA: Seriously, though; I really think you should. For your own sake.

MRS. ELVSTED: No, but Hedda — !

LØVBORG: Why so?

HEDDA: Or rather for people's sake.

LØVBORG: Oh?

HEDDA: For else they might think you don't really trust yourself — That you lack self-confidence —

MRS. ELVSTED (*softly*): Don't, Hedda!

LØVBORG: People may think whatever they like for all I care — for the time being.

MRS. ELVSTED (*happy*): Exactly!

HEDDA: I could easily tell from watching Judge Brack just now.

LØVBORG: Tell what?

HEDDA: He smiled so contemptuously when you didn't dare to join them in there.

LØVBORG: Didn't I dare to! It's just that I'd much rather stay here and talk with you!

MRS. ELVSTED: But that's only natural, Hedda.

HEDDA: The Judge had no way of knowing that. And I also noticed he smiled and looked at Tesman when you didn't dare to go to his silly old party.

LØVBORG: Didn't dare! Are you saying I didn't dare?

HEDDA: *I* am not. But that's how Judge Brack understood it.

LØVBORG: Let him.

HEDDA: So you're not going?

LØVBORG: I'm staying here with you and Thea.

MRS. ELVSTED: Of course, he is, Hedda!

HEDDA (*smiles, nods approvingly*): That's what I call firm foundations. Principled forever; that's the way a man ought to be! (*Turning to* MRS. ELVSTED, *stroking her cheek.*) What did I tell you this morning — when you came here, quite beside yourself — ?

LØVBORG (*puzzled*): Beside herself?

MRS. ELVSTED (*in terror*): Hedda — Hedda — don't!

HEDDA: Now do you see? There was no need at all for that mortal fear of yours — (*Interrupting herself.*) There, now! Now we can all three relax and enjoy ourselves.

LØVBORG (*startled*): What's all this, Mrs. Tesman?

MRS. ELVSTED: Oh, God, Hedda — what are you saying? What are you doing?

HEDDA: Please be quiet. That horrible Judge is looking at you.

LØVBORG: In mortal fear? So that's it. For my sake.

MRS. ELVSTED (*softly, wailing*): Oh, Hedda — if you only knew how utterly miserable you have made me!

LØVBORG (*stares at her for a moment. His face is distorted*): So that was the comrade's happy confidence in me!

MRS. ELVSTED: Oh, my dearest friend — listen to me first — !

LØVBORG (*picks up one of the glasses of punch, raises it, says hoarsely*): Here's to you, Thea! (*Empties the glass, puts it down, picks up the other one.*)

MRS. ELVSTED (*softly*): Hedda, Hedda — why did you want to do this?

HEDDA: Want to! I! Are you mad?

LØVBORG: And here's to you, too, Mrs. Tesman! Thanks for telling me the truth. Long live the truth! (*He drains the glass and is about to fill it again.*)

HEDDA (*restrains him*): That's enough for now. Remember you are going to a party.

MRS. ELVSTED: No, no, no!

HEDDA: Shhh! They are looking at you.

LØVBORG (*puts his glass down*): Listen, Thea — tell me the truth —

MRS. ELVSTED: I will, I will!

LØVBORG: Did your husband know you were coming after me?

MRS. ELVSTED (*wringing her hands*): Oh, Hedda — do you hear what he's asking?

LØVBORG: Did the two of you agree that you were to come here and look after me? Maybe it was his idea, even? Did he send you? Ah, I know what it was — he missed me in the office, didn't he? Or was it at the card table?

MRS. ELVSTED (*softly, in agony*): Oh, Løvborg, Løvborg!

LØVBORG (*grabs a glass and is about to fill it*): Here's to the old Commissioner, too!

HEDDA (*stops him*): No more now. You're supposed to read aloud for Tesman tonight — remember?

LØVBORG (*calm again, puts the glass down*): This was silly of me, Thea. I'm sorry. Taking it this way. Please, don't be angry with me. You'll see — both you and all those others — that even if I have been down — ! With your help, Thea — dear comrade.

MRS. ELVSTED (*beaming*): Oh, thank God — !

(*In the meantime,* BRACK *has looked at his watch. He and* TESMAN *get up and come forward.*)

BRACK (*picking up his coat and hat*): Well, Mrs. Tesman; our time is up.

HEDDA: I suppose it is.

LØVBORG (*rising*): Mine, too, Judge.

MRS. ELVSTED (*softly, pleadingly*): Oh, Løvborg — don't do it!

HEDDA (*pinches her arm*): They can hear you!

MRS. ELVSTED (*with a soft exclamation*): Ouch!

LØVBORG (*to* BRACK): You were good enough to ask me —

BRACK: So you're coming, after all?

LØVBORG: If I may.

BRACK: I'm delighted.

LØVBORG (*picks up his manuscript and says*

to TESMAN): For there are a couple of things here I'd like to show you before I send it off.

TESMAN: Just think! Isn't that nice! But — dearest Hedda — ? In that case, how are you going to get Mrs. Elvsted home? Hm?

HEDDA: We'll manage somehow.

LØVBORG (*looking at the two women*): Mrs. Elvsted? I'll be back to pick her up, of course. (*Coming closer.*) About ten o'clock, Mrs. Tesman? Is that convenient?

HEDDA: Certainly. That will be fine.

TESMAN: Then everything is nice and settled. But don't expect me that early, Hedda.

HEDDA: You just stay as long as — as long as you want to, dear.

MRS. ELVSTED (*in secret fear*): I'll be waiting for you here, then, Mr. Løvborg.

LØVBORG (*hat in hand*): Of course, Mrs. Elvsted.

BRACK: All aboard the pleasure train, gentlemen! I hope we'll have a lively evening — as a certain fair lady would say.

HEDDA: Ah — if only the fair lady could be present. Invisibly.

BRACK: Why invisibly?

HEDDA: To listen to some of your unadulterated liveliness, Judge.

BRACK (*laughs*): I shouldn't advise the fair lady to do that!

TESMAN (*also laughing*): You're a good one, Hedda! Just think!

BRACK: Well —'good night, ladies!

LØVBORG (*with a bow*): Till about ten, then.

(BRACK, LØVBORG, and TESMAN *go out, right. At the same time* BERTE *enters from the inner room with a lighted lamp, which she places on the table, front center. She goes out the same way.*)

MRS. ELVSTED (*has risen and paces restlessly up and down*): Hedda, Hedda — how do you think all this will end?

HEDDA: At ten o'clock he'll be here. I see him already. With vine leaves in his hair. Flushed and confident.

MRS. ELVSTED: I only hope you're right.

HEDDA: For then, you see, he'll have mastered himself. And be a free man for all the days of his life.

MRS. ELVSTED: Dear God — how I hope you are right! That he'll come back like that.

HEDDA: That is the way he will come. No other way. (*She rises and goes closer to* MRS. ELVSTED.) *You* may doubt as long as you like. I believe in him. And now we'll see —

MRS. ELVSTED: There is something behind all this, Hedda. Some hidden purpose.

HEDDA: Yes, there is! For once in my life I want to have power over a human destiny.

MRS. ELVSTED: But don't you already?

HEDDA: I don't and I never have.

MRS. ELVSTED: But your husband — ?

HEDDA: You think that's worth the trouble? Oh, if you knew how poor I am! And you got to be so rich! (*Embraces her passionately.*) I think I'll have to burn your hair off, after all!

MRS. ELVSTED: Let me go! Let me go! You scare me, Hedda!

BERTE (*in the doorway*): Supper is served, ma'am.

HEDDA: Good. We're coming.

MRS. ELVSTED: No, no, no! I'd rather go home by myself! Right now!

HEDDA: Nonsense! You'll have your cup of tea first, you little silly. And then — at ten o'clock — Eilert Løvborg comes — with vine leaves in his hair! (*She almost pulls* MRS. ELVSTED *toward the doorway.*)

ACT III

The same room at the TESMANS'. *The doorway and the French windows both have their portieres closed. The lamp, turned half down, is still on the table. The stove is open. Some dying embers can be seen.* MRS. ELVSTED, *wrapped in a big shawl, is in the easy chair near the stove, her feet on a footstool.* HEDDA, *also dressed, is lying on the sofa, covered by a blanket.*

MRS. ELVSTED (*after a while suddenly sits up, listens anxiously; then she wearily sinks back in her chair, whimpers softly*): Oh my God, my God — not yet!

(BERTE *enters cautiously, right, carrying a letter.*)

MRS. ELVSTED (*turns and whispers tensely*): Well — has anybody been here?

BERTE (*in a low voice*): Yes. Just now there was a girl with this letter.

MRS. ELVSTED (*quickly, reaches for it*): A letter! Give it to me.

BERTE: No, ma'am. It's for the Doctor.

MRS. ELVSTED: I see.

BERTE: Miss Tesman's maid brought it. I'll leave it here on the table.

MRS. ELVSTED: All right.

BERTE (*puts the letter down*): I'd better put out the lamp. It just reeks.

MRS. ELVSTED: Yes, do that. It must be daylight soon, anyway.

BERTE (*putting out the lamp*): It's light already, ma'am.

MRS. ELVSTED: Light already! And still not back!

BERTE: No, so help us. Not that I didn't expect as much —

MRS. ELVSTED: You did?

BERTE: Yes, when I saw a certain character was back in town. Taking them off with him. We sure heard enough about him in the old days!

MRS. ELVSTED: Not so loud. You are waking up Mrs. Tesman.

BERTE (*looks toward the sofa, sighs*): God forbid — ! Let her sleep, poor thing. Do you want me to get the fire going again?

MRS. ELVSTED: Not on my account, thank you.

BERTE: All right. (*Exits quietly, right.*)

HEDDA (*awakened by the closing door*): What's that?

MRS. ELVSTED: Just the maid.

HEDDA (*looks around*): Why in here — ? Oh, I remember! (*Sits up, rubs her eyes, stretches.*) What time is it, Thea?

MRS. ELVSTED (*looks at her watch*): Past seven.

HEDDA: When did Tesman get home?

MRS. ELVSTED: He didn't.

HEDDA: Not home yet!

MRS. ELVSTED (*getting up*): Nobody's come.

HEDDA: And we waited till four!

MRS. ELVSTED (*wringing her hands*): And *how* we waited!

HEDDA (*her hand covering a yawn*): We — ll. We could have saved ourselves that trouble.

MRS. ELVSTED: Did you get any sleep at all?

HEDDA: Yes, I slept pretty well, I think. Didn't you?

MRS. ELVSTED: Not a wink. I just couldn't, Hedda! It was just impossible.

HEDDA (*rises, walks over to her*): Well, now! There's nothing to worry about, for heaven's sake. I know exactly what's happened.

MRS. ELVSTED: Then tell me please. Where do you think they are?

HEDDA: Well, first of all, I'm sure they were terribly late leaving the Judge's —

MRS. ELVSTED: Dear, yes. I'm sure you're right. Still —

HEDDA: — and so Tesman didn't want to wake us up in the middle of the night. (*Laughs.*) Maybe he didn't want us to see him, either — after a party like that.

MRS. ELVSTED: But where do you think he has gone?

HEDDA: To the aunts', of course. His old room is still there, all ready for him.

MRS. ELVSTED: No, he can't be there. Just a few minutes ago there came a letter for him from Miss Tesman. It's over there.

HEDDA: Oh? (*Looks at the envelope.*) So it is — Auntie Julle herself. In that case, I suppose he's still at Brack's. And there's Eilert Løvborg, too — reading aloud, with vine leaves in his hair.

MRS. ELVSTED: Oh Hedda — you're only saying things you don't believe yourself.

HEDDA: My, what a little imbecile you really are, Thea!

MRS. ELVSTED: Yes, I suppose I am.

HEDDA: And you look dead tired, too.

MRS. ELVSTED: I *am* dead tired.

HEDDA: Why don't you do as I say. Go into my room and lie down.

MRS. ELVSTED: No, no — I wouldn't be able to go to sleep, anyway.

HEDDA: Of course, you would.

MRS. ELVSTED: And your husband is bound to be home any minute now. And I have to know right away.

HEDDA: I'll let you know as soon as he gets here.

MRS. ELVSTED: You promise me that, Hedda?

HEDDA: I do. You just go to sleep.

MRS. ELVSTED: Thanks. At least I'll try. (*Exits through inner room.*)

(HEDDA *goes to the French doors, opens the portieres. The room is now in full daylight. She picks up a little hand mirror from the desk, looks at herself, smooths her hair. Walks over to door, right, rings the bell for the maid.* BERTE *presently appears.*)

BERTE: You want something, ma'am?

HEDDA: Yes. You'll have to start the fire again. I'm cold.

BERTE: Yes, ma'am! I'll get it warm in no time. (*Rakes the embers together and puts in another piece of wood. Then she suddenly listens.*) There's the doorbell, ma'am.

HEDDA: All right. See who it is. I'll take care of the stove myself.

BERTE: You'll have a nice blaze going in a minute. (*Exits right.*)

(HEDDA *kneels on the footstool and puts in more pieces of wood. Presently* TESMAN *enters, right. He looks tired and somber. He tiptoes toward the doorway and is about to disappear between the portieres.*)

HEDDA (*by the stove, without looking up*): Good morning.

TESMAN (*turning*): Hedda! (*Comes closer.*) For heaven's sake — you up already! Hm?

HEDDA: Yes, I got up very early this morning.

TESMAN: And I was sure you'd still be sound asleep! Just think!

HEDDA: Not so loud. Mrs. Elvsted is asleep in my room.

TESMAN: Mrs. Elvsted stayed here all night?

HEDDA: Yes. Nobody came for her, you know.

TESMAN: No, I suppose —

HEDDA (*closes the stove, rises*): Well, did you have a good time at the Judge's?

TESMAN: Were you worried about me? Hm?

HEDDA: I'd never dream of worrying about you. I asked if you had a good time.

TESMAN: Yes, indeed. Nice for a change anyway. But I think I liked it best early in the evening. For then Eilert read to me. Just think — we were more than an hour early! And Brack, of course, had things to see to. So Eilert read.

HEDDA (*sits down at the right side of the table*): So? Tell me all about it.

TESMAN (*sits down on an ottoman near the stove*): Oh Hedda, you'll never believe what a book that will be! It must be just the most remarkable thing ever written! Just think!

HEDDA: Yes, but I don't really care about that —

TESMAN: I must tell you, Hedda — I have a confession to make. As he was reading — something ugly came over me —

HEDDA: Ugly?

TESMAN: I sat there envying Eilert for being able to write like that! Just think, Hedda!

HEDDA: All right. I'm thinking!

TESMAN: And yet, with all his gifts — he's incorrigible, after all.

HEDDA: I suppose you mean he has more courage for life than the rest of you?

TESMAN: No, no — I don't mean that. I mean that he's incapable of exercising moderation in his pleasures.

HEDDA: What happened — in the end?

TESMAN: Well — I would call it bacchanal, Hedda.

HEDDA: Did he have vine leaves in his hair?

TESMAN: Vine leaves? No, I didn't notice any vine leaves. But he gave a long, muddled speech in honor of the woman who had inspired him in his work. Those were his words.

HEDDA: Did he mention her name?

TESMAN: No, he didn't. But I'm sure it must be Mrs. Elvsted. You just wait and see if I'm not right!

HEDDA: And where did you and he part company?

TESMAN: On the way back to town. We left — the last of us did — at the same time. And Brack came along, too, to get some fresh air. Then we decided we'd better see Eilert home. You see, he had had altogether too much to drink.

HEDDA: I can imagine.

TESMAN: But then the strangest thing of all happened, Hedda! Or maybe I should say the saddest. I'm almost ashamed — on Eilert's behalf — even talking about it.

HEDDA: Well — ?

TESMAN: You see, on the way back I happened to be behind the others a little. Just for a minute or two — you know —

HEDDA: All right, all right — !

TESMAN: And when I hurried to catch up with them, can you guess what I found by the roadside? Hm?

HEDDA: How can I possibly — ?

TESMAN: You mustn't tell this to a living soul, Hedda! Do you hear! Promise me that, for Eilert's sake. (*Pulls a parcel out of his coat pocket.*) Just think — I found this!

HEDDA: Isn't that what he had with him here yesterday?

TESMAN: Yes! It's his whole, precious, irreplaceable manuscript! And he had dropped it — just like that! Without even noticing! Just think, Hedda! Isn't that awfully sad?

HEDDA: But why didn't you give it back to him?

TESMAN: In the condition he was in! Dear — I just didn't dare to.

HEDDA: And you didn't tell any of the others that you had found it, either?

TESMAN: Of course not. I didn't want to, for Eilert's sake — don't you see?

HEDDA: So nobody knows that you have Eilert Løvborg's papers?

TESMAN: Nobody. And nobody must know, either.

HEDDA: And what did you and he talk about afterwards?

TESMAN: I didn't have a chance to talk to him at all after that. For when we came into town, he and a couple of the others simply vanished. Just think!

HEDDA: Oh? I expect they took him home.

TESMAN: I suppose that must be it. And Brack took off on his own, too.

HEDDA: And what have you been doing with yourself since then?

TESMAN: Well, you see, I and some of the others went home with one of the younger fellows and had a cup of early morning coffee. Or night coffee maybe, rather. Hm? And now, after I've rested a bit and poor Eilert's had some sleep, I'll take this back to him.

HEDDA (reaches for the parcel): No — don't do that! Not right away, I mean. Let me look at it first.

TESMAN: Dearest Hedda — honestly, I just don't dare to.

HEDDA: Don't you dare to?

TESMAN: No, for I'm sure you realize how utterly desperate he'll be when he wakes up and finds that the manuscript is gone. For he hasn't a copy, you know. He said so himself.

HEDDA (looks searchingly at him): But can't a thing like that be written over again?

TESMAN: Hardly. I really don't think so. For, you see — the inspiration —

HEDDA: Yes, I daresay that's the main thing. (Casually.) By the way, here's a letter for you.

TESMAN: Imagine!

HEDDA (gives it to him): It came early this morning.

TESMAN: It's from Aunt Julle, Hedda! I wonder what it can be. (Puts the manuscript down on the other ottoman, opens the letter, skims the content, jumps up.) Oh Hedda! She says here that poor Aunt Rina is dying!

HEDDA: You know we had to expect that.

TESMAN: And if I want to see her again I had better hurry. I'll rush over right away.

HEDDA (suppressing a smile): You'll rush?

TESMAN: Dearest Hedda of mine — if only you could bring yourself to come along! Hm?

HEDDA (rises, weary, with an air of refusal): No, no. You mustn't ask me that. I don't want to look at death and disease. I don't want anything to do with ugliness.

TESMAN: Well, all right — (Rushing around.) My hat? My coat? Oh — out here in the hall. I just hope I won't be too late, Hedda. Hm?

HEDDA: Oh I'm sure that if you rush —

(BERTE appears in the door, right.)

BERTE: Judge Brack is here and wants to know if he may see you.

TESMAN: At this hour! No, no. I can't possibly see him now!

HEDDA: But I can. (To BERTE.) Tell the Judge please to come in.

(BERTE exits.)

HEDDA (with a quick whisper): Tesman! The package! (She grabs it from the ottoman.)

TESMAN: Yes! Give it to me!

HEDDA: No, no. I'll hide it for you till later.

(She walks over to the desk and sticks the parcel in among the books on the shelf. In his hurry TESMAN is having difficulties getting his gloves on. JUDGE BRACK enters, right.)

HEDDA (nods to him): If you aren't an early bird —

BRACK: Yes, don't you think so? (To TESMAN.) You're going out, too?

TESMAN: Yes, I must go and see the aunts. Just think, the invalid — she's dying!

BRACK: Oh, I'm terribly sorry! In that case, don't let me keep you. At such a moment —

TESMAN: Yes, I really must run. Goodbye, goodbye! (Hurries out, right.)

HEDDA (approaching BRACK): It appears that things were quite lively last night over at your house.

BRACK: Indeed, Mrs. Tesman — I didn't get to bed at all.

HEDDA: You didn't either?

BRACK: As you see. But tell me — what has Tesman told you about the night's adventures?

HEDDA: Just some tiresome story about having coffee with somebody someplace —

BRACK: I believe I know all about that coffee. Eilert Løvborg wasn't one of them, was he?

HEDDA: No, they had taken him home first.

BRACK: Tesman, too?

HEDDA: No. Some of the others, he said.

BRACK (*smiles*): Jørgen Tesman is really an ingenuous soul, you know.

HEDDA: He certainly is. But why do you say that? Is there something more to all this?

BRACK: Yes, there is.

HEDDA: Well! In that case, why don't we make ourselves comfortable, Judge. You'll tell your story better, too.

(*She sits down at the left side of the table,* BRACK *near her at the adjacent side.*)

HEDDA: All right?

BRACK: For reasons of my own I wanted to keep track of my guests' movements last night. Or, rather — some of my guests.

HEDDA: Eilert Løvborg was one of them, perhaps?

BRACK: As a matter of fact — he was.

HEDDA: Now you are really making me curious.

BRACK: Do you know where he and a couple of the others spent the rest of the night, Mrs. Tesman?

HEDDA: No — tell me. If it can be told.

BRACK: Oh, certainly. They turned up at an exceptionally gay early morning gathering.

HEDDA: Of the lively kind?

BRACK: Of the liveliest.

HEDDA: A little more about this, Judge.

BRACK: Løvborg had been invited beforehand. I knew about that. But he had declined. He is a reformed character, you know.

HEDDA: As of his stay with the Elvsteds — yes. But he went after all?

BRACK: Well, yes, you see, Mrs. Tesman — unfortunately, the spirit moved him over at my house last evening.

HEDDA: Yes, I understand he became inspired.

BRACK: Quite violently inspired. And that, I gather, must have changed his mind. You know, we men don't always have as much integrity as we ought to have.

HEDDA: Oh, I'm sure you're an exception, Judge Brack. But about Løvborg — ?

BRACK: To make a long story short — he ended up at Miss Diana's establishment.

HEDDA: Miss Diana's?

BRACK: She was the hostess at this gathering — a select circle of intimate friends, male and female.

HEDDA: Is she a redhead, by any chance?

BRACK: That's correct.

HEDDA: And a singer — of sorts?

BRACK: Yes — that, too. And a mighty huntress — of men, Mrs. Tesman. You seem to have heard of her. Eilert Løvborg used to be one of her most devoted protectors in his more affluent days.

HEDDA: And how did it all end?

BRACK: Not in a very friendly fashion, apparently. It seems that after the tenderest reception Miss Diana resorted to brute force —

HEDDA: Against Løvborg?

BRACK: Yes. He accused her or her women friends of having stolen something of his. Said his wallet was gone. And other things, too. In brief, he's supposed to have started a pretty wicked row.

HEDDA: And — ?

BRACK: Well — there was a general free-for-all — men and women both. Fortunately, the police stepped in —

HEDDA: The police — !

BRACK: Yes. But I'm afraid this will be an expensive escapade for Eilert Løvborg, crazy fool that he is.

HEDDA: Well!

BRACK: It appears that he made quite violent objection — struck an officer in the car and tore his coat. So they had to take him along.

HEDDA: How do you know all this?

BRACK: From the police.

HEDDA (*staring straight ahead*): So that's how it was. No vine leaves in his hair.

BRACK: Vine leaves, Mrs. Tesman?

HEDDA (*changing her tone*): But tell me, Judge Brack — why did you keep such a close watch on Eilert Løvborg?

BRACK: Well — for one thing, it is obviously of some concern to me if he testifies that he came straight from my party.

HEDDA: So you think there will be an investigation?

BRACK: Naturally. But I suppose that doesn't really matter too much. However, as a friend of the house I considered it my duty to give you and Tesman a full account of his nighttime exploits.

HEDDA: Yes, but why?

BRACK: Because I very strongly suspect that he intends to use you as a kind of screen.

HEDDA: Really! Why do you think that?

BRACK: Oh, come now, Mrs. Tesman! We can use our eyes, can't we? This Mrs. Elvsted — she isn't leaving town right away you know.

HEDDA: Well, even if there should be something going on between those two, I'd think there would be plenty of other places they could meet.

BRACK: But no home. After last night, every respectable house will once again be closed to Eilert Løvborg.

HEDDA: And so should mine, you mean?

BRACK: Yes. I admit I would find it more than embarrassing if the gentleman were to become a daily guest here, Mrs. Tesman. If he, as an outsider — a highly dispensable outsider — if he were to intrude himself —

HEDDA: — into the triangle?

BRACK: Precisely. It would amount to homelessness for me.

HEDDA (smiling): Sole cock-o'-the-walk — so, that's your goal, is it, Judge?

BRACK (nods slowly, lowers his voice): Yes. That is my goal. And for that I will fight with every means at my disposal.

HEDDA (her smile fading): You're really a dangerous person, you know — when you come right down to it.

BRACK: You think so?

HEDDA: Yes. I am beginning to think so now. And I must say I am exceedingly glad you don't have any kind of hold on me.

BRACK (with a noncommittal laugh): Well, well, Mrs. Tesman! Maybe there is something to what you are saying, at that. Who knows what I might do if I did.

HEDDA: Really, now, Judge Brack! Are you threatening me?

BRACK (rising): — Nonsense! For the triangle, you see — is best maintained on a voluntary basis.

HEDDA: My sentiments, exactly.

BRACK: Well, I have said what I came to say. And now I should get back to town. Goodbye, Mrs. Tesman! (Walks toward the French doors.)

HEDDA (rises): You're going through the garden?

BRACK: Yes. For me that's a short cut.

HEDDA: Yes, and then it's a back way.

BRACK: Quite true. I have nothing against back ways. There are times when they are most intriguing.

HEDDA: You mean when real ammunition is used?

BRACK (in the doorway, laughs back at her): Oh good heavens! I don't suppose one shoots one's tame roosters!

HEDDA (laughs also): No — not if one has only one — !

(They nod to each other, both still laughing. He leaves. She closes the door behind him. For a few moments she remains by the door, quite serious now, looking into the garden. Then she walks over to the doorway and opens the portieres wide enough to look into the inner room. Goes to the desk, pulls LØVBORG's manuscript from the bookshelf and is about to read it when BERTE's voice, very loud, is heard from the hall, right. HEDDA turns around, listens. She hurriedly puts the manuscript into the drawer of the desk and puts the key down on its top. EILERT LØVBORG, wearing his coat and with his hat in his hand, flings open the door, right. He looks somewhat confused and excited.)

LØVBORG (turned toward the invisible BERTE in the hall): — And I say I must! You can't stop me! (He closes the door, turns, sees HEDDA, immediately controls himself, greets her.)

HEDDA (by the desk): Well, well, Mr. Løvborg — aren't you a trifle late coming for Thea?

LØVBORG: Or a trifle early for calling on you. I apologize.

HEDDA: How do you know she is still here?

LØVBORG: The people she is staying with told me she's been gone all night.

HEDDA (walks over to the table): Did they seem — strange — when they said it?

LØVBORG (puzzled): Strange?

HEDDA: I mean, did they seem to find it a little — unusual?

LØVBORG (suddenly understands): Ah, I see what you mean! Of course! I'm dragging her down with me. No, as a matter of fact, I didn't notice anything. I suppose Tesman isn't up yet?

HEDDA: I — I don't think so —

LØVBORG: When did he get home?

HEDDA: Very late.

LØVBORG: Did he tell you anything?

HEDDA: Yes, he said you'd all had quite a time over at Brack's.

LØVBORG: Just that?

HEDDA: I think so. But I was so awfully sleepy —

(MRS. ELVSTED enters through portieres in the rear.)

MRS ELVSTED (toward him): Oh, Løvborg! At last!

LØVBORG: Yes, at last. And too late.

MRS. ELVSTED (*in fear*): What is too late?

LØVBORG: Everything is too late now. It's all over with me.

MRS. ELVSTED: Oh no, no! Don't say things like that!

LØVBORG: You'll say the same yourself when you hear —

MRS. ELVSTED: I don't want to hear — !

HEDDA: Maybe you'd rather talk with her alone? I'll leave.

LØVBORG: No stay — you, too. I beg you to.

MRS. ELVSTED: But I don't want to listen, do you hear?

LØVBORG: It isn't last night I want to talk about.

MRS. ELVSTED: What about, then?

LØVBORG: We'll have to part, Thea.

MRS. ELVSTED: Part!

HEDDA (*involuntarily*): I knew it!

LØVBORG: For I don't need you any more.

MRS. ELVSTED: And you can stand there and tell me a thing like that! Don't need me! Why can't I help you the way I did before? Aren't we going to keep on working together?

LØVBORG: I don't intend to work any more.

MRS. ELVSTED (*desperately*): What am I going to do with my life, then?

LØVBORG: You'll have to try to live your life as if you'd never known me.

MRS. ELVSTED: But I can't do that!

LØVBORG: Try, Thea. Go back home.

MRS. ELVSTED (*agitated*): Never again! Where you are I want to be! And you can't chase me away just like that. I want to stay right here! Be with you when the book appears.

HEDDA (*in a tense whisper*): Ah — yes — the book!

LØVBORG (*looks at her*): My book — and Thea's. For that's what it is.

MRS. ELVSTED: That's what I feel, too. And that's why I have the right to be with you when it comes out. I want to see all the honor and all the fame you'll get. And the joy — I want to share the joy, too.

LØVBORG: Thea, our book is never going to come out.

HEDDA: Ah!

MRS. ELVSTED: It won't!

LØVBORG: *Can't* ever appear.

MRS. ELVSTED (*with fearful suspicion*): Løvborg, what have you done with the manuscript?

HEDDA (*watching him tensely*): Yes — what about the manuscript?

MRS. ELVSTED: Where is it?

LØVBORG: Oh Thea — please, don't ask me about that!

MRS. ELVSTED: Yes, yes — I want to be told! I have the right to know — right now!

LØVBORG: All right. I've torn it to pieces.

MRS. ELVSTED (*screams*): Oh, no! No!

HEDDA (*involuntarily*): But that's not — !

LØVBORG (*looks at her*): Not true, you think?

HEDDA (*composing herself*): Well, of course, if you say so. You should know. It just sounds so — so unbelievable.

LØVBORG: All the same, it's true.

MRS. ELVSTED (*hands clenched*): Oh God — Oh God, Hedda. He has torn his own work to pieces!

LØVBORG: I have torn my whole life to pieces, so why not my life's work as well?

MRS. ELVSTED: And that's what you did last night?

LØVBORG: Yes, I tell you! In a thousand pieces. And scattered them in the fjord. Far out — where the water is clean and salty. Let them drift there, with wind and current. Then they'll sink. Deep, deep down. Like me, Thea.

MRS. ELVSTED: Do you know, Løvborg — this thing you've done to the book — all the rest of my life I'll think of it as killing a little child.

LØVBORG: You are right. It is like murdering a child.

MRS. ELVSTED: But then, how could you? For the child was mine, too!

HEDDA (*almost soundlessly*): The child —

MRS. ELVSTED (*with a deep sigh*): So it's all over. I'll go now, Hedda.

HEDDA: But you aren't leaving town?

MRS. ELVSTED: Oh, I don't know myself what I'll do. There's only darkness before me. (*Exits, right.*)

HEDDA (*waits for a moment*): Aren't you going to see her home, Mr. Løvborg?

LØVBORG: I? Through the streets? Letting people see her with me?

HEDDA: Of course, I don't know what else may have happened last night. But is it really so absolutely irreparable — ?

LØVBORG: Last night is not the end of it. That I know. And yet, I don't really care for that kind of life any more. Not again. She has broken all the courage for life and all the defiance that was in me.

HEDDA (*staring ahead*): So that sweet little goose has had her hand in a human destiny. (*Looks at him.*) But that you could be so heartless, even so!

LØVBORG: Don't tell me I was heartless!

HEDDA: To ruin everything that's filled her soul for such a long time! You don't call that heartless!

LØVBORG: Hedda — to you I can tell the truth.

HEDDA: The truth?

LØVBORG: But first promise me — give me your word you'll never let Thea know what I'm going to tell you now.

HEDDA: You have it.

LØVBORG: All right. It isn't true, what I just told her.

HEDDA: About the manuscript?

LØVBORG: Yes. I have not torn it up. Not thrown it in the sea, either.

HEDDA: But then — where is it?

LØVBORG: I've destroyed it just the same. Really, I have, Hedda!

HEDDA: I don't understand.

LØVBORG: Thea said that what I had done seemed to her like murdering a child.

HEDDA: Yes — she did.

LØVBORG: But killing a child, that's not the worst thing a father can do to it.

HEDDA: No?

LØVBORG: No. And the worst is what I don't want Thea to know.

HEDDA: What *is* the worst?

LØVBORG: Hedda — suppose a man, say, early in the morning, after a stupid, drunken night — suppose he comes home to his child's mother and says: Listen, I've been in such and such a place. I've been here — and I've been there. And I had our child with me. In all those places. And the child is lost. Gone. Vanished. I'll be damned if I know where it is. Who's got hold of it —

HEDDA: Yes — but when all is said and done — it is only a book, you know.

LØVBORG: Thea's pure soul was in that book.

HEDDA: I realize that.

LØVBORG: Then you surely also realize that she and I can have no future together.

HEDDA: Where do you go from here?

LØVBORG: Nowhere. Just finish everything off. The sooner the better.

HEDDA (*a step closer*): Listen — Eilert Løvborg — Couldn't you make sure it's done beautifully?

LØVBORG: Beautifully? (*Smiles.*) With vine leaves in the hair, as you used to say.

HEDDA: Oh no. I don't believe in vine leaves any more. But still beautifully! For once. Goodbye. Go now. And don't come back.

LØVBORG: Goodbye, Mrs. Tesman. Give my regards to Jørgen Tesman. (*He is about to leave.*)

HEDDA: Wait! I want to give you something — a remembrance. (*Goes to the desk, opens the drawer, takes out the gun case. Returns to* LØVBORG *with one of the revolvers.*)

LØVBORG: The gun? That's the remembrance?

HEDDA (*nods slowly*): Do you recognize it? It was pointed at you once.

LØVBORG: You should have used it then.

HEDDA: Take it! *You* use it.

LØVBORG (*pockets the gun*): Thanks!

HEDDA: And beautifully, Eilert Løvborg! That's all I ask!

LØVBORG: Goodbye, Hedda Gabler. (*Exits, right.*)

(HEDDA *listens by the door for a moment. Then she crosses to the desk, takes out the manuscript, glances inside the cover, pulls some of the pages halfway out and looks at them. Carries the whole manuscript over to the chair by the stove. She sits down with the parcel in her lap. After a moment she opens the stove and then the manuscript.*)

HEDDA (*throws a bundle of sheets into the fire, whispers*): Now I'm burning your child, Thea. You — curlyhead! (*Throws more sheets in.*) Your and Eilert Løvborg's child. (*Throws all the rest of the manuscript into the stove.*) I am burning — I am burning your child.

ACT IV

The same rooms at the TESMANS'. *Evening. The front room is dark. The inner room is lighted by the ceiling lamp over the table. Portieres cover the French doors.*

HEDDA, *in black, is walking up and down in the dark of the front room. She goes into the inner room, turning left in the doorway. She is heard playing a few bars on the piano. She reappears and comes forward again.* BERTE *enters from the right side of the inner room. She carries a lighted lamp, which she puts down on the table in front of the corner sofa. Her eyes show signs of weeping; she wears black ribbons on her uniform. She exits quietly, right.* HEDDA *goes over to the French windows, looks between the portieres into the dark. Presently* MISS TESMAN, *in mourning, with hat and veil, enters, right.* HEDDA *walks over to meet her, gives her her hand.*

MISS TESMAN: Yes, my dearest Hedda — here you see me in my garb of grief. For now at last my poor sister has fought her fight to the end.

HEDDA: I already know — as you see. Tesman sent word.

MISS TESMAN: Yes, he promised he'd do that. But I thought that to you, Hedda — here in the house of life — I really ought to bring you the tidings of death myself.

HEDDA: That is very kind of you.

MISS TESMAN: Ah, but Rina shouldn't have died just now. There should be no mourning in Hedda's house at this time.

HEDDA (*changing the topic*): I understand she had a very quiet end.

MISS TESMAN: Oh so beautiful, so peaceful! She left us so quietly! And then the unspeakable happiness of seeing Jørgen one more time! To say goodbye to him to her heart's content! Isn't he back yet?

HEDDA: No. He wrote I mustn't expect him back very soon. But do sit down.

MISS TESMAN: No — no, thanks, my dear, blessed Hedda. Not that I wouldn't like to. But I don't have much time. I must go back and prepare her as best I can. I want her to look right pretty when she goes into her grave.

HEDDA: Is there anything I can help you with?

MISS TESMAN: I won't have you as much as think of it! That's not for Hedda Tesman to lend a hand to. Or lend thoughts to either. Not now, of all times!

HEDDA: Oh — thoughts! We can't always control our thoughts —

MISS TESMAN (*still preoccupied*): Ah yes — such is life. At home we're making a shroud for Rina. And here, too, there'll be sewing to do soon, I expect. But of quite a different kind, thank God!

(TESMAN *enters, right.*)

HEDDA: Finally!

TESMAN: You here, Aunt Julle? With Hedda? Just think!

MISS TESMAN: I am just about to leave, Jørgen dear. Well — did you do all the things you promised me you'd do?

TESMAN: No, I'm afraid I forgot half of them, Auntie. I'd better run in again tomorrow. I'm all confused today. I can't seem to keep my thoughts together.

MISS TESMAN: But dearest Jørgen — you mustn't take it this way!

TESMAN: Oh, I mustn't? How do you mean?

MISS TESMAN: You ought to be joyful in the midst of your sorrow. Glad for what's happened. The way I am.

TESMAN: Oh yes, of course. You're thinking of Aunt Rina.

HEDDA: You're going to feel lonely now, Miss Tesman.

MISS TESMAN: The first few days, yes. But I hope that won't last long. Dear Rina's little parlor won't be empty for long, if I can help it!

TESMAN: Oh? And who do you want to move in there? Hm?

MISS TESMAN: Ah — it's not very hard to find some poor soul who needs nursing and comfort.

HEDDA: And you really want to take on such a burden all over again?

MISS TESMAN: Heavens! God forgive you, child — burden? It has not been a burden to me.

HEDDA: Still — a stranger, who —

MISS TESMAN: Oh, it's easy to make friends with sick people. And I need somebody to live for, too. Well, the Lord be praised, maybe soon there'll be a thing or two an old aunt can turn her hand to here.

HEDDA: Oh, never mind us —

TESMAN: Yes, just think — how lovely it would be for the three of us, if only —

HEDDA: If only — ?

TESMAN (*uneasy*): Oh, nothing. I daresay it will all work out. Let's hope it will, hm?

MISS TESMAN: Well, well. I can see that you two have something to talk about. (*With a smile.*) And perhaps Hedda has something to tell you, Jørgen! Goodbye! I'm going home to Rina, now. (*Turns round in the door.*) Dear, dear — how strange to think — Now Rina is both with me and with Jochum!

TESMAN: Yes, just think, Aunt Julle! Hm?

(MISS TESMAN *exits, right.*)

HEDDA (*coldly scrutinizing* TESMAN): I wouldn't be at all surprised if you aren't more affected by this death than she is.

TESMAN: Oh, it isn't just Aunt Rina's death, Hedda. It's Eilert I worry about.

HEDDA (*quickly*): Any news about him?

TESMAN: I went over to his room this afternoon to tell him the manuscript is safe.

HEDDA: Well? And didn't you see him?

TESMAN: No. He wasn't home. But I ran into Mrs. Elvsted and she told me he'd been here early this morning.

HEDDA: Yes, right after you'd left.

TESMAN: And he said he'd torn up the manuscript? Did he really say that?

HEDDA: Yes. So he claimed.

TESMAN: But dear God — in that case he really must have been out of his mind! So I assume you didn't give it to him either, hm, Hedda?

HEDDA: No. He didn't get it.

TESMAN: But you told him we had it, of course?

HEDDA: No. (*Quickly.*) Did you tell Mrs. Elvsted?

TESMAN: No, I didn't want to. But you ought to have told him, Hedda. Just think — what if he does something rash — something to hurt himself! Give me the manuscript, Hedda! I want to rush down to him with it right this minute. Where is it?

HEDDA (*cold motionless, one arm resting on the chair*): I haven't got it any more.

TESMAN: You haven't got it! What do you mean by that?

HEDDA: I burned it — the whole thing.

TESMAN (*jumps up*): Burned it! Burned Eilert's book!

HEDDA: Don't shout. The maid might hear you.

TESMAN: Burned it? But good God — no, no, no — ! This can't be — !

HEDDA: It is, all the same.

TESMAN: But do you realize what you've done, Hedda? It's illegal! Willful destruction of lost property! You just ask Judge Brack! He'll tell you!

HEDDA: You'd better not talk about this to anyone — the Judge or anybody else.

TESMAN: But how could you do a thing like that! I never heard anything like it! What came over you? What can possibly have been going on in your head? Answer me! Hm?

HEDDA (*suppresses an almost imperceptible smile*): I did it for your sake, Jørgen.

TESMAN: For my sake!

HEDDA: When you came back this morning and told me he had read aloud to you —

TESMAN: Yes, yes! What then?

HEDDA: You admitted you were jealous of him for having written such a book.

TESMAN: But good gracious — ! I didn't mean it as seriously as all that!

HEDDA: All the same. I couldn't stand the thought that somebody else was to overshadow you.

TESMAN (*in an outburst of mingled doubt and joy*): Hedda — oh Hedda! Is it true what you're saying. But — but — but — I never knew you loved me like that! Just think!

HEDDA: In that case, I might as well tell you — that — just at this time — (*Breaks off, vehemently.*) No, no! You can ask Aunt Julle. She'll tell you.

TESMAN: I almost think I know what you mean, Hedda! (*Claps his hands.*) For goodness' sake! Can that really be so! Hm?

HEDDA: Don't shout so! The maid can hear you.

TESMAN (*laughing with exuberant joy*): The maid! Well, if you don't take the prize, Hedda! The maid — but that's Berte! I'm going to tell Berte myself this very minute!

HEDDA (*her hands clenched in despair*): Oh I'll die — I'll die, in all this!

TESMAN: In what, Hedda? Hm?

HEDDA (*cold and composed*): In all this — ludicrousness, Jørgen.

TESMAN: Ludicrous? That I'm so happy? Still — maybe I oughtn't to tell Berte, after all.

HEDDA: Oh, go ahead. What difference does it make?

TESMAN: No, not yet. But on my word — Aunt Julle must be told. And that you've started to call me "Jørgen," too! Just think! She'll be ever so happy — Aunt Julle will!

HEDDA: Even when you tell her that I have burned Eilert Løvborg's papers?

TESMAN: No, oh no! That's true! That about the manuscript — nobody must know about that. But to think that you'd burn for me, Hedda — I certainly want to tell *that* to Aunt Julle! I wonder now — is that sort of thing usual with young wives, hm?

HEDDA: Why don't you ask Aunt Julle about that, too?

TESMAN: I shall — I certainly shall, when I get the chance. (*Looks uneasy and disturbed again.*) But the manuscript! Good God — I don't dare to think what this is going to do to poor Eilert!

(MRS. ELVSTED, *dressed as on her first visit wearing hat and coat, enters, right.*)

MRS. ELVSTED (*gives a hurried greeting, is obviously upset*): Oh Hedda, you must forgive me for coming here again!

HEDDA: What has happened, Thea?

TESMAN: Something to do with Eilert Løvborg again? Hm?

MRS. ELVSTED: Yes, yes — I'm so terribly afraid something's happened to him.

HEDDA (*seizing her arm*): Ah — you think so?

TESMAN: Oh dear — why do you think that, Mrs. Elvsted?

MRS. ELVSTED: I heard them talking about him in the boarding house, just as I came in. And people are saying the most incredible things about him today.

TESMAN: Yes, imagine! I heard that, too! And I can testify that he went straight home to bed! Just think!

HEDDA: And what did they say in the boarding house?

MRS. ELVSTED: Oh, I didn't find out anything. Either they didn't know any details or — They all became silent when they saw me. And I didn't dare to ask.

TESMAN (*pacing the floor uneasily*): We'll just have to hope — to hope that you heard wrong, Mrs. Elvsted!

MRS. ELVSTED: No, no. I'm sure it was he they were talking about. And somebody said something about the hospital or —

TESMAN: The hospital — !

HEDDA: Surely, that can't be so!

MRS. ELVSTED: I got so terribly frightened! So I went up to his room and asked for him there.

HEDDA: Could you bring yourself to do that, Thea?

MRS. ELVSTED: What else could I do? For I felt I just couldn't stand the uncertainty any longer.

TESMAN: But I suppose you didn't find him in, either, did you? Hm?

MRS. ELVSTED: No. And the people there didn't know anything about him. He hadn't been home since yesterday afternoon, they said.

TESMAN: Yesterday! Just think! How could they say that!

MRS. ELVSTED: I don't know what else *to*

think — something bad must have happened to him!

TESMAN: Hedda, dear — ? What if I were to walk downtown and ask around for him — ?

HEDDA: No, no — don't you go and get mixed up in all this.

(JUDGE BRACK, *hat in hand, enters through the door, right, which* BERTE *opens and closes for him. He looks serious and greets the others in silence.*)

TESMAN: So here you are, Judge, hm?

BRACK: Yes. I had to see you this evening.

TESMAN: I can see you have got Aunt Julle's message.

BRACK: That, too — yes.

TESMAN: Isn't it sad, though?

BRACK: Well, my dear Tesman — that depends on how you look at it.

TESMAN (*looks at him uncertainly*): Has something else happened?

BRACK: Yes.

HEDDA (*tense*): Something sad, Judge Brack?

BRACK: That, too, depends on how you look at it, Mrs. Tesman.

MRS. ELVSTED (*bursting out*): Oh, I'm sure it has something to do with Eilert Løvborg!

BRACK (*looks at her for a moment*): Why do you think that, Mrs. Elvsted? Maybe you already know something — ?

MRS. ELVSTED (*confused*): No, no; not at all. It's just —

TESMAN: For heaven's sake, Brack, out with it!

BRACK (*shrugging his shoulders*): Well — unfortunately, Eilert Løvborg's in the hospital. Dying.

MRS. ELVSTED (*screams*): Oh God, oh God!

TESMAN: In the hospital! And dying!

HEDDA (*without thinking*): So soon — !

MRS. ELVSTED (*wailing*): And we didn't even part as friends, Hedda!

HEDDA (*whispers*): Thea, Thea — for heaven's sake — !

MRS. ELVSTED (*paying no attention to her*): I want to see him! I want to see him alive!

BRACK: Won't do you any good, Mrs. Elvsted. Nobody can see him.

MRS. ELVSTED: Then tell me what's happened to him! What?

TESMAN: For, surely, he hasn't himself — !

HEDDA: I'm sure he has.

TESMAN: Hedda! How can you — !

BRACK (*observing her all this time*): I am sorry to say that your guess is absolutely correct, Mrs. Tesman.

MRS. ELVSTED: Oh, how awful!

TESMAN: Did it himself! Just think!

HEDDA: Shot himself!

BRACK: Right again, Mrs. Tesman.

MRS. ELVSTED (*trying to pull herself together*): When did this happen, Judge?

BRACK: This afternoon. Between three and four.

TESMAN: But dear me — where can he have done a thing like that? Hm?

BRACK (*a little uncertain*): Where? Well — I suppose in his room. I don't really know —

MRS. ELVSTED: No, it can't have been there. For I was up there sometime between six and seven.

BRACK: Well, then, some other place. I really can't say. All I know is that he was found. He had shot himself — in the chest.

MRS. ELVSTED: Oh, how horrible to think! That he was to end like that!

HEDDA (*to* BRACK): In the chest?

BRACK: Yes — as I just told you.

HEDDA: Not the temple?

BRACK: In the chest, Mrs. Tesman.

HEDDA: Well, well — the chest is a good place, too.

BRACK: How is that, Mrs. Tesman?

HEDDA (*turning him aside*): Oh — nothing.

TESMAN: And you say the wound is fatal? Hm?

BRACK: No doubt about it — absolutely fatal. He's probably dead already.

MRS. ELVSTED: Yes, yes! I feel you're right! It's over! It's all over! Oh, Hedda!

TESMAN: But tell me — how do *you* know all this?

BRACK (*tersely*): A man on the force told me. One I had some business with.

HEDDA (*loudly*): At last a deed!

TESMAN (*appalled*): Oh dear — what are you saying, Hedda!

HEDDA: I am saying there is beauty in this.

BRACK: Well, now — Mrs. Tesman —

TESMAN: Beauty — ! Just think!

MRS. ELVSTED: Oh, Hedda — how can you talk about beauty in a thing like this!

HEDDA: Eilert Løvborg has settled his account with himself. He has had the courage to do — what had to be done.

MRS. ELVSTED: But you mustn't believe it happened that way! He did it when he was not himself!

TESMAN: In despair! That's how!

HEDDA: He did not. I am certain of that.

MRS. ELVSTED: Yes he did! He was not himself! That's the way he tore up the book, too!

BRACK (*puzzled*): The book? You mean the manuscript? Has he torn it up?

MRS. ELVSTED: Yes, last night.

TESMAN (*whispers*): Oh, Hedda — we'll never get clear of all this!

BRACK: That is strange.

TESMAN (*walking the floor*): To think that this was to be the end of Eilert! Not to leave behind him anything that would have preserved his name —

MRS. ELVSTED: Oh, if only it could be put together again!

TESMAN: Yes, if only it could. I don't know what I wouldn't give —

MRS. ELVSTED: Maybe it can, Mr. Tesman.

TESMAN: What do you mean?

MRS. ELVSTED (*searching her dress pocket*): Look. I have kept these little slips he dictated from.

HEDDA (*a step closer*): Ah — !

TESMAN: You've kept them, Mrs. Elvsted? Hm?

MRS. ELVSTED: Yes. Here they are. I took them with me when I left. And I've had them in my pocket ever since —

TESMAN: Please, let me see —

MRS. ELVSTED (*gives him a pile of small paper slips*): But it's such a mess. Without any kind of system or order — !

TESMAN: But just think if we could make sense out of them, all the same! Perhaps if we helped each other —

MRS. ELVSTED: Oh yes! Let's try, anyway!

TESMAN: It will work! It *has* to work! I'll stake my whole life on this!

HEDDA: You, Jørgen? Your life?

TESMAN: Yes, or at any rate all the time I can set aside. My own collections can wait. Hedda, you understand — don't you? Hm? This is something I owe Eilert's memory.

HEDDA: Maybe so.

TESMAN: And now, my dear Mrs. Elvsted, we want to get to work. Good heavens, there's no point brooding over what's happened. Hm? We'll just have to acquire sufficient peace of mind to —

MRS. ELVSTED: All right, Mr. Tesman. I'll try to do my best.

TESMAN: Very well, then. Come over here. Let's look at these slips right away. Where can we sit? Here? No, it's better in the other room. If you'll excuse us, Judge! Come along, Mrs. Elvsted.

MRS. ELVSTED: Oh dear God — if only it were possible — !

(TESMAN *and* MRS. ELVSTED *go into the inner room. She takes off her hat and coat. Both sit down at the table under the hanging lamp and absorb themselves in the slips.* HEDDA *walks over toward the stove and sits down in the easy chair. After a while,* BRACK *walks over to her.*)

HEDDA (*in a low voice*): Ah, Judge — what a liberation there is in this thing with Eilert Løvborg!

BRACK: Liberation, Mrs. Tesman? Well, yes, for him perhaps one may say there was liberation of a kind —

HEDDA: I mean for me. There is liberation in knowing that there is such a thing in the world as an act of free courage. Something which becomes beautiful by its very nature.

BRACK (*smiles*): Well — dear Mrs. Tesman —

HEDDA: Oh I know, what you're going to say! For you see — you really are a kind of specialist, too!

BRACK (*looks at her fixedly*): Eilert Løvborg has meant more to you than perhaps you're willing to admit, even to yourself. Or am I wrong?

HEDDA: I won't answer such questions. All I know is that Eilert Løvborg had the courage to live his own life. And then now — this — magnificence! The beauty of it! Having the strength and the will to get up and leave life's feast — so early —

BRACK: Believe me, Mrs. Tesman, this pains me, but I see it is necessary that I destroy a pretty illusion —

HEDDA: An illusion?

BRACK: Which could not have been maintained for very long, anyway.

HEDDA: And what is that?

BRACK: He didn't shoot himself — of his own free will.

HEDDA: Not of his own — !

BRACK: No. To tell the truth, the circumstances of Eilert Løvborg's death aren't exactly what I said they were.

HEDDA (*tense*): You've held something back? What?

BRACK: For the sake of poor Mrs. Elvsted I used a few euphemisms.

HEDDA: What?

BRACK: First — he is already dead.

HEDDA: In the hospital.

BRACK: Yes. And without regaining consciousness.

HEDDA: What else haven't you told?

BRACK: That fact that it didn't happen in his room.

HEDDA: Well, does that really make much difference?

BRACK: Some. You see — Eilert Løvborg was found shot in Miss Diana's bedroom.

HEDDA (*is about to jump up, but sinks back*): That's impossible, Judge Brack! He can't have been there again today!

BRACK: He was there this afternoon. He came to claim something he said they had taken from him. Spoke some gibberish about a lost child —

HEDDA: So that's why — !

BRACK: I thought maybe he meant his manuscript. But now I hear he has destroyed that himself. So I suppose it must have been something else.

HEDDA: I suppose. So it was there — so they found him there?

BRACK: Yes. With a fired gun in his pocket. Mortally wounded.

HEDDA: Yes — in the chest.

BRACK: No — in the guts.

HEDDA (*looks at him with an expression of disgust*): That, too! What is this curse that turns everything I touch into something ludicrous and low!

BRACK: There is something else, Mrs. Tesman. Something I'd call — nasty.

HEDDA: And what is that.

BRACK: The gun they found —

HEDDA (*breathless*): What about it?

BRACK: He must have stolen it.

HEDDA (*jumps up*): Stolen! That's not true! He didn't!

BRACK: Anything else is impossible. He *must* have stolen it. — Shhh!

(TESMAN *and* MRS. ELVSTED *have risen from the table and come forward into the front room.*)

TESMAN (*with papers in both hands*): D'you know, Hedda — you can hardly see in there with that lamp! Just think!

HEDDA: I am thinking.

TESMAN: I wonder if you'd let us use your desk, hm?

HEDDA: Certainly, if you like. (*Adds quickly.*) Wait a minute, though! Let me clear it off a bit first.

TESMAN: Ah, there's no need for that, Hedda. There's plenty of room.

HEDDA: No, no. I want to straighten it up. I'll carry all this in here. I'll put it on top of the piano for the time being.

(*She has pulled an object, covered by note paper, out of the bookcase. She puts several other sheets of paper on top of it and carries the whole pile into the left part of the inner room.* TESMAN *puts the papers down on the desk and moves the lamp from the corner table over to the desk. He and* MRS. ELVSTED *sit down and resume their work.* HEDDA *returns.*)

HEDDA (*behind* MRS. ELVSTED's *chair, softly ruffling her hair*): Well, little Thea — how is Eilert Løvborg's memorial coming along?

MRS. ELVSTED (*looks up at her, discouraged*): Oh God — I'm sure it's going to be terribly hard to make anything out of all this.

TESMAN: But we have to. We just don't have a choice. And putting other people's papers in order — that's just the thing for me.

(HEDDA *walks over to the stove and sits down on one of the ottomans.* BRACK *stands over her, leaning on the easy chair.*)

HEDDA (*whispers*): What were you saying about the gun?

BRACK (*also softly*): That he must have stolen it.

HEDDA: Why, necessarily?

BRACK: Because any other explanation ought to be out of the question, Mrs. Tesman.

HEDDA: Oh?

BRACK (*looks at her for a moment*): Eilert Løvborg was here this morning, of course. Isn't that so?

HEDDA: Yes.

BRACK: Were you alone with him?

HEDDA: Yes, for a while.

BRACK: You didn't leave the room while he was here?

HEDDA: No.

BRACK: Think. Not at all? Not even for a moment?

HEDDA: Well — maybe just for a moment — out in the hall.

BRACK: And where was the gun case?

HEDDA: In the —

BRACK: Mrs. Tesman?

HEDDA: On the desk.

BRACK: Have you looked to see if both guns are still there?

HEDDA: No.

BRACK: You needn't bother. I saw the gun they found on Løvborg, and I knew it immediately. From yesterday — and from earlier occasions, too.

HEDDA: Perhaps you have it?

BRACK: No, the police do.

HEDDA: What are the police going to do with it?

BRACK: Try to find the owner.

HEDDA: Do you think they will?

BRACK (*leans over her, whispers*): No, Hedda Gabler — not as long as I keep quiet.

HEDDA (*with a hunted look*): And if you don't?

BRACK (*shrugs his shoulders*): Of course, there's always the chance that the gun was stolen.

HEDDA (*firmly*): Rather die!

BRACK (*smiles*): People *say* things like that. They don't *do* them.

HEDDA (*without answering*): And if the gun was not stolen — and if they find the owner — then what happens?

BRACK: Well, Hedda — then comes the scandal!

HEDDA: The scandal!

BRACK: Yes — the scandal. That you are so afraid of. You will of course be required to testify. Both you and Miss Diana. Obviously, she'll have to explain how the whole thing happened. Whether it was accidental or homicide. Did he try to pull the gun out of his pocket to threaten her? And did it fire accidentally? Or did she grab the gun away from him, shoot him, and put it back in his pocket? She might just possibly have done that. She's a pretty tough girl — Miss Diana.

HEDDA: But this whole disgusting mess has nothing to do with me.

BRACK: Quite so. But you'll have to answer the question: Why did you give Eilert Løvborg the gun? And what inferences will be drawn from the fact that you did?

HEDDA (*lowers her head*): That's true. I hadn't thought of that.

BRACK: Well — luckily, there's nothing to worry about as long as I don't say anything.

HEDDA (*looks up at him*): So then I'm in your power, Judge. From now on you can do anything you like with me.

BRACK (*in an even softer whisper*): Dearest Hedda — believe me, I'll not misuse my position.

HEDDA: In your power, all the same. Dependent on your will. Servant to your demands. Not free. Not free! (*Rises suddenly.*) No — I can't stand that thought! Never!

BRACK (*looks at her, half mockingly*): Most people submit to the inevitable.

HEDDA (*returning his glance*): Perhaps. (*Walks over to the desk. Suppresses a smile and mimics* TESMAN's *way of speaking.*) Well? Do you think you can do it, Jørgen? Hm?

TESMAN: Lord knows, Hedda. Anyway, I can already see it will take months.

HEDDA (*still mimicking*): Just think! (*Runs her hands lightly through* MRS. ELVSTED's *hair.*) Doesn't this seem strange to you, Thea? Sitting here with Tesman — just the way you used to with Eilert Løvborg?

MRS. ELVSTED: Oh dear — if only I could inspire your husband, too!

HEDDA: Oh, I'm sure that will come — in time.

TESMAN: Well, yes — do you know, Hedda? I really think I begin to feel something of the kind. But why don't you go and talk to the Judge again.

HEDDA: Isn't there anything you two can use me for?

TESMAN: No, not a thing, dear. (*Turns around.*) From now on, you must be good enough to keep Hedda company, my dear Judge!

BRACK (*glancing at* HEDDA): I'll be only too delighted.

HEDDA: Thank you. But I'm tired tonight. I think I'll go and lie down for a while.

TESMAN: Yes, you do that, dear; why don't you? Hm?

(HEDDA *goes into the inner room, closes the portieres behind her. Brief pause. Suddenly, she is heard playing a frenzied dance tune on the piano.*)

MRS. ELVSTED (*jumps up*): Oh God! What's that!

TESMAN (*running to the doorway*): But dearest Hedda — you mustn't play dance music tonight, for goodness' sake! Think of Aunt Rina! And Eilert, too!

HEDDA (*peeks in from between the portieres*): And Aunt Julle. And everybody. I'll be quiet. (*She pulls the portieres shut again.*)

TESMAN (*back at the desk*): I don't think it's good for her to see us at such a melancholy task. I'll tell you what, Mrs. Elvsted. You move in with Aunt Julle, and then I'll come over in the evenings. Then we can sit and work over there. Hm?

MRS. ELVSTED: Maybe that would be better —

HEDDA (*from inner room*): I hear every word you're saying, Tesman. And how am I going to spend my evenings?

TESMAN (*busy with the papers*): Oh, I'm sure Judge Brack will be good enough to come out and see you, anyway.

BRACK (*in the easy chair, calls out gaily*): Every single night, as far as I'm concerned, Mrs. Tesman! I'm sure we're going to have a lovely time, you and I!

HEDDA (*loud and clear*): Yes, don't you think that would be nice, Judge Brack? You — sole cock-o'-the-walk —

(*A shot is heard from the inner room,* TESMAN, MRS. ELVSTED, *and* JUDGE BRACK *all jump up.*)

TESMAN: There she is, fooling with those guns again.

(*He pulls the portieres apart and runs inside.* MRS. ELVSTED *also.* HEDDA, *lifeless, is lying on the sofa. Cries and confusion,* BERTE, *flustered, enters, right.*)

TESMAN (*shouts to* BRACK): She's shot herself! In the temple! Just think!

BRACK (*half stunned in the easy chair*): But, merciful God — ! One just doesn't *do* that!

Before he was forty Ibsen had written two masterpieces of poetic drama, *Brand* (1866) and *Peer Gynt* (1867). But a few years later he came to feel, along with many others, that the future of dramatic literature was not in poetic language, but in language that closely resembled ordinary speech.* He devoted his subsequent efforts to prose drama, and we find him, in his letters, occasionally prophesying that poetic drama has no future, and warning his translators to avoid all expressions that depart from "everyday speech." In the 1870's and 1880's he wrote the so-called "problem plays" (including *A Doll's House*, *Ghosts*, and *An Enemy of the People*) that for the next seventy-five years made his name familiar to the English-speaking world. A problem play, or "play of ideas," or *pièce à thèse*, is concerned with some troublesome social institution, its author hoping to arouse the audience to do something about the problem (for example, to modify the divorce laws, to extend the ballot, to alter the tax structure). The more successful the play, the more it insures its own demise, for when the social institutions have been altered and the problem has been solved, the play has no relevance to experience; it is merely a thing of historical importance, a museum curio. The violent reviews that *Ghosts* and some of Ibsen's other plays engendered are evidence that more was at stake than aesthetic matters; discussions of the plays inevitably became discussions of divorce, venereal disease, incest, etc. Almost a century has passed, and readers have found that Ibsen has something more to offer than thoughts on how to improve society.

In December 1890, a few weeks after he finished *Hedda Gabler*, Ibsen made the point that "it was not really my intention to deal in this play with so-called problems. What I principally wanted to do was to depict human beings, human emotions, and human destinies, upon a groundwork of certain of the social conditions and principles of the present day." We get some idea of what Ibsen meant by "the social conditions and principles of the present day" from another jotting he made while he was getting the play into shape: "Tesman represents propriety. Hedda represents *ennui*. Mrs. R. [i.e., Mrs. Elvsted] modern nervousness and hysteria. Brack the representative of bourgeois society." This early summary does not, of course, correspond exactly to the finished play, but it gives us some idea of the direction Ibsen was taking. "Propriety," "*ennui*," "nervousness and hysteria," and even "bourgeois society" are not problems that can be solved by legislation or by any other form of tinkering. The play, after all, is not about a society that foolishly restrains energetic women from putting their energy to use — though it is in part about the

---

* Prose, and indeed prose clearly imitative of speech, had, of course, been occasionally used much earlier, even during the Renaissance, but prose tragedy with its middle-class figures was for a long while a poor relation of poetic tragedy. With the increasing power of the middle class and the rise of science (which not only helped to enlarge the middle class but also helped to popularize the view that all matter is equally interesting and presumably equally fit for literature), the days of "heroic" tragedy were numbered. Probably Darwin's *Origin of Species* (1859) was the *coup de grâce*; one could hardly take a very high view of creatures that had survived because accidental variations made them more suited to their environment than other creatures.

social conventions (especially aristocratic pride) that Hedda cannot abandon. The other jottings show even more clearly that Ibsen was concerned with unchanging experiences rather than with transitory problems. Here are two of them:

> They aren't all created to be mothers.
> The daemon in Hedda is that she wants to influence another human being, but once that has happened, she despises him.

Hedda wishes to influence someone, to shape a human destiny. Her own destiny, like everyone else's, has been partly shaped by the circumstances of her birth. She is the daughter of an aristocrat, General Gabler (in a letter Ibsen called attention to the fact that the play is entitled *Hedda Gabler*, and not, despite her marriage to Jørgen Tesman, *Hedda Tesman*). Her aristocratic background has given her leisure but no direction, energy but no channel for it, and we see her becoming increasingly desperate. Having married rashly, she now feels her identity is threatened. The point is obvious, but it is worth quoting Ibsen's own description, from a letter: "Jørgen Tesman, his old aunts, and the faithful servant Berte together form a picture of complete unity. They think alike, they share the same memories and have the same outlook on life. To Hedda they appear like a strange and hostile power, aimed at her very being." Tesman is a bore, scarcely worth shaping, and the aunt and the maid are no challenge. Yet this family group frightens Hedda because (she thinks) it would lessen her identity if it absorbed her. Her distress at the thought of having a child is a further indication that although she yearns to shape a human destiny, she does not want to become involved in any sort of relationship in which she herself may be shaped; that is, she evades responsibilities. Presumably when she rejected Eilert Løvborg's overtures, she did so not only because she feared scandal, but also because she feared the relationship itself. Now she seeks to fulfill herself by controlling Løvborg's life to the point that he will be a Dionysian figure who will kill himself "beautifully." Hedda apparently has in mind something of the romantic view of Greek tragedy that Ibsen himself had held twenty-five years earlier, when he rhapsodized over a statue of "the Tragic Muse," with its "laurel-crowned head with something supernaturally exuberant and bacchantic about it."

In Ibsen's world, as everywhere, people impinge upon each other and relationships are necessarily established. Miss Tesman's life, for example, is intertwined with the invalid Aunt Rina's, and when Rina dies, a replacement must be found: "Ah — it's not very hard to find some poor soul who needs nursing and comfort." To Hedda's question, "And you really want to take on such a burden all over again?" Miss Tesman replies, "Heavens! God forgive you, child — burden? It has not been a burden to me." Similarly, Mrs. Elvsted and Løvborg require each other, and are shaped by each other as they shape each other, and Tesman is at his best when he is bringing to completion someone else's work. The play is built on a groundwork of "social conditions and principles" of nineteenth-century Norwegian life, but these conditions themselves, as

Ibsen presents them, are rooted in elementary facts of life and are not out-moded institutions that needlessly create problems. (In *Peer Gynt* Ibsen had earlier represented this matter of interrelationships with a brilliant image. Peer wishes "to be himself," but he finds he has no individuality when apart from others. He peels an onion, to get at the core, and finds that after all layers — or relationships — are removed, there is nothing left.) Hedda seeks power divorced from responsibility, which means that finally her power must be directed against herself. The attempt to have Løvborg do some "beautiful" deed in defiance of society fails because she cannot have full power over Løvborg unless she gives something of herself to him. When Løvborg is dead, and Tesman and Mrs. Elvsted are occupied with each other, and Hedda is at Judge Brack's mercy, Hedda releases her energy against herself, killing herself "beautifully." Judge Brack's final comment, "One just doesn't *do* that!" is the sort of scandalized remark that Hedda had feared all her life, the voice of society, a society that does not know the depths of Hedda's anguish, a society that holds itself together by dull virtues, petty vices, and all sorts of dodges. But society does help men to survive, and to reject it is to annihilate oneself.

THE GHOST SONATA

August Strindberg

Translated by Elizabeth Sprigge

August Strindberg (1849–1912) was born in Sweden, two months after the marriage of his parents (who already had three children). After a desperately unhappy childhood and youth, he turned to play writing; King Charles XV of Sweden was impressed by one drama and granted Strindberg a small scholarship to the university. After the king's death, Strindberg worked in the Royal Library, where he studied Chinese. He married a divorced baroness in 1877, but the marriage ended in divorce in 1891. His second marriage, to an Austrian girl, also ended in divorce (in 1894). After a period in a mental hospital he married and divorced a third time. Among his voluminous writings are novels, short stories, autobiographies, essays, and plays, the most notable of which include *The Father* (1887), *Miss Julie* (1888), *A Dream Play* (1901), and *The Ghost Sonata* (1907).

CHARACTERS

THE OLD MAN, *Hummel, a Company Director*
THE STUDENT, *Arkenholtz*
THE MILKMAID, *an apparition*
THE CARETAKER'S WIFE
THE CARETAKER
THE LADY IN BLACK, *the daughter of the Caretaker's Wife and the Dead Man. Also referred to as the Dark Lady*
THE COLONEL
THE MUMMY, *the Colonel's wife*

THE GIRL, *the Colonel's daughter, actually the daughter of the Old Man*
THE ARISTOCRAT, *Baron Skanskorg. Engaged to the Lady in Black*
JOHANSSON, *the Old Man's servant*
BENGTSSON, *the Colonel's servant*
THE FIANCÉE, *a white-haired old woman, once betrothed to the Old Man*
THE COOK
A MAIDSERVANT
BEGGARS

Serafina Hovhaness as the Mummy and Joseph Leberman as the Old Man in the Living Theater production of *The Ghost Sonata*, directed by Judith Malina, New York, 1954. (Photograph: © Alix Jeffry.)

SCENE I

Outside the house. The corner of the façade of a modern house, showing the ground floor above, and the street in front. The ground floor terminates on the right in the Round Room, above which, on the first floor, is a balcony with a flagstaff. The windows of the Round Room face the street in front of the house, and at the corner look on to the suggestion of a side-street running toward the back. At the beginning of the scene the blinds of the Round Room are down. When, later, they are raised, the white marble statue of a young woman can be seen, surrounded with palms and brightly lighted by rays of sunshine.

To the left of the Round Room is the Hyacinth Room; its window filled with pots of hyacinths, blue, white and pink. Further left, at the back, is an imposing double front door with laurels in tubs on either side of it. The doors are wide open, showing a staircase of white marble with a banister of mahogany and brass. To the left of the front door is another ground-floor window, with a window-mirror.[1] On the balcony rail in the corner above the Round Room are a blue silk quilt and two white pillows. The windows to the left of this are hung with white sheets.[2]

In the foreground, in front of the house, is a green bench; to the right a street drinking-fountain, to the left an advertisement column.

It is a bright Sunday morning, and as the curtain rises the bells of several churches, some near, some far away, are ringing.

On the staircase the LADY IN BLACK stands motionless.

The CARETAKER'S WIFE sweeps the doorstep, then polishes the brass on the door and waters the laurels.

In a wheelchair by the advertisement column sits the OLD MAN, reading a newspaper. His hair and beard are white and he wears spectacles.

The MILKMAID comes round the corner on the right, carrying milk bottles in a wire basket. She is wearing a summer dress with brown shoes, black stockings and a white cap. She takes off her cap and hangs it on the fountain, wipes the perspiration from her forehead, washes her hands and arranges her hair, using the water as a mirror.

A steamship bell is heard, and now and then the silence is broken by the deep notes of an organ in a nearby church.

After a few moments, when all is silent and the MILKMAID has finished her toilet, the STUDENT enters from the left. He has had a sleepless night and is unshaven. He goes straight up to the fountain. There is a pause before he speaks.

STUDENT: May I have the cup?

(The MILKMAID clutches the cup to her.)

Haven't you finished yet?

(The MILKMAID looks at him with horror.)

OLD MAN (to himself): Who's he talking to? I don't see anybody. Is he crazy? (He goes on watching them in great astonishment.)

STUDENT (to the MILKMAID): What are you staring at? Do I look so terrible? Well, I've had no sleep, and of course you think I've been making a night of it . . .

(The MILKMAID stays just as she is.)

You think I've been drinking, eh? Do I smell of liquor?

(The MILKMAID does not change.)

I haven't shaved, I know. Give me a drink of water, girl. I've earned it. (Pause.) Oh well, I suppose I'll have to tell you. I spent the whole night dressing wounds and looking after the injured. You see, I was there when that house collapsed last night. Now you know.

(The MILKMAID rinses the cup and gives him a drink.)

The Ghost Sonata by Strindberg. Reprinted by permission of Curtis Brown, Ltd. Copyright © 1955 by Elizabeth Sprigge.

[1] Set at an angle inside the window, so as to show what is going on in the street. [Translator's note.]

[2] Sign of mourning. [Translator's note.]

Thanks.

(*The* MILKMAID *stands motionless. Slowly.*)

Will you do me a great favor? (*Pause.*) The thing is, my eyes, as you can see, are inflamed, but my hands have been touching wounds and corpses, so it would be dangerous to put them near my eyes. Will you take my handkerchief — it's quite clean — and dip it in the fresh water and bathe my eyes? Will you do this? Will you play the good Samaritan?

(*The* MILKMAID *hesitates, but does as he bids.*)

Thank you, my dear. (*He takes out his purse. She makes a gesture of refusal.*) Forgive my stupidity, but I'm only half-awake. . . .

(*The* MILKMAID *disappears.*)

OLD MAN (*to the* STUDENT): Excuse me speaking to you, but I heard you say you were at the scene of the accident last night. I was just reading about it in the paper.

STUDENT: Is it in the paper already?

OLD MAN: The whole thing, including your portrait. But they regret that they have been unable to find out the name of the splendid young student. . . .

STUDENT: Really? (*Glances at the paper.*) Yes, that's me. Well I never!

OLD MAN: Who was it you were talking to just now?

STUDENT: Didn't you see? (*Pause.*)

OLD MAN: Would it be impertinent to inquire — what in fact your name is?

STUDENT: What would be the point? I don't care for publicity. If you get any praise, there's always disapproval too. The art of running people down has been developed to such a pitch. . . . Besides, I don't want any reward.

OLD MAN: You're well off, perhaps.

STUDENT: No, indeed. On the contrary, I'm very poor.

OLD MAN: Do you know, it seems to me I've heard your voice before. When I was young I had a friend who pronounced certain words just as you do. I've never met anyone else with quite that pronunciation. Only him — and you. Are you by any chance related to Mr. Arkenholtz, the merchant?

STUDENT: He was my father.

OLD MAN: Strange are the paths of fate. I saw you when you were an infant, under very painful circumstances.

STUDENT: Yes, I understand I came into the world in the middle of a bankruptcy.

OLD MAN: Just that.

STUDENT: Perhaps I might ask your name.

OLD MAN: I am Mr. Hummel.

STUDENT: Are you the? . . . I remember that . . .

OLD MAN: Have you often heard my name mentioned in your family?

STUDENT: Yes.

OLD MAN: And mentioned perhaps with a certain aversion?

(*The* STUDENT *is silent.*)

Yes, I can imagine it. You were told, I suppose, that I was the man who ruined your father? All who ruin themselves through foolish speculations consider they were ruined by those they couldn't fool. (*Pause.*) Now these are the facts. Your father robbed me of seventeen thousand crowns — the whole of my savings at that time.

STUDENT: It's queer that the same story can be told in two such different ways.

OLD MAN: You surely don't believe I'm telling you what isn't true?

STUDENT: What am I to believe? My father didn't lie.

OLD MAN: That is so true. A father never lies. But I too am a father, and so it follows . . .

STUDENT: What are you driving at?

OLD MAN: I saved your father from disaster, and he repaid me with all the frightful hatred that is born of an obligation to be grateful. He taught his family to speak ill of me.

STUDENT: Perhaps you made him ungrateful by poisoning your help with unnecessary humiliation.

OLD MAN: All help is humiliating, sir.

STUDENT: What do you want from me?

OLD MAN: I'm not asking for the money, but if you will render me a few small services, I shall consider myself well paid. You see that I am a cripple. Some say it is my own fault; others lay the blame on my parents. I prefer to blame life itself, with its pitfalls. For if you escape one snare, you fall headlong into another. In any case, I am unable to climb stairs or ring doorbells, and that is why I am asking you to help me.

STUDENT: What can I do?

OLD MAN: To begin with, push my chair so

that I can read those playbills. I want to see what is on tonight.

STUDENT (*pushing the chair*): Haven't you got an attendant?

OLD MAN: Yes, but he has gone on an errand. He'll be back soon. Are you a medical student?

STUDENT: No, I am studying languages, but I don't know at all what I'm going to do.

OLD MAN: Aha! Are you good at mathematics?

STUDENT: Yes, fairly.

OLD MAN: Good. Perhaps you would like a job.

STUDENT: Yes, why not?

OLD MAN: Splendid. (*He studies the playbills.*) They are doing *The Valkyrie* for the matinée. That means the Colonel will be there with his daughter, and as he always sits at the end of the sixth row, I'll put you next to him. Go to that telephone kiosk please and order a ticket for seat eighty-two in the sixth row.

STUDENT: Am I to go to the Opera in the middle of the day?

OLD MAN: Yes. Do as I tell you and things will go well with you. I want to see you happy, rich and honored. Your début last night as the brave rescuer will make you famous by tomorrow and then your name will be worth something.

STUDENT (*going to the telephone kiosk*): What an odd adventure!

OLD MAN: Are you a gambler?

STUDENT: Yes, unfortunately.

OLD MAN: We'll make it fortunately. Go on now, telephone.

(*The STUDENT goes. The OLD MAN reads his paper. The LADY IN BLACK comes out on to the pavement and talks to the CARETAKER'S WIFE. The OLD MAN listens, but the audience hears nothing. The STUDENT returns.*)

Did you fix it up?

STUDENT: It's done.

OLD MAN: You see that house?

STUDENT: Yes, I've been looking at it a lot. I passed it yesterday when the sun was shining on the windowpanes, and I imagined all the beauty and elegance there must be inside. I said to my companion: "Think of living up there in the top flat, with a beautiful young wife, two pretty little children and an income of twenty thousand crowns a year."

OLD MAN: So that's what you said. That's

what you said. Well, well! I too am very fond of this house.

STUDENT: Do you speculate in houses?

OLD MAN: Mm — yes. But not in the way you mean.

STUDENT: Do you know the people who live here?

OLD MAN: Every one of them. At my age one knows everybody, and their parents and grandparents too, and one's always related to them in some way or other. I am just eighty, but no one knows me — not really. I take an interest in human destiny.

(*The blinds of the Round Room are drawn up. The COLONEL is seen, wearing mufti. He looks at the thermometer outside one of the windows, then turns back into the room and stands in front of the marble statue.*)

Look, that's the Colonel, whom you will sit next to this afternoon.

STUDENT: Is he — the Colonel? I don't understand any of this, but it's like a fairy story.

OLD MAN: My whole life's like a book of fairy stories, sir. And although the stories are different, they are held together by one thread, and the main theme constantly recurs.

STUDENT: Who is that marble statue of?

OLD MAN: That, naturally, is his wife.

STUDENT: Was she such a wonderful person?

OLD MAN: Er . . . yes.

STUDENT: Tell me.

OLD MAN: We can't judge people, young man. If I were to tell you that she left him, that he beat her, that she returned to him and married him a second time, and that now she is sitting inside there like a mummy, worshiping her own statue — then you would think me crazy.

STUDENT: I don't understand.

OLD MAN: I didn't think you would. Well, then we have the window with the hyacinths. His daughter lives there. She has gone out for a ride, but she will be home soon.

STUDENT: And who is the dark lady talking to the caretaker?

OLD MAN: Well, that's a bit complicated, but it is connected with the dead man, up there where you see the white sheets.

STUDENT: Why, who was he?

OLD MAN: A human being like you or me, but the most conspicuous thing about him was his vanity. If you were a Sunday child, you would see him presently come out of that door to look at the Consulate flag flying at half-mast. He was, you understand, a Consul, and he reveled in coronets and lions and plumed hats and colored ribbons.

STUDENT: Sunday child, you say? I'm told I was born on a Sunday.

OLD MAN: No, were you really? I might have known it. I saw it from the color of your eyes. Then you can see what others can't. Have you noticed that?

STUDENT: I don't know what others do see, but at times. . . . Oh, but one doesn't talk of such things!

OLD MAN: I was almost sure of it. But you can talk to me, because I understand such things.

STUDENT: Yesterday, for instance . . . I was drawn to that obscure little street where later on the house collapsed. I went there and stopped in front of that building which I had never seen before. Then I noticed a crack in the wall. . . . I heard the floor boards snapping. . . . I dashed over and picked up a child that was passing under the wall. . . . The next moment the house collapsed. I was saved, but in my arms, which I thought held the child, was nothing at all.

OLD MAN: Yes, yes, just as I thought. Tell me something. Why were you gesticulating that way just now by the fountain? And why were you talking to yourself?

STUDENT: Didn't you see the milkmaid I was talking to?

OLD MAN (in horror): Milkmaid?

STUDENT: Surely. The girl who handed me the cup.

OLD MAN: Really? So that's what was going on. Ah well, I haven't second sight, but there are things I can do.

(The FIANCÉE is now seen to sit down by the window which has the window-mirror.)

Look at that old woman in the window. Do you see her? Well, she was my fiancée once, sixty years ago. I was twenty. Don't be alarmed. She doesn't recognize me. We see one another every day, and it makes no impression on me, although once we vowed to love one another eternally. Eternally!

STUDENT: How foolish you were in those days! We never talk to our girls like that.

OLD MAN: Forgive us, young man. We didn't know any better. But can you see that that old woman was once young and beautiful?

STUDENT: It doesn't show. And yet there's some charm in her looks. I can't see her eyes.

(The CARETAKER'S WIFE comes out with a basket of chopped fir branches.[3])

OLD MAN: Ah, the caretaker's wife! That dark lady is her daughter by the dead man. That's why her husband was given the job of caretaker. But the dark lady has a suitor, who is an aristocrat with great expectations. He is in the process of getting a divorce — from his present wife, you understand. She's presenting him with a stone mansion in order to be rid of him. This aristocratic suitor is the son-in-law of the dead man, and you can see his bedclothes being aired on the balcony upstairs. It is complicated, I must say.

STUDENT: It's fearfully complicated.

OLD MAN: Yes, that it is, internally and externally, although it looks quite simple.

STUDENT: But then who was the dead man?

OLD MAN: You asked me that just now, and I answered. If you were to look round the corner, where the tradesmen's entrance is, you would see a lot of poor people whom he used to help — when it suited him.

STUDENT: He was a kind man then.

OLD MAN: Yes — sometimes.

STUDENT: Not always?

OLD MAN: No-o. That's the way of people. Now, sir, will you push my chair a little, so that it gets into the sun. I'm horribly cold. When you're never able to move about, the blood congeals. I'm going to die soon, I know that, but I have a few things to do first. Take my hand and feel how cold I am.

STUDENT (taking it): Yes, inconceivably. (He shrinks back, trying in vain to free his hand.)

OLD MAN: Don't leave me. I am tired now and lonely, but I haven't always been like this, you know. I have an enormously long life behind me, enormously long. I have made people unhappy and people have made me unhappy — the one cancels out the other — but before I die I want to see you happy. Our fates are entwined through your father — and other things.

STUDENT: Let go of my hand. You are taking all my strength. You are freezing me.

[3] It was customary in Sweden to strew the ground with these for a funeral. [Translator's note.]

What do you want with me?

OLD MAN (*letting go*): Be patient and you shall see and understand. Here comes the young lady.

(*They watch the* GIRL *approaching, though the audience cannot yet see her.*)

STUDENT: The Colonel's daughter?

OLD MAN: His daughter — yes. Look at her. Have you ever seen such a masterpiece?

STUDENT: She is like the marble statue in there.

OLD MAN: That's her mother, you know.

STUDENT: You are right. Never have I seen such a woman of woman born. Happy the man who may lead her to the altar and his home.

OLD MAN: You can see it. Not everyone recognizes her beauty. So, then, it is written.

(*The* GIRL *enters, wearing an English riding habit. Without noticing anyone she walks slowly to the door, where she stops to say a few words to the* CARETAKER'S WIFE. *Then she goes into the house. The* STUDENT *covers his eyes with his hand.*)

OLD MAN: Are you weeping?

STUDENT: In the face of what's hopeless there can be nothing but despair.

OLD MAN: I can open doors and hearts, if only I find an arm to do my will. Serve me and you shall have power.

STUDENT: Is it a bargain? Am I to sell my soul?

OLD MAN: Sell nothing. Listen. All my life I have *taken*. Now I have a craving to give — give. But no one will accept. I am rich, very rich, but I have no heirs, except for a good-for-nothing who torments the life out of me. Become my son. Inherit me while I am still alive. Enjoy life so that I can watch, at least from a distance.

STUDENT: What am I to do?

OLD MAN: First go to *The Valkyrie*.

STUDENT: That's settled. What else?

OLD MAN: This evening you must be in there — in the Round Room.

STUDENT: How am I to get there?

OLD MAN: By way of *The Valkyrie*.

STUDENT: Why have you chosen me as your medium? Did you know me before?

OLD MAN: Yes, of course. I have had my eye on you for a long time. But now look up there at the balcony. The maid is hoisting the flag to half-mast for the Consul. And now she is turning the bedclothes. Do you see that blue quilt? It was made for two to sleep under, but now it covers only one.

(*The* GIRL, *having changed her dress, appears in the window and waters the hyacinths.*)

There is my little girl. Look at her, look! She is talking to the flowers. Is she not like that blue hyacinth herself? She gives them drink — nothing but pure water, and they transform the water into color and fragrance. Now here comes the Colonel with the newspaper. He is showing her the bit about the house that collapsed. Now he's pointing to your portrait. She's not indifferent. She's reading of your brave deed. . . .

I believe it's clouding over. If it turns to rain I shall be in a pretty fix, unless Johansson comes back soon.

(*It grows cloudy and dark. The* FIANCÉE *at the window-mirror closes her window.*)

Now my fiancée is closing the window. Seventy-nine years old. The window-mirror is the only mirror she uses, because in it she sees not herself, but the world outside — in two directions. But the world can see her; she hasn't thought of that. Anyhow she's a handsome old woman.

(*Now the* DEAD MAN, *wrapped in a winding sheet, comes out of the door.*)

STUDENT: Good God, what do I see?

OLD MAN: What do you see?

STUDENT: Don't *you* see? There, in the doorway, the dead man?

OLD MAN: I see nothing, but I expected this. Tell me.

STUDENT: He is coming out into the street. (*Pause.*) Now he is turning his head and looking up at the flag.

OLD MAN: What did I tell you? You may be sure he'll count the wreaths and read the visiting cards. Woe to him who's missing.

STUDENT: Now he's turning the corner.

OLD MAN: He's gone to count the poor at the back door. The poor are in the nature of a decoration, you see. "Followed by the blessings of many." Well, he's not going to have my blessing. Between ourselves he was a great scoundrel.

STUDENT: But charitable.

OLD MAN: A charitable scoundrel, always thinking of his grand funeral. When he knew his end was near, he cheated the State out of fifty thousand crowns. Now his daughter has relations with another woman's husband and is wondering about the Will. Yes, the scoundrel can hear every word we're saying, and he's welcome to it. Ah, here comes Johansson!

(JOHANSSON *enters*.)

Report!

(JOHANSSON *speaks, but the audience does not hear*.)

Not at home, eh? You are an ass. And the telegram? Nothing? Go on.... At six this evening? That's good. Special edition, you say? With his name in full. Arkenholtz, a student, born ... parents ... That's splendid.... I think it's beginning to rain.... What did he say about it? So — so. He wouldn't? Well, he must. Here comes the aristocrat. Push me round the corner, Johansson, so I can hear what the poor are saying. And, Arkenholtz, you wait for me here. Understand? (*To* JOHANSSON.) Hurry up now, hurry up.

(JOHANSSON *wheels the chair round the corner. The* STUDENT *remains watching the* GIRL, *who is now loosening the earth round the hyacinths. The* ARISTOCRAT, *wearing mourning, comes in and speaks to the* DARK LADY, *who has been walking to and fro on the pavement*.)

ARISTOCRAT: But what can we do about it? We shall have to wait.
LADY: I can't wait.
ARISTOCRAT: You can't? Well then, go into the country.
LADY: I don't want to do that.
ARISTOCRAT: Come over here or they will hear what we are saying.

(*They move toward the advertisement column and continue their conversation inaudibly.* JOHANSSON *returns*.)

JOHANSSON (*to the* STUDENT): My master asks you not to forget that other thing, sir.
STUDENT (*hesitating*): Look here ... first of all tell me ... who is your master?
JOHANSSON: Well, he's so many things, and he has been everything.
STUDENT: Is he a wise man?

JOHANSSON: Depends what that is. He says all his life he's been looking for a Sunday child, but that may not be true.
STUDENT: What does he want? He's grasping, isn't he?
JOHANSSON: It's power he wants. The whole day long he rides round in his chariot like the god Thor himself. He looks at houses, pulls them down, opens up new streets, builds squares.... But he breaks into houses too, sneaks through windows, plays havoc with human destinies, kills his enemies — and never forgives. Can you imagine it, sir? This miserable cripple was once a Don Juan — although he always lost his women.
STUDENT: How do you account for that?
JOHANSSON: You see he's so cunning he makes the women leave him when he's tired of them. But what he's most like now is a horse thief in the human market. He steals human beings in all sorts of different ways. He literally stole me out of the hands of the law. Well, as a matter of fact I'd made a slip — hm, yes — and only he knew about it. Instead of getting me put in jail, he turned me into a slave. I slave — for my food alone, and that's none of the best.
STUDENT: Then what is it he means to do in this house?
JOHANSSON: I'm not going to talk about that. It's too complicated.
STUDENT: I think I'd better get away from it all.

(*The* GIRL *drops a bracelet out the window*.)

JOHANSSON: Look! The young lady has dropped her bracelet out of the window.

(*The* STUDENT *goes slowly over, picks up the bracelet and returns it to the* GIRL, *who thanks him stiffly. The* STUDENT *goes back to* JOHANSSON.)

So you mean to get away. That's not so easy as you think, once he's got you in his net. And he's afraid of nothing between heaven and earth — yes, of one thing he is — of one person rather....
STUDENT: Don't tell me. I think perhaps I know.
JOHANSSON: How can you know?
STUDENT: I'm guessing. Is it a little milkmaid he's afraid of?

JOHANSSON: He turns his head the other way whenever he meets a milk cart. Besides, he talks in his sleep. It seems he was once in Hamburg. . . .

STUDENT: Can one trust this man?

JOHANSSON: You can trust him — to do anything.

STUDENT: What's he doing now round the corner?

JOHANSSON: Listening to the poor. Sowing a little word, loosening one stone at a time, till the house falls down — metaphorically speaking. You see I'm an educated man. I was once a book-seller. . . . Do you still mean to go away?

STUDENT: I don't like to be ungrateful. He saved my father once, and now he only asks a small service in return.

JOHANSSON: What is that?

STUDENT: I am to go to *The Valkyrie*.

JOHANSSON: That's beyond me. But he's always up to new tricks. Look at him now, talking to that policeman. He is always thick with the police. He uses them, gets them involved in his interests, holds them with false promises and expectations, while all the time he's pumping them. You'll see that before the day is over he'll be received in the Round Room.

STUDENT: What does he want there? What connection has he with the Colonel?

JOHANSSON: I think I can guess, but I'm not sure. You'll see for yourself once you're in there.

STUDENT: I shall never be in there.

JOHANSSON: That depends on yourself. Go to *The Valkyrie*.

STUDENT: Is that the way?

JOHANSSON: Yes, if he said so. Look. Look at him in his war chariot, drawn in triumph by the beggars, who get nothing for their pains but the hint of a treat at his funeral.

(*The* OLD MAN *appears standing up in his wheel-chair, drawn by one of the beggars and followed by the rest.*)

OLD MAN: Hail the noble youth who, at the risk of his own life, saved so many others in yesterday's accident. Three cheers for Arkenholtz!

(*The* BEGGARS *bare their heads but do not cheer. The* GIRL *at the window waves her handkerchief. The* COLONEL *gazes from the window of the Round Room. The* OLD

WOMAN *rises at her window. The* MAID *on the balcony hoists the flag to the top.*)

Clap your hands, citizens. True, it is Sunday, but the ass in the pit and the ear in the corn field will absolve us. And although I am not a Sunday child, I have the gift of prophecy and also that of healing. Once I brought a drowned person back to life. That was in Hamburg on a Sunday morning just like this. . . .

(*The* MILKMAID *enters, seen only by the* STU-DENT *and the* OLD MAN. *She raises her arms like one who is drowning and gazes fixedly at the* OLD MAN. *He sits down, then crumples up, stricken with horror.*)

Johansson! Take me away! Quick! . . . . Arkenholtz, don't forget *The Valkyrie*.

STUDENT: What is all this?

JOHANSSON: We shall see. We shall see.

SCENE II

Inside the Round Room. At the back is a white porcelain stove. On either side of it are a mirror, a pendulum clock and candelabra. On the right of the stove is the entrance to the hall beyond which is a glimpse of a room furnished in green and mahogany. On the left of the stove is the door to a cupboard, papered like the wall. The statue, shaded by palms, has a curtain which can be drawn to conceal it.

A door on the left leads into the Hyacinth Room, where the GIRL *sits reading. The back of the* COLONEL *can be seen, as he sits in the Green Room, writing.* BENGTS-SON, *the Colonel's servant, comes in from the hall. He is wearing livery, and is followed by* JOHANSSON, *dressed as a waiter.*

BENGTSSON: Now you'll have to serve the tea, Johansson, while I take the coats. Have you ever done it before?

JOHANSSON: It's true I push a war chariot in the daytime, as you know, but in the evenings I go as a waiter to receptions and so forth. It's always been my dream to get into this house. They're queer people here, aren't they?

BENGTSSON: Ye-es. A bit out of the ordinary anyhow.

JOHANSSON: Is it to be a musical party or what?

BENGTSSON: The usual ghost supper, as we call it. They drink tea and don't say a word — or else the Colonel does all the talking. And they crunch their biscuits, all at the same time. It sounds like rats in an attic.

JOHANSSON: Why do you call it the ghost supper?

BENGTSSON: They look like ghosts. And they've kept this up for twenty years, always the same people saying the same things or saying nothing at all for fear of being found out.

JOHANSSON: Isn't there a mistress of the house?

BENGTSSON: Oh yes, but she's crazy. She sits in a cupboard because her eyes can't bear the light. (*He points to the papered door.*) She sits in there.

JOHANSSON: In there?

BENGTSSON: Well, I told you they were a bit out of the ordinary.

JOHANSSON: But then — what does she look like?

BENGTSSON: Like a mummy. Do you want to have a look at her? (*He opens the door.*) There she is.

(*The figure of the* COLONEL'S WIFE *is seen, white and shrivelled into a* MUMMY.)

JOHANSSON: Oh my God!

MUMMY (*babbling*): Why do you open the door? Haven't I told you to keep it closed?

BENGTSSON (*in a wheedling tone*): Ta, ta, ta, ta. Be a good girl now, then you'll get something nice. Pretty Polly.

MUMMY (*parrot-like*): Pretty Polly. Are you there, Jacob? Currrrr!

BENGTSSON: She thinks she's a parrot, and maybe she's right. (*To the* MUMMY.) Whistle for us, Polly.

(*The* MUMMY *whistles.*)

JOHANSSON: Well, I've seen a few things in my day, but this beats everything.

BENGTSSON: You see, when a house gets old, it grows moldy, and when people stay a long time together and torment each other they go mad. The mistress of the house — shut up, Polly! — that mummy there, has been living here for forty years — same husband, same furniture, same relatives, same friends. (*He closes the papered door.*) And the goings-on in this house — well, they're beyond me. Look at that statue — that's her when she was young.

JOHANSSON: Good Lord! Is that the mummy?

BENGTSSON: Yes. It's enough to make you weep. And somehow, carried away by her own imagination or something, she's got to be a bit like a parrot — the way she talks and the way she can't stand cripples or sick people. She can't stand the sight of her own daughter, because she's sick.

JOHANSSON: Is the young lady sick?

BENGTSSON: Didn't you know that?

JOHANSSON: No. And the Colonel, who is he?

BENGTSSON: You'll see.

JOHANSSON (*looking at the statue*): It's horrible to think that . . . How old is she now?

BENGTSSON: Nobody knows. But it's said that when she was thirty-five she looked nineteen, and that's what she made the Colonel believe she was — here in this very house. Do you know what that black Japanese screen by the couch is for? They call it the death-screen, and when someone's going to die, they put it round — same as in a hospital.

JOHANSSON: What a horrible house! And the student was longing to get in, as if it were paradise.

BENGTSSON: What student? Oh, I know. The one who's coming here this evening. The Colonel and the young lady happened to meet him at the Opera, and both of them took a fancy to him. Hm. Now it's my turn to ask questions. Who is your master — the man in the wheelchair?

JOHANSSON: Well, he . . . er . . . Is he coming here too?

BENGTSSON: He hasn't been invited.

JOHANSSON: He'll come uninvited — if need be.

(*The* OLD MAN *appears in the hall on crutches, wearing a frock-coat and top-hat. He steals forward and listens.*)

BENGTSSON: He's a regular old devil, isn't he?

JOHANSSON: Up to the ears.

BENGTSSON: He looks like old Nick himself.

JOHANSSON: And he must be a wizard too, for he goes through locked doors.

(*The* OLD MAN *comes forward and takes hold of* JOHANSSON *by the ear.*)

OLD MAN: Rascal — take care! (*To* BENGTSSON.) Tell the Colonel I am here.

BENGTSSON: But we are expecting guests.

OLD MAN: I know. But my visit is as good as expected, if not exactly looked forward to.

BENGTSSON: I see. What name shall I say? Mr. Hummel?

OLD MAN: Exactly. Yes.

(BENGTSSON *crosses the hall to the Green Room, the door of which he closes behind him.*)

(*To* JOHANSSON.) Get out!

(JOHANSSON *hesitates.*)

Get out!

(JOHANSSON *disappears into the hall. The* OLD MAN *inspects the room and stops in front of the statue in much astonishment.*)

Amelia! It is she — she!

MUMMY (*from the cupboard*): Prrr-etty Polly.

(*The* OLD MAN *starts.*)

OLD MAN: What was thát? Is there a parrot in the room? I don't see it.

MUMMY: Are you there, Jacob?

OLD MAN: The house is haunted.

MUMMY: Jacob!

OLD MAN: I'm scared. So these are the kind of secrets they guard in this house. (*With his back turned to the cupboard he stands looking at a portrait.*) There he is — he!

(*The* MUMMY *comes out behind the* OLD MAN *and gives a pull at his wig.*)

MUMMY: Currrrr! Is it . . . ? Currrrr!

OLD MAN (*jumping out of his skin*): God in heaven! Who is it?

MUMMY (*in a natural voice*): Is it Jacob?

OLD MAN: Yes, my name is Jacob.

MUMMY (*with emotion*): And my name is Amelia.

OLD MAN: No, no, no . . . Oh my God!

MUMMY: That's how I look. Yes. (*Pointing to the statue.*) And that's how I *did* look. Life opens one's eyes, does it not? I live mostly in the cupboard to avoid seeing and being seen. . . . But, Jacob, what do you want here?

OLD MAN: My child. Our child.

MUMMY: There she is.

OLD MAN: Where?

MUMMY: There — in the Hyacinth Room.

OLD MAN (*looking at the* GIRL): Yes, that is she. (*Pause.*) And what about her father — the Colonel, I mean — your husband?

MUMMY: Once, when I was angry with him, I told him everything.

OLD MAN: Well . . . ?

MUMMY: He didn't believe me. He just said: "That's what all wives say when they want to murder their husbands." It was a terrible crime none the less. It has falsified his whole life — his family tree too. Sometimes I take a look in the Peerage, and then I say to myself: Here she is, going about with a false birth certificate like some servant girl, and for such things people are sent to the reformatory.

OLD MAN: Many do it. I seem to remember your own date of birth was given incorrectly.

MUMMY: My mother made me do that. I was not to blame. And in our crime, *you* played the biggest part.

OLD MAN: No. Your husband caused that crime, when he took my fiancée from me. I was born one who cannot forgive until he has punished. That was to me an imperative duty — and is so still.

MUMMY: What are you expecting to find in this house? What do you want? How did you get in? Is it to do with my daughter? If you touch her, you shall die.

OLD MAN: I mean well by her.

MUMMY: Then you must spare her father.

OLD MAN: No.

MUMMY: Then you shall die. In this room, behind that screen.

OLD MAN: That may be. But I can't let go once I've got my teeth into a thing.

MUMMY: You want to marry her to that student. Why? He is nothing and has nothing.

OLD MAN: He will be rich, through me.

MUMMY: Have you been invited here tonight?

OLD MAN: No, but I propose to get myself an invitation to this ghost supper.

MUMMY: Do you know who is coming?

OLD MAN: Not exactly.

MUMMY: The Baron. The man who lives up above — whose father-in-law was buried this afternoon.

OLD MAN: The man who is getting a divorce in order to marry the daughter of the Caretaker's wife . . . The man who used to be — your lover.

MUMMY: Another guest will be your former fiancée, who was seduced by my husband.

OLD MAN: A select gathering.

MUMMY: Oh God, if only we might die, might die!

OLD MAN: Then why have you stayed together?

MUMMY: Crime and secrets and guilt bind us together. We have broken our bonds and gone our own ways, times without number, but we are always drawn together again.

OLD MAN: I think the Colonel is coming.

MUMMY: Then I will go in to Adèle. (*Pause.*) Jacob, mind what you do. Spare him. (*Pause. She goes into the Hyacinth Room and disappears.*)

(*The* COLONEL *enters, cold and reserved, with a letter in his hand.*)

COLONEL: Be seated, please.

(*Slowly the* OLD MAN *sits down. Pause. The* COLONEL *stares at him.*)

You wrote this letter, sir?

OLD MAN: I did.

COLONEL: Your name is Hummel?

OLD MAN: It is. (*Pause.*)

COLONEL: As I understand, you have bought in all my unpaid promissory notes. I can only conclude that I am in your hands. What do you want?

OLD MAN: I want payment, in one way or another.

COLONEL: In what way?

OLD MAN: A very simple one. Let us not mention the money. Just bear with me in your house as a guest.

COLONEL: If so little will satisfy you . . .

OLD MAN: Thank you.

COLONEL: What else?

OLD MAN: Dismiss Bengtsson.

COLONEL: Why should I do that? My devoted servant, who has been with me a lifetime, who has the national medal for long and faithful service — why should I do that?

OLD MAN: That's how you see him — full of excellent qualities. He is not the man he appears to be.

COLONEL: Who is?

OLD MAN (*taken aback*): True. But Bengtsson must go.

COLONEL: Are you going to run my house?

OLD MAN: Yes. Since everything here belongs to me — furniture, curtains, dinner service, linen . . . and more too.

COLONEL: How do you mean — more?

OLD MAN: Everything. I own everything here. It is mine.

COLONEL: Very well, it is yours. But my family escutcheon and my good name remain my own.

OLD MAN: No, not even those. (*Pause.*) You are not a nobleman.

COLONEL: How dare you!

OLD MAN (*producing a document*): If you read this extract from *The Armorial Gazette*, you will see that the family whose name you are using has been extinct for a hundred years.

COLONEL: I have heard rumors to this effect, but I inherited the name from my father. (*Reads.*) It is true. You are right. I am not a nobleman. Then I must take off my signet ring. It is true, it belongs to you. (*Gives it to him.*) There you are.

OLD MAN (*pocketing the ring*): Now we will continue. You are not a Colonel either.

COLONEL: I am not . . . ?

OLD MAN: No. You once held the temporary rank of Colonel in the American Volunteer Force, but after the war in Cuba and the reorganization of the Army, all such titles were abolished.

COLONEL: Is this true?

OLD MAN (*indicating his pocket*): Do you want to read it?

COLONEL: No, that's not necessary. Who are you, and what right have you to sit there stripping me in this fashion?

OLD MAN: You will see. But as far as stripping you goes . . . do you know who you are?

COLONEL: How dare you?

OLD MAN: Take off that wig and have a look at yourself in the mirror. But take your teeth out at the same time and shave off your moustache. Let Bengtsson unlace your metal stays and perhaps a certain X.Y.Z., a lackey, will recognize himself. The fellow who was a cupboard lover in a certain kitchen . . .

(*The* COLONEL *reaches for the bell on the table, but* HUMMEL *checks him.*)

Don't touch that bell, and don't call Bengtsson. If you do, I'll have him arrested. (*Pause.*) And now the guests are beginning to arrive. Keep your composure and we will continue to play our old parts for a while.

COLONEL: Who are you? I recognize your voice and eyes.

OLD MAN: Don't try to find out. Keep silent and obey.

(*The* STUDENT *enters and bows to the* COL-ONEL.)

STUDENT: How do you do, sir.

COLONEL: Welcome to my house, young man. Your splendid behavior at that great disaster has brought your name to everybody's lips, and I count it an honor to receive you in my home.

STUDENT: My humble descent, sir . . . Your illustrious name and noble birth. . . .

COLONEL: May I introduce Mr. Arkenholtz — Mr. Hummel. If you will join the ladies in here, Mr. Arkenholtz — I must conclude my conversation with Mr. Hummel.

(*He shows the* STUDENT *into the Hyacinth Room, where he remains visible, talking shyly to the* GIRL.)

A splendid young man, musical, sings, writes poetry. If he only had blue blood in him, if he were of the same station, I don't think I should object . . .

OLD MAN: To what?

COLONEL: To my daughter . . .

OLD MAN: *Your* daughter! But apropos of that, why does she spend all her time in there?

COLONEL: She insists on being in the Hyacinth Room except when she is out-of-doors. It's a peculiarity of hers. Ah, here comes Miss Beatrice von Holsteinkrona — a charming woman, a pillar of the Church, with just enough money of her own to suit her birth and position.

OLD MAN (*to himself*): My fiancée.

(*The* FIANCÉE *enters, looking a little crazy.*)

COLONEL: Miss Holsteinkrona — Mr. Hummel.

(*The* FIANCÉE *curtseys and takes a seat. The* ARISTOCRAT *enters and seats himself. He wears mourning and looks mysterious.*)

Baron Skanskorg . . .

OLD MAN (*aside, without rising*): That's the jewel-thief, I think. (*To the* COLONEL.) If you bring in the Mummy, the party will be complete.

COLONEL (*at the door of the Hyacinth Room*): Polly!

MUMMY (*entering*): Currrrr . . . !

COLONEL: Are the young people to come in too?

OLD MAN: No, not the young people. They shall be spared.

(*They all sit silent in a circle.*)

COLONEL: Shall we have the tea brought in?

OLD MAN: What's the use? No one wants tea. Why should we pretend about it?

COLONEL: Then shall we talk?

OLD MAN: Talk of the weather, which we know? Inquire about each other's health, which we know just as well? I prefer silence — then one can hear thoughts and see the past. Silence cannot hide anything — but words can. I read the other day that differences of language originated among savages for the purpose of keeping one tribe's secrets hidden from another. Every language therefore is a code, and he who finds the key can understand every language in the world. But this does not prevent secrets from being exposed without a key, specially when there is a question of paternity to be proved. Proof in a Court of Law is another matter. Two false witnesses suffice to prove anything about which they are agreed, but one does not take witnesses along on the kind of explorations I have in mind. Nature herself has instilled in human beings a sense of modesty which tries to hide what should be hidden, but we slip into situations unintentionally, and by chance sometimes the deepest secret is divulged — the mask torn from the impostor, the villain exposed. . . .

(*Pause. All look at each other in silence.*)

What a silence there is now!

(*Long silence.*)

Here, for instance, in this honorable house, in this elegant home, where beauty, wealth and culture are united. . . .

(*Long silence.*)

All of us now sitting here know who we are — do we not? There's no need for me to tell you. And you know me, although you pretend ignorance. (*He indicates the Hyacinth Room.*) In there is my daughter. *Mine* — you know that too. She had lost the desire to live, without knowing why. The fact is she was withering away in this air charged with crime and deceit and falseness of every kind. That is why I looked for a friend for her in whose company she might enjoy the light and warmth of noble deeds.

(*Long silence.*)

That was my mission in this house: to pull up the weeds, to expose the crimes, to settle all accounts, so that those young people might start afresh in this home, which is my gift to them.

(*Long silence.*)

Now I am going to grant safe-conduct, to each of you in his and her proper time and turn. Whoever stays I shall have arrested.

(*Long silence.*)

Do you hear the clock ticking like a death-watch beetle in the wall? Do you hear what it says? "It's time, it's time, it's time." When it strikes, in a few moments, your time will be up. Then you can go, but not before. It's raising its arm against you before it strikes. Listen! It is warning you. "The clock can strike." And I can strike too. (*He strikes the table with one of his crutches.*) Do you hear?

(*Silence. The* MUMMY *goes up to the clock and stops it, then speaks in a normal and serious voice.*)

MUMMY: But I can stop time in its course. I can wipe out the past and undo what is done. But not with bribes, not with threats — only through suffering and repentance. (*She goes up to the* OLD MAN.) We are miserable human beings, that we know. We have erred and we have sinned, we are like all the rest. We are not what we seem, because at bottom we are better than ourselves, since we detest our sins. But when you, Jacob Hummel, with your false name, choose to sit in judgment over us, you prove yourself worse than us miserable sinners. For you are not the one you appear to be. You are a thief of human souls. You stole me once with false promises. You murdered the Consul who was buried today; you strangled him with debts. You have stolen the student, binding him by the pretense of a claim on his father, who never owed you a farthing.

(*Having tried to rise and speak, the* OLD MAN *sinks back in his chair and crumples up more and more as she goes on.*)

But there is one dark spot in your life which I am not quite sure about, although I have my suspicions. I think Bengtsson knows. (*She rings the bell on the table.*)

OLD MAN: No, not Bengtsson, not him.

MUMMY: So he does know. (*She rings again.*)

(*The* MILKMAID *appears in the hallway door, unseen by all but the* OLD MAN, *who shrinks back in horror. The* MILKMAID *vanishes as* BENGTSSON *enters.*)

Do you know this man, Bengtsson?

BENGTSSON: Yes, I know him and he knows me. Life, as you are aware, has its ups and downs. I have been in his service; another time he was in mine. For two whole years he was a sponger in my kitchen. As he had to be away by three, the dinner was got ready at two, and the family had to eat the warmed-up leavings of that brute. He drank the soup stock, which the cook then filled up with water. He sat out there like a vampire, sucking the marrow out of the house, so that we became like skeletons. And he nearly got us put in prison when we called the cook a thief. Later I met this man in Hamburg under another name. He was a usurer then, a blood-sucker. But while he was there he was charged with having lured a young girl out on to the ice so as to drown her, because she had seen him commit a crime he was afraid would be discovered. . . .

(*The* MUMMY *passes her hand over the* OLD MAN*'s face.*)

MUMMY: *This* is you. Now give up the notes and the Will.

(*JOHANSSON appears in the hallway door and watches the scene with great interest, knowing he is now to be freed from slavery. The* OLD MAN *produces a bundle of papers and throws it on the table. The* MUMMY *goes over and strokes his back.*)

Parrot. Are you there, Jacob?

OLD MAN (*like a parrot*): Jacob is here. Pretty Polly. Currrrr!

MUMMY: May the clock strike?

OLD MAN (*with a clucking sound*): The clock may strike. (*Imitating a cuckoo clock.*) Cuckoo, cuckoo, cuckoo. . . .

(*The* MUMMY *opens the cupboard door.*)

MUMMY: Now the clock has struck. Rise, and enter the cupboard where I have spent twenty years repenting our crime. A rope is hanging there, which you can take as the one with which you strangled the Consul, and with which you meant to strangle your benefactor. . . . Go!

(*The* OLD MAN *goes in to the cupboard. The* MUMMY *closes the door.*)

Bengtsson! Put up the screen — the death-screen.

(BENGTSSON *places the screen in front of the door.*)

It is finished. God have mercy on his soul.
ALL: Amen. (*Long silence.*)

(*The* GIRL *and the* STUDENT *appear in the Hyacinth Room. She has a harp, on which she plays a prelude, and then accompanies the* STUDENT'S *recitation.*)

STUDENT:
    I saw the sun. To me it seemed
    that I beheld the Hidden.
    Men must reap what they have sown;
    blest is he whose deeds are good.
    Deeds which you have wrought in fury,
    cannot in evil find redress.
    Comfort him you have distressed
    with loving-kindness — this will heal.
    No fear has he who does no ill.
    Sweet is innocence.

SCENE III

Inside the Hyacinth Room. The general effect of the room is exotic and oriental. There are hyacinths everywhere, of every color, some in pots, some with the bulbs in glass vases and the roots going down into the water.

On top of the tiled stove is a large seated Buddha, in whose lap rests a bulb from which rises the stem of a shallot (Allium ascalonicum), *bearing its globular cluster of white, starlike flowers.*

On the right is an open door, leading into the Round Room, where the COLONEL *and the* MUMMY *are seated, inactive and silent. A part of the death-screen is also visible.*

On the left is a door to the pantry and kitchen.

The STUDENT *and the* GIRL (Adèle) *are beside the table; he standing, she seated with her harp.*

GIRL: Now sing to my flowers.
STUDENT: Is this the flower of your soul?
GIRL: The one and only. Do you too love the hyacinth?
STUDENT: I love it above all other flowers — its virginal shape rising straight and slender out of the bulb, resting on the water and sending its pure white roots down into the colorless fluid. I love its colors: the snow-white, pure as innocence, the yellow honey-sweet, the youthful pink, the ripe red, but best of all the blue — the dewy blue, deep-eyed and full of faith. I love them all, more than gold or pearls. I have loved them ever since I was a child, have worshipped them because they have all the fine qualities I lack. . . . And yet . . .
GIRL: Go on.
STUDENT: My love is not returned, for these beautiful blossoms hate me.
GIRL: How do you mean?
STUDENT: Their fragrance, strong and pure as the early winds of spring which have passed over melting snows, confuses my senses, deafens me, blinds me, thrusts me out of the room, bombards me with poisoned arrows that wound my heart and set my head on fire. Do you know the legend of that flower?
GIRL: Tell it to me.
STUDENT: First its meaning. The bulb is the earth, resting on the water or buried in the soil. Then the stalk rises, straight as the axis of the world, and at the top are the six-pointed star-flowers.
GIRL: Above the earth — the stars. Oh, that is wonderful! Where did you learn this? How did you find it out?
STUDENT: Let me think . . . In your eyes. And so, you see, it is an image of the Cosmos. This is why Buddha sits holding the earth-bulb, his eyes brooding as he watches it grow, outward and upward, transforming itself into a heaven. This poor earth will become a heaven. It is for this that Buddha waits.
GIRL: I see it now. Is not the snowflake six-pointed too like the hyacinth flower?
STUDENT: You are right. The snowflakes must be falling stars.
GIRL: And the snowdrop is a snow-star, grown out of snow.
STUDENT: But the largest and most beautiful of all the stars in the firmament, the golden-red Sirius, is the narcissus with its gold and red chalice and its six white rays.
GIRL: Have you seen the shallot in bloom?
STUDENT: Indeed I have. It bears its blossoms within a ball, a globe like the celestial one, strewn with white stars.
GIRL: Oh how glorious! Whose thought was that?
STUDENT: Yours.

GIRL: Yours.

STUDENT: Ours. We have given birth to it together. We are wedded.

GIRL: Not yet.

STUDENT: What's still to do?

GIRL: Waiting, ordeals, patience.

STUDENT: Very well. Put me to the test. (*Pause.*) Tell me. Why do your parents sit in there so silently, not saying a single word?

GIRL: Because they have nothing to say to each other, and because neither believes what the other says. This is how my father puts it: What's the point of talking, when neither of us can fool the other?

STUDENT: What a horrible thing to hear!

GIRL: Here comes the Cook. Look at her, how big and fat she is.

(*They watch the* COOK, *although the audience cannot yet see her.*)

STUDENT: What does she want?

GIRL: To ask me about the dinner. I have to do the housekeeping as my mother's ill.

STUDENT: What have we to do with the kitchen?

GIRL: We must eat. Look at the Cook. I can't bear the sight of her.

STUDENT: Who is that ogress?

GIRL: She belongs to the Hummel family of vampires. She is eating us.

STUDENT: Why don't you dismiss her?

GIRL: She won't go. We have no control over her. We've got her for our sins. Can't you see that we are pining and wasting away?

STUDENT: Don't you get enough to eat?

GIRL: Yes, we get many dishes, but all the strength has gone. She boils the nourishment out of the meat and gives us the fibre and water, while she drinks the stock herself. And when there's a roast, she first boils out the marrow, eats the gravy and drinks the juices herself. Everything she touches loses its savor. It's as if she sucked with her eyes. We get the grounds when she has drunk the coffee. She drinks the wine and fills the bottles up with water.

STUDENT: Send her packing.

GIRL: We can't.

STUDENT: Why not?

GIRL: We don't know. She won't go. No one has any control over her. She has taken all our strength from us.

STUDENT: May I get rid of her?

GIRL: No. It must be as it is. Here she is. She will ask me what is to be for dinner. I shall tell her. She will make objections and get her own way.

STUDENT: Let her do the ordering herself then.

GIRL: She won't do that.

STUDENT: What an extraordinary house! It is bewitched.

GIRL: Yes. But now she is turning back, because she has seen you.

COOK (*in the doorway*): No, that wasn't the reason. (*She grins, showing all her teeth.*)

STUDENT: Get out!

COOK: When it suits me. (*Pause.*) It does suit me now. (*She disappears.*)

GIRL: Don't lose your temper. Practice patience. She is one of the ordeals we have to go through in this house. You see, we have a housemaid too, whom we have to clean up after.

STUDENT: I am done for. *Cor in aethere.*[4] Music!

GIRL: Wait.

STUDENT: Music!

GIRL: Patience. This room is called the room of ordeals. It looks beautiful, but it is full of defects.

STUDENT: Really? Well, such things must be seen to. It is very beautiful, but a little cold. Why don't you have a fire?

GIRL: Because it smokes.

STUDENT: Can't you have the chimney swept?

GIRL: It doesn't help. You see that writing-desk there?

STUDENT: An unusually fine piece.

GIRL: But it wobbles. Every day I put a piece of cork under that leg, and every day the housemaid takes it away when she sweeps and I have to cut a new piece. The penholder is covered with ink every morning and so is the inkstand. I have to clean them up every morning after that woman, as sure as the sun rises. (*Pause.*) What's the worst job you can think of?

STUDENT: To count the washing. Ugh!

GIRL: That I have to do. Ugh!

STUDENT: What else?

GIRL: To be waked in the middle of the night and have to get up and see to the window, which the housemaid has left banging.

STUDENT: What else?

---

4 Heart in air. [Editor's note.]

GIRL: To get up on a ladder and tie the cord on the damper[5] which the housemaid has torn off.

STUDENT: What else?

GIRL: To sweep after her, to dust after her, to light the fire in the stove when all she's done is throw in some wood. To see to the damper, to wipe the glasses, to lay the table over again, to open the bottles, to see that the rooms are aired, to remake my bed, to rinse the water-bottle when it's green with sediment, to buy matches and soap which are always lacking, to wipe the chimneys and trim the wicks to keep the lamps from smoking — and so that they don't go out when we have company, I have to fill them myself. . . .

STUDENT: Music!

GIRL: Wait. The labor comes first. The labor of keeping the dirt of life at a distance.

STUDENT: But you are wealthy and have two servants.

GIRL: It doesn't help. Even if we had three. Living is hard work, and sometimes I grow tired. (*Pause.*) Think then if there were a nursery as well.

STUDENT: The greatest of joys.

GIRL: And the costliest. Is life worth so much hardship?

STUDENT: That must depend on the reward you expect for your labors. I would not shrink from anything to win your hand.

GIRL: Don't say that. You can never have me.

STUDENT: Why not?

GIRL: You mustn't ask. (*Pause.*)

STUDENT: You dropped your bracelet out of the window. . . .

GIRL: Because my hand has grown so thin. (*Pause.*)

(*The* COOK *appears with a Japanese bottle in her hand.*)

There she is — the one who devours me and all of us.

STUDENT: What has she in her hand?

GIRL: It is the bottle of coloring matter that has letters like scorpions on it. It is the soy which turns water into soup and takes the place of gravy. She makes cabbage soup with it — and mock-turtle soup too.

STUDENT (*to* COOK): Get out!

COOK: You drain us of sap, and we drain

[5] Damper to the big stove. [Translator's note.]

you. We take the blood and leave you the water, but colored . . . colored. I am going now, but all the same I shall stay, as long as I please. (*She goes out.*)

STUDENT: Why did Bengtsson get a medal?

GIRL: For his great merits.

STUDENT: Has he no defects?

GIRL: Yes, great ones. But you don't get a medal for them.

(*They smile.*)

STUDENT: You have many secrets in this house.

GIRL: As in all others. Permit us to keep ours.

STUDENT: Don't you approve of candor?

GIRL: Yes — within reason.

STUDENT: Sometimes I'm seized with a raging desire to say all I think. But I know the world would go to pieces if one were completely candid. (*Pause.*) I went to a funeral the other day . . . in church. It was very solemn and beautiful.

GIRL: Was it Mr. Hummel's?

STUDENT: My false benefactor's — yes. At the head of the coffin stood an old friend of the deceased. He carried the mace. I was deeply impressed by the dignified manner and moving words of the clergyman. I cried. We all cried. Afterwards we went to a tavern, and there I learned that the man with the mace had been in love with the dead man's son. . . .

(*The* GIRL *stares at him, trying to understand.*)

And that the dead man had borrowed money from his son's admirer. (*Pause.*) Next day the clergyman was arrested for embezzling the church funds. A pretty story.

GIRL: Oh . . . ! (*Pause.*)

STUDENT: Do you know how I am thinking about you now?

GIRL: Don't tell me, or I shall die.

STUDENT: I must, or I shall die.

GIRL: It is in asylums that people say everything they think.

STUDENT: Exactly. My father finished up in an asylum.

GIRL: Was he ill?

STUDENT: No, he was well, but he was mad. You see, he broke out once — in these circumstances. Like all of us, he was surrounded with a circle of acquaintances; he called them friends for short. They were a lot of rotters, of course, as most people are, but he had to have some society — he couldn't get on all alone. Well, as you know, in everyday life no one tells people what he thinks of them, and he didn't either. He knew perfectly well what frauds they were — he'd sounded the depths of their deceit — but as he was a wise and well-bred man, he was always courteous to them. Then one day he gave a big party. It was in the evening and he was tired by the day's work and by the strain of holding his tongue and at the same time talking rubbish with his guests. . . .

(*The* GIRL *is frightened.*)

Well, at the dinner table he rapped for silence, raised his glass, and began to speak. Then something loosed the trigger. He made an enormous speech in which he stripped the whole company naked, one after the other, and told them of all their treachery. Then, tired out, he sat down on the table and told them all to go to hell.

GIRL: Oh!

STUDENT: I was there, and I shall never forget what happened then. Father and Mother came to blows, the guests rushed for the door . . . and my father was taken to a madhouse, where he died. (*Pause.*) Water that is still too long stagnates, and so it is in this house too. There is something stagnating here. And yet I thought it was paradise itself that first time I saw you coming in here. There I stood that Sunday morning, gazing in. I saw a Colonel who was no Colonel. I had a benefactor who was a thief and had to hang himself. I saw a mummy who was not a mummy and an old maid — what of the maidenhood, by the way? Where is beauty to be found? In nature, and in my own mind, when it is in its Sunday clothes. Where are honor and faith? In fairy-tales and children's fancies. Where is anything that fulfills its promise? In my imagination. Now your flowers have poisoned me and I have given the poison back to you. I asked you to become my wife in a home full of poetry and song and music. Then the Cook came. . . . *Sursum Corda!* [6] Try once more to strike fire and glory out of the golden harp. Try, I beg you, I implore you on my knees. (*Pause.*) Then I will do it myself. (*He picks up the harp, but the strings give no sound.*) It is dumb and deaf. To think that the

most beautiful flowers are so poisonous, are the most poisonous. The curse lies over the whole of creation, over life itself. Why will you not be my bride? Because the very life-spring within you is sick . . . now I can feel that vampire in the kitchen beginning to suck me. I believe she is a Lamia, one of those that suck the blood of children. It is always in the kitchen quarters that the seed-leaves of the children are nipped, if it has not already happened in the bedroom. There are poisons that destroy the sight and poisons that open the eyes. I seem to have been born with the latter kind, for I cannot see what is ugly as beautiful, nor call evil good. I cannot. Jesus Christ descended into hell. That was His pilgrimage on earth — to this madhouse, this prison, this charnel-house, this earth. And the madmen killed Him when He wanted to set them free; but the robber they let go. The robber always gets the sympathy. Woe! Woe to us all. Saviour of the world, save us! We perish.

(*And now the* GIRL *has drooped, and it is seen that she is dying. She rings.* BENGTSSON *enters.*)

GIRL: Bring the screen. Quick. I am dying.

(BENGTSSON *comes back with the screen, opens it and arranges it in front of the* GIRL.)

STUDENT: The Liberator is coming. Welcome, pale and gentle one. Sleep, you lovely, innocent, doomed creature, suffering for no fault of your own. Sleep without dreaming, and when you wake again . . . may you be greeted by a sun that does not burn, in a home without dust, by friends without stain, by a love without flaw. You wise and gentle Buddha, sitting there waiting for a Heaven to sprout from the earth, grant us patience in our ordeal and purity of will, so that this hope may not be confounded.

(*The strings of the harp hum softly and a white light fills the room.*)

> I saw the sun. To me it seemed
> that I beheld the Hidden.
> Men must reap what they have sown;
> blest is he whose deeds are good.
> Deeds which you have wrought in fury,
> cannot in evil find redress.
> Comfort him you have distressed
> with loving-kindness — this will heal.

[6] Lift up your hearts. [Editor's note.]

No fear has he who does no ill.
Sweet is innocence.

(*A faint moaning is heard behind the screen.*)

You poor little child, child of this world of illusion, guilt, suffering, and death, this world of endless change, disappointment, and pain. May the Lord of Heaven be merciful to you upon your journey.

(*The room disappears. Böcklin's picture* The Island of the Dead *is seen in the distance, and from the island comes music, soft, sweet, and melancholy.*)

Some of Strindberg's best-known plays, such as *The Father* (1887) and *Miss Julie* (1888), are part of a nineteenth-century movement called "naturalism." As we suggest in a longish entry in the Glossary (page 827), naturalism supposedly offered an objective or dispassionately scientific (as opposed to a fancifully romantic) view of life. But in fact, most naturalists saw life through a rather special sort of lens, for the scientific idea that influenced them was the theory of evolution, and they usually saw human beings as creatures largely determined — destined, one might say — by their heredity and their environment. To a great extent, then, the naturalists resemble the Greek tragic dramatists, for they reintroduced into literature (though they did not quite see it that way) the ancient idea of fate.

True, great differences between the Greeks and the naturalists are immediately apparent: for example, Greek drama is in verse, whereas naturalistic drama is in prose, attempting to imitate ordinary language. And Greek drama deals with heroes, people of high stature in their societies, whereas naturalistic drama often deals with middle-class or even lower-class figures. But the naturalists, though they set forth the language and deeds of ordinary people, like the Greeks reveal the invisible or mysterious forces working in and around their figures. Eugene O'Neill, for example, a second-generation naturalist and disciple of Strindberg, in *Long Day's Journey into Night* has a character say, "None of us can help the things that life has done to us. They're done before you realize it, and once they're done they make you do other things until at last everything comes between you and what you'd like to be, and you've lost your true self forever." It is not surprising, then, that the greatest naturalists, including Strindberg, grew dissatisfied with drama that seemed to show realistically, in the language of ordinary talk, the doings of characters very like one's family and acquaintances. And so we find Strindberg moving beyond naturalism (which we can now define, roughly, as the presentation of a realistic surface fused with a deterministic view of character and action) to a more obviously theatrical and allegorical drama. As Strindberg became increasingly obsessed with the inner workings of things, he abandoned the emphasis on the close or realistic presentation of the familiar surface, and more vividly emphasized the strange discoveries that he made through his insistent and untrammeled pursuit of what he saw as the truth. That is, his naturalism, which insisted on the unprejudiced study of human nature, came to take the form of highly unconventional presentations of exciting worlds unseen by the previous generation of writers. In the preface to *A Dream Play*, he writes:

> The writer has tried to imitate the disjointed but apparently logical form of a dream. Anything may happen: everything is possible and probable. Time and space do not exist.... The characters are split, doubled, and multiplied: they evaporate and are condensed, are diffused and concentrated. But a single consciousness holds sway over them all — that of the dreamer.

Behind this antirealistic creed is, paradoxically, the naturalistic passionate devotion to the truth, passionate insistence that the conventional form (so venerated by conventional playwrights) must yield to the content. And so Strindberg, a father of naturalism in the 1880s, becomes at the turn of the century the first Expressionist, the first dramatist whose concern with truth led him to set forth on the stage *in a highly subjective form* the reality that really mattered: not the way in which people exchange small talk but their underlying passions and their innermost fantasies and motives. Traditional recipes for plot, for characterization, and for dialogue were jettisoned by a passion to tell the truth as his own consciousness saw it; the only way to tell this truth in a play was to people the stage with characters who, on the surface, did not seem at all real. And so we have in *The Ghost Sonata* such characters as a man who seems helpful but whose hand is icy (he destroys all whom he clasps to him), a woman who appears as a mummy and who lives in a closet (though physically alive, she has been robbed of her life and her soul), and a cook who steals all the nourishment out of the food she prepares for her employers. We get, in short, Strindberg's view of bourgeois society, not as it seems in a family photograph or in a conventional play about middle-class life, but as he felt it.

But not quite. Although Strindberg's play is an exposure of the parasitic nature of bourgeois society, it is also a revelation (and here we go back to ancient Greek drama) of the eternal mysterious forces — invisible to most people — that surround or underlie our existence. After all, even Sophocles' *Oedipus the King*, relatively unusual (among Greek plays) in its emphasis on character, is far more than a play about a particular kind of man doing deeds that arise entirely out of his personality and that cause his subsequent great suffering. *Oedipus the King* has a cosmic background, evident not only in the references to gods and oracles, but also in the idea of a mysterious moral pollution that can be incurred regardless of motive. The Greek word for this pollution is *miasma*; but the modern English word "miasma," meaning a physically poisonous atmosphere, misses the effect of the Greek word, for the English word refers to a physical or natural world, and the Greek word refers to a spiritual condition.

It is a miasmal world that Strindberg gives us, not merely a world of physical cause and effect. In the first scene of *The Ghost Sonata* we see "the

façade of a modern house, and the street in front." The Student says that
when he first saw the house — on a Sunday, the first day of Creation — he
"imagined all the beauty and elegance there must be inside," and he said to
a friend, "Think of living up there in the top flat, with a beautiful young
wife, two pretty little children and an income of twenty thousand crowns a
year." But this view of paradise does not last; in the second scene we learn
from the Old Man, Hummel, that the beautiful and delicate Girl who lives
in the house is "withering away in this air charged with crime and deceit and
falseness of every kind." And Hummel himself is a deceiver, not merely a
dishonest businessman such as we might find in a play by Ibsen or in Arthur
Miller's *All My Sons*, but one who "steals human beings." (Even in the first
scene the Student, alarmed when the friendly Hummel placed his hand on
him, says: "You are taking all my strength. You are freezing me!") In the
third scene we penetrate yet further into the mystery of existence when we
learn that the Cook flourishes by robbing her employers. This bloated Cook
is a realistic figure if we consider only her dialogue, but clearly she is, like
Hummel, a sort of vampire. Finally the Student is forced to perceive the hell
that is within the house that he had thought was a paradise.*

At the end of the play the Student prays to the Buddha, and a harp,
which a few minutes earlier had not responded to the Girl's touch, now mysteriously plays; the Girl dies, the room disappears, and a vision of beauty and
death, Arnold Böcklin's painting *The Island of the Dead*, appears.

The play ends, then, with a religous vision. It is often said that religion
and tragedy are incompatible, for religion (so the argument runs) obliterates
tragic suffering by offering heaven in compensation. A related argument holds
that religious creeds, by exalting the cosmic principle above the human sufferer, deemphasize human suffering and thus show us figures who cannot be
regarded as tragic heroes. But perhaps too much critical writing has assumed
that tragedy and religion are irreconcilable; indeed, the Greeks, who performed their tragic plays in a festival in honor of the god Dionysus (the priest
of Dionysus occupied the seat of honor, and the altar of Dionysus was in
full sight) would have found such a view baffling, for Greek tragedy sees human existence as surrounded by a mysterious world of the gods. True, *The
Ghost Sonata* does not show us the heroic assertion that much criticism has
come to say is necessary in tragedy, but perhaps this dogma needs to be re-
examined. If we can be content to say, with John Milton, that tragedy deals
with "fate, and chance, and change in human life" — that is, with doom (the
doom of being born into a world of suffering, and the doom of death), with
inevitable accidents (we cannot control the circumstances that impinge on
us), and with reversals (the Student comes to perceive the corruption be-

---

* A word about the title of the play: Strindberg did not explain why he called the play a
sonata, but presumably he felt that it was constructed in sonata form, a musical form
usually in three movements (ABA) that are independent in key, mood, and tempo. Notice
that the Student appears in the first and third scenes, but not in the second; notice, too,
the pronounced difference in tone among the three scenes.

neath the attractive façade, the powerful Hummel is stripped of his power and ends by having to hang himself, the Student's love for the Girl drives him to tell her the truth, but the truth kills her), perhaps we will have no trouble seeing *The Ghost Sonata* as a true (if puzzling) tragedy. The Mummy declares that through "suffering and repentance" she "can wipe out the past and undo what is done," but despite the soft music and the vision of the peaceful Island of the Dead at the end of the play, we do not feel that the world of deceit and of inescapable guilt and suffering is dissolved into a non-tragic heavenly vision. "We are wedded," the Student says to the Girl, but it is not to be, for she soon dies. Surely even at the end of *The Ghost Sonata* we are not in a world very different from the world that the Chorus speaks of at the end of *Oedipus the King*: "... speak of no man's happiness / Till, without sorrow, he hath passed the goal of life."

RIDERS TO THE SEA

John Millington Synge

John Millington Synge (1871–1909) was born in Dublin of Protestant English stock. After his graduation from Trinity College, Dublin, where he specialized in languages — Gaelic, Latin, Greek, Hebrew — he went to Paris and tried to eke out a living by writing criticism of French literature. William Butler Yeats, in Paris in 1896, urged him to return to Ireland that he might steep himself in the speech of the common people and record a life never described in literature. Synge took the advice and then in his few remaining years wrote six plays, three of which are masterpieces: *Riders to the Sea* (1904), *The Playboy of the Western World* (1907) and *Deidre of the Sorrows* (1909). He died of cancer in his thirty-eighth year.

CHARACTERS

MAURYA, *an old woman*
BARTLEY, *her son*
CATHLEEN, *her daughter*
NORA, *a younger daughter*
MEN *and* WOMEN

A scene from the Abbey Theatre production of *Riders to the Sea*, Dublin, 1980. (Photograph: Rod Tuach/The Abbey Theatre.)

Scene: An Island off the West of Ireland.

Cottage kitchen, with nets, oilskins, spin-ning-wheel, some new boards standing by the wall, etc. CATHLEEN, *a girl of about twenty, finishes kneading cake, and puts it down in the pot-oven by the fire; then wipes her hands, and begins to spin at the wheel.* NORA, *a young girl, puts her head in at the door.*

NORA (*in a low voice*): Where is she?
CATHLEEN: She's lying down, God help her, and maybe sleeping, if she's able.

(NORA *comes in softly, and takes a bundle from under her shawl.*)

CATHLEEN (*spinning the wheel rapidly*): What is it you have?
NORA: The young priest is after bringing them. It's a shirt and a plain stocking were got off a drowned man in Donegal.

(CATHLEEN *stops her wheel with a sudden movement, and leans out to listen.*)

NORA: We're to find out if it's Michael's they are, some time herself will be down look-ing by the sea.
CATHLEEN: How would they be Michael's, Nora? How would he go the length of that way to the far north?
NORA: The young priest says he's known the like of it. "If it's Michael's they are," says he, "you can tell herself he's got a clean burial by the grace of God, and if they're not his, let no one say a word about them, for she'll be get-ting her death," says he, "with crying and la-menting."

(*The door which* NORA *half closed is blown open by a gust of wind.*)

CATHLEEN (*looking out anxiously*): Did you ask him would he stop Bartley going this day with the horses to the Galway fair?
NORA: "I won't stop him," says he, "but let you not be afraid. Herself does be saying pray-ers half through the night, and the Almighty God won't leave her destitute," says he, "with no son living."
CATHLEEN: Is the sea bad by the white rocks, Nora?
NORA: Middling bad, God help us. There's a great roaring in the west, and it's worse it'll be getting when the tide's turned to the wind. (*She goes over to the table with the bundle.*) Shall I open it now?
CATHLEEN: Maybe she'd wake up on us, and come in before we'd done. (*Coming to the table.*) It's a long time we'll be, and the two of us crying.
NORA (*goes to the inner door and listens*): She's moving about on the bed. She'll be com-ing in a minute.
CATHLEEN: Give me the ladder, and I'll put them up in the turf-loft, the way she won't know of them at all, and maybe when the tide turns she'll be going down to see would he be floating from the east.

(*They put the ladder against the gable of the chimney;* CATHLEEN *goes up a few steps and hides the bundle in the turf-loft.* MAURYA *comes from the inner room.*)

MAURYA (*looking up at* CATHLEEN *and speak-ing querulously*): Isn't it turf enough you have for this day and evening?
CATHLEEN: There's a cake baking at the fire for a short space (*throwing down the turf*), and Bartley will want it when the tide turns if he goes to Connemara.

(NORA *picks up the turf and puts it round the pot-oven.*)

MAURYA (*sitting down on a stool at the fire*): He won't go this day with the wind rising from the south and west. He won't go this day, for the young priest will stop him surely.
NORA: He'll not stop him, mother, and I heard Eamon Simon and Stephen Pheety and Colum Shawn saying he would go.
MAURYA: Where is he itself?
NORA: He went down to see would there be another boat sailing in the week, and I'm thinking it won't be long till he's here now, for the tide's turning at the green head, and the hooker's[1] tacking from the east.

From *The Complete Works of John M. Synge* (New York: Random House, 1935).

[1] Fishing vessel.

CATHLEEN: I hear some one passing the big stones.

NORA (*looking out*): He's coming now, and he in a hurry.

BARTLEY (*comes in and looks round the room. Speaking sadly and quietly*): Where is the bit of new rope, Cathleen, was bought in Connemara?

CATHLEEN (*coming down*): Give it to him, Nora; it's on a nail by the white boards. I hung it up this morning, for the pig with the black feet was eating it.

NORA (*giving him a rope*): Is that it, Bartley?

MAURYA: You'd do right to leave that rope, Bartley, hanging by the boards. (BARTLEY *takes the rope.*) It will be wanting in this place, I'm telling you, if Michael is washed up to-morrow morning, or the next morning, or any morning in the week, for it's a deep grave we'll make him by the grace of God.

BARTLEY (*beginning to work with the rope*): I've no halter the way I can ride down on the mare, and I must go now quickly. This is the one boat going for two weeks or beyond it, and the fair will be a good fair for horses I heard them saying below.

MAURYA: It's a hard thing they'll be saying below if the body is washed up and there's no man in it to make the coffin, and I after giving a big price for the finest white boards you'd find in Connemara.

(*She looks round at the boards.*)

BARTLEY: How would it be washed up, and we after looking each day for nine days, and a strong wind blowing a while back from the west and south?

MAURYA: If it isn't found itself, that wind is raising the sea, and there was a star up against the moon, and it rising in the night. If it was a hundred horses, or a thousand horses you had itself, what is the price of a thousand horses against a son where there is one son only?

BARTLEY (*working at the halter, to CATHLEEN*): Let you go down each day, and see the sheep aren't jumping in on the rye, and if the jobber comes you can sell the pig with the black feet if there is a good price going.

MAURYA: How would the like of her get a good price for a pig?

BARTLEY (*to CATHLEEN*): If the west wind holds with the last bit of the moon let you

and Nora get up weed[2] enough for another cock for the kelp. It's hard set we'll be from this day with no one in it but one man to work.

MAURYA: It's hard set we'll be surely the day you're drownd'd with the rest. What way will I live and the girls with me, and I an old woman looking for the grave?

(BARTLEY *lays down the halter, takes off his old coat, and puts on a newer one of the same flannel.*)

BARTLEY (*to NORA*): Is she coming to the pier?

NORA (*looking out*): She's passing the green head and letting fall her sails.

BARTLEY (*getting his purse and tobacco*): I'll have half an hour to go down, and you'll see me coming again in two days, or in three days, or maybe in four days if the wind is bad.

MAURYA (*turning round to the fire, and putting her shawl over her head*): Isn't it a hard and cruel man won't hear a word from an old woman, and she holding him from the sea?

CATHLEEN: It's the life of a young man to be going on the sea, and who would listen to an old woman with one thing and she saying it over?

BARTLEY (*taking the halter*): I must go now quickly. I'll ride down on the red mare, and the gray pony'll run behind me. . . . The blessing of God on you.

(*He goes out.*)

MAURYA (*crying out as he is in the door*): He's gone now, God spare us, and we'll not see him again. He's gone now, and when the black night is falling I'll have no son left me in the world.

CATHLEEN: Why wouldn't you give him your blessing and he looking round in the door? Isn't it sorrow enough is on every one in this house without your sending him out with an unlucky word behind him, and a hard word in his ear?

(MAURYA *takes up the tongs and begins raking the fire aimlessly without looking round.*)

NORA (*turning towards her*): You're taking away the turf from the cake.

CATHLEEN (*crying out*): The Son of God

2 Seaweed (used for fertilizer).

forgive us, Nora, we're after forgetting his bit of bread.

(*She comes over to the fire.*)

NORA: And it's destroyed he'll be going till dark night, and he after eating nothing since the sun went up.

CATHLEEN (*turning the cake out of the oven*): It's destroyed he'll be, surely. There's no sense left on any person in a house where an old woman will be talking for ever.

(MAURYA *sways herself on her stool.*)

CATHLEEN (*cutting off some of the bread and rolling it in a cloth; to* MAURYA): Let you go down now to the spring well and give him this and he passing. You'll see him then and the dark word will be broken, and you can say "God speed you," the way he'll be easy in his mind.

MAURYA (*taking the bread*): Will I be in it as soon as himself?

CATHLEEN: If you go now quickly.

MAURYA (*standing up unsteadily*): It's hard set I am to walk.

CATHLEEN (*looking at her anxiously*): Give her the stick, Nora, or maybe she'll slip on the big stones.

NORA: What stick?

CATHLEEN: The stick Michael brought from Connemara.

MAURYA (*taking a stick* NORA *gives her*): In the big world the old people do be leaving things after them for their sons and children, but in this place it is the young men do be leaving things behind for them that do be old.

(*She goes out slowly.* NORA *goes over to the ladder.*)

CATHLEEN: Wait, Nora, maybe she'd turn back quickly. She's that sorry, God help her, you wouldn't know the thing she'd do.

NORA: Is she gone round by the bush?

CATHLEEN (*looking out*): She's gone now. Throw it down quickly, for the Lord knows when she'll be out of it again.

NORA (*getting the bundle from the loft*): The young priest said he'd be passing tomorrow, and we might go down and speak to him below if it's Michael's they are surely.

CATHLEEN (*taking the bundle*): Did he say what way they were found?

NORA (*coming down*): "There were two men," says he, "and they rowing round with poteen[3] before the cocks crowed, and the oar of one of them caught the body, and they passing the black cliffs of the north."

CATHLEEN (*trying to open the bundle*): Give me a knife, Nora, the string's perished with the salt water, and there's a black knot on it you wouldn't loosen in a week.

NORA (*giving her a knife*): I've heard tell it was a long way to Donegal.

CATHLEEN (*cutting the string*): It is surely. There was a man here a while ago — the man sold us that knife — and he said if you set off walking from the rocks beyond, it would be in seven days you'd be in Donegal.

NORA: And what time would a man take, and he floating?

(CATHLEEN *opens the bundle and takes out a bit of a stocking. They look at them eagerly.*)

CATHLEEN (*in a low voice*): The Lord spare us, Nora! isn't it a queer hard thing to say if it's his they are surely?

NORA: I'll get his shirt off the hook the way we can put the one flannel on the other. (*She looks through some clothes hanging in the corner.*) It's not with them, Cathleen, and where will it be?

CATHLEEN: I'm thinking Bartley put it on him in the morning, for his own shirt was heavy with the salt in it. (*Pointing to the corner.*) There's a bit of a sleeve was of the same stuff. Give me that and it will do.

(NORA *brings it to her and they compare the flannel.*)

CATHLEEN: It's the same stuff, Nora; but if it is itself aren't there great rolls of it in the shops of Galway, and isn't it many another man may have a shirt of it as well as Michael himself?

NORA (*who has taken up the stocking and counted the stitches, crying out*): It's Michael, Cathleen, it's Michael; God spare his soul, and what will herself say when she hears this story, and Bartley on the sea?

CATHLEEN (*taking the stocking*): It's a plain stocking.

NORA: It's the second one of the third pair

---

[3] Illegal whiskey.

I knitted, and I put up three score stitches, and I dropped four of them.

CATHLEEN (*counts the stitches*): It's that number is in it. (*Crying out.*) Ah, Nora, isn't it a bitter thing to think of him floating that way to the far north, and no one to keen him but the black hags that do be flying on the sea?

NORA (*swinging herself half round, and throwing out her arms on the clothes*): And isn't it a pitiful thing when there is nothing left of a man who was a great rower and fisher, but a bit of an old shirt and a plain stocking?

CATHLEEN (*after an instant*): Tell me is herself coming, Nora? I hear a little sound on the path.

NORA (*looking out*): She is, Cathleen. She's coming up to the door.

CATHLEEN: Put these things away before she'll come in. Maybe it's easier she'll be after giving her blessing to Bartley, and we won't let on we've heard anything the time he's on the sea.

NORA (*helping* CATHLEEN *to close the bundle*): We'll put them here in the corner.

(*They put them into a hole in the chimney corner.* CATHLEEN *goes back to the spinning-wheel.*)

NORA: Will she see it was crying I was?

CATHLEEN: Keep your back to the door the way the light'll not be on you.

(NORA *sits down at the chimney corner, with her back to the door.* MAURYA *comes in very slowly, without looking at the girls, and goes over to her stool at the other side of the fire. The cloth with the bread is still in her hand. The girls look at each other, and* NORA *points to the bundle of bread.*)

CATHLEEN (*after spinning for a moment*): You didn't give him his bit of bread?

(MAURYA *begins to keen softly, without turning round.*)

CATHLEEN: Did you see him riding down?

(MAURYA *goes on keening.*)

CATHLEEN (*a little impatiently*): God forgive you; isn't it a better thing to raise your voice and tell what you seen, than to be making lamentation for a thing that's done? Did you see Bartley, I'm saying to you.

MAURYA (*with a weak voice*): My heart's broken from this day.

CATHLEEN (*as before*): Did you see Bartley?

MAURYA: I seen the fearfulest thing.

CATHLEEN (*leaves her wheel and looks out*): God forgive you; he's riding the mare now over the green head, and the gray pony behind him.

MAURYA (*starts, so that her shawl falls back from her head and shows her white tossed hair. With a frightened voice*): The gray pony behind him. . . .

CATHLEEN (*coming to the fire*): What is it ails you, at all?

MAURYA (*speaking very slowly*): I've seen the fearfulest thing any person has seen, since the day Bride Dara seen the dead man with the child in his arms.

CATHLEEN *and* NORA: Uah.

(*They crouch down in front of the old woman at the fire.*)

NORA: Tell us what it is you seen.

MAURYA: I went down to the spring well, and I stood there saying a prayer to myself. Then Bartley came along, and he riding on the red mare with the gray pony behind him. (*She puts up her hands, as if to hide something from her eyes.*) The Son of God spare us, Nora!

CATHLEEN: What is it you seen?

MAURYA: I seen Michael himself.

CATHLEEN (*speaking softly*): You did not, mother. It wasn't Michael you seen, for his body is after being found in the far north, and he's got a clean burial by the grace of God.

MAURYA (*a little defiantly*): I'm after seeing him this day, and he riding and galloping. Bartley came first on the red mare; and I tried to say "God speed you," but something choked the words in my throat. He went by quickly; and "the blessing of God on you," says he, and I could say nothing. I looked up then, and I crying, at the gray pony, and there was Michael upon it — with fine clothes on him, and new shoes on his feet.

CATHLEEN (*begins to keen*): It's destroyed we are from this day. It's destroyed, surely.

NORA: Didn't the young priest say the Almighty God won't leave her destitute with no son living?

MAURYA (*in a low voice, but clearly*): It's little the like of him knows of the sea. . . . Bartley will be lost now, and let you call in Eamon and make me a good coffin out of the white boards, for I won't live after them. I've had a husband, and a husband's father, and six sons in this house — six fine men, though it was a hard birth I had with every one of them and they coming to the world — and some of them were found and some of them were not found, but they're gone now the lot of them.... There were Stephen, and Shawn, were lost in the great wind, and found after in the Bay of Gregory of the Golden Mouth, and carried up the two of them on one plank, and in by that door.

(*She pauses for a moment, the girls start as if they heard something through the door that is half open behind them.*)

NORA (*in a whisper*): Did you hear that, Cathleen? Did you hear a noise in the northeast?

CATHLEEN (*in a whisper*): There's some one after crying out by the seashore.

MAURYA (*continues without hearing anything*): There was Sheamus and his father, and his own father again, were lost in a dark night, and not a stick or sign was seen of them when the sun went up. There was Patch after was drowned out of a curragh[4] that turned over. I was sitting here with Bartley, and he a baby, lying on my two knees, and I seen two women, and three women, and four women coming in, and they crossing themselves, and not saying a word. I looked out then, and there were men coming after them, and they holding a thing in the half of a red sail, and water dripping out of it — it was a dry day, Nora — and leaving a track to the door.

(*She pauses again with her hand stretched out towards the door. It opens softly and old women begin to come in, crossing themselves on the threshold, and kneeling down in front of the stage with their backs to the people, and the white waist-bands of the red petticoats they wear over their heads just seen from behind.*)

MAURYA (*half in a dream, to* CATHLEEN): Is it Patch, or Michael, or what is it at all?

CATHLEEN: Michael is after being found in the far north, and when he is found there how could he be here in this place?

4 A fragile, open boat.

MAURYA: There does be a power of young men floating round in the sea, and what way would they know if it was Michael they had, or another man like him, for when a man is nine days in the sea, and the wind blowing, it's hard set his own mother would be to say what man was in it.

CATHLEEN: It's Michael, God spare him, for they're after sending us a bit of his clothes from the far north.

(*She reaches out and hands* MAURYA *the clothes that belonged to Michael.* MAURYA *stands up slowly, and takes them in her hands.* NORA *looks out.*)

NORA: They're carrying a thing among them and there's water dripping out of it and leaving a track by the big stones.

CATHLEEN (*in a whisper to the women who have come in*): Is it Bartley it is?

ONE OF THE WOMEN: It is surely, God rest his soul.

(*Two younger women come in and pull out the table. Then men carry in the body of* BARTLEY, *laid on a plank, with a bit of a sail over it, and lay it on the table.*)

CATHLEEN (*to the women, as they are doing so*): What way was he drowned?

ONE OF THE WOMEN: The gray pony knocked him over into the sea, and he was washed out where there is a great surf on the white rocks.

(MAURYA *has gone over and knelt down at the head of the table. The women are keening softly and swaying themselves with a slow movement.* CATHLEEN *and* NORA *kneel at the other end of the table. The men kneel near the door.*)

MAURYA (*raising her head and speaking as if she did not see the people around her*): They're all gone now, and there isn't anything more the sea can do to me.... I'll have no call now to be up crying and praying when the wind breaks from the south, and you can hear the surf is in the east, and the surf is in the west, making a great stir with the two noises, and they hitting one on the other. I'll have no call now to be going down and getting Holy Water in the dark nights after Samhain,[5] and I won't care what way the sea is when the other women will be keening. (*To* NORA.) Give me the Holy Water, Nora, there's a small cup still on the dresser.

(NORA *gives it to her.*)

MAURYA (*drops Michael's clothes across* BARTLEY's *feet, and sprinkles the Holy Water over him*): It isn't that I haven't prayed for you, Bartley, to the Almighty God. It isn't that I haven't said prayers in the dark night till you wouldn't know what I'd be saying; but it's a great rest I'll have now, and it's time surely. It's a great rest I'll have now, and great sleeping in the long nights after Samhain, if it's only a bit of wet flour we do have to eat, and maybe a fish that would be stinking.

(*She kneels down again, crossing herself, and saying prayers under her breath.*)

CATHLEEN (*to an* OLD MAN): Maybe yourself and Eamon would make a coffin when the sun rises. We have fine white boards herself bought, God help her, thinking Michael would be found, and I have a new cake you can eat while you'll be working.

THE OLD MAN (*looking at the boards*): Are there nails with them?

CATHLEEN: There are not, Colum; we didn't think of the nails.

ANOTHER MAN: It's a great wonder she wouldn't think of the nails, and all the coffins she's seen made already.

CATHLEEN: It's getting old she is, and broken.

[5] All Souls' Day, November 1.

(MAURYA *stands up again very slowly and spreads out the pieces of Michael's clothes beside the body, sprinkling them with the last of the Holy Water.*)

NORA (*in a whisper to* CATHLEEN): She's quiet now and easy; but the day Michael was drowned you could hear her crying out from this to the spring well. It's fonder she was of Michael, and would any one have thought that?

CATHLEEN (*slowly and clearly*): An old woman will be soon tired with anything she will do, and isn't it nine days herself is after crying and keening, and making great sorrow in the house?

MAURYA (*puts the empty cup mouth downwards on the table, and lays her hands together on* BARTLEY's *feet*): They're all together this time, and the end is come. May the Almighty God have mercy on Bartley's soul, and on Michael's soul, and on the souls of Sheamus and Patch, and Stephen and Shawn (*bending her head*); and may He have mercy on my soul, Nora, and on the soul of every one is left living in the world.

(*She pauses, and the keen rises a little more loudly from the women, then sinks away.*)

MAURYA (*continuing*): Michael has a clean burial in the far north, by the grace of the Almighty God. Bartley will have a fine coffin out of the white boards, and a deep grave surely. What more can we want than that? No man at all can be living for ever, and we must be satisfied.

(*She kneels down again and the curtain falls slowly.*)

Synge first visited the Aran Islands (three rocky places off the west coast of Ireland, inhabited by Gaelic-speaking fishermen) in the summer of 1898. From this visit and subsequent ones he derived the material for *The Aran Islands*, an account of life there, full of observations and bits of folklore he had picked up. In it one can find something of the origins of *Riders to the Sea*: descriptions of bringing horses across the sound, including an account of an old woman who had a vision of her drowned son riding on a horse; a reference to a coffin untimely made out of boards prepared for another person; and a reference to a body that floated ashore some weeks after the man drowned.

In writing the play Synge chose among the innumerable things he saw and heard, selecting (as any artist does) from the welter or chaos of experience to put together a unified story. One need not compare *Riders to the Sea* (in which everything is related to everything else) with *The Aran Islands* (in which we have a wonderful grab bag of scarcely related details) to see that the careful arrangement of physical happenings and dialogue gives us more than a slice of life, more than a picture of a certain kind of Irish life. Synge's art extends beyond his plot to his language. The islanders spoke Gaelic, and Synge claimed that his English was close to a translation of their language; but the speeches — as distinct from the words — are Synge's, just as Macbeth's "I am in blood / Stepped in so far, that, should I wade no more, / Returning were as tedious as go o'er" is Shakespeare's creation although the individual words are pretty much the property of any literate American or Englishman. The speeches Synge creates, no less than his plot, belong to the world of art, though the speeches and the events are made up of the materials of Aran life.

Synge chose the peasant idiom because it seemed to him to have beauty and even grandeur, while at the same time it was rooted in people who lived an elemental existence. He saw no need to choose between beauty and truth: beauty without truth led writers of the late nineteenth century (he believed) to highly wrought yet trivial or even meaningless verse, and truth without beauty to dull pictures of humankind's insignificance. It is partly by making "every speech . . . as fully flavored as a nut or apple" that Synge produced a work that (although it deals with multiple deaths) is not depressing but is, like every work of art, stimulating: "Let you go down each day, and see the sheep aren't jumping in on the rye, and if the jobber comes you can sell the pig with the black feet if there is a good price going." Even the speeches on the inevitable end of humankind have, while they call attention to a person's ignominious remains, richness and dignity: "And isn't it a pitiful thing when there is nothing left of a man who was a great rower and fisher, but a bit of an old shirt and a plain stocking?" Throughout the play this artful use of language communicates a picture of heroism and humbleness that is reassuring as well as grievous, nowhere more so than in Maurya's final speech, which calls attention to the hardness of life and the inevitability of death in such a way as almost to offer a kind of reassurance.

Early in the play Maurya spoke "querulously" and raked the fire "aimlessly." Finally, after the death of Bartley, Maurya derives some comfort from the thought that "Bartley will have a fine coffin out of the white boards," and Michael "a clean burial in the far north." She has been "hard set," known despair, seen the worst that can happen ("They're all gone now, and there isn't anything more the sea can do to me"), and now from the vantage point of one stripped of all that one has cherished, she can utter with dignity the most terrible facts of life. This is the heart of Synge's drama. The word "drama" is from the Greek verb *dran*, "to do," "to accomplish"; in *Riders to the Sea* the thing accomplished is not only the identification of Michael's clothing and the death of Bartley, but the shift in Maurya's mind.

We have been talking at some length about *Riders to the Sea* as a drama, but we have said nothing about it as a tragedy. Two of Synge's fellow Irishmen have left brief interesting comments on the play, especially on the play's relation to classical tragedy. William Butler Yeats, Synge's older contemporary, called it "quite Greek"; but James Joyce, Synge's younger contemporary, who regarded himself as one who adhered to Aristotle's *Poetics*, after reading *Riders to the Sea* sniffily remarked that "Synge isn't an Aristotelian." Joyce was especially bothered by the brevity of the play; he called it "dwarf-drama," and later, in a program note to a production of the play, he wondered "whether a brief tragedy be possible or not (a point on which Aristotle had some doubts)," though he did go on to say that *Riders to the Sea* is "the work of a tragic poet." One might learn something by considering the play in the light of some of Aristotle's remarks. This is not to say that if the play doesn't hew to Aristotle's prescriptions it is defective — and indeed Aristotle is sometimes confusing and sometimes contradictory. Still, here are a few of his comments, extracted from the fuller text of *The Poetics* that we print on pages 428–33. You may want to evaluate their relevance to *Riders to the Sea*, partly in an effort to see the strengths or weaknesses of the play, partly in an effort to see the strengths or weaknesses of *The Poetics*.

1. "Tragedy [imitates] persons [who are] above [the level of our world]" (page 428).
2. "Tragedy . . . is an imitation of an action of high importance, complete and of some amplitude; in language enhanced by . . . beauties. . . . By the beauties enhancing the language I mean rhythm and melody" (page 429).
3. "[One of] the chief means by which tragedy moves us [is] Irony of events. . . . Irony is a reversal in the course of events, . . . and, as I say, in accordance with probability or necessity" (page 431).
4. ". . . tragedy is an imitation of a whole and complete action of some amplitude. . . . as to amplitude, the invariable rule dictated by the nature of the action is the fuller the more beautiful so long as the outline remains clear" (page 430).
5. ". . . it is not the poet's business to tell what has happened, but the kind of things that would happen — what is possible according to probability or necessity" (page 430).
6. "The action imitated must contain incidents that evoke fear and pity, besides being a complete action; but this effect is accentuated when these incidents occur logically as well as unexpectedly, which will be more sensational if they happen arbitrarily, by chance" (page 431).
7. ". . . tragedy, to be at its finest, . . . should . . . imitate fearful and pitiful events. . . . pity is induced by undeserved misfortune, and fear by the misfortunes of normal people" (page 432).
8. "[Tragedy shows] the kind of man who neither is distinguished for excellence and virtue, nor comes to grief on account of baseness and vice, but on account of some error" (page 432).

DESIRE UNDER THE ELMS

Eugene O'Neill

Eugene O'Neill (1888–1953), the son of an actor, was born in a hotel room near Broadway and spent his early years traveling with his parents throughout the United States. He entered Princeton University in 1906 but left before the end of his first year. In 1909 he traveled to Honduras looking for gold, contracted malaria, and returned to the United States in 1910. After touring briefly with his father's company, he shipped to Buenos Aires, jumped ship there, did odd jobs, shipped to South Africa, and returned to the United States in 1911. The following year he learned that he had tuberculosis. In a sanatorium he began seriously reading plays, and in 1916 he joined the Provincetown Players, who put on some of his one-act plays. His first major play, *The Emperor Jones* (1920), produced by the Provincetown Players in New York, was followed in rapid succession by such plays as *Anna Christie* (1921), *Desire Under the Elms* (1924), *Strange Interlude* (1928), and *Ah, Wilderness!* (1933). In time he was awarded four Pulitzer Prizes (one, posthumous, was for *Long Day's Journey into Night*, written in 1940, but not produced until 1955), and a Nobel Prize.

CHARACTERS

EPHRAIM CABOT

SIMEON
PETER } *His sons*
EBEN

ABBIE PUTNAM

YOUNG GIRL, TWO FARMERS,
THE FIDDLER, A SHERIFF,
and other folk from the
neighboring farms.

The action of the entire play takes place in, and immediately outside of, the Cabot farmhouse in New England, in the year 1850. The south end of the house faces front to a stone wall with a wooden gate at center opening on a country road. The house is in good condition but in need of paint. Its walls are a sickly grayish, the green of the shutters faded. Two enormous elms are on each side of the house. They bend their trailing branches down over the roof. They appear to protect and at the same time subdue. There is a sinister maternity in their aspect, a crushing, jealous absorption. They have developed from their intimate contact with the life of man in the house an appalling humaneness. They brood oppressively over the house. They are like exhausted women resting their sagging breasts and hands and hair on its roof, and when it rains their tears trickle down monotonously and rot on the shingles.

Mary Morris as Abbie, Walter Huston as Cabot, and Charles Ellis as Eben in the Provincetown Players production of *Desire Under the Elms*, directed by Robert Edmond Jones, New York, 1925. (Photograph: Museum of the City of New York.)

There is a path running from the gate around the right corner of the house to the front door. A narrow porch is on this side. The end wall facing us has two windows in its upper story, two larger ones on the floor below. The two upper are those of the father's bedroom and that of the brothers. On the left, ground floor, is the kitchen — on the right, the parlor, the shades of which are always drawn down.

PART I

SCENE I

Exterior of the farmhouse. It is sunset of a day at the beginning of summer in the year 1850. There is no wind and everything is still. The sky above the roof is suffused with deep colors, the green of the elms glows, but the house is in shadow, seeming pale and washed out by contrast.

A door opens and EBEN CABOT *comes to the end of the porch and stands looking down the road to the right. He has a large bell in his hand and this he swings mechanically, awakening a deafening clangor. Then he puts his hands on his hips and stares up at the sky. He sighs with a puzzled awe and blurts out with halting appreciation.*

EBEN: God! Purty! (*His eyes fall and he stares about him frowningly. He is twenty-five, tall and sinewy. His face is well-formed, good-looking, but its expression is resentful and defensive. His defiant, dark eyes remind one of a wild animal's in captivity. Each day is a cage*

Copyright 1924 and renewed 1952 by Eugene O'Neill. Reprinted from *The Plays of Eugene O'Neill,* by Eugene O'Neill, by permission of Random House, Inc. *Caution:* Professionals and amateurs are hereby warned that this play, being fully protected under the Copyright Laws of the United States of America, the British Commonwealth, including the Dominion of Canada, and all other countries of the Berne and Universal Copyright Conventions, is subject to royalty. All rights, including professional, amateur, motion picture, recitation, lecturing, public reading, radio and television broadcasting, and the rights of translation into foreign languages, are strictly reserved. Particular emphasis is laid on the question of readings, permission for which must be secured in writing from the author's agent: Richard J. Madden Play Company, Inc., 52 Vanderbilt Ave., New York, New York.

in which he finds himself trapped but inwardly unsubdued. There is a fierce repressed vitality about him. He has black hair, mustache, a thin curly trace of beard. He is dressed in rough farm clothes.

(*He spits on the ground with intense disgust, turns and goes back into the house.*

(SIMEON *and* PETER *come in from their work in the fields. They are tall men, much older than their half-brother [*SIMEON *is thirty-nine and* PETER *thirty-seven], built on a squarer, simpler model, fleshier in body, more bovine and homelier in face, shrewder and more practical. Their shoulders stoop a bit from years of farm work. They clump heavily along in their clumsy thick-soled boots caked with earth. Their clothes, their faces, hands, bare arms and throats are earth-stained. They smell of earth. They stand together for a moment in front of the house and, as if with the one impulse, stare dumbly up at the sky, leaning on their hoes. Their faces have a compressed, unresigned expression. As they look upward, this softens.*)

SIMEON (*grudgingly*): Purty.

PETER: Ay-eh.

SIMEON (*suddenly*): Eighteen years ago.

PETER: What?

SIMEON: Jenn. My woman. She died.

PETER: I'd fergot.

SIMEON: I rec'lect — now an' agin. Makes it lonesome. She'd hair long's a hoss' tail — an' yaller like gold!

PETER: Waal — she's gone. (*This with indifferent finality — then after a pause.*) They's gold in the West, Sim.

SIMEON (*still under the influence of sunset — vaguely*): In the sky!

PETER: Waal — in a manner o' speakin' — thar's the promise. (*Growing excited.*) Gold in the sky — in the West — Golden Gate — Californi-a! — Goldest West! — fields o' gold!

SIMEON (*excited in his turn*): Fortunes layin'

just atop o' the ground waitin' t' be picked! Solomon's mines, they says! (*For a moment they continue looking up at the sky — then their eyes drop.*)

PETER (*with sardonic bitterness*): Here — it's stones atop o' the ground — stones atop o' stones — makin' stone walls — year atop o' year — him 'n' yew 'n' me 'n' then Eben — makin' stone walls fur him to fence us in!

SIMEON: We've wuked. Give our strength. Give our years. Plowed 'em under in the ground, — (*he stamps rebelliously*) — rottin' — makin' soil for his crops! (*A pause.*) Waal — the farm pays good for hereabouts.

PETER: If we plowed in Californi-a, they'd be lumps o' gold in the furrow!

SIMEON: Californi-a's t'other side o' earth, a'most. We got t' calc'late —

PETER (*after a pause*): 'Twould be hard fur me, too, to give up what we've 'arned here by our sweat. (*A pause. EBEN sticks his head out of the dining-room window, listening.*)

SIMEON: Ay-eh. (*A pause.*) Mebbe — he'll die soon.

PETER (*doubtfully*): Mebbe.

SIMEON: Mebbe — fur all we knows — he's dead now.

PETER: Ye'd need proof.

SIMEON: He's been gone two months — with no word.

PETER: Left us in the fields an evenin' like this. Hitched up an' druv off into the West. That's plum onnateral. He hain't never been off this farm 'ceptin' t' the village in thirty year or more, not since he married Eben's maw. (*A pause. Shrewdly.*) I calc'late we might git him declared crazy by the court.

SIMEON: He skinned 'em too slick. He got the best o' all on 'em. They'd never b'lieve him crazy. (*A pause.*) We got t' wait — till he's under ground.

EBEN (*with a sardonic chuckle*): Honor thy father! (*They turn, startled, and stare at him. He grins, then scowls.*) I pray he's died. (*They stare at him. He continues matter-of-factly.*) Supper's ready.

SIMEON *and* PETER (*together*): Ay-eh.

EBEN (*gazing up at the sky*): Sun's downin' purty.

SIMEON *and* PETER (*together*): Ay-eh. They's gold in the West.

EBEN: Ay-eh. (*Pointing.*) Yonder atop o' the hill pasture, ye mean?

SIMEON *and* PETER (*together*): In Californi-a!

EBEN: Hunh? (*Stares at them indifferently for a second, then drawls.*) Waal — supper's gittin' cold. (*He turns back into kitchen.*)

SIMEON (*startled — smacks his lips*): I air hungry!

PETER (*sniffing*): I smells bacon!

SIMEON (*with hungry appreciation*): Bacon's good!

PETER (*in same tone*): Bacon's bacon! (*They turn, shouldering each other, their bodies bumping and rubbing together as they hurry clumsily to their food, like two friendly oxen toward their evening meal. They disappear around the right corner of house and can be heard entering the door.*)

CURTAIN

SCENE II

The color fades from the sky. Twilight begins. The interior of the kitchen is now visible. A pine table is at center, a cookstove in the right rear corner, four rough wooden chairs, a tallow candle on the table. In the middle of the rear wall is fastened a big advertizing poster with a ship in full sail and the word "California" in big letters. Kitchen utensils hang from nails. Everything is neat and in order but the atmosphere is of a men's camp kitchen rather than that of a home.

Places for three are laid. EBEN takes boiled potatoes and bacon from the stove and puts them on the table, also a loaf of bread and a crock of water. SIMEON and PETER shoulder in, slump down in their chairs without a word. EBEN joins them. The three eat in silence for a moment, the two elder as naturally unrestrained as beasts of the field, EBEN picking at his food without appetite, glancing at them with a tolerant dislike.

SIMEON (*suddenly turns to EBEN*): Looky here! Ye'd oughtn't t' said that, Eben.

PETER: 'Twa'n't righteous.

EBEN: What?

SIMEON: Ye prayed he'd died.

EBEN: Waal — don't yew pray it? (*A pause.*)

PETER: He's our Paw.

EBEN (*violently*): Not mine!

SIMEON (*dryly*): Ye'd not let no one else say that about yer Maw! Ha! (*He gives one abrupt sardonic guffaw. PETER grins.*)

EBEN (*very pale*): I meant — I hain't his'n — I hain't like him — he hain't me!

PETER (*dryly*): Wait till ye've growed his age!

EBEN (*intensely*): I'm Maw — every drop o' blood! (*A pause. They stare at him with indifferent curiosity.*)

PETER (*reminiscently*): She was good t' Sim 'n' me. A good step-maw's scurse.

SIMEON: She was good t' everyone.

EBEN (*greatly moved, gets to his feet and makes an awkward bow to each of them — stammering*): I be thankful t' ye. I'm her — her heir. (*He sits down in confusion.*)

PETER (*after a pause — judicially*): She was good even t' him.

EBEN (*fiercely*): An' fur thanks he killed her!

SIMEON (*after a pause*): No one never kills nobody. It's allus some thin'. That's the murderer.

EBEN: Didn't he slave Maw t' death?

PETER: He's slaved himself t' death. He's slaved Sim 'n' me 'n' yew t' death — on'y none o' us hain't died — yit.

SIMEON: It's somethin' — drivin' him — t' drive us!

EBEN (*vengefully*): Waal — I hold him t' jedgment! (*Then scornfully.*) Somethin'! What's somethin'?

SIMEON: Dunno.

EBEN (*sardonically*): What's drivin' yew to Californi-a, mebbe? (*They look at him in surprise.*) Oh, I've heerd ye! (*Then, after a pause.*) But ye'll never go t' the gold fields!

PETER (*assertively*): Mebbe!

EBEN: Whar'll ye git the money?

PETER: We kin walk. It's an a'mighty ways — Californi-a — but if yew was t' put all the steps we've walked on this farm end t' end we'd be in the moon!

EBEN: The Injuns'll skulp ye on the plains.

SIMEON (*with grim humor*): We'll mebbe make 'em pay a hair fur a hair!

EBEN (*decisively*): But t'aint that. Ye won't never go because ye'll wait here fur yer share o' the farm, thinkin' allus he'll die soon.

SIMEON (*after a pause*): We've a right.

PETER: Two-thirds belong t' us.

EBEN (*jumping to his feet*): Ye've no right! She wa'n't yewr Maw! It was her farm! Didn't he steal it from her? She's dead. It's my farm.

SIMEON (*sardonically*): Tell that t' Paw — when he comes! I'll bet ye a dollar he'll laugh — fur once in his life. Ha! (*He laughs himself in one single mirthless bark.*)

PETER (*amused in turn, echoes his brother*): Ha!

SIMEON (*after a pause*): What've ye got held agin us, Eben? Year arter year it's skulked in yer eye — somethin'.

PETER: Ay-eh.

EBEN: Ay-eh. They's somethin'. (*Suddenly exploding.*) Why didn't ye never stand between him 'n' my Maw when he was slavin' her to her grave — t' pay her back fur the kindness she done t' yew? (*There is a long pause. They stare at him in surprise.*)

SIMEON: Waal — the stock's got t' be watered.

PETER: 'R they was woodin' t' do.

SIMEON: 'R plowin'.

PETER: 'R hayin'.

SIMEON: 'R spreadin' manure.

PETER: 'R weedin'.

SIMEON: 'R prunin'.

PETER: 'R milkin'.

EBEN (*breaking in harshly*): An' makin' walls — stone atop o' stone — makin' walls till yer heart's a stone ye heft up out o' the way o' growth onto a stone wall t' wall in yer heart!

SIMEON (*matter-of-factly*): We never had no time t' meddle.

PETER (*to EBEN*): Yew was fifteen afore yer Maw died — an' big fur yer age. Why didn't ye never do nothin'?

EBEN (*harshly*): They was chores t' do, wa'n't they? (*A pause — then slowly.*) It was on'y arter she died I come to think o' it. Me cookin' — doin' her work — that made me know her, suffer her sufferin' — she'd come back t' help — come back t' bile potatoes — come back t' fry bacon — come back t' bake biscuits — come back all cramped up t' shake the fire, an' carry ashes, her eyes weepin' an' bloody with smoke an' cinders same's they used t' be. She still comes back — stands by the stove thar in the evenin' — she can't find it nateral sleepin' an' restin' in peace. She can't git used t' bein' free — even in her grave.

SIMEON: She never complained none.

EBEN: She'd got too tired. She'd got too used t' bein' too tired. That was what he done. (*With vengeful passion.*) An' sooner'r later, I'll meddle. I'll say the thin's I didn't say then t' him! I'll yell 'em at the top o' my lungs. I'll see t' it my Maw gits some rest an' sleep in her grave! (*He sits down again, relapsing into a brooding silence. They look at him with a queer indifferent curiosity.*)

PETER (*after a pause*): Whar in tarnation d'ye s'pose he went, Sim?

SIMEON: Dunno. He druv off in the buggy, all spick an' span, with the mare all breshed an' shiny, druv off clackin' his tongue an' wavin' his whip. I remember it right well. I was finishin' plowin', it was spring an' May an' sunset, an' gold in the West, an' he druv off into it. I yells "Whar ye goin', Paw?" an' he hauls up by the stone wall a jiffy. His old snake's eyes was glitterin' in the sun like he'd been drinkin' a jugful an' he says with a mule's grin: "Don't ye run away till I come back!"

PETER: Wonder if he knowed we was wantin' fur Californi-a?

SIMEON: Mebbe. I didn't say nothin' and he says, lookin' kinder queer an' sick: "I been hearin' the hens cluckin' an' the roosters crowin' all the durn day. I been listenin' t' the cows lowin' an' everythin' else kickin' up till I can't stand it no more. It's spring an' I'm feelin' damned," he says. "Damned like an old bare hickory tree fit on'y fur burnin'," he says. An' then I calc'late I must've looked a mite hopeful, fur he adds real spry and vicious: "But don't git no fool idee I'm dead. I've sworn t' live a hundred an' I'll do it, if on'y t' spite yer sinful greed! An' now I'm ridin' out t' learn God's message t' me in the spring, like the prophets done. An' yew git back t' yer plowin'," he says. An' he druv off singin' a hymn. I thought he was drunk — 'r I'd stopped him goin'.

EBEN (*scornfully*): No, ye wouldn't! Ye're scared o' him. He's stronger — inside — than both o' ye put together!

PETER (*sardonically*): An' yew — be yew Samson?

EBEN: I'm gittin' stronger. I kin feel it growin' in me — growin' an' growin' — till it'll bust out — ! (*He gets up and puts on his coat and a hat. They watch him, gradually breaking into grins. EBEN avoids their eyes sheepishly.*) I'm goin' out fur a spell — up the road.

PETER: T' the village?

SIMEON: T' the village?

SIMEON: T' see Minnie?

EBEN (*defiantly*): Ay-eh?

PETER (*jeeringly*): The Scarlet Woman!

SIMEON: Lust — that's what's growin' in ye!

EBEN: Waal — she's purty!

PETER: She's been purty fur twenty year!

SIMEON: A new coat o' paint'll make a heifer out of forty.

EBEN: She hain't forty!

PETER: If she hain't, she's teeterin' on the edge.

EBEN (*desperately*): What d'yew know —

PETER: All they is . . . Sim knew her — an' then me arter —

SIMEON: An' Paw kin tell yew somethin' too! He was fust!

EBEN: D'ye mean t' say he . . . ?

SIMEON (*with a grin*): Ay-eh! We air his heirs in everythin'!

EBEN (*intensely*): That's more to it! That grows on it! It'll bust soon! (*Then violently.*) I'll go smash my fist in her face! (*He pulls open the door in rear violently.*)

SIMEON (*with a wink at PETER — drawlingly*): Mebbe — but the night's wa'm — purty — by the time ye git thar mebbe ye'll kiss her instead!

PETER: Sart'n he will! (*They both roar with coarse laughter. EBEN rushes out and slams the door — then the outside front door — comes around the corner of the house and stands still by the gate, staring up at the sky.*)

SIMEON (*looking after him*): Like his Paw.

PETER: Dead spit an' image!

SIMEON: Dog'll eat dog!

PETER: Ay-eh. (*Pause. With yearning.*) Mebbe a year from now we'll be in Californi-a.

SIMEON: Ay-eh. (*A pause. Both yawn.*) Let's git t' bed. (*He blows out the candle. They go out door in rear. EBEN stretches his arms up to the sky — rebelliously.*)

EBEN: Waal — thar's a star, an' somewhar's they's him, an' here's me, an' thar's Min up the road — in the same night. What if I does kiss her? She's like t'night, she's soft 'n' wa'm, her eyes kin wink like a star, her mouth's wa'm, her arms're wa'm, she smells like a wa'm plowed field, she's purty . . . Ay-eh! By God A'mighty she's purty, an' I don't give a damn how many sins she's sinned afore mine or who she's sinned 'em with, my sin's as purty as any one of 'em! (*He strides off down the road to the left.*)

CURTAIN

SCENE III

It is the pitch darkness just before dawn. EBEN comes in from the left and goes around to the porch, feeling his way, chuckling bitterly and cursing half-aloud to himself.

EBEN: The cussed old miser! (*He can be heard going in the front door. There is a pause as he goes upstairs, then a loud knock on the bedroom door of the brothers.*) Wake up!

SIMEON (*startledly*): Who's thar?

EBEN (*pushing open the door and coming in, a lighted candle in his hand. The bedroom of the brothers is revealed. Its ceiling is the sloping roof. They can stand upright only close to the center dividing wall of the upstairs. SIMEON and PETER are in a double bed, front. EBEN's cot is to the rear. EBEN has a mixture of silly grin and vicious scowl on his face.*) I be!

PETER (*angrily*): What in hell's-fire . . . ?

EBEN: I got news fur ye! Ha! (*He gives one abrupt sardonic guffaw.*)

SIMEON (*angrily*): Couldn't ye hold it 'til we'd got our sleep?

EBEN: It's nigh sunup. (*Then explosively.*) He's gone an' married agen!

SIMEON *and* PETER (*explosively*): Paw?

EBEN: Got himself hitched to a female 'bout thirty-five — an' purty, they says . . .

SIMEON (*aghast*): It's a durn lie!

PETER: Who says?

SIMEON: They been stringin' ye!

EBEN: Think I'm a dunce, do ye? The hull village says. The preacher from New Dover, he brung the news — told it t' our preacher — New Dover, that's whar the old loon got himself hitched — that's whar the woman lived —

PETER (*no longer doubting — stunned*): Waal . . . !

SIMEON (*the same*): Waal . . . !

EBEN (*sitting down on a bed — with vicious hatred*): Ain't he a devil out o' hell? It's jest t' spite us — the damned old mule!

PETER (*after a pause*): Everythin'll go t' her now.

SIMEON: Ay-eh. (*A pause — dully.*) Waal — if it's done —

PETER: It's done us. (*Pause — then persuasively.*) They's gold in the fields o' Californi-a, Sim. No good a-stayin' here now.

SIMEON: Jest what I was a-thinkin'. (*Then with decision.*) S'well fust's last! Let's light out and git this mornin'.

PETER: Suits me.

EBEN: Ye must like walkin'.

SIMEON (*sardonically*): If ye'd grow wings on us we'd fly thar!

EBEN: Ye'd like ridin' better — on a boat, wouldn't ye? (*Fumbles in his pocket and takes out a crumpled sheet of foolscap.*) Waal, if ye

sign this ye kin ride on a boat. I've had it writ out an' ready in case ye'd ever go. It says fur three hundred dollars t' each ye agree yewr shares o' the farm is sold t' me. (*They look suspiciously at the paper. A pause.*)

SIMEON (*wonderingly*): But if he's hitched agen —

PETER: An' whar'd yew git that sum o' money, anyways?

EBEN (*cunningly*): I know whar it's hid. I been waitin' — Maw told me. She knew whar it lay fur years, but she was waitin' . . . It's her'n — the money he hoarded from her farm an' hid from Maw. It's my money by rights now.

PETER: Whar's it hid?

EBEN (*cunningly*): Whar yew won't never find it without me. Maw spied on him — 'r she'd never knowed. (*A pause. They look at him suspiciously, and he at them.*) Waal, is it fa'r trade?

SIMEON: Dunno.

PETER: Dunno.

SIMEON (*looking at window*): Sky's grayin'.

PETER: Ye better start the fire, Eben.

SIMEON: An' fix some vittles.

EBEN: Ay-eh. (*Then with a forced jocular heartiness.*) I'll git ye a good one. If ye're startin' t' hoof it t' Californi-a ye'll need somethin' that'll stick t' yer ribs. (*He turns to the door, adding meaningly.*) But ye kin ride on a boat if ye'll swap. (*He stops at the door and pauses. They stare at him.*)

SIMEON (*suspiciously*): Whar was ye all night?

EBEN (*defiantly*): Up t' Min's. (*Then slowly.*) Walkin' thar, fust I felt 's if I'd kiss her; then I got a-thinkin' o' what ye'd said o' him an' her an' I says, I'll bust her nose fur that! Then I got t' the village an' heerd the news an' I got madder'n hell an' run all the way t' Min's not knowin' what I'd do — (*He pauses — then sheepishly but more defiantly.*) Waal — when I seen her, I didn't hit her — nor I didn't kiss her nuther — I begun t' beller like a calf an' cuss at the same time, I was so durn mad — an' she got scared — an' I jest grabbed holt an' tuk her! (*Proudly.*) Yes, sirree! I tuk her. She may've been his'n — an' your'n, too — but she's mine now!

SIMEON (*dryly*): In love, air yew?

EBEN (*with lofty scorn*): Love! I don't take no stock in sech slop!

PETER (*winking at* SIMEON): Mebbe Eben's aimin' t' marry, too.

SIMEON: Min'd make a true faithful he'p-meet! (*They snicker.*)

EBEN: What do I care fur her — 'ceptin' she's round an' wa'm? The p'int is she was his'n — an' now she b'longs t' me! (*He goes to the door — then turns — rebelliously.*) An' Min hain't sech a bad un. They's worse'n Min in the world, I'll bet ye! Wait'll we see this cow the Old Man's hitched t'! She'll beat Min, I got a notion! (*He starts to go out.*)

SIMEON (*suddenly*): Mebbe ye'll try t' make her your'n, too?

PETER: Ha! (*He gives a sardonic laugh of relish at this idea.*)

EBEN (*spitting with disgust*): Her — here — sleepin' with him — stealin' my Maw's farm! I'd as soon pet a skunk 'r kiss a snake! (*He goes out. The two stare after him suspiciously. A pause. They listen to his steps receding.*)

PETER: He's startin' the fire.

SIMEON: I'd like t' ride t' Californi-a — but —

PETER: Min might o' put some scheme in his head.

SIMEON: Mebbe it's all a lie 'bout Paw marryin'. We'd best wait an' see the bride.

PETER: An' don't sign nothin' till we does!

SIMEON: Nor till we've tested it's good money! (*Then with a grin.*) But if Paw's hitched we'd be sellin' Eben somethin' we'd never git nohow!

PETER: We'll wait an' see. (*Then with sudden vindictive anger.*) An' till he comes, let's yew 'n' me not wuk a lick, let Eben tend to thin's if he's a mind t', let's us jest sleep an' eat an' drink likker an' let the hull damned farm go t' blazes!

SIMEON (*excitedly*): By God, we've 'arned a rest! We'll play rich fur a change. I hain't a-going to stir outa bed till breakfast's ready.

PETER: An' on the table!

SIMEON (*after a pause — thoughtfully*): What d'ye calc'late she'll be like — our new Maw? Like Eben thinks?

PETER: More'n' likely.

SIMEON (*vindictively*): Waal — I hope she's a she-devil that'll make him wish he was dead an' livin' in the pit o' hell fur comfort!

PETER (*fervently*): Amen!

SIMEON (*imitating his father's voice*): "I'm ridin' out t' learn God's message t' me in the spring like the prophets done," he says. I'll bet right then an' thar he knew plumb well he was goin' whorin', the stinkin' old hypocrite!

CURTAIN

SCENE IV

Same as Scene II — shows the interior of the kitchen with a lighted candle on table. It is gray dawn outside. SIMEON *and* PETER *are just finishing their breakfast.* EBEN *sits before his plate of untouched food, brooding frowningly.*

PETER (*glancing at him rather irritably*): Lookin' glum don't help none.

SIMEON (*sarcastically*): Sorrowin' over his lust o' the flesh!

PETER (*with a grin*): Was she yer fust?

EBEN (*angrily*): None o' yer business. (*A pause.*) I was thinkin' o' him. I got a notion he's gittin' near — I kin feel him comin' on like yew kin feel malaria chill afore it takes ye.

PETER: It's too early yet.

SIMEON: Dunno. He'd like t' catch us nappin' — jest t' have somethin' t' hoss us 'round over.

PETER (*mechanically gets to his feet.* SIMEON *does the same*): Waal — let's git t' wuk. (*They both plod mechanically toward the door before they realize. Then they stop short.*)

SIMEON (*grinning*): Ye're a cussed fool, Pete — and I be wuss! Let him see we hain't wukin'! We don't give a durn!

PETER (*as they go back to the table*): Not a damned durn! It'll serve t' show him we're done with him. (*They sit down again.* EBEN *stares from one to the other with surprise.*)

SIMEON (*grins at him*): We're aimin' t' start bein' lilies o' the field.

PETER: Nary a toil 'r spin 'r lick o' wuk do we put in!

SIMEON: Ye're sole owner — till he comes — that's what ye wanted. Waal, ye got t' be sole hand, too.

PETER: The cows air bellerin'. Ye better hustle at the milkin'.

EBEN (*with excited joy*): Ye mean ye'll sign the paper?

SIMEON (*dryly*): Mebbe.

PETER: Mebbe.

SIMEON: We're considerin'. (*Peremptorily.*) Ye better git t' wuk.

EBEN (*with queer excitement*): It's Maw's farm agen! It's my farm! Them's my cows! I'll milk my durn fingers off fur cows o' mine! (*He goes out door in rear, they stare after him indifferently.*)

SIMEON: Like his Paw.

PETER: Dead spit 'n' image!

SIMEON: Waal — let dog eat dog! (EBEN *comes out of front door and around the corner of the house. The sky is beginning to grow flushed with sunrise.* EBEN *stops by the gate and stares around him with glowing, possessive eyes. He takes in the whole farm with his embracing glance of desire.*)

EBEN: It's purty! It's damned purty! It's mine! (*He suddenly throws his head back boldly and glares with hard, defiant eyes at the sky.*) Mine, d'ye hear? Mine! (*He turns and walks quickly off left, rear, toward the barn. The two brothers light their pipes.*)

SIMEON (*putting his muddy boots up on the table, tilting back his chair, and puffing defiantly*): Waal — this air solid comfort — fur once.

PETER: Ay-eh. (*He follows suit. A pause. Unconsciously they both sigh.*)

SIMEON (*suddenly*): He never was much o' a hand at milkin', Eben wa'n't.

PETER (*with a snort*): His hands air like hoofs! (*A pause.*)

SIMEON: Reach down the jug thar! Let's take a swaller. I'm feelin' kind o' low.

PETER: Good idee! (*He does so — gets two glasses — they pour out drinks of whisky.*) Here's t' the gold in Californi-a!

SIMEON: An' luck t' find it! (*They drink — puff resolutely — sigh — take their feet down from the table.*)

PETER: Likker don't 'pear t' sot right.

SIMEON: We hain't used t' it this early. (*A pause. They become very restless.*)

PETER: Gittin' close in this kitchen.

SIMEON (*with immense relief*): Let's git a breath o' air. (*They arise briskly and go out rear — appear around house and stop by the gate. They stare up at the sky with a numbed appreciation.*)

PETER: Purty!

SIMEON: Ay-eh. Gold's t' the East now.

PETER: Sun's startin' with us fur the Golden West.

SIMEON (*staring around the farm, his compressed face tightened, unable to conceal his emotion*): Waal — it's our last mornin' — mebbe.

PETER (*the same*): Ay-eh.

SIMEON (*stamps his foot on the earth and addresses it desperately*): Waal — ye've thirty year o' me buried in ye — spread out over ye — blood an' bone an' sweat — rotted away — fertilizin' ye — richin' yer soul — prime manure, by God, that's what I been t' ye!

PETER: Ay-eh! An' me!

SIMEON: An' yew, Peter. (*He sighs — then spits.*) Waal — no use'n cryin' over spilt milk.

PETER: They's gold in the West — an' freedom, mebbe. We been slaves t' stone walls here.

SIMEON (*defiantly*): We hain't nobody's slaves from this out — nor no thin's slaves nuther. (*A pause — restlessly.*) Speakin' o' milk, wonder how Eben's managin'?

PETER: I s'pose he's managin'.

SIMEON: Mebbe we'd ought t' help — this once.

PETER: Mebbe. The cows knows us.

SIMEON: An' likes us. They don't know him much.

PETER: An' the hosses, an' pigs, an' chickens. They don't know him much.

SIMEON: They knows us like brothers — an' likes us! (*Proudly.*) Hain't we raised 'em t' be fust-rate, number one prize stock?

PETER: We hain't — not no more.

SIMEON (*dully*): I was fergittin'. (*Then resignedly.*) Waal, let's go help Eben a spell an' git waked up.

PETER: Suits me. (*They are starting off down left, rear, for the barn when* EBEN *appears from there hurrying toward them, his face excited.*)

EBEN (*breathlessly*): Waal — thar they be! The old mule an' the bride! I seen 'em from the barn down below at the turnin'.

PETER: How could ye tell that far?

EBEN: Hain't I as far-sight as he's near-sight? Don't I know the mare 'n' buggy, an' two people settin' in it? Who else . . . ? An' I tell ye I kin feel 'em a-comin', too! (*He squirms as if he had the itch.*)

PETER (*beginning to be angry*): Waal — let him do his own unhitchin'!

SIMEON (*angry in his turn*): Let's hustle in an' git our bundles an' be a-goin' as he's a-comin'. I don't want never t' step inside the door agen arter he's back. (*They both start back around the corner of the house.* EBEN *follows them.*)

EBEN (*anxiously*): Will ye sign it afore ye go?

PETER: Let's see the color o' the old skinflint's money an' we'll sign. (*They disappear left. The two brothers clump upstairs to get their bundles.* EBEN *appears in the kitchen, runs to window, peers out, comes back and pulls up a strip of flooring in under stove, takes out a canvas bag and puts it on table, then sets the floorboard back in place. The two brothers appear a moment after. They carry old carpetbags.*)

EBEN (*puts his hand on bag guardingly*): Have ye signed?

SIMEON (*shows paper in his hand*): Ay-eh. (*Greedily.*) Be that the money?

EBEN (*opens bag and pours out pile of twenty-dollar gold pieces*): Twenty-dollar pieces — thirty of 'em. Count 'em. (*Peter does so, arranging them in stacks of five, biting one or two to test them.*)

PETER: Six hundred. (*He puts them in bag and puts it inside his shirt carefully.*)

SIMEON (*handing paper to* EBEN): Har ye be.

EBEN (*after a glance, folds it carefully and hides it under his shirt — gratefully*): Thank yew.

PETER: Thank yew fur the ride.

SIMEON: We'll send ye a lump o' gold fur Christmas. (*A pause.* EBEN *stares at them and they at him.*)

PETER (*awkwardly*): Waal — we're a-goin'.

SIMEON: Comin' out t' the yard?

EBEN: No. I'm waitin' in here a spell. (*Another silence. The brothers edge awkwardly to door in rear — then turn and stand.*)

SIMEON: Waal — good-by.

PETER: Good-by.

EBEN: Good by. (*They go out. He sits down at the table, faces the stove and pulls out the paper. He looks from it to the stove. His face, lighted up by the shaft of sunlight from the window, has an expression of trance. His lips move. The two brothers come out to the gate.*)

PETER (*looking off toward barn*): Thar he be — unhitchin'.

SIMEON (*with a chuckle*): I'll bet ye he's riled!

PETER: An' thar she be.

SIMEON: Let's wait 'n' see what our new Maw looks like.

PETER (*with a grin*): An' give him our partin' cuss!

SIMEON (*grinning*): I feel like raisin' fun. I feel light in my head an' feet.

PETER: Me, too. I feel like laffin' till I'd split up the middle.

SIMEON: Reckon it's the likker?

PETER: No. My feet feel itchin' t' walk an' walk — an' jump high over thin's — an'. . . .

SIMEON: Dance? (*A pause.*)

PETER (*puzzled*): It's plumb onnateral.

SIMEON (*a light coming over his face*): I calc'late it's 'cause school's out. It's holiday. Fur once we're free!

PETER (*dazedly*): Free?

SIMEON: The halter's broke — the harness is busted — the fence bars is down — the stone walls air crumblin' an' tumblin'! We'll be kickin' up an' tearin' away down the road!

PETER (*drawing a deep breath — oratorically*): Anybody that wants this stinkin' old rock-pile of a farm kin hev it. T'ain't our'n, no sirree!

SIMEON (*takes the gate off its hinges and puts it under his arm*): We harby 'bolishes shet gates, an' open gates, an' all gates, by thunder!

PETER: We'll take it with us fur luck an' let 'er sail free down some river.

SIMEON (*as a sound of voices comes from left, rear*): Har they comes! (*The two brothers congeal into two stiff, grim-visaged statues.* EPHRAIM CABOT *and* ABBIE PUTNAM *come in.* CABOT *is seventy-five, tall and gaunt, with great, wiry, concentrated power, but stooped-shouldered from toil. His face is as hard as if it were hewn out of a boulder, yet there is a weakness in it, a petty pride in its own narrow strength. His eyes are small, close together, and extremely near-sighted, blinking continually in the effort to focus on objects, their stare having a straining, ingrowing quality. He is dressed in his dismal black Sunday suit.* ABBIE *is thirty-five, buxom, full of vitality. Her round face is pretty but marred by its rather gross sensuality. There is strength and obstinacy in her jaw, a hard determination in her eyes, and about her whole personality the same unsettled, untamed, desperate quality which is so apparent in* EBEN.)

CABOT (*as they enter — a queer strangled emotion in his dry cracking voice*): Har we be t' hum, Abbie.

ABBIE (*with lust for the word*): Hum! (*Her eyes gloating on the house without seeming to see the two stiff figures at the gate.*) It's purty — purty! I can't b'lieve it's r'ally mine.

CABOT (*sharply*): Yewr'n? Mine! (*He stares at her penetratingly, she stares back. He adds relentingly.*) Our'n — mebbe! It was lonesome too long. I was growin' old in the spring. A hum's got t' hev a woman.

ABBIE (*her voice taking possession*): A woman's got t' hev a hum!

CABOT (*nodding uncertainly*): Ay-eh. (*Then irritably.*) Whar be they? Ain't thar nobody about — 'r wukin' — 'r nothin'?

ABBIE (*sees the brothers. She returns their stare of cold appraising contempt with interest — slowly*): Thar's two men loafin' at the gate an' starin' at me like a couple o' strayed hogs.

CABOT (*straining his eyes*): I kin see 'em — but I can't make out. . . .

SIMEON: It's Simeon.

PETER: It's Peter.

CABOT (*exploding*): Why hain't ye wukin'?

SIMEON (*dryly*): We're waitin' t' welcome ye hum — yew an' the bride!

CABOT (*confusedly*): Huh? Waal — this be yer new Maw, boys. (*She stares at them and they at her.*)

SIMEON (*turns away and spits contemptuously*): I see her!

PETER (*spits also*): An' I see her!

ABBIE (*with the conqueror's conscious superiority*): I'll go in an' look at *my* house. (*She goes slowly around to porch.*)

SIMEON (*with a snort*): Her house!

PETER (*calls after her*): Ye'll find Eben inside. Ye better not tell him it's *yewr* house.

ABBIE (*mouthing the name*): Eben. (*Then quietly*) I'll tell Eben.

CABOT (*with a contemptuous sneer*): Ye needn't heed Eben. Eben's a dumb fool — like his Maw — soft an' simple!

SIMEON (*with his sardonic burst of laughter*): Ha! Eben's a chip o' yew — spit 'n' image — hard 'n' bitter's a hickory tree! Dog'll eat dog. He'll eat ye yet, old man!

CABOT (*commandingly*): Ye git t' wuk!

SIMEON (*as ABBIE disappears in house — winks at PETER and says tauntingly*): So that thar's our new Maw, be it? Whar in hell did ye dig her up? (*He and PETER laugh.*)

PETER: Ha! Ye'd better turn her in the pen with the other sows. (*They laugh uproariously, slapping their thighs.*)

CABOT (*so amazed at their effrontery that he stutters in confusion*): Simeon! Peter! What's come over ye? Air ye drunk?

SIMEON: We're free, old man — free o' yew an' the hull damned farm! (*They grow more and more hilarious and excited.*)

PETER: An' we're startin' out fur the gold fields o' Californi-a!

SIMEON: Ye kin take this place an' burn it!

PETER: An' bury it — fur all we cares!

SIMEON: We're free, old man! (*He cuts a caper.*)

PETER: Free! (*He gives a kick in the air.*)

SIMEON (*in a frenzy*): Whoop!

PETER: Whoop! (*They do an absurd Indian war dance about the old man who is petrified between rage and the fear that they are insane.*)

SIMEON: We're free as Injuns! Lucky we don't skulp ye!

PETER: An' burn yer barn an' kill the stock!

SIMEON: An' rape yer new woman! Whoop! (*He and PETER stop their dance, holding their sides, rocking with wild laughter.*)

CABOT (*edging away*): Lust fur gold — fur the sinful, easy gold o' Californi-a! It's made ye mad!

SIMEON (*tauntingly*): Wouldn't ye like us to send ye back some sinful gold, ye old sinner?

PETER: They's gold besides what's in Californi-a! (*He retreats back beyond the vision of the old man and takes the bag of money and flaunts it in the air above his head, laughing.*)

SIMEON: And sinfuller, too!

PETER: We'll be voyagin' on the sea! Whoop! (*He leaps up and down.*)

SIMEON: Livin' free! Whoop! (*He leaps in turn.*)

CABOT (*suddenly roaring with rage*): My cuss on ye!

SIMEON: Take our'n in trade fur it! Whoop!

CABOT: I'll hev ye both chained up in the asylum!

PETER: Ye old skinflint! Good-by!

SIMEON: Ye old blood sucker! Good-by!

CABOT: Go afore I . . . !

PETER: Whoop! (*He picks a stone from the road. SIMEON does the same.*)

SIMEON: Maw'll be in the parlor.

PETER: Ay-eh! One! Two!

CABOT (*frightened*): What air ye . . . ?

PETER: Three! (*They both throw, the stones hitting the parlor window with a crash of glass, tearing the shade.*)

SIMEON: Whoop!

PETER: Whoop!

CABOT (*in a fury now, rushing toward them*): If I kin lay hands on ye — I'll break yer bones fur ye! (*But they beat a capering retreat before him, SIMEON with the gate still under his arm. CABOT comes back, panting with impotent rage.*)

Their voices as they go off take up the song of the gold-seekers to the old tune of "Oh, Susannah!"

"I jumped aboard the Liza ship,
And traveled on the sea,
And every time I thought of home
I wished it wasn't me!
Oh! Californi-a,
That's the land fur me!
I'm off to Californi-a!
With my wash bowl on my knee."

(*In the meantime, the window of the upper bedroom on right is raised and* ABBIE *sticks her head out. She looks down at* CABOT — *with a sigh of relief.*)

ABBIE: Waal — that's the last o' them two, hain't it? (*He doesn't answer. Then in possessive tones.*) This here's a nice bedroom, Ephraim. It's a r'al nice bed. Is it my room, Ephraim?

CABOT (*grimly — without looking up*): Our'n! (*She cannot control a grimace of aversion and pulls back her head slowly and shuts the window. A sudden horrible thought seems to enter* CABOT's *head.*) They been up to somethin'! Mebbe — mebbe they've pizened the stock — 'r somethin'! (*He almost runs off down toward the barn. A moment later the kitchen door is slowly pushed open and* ABBIE *enters. For a moment she stands looking at* EBEN. *He does not notice her at first. Her eyes take him in penetratingly with a calculating appraisal of his strength as against hers. But under this her desire is dimly awakened by his youth and good looks. Suddenly he becomes conscious of her presence and looks up. Their eyes meet. He leaps to his feet, glowering at her speechlessly.*)

ABBIE (*in her most seductive tones which she uses all through this scene*): Be you — Eben? I'm Abbie — (*She laughs.*) I mean, I'm yer new Maw.

EBEN (*viciously*): No, damn ye!

ABBIE (*as if she hadn't heard — with a queer smile*): Yer Paw's spoke a lot o' yew. . . .

EBEN: Ha!

ABBIE: Ye mustn't mind him. He's an old man. (*A long pause. They stare at each other.*) I don't want t' pretend playin' Maw t' ye, Eben. (*Admiringly.*) Ye're too big an' too strong fur that. I want t' be frens with ye. Mebbe with me fur a fren ye'd find ye'd like livin' here better. I kin make it easy fur ye with him, mebbe. (*With a scornful sense of power.*) I

calc'late I kin git him t' do most anythin' fur me.

EBEN (*with bitter scorn*): Ha! (*They stare again,* EBEN *obscurely moved, physically attracted to her — in forced stilted tones.*) Yew kin go t' the devil!

ABBIE (*calmly*): If cussin' me does ye good, cuss all ye've a mind t'. I'm all prepared t' have ye agin me — at fust. I don't blame ye nuther. I'd feel the same at any stranger comin' t' take my Maw's place. (*He shudders. She is watching him carefully.*) Yew must've cared a lot fur yewr Maw, didn't ye? My Maw died afore I'd growed. I don't remember her none. (*A pause.*) But yew won't hate me long, Eben. I'm not the wust in the world — an' yew an' me've got a lot in common. I kin tell that by lookin' at ye. Waal — I've had a hard life, too — oceans o' trouble an' nuthin' but wuk fur reward. I was a orphan early an' had t' wuk fur others in other folks' hums. Then I married an' he turned out a drunken spreer an' so he had to wuk fur others an' me too agen in other folks' hums, an' the baby died, an' my husband got sick an' died too, an' I was glad sayin' now I'm free fur once, on'y I diskivered right away all I was free fur was t' wuk agen in other folks' hums, doin' other folks' wuk till I'd most give up hope o' ever doin' my own wuk in my own hum, an' then your Paw come. . . . (CABOT *appears returning from the barn. He comes to the gate and looks down the road the brothers have gone. A faint strain of their retreating voices is heard:* "Oh, Californi-a! That's the place for me." *He stands glowering, his fist clenched, his face grim with rage.*)

EBEN (*fighting against his growing attraction and sympathy — harshly*): An' bought yew — like a harlot! (*She is stung and flushes angrily. She has been sincerely moved by the recital of her troubles. He adds furiously.*) An' the price he's payin' ye — this farm — was my Maw's, damn ye! — an' mine now!

ABBIE (*with a cool laugh of confidence*): Yewr'n? We'll see 'bout that! (*Then strongly.*) Waal — what if I did need a hum? What else'd I marry an old man like him fur?

EBEN (*maliciously*): I'll tell him ye said that!

ABBIE (*smiling*): I'll say ye're lyin' a-purpose — an' he'll drive ye off the place!

EBEN: Ye devil!

ABBIE (*defying him*): This be my farm — this be my hum — this be my kitchen — !

EBEN (*furiously, as if he were going to attack her*): Shut up, damn ye!

ABBIE (*walks up to him — a queer coarse expression of desire in her face and body — slowly*): An' upstairs — that be my bedroom — an' my bed! (*He stares into her eyes, terribly confused and torn. She adds softly.*) I hain't bad nor mean — 'ceptin' fur an enemy — but I got t' fight fur what's due me out o' life, if I ever 'spect t' git it. (*Then putting her hand on his arm — seductively.*) Let's yew 'n' me be frens, Eben.

EBEN (*stupidly — as if hypnotized*): Ay-eh. (*Then furiously flinging off her arm.*) No, ye durned old witch! I hate ye! (*He rushes out the door.*)

ABBIE (*looks after him smiling satisfiedly — then half to herself, mouthing the words*): Eben's nice. (*She looks at the table, proudly.*) I'll wash up *my* dishes now. (EBEN *appears outside, slamming the door behind him. He comes around corner, stops on seeing his father, and stands staring at him with hate.*)

CABOT (*raising his arms to heaven in the fury he can no longer control*): Lord God o' Hosts, smite the undutiful sons with Thy wust cuss!

EBEN (*breaking in violently*): Yew 'n' yewr God! Allus cussin' folks — allus naggin' 'em!

CABOT (*oblivious to him — summoningly*): God o' the old! God o' the lonesome!

EBEN (*mockingly*): Naggin' His sheep t' sin! T' hell with yewr God! (CABOT *turns. He and* EBEN *glower at each other.*)

CABOT (*harshly*): So it's yew. I might've knowed it. (*Shaking his finger threateningly at him.*) Blasphemin' fool! (*Then quickly.*) Why hain't ye t' wuk?

EBEN: Why hain't yew? They've went. I can't wuk it all alone.

CABOT (*contemptuously*): Nor noways! I'm wuth ten o' ye yit, old's I be! Ye'll never be more'n half a man! (*Then, matter-of-factly.*) Waal — let's git t' the barn. (*They go. A last faint note of the "Californi-a" song is heard from the distance.* ABBIE *is washing her dishes.*)

CURTAIN

PART II

SCENE I

The exterior of the farmhouse, as in Part I — a hot Sunday afternoon two months later.

ABBIE, *dressed in her best, is discovered sitting in a rocker at the end of the porch. She rocks listlessly, enervated by the heat, staring in front of her with bored, half-closed eyes.*

EBEN *sticks his head out of his bedroom window. He looks around furtively and tries to see — or hear — if anyone is on the porch, but although he has been careful to make no noise,* ABBIE *has sensed his movement. She stops rocking, her face grows animated and eager, she waits attentively.* EBEN *seems to feel her presence, he scowls back his thoughts of her and spits with exaggerated disdain — then withdraws back into the room.* ABBIE *waits, holding her breath as she listens with passionate eagerness for every sound within the house.*

EBEN *comes out. Their eyes meet. His falter, he is confused, he turns away and slams the door resentfully. At this gesture,* ABBIE *laughs tantalizingly, amused but at the same time piqued and irritated. He scowls, strides off the porch to the path and starts to walk past her to the road with a grand swagger of ignoring her existence. He is dressed in his store suit, spruced up, his face shines from soap and water.* ABBIE *leans forward on her chair, her eyes hard and angry now, and, as he passes her, gives a sneering, taunting chuckle.*

EBEN (*stung — turns on her furiously*): What air yew cacklin' 'bout?

ABBIE (*triumphant*): Yew!

EBEN: What about me?

ABBIE: Ye look all slicked up like a prize bull.

EBEN (*with a sneer*): Waal — ye hain't so durned purty yerself, be ye? (*They stare into each other's eyes, his held by hers in spite of himself, hers glowingly possessive. Their physical attraction becomes a palpable force quivering in the hot air.*)

ABBIE (*softly*): Ye don't mean that, Eben. Ye may think ye mean it, mebbe, but ye don't. Ye can't. It's agin nature, Eben. Ye been fightin' yer nature ever since the day I come — tryin' t' tell yerself I hain't purty t'ye. (*She laughs a low humid laugh without taking her eyes from his. A pause — her body squirms desirously — she murmurs languorously.*) Hain't the sun strong an' hot? Ye kin feel it burnin' into the earth — Nature — makin' thin's grow — bigger 'n' bigger — burnin' inside ye — makin' ye want t' grow — into somethin' else — till ye're jined with it — an' it's your'n — but it owns ye, too — an' makes ye grow bigger — like a tree — like them elums — (*She laughs again softly, holding his eyes. He takes a step toward her, compelled against his will.*) Nature'll beat ye, Eben. Ye might's well own up t' it fust 's last.

EBEN (*trying to break from her spell — confusedly*): If Paw'd hear ye goin' on.... (*Resentfully.*) But ye've made such a damned idjit out o' the old devil ...! (ABBIE *laughs.*)

ABBIE: Waal — hain't it easier fur yew with him changed softer?

EBEN (*defiantly*): No. I'm fightin' him — fightin' yew — fightin' fur Maw's rights t' her hum! (*This breaks her spell for him. He glowers at her.*) An' I'm onto ye. Ye hain't foolin' me a mite. Ye're aimin' t' swaller up everythin' an' make it your'n. Waal, you'll find I'm a heap sight bigger hunk nor yew kin chew! (*He turns from her with a sneer.*)

ABBIE (*trying to regain her ascendancy — seductively*): Eben!

EBEN: Leave me be! (*He starts to walk away.*)

ABBIE (*more commandingly*): Eben!

EBEN (*stops — resentfully*): What d'ye want?

ABBIE (*trying to conceal a growing excitement*): Whar air ye goin'?

EBEN (*with malicious nonchalance*): Oh — up the road a spell.

ABBIE: T' the village?

EBEN (*airily*): Mebbe.

ABBIE (*excitedly*): T' see that Min, I s'pose?

EBEN: Mebbe.

ABBIE (*weakly*): What d'ye want t' waste time on her fur?

EBEN (*revenging himself now — grinning at her*): Ye can't beat Nature, didn't ye say? (*He laughs and again starts to walk away.*)

ABBIE (*bursting out*): An ugly old hake!

EBEN (*with a tantalizing sneer*): She's purtier'n yew be!

ABBIE: That every wuthless drunk in the country has....

EBEN (*tauntingly*): Mebbe — but she's better'n yew. She owns up fa'r 'n' squar' t' her doin's.

ABBIE (*furiously*): Don't ye dare compare....

EBEN: She don't go sneakin' an' stealin' — what's mine.

ABBIE (*savagely seizing on his weak point*): Your'n? Yew mean — my farm?

EBEN: I mean the farm yew sold yerself fur like any other old whore — my farm!

ABBIE (*stung — fiercely*): Ye'll never live t' see the day when even a stinkin' weed on it 'll belong t' ye! (*Then in a scream.*) Git out o' my sight! Go on t' yer slut — disgracin' yer Paw 'n' me! I'll git yer Paw t' horsewhip ye off the place if I want t'! Ye're only livin' here 'cause I tolerate ye! Git along! I hate the sight o' ye! (*She stops panting and glaring at him.*)

EBEN (*returning her glance in kind*): An' I hate the sight o' yew! (*He turns and strides off up the road. She follows his retreating figure with concentrated hate. Old* CABOT *appears coming up from the barn. The hard, grim expression of his face has changed. He seems in some queer way softened, mellowed. His eyes have taken on a strange, incongruous dreamy quality. Yet there is no hint of physical weakness about him — rather he looks more robust and younger.* ABBIE *sees him and turns away quickly with unconcealed aversion. He comes slowly up to her.*)

CABOT (*mildly*): War yew an' Eben quarrelin' agen?

ABBIE (*shortly*): No.

CABOT: Ye was talkin' a'mighty loud. (*He sits down on the edge of porch.*)

ABBIE (*snappishly*): If ye heerd us they hain't no need askin' questions.

CABOT: I didn't hear what ye said.

ABBIE (*relieved*): Waal — it wa'n't nothin' t' speak on.

CABOT (*after a pause*): Eben's queer.

ABBIE (*bitterly*): He's the dead spit 'n' image o' yew!

CABOT (*queerly interested*): D'ye think so, Abbie? (*After a pause, ruminatingly.*) Me 'n' Eben's allus fit 'n' fit. I never could b'ar him noways. He's so thunderin' soft — like his Maw.

ABBIE (*scornfully*): Ay-eh! 'Bout as soft as yew be!

CABOT (*as if he hadn't heard*): Mebbe I been too hard on him.

ABBIE (*jeeringly*): Waal — ye're gittin' soft now — soft as slop! That's what Eben was sayin'.

CABOT (*his face instantly grim and ominous*): Eben was sayin'? Waal, he'd best not do nothin' t' try me 'r he'll soon diskiver.... (*A pause. She keeps her face turned away. His gradually softens. He stares up at the sky.*) Purty, hain't it?

ABBIE (*crossly*): I don't see nothin' purty.

CABOT: The sky. Feels like a wa'm field up thar.

ABBIE (*sarcastically*): Air yew aimin' t' buy

up over the farm too? (*She snickers contemptuously.*)

CABOT (*strangely*): I'd like t' own my place up thar. (*A pause.*) I'm gittin' old, Abbie. I'm gittin' ripe on the bough. (*A pause. She stares at him mystified. He goes on.*) It's allus lonesome cold in the house — even when it's bilin' hot outside. Hain't yew noticed?

ABBIE: No.

CABOT: It's wa'm down t' the barn — nice smellin' an' warm — with the cows. (*A pause.*) Cows is queer.

ABBIE: Like yew?

CABOT: Like Eben. (*A pause.*) I'm gittin' t' feel resigned t' Eben — jest as I got t' feel 'bout his Maw. I'm gittin' t' learn to b'ar his softness — jest like her'n. I calc'late I c'd a'most take t' him — if he wa'n't sech a dumb fool! (*A pause.*) I s'pose it's old age a'creepin' in my bones.

ABBIE (*indifferently*): Waal — ye hain't dead yet.

CABOT (*roused*): No, I hain't, yew bet — not by a hell of a sight — I'm sound 'n' tough as hickory! (*Then moodily.*) But arter three score and ten the Lord warns ye t' prepare. (*A pause.*) That's why Eben's come in my head. Now that his cussed sinful brothers is gone their path t' hell, they's no one left but Eben.

ABBIE (*resentfully*): They's me, hain't they? (*Agitatedly.*) What's all this sudden likin' ye've tuk to Eben? Why don't ye say nothin' 'bout me? Hain't I yer lawful wife?

CABOT (*simply*): Ay-eh. Ye be. (*A pause — he stares at her desirously — his eyes grow avid — then with a sudden movement he seizes her hands and squeezes them, declaiming in a queer camp-meeting preacher's tempo.*) Yew air my Rose o' Sharon! Behold, yew air fair; yer eyes air doves; yer lips air like scarlet; yer two breasts air like two fawns; yer navel be like a round goblet; yer belly be like a heap o' wheat.... (*He covers her hand with kisses. She does not seem to notice. She stares before her with hard angry eyes.*)

ABBIE (*jerking her hands away — harshly*): So ye're plannin' t' leave the farm t' Eben, air ye?

CABOT (*dazedly*): Leave ...? (*Then with resentful obstinacy.*) I hain't a-givin' it t' no one!

ABBIE (*remorselessly*): Ye can't take it with ye.

CABOT (*thinks a moment — then reluctantly*): No, I calc'late not. (*After a pause — with a strange passion.*) But if I could, I would, by the Etarnal! 'R if I could, in my dyin' hour, I'd set it afire an' watch it burn — this house an' every ear o' corn an' every tree down t' the last blade o' hay! I'd sit an' know it was all a-dying with me an' no one else'd ever own what was mine, what I'd made out o' nothin' with my own sweat 'n' blood! (*A pause — then he adds with a queer affection.*) 'Ceptin' the cows. Them I'd turn free.

ABBIE (*harshly*): An' me?

CABOT (*with a queer smile*): Ye'd be turned free, too.

ABBIE (*furiously*): So that's the thanks I git fur marryin' ye — t' have ye change kind to Eben who hates ye, an' talk o' turnin' me out in the road.

CABOT (*hastily*): Abbie! Ye know I wa'n't....

ABBIE (*vengefully*): Just let me tell ye a thing or two 'bout Eben! Whar's he gone? T' see that harlot, Min! I tried fur t' stop him. Disgracin' yew an' me — on the Sabbath, too!

CABOT (*rather guiltily*): He's a sinner — nateral-born. It's lust eatin' his heart.

ABBIE (*enraged beyond endurance — wildly vindictive*): An' his lust fur me! Kin ye find excuses fur that?

CABOT (*stares at her — after a dead pause*): Lust — fur yew?

ABBIE (*defiantly*): He was tryin' t' make love t' me — when ye heerd us quarrelin'.

CABOT (*stares at her — then a terrible expression of rage comes over his face — he springs to his feet shaking all over*): By the A'mighty God — I'll end him!

ABBIE (*frightened now for EBEN*): No! Don't ye!

CABOT (*violently*): I'll git the shotgun an' blow his soft brains t' the top o' them elums!

ABBIE (*throwing her arms around him*): No, Ephraim!

CABOT (*pushing her away violently*): I will, by God!

ABBIE (*in a quieting tone*): Listen, Ephraim. 'Twa'n't nothin' bad — on'y a boy's foolin' — 'twa'n't meant serious — jest jokin' an' teasin'....

CABOT: Then why did ye say — lust?

ABBIE: It must hev sounded wusser'n I meant. An' I was mad at thinkin' — ye'd leave him the farm.

CABOT (*quieter but still grim and cruel*): Waal then, I'll horsewhip him off the place if that much'll content ye.

ABBIE (*reaching out and taking his hand*):

No. Don't think o' me! Ye mustn't drive him off. 'Tain't sensible. Who'll ye get to help ye on the farm? They's no one hereabouts.

CABOT (*considers this — then nodding his appreciation*): Ye got a head on ye. (*Then irritably.*) Waal, let him stay. (*He sits down on the edge of the porch. She sits beside him. He murmurs contemptuously.*) I oughtn't t' git riled so — at that 'ere fool calf. (*A pause.*) But har's the p'int. What son o' mine'll keep on here t' the farm — when the Lord does call me? Simeon an' Peter air gone t' hell — an' Eben's follerin' 'em.

ABBIE: They's me.

CABOT: Ye're on'y a woman.

ABBIE: I'm yewr wife.

CABOT: That hain't me. A son is me — my blood — mine. Mine ought t' git mine. An' then it's still mine — even though I be six foot under. D'ye see?

ABBIE (*giving him a look of hatred*): Ay-eh. I see. (*She becomes very thoughtful, her face growing shrewd, her eyes studying* CABOT *craftily.*)

CABOT: I'm gittin' old — ripe on the bough. (*Then with a sudden forced reassurance.*) Not but what I hain't a hard nut t' crack even yet — an' fur many a year t' come! By the Eternal, I kin break most o' the young fellers' backs at any kind o' work any day o' the year!

ABBIE (*suddenly*): Mebbe the Lord'll give us a son.

CABOT (*turns and stares at her eagerly*): Ye mean — a son — t' me 'n' yew?

ABBIE (*with a cajoling smile*): Ye're a strong man yet, hain't ye? 'Tain't noways impossible, be it? We know that. Why d'ye stare so? Hain't ye never thought o' that afore? I been thinkin' o' it all along. Ay-eh — an' I been prayin' it'd happen, too.

CABOT (*his face growing full of joyous pride and a sort of religious ecstasy*): Ye been prayin', Abbie? — fur a son? — t' us?

ABBIE: Ay-eh. (*With a grim resolution.*) I want a son now.

CABOT (*excitedly clutching both of her hands in his*): It'd be the blessin' o' God, Abbie — the blessin' o' God A'mighty on me — in my old age — in my lonesomeness! They hain't nothin' I wouldn't do fur ye then, Abbie. Ye'd hev on'y t' ask it — anythin' ye'd a mind t'!

ABBIE (*interrupting*): Would ye will the farm t' me then — t' me an' it . . . ?

CABOT (*vehemently*): I'd do anythin' ye axed, I tell ye! I swar it! May I be everlastin' damned t' hell if I wouldn't! (*He sinks to his knees pulling her down with him. He trembles all over with the fervor of his hopes.*) Pray t' the Lord agen, Abbie. It's the Sabbath! I'll jine ye! Two prayers air better nor one "An' God hearkened unto Rachel"! An' God hearkened unto Abbie! Pray, Abbie! Pray fur him to hearken! (*He bows his head, mumbling. She pretends to do likewise but gives him a side glance of scorn and triumph.*)

CURTAIN

SCENE II

About eight in the evening. The interior of the two bedrooms on the top floor is shown. EBEN *is sitting on the side of his bed in the room on the left. On account of the heat he has taken off everything but his undershirt and pants. His feet are bare. He faces front, brooding moodily, his chin propped on his hands, a desperate expression on his face.*

In the other room CABOT *and* ABBIE *are sitting side by side on the edge of their bed, an old four-poster with feather mattress. He is in his night shirt, she in her nightdress. He is still in the queer, excited mood into which the notion of a son has thrown him. Both rooms are lighted dimly and flickeringly by tallow candles.*

CABOT: The farm needs a son.

ABBIE: I need a son.

CABOT: Ay-eh. Sometimes ye air the farm an' sometimes the farm be yew. That's why I clove t' ye in my lonesomeness. (*A pause. He pounds his knee with his fist.*) Me an' the farm has got t' beget a son!

ABBIE: Ye'd best go t' sleep. Ye're gittin' thin's all mixed.

CABOT (*with an impatient gesture*): No, I hain't. My mind's clear's a well. Ye don't know me, that's it. (*He stares hopelessly at the floor.*)

ABBIE (*indifferently*): Mebbe. (*In the next room* EBEN *gets up and paces up and down distractedly.* ABBIE *hears him. Her eyes fasten on the intervening wall with concentrated attention.* EBEN *stops and stares. Their hot glances seem to meet through the wall. Unconsciously he stretches out his arms for her and she half rises. Then aware, he mutters a curse at himself and flings himself face downward on the bed, his clenched fists above his head, his face buried in the pillow.* ABBIE *relaxes with a faint sigh but her eyes remain fixed on the wall; she listens with all her attention for some movement from* EBEN.)

CABOT (*suddenly raises his head and looks at her — scornfully*): Will ye ever know me — 'r will any man 'r woman? (*Shaking his head.*) No. I calc'late 't wa'n't t' be. (*He turns away.* ABBIE *looks at the wall. Then, evidently unable to keep silent about his thoughts without looking at his wife, he puts out his hand and clutches her knee. She starts violently, looks at him, sees he is not watching her, concentrates again on the wall and pays no attention to what he says.*) Listen, Abbie. When I come here fifty odd year ago — I was jest twenty an' the strongest an' hardest ye ever seen — ten times as strong an' fifty times as hard as Eben. Waal — this place was nothin' but fields o' stones. Folks laughed when I tuk it. They couldn't know what I knowed. When ye kin make corn sprout out o' stones, God's livin' in yew! They wa'n't strong enuf fur that! They reckoned God was easy. They laughed. They don't laugh no more. Some died hereabouts. Some went West an' died. They're all under ground — fur follerin' arter an easy God. God hain't easy. (*He shakes his head slowly.*) An' I growed hard. Folks kept allus sayin' he's a hard man like 'twas sinful t' be hard, so's at last I said back at 'em: Waal then, by thunder, ye'll git me hard an' see how ye like it! (*Then suddenly.*) But I give in t' weakness once. 'Twas arter I'd been here two year. I got weak — despairful — they was so many stones. They was a party leavin', givin' up, goin' West. I jined 'em. We tracked on 'n on. We come t' broad medders, plains, whar the soil was black an' rich as gold. Nary a stone. Easy. Ye'd on'y to plow an' sow an' then set an' smoke yer pipe an' watch thin's grow. I could o' been a rich man — but somethin' in me fit me an' fit me — the voice o' God sayin': "This hain't wuth nothin' t' Me. Git ye back t' hum!" I got afeerd o' that voice an' I lit out back t' hum here, leavin' my claim an' crops t' whoever'd a mind t' take 'em. Ay-eh. I actoolly give up what was rightful mine! God's hard, not easy! God's in the stones! Build my church on a rock — out o' stones an' I'll be in them! That's what He meant t' Peter! (*He sighs heavily — a pause.*) Stones. I picked 'em up an' piled 'em into walls. Ye kin read the years o' my life in them walls, every day a hefted stone, climbin' over the hills up and down, fencin' in the fields that was mine, whar I'd made thin's grow out o' nothin' — like the will o' God, like the servant o' His hand. It wa'n't easy. It was hard an' He made me hard fur it. (*He pauses.*) All the time I kept gittin' lonesomer. I tuk a wife. She bore Simeon an' Peter. She was a good woman. She wuked hard. We was married twenty year. She never knowed me. She helped but she never knowed what she was helpin'. I was allus lonesome. She died. After that it wa'n't so lonesome fur a spell. (*A pause.*) I lost count o' the years. I had no time t' fool away countin' 'em. Sim an' Peter helped. The farm growed. It was all mine! When I thought o' that I didn't feel lonesome. (*A pause.*) But ye can't hitch yer mind t' one thin' day an' night. I tuk another wife — Eben's Maw. Her folks was contestin' me at law over my deeds t' the farm — my farm! That's why Eben keeps a-talkin' his fool talk o' this bein' his Maw's farm. She bore Eben. She was purty — but soft. She tried t' be hard. She couldn't. She never knowed me nor nothin'. It was lonesomer 'n hell with her. After a matter o' sixteen odd years, she died. (*A pause.*) I lived with the boys. They hated me 'cause I was hard. I hated them 'cause they was soft. They coveted the farm without knowin' what it meant. It made me bitter 'n wormwood. It aged me — them coveting what I'd made fur mine. Then this spring the call come — the voice o' God cryin' in my wilderness, in my lonesomeness — t' go out an' seek an' find! (*Turning to her with strange passion.*) I sought ye an' I found ye! Yew air my Rose o' Sharon! Yer eyes air like.... (*She has turned a blank face, resentful eyes to his. He stares at her for a moment — then harshly.*) Air ye any the wiser fur all I've told ye?

ABBIE (*confusedly*): Mebbe.

CABOT (*pushing her away from him — angrily*): Ye don't know nothin' — nor never will. If ye don't hev a son t' redeem ye.... (*This in a tone of cold threat.*)

ABBIE (*resentfully*): I've prayed, hain't I?

CABOT (*bitterly*): Pray agen — fur understandin'!

ABBIE (*a veiled threat in her tone*): Ye'll have a son out o' me, I promise ye.

CABOT: How kin ye promise?

ABBIE: I got second-sight mebbe. I kin foretell. (*She gives a queer smile.*)

CABOT: I believe ye have. Ye give me the

chills sometimes. (*He shivers.*) It's cold in this house. It's oneasy. They's thin's pokin' about in the dark — in the corners. (*He pulls on his trousers, tucking in his night shirt, and pulls on his boots.*)

ABBIE (*surprised*): Whar air ye goin'?

CABOT (*queerly*): Down whar it's restful — whar it's warm down t' the barn. (*Bitterly.*) I kin talk t' the cows. They know. They know the farm an' me. They'll give me peace. (*He turns to go out the door.*)

ABBIE (*a bit frightenedly*): Air ye ailin' tonight, Ephraim?

CABOT: Growin'. Growin' ripe on the bough. (*He turns and goes, his boots clumping down the stairs.* EBEN *sits up with a start, listening.* ABBIE *is conscious of his movement and stares at the wall.* CABOT *comes out of the house around the corner and stands by the gate, blinking at the sky. He stretches up his hands in a tortured gesture.*) God A'mighty, call from the dark! (*He listens as if expecting an answer. Then his arms drop, he shakes his head and plods off toward the barn.* EBEN *and* ABBIE *stare at each other through the wall.* EBEN *sighs heavily and* ABBIE *echoes it. Both become terribly nervous, uneasy. Finally* ABBIE *gets up and listens, her ear to the wall. He acts as if he saw every move she was making, he becomes resolutely still. She seems driven into a decision — goes out the door in rear determinedly. His eyes follow her. Then as the door of his room is opened softly, he turns away, waits in an attitude of strained fixity.* ABBIE *stands for a second staring at him, her eyes burning with desire. Then with a little cry she runs over and throws her arms about his neck, she pulls his head back and covers his mouth with kisses. At first, he submits dumbly; then he puts his arms about her neck and returns her kisses, but finally, suddenly aware of his hatred, he hurls her away from him, springing to his feet. They stand speechless and breathless, panting like two animals.*)

ABBIE (*at last — painfully*): Ye shouldn't, Eben — ye shouldn't — I'd make ye happy!

EBEN (*harshly*): I don't want t' be happy — from yew!

ABBIE (*helplessly*): Ye do, Eben! Ye do! Why d'ye lie?

EBEN (*viciously*): I don't take t'ye, I tell ye! I hate the sight o' ye!

ABBIE (*with an uncertain troubled laugh*): Waal, I kissed ye anyways — an' ye kissed back — yer lips was burnin' — ye can't lie 'bout that! (*Intensely.*) If ye don't care, why did ye kiss me back — why was yer lips burnin'?

EBEN (*wiping his mouth*): It was like pizen on 'em. (*Then tauntingly.*) When I kissed ye back, mebbe I thought 'twas someone else.

ABBIE (*wildly*): Min?

EBEN: Mebbe.

ABBIE (*torturedly*): Did ye go t' see her? Did ye r'ally go? I thought ye mightn't. Is that why ye throwed me off jest now?

EBEN (*sneeringly*): What if it be?

ABBIE (*raging*): Then ye're a dog, Eben Cabot!

EBEN (*threateningly*): Ye can't talk that way t' me!

ABBIE (*with a shrill laugh*): Can't I? Did ye think I was in love with ye — a weak thin' like yew? Not much! I on'y wanted ye fur a purpose o' my own — an' I'll hev ye fur it yet 'cause I'm stronger 'n yew be!

EBEN (*resentfully*): I knowed well it was on'y part o' yer plan t' swaller everythin'!

ABBIE (*tauntingly*): Mebbe!

EBEN (*furious*): Git out o' my room!

ABBIE: This air my room an' ye're on'y hired help!

EBEN (*threateningly*): Git out afore I murder ye!

ABBIE (*quite confident now*): I hain't a mite afeerd. Ye want me, don't ye? Yes, ye do! An' yer Paw's son'll never kill what he wants! Look at yer eyes! They's lust fur me in 'em, burnin' 'em up! Look at yer lips now! They're tremblin' an' longin' t' kiss me, an' yer teeth t' bite! (*He is watching her now with a horrible fascination. She laughs a crazy triumphant laugh.*) I'm a-goin' t' make all o' this hum my hum! They's one room hain't mine yet, but it's a-goin' t' be tonight. I'm a-goin' down now an' light up! (*She makes him a mocking bow.*) Won't ye come courtin' me in the best parlor, Mister Cabot?

EBEN (*staring at her — horribly confused — dully*): Don't ye dare! It hain't been opened since Maw died an' was laid out thar! Don't ye . . . ! (*But her eyes are fixed on his so burningly that his will seems to wither before hers. He stands swaying toward her helplessly.*)

ABBIE (*holding his eyes and putting all her will into her words as she backs out the door*): I'll expect ye afore long, Eben.

EBEN (*stares after her for a while, walking toward the door. A light appears in the parlor window. He murmurs*): In the parlor? (*This seems to arouse connotations for he comes back and puts on his white shirt, collar, half ties the tie mechanically, puts on coat, takes his hat, stands barefooted looking about him in bewilderment, mutters wonderingly*): Maw! Whar air yew? (*Then goes slowly toward the door in rear.*)

CURTAIN

SCENE III

A few minutes later. The interior of the parlor is shown. A grim, repressed room like a tomb in which the family has been interred alive. ABBIE *sits on the edge of the horsehair sofa. She has lighted all the candles and the room is revealed in all its preserved ugliness. A change has come over the woman. She looks awed and frightened now, ready to run away.*

The door is opened and EBEN *appears. His face wears an expression of obsessed confusion. He stands staring at her, his arms hanging disjointedly from his shoulders, his feet bare, his hat in his hand.*

ABBIE (*after a pause — with a nervous, formal politeness*): Won't ye set?

EBEN (*dully*): Ay-eh. (*Mechanically he places his hat carefully on the floor near the door and sits stiffly beside her on the edge of the sofa. A pause. They both remain rigid, looking straight ahead with eyes full of fear.*)

ABBIE: When I fust come in — in the dark — they seemed somethin' here.

EBEN (*simply*): Maw.

ABBIE: I kin still feel — somethin'. . . .

EBEN: It's Maw.

ABBIE: At fust I was feered o' it. I wanted t' yell an' run. Now — since yew come — seems like it's growin' soft an' kind t' me. (*Addressing the air — queerly.*) Thank yew.

EBEN: Maw allus loved me.

ABBIE: Mebbe it knows I love yew, too. Mebbe that makes it kind t' me.

EBEN (*dully*): I dunno. I should think she'd hate ye.

ABBIE (*with certainty*): No. I kin feel it don't — not no more.

EBEN: Hate ye fur stealin' her place — here in her hum — settin' in her parlor whar she was laid — (*He suddenly stops, staring stupidly before him.*)

ABBIE: What is it, Eben?

EBEN (*in a whisper*): Seems like Maw didn't want me t' remind ye.

ABBIE (*excitedly*): I knowed, Eben! It's kind t' me! It don't b'ar me no grudges fur what I never knowed an' couldn't help!

EBEN: Maw b'ars him a grudge.

ABBIE: Waal, so does all o' us.

EBEN: Ay-eh. (*With passion.*) I does, by God!

ABBIE (*taking one of his hands in hers and patting it*): Thar! Don't get riled thinkin' o' him. Think o' yer Maw who's kind t' us. Tell me about yer Maw, Eben.

EBEN: They hain't nothin' much. She was kind. She was good.

ABBIE (*putting one arm over his shoulder. He does not seem to notice — passionately*): I'll be kind an' good t' ye!

EBEN: Sometimes she used t' sing fur me.

ABBIE: I'll sing fur ye!

EBEN: This was her hum. This was her farm.

ABBIE: This is my hum! This is my farm!

EBEN: He married her t' steal 'em. She was soft an' easy. He couldn't 'preciate her.

ABBIE: He can't 'preciate me!

EBEN: He murdered her with his hardness.

ABBIE: He's murderin' me!

EBEN: She died. (*A pause.*) Sometimes she used to sing fur me. (*He bursts into a fit of sobbing.*)

ABBIE (*both her arms around him — with wild passion*): I'll sing fur ye! I'll die fur ye! (*In spite of her overwhelming desire for him, there is a sincere maternal love in her manner and voice — a horribly frank mixture of lust and mother love.*) Don't cry, Eben! I'll take yer Maw's place! I'll be everythin' she was t' ye! Let me kiss ye, Eben! (*She pulls his head around. He makes a bewildered pretense of resistance. She is tender.*) Don't be afeered! I'll kiss ye pure, Eben — same 's if I was a Maw t' ye — an' ye kin kiss me back 's if yew was my son — my boy — sayin' good-night t' me! Kiss me, Eben. (*They kiss in restrained fashion. Then suddenly wild passion overcomes her. She kisses him lustfully again and again and he flings his arms about her and returns her kisses. Suddenly, as in the bedroom, he frees himself from her violently and springs to his feet. He is trembling all over, in a strange state of terror.* ABBIE *strains her arms toward him with fierce pleading.*) Don't ye leave me, Eben! Can't ye see it hain't enuf — lovin' ye like a

Maw — can't ye see it's got t' be that an' more — much more — a hundred times more — fur me t' be happy — fur yew t' be happy?

EBEN (*to the presence he feels in the room*): Maw! Maw! What d'ye want? What air ye tellin' me?

ABBIE: She's tellin' ye t' love me. She knows I love ye an' I'll be good t' ye. Can't ye feel it? Don't ye know? She's tellin' ye t' love me, Eben!

EBEN: Ay-eh. I feel — mebbe she — but — I can't figger out — why — when ye've stole her place — here in her hum — in the parlor whar she was —

ABBIE (*fiercely*): She knows I love ye!

EBEN (*his face suddenly lighting up with a fierce, triumphant grin*): I see it! I see why. It's her vengeance on him — so's she kin rest quiet in her grave!

ABBIE (*wildly*): Vengeance o' God on the hull o' us! What d'we give a durn? I love ye, Eben! God knows I love ye! (*She stretches out her arms for him.*)

EBEN (*throws himself on his knees beside the sofa and grabs her in his arms — releasing all his pent-up passion*): An' I love yew, Abbie! — now I kin say it! I been dyin' fur want o' ye — every hour since ye come! I love ye! (*Their lips meet in a fierce, bruising kiss.*)

CURTAIN

SCENE IV

Exterior of the farmhouse. It is just dawn. The front door at right is opened and EBEN *comes out and walks around to the gate. He is dressed in his working clothes. He seems changed. His face wears a bold and confident expression, he is grinning to himself with evident satisfaction. As he gets near the gate, the window of the parlor is heard opening and the shutters are flung back and* ABBIE *sticks her head out. Her hair tumbles over her shoulders in disarray, her face is flushed, she looks at* EBEN *with tender, languorous eyes and calls softly.*

ABBIE: Eben. (*As he turns — playfully.*) Jest one more kiss afore ye go. I'm goin' to miss ye fearful all day.

EBEN: An' me yew, ye kin bet! (*He goes to her. They kiss several times. He draws away, laughingly.*) Thar. That's enuf, hain't it? Ye won't hev none left fur next time.

ABBIE: I got a million o' 'em left fur yew! (*Then a bit anxiously.*) D'ye r'ally love me, Eben?

EBEN (*emphatically*): I like ye better'n any gal I ever knowed! That's gospel!

ABBIE: Likin' hain't lovin'.

EBEN: Waal then — I love ye. Now air yew satisfied?

ABBIE: Ay-eh, I be. (*She smiles at him adoringly.*)

EBEN: I better git t' the barn. The old critter's liable t' suspicion an' come sneakin' up.

ABBIE (*with a confident laugh*): Let him! I kin allus pull the wool over his eyes. I'm goin' t' leave the shutters open and let in the sun 'n' air. This room's been dead long enuf. Now it's goin' t' be my room!

EBEN (*frowning*): Ay-eh.

ABBIE (*hastily*): I meant — our room.

EBEN: Ay-eh.

ABBIE: We made it our'n last night, didn't we? We give it life — our lovin' did. (*A pause.*)

EBEN (*with a strange look*): Maw's gone back t' her grave. She kin sleep now.

ABBIE: May she rest in peace! (*Then tenderly rebuking.*) Ye oughtn't t' talk o' sad thin's — this mornin'.

EBEN: It jest come up in my mind o' itself.

ABBIE: Don't let it. (*He doesn't answer. She yawns.*) Waal, I'm a-goin' t' steal a wink o' sleep. I'll tell the Old Man I hain't feelin' pert. Let him git his own vittles.

EBEN: I see him comin' from the barn. Ye better look smart an' git upstairs.

ABBIE: Ay-eh. Good-by. Don't ferget me. (*She throws him a kiss. He grins — then squares his shoulders and awaits his father confidently.* CABOT *walks slowly up from the left, staring up at the sky with a vague face.*)

EBEN (*jovially*): Mornin', Paw. Star-gazin' in daylight?

CABOT: Purty, hain't it?

EBEN (*looking around him possessively*): It's a durned purty farm.

CABOT: I mean the sky.

EBEN (*grinning*): How d'ye know? Them eyes o' your'n can't see that fur. (*This tickles his humor and he slaps his thigh and laughs.*) Ho-ho! That's a good un!

CABOT (*grimly sarcastic*): Ye're feelin' right chipper, hain't ye? Whar'd ye steal the likker?

EBEN (*good-naturedly*): 'Tain't likker. Jest life. (*Suddenly holding out his hand — soberly.*) Yew 'n' me is quits. Let's shake hands.

CABOT (*suspiciously*): What's come over ye?

EBEN: Then don't. Mebbe it's jest as well. (*A moment's pause.*) What's come over me? (*Queerly.*) Didn't ye feel her passin' — goin' back t' her grave?

CABOT (*dully*): Who?

EBEN: Maw. She kin rest now an' sleep content. She's quit with ye.

CABOT (*confusedly*): I rested. I slept good — down with the cows. They know how t' sleep. They're teachin' me.

EBEN (*suddenly jovial again*): Good fur the cows! Waal — ye better git t' work.

CABOT (*grimly amused*): Air ye bossin' me, ye calf?

EBEN (*beginning to laugh*): Ay-eh! I'm bossin' yew! Ha-ha-ha! See how ye like it! Ha-ha-ha! I'm the prize rooster o' this roost. Ha-ha-ha! (*He goes off toward the barn laughing.*)

CABOT (*looks after him with scornful pity*): Soft-headed. Like his Maw. Dead spit 'n' image. No hope in him! (*He spits with contemptuous disgust.*) A born fool! (*Then matter-of-factly.*) Waal — I'm gittin' peckish. (*He goes toward door.*)

CURTAIN

PART III

SCENE I

A *night in late spring the following year. The kitchen and the two bedrooms upstairs are shown. The two bedrooms are dimly lighted by a tallow candle in each.* EBEN *is sitting on the side of the bed in his room, his chin propped on his fists, his face a study of the struggle he is making to understand his conflicting emotions. The noisy laughter and music from below where a kitchen dance is in progress annoy and distract him. He scowls at the floor.*

In the next room a cradle stands beside the double bed.

In the kitchen all is festivity. The stove has been taken down to give more room to the dancers. The chairs, with wooden benches added, have been pushed back against the walls. On these are seated, squeezed in tight against one another, farmers and their wives and their young folks of both sexes from the neighboring farms. They are all chattering and laughing loudly. They evidently have some secret joke in common. There is no end of winking, of nudging, of meaning nods of the head toward CABOT *who, in a state of extreme hilarious excitement increased by the amount he has drunk, is standing near the rear door where there is a small keg of whisky and serving drinks to all the men. In the left corner, front, dividing the attention with her husband,* ABBIE *is sitting in a rocking chair, a shawl wrapped about her shoulders. She is very pale, her face is thin and drawn, her eyes are fixed anxiously on the open door in rear as if waiting for someone.*

The musician is tuning up his fiddle, seated in the far right corner. He is a lanky young fellow with a long, weak face. His pale eyes blink incessantly and he grins about him slyly with a greedy malice.

ABBIE (*suddenly turning to a young girl on her right*): Whar's Eben?

YOUNG GIRL (*eying her scornfully*): I dunno, Mrs. Cabot. I hain't seen Eben in ages. (*Meaningly.*) Seems like he's spent most o' his time t' hum since yew come.

ABBIE (*vaguely*): I tuk his Maw's place.

YOUNG GIRL: Ay-eh. So I've heerd. (*She turns away to retail this bit of gossip to her mother sitting next to her.* ABBIE *turns to her left to a big stoutish middle-aged man whose flushed face and starting eyes show the amount of "likker" he has consumed.*)

ABBIE: Ye hain't seen Eben, hev ye?

MAN: No, I hain't. (*Then he adds with a wink.*) If yew hain't, who would?

ABBIE: He's the best dancer in the county. He'd ought t' come an' dance.

MAN (*with a wink*): Mebbe he's doin' the dutiful an' walkin' the kid t' sleep. It's a boy, hain't it?

ABBIE (*nodding vaguely*): Ay-eh — born two weeks back — purty's a picter.

MAN: They all is — t' their Maws. (*Then in a whisper, with a nudge and a leer.*) Listen, Abbie — if ye ever git tired o' Eben, remember me! Don't fergit now! (*He looks at her uncomprehending face for a second — then grunts disgustedly.*) Waal — guess I'll likker agin. (*He goes over and joins* CABOT *who is arguing noisily with an old farmer over cows. They all drink.*)

ABBIE (*this time appealing to nobody in particular*): Wonder what Eben's a-doin'? (*Her remark is repeated down the line with many a guffaw and titter until it reaches the fiddler. He fastens his blinking eyes on* ABBIE.)

FIDDLER (*raising his voice*): Bet I kin tell ye, Abbie, what Eben's doin'! He's down t' the church offerin' up prayers o' thanksgivin'. (*They all titter expectantly.*)

A MAN: What fur? (*Another titter.*)

FIDDLER: 'Cause unto him a — (*He hesitates just long enough*) brother is born! (*A roar of laughter. They all look from* ABBIE *to* CABOT. *She is oblivious, staring at the door.* CABOT, *although he hasn't heard the words, is irritated by the laughter and steps forward, glaring about him. There is an immediate silence.*)

CABOT: What're ye all bleatin' about — like a flock o' goats? Why don't ye dance, damn ye? I axed ye here t' dance — t' eat, drink an' be merry — an' thar ye set cacklin' like a lot o' wet hens with the pip! Ye've swilled my likker an' guzzled my vittles like hogs, hain't ye? Then dance fur me, can't ye? That's fa'r an' squar', hain't it? (*A grumble of resentment goes around but they are all evidently in too much awe of him to express it openly.*)

FIDDLER (*slyly*): We're waitin' fur Eben. (*A suppressed laugh.*)

CABOT (*with a fierce exultation*): T'hell with Eben! Eben's done fur now! I got a new son! (*His mood switching with drunken suddenness*) But ye needn't t' laugh at Eben, none o' ye! He's my blood, if he be a dumb fool. He's better nor any o' yew! He kin do a day's work a'most up t' what I kin — an' that'd put any o' yew pore critters t' shame!

FIDDLER: An' he kin do a good night's work too! (*A roar of laughter.*)

CABOT: Laugh, ye damn fools! Ye're right jist the same, Fiddler. He kin work day an' night too, like I kin, if need be!

OLD FARMER (*from behind the keg where he is weaving drunkenly back and forth — with great simplicity*): They hain't many t' touch ye, Ephraim — a son at seventy-six. That's a hard man fur ye! I be on'y sixty-eight an' I couldn't do it. (*A roar of laughter in which* CABOT *joins uproariously.*)

CABOT (*slapping him on the back*): I'm sorry fur ye, Hi. I'd never suspicion sech weakness from a boy like yew!

OLD FARMER: An' I never reckoned yew had it in ye nuther, Ephraim. (*There is another laugh.*)

CABOT (*suddenly grim*): I got a lot in me — a hell of a lot — folks don't know on. (*Turning to the fiddler.*) Fiddle 'er up, durn ye! Give 'em somethin' t' dance t'! What air ye, an ornament? Hain't this a celebration? Then grease yer elbow an' go it!

FIDDLER (*seizes a drink which the* OLD FARMER *holds out to him and downs it*): Here goes! (*He starts to fiddle "Lady of the Lake." Four young fellows and four girls form in two lines and dance a square dance. The* FIDDLER *shouts directions for the different movements, keeping his words in the rhythm of the music and interspersing them with jocular personal remarks to the dancers themselves. The people seated along the walls stamp their feet and clap their hands in unison.* CABOT *is especially active in this respect. Only* ABBIE *remains apathetic, staring at the door as if she were alone in a silent room.*)

FIDDLER: Swing your partner t' the right! That's it, Jim! Give her a b'ar hug! Her Maw hain't lookin'. (*Laughter.*) Change partners! That suits ye, don't it, Essie, now ye got Reub afore ye? Look at her redden up, will ye? Waal, life is short an' so's love, as the feller says. (*Laughter.*)

CABOT (*excitedly, stamping his foot*): Go it, boys! Go it, gals!

FIDDLER (*with a wink at the others*): Ye're the spryest seventy-six ever I sees, Ephraim! Now if ye'd on'y good eyesight...! (*Suppressed laughter. He gives* CABOT *no chance to retort but roars.*) Promenade! Ye're walkin' like a bride down the aisle, Sarah! Waal, while they's life they's allus hope, I've heerd tell. Swing your partner to the left! Gosh A'mighty, look at Johnny Cook high-steppin'! They hain't goin' t'be much strength left fur howin' in the corn lot t'morrow. (*Laughter.*)

CABOT: Go it! Go it! (*Then suddenly, unable to restrain himself any longer, he prances into the midst of the dancers, scattering them, waving his arms about wildly.*) Ye're all hoofs! Git out o' my road! Give me room! I'll show ye dancin'. Ye're all too soft! (*He pushes them roughly away. They crowd back toward the walls, muttering, looking at him resentfully.*)

FIDDLER (*jeeringly*): Go it, Ephraim! Go it! (*He starts "Pop Goes the Weasel," increasing the tempo with every verse until at the end he is fiddling crazily as fast as he can go.*)

CABOT (*starts to dance, which he does very well and with tremendous vigor. Then he begins to improvise, cuts incredibly grotesque capers, leaping up and cracking his heels together, prancing around in a circle with body bent in an Indian war dance, then suddenly straightening up and kicking as high as he can with both legs. He is like a monkey on a string. And all the while he intersperses his antics with shouts and derisive comments*): Whoop! Here's dancin' fur ye! Whoop! See that! Seventy-six, if I'm a day! Hard as iron yet! Beatin' the young 'uns like I allus done! Look at me! I'd invite ye t' dance on my hundredth birthday on'y ye'll all be dead by then. Ye're a sickly generation! Yer hearts air pink, not red! Yer veins is full o' mud an' water! I be the on'y man in the county! Whoop! See that! I'm a Injun! I've killed Injuns in the West afore ye was born — an' skulped 'em too! They's a arrer wound on my backside I c'd show ye! The hull tribe chased me. I outrun 'em all — with the arrer stuck in me! An' I tuk vengeance on 'em. Ten eyes fur an eye, that was my motter! Whoop! Look at me! I kin kick the ceilin' off the room! Whoop!

FIDDLER (*stops playing — exhaustedly*): God A'mighty, I got enuf. Ye got the devil's strength in ye.

CABOT (*delightedly*): Did I beat yew, too? Wa'al, ye played smart. Hev a swig. (*He pours whisky for himself and FIDDLER. They drink. The others watch CABOT silently with cold, hostile eyes. There is a dead pause. The FIDDLER rests. CABOT leans against the keg, panting, glaring around him confusedly. In the room above, EBEN gets to his feet and tiptoes out the door in rear, appearing a moment later in the other bedroom. He moves silently, even frightenedly, toward the cradle and stands there looking down at the baby. His face is as vague as his reactions are confused, but there is a trace of tenderness, of interested discovery. At the same moment that he reaches the cradle ABBIE seems to sense something. She gets up weakly and goes to CABOT.*)

ABBIE: I'm goin' up t' the baby.

CABOT (*with real solicitation*): Air ye able fur the stairs? D'ye want me t' help ye, Abbie?

ABBIE: No. I'm able. I'll be down agen soon.

CABOT: Don't ye git wore out! He needs ye, remember — our son does! (*He grins affectionately, patting her on the back. She shrinks from his touch.*)

ABBIE (*dully*): Don't — tech me. I'm goin' — up. (*She goes. CABOT looks after her. A whisper goes around the room. CABOT turns. It ceases. He wipes his forehead streaming with sweat. He is breathing pantingly.*)

CABOT: I'm a-goin' out t' git fresh air. I'm feelin' a mite dizzy. Fiddle up thar! Dance, all o' ye! Here's likker fur them as wants it. Enjoy yerselves. I'll be back. (*He goes, closing the door behind him.*)

FIDDLER (*sarcastically*): Don't hurry none on our account! (*A suppressed laugh. He imitates ABBIE.*) Whar's Eben? (*More laughter.*)

A WOMAN (*loudly*): What's happened in this house is plain as the nose on yer face! (*ABBIE appears in the doorway upstairs and stands looking in surprise and adoration at EBEN who does not see her.*)

A MAN: Ssshh! He's li-ble t' be listenin' at the door. That'd be like him. (*Their voices die to an intensive whispering. Their faces are concentrated on this gossip. A noise as of dead leaves in the wind comes from the room. CABOT has come out from the porch and stands by the gate, leaning on it, staring at the sky blinkingly. ABBIE comes across the room silently. EBEN does not notice her until quite near.*)

EBEN (*starting*): Abbie!

ABBIE: Ssshh! (*She throws her arms around him. They kiss — then bend over the cradle together.*) Ain't he purty? — dead spit 'n' image o' yew!

EBEN (*pleased*): Air he? I can't tell none.

ABBIE: E-zactly like!

EBEN (*frowningly*): I don't like this. I don't like lettin' on what's mine's his'n. I been doin' that all my life. I'm gittin' t' the end o' b'arin' it!

ABBIE (*putting her finger on his lips*): We're doin' the best we kin. We got t' wait. Somethin's bound t' happen. (*She puts her arms around him.*) I got t' go back.

EBEN: I'm goin' out. I can't b'ar it with the fiddle playin' an' the laughin'.

ABBIE: Don't git feelin' low. I love ye, Eben. Kiss me. (*He kisses her. They remain in each other's arms.*)

CABOT (*at the gate, confusedly*): Even the music can't drive it out — somethin'. Ye kin feel it droppin' off the elums, climbin' up the roof, sneakin' down the chimney, pokin' in the corners! They's no peace in houses, they's no rest livin' with folks. Somethin's always livin' with ye. (*With a deep sigh.*) I'll go t' the barn an' rest a spell. (*He goes wearily toward the barn.*)

FIDDLER (*tuning up*): Let's celebrate the old skunk gittin' fooled! We kin have some fun now he's went. (*He starts to fiddle "Turkey in the Straw." There is real merriment now. The young folks get up to dance.*)

CURTAIN

SCENE II

A half-hour later — Exterior — EBEN *is standing by the gate looking up at the sky, an expression of dumb pain bewildered by itself on his face.* CABOT *appears, returning from the barn, walking wearily, his eyes on the ground. He sees* EBEN *and his whole mood immediately changes. He becomes excited, a cruel, triumphant grin comes to his lips, he strides up and slaps* EBEN *on the back. From within comes the whining of the fiddle and the noise of stamping feet and laughing voices.*

CABOT: So har ye be!

EBEN (*startled, stares at him with hatred for a moment — then dully*): Ay-ch.

CABOT (*surveying him jeeringly*): Why hain't ye been in t' dance? They was all axin' fur ye.

EBEN: Let 'em ax!

CABOT: They's a hull passel o' purty gals.

EBEN: T'hell with 'em!

CABOT: Ye'd ought t' be marryin' one o' 'em soon.

EBEN: I hain't marryin' no one.

CABOT: Ye might 'arn a share o' a farm that way.

EBEN (*with a sneer*): Like yew did, ye mean? I hain't that kind.

CABOT (*stung*): Ye lie! 'Twas yer Maw's folks aimed t' steal my farm from me.

EBEN: Other folks don't say so. (*After a pause — defiantly.*) An' I got a farm, anyways!

CABOT (*derisively*): Whar?

EBEN (*stamps a foot on the ground*): Har!

CABOT (*throws his head back and laughs coarsely*): Ho-ho! Ye hev, hev ye? Waal, that's a good un!

EBEN (*controlling himself — grimly*): Ye'll see!

CABOT (*stares at him suspiciously, trying to make him out — a pause — then with scornful confidence*): Ay-eh. I'll see. So'll ye. It's ye that's blind — blind as a mole underground. (EBEN *suddenly laughs, one short sardonic bark:* "Ha." *A pause.* CABOT *peers at him with renewed suspicion.*) Whar air ye hawin' 'bout? (EBEN *turns away without answering.* CABOT *grows angry.*) God A'mighty, yew air a dumb dunce! They's nothin' in that thick skull o' your'n but noise — like a empty keg it be! (EBEN *doesn't seem to hear.* CABOT's *rage grows.*) Yewr farm! God A'mighty! If ye wa'n't a born donkey ye'd know ye'll never own stick nor stone on it, specially now arter him bein' born. It's his'n, I tell ye — his'n arter I die — but I'll live a hundred jest t' fool ye all — an' he'll be growed then — yewr age a'most! (EBEN *laughs again his sardonic "Ha." This drives* CABOT *into a fury.*) Ha? Ye think ye kin git 'round that someways, do ye? Waal, it'll be her'n, too — Abbie's — ye won't git 'round her — she knows yer tricks — she'll be too much fur ye — she wants the farm her'n — she was afeerd o' ye — she told me ye was sneakin' 'round tryin' t' make love t' her t' git her on yer side . . . ye . . . ye mad fool, ye! (*He raises his clenched fists threateningly.*)

EBEN (*is confronting him choking with rage*): Ye lie, ye old skunk! Abbie never said no sech thing!

CABOT (*suddenly triumphant when he sees how shaken* EBEN *is*): She did. An' I says, I'll blow his brains t' the top o' them elums — an' she says no, that hain't sense, who'll ye git t'help ye on the farm in his place — an' then she says yew'n me ought t' have a son — I know we kin, she says — an' I says, if we do, ye kin have anythin' I've got ye've a mind t'. An' she says, I wants Eben cut off so's this farm'll be mine when ye die! (*With terrible gloating.*) An' that's what's happened, hain't it? An' the farm's her'n! An' the dust o' the road — that's you'rn! Ha! Now who's hawin'?

EBEN (*has been listening, petrified with grief and rage — suddenly laughs wildly and brokenly*): Ha-ha-ha! So that's her sneakin' game — all along! — like I suspicioned at fust — t'swaller it all — an' me, too . . . ! (*Madly.*) I'll murder her! (*He springs toward the porch but* CABOT *is quicker and gets in between.*)

CABOT: No, ye don't!

EBEN: Git out o' my road! (*He tries to throw* CABOT *aside. They grapple in what becomes immediately a murderous struggle. The old man's concentrated strength is too much for* EBEN. CABOT *gets one hand on his throat and presses him back across the stone wall. At the same moment,* ABBIE *comes out on the porch. With a stifled cry she runs toward them.*)

ABBIE: Eben! Ephraim! (*She tugs at the hand on* EBEN's *throat.*) Let go, Ephraim! Ye're chokin' him!

CABOT (*removes his hand and flings* EBEN *sideways full length on the grass, gasping and choking. With a cry,* ABBIE *kneels beside him, trying to take his head on her lap, but he pushes her away.* CABOT *stands looking down with fierce triumph*): Ye needn't t've fret, Abbie, I wa'n't aimin' t' kill him. He hain't wuth hangin' fur — not by a hell of a sight! (*More and more triumphantly.*) Seventy-six an' him not thirty yit — an' look whar he be fur thinkin' his Paw was easy! No, by God, I hain't easy! An' him upstairs, I'll raise him t' be like me! (*He turns to leave them.*) I'm goin' in an' dance! — sing an' celebrate! (*He walks to the porch — then turns with a great grin.*) I don't calc'late it's left in him, but if he gits pesky, Abbie, ye jest sing out. I'll come a-runnin' an' by the Etarnal, I'll put him across my knee an' birch him! Ha-ha-ha! (*He goes into the house laughing. A moment later his loud "whoop" is heard.*)

ABBIE (*tenderly*): Eben. Air ye hurt? (*She tires to kiss him but he pushes her violently away and struggles to a sitting position.*)

EBEN (*gaspingly*): T' hell — with ye!

ABBIE (*not believing her ears*): It's me, Eben — Abbie — don't ye know me?

EBEN (*glowering at her with hatred*): Ay-eh — I know ye — now! (*He suddenly breaks down, sobbing weakly.*)

ABBIE (*fearfully*): Eben — what's happened t' ye — why did ye look at me 's if ye hated me?

EBEN (*violently, between sobs and gasps*): I do hate ye! Ye're a whore — a damn trickin' whore!

ABBIE (*shrinking back horrified*): Eben! Ye don't know what ye're sayin'!

EBEN (*scrambling to his feet and following her — accusingly*): Ye're nothin' but a stinkin' passel o' lies! Ye've been lyin' t' me every word ye spoke, day an' night, since we fust — done it. Ye've kept sayin' ye loved me. . . .

ABBIE (*frantically*): I do love ye! (*She takes his hand but he flings hers away.*)

EBEN (*unheeding*): Ye've made a fool o' me — a sick, dumb fool — a-purpose! Ye've been on'y playin' yer sneakin', stealin' game all along — gittin' me t' lie with ye so's ye'd

hev a son he'd think was his'n, an' makin' him promise he'd give ye the farm and let me eat dust, if ye git him a son! (*Staring at her with anguished, bewildered eyes.*) They must be a devil livin' in ye! T'aint human t' be as bad as that be!

ABBIE (*stunned — dully*): He told yew . . . ?

EBEN: Hain't it true? It hain't no good in yew lyin'.

ABBIE (*pleadingly*): Eben, listen — ye must listen — it was long ago — afore we done nothin' — yew was scornin' me — goin' t' see Min — when I was lovin' ye — an' I said it t' him t' git vengeance on ye!

EBEN (*unheedingly. With tortured passion*): I wish ye was dead! I wish I was dead along with ye afore this come! (*Ragingly.*) But I'll git my vengeance too! I'll pray Maw t' come back t' help me — t' put her cuss on yew an' him!

ABBIE (*brokenly*): Don't ye, Eben! Don't ye! (*She throws herself on her knees before him, weeping.*) I didn't mean t' do bad t' ye! Fergive me, won't ye?

EBEN (*not seeming to hear her — fiercely*): I'll git squar' with the old skunk — an' yew! I'll tell him the truth 'bout the son he's so proud o'! Then I'll leave ye here t' pizen each other — with Maw comin' out o' her grave at nights — an' I'll go t' the gold fields o' Californi-a whar Sim an' Peter be!

ABBIE (*terrified*): Ye won't — leave me? Ye can't!

EBEN (*with fierce determination*): I'm a-goin', I tell ye! I'll git rich thar an' come back an' fight him fur the farm he stole — an' I'll kick ye both out in the road — t' beg an' sleep in the woods — an' yer son along with ye — t' starve an' die! (*He is hysterical at the end.*)

ABBIE (*with a shudder — humbly*): He's yewr son, too, Eben.

EBEN (*torturedly*): I wish he never was born! I wish he'd die this minit! I wish I'd never sot eyes on him! It's him — yew havin' him — a-purpose t' steal — that's changed everythin'!

ABBIE (*gently*): Did ye believe I loved ye — afore he come?

EBEN: Ay-eh — like a dumb ox!

ABBIE: An' ye don't believe no more?

EBEN: B'lieve a lyin' thief! Ha!

ABBIE (*shudders — then humbly*): An' did ye r'ally love me afore?

EBEN (*brokenly*): Ay-eh — an' ye was trickin' me!

ABBIE: An' ye don't love me now!

EBEN (*violently*): I hate ye, I tell ye!

ABBIE: An' ye're truly goin' West — goin' t' leave me — all account o' him being born?

EBEN: I'm a-goin' in the mornin' — or may God strike me t' hell!

ABBIE (*after a pause — with a dreadful cold intensity — slowly*): If that's what his comin 's done t' me — killin' yewr love — takin' yew away — my on'y joy — the on'y joy I ever knowed — like heaven t' me — purtier'n heaven — then I hate him, too, even if I be his Maw!

EBEN (*bitterly*): Lies! Ye love him! He'll steal the farm fur ye! (*Brokenly.*) But t'ain't the farm so much — not no more — it's yew foolin' me — gittin' me t' love ye — lyin' yew loved me — jest t' git a son t' steal!

ABBIE (*distractedly*): He won't steal! I'd kill him fust! I do love ye! I'll prove t' ye . . . !

EBEN (*harshly*): T'ain't no use lyin' no more. I'm deaf t' ye! (*He turns away.*) I hain't seein' ye agen. Good-by!

ABBIE (*pale with anguish*): Hain't ye even goin' t' kiss me — not once — arter all we loved?

EBEN (*in a hard voice*): I hain't wantin' t' kiss ye never agen! I'm wantin' t' forgit I ever sot eyes on ye!

ABBIE: Eben! — ye mustn't — wait a spell — I want t' tell ye. . . .

EBEN: I'm a-goin' in t' git drunk. I'm a-goin' t' dance.

ABBIE (*clinging to his arm — with passionate earnestness*): If I could make it — 's if he'd never come up between us — if I could prove t' ye I wa'n't schemin' t' steal from ye — so's everythin' could be jest the same with us, lovin' each other jest the same, kissin' an' happy the same's we've been happy afore he come — if I could do it — ye'd love me agen, wouldn't ye? Ye'd kiss me agen? Ye wouldn't never leave me, would ye?

EBEN (*moved*): I calc'late not. (*Then shaking her hand off his arm — with a bitter smile.*) But ye hain't God, be ye?

ABBIE (*exultantly*): Remember ye've promised! (*Then with strange intensity.*) Mebbe I kin take back one thin' God does!

EBEN (*peering at her*): Ye're gittin' cracked, hain't ye? (*Then going towards door.*) I'm a-goin' t' dance.

ABBIE (*calls after him intensely*): I'll prove t' ye! I'll prove I love ye better'n. . . . (*He*

goes in the door, not seeming to hear. She remains standing where she is, looking after him — then she finishes desperately.*) Better'n everythin' else in the world!

SCENE III

Just before dawn in the morning — shows the kitchen and CABOT's *bedroom. In the kitchen, by the light of a tallow candle on the table,* EBEN *is sitting, his chin propped on his hands, his drawn face blank and expressionless. His carpetbag is on the floor beside him. In the bedroom, dimly lighted by a small whale-oil lamp,* CABOT *lies asleep.* ABBIE *is bending over the cradle, listening, her face full of terror yet with an undercurrent of desperate triumph. Suddenly, she breaks down and sobs, appears about to throw herself on her knees beside the cradle; but the old man turns restlessly, groaning in his sleep, and she controls herself, and, shrinking away from the cradle with a gesture of horror, backs swiftly toward the door in rear and goes out. A moment later she comes into the kitchen and, running to* EBEN, *flings her arms about his neck and kisses him wildly. He hardens himself, he remains unmoved and cold, he keeps his eyes straight ahead.*

ABBIE (*hysterically*): I done it, Eben! I told ye I'd do it! I've proved I love ye — better'n everythin' — so's ye can't never doubt me no more!

EBEN (*dully*): Whatever ye done, it hain't no good now.

ABBIE (*wildly*): Don't ye say that! Kiss me, Eben, won't ye? I need ye t' kiss me arter what I done! I need ye t' say ye love me!

EBEN (*kisses her without emotion — dully*): That's fur good-by. I'm a-goin' soon.

ABBIE: No! No! Ye won't go — not now!

EBEN (*going on with his own thoughts*): I been a-thinkin' — an' I hain't goin' t' tell Paw nothin'. I'll leave Maw t' take vengeance on ye. If I told him, the old skunk'd jest be stinkin' mean enuf to take it out on that baby. (*His voice showing emotion in spite of him.*) An' I don't want nothin' bad t' happen t' him. He hain't t' blame fur yew. (*He adds with a certain queer pride.*) An' he looks like me! An' by God, he's mine! An' some day I'll be a-comin' back an' ...!

ABBIE (*too absorbed in her own thoughts to listen to him — pleadingly*): They's no cause fur ye t' go now — they's no sense — it's all the same's it was — they's nothin' come b'tween us now — arter what I done!

EBEN (*something in her voice arouses him. He stares at her a bit frightenedly*): Ye look mad, Abbie. What did ye do?

ABBIE: I — I killed him, Eben.

EBEN (*amazed*): Ye killed him?

ABBIE (*dully*): Ay-eh.

EBEN (*recovering from his astonishment — savagely*): An' serves him right! But we got t' do somethin' quick t' make it look 's if the old skunk'd killed himself when he was drunk. We kin prove by 'em all how drunk he got.

ABBIE (*wildly*): No! No! Not him! (*Laughing distractedly.*) But that's what I ought t' done, hain't it? I oughter killed him instead! Why didn't ye tell me?

EBEN (*appalled*): Instead? What d'ye mean?

ABBIE: Not him.

EBEN (*his face grown ghastly*): Not — not that baby!

ABBIE (*dully*): Ay-eh!

EBEN (*falls to his knees as if he'd been struck — his voice trembling with horror*): Oh, God A'mighty! A'mighty God! Maw, whar was ye, why didn't ye stop her?

ABBIE (*simply*): She went back t' her grave that night we fust done it, remember? I hain't felt her about since. (*A pause.* EBEN *hides his head in his hands, trembling all over as if he had the ague. She goes on dully.*) I left the piller over his little face. Then he killed himself. He stopped breathin'. (*She begins to weep softly.*)

EBEN (*rage beginning to mingle with grief*): He looked like me. He was mine, damn ye!

ABBIE (*slowly and brokenly*): I didn't want t' do it. I hated myself fur doin' it. I loved him. He was so purty — dead spit 'n' image o' yew. But I loved yew more — an' yew was goin' away — far off whar I'd never see ye agen, never kiss ye, never feel ye pressed agin me agen — an' ye said ye hated me fur havin' him — ye said ye hated him an' wished he was dead — ye said if it hadn't been fur him comin' it'd be the same's afore between us.

EBEN (*unable to endure this, springs to his feet in a fury, threatening her, his twitching fingers seeming to reach out for her throat*): Ye lie! I never said — I never dreamed ye'd — I'd cut off my head afore I'd hurt his finger!

ABBIE (*piteously, sinking on her knees*): Eben, don't ye look at me like that — hatin' me — not after what I done fur ye — fur us — so's we could be happy agen —

EBEN (*furiously now*): Shut up, or I'll kill ye! I see yer game now — the same old sneakin' trick — ye're aimin' t' blame me fur the murder ye done!

ABBIE (*moaning — putting her hands over her ears*): Don't ye, Eben! Don't ye! (*She grasps his legs.*)

EBEN (*his mood suddenly changing to horror, shrinks away from her*): Don't ye tech me! Ye're pizen! How could ye — t' murder a pore little critter — Ye must've swapped yer soul t' hell! (*Suddenly raging.*) Ha! I kin see why ye done it! Not the lies ye jest told — but 'cause ye wanted t' steal agen — steal the last thin' ye'd left me — my part o' him — no, the hull o' him — ye saw he looked like me — ye knowed he was all mine — an' ye couldn't b'ar it — I know ye! Ye killed him fur bein' mine! (*All this has driven him almost insane. He makes a rush past her for the door — then turns — shaking both fists at her, violently.*) But I'll take vengeance now! I'll git the Sheriff! I'll tell him everythin'! Then I'll sing "I'm off to Californi-a!" an' go — gold — Golden Gate — gold sun — fields o' gold in the West! (*This last he half shouts, half croons incoherently, suddenly breaking off passionately.*) I'm a-goin' fur the Sheriff t' come an' git ye! I want ye tuk away, locked up from me! I can't stand t' luk at ye! Murderer an' thief 'r not, ye still tempt me! I'll give ye up t' the Sheriff. (*He turns and runs out, around the corner of house, panting and sobbing, and breaks into a swerving sprint down the road.*)

ABBIE (*struggling to her feet, runs to the door, calling after him*): I love ye, Eben! I love ye! (*She stops at the door weakly, swaying, about to fall.*) I don't care what ye do — if ye'll on'y love me agen — (*She falls limply to the floor in a faint.*)

CURTAIN

SCENE IV

About an hour later. Same as Scene III. Shows the kitchen and CABOT's *bedroom. It is after dawn. The sky is brilliant with the sunrise. In the kitchen,* ABBIE *sits at the table, her body limp and exhausted, her head bowed down over her arms, her face hidden. Upstairs,* CABOT *is still asleep but awakens with a start. He looks toward the window and gives a snort of surprise and irritation — throws back the covers and begins hurriedly pulling on his clothes. Without looking behind him, he begins talking to* ABBIE *whom he supposes beside him.*

CABOT: Thunder 'n' lightin', Abbie! I hain't slept this late in fifty year! Looks 's if the sun was full riz a'most. Must've been the dancin' an' likker. Must be gittin' old. I hope Eben's t' wuk. Ye might've tuk the trouble t' rouse me, Abbie. (*He turns — sees no one there — surprised.*) Waal — whar air she? Gittin' vittles, I calc'late. (*He tiptoes to the cradle and peers down — proudly.*) Mornin', sonny. Purty's a picture! Sleepin' sound. He don't beller all night like most o' 'em. (*He goes quietly out the door in rear — a few moments later enters kitchen — sees* ABBIE — *with satisfaction.*) So thar ye be. Ye got any vittles cooked?

ABBIE (*without moving*): No.

CABOT (*coming to her, almost sympathetically*): Ye feelin' sick?

ABBIE: No.

CABOT (*pats her on shoulder. She shudders*): Ye'd best lie down a spell. (*Half jocularly.*) Yer son'll be needin' ye soon. He'd ought t' wake up with a gnashin' appetite, the sound way he's sleepin'.

ABBIE (*shudders — then in a dead voice*): He hain't never goin' t' wake up.

CABOT (*jokingly*): Takes after me this mornin'. I hain't slept so late in . . .

ABBIE: He's dead.

CABOT (*stares at her — bewilderedly*): What. . . .

ABBIE: I killed him.

CABOT (*stepping back from her — aghast*): Air ye drunk — 'r crazy — 'r . . . !

ABBIE (*suddenly lifts her head and turns on him — wildly*): I killed him, I tell ye! I smothered him. Go up an' see if ye don't b'lieve me! (CABOT *stares at her a second, then bolts out the rear door — can be heard bounding up the stairs — and rushes into the bedroom and over to the cradle.* ABBIE *has sunk back lifelessly into her former position.* CABOT *puts his hand down on the body in the crib.*

An expression of fear and horror comes over his face.)

CABOT (*shrinking away — tremblingly*): God A'mighty! God A'mighty. (*He stumbles out the door — in a short while returns to the kitchen — comes to* ABBIE, *the stunned expression still on his face — hoarsely.*) Why did ye do it? Why? (*As she doesn't answer, he grabs her violently by the shoulder and shakes her.*) I ax ye why ye done it! Ye'd better tell me 'r . . . !

ABBIE (*gives him a furious push which sends him staggering back and springs to her feet — with wild rage and hatred*): Don't ye dare tech me! What right hev ye t' question me 'bout him? He wa'n't yewr son! Think I'd have a son by yew? I'd die fust! I hate the sight o' ye an' allus did! It's yew I should've murdered, if I'd had good sense! I hate ye! I love Eben. I did from the fust. An' he was Eben's son — mine an' Eben's — not your'n!

CABOT (*stands looking at her dazedly — a pause — finding his words with an effort — dully*): That was it — what I felt — pokin' round the corners — while ye lied — holdin' yerself from me — sayin' ye'd a'ready conceived — (*He lapses into crushed silence — then with a strange emotion*) He's dead, sart'n. I felt his heart. Pore little critter! (*He blinks back one tear, wiping his sleeve across his nose.*)

ABBIE (*hysterically*): Don't ye! Don't ye! (*She sobs unrestrainedly.*)

CABOT (*with a concentrated effort that stiffens his body into a rigid line and hardens his face into a stony mask — through his teeth to himself*): I got t' be — like a stone — a rock o' jedgment! (*A pause. He gets complete control over himself — harshly.*) If he was Eben's, I be glad he air gone! An' mebbe I suspicioned it all along. I felt they was somethin' onnateral — somewhars — the house got so lonesome — an' cold — drivin' me down t' the barn — t' the beasts o' the field. . . . Ay-eh. I must've suspicioned — somethin'. Ye didn't fool me — not altogether, leastways — I'm too old a bird — growin' ripe on the bough. . . . (*He becomes aware he is wandering, straightens again, looks at* ABBIE *with a cruel grin.*) So ye'd like t' hev murdered me 'stead o' him, would ye? Waal, I'll live to a hundred! I'll live t' see ye hung! I'll deliver ye up t' the jedgment o' God an' the law! I'll git the Sheriff now. (*Starts for the door.*)

ABBIE (*dully*): Ye needn't. Eben's gone fur him.

CABOT (*amazed*): Eben — gone fur the Sheriff?

ABBIE: Ay-eh.

CABOT: T' inform agen ye?

ABBIE: Ay-eh.

CABOT (*considers this — a pause — then in a hard voice*): Waal, I'm thankful fur him savin' me the trouble. I'll git t' wuk. (*He goes to the door — then turns — in a voice full of strange emotion.*) He'd ought t' been my son, Abbie. Ye'd ought t' loved me. I'm a man. If ye'd loved me, I'd never told no Sheriff on ye no matter what ye did, if they was t' brile me alive!

ABBIE (*defensively*): They's more to it nor yew know, makes him tell.

CABOT (*dryly*): Fur yewr sake, I hope they be. (*He goes out — comes around to the gate — stares up at the sky. His control relaxes. For a moment he is old and weary. He murmurs despairingly.*) God A'mighty, I be lonesomer'n ever! (*He hears running footsteps from the left, immediately is himself again. EBEN runs in, panting exhaustedly, wild-eyed and mad looking. He lurches through the gate. CABOT grabs him by the shoulder. EBEN stares at him dumbly.*) Did ye tell the Sheriff?

EBEN (*nodding stupidly*): Ay-eh.

CABOT (*gives him a push away that sends him sprawling — laughing with withering contempt*): Good fur ye! A prime chip o' yer Maw ye be! (*He goes toward the barn, laughing harshly. EBEN scrambles to his feet. Suddenly CABOT turns — grimly threatening.*) Git off this farm when the Sheriff takes her — or, by God, he'll have t' come back an' git me fur murder, too! (*He stalks off. EBEN does not appear to have heard him. He runs to the door and comes into the kitchen. ABBIE looks up with a cry of anguished joy. EBEN stumbles over and throws himself on his knees beside her — sobbing brokenly.*)

EBEN: Fergive me!

ABBIE (*happily*): Eben! (*She kisses him and pulls his head over against her breast.*)

EBEN: I love ye! Fergive me!

ABBIE (*ecstatically*): I'd fergive ye all the sins in hell fur sayin' that! (*She kisses his head, pressing it to her with a fierce passion of possession.*)

EBEN (*brokenly*): But I told the Sheriff. He's comin' fur ye!

ABBIE: I kin b'ar what happens t' me — now!

EBEN: I woke him up. I told him. He says, wait 'til I git dressed. I was waiting. I got to thinkin' o' yew. I got to thinkin' how I'd loved ye. It hurt like somethin' was bustin' in my chest an' head. I got t' cryin'. I knowed sudden I loved ye yet, an' allus would love ye!

ABBIE (*caressing his hair — tenderly*): My boy, hain't ye?

EBEN: I begun t' run back. I cut across the fields an' through the woods. I thought ye might have time t' run away — with me — an' . . .

ABBIE (*shaking her head*): I got t' take my punishment — t' pay fur my sin.

EBEN: Then I want t' share it with ye.

ABBIE: Ye didn't do nothin'.

EBEN: I put it in yer head. I wisht he was dead! I as much as urged ye t' do it!

ABBIE: No. It was me alone!

EBEN: I'm as guilty as yew be! He was the child o' our sin.

ABBIE (*lifting her head as if defying God*): I don't repent that sin! I hain't askin' God t' fergive that!

EBEN: Nor me — but it led up t' the other — an' the murder ye did, ye did 'count o' me — an' it's my murder, too, I'll tell the Sheriff — an' if ye deny it, I'll say we planned it t'gether — an' they'll all b'lieve me, fur they suspicion everythin' we've done, an' it'll seem likely an' true to 'em. An' it is true — way down. I did help ye — somehow.

ABBIE (*laying her head on his — sobbing*): No! I don't want yew t' suffer!

EBEN: I got t' pay fur my part o' the sin! An' I'd suffer wust leavin' ye, goin' West, thinkin' o' ye day an' night, bein' out when yew was in — (*Lowering his voice.*) 'r bein' alive when yew was dead. (*A pause.*) I want t' share with ye, Abbie — prison 'r death 'r hell 'r anythin'! (*He looks into her eyes and forces a trembling smile.*) If I'm sharin' with ye, I won't feel lonesome, leastways.

ABBIE (*weakly*): Eben! I won't let ye! I can't let ye!

EBEN (*kissing her — tenderly*): Ye can't he'p yerself. I got ye beat fur once!

ABBIE (*forcing a smile — adoringly*): I hain't beat — s'long's I got ye!

EBEN (*hears the sound of feet outside*): Ssshh! Listen! They've come t' take us!

ABBIE: No, it's him. Don't give him no chance to fight ye, Eben. Don't say nothin' — no matter what he says. An' I won't neither. (*It is* CABOT. *He comes up from the barn in a great state of excitement and strides into the house and then into the kitchen.* EBEN *is kneeling beside* ABBIE, *his arm around her, hers around him. They stare straight ahead.*)

CABOT (*stares at them, his face hard. A long pause — vindictively*): Ye make a slick pair o' murderin' turtle doves! Ye'd ought t' be both hung on the same limb an' left thar t' swing in the breeze an' rot — a warnin' t' old fools like me t' b'ar their lonesomeness alone — an' fur young fools like ye t' hobble their lust. (*A pause. The excitement returns to his face, his eyes snap, he looks a bit crazy.*) I couldn't work today. I couldn't take no interest. T' hell with the farm! I'm leavin' it! I've turned the cows an' other stock loose! I've druv 'em into the woods whar they kin be free! By freein' 'em, I'm freein' myself! I'm quittin' here today! I'll set fire t' house an' barn an' watch 'em burn, an' I'll leave yer Maw t' haunt the ashes, an' I'll will the fields back t' God, so that nothin' human kin never touch 'em! I'll be a-goin' to Californi-a — t' jine Simeon an' Peter — true sons o' mine if they be dumb fools — an' the Cabots'll find Solomon's Mines t'gether! (*He suddenly cuts a mad caper.*) Whoop! What was the song they sung? "Oh, Californi-a! That's the land fur me." (*He sings this — then gets on his knees by the floorboard under which the money was hid.*) An' I'll sail thar on one o' the finest clippers I kin find! I've got the money! Pity ye didn't know whar this was hidden so's ye could steal.... (*He has pulled up the board. He stares — feels — stares again. A pause of dead silence. He slowly turns, slumping into a sitting position on the floor, his eyes like those of a dead fish, his face the sickly green of an attack of nausea. He swallows painfully several times — forces a weak smile at last.*) So — ye did steal it!

EBEN (*emotionlessly*): I swapped it t' Sim an' Peter fur their share o' the farm — t' pay their passage t' Californi-a.

CABOT (*with one sardonic*): Ha! (*He begins to recover. Gets slowly to his feet — strangely.*) I calc'late God give it t' 'em — not yew! God's hard, not easy! Mebbe they's easy gold in the West but it hain't God's gold. It hain't fur me. I kin hear His voice warnin' me agen t' be hard an' stay on my farm. I kin see his hand usin' Eben t' steal t' keep me from weakness. I kin feel I be in the palm o' His hand, His fingers guidin' me. (*A pause — then he mutters sadly.*) It's a-goin' t' be lonesomer now than ever it war afore — an' I'm gittin' old, Lord — ripe on the bough.... (*Then stiffening.*) Waal — what d'ye want? God's lonesome, hain't He? God's hard an' lonesome! (*A pause. The* SHERIFF *with two men comes up the road from the left. They move cautiously to the door. The* SHERIFF *knocks on it with the butt of his pistol.*)

SHERIFF: Open in the name o' the law! (*They start.*)

CABOT: They've come fur ye. (*He goes to the rear door.*) Come in, Jim! (*The three men enter.* CABOT *meets them in doorway.*) Jest a minit, Jim. I got 'em safe here. (*The* SHERIFF *nods. He and his companions remain in the doorway.*)

EBEN (*suddenly calls*): I lied this mornin', Jim. I helped her to do it. Ye kin take me, too.

ABBIE (*brokenly*): No!

CABOT: Take 'em both. (*He comes forward — stares at* EBEN *with a trace of grudging admiration.*) Purty good — fur yew! Waal, I got t' round up the stock. Good-by.

EBEN: Good-by.

ABBIE: Good-by. (CABOT *turns and strides past the men — comes out and around the corner of the house, his shoulders squared, his face stony, and stalks grimly toward the barn. In the meantime the* SHERIFF *and men have come into the room.*)

SHERIFF (*embarrassedly*): Waal — we'd best start.

ABBIE: Wait. (*Turns to* EBEN.) I love ye, Eben.

EBEN: I love ye, Abbie. (*They kiss. The three men grin and shuffle embarrassedly.* EBEN *takes* ABBIE's *hand. They go out the door in rear, the men following, and come from the house, walking hand in hand to the gate.* EBEN *stops there and points to the sunrise sky.*) Sun's a-rizin'. Purty, hain't it?

ABBIE: Ay-eh. (*They both stand for a moment looking up raptly in attitudes strangely aloof and devout.*)

SHERIFF (*looking around at the farm enviously — to his companion*): It's a jim-dandy farm, no denyin'. Wished I owned it!

CURTAIN

Although tragic drama traditionally depicted the fall of kings and princes, as early as the sixteenth century there were tragedies with middle-class protagonists. Playwrights sought to justify their new tragedies against conservative critical theory. The standard argument in favor of the older heroic tragedy is that only the fall of a great man can excite pity and fear, whereas the fall of an ordinary man — someone like ourselves — is not awe-inspiring but merely pathetic. Great passions, the argument runs, are found only in great people; a king, for example, can avenge his honor, but a shopkeeper has no honor to avenge. More specifically, the fall of a great hero is more tragic than the fall of an ordinary citizen because it is a bigger fall, and because it necessarily has greater reverberations. When a king falls, a kingdom trembles.

On the other hand, advocates of bourgeois tragedy generally insist that tragic drama derives much of its impact from our sympathy for (or identification with) the tragic hero, and this identification is, presumably, more likely to be achieved when the hero resembles us. Furthermore, democratic supporters of middle-class tragedy say, all people are potentially great, and rank is irrelevant to largeness of spirit.

Paradoxically, O'Neill's characters achieve their greatness through passions that might be thought of as base. When *Desire Under the Elms* was first produced, it was denounced for its depiction of greed, lechery, adultery, and murder, and the entire cast of the Los Angeles production was arrested for publicly performing "filth." But whatever grandeur the characters have is rooted in their primal feelings. Thus Eben's stepmother, Abbie, drawn irresistibly to her stepson and sensing his passionate interest in her, says, "Hain't the sun strong an' hot? Ye kin feel it burnin' into the earth — Nature — makin' thin's grow — bigger 'n' bigger — burnin' inside ye — makin' ye want t' grow — into somethin' else — till ye're jined with it — an' its your'n — but it owns ye, too — an' makes ye grow bigger — like a tree — like them elums — (*She laughs again softly, holding his eyes. He takes a step toward her, compelled against his will.*) Nature'll beat ye, Eben. Ye might's well own up t' it fust 's last." Or consider these words of Ephraim's, Abbie's husband and Eben's father. He is talking about his passionate devotion to his rocky New England farm: "When ye kin make corn sprout out o' stones, God's livin' in yew! . . . God's hard, not easy! God's in the stones! Build my church on a rock — out o' stones an' I'll be in them! That's what He meant t' Peter!"

One critic, assuming that O'Neill accepted the view that Aristotle's word *hamartia* refers to a tragic flaw, argues that Ephraim "has dedicated his entire life to God, who is, of course, only an image of his own ego." Really "only an image of his own ego"? We shall let the reader decide whether or not Ephraim's devotion to God is, in the context of the play, a tragic fault, but we want to take advantage of this space to give the reader three quotations by O'Neill. These may help the reader to understand, if not what O'Neill accomplished, at least what he intended. The first dates from 1921, a few years before *Desire Under the Elms*; the second is an undated remark made in conversation; the third, from 1925, was made in response to reviews of *Desire Under the Elms.*

I have been accused of unmitigated gloom. Is this a pessimistic view of life? I do not think so. There is a skin deep optimism and another higher optimism, not skin deep, which is usually confounded with pessimism. To me, the tragic alone has that significant beauty which is truth. It is the meaning of life — and the hope. The noblest is eternally the most tragic. The people who succeed and do not push on to a greater failure are the spiritual middle classers. Their stopping at success is the proof of their compromising insignificance. How pretty their dreams must have been! The man who pursues the mere attainable should be sentenced to get it — and keep it. Let him rest on his laurels and enthrone him in a Morris chair, in which laurels and hero may wither away together. Only through the unattainable does man achieve a hope worth living and dying for — and so attain himself. He with the spiritual guerdon of a hope in hopelessness, is nearest to the stars and the rainbow's foot.*

Most modern plays are concerned with the relation between man and man, but that does not interest me at all. I am interested only in the relation between man and God.

It's not in me to pose much as a "misunderstood one," but it does seem discouragingly (that is, if one lacked a sense of ironic humor!) evident to me that most of my critics don't want to see what I'm trying to do or how I'm trying to do it, although I flatter myself that end and means are characteristic, individual and positive enough not to be mistaken for anyone else's, or for those of any "modern" or "pre-modern" school. To be called a "sordid realist" one day, a "grim, pessimistic Naturalist" the next, a "lying Moral Romanticist" the next, etc. is quite perplexing — not to add the *Times* editorial that settled *Desire* once and for all by calling it a "Neo-Primitive," a Matisse of the drama, as it were! So I'm really longing to explain and try and convince some sympathetic ear that I've tried to make myself a melting pot for all these methods, seeing some virtues for my ends in each of them, and thereby, if there is enough real fire in me, boil down to my own technique. But where I feel myself most neglected is just where I set most store by myself — as a bit of a poet, who has labored with the spoken word to evolve original rhythms of beauty, where beauty apparently isn't — *Jones, Ape, God's Chillun, Desire*, etc. — and to see the transfiguring nobility of tragedy, in as near the Greek sense as one can grasp it, in seemingly the most ignoble, debased lives. And just here is where I am a most confirmed mystic, too, for I'm always, always trying to interpret Life in terms of lives, never just lives in terms of character. I'm always acutely conscious of the Force behind — Fate, God, our biological past creating our present, whatever one calls it — Mystery certainly — and of the one eternal tragedy of Man in his glorious, self-destructive struggle to make the Force express him instead of being, as an animal is, an infinitesimal incident in its expression. And my profound conviction is that

* *New York Tribune,* February 13, 1921.

this is the only subject worth writing about and that it is possible — or can be — to develop a tragic expression in terms of transfigured modern values and symbols in the theater which may to some degree bring home to members of a modern audience their ennobling identity with the tragic figures on the stage. Of course, this is very much of a dream, but where the theater is concerned, one must have a dream, and the Greek dream in tragedy is the noblest ever!*

* From Arthur Hobson Quinn, *A History of the American Drama,* II. Copyright 1936 by Arthur Hobson Quinn. Reprinted by permission of the Estate of Helen McKee Quinn.

DEATH OF A SALESMAN

Certain private conversations in two acts and a requiem

Arthur Miller

Arthur Miller was born in New York in 1915. In 1938 he graduated from the University of Michigan, where he won several prizes for drama. Six years later he had his first Broadway production, *The Man Who Had All the Luck*, but the play was unlucky and closed after four days. By the time of his first commercial success, *All My Sons* (1947), he had already written eight or nine plays. In 1949 he won a Pulitzer prize with *Death of a Salesman* and achieved an international reputation. Among his other works are an adaptation (1950) of Ibsen's *Enemy of the People* and a play about the Salem witch trials, *The Crucible* (1953), both containing political implications, and *The Misfits* (1961, a screen-play), *After the Fall* (1964), and *Incident at Vichy* (1965).

The action takes place in WILLY LOMAN's *house and yard and in various places he visits in the New York and Boston of today.*

Throughout the play, in the stage directions, left and right mean stage left and stage right.

Design for Act I of *Death of a Salesman*. Painting by Jo Mielziner. (Photograph: Smithsonian Institution, Peter A. Juley & Sons Collection.)

ACT I

A melody is heard, played upon a flute. It is small and fine, telling of grass and trees and the horizon. The curtain rises.

Before us is the Salesman's house. We are aware of towering, angular shapes behind it, surrounding it on all sides. Only the blue light of the sky falls upon the house and forestage; the surrounding area shows an angry glow of orange. As more light appears, we see a solid vault of apartment houses around the small, fragile-seeming home. An air of the dream clings to the place, a dream rising out of reality. The kitchen at center seems actual enough, for there is a kitchen table with three chairs, and a refrigerator. But no other fixtures are seen. At the back of the kitchen there is a draped entrance, which leads to the living-room. To the right of the kitchen, on a level raised two feet, is a bedroom furnished only with a brass bedstead and a straight chair. On a shelf over the bed a silver athletic trophy stands. A window opens onto the apartment house at the side.

Behind the kitchen, on a level raised six and a half feet, is the boys' bedroom, at present barely visible. Two beds are dimly seen, and at the back of the room a dormer window. (This bedroom is above the unseen living-room.) At the left a stairway curves up to it from the kitchen.

The entire setting is wholly or, in some places, partially transparent. The roof-line of the house is one-dimensional; under and over it we see the apartment buildings. Before the house lies an apron, curving beyond the forestage into the orchestra. This forward area serves as the back yard as well as the locale of all WILLY's *imaginings and of his city scenes. Whenever the action is in the present the actors observe the imaginary wall-lines, entering the house only through its door at the left. But in the scenes of the past these boundaries are broken, and characters enter or leave a room by stepping "through" a wall onto the forestage.*

From the right, WILLY LOMAN, *the Salesman, enters, carrying two large sample cases. The flute plays on. He hears but is not aware of it. He is past sixty years of age, dressed quietly. Even as he crosses the stage to the doorway of the house, his exhaustion is apparent. He unlocks the door, comes into the kitchen, and thankfully lets his burden down, feeling the soreness of his palms. A word-sigh escapes his lips — it might be "Oh, boy, oh, boy." He closes the door, then carries his cases out into the living-room, through the draped kitchen doorway.*

LINDA, *his wife, has stirred in her bed at the right. She gets out and puts on a robe, listening. Most often jovial, she has developed an iron repression of her exceptions to* WILLY's *behavior — she more than loves him, she admires him, as though his mercurial nature, his temper, his massive dreams and little cruelties, served her only as sharp reminders of the turbulent longings within him, longings which she shares but lacks the temperament to utter and follow to their end.*

Death of a Salesman by Arthur Miller. Copyright 1949 by Arthur Miller, copyright renewed © 1977 by Arthur Miller. Reprinted by permission of Viking Penguin Inc.

Caution: This play in its printed form is designed for the reading public only. All dramatic rights in it are fully protected by copyright, and no public or private performance — professional or amateur — may be given without the written permission of the author and the payment of royalty. As the courts have also ruled that the public reading of a play constitutes a public performance, no such reading may be given except under the conditions stated above. Communication should be addressed to the author's representative, International Creative Management, Inc., 40 W. 57th Street, New York, N.Y. 10019.

LINDA (*hearing* WILLY *outside the bedroom, calls with some trepidation*): Willy!

WILLY: It's all right. I came back.

LINDA: Why? What happened? (*Slight pause.*) Did something happen, Willy?

WILLY: No, nothing happened.

LINDA: You didn't smash the car, did you?

WILLY (*with casual irritation*): I said nothing happened. Didn't you hear me?

LINDA: Don't you feel well?

WILLY: I am tired to the death. (*The flute*

has faded away. He sits on the bed beside her, a little numb.) I couldn't make it. I just couldn't make it, Linda.

LINDA (*very carefully, delicately*): Where were you all day? You look terrible.

WILLY: I got as far as a little above Yonkers. I stopped for a cup of coffee. Maybe it was the coffee.

LINDA: What?

WILLY (*after a pause*): I suddenly couldn't drive any more. The car kept going off onto the shoulder, y'know?

LINDA (*helpfully*): Oh. Maybe it was the steering again. I don't think Angelo knows the Studebaker.

WILLY: No, it's me, it's me. Suddenly I realize I'm goin' sixty miles an hour and I don't remember the last five minutes. I'm — I can't seem to — keep my mind to it.

LINDA: Maybe it's your glasses. You never went for your new glasses.

WILLY: No, I see everything. I came back ten miles an hour. It took me nearly four hours from Yonkers.

LINDA (*resigned*): Well, you'll just have to take a rest, Willy, you can't continue this way.

WILLY: I just got back from Florida.

LINDA: But you didn't rest your mind. Your mind is overactive, and the mind is what counts, dear.

WILLY: I'll start out in the morning. Maybe I'll feel better in the morning. (*She is taking off his shoes.*) These goddam arch supports are killing me.

LINDA: Take an aspirin. Should I get you an aspirin? It'll soothe you.

WILLY (*with wonder*): I was driving along, you understand? And I was fine. I was even observing the scenery. You can imagine, me looking at scenery, on the road every week of my life. But it's so beautiful up there, Linda, the trees are so thick, and the sun is warm. I opened the windshield and just let the warm air bathe over me. And then all of a sudden I'm goin' off the road! I'm tellin' ya, I absolutely forgot I was driving. If I'd've gone the other way over the white line I might've killed somebody. So I went on again — and five minutes later I'm dreamin' again, and I nearly — (*He presses two fingers against his eyes.*) I have such thoughts, I have such strange thoughts.

LINDA: Willy, dear. Talk to them again.

There's no reason why you can't work in New York.

WILLY: They don't need me in New York. I'm the New England man. I'm vital in New England.

LINDA: But you're sixty years old. They can't expect you to keep traveling every week.

WILLY: I'll have to send a wire to Portland. I'm supposed to see Brown and Morrison tomorrow morning at ten o'clock to show the line. Goddammit, I could sell them! (*He starts putting on his jacket.*)

LINDA (*taking the jacket from him*): Why don't you go down to the place tomorrow and tell Howard you've simply got to work in New York? You're too accommodating, dear.

WILLY: If old man Wagner was alive I'd a been in charge of New York now! That man was a prince, he was a masterful man. But that boy of his, that Howard, he don't appreciate. When I went north the first time, the Wagner Company didn't know where New England was!

LINDA: Why don't you tell those things to Howard, dear?

WILLY (*encouraged*): I will, I definitely will. Is there any cheese?

LINDA: I'll make you a sandwich.

WILLY: No, go to sleep. I'll take some milk. I'll be up right away. The boys in?

LINDA: They're sleeping. Happy took Biff on a date tonight.

WILLY (*interested*): That so?

LINDA: It was so nice to see them shaving together, one behind the other, in the bathroom. And going out together. You notice? The whole house smells of shaving lotion.

WILLY: Figure it out. Work a lifetime to pay off a house. You finally own it, and there's nobody to live in it.

LINDA: Well, dear, life is a casting off. It's always that way.

WILLY: No, no, some people — some people accomplish something. Did Biff say anything after I went this morning?

LINDA: You shouldn't have criticized him, Willy, especially after he just got off the train. You mustn't lose your temper with him.

WILLY: When the hell did I lose my temper? I simply asked him if he was making any money. Is that a criticism?

LINDA: But, dear, how could he make any money?

WILLY (*worried and angered*): There's such an undercurrent in him. He became a moody man. Did he apologize when I left this morning?

LINDA: He was crestfallen, Willy. You know how he admires you. I think if he finds himself, then you'll both be happier and not fight any more.

WILLY: How can he find himself on a farm? Is that a life? A farmhand? In the beginning, when he was young, I thought, well, a young man, it's good for him to tramp around, take a lot of different jobs. But it's more than ten years now and he has yet to make thirty-five dollars a week!

LINDA: He's finding himself, Willy.

WILLY: Not finding yourself at the age of thirty-four is a disgrace!

LINDA: Shh!

WILLY: The trouble is he's lazy, goddammit!

LINDA: Willy, please!

WILLY: Biff is a lazy bum!

LINDA: They're sleeping. Get something to eat. Go on down.

WILLY: Why did he come home? I would like to know what brought him home.

LINDA: I don't know. I think he's still lost, Willy. I think he's very lost.

WILLY: Biff Loman is lost. In the greatest country in the world a young man with such — personal attractiveness, gets lost. And such a hard worker. There's one thing about Biff — he's not lazy.

LINDA: Never.

WILLY (*with pity and resolve*): I'll see him in the morning; I'll have a nice talk with him. I'll get him a job selling. He could be big in no time. My God! Remember how they used to follow him around in high school? When he smiled at one of them their faces lit up. When he walked down the street . . . (*He loses himself in reminiscences.*)

LINDA (*trying to bring him out of it*): Willy, dear, I got a new kind of American-type cheese today. It's whipped.

WILLY: Why do you get American when I like Swiss?

LINDA: I just thought you'd like a change —

WILLY: I don't want a change! I want Swiss cheese. Why am I always being contradicted?

LINDA (*with a covering laugh*): I thought it would be a surprise.

WILLY: Why don't you open a window in here, for God's sake?

LINDA (*with infinite patience*): They're all open, dear.

WILLY: The way they boxed us in here. Bricks and windows, windows and bricks.

LINDA: We should've bought the land next door.

WILLY: The street is lined with cars. There's not a breath of fresh air in the neighborhood. The grass don't grow any more, you can't raise a carrot in the back yard. They should've had a law against apartment houses. Remember those two beautiful elm trees out there? When I and Biff hung the swing between them?

LINDA: Yeah, like being a million miles from the city.

WILLY: They should've arrested the builder for cutting those down. They massacred the neighborhood. (*Lost.*) More and more I think of those days, Linda. This time of year it was lilac and wisteria. And then the peonies would come out, and the daffodils. What fragrance in this room!

LINDA: Well, after all, people had to move somewhere.

WILLY: No, there's more people now.

LINDA: I don't think there's more people. I think —

WILLY: There's more people! That's what's ruining this country! Population is getting out of control. The competition is maddening! Smell the stink from that apartment house! And another one on the other side . . . How can they whip cheese?

(*On* WILLY'S *last line,* BIFF *and* HAPPY *raise themselves up in their beds, listening.*)

LINDA: Go down, try it. And be quiet.

WILLY (*turning to* LINDA, *guiltily*): You're not worried about me, are you, sweetheart?

BIFF: What's the matter?

HAPPY: Listen!

LINDA: You've got too much on the ball to worry about.

WILLY: You're my foundation and my support, Linda.

LINDA: Just try to relax, dear. You make mountains out of molehills.

WILLY: I won't fight with him any more. If he wants to go back to Texas, let him go.

LINDA: He'll find his way.

WILLY: Sure. Certain men just don't get started till later in life. Like Thomas Edison, I think. Or B. F. Goodrich. One of them was deaf. (*He starts for the bedroom doorway.*) I'll put my money on Biff.

LINDA: And Willy — if it's warm Sunday we'll drive in the country. And we'll open the windshield, and take lunch.

WILLY: No, the windshields don't open on the new cars.

LINDA: But you opened it today.

WILLY: Me? I didn't. (*He stops.*) Now isn't that peculiar! Isn't that a remarkable — (*He breaks off in amazement and fright as the flute is heard distantly.*)

LINDA: What, darling?

WILLY: That is the most remarkable thing.

LINDA: What, dear?

WILLY: I was thinking of the Chevvy. (*Slight pause.*) Nineteen twenty-eight ... when I had that red Chevvy — (*Breaks off.*) That funny? I coulda sworn I was driving that Chevvy today.

LINDA: Well, that's nothing. Something must've reminded you.

WILLY: Remarkable. Ts. Remember those days? The way Biff used to simonize that car? The dealer refused to believe there was eighty thousand miles on it. (*He shakes his head.*) Heh! (*To Linda.*) Close your eyes, I'll be right up. (*He walks out of the bedroom.*)

HAPPY (*to* BIFF): Jesus, maybe he smashed up the car again!

LINDA (*calling after* WILLY): Be careful on the stairs, dear! The cheese is on the middle shelf! (*She turns, goes over to the bed, takes his jacket, and goes out of the bedroom.*)

(*Light has risen on the boys' room. Unseen, WILLY is heard talking to himself, "Eighty thousand miles," and a little laugh. BIFF gets out of bed, comes downstage a bit, and stands attentively. BIFF is two years older than his brother HAPPY, well built, but in these days bears a worn air and seems less self-assured. He has succeeded less, and his dreams are stronger and less acceptable than HAPPY'S. HAPPY is tall, powerfully made. Sexuality is like a visible color on him, or a scent that many women have discovered. He, like his brother, is lost, but in a different way, for he has never allowed himself to turn his face toward defeat and is thus more confused and hard-skinned, although seemingly more content.*)

HAPPY (*getting out of bed*): He's going to get his license taken away if he keeps that up.

I'm getting nervous about him, y'know, Biff?

BIFF: His eyes are going.

HAPPY: No, I've driven with him. He sees all right. He just doesn't keep his mind on it. I drove into the city with him last week. He stops at a green light and then it turns red and he goes. (*He laughs.*)

BIFF: Maybe he's color-blind.

HAPPY: Pop? Why he's got the finest eye for color in the business. You know that.

BIFF (*sitting down on his bed*): I'm going to sleep.

HAPPY: You're not still sour on Dad, are you, Biff?

BIFF: He's all right, I guess.

WILLY (*underneath them, in the living-room*): Yes, sir, eighty thousand miles — eighty-two thousand!

BIFF: You smoking?

HAPPY (*holding out a pack of cigarettes*): Want one?

BIFF (*taking a cigarette*): I can never sleep when I smell it.

WILLY: What a simonizing job, heh!

HAPPY (*with deep sentiment*): Funny, Biff, y'know? Us sleeping in here again? The old beds. (*He pats his bed affectionately.*) All the talk that went across those two beds, huh? Our whole lives.

BIFF: Yeah. Lotta dreams and plans.

HAPPY (*with a deep and masculine laugh*): About five hundred women would like to know what was said in this room.

(*They share a soft laugh.*)

BIFF: Remember that big Betsy something — what the hell was her name — over on Bushwick Avenue?

HAPPY (*combing his hair*): With the collie dog!

BIFF: That's the one. I got you in there, remember?

HAPPY: Yeah, that was my first time — I think. Boy, there was a pig! (*They laugh, almost crudely.*) You taught me everything I know about women. Don't forget that.

BIFF: I bet you forgot how bashful you used to be. Especially with girls.

HAPPY: Oh, I still am, Biff.

BIFF: Oh, go on.

HAPPY: I just control it, that's all. I think I got less bashful and you got more so. What happened, Biff? Where's the old humor, the old confidence? (*He shakes* BIFF's *knee.* BIFF

gets up and moves restlessly about the room.)
What's the matter?

BIFF: Why does Dad mock me all the time?

HAPPY: He's not mocking you, he —

BIFF: Everything I say there's a twist of mockery on his face. I can't get near him.

HAPPY: He just wants you to make good, that's all. I wanted to talk to you about Dad for a long time, Biff. Something's — happening to him. He — talks to himself.

BIFF: I noticed that this morning. But he always mumbled.

HAPPY: But not so noticeable. It got so embarrassing I sent him to Florida. And you know something? Most of the time he's talking to you.

BIFF: What's he say about me?

HAPPY: I can't make it out.

BIFF: What's he say about me?

HAPPY: I think the fact that you're not settled, that you're still kind of up in the air . . .

BIFF: There's one or two other things depressing him, Happy.

HAPPY: What do you mean?

BIFF: Never mind. Just don't lay it all to me.

HAPPY: But I think if you just got started — I mean — is there any future for you out there?

BIFF: I tell ya, Hap, I don't know what the future is. I don't know — what I'm supposed to want.

HAPPY: What do you mean?

BIFF: Well, I spent six or seven years after high school trying to work myself up. Shipping clerk, salesman, business of one kind or another. And it's a measly manner of existence. To get on that subway on the hot mornings in summer. To devote your whole life to keeping stock, or making phone calls, or selling or buying. To suffer fifty weeks of the year for the sake of a two-week vacation, when all you really desire is to be outdoors, with your shirt off. And always to have to get ahead of the next fella. And still — that's how you build a future.

HAPPY: Well, you really enjoy it on a farm? Are you content out there?

BIFF (*with rising agitation*): Hap, I've had twenty or thirty different kinds of jobs since I left home before the war, and it always turns out the same. I just realized it lately. In Nebraska when I herded cattle, and the Da-kotas, and Arizona, and now in Texas. It's why I came home now, I guess, because I realized it. This farm I work on, it's spring there now, see? And they've got about fifteen new colts. There's nothing more inspiring or — beautiful than the sight of a mare and a new colt. And it's cool there now, see? Texas is cool now, and it's spring. And whenever spring comes to where I am, I suddenly get the feeling, my God, I'm not gettin' anywhere! What the hell am I doing, playing around with horses, twenty-eight dollars a week! I'm thirty-four years old, I oughta be makin' my future. That's when I come running home. And now, I get here, and I don't know what to do with myself. (*After a pause.*) I've always made a point of not wasting my life, and everytime I come back here I know that all I've done is to waste my life.

HAPPY: You're a poet, you know that, Biff? You're a — you're an idealist!

BIFF: No, I'm mixed up very bad. Maybe I oughta get married. Maybe I oughta get stuck into something. Maybe that's my trouble. I'm like a boy. I'm not married, I'm not in business, I just — I'm like a boy. Are you content, Hap? You're a success, aren't you? Are you content?

HAPPY: Hell, no!

BIFF: Why? You're making money, aren't you?

HAPPY (*moving about with energy, expressiveness*): All I can do now is wait for the merchandise manager to die. And suppose I get to be merchandise manager? He's a good friend of mine, and he just built a terrific estate on Long Island. And he lived there about two months and sold it, and now he's building another one. He can't enjoy it once it's finished. And I know that's just what I would do. I don't know what the hell I'm workin' for. Sometimes I sit in my apartment — all alone. And I think of the rent I'm paying. And it's crazy. But then, it's what I always wanted. My own apartment, a car, and plenty of women. And still, goddammit, I'm lonely.

BIFF (*with enthusiasm*): Listen, why don't you come out West with me?

HAPPY: You and I, heh?

BIFF: Sure, maybe we could buy a ranch. Raise cattle, use our muscles. Men built like we are should be working out in the open.

HAPPY (*avidly*): The Loman Brothers, heh?

BIFF (*with vast affection*): Sure, we'd be known all over the counties!

HAPPY (*enthralled*): That's what I dream about, Biff. Sometimes I want to just rip my clothes off in the middle of the store and outbox that goddam merchandise manager. I mean I can outbox, outrun, and outlift anybody in that store, and I have to take orders from those common, petty sons-of-bitches till I can't stand it any more.

BIFF: I'm tellin' you, kid, if you were with me I'd be happy out there.

HAPPY (*enthused*): See, Biff, everybody around me is so false that I'm constantly lowering my ideals . . .

BIFF: Baby, together we'd stand up for one another, we'd have someone to trust.

HAPPY: If I were around you —

BIFF: Hap, the trouble is we weren't brought up to grub for money. I don't know how to do it.

HAPPY: Neither can I!

BIFF: Then let's go!

HAPPY: The only thing is — what can you make out there?

BIFF: But look at your friend. Builds an estate and then hasn't the peace of mind to live in it.

HAPPY: Yeah, but when he walks into the store the waves part in front of him. That's fifty-two thousand dollars a year coming through the revolving door, and I got more in my pinky finger than he's got in his head.

BIFF: Yeah, but you just said —

HAPPY: I gotta show some of those pompous, self-important executives over there that Hap Loman can make the grade. I want to walk into the store the way he walks in. Then I'll go with you, Biff. We'll be together yet, I swear. But take those two we had tonight. Now weren't they gorgeous creatures?

BIFF: Yeah, yeah, most gorgeous I've had in years.

HAPPY: I get that any time I want, Biff. Whenever I feel disgusted. The only trouble is, it gets like bowling or something. I just keep knockin' them over and it doesn't mean anything. You still run around a lot?

BIFF: Naa. I'd like to find a girl — steady, somebody with substance.

HAPPY: That's what I long for.

BIFF: Go on! You'd never come home.

HAPPY: I would! Somebody with character, with resistance! Like Mom, y'know? You're gonna call me a bastard when I tell you this. That girl Charlotte I was with tonight is engaged to be married in five weeks. (*He tries on his new hat.*)

BIFF: No kiddin'!

HAPPY: Sure, the guy's in line for the vice-presidency of the store. I don't know what gets into me, maybe I just have an overdeveloped sense of competition or something, but I went and ruined her, and furthermore I can't get rid of her. And he's the third executive I've done that to. Isn't that a crummy characteristic? And to top it all, I go to their weddings! (*Indignantly, but laughing.*) Like I'm not supposed to take bribes. Manufacturers offer me a hundred-dollar bill now and then to throw an order their way. You know how honest I am, but it's like this girl, see. I hate myself for it. Because I don't want the girl, and, still, I take it and — I love it!

BIFF: Let's go to sleep.

HAPPY: I guess we didn't settle anything, heh?

BIFF: I just got one idea that I think I'm going to try.

HAPPY: What's that?

BIFF: Remember Bill Oliver?

HAPPY: Sure, Oliver is very big now. You want to work for him again?

BIFF: No, but when I quit he said something to me. He put his arm on my shoulder, and he said, "Biff, if you ever need anything, come to me."

HAPPY: I remember that. That sounds good.

BIFF: I think I'll go to see him. If I could get ten thousand or even seven or eight thousand dollars I could buy a beautiful ranch.

HAPPY: I bet he'd back you. 'Cause he thought highly of you, Biff. I mean, they all do. You're well liked, Biff. That's why I say to come back here, and we both have the apartment. And I'm tellin' you, Biff, any babe you want . . .

BIFF: No, with a ranch I could do the work I like and still be something. I just wonder though. I wonder if Oliver still thinks I stole that carton of basketballs.

HAPPY: Oh, he probably forgot that long ago. It's almost ten years. You're too sensitive. Anyway, he didn't really fire you.

BIFF: Well, I think he was going to. I think that's why I quit. I was never sure whether he knew or not. I know he thought the world of me, though. I was the only one he'd let lock up the place.

WILLY (*below*): You gonna wash the engine, Biff?

HAPPY: Shh!

(BIFF *looks at* HAPPY, *who is gazing down, listening.* WILLY *is mumbling in the parlor.*)

HAPPY: You hear that?

(*They listen.* WILLY *laughs warmly.*)

BIFF (*growing angry*): Doesn't he know Mom can hear that?

WILLY: Don't get your sweater dirty, Biff!

(*A look of pain crosses* BIFF's *face.*)

HAPPY: Isn't that terrible? Don't leave again, will you? You'll find a job here. You gotta stick around. I don't know what to do about him, it's getting embarrassing.

WILLY: What a simonizing job!

BIFF: Mom's hearing that!

WILLY: No kiddin', Biff, you got a date? Wonderful!

HAPPY: Go on to sleep. But talk to him in the morning, will you?

BIFF (*reluctantly getting into bed*): With her in the house. Brother!

HAPPY (*getting into bed*): I wish you'd have a good talk with him.

(*The light on their room begins to fade.*)

BIFF (*to himself in bed*): That selfish, stupid . . .

HAPPY: Sh . . . Sleep, Biff.

(*Their light is out. Well before they have finished speaking,* WILLY's *form is dimly seen below in the darkened kitchen. He opens the refrigerator, searches in there, and takes out a bottle of milk. The apartment houses are fading out, and the entire house and surroundings become covered with leaves. Music insinuates itself as the leaves appear.*)

WILLY: Just wanna be careful with those girls, Biff, that's all. Don't make any promises. No promises of any kind. Because a girl, y'know, they always believe what you tell 'em, and you're very young, Biff, you're too young to be talking seriously to girls.

(*Light rises on the kitchen.* WILLY, *talking, shuts the refrigerator door and comes downstage to the kitchen table. He pours milk into a glass. He is totally immersed in himself, smiling faintly.*)

WILLY: Too young entirely, Biff. You want to watch your schooling first. Then when you're all set, there'll be plenty of girls for a boy like you. (*He smiles broadly at a kitchen chair.*) That so? The girls pay for you? (*He laughs.*) Boy, you must really be makin' a hit.

(WILLY *is gradually addressing — physically — a point offstage, speaking through the wall of the kitchen, and his voice has been rising in volume to that of a normal conversation.*)

WILLY: I been wondering why you polish the car so careful. Ha! Don't leave the hubcaps, boys. Get the chamois to the hubcaps. Happy, use newspaper on the windows, it's the easiest thing. Show him how to do it, Biff! You see, Happy? Pad it up, use it like a pad. That's it, that's it, good work. You're doin' all right, Hap. (*He pauses, then nods in approbation for a few seconds, then looks upward.*) Biff, first thing we gotta do when we get time is clip that big branch over the house. Afraid it's gonna fall in a storm and hit the roof. Tell you what. We get a rope and sling her around, and then we climb up there with a couple of saws and take her down. Soon as you finish the car, boys, I wanna see ya. I got a surprise for you, boys.

BIFF (*offstage*): Whatta ya got, Dad?

WILLY: No, you finish first. Never leave a job till you're finished — remember that. (*Looking toward the "big trees."*) Biff, up in Albany I saw a beautiful hammock. I think I'll buy it next trip, and we'll hang it right between those two elms. Wouldn't that be something! Just swingin' there under those branches. Boy, that would be . . .

(YOUNG BIFF *and* YOUNG HAPPY *appear from the direction* WILLY *was addressing.* HAPPY *carries rags and a pail of water.* BIFF, *wearing a sweater with a block "S," carries a football.*)

BIFF (*pointing in the direction of the car offstage*): How's that, Pop, professional?

WILLY: Terrific. Terrific job, boys. Good work, Biff.

HAPPY: Where's the surprise, Pop?

WILLY: In the back seat of the car.

HAPPY: Boy! (*He runs off.*)

BIFF: What is it, Dad? Tell me, what'd you buy?

WILLY (*laughing, cuffs him*): Never mind, something I want you to have.

BIFF (*turns and starts off*): What is it, Hap?

HAPPY (*offstage*): It's a punching bag!

BIFF: Oh, Pop!

WILLY: It's got Gene Tunney's signature on it!

(HAPPY *runs onstage with a punching bag.*)

BIFF: Gee, how'd you know we wanted a punching bag?

WILLY: Well, it's the finest thing for the timing.

HAPPY (*lies down on his back and pedals with his feet*): I'm losing weight, you notice, Pop?

WILLY (*to* HAPPY): Jumping rope is good too.

BIFF: Did you see the new football I got?

WILLY (*examining the ball*): Where'd you get a new ball?

BIFF: The coach told me to practice my passing.

WILLY: That so? And he gave you the ball, heh?

BIFF: Well, I borrowed it from the locker room. (*He laughs confidentially.*)

WILLY (*laughing with him at the theft*): I want you to return that.

HAPPY: I told you he wouldn't like it!

BIFF (*angrily*): Well, I'm bringing it back!

WILLY (*stopping the incipient argument, to* HAPPY): Sure, he's gotta practice with a regulation ball, doesn't he? (*To* BIFF.) Coach'll probably congratulate you on your initiative!

BIFF: Oh, he keeps congratulating my initiative all the time, Pop.

WILLY: That's because he likes you. If somebody else took that ball there'd be an uproar. So what's the report, boys, what's the report?

BIFF: Where'd you go this time, Dad? Gee we were lonesome for you.

WILLY (*pleased, puts an arm around each boy and they come down to the apron*): Lonesome, heh?

BIFF: Missed you every minute.

WILLY: Don't say? Tell you a secret, boys. Don't breathe it to a soul. Someday I'll have my own business, and I'll never have to leave home any more.

HAPPY: Like Uncle Charley, heh?

WILLY: Bigger than Uncle Charley! Because Charley is not — liked. He's liked, but he's not — well liked.

BIFF: Where'd you go this time, Dad?

WILLY: Well, I got on the road, and I went north to Providence. Met the Mayor.

BIFF: The Mayor of Providence!

WILLY: He was sitting in the hotel lobby.

BIFF: What'd he say?

WILLY: He said, "Morning!" And I said, "You got a fine city here, Mayor." And then he had coffee with me. And then I went to Waterbury. Waterbury is a fine city. Big clock city, the famous Waterbury clock. Sold a nice bill there. And then Boston — Boston is the cradle of the Revolution. A fine city. And a couple of other towns in Mass., and on to Portland and Bangor and straight home!

BIFF: Gee, I'd love to go with you sometime, Dad.

WILLY: Soon as summer comes.

HAPPY: Promise?

WILLY: You and Hap and I, and I'll show you all the towns. America is full of beautiful towns and fine, upstanding people. And they know me, boys, they know me up and down New England. The finest people. And when I bring you fellas up, there'll be open sesame for all of us, 'cause one thing, boys: I have friends. I can park my car in any street in New England, and the cops protect it like their own. This summer, heh?

BIFF AND HAPPY (*together*): Yeah! You bet!

WILLY: We'll take our bathing suits.

HAPPY: We'll carry your bags, Pop!

WILLY: Oh, won't that be something! Me comin' into the Boston stores with you boys carryin' my bags. What a sensation!

(BIFF *is prancing around, practicing passing the ball.*)

WILLY: You nervous, Biff, about the game?

BIFF: Not if you're gonna be there.

WILLY: What do they say about you in school, now that they made you captain?

HAPPY: There's a crowd of girls behind him everytime the classes change.

BIFF (*taking* WILLY'*s hand*): This Saturday, Pop, this Saturday — just for you, I'm going to break through for a touchdown.

HAPPY: You're supposed to pass.

BIFF: I'm takin' one play for Pop. You watch me, Pop, and when I take off my helmet, that means I'm breakin' out. Then you watch me crash through that line!

WILLY (kisses BIFF): Oh, wait'll I tell this in Boston!

(BERNARD enters in knickers. He is younger than BIFF, earnest and loyal, a worried boy.)

BERNARD: Biff, where are you? You're supposed to study with me today.

WILLY: Hey, looka Bernard. What're you lookin' so anemic about, Bernard?

BERNARD: He's gotta study, Uncle Willy. He's got Regents next week.

HAPPY (tauntingly, spinning BERNARD around): Let's box, Bernard!

BERNARD: Biff! (He gets away from HAPPY.) Listen, Biff, I heard Mr. Birnbaum say that if you don't start studyin' math he's gonna flunk you, and you won't graduate. I heard him!

WILLY: You better study with him, Biff. Go ahead now.

BERNARD: I heard him!

BIFF: Oh, Pop, you didn't see my sneakers! (He holds up a foot for WILLY to look at.)

WILLY: Hey, that's a beautiful job of printing!

BERNARD (wiping his glasses): Just because he printed University of Virginia on his sneakers doesn't mean they've got to graduate him, Uncle Willy!

WILLY (angrily): What're you talking about? With scholarships to three universities they're gonna flunk him?

BERNARD: But I heard Mr. Birnbaum say —

WILLY: Don't be a pest, Bernard! (To his boys.) What an anemic!

BERNARD: Okay, I'm waiting for you in my house, Biff.

(Bernard goes off. THE LOMANS laugh.)

WILLY: Bernard is not well liked, is he?

BIFF: He's liked, but he's not well liked.

HAPPY: That's right, Pop.

WILLY: That's just what I mean. Bernard can get the best marks in school, y'understand, but when he gets out in the business world, y'understand, you are going to be five times ahead of him. That's why I thank Almighty God you're both built like Adonises. Because the man who makes an appearance in the business world, the man who creates personal interest, is the man who gets ahead. Be liked and you will never want. You take me, for instance. I never have to wait in line to see a buyer. "Willy Loman is here!" That's all they have to know, and I go right through.

BIFF: Did you knock them dead, Pop?

WILLY: Knocked 'em cold in Providence, slaughtered 'em in Boston.

HAPPY (on his back, pedaling again): I'm losing weight, you notice, Pop?

(LINDA enters, as of old, a ribbon in her hair, carrying a basket of washing.)

LINDA (with youthful energy): Hello, dear!

WILLY: Sweetheart!

LINDA: How'd the Chevvy run?

WILLY: Chevrolet, Linda, is the greatest car ever built. (To the boys.) Since when do you let your mother carry wash up the stairs?

BIFF: Grab hold there, boy!

HAPPY: Where to, Mom?

LINDA: Hang them up on the line. And you better go down to your friends, Biff. The cellar is full of boys. They don't know what to do with themselves.

BIFF: Ah, when Pop comes home they can wait!

WILLY (laughs appreciatively): You better go down and tell them what to do, Biff.

BIFF: I think I'll have them sweep out the furnace room.

WILLY: Good work, Biff.

BIFF (goes through wall-line of kitchen to doorway at back and calls down): Fellas! Everybody sweep out the furnace room! I'll be right down!

VOICES: All right! Okay, Biff.

BIFF: George and Sam and Frank, come out back! We're hangin' up the wash! Come on, Hap, on the double! (He and HAPPY carry out the basket.)

LINDA: The way they obey him!

WILLY: Well, that's training, the training. I'm tellin' you, I was sellin' thousands and thousands, but I had to come home.

LINDA: Oh, the whole block'll be at that game. Did you sell anything?

WILLY: I did five hundred gross in Providence and seven hundred gross in Boston.

LINDA: No! Wait a minute, I've got a pencil. (She pulls pencil and paper out of her apron pocket.) That makes your commission ... Two hundred — my God! Two hundred and twelve dollars!

WILLY: Well, I didn't figure it yet, but ...

LINDA: How much did you do?

WILLY: Well, I — I did — about a hundred and eighty gross in Providence. Well, no — it came to — roughly two hundred gross on the whole trip.

LINDA (*without hesitation*): Two hundred gross. That's ... (*She figures.*)

WILLY: The trouble was that three of the stores were half closed for inventory in Boston. Otherwise I woulda broke records.

LINDA: Well, it makes seventy dollars and some pennies. That's very good.

WILLY: What do we owe?

LINDA: Well, on the first there's sixteen dollars on the refrigerator —

WILLY: Why sixteen?

LINDA: Well, the fan belt broke, so it was a dollar eighty.

WILLY: But it's brand new.

LINDA: Well, the man said that's the way it is. Till they work themselves in, y'know.

(*They move through the wall-line into the kitchen.*)

WILLY: I hope we didn't get stuck on that machine.

LINDA: They got the biggest ads of any of them!

WILLY: I know, it's a fine machine. What else?

LINDA: Well, there's nine-sixty for the washing machine. And for the vacuum cleaner there's three and a half due on the fifteenth. Then the roof, you got twenty-one dollars remaining.

WILLY: It don't leak, does it?

LINDA: No, they did a wonderful job. Then you owe Frank for the carburetor.

WILLY: I'm not going to pay that man! That goddam Chevrolet, they ought to prohibit the manufacture of that car!

LINDA: Well, you owe him three and a half. And odds and ends, comes to around a hundred and twenty dollars by the fifteenth.

WILLY: A hundred and twenty dollars! My God, if business don't pick up I don't know what I'm gonna do!

LINDA: Well, next week you'll do better.

WILLY: Oh, I'll knock 'em dead next week. I'll go to Hartford. I'm very well liked in

Hartford. You know, the trouble is, Linda, people don't seem to take to me.

(*They move onto the forestage.*)

LINDA: Oh, don't be foolish.

WILLY: I know it when I walk in. They seem to laugh at me.

LINDA: Why? Why would they laugh at you? Don't talk that way, Willy.

(WILLY *moves to the edge of the stage.* LINDA *goes into the kitchen and starts to darn stockings.*)

WILLY: I don't know the reason for it, but they just pass me by. I'm not noticed.

LINDA: But you're doing wonderful, dear. You're making seventy to a hundred dollars a week.

WILLY: But I gotta be at it ten, twelve hours a day. Other men — I don't know — they do it easier. I don't know why — I can't stop myself — I talk too much. A man oughta come in with a few words. One thing about Charley. He's a man of few words, and they respect him.

LINDA: You don't talk too much, you're just lively.

WILLY (*smiling*): Well, I figure, what the hell, life is short, a couple of jokes. (*To himself.*) I joke too much! (*The smile goes.*)

LINDA: Why? You're —

WILLY: I'm fat. I'm very — foolish to look at, Linda. I didn't tell you, but Christmas time I happened to be calling on F. H. Stewarts, and a salesman I know, as I was going in to see the buyer I heard him say something about — walrus. And I — I cracked him right across the face. I won't take that. I simply will not take that. But they do laugh at me. I know that.

LINDA: Darling ...

WILLY: I gotta overcome it. I know I gotta overcome it. I'm not dressing to advantage, maybe.

LINDA: Willy, darling, you're the handsomest man in the world —

WILLY: Oh, no, Linda.

LINDA: To me you are. (*Slight pause.*) The handsomest.

(*From the darkness is heard the laughter of a woman.* WILLY *doesn't turn to it, but it continues through* LINDA's *lines.*)

LINDA: And the boys, Willy. Few men are idolized by their children the way you are.

(*Music is heard as behind a scrim, to the left of the house,* THE WOMAN, *dimly seen, is dressing.*)

WILLY (*with great feeling*): You're the best there is, Linda, you're a pal, you know that? On the road — on the road I want to grab you sometimes and just kiss the life outa you.

(*The laughter is loud now, and he moves into a brightening area at the left, where* THE WOMAN *has come from behind the scrim and is standing, putting on her hat, looking into a "mirror" and laughing.*)

WILLY: 'Cause I get so lonely — especially when business is bad and there's nobody to talk to. I get the feeling that I'll never sell anything again, that I won't make a living for you, or a business, a business for the boys. (*He talks through* THE WOMAN'*s subsiding laughter;* THE WOMAN *primps at the "mirror."*) There's so much I want to make for —

THE WOMAN: Me? You didn't make me, Willy. I picked you.

WILLY (*pleased*): You picked me?

THE WOMAN (*who is quite proper-looking,* WILLY'*s age*): I did. I've been sitting at that desk watching all the salesmen go by, day in, day out. But you've got such a sense of humor, and we do have such a good time together, don't we?

WILLY: Sure, sure. (*He takes her in his arms.*) Why do you have to go now?

THE WOMAN: It's two o'clock . . .

WILLY: No, come on in! (*He pulls her.*)

THE WOMAN: . . . my sisters'll be scandalized. When'll you be back?

WILLY: Oh, two weeks about. Will you come up again?

THE WOMAN: Sure thing. You do make me laugh. It's good for me. (*She squeezes his arm, kisses him.*) And I think you're a wonderful man.

WILLY: You picked me, heh?

THE WOMAN: Sure. Because you're so sweet. And such a kidder.

WILLY: Well, I'll see you next time I'm in Boston.

THE WOMAN: I'll put you right through to the buyers.

WILLY (*slapping her bottom*): Right. Well, bottoms up!

THE WOMAN (*slaps him gently and laughs*): You just kill me, Willy. (*He suddenly grabs her and kisses her roughly.*) You kill me. And thanks for the stockings. I love a lot of stockings. Well, good night.

WILLY: Good night. And keep your pores open!

THE WOMAN: Oh, Willy!

(THE WOMAN *bursts out laughing, and* LINDA'*s laughter blends in.* THE WOMAN *disappears into the dark. Now the area at the kitchen table brightens.* LINDA *is sitting where she was at the kitchen table, but now is mending a pair of her silk stockings.*)

LINDA: You are, Willy. The handsomest man. You've got no reason to feel that —

WILLY (*coming out of* THE WOMAN'*s dimming area and going over to* LINDA): I'll make it all up to you, Linda, I'll —

LINDA: There's nothing to make up, dear. You're doing fine, better than —

WILLY (*noticing her mending*): What's that?

LINDA: Just mending my stockings. They're so expensive —

WILLY (*angrily, taking them from her*): I won't have you mending stockings in this house! Now throw them out!

(LINDA *puts the stockings in her pocket.*)

BERNARD (*entering on the run*): Where is he? If he doesn't study!

WILLY (*moving to the forestage, with great agitation*): You'll give him the answers!

BERNARD: I do, but I can't on a Regents! That's a state exam! They're liable to arrest me!

WILLY: Where is he? I'll whip him, I'll whip him!

LINDA: And he'd better give back that football, Willy, it's not nice.

WILLY: Biff! Where is he? Why is he taking everything?

LINDA: He's too rough with the girls, Willy. All the mothers are afraid of him!

WILLY: I'll whip him!

BERNARD: He's driving the car without a license!

(THE WOMAN'*s laugh is heard.*)

WILLY: Shut up!

LINDA: All the mothers —

WILLY: Shut up!

BERNARD (*backing quietly away and out*): Mr. Birnbaum says he's stuck up.

WILLY: Get outa here!

BERNARD: If he doesn't buckle down he'll flunk math! (*He goes off.*)

LINDA: He's right, Willy, you've gotta —

WILLY (*exploding at her*): There's nothing the matter with him! You want him to be a worm like Bernard? He's got spirit, personality ...

(*As he speaks,* LINDA, *almost in tears, exits into the living-room.* WILLY *is alone in the kitchen, wilting and staring. The leaves are gone. It is night again, and the apartment houses look down from behind.*)

WILLY: Loaded with it. Loaded! What is he stealing? He's giving it back, isn't he? Why is he stealing? What did I tell him? I never in my life told him anything but decent things.

(HAPPY *in pajamas has come down the stairs;* WILLY *suddenly becomes aware of* HAPPY's *presence.*)

HAPPY: Let's go now, come on.

WILLY (*sitting down at the kitchen table*): Huh! Why did she have to wax the floors herself? Everytime she waxes the floors she keels over. She knows that!

HAPPY: Shh! Take it easy. What brought you back tonight?

WILLY: I got an awful scare. Nearly hit a kid in Yonkers. God! Why didn't I go to Alaska with my brother Ben that time! Ben! That man was a genius, that man was success incarnate! What a mistake! He begged me to go.

HAPPY: Well, there's no use in —

WILLY: You guys! There was a man started with the clothes on his back and ended up with diamond mines!

HAPPY: Boy, someday I'd like to know how he did it.

WILLY: What's the mystery? The man knew what he wanted and went out and got it! Walked into a jungle, and comes out, the age of twenty-one, and he's rich! The world is an oyster, but you don't crack it open on a mattress!

HAPPY: Pop, I told you I'm gonna retire you for life.

WILLY: You'll retire me for life on seventy goddam dollars a week? And your women and your car and your apartment, and you'll retire me for life! Christ's sake, I couldn't get past Yonkers today! Where are you guys, where are you? The woods are burning! I can't drive a car!

(CHARLEY *has appeared in the doorway. He is a large man, slow of speech, laconic, immovable. In all he says, despite what he says, there is pity, and, now, trepidation. He has a robe over pajamas, slippers on his feet. He enters the kitchen.*)

CHARLEY: Everything all right?

HAPPY: Yeah, Charley, everything's ...

WILLY: What's the matter?

CHARLEY: I heard some noise. I thought something happened. Can't we do something about the walls? You sneeze in here, and in my house hats blow off.

HAPPY: Let's go to bed, Dad. Come on.

(CHARLEY *signals to* HAPPY *to go.*)

WILLY: You go ahead, I'm not tired at the moment.

HAPPY (*to* WILLY): Take it easy, huh? (*He exits.*)

WILLY: What're you doin' up?

CHARLEY (*sitting down at the kitchen table opposite* WILLY): Couldn't sleep good. I had a heartburn.

WILLY: Well, you don't know how to eat.

CHARLEY: I eat with my mouth.

WILLY: No, you're ignorant. You gotta know about vitamins and things like that.

CHARLEY: Come on, let's shoot. Tire you out a little.

WILLY (*hesitantly*): All right. You got cards?

CHARLEY (*taking a deck from his pocket*): Yeah, I got them. Someplace. What is it with those vitamins?

WILLY (*dealing*): They build up your bones. Chemistry.

CHARLEY: Yeah, but there's no bones in a heartburn.

WILLY: What are you talkin' about? Do you know the first thing about it?

CHARLEY: Don't get insulted.

WILLY: Don't talk about something you don't know anything about.

(*They are playing. Pause.*)

CHARLEY: What're you doin' home?

WILLY: A little trouble with the car.

CHARLEY: Oh. (*Pause.*) I'd like to take a trip to California.

WILLY: Don't say.

CHARLEY: You want a job?

WILLY: I got a job, I told you that. (*After a slight pause.*) What the hell are you offering me a job for?

CHARLEY: Don't get insulted.

WILLY: Don't insult me.

CHARLEY: I don't see no sense in it. You don't have to go on this way.

WILLY: I got a good job. (*Slight pause.*) What do you keep comin' in here for?

CHARLEY: You want me to go?

WILLY (*after a pause, withering*): I can't understand it. He's going back to Texas again. What the hell is that?

CHARLEY: Let him go.

WILLY: I got nothin' to give him, Charley, I'm clean, I'm clean.

CHARLEY: He won't starve. None a them starve. Forget about him.

WILLY: Then what have I got to remember?

CHARLEY: You take it too hard. To hell with it. When a deposit bottle is broken you don't get your nickel back.

WILLY: That's easy enough for you to say.

CHARLEY: That ain't easy for me to say.

WILLY: Did you see the ceiling I put up in the living-room?

CHARLEY: Yeah, that's a piece of work. To put up a ceiling is a mystery to me. How do you do it?

WILLY: What's the difference?

CHARLEY: Well, talk about it.

WILLY: You gonna put up a ceiling?

CHARLEY: How could I put up a ceiling?

WILLY: Then what the hell are you bothering me for?

CHARLEY: You're insulted again.

WILLY: A man who can't handle tools is not a man. You're disgusting.

CHARLEY: Don't call me disgusting, Willy.

(UNCLE BEN, *carrying a valise and an umbrella, enters the forestage from around the right corner of the house. He is a stolid man, in his sixties, with a mustache and an authoritative air. He is utterly certain of his destiny, and there is an aura of far places about him. He enters exactly as* WILLY *speaks.*)

WILLY: I'm getting awfully tired, Ben.

(BEN's *music is heard.* BEN *looks around at everything.*)

CHARLEY: Good, keep playing; you'll sleep better. Did you call me Ben?

(BEN *looks at his watch.*)

WILLY: That's funny. For a second there you reminded me of my brother Ben.

BEN: I only have a few minutes. (*He strolls, inspecting the place.* WILLY *and* CHARLEY *continue playing.*)

CHARLEY: You never heard from him again, heh? Since that time?

WILLY: Didn't Linda tell you? Couple of weeks ago we got a letter from his wife in Africa. He died.

CHARLEY: That so.

BEN (*chuckling*): So this is Brooklyn, eh?

CHARLEY: Maybe you're in for some of his money.

WILLY: Naa, he had seven sons. There's just one opportunity I had with that man . . .

BEN: I must make a train, William. There are several properties I'm looking at in Alaska.

WILLY: Sure, sure! If I'd gone with him to Alaska that time, everything would've been totally different.

CHARLEY: Go on, you'd froze to death up there.

WILLY: What're you talking about?

BEN: Opportunity is tremendous in Alaska, William. Surprised you're not up there.

WILLY: Sure, tremendous.

CHARLEY: Heh?

WILLY: There was the only man I ever met who knew the answers.

CHARLEY: Who?

BEN: How are you all?

WILLY (*taking a pot, smiling*): Fine, fine.

CHARLEY: Pretty sharp tonight.

BEN: Is Mother living with you?

WILLY: No, she died a long time ago.

CHARLEY: Who?

BEN: That's too bad. Fine specimen of a lady, Mother.

WILLY (*to* CHARLEY): Heh?

BEN: I'd hoped to see the old girl.

CHARLEY: Who died?

BEN: Heard anything from Father, have you?

WILLY (*unnerved*): What do you mean, who died?

CHARLEY (*taking a pot*): What're you talkin' about?

BEN (*looking at his watch*): William, it's half-past eight!

WILLY (*as though to dispel his confusion he*

angrily stops CHARLEY'S *hand*): That's my build!

CHARLEY: I put the ace —

WILLY: If you don't know how to play the game I'm not gonna throw my money away on you!

CHARLEY (*rising*): It was my ace, for God's sake!

WILLY: I'm through, I'm through!

BEN: When did Mother die?

WILLY: Long ago. Since the beginning you never knew how to play cards.

CHARLEY (*picks up the cards and goes to the door*): All right! Next time I'll bring a deck with five aces.

WILLY: I don't play that kind of game!

CHARLEY (*turning to him*): You ought to be ashamed of yourself!

WILLY: Yeah?

CHARLEY: Yeah! (*He goes out.*)

WILLY (*slamming the door after him*): Ignoramus!

BEN (*as* WILLY *comes toward him through the wall-line of the kitchen*): So you're William.

WILLY (*shaking* BEN'S *hand*): Ben! I've been waiting for you so long! What's the answer? How did you do it?

BEN: Oh, there's a story in that.

(LINDA *enters the forestage, as of old, carrying the wash basket.*)

LINDA: Is this Ben?

BEN (*gallantly*): How do you do, my dear.

LINDA: Where've you been all these years? Willy's always wondered why you —

WILLY (*pulling* BEN *away from her impatiently*): Where is Dad? Didn't you follow him? How did you get started?

BEN: Well, I don't know how much you remember.

WILLY: Well, I was just a baby, of course, only three or four years old —

BEN: Three years and eleven months.

WILLY: What a memory, Ben!

BEN: I have many enterprises, William, and I have never kept books.

WILLY: I remember I was sitting under the wagon in — was it Nebraska?

BEN: It was South Dakota, and I gave you a bunch of wild flowers.

WILLY: I remember you walking away down some open road.

BEN (*laughing*): I was going to find Father in Alaska.

WILLY: Where is he?

BEN: At that age I had a very faulty view of geography, William. I discovered after a few days that I was heading due south, so instead of Alaska, I ended up in Africa.

LINDA: Africa!

WILLY: The Gold Coast!

BEN: Principally diamond mines.

LINDA: Diamond mines!

BEN: Yes, my dear. But I've only a few minutes —

WILLY: No! Boys! Boys! (YOUNG BIFF *and* HAPPY *appear.*) Listen to this. This is your Uncle Ben, a great man! Tell my boys, Ben!

BEN: Why, boys, when I was seventeen I walked into the jungle, and when I was twenty-one I walked out. (*He laughs.*) And by God I was rich.

WILLY (*to the boys*): You see what I been talking about? The greatest things can happen!

BEN (*glancing at his watch*): I have an appointment in Ketchikan Tuesday week.

WILLY: No, Ben! Please tell about Dad. I want my boys to hear. I want them to know the kind of stock they spring from. All I remember is a man with a big beard, and I was in Mamma's lap, sitting around a fire, and some kind of high music.

BEN: His flute. He played the flute.

WILLY: Sure, the flute, that's right!

(*New music is heard, a high, rollicking tune.*)

BEN: Father was a very great and a very wild-hearted man. We would start in Boston, and he'd toss the whole family into the wagon, and then he'd drive the team right across the country; through Ohio, and Indiana, Michigan, Illinois, and all the Western states. And we'd stop in the towns and sell the flutes that he'd made on the way. Great inventor, Father. With one gadget he made more in a week than a man like you could make in a lifetime.

WILLY: That's just the way I'm bringing them up, Ben — rugged, well liked, all-around.

BEN: Yeah? (*To* BIFF.) Hit that, boy — hard as you can. (*He pounds his stomach.*)

BIFF: Oh, no, sir!

BEN (*taking boxing stance*): Come on, get to me! (*He laughs.*)

WILLY: Go to it, Biff! Go ahead, show him!

BIFF: Okay! (*He cocks his fists and starts in.*)

LINDA (*to* WILLY): Why must he fight, dear?

BEN (*sparring with* BIFF): Good boy! Good boy!

WILLY: How's that, Ben, heh?

HAPPY: Give him the left, Biff!

LINDA: Why are you fighting?

BEN: Good boy! (*Suddenly comes in, trips* BIFF, *and stands over him, the point of his umbrella poised over* BIFF's *eye.*)

LINDA: Look out, Biff!

BIFF: Gee!

BEN (*patting* BIFF's *knee*): Never fight fair with a stranger, boy. You'll never get out of the jungle that way. (*Taking* LINDA's *hand and bowing.*) It was an honor and a pleasure to meet you, Linda.

LINDA (*withdrawing her hand coldly, frightened*): Have a nice — trip.

BEN (*to* WILLY): And good luck with your — what do you do?

WILLY: Selling.

BEN: Yes. Well . : . (*He raises his hand in farewell to all.*)

WILLY: No, Ben, I don't want you to think . . . (*He takes* BEN's *arm to show him.*) It's Brooklyn, I know, but we hunt too.

BEN: Really, now.

WILLY: Oh, sure, there's snakes and rabbits and — that's why I moved out here. Why, Biff can fell any one of these trees in no time! Boys! Go right over to where they're building the apartment house and get some sand. We're gonna rebuild the entire front stoop right now! Watch this, Ben!

BIFF: Yes, sir! On the double, Hap!

HAPPY (*as he and* BIFF *run off*): I lost weight, Pop, you notice?

(CHARLEY *enters in knickers, even before the boys are gone.*)

CHARLEY: Listen, if they steal any more from that building the watchman'll put the cops on them!

LINDA (*to* WILLY): Don't let Biff . . .

(BEN *laughs lustily.*)

WILLY: You shoulda seen the lumber they brought home last week. At least a dozen six-by-tens worth all kinds a money.

CHARLEY: Listen, if that watchman —

WILLY: I gave them hell, understand. But I got a couple of fearless characters there.

CHARLEY: Willy, the jails are full of fearless characters.

BEN (*clapping* WILLY *on the back, with a laugh at* CHARLEY): And the stock exchange, friend!

WILLY (*joining in* BEN's *laughter*): Where are the rest of your pants?

CHARLEY: My wife bought them.

WILLY: Now all you need is a golf club and you can go upstairs and go to sleep. (*To* BEN.) Great athlete! Between him and his son Bernard they can't hammer a nail!

BERNARD (*rushing in*): The watchman's chasing Biff!

WILLY (*angrily*): Shut up! He's not stealing anything!

LINDA (*alarmed, hurrying off left*): Where is he? Biff, dear! (*She exits.*)

WILLY (*moving toward the left, away from* BEN): There's nothing wrong. What's the matter with you?

BEN: Nervy boy. Good!

WILLY (*laughing*): Oh, nerves of iron, that Biff!

CHARLEY: Don't know what it is. My New England man comes back and he's bleedin', they murdered him up there.

WILLY: It's contacts, Charley, I got important contacts!

CHARLEY (*sarcastically*): Glad to hear it, Willy. Come in later, we'll shoot a little casino. I'll take some of your Portland money. (*He laughs at* WILLY *and exists.*)

WILLY (*turning to* BEN): Business is bad, it's murderous. But not for me, of course.

BEN: I'll stop by on my way back to Africa.

WILLY (*longingly*): Can't you stay a few days? You're just what I need, Ben, because I — I have a fine position here, but I — well, Dad left when I was such a baby and I never had a chance to talk to him and I still feel — kind of temporary about myself.

BEN: I'll be late for my train.

(*They are at opposite ends of the stage.*)

WILLY: Ben, my boys — can't we talk? They'd go into the jaws of hell for me, see, but I —

BEN: William, you're being first-rate with your boys. Outstanding, manly chaps!

WILLY (*hanging on to his words*): Oh, Ben, that's good to hear! Because sometimes I'm afraid that I'm not teaching them the right kind of — Ben, how should I teach them?

BEN (*giving great weight to each word, and with a certain vicious audacity*): William, when I walked into the jungle, I was seventeen. When I walked out I was twenty-one. And, by God, I was rich! (*He goes off into darkness around the right corner of the house.*)

WILLY: . . . was rich! That's just the spirit I want to imbue them with! To walk into a jungle! I was right! I was right! I was right!

(BEN *is gone, but* WILLY *is still speaking to him as* LINDA, *in nightgown and robe, enters the kitchen, glances around for* WILLY, *then goes to the door of the house, looks out and sees him. Comes down to his left. He looks at her.*)

LINDA: Willy, dear? Willy?

WILLY: I was right!

LINDA: Did you have some cheese? (*He can't answer.*) It's very late, darling. Come to bed, heh?

WILLY (*looking straight up*): Gotta break your neck to see a star in this yard.

LINDA: You coming in?

WILLY: Whatever happened to that diamond watch fob? Remember? When Ben came from Africa that time? Didn't he give me a watch fob with a diamond in it?

LINDA: You pawned it, dear. Twelve, thirteen years ago. For Biff's radio correspondence course.

WILLY: Gee, that was a beautiful thing. I'll take a walk.

LINDA: But you're in your slippers.

WILLY (*starting to go around the house at the left*): I was right! I was! (*Half to* LINDA, *as he goes, shaking his head.*) What a man! There was a man worth talking to. I was right!

LINDA (*calling after* WILLY): But in your slippers, Willy!

(WILLY *is almost gone when* BIFF, *in his pajamas, comes down the stairs and enters the kitchen.*)

BIFF: What is he doing out there?

LINDA: Sh!

BIFF: God Almighty, Mom, how long has he been doing this?

LINDA: Don't, he'll hear you.

BIFF: What the hell is the matter with him?

LINDA: It'll pass by morning.

BIFF: Shouldn't we do anything?

LINDA: Oh, my dear, you should do a lot of things, but there's nothing to do, so go to sleep.

(HAPPY *comes down the stairs and sits on the steps.*)

HAPPY: I never heard him so loud, Mom.

LINDA: Well, come around more often; you'll hear him. (*She sits down at the table and mends the lining of* WILLY's *jacket.*)

BIFF: Why didn't you ever write me about this, Mom?

LINDA: How would I write to you? For over three months you had no address.

BIFF: I was on the move. But you know I thought of you all the time. You know that, don't you, pal?

LINDA: I know, dear, I know. But he likes to have a letter. Just to know that there's still a possibility for better things.

BIFF: He's not like this all the time, is he?

LINDA: It's when you come home he's always the worst.

BIFF: When I come home?

LINDA: When you write you're coming, he's all smiles, and talks about the future, and — he's just wonderful. And then the closer you seem to come, the more shaky he gets, and then, by the time you get here, he's arguing, and he seems angry at you. I think it's just that maybe he can't bring himself to — to open up to you. Why are you so hateful to each other? Why is that?

BIFF (*evasively*): I'm not hateful, Mom.

LINDA: But you no sooner come in the door than you're fighting!

BIFF: I don't know why. I mean to change. I'm tryin', Mom, you understand?

LINDA: Are you home to stay now?

BIFF: I don't know. I want to look around, see what's doin'.

LINDA: Biff, you can't look around all your life, can you?

BIFF: I just can't take hold, Mom. I can't take hold of some kind of a life.

LINDA: Biff, a man is not a bird, to come and go with the springtime.

BIFF: Your hair . . . (*He touches her hair.*) Your hair got so gray.

LINDA: Oh, it's been gray since you were in high school. I just stopped dyeing it, that's all.

BIFF: Dye it again, will ya? I don't want my pal looking old. (*He smiles.*)

LINDA: You're such a boy! You think you can go away for a year and . . . You've got to get it into your head now that one day you'll knock on this door and there'll be strange people here —

BIFF: What are you talking about? You're not even sixty, Mom.

LINDA: But what about your father?

BIFF (*lamely*): Well, I meant him too.

HAPPY: He admires Pop.

LINDA: Biff, dear, if you don't have any feeling for him, then you can't have any feeling for me.

BIFF: Sure I can, Mom.

LINDA: No. You can't just come to see me, because I love him. (*With a threat, but only a threat, of tears.*) He's the dearest man in the world to me, and I won't have anyone making him feel unwanted and low and blue. You've got to make up your mind now, darling, there's no leeway any more. Either he's your father and you pay him that respect, or else you're not to come here. I know he's not easy to get along with — nobody knows that better than me — but . . .

WILLY (*from the left, with a laugh*): Hey, hey, Biffo!

BIFF (*starting to go out after* WILLY): What the hell is the matter with him? (HAPPY *stops him.*)

LINDA: Don't — don't go near him!

BIFF: Stop making excuses for him! He always, always wiped the floor with you. Never had an ounce of respect for you.

HAPPY: He's always had respect for —

BIFF: What the hell do you know about it?

HAPPY (*surlily*): Just don't call him crazy!

BIFF: He's got no character — Charley wouldn't do this. Not in his own house — spewing out that vomit from his mind.

HAPPY: Charley never had to cope with what he's got to.

BIFF: People are worse off than Willy Loman. Believe me, I've seen them!

LINDA: Then make Charley your father, Biff. You can't do that, can you? I don't say he's a great man. Willy Loman never made a lot of money. His name was never in the paper. He's not the finest character that ever lived. But he's a human being, and a terrible thing is happening to him. So attention must be paid. He's not to be allowed to fall into his grave like an old dog. Attention, attention must be finally paid to such a person. You called him crazy —

BIFF: I didn't mean —

LINDA: No, a lot of people think he's lost his — balance. But you don't have to be very smart to know what his trouble is. The man is exhausted.

HAPPY: Sure!

LINDA: A small man can be just as exhausted as a great man. He works for a company thirty-six years this March, opens up unheard-of territories to their trademark, and now in his old age they take his salary away.

HAPPY (*indignantly*): I didn't know that, Mom.

LINDA: You never asked, my dear! Now that you get your spending money someplace else you don't trouble your mind with him.

HAPPY: But I gave you money last —

LINDA: Christmas time, fifty dollars! To fix the hot water it cost ninety-seven fifty! For five weeks he's been on straight commission, like a beginner, an unknown!

BIFF: Those ungrateful bastards!

LINDA: Are they any worse than his sons? When he brought them business, when he was young, they were glad to see him. But now his old friends, the old buyers that loved him so and always found some order to hand him in a pinch — they're all dead, retired. He used to be able to make six, seven calls a day in Boston. Now he takes his valises out of the car and puts them back and takes them out again and he's exhausted. Instead of walking he talks now. He drives seven hundred miles, and when he gets there no one knows him any more, no one welcomes him. And what goes through a man's mind, driving seven hundred miles home without having earned a cent? Why shouldn't he talk to himself? Why? When he has to go to Charley and borrow fifty dollars a week and pretend to me that it's his pay? How long can that go on? How long? You see what I'm sitting here and waiting for? And you tell me he has no character? The man who never worked a day but for your benefit? When does he get the medal for that? Is this his reward — to turn around at the age of sixty-three and find his sons, who he loved better than his life, one a philandering bum —

HAPPY: Mom!

LINDA: That's all you are, my baby! (*To* BIFF.) And you! What happened to the love you had for him? You were such pals! How you used to talk to him on the phone every night! How lonely he was till he could come home to you!

BIFF: All right, Mom. I'll live here in my room, and I'll get a job. I'll keep away from him, that's all.

LINDA: No, Biff. You can't stay here and fight all the time.

BIFF: He threw me out of this house, remember that.

LINDA: Why did he do that? I never knew why.

BIFF: Because I know he's a fake and he doesn't like anybody around who knows!

LINDA: Why a fake? In what way? What do you mean?

BIFF: Just don't lay it all at my feet. It's between me and him — that's all I have to say. I'll chip in from now on. He'll settle for half my pay check. He'll be all right. I'm going to bed. (*He starts for the stairs.*)

LINDA: He won't be all right.

BIFF (*turning on the stairs, furiously*): I hate this city and I'll stay here. Now what do you want?

LINDA: He's dying, Biff.

(HAPPY *turns quickly to her, shocked.*)

BIFF (*after a pause*): Why is he dying?

LINDA: He's been trying to kill himself.

BIFF (*with great horror*): How?

LINDA: I live from day to day.

BIFF: What're you talking about?

LINDA: Remember I wrote you that he smashed up the car again? In February?

BIFF: Well?

LINDA: The insurance inspector came. He said that they have evidence. That all these accidents in the last year — weren't — weren't — accidents.

HAPPY: How can they tell that? That's a lie.

LINDA: It seems there's a woman . . . (*She takes a breath as —*)

 BIFF (*sharply but contained*): What woman?
 LINDA (*simultaneously*): . . . and this woman . . .

LINDA: What?

BIFF: Nothing. Go ahead.

LINDA: What did you say?

BIFF: Nothing. I just said what woman?

HAPPY: What about her?

LINDA: Well, it seems she was walking down the road and saw his car. She says that he wasn't driving fast at all, and that he didn't

skid. She says he came to that little bridge, and then deliberately smashed into the railing, and it was only the shallowness of the water that saved him.

BIFF: Oh, no, he probably just fell asleep again.

LINDA: I don't think he fell asleep.

BIFF: Why not?

LINDA: Last month . . . (*With great difficulty.*) Oh, boys, it's so hard to say a thing like this! He's just a big stupid man to you, but I tell you there's more good in him than in many other people. (*She chokes, wipes her eyes.*) I was looking for a fuse. The lights blew out, and I went down the cellar. And behind the fuse box — it happened to fall out — was a length of rubber pipe — just short.

HAPPY: No kidding?

LINDA: There's a little attachment on the end of it. I knew right away. And sure enough, on the bottom of the water heater there's a new little nipple on the gas pipe.

HAPPY (*angrily*): That — jerk.

BIFF: Did you have it taken off?

LINDA: I'm — I'm ashamed to. How can I mention it to him? Every day I go down and take away that little rubber pipe. But, when he comes home, I put it back where it was. How can I insult him that way? I don't know what to do. I live from day to day, boys. I tell you, I know every thought in his mind. It sounds so old-fashioned and silly, but I tell you he put his whole life into you and you've turned your backs on him. (*She is bent over in the chair, weeping, her face in her hands.*) Biff, I swear to God! Biff, his life is in your hands!

HAPPY (*to* BIFF): How do you like that damned fool!

BIFF (*kissing her*): All right, pal, all right. It's all settled now. I've been remiss. I know that, Mom. But now I'll stay, and I swear to you, I'll apply myself. (*Kneeling in front of her, in a fever of self-reproach.*) It's just — you see, Mom, I don't fit in business. Not that I won't try. I'll try, and I'll make good.

HAPPY: Sure you will. The trouble with you in business was you never tried to please people.

BIFF: I know, I —

HAPPY: Like when you worked for Harrison's. Bob Harrison said you were tops, and then you go and do some damn fool thing like whistling whole songs in the elevator like a comedian.

BIFF (*against* HAPPY): So what? I like to whistle sometimes.

HAPPY: You don't raise a guy to a responsible job who whistles in the elevator!

LINDA: Well, don't argue about it now.

HAPPY: Like when you'd go off and swim in the middle of the day instead of taking the line around.

BIFF (*his resentment rising*): Well, don't you run off? You take off sometimes, don't you? On a nice summer day?

HAPPY: Yeah, but I cover myself!

LINDA: Boys!

HAPPY: If I'm going to take a fade the boss can call any number where I'm supposed to be and they'll swear to him that I just left. I'll tell you something that I hate to say, Biff, but in the business world some of them think you're crazy.

BIFF (*angered*): Screw the business world!

HAPPY: All right, screw it! Great, but cover yourself!

LINDA: Hap, Hap!

BIFF: I don't care what they think! They've laughed at Dad for years, and you know why? Because we don't belong in this nut-house of a city! We should be mixing cement on some open plain, or — or carpenters. A carpenter is allowed to whistle!

(WILLY *walks in from the entrance of the house, at left.*)

WILLY: Even your grandfather was better than a carpenter. (*Pause. They watch him.*) You never grew up. Bernard does not whistle in the elevator, I assure you.

BIFF (*as though to laugh* WILLY *out of it*): Yeah, but you do, Pop.

WILLY: I never in my life whistled in an elevator! And who in the business world thinks I'm crazy?

BIFF: I didn't mean it like that, Pop. Now don't make a whole thing out of it, will ya?

WILLY: Go back to the West! Be a carpenter, a cowboy, enjoy yourself!

LINDA: Willy, he was just saying —

WILLY: I heard what he said!

HAPPY (*trying to quiet* WILLY): Hey, Pop, come on now . . .

WILLY (*continuing over* HAPPY's *line*): They laugh at me, heh? Go to Filene's, go to the Hub, go to Slattery's, Boston. Call out the name Willy Loman and see what happens! Big shot!

BIFF: All right, Pop.

WILLY: Big!

BIFF: All right!

WILLY: Why do you always insult me?

BIFF: I didn't say a word. (*To* LINDA.) Did I say a word?

LINDA: He didn't say anything, Willy.

WILLY (*going to the doorway of the living-room*): All right, good night, good night.

LINDA: Willy, dear, he just decided . . .

WILLY (*to* BIFF): If you get tired hanging around tomorrow, paint the ceiling I put up in the living-room.

BIFF: I'm leaving early tomorrow.

HAPPY: He's going to see Bill Oliver, Pop.

WILLY (*interestedly*): Oliver? For what?

BIFF (*with reserve, but trying, trying*): He always said he'd stake me. I'd like to go into business, so maybe I can take him up on it.

LINDA: Isn't that wonderful?

WILLY: Don't interrupt. What's wonderful about it? There's fifty men in the City of New York who'd stake him. (*To* BIFF.) Sporting goods?

BIFF: I guess so. I know something about it and —

WILLY: He knows something about it! You know sporting goods better than Spalding, for God's sake! How much is he giving you?

BIFF: I don't know, I didn't even see him yet, but —

WILLY: Then what're you talkin' about?

BIFF (*getting angry*): Well, all I said was I'm gonna see him, that's all!

WILLY (*turning away*): Ah, you're counting your chickens again.

BIFF (*starting left for the stairs*): Oh, Jesus, I'm going to sleep!

WILLY (*calling after him*): Don't curse in this house!

BIFF (*turning*): Since when did you get so clean?

HAPPY (*trying to stop them*): Wait a . . .

WILLY: Don't use that language to me! I won't have it!

HAPPY (*grabbing* BIFF, *shouts*): Wait a minute! I got an idea. I got a feasible idea. Come here, Biff, let's talk this over now, let's talk some sense here. When I was down in Florida last time, I thought of a great idea to sell sporting goods. It just came back to me. You and I, Biff — we have a line, the Loman Line. We train a couple of weeks, and put on a couple of exhibitions, see?

WILLY: That's an idea!

HAPPY: Wait! We form two basketball teams, see? Two water-polo teams. We play each other. It's a million dollars' worth of publicity. Two brothers, see? The Loman Brothers. Displays in the Royal Palms — all the hotels. And banners over the ring and the basketball court: "Loman Brothers." Baby, we could sell sporting goods!

WILLY: That is a one-million-dollar idea!

LINDA: Marvelous!

BIFF: I'm in great shape as far as that's concerned.

HAPPY: And the beauty of it is, Biff, it wouldn't be like a business. We'd be out playin' ball again . . .

BIFF (*enthused*): Yeah, that's . . .

WILLY: Million-dollar . . .

HAPPY: And you wouldn't get fed up with it, Biff. It'd be the family again. There'd be the old honor, and comradeship, and if you wanted to go off for a swim or somethin' — well, you'd do it! Without some smart cooky gettin' up ahead of you!

WILLY: Lick the world! You guys together could absolutely lick the civilized world.

BIFF: I'll see Oliver tomorrow. Hap, if we could work that out . . .

LINDA: Maybe things are beginning to —

WILLY (*wildly enthused, to* LINDA): Stop interrupting! (*To* BIFF.) But don't wear sport jacket and slacks when you see Oliver.

BIFF: No, I'll —

WILLY: A business suit, and talk as little as possible, and don't crack any jokes.

BIFF: He did like me. Always liked me.

LINDA: He loved you!

WILLY (*to* LINDA): Will you stop! (*To* BIFF.) Walk in very serious. You are not applying for a boy's job. Money is to pass. Be quiet, fine, and serious. Everybody likes a kidder, but nobody lends him money.

HAPPY: I'll try to get some myself, Biff. I'm sure I can.

WILLY: I see great things for you kids, I think your troubles are over. But remember, start big and you'll end big. Ask for fifteen. How much you gonna ask for?

BIFF: Gee, I don't know —

WILLY: And don't say "Gee." "Gee" is a boy's word. A man walking in for fifteen thousand dollars does not say "Gee!"

BIFF: Ten, I think, would be top though.

WILLY: Don't be so modest. You always started too low. Walk in with a big laugh. Don't look worried. Start off with a couple of your good stories to lighten things up. It's not what you say, it's how you say it — because personality always wins the day.

LINDA: Oliver always thought the highest of him —

WILLY: Will you let me talk?

BIFF: Don't yell at her, Pop, will ya?

WILLY (*angrily*): I was talking, wasn't I?

BIFF: I don't like you yelling at her all the time, and I'm tellin' you, that's all.

WILLY: What're you, takin' over this house?

LINDA: Willy —

WILLY (*turning on her*): Don't take his side all the time, goddammit!

BIFF (*furiously*): Stop yelling at her!

WILLY (*suddenly pulling on his cheek, beaten down, guilt ridden*): Give my best to Bill Oliver — he may remember me. (*He exits through the living-room doorway.*)

LINDA (*her voice subdued*): What'd you have to start that for? (BIFF *turns away.*) You see how sweet he was as soon as you talked hopefully? (*She goes over to* BIFF.) Come up and say good night to him. Don't let him go to bed that way.

HAPPY: Come on, Biff, let's buck him up.

LINDA: Please, dear. Just say good night. It takes so little to make him happy. Come. (*She goes through the living-room doorway, calling upstairs from within the living-room.*) Your pajamas are hanging in the bathroom, Willy!

HAPPY (*looking toward where* LINDA *went out*): What a woman! They broke the mold when they made her. You know that, Biff?

BIFF: He's off salary. My God, working on commission!

HAPPY: Well, let's face it: he's no hot-shot selling man. Except that sometimes, you have to admit, he's a sweet personality.

BIFF (*deciding*): Lend me ten bucks, will ya? I want to buy some new ties.

HAPPY: I'll take you to a place I know. Beautiful stuff. Wear one of my striped shirts tomorrow.

BIFF: She got gray. Mom got awful old. Gee, I'm gonna go in to Oliver tomorrow and knock him for a —

HAPPY: Come on up. Tell that to Dad. Let's give him a whirl. Come on.

BIFF (*steamed up*): You know, with ten thousand bucks, boy!

HAPPY (*as they go into the living-room*): That's the talk, Biff, that's the first time I've heard the old confidence out of you! (*From within the living-room, fading off.*) You're gonna live with me, kid, and any babe you want just say the word . . . (*The last lines are hardly heard. They are mounting the stairs to their parents' bedroom.*)

LINDA (*entering her bedroom and addressing* WILLY, *who is in the bathroom. She is straightening the bed for him*): Can you do anything about the shower? It drips.

WILLY (*from the bathroom*): All of a sudden everything falls to pieces! Goddam plumbing, oughta be sued, those people. I hardly finished putting it in and the thing . . . (*His words rumble off.*)

LINDA: I'm just wondering if Oliver will remember him. You think he might?

WILLY (*coming out of the bathroom in his pajamas*): Remember him? What's the matter with you, you crazy? If he'd've stayed with Oliver he'd be on top by now! Wait'll Oliver gets a look at him. You don't know the average caliber any more. The average young man today — (*he is getting into bed*) — is got a caliber of zero. Greatest thing in the world for him was to bum around.

(BIFF *and* HAPPY *enter the bedroom. Slight pause.*)

WILLY (*stops short, looking at* BIFF): Glad to hear it, boy.

HAPPY: He wanted to say good night to you, sport.

WILLY (*to* BIFF): Yeah. Knock him dead, boy. What'd you want to tell me?

BIFF: Just take it easy, Pop. Good night. (*He turns to go.*)

WILLY (*unable to resist*): And if anything falls off the desk while you're talking to him — like a package or something — don't you pick it up. They have office boys for that.

LINDA: I'll make a big breakfast —

WILLY: Will you let me finish? (*To* BIFF.) Tell him you were in the business in the West. Not farm work.

BIFF: All right, Dad.

LINDA: I think everything —

WILLY (*going right through her speech*): And don't undersell yourself. No less than fifteen thousand dollars.

BIFF (*unable to bear him*): Okay. Good night, Mom. (*He starts moving.*)

WILLY: Because you got a greatness in you, Biff, remember that. You got all kinds a greatness . . . (*He lies back, exhausted.* BIFF *walks out.*)

LINDA (*calling after* BIFF): Sleep well, darling!

HAPPY: I'm gonna get married, Mom. I wanted to tell you.

LINDA: Go to sleep, dear.

HAPPY (*going*): I just wanted to tell you.

WILLY: Keep up the good work. (HAPPY *exits.*) God . . . remember that Ebbets Field game? The championship of the city?

LINDA: Just rest. Should I sing to you?

WILLY: Yeah. Sing to me. (LINDA *hums a soft lullaby.*) When that team came out — he was the tallest, remember?

LINDA: Oh, yes. And in gold.

(BIFF *enters the darkened kitchen, takes a cigarette, and leaves the house. He comes downstage into a golden pool of light. He smokes, staring at the night.*)

WILLY: Like a young god. Hercules — something like that. And the sun, the sun all around him. Remember how he waved to me? Right up from the field, with the representatives of three colleges standing by? And the buyers I brought, and the cheers when he came out — Loman, Loman, Loman! God Almighty, he'll be great yet. A star like that, magnificent, can never really fade away!

(*The light on* WILLY *is fading. The gas heater begins to glow through the kitchen wall, near the stairs, a blue flame beneath red coils.*)

LINDA (*timidly*): Willy dear, what has he got against you?

WILLY: I'm so tired. Don't talk any more.

(BIFF *slowly returns to the kitchen. He stops, stares toward the heater.*)

LINDA: Will you ask Howard to let you work in New York?

WILLY: First thing in the morning. Everything'll be all right.

(BIFF *reaches behind the heater and draws out a length of rubber tubing. He is horrified and turns his head toward* WILLY'S *room, still dimly lit, from which the strains of* LINDA'S *desperate but monotonous humming rise.*)

WILLY (*staring through the window into the*

moonlight): Gee, look at the moon moving between the buildings!

(BIFF *wraps the tubing around his hand and quickly goes up the stairs.*)

CURTAIN

ACT II

Music is heard, gay and bright. The curtain rises as the music fades away. WILLY, *in shirt sleeves, is sitting at the kitchen table, sipping coffee, his hat in his lap.* LINDA *is filling his cup when she can.*

WILLY: Wonderful coffee. Meal in itself.

LINDA: Can I make you some eggs?

WILLY: No. Take a breath.

LINDA: You look so rested, dear.

WILLY: I slept like a dead one. First time in months. Imagine, sleeping till ten on a Tuesday morning. Boys left nice and early, heh?

LINDA: They were out of here by eight o'clock.

WILLY: Good work!

LINDA: It was so thrilling to see them leaving together. I can't get over the shaving lotion in this house!

WILLY (*smiling*): Mmm —

LINDA: Biff was very changed this morning. His whole attitude seemed to be hopeful. He couldn't wait to get downtown to see Oliver.

WILLY: He's heading for a change. There's no question, there simply are certain men that take longer to get — solidified. How did he dress?

LINDA: His blue suit. He's so handsome in that suit. He could be a — anything in that suit!

(WILLY *gets up from the table.* LINDA *holds his jacket for him.*)

WILLY: There's no question, no question at all. Gee, on the way home tonight I'd like to buy some seeds.

LINDA (*laughing*): That'd be wonderful. But not enough sun gets back there. Nothing'll grow any more.

WILLY: You wait, kid, before it's all over we're gonna get a little place out in the country, and I'll raise some vegetables, a couple of chickens . . .

LINDA: You'll do it yet, dear.

(WILLY *walks out of his jacket.* LINDA *follows him.*)

WILLY: And they'll get married, and come for a weekend. I'd build a little guest house. 'Cause I got so many fine tools, all I'd need would be a little lumber and some peace of mind.

LINDA (*joyfully*): I sewed the lining . . .

WILLY: I could build two guest houses, so they'd both come. Did he decide how much he's going to ask Oliver for?

LINDA (*getting him into the jacket*): He didn't mention it, but I imagine ten or fifteen thousand. You going to talk to Howard today?

WILLY: Yeah. I'll put it to him straight and simple. He'll just have to take me off the road.

LINDA: And Willy, don't forget to ask for a little advance, because we've got the insurance premium. It's the grace period now.

WILLY: That's a hundred . . . ?

LINDA: A hundred and eight, sixty-eight. Because we're a little short again.

WILLY: Why are we short?

LINDA: Well, you had the motor job on the car . . .

WILLY: That goddam Studebaker!

LINDA: And you got one more payment on the refrigerator . . .

WILLY: But it just broke again!

LINDA: Well, it's old, dear.

WILLY: I told you we should've bought a well-advertised machine. Charley bought a General Electric and it's twenty years old and it's still good, that son-of-a-bitch.

LINDA: But, Willy —

WILLY: Whoever heard of a Hastings refrigerator? Once in my life I would like to own something outright before it's broken! I'm always in a race with the junkyard! I just finished paying for the car and it's on its last legs. The refrigerator consumes belts like a goddam maniac. They time those things. They time them so when you finally paid for them, they're used up.

LINDA (*buttoning up his jacket as he unbuttons it*): All told, about two hundred dollars would carry us, dear. But that includes the last payment on the mortgage. After this payment, Willy, the house belongs to us.

WILLY: It's twenty-five years!

LINDA: Biff was nine years old when we bought it.

WILLY: Well, that's a great thing. To weather a twenty-five year mortgage is —

LINDA: It's an accomplishment.

WILLY: All the cement, the lumber, the reconstruction I put in this house! There ain't a crack to be found in it any more.

LINDA: Well, it served its purpose.

WILLY: What purpose? Some stranger'll come along, move in, and that's that. If only Biff would take this house, and raise a family ... (*He starts to go.*) Good-by, I'm late.

LINDA (*suddenly remembering*): Oh, I forgot! You're supposed to meet them for dinner.

WILLY: Me?

LINDA: At Frank's Chop House on Forty-eighth near Sixth Avenue.

WILLY: Is that so! How about you?

LINDA: No, just the three of you. They're gonna blow you to a big meal!

WILLY: Don't say! Who thought of that?

LINDA: Biff came to me this morning, Willy, and he said, "Tell Dad, we want to blow him to a big meal." Be there six o'clock. You and your two boys are going to have dinner.

WILLY: Gee whiz! That's really somethin'. I'm gonna knock Howard for a loop, kid. I'll get an advance, and I'll come home with a New York job. Goddammit, now I'm gonna do it!

LINDA: Oh, that's the spirit, Willy!

WILLY: I will never get behind a wheel the rest of my life!

LINDA: It's changing, Willy, I can feel it changing!

WILLY: Beyond a question. G'by, I'm late. (*He starts to go again.*)

LINDA (*calling after him as she runs to the kitchen table for a handkerchief*): You got your glasses?

WILLY (*feels for them, then comes back in*): Yeah, yeah, got my glasses.

LINDA (*giving him the handkerchief*): And a handkerchief.

WILLY: Yeah, handkerchief.

LINDA: And your saccharine?

WILLY: Yeah, my saccharine.

LINDA: Be careful on the subway stairs.

(*She kisses him, and a silk stocking is seen hanging from her hand. WILLY notices it.*)

WILLY: Will you stop mending stockings? At least while I'm in the house. It gets me nervous. I can't tell you. Please.

(LINDA *hides the stocking in her hand as she follows* WILLY *across the forestage in front of the house.*)

LINDA: Remember, Frank's Chop House.

WILLY (*passing the apron*): Maybe beets would grow out there.

LINDA (*laughing*): But you tried so many times.

WILLY: Yeah. Well, don't work hard today. (*He disappears around the right corner of the house.*)

LINDA: Be careful!

(*As* WILLY *vanishes,* LINDA *waves to him. Suddenly the phone rings. She runs across the stage and into the kitchen and lifts it.*)

LINDA: Hello? Oh, Biff! I'm so glad you called, I just ... Yes, sure, I just told him. Yes, he'll be there for dinner at six o'clock, I didn't forget. Listen, I was just dying to tell you. You know that little rubber pipe I told you about? That he connected to the gas heater? I finally decided to go down the cellar this morning and take it away and destroy it. But it's gone! Imagine? He took it away himself, it isn't there! (*She listens.*) When? Oh, then you took it. Oh — nothing, it's just that I'd hoped he'd taken it away himself. Oh, I'm not worried, darling, because this morning he left in such high spirits, it was like the old days! I'm not afraid any more. Did Mr. Oliver see you? ... Well, you wait there then. And make a nice impression on him, darling. Just don't perspire too much before you see him. And have a nice time with Dad. He may have big news too! ... That's right, a New York job. And be sweet to him tonight, dear. Be loving to him. Because he's only a little boat looking for a harbor. (*She is trembling with sorrow and joy.*) Oh, that's wonderful, Biff, you'll save his life. Thanks, darling. Just put your arm around him when he comes into the restaurant. Give him a smile. That's the boy ... Good-by, dear. ... You got your comb? ... That's fine. Good-by, Biff dear.

(*In the middle of her speech,* HOWARD WAGNER, *thirty-six, wheels on a small typewriter table on which is a wire-recording machine and proceeds to plug it in. This is on the left forestage. Light slowly fades on* LINDA *as it rises on* HOWARD. HOWARD *is intent on threading the machine and only glances over his shoulder as* WILLY *appears.*)

WILLY: Pst! Pst!

HOWARD: Hello, Willy, come in.

WILLY: Like to have a little talk with you, Howard.

HOWARD: Sorry to keep you waiting. I'll be with you in a minute.

WILLY: What's that, Howard?

HOWARD: Didn't you ever see one of these? Wire recorder.

WILLY: Oh. Can we talk a minute?

HOWARD: Records things. Just got delivery yesterday. Been driving me crazy, the most terrific machine I ever saw in my life. I was up all night with it.

WILLY: What do you do with it?

HOWARD: I bought it for dictation, but you can do anything with it. Listen to this. I had it home last night. Listen to what I picked up. The first one is my daughter. Get this. (*He flicks the switch and "Roll out the Barrel" is heard being whistled.*) Listen to that kid whistle.

WILLY: That is lifelike, isn't it?

HOWARD: Seven years old. Get that tone.

WILLY: Ts, ts. Like to ask a little favor if you . . .

(*The whistling breaks off, and the voice of* HOWARD'S DAUGHTER *is heard.*)

HIS DAUGHTER: "Now you, Daddy."

HOWARD: She's crazy for me! (*Again the same song is whistled.*) That's me! Ha! (*He winks.*)

WILLY: You're very good!

(*The whistling breaks off again. The machine runs silent for a moment.*)

HOWARD: Sh! Get this now, this is my son.

HIS SON: "The capital of Alabama is Montgomery; the capital of Arizona is Phoenix; the capital of Arkansas is Little Rock; the capital of California is Sacramento . . ." (*And on, and on.*)

HOWARD (*holding up five fingers*): Five years old, Willy!

WILLY: He'll make an announcer some day!

HIS SON (*continuing*): "The capital . . ."

HOWARD: Get that — alphabetical order! (*The machine breaks off suddenly.*) Wait a minute. The maid kicked the plug out.

WILLY: It certainly is a —

HOWARD: Sh, for God's sake!

HIS SON: "It's nine o'clock, Bulova watch time. So I have to go to sleep."

WILLY: That really is —

HOWARD: Wait a minute! The next is my wife.

(*They wait.*)

HOWARD'S VOICE: "Go on, say something." (*Pause.*) "Well, you gonna talk?"

HIS WIFE: "I can't think of anything."

HOWARD'S VOICE: "Well, talk — it's turning."

HIS WIFE (*shyly, beaten*): "Hello." (*Silence.*) "Oh, Howard, I can't talk into this . . ."

HOWARD (*snapping the machine off*): That was my wife.

WILLY: That is a wonderful machine. Can we —

HOWARD: I tell you, Willy, I'm gonna take my camera, and my bandsaw, and all my hobbies, and out they go. This is the most fascinating relaxation I ever found.

WILLY: I think I'll get one myself.

HOWARD: Sure, they're only a hundred and a half. You can't do without it. Supposing you wanna hear Jack Benny, see? But you can't be at home at that hour. So you tell the maid to turn the radio on when Jack Benny comes on, and this automatically goes on with the radio . . .

WILLY: And when you come home you . . .

HOWARD: You can come home twelve o'clock, one o'clock, any time you like, and you get yourself a Coke and sit yourself down, throw the switch, and there's Jack Benny's program in the middle of the night!

WILLY: I'm definitely going to get one. Because lots of time I'm on the road, and I think to myself, what I must be missing on the radio!

HOWARD: Don't you have a radio in the car?

WILLY: Well, yeah, but who ever thinks of turning it on?

HOWARD: Say, aren't you supposed to be in Boston?

WILLY: That's what I want to talk to you about, Howard. You got a minute? (*He draws a chair in from the wing.*)

HOWARD: What happened? What're you doing here?

WILLY: Well . . .

HOWARD: You didn't crack up again, did you?

WILLY: Oh, no. No . . .

HOWARD: Geez, you had me worried there for a minute. What's the trouble?

WILLY: Well, tell you the truth, Howard. I've come to the decision that I'd rather not travel any more.

HOWARD: Not travel! Well, what'll you do?

WILLY: Remember, Christmas time, when you had the party here? You said you'd try to think of some spot for me here in town.

HOWARD: With us?

WILLY: Well, sure.

HOWARD: Oh, yeah, yeah. I remember. Well, I couldn't think of anything for you, Willy.

WILLY: I tell ya, Howard. The kids are all grown up, y'know. I don't need much any more. If I could take home — well, sixty-five dollars a week, I could swing it.

HOWARD: Yeah, but Willy, see I —

WILLY: I tell ya why, Howard. Speaking frankly and between the two of us, y'know — I'm just a little tired.

HOWARD: Oh, I could understand that, Willy. But you're a road man, Willy, and we do a road business. We've only got a half-dozen salesmen on the floor here.

WILLY: God knows, Howard, I never asked a favor of any man. But I was with the firm when your father used to carry you in here in his arms.

HOWARD: I know that, Willy, but —

WILLY: Your father came to me the day you were born and asked me what I thought of the name of Howard, may he rest in peace.

HOWARD: I appreciate that, Willy, but there just is no spot here for you. If I had a spot I'd slam you right in, but I just don't have a single solitary spot.

(*He looks for his lighter.* WILLY *has picked it up and gives it to him. Pause.*)

WILLY (*with increasing anger*): Howard, all I need to set my table is fifty dollars a week.

HOWARD: But where am I going to put you, kid?

WILLY: Look, it isn't a question of whether I can sell merchandise, is it?

HOWARD: No, but it's a business, kid, and everybody's gotta pull his own weight.

WILLY (*desperately*): Just let me tell you a story, Howard —

HOWARD: 'Cause you gotta admit, business is business.

WILLY (*angrily*): Business is definitely business, but just listen for a minute. You don't understand this. When I was a boy — eighteen, nineteen — I was already on the road. And there was a question in my mind as to whether selling had a future for me. Because in those days I had a yearning to go to Alaska. See, there were three gold strikes in one month in Alaska, and I felt like going out. Just for the ride, you might say.

HOWARD (*barely interested*): Don't say.

WILLY: Oh, yeah, my father lived many years in Alaska. He was an adventurous man. We've got quite a little streak of self-reliance in our family. I thought I'd go out with my older brother and try to locate him, and maybe settle in the North with the old man. And I was almost decided to go, when I met a salesman in the Parker House. His name was Dave Singleman. And he was eighty-four years old, and he'd drummed merchandise in thirty-one states. And old Dave, he'd go up to his room, y'understand, put on his green velvet slippers — I'll never forget — and pick up his phone and call the buyers, and without ever leaving his room, at the age of eighty-four, he made his living. And when I saw that, I realized that selling was the greatest career a man could want. 'Cause what could be more satisfying than to be able to go, at the age of eighty-four, into twenty or thirty different cities, and pick up a phone, and be remembered and loved and helped by so many different people? Do you know? when he died — and by the way he died the death of a salesman, in his green velvet slippers in the smoker of the New York, New Haven and Hartford, going into Boston — when he died, hundreds of salesmen and buyers were at his funeral. Things were sad on a lotta trains for months after that. (*He stands up.* HOWARD *has not looked at him.*) In those days there was personality in it, Howard. There was respect, and comradeship, and gratitude in it. Today, it's all cut and dried, and there's no chance for bringing friendship to bear — or personality. You see what I mean? They don't know me any more.

HOWARD (*moving away, to the right*): That's just the thing, Willy.

WILLY: If I had forty dollars a week — that's all I'd need. Forty dollars, Howard.

HOWARD: Kid, I can't take blood from a stone, I —

WILLY (*desperation is on him now*): Howard, the year Al Smith was nominated, your father came to me and —

HOWARD (*starting to go off*): I've got to see some people, kid.

WILLY (*stopping him*): I'm talking about your father! There were promises made across this desk! You mustn't tell me you've got people to see — I put thirty-four years into this firm, Howard, and now I can't pay my insurance! You can't eat the orange and throw the peel away — a man is not a piece of fruit! (*After a pause.*) Now pay attention. Your father — in 1928 I had a big year. I averaged a hundred and seventy dollars a week in commissions.

HOWARD (*impatiently*): Now, Willy, you never averaged —

WILLY (*banging his hand on the desk*): I averaged a hundred and seventy dollars a week in the year of 1928! And your father came to me — or rather, I was in the office here — it was right over this desk — and he put his hand on my shoulder —

HOWARD (*getting up*): You'll have to excuse me, Willy, I gotta see some people. Pull yourself together. (*Going out.*) I'll be back in a little while.

(*On* HOWARD'S *exit, the light on his chair grows very bright and strange.*)

WILLY: Pull myself together! What the hell did I say to him! My God, I was yelling at him! How could I! (WILLY *breaks off, staring at the light, which occupies the chair, animating it. He approaches this chair, standing across the desk from it.*) Frank, Frank, don't you remember what you told me that time? How you put your hand on my shoulder, and Frank . . . (*He leans on the desk and as he speaks the dead man's name he accidentally switches on the recorder, and instantly —*)

HOWARD'S SON: ". . . of New York is Albany. The capital of Ohio is Cincinnati, the capital of Rhode Island is . . ." (*The recitation continues.*)

WILLY (*leaping away with fright, shouting*): Ha! Howard! Howard! Howard!

HOWARD (*rushing in*): What happened?

WILLY (*pointing at the machine, which continues nasally, childishly, with the capital cities*): Shut it off! Shut it off!

HOWARD (*pulling the plug out*): Look, Willy . . .

WILLY (*pressing his hands to his eyes*): I gotta get myself some coffee. I'll get some coffee . . .

(WILLY *starts to walk out.* HOWARD *stops him.*)

HOWARD (*rolling up the cord*): Willy, look . . .

WILLY: I'll go to Boston.

HOWARD: Willy, you can't go to Boston for us.

WILLY: Why can't I go?

HOWARD: I don't want you to represent us. I've been meaning to tell you for a long time now.

WILLY: Howard, are you firing me?

HOWARD: I think you need a good long rest, Willy.

WILLY: Howard —

HOWARD: And when you feel better, come back, and we'll see if we can work something out.

WILLY: But I gotta earn money, Howard. I'm in no position to —

HOWARD: Where are your sons? Why don't your sons give you a hand?

WILLY: They're working on a very big deal.

HOWARD: This is no time for false pride, Willy. You go to your sons and you tell them that you're tired. You've got two great boys, haven't you?

WILLY: Oh, no question, no question, but in the meantime . . .

HOWARD: Then that's that, heh?

WILLY: All right, I'll go to Boston tomorrow.

HOWARD: No, no.

WILLY: I can't throw myself on my sons. I'm not a cripple!

HOWARD: Look, kid, I'm busy this morning.

WILLY (*grasping* HOWARD'S *arm*): Howard, you've got to let me go to Boston!

HOWARD (*hard, keeping himself under control*): I've got a line of people to see this morning. Sit down, take five minutes, and pull yourself together, and then go home, will ya? I need the office, Willy. (*He starts to go, turns, remembering the recorder, starts to push off the table holding the recorder.*) Oh, yeah. Whenever you can this week, stop by and drop off the samples. You'll feel better, Willy, and then come back and we'll talk. Pull yourself together, kid, there's people outside.

(HOWARD *exits, pushing the table off left.* WILLY *stares into space, exhausted. Now the music is heard —* BEN'S *music — first distantly, then closer, closer. As* WILLY *speaks,* BEN *enters from the right. He carries valise and umbrella.*)

WILLY: Oh, Ben, how did you do it? What

is the answer? Did you wind up the Alaska deal already?

BEN: Doesn't take much time if you know what you're doing. Just a short business trip. Boarding ship in an hour. Wanted to say good-by.

WILLY: Ben, I've got to talk to you.

BEN (*glancing at his watch*): Haven't the time, William.

WILLY (*crossing the apron to* BEN): Ben, nothing's working out. I don't know what to do.

BEN: Now, look here, William. I've bought timberland in Alaska and I need a man to look after things for me.

WILLY: God, timberland! Me and my boys in those grand outdoors!

BEN: You've a new continent at your doorstep, William. Get out of these cities, they're full of talk and time payments and courts of law. Screw on your fists and you can fight for a fortune up there.

WILLY: Yes, yes! Linda, Linda!

(LINDA *enters as of old, with the wash.*)

LINDA: Oh, you're back?

BEN: I haven't much time.

WILLY: No, wait! Linda, he's got a proposition for me in Alaska.

LINDA: But you've got — (*To* BEN.) He's got a beautiful job here.

WILLY: But in Alaska, kid, I could —

LINDA: You're doing well enough, Willy!

BEN (*to* LINDA): Enough for what, my dear?

LINDA (*frightened of* BEN *and angry at him*): Don't say those things to him! Enough to be happy right here, right now. (*To* WILLY, *while* BEN *laughs.*) Why must everybody conquer the world? You're well liked, and the boys love you, and someday — (*to* BEN) — why, old man Wagner told him just the other day that if he keeps it up he'll be a member of the firm, didn't he, Willy?

WILLY: Sure, sure. I am building something with this firm, Ben, and if a man is building something he must be on the right track, mustn't he?

BEN: What are you building? Lay your hand on it. Where is it?

WILLY (*hesitantly*): That's true, Linda, there's nothing.

LINDA: Why? (*To* BEN.) There's a man eighty-four years old —

WILLY: That's right, Ben, that's right. When I look at that man I say, what is there to worry about?

BEN: Bah!

WILLY: It's true, Ben. All he has to do is go into any city, pick up the phone, and he's making his living and you know why?

BEN (*picking up his valise*): I've got to go.

WILLY (*holding* BEN *back*): Look at this boy!

(BIFF, *in his high school sweater, enters carrying suitcase.* HAPPY *carries* BIFF's *shoulder guards, gold helmet, and football pants.*)

WILLY: Without a penny to his name, three great universities are begging for him, and from there the sky's the limit, because it's not what you do, Ben. It's who you know and the smile on your face! It's contacts, Ben, contacts! The whole wealth of Alaska passes over the lunch table at the Commodore Hotel, and that's the wonder, the wonder of this country, that a man can end with diamonds here on the basis of being liked! (*He turns to* BIFF.) And that's why when you get out on that field today it's important. Because thousands of people will be rooting for you and loving you. (*To* BEN, *who has again begun to leave.*) And Ben! when he walks into a business office his name will sound out like a bell and all the doors will open to him! I've seen it, Ben, I've seen it a thousand times! You can't feel it with your hand like timber, but it's there!

BEN: Good-by, William.

WILLY: Ben, am I right? Don't you think I'm right? I value your advice.

BEN: There's a new continent at your doorstep, William. You could walk out rich. Rich! (*He is gone.*)

WILLY: We'll do it here, Ben! You hear me? We're gonna do it here!

(YOUNG BERNARD *rushes in. The gay music of the boys is heard.*)

BERNARD: Oh, gee, I was afraid you left already!

WILLY: Why? What time is it?

BERNARD: It's half-past one!

WILLY: Well, come on, everybody! Ebbets Field next stop! Where's the pennants? (*He rushes through the wall-line of the kitchen and out into the living-room.*)

LINDA (*to* BIFF): Did you pack fresh underwear?

BIFF (*who has been limbering up*): I want to go!

BERNARD: Biff, I'm carrying your helmet, ain't I?

HAPPY: No, I'm carrying the helmet.

BERNARD: Oh, Biff, you promised me.

HAPPY: I'm carrying the helmet.

BERNARD: How am I going to get in the locker room?

LINDA: Let him carry the shoulder guards. (*She puts her coat and hat on in the kitchen.*)

BERNARD: Can I, Biff? 'Cause I told everybody I'm going to be in the locker room.

HAPPY: In Ebbets Field it's the clubhouse.

BERNARD: I meant the clubhouse. Biff!

HAPPY: Biff!

BIFF (*grandly, after a slight pause*): Let him carry the shoulder guards.

HAPPY (*as he gives* BERNARD *the shoulder guards*): Stay close to us now.

(WILLY *rushes in with the pennants.*)

WILLY (*handing them out*): Everybody wave when Biff comes out on the field. (HAPPY *and* BERNARD *run off.*) You set now, boy?

(*The music has died away.*)

BIFF: Ready to go, Pop. Every muscle is ready.

WILLY (*at the edge of the apron*): You realize what this means?

BIFF: That's right, Pop.

WILLY (*feeling* BIFF'S *muscles*): You're comin' home this afternoon captain of the All-Scholastic Championship Team of the City of New York.

BIFF: I got it, Pop. And remember, pal, when I take off my helmet, that touchdown is for you.

WILLY: Let's go! (*He is starting out, with his arm around* BIFF, *when* CHARLEY *enters, as of old, in knickers.*) I got no room for you, Charley.

CHARLEY: Room? For what?

WILLY: In the car.

CHARLEY: You goin' for a ride? I wanted to shoot some casino.

WILLY (*furiously*): Casino! (*Incredulously.*) Don't you realize what today is?

LINDA: Oh, he knows, Willy. He's just kidding you.

WILLY: That's nothing to kid about!

CHARLEY: No, Linda, what's goin' on?

LINDA: He's playing in Ebbets Field.

CHARLEY: Baseball in this weather?

WILLY: Don't talk to him. Come on, come on! (*He is pushing them out.*)

CHARLEY: Wait a minute, didn't you hear the news?

WILLY: What?

CHARLEY: Don't you listen to the radio? Ebbets Field just blew up.

WILLY: You go to hell! (CHARLEY *laughs. Pushing them out.*) Come on, come on! We're late.

CHARLEY (*as they go*): Knock a homer, Biff, knock a homer!

WILLY (*the last to leave, turning to* CHARLEY): I don't think that was funny, Charley. This is the greatest day of his life.

CHARLEY: Willy, when are you going to grow up?

WILLY: Yeah, heh? When this game is over, Charley, you'll be laughing out of the other side of your face. They'll be calling him another Red Grange. Twenty-five thousand a year.

CHARLEY (*kidding*): Is that so?

WILLY: Yeah, that's so.

CHARLEY: Well, then, I'm sorry, Willy. But tell me something.

WILLY: What?

CHARLEY: Who is Red Grange?

WILLY: Put up your hands. Goddam you, put up your hands!

(CHARLEY, *chuckling, shakes his head and walks away, around the left corner of the stage.* WILLY *follows him. The music rises to a mocking frenzy.*)

WILLY: Who the hell do you think you are, better than everybody else? You don't know everything, you big, ignorant, stupid . . . Put up your hands!

(*Light rises, on the right side of the forestage, on a small table in the reception room of* CHARLEY'S *office. Traffic sounds are heard.* BERNARD, *now mature, sits whistling to himself. A pair of tennis rackets and an overnight bag are on the floor beside him.*)

WILLY (*offstage*): What are you walking away for? Don't walk away! If you're going to say something say it to my face! I know you laugh at me behind my back. You'll laugh out of the other side of your goddam face after this game. Touchdown! Touchdown! Eighty thousand people! Touchdown! Right between the goal posts.

(BERNARD *is a quiet, earnest, but self-assured young man.* WILLY'*s voice is coming from right upstage now.* BERNARD *lowers his feet off the table and listens.* JENNY, *his father's secretary, enters.*)

JENNY (*distressed*): Say, Bernard, will you go out in the hall?

BERNARD: What is that noise? Who is it?

JENNY: Mr. Loman. He just got off the elevator.

BERNARD (*getting up*): Who's he arguing with?

JENNY: Nobody. There's nobody with him. I can't deal with him any more, and your father gets all upset everytime he comes. I've got a lot of typing to do, and your father's waiting to sign it. Will you see him?

WILLY (*entering*): Touchdown! Touch — (*He sees* JENNY.) Jenny, Jenny, good to see you. How're ya? Workin'? Or still honest?

JENNY: Fine. How've you been feeling?

WILLY: Not much any more, Jenny. Ha, ha! (*He is surprised to see the rackets.*)

BERNARD: Hello, Uncle Willy.

WILLY (*almost shocked*): Bernard! Well, look who's here! (*He comes quickly, guiltily, to* BERNARD *and warmly shakes his hand.*)

BERNARD: How are you? Good to see you.

WILLY: What are you doing here?

BERNARD: Oh, just stopped by to see Pop. Get off my feet till my train leaves. I'm going to Washington in a few minutes.

WILLY: Is he in?

BERNARD: Yes, he's in his office with the accountant. Sit down.

WILLY (*sitting down*): What're you going to do in Washington?

BERNARD: Oh, just a case I've got there, Willy.

WILLY: That so? (*Indicating the rackets.*) You going to play tennis there?

BERNARD: I'm staying with a friend who's got a court.

WILLY: Don't say. His own tennis court. Must be fine people, I bet.

BERNARD: They are, very nice. Dad tells me Biff's in town.

WILLY (*with a big smile*): Yeah, Biff's in. Working on a very big deal, Bernard.

BERNARD: What's Biff doing?

WILLY: Well, he's been doing very big things in the West. But he decided to establish himself here. Very big. We're having dinner. Did I hear your wife had a boy?

BERNARD: That's right. Our second.

WILLY: Two boys! What do you know!

BERNARD: What kind of a deal has Biff got?

WILLY: Well, Bill Oliver — very big sporting-goods man — he wants Biff very badly. Called him in from the West. Long distance, carte blanche, special deliveries. Your friends have their own private tennis court.

BERNARD: You still with the old firm, Willy?

WILLY (*after a pause*): I'm — I'm overjoyed to see how you made the grade, Bernard, overjoyed. It's an encouraging thing to see a young man really — really — Looks very good for Biff — very — (*He breaks off, then.*) Bernard — (*He is so full of emotion, he breaks off again.*)

BERNARD: What is it, Willy?

WILLY (*small and alone*): What — what's the secret?

BERNARD: What secret?

WILLY: How — how did you? Why didn't he ever catch on?

BERNARD: I wouldn't know that, Willy.

WILLY (*confidentially, desperately*): You were his friend, his boyhood friend. There's something I don't understand about it. His life ended after that Ebbets Field game. From the age of seventeen nothing good ever happened to him.

BERNARD: He never trained himself for anything.

WILLY: But he did, he did. After high school he took so many correspondence courses. Radio mechanics; television; God knows what, and never made the slightest mark.

BERNARD (*taking off his glasses*): Willy, do you want to talk candidly?

WILLY (*rising, faces* BERNARD): I regard you as a very brilliant man, Bernard. I value your advice.

BERNARD: Oh, the hell with the advice, Willy. I couldn't advise you. There's just one thing I've always wanted to ask you. When he was supposed to graduate, and the math teacher flunked him —

WILLY: Oh, that son-of-a-bitch ruined his life.

BERNARD: Yeah, but, Willy, all he had to do was go to summer school and make up that subject.

WILLY: That's right, that's right.

BERNARD: Did you tell him not to go to summer school?

WILLY: Me? I begged him to go. I ordered him to go!

BERNARD: Then why wouldn't he go?

WILLY: Why? Why! Bernard, that question has been trailing me like a ghost for the last fifteen years. He flunked the subject, and laid down and died like a hammer hit him!

BERNARD: Take it easy, kid.

WILLY: Let me talk to you — I got nobody to talk to. Bernard, Bernard, was it my fault? Y'see? It keeps going around in my mind, maybe I did something to him. I got nothing to give him.

BERNARD: Don't take it so hard.

WILLY: Why did he lay down? What is the story there? You were his friend!

BERNARD: Willy, I remember, it was June, and our grades came out. And he'd flunked math.

WILLY: That son-of-a-bitch!

BERNARD: No, it wasn't right then. Biff just got very angry, I remember, and he was ready to enroll in summer school.

WILLY (surprised): He was?

BERNARD: He wasn't beaten by it at all. But then, Willy, he disappeared from the block for almost a month. And I got the idea that he'd gone up to New England to see you. Did he have a talk with you then?

(WILLY stares in silence.)

BERNARD: Willy?

WILLY (with a strong edge of resentment in his voice): Yeah, he came to Boston. What about it?

BERNARD: Well, just that when he came back — I'll never forget this, it always mystifies me. Because I'd thought so well of Biff, even though he'd always taken advantage of me. I loved him, Willy, y'know? And he came back after that month and took his sneakers — remember those sneakers with "University of Virginia" printed on them? He was so proud of those, wore them every day. And he took them down in the cellar, and burned them up

in the furnace. We had a fist fight. It lasted at least half an hour. Just the two of us, punching each other down the cellar, and crying right through it. I've often thought of how strange it was that I knew he'd given up his life. What happened in Boston, Willy?

(WILLY looks at him as at an intruder.)

BERNARD: I just bring it up because you asked me.

WILLY (angrily): Nothing. What do you mean, "What happened?" What's that got to do with anything?

BERNARD: Well, don't get sore.

WILLY: What are you trying to do, blame it on me? If a boy lays down is that my fault?

BERNARD: Now, Willy, don't get —

WILLY: Well, don't — don't talk to me that way! What does that mean, "What happened?"

(CHARLEY enters. He is in his vest, and he carries a bottle of bourbon.)

CHARLEY: Hey, you're going to miss that train. (He waves the bottle.)

BERNARD: Yeah, I'm going. (He takes the bottle.) Thanks, Pop. (He picks up his rackets and bag.) Good-by, Willy, and don't worry about it. You know, "If at first you don't succeed . . ."

WILLY: Yes, I believe in that.

BERNARD: But sometimes, Willy, it's better for a man just to walk away.

WILLY: Walk away?

BERNARD: That's right.

WILLY: But if you can't walk away?

BERNARD (after a slight pause): I guess that's when it's tough. (Extending his hand.) Good-by, Willy.

WILLY (shaking BERNARD's hand): Good-by, boy.

CHARLEY (an arm on BERNARD's shoulder): How do you like this kid? Gonna argue a case in front of the Supreme Court.

BERNARD (protesting): Pop!

WILLY (genuinely shocked, pained, and happy): No! The Supreme Court!

BERNARD: I gotta run. 'By, Dad!

CHARLEY: Knock 'em dead, Bernard!

(BERNARD goes off.)

WILLY (as CHARLEY takes out his wallet): The Supreme Court! And he didn't even mention it!

CHARLEY (*counting out money on the desk*): He don't have to — he's gonna do it.

WILLY: And you never told him what to do, did you? You never took any interest in him.

CHARLEY: My salvation is that I never took any interest in anything. There's some money — fifty dollars. I got an accountant inside.

WILLY: Charley, look . . . (*With difficulty.*) I got my insurance to pay. If you can manage it — I need a hundred and ten dollars.

(CHARLEY *doesn't reply for a moment; merely stops moving.*)

WILLY: I'd draw it from my bank but Linda would know, and I . . .

CHARLEY: Sit down, Willy.

WILLY (*moving toward the chair*): I'm keeping an account of everything, remember. I'll pay every penny back. (*He sits.*)

CHARLEY: Now listen to me, Willy.

WILLY: I want you to know I appreciate . . .

CHARLEY (*sitting down on the table*): Willy, what're you doin'? What the hell is goin' on in your head?

WILLY: Why? I'm simply . . .

CHARLEY: I offered you a job. You can make fifty dollars a week. And I won't send you on the road.

WILLY: I've got a job.

CHARLEY: Without pay? What kind of a job is a job without pay? (*He rises.*) Now, look, kid, enough is enough. I'm no genius but I know when I'm being insulted.

WILLY: Insulted!

CHARLEY: Why don't you want to work for me?

WILLY: What's the matter with you? I've got a job.

CHARLEY: Then what're you walkin' in here every week for?

WILLY (*getting up*): Well, if you don't want me to walk in here —

CHARLEY: I am offering you a job.

WILLY: I don't want your goddam job!

CHARLEY: When the hell are you going to grow up?

WILLY (*furiously*): You big ignoramus, if you say that to me again I'll rap you one! I don't care how big you are! (*He's ready to fight.*)

(*Pause.*)

CHARLEY (*kindly, going to him*): How much do you need, Willy?

WILLY: Charley, I'm strapped. I'm strapped. I don't know what to do. I was just fired.

CHARLEY: Howard fired you?

WILLY: That snotnose. Imagine that? I named him. I named him Howard.

CHARLEY: Willy, when're you gonna realize that them things don't mean anything? You named him Howard, but you can't sell that. The only thing you got in this world is what you can sell. And the funny thing is that you're a salesman, and you don't know that.

WILLY: I've always tried to think otherwise, I guess. I always felt that if a man was impressive, and well liked, that nothing —

CHARLEY: Why must everybody like you? Who liked J. P. Morgan? Was he impressive? In a Turkish bath he'd look like a butcher. But with his pockets on he was very well liked. Now listen, Willy, I know you don't like me, and nobody can say I'm in love with you, but I'll give you a job because — just for the hell of it, put it that way. Now what do you say?

WILLY: I — I just can't work for you, Charley.

CHARLEY: What're you, jealous of me?

WILLY: I can't work for you, that's all, don't ask me why.

CHARLEY (*angered, takes out more bills*): You been jealous of me all your life, you damned fool! Here, pay your insurance. (*He puts the money in* WILLY's *hand.*)

WILLY: I'm keeping strict accounts.

CHARLEY: I've got some work to do. Take care of yourself. And pay your insurance.

WILLY (*moving to the right*): Funny, y'know? After all the highways, and the trains, and the appointments, and the years, you end up worth more dead than alive.

CHARLEY: Willy, nobody's worth nothin' dead. (*After a slight pause.*) Did you hear what I said?

(WILLY *stands still, dreaming.*)

CHARLEY: Willy!

WILLY: Apologize to Bernard for me when you see him. I didn't mean to argue with him. He's a fine boy. They're all fine boys, and they'll end up big — all of them. Someday they'll all play tennis together. Wish me luck, Charley. He saw Bill Oliver today.

CHARLEY: Good luck.

WILLY (*on the verge of tears*): Charley, you're the only friend I got. Isn't that a remarkable thing? (*He goes out.*)

CHARLEY: Jesus!

(CHARLEY *stares after him a moment and follows. All light blacks out. Suddenly raucous music is heard, and a red glow rises behind the screen at right.* STANLEY, *a young waiter, appears, carrying a table, followed by* HAPPY, *who is carrying two chairs.*)

STANLEY (*putting the table down*): That's all right, Mr. Loman, I can handle it myself. (*He turns and takes the chairs from* HAPPY *and places them at the table.*)

HAPPY (*glancing around*): Oh, this is better.

STANLEY: Sure, in the front there you're in the middle of all kinds a noise. Whenever you got a party, Mr. Loman, you just tell me and I'll put you back here. Y'know, there's a lotta people they don't like it private, because when they go out they like to see a lotta action around them because they're sick and tired to stay in the house by theirself. But I know you, you ain't from Hackensack. You know what I mean?

HAPPY (*sitting down*): So how's it coming, Stanley?

STANLEY: Ah, it's a dog's life. I only wish during the war they'd a took me in the Army. I coulda been dead by now.

HAPPY: My brother's back, Stanley.

STANLEY: Oh, he come back, heh? From the Far West.

HAPPY: Yeah, big cattle man, my brother, so treat him right. And my father's coming too.

STANLEY: Oh, your father too!

HAPPY: You got a couple of nice lobsters?

STANLEY: Hundred per cent, big.

HAPPY: I want them with the claws.

STANLEY: Don't worry, I don't give you no mice. (HAPPY *laughs.*) How about some wine? It'll put a head on the meal.

HAPPY: No. You remember, Stanley, that recipe I brought you from overseas? With the champagne in it?

STANLEY: Oh, yeah, sure. I still got it tacked up yet in the kitchen. But that'll have to cost a buck apiece anyways.

HAPPY: That's all right.

STANLEY: What'd you, hit a number or somethin'?

HAPPY: No, it's a little celebration. My brother is — I think he pulled off a big deal today. I think we're going into business together.

STANLEY: Great! That's the best for you. Because a family business, you know what I mean? — that's the best.

HAPPY: That's what I think.

STANLEY: 'Cause what's the difference? Somebody steals? It's in the family. Know what I mean? (*Sotto voce.*) Like this bartender here. The boss is goin' crazy what kinda leak he's got in the cash register. You put it in but it don't come out.

HAPPY (*raising his head*): Sh!

STANLEY: What?

HAPPY: You notice I wasn't lookin' right or left, was I?

STANLEY: No.

HAPPY: And my eyes are closed.

STANLEY: So what's the — ?

HAPPY: Strudel's comin'.

STANLEY (*catching on, looks around*): Ah, no, there's no —

(*He breaks off as a furred, lavishly dressed* GIRL *enters and sits at the next table. Both follow her with their eyes.*)

STANLEY: Geez, how'd ya know?

HAPPY: I got radar or something. (*Staring directly at her profile.*) Oooooooo . . . Stanley.

STANLEY: I think that's for you, Mr. Loman.

HAPPY: Look at that mouth. Oh, God. And the binoculars.

STANLEY: Geez, you got a life, Mr. Loman.

HAPPY: Wait on her.

STANLEY (*going to* THE GIRL's *table*): Would you like a menu, ma'am?

GIRL: I'm expecting someone, but I'd like a —

HAPPY: Why don't you bring her — excuse me, miss, do you mind? I sell champagne, and I'd like you to try my brand. Bring her a champagne, Stanley.

GIRL: That's awfully nice of you.

HAPPY: Don't mention it. It's all company money. (*He laughs.*)

GIRL: That's a charming product to be selling, isn't it?

HAPPY: Oh, gets to be like everything else. Selling is selling, y'know.

GIRL: I suppose.

HAPPY: You don't happen to sell, do you?

GIRL: No, I don't sell.

HAPPY: Would you object to a compliment from a stranger? You ought to be on a magazine cover.

GIRL (*looking at him a little archly*): I have been.

(STANLEY *comes in with a glass of champagne.*)

HAPPY: What'd I say before, Stanley? You see? She's a cover girl.

STANLEY: Oh, I could see, I could see.

HAPPY (to THE GIRL): What magazine?

GIRL: Oh, a lot of them. (*She takes the drink.*) Thank you.

HAPPY: You know what they say in France, don't you? "Champagne is the drink of the complexion" — Hya, Biff!

(BIFF *has entered and sits with* HAPPY.)

BIFF: Hello, kid. Sorry I'm late.

HAPPY: I just got here. Uh, Miss — ?

GIRL: Forsythe.

HAPPY: Miss Forsythe, this is my brother.

BIFF: Is Dad here?

HAPPY: His name is Biff. You might've heard of him. Great football player.

GIRL: Really? What team?

HAPPY: Are you familiar with football?

GIRL: No, I'm afraid I'm not.

HAPPY: Biff is quarterback with the New York Giants.

GIRL: Well, that is nice, isn't it? (*She drinks.*)

HAPPY: Good health.

GIRL: I'm happy to meet you.

HAPPY: That's my name. Hap. It's really Harold, but at West Point they called me Happy.

GIRL (*now really impressed*): Oh, I see. How do you do? (*She turns her profile.*)

BIFF: Isn't Dad coming?

HAPPY: You want her?

BIFF: Oh, I could never make that.

HAPPY: I remember the time that idea would never come into your head. Where's the old confidence, Biff?

BIFF: I just saw Oliver —

HAPPY: Wait a minute. I've got to see that old confidence again. Do you want her? She's on call.

BIFF: Oh, no. (*He turns to look at* THE GIRL.)

HAPPY: I'm telling you. Watch this. (*Turning to* THE GIRL.) Honey? (*She turns to him.*) Are you busy?

GIRL: Well, I am . . . but I could make a phone call.

HAPPY: Do that, will you, honey? And see if you can get a friend. We'll be here for a while. Biff is one of the greatest football players in the country.

GIRL (*standing up*): Well, I'm certainly happy to meet you.

HAPPY: Come back soon.

GIRL: I'll try.

HAPPY: Don't try, honey, try hard.

(THE GIRL *exits.* STANLEY *follows, shaking his head in bewildered admiration.*)

HAPPY: Isn't that a shame now? A beautiful girl like that? That's why I can't get married. There's not a good woman in a thousand. New York is loaded with them, kid!

BIFF: Hap, look —

HAPPY: I told you she was on call!

BIFF (*strangely unnerved*): Cut it out, will ya? I want to say something to you.

HAPPY: Did you see Oliver?

BIFF: I saw him all right. Now look, I want to tell Dad a couple of things and I want you to help me.

HAPPY: What? Is he going to back you?

BIFF: Are you crazy? You're out of your goddam head, you know that?

HAPPY: Why? What happened?

BIFF (*breathlessly*): I did a terrible thing today, Hap. It's been the strangest day I ever went through. I'm all numb, I swear.

HAPPY: You mean he wouldn't see you?

BIFF: Well, I waited six hours for him, see? All day. Kept sending my name in. Even tried to date his secretary so she'd get me to him, but no soap.

HAPPY: Because you're not showin' the old confidence, Biff. He remembered you, didn't he?

BIFF (*stopping* HAPPY *with a gesture*): Finally, about five o'clock, he comes out. Didn't remember who I was or anything. I felt like such an idiot, Hap.

HAPPY: Did you tell him my Florida idea?

BIFF: He walked away. I saw him for one minute. I got so mad I could've torn the walls down! How the hell did I ever get the idea I was a salesman there? I even believed myself that I'd been a salesman for him! And then he gave me one look and — I realized what a ridiculous lie my whole life has been! We've been talking in a dream for fifteen years. I was a shipping clerk.

HAPPY: What'd you do?

BIFF (*with great tension and wonder*): Well, he left, see. And the secretary went out. I was all alone in the waiting-room. I don't know what came over me, Hap. The next thing I know I'm in his office — paneled walls, everything. I can't explain it. I — Hap, I took his fountain pen.

HAPPY: Geez, did he catch you?

BIFF: I ran out. I ran down all eleven flights. I ran and ran and ran.

HAPPY: That was an awful dumb — what'd you do that for?

BIFF (*agonized*): I don't know, I just — wanted to take something, I don't know. You gotta help me, Hap, I'm gonna tell Pop.

HAPPY: You crazy? What for?

BIFF: Hap, he's got to understand that I'm not the man somebody lends that kind of money to. He thinks I've been spiting him all these years and it's eating him up.

HAPPY: That's just it. You tell him something nice.

BIFF: I can't.

HAPPY: Say you got a lunch date with Oliver tomorrow.

BIFF: So what do I do tomorrow?

HAPPY: You leave the house tomorrow and come back at night and say Oliver is thinking it over. And he thinks it over for a couple of weeks, and gradually it fades away and nobody's the worse.

BIFF: But it'll go on forever!

HAPPY: Dad is never so happy as when he's looking forward to something!

(WILLY *enters.*)

HAPPY: Hello, scout!

WILLY: Gee, I haven't been here in years!

(STANLEY *has followed* WILLY *in and sets a chair for him.* STANLEY *starts off but* HAPPY *stops him.*)

HAPPY: Stanley!

(STANLEY *stands by, waiting for an order.*)

BIFF (*going to* WILLY *with guilt, as to an invalid*): Sit down, Pop. You want a drink?

WILLY: Sure, I don't mind.

BIFF: Let's get a load on.

WILLY: You look worried.

BIFF: N-no. (*To* STANLEY.) Scotch all around. Make it doubles.

STANLEY: Doubles, right. (*He goes.*)

WILLY: You had a couple already, didn't you?

BIFF: Just a couple, yeah.

WILLY: Well, what happened, boy?

(*Nodding affirmatively, with a smile.*) Everything go all right?

BIFF (*takes a breath, then reaches out and grasps* WILLY's *hand*): Pal . . . (*He is smiling bravely, and* WILLY *is smiling too.*) I had an experience today.

HAPPY: Terrific, Pop.

WILLY: That so? What happened?

BIFF (*high, slightly alcoholic, above the earth*): I'm going to tell you everything from first to last. It's been a strange day. (*Silence. He looks around, composes himself as best he can, but his breath keeps breaking the rhythm of his voice.*) I had to wait quite a while for him, and —

WILLY: Oliver?

BIFF: Yeah, Oliver. All day, as a matter of cold fact. And a lot of — instances — facts, Pop, facts about my life came back to me. Who was it, Pop? Who ever said I was a salesman with Oliver?

WILLY: Well, you were.

BIFF: No, Dad, I was a shipping clerk.

WILLY: But you were practically —

BIFF (*with determination*): Dad, I don't know who said it first, but I was never a salesman for Bill Oliver.

WILLY: What're you talking about?

BIFF: Let's hold on to the facts tonight, Pop. We're not going to get anywhere bullin' around. I was a shipping clerk.

WILLY (*angrily*): All right, now listen to me —

BIFF: Why don't you let me finish?

WILLY: I'm not interested in stories about the past or any crap of that kind because the woods are burning, boys, you understand? There's a big blaze going on all around. I was fired today.

BIFF (*shocked*): How could you be?

WILLY: I was fired, and I'm looking for a little good news to tell your mother, because the woman has waited and the woman has suffered. The gist of it is that I haven't got a story left in my head, Biff. So don't give me a lecture about facts and aspects. I am not interested. Now what've you got to say to me?

(STANLEY *enters with three drinks. They wait until he leaves.*)

WILLY: Did you see Oliver?

BIFF: Jesus, Dad!

WILLY: You mean you didn't go up there?

HAPPY: Sure he went up there.

BIFF: I did. I — saw him. How could they fire you?

WILLY (*on the edge of his chair*): What kind of a welcome did he give you?

BIFF: He won't even let you work on commission?

WILLY: I'm out! (*Driving.*) So tell me, he gave you a warm welcome?

HAPPY: Sure, Pop, sure!

BIFF (*driven*): Well, it was kind of —

WILLY: I was wondering if he'd remember you. (*To* HAPPY.) Imagine, man doesn't see him for ten, twelve years and gives him that kind of a welcome!

HAPPY: Damn right!

BIFF (*trying to return to the offensive*): Pop, look —

WILLY: You know why he remembered you, don't you? Because you impressed him in those days.

BIFF: Let's talk quietly and get this down to the facts, huh?

WILLY (*as though* BIFF *had been interrupting*): Well, what happened? It's great news, Biff. Did he take you into his office or'd you talk in the waiting-room?

BIFF: Well, he came in, see, and —

WILLY (*with a big smile*): What'd he say? Betcha he threw his arm around you.

BIFF: Well, he kinda —

WILLY: He's a fine man. (*To* HAPPY.) Very hard man to see, y'know.

HAPPY (*agreeing*): Oh, I know.

WILLY (*to* BIFF): Is that where you had the drinks?

BIFF: Yeah, he gave me a couple of — no, no!

HAPPY (*cutting in*): He told him my Florida idea.

WILLY: Don't interrupt. (*To* BIFF.) How'd he react to the Florida idea?

BIFF: Dad, will you give me a minute to explain?

WILLY: I've been waiting for you to explain since I sat down here! What happened? He took you into his office and what?

BIFF: Well — I talked. And — and he listened, see.

WILLY: Famous for the way he listens, y'know. What was his answer?

BIFF: His answer was — (*He breaks off, suddenly angry.*) Dad, you're not letting me tell you what I want to tell you!

WILLY (*accusing, angered*): You didn't see him, did you?

BIFF: I did see him!

WILLY: What'd you insult him or something? You insulted him, didn't you?

BIFF: Listen, will you let me out of it, will you just let me out of it!

HAPPY: What the hell!

WILLY: Tell me what happened!

BIFF (*to* HAPPY): I can't talk to him!

(*A single trumpet note jars the ear. The light of green leaves stains the house, which holds the air of night and a dream.* YOUNG BERNARD *enters and knocks on the door of the house.*)

YOUNG BERNARD (*frantically*): Mrs. Loman, Mrs. Loman!

HAPPY: Tell him what happened!

BIFF (*to* HAPPY): Shut up and leave me alone!

WILLY: No, no! You had to go and flunk math!

BIFF: What math? What're you talking about?

YOUNG BERNARD: Mrs. Loman, Mrs. Loman!

(LINDA *appears in the house, as of old.*)

WILLY (*wildly*): Math, math, math!

BIFF: Take it easy, Pop!

YOUNG BERNARD: Mrs. Loman!

WILLY (*furiously*): If you hadn't flunked you'd've been set by now!

BIFF: Now, look, I'm gonna tell you what happened, and you're going to listen to me.

YOUNG BERNARD: Mrs. Loman!

BIFF: I waited six hours —

HAPPY: What the hell are you saying?

BIFF: I kept sending in my name but he wouldn't see me. So finally he . . . (*He continues unheard as light fades low on the restaurant.*)

YOUNG BERNARD: Biff flunked math!

LINDA: No!

YOUNG BERNARD: Birnbaum flunked him! They won't graduate him!

LINDA: But they have to. He's gotta go to the university. Where is he? Biff! Biff!

YOUNG BERNARD: No, he left. He went to Grand Central.

LINDA: Grand — You mean he went to Boston!

YOUNG BERNARD: Is Uncle Willy in Boston?

LINDA: Oh, maybe Willy can talk to the teacher. Oh, the poor, poor boy!

(*Light on house area snaps out.*)

BIFF (*at the table, now audible, holding up a gold fountain pen*): ... so I'm washed up with Oliver, you understand? Are you listening to me?

WILLY (*at a loss*): Yeah, sure. If you hadn't flunked —

BIFF: Flunked what? What're you talking about?

WILLY: Don't blame everything on me! I didn't flunk math — you did! What pen?

HAPPY: That was awful dumb, Biff, a pen like that is worth —

WILLY (*seeing the pen for the first time*): You took Oliver's pen?

BIFF (*weakening*): Dad, I just explained it to you.

WILLY: You stole Bill Oliver's fountain pen!

BIFF: I didn't exactly steal it! That's just what I've been explaining to you!

HAPPY: He had it in his hand and just then Oliver walked in, so he got nervous and stuck it in his pocket!

WILLY: My God, Biff!

BIFF: I never intended to do it, Dad!

OPERATOR'S VOICE: Standish Arms, good evening!

WILLY (*shouting*): I'm not in my room!

BIFF (*frightened*): Dad, what's the matter? (*He and* HAPPY *stand up.*)

OPERATOR: Ringing Mr. Loman for you!

WILLY: I'm not there, stop it!

BIFF (*horrified, gets down on one knee before* WILLY): Dad, I'll make good, I'll make good. (WILLY *tries to get to his feet.* BIFF *holds him down.*) Sit down now.

WILLY: No, you're no good, you're no good for anything.

BIFF: I am, Dad, I'll find something else, you understand? Now don't worry about anything. (*He holds up* WILLY's *face.*) Talk to me, Dad.

OPERATOR: Mr. Loman does not answer. Shall I page him?

WILLY (*attempting to stand, as though to rush and silence the* OPERATOR): No, no, no!

HAPPY: He'll strike something, Pop.

WILLY: No, no ...

BIFF (*desperately, standing over* WILLY): Pop, listen! Listen to me! I'm telling you something good. Oliver talked to his partner about the Florida idea. You listening? He — he talked to his partner, and he came to me ... I'm going to be all right, you hear? Dad, listen to me, he said it was just a question of the amount!

WILLY: Then you ... got it?

HAPPY: He's gonna be terrific, Pop!

WILLY (*trying to stand*): Then you got it, haven't you? You got it! You got it!

BIFF (*agonized, holds* WILLY *down*): No, no. Look, Pop. I'm supposed to have lunch with them tomorrow. I'm just telling you this so you'll know that I can still make an impression, Pop. And I'll make good somewhere, but I can't go tomorrow, see?

WILLY: Why not? You simply —

BIFF: But the pen, Pop!

WILLY: You give it to him and tell him it was an oversight!

HAPPY: Sure, have lunch tomorrow!

BIFF: I can't say that —

WILLY: You were doing a crossword puzzle and accidentally used his pen!

BIFF: Listen, kid, I took those balls years ago, now I walk in with his fountain pen? That clinches it, don't you see? I can't face him like that! I'll try elsewhere.

PAGE'S VOICE: Paging Mr. Loman!

WILLY: Don't you want to be anything?

BIFF: Pop, how can I go back?

WILLY: You don't want to be anything, is that what's behind it?

BIFF (*now angry at* WILLY *for not crediting his sympathy*): Don't take it that way! You think it was easy walking into that office after what I'd done to him? A team of horses couldn't have dragged me back to Bill Oliver!

WILLY: Then why'd you go?

BIFF: Why did I go? Why did I go! Look at you! Look at what's become of you!

(*Off left,* THE WOMAN *laughs.*)

WILLY: Biff, you're going to go to that lunch tomorrow, or —

BIFF: I can't go. I've got no appointment!

HAPPY: Biff, for ...!

WILLY: Are you spiting me?

BIFF: Don't take it that way! Goddammit!

WILLY (*strikes* BIFF *and falters away from the table*): You rotten little louse! Are you spiting me?

THE WOMAN: Someone's at the door, Willy!

BIFF: I'm no good, can't you see what I am?

HAPPY (*separating them*): Hey, you're in a restaurant! Now cut it out, both of you! (THE GIRLS *enter*.) Hello, girls, sit down.

(THE WOMAN *laughs, off left.*)

MISS FORSYTHE: I guess we might as well. This is Letta.

THE WOMAN: Willy, are you going to wake up?

BIFF (*ignoring* WILLY): How're ya, miss, sit down. What do you drink?

MISS FORSYTHE: Letta might not be able to stay long.

LETTA: I gotta get up very early tomorrow. I got jury duty. I'm so excited! Were you fellows ever on a jury?

BIFF: No, but I been in front of them! (THE GIRLS *laugh*.) This is my father.

LETTA: Isn't he cute? Sit down with us, Pop.

HAPPY: Sit him down, Biff!

BIFF (*going to him*): Come on, slugger, drink us under the table. To hell with it! Come on, sit down, pal.

(On BIFF's *last insistence,* WILLY *is about to sit.*)

THE WOMAN (*now urgently*): Willy, are you going to answer the door!

(THE WOMAN's *call pulls* WILLY *back. He starts right, befuddled.*)

BIFF: Hey, where are you going?

WILLY: Open the door.

BIFF: The door?

WILLY: The washroom . . . the door . . . where's the door?

BIFF (*leading* WILLY *to the left*): Just go straight down.

(WILLY *moves left.*)

THE WOMAN: Willy, Willy, are you going to get up, get up, get up, get up?

(WILLY *exits left.*)

LETTA: I think it's sweet you bring your daddy along.

MISS FORSYTHE: Oh, he isn't really your father!

BIFF (*at left, turning to her resentfully*): Miss Forsythe, you've just seen a prince walk by. A fine, troubled prince. A hard-working, unappreciated prince. A pal, you understand? A good companion. Always for his boys.

LETTA: That's so sweet.

HAPPY: Well, girls, what's the program? We're wasting time. Come on, Biff. Gather round. Where would you like to go?

BIFF: Why don't you do something for him?

HAPPY: Me!

BIFF: Don't you give a damn for him, Hap?

HAPPY: What're you talking about? I'm the one who —

BIFF: I sense it, you don't give a good goddam about him. (He takes the rolled-up hose from his pocket and puts it on the table in front of HAPPY.) Look what I found in the cellar, for Christ's sake. How can you bear to let it go on?

HAPPY: Me? Who goes away? Who runs off and —

BIFF: Yeah, but he doesn't mean anything to you. You could help him — I can't! Don't you understand what I'm talking about? He's going to kill himself, don't you know that?

HAPPY: Don't I know it! Me!

BIFF: Hap, help him! Jesus . . . help him . . . Help me, help me, I can't bear to look at his face! (*Ready to weep, he hurries out, up right.*)

HAPPY (*starting after him*): Where are you going?

MISS FORSYTHE: What's he so mad about?

HAPPY: Come on, girls, we'll catch up with him.

MISS FORSYTHE (*as* HAPPY *pushes her out*): Say, I don't like that temper of his!

HAPPY: He's just a little overstrung, he'll be all right!

WILLY (*off left, as* THE WOMAN *laughs*): Don't answer! Don't answer!

LETTA: Don't you want to tell your father —

HAPPY: No, that's not my father. He's just a guy. Come on, we'll catch Biff, and, honey, we're going to paint this town! Stanley, where's the check! Hey, Stanley!

(*They exit.* STANLEY *looks toward left.*)

STANLEY (*calling to* HAPPY *indignantly*): Mr. Loman! Mr. Loman!

(STANLEY *picks up a chair and follows them off. Knocking is heard off left.* THE WOMAN *enters, laughing.* WILLY *follows her. She is in a black slip; he is buttoning his shirt. Raw, sensuous music accompanies their speech.*)

WILLY: Will you stop laughing? Will you stop?

THE WOMAN: Aren't you going to answer the door? He'll wake the whole hotel.

WILLY: I'm not expecting anybody.

THE WOMAN: Whyn't you have another drink, honey, and stop being so damn self-centered?

WILLY: I'm so lonely.

THE WOMAN: You know you ruined me, Willy? From now on, whenever you come to the office, I'll see that you go right through to the buyers. No waiting at my desk any more, Willy. You ruined me.

WILLY: That's nice of you to say that.

THE WOMAN: Gee, you are self-centered! Why so sad? You are the saddest self-centeredest soul I ever did see-saw. (*She laughs. He kisses her.*) Come on inside, drummer boy. It's silly to be dressing in the middle of the night. (*As knocking is heard.*) Aren't you going to answer the door?

WILLY: They're knocking on the wrong door.

THE WOMAN: But I felt the knocking. And he heard us talking in here. Maybe the hotel's on fire!

WILLY (*his terror rising*): It's a mistake.

THE WOMAN: Then tell him to go away!

WILLY: There's nobody there.

THE WOMAN: It's getting on my nerves, Willy. There's somebody standing out there and it's getting on my nerves!

WILLY (*pushing her away from him*): All right, stay in the bathroom here, and don't come out. I think there's a law in Massachusetts about it, so don't come out. It may be that new room clerk. He looked very mean. So don't come out. It's a mistake, there's no fire.

(*The knocking is heard again. He takes a few steps away from her, and she vanishes into the wing. The light follows him, and now he is facing* YOUNG BIFF, *who carries a suitcase.* BIFF *steps toward him. The music is gone.*)

BIFF: Why didn't you answer?

WILLY: Biff! What are you doing in Boston?

BIFF: Why didn't you answer? I've been knocking for five minutes, I called you on the phone —

WILLY: I just heard you. I was in the bathroom and had the door shut. Did anything happen home?

BIFF: Dad — I let you down.

WILLY: What do you mean?

BIFF: Dad . . .

WILLY: Biffo, what's this about? (*Putting his arm around* BIFF.) Come on, let's go downstairs and get you a malted.

BIFF: Dad, I flunked math.

WILLY: Not for the term?

BIFF: The term. I haven't got enough credits to graduate.

WILLY: You mean to say Bernard wouldn't give you the answers?

BIFF: He did, he tried, but I only got a sixty-one.

WILLY: And they wouldn't give you four points?

BIFF: Birnbaum refused absolutely. I begged him, Pop, but he won't give me those points. You gotta talk to him before they close the school. Because if he saw the kind of man you are, and you just talked to him in your way, I'm sure he'd come through for me. The class came right before practice, see, and I didn't go enough. Would you talk to him? He'd like you, Pop. You know the way you could talk.

WILLY: You're on. We'll drive right back.

BIFF: Oh, Dad, good work! I'm sure he'll change it for you!

WILLY: Go downstairs and tell the clerk I'm checkin' out. Go right down.

BIFF: Yes, sir! See, the reason he hates me, Pop — one day he was late for class so I got up at the blackboard and imitated him. I crossed my eyes and talked with a lithp.

WILLY (*laughing*): You did? The kids like it?

BIFF: They nearly died laughing!

WILLY: Yeah? What'd you do?

BIFF: The thquare root of thixthy twee is . . . (WILLY *bursts out laughing;* BIFF *joins him.*) And in the middle of it he walked in!

(WILLY *laughs and* THE WOMAN *joins in offstage.*)

WILLY (*without hesitation*): Hurry downstairs and —

BIFF: Somebody in there?

WILLY: No, that was next door.

(THE WOMAN *laughs offstage.*)

BIFF: Somebody got in your bathroom!

WILLY: No, it's the next room, there's a party —

THE WOMAN (*enters, laughing. She lisps*

this): Can I come in? There's something in the bathtub, Willy, and it's moving!

(WILLY *looks at* BIFF, *who is staring open-mouthed and horrified at* THE WOMAN.)

WILLY: Ah — you better go back to your room. They must be finished painting by now. They're painting her room so I let her take a shower here. Go back, go back . . . (*He pushes her.*)

THE WOMAN (*resisting*): But I've got to get dressed, Willy, I can't —

WILLY: Get out of here! Go back, go back . . . (*Suddenly striving for the ordinary.*) This is Miss Francis, Biff, she's a buyer. They're painting her room. Go back, Miss Francis, go back . . .

THE WOMAN: But my clothes, I can't go out naked in the hall!

WILLY (*pushing her offstage*): Get outa here! Go back, go back!

(BIFF *slowly sits down on his suitcase as the argument continues offstage.*)

THE WOMAN: Where's my stockings? You promised me stockings, Willy!

WILLY: I have no stockings here!

THE WOMAN: You had two boxes of size nine sheers for me, and I want them!

WILLY: Here, for God's sake, will you get outa here!

THE WOMAN (*enters holding a box of stockings*): I just hope there's nobody in the hall. That's all I hope. (*To* BIFF.) Are you football or baseball?

BIFF: Football.

THE WOMAN (*angry, humiliated*): That's me too. G'night. (*She snatches her clothes from* WILLY, *and walks out.*)

WILLY (*after a pause*): Well, better get going. I want to get to the school first thing in the morning. Get my suits out of the closet. I'll get my valise. (BIFF *doesn't move.*) What's the matter? (BIFF *remains motionless, tears falling.*) She's a buyer. Buys for J. H. Simmons. She lives down the hall — they're painting. You don't imagine — (*He breaks off. After a pause.*) Now listen, pal, she's just a buyer. She sees merchandise in her room and they have to keep it looking just so . . . (*Pause. Assuming command.*) All right, get my suits. (BIFF *doesn't move.*) Now stop crying and do as I say. I gave you an order. Biff, I gave you an order! Is that what you do when I give you

an order? How dare you cry! (*Putting his arm around* BIFF.) Now look, Biff, when you grow up you'll understand about these things. You mustn't — you mustn't overemphasize a thing like this. I'll see Birnbaum first thing in the morning.

BIFF: Never mind.

WILLY (*getting down beside* BIFF): Never mind! He's going to give you those points. I'll see to it.

BIFF: He wouldn't listen to you.

WILLY: He certainly will listen to me. You need those points for the U. of Virginia.

BIFF: I'm not going there.

WILLY: Heh? If I can't get him to change that mark you'll make it up in summer school. You've got all summer to —

BIFF (*his weeping breaking from him*): Dad . . .

WILLY (*infected by it*): Oh, my boy . . .

BIFF: Dad . . .

WILLY: She's nothing to me, Biff. I was lonely, I was terribly lonely.

BIFF: You — you gave her Mama's stockings! (*His tears break through and he rises to go.*)

WILLY (*grabbing for* BIFF): I gave you an order!

BIFF: Don't touch me, you — liar!

WILLY: Apologize for that!

BIFF: You fake! You phony little fake! You fake! (*Overcome, he turns quickly and weeping fully goes out with his suitcase.* WILLY *is left on the floor on his knees.*)

WILLY: I gave you an order! Biff, come back here or I'll beat you! Come back here! I'll whip you!

(STANLEY *comes quickly in from the right and stands in front of* WILLY.)

WILLY (*shouts at* STANLEY): I gave you an order . . .

STANLEY: Hey, let's pick it up, pick it up, Mr. Loman. (*He helps* WILLY *to his feet.*) Your boys left with the chippies. They said they'll see you home.

(*A second waiter watches some distance away.*)

WILLY: But we were supposed to have dinner together.

(*Music is heard,* WILLY's *theme.*)

STANLEY: Can you make it?

WILLY: I'll — sure, I can make it. (*Suddenly*

concerned about his clothes.) Do I — I look all right?

STANLEY: Sure, you look all right. (*He flicks a speck off* WILLY'S *lapel.*)

WILLY: Here — here's a dollar.

STANLEY: Oh, your son paid me. It's all right.

WILLY (*putting it in* STANLEY'S *hand*): No, take it. You're a good boy.

STANLEY: Oh, no, you don't have to . . .

WILLY: Here — here's some more, I don't need it any more. (*After a slight pause.*) Tell me — is there a seed store in the neighborhood?

STANLEY: Seeds? You mean like to plant?

(*As* WILLY *turns,* STANLEY *slips the money back into his jacket pocket.*)

WILLY: Yes. Carrots, peas . . .

STANLEY: Well, there's hardware stores on Sixth Avenue, but it may be too late now.

WILLY (*anxiously*): Oh, I'd better hurry. I've got to get some seeds. (*He starts off to the right.*) I've got to get some seeds, right away. Nothing's planted. I don't have a thing in the ground.

(WILLY *hurries out as the light goes down.* STANLEY *moves over to the right after him, watches him off. The other waiter has been staring at* WILLY.)

STANLEY (*to the waiter*): Well, whatta you looking at?

(*The waiter picks up the chairs and moves off right.* STANLEY *takes the table and follows him. The light fades on this area. There is a long pause, the sound of the flute coming over. The light gradually rises on the kitchen, which is empty.* HAPPY *appears at the door of the house, followed by* BIFF. HAPPY *is carrying a large bunch of long-stemmed roses. He enters the kitchen, looks around for* LINDA. *Not seeing her, he turns to* BIFF, *who is just outside the house door, and makes a gesture with his hands, indicating "Not here, I guess." He looks into the living-room and freezes. Inside,* LINDA, *unseen, is seated,* WILLY'S *coat on her lap. She rises ominously and quietly and moves toward* HAPPY, *who backs up into the kitchen, afraid.*)

HAPPY: Hey, what're you doing up? (LINDA *says nothing but moves toward him implacably.*) Where's Pop? (*He keeps backing to the right, and now* LINDA *is in full view in the doorway to the living-room.*) Is he sleeping?

LINDA: Where were you?

HAPPY (*trying to laugh it off*): We met two girls, Mom, very fine types. Here, we brought you some flowers. (*Offering them to her.*) Put them in your room, Ma.

(*She knocks them to the floor at* BIFF'S *feet. He has now come inside and closed the door behind him. She stares at* BIFF, *silent.*)

HAPPY: Now what'd you do that for? Mom, I want you to have some flowers —

LINDA (*cutting* HAPPY *off, violently to* BIFF): Don't you care whether he lives or dies?

HAPPY (*going to the stairs*): Come upstairs, Biff.

BIFF (*with a flare of disgust, to* HAPPY): Go away from me! (*To* LINDA.) What do you mean, lives or dies? Nobody's dying around here, pal.

LINDA: Get out of my sight! Get out of here!

BIFF: I wanna see the boss.

LINDA: You're not going near him!

BIFF: Where is he? (*He moves into the living-room and* LINDA *follows.*)

LINDA (*shouting after* BIFF): You invite him for dinner. He looks forward to it all day — (BIFF *appears in his parents' bedroom, looks around, and exits*) — and then you desert him there. There's no stranger you'd do that to!

HAPPY: Why? He had a swell time with us. Listen, when I — (LINDA *comes back into the kitchen*) — desert him I hope I don't outlive the day!

LINDA: Get out of here!

HAPPY: Now look, Mom . . .

LINDA: Did you have to go to women tonight? You and your lousy rotten whores!

(BIFF *re-enters the kitchen.*)

HAPPY: Mom, all we did was follow Biff around trying to cheer him up! (*To* BIFF.) Boy, what a night you gave me!

LINDA: Get out of here, both of you, and don't come back! I don't want you tormenting him any more. Go on now, get your things together! (*To* BIFF.) You can sleep in his apartment. (*She starts to pick up the flowers and stops herself.*) Pick up this stuff, I'm not your maid any more. Pick it up, you bum, you!

(HAPPY *turns his back to her in refusal.* BIFF *slowly moves over and gets down on his knees, picking up the flowers.*)

LINDA: You're a pair of animals! Not one, not another living soul would have had the cruelty to walk out on that man in a restaurant!

BIFF (*not looking at her*): Is that what he said?

LINDA: He didn't have to say anything. He was so humiliated he nearly limped when he came in.

HAPPY: But, Mom, he had a great time with us —

BIFF (*cutting him off violently*): Shut up!

(*Without another word,* HAPPY *goes upstairs.*)

LINDA: You! You didn't even go in to see if he was all right!

BIFF (*still on the floor in front of* LINDA, *the flowers in his hand; with self-loathing*): No. Didn't. Didn't do a damned thing. How do you like that, heh? Left him babbling in a toilet.

LINDA: You louse. You . . .

BIFF: Now you hit it on the nose! (*He gets up, throws the flowers in the wastebasket.*) The scum of the earth, and you're looking at him!

LINDA: Get out of here!

BIFF: I gotta talk to the boss, Mom. Where is he?

LINDA: You're not going near him. Get out of this house!

BIFF (*with absolute assurance, determination*): No. We're gonna have an abrupt conversation, him and me.

LINDA: You're not talking to him!

(*Hammering is heard from outside the house, off right.* BIFF *turns toward the noise.*)

LINDA (*suddenly pleading*): Will you please leave him alone?

BIFF: What's he doing out there?

LINDA: He's planting the garden!

BIFF (*quietly*): Now? Oh, my God!

(BIFF *moves outside,* LINDA *following. The light dies down on them and comes up on the center of the apron as* WILLY *walks into*

it. *He is carrying a flashlight, a hoe, and a handful of seed packets. He raps the top of the hoe sharply to fix it firmly, and then moves to the left, measuring off the distance with his foot. He holds the flashlight to look at the seed packets, reading off the instructions. He is in the blue of night.*)

WILLY: Carrots . . . quarter-inch apart. Rows . . . one-foot rows. (*He measures it off.*) One foot. (*He puts down a package and measures off.*) Beets. (*He puts down another package and measures again.*) Lettuce. (*He reads the package, puts it down.*) One foot — (*He breaks off as* BEN *appears at the right and moves slowly down to him.*) What a proposition, ts, ts. Terrific, terrific. 'Cause she's suffered, Ben, the woman has suffered. You understand me? A man can't go out the way he came in, Ben, a man has got to add up to something. You can't, you can't — (*Ben moves toward him as though to interrupt.*) You gotta consider, now. Don't answer so quick. Remember, it's a guaranteed twenty-thousand-dollar proposition. Now look, Ben, I want you to go through the ins and outs of this thing with me. I've got nobody to talk to, Ben, and the woman has suffered, you hear me?

BEN (*standing still, considering*): What's the proposition?

WILLY: It's twenty thousand dollars on the barrelhead. Guaranteed, gilt-edged, you understand?

BEN: You don't want to make a fool of yourself. They might not honor the policy.

WILLY: How can they dare refuse? Didn't I work like a coolie to meet every premium on the nose? And now they don't pay off? Impossible!

BEN: It's called a cowardly thing, William.

WILLY: Why? Does it take more guts to stand here the rest of my life ringing up a zero?

BEN (*yielding*): That's a point, William. (*He moves, thinking, turns.*) And twenty thousand — that *is* something one can feel with the hand, it is there.

WILLY (*now assured, with rising power*): Oh, Ben, that's the whole beauty of it! I see it like a diamond, shining in the dark, hard and rough, that I can pick up and touch in my hand. Not like — like an appointment! This would not be another damned-fool appointment, Ben, and it changes all the aspects.

Because he thinks I'm nothing, see, and so he spites me. But the funeral — (*Straightening up.*) Ben, that funeral will be massive! They'll come from Maine, Massachusetts, Vermont, New Hampshire! All the old-timers with the strange license plates — that boy will be thunder-struck, Ben, because he never realized — I am known! Rhode Island, New York, New Jersey — I am known, Ben, and he'll see it with his eyes once and for all. He'll see what I am, Ben! He's in for a shock, that boy!

BEN (*coming down to the edge of the garden*): He'll call you a coward.

WILLY (*suddenly fearful*): No, that would be terrible.

BEN: Yes. And a damned fool.

WILLY: No, no, he mustn't, I won't have that! (*He is broken and desperate.*)

BEN: He'll hate you, William.

(*The gay music of the boys is heard.*)

WILLY: Oh, Ben, how do we get back to all the great times? Used to be so full of light, and comradeship, the sleigh-riding in winter, and the ruddiness on his cheeks. And always some kind of good news coming up, always something nice coming up ahead. And never even let me carry the valises in the house, and simonizing, simonizing that little red car! Why, why can't I give him something and not have him hate me?

BEN: Let me think about it. (*He glances at his watch.*) I still have a little time. Remarkable proposition, but you've got to be sure you're not making a fool of yourself.

(*BEN drifts off upstage and goes out of sight. BIFF comes down from the left.*)

WILLY (*suddenly conscious of BIFF, turns and looks up at him, then begins picking up the packages of seeds in confusion*): Where the hell is that seed? (*Indignantly.*) You can't see nothing out here! They boxed in the whole goddam neighborhood!

BIFF: There are people all around here. Don't you realize that?

WILLY: I'm busy. Don't bother me.

BIFF (*taking the hoe from WILLY*): I'm saying good-by to you, Pop. (*WILLY looks at him, silent, unable to move.*) I'm not coming back any more.

WILLY: You're not going to see Oliver tomorrow?

BIFF: I've got no appointment, Dad.

WILLY: He put his arm around you, and you've got no appointment?

BIFF: Pop, get this now, will you? Everytime I've left it's been a fight that sent me out of here. Today I realized something about myself and I tried to explain it to you and I — I think I'm just not smart enough to make any sense out of it for you. To hell with whose fault it is or anything like that. (*He takes WILLY's arm.*) Let's just wrap it up, heh? Come on in, we'll tell Mom. (*He gently tries to pull WILLY to left.*)

WILLY (*frozen, immobile, with guilt in his voice*): No, I don't want to see her.

BIFF: Come on! (*He pulls again, and WILLY tries to pull away.*)

WILLY (*highly nervous*): No, no, I don't want to see her.

BIFF (*tries to look into WILLY's face, as if to find the answer there*): Why don't you want to see her?

WILLY (*more harshly now*): Don't bother me, will you?

BIFF: What do you mean, you don't want to see her? You don't want them calling you yellow, do you? This isn't your fault; it's me, I'm a bum. Now come inside! (*WILLY strains to get away.*) Did you hear what I said to you?

(*WILLY pulls away and quickly goes by himself into the house. BIFF follows.*)

LINDA (*to WILLY*): Did you plant, dear?

BIFF (*at the door, to LINDA*): All right, we had it out. I'm going and I'm not writing any more.

LINDA (*going to WILLY in the kitchen*): I think that's the best way, dear. 'Cause there's no use drawing it out, you'll just never get along.

(*WILLY doesn't respond.*)

BIFF: People ask where I am and what I'm doing, you don't know, and you don't care. That way it'll be off your mind and you can start brightening up again. All right? That clears it, doesn't it? (*WILLY is silent, and BIFF goes to him.*) You gonna wish me luck, scout? (*He extends his hand.*) What do you say?

LINDA: Shake his hand, Willy.

WILLY (*turning to her, seething with hurt*): There's no necessity to mention the pen at all, y'know.

BIFF (*gently*): I've got no appointment, Dad.

WILLY (*erupting fiercely*): He put his arm around . . . ?

BIFF: Dad, you're never going to see what I am, so what's the use of arguing? If I strike oil I'll send you a check. Meantime forget I'm alive.

WILLY (*to* LINDA): Spite, see?

BIFF: Shake hands, Dad.

WILLY: Not my hand.

BIFF: I was hoping not to go this way.

WILLY: Well, this is the way you're going. Good-by.

(BIFF *looks at him a moment, then turns sharply and goes to the stairs.*)

WILLY (*stops him with*): May you rot in hell if you leave this house!

BIFF (*turning*): Exactly what is it that you want from me?

WILLY: I want you to know, on the train, in the mountains, in the valleys, wherever you go, that you cut down your life for spite!

BIFF: No, no.

WILLY: Spite, spite, is the word of your undoing! And when you're down and out, remember what did it. When you're rotting somewhere beside the railroad tracks, remember, and don't you dare blame it on me!

BIFF: I'm not blaming it on you!

WILLY: I won't take the rap for this, you hear?

(HAPPY *comes down the stairs and stands on the bottom step, watching.*)

BIFF: That's just what I'm telling you!

WILLY (*sinking into a chair at the table, with full accusation*): You're trying to put a knife in me — don't think I don't know what you're doing!

BIFF: All right, phony! Then let's lay it on the line. (*He whips the rubber tube out of his pocket and puts it on the table.*)

HAPPY: You crazy —

LINDA: Biff! (*She moves to grab the hose, but* BIFF *holds it down with his hand.*)

BIFF: Leave it there! Don't move it!

WILLY (*not looking at it*): What is that?

BIFF: You know goddam well what that is.

WILLY (*caged, wanting to escape*): I never saw that.

BIFF: You saw it. The mice didn't bring it into the cellar! What is this supposed to do, make a hero out of you? This supposed to make me sorry for you?

WILLY: Never heard of it.

BIFF: There'll be no pity for you, you hear it? No pity!

WILLY (*to* LINDA): You hear the spite!

BIFF: No, you're going to hear the truth — what you are and what I am!

LINDA: Stop it!

WILLY: Spite!

HAPPY (*coming down toward* BIFF): You cut it now!

BIFF (*to* HAPPY): The man don't know who we are! The man is gonna know! (*To* WILLY.) We never told the truth for ten minutes in this house!

HAPPY: We always told the truth!

BIFF (*turning on him*): You big blow, are you the assistant buyer? You're one of the two assistants to the assistant, aren't you?

HAPPY: Well, I'm practically —

BIFF: You're practically full of it! We all are! And I'm through with it. (*To* WILLY.) Now hear this, Willy, this is me.

WILLY: I know you!

BIFF: You know why I had no address for three months? I stole a suit in Kansas City and I was in jail. (*To* LINDA, *who is sobbing.*) Stop crying. I'm through with it.

(LINDA *turns away from them, her hands covering her face.*)

WILLY: I suppose that's my fault!

BIFF: I stole myself out of every good job since high school!

WILLY: And whose fault is that?

BIFF: And I never got anywhere because you blew me so full of hot air I could never stand taking orders from anybody! That's whose fault it is!

WILLY: I hear that!

LINDA: Don't, Biff!

BIFF: It's goddam time you heard that! I had to be boss big shot in two weeks, and I'm through with it!

WILLY: Then hang yourself! For spite, hang yourself!

BIFF: No! Nobody's hanging himself, Willy! I ran down eleven flights with a pen in my hand today. And suddenly I stopped, you hear me? And in the middle of that office building, do you hear this? I stopped in the middle of that building and I saw — the sky. I saw the things that I love in this world. The work and the food and time to sit and smoke. And I looked at the pen and said to myself, what the hell am I grabbing this for? Why am I trying to become what I don't want to be? What am I doing in an office, making a contemptuous, begging fool of myself, when all I want is out there, waiting for me the minute I say I know who I am! Why can't I say that, Willy? (*He tries to make* WILLY *face him, but* WILLY *pulls away and moves to the left.*)

WILLY (*with hatred, threateningly*): The door of your life is wide open!

BIFF: Pop! I'm a dime a dozen, and so are you!

WILLY (*turning on him now in an uncontrolled outburst*): I am not a dime a dozen! I am Willy Loman, and you are Biff Loman!

(BIFF *starts for* WILLY, *but is blocked by* HAPPY. *In his fury,* BIFF *seems on the verge of attacking his father.*)

BIFF: I am not a leader of men, Willy, and neither are you. You were never anything but a hard-working drummer who landed in the ash can like all the rest of them! I'm one dollar an hour, Willy! I tried seven states and couldn't raise it. A buck an hour! Do you gather my meaning? I'm not bringing home any prizes any more, and you're going to stop waiting for me to bring them home!

WILLY (*directly to* BIFF): You vengeful, spiteful mut!

(BIFF *breaks from* HAPPY. WILLY, *in fright, starts up the stairs.* BIFF *grabs him.*)

BIFF (*at the peak of his fury*): Pop, I'm nothing! I'm nothing, Pop. Can't you understand that? There's no spite in it any more. I'm just what I am, that's all.

(BIFF'*s fury has spent itself, and he breaks down, sobbing, holding on to* WILLY, *who dumbly fumbles for* BIFF'*s face.*)

WILLY (*astonished*): What're you doing? What're you doing? (*To* LINDA.) Why is he crying?

BIFF (*crying, broken*): Will you let me go, for Christ's sake? Will you take that phony dream and burn it before something happens? (*Struggling to contain himself, he pulls away and moves to the stairs.*) I'll go in the morning. Put him — put him to bed. (*Exhausted,* BIFF *moves up the stairs to his room.*)

WILLY (*after a long pause, astonished, ele-* vated): Isn't that — isn't that remarkable? Biff — he likes me!

LINDA: He loves you, Willy!

HAPPY (*deeply moved*): Always did, Pop.

WILLY: Oh, Biff! (*Staring wildly.*) He cried! Cried to me. (*He is choking with his love, and now cries out his promise.*) That boy — that boy is going to be magnificent!

(BEN *appears in the light just outside the kitchen.*)

BEN: Yes, outstanding, with twenty thousand behind him.

LINDA (*sensing the racing of his mind, fearfully, carefully*): Now come to bed, Willy. It's all settled now.

WILLY (*finding it difficult not to rush out of the house*): Yes, we'll sleep. Come on. Go to sleep, Hap.

BEN: And it does take a great kind of a man to crack the jungle.

(*In accents of dread,* BEN'*s idyllic music starts up.*)

HAPPY (*his arm around* LINDA): I'm getting married, Pop, don't forget it. I'm changing everything. I'm gonna run that department before the year is up. You'll see, Mom. (*He kisses her.*)

BEN: The jungle is dark but full of diamonds, Willy.

(WILLY *turns, moves, listening to* BEN.)

LINDA: Be good. You're both good boys, just act that way, that's all.

HAPPY: 'Night, Pop. (*He goes upstairs.*)

LINDA (*to* WILLY): Come, dear.

BEN (*with greater force*): One must go in to fetch a diamond out.

WILLY (*to* LINDA, *as he moves slowly along the edge of the kitchen, toward the door*): I just want to get settled down, Linda. Let me sit alone for a little.

LINDA (*almost uttering her fear*): I want you upstairs.

WILLY (*taking her in his arms*): In a few minutes, Linda. I couldn't sleep right now. Go on, you look awful tired. (*He kisses her.*)

BEN: Not like an appointment at all. A diamond is rough and hard to the touch.

WILLY: Go on now. I'll be right up.

LINDA: I think this is the only way, Willy.

WILLY: Sure, it's the best thing.

BEN: Best thing!

WILLY: The only way. Everything is gonna be — go on, kid, get to bed. You look so tired.

LINDA: Come right up.

WILLY: Two minutes.

(LINDA *goes into the living-room, then reappears in her bedroom.* WILLY *moves just outside the kitchen door.*)

WILLY: Loves me. (*Wonderingly.*) Always loved me. Isn't that a remarkable thing? Ben, he'll worship me for it!

BEN (*with promise*): It's dark there, but full of diamonds.

WILLY: Can you imagine that magnificence with twenty thousand dollars in his pocket?

LINDA (*calling from her room*): Willy! Come up!

WILLY (*calling into the kitchen*): Yes! Yes. Coming! It's very smart, you realize that, don't you, sweetheart? Even Ben sees it. I gotta go, baby. 'By! 'By! (*Going over to* BEN, *almost dancing.*) Imagine? When the mail comes he'll be ahead of Bernard again!

BEN: A perfect proposition all around.

WILLY: Did you see how he cried to me? Oh, if I could kiss him, Ben!

BEN: Time, William, time!

WILLY: Oh, Ben, I always knew one way or another we were gonna make it, Biff and I!

BEN (*looking at his watch*): The boat. We'll be late. (*He moves slowly off into the darkness.*)

WILLY (*elegiacally, turning to the house*): Now when you kick off, boy, I want a seventy-yard boot, and get right down the field under the ball, and when you hit, hit low and hit hard, because it's important, boy. (*He swings around and faces the audience.*) There's all kinds of important people in the stands, and the first thing you know ... (*Suddenly realizing he is alone.*) Ben! Ben, where do I ...? (*He makes a sudden movement of search.*) Ben, how do I ...?

LINDA (*calling*): Willy, you coming up?

WILLY (*uttering a gasp of fear, whirling about as if to quiet her*): Sh! (*He turns around as if to find his way; sounds, faces, voices, seem to be swarming in upon him and he flicks at them, crying*) Sh! Sh! (*Suddenly music, faint and high, stops him. It rises in intensity, almost to an unbearable scream. He goes up and down on his toes, and rushes off around the house.*) Shhh!

LINDA: Willy?

(*There is no answer.* LINDA *waits.* BIFF *gets up off his bed. He is still in his clothes.* HAPPY *sits up.* BIFF *stands listening.*)

LINDA (*with real fear*): Willy, answer me! Willy!

(*There is the sound of a car starting and moving away at full speed.*)

LINDA: No!

BIFF (*rushing down the stairs*): Pop!

(*As the car speeds off, the music crashes down in a frenzy of sound, which becomes the soft pulsation of a single cello string.* BIFF *slowly returns to his bedroom. He and* HAPPY *gravely don their jackets.* LINDA *slowly walks out of her room. The music has developed into a dead march. The leaves of day are appearing over everything.* CHARLEY *and* BERNARD, *somberly dressed, appear and knock on the kitchen door.* BIFF *and* HAPPY *slowly descend the stairs to the kitchen as* CHARLEY *and* BERNARD *enter. All stop a moment when* LINDA, *in clothes of mourning, bearing a little bunch of roses, comes through the draped doorway into the kitchen. She goes to* CHARLEY *and takes his arm. Now all move toward the audience, through the wall-line of the kitchen. At the limit of the apron,* LINDA *lays down the flowers, kneels, and sits back on her heels. All stare down at the grave.*)

REQUIEM

CHARLEY: It's getting dark, Linda.

(LINDA *doesn't react. She stares at the grave.*)

BIFF: How about it, Mom? Better get some rest, heh? They'll be closing the gate soon.

(LINDA *makes no move. Pause.*)

HAPPY (*deeply angered*): He had no right to do that. There was no necessity for it. We would've helped him.

CHARLEY (*grunting*): Hmmm.

BIFF: Come along, Mom.

LINDA: Why didn't anybody come?

CHARLEY: It was a very nice funeral.

LINDA: But where are all the people he knew? Maybe they blame him.

CHARLEY: Naa. It's a rough world, Linda. They wouldn't blame him.

LINDA: I can't understand it. At this time especially. First time in thirty-five years we were just about free and clear. He only needed a little salary. He was even finished with the dentist.

CHARLEY: No man only needs a little salary.

LINDA: I can't understand it.

BIFF: There were a lot of nice days. When he'd come home from a trip; or on Sundays, making the stoop; finishing the cellar; putting on the new porch; when he built the extra bathroom; and put up the garage. You know something, Charley, there's more of him in that front stoop than in all the sales he ever made.

CHARLEY: Yeah. He was a happy man with a batch of cement.

LINDA: He was so wonderful with his hands.

BIFF: He had the wrong dreams. All, all, wrong.

HAPPY (almost ready to fight BIFF): Don't say that!

BIFF: He never knew who he was.

CHARLEY (stopping HAPPY's movement and reply. To BIFF): Nobody dast blame this man. You don't understand: Willy was a salesman. And for a salesman, there is no rock bottom to the life. He don't put a bolt to a nut, he don't tell you the law or give you medicine. He's a man way out there in the blue, riding on a smile and a shoeshine. And when they start not smiling back — that's an earthquake. And then you get yourself a couple of spots on your hat, and you're finished. Nobody dast blame this man. A salesman is got to dream, boy. It comes with the territory.

BIFF: Charley, the man didn't know who he was.

HAPPY (infuriated): Don't say that!

BIFF: Why don't you come with me, Happy?

HAPPY: I'm not licked that easily. I'm staying right in this city, and I'm gonna beat this racket! (He looks at BIFF, his chin set.) The Loman Brothers!

BIFF: I know who I am, kid.

HAPPY: All right, boy. I'm gonna show you and everybody else that Willy Loman did not die in vain. He had a good dream. It's the only dream you can have — to come out number-one man. He fought it out here, and this is where I'm gonna win it for him.

BIFF (with a hopeless glance at HAPPY, bends toward his mother): Let's go, Mom.

LINDA: I'll be with you in a minute. Go on, Charley. (He hesitates.) I want to, just for a minute. I never had a chance to say good-by.

(CHARLEY moves away, followed by HAPPY. BIFF remains a slight distance up and left of LINDA. She sits there, summoning herself. The flute begins, not far away, playing behind her speech.)

LINDA: Forgive me, dear. I can't cry. I don't know what it is, but I can't cry. I don't understand it. Why did you ever do that? Help me, Willy, I can't cry. It seems to me that you're just on another trip. I keep expecting you. Willy, dear, I can't cry. Why did you do it? I search and search and I search, and I can't understand it, Willy. I made the last payment on the house today. Today, dear. And there'll be nobody home. (A sob rises in her throat.) We're free and clear. (Sobbing more fully, released.) We're free. (BIFF comes slowly toward her.) We're free . . . We're free . . .

(BIFF lifts her to her feet and moves out up right with her in his arms. LINDA sobs quietly. BERNARD and CHARLEY come together and follow them, followed by HAPPY. Only the music of the flute is left on the darkening stage as over the house the hard towers of the apartment buildings rise into sharp focus, and —)

THE CURTAIN FALLS

For the ancient Greeks, at least for Aristotle, *pathos* was the destructive or painful act common in tragedy; but in English "pathos" refers to an element in art or life that evokes tenderness or sympathetic pity. Modern English critical usage distinguishes between tragic figures and pathetic figures by recognizing some element either of strength or of regeneration in the former that is not in the latter. The tragic protagonist perhaps acts so that he brings his destruction upon himself, or if his destruction comes from outside, he resists it, and in either case he comes to at least a partial understanding of the causes of his suffering. The pathetic figure, however, is largely passive, an unknowing and unresisting innocent. In such a view Macbeth is tragic, Duncan pathetic; Lear is tragic, Cordelia pathetic; Othello is tragic, Desdemona pathetic; Hamlet is tragic (the situation is not of his making, but he does what he can to alter it), Ophelia pathetic. (Note, by the way, that of the four pathetic figures named, the first is old and the remaining three are women. Pathos is more likely to be evoked by persons assumed to be relatively defenseless than by the able-bodied.)

The guardians of critical terminology, then, have tended to insist that "tragedy" be reserved for a play showing action that leads to suffering which in turn leads to knowledge. They get very annoyed when a newspaper describes as a tragedy the death of a promising high school football player in an automobile accident, and they insist that such a death is pathetic not tragic; it is unexpected, premature, and deeply regrettable, but it does not give us a sense of man's greatness achieved through understanding the sufferings that a sufferer has at least in some degree chosen. Probably critics hoard the term "tragedy" because it is also a word of praise: to call a play a comedy or a problem play is not to imply anything about its merits, but to call a play a tragedy is tantamount to calling it an important or even a great play. In most of the best-known Greek tragedies the protagonist either does some terrible deed, or resists mightily. But Greek drama has its pathetic figures too, figures who do not so much act as suffer. Euripides' *The Trojan Women* is perhaps the greatest example of a play which does not allow its heroes to choose and to act but only to undergo, to be in agony. When we think of pathetic figures in Greek drama, however, we probably think chiefly of the choruses, groups of rather commonplace persons who do not perform a tragic deed but who suffer in sympathy with the tragic hero, who lament the hardness of the times, and who draw the spectators into the range of the hero's suffering.

That the spectators were not themselves heroic figures seems to have been assumed by the Greeks and by the Elizabethans; at least there are usually these lesser choral figures, nameless citizens, who interpret the action and call attention to the fact that even highly placed great heroes are not exempt from pain: indeed, high place and strenuous activity invite pain: the lofty pine tree, or the mariner who ventures far from the coast, is more likely to meet destruction than the lowly shrub or the fair-weather sailor. For Greeks of the fifth century B.C., and for Elizabethans, high place was not a mere matter of rank, but of worth. In both ages, it was of course known that a king may be unkingly, but it was assumed that kingship required a special nature — though that nature was not always forthcoming. Put it this way: tragedy deals with kings not because they are men with a certain title (though of course the title does give them special power), but because they are men with a certain nature. This nature is an extraordinary capacity for action and for feeling; when they make an error its consequences are enormous, and they themselves feel it as lesser people would not. When Oedipus is polluted, all of Thebes feels it. Arthur Miller is somewhat misleading when he argues (p. 306) that because Oedipus has given his name to a complex that the common man may have, the common man is therefore "as apt a subject for tragedy." It is not Oedipus' "complex" but his unique importance that is the issue in the play. Moreover, even if one argues that a man of no public importance may suffer as much as a man of public importance (and surely no one doubts this), one may be faced with the fact that the unimportant man by his ordinariness is not particularly good material for drama, and we are here concerned with drama rather than with life. In *Death of a Salesman* Willy Loman's wife says, rightly, "A small man can be just as exhausted as a great man." Yes, but is his exhaustion itself interesting, and do his activities (and this includes the words he utters) before his exhaustion have interesting dramatic possibilities? Isn't there a colorlessness that may weaken the play, an impoverishment of what John Milton called "gorgeous tragedy"?

Inevitably the rise of the bourgeoisie brought about the rise of bourgeois drama, and in the eighteenth century we get a fair number of tragedies with prologues that insist that characters like ourselves deserve our *pity*:

> No fustian hero rages here tonight,
> No armies fall, to fix a tyrant's right.
> From lower life we draw our scene's distress:
> — Let not your equals move your pity less.
>
> George Lillo, *Fatal Curiosity* (1733)

Note the deflation of older tragedy, the implication that its heroes were "fustian" (bombastic, pretentious) rather than genuinely heroic persons of deep feelings and high aspirations. Or, to put it differently, older tragedy in the bourgeois view dealt with persons of high rank, but rank (in this view) is not significant; therefore one may as well show persons of middle rank with whom the middle-class audience may readily identify. At the same time, the dismissal of heroic activities ("no fustian hero *rages*," "no armies *fall*") and the substitution of "distress" indicates that we are well on the road to The Hero As Victim.

And we have kept on that road. As early as the sixteenth century Copernicus had shown that man and his planet were not the center of the universe, but the thought did not distress the bulk of men until much later. In 1859 Darwin published *The Origin of Species*, arguing that man was not a special creation but a creature that had evolved because "accidental variations" had aided him in the struggle for survival. At about the same time, Marx (who wished to dedicate *Capital* to Darwin) argued that economic forces guided men's lives. Early in the twentieth century Freud seemed to argue that men are conditioned by infantile experiences and are enslaved by the dark forces of the id. All in all, by the time of the Depression of the 1930's, it was difficult to have much confidence in man's ability to shape his destiny. The human condition was a sorry one; man was an insignificant lust-ridden, soulless creature in a terrifying materialistic universe. He was no Oedipus whose moral pollution infected a great city, no Brutus whose deed might bring civil war to Rome. He was really not much of anything, except perhaps to a few who immediately depended upon him.

Arthur Miller accurately noted (*Theatre Arts*, October, 1953) that American drama "has been a steady year by year documentation of the frustration of man," and it is evident that Miller has set out to restore a sense of importance if not greatness to the individual. In "Tragedy and the Common Man," published in the same year that *Death of a Salesman* was produced and evidently a defense of the play, he argues on behalf of the common man as a tragic figure and he insists that tragedy and pathos are very different: "Pathos truly is the mode of the pessimist.... The plays we revere, century after century, are the tragedies. In them, and in them alone, lies the belief — optimistic, if you will — in the perfectibility of man." Elsewhere (*Harper's*, August 1958) he has said that pathos is an oversimplification and therefore is the "counterfeit of meaning." Curiously, however, many spectators and readers find that by Miller's own terms Willy Loman fails to be a tragic figure; he seems to them pathetic rather than tragic, a victim rather than a man who acts and who wins our esteem. True, he is partly the victim of his own actions (although he could have chosen to be a carpenter, he chose to live by the bourgeois code that values a white collar), but he seems in larger part to be a victim of the system itself, a system of ruthless competition that has no place for the man who can no longer produce. (Here is an echo of the social-realist drama of the 'thirties.) Willy had believed in this system; and although his son Biff comes to the realization that Willy "had the wrong dreams," Willy himself seems not to achieve this insight. Of course he knows that he is out of a job, that the system does not value him any longer, but he still seems not to question the values he had subscribed to. Even in the last minutes of the play, when he is planning his suicide in order to provide money for his family — really for Biff — he says such things as "Can you imagine his magnificence with twenty thousand dollars in his pocket?" and "When the mail comes he'll be ahead of Bernard again." In the preface to his *Collected Plays* Miller comments on the "exultation" with which Willy faces the end, but it is questionable whether an audience shares it. Many people find that despite the gulf in rank, they can share King Lear's feelings more easily than Willy's.

Perhaps, however, tradition has been too arbitrary in its use of the word "tragedy." Perhaps we should be as liberal as the ancient Greeks were, who did not withhold it from any play that was serious and dignified.

DUTCHMAN

LeRoi Jones (Imamu Amiri Baraka)

LeRoi Jones (born in 1934), who has taken the name Imamu Amiri Baraka, was born in Newark, N.J., attended Rutgers, and graduated from Howard University. After his graduation he served for three years in the United States Air Force, and then did graduate work at the New School for Social Research and at Columbia. In addition to writing plays, poems, stories, essays, and a book on black music, he founded the Black Arts Repertory Theatre/School. *Dutchman*, produced off Broadway in 1964, was made into a film in 1967. During the Newark riots of 1967, Jones was arrested and charged with illegal possession of weapons. He was convicted in 1968 and was sentenced to two and one-half to three years in jail but he appealed and his appeal was upheld. He continues to be active as a writer and an educator in Newark.

CHARACTERS

CLAY, *twenty-year-old Negro*
LULA, *thirty-year-old white woman*
RIDERS OF COACH, *white and black*
YOUNG NEGRO
CONDUCTOR

In the flying underbelly of the city. Steaming hot, and summer on top, outside. Underground. The subway heaped in modern myth.

Opening scene is a man sitting in a subway seat, holding a magazine but looking vacantly just above its wilting pages. Occasionally he looks blankly toward the window on his right. Dim lights and darkness whistling by against the glass. (Or paste the lights, as admitted props, right on the subway windows. Have them move, even dim and flicker. But give the sense of speed. Also stations, whether the train is stopped or the glitter and activity of these stations merely flashes by the windows.)

The man is sitting alone. That is, only his seat is visible, though the rest of the car is outfitted as a complete subway car. But only his seat is shown. There might be, for a time, as the play begins, a loud

Calvin Lockhart as Clay and Tony Robbins as Lula in the Hampstead Theatre Club production directed by Charles Jarrott, London, 1967. (Photograph: © 1972 John Haynes.)

scream of the actual train. And it can recur throughout the play, or continue on a lower key once the dialogue starts.

The train slows after a time, pulling to a brief stop at one of the stations. The man looks idly up, until he sees a woman's face staring at him through the window; when it realizes that the man has noticed the face, it begins very premeditatedly to smile. The man smiles too, for a moment, without a trace of self-consciousness. Almost an instinctive though undesirable response. Then a kind of awkwardness or embarrassment sets in, and the man makes to look away, is further embarrassed, so he brings back his eyes to where the face was, but by now the train is moving again, and the face would seem to be left behind by the way the man turns his head to look back through the other windows at the slowly fading platform. He smiles then; more comfortably confident, hoping perhaps that his memory of this brief encounter will be pleasant. And then he is idle again.

SCENE I

Train roars. Lights flash outside the windows.

LULA *enters from the rear of the car in bright, skimpy summer clothes and sandals. She carries a net bag full of paper books, fruit, and other anonymous articles. She is wearing sunglasses, which she pushes up on her forehead from time to time.* LULA *is a tall, slender, beautiful woman with long red hair hanging straight down her back, wearing only loud lipstick in somebody's good taste. She is eating an apple, very daintily. Coming down the car toward* CLAY.

She stops beside CLAY's *seat and hangs languidly from the strap, still managing to eat the apple. It is apparent that she is going to sit in the seat next to* CLAY, *and that she is only waiting for him to notice her before she sits.*

CLAY *sits as before, looking just beyond his magazine, now and again pulling the magazine slowly back and forth in front of his face in a hopeless effort to fan himself. Then he sees the woman hanging there beside him and he looks up into her face, smiling quizzically.*

LULA: Hello.
CLAY: Uh, hi're you?
LULA: I'm going to sit down.... O.K.?

Reprinted by permission of the Sterling Lord Agency. Copyright © 1964 by LeRoi Jones.

CLAY: Sure.

LULA (*swings down onto the seat, pushing her legs straight out as if she is very weary*): Oooof! Too much weight.

CLAY: Ha, doesn't look like much to me. (*Leaning back against the window, a little surprised and maybe stiff.*)

LULA: It's so anyway.

(*And she moves her toes in the sandals, then pulls her right leg up on the left knee, better to inspect the bottoms of the sandals and the back of her heel. She appears for a second not to notice that* CLAY *is sitting next to her or that she has spoken to him just a second before.* CLAY *looks at the magazine, then out the black window. As he does this, she turns very quickly toward him.*)

Weren't you staring at me through the window?

CLAY (*wheeling around and very much stiffened*): What?

LULA: Weren't you staring at me through the window? At the last stop?

CLAY: Staring at you? What do you mean?

LULA: Don't you know what staring means?

CLAY: I saw you through the window ... if that's what it means. I don't know if I was staring. Seems to me you were staring through the window at me.

LULA: I was. But only after I'd turned around and saw you staring through that window down in the vicinity of my ass and legs.

CLAY: Really?

LULA: Really. I guess you were just taking those idle potshots. Nothing else to do. Run your mind over people's flesh.

CLAY: Oh boy. Wow, now I admit I was looking in your direction. But the rest of that weight is yours.

LULA: I suppose.

CLAY: Staring through train windows is weird business. Much weirder than staring very sedately at abstract asses.

LULA: That's why I came looking through the window . . . so you'd have more than that to go on. I even smiled at you.

CLAY: That's right.

LULA: I even got into this train, going some other way than mine. Walked down the aisle . . . searching you out.

CLAY: Really? That's pretty funny.

LULA: That's pretty funny. . . . God, you're dull.

CLAY: Well, I'm sorry, lady, but I really wasn't prepared for party talk.

LULA: No, you're not. What are you prepared for? (*Wrapping the apple core in a Kleenex and dropping it on the floor.*)

CLAY (*takes her conversation as pure sex talk. He turns to confront her squarely with this idea*): I'm prepared for anything. How about you?

LULA (*laughing loudly and cutting it off abruptly*): What do you think you're doing?

CLAY: What?

LULA: You think I want to pick you up, get you to take me somewhere and screw me, huh?

CLAY: Is that the way I look?

LULA: You look like you been trying to grow a beard. That's exactly what you look like. You look like you live in New Jersey with your parents and are trying to grow a beard. That's what. You look like you've been reading Chinese poetry and drinking lukewarm sugarless tea. (*Laughs, uncrossing and recrossing her legs.*) You look like death eating a soda cracker.

CLAY (*cocking his head from one side to the other, embarrassed and trying to make some comeback, but also intrigued by what the woman is saying . . . even the sharp city coarseness of her voice, which is still a kind of gentle sidewalk throb*): Really? I look like all that?

LULA: Not all of it. (*She feints a seriousness to cover an actual somber tone.*) I lie a lot. (*Smiling.*) It helps me control the world.

CLAY (*relieved and laughing louder than the humor*): Yeah, I bet.

LULA: But it's true, most of it, right? Jersey? Your bumpy neck?

CLAY: How'd you know all that? Huh? Really, I mean about Jersey . . . and even the beard. I met you before? You know Warren Enright?

LULA: You tried to make it with your sister when you were ten.

(CLAY *leans back hard against the back of the seat, his eyes opening now, still trying to look amused.*)

But I succeeded a few weeks ago. (*She starts to laugh again.*)

CLAY: What're you talking about? Warren tell you that? You're a friend of Georgia's?

LULA: I told you I lie. I don't know your sister. I don't know Warren Enright.

CLAY: You mean you're just picking these things out of the air?

LULA: Is Warren Enright a tall skinny black boy with a phony English accent?

CLAY: I figured you knew him.

LULA: But I don't. I just figured you would know somebody like that. (*Laughs.*)

CLAY: Yeah, yeah.

LULA: You're probably on your way to his house now.

CLAY: That's right.

LULA (*putting her hand on* CLAY'S *closest knee, drawing it from the knee up to the thigh's hinge, then removing it, watching his face very closely, and continuing to laugh, perhaps more gently than before*): Dull, dull, dull. I bet you think I'm exciting.

CLAY: You're O.K.

LULA: Am I exciting you now?

CLAY: Right. That's not what's supposed to happen?

LULA: How do I know? (*She returns her hand, without moving it, then takes it away and plunges it in her bag to draw out an apple.*) You want this?

CLAY: Sure.

LULA (*she gets one out of the bag for herself*): Eating apples together is always the first step. Or walking up uninhabited Seventh Avenue in the twenties on weekends. (*Bites and giggles, glancing at* CLAY *and speaking in loose sing-song.*) Can get you involved . . . boy! Get us involved. Um-huh. (*Mock seriousness.*) Would you like to get involved with me, Mister Man?

CLAY (*trying to be as flippant as* LULA, *whacking happily at the apple*): Sure. Why not? A beautiful woman like you. Huh, I'd be a fool not to.

LULA: And I bet you're sure you know what you're talking about. (*Taking him a little roughly by the wrist, so he cannot eat the apple, then shaking the wrist.*) I bet you're sure of almost everything anybody ever asked you about . . . right? (*Shakes his wrist harder.*) Right?

CLAY: Yeah, right. . . . Wow, you're pretty strong, you know? Whatta you, a lady wrestler or something?

LULA: What's wrong with lady wrestlers? And don't answer because you never knew any. Huh. (*Cynically.*) That's for sure. They don't have any lady wrestlers in that part of Jersey. That's for sure.

CLAY: Hey, you still haven't told me how you know so much about me.

LULA: I told you I didn't know anything about *you* . . . you're a well-known type.

CLAY: Really?

LULA: Or at least I know the type very well. And your skinny English friend too.

CLAY: Anonymously?

LULA (*settles back in seat, single-mindedly finishing her apple and humming snatches of rhythm and blues song*): What?

CLAY: Without knowing us specifically?

LULA: Oh boy. (*Looking quickly at* CLAY.) What a face. You know, you could be a handsome man.

CLAY: I can't argue with you.

LULA (*vague, off-center response*): What?

CLAY (*raising his voice, thinking the train noise has drowned part of his sentence*): I can't argue with you.

LULA: My hair is turning gray. A gray hair for each year and type I've come through.

CLAY: Why do you want to sound so old?

LULA: But it's always gentle when it starts. (*Attention drifting.*) Hugged against tenements, day or night.

CLAY: What?

LULA (*refocusing*): Hey, why don't you take me to that party you're going to?

CLAY: You must be a friend of Warren's to know about the party.

LULA: Wouldn't you like to take me to the party? (*Imitates clinging vine.*) Oh, come on, ask me to your party.

CLAY: Of course I'll ask you to come with me to the party. And I'll bet you're a friend of Warren's.

LULA: Why not be a friend of Warren's? Why not? (*Taking his arm.*) Have you asked me yet?

CLAY: How can I ask you when I don't know your name?

LULA: Are you talking to my name?

CLAY: What is it, a secret?

LULA: I'm Lena the Hyena.

CLAY: The famous woman poet?

LULA: Poetess! The same!

CLAY: Well, you know so much about me . . . what's my name?

LULA: Morris the Hyena.

CLAY: The famous woman poet?

LULA: The same. (*Laughing and going into her bag.*) You want another apple?

CLAY: Can't make it, lady. I only have to keep one doctor away a day.

LULA: I bet your name is . . . something like . . . uh, Gerald or Walter. Huh?

CLAY: God, no.

LULA: Lloyd, Norman? One of those hopeless colored names creeping out of New Jersey. Leonard? Gag. . . .

CLAY: Like Warren?

LULA: Definitely. Just exactly like Warren. Or Everett.

CLAY: Gag. . . .

LULA: Well, for sure, it's not Willie.

CLAY: It's Clay.

LULA: Clay? Really? Clay what?

CLAY: Take your pick. Jackson, Johnson, or Williams.

LULA: Oh, really? Good for you. But it's got to be Williams. You're too pretentious to be a Jackson or Johnson.

CLAY: Thass right.

LULA: But Clay's O.K.

CLAY: So's Lena.

LULA: It's Lula.

CLAY: Oh?

LULA: Lula the Hyena.

CLAY: Very good.

LULA (*starts laughing again*): Now you say to me, "Lula, Lula, why don't you go to this party with me tonight?" It's your turn, and let those be your lines.

CLAY: Lula, why don't you go to this party with me tonight, huh?

LULA: Say my name twice before you ask, and no huh's.

CLAY: Lula, Lula, why don't you go to this party with me tonight?

LULA: I'd like to go, Clay, but how can you ask me to go when you barely know me?

CLAY: That is strange, isn't it?

LULA: What kind of reaction is that? You're supposed to say, "Aw, come on, we'll get to know each other better at the party."

CLAY: That's pretty corny.

LULA: What are you into anyway? (*Looking at him half sullenly but still amused.*) What thing are you playing at, Mister? Mister Clay Williams? (*Grabs his thigh, up near the crotch.*) What are *you* thinking about?

CLAY: Watch it now, you're gonna excite me for real.

LULA (*taking her hand away and throwing her apple core through the window*): I bet. (*She slumps in the seat and is heavily silent.*)

CLAY: I thought you knew everything about me? What happened?

(LULA *looks at him, then looks slowly away, then over where the other aisle would be. Noise of the train. She reaches in her bag and pulls out one of the paper books. She puts it on her leg and thumbs the pages listlessly.* CLAY *cocks his head to see the title of the book. Noise of the train.* LULA *flips pages and her eyes drift. Both remain silent.*)

Are you going to the party with me, Lula?

LULA (*bored and not even looking*): I don't even know you.

CLAY: You said you know my type.

LULA (*strangely irritated*): Don't get smart with me, Buster. I know you like the palm of my hand.

CLAY: The one you eat the apples with?

LULA: Yeh. And the one I open doors late Saturday evening with. That's my door. Up at the top of the stairs. Five flights. Above a lot of Italians and lying Americans. And scrape carrots with. Also . . . (*looks at him*) the same hand I unbutton my dress with, or let my skirt fall down. Same hand. Lover.

CLAY: Are you angry about anything? Did I say something wrong?

LULA: Everything you say is wrong. (*Mock smile.*) That's what makes you so attractive. Ha. In that funnybook jacket with all the buttons. (*More animate, taking hold of his jacket.*) What've you got that jacket and tie on in all this heat for? And why're you wearing a jacket and tie like that? Did your people ever burn witches or start revolutions over the price of tea? Boy, those narrow-shoulder clothes come from a tradition you ought to feel oppressed by. A three-button suit. What right do you have to be wearing a three-button suit and striped tie? Your grandfather was a slave, he didn't go to Harvard.

CLAY: My grandfather was a night watchman.

LULA: And you went to a colored college where everybody thought they were Averell Harriman.

CLAY: All except me.

LULA: And who did you think you were? Who do you think you are now?

CLAY (*laughs as if to make light of the whole trend of the conversation*): Well, in college I thought I was Baudelaire. But I've slowed down since.

LULA: I bet you never once thought you were a black nigger.

(*Mock serious, then she howls with laughter.* CLAY *is stunned but after initial reaction, he quickly tries to appreciate the humor.* LULA *almost shrieks.*)

A black Baudelaire.

CLAY: That's right.

LULA: Boy, are you corny. I take back what I said before. Everything you say is not wrong. It's perfect. You should be on television.

CLAY: You act like you're on television already.

LULA: That's because I'm an actress.

CLAY: I thought so.

LULA: Well, you're wrong. I'm no actress. I told you I always lie. I'm nothing, honey, and don't you ever forget it. (*Lighter.*) Although my mother was a Communist. The only person in my family ever to amount to anything.

CLAY: My mother was a Republican.

LULA: And your father voted for the man rather than the party.

CLAY: Right!

LULA: Yea for him. Yea, yea for him.

CLAY: Yea!

LULA: And yea for America where he is free to vote for the mediocrity of his choice! Yea!

CLAY: Yea!

LULA: And yea for both your parents who even though they differ about so crucial a matter as the body politic still forged a union of love and sacrifice that was destined to flower at the birth of the noble Clay ... what's your middle name?

CLAY: Clay.

LULA: A union of love and sacrifice that was destined to flower at the birth of the noble Clay Clay Williams. Yea! And most of all yea yea for you, Clay Clay. The Black Baudelaire! Yes! (*And with knifelike cynicism.*) My Christ. My Christ.

CLAY: Thank you, ma'am.

LULA: May the people accept you as a ghost of the future. And love you, that you might not kill them when you can.

CLAY: What?

LULA: You're a murderer, Clay, and you know it. (*Her voice darkening with significance.*) You know goddamn well what I mean.

CLAY: I do?

LULA: So we'll pretend the air is light and full of perfume.

CLAY (*sniffing at her blouse*): It is.

LULA: And we'll pretend the people cannot see you. That is, the citizens. And that you are free of your own history. And I am free of my history. We'll pretend that we are both anonymous beauties smashing along through the city's entrails. (*She yells as loud as she can.*) GROOVE!

BLACK

SCENE II

Scene is the same as before, though now there are other seats visible in the car. And throughout the scene other people get on the subway. There are maybe one or two seated in the car as the scene opens, though neither CLAY *nor* LULA *notices them.* CLAY's *tie is open.* LULA *is hugging his arm.*

CLAY: The party!

LULA: I know it'll be something good. You can come in with me, looking casual and significant. I'll be strange, haughty, and silent, and walk with long slow strides.

CLAY: Right.

LULA: When you get drunk, pat me once, very lovingly on the flanks, and I'll look at you cryptically, licking my lips.

CLAY: It sounds like something we can do.

LULA: You'll go around talking to young men about your mind, and to old men about your plans. If you meet a very close friend who is also with someone like me, we can stand together, sipping our drinks and exchanging codes of lust. The atmosphere will be slithering in love and half-love and very open moral decision.

CLAY: Great. Great.

LULA: And everyone will pretend they don't know your name, and then ... (*she pauses heavily*) later, when they have to, they'll claim a friendship that denies your sterling character.

CLAY (*kissing her neck and fingers*): And then what?

LULA: Then? Well, then we'll go down the street, late night, eating apples and winding very deliberately toward my house.

CLAY: Deliberately?

LULA: I mean, we'll look in all the shopwindows, and make fun of the queers. Maybe we'll meet a Jewish Buddhist and flatten his conceits over some very pretentious coffee.

CLAY: In honor of whose God?

LULA: Mine.

CLAY: Who is ... ?

LULA: Me ... and you?

CLAY: A corporate Godhead.

LULA: Exactly. Exactly. (*Notices one of the other people entering.*)

CLAY: Go on with the chronicle. Then what happens to us?

LULA (*a mild depression, but she still makes her description triumphant and increasingly direct*): To my house, of course.

CLAY: Of course.

LULA: And up the narrow steps of the tenement.

CLAY: You live in a tenement?

LULA: Wouldn't live anywhere else. Reminds me specifically of my novel form of insanity.

CLAY: Up the tenement stairs.

LULA: And with my apple-eating hand I push open the door and lead you, my tender big-eyed prey, into my ... God, what can I call it ... into my hovel.

CLAY: Then what happens?

LULA: After the dancing and games, after the long drinks and long walks, the real fun begins.

CLAY: Ah, the real fun. (*Embarrassed, in spite of himself.*) Which is ... ?

LULA (*laughs at him*): Real fun in the dark house. Hah! Real fun in the dark house, high up above the street and the ignorant cowboys. I lead you in, holding your wet hand gently in my hand . . .

CLAY: Which is not wet?

LULA: Which is dry as ashes.

CLAY: And cold?

LULA: Don't think you'll get out of your responsibility that way. It's not cold at all. You Fascist! Into my dark living room. Where we'll sit and talk endlessly, endlessly.

CLAY: About what?

LULA: About what? About your manhood, what do you think? What do you think we've been talking about all this time?

CLAY: Well, I didn't know it was that. That's for sure. Every other thing in the world but that. (*Notices another person entering, looks quickly, almost involuntarily up and down the car, seeing the other people in the car.*) Hey, I didn't even notice when those people got on.

LULA: Yeah, I know.

CLAY: Man, this subway is slow.

LULA: Yeah, I know.

CLAY: Well, go on. We were talking about my manhood.

LULA: We still are. All the time.

CLAY: We were in your living room.

LULA: My dark living room. Talking endlessly.

CLAY: About my manhood.

LULA: I'll make you a map of it. Just as soon as we get to my house.

CLAY: Well, that's great.

LULA: One of the things we do while we talk. And screw.

CLAY (*trying to make his smile broader and less shaky*): We finally got there.

LULA: And you'll call my rooms black as a grave. You'll say, "This place is like Juliet's tomb."

CLAY (*laughs*): I might.

LULA: I know. You've probably said it before.

CLAY: And is that all? The whole grand tour?

LULA: Not all. You'll say to me very close to my face, many, many times, you'll say, even whisper, that you love me.

CLAY: Maybe I will.

LULA: And you'll be lying.

CLAY: I wouldn't lie about something like that.

LULA: Hah. It's the only kind of thing you will lie about. Especially if you think it'll keep me alive.

CLAY: Keep you alive? I don't understand.

LULA (*bursting out laughing, but too shrilly*): Don't understand? Well, don't look at me. It's the path I take, that's all. Where both feet take me when I set them down. One in front of the other.

CLAY: Morbid. Morbid. You sure you're not an actress? All that self-aggrandizement.

LULA: Well, I told you I wasn't an actress . . . but I also told you I lie all the time. Draw your own conclusions.

CLAY: Morbid. Morbid. You sure you're not an actress? All scribed? There's no more?

LULA: I've told you all I know. Or almost all.

CLAY: There's no funny parts?

LULA: I thought it was all funny.

CLAY: But you mean peculiar, not ha-ha.

LULA: You don't know what I mean.

CLAY: Well, tell me the almost part then. You said almost all. What else? I want the whole story.

LULA (*searching aimlessly through her bag. She begins to talk breathlessly, with a light and silly tone*): All stories are whole stories. All of 'em. Our whole story . . . nothing but change. How could things go on like that forever? Huh? (*Slaps him on the shoulder, begins finding things in her bag, taking them out and throwing them over her shoulder into the aisle.*) Except I do go on as I do. Apples and long walks with deathless intelligent lovers. But you mix it up. Look out the window, all the time. Turning pages. Change change change. Till, shit, I don't know you. Wouldn't, for that matter. You're too serious. I bet you're even too serious to be psychoanalyzed. Like all those Jewish poets from Yonkers, who leave their mothers looking for other mothers, or others' mothers, on whose baggy tits they lay their fumbling heads. Their poems are always funny, and all about sex.

CLAY: They sound great. Like movies.

LULA: But you change. (*Blankly.*) And things work on you till you hate them.

(*More people come into the train. They come closer to the couple, some of them not sitting, but swinging drearily on the straps, staring at the two with uncertain interest.*)

CLAY: Wow. All these people, so suddenly. They must all come from the same place.

LULA: Right. That they do.

CLAY: Oh? You know about them too?

LULA: Oh yeah. About them more than I know about you. Do they frighten you?

CLAY: Frighten me? Why should they frighten me?

LULA: 'Cause you're an escaped nigger.

CLAY: Yeah?

LULA: 'Cause you crawled through the wire and made tracks to my side.

CLAY: Wire?

LULA: Don't they have wire around plantations?

CLAY: You must be Jewish. All you can think about is wire. Plantations didn't have any wire. Plantations were big open white-washed places like heaven, and everybody on 'em was grooved to be there. Just strummin' and hummin' all day.

LULA: Yes, yes.

CLAY: And that's how the blues was born.

LULA: Yes, yes. And that's how the blues was born. (*Begins to make up a song that becomes quickly hysterical. As she sings she rises from her seat, still throwing things out of her bag into the aisle, beginning a rhythmical shudder and twistlike wiggle, which she continues up and down the aisle, bumping into many of the standing people and tripping over the feet of those sitting. Each time she runs into a person she lets out a very vicious piece of profanity, wiggling and stepping all the time.*) And that's how the blues was born. Yes. Yes. Son of a bitch, get out of the way. Yes. Quack. Yes. Yes. And that's how the blues was born. Ten little niggers sitting on a limb, but none of them ever looked like him. (*Points to CLAY, returns toward the seat, with her hands extended for him to rise and dance with her.*) And that's how blues was born. Yes. Come on, Clay. Let's do the nasty. Rub bellies. Rub bellies.

CLAY (*waves his hands to refuse. He is embarrassed, but determined to get a kick out of the proceedings*): Hey, what was in those apples? Mirror, mirror on the wall, who's the fairest one of all? Snow White, baby, and don't you forget it.

LULA (*grabbing for his hands, which he draws away*): Come on, Clay. Let's rub bellies on the train. The nasty. The nasty. Do the gritty grind, like your ol' rag-head mammy. Grind till you lose your mind. Shake it, shake it, shake it, shake it! OOOOweeee! Come on, Clay. Let's do the choochoo train shuffle, the navel scratcher.

CLAY: Hey, you coming on like the lady who smoked up her grass skirt.

LULA (*becoming annoyed that he will not dance, and becoming more animated as if to embarrass him still further*): Come on, Clay . . . let's do the thing. Uhh! Uhh! Clay! Clay! You middle-class black bastard. Forget your social-working mother for a few seconds and let's knock stomachs. Clay, you liver-lipped white man. You would-be Christian. You ain't no nigger, you're just a dirty white man. Get up, Clay. Dance with me, Clay.

CLAY: Lula! Sit down, now. Be cool.

LULA (*mocking him, in wild dance*): Be cool. Be cool. That's all you know . . . shaking that wildroot cream-oil on your knotty head, jackets buttoning up to your chin, so full of white man's words. Christ. God. Get up and scream at these people. Like scream meaningless shit in these hopeless faces. (*She screams at people in train, still dancing.*) Red trains cough Jewish underwear for keeps! Expanding smells of silence. Gravy snot whistling like sea birds. Clay. Clay, you got to break out. Don't sit there dying the way they want you to die. Get up.

CLAY: Oh, sit the fuck down. (*He moves to restrain her.*) Sit down, goddamn it.

LULA (*twisting out of his reach*): Screw yourself, Uncle Tom. Thomas Woolly-Head. (*Begins to dance a kind of jig, mocking CLAY with loud forced humor.*) There is Uncle Tom . . . I mean, Uncle Thomas Woolly-Head. With old white matted mane. He hobbles on his wooden cane. Old Tom. Old Tom. Let the white man hump his ol' mama, and he jes' shuffle off in the woods and hide his gentle gray head. Ol' Thomas Woolly-Head.

(*Some of the other riders are laughing now. A drunk gets up and joins LULA in her dance, singing, as best he can, her "song." CLAY gets up out of his seat and visibly scans the faces of the other riders.*)

CLAY: Lula! Lula!

(*She is dancing and turning, still shouting as loud as she can. The drunk too is shouting, and waving his hands wildly.*)

Lula . . . you dumb bitch. Why don't you stop it? (*He rushes half stumbling from his seat, and grabs one of her flailing arms.*)

LULA: Let me go! You black son of a bitch. (*She struggles against him.*) Let me go! Help!

(CLAY *is dragging her toward her seat, and the drunk seeks to interfere. He grabs* CLAY *around the shoulders and begins wrestling with him.* CLAY *clubs the drunk to the floor without releasing* LULA, *who is still screaming.* CLAY *finally gets her to the seat and throws her into it.*)

CLAY: Now you shut the hell up. (*Grabbing her shoulders.*) Just shut up. You don't know what you're talking about. You don't know anything. So just keep your stupid mouth closed.

LULA: You're afraid of white people. And your father was. Uncle Tom Big Lip!

CLAY (*slaps her as hard as he can, across the mouth.* LULA's *head bangs against the back of the seat. When she raises it again,* CLAY *slaps her again*): Now shut up and let me talk.

(*He turns toward the other riders, some of whom are sitting on the edge of their seats. The drunk is on one knee, rubbing his head, and singing softly the same song. He shuts up too when he sees* CLAY *watching him. The others go back to newspapers or stare out the windows.*)

Shit, you don't have any sense, Lula, nor feelings either. I could murder you now. Such a tiny ugly throat. I could squeeze it flat, and watch you turn blue, on a humble. For dull kicks. And all these weak-faced ofays squatting around here, staring over their papers at me. Murder them too. Even if they expected it. That man there ... (*Points to well-dressed man.*) I could rip that *Times* right out of his hand, as skinny and middle-classed as I am, I could rip that paper out of his hand and just as easily rip out his throat. It takes no great effort. For what? To kill you soft idiots? You don't understand anything but luxury.

LULA: You fool!

CLAY (*pushing her against the seat*): I'm not telling you again, Tallulah Bankhead! Luxury. In your face and your fingers. You telling me what I ought to do. (*Sudden scream frightening the whole coach.*) Well, don't! Don't you tell me anything! If I'm a middle-class fake white man ... let me be. And let me be in the way I want. (*Through his teeth.*) I'll rip your lousy breasts off! Let me be who I feel

like being. Uncle Tom. Thomas. Whoever. It's none of your business. You don't know anything except what's there for you to see. An act. Lies. Device. Not the pure heart, the pumping black heart. You don't ever know that. And I sit here, in this buttoned-up suit, to keep myself from cutting all your throats. I mean wantonly. You great liberated whore! You fuck some black man, and right away you're an expert on black people. What a lotta shit that is. The only thing you know is that you come if he bangs you hard enough. And that's all. The belly rub? You wanted to do the belly rub? Shit, you don't even know how. You don't know how. That ol' dipty-dip shit you do, rolling your ass like an elephant. That's not my kind of belly rub. Belly rub is not Queens. Belly rub is dark places, with big hats and overcoats held up with one arm. Belly rub hates you. Old bald-headed four-eyed ofays popping their fingers ... and don't know yet what they're doing. They say, "I love Bessie Smith." And don't even understand that Bessie Smith is saying, "Kiss my ass, kiss my black unruly ass." Before love, suffering, desire, anything you can explain, she's saying, and very plainly, "Kiss my black ass." And if you don't know that, it's you that's doing the kissing.

Charlie Parker? Charlie Parker. All the hip white boys scream for Bird. And Bird saying, "Up your ass, feeble-minded ofay! Up your ass." And they sit there talking about the tortured genius of Charlie Parker. Bird would've played not a note of music if he just walked up to East Sixty-seventh Street and killed the first ten white people he saw. Not a note! And I'm the great would be poet. Yes. That's right! Poet. Some kind of bastard literature ... all it needs is a simple knife thrust. Just let me bleed you, you loud whore, and one poem vanished. A whole people of neurotics, struggling to keep from being sane. And the only thing that would cure the neurosis would be your murder. Simple as that. I mean if I murdered you, then other white people would begin to understand me. You understand? No. I guess not. If Bessie Smith had killed some white people she wouldn't have needed that music. She could have talked very straight and plain about the world. No metaphors. No grunts. No wiggles in the dark of her soul. Just straight two and two are four. Money. Power. Luxury. Like that. All of them. Crazy niggers turning their backs on sanity.

When all it needs is that simple act. Murder. Just murder! Would make us all sane.

(*Suddenly weary.*) Ahhh. Shit. But who needs it? I'd rather be a fool. Insane. Safe with my words, and no deaths, and clean, hard thoughts, urging me to new conquests. My people's madness. Hah! That's a laugh. My people. They don't need me to claim them. They got legs and arms of their own. Personal insanities. Mirrors. They don't need all those words. They don't need any defense. But listen, though, one more thing. And you tell this to your father, who's probably the kind of man who needs to know at once. So he can plan ahead. Tell him not to preach so much rationalism and cold logic to these niggers. Let them alone. Let them sing curses at you in code and see your filth as simple lack of style. Don't make the mistake, through some irresponsible surge of Christian charity, of talking too much about the advantages of Western rationalism, or the great intellectual legacy of the white man, or maybe they'll begin to listen. And then, maybe one day, you'll find they actually do understand exactly what you are talking about, all these fantasy people. All these blues people. And on that day, as sure as shit, when you really believe you can "accept" them into your fold, as half-white trusties late of the subject peoples. With no more blues, except the very old ones, and not a watermelon in sight, the great missionary heart will have triumphed, and all of those ex-coons will be stand-up Western men, with eyes for clean hard useful lives, sober, pious and sane, and they'll murder you. They'll murder you, and have very rational explanations. Very much like your own. They'll cut your throats, and drag you out to the edge of your cities so the flesh can fall away from your bones, in sanitary isolation.

LULA (*her voice takes on a different, more businesslike quality*): I've heard enough.

CLAY (*reaching for his books*): I bet you have. I guess I better collect my stuff and get off this train. Looks like we won't be acting out that little pageant you outlined before.

LULA: No. We won't. You're right about that, at least. (*She turns to look quickly around the rest of the car.*) All right!

(*The others respond.*)

CLAY (*bending across the girl to retrieve his belongings*): Sorry, baby, I don't think we could make it.

(*As he is bending over her, the girl brings up a small knife and plunges it into* CLAY's *chest. Twice. He slumps across her knees, his mouth working stupidly.*)

LULA: Sorry is right. (*Turning to the others in the car who have already gotten up from their seats.*) Sorry is the rightest thing you've said. Get this man off me! Hurry, now!

(*The others come and drag* CLAY's *body down the aisle.*)

Open the door and throw his body out.

(*They throw him off.*)

And all of you get off at the next stop.

(LULA *busies herself straightening her things. Getting everything in order. She takes out a notebook and makes a quick scribbling note. Drops it in her bag. The train apparently stops and all the others get off, leaving her alone in the coach.*
Very soon a young Negro of about twenty comes into the coach, with a couple of books under his arm. He sits a few seats in back of* LULA. *When he is seated she turns and gives him a long slow look. He looks up from his book and drops the book on his lap. Then an old Negro conductor comes into the car, doing a sort of restrained soft shoe, and half mumbling the words of some song. He looks at the young man, briefly, with a quick greeting.*)

CONDUCTOR: Hey, brother!
YOUNG MAN: Hey.

(*The conductor continues down the aisle with his little dance and the mumbled song.* LULA *turns to stare at him and follows his movements down the aisle. The conductor tips his hat when he reaches her seat, and continues out the car.*)

CURTAIN

Near the end of the nineteenth century, Joseph Conrad wrote:

My task which I am trying to achieve is, by the power of the written word, to make you hear, to make you feel — it is, before all, to make you see. That — and no more, and it is everything.

To make an audience see has been the aim of many writers, but LeRoi Jones argues, in several essays in a collection entitled *Home*, that the black writer, such as Jones, who by his very status as outsider may be equipped to see American society with special clarity, will inevitably be opposed by the white Establishment, which regularly demands that writers see only what glorifies the Establishment. Not surprisingly, Jones has been harassed by public officials who claim that his revolutionary vision is a threat to public morality.

Jones admits the charge. Several quotations from "The Revolutionary Theatre" (included in *Home*) will give the gist of his position:

The Revolutionary Theatre should force change; it should be change. ... The Revolutionary Theatre must EXPOSE! Show up the insides of these humans, look into black skulls. White men will cower before this theatre because it hates them. Because they themselves have been trained to hate.

The Revolutionary Theatre must take dreams and give them a reality. ... It must be food for all those who need food, and daring propaganda for the beauty of the Human Mind. It is a political theatre, a weapon to help in the slaughter of these dim-witted fatbellied white guys who somehow believe that the rest of the world is here for them to slobber on.

Our theatre will show victims so that their brothers in the audience will be better able to understand that they are the brothers of victims, and that they themselves are victims if they are blood brothers.*

Finally, here is a passage from the short essay that concludes *Home*:

The Black Artist's role in America is to aid in the destruction of America as he knows it. His role is to report and reflect so precisely the nature of the society, that other men will be moved by the exactness of his rendering and, if they are black men, grow strong through this moving, having seen their own strength, and weakness; and if they are white men, tremble, curse, and go mad, because they will be drenched with the filth of their evil.

Jones thus assumes that art is enormously potent, and in so doing he takes his place in a tradition that can be traced back to Chekhov (who said that he wrote his plays in order to make people see that their lives were dreary and to make them create a better life for themselves), back to Shakespeare (whose Hamlet had heard that "guilty creatures sitting at a play" may see their own image on the stage and may be moved to "proclaim" their malefactions), and finally back to Plato, who in the fourth century B.C. argued that the tragic

* The four extracts on this page and the one on page 246 are reprinted from LeRoi Jones's *Home*, pages 210–11, 211–12, 213, 251, and 188, by permission of The Sterling Lord Agency, Inc. Copyright © 1961, 1962, 1963, 1964, 1965, 1966 by LeRoi Jones.

dramatists should be barred from the ideal commonwealth precisely because they have the power to stir up pity and terror in men and thus to obscure men's rational faculty. For Plato the emotional effect of dramatic art is harmful. People ought not to be stirred by such emotions. (If this seems hopelessly old fashioned, one can reflect that probably some such thinking plays a part in our own prohibition of such entertainments as bull fighting and public executions.) Aristotle apparently tried to reply to Plato by arguing that the playwrights arouse pity and terror for the sake of moral well-being. There is a good deal of uncertainty about the meaning of Aristotle's remarks on the catharsis of pity and terror, but perhaps he meant that spectators were educated by being shown on the stage the proper objects of these emotions, or perhaps he meant that these emotions are expended harmlessly in the theater and thus the spectators are healthier when they leave the theater — rather as a boxing match or a prize fight may drain off the aggressions of the spectators who otherwise might expend their aggression outside of the stadium. In any case, the doctrine of catharsis, though much disputed, tends to be seen as counter-revolutionary; it stimulates the passions in order to diminish them, making spectators more willing to accept the affairs of the daily world.

Acceptance of the daily world is intolerable to Jones, for whom psychic health depends not on calm acceptance but on drastically changed social conditions. So Jones shows us an intolerable society, and in *Dutchman* he does this not by abstract preaching (though his essays are full of such preaching) but by vividly setting forth on the stage characters engaged in a human relationship. Jones has denied that Clay and Lula are symbols: they are, he says, real people in a real world. At the same time, however, he admits that these characters are not only individuals but are recognizable human types:

> Lula, for all her alleged insanity, just barely reflects the insanity of this hideous place. And Clay is a young boy trying desperately to become a man. *Dutchman* is about the difficulty of becoming a man in America. It is very difficult, to be sure, if you are black, but I think it is now much harder to become one if you're white. In fact, you will find very few white American males with the slightest knowledge of what manhood involves. They are too busy running the world, or running from it.

Let us begin with Lula. Jones presents her in such a way that we see her, we know her, and he does this as a dramatist must, by endowing the character with gestures and with language that ring true. Early in the play we see her as a vivid rendition of a fairly common type, someone whose precise kind of vulgarity is especially revealed in pretentiousness. She says that Clay was staring "in the vicinity of my ass" (not "at my ass"), and before she tosses her apple core onto the floor of the subway car she wraps it in a Kleenex. Through such bits of dialogue and such gestures a very real human being is rendered visible to us — but our perception of her reality is partly indebted to our recognition of her as a type. Moreover, she is not just one of millions of people whose special sort of coarseness reveals itself in ludicrous attempts at being genteel: she is also a *femme fatale*, a woman who seeks out victims, an Eve tempting Adam with her apple — specifically, the white woman who, surrounded by a myth of purity, lures black men to their destruction. Early in her conversation with Clay, Lula admits that she sought him out, and that she often lies because "it helps me to control the world." We can say that Lula — while never ceasing to be a specific woman who encounters a specific man on the subway — at least in part stands for, or, perhaps better, embodies the white society that Jones sees as enslaving all blacks.

And what of Clay, the black man? Jones said that "Clay is a young boy trying desperately to become a man." Just because Jones said so in an essay does not make it true in the play, but when we return to the play we can see ample evidence. Lula immediately sees Clay's effort to mature: "You look like you live in New Jersey with your parents and are trying to grow a beard." Again the specific details embody a type. She knows him well because he is, as she says, "a well-known type," and she later calls to Clay's attention that they have all the while been talking (however indirectly) about his manhood. The kind of man Clay wants to be is clear to Lula and to us, from his clothing:

> Boy, those narrow-shoulder clothes come from a tradition you ought to feel oppressed by. A three-button suit. What right do you have to be wearing a three-button suit and striped tie? Your grandfather was a slave, he didn't go to Harvard.

Clay is, Lula says, a "middle-class black bastard. . . . You ain't no nigger, you're just a dirty white man." Clay half knows that he is trying to surrender his black identity, and he also knows that he embodies the slave's murderous impulses toward his white oppressor. But Clay's bourgeois aspirations enslave him, and rather than achieve manhood by murdering his oppressor (so Jones seems to see it) Clay makes the mistake of thinking that murder can be avoided. "I sit here, in this buttoned up suit, to keep myself from cutting your throats." Clay, self-imprisoned in the white man's clothes, thinks he is achieving manhood but he is ensuring his own destruction. The white oppressor, having none of Clay's illusions, knows that in white America the whites must murder the blacks (deprive them of "manhood") or the whites will be murdered by the blacks.

This commentary has become increasingly abstract, and a reader does well to remember that the play is about individuals as well as about ideas. But ideas are not antithetical to individuals and to realities, and the individuals and the realistic details that fill the play are endowed with metaphoric implications that insistently point beyond themselves. The very first line of the first stage direction is metaphoric: the play is set "in the flying underbelly of the city." The subway is the belly, the guts, of the city, invisible to the eye that dwells on the surface but real and teeming, like the passions that churn within an individual and like the political, social, and economic structures that, though invisible to many, dominate men's lives. The stage direction also tells that from time to time there is "a loud scream" of a train. Such screams are not only bits of realism, representations of trains; the title forces us, on reflection, toward a symbolic reading.

There is no Dutchman in the play; in fact the word is never used within the play. But, in conjunction with the description of the locale — "the *flying* underbelly of the city . . . the subway heaped in modern *myth*" — is it fanciful to see the endlessly shuttling subway as a modern version of the ship of the mythical flying Dutchman, who was condemned to sail the stormy seas until redeemed by the love of a pure woman? Both Lula and Clay are condemned to restlessness; Clay thinks he can find peace in the white man's world but he finds only the loss of identity; Lula's fate is that she is condemned to go on riding the subway, murdering one black after another.

EQUUS

Peter Shaffer

Peter Shaffer (b. 1926) is an Englishman who, after studying at Cambridge University, worked for three years in the United States. He returned to England, where he wrote his first play, *Five Finger Exercise* (produced in New York in 1959). Among his other plays are *The Royal Hunt of the Sun* (1964), *Black Comedy* (1965), and of course *Equus* (1973), which when produced in New York won the Tony Award for the best play of the year.

CHARACTERS

MARTIN DYSART, *a psychiatrist*   DORA STRANG, *his mother*   HARRY DALTON, *a stable owner*
ALAN STRANG   HESTHER SALOMON, *a magistrate*   A YOUNG HORSEMAN
FRANK STRANG, *his father*   JILL MASON   A NURSE

SIX ACTORS — *including the* YOUNG HORSEMAN, *who also plays* NUGGET — *appear as* HORSES.

THE HORSES: The actors wear track-suits of chestnut velvet. On their feet are light strutted hooves, about four inches high, set on metal horse-shoes. On their hands are gloves of the same colour. On their heads are tough masks made of alternating bands of silver wire and leather: their eyes are outlined by leather blinkers. The actors' own heads are seen beneath them: no attempt should be made to conceal them.

Any literalism which could suggest the cosy familiarity of a domestic animal — or worse, a pantomime horse — should be avoided. The actors should never crouch on all fours, or even bend forward. They must always — except on the one occasion where NUGGET is ridden — stand upright, as if the body of the horse extended invisibly behind them. Animal effect must be created entirely mimetically, through the use of legs, knees, neck, face, and the turn of the head which can move the mask above it through all the gestures of equine wariness and pride. Great care must also be taken that the masks are put on before the audience with very precise timing — the actors watching each other, so that the masking has an exact and ceremonial effect.

THE CHORUS: References are made in the text to the Equus Noise. I have in mind a choric effect, made by all the actors sitting round upstage, and composed of humming, thumping, and stamping — though never of neighing or whinnying. This Noise heralds or illustrates the presence of Equus the God.

Peter Firth as Alan in the New York production of *Equus*, directed by John Dexter, 1974. (Photograph: Van Williams.)

A Note on the Play — One weekend over two years ago, I was driving with a friend through bleak countryside. We passed a stable. Suddenly he was reminded by it of an alarming crime which he had heard about recently at a dinner party in London. He knew only one horrible detail, and his complete mention of it could barely have lasted a minute — but it was enough to arouse in me an intense fascination.

The act had been committed several years before by a highly disturbed young man. It had deeply shocked a local bench of magistrates. It lacked, finally, any coherent explanation.

A few months later my friend died. I could not verify what he had said, or ask him to expand it. He had given me no name, no place, and no time. I don't think he knew them. All I possessed was his report of a dreadful event, and the feeling it engendered in me. I knew very strongly that I wanted to interpret it in some entirely personal way. I had to create a mental world in which the deed could be made comprehensible.

Every person and incident in *Equus* is of my own invention, save the crime itself: and even that I modified to accord with what I feel to be acceptable theatrical proportion. I am grateful now that I have never received confirmed details of the real story, since my concern has been more and more with a different kind of exploration.

I have been lucky, in doing final work on the play, to have enjoyed the advice and expert comment of a distinguished child psychiatrist. Through him I have tried to keep things real in a more naturalistic sense. I have also come to perceive that psychiatrists are an immensely varied breed, professing immensely varied methods and techniques. MARTIN DYSART is simply one doctor in one hospital. I must take responsibility for him, as I do for his patient.

The Set — A square of wood set on a circle of wood.

The square resembles a railed boxing ring. The rail, also of wood, encloses three sides. It is perforated on each side by an opening. Under the rail are a few vertical slats, as if in a fence. On the downstage side there is no rail. The whole square is set on ball bearings, so that by slight pressure from actors standing round it on the circle, it can be made to turn round smoothly by hand.

On the square are set three little plain benches, also of wood. They are placed parallel with the rail, against the slats, but can be moved out by the actors to stand at right angles to them.

Set into the floor of the square, and flush with it, is a thin metal pole, about a yard high. This can be raised out of the floor, to stand upright. It acts as a support for the actor playing NUGGET, when he is ridden.

In the area outside the circle stand benches. Two downstage left and right, are curved to accord with the circle. The left one is used by DYSART as a listening and observing post when he is out of the square, and also by ALAN as his hospital bed. The right one is used by ALAN's parents, who sit side by side on it. (Viewpoint is from the main body of the audience.)

Further benches stand upstage, and accommodate the other actors. All the cast of *Equus* sits on stage the entire evening. They get up to perform their scenes, and return when they are done to their places around the set. They are witnesses, assistants — and especially a CHORUS.

Upstage, forming a backdrop to the whole, are tiers of seats in the fashion of a dissecting theatre, formed into two railed-off blocks, pierced by a central tunnel. In these blocks sit members of the audience. During the play, DYSART addresses them directly from time to time, as he addresses the main body of the theatre. No other actor ever refers to them.

To left and right, downstage, stand two ladders on which are suspended horse masks.

The colour of all benches is olive green.

Above the stage hangs a battery of lights, set in a huge metal ring. Light cues, in this version, will be only of the most general description.

The main action of the play takes place in Rokeby Psychiatric Hospital in Southern England.

The time is the present.

The play is divided into numbered scenes, indicating a change of time or locale or mood. The action, however, is continuous.

ACT 1

SCENE 1

Darkness.
Silence.
Dim light up on the square. In a spotlight stands ALAN STRANG, *a lean boy of seventeen, in sweater and jeans. In front of him, the horse* NUGGET. ALAN's *pose represents a contour of great tenderness: his head is pressed against the shoulder of the horse, his hands stretching up to fondle its head.*

Equus by Peter Shaffer is reprinted here by permission of Atheneum Publishers of New York and Andre Deutsch Limited of London. Copyright © 1974 by Peter Shaffer. *Caution:* Professionals and amateurs are hereby warned that this play, *Equus*, being fully protected under the Copyright Laws of the United States of America, the British Empire, including the Dominion of Canada, and all other countries of the Berne and Universal Copyright Conventions, is subject to royalty. All rights, including professional, amateur, motion picture, recitation, lecturing, public reading, radio and television broadcasting, and the rights of translation into foreign languages, are strictly reserved. Particular emphasis is laid on the question of readings, permission for which must be secured from the author's agent in writing. All inquiries should be addressed to The Lantz Office, 114 East 55 Street, New York, New York 10022.

The horse in turn nuzzles his neck.
The flame of a cigarette lighter jumps in the dark. Lights come up slowly on the circle. On the left bench, downstage, MARTIN DYSART, *smoking. A man in his mid-forties.*

DYSART: With one particular horse, called Nugget, he embraces. The animal digs its sweaty brow into his cheek, and they stand in the dark for an hour — like a necking couple. And of all nonsensical things — I keep thinking about the *horse!* Not the boy: the horse, and what it may be trying to do. I keep seeing that huge head kissing him with its chained mouth. Nudging through the metal some desire absolutely irrelevant to filling its belly or propagating its own kind. What desire could that be? Not to stay a horse any longer? Not to remain reined up for ever in those particular genetic strings? Is it possible, at certain moments we cannot imagine, a horse can add its sufferings together — the non-stop jerks and jabs that are its daily life — and turn them into grief? What use is grief to a horse?

(ALAN *leads* NUGGET *out of the square and they disappear together up the tunnel, the horse's hooves scraping delicately on the wood.*

DYSART *rises, and addresses both the large audience in the theatre and the smaller one on stage.*)

You see, I'm lost. What use, I should be asking, are questions like these to an overworked psychiatrist in a provincial hospital? They're worse than useless: they are, in fact, subversive.

(*He enters the square. The light grows brighter.*)

The thing is, I'm desperate. You see, I'm wearing that horse's head myself. That's the feeling. All reined up in old language and old assumptions, straining to jump clean-hoofed on to a whole new track of being I only suspect is there. I can't see it, because my educated, average head is being held at the wrong angle. I can't jump because the bit forbids it, and my own basic force — my horsepower, if you like — is too little. The only thing I know for sure is this: a horse's head is finally unknowable to me. Yet I handle children's heads — which I must presume to be more complicated, at least in the area of my chief concern. . . . In a way, it has nothing to do with this boy. The doubts have been there for years, piling up steadily in this dreary place. It's only the extremity of this case that's made them active. I know that. The *extremity* is the point! All the same, whatever the reason, they are now, these doubts, not just vaguely worrying — but intolerable . . . I'm sorry. I'm not making much sense. Let me start properly: in order. It began one Monday last month, with Hesther's visit.

SCENE 2

The light gets warmer.
He sits. NURSE *enters the square.*

NURSE: Mrs. Salomon to see you, Doctor.
DYSART: Show her in, please.

(NURSE *leaves and crosses to where* HESTHER *sits.*)

Some days I blame Hesther. She brought him to see me. But of course that's nonsense. What is he but a last straw? a last symbol? If it hadn't been him, it would have been the next patient, or the next. At least, I suppose so.

(HESTHER *enters the square: a woman in her mid-forties.*)

HESTHER: Hallo, Martin.

(DYSART *rises and kisses her on the cheek.*)

DYSART: Madam Chairman! Welcome to the torture chamber!
HESTHER: It's good of you to see me right away.
DYSART: You're a welcome relief. Take a couch.
HESTHER: It's been a day?
DYSART: No — just a fifteen year old schizophrenic, and a girl of eight thrashed into catatonia by her father. Normal, really . . . You're in a state.
HESTHER: Martin, this is the most shocking case I ever tried.
DYSART: So you said on the phone.
HESTHER: I mean it. My bench wanted to send the boy to prison. For life, if they could manage it. It took me two hours solid arguing to get him sent to you instead.
DYSART: Me?
HESTHER: I mean, to hospital.
DYSART: Now look, Hesther. Before you say anything else, I can take no more patients at the moment. I can't even cope with the ones I have.
HESTHER: You must.
DYSART: Why?
HESTHER: Because most people are going to be disgusted by the whole thing. Including doctors.
DYSART: May I remind you I share this room with two highly competent psychiatrists?
HESTHER: Bennett and Thoroughgood. They'll be as shocked as the public.
DYSART: That's an absolutely unwarrantable statement.
HESTHER: Oh, they'll be cool and exact. And underneath they'll be revolted, and immovably English. Just like my bench.
DYSART: Well, what am I? Polynesian?
HESTHER: You know exactly what I mean!
. . . (*Pause.*) Please, Martin. It's vital. You're this boy's only chance.
DYSART: Why? What's he done? Dosed some little girl's Pepsi with Spanish Fly? What could possibly throw your bench into two-hour convulsions?
HESTHER: He blinded six horses with a metal spike.

(*A long pause.*)

DYSART: Blinded?

HESTHER: Yes.

DYSART: All at once, or over a period?

HESTHER: All on the same night.

DYSART: Where?

HESTHER: In a riding stable near Winchester. He worked there at weekends.

DYSART: How old?

HESTHER: Seventeen.

DYSART: What did he say in Court?

HESTHER: Nothing. He just sang.

DYSART: Sang?

HESTHER: Any time anyone asked him anything.

(*Pause.*)

Please take him, Martin. It's the last favour I'll ever ask you.

DYSART: No, it's not.

HESTHER: No, it's not — and he's probably abominable. All I know is, he needs you badly. Because there really is nobody within a hundred miles of your desk who can handle him. And perhaps understand what this is about. Also . . . .

DYSART: What?

HESTHER: There's something very special about him.

DYSART: In what way?

HESTHER: Vibrations.

DYSART: You and your vibrations.

HESTHER: They're quite startling. You'll see.

DYSART: When does he get here?

HESTHER: Tomorrow morning. Luckily there was a bed in Neville Ward. I know this is an awful imposition, Martin. Frankly I didn't know what else to do.

(*Pause.*)

DYSART: Can you come in and see me on Friday?

HESTHER: Bless you!

DYSART: If you come after work I can give you a drink. Will 6:30 be all right?

HESTHER: You're a dear. You really are.

DYSART: Famous for it.

HESTHER: Goodbye.

DYSART: By the way, what's his name?

HESTHER: Alan Strang.

(*She leaves and returns to her seat.*)

DYSART (*to audience*): What did I expect of him? Very little, I promise you. One more dented little face. One more adolescent freak. The usual unusual. One great thing about being in the adjustment business: you're never short of customers.

(NURSE *comes down the tunnel, followed by* ALAN. *She enters the square.*)

NURSE: Alan Strang, Doctor.

(*The boy comes in.*)

DYSART: Hallo. My name's Martin Dysart. I'm pleased to meet you.

(*He puts out his hand.* ALAN *does not respond in any way.*)

That'll be all, Nurse, thank you.

SCENE 3

NURSE *goes out and back to her place.* DYSART *sits, opening a file.*

So: did you have a good journey? I hope they gave you lunch at least. Not that there's much to choose between a British Rail meal and one here.

(ALAN *stands staring at him.*)

DYSART: Won't you sit down?

(*Pause. He does not.* DYSART *consults his file.*)

Is this your full name? Alan Strang?

(*Silence.*)

And you're seventeen. Is that right? Seventeen? . . . Well?

ALAN (*singing low*):
      Double your pleasure,
      Double your fun
      With Doublemint, Doublemint
      Doublemint gum.

DYSART (*unperturbed*): Now, let's see. You work in an electrical shop during the week. You live with your parents, and your father's a printer. What sort of things does he print?

ALAN (*singing louder*):
      Double your pleasure
      Double your fun
      With Doublemint, Doublemint
      Doublemint gum.

DYSART: I mean does he do leaflets and calendars? Things like that?

(*The boy approaches him, hostile.*)

ALAN (*singing*):
  Try the taste of Martini
  The most beautiful drink in the world.
  It's the right one —
  The bright one —
  That's Martini!
DYSART: I wish you'd sit down, if you're going to sing. Don't you think you'd be more comfortable?

(*Pause.*)

ALAN (*singing*):
There's only one T in Typhoo!
In packets and in teabags too.
Any way you make it, you'll find it's true:
There's only one T in Typhoo!
DYSART (*appreciatively*): Now that's a good song. I like it better than the other two. Can I hear that one again?

(ALAN *starts away from him, and sits on the upstage bench.*)

ALAN (*singing*):
  Double your pleasure
  Double your fun
  With Doublemint, Doublemint
  Doublemint gum.
DYSART (*smiling*): You know I was wrong. I really do think that one's better. It's got such a catchy tune. Please do that one again.

(*Silence. The boy glares at him.*)

I'm going to put you in a private bedroom for a little while. There are one or two available, and they're rather more pleasant than being in a ward. Will you please come and see me tomorrow? . . . (*He rises.*) By the way, which parent is it who won't allow you to watch television? Mother or father? Or is it both? (*Calling out of the door.*) Nurse!

(ALAN *stares at him.* NURSE *comes in.*)

NURSE: Yes, Doctor?
DYSART: Take Strang here to Number Three, will you? He's moving in there for a while.
NURSE: Very good, Doctor.
DYSART (*to* ALAN): You'll like that room. It's nice.

(*The boy sits staring at* DYSART. DYSART *returns the stare.*)

NURSE: Come along, young man. This way. . . . I said this way, please.

(*Reluctantly* ALAN *rises and goes to* NURSE, *passing dangerously close to* DYSART, *and out through the left door.* DYSART *looks after him, fascinated.*)

SCENE 4

NURSE *and patient move on to the circle, and walk downstage to the bench where the doctor first sat, which is to serve also as* ALAN's *bed.*

NURSE: Well now: isn't this nice? You're lucky to be in here, you know, rather than the ward. That ward's a noisy old place.
ALAN (*singing*):
  Let's go where you wanna go — Texaco!
NURSE (*contemplating him*): I hope you're not going to make a nuisance of yourself. You'll have a much better time of it here, you know, if you behave yourself.
ALAN: Fuck off.
NURSE (*tight*): That's the bell there. The lav's down the corridor.

(*She leaves him, and goes back to her place.* ALAN *lies down.*)

SCENE 5

DYSART *stands in the middle of the square and addresses the audience. He is agitated.*

DYSART: That night, I had this very explicit dream. In it I'm a chief priest in Homeric Greece. I'm wearing a wide gold mask, all noble and bearded, like the so-called Mask of Agamemnon found at Mycenae. I'm standing by a thick round stone and holding a sharp knife. In fact, I'm officiating at some immensely important ritual sacrifice, on which depends the fate of the crops or of a military expedition. The sacrifice is a herd of children: about five hundred boys and girls. I can see them stretching away in a long queue, right across the plain of Argos. I know it's Argos because of the red soil. On either side of me stand two assistant priests, wearing masks as well: lumpy, pop-eyed masks, such as also were found at Mycenae. They are enormously strong, these other priests, and absolutely tireless. As each child steps forward, they grab it from behind and throw it over the stone. Then with a surgical skill which amazes even me, I fit in the knife and slice elegantly down to the navel, just like a seamstress following a pattern. I part the flaps, sever the inner tubes, yank them out and throw them hot and steaming on to the floor. The other two then study the pattern they make, as if they were reading hieroglyphics. It's obvious to me that I'm tops as chief priest. It's this unique talent for carving that has got me where I am. The only thing is, unknown to them, I've started to feel distinctly nauseous. And with each victim, it's getting worse. My face is going green behind the mask. Of course, I redouble my efforts to look professional — cutting and snipping for all I'm worth: mainly because I know that if ever those two assistants so much as glimpse my distress — and the implied doubt that this repetitive and smelly work is doing any social good at all — I will be the next across the stone. And then, of course — the damn mask begins to slip. The priests both turn and look at it — it slips some more — they see the green sweat running down my face — their gold pop-eyes suddenly fill up with blood — they tear the knife out of my hand . . . and I wake up.

SCENE 6

HESTHER *enters the square. Light grows warmer.*

HESTHER: That's the most indulgent thing I ever heard.
DYSART: You think?
HESTHER: Please don't be ridiculous. You've done the most superb work with children. You must know that.
DYSART: Yes, but do the children?
HESTHER: Really!
DYSART: I'm sorry.
HESTHER: So you should be.
DYSART: I don't know why you listen. It's just professional menopause. Everyone gets it sooner or later. Except you.
HESTHER: Oh, of course. I feel totally fit to be a magistrate all the time.
DYSART: No, you don't — but then that's you feeling unworthy to fill a job. I feel the job is unworthy to fill me.
HESTHER: Do you seriously?
DYSART: More and more. I'd like to spend the next ten years wandering very slowly around the *real* Greece. . . . Anyway, all this dream nonsense is your fault.

HESTHER: Mine?
DYSART: It's that lad of yours who started it off. Do you know it's his face I saw on every victim across the stone?
HESTHER: Strang?
DYSART: He has the strangest stare I ever met.
HESTHER: Yes.
DYSART: It's exactly like being accused. Violently accused. But what of? . . . Treating him is going to be unsettling. Especially in my present state. His singing was direct enough. His speech is more so.
HESTHER (*surprised*): He's talking to you, then?
DYSART: Oh yes. It took him two more days of commercials, and then he snapped. Just like that — I suspect it has something to do with his nightmares.

(NURSE *walks briskly round the circle, a blanket over her arm, a clipboard of notes in her hand.*)

HESTHER: He has nightmares?
DYSART: Bad ones.
NURSE: We had to give him a sedative or two, Doctor. Last night it was exactly the same.
DYSART (*to* NURSE): What does he do? Call out?
NURSE (*to desk*): A lot of screaming, Doctor.
DYSART (*to* NURSE): Screaming?
NURSE: One word in particular.
DYSART (*to* NURSE): You mean a special word?
NURSE: Over and over again. (*Consulting clipboard.*) It sounds like "Ek."
HESTHER: Ek?
NURSE: Yes, Doctor. Ek. . . . "Ek!" he goes. "Ek!"
HESTHER: How weird.
NURSE: When I woke him up he clung to me like he was going to break my arm.

(*She stops at* ALAN's *bed. He is sitting up. She puts the blanket over him, and returns to her place.*)

DYSART: And then he burst in — just like that — without knocking or anything. Fortunately, I didn't have a patient with me.
ALAN (*jumping up*): Dad!
HESTHER: What?

DYSART: The answer to a question I'd asked him two days before. Spat out with the same anger as he sang the commercials.

HESTHER: Dad what?

ALAN: Who hates telly.

(*He lies downstage on the circle, as if watching television.*)

HESTHER: You mean his dad forbids him to watch?

DYSART: Yes.

ALAN: It's a dangerous drug.

HESTHER: Oh, really!

(FRANK *stands up and enters the scene downstage. A man in his fifties.*)

FRANK (*to* ALAN): It may not look like that, but that's what it is. Absolutely fatal mentally, if you receive my meaning.

(DORA *follows him on. She is also middle-aged.*)

DORA: That's a little extreme, dear, isn't it?

FRANK: You sit in front of that thing long enough, you'll become stupid for life — like most of the population. (*To* ALAN.) The thing is, it's a *swiz.* It seems to be offering you something, but actually it's taking something away. Your intelligence and your concentration, every minute you watch it. That's a true swiz, do you see?

(*Seated on the floor,* ALAN *shrugs.*)

I don't want to sound like a spoilsport, old chum — but there really is no substitute for reading. What's the matter: don't you like it?

ALAN: It's all right.

FRANK: I know you think it's none of my beeswax, but it really is you know . . . Actually, it's a disgrace when you come to think of it. You the son of a printer, and never opening a book! If all the world was like you, I'd be out of a job, if you receive my meaning!

DORA: All the same, times change, Frank.

FRANK (*reasonably*): They change if you let them change, Dora. Please return that set in the morning.

ALAN (*crying out*): No!

DORA: Frank! No!

FRANK: I'm sorry, Dora, but I'm not having that thing in the house a moment longer. I told you I didn't want it to begin with.

DORA: But, dear, everyone watches television these days!

FRANK: Yes, and what do they watch? Mindless violence! Mindless jokes! Every five minutes some laughing idiot selling you something you don't want, just to bolster up the economic system. (*To* ALAN.) I'm sorry, old chum.

(*He leaves the scene and sits again in his place.*)

HESTHER: He's a Communist, then?

DYSART: Old-type Socialist, I'd say. Relentlessly self-improving.

HESTHER: They're *both* older than you'd expect.

DYSART: So I gather.

DORA (*looking after* FRANK): Really, dear, you are very extreme!

(*She leaves the scene too, and again sits beside her husband.*)

HESTHER: She's an ex-school teacher, isn't she?

DYSART: Yes. The boy's proud of that. We got on to it this afternoon.

ALAN (*belligerently, standing up*): She knows more than you.

(HESTHER *crosses and sits by* DYSART. *During the following, the boy walks round the circle, speaking to* DYSART *but not looking at him.* DYSART *replies in the same manner.*)

DYSART (*to* ALAN): Does she?

ALAN: I bet I do too. I bet I know more history than you.

DYSART (*to* ALAN): Well, I bet you don't.

ALAN: All right: who was the Hammer of the Scots?

DYSART (*to* ALAN): I don't know: who?

ALAN: King Edward the First. Who never smiled again?

DYSART (*to* ALAN): I don't know: who?

ALAN: You don't know anything, do you? It was Henry the First. I know all the Kings.

DYSART (*to* ALAN): And who's your favourite?

ALAN: John.

DYSART (*to* ALAN) Why?

ALAN: Because he put out the eyes of that smarty little —

(*Pause.*)

(Sensing he has said something wrong.) Well, he didn't really. He was prevented, because the gaoler was merciful!

HESTHER: Oh dear.

ALAN: *He was prevented!*

DYSART: Something odder was to follow.

ALAN: Who said "Religion is the opium of the people"?

HESTHER: Good Lord!

(ALAN giggles.)

DYSART: The odd thing was, he said it with a sort of guilty snigger. The sentence is obviously associated with some kind of tension.

HESTHER: What did you say?

DYSART: I gave him the right answer. *(To* ALAN.*)* Karl Marx.

ALAN: No.

DYSART *(to* ALAN*)*: Then who?

ALAN: Mind your own beeswax.

DYSART: It's probably his dad. He may say it to provoke his wife.

HESTHER: And you mean she's religious?

DYSART: She could be. I tried to discover — none too successfully.

ALAN: Mind your own beeswax!

(ALAN goes back to bed and lies down in the dark.)

DYSART: However, I shall find out on Sunday.

HESTHER: What do you mean?

DYSART *(getting up)*: I want to have a look at his home, so I invited myself over.

HESTHER: Did you?

DYSART: If there's any tension over religion, it should be evident on a Sabbath evening! I'll let you know.

(He kisses her cheek and they part, both leaving the square. HESTHER *sits in her place again;* DYSART *walks round the circle, and greets* DORA *who stands waiting for him downstage.)*

SCENE 7

DYSART *(shaking hands)*: Mrs. Strang.

DORA: Mr. Strang's still at the Press, I'm afraid. He should be home in a minute.

DYSART: He works Sundays as well?

DORA: Oh, yes. He doesn't set much store by Sundays.

DYSART: Perhaps you and I could have a little talk before he comes in.

DORA: Certainly. Won't you come into the living room?

(She leads the way into the square. She is very nervous.)

Please. . . .

(She motions him to sit, then holds her hands tightly together.)

DYSART: Mrs. Strang, have you any idea how this thing could have occurred?

DORA: I can't imagine, Doctor. It's all so unbelievable! . . . Alan's always been such a gentle boy. He loves animals! Especially horses.

DYSART: Especially?

DORA: Yes. He even has a photograph of one up in his bedroom. A beautiful white one, looking over a gate. His father gave it to him a few years ago, off a calendar he'd printed — and he's never taken it down . . . And when he was seven or eight, I used to have to read him the same book over and over, all *about* a horse.

DYSART: Really?

DORA: Yes: it was called Prince, and no one could ride him.

(ALAN calls from his bed, not looking at his mother.)

ALAN *(excited, younger voice)*: Why not? . . . Why not? . . . Say it! In his voice!

DORA: He loved the idea of animals talking.

DYSART: Did he?

ALAN: *Say it! Say it! . . . Use his voice!*

DORA *("proud" voice)*: "Because I am faithful!"

(ALAN giggles.)

"My name is Prince, and I'm a Prince among horses! Only my young Master can ride me! Anyone else — I'll *throw off!*"

(ALAN giggles louder.)

And then I remember I used to tell him a funny thing about falling off horses. Did you know that when Christian cavalry first appeared in the New World, the pagans thought horse and rider was one person?

DYSART: Really?

ALAN *(sitting up, amazed)*: One person?

DORA: Actually they thought it must be a god.

ALAN: *A god!*

DORA: It was only when one rider fell off, they realized the truth.

DYSART: That's fascinating. I never heard that before. . . . Can you remember anything else like that you may have told him about horses?

DORA: Well, not really. They're in the Bible, of course. "He saith among the trumpets, Ha, ha."

DYSART: Ha, ha?

DORA: The Book of Job. Such a noble passage. *You* know — (*Quoting.*) "Hast thou given the horse strength?"

ALAN (*responding*): "Hast thou clothed his neck with thunder?"

DORA (*to* ALAN): "The glory of his nostrils is terrible!"

ALAN: "He swallows the ground with fierceness and rage!"

DORA: "He saith among the trumpets —"

ALAN (*trumpeting*): "Ha! Ha!"

DORA (*to* DYSART): Isn't that splendid?

DYSART: It certainly is.

ALAN (*trumpeting*): Ha! Ha!

DORA: And then, of course, we saw an awful lot of Westerns on the television. He couldn't have enough of those.

DYSART: But surely you don't have a set, do you? I understood Mr. Strang doesn't approve.

DORA (*conspiratorially*): He doesn't . . . I used to let him slip off in the afternoons to a friend next door.

DYSART (*smiling*): You mean without his father's knowledge?

DORA: What the eye does not see, the heart does not grieve over, does it? Anyway, Westerns are harmless enough, surely?

(FRANK *stands up and enters the square.* ALAN *lies back under the blanket.*)

(*To* FRANK.) Oh, hallo dear. This is Dr. Dysart.

FRANK (*shaking hands*): How d'you do?

DYSART: How d'you do?

DORA: I was just telling the Doctor, Alan's always adored horses.

FRANK (*tight*): We assumed he did.

DORA: You know he did, dear. Look how he liked that photograph you gave him.

FRANK (*startled*): What about it?

DORA: Nothing dear. Just that he pestered you to have it as soon as he saw it. Do you remember? (*To* DYSART.) We've always been a horsey family. At least my side of it has. My grandfather used to ride every morning on the downs behind Brighton, all dressed up in bowler hat and jodhpurs! He used to look splendid. Indulging in equitation, he called it.

(FRANK *moves away from them and sits wearily.*)

ALAN (*trying the word*): Equitation. . . .

DORA: I remember I told him how that came from *equus*, the Latin word for horse. Alan was fascinated by that word, I know. I suppose because he'd never come across one with two U's together before.

ALAN (*savouring it*): *Equus!*

DORA: I always wanted the boy to ride himself. He'd have so enjoyed it.

DYSART: But surely he did?

DORA: No.

DYSART: Never?

DORA: He didn't care for it. He was most definite about not wanting to.

DYSART: But he must have had to at the stables? I mean, it would be part of the job.

DORA: You'd have thought so, but no. He absolutely wouldn't, would he, dear?

FRANK (*dryly*): It seems he was perfectly happy raking out manure.

DYSART: Did he ever give a reason for this?

DORA: No. I must say we both thought it most peculiar, but he wouldn't discuss it. I mean, you'd have thought he'd be longing to get out in the air after being cooped up all week in that dreadful shop. Electrical and kitchenware! Isn't *that* an environment for a sensitive boy, Doctor? . . .

FRANK: Dear, have you offered the doctor a cup of tea?

DORA: Oh dear, no, I haven't . . . And you must be dying for one.

DYSART: That would be nice.

DORA: Of course it would. . . . Excuse me . . .

(*She goes out — but lingers on the circle, eavesdropping near the right door.* ALAN *stretches out under his blanket and sleeps.* FRANK *gets up.*)

FRANK: My wife has romantic ideas, if you receive my meaning.

DYSART: About her family?

FRANK: She thinks she married beneath her. I daresay she did. I don't understand these things myself.

DYSART: Mr. Strang, I'm fascinated by the fact that Alan wouldn't ride.

FRANK: Yes, well that's him. He's always been a weird lad, I have to be honest. Can you imagine spending your weekends like that — just cleaning out stalls — with all the things that he could have been doing in the way of Further Education?

DYSART: Except he's hardly a scholar.

FRANK: How do we know? He's never really tried. His mother indulged him. She doesn't care if he can hardly write his own name, and she a school teacher that was. Just as long as he's happy, she says . . .

(DORA *wrings her hands in anguish.*
FRANK *sits again.*)

DYSART: Would you say she was closer to him than you are?

FRANK: They've always been thick as thieves. I can't say I entirely approve — especially when I hear her whispering that Bible to him hour after hour, up there in his room.

DYSART: Your wife is religious?

FRANK: Some might say excessively so. Mind you that's her business. But when it comes to dosing it down the boy's throat — well, frankly, he's my son as well as hers. She doesn't see that. Of course, that's the funny thing about religious people. They always think their susceptibilities are more important than non-religious.

DYSART: And you're non-religious, I take it?

FRANK: I'm an atheist, and I don't mind admitting it. If you want my opinion, it's the Bible that's responsible for all this.

DYSART: Why?

FRANK: Well, look at it yourself. A boy spends night after night having this stuff read into him: an innocent man tortured to death — thorns driven into his head — nails into his hands — a spear jammed through his ribs. It can mark anyone for life, that kind of thing. I'm not joking. The boy was absolutely fascinated by all that. He was always mooning over religious pictures. I mean real kinky ones, if you receive my meaning. I had to put a stop to it once or twice! . . . (*Pause.*) Bloody religion — it's our only real problem in this house, but it's insuperable: I don't mind admitting it.

(*Unable to stand any more,* DORA *comes in again.*)

DORA (*pleasantly*): You must excuse my husband, Doctor. This one subject is something of an obsession with him, isn't it, dear? You must admit.

FRANK: Call it what you like. All that stuff to me is just bad sex.

DORA: And what has that got to do with Alan?

FRANK: Everything! . . . (*Seriously.*) Everything, Dora!

DORA: I don't understand. What are you saying?

(*He turns away from her.*)

DYSART (*calmingly*): Mr. Strang, exactly how informed do you judge your son to *be* about sex?

FRANK (*tight*): I don't know.

DYSART: You didn't actually instruct him yourself?

FRANK: Not in so many words, no.

DYSART: Did *you*, Mrs. Strang?

DORA: Well, I spoke a little, yes. I had to. I've been a teacher, Doctor, and I know what happens if you don't. They find out through magazines and dirty books.

DYSART: What sort of thing did you tell him? I'm sorry if this is embarrassing.

DORA: I told him the biological facts. But I also told him what I believed. That sex is not *just* a biological matter, but spiritual as well. That if God willed, he would fall in love one day. That his task was to prepare himself for the most important happening of his life. And after that, if he was lucky, he might come to know a higher love still . . . I simply . . . don't understand. . . . *Alan!* . . .

(*She breaks down in sobs.*
Her husband gets up and goes to her.)

FRANK (*embarrassed*): There now. There now, Dora. Come on!

DORA (*with sudden desperation*): All right — laugh! Laugh, as usual!

FRANK (*kindly*): No one's laughing, Dora.

(*She glares at him. He puts his arms round her shoulders.*)

No one's laughing, are they, Doctor?

(Tenderly, he leads his wife out of the square, and they resume their places on the bench.
Lights grow much dimmer.)

SCENE 8

A strange noise begins. ALAN *begins to murmur from his bed. He is having a bad nightmare, moving his hands and body as if frantically straining to tug something back.* DYSART *leaves the square as the boy's cries increase.*

ALAN: Ek! . . . Ek! . . . Ek! . . .

(Cries of Ek! on tape fill the theatre, from all around.
DYSART *reaches the foot of* ALAN's *bed as the boy gives a terrible cry —)*

EK!

(— and wakes up. The sounds snap off. ALAN *and the* DOCTOR *stare at each other. Then abruptly* DYSART *leaves the area and re-enters the square.)*

SCENE 9

Lights grow brighter.
DYSART *sits on his bench, left, and opens his file.* ALAN *gets out of bed, leaves his blanket, and comes in. He looks truculent.*

DYSART: Hallo. How are you this morning?

*(*ALAN *stares at him.)*

Come on: sit down.

*(*ALAN *crosses the stage and sits on the bench, opposite.)*

Sorry if I gave you a start last night. I was collecting some papers from my office, and I thought I'd look in on you. Do you dream often?
ALAN: Do *you?*
DYSART: It's my job to ask the questions. Yours to answer them.
ALAN: Says who?
DYSART: Says me. Do you dream often?
ALAN: Do *you?*
DYSART: Look — Alan.
ALAN: I'll answer if you answer. In turns.

(Pause.)

DYSART: Very well. Only we have to speak the truth.
ALAN *(mocking)*: Very well.
DYSART: So. Do you dream often?
ALAN: Yes. Do you?
DYSART: Yes. Do you have a special dream?
ALAN: No. Do you?
DYSART: Yes. What was your dream about last night?
ALAN: Can't remember. What's yours about?
DYSART: I said the truth.
ALAN: That is the truth. What's yours about? The special one.
DYSART: Carving up children.

*(*ALAN *smiles.)*

My turn!
ALAN: What?
DYSART: What is your first memory of a horse?
ALAN: What d'you mean?
DYSART: The first time one entered your life, in any way.
ALAN: Can't remember.
DYSART: Are you sure?
ALAN: Yes.
DYSART: You have no recollection of the first time you noticed a horse?
ALAN: I told you. Now it's my turn. Are you married?
DYSART *(controlling himself)*: I am.
ALAN: Is she a doctor too?
DYSART: It's my turn.
ALAN: Yes, well what?
DYSART: What is Ek?

(Pause.)

You shouted it out last night in your sleep. I thought you might like to talk about it.
ALAN *(singing)*:
          Double your pleasure,
          Double your fun!
DYSART: Come on, now. You can do better than that.
ALAN *(singing louder)*:
          With Doublemint, Doublemint
          Doublemint gum!
DYSART: All right. Good morning.
ALAN: What d'you mean?
DYSART: We're finished for today.
ALAN: But I've only had ten minutes.
DYSART: Too bad.

(He picks up a file and studies it.
ALAN *lingers.)*

Didn't you hear me? I said, Good morning.

ALAN: That's not fair!

DYSART: No?

ALAN *(savagely)*: The Government pays you twenty quid an hour to see me. I know. I heard downstairs.

DYSART: Well, go back there and hear some more.

ALAN: *That's not fair!*

(He springs up, clenching his fists in a sudden violent rage.)

You're a — you're a — You're a swiz! . . . Bloody swiz! . . . Fucking swiz!

DYSART: Do I have to call Nurse?

ALAN: She puts a finger on me, I'll bash her!

DYSART: She'll bash you much harder, I can assure you. Now go away.

(He reads his file. ALAN stays where he is, emptily clenching his hands. He turns away.
A pause.
A faint hum starts from the CHORUS.)

ALAN *(suddenly)*: On a beach. . . .

SCENE 10

He steps out of the square, upstage, and begins to walk round the circle. Warm light glows on it.

DYSART: What?

ALAN: Where I saw a horse, Swizzy.

(Lazily he kicks at the sand, and throws stones at the sea.)

DYSART: How old were you?

ALAN: How should I know? . . . Six.

DYSART: Well, go on. What were you doing there?

ALAN: Digging.

(He throws himself on the ground, downstage centre of the circle, and starts scuffing with his hands.)

DYSART: A sandcastle?

ALAN: Well, what else?

DYSART *(warningly)*: And?

ALAN: Suddenly I heard this noise. Coming up behind me.

(A young HORSEMAN issues in slow motion out of the tunnel. He carries a riding crop with which he is urging on his invisible horse, down the right side of the circle. The hum increases.)

DYSART: What noise?

ALAN: Hooves. Splashing.

DYSART: Splashing?

ALAN: The tide was out and he was galloping.

DYSART: Who was?

ALAN: This fellow. Like a college chap. He was on a big horse — urging him on. I thought he hadn't seen me. I called out: Hey!

(The HORSEMAN goes into natural time, charging fast round the downstage corner of the square straight at ALAN.)

and they just swerved in time!

HORSEMAN *(reining back)*: Whoa! . . . Whoa there! *Whoa!* . . . Sorry! I didn't see you! . . . Did I scare you?

ALAN: No!

HORSEMAN *(looking down on him)*: That's a terrific castle!

ALAN: What's his name?

HORSEMAN: Trojan. You can stroke him, if you like. He won't mind.

(Shyly ALAN stretches up on tip-toe, and pats an invisible shoulder.)

(Amused.) You can hardly reach down there. Would you like to come up?

(ALAN nods, eyes wide.)

All right. Come round this side. You always mount a horse from the left. I'll give you a lift. O.K.?

(ALAN goes round on the other side.)

Here we go, now. Just do nothing. Upsadaisy!

(ALAN sets his foot on the HORSEMAN's thigh, and is lifted by him up on to his shoulders.
The hum from the CHORUS becomes exultant. Then stops.)

All right?

(ALAN nods.)

Good. Now all you do is hold onto his mane.

(*He holds up the crop, and* ALAN *grips on to it.*)

Tight now. And grip with your knees. All right? All set? . . . Come on, then, Trojan. Let's go!

(*The* HORSEMAN *walks slowly upstage round the circle, with* ALAN's *legs tight round his neck.*)

DYSART: How was it? Was it wonderful?

(ALAN *rides in silence.*)

Can't you remember?
HORSEMAN: Do you want to go faster?
ALAN: Yes!
HORSEMAN: O.K. All you have to do is say "Come on, Trojan – bear me away!" . . . Say it, then!
ALAN: Bear me away!

(*The* HORSEMAN *starts to run with* ALAN *round the circle.*)

DYSART: You went fast?
ALAN: Yes!
DYSART: Weren't you frightened?
ALAN: No!
HORSEMAN: Come on now, Trojan! Bear us away! Hold on! Come on now! . . .

(*He runs faster.* ALAN *begins to laugh. Then suddenly, as they reach again the right downstage corner,* FRANK *and* DORA *stand up in alarm.*)

DORA: Alan!
FRANK: Alan!
DORA: Alan, stop!

(FRANK *runs round after them.* DORA *follows behind.*)

FRANK: Hey, you! *You!* . . .
HORSEMAN: Whoa, boy! . . .Whoa! . . .

(*He reins the horse round, and wheels to face the parents. This all goes fast.*)

FRANK: What do you imagine you are doing?
HORSEMAN (*ironic*): "Imagine"?
FRANK: What is my son doing up there?
HORSEMAN: Water-skiing!

(DORA *joins them, breathless.*)

DORA: Is he all right, Frank? . . . He's not hurt?
FRANK: Don't you think you should ask permission before doing a stupid thing like that?
HORSEMAN: What's stupid?
ALAN: It's lovely, dad!
DORA: Alan, come down here!
HORSEMAN: The boy's perfectly safe. Please don't be hysterical.
FRANK: Don't you be la-di-da with me, young man! Come down here, Alan. You heard what your mother said.
ALAN: No.
FRANK: Come down at once. Right this moment.
ALAN: No . . . NO!
FRANK (*in a fury*): I said – this moment!

(*He pulls* ALAN *from the* HORSEMAN's *shoulders. The boy shrieks, and falls to the ground.*)

HORSEMAN: Watch it!
DORA: Frank!

(*She runs to her son, and kneels. The* HORSEMAN *skitters.*)

HORSEMAN: Are you mad? D'you want to terrify the horse?
DORA: He's grazed his knee. Frank – the boy's hurt!
ALAN: I'm not! I'm *not*!
FRANK: What's your name?
HORSEMAN: Jesse James.
DORA: Frank, he's bleeding!
FRANK: I intend to report you to the police for endangering the lives of children.
HORSEMAN: Go right ahead!
DORA: Can you stand, dear?
ALAN: Oh, *stop* it! . . .
FRANK: You're a public menace, d'you know that? How dare you pick up children and put them on dangerous animals.
HORSEMAN: Dangerous?
FRANK: Of course dangerous. Look at his eyes. They're rolling.
HORSEMAN: So are yours!
FRANK: In my opinion that is a dangerous animal. In my considered opinion you are both dangers to the safety of this beach.
HORSEMAN: And in my opinion, you're a stupid fart!
DORA: Frank, leave it!
FRANK: What did you say?

DORA: It's not important, Frank — really!

FRANK: *What did you say?*

HORSEMAN: Oh bugger off! Sorry, chum! Come on, Trojan!

(*He urges his horse straight at them, then wheels it and gallops off round the right side of the circle and away up the tunnel, out of sight. The parents cry out, as they are covered with sand and water. Frank runs after him, and round the left side of the circle, with his wife following after.*)

ALAN: Splash, splash, splash! All three of us got covered with water! Dad got absolutely soaked!

FRANK (*shouting after the* HORSEMAN): Hooligan! Filthy hooligan!

ALAN: I wanted to laugh!

FRANK: Upper class riff-raff! That's all they are, people who go riding! That's what they *want* — trample on ordinary people!

DORA: Don't be absurd, Frank.

FRANK: It's why they do it. It's why they bloody do it!

DORA (*amused*): Look at you. You're covered!

FRANK: Not as much as you. There's sand all over your hair!

(*She starts to laugh.*)

(*Shouting.*) Hooligan! Bloody hooligan!

(*She starts to laugh more. He tries to brush the sand out of her hair.*)

What are you laughing at? It's not funny. It's not funny at all, Dora!

(*She goes off, right, still laughing.* ALAN *edges into the square, still on the ground.*)

It's just not funny! . . .

(FRANK *returns to his place on the beach, sulky. Abrupt silence.*)

ALAN: And that's all I remember.

DYSART: And a lot, too. Thank you. . . . You know, I've never been on a horse in my life.

ALAN (*not looking at him*): Nor me.

DYSART: You mean, after that?

ALAN: Yes.

DYSART: But you must have done at the stables?

ALAN: No.

DYSART: Never?

ALAN: No.

DYSART: How come?

ALAN: I didn't care to.

DYSART: Did it have anything to do with falling off like that, all those years ago?

ALAN (*tight*): I just didn't care to, that's all.

DYSART: Do you think of that scene often?

ALAN: I suppose.

DYSART: Why, do you think?

ALAN: 'Cos it's funny.

DYSART: Is that all?

ALAN: What else? My turn. . . . I told you a secret: now you tell me one.

DYSART: All right. I have patients who've got things to tell me, only they're ashamed to say them to my face. What do you think I do about that?

ALAN: What?

DYSART: I give them this little tape recorder.

(*He takes a small tape recorder and microphone from his pocket.*)

They go off to another room, and send me the tape through Nurse. They don't have to listen to it with me.

ALAN: That's stupid.

DYSART: All you do is press this button, and speak into this. It's very simple. Anyway, your time's up for today. I'll see you tomorrow.

ALAN (*getting up*): Maybe.

DYSART: Maybe?

ALAN: If I feel like it.

(*He is about to go out. Then suddenly he returns to* DYSART *and takes the machine from him.*)

It's stupid.

(*He leaves the square and goes back to his bed.*)

SCENE 11

DORA (*calling out*): Doctor!

(DORA *re-enters and comes straight on to the square from the right. She wears an overcoat, and is nervously carrying a shopping bag.*)

DYSART: That same evening, his mother appeared.

DORA: Hallo, Doctor.

DYSART: Mrs. Strang!

DORA: I've been shopping in the neighbour-hood. I thought I might just look in.

DYSART: Did you want to see Alan?

DORA (uncomfortably): No, no . . . Not just at the moment. Actually, it's more you I wanted to see.

DYSART: Yes?

DORA: You see, there's something Mr. Strang and I thought you ought to know. We dis-cussed it, and it might just be important.

DYSART: Well, come and sit down.

DORA: I can't stay more than a moment. I'm late as it is. Mr. Strang will be wanting his dinner.

DYSART: Ah. (Encouragingly.) So, what was it you wanted to tell me?

(She sits on the upstage bench.)

DORA: Well, do you remember that photo-graph I mentioned to you. The one Mr. Strang gave Alan to decorate his bedroom a few years ago?

DYSART: Yes. A horse looking over a gate, wasn't it?

DORA: That's right. Well, actually, it took the place of another kind of picture alto-gether.

DYSART: What kind?

DORA: It was a reproduction of Our Lord on his way to Calvary. Alan found it in Reeds Art Shop, and fell absolutely in love with it. He insisted on buying it with his pocket money, and hanging it at the foot of his bed where he could see it last thing at night. My husband was very displeased.

DYSART: Because it was religious?

DORA: In all fairness I must admit it was a little extreme. The Christ was loaded down with chains, and the centurions were really laying on the stripes. It certainly would not have been my choice, but I don't believe in interfering too much with children, so I said nothing.

DYSART: But Mr. Strang did?

DORA: He stood it for a while, but one day we had one of our tiffs about religion, and he went straight upstairs, tore it off the boy's wall and threw it in the dustbin. Alan went quite hysterical. He cried for days without stopping — and he was not a crier, you know.

DYSART: But he recovered when he was given the photograph of the horse in its place?

DORA: He certainly seemed to. At least, he

hung it in exactly the same position, and we had no more of that awful weeping.

DYSART: Thank you, Mrs. Strang. That is interesting . . . Exactly how long ago was that? Can you remember?

DORA: It must be five years ago, Doctor. Alan would have been about twelve. How is he, by the way?

DYSART: Bearing up.

(She rises.)

DORA: Please give him my love.

DYSART: You can see him any time you want, you know.

DORA: Perhaps if I could come one after-noon without Mr. Strang. He and Alan don't exactly get on at the moment, as you can imagine.

DYSART: Whatever you decide, Mrs. Strang . . . Oh, one thing.

DORA: Yes?

DYSART: Could you describe that photo-graph of the horse in a little more detail for me? I presume it's still in his bedroom?

DORA: Oh, yes. It's a most remarkable pic-ture, really. You very rarely see a horse taken from that angle — absolutely head on. That's what makes it so interesting.

DYSART: Why? What does it look like?

DORA: Well, it's most extraordinary. It comes out all eyes.

DYSART: Staring straight at you?

DORA: Yes, that's right . . .

(An uncomfortable pause.)

I'll come and see him one day very soon, Doctor. Goodbye.

(She leaves, and resumes her place by her husband.)

DYSART (to audience): It was then — that moment — I felt real alarm. What was it? The shadow of a giant head across my desk? . . . At any rate, the feeling got worse with the stable-owner's visit.

SCENE 12

DALTON comes in to the square: heavy-set: mid-fifties.

DALTON: Dr. Dysart?

DYSART: Mr. Dalton. It's very good of you to come.

DALTON: It is, actually. In my opinion the boy should be in prison. Not in a hospital at the tax-payers' expense.

DYSART: Please sit down.

(DALTON *sits*.)

This must have been a terrible experience for you.

DALTON: Terrible? I don't think I'll ever get over it. Jill's had a nervous breakdown.

DYSART: Jill?

DALTON: The girl who worked for me. Of course, she feels responsible in a way. Being the one who introduced him in the first place.

DYSART: He was introduced to the stable by a girl?

DALTON: Jill Mason, He met her somewhere, and asked for a job. She told him to come and see me. I wish to Christ she never had.

DYSART: But when he first appeared he didn't seem in any way peculiar?

DALTON: No, he was bloody good. He'd spend hours with the horses cleaning and grooming them, way over the call of duty. I thought he was a real find.

DYSART: Apparently, during the whole time he worked for you, he never actually rode.

DALTON: That's true.

DYSART: Wasn't that peculiar?

DALTON: Very . . . *If* he didn't.

DYSART: What do you mean?

(DALTON *rises*.)

DALTON: Because on and off, that whole year, I had the feeling the horses were being taken out at night.

DYSART: At night?

DALTON: There were just odd things I noticed. I mean too often one or other of them would be sweaty first thing in the morning, when it wasn't sick. Very sweaty, too. And its stall wouldn't be near as mucky as it should be if it had been in all night. I never paid it much mind at the time. It was only when I realised I'd been hiring a loony, I came to wonder if he hadn't been riding all the time, behind our backs.

DYSART: But wouldn't you have noticed if things had been disturbed?

DALTON: Nothing ever was. Still, he's a neat worker. That wouldn't prove anything.

DYSART: Aren't the stables locked at night?

DALTON: Yes.

DYSART: And someone sleeps on the premises?

DALTON: Me and my son.

DYSART: Two people?

DALTON: I'm sorry, Doctor. It's obviously just my fancy. I tell you, this thing has shaken me so bad, I'm liable to believe anything. If there's nothing else, I'll be going.

DYSART: Look: even if you were right, why should anyone do that? Why would any boy prefer to ride by himself at night, when he could go off with others during the day.

DALTON: Are you asking me? He's a loony, isn't he?

(DALTON *leaves the square and sits again in his place*. DYSART *watches him go*.)

ALAN: It was *sexy*.

DYSART: His tape arrived that evening.

SCENE 13

ALAN *is sitting on his bed holding the tape-recorder*. NURSE *approaches briskly, takes the machine from him — gives it to* DYSART *in the square — and leaves again, resuming her seat*. DYSART *switches on the tape*.

ALAN: That's what you want to know, isn't it? All right: it was. I'm talking about the beach. That time when I was a kid. What I told you about. . . .

(*Pause. He is in great emotional difficulty.*
DYSART *sits on the left bench listening, file in hand.* ALAN *rises and stands directly behind him, but on the circle, as if recording the ensuing speech. He never, of course, looks directly at the* DOCTOR.)

I was pushed forward on the horse. There was sweat on my legs from his neck. The fellow held me tight, and let me turn the horse which way I wanted. All that power going any way you wanted . . . His sides were all warm, and the smell . . . Then suddenly I was on the ground, where Dad pulled me. I could have bashed him . . .

(*Pause.*)

Something else. When the horse first appeared, I looked up into his mouth. It was huge. There was this chain in it. The fellow pulled it, and cream dripped out. I said "Does it hurt?" And he said — the horse said — said —

(*He stops, in anguish.* DYSART *makes a note in his file.*)

(*Desperately.*) It was always the same, after that. Every time I heard one clop by, I had to run and see. Up a country lane or anywhere. They sort of pulled me. I couldn't take my eyes off them. Just to watch their skins. The way their necks twist, and sweat shines in the folds . . . (*Pause.*) I can't remember when it started. Mum reading to me about Prince who no one could ride, except one boy. Or the white horse in Revelations. "He that sat upon him was called Faithful and True. His eyes were as flames of fire, and he had a name written that no man knew but himself" . . . Words like reins. Stirrup. Flanks . . . "Dashing his spurs against his charger's flanks!" . . . Even the words made me feel — . . . Years, I never told anyone. Mum wouldn't understand. She likes "Equitation." Bowler hats and jodhpurs! "My grandfather dressed for the horse," she says. What does that mean? The horse isn't dressed. It's the most naked thing you ever saw! More than a dog or a cat or anything. Even the most broken down old nag has got its *life*! To put a bowler on it is *filthy*! . . . Putting them through their paces! Bloody gymkhanas! . . . No one understands! . . . Except cowboys. They do. I wish I was a cowboy. They're free. They just swing up and then it's miles of grass . . . I bet all cowboys are *orphans*! . . . I bet they are!

NURSE: Mr. Strang to see you, Doctor.

DYSART (*in surprise*): Mr. Strang? Show him up, please.

ALAN: No one ever says to cowboys "Receive my meaning"! They wouldn't dare. Or "God" all the time. (*Mimicking his mother.*) "God sees you, Alan. God's got eyes everywhere — "

(*He stops abruptly.*)

I'm not doing any more! . . . I hate this! . . . You can whistle for anymore. I've had it!

(*He returns angrily to his bed, throwing the blanket over him.* DYSART *switches off the tape.*)

SCENE 14

FRANK STRANG *comes into the square, his hat in his hand. He is nervous and embarrassed.*

DYSART (*welcoming*): Hallo, Mr. Strang.

FRANK: I was passing. I hope it's not too late.

DYSART: Of course not. I'm delighted to see you.

FRANK: My wife doesn't know I'm here. I'd be grateful to you if you didn't enlighten her, if you receive my meaning.

DYSART: Everything that happens in this room is confidential, Mr. Strang.

FRANK: I hope so . . . I hope so . . .

DYSART (*gently*): Do you have something to tell me?

FRANK: As a matter of fact I have. Yes.

DYSART: Your wife told me about the photograph.

FRANK: I know, it's not that! It's *about* that, but it's — worse. . . . I wanted to tell you the other night, but I couldn't in front of Dora. Maybe I should have. It might show her where all that stuff leads to, she drills into the boy behind my back.

DYSART: What kind of thing is it?

FRANK: Something I witnessed.

DYSART: Where?

FRANK: At home. About eighteen months ago.

DYSART: Go on.

FRANK: It was late. I'd gone upstairs to fetch something. The boy had been in bed hours, or so I thought.

DYSART: Go on.

FRANK: As I came along the passage I saw the door of his bedroom was ajar. I'm sure he didn't know it was. From inside I heard the sound of this chanting.

DYSART: Chanting?

FRANK: Like the Bible. One of those lists his mother's always reading to him.

DYSART: What kind of list?

FRANK: Those Begats. So-and-so begat, you know. Genealogy.

DYSART: Can you remember what Alan's list sounded like?

FRANK: Well, the *sort* of thing. I stood there absolutely astonished. The first word I heard was . . .

ALAN (*rising and chanting*): Prince!

DYSART: Prince?

FRANK: Prince begat Prance. That sort of nonsense.

(ALAN *moves slowly to the center of the circle, downstage.*)

ALAN: And Prance begat Prankus! And Prankus begat Flankus!

FRANK: I looked through the door, and he was standing in the moonlight in his pyjamas, right in front of that big photograph.

DYSART: The horse with the huge eyes?

FRANK: Right.

ALAN: Flankus begat Spankus. And Spankus begat Spunkus the Great, who lived three score years!

FRANK: It was all like that. I can't remember the exact names, of course. Then suddenly he knelt down.

DYSART: In front of the photograph?

FRANK: Yes. Right there at the foot of his bed.

ALAN (*kneeling*): And Legwus begat Neckwus. And Neckwus begat Fleckwus, the King of Spit. And Fleckwus spoke out of his chinkle-chankle!

(*He bows himself to the ground.*)

DYSART: What?

FRANK: I'm sure that was the word. I've never forgotten it. Chinkle-chankle.

(ALAN *raises his head and extends his hands up in glory.*)

ALAN: And he said "Behold – I give you Equus, my only begotten son!"

DYSART: Equus?

FRANK: Yes. No doubt of that. He repeated that word several times. "Equus my only begotten son."

ALAN (*reverently*): Ek . . . wus!

DYSART (*suddenly understanding: almost "aside"*): Ek . . . Ek . . .

FRANK (*embarrassed*): And then . . .

DYSART: Yes: what?

FRANK: He took a piece of string out of his pocket. Made up into a noose. And put it in his mouth.

(ALAN *bridles himself with invisible string, and pulls it back.*)

And then with his other hand he picked up a coat hanger. A wooden coat hanger, and – and –

DYSART: Began to beat himself?

(ALAN, *in mime, begins to thrash himself, increasing the strokes in speed and viciousness.*)
(*Pause.*)

FRANK: You see why I couldn't tell his mother. . . . Religion. Religion's at the bottom of all this!

DYSART: What did you do?

FRANK: Nothing. I coughed – and went back downstairs.

(*The boy starts guiltily – tears the string from his mouth – and scrambles back to bed.*)

DYSART: Did you ever speak to him about it later? Even obliquely?

FRANK (*unhappily*): I can't speak of things like that, Doctor. It's not in my nature.

DYSART (*kindly*): No. I see that.

FRANK: But I thought you ought to know. So I came.

DYSART (*warmly*): Yes. I'm very grateful to you. Thank you.

(*Pause.*)

FRANK: Well, that's it. . . .

DYSART: Is there anything else?

FRANK (*even more embarrassed*): There is actually. One thing.

DYSART: What's that?

FRANK: On the night that he did it – that awful thing in the stable –

DYSART: Yes?

FRANK: That very night, he was out with a girl.

DYSART: How d'you know that?

FRANK: I just know.

DYSART (*puzzled*): Did he tell you?

FRANK: I can't say any more.

DYSART: I don't quite understand.

FRANK: Everything said in here is confidential, you said.

DYSART: Absolutely.

FRANK: Then ask him. Ask him about taking a girl out, that very night he did it. . . . (*Abruptly.*) Goodbye, Doctor.

(*He goes.* DYSART *looks after him.* FRANK *resumes his seat.*)

Scene 15

ALAN *gets up and enters the square.*

DYSART: Alan! Come in. Sit down. (*Pleasantly.*) What did you do last night?

ALAN: Watched telly.

DYSART: Any good?

ALAN: All right.

DYSART: Thanks for the tape. It was excellent.

ALAN: I'm not making any more.

DYSART: One thing I didn't quite understand. You began to say something about the horse on the beach talking to you.

ALAN: That's stupid. Horses don't talk.

DYSART: So I believe.

ALAN: I don't know what you mean.

DYSART: Never mind. Tell me something else. Who introduced you to the stable to begin with?

(*Pause.*)

ALAN: Someone I met.

DYSART: Where?

ALAN: Bryson's.

DYSART: The shop where you worked?

ALAN: Yes.

DYSART: That's a funny place for you to be. Whose idea was that?

ALAN: Dad.

DYSART: I'd have thought he'd have wanted you to work with him.

ALAN: I haven't the aptitude. And printing's a failing trade. If you receive my meaning.

DYSART (*amused*): I see . . . What did your mother think?

ALAN: Shops are common.

DYSART: And you?

ALAN: I loved it.

DYSART: Really?

ALAN (*sarcastic*): Why not? You get to spend every minute with electrical things. It's fun.

(NURSE, DALTON *and the actors playing horses call out to him as* CUSTOMERS, *seated where they are. Their voices are aggressive and demanding. There is a constant background mumbling, made up of trade names, out of which can clearly be distinguished the italicized words, which are shouted out.*)

CUSTOMER: *Philco!*

ALAN (*to* DYSART): Of course it might just drive you off your chump.

CUSTOMER: I want to buy a hot-plate. I'm told the *Philco* is a good make!

ALAN: I think it is, madam.

CUSTOMER: Remington ladies' shavers?

ALAN: I'm not sure, madam.

CUSTOMER: *Robex* tableware?

CUSTOMER: *Croydex?*

CUSTOMER: *Volex?*

CUSTOMER: *Pifco* automatic toothbrushes?

ALAN: I'll find out, sir.

CUSTOMER: *Beautiflor!*

CUSTOMER: *Windowlene!*

CUSTOMER: I want a *Philco* transistor radio!

CUSTOMER: This isn't a *Remington!* I wanted a *Remington!*

ALAN: Sorry.

CUSTOMER: Are you a dealer for *Hoover?*

ALAN: Sorry.

CUSTOMER: I wanted the heat retaining *Pifco!*

ALAN: *Sorry!*

(JILL *comes into the square; a girl in her early twenties, pretty and middle class. She wears a sweater and jeans. The mumbling stops.*)

JILL: Hallo.

ALAN: Hallo.

JILL: Have you any blades for a clipping machine?

ALAN: Clipping?

JILL: To clip horses.

(*Pause. He stares at her, open-mouthed.*)

What's the matter?

ALAN: You work at Dalton's stables. I've seen you.

(*During the following, he mimes putting away a pile of boxes on a shelf in the shop.*)

JILL: I've seen you too, haven't I? You're the boy who's always staring into the yard around lunch-time.

ALAN: Me?

JILL: You're there most days.

ALAN: Not me.

JILL (*amused*): Of course it's you. Mr. Dalton was only saying the other day: "Who's that boy keeps staring in at the door?" Are you looking for a job or something?

ALAN (*eagerly*): Is there one?

JILL: I don't know.

ALAN: I can only do weekends.

JILL: That's when most people ride. We can always use extra hands. It'd mainly be mucking out.

ALAN: I don't mind.

JILL: Can you ride?

ALAN: No . . . No . . . I don't want to.

(*She looks at him curiously.*)

Please.

JILL: Come up on Saturday. I'll introduce you to Mr. Dalton.

(*She leaves the square.*)

DYSART: When was this? About a year ago?
ALAN: I suppose.
DYSART: And she did?
ALAN: Yes.

(*Briskly he moves the three benches to form three stalls in the stable.*)

SCENE 16

Rich light falls on the square.
An exultant humming from the CHORUS.
Tramping is heard. Three actors playing horses rise from their places. Together they unhook three horse masks from the ladders to left and right, put them on with rigid timing, and walk with swaying horse-motion into the square. Their metal hooves stamp on the wood. Their masks turn and toss high above their heads — as they will do sporadically throughout all horse scenes — making the steel gleam in the light.
For a moment they seem to converge on the boy as he stands in the middle of the stable, but then they swiftly turn and take up positions as if tethered by the head, with their invisible rumps towards him, one by each bench. ALAN *is sunk in this glowing world of horses. Lost in wonder, he starts almost involuntarily to kneel on the floor in reverence — but is sharply interrupted by the cheery voice of* DALTON, *coming into the stable, followed by* JILL. *The boy straightens up guiltily.*

DALTON: First thing to learn is drill. Learn it and keep to it. I want this place neat, dry and clean at all times. After you've mucked out, Jill will show you some grooming. What we call strapping a horse.
JILL: I think Trooper's got a stone.
DALTON: Yes? Let's see.

(*He crosses to the horse by the left bench, who is balancing one hoof on its tip. He picks up the hoof.*)

You're right. (*To* ALAN.) See this? This V here. It's what's called a frog. Sort of shock-absorber. Once you pierce that, it take ages to

heal — so you want to watch for it. You clean it out with this. What we call a hoof-pick.

(*He takes from his pocket an invisible pick.*)

Mind how you go with it. It's very sharp. Use it like this.

(*He quickly takes the stone out.*)

See?

(ALAN *nods, fascinated.*)

You'll soon get the hang of it. Jill will look after you. What she doesn't know about stables, isn't worth knowing.
JILL (*pleased*): Oh yes, I'm sure!
DALTON (*handing* ALAN *the pick*): Careful how you go with that. The main rule is: anything you don't know — ask. Never pretend you know something when you don't. (*Smiling.*) Actually, the main rule is: enjoy yourself. All right?
ALAN: Yes, sir.
DALTON: Good lad. See you later.

(*He nods to them cheerfully, and leaves the square.* ALAN *clearly puts the invisible hoof-pick on the rail, downstage left.*)

JILL: All right, let's start on some grooming. Why don't we begin with him? He looks as if he needs it.

(*They approach* NUGGET, *who is standing to the right. She pats him.* ALAN *sits and watches her.*)

This is Nugget. He's my favorite. He's as gentle as a baby, aren't you? But terribly fast if you want him to be.

(*During the following, she mimes both the actions and the objects, which she picks up from the right bench.*)

Now this is the dandy, and we start with that. Then you move on to the body brush. This is the most important, and you use it with this curry-comb. Now you always groom the same way: from the ears downward. Don't be afraid to do it hard. The harder you do it, the more the horse loves it. Push it right through the coat: like this.

(*The boy watches in fascination as she brushes the invisible body of* NUGGET, *scraping the dirt and hair off on to the invisible curry-comb. Now and then the horse mask moves very slightly in pleasure.*)

Down towards the tail and right through the coat. See how he loves it? I'm giving you a lovely massage, boy, aren't I? . . . You try.

(*She hands him the brush. Gingerly he rises and approaches* NUGGET. *Embarrassed and excited, he copies her movements, inexpertly.*)

Keep it nice and easy. Never rush. Down towards the tail and right through the coat. That's it. Again. Down towards the tail and right through the coat. . . . Very good. Now you keep that up for fifteen minutes and then do old Trooper. Will you?

(ALAN *nods.*)

You've got a feel for it. I can tell. It's going to be nice teaching you. See you later.

(*She leaves the square and resumes her place.* ALAN *is left alone with the horses.*
They all stamp. He approaches NUGGET *again, and touches the horse's shoulder. The mask turns sharply in his direction. The boy pauses, then moves his hand gently over the outline of the neck and back. The mask is re-assured. It stares ahead unmoving. Then* ALAN *lifts his palm to his face and smells it deeply, closing his eyes.*
DYSART *rises from his bench, and begins to walk slowly upstage round the circle.*)

DYSART: Was that good? Touching them.

(ALAN *gives a faint groan.*)

ALAN: Mmm.
DYSART: It must have been marvelous, being near them at last . . . Stroking them . . . Making them fresh and glossy . . . Tell me . . .

(*Silence.* ALAN *begins to brush* NUGGET.)

How about the girl? Did you like her?
ALAN (*tight*): All right.
DYSART: Just all right?

(ALAN *changes his position, moving round* NUGGET's *rump so that his back is to the audience. He brushes harder.* DYSART *comes downstage around the circle, and finally back to his bench.*)

Was she friendly?

ALAN: Yes.
DYSART: Or stand-offish?
ALAN: Yes.
DYSART: Well which?
ALAN: What?
DYSART: Which was she?

(ALAN *brushes harder.*)

Did you take her out? Come on now: tell me. Did you have a date with her?
ALAN: What?
DYSART (*sitting*): Tell me if you did.

(*The boy suddenly explodes in one of his rages.*)

ALAN (*yelling*): TELL ME!

(*All the masks toss at the noise.*)

DYSART: What?
ALAN: *Tell me, tell me, tell me, tell me!*

(ALAN *storms out of the square, and down-stage to where* DYSART *sits. He is raging. During the ensuing, the horses leave by all three openings.*)

On and on, sitting there! Nosey Parker! That's all you are! Bloody Nosey Parker! Just like Dad. On and on and bloody on! Tell me, tell me, tell me . . . Answer this. Answer that. Never stop! —

(*He marches round the circle and back into the square.* DYSART *rises and enters it from the other side.*)

SCENE 17

Lights brighten.

DYSART: I'm sorry.

(ALAN *slams about what is now the office again, replacing the benches to their usual position.*)

ALAN: All right, it's my turn now. You tell me! Answer me!
DYSART: We're not playing that game now.
ALAN: We're playing what I say.
DYSART: All right. What do you want to know?

(*He sits.*)

ALAN: Do *you* have dates?
DYSART: I told you. I'm married.

(ALAN *approaches him, very hostile.*)

ALAN: I know. Her name's Margaret. She's a dentist! You see, I found out! What made you go with her? Did you use to bite her hands when she did you in the chair?

(*The boy sits next to him, close.*)

DYSART: That's not very funny.
ALAN: Do you have girls behind her back?
DYSART: No.
ALAN: Then what? Do you fuck her?
DYSART: That's enough now.

(*He rises and moves away.*)

ALAN: Come on, tell me! Tell me, tell me!
DYSART: I said that's enough now.

(ALAN *rises too and walks around him.*)

I bet you don't. I bet you never touch her. Come on, tell me. You've got no kids, have you? Is that because you don't fuck?
DYSART (*sharp*): Go to your room. Go on: quick march.

(*Pause.* ALAN *moves away from him, insolently takes up a packet of* DYSART's *cigarettes from the bench, and extracts one.*)

Give me those cigarettes.

(*The boy puts one in his mouth.*)

(*Exploding.*) Alan, *give them to me!*

(*Reluctantly* ALAN *shoves the cigarette back in the packet, turns and hands it to him.*)

Now go!

(ALAN *bolts out of the square, and back to his bed.* DYSART, *unnerved, addresses the audience.*)

Brilliant! Absolutely brilliant! The boy's on the run, so he gets defensive. What am *I*, then? . . . Wicked little bastard — he knew exactly what questions to try. He'd actually marched himself round the hospital, making enquiries about my wife. Wicked and — of course, perceptive. Ever since I made that crack about carving up children, he's been aware of me in an absolutely specific way. Of course, there's nothing novel in that. Advanced neurotics can

be dazzling at that game. They aim unswervingly at your area of maximum vulnerability. . . . Which I suppose is as good a way as any of describing Margaret.

(*He sits.* HESTHER *enters the square. Light grows warmer.*)

SCENE 18

HESTHER: Now stop it.
DYSART: Do I embarrass you?
HESTHER: I suspect you're about to.

(*Pause.*)

DYSART: My wife doesn't understand me, Your Honour.
HESTHER: Do you understand her?
DYSART: No. Obviously I never did.
HESTHER: I'm sorry. I've never liked to ask but I've always imagined you weren't exactly compatible.

(*She moves to sit opposite.*)

DYSART: We were. It actually worked for a bit. I mean for both of us. We worked for each other, she actually for me through a kind of briskness. A clear, red-headed, inaccessible briskness which kept me keyed up for months. Mind you, if you're kinky for Northern Hygienic, as I am, you can't find anything much more compelling than a Scottish Lady Dentist.
HESTHER: It's *you* who are wicked, you know!
DYSART: Not at all: She got exactly the same from me. Antiseptic proficiency. I was like that in those days. We suited each other admirably. I see us in our wedding photo: Doctor and Doctor Mac Brisk. We were brisk in our wooing, brisk in our wedding, brisk in our disappointment. We turned from each other briskly into our separate surgeries: and now there's damn all.
HESTHER: You have no children, have you?
DYSART: No, we didn't go in for them. Instead, she sits beside our salmon-pink, glazed brick fireplace, and knits things for orphans in a home she helps with. And I sit opposite, turning the pages of art books on Ancient Greece. Occasionally, I still trail a faint scent of my enthusiasm across her path. I pass her a picture of the sacred acrobats of Crete leaping through the horns of running bulls — and she'll say: "Och, Martin, what an *absurred* thing to be doing! The Highland Games, now there's

norrmal sport!" Or she'll observe, just after
I've told her a story from the Iliad: "You
know, when you come to think of it, Agamemnon and that lot were nothing but a bunch of
ruffians from the Gorbals, only with fancy
names!" (*He rises.*) You get the picture. She's
turned into a Shrink. The familiar domestic
monster. Margaret Dysart: the Shrink's Shrink.

HESTHER: That's cruel, Martin.

DYSART: Yes. Do you know what it's like for
two people to live in the same house as if they
were in different parts of the world? Mentally,
she's always in some drizzly kirk of her own
inheriting: and I'm in some Doric temple —
clouds tearing through pillars — eagles bearing
prophecies out of the sky. She finds all that
repulsive. All my wife has ever taken from the
Mediterranean — from that whole vast intuitive
culture — are four bottles of Chianti to make
into lamps, and two china condiment donkeys
labelled Sally and Peppy.

(*Pause.*)

(*More intimately.*) I wish there was one person in my life I could show. One instinctive,
absolutely unbrisk person I could take to
Greece, and stand in front of certain shrines
and sacred streams and say "Look! Life is only
comprehensible through a thousand local
Gods." And not just the old dead ones with
names like Zeus — no, but living Geniuses of
Place and Person! And not just Greece but
modern England! Spirits of certain trees, certain curves of brick wall, certain chip shops, if
you like, and slate roofs — just as of certain
frowns in people and slouches . . . I'd say to
them — "Worship as many as you can see —
and more will appear!" . . . If I had a son, I
bet you he'd come out exactly like his mother.
Utterly worshipless. Would you like a drink?

HESTHER: No, thanks. Actually, I've got to
be going. As usual . . .

DYSART: Really?

HESTHER: Really. I've got an Everest of
papers to get through before bed.

DYSART: You never stop, do you?

HESTHER: Do you?

DYSART: This boy, with his stare. He's trying
to save himself through me.

HESTHER: I'd say so.

DYSART: What am I trying to do to him?

HESTHER: Restore him, surely?

DYSART: To what?

HESTHER: A normal life.

DYSART: Normal?

HESTHER: It still means something.

DYSART: Does it?

HESTHER: Of course.

DYSART: You mean a normal boy has one
head: a normal head has two ears?

HESTHER: You know I don't.

DYSART: Then what else?

HESTHER (*lightly*): Oh, stop it.

DYSART: No, what? You tell me.

HESTHER (*rising: smiling*): I won't be put
on the stand like this, Martin. You're really
disgraceful! . . . (*Pause.*) You know what I
mean by a normal smile in a child's eyes, and
one that isn't — even if I can't exactly define
it. Don't you?

DYSART: Yes.

HESTHER: Then we have a duty to that,
surely? Both of us.

DYSART: Touché. . . . I'll talk to you.

HESTHER: Dismissed?

DYSART: You said you had to go.

HESTHER: I do. . . . (*She kisses his cheek.*)
Thank you for what you're doing. . . . You're
going through a rotten patch at the moment.
I'm sorry . . . I suppose one of the few things
one can do is simply hold on to priorities.

DYSART: Like what?

HESTHER: Oh — children before grown-ups.
Things like that.

(*He contemplates her.*)

DYSART: You're really quite splendid.

HESTHER: Famous for it. Goodnight.

(*She leaves him.*)

DYSART (*to himself — or to the audience*):
Normal! . . . Normal!

SCENE 19

ALAN *rises and enters the square. He is
subdued.*

DYSART: Good afternoon.

ALAN: Afternoon.

DYSART: I'm sorry about our row yesterday.

ALAN: It was stupid.

DYSART: It was.

ALAN: What I said, I mean.

DYSART: How are you sleeping?

(ALAN *shrugs.*)

You're not feeling well, are you?

ALAN: All right.

DYSART: Would you like to play a game? It could make you feel better.

ALAN: What kind?

DYSART: It's called *Blink*. You have to fix your eyes on something: say, that little stain over there on the wall — and I tap this pen on the desk. The first time I tap it, you close your eyes. The next time you open them. And so on. Close, open, close, open, till I say Stop.

ALAN: How can that make you feel better?

DYSART: It relaxes you. You'll feel as though you're talking to me in your sleep.

ALAN: It's stupid.

DYSART: You don't have to do it, if you don't want to.

ALAN: I didn't say I didn't want to.

DYSART: Well?

ALAN: I don't mind.

DYSART: Good. Sit down and start watching that stain. Put your hands by your sides, and open the fingers wide.

(*He opens the left bench and* ALAN *sits on the end of it.*)

The thing is to feel comfortable, and relax absolutely. . . . Are you looking at the stain?

ALAN: Yes.

DYSART: Right. Now try and keep your mind as blank as possible.

ALAN: That's not difficult.

DYSART: Ssh. Stop talking . . . On the first tap, close. On the second, open. Are you ready?

(ALAN *nods.* DYSART *taps his pen on the wooden rail.* ALAN *shuts his eyes.* DYSART *taps again.* ALAN *opens them. The taps are evenly spaced. After four of them the sound cuts out, and is replaced by a louder, metallic sound, on tape.* DYSART *talks through this, to the audience — the light changes to cold — while the boy sits in front of him, staring at the wall, opening and shutting his eyes.*)

The Normal is the good smile in a child's eyes — all right. It is also the dead stare in a million adults. It both sustains and kills — like a God. It is the Ordinary made beautiful: it is also the Average made lethal. The Normal is the indispensable, murderous God of Health, and I am his Priest. My tools are very delicate. My compassion is honest. I have honestly assisted children in this room. I have talked away terrors and relieved many agonies. But also — beyond question — I have cut from them parts of individuality repugnant to this God, in both his aspects. Parts sacred to rarer and more wonderful Gods. And at what length . . . Sacrifices to Zeus took at the most surely, sixty seconds each. Sacrifices to the Normal can take as long as sixty months.

(*The natural sound of the pencil resumes. Light changes back.*)

(*To* ALAN.) Now your eyes are feeling heavy. You want to sleep, don't you? You want a long, deep sleep. Have it. Your head is heavy. Very heavy. Your shoulders are heavy. Sleep.

(*The pencil stops.* ALAN's *eyes remain shut and his head has sunk on his chest.*)

Can you hear me?

ALAN: Mmm.

DYSART: You can speak normally. Say Yes, if you can.

ALAN: Yes.

DYSART: Good boy. Now raise your head, and open your eyes.

(*He does so.*)

Now, Alan, you're going to answer questions I'm going to ask you. Do you understand?

ALAN: Yes.

DYSART: And when you wake up, you are going to remember everything you tell me. All right?

ALAN: Yes.

DYSART: Good. Now I want you to think back in time. You are on that beach you told me about. The tide has gone out, and you're making sandcastles. Above you, staring down at you, is that great horse's head, and the cream dropping from it. Can you see that?

ALAN: Yes.

DYSART: You ask him a question. "Does the chain hurt?"

ALAN: Yes.

DYSART: Do you ask him aloud?

ALAN: No.

DYSART: And what does the horse say back?

ALAN: "Yes."

DYSART: Then what do you say?

ALAN: "I'll take it out for you."

DYSART: And he says?

ALAN: "It never comes out. They have me in chains."
DYSART: Like Jesus?
ALAN: Yes!
DYSART: Only his name isn't Jesus, is it?
ALAN: No.
DYSART: What is it?
ALAN: No one knows but him and me.
DYSART: You can tell me, Alan. Name him.
ALAN: Equus.
DYSART: Thank you. Does he live in all horses or just some?
ALAN: All.
DYSART: Good boy. Now: you leave the beach. You're in your bedroom at home. You're twelve years old. You're in front of the picture. You're looking at Equus from the foot of your bed. Would you like to kneel down?
ALAN: Yes.
DYSART (encouragingly): Go on, then.

(ALAN kneels.)

Now tell me. Why is Equus in chains?
ALAN: For the sins of the world.
DYSART: What does he say to you?
ALAN: "I see you." "I will save you."
DYSART: How?
ALAN: "Bear you away. Two shall be one."
DYSART: Horse and rider shall be one beast?
ALAN: One person!
DYSART: Go on.
ALAN: "And my chinkle-chankle shall be in thy hand."
DYSART: Chinkle-chankle? That's his mouth chain?
ALAN: Yes.
DYSART: Good. You can get up . . . Come on.

(ALAN rises.)

Now: think of the stable. What is the stable? His Temple? His Holy of Holies?
ALAN: Yes.
DYSART: Where you wash him? Where you tend him, and brush him with many brushes?
ALAN: Yes.
DYSART: And there he spoke to you, didn't he? He looked at you with his gentle eyes, and spake unto you?
ALAN: Yes.
DYSART: What did he say? "Ride me? Mount me, and ride me forth at night?"
ALAN: Yes.

DYSART: And you obeyed?
ALAN: Yes.
DYSART: How did you learn? By watching others?
ALAN: Yes.
DYSART: It must have been difficult. You bounced about?
ALAN: Yes.
DYSART: But he showed you, didn't he? Equus showed you the way.
ALAN: No!
DYSART: He didn't?
ALAN: He showed me nothing! He's a mean bugger! Ride — or fall! That's Straw Law.
DYSART: Straw Law?
ALAN: He was born in the straw, and this is his law.
DYSART: But you managed? You mastered him?
ALAN: Had to!
DYSART: And then you rode in secret?
ALAN: Yes.
DYSART: How often?
ALAN: Every three weeks. More, people would notice.
DYSART: On a particular horse?
ALAN: No.
DYSART: How did you get into the stable?
ALAN: Stole a key. Had it copied at Bryson's.
DYSART: Clever boy.

(ALAN smiles.)

Then you'd slip out of the house?
ALAN: Midnight! On the stroke!
DYSART: How far's the stable?
ALAN: Two miles.

(Pause.)

DYSART: Let's do it! Let's go riding! . . . Now!

(He stands up, and pushes in his bench.)

You are there now, in front of the stable door.

(ALAN turns upstage.)

That key's in your hand. Go and open it.

SCENE 20

ALAN moves upstage, and mimes opening the door.
Soft light on the circle.
Humming from the CHORUS: the Equus noise.

The horse-actors enter, raise high their masks, and put them on all together. They stand around the circle — NUGGET in the mouth of the tunnel.

DYSART: Quietly as possible. Dalton may still be awake. Sssh . . . Quietly . . . Good. Now go in.

(ALAN steps secretly out of the square through the central opening on to the circle, now glowing with a warm light. He looks about him. The horses stamp uneasily: their masks turn towards him.)

You are on the inside now. All the horses are staring at you. Can you see them?

ALAN *(excited)*: Yes!
DYSART: Which one are you going to take?
ALAN: Nugget.

(ALAN reaches up and mimes leading NUGGET carefully round the circle downstage with a rope, past all the horses on the right.)

DYSART: What colour is Nugget?
ALAN: Chestnut.

(The horse picks his way with care. ALAN halts him at the corner of the square.)

DYSART: What do you do, first thing?
ALAN: Put on his sandals.
DYSART: Sandals?

(He kneels, downstage centre.)

ALAN: Sandals of majesty! . . . Made of sack.

(He picks up the invisible sandals, and kisses them devoutly.)

Tie them round his hooves.

(He taps NUGGET's right leg: the horse raises it and the boy mimes tying the sack round it.)

DYSART: All four hooves?
ALAN: Yes.
DYSART: Then?
ALAN: Chinkle-chankle.

(He mimes picking up the bridle and bit.)

He doesn't like it so late, but he takes it for my sake. He bends for me. He stretches forth his neck to it.

(NUGGET bends his head down. ALAN first ritually puts the bit into his own mouth, then crosses, and transfers it into NUGGET's. He reaches up and buckles on the bridle. Then he leads him by the invisible reins, across the front of the stage and up round the left side of the circle. NUGGET follows obediently.)

ALAN: Buckle and lead out.
DYSART: No saddle?
ALAN: Never.
DYSART: Go on.
ALAN: Walk down the path behind. He's quiet. Always is, this bit. Meek and mild legs. At least till the field. Then there's trouble.

(The horse jerks back. The mask tosses.)

DYSART: What kind?
ALAN: Won't go in.
DYSART: Why not?
ALAN: It's his place of Ha Ha.
DYSART: What?
ALAN: Ha Ha.
DYSART: Make him go into it.
ALAN *(whispering fiercely)*: Come on! . . . Come on! . . .

(He drags the horse into the square as DYSART steps out of it.)

SCENE 21

NUGGET *comes to a halt staring diagonally down what is now the field. The Equus noise dies away. The boy looks about him.*

DYSART *(from the circle)*: Is it a big field?
ALAN: Huge!
DYSART: What's it like?
ALAN: Full of mist. Nettles on your feet.

(He mimes taking off his shoes — and the sting.)

Ah!
DYSART *(going back to his bench)*: You take your shoes off?
ALAN: Everything.
DYSART: All your clothes?
ALAN: Yes.

(He mimes undressing completely in front of the horse. When he is finished and obviously quite naked, he throws out his arms

and shows himself fully to his God, bowing his head before NUGGET.)

DYSART: Where do you leave them?
ALAN: Tree hole near the gate. No one could find them.

(*He walks upstage and crouches by the bench, stuffing the invisible clothes beneath it.* DYSART *sits again on the left bench, downstage beyond the circle.*)

DYSART: How does it feel now?
ALAN (*holds himself*): Burns.
DYSART: Burns?
ALAN: The mist!
DYSART: Go on. Now what?
ALAN: The Manbit.

(*He reaches again under the bench and draws out an invisible stick.*)

DYSART: Manbit?
ALAN: The stick for my mouth.
DYSART: Your mouth?
ALAN: To bite on.
DYSART: Why? What for?
ALAN: So's it won't happen too quick.
DYSART: Is it always the same stick?
ALAN: Course. Sacred stick. Keep it in the hole. The Ark of the Manbit.
DYSART: And now what? . . . What do you do now?

(*Pause. He rises and approaches* NUGGET.)

ALAN: Touch him!
DYSART: Where?
ALAN (*in wonder*): All over. Everywhere. Belly. Ribs. His ribs are of ivory. Of great value! . . . His flank is cool. His nostrils open for me. His eyes shine. They can see in the dark . . . *Eyes!* —

(*Suddenly he dashes in distress to the farthest corner of the square.*)

DYSART: Go on! . . . Then?

(*Pause.*)

ALAN: Give sugar.
DYSART: A lump of sugar?

(ALAN *returns to* NUGGET.)

ALAN: His Last Supper.
DYSART: Last before what?
ALAN: Ha Ha.

(*He kneels before the horse, palms upward and joined together.*)

DYSART: Do you say anything when you give it to him?
ALAN (*offering it*): Take my sins. Eat them for my sake . . . He always does.

(NUGGET *bows the mask into* ALAN's *palm, then takes a step back to eat.*)

And then he's ready.
DYSART: You can get up on him now?
ALAN: Yes!
DYSART: Do it, then. Mount him.

(ALAN, *lying before* NUGGET, *stretches out on the square. He grasps the top of the thin metal pole embedded in the wood. He whispers his God's name ceremonially.*)

ALAN: Equus! . . . Equus! . . . Equus!

(*He pulls the pole upright. The actor playing* NUGGET *leans forward and grabs it. At the same instant all the other horses lean forward around the circle, each placing a gloved hand on the rail.* ALAN *rises and walks right back to the upstage corner, left.*)

Take me!

(*He runs and jumps high on to* NUGGET's *back.*)

(*crying out*) Ah!
DYSART: What is it?
ALAN: Hurts!
DYSART: Hurts?
ALAN: Knives in his skin! Little knives — all inside my legs.

(NUGGET *mimes restiveness.*)

ALAN: Stay, Equus. No one said Go! . . . That's it. He's good. Equus the Godslave, Faithful and True. Into my hands he commends himself — naked in his chinkle-chankle. (*He punches.*) Stop it! . . . He wants to go so badly.
DYSART: Go, then. Leave me behind. Ride away now, Alan. Now! . . . Now you are alone with Equus.

(ALAN *stiffens his body.*)

ALAN: (*ritually*) Equus — son of Fleckwus — son of Neckwus — *Walk.*

(*A hum from the* CHORUS.
*Very slowly the horses standing on the circle
begin to turn the square by gently pushing
the wooden rail.* ALAN *and his mount start
to revolve. The effect, immediately, is of a
statue being slowly turned round on a plinth.
During the ride however the speed increases,
and the light decreases until it is only a
fierce spotlight on horse and rider, with the
overspill glinting on the other masks leaning
in towards them.*)

Here we go. The King rides out on Equus,
mightiest of horses. Only I can ride him. He
lets me turn him this way and that. His neck
comes out of my body. It lifts in the dark.
Equus, my Godslave! . . . Now the King
commands you. Tonight, we ride against them
all.

DYSART: Who's all?

ALAN: My foes and His.

DYSART: Who are your foes?

ALAN: The Hosts of Hoover. The Hosts of
Philco. The Hosts of Pifco. The House of
Remington and all its tribe!

DYSART: Who are His foes?

ALAN: The Hosts of Jodhpur. The Hosts of
Bowler and Gymkhana. All those who show
him off for their vanity. Tie rosettes on his
head for their vanity! Come on, Equus. Let's
get them! . . . *Trot!*

(*The speed of the turning square increases.*)

Stead-y! Stead-y! Stead-y! Stead-y! Cowboys are
watching! Take off their stetsons. They know
who we are. They're admiring us! Bowing low
unto us! Come on now — show them! *Canter!*
. . . CANTER!

(*He whips* NUGGET.)

And Equus the Mighty rose against All!
His enemies scatter, his enemies fall!
TURN!
Trample them, trample them,
Trample them, trample them,
TURN!
TURN!!
TURN!!!

(*The Equus noise increases in volume.*)

(*Shouting.*) WEE! . . . WAA! . . . WON-
DERFUL! . . .
I'm stiff! Stiff in the wind!

My mane, stiff in the wind!
My flanks! My hooves!
Mane on my legs, on my flanks, like whips!
Raw!
Raw!
I'm raw! Raw!
Feel me on you! *On* you! *On* you! *On* you!
I want to be *in* you!
I want to BE you forever and ever! —
Equus, I love you!
Now! —
Bear me away!
Make us One Person!

(*He rides Equus frantically.*)

*One Person! One Person! One Person! One
Person!*

(*He rises up on the horse's back, and calls
like a trumpet.*)

Ha-HA! . . . Ha-HA! . . . Ha HA!

(*The trumpet turns to great cries.*)

HA-HA! HA-HA! HA-HA! HA-HA! HA! . . .
HA! . . . HAAAAA!

(*He twists like a flame.
Silence.
The turning square comes to a stop in the
same position it occupied at the opening of
the Act.
Slowly the boy drops off the horse's back on
to the ground.
He lowers his head and kisses* NUGGET'S
*hoof.
Finally he flings back his head and cries up
to him:*)

AMEN!

(NUGGET *snorts, once.*)

BLACKOUT

ACT 2

SCENE 22

*Darkness.
Lights come slowly up on* ALAN *kneeling in
the night at the hooves of* NUGGET. *Slowly
he gets up, climbing lovingly up the body
of the horse until he can stand and kiss it.*
DYSART *sits on the downstage bench where
he began Act 1.*

DYSART: With one particular horse, called Nugget, he embraces. He showed me how he stands with it afterwards in the night, one hand on its chest, one on its neck, like a frozen tango dancer, inhaling its cold sweet breath. "Have you noticed," he said, "about horses: how they'll stand one hoof on its end, like those girls in the ballet?"

(ALAN *leads* NUGGET *out of the square.* DYSART *rises. The horse walks away up the tunnel and disappears. The boy comes down-stage and sits on the bench* DYSART *has vacated.* DYSART *crosses downstage and moves slowly up round the circle, until he reaches the central entrance to the square.*)

Now he's gone off to rest, leaving me alone with Equus. I can hear the creature's voice. It's calling me out of the black cave of the Pysche. I shove in my dim little torch, and there he stands — waiting for me. He raises his matted head. He opens his great square teeth, and says — (*Mocking.*) "Why? . . . Why Me? . . . Why — ultimately — Me? . . . Do you really imagine you can account for Me? Totally, in-fallibly, inevitably account for Me? . . . Poor Doctor Dysart!"

(*He enters the square.*)

Of course I've stared at such images before. Or been stared at by them, whichever way you look at it. And weirdly often now with me the feeling is that *they* are staring at *us* — that in some quite palpable way they precede us. Meaningless, but unsettling . . . In either case, this one is the most alarming yet. It asks questions I've avoided all my professional life. (*Pause.*) A child is born into a world of phenomena all equal in their power to enslave. It sniffs — it sucks — it strokes its eyes over the whole uncountable range. Suddenly one strikes. Why? Moments snap together like magnets, forging a chain of shackles. Why? I can trace them. I can even, with time, pull them apart again. But why at the start they were ever magnetized at all — just those partic-ular moments of experience and no others — I don't know. *And nor does anyone else.* Yet *if* I don't know — if I can never know that — then what am I doing here? I don't mean clinically doing or socially doing — I mean *fundamentally!* These questions, these Whys, are fundamental — yet they have no place in a consulting room. So then, do I? . . . This is the feeling more and more with me — No Place. Displacement. . . . "Account for me," says staring Equus. "First account for Me! . . ." I fancy this is more than menopause.

(NURSE *rushes in.*)

NURSE: Doctor! . . . Doctor! There's a terrible scene with the Strang boy. His mother came to visit him, and I gave her the tray to take in. He threw it at her. She's saying the most dreadful things.

(ALAN *springs up, down left.* DORA *springs up, down right. They face each other across the bottom end of the stage. It is observable that at the start of this Act* FRANK *is not sitting beside his wife on their bench. It is hopefully not observable that he is placed among the audience upstage, in the gloom, by the central tunnel.*)

DORA: Don't you dare! *Don't you dare!*
DYSART: Is she still there?
NURSE: Yes!

(*He quickly leaves the square, followed by the* NURSE. DORA *moves towards her son.*)

DORA: Don't you look at me like that! I'm not a doctor, you know, who'll take anything. Don't you dare give me that stare, young man!

(*She slaps his face.* DYSART *joins them.*)

DYSART: Mrs. Strang!
DORA: I know your stares. They don't work on me!
DYSART (*to her*): Leave this room.
DORA: What did you say?
DYSART: I tell you to leave here at once.

(DORA *hesitates. Then:*)

DORA: Goodbye, Alan.

(*She walks past her son, and round into the square.* DYSART *follows her. Both are very upset.* ALAN *returns to his bench and* NURSE *to her place.*)

SCENE 23

Lights up on the square.

DYSART: I must ask you never to come here again.

DORA: Do you think I want to? Do you think I want to?

DYSART: Mrs. Strang, what on earth has got into you? Can't you see the boy is highly distressed?

DORA (ironic): Really?

DYSART: Of course! He's at a most delicate stage of treatment. He's totally exposed. Ashamed. Everything you can imagine!

DORA (exploding): And me? What about me? . . . What do you think I am? . . . I'm a parent, of course — so it doesn't count. That's a dirty word in here, isn't it, "parent"?

DYSART: You know that's not true.

DORA: Oh, I know. I know, all right! I've heard it all my life. It's our fault. Whatever happens, we did it. Alan's just a little victim. He's really done nothing at all! (Savagely.) What do you have to do in this world to get any sympathy — blind animals?

DYSART: Sit down, Mrs. Strang.

DORA (ignoring him: more and more urgently): Look, Doctor: you don't have to live with this. Alan is one patient to you: one out of many. He's my son. I lie awake every night thinking about it. Frank lies there beside me. I can hear him. Neither of us sleeps all night. You come to us and say Who forbids television? who does what behind whose back? — as if we're criminals. Let me tell you something. We're not criminals. We've done nothing wrong. We loved Alan. We gave him the best love we could. All right, we quarrel sometimes — all parents quarrel — we always make it up. My husband is a good man. He's an upright man, religion or no religion. He cares for his home, for the world, and for his boy. Alan had love and care and treats, and as much fun as any boy in the world. I know about loveless homes: I was a teacher. Our home wasn't loveless. I know about privacy too — not invading a child's privacy. All right, Frank may be at fault there — he digs into him too much — but nothing in excess. He's not a bully. . . . (Gravely.) No, doctor. Whatever's happened has happened because of Alan. Alan is himself. Every soul is itself. If you added up everything we ever did to him, from his first day on earth to this, you wouldn't find why he did this terrible thing — because that's him: not just all of our things added up. Do you understand what I'm saying? I want you to understand, because I lie awake and awake thinking it out, and I want you to know that I deny it

absolutely what he's doing now, staring at me, attacking me for what he's done, for what he is! (Pause: calmer.) You've got your words, and I've got mine. You call it a complex, I suppose. But if you knew God, Doctor, you would know about the Devil. You'd know the Devil isn't made by what mummy says and daddy says. The Devil's there. It's an old-fashioned word, but a true thing . . . I'll go. What I did in there was inexcusable. I only know he was my little Alan, and then the Devil came.

(She leaves the square, and resumes her place. DYSART watches her go, then leaves himself by the opposite entrance, and approaches ALAN.)

SCENE 24

Seated on his bench, the boy glares at him.

DYSART: I thought you liked your mother.

(Silence.)

She doesn't know anything, you know. I haven't told her what you told me. You do know that, don't you?

ALAN: It was lies anyway.

DYSART: What?

ALAN: You and your pencil. Just a con trick, that's all.

DYSART: What do you mean?

ALAN: Made me say a lot of lies.

DYSART: Did it? . . . Like what?

ALAN: All of it. Everything I said. Lot of lies.

(Pause.)

DYSART: I see.

ALAN: You ought to be locked up. Your bloody tricks.

DYSART: I thought you liked tricks.

ALAN: It'll be the drug next. I know.

(DYSART turns, sharply.)

DYSART: What drug?

ALAN: I've heard. I'm not ignorant. I know what you get up to in here. Shove needles in people, pump them full of truth drug, so they can't help saying things. That's next, isn't it?

(Pause.)

DYSART: Alan, do you know why you're here?

ALAN: So you can give me truth drugs.

(*He glares at him.*
DYSART *leaves abruptly, and returns to the square.*)

SCENE 25

HESTHER *comes in simultaneously from the other side.*

DYSART (*agitated*): He actually thinks they exist! And of course he wants one.
HESTHER: It doesn't sound like that to me.
DYSART: Of course he does. Why mention them otherwise? He wants a way to speak. To finally tell me what happened in that stable. Tape's too isolated, and hypnosis is a trick. At least that's the pretence.
HESTHER: Does he still say that today?
DYSART: I haven't seen him. I cancelled his appointment this morning, and let him stew in his own anxiety. Now I am almost tempted to play a real trick on him.
HESTHER (*sitting*): Like what?
DYSART: The old placebo.
HESTHER: You mean a harmless pill?
DYSART: Full of *alleged* Truth Drug. Probably an aspirin.
HESTHER: But he'd deny it afterwards. Same thing all over.
DYSART: No. Because he's ready to abreact.
HESTHER: Abreact?
DYSART: Live it all again. He won't be able to deny it after that, because he'll have shown me. Not just told me – but acted it out in front of me.
HESTHER: Can you get him to do that?
DYSART: I think so. He's nearly done it already. Under all that glowering, he trusts me. Do you realise that?
HESTHER (*warmly*): I'm sure he does.
DYSART: Poor bloody fool.
HESTHER: Don't start that again.

(*Pause.*)

DYSART (*quietly*): Can you think of anything worse one can do to anybody than take away their worship?
HESTHER: Worship?
DYSART: Yes, that word again!
HESTHER: Aren't you being a little extreme?
DYSART: Extremity's the point.
HESTHER: Worship isn't destructive, Martin. I know that.

DYSART: I don't. I only know it's the core of his life. What else has he got? Think about him. He can hardly read. He knows no physics or engineering to make the world real for him. No paintings to show him how others have enjoyed it. No music except television jingles. No history except tales from a desperate mother. No friends. Not one kid to give him a joke, or make him know himself more moderately. He's a modern citizen for whom society doesn't exist. He lives *one hour* every three weeks – howling in a mist. And after the service kneels to a slave who stands over him obviously and unthrowably his master. With my body I thee worship! . . . Many men have less vital with their wives.

(*Pause.*)

HESTHER: All the same, they don't usually blind their wives, do they?
DYSART: Oh, come on!
HESTHER: Well, do they?
DYSART (*sarcastically*): You mean he's dangerous? A violent, dangerous madman who's going to run round the country doing it again and again?
HESTHER: I mean he's in pain, Martin. He's been in pain for most of his life. That much, at least, you *know*.
DYSART: Possibly.
HESTHER: *Possibly?!* . . . That cut-off little figure you just described must have been in pain for years.
DYSART (*doggedly*): Possibly.
HESTHER: And you can take it away.
DYSART: Still – possibly.
HESTHER: Then that's enough. That simply has to be enough for you, surely?
DYSART: No!
HESTHER: Why not?
DYSART: Because it's his.
HESTHER: I don't understand.
DYSART: His pain. His own. He made it.

(*Pause.*)

(*Earnestly.*) Look . . . to go through life and call it yours – *your life* – you first have to get your own pain. Pain that's unique to you. You can't just dip into the common bin and say "That's enough!" . . . He's done that. All right, he's sick. He's full of misery and fear. He was dangerous, and could be again, though I doubt it. But that boy has known a passion more ferocious than I have felt in any second of my life. And let me tell you something: I envy it.

HESTHER: You can't.

DYSART (*vehemently*): Don't you see? That's the Accusation! That's what his stare has been saying to me all the time. "*At least I galloped! When did you?*" . . . (*Simply.*) I'm jealous, Hester. Jealous of Alan Strang.

HESTHER: That's absurd.

DYSART: Is it? . . . I go on about my wife. That smug woman by the fire. Have you thought of the fellow on the other side of it? The finicky, critical husband looking through his art books on mythical Greece. What worship has *he* ever known? Real worship! Without worship you shrink, it's as brutal as that . . . I shrank my *own* life. No one can do it for you. I settled for being pallid and provincial, out of my own eternal timidity. The old story of bluster, and do bugger-all . . . I imply that we can't have children: but actually, it's only me. I had myself tested behind her back. The lowest sperm count you could find. And I never told her. That's all I need — her sympathy mixed with resentment . . . I tell everyone Margaret's the puritan, I'm the pagan. Some pagan! Such wild returns I make to the womb of civilization. Three weeks a year in the Peleponnese, every bed booked in advance, every meal paid for by vouchers, cautious jaunts in hired Fiats, suitcase crammed with Kao-Pectate! Such a fantastic surrender to the primitive. And I use that word endlessly: "primitive." "Oh, the primitive world," I say. "What instinctual truths were lost with it!" And while I sit there, baiting a poor unimaginative woman with the word, that freaky boy tries to conjure the reality! I sit looking at pages of centaurs trampling the soil of Argos — and outside my window he is trying to *become one*, in a Hampshire field! . . . I watch that woman knitting, night after night — a woman I haven't *kissed* in six years — and he stands in the dark for an hour, sucking the sweat off his God's hairy cheek! (*Pause.*) Then in the morning, I put away my books on the cultural shelf, close up the kodachrome snaps of Mount Olympus, touch my reproduction statue of Dionysus for luck — and go off to hospital to treat him for insanity. Do you see?

HESTHER: The boy's in pain, Martin. That's all I see. In the end . . . I'm sorry.

(*He looks at her.* ALAN *gets up from his bench and stealthily places an envelope in the left-hand entrance of the square, then goes back and sits with his back to the audience, as if watching television.* HESTHER *rises.*)

HESTHER: That stare of his. Have you thought it might not be accusing you at all?

DYSART: What then?

HESTHER: Claiming you.

DYSART: For what?

HESTHER (*mischievously*): A new God.

(*Pause.*)

DYSART: Too conventional, for him. Finding a religion in Psychiatry is really for very ordinary patients.

(*She laughs.*)

HESTHER: Maybe he just wants a new Dad. Or is that too conventional too? . . . Since you're questioning your profession anyway, perhaps you ought to try it and see.

DYSART (*amused*): I'll talk to you.

HESTHER: Goodbye.

(*She smiles, and leaves him.*)

SCENE 26

DYSART *becomes aware of the letter lying on the floor. He picks it up, opens and reads it.*

ALAN (*speaking stiffly, as* DYSART *reads*): "It is all true, what I said after you tapped the pencil. I'm sorry if I said different. Post Scriptum: I know why I'm in here."

(*Pause.*)

DYSART (*calling, joyfully*): Nurse!

(NURSE *comes in.*)

NURSE: Yes, Doctor?

DYSART (*trying to conceal his pleasure*): Good evening!

NURSE: You're in late tonight.

DYSART: Yes! . . . Tell me, is the Strang boy in bed yet?

NURSE: Oh, no, Doctor. He's bound to be upstairs looking at television. He always watches to the last possible moment. He doesn't like going to his room at all.

DYSART: You mean he's still having nightmares?

NURSE: He had a bad one last night.

DYSART: Would you ask him to come down here, please?

NURSE (*faint surprise*): Now?

DYSART: I'd like a word with him.

NURSE (*puzzled*): Very good, Doctor.

DYSART: If he's not back in his room by lights out, tell Night Nurse not to worry. I'll see he gets back to bed all right. And would you phone my home and tell my wife I may be in late?

NURSE: Yes, Doctor.

DYSART: Ask him to come straight away, please.

(NURSE *goes to the bench, taps* ALAN *on the shoulder, whispers her message in his ear, and returns to her place.* ALAN *stands up and pauses for a second — then steps into the square.*)

SCENE 27

He stands in the doorway, depressed.

DYSART: Hallo.

ALAN: Hallo.

DYSART: I got your letter. Thank you. (*Pause.*) Also the Post Scriptum.

ALAN (*defensively*): That's the right word. My mum told me. It's Latin for "After-writing."

DYSART: How are you feeling?

ALAN: All right.

DYSART: I'm sorry I didn't see you today.

ALAN: You were fed up with me.

DYSART: Yes. (*Pause.*) Can I make it up to you now?

ALAN: What d'you mean?

DYSART: I thought we'd have a session.

ALAN (*startled*): Now?

DYSART: Yes! At dead of night! . . . Better than going to sleep, isn't it?

(*The boy flinches.*)

Alan — look. Everything I say has a trick or a catch. Everything I do is a trick or a catch. That's all I know to do. But they work — and you know that. Trust me.

(*Pause.*)

ALAN: You got another trick, then?

DYSART: Yes.

ALAN: A truth drug?

DYSART: If you like.

ALAN: What's it do?

DYSART: Make it easier for you to talk.

ALAN: Like you can't help yourself?

DYSART: That's right. Like you have to speak the truth at all costs. And all of it.

(*Pause.*)

ALAN (*slyly*): Comes in a needle, doesn't it?

DYSART: No.

ALAN: Where is it?

DYSART (*indicating his pocket*): In here.

ALAN: Let's see.

(DYSART *solemnly takes a bottle of pills out of his pocket.*)

DYSART: There.

ALAN (*suspicious*): That really it?

DYSART: It is . . . Do you want to try it?

ALAN: No.

DYSART: I think you do.

ALAN: I don't. Not at all.

DYSART: Afterwards you'd sleep. You'd have no bad dreams all night. Probably many nights, from then on . . .

(*Pause.*)

ALAN: How long's it take to work?

DYSART: It's instant. Like coffee.

ALAN (*half believing*): It isn't!

DYSART: I promise you . . . Well?

ALAN: Can I have a fag?

DYSART: Pill first. Do you want some water?

ALAN: No.

(DYSART *shakes one out on to his palm.* ALAN *hesitates for a second — then takes it and swallows it.*)

DYSART: Then you can chase it down with this. Sit down.

(*He offers him a cigarette, and lights it for him.*)

ALAN (*nervous*): What happens now?

DYSART: We wait for it to work.

ALAN: What'll I feel first?

DYSART: Nothing much. After a minute, about a hundred green snakes should come out of that cupboard singing the Hallelujah Chorus.

ALAN (*annoyed*): I'm serious!

DYSART (*earnestly*): You'll feel nothing.

Nothing's going to happen now but what you want to happen. You're not going to say anything to me but what you want to say. Just relax. Lie back and finish your fag.

(ALAN *stares at him. Then accepts the situation, and lies back.*)

DYSART: Good boy.
ALAN: I bet this room's heard some funny things.
DYSART: It certainly has.
ALAN: I like it.
DYSART: This room?
ALAN: Don't you?
DYSART: Well, there's not much to like, is there?
ALAN: How long am I going to be in here?
DYSART: It's hard to say. I quite see you want to leave.
ALAN: No.
DYSART: You don't?
ALAN: Where would I go?
DYSART: Home. . . .

(*The boy looks at him.* DYSART *crosses and sits on the rail upstage, his feet on the bench. A pause.*)

Actually, I'd like to leave this room and never see it again in my life.
ALAN (*surprise*): Why?
DYSART: I've been in it too long.
ALAN: Where would you go?
DYSART: Somewhere.
ALAN: Secret?
DYSART: Yes. There's a sea — a great sea — I love . . . It's where the Gods used to go to bathe.
ALAN: What Gods?
DYSART: The old ones. Before they died.
ALAN: Gods don't die.
DYSART: Yes, they do.

(*Pause.*)

There's a village I spent one night in, where I'd like to live. It's all white.
ALAN: How would you Nosey Parker, though? You wouldn't have a room for it any more.
DYSART: I wouldn't mind. I don't actually enjoy being a Nosey Parker, you know.
ALAN: Then why do it?
DYSART: Because you're unhappy.
ALAN: So are you.

(DYSART *looks at him sharply.* ALAN *sits up in alarm.*)

Oooh, I didn't mean that!
DYSART: Didn't you?
ALAN: Here — is that how it works? Things just slip out, not feeling anything?
DYSART: That's right.
ALAN: But it's so quick!
DYSART: I told you: it's instant.
ALAN (*delighted*): It's wicked, isn't it? I mean, you can say anything under it.
DYSART: Yes.
ALAN: Ask me a question.
DYSART: Tell me about Jill.

(*Pause. The boy turns away.*)

ALAN: There's nothing to tell.
DYSART: Nothing?
ALAN: No.
DYSART: Well, for example — is she pretty? You've never described her.
ALAN: She's all right.
DYSART: What colour hair?
ALAN: Dunno.
DYSART: Is it long or short?
ALAN: Dunno.
DYSART (*lightly*): You must know that.
ALAN: I don't remember. *I don't!*

(DYSART *rises and comes down to him. He takes the cigarette out of his hand.*)

DYSART (*firmly*): Lie back . . . Now listen. You have to do this. And now. You are going to tell me everything that happened with this girl. And not just *tell* me — *show* me. Act it out, if you like — even more than you did when I tapped the pencil. I want you to feel free to do absolutely anything in this room. The pill will help you. I will help you. . . . Now, where does she live?

(*A long pause.*)

ALAN (*tight*): Near the stables. About a mile.

(DYSART *steps down out of the square as* JILL *enters it. He sits again on the downstage bench.*)

SCENE 28

The light grows warmer.

JILL: It's called The China Pantry.

(She comes down and sits casually on the rail. Her manner is open and lightly provocative. During these scenes ALAN *acts directly with her, and never looks over at* DYSART *when he replies to him.)*

When Daddy disappeared, she was left without a bean. She had to earn her own living. I must say she did jolly well, considering she was never trained in business.

DYSART: What do you mean, "disappeared"?

ALAN (*to* DYSART): He ran off. No one ever saw him again.

JILL: Just left a note on her dressing table saying "Sorry. I've had it." Just like that. She never got over it. It turned her right off men. All my dates have to be sort of secret. I mean, she knows about them, but I can't ever bring anyone back home. She's so rude to them.

ALAN (*to* DYSART): She was always looking.

DYSART: At you?

ALAN (*to* DYSART): Saying stupid things.

(She jumps off the bench.)

JILL: You've got super eyes.

ALAN (*to* DYSART): Anyway, *she* was the one who had them.

(She sits next to him. Embarrassed, the boy tries to move away as far as he can.)

JILL: There was an article in the paper last week saying what points about boys fascinate girls. They said Number One is bottoms. I think it's eyes every time.... They fascinate you too, don't they?

ALAN: Me?

JILL (*sly*): Or is it only horses' eyes?

ALAN (*startled*): What d'you mean?

JILL: I saw you staring into Nugget's eyes yesterday for ages. I spied on you through the door!

ALAN (*hotly*): There must have been something in it!

JILL: You're a real Man of Mystery, aren't you?

ALAN (*to* DYSART): Sometimes, it was like she knew.

DYSART: Did you ever hint?

ALAN (*to* DYSART): Course not!

JILL: I love horses' eyes. The way you can see yourself in them. D'you find them sexy?

ALAN (*outraged*): What? !

JILL: Horses.

ALAN: Don't be daft!

(He springs up, and away from her.)

JILL: Girls do. I mean, they go through a period when they pat them and kiss them a lot. I know *I* did. I suppose it's just a substitute, really.

ALAN (*to* DYSART): That kind of thing, all the time. Until one night . . .

DYSART: Yes? What?

ALAN (*to* DYSART: *defensively*): She did it! Not me. It was her idea, the whole thing! . . . She got me into it!

DYSART: What are you saying? "One night": go on from there.

(A pause.)

ALAN (*to* DYSART): Saturday night. We were just closing up.

JILL: How would you like to take me out?

ALAN: What?

JILL (*coolly*): How would you like to take me out tonight?

ALAN: I've got to go home.

JILL: What for?

(He tries to escape upstage.)

ALAN: They expect me.

JILL: Ring up and say you're going out.

ALAN: I can't.

JILL: Why?

ALAN: They expect me.

JILL: Look. Either we go out together and have some fun, or you go back to your boring home, *as usual*, and I go back to mine. That's the situation, isn't it?

ALAN: Well . . . where would we go?

JILL: The pictures! There's a skinflick over in Winchester! I've never seen one, have you?

ALAN: No.

JILL: Wouldn't you like to? *I* would. All those heavy Swedes, panting at each other! . . . What d'you say?

ALAN (*grinning*): Yeh! . . .

JILL: Good! . . .

(He turns away.)

DYSART: Go on, please.

(He steps off the square.)

ALAN (*to* DYSART): I'm tired now!

DYSART: Come on now. You can't stop there.

(*He storms round the circle to* DYSART, *and faces him directly.*)

ALAN: I'm *tired!* I want to go to bed!
DYSART (*sharply*): Well, you can't. I want to hear about the film.
ALAN (*hostile*): Hear what? . . . *What?* . . . It was bloody awful!

(*The actors playing horses come swiftly on to the square, dressed in sports coats or raincoats. They move the benches to be parallel with the audience, and sit on them — staring out front.*)

DYSART: Why?
ALAN: Nosey Parker!
DYSART: *Why?*
ALAN: *Because!* . . . Well — we went into the Cinema!

SCENE 29

A burst of Rock music, instantly fading down. Lights darken.
ALAN *re-enters the square.* JILL *rises and together they grope their way to the downstage bench, as if in a dark auditorium.*

ALAN (*to* DYSART): The whole place was full of men. Jill was the only girl.

(*They push by a patron seated at the end, and sit side by side, staring up at the invisible screen, located above the heads of the main audience. A spotlight hits the boy's face.*)

We sat down and the film came on. It was daft. Nothing happened for ages. There was this girl Brita, who was sixteen. She went to stay in this house, where there was an older boy. He kept giving her looks, but she ignored him completely. In the end she took a shower. She went into the bathroom and took off all her clothes. The lot. Very slowly. . . . What she didn't know was the boy was looking through the door all the time. . . . (*He starts to become excited.*) It was fantastic! The water fell on her breasts, bouncing down her. . . .

(FRANK *steps into the square furtively from the back, hat in hand, and stands looking about for a place.*)

DYSART: Was that the first time you'd seen a girl naked?

ALAN (*to* DYSART): Yes! You couldn't see everything, though. . . . (*Looking about him.*) All round me they were all looking. All the men — staring up like they were in church. Like they were a sort of congregation. And then — (*He sees his father.*) Ah!

(*At the same instant* FRANK *sees him.*)

FRANK: Alan!
ALAN: God!
JILL: What is it?
ALAN: *Dad!*
JILL: *Where?*
ALAN: At the back! *He saw me!*
JILL: You sure?
ALAN: Yes!
FRANK (*calling*): Alan!
ALAN: Oh God!

(*He tries to hide his face in the girl's shoulder. His father comes down the aisle towards him.*)

FRANK: Alan! You can hear me! Don't pretend!
PATRONS: Ssssh!
FRANK (*approaching the row of seats*): Do I have to come and fetch you out? . . . Do I? . . .

(*Cries of "Sssh!" and "Shut up!"*)

Do I, Alan?
ALAN (*through gritted teeth*): Oh, fuck!

(*He gets up as the noise increases.* JILL *gets up too and follows him.*)

DYSART: You went?
ALAN (*to* DYSART): What else could I do? He kept shouting. Everyone was saying Shut up!

(*They go out, right, through the group of* PATRONS — *who rise protesting as they pass, quickly replace the benches and leave the square.*
DYSART *enters it.*)

SCENE 30

Light brightens from the cinema, but remains cold: streets at night.
The three walk round the circle downstage in a line: FRANK *leading, wearing his hat. He halts in the middle of the left rail, and*

stands staring straight ahead of him, rigid with embarrassment.
ALAN *is very agitated.*

ALAN (*to* DYSART): We went into the street, all three of us. It was weird. We just stood there by the bus stop — like we were three people in a queue, and we didn't know each other. Dad was all white and sweaty. He didn't look at us at all. It must have gone on for about five minutes. I tried to speak. I said — (*To his father.*) I — I — I've never been there before. Honest . . . Never . . . (*To* DYSART.) He didn't seem to hear. Jill tried.
JILL: It's true. Mr. Strang. It wasn't Alan's idea to go there. It was mine.
ALAN (*to* DYSART): He just went on staring, straight ahead. It was awful.
JILL: I'm not shocked by films like that. I think they're just silly.
ALAN (*to* DYSART): The bus wouldn't come. We just stood and stood. . . . Then suddenly he spoke.

(FRANK *takes off his hat.*)

FRANK (*stiffly*): I'd like you to know something. Both of you. I came here tonight to see the Manager. He asked me to call on him for business purposes. I happen to be a printer, Miss. A picture house needs posters. That's entirely why I'm here. To discuss posters. While I was waiting I happened to glance in, that's all. I can only say I'm going to complain to the council. I had no idea they showed films like this. I'm certainly going to refuse my services.
JILL (*kindly*): Yes, of course.
FRANK: So long as that's understood.
ALAN (*to* DYSART): Then the bus came along.
FRANK: Come along now, Alan.

(*He moves away downstage.*)

ALAN: No.
FRANK (*turning*): No fuss, please. Say Goodnight to the young lady.
ALAN (*timid but firm*): No. I'm stopping here . . . I've got to see her home . . . It's proper.

(*Pause.*)

FRANK (*as dignified as possible*): Very well. I'll see you when you choose to return. Very well then . . . Yes . . .

(*He walks back to his original seat, next to his wife. He stares across the square at his son — who stares back at him. Then, slowly, he sits.*)

ALAN (*to* DYSART): And he got in, and we didn't. He sat down and looked at me through the glass. And I saw . . .
DYSART (*soft*): What?
ALAN (*to* DYSART): His face. It was scared.
DYSART: Of you?
ALAN (*to* DYSART): It was terrible. We had to walk home. Four miles. I got the shakes.
DYSART: You were scared too?
ALAN (*to* DYSART): It was like a hole had been drilled in my tummy. A hole — right here. And the air was getting in!

(*He starts to walk upstage, round the circle.*)

SCENE 31

The girl stays still.

JILL (*aware of other people looking*): Alan . . .
ALAN (*to* DYSART): People kept turning round in the street to look.
JILL: Alan!
ALAN (*to* DYSART): I kept seeing him, just as he drove off. Scared of me. . . . And me scared of *him*. . . . I kept thinking — all those airs he put on! . . . "Receive my meaning. Improve your mind!" . . . All those nights he said he'd be in late. "Keep my supper hot, Dora!" "Your poor father: he works so hard!" . . . Bugger! Old bugger! . . . Filthy old bugger!

(*He stops, clenching his fists.*)

JILL: Hey! Wait for me!

(*She runs after him. He waits.*)

What are you thinking about?
ALAN: Nothing.
JILL: Mind my own beeswax?

(*She laughs.*)

ALAN (*to* DYSART): And suddenly she began to laugh.
JILL: I'm sorry. But it's pretty funny, when you think of it.
ALAN (*bewildered*): What?

JILL: Catching him like that! I mean, it's terrible – but it's very funny.

ALAN: Yeh!

(*He turns from her.*)

JILL: No, wait! . . . I'm sorry. I know you're upset. But it's not the end of the world, is it? I mean, what was he doing? Only what we were. Watching a silly film. It's a case of like father like son, I'd say! . . . I mean, when that girl was taking a shower, you were pretty interested, weren't you?

(*He turns round and looks at her.*)

We keep saying old people are square. Then when they suddenly aren't – we don't like it!

DYSART: What did you think about that?

ALAN (*to* DYSART): I don't know. I kept looking at all the people in the street. They were mostly men coming out of pubs. I suddenly thought – *they all do it! All of them!* . . . They're not just Dads – they're people with pricks! . . . And Dad – he's just not Dad either. He's a man with a prick too. You know, I'd never thought about it.

(*Pause.*)

We went into the country.

(*He walks again.* JILL *follows. They turn the corner and come downstage, right.*)

We kept walking. I just thought about Dad, and how he was nothing special – just a poor old sod on his own.

(*He stops.*)

(To JILL: *realising it.*) Poor old sod!

JILL: That's right!

ALAN (*grappling with it*): I mean, what else has he got? . . . He's got mum, of course, but well – she – she – she ——

JILL: She doesn't give him anything?

ALAN: That's right. I bet you . . . She doesn't give him anything. That's right . . . That's really right! . . . She likes Ladies and Gentlemen. Do you understand what I mean?

JILL (*mischievously*): Ladies and gentlemen aren't naked?

ALAN: That's right! Never! . . . *Never!* That would be disgusting! She'd have to put bowler hats on them! . . . Jodhpurs!

(JILL *laughs.*)

DYSART: Was that the first time you ever thought anything like that about your mother? . . . I mean, that she was unfair to your dad?

ALAN (*to* DYSART): Absolutely!

DYSART: How did you feel?

ALAN (*to* DYSART): Sorry. I mean for him. Poor old sod, that's what I felt – he's just like me! He hates ladies and gents just like me! Posh things – and la-di-da. He goes off by himself at night, and does his own secret thing which no one'll know about, just like me! There's no difference – he's just the same as me – just the same! –

(*He stops in distress, then bolts back a little upstage.*)

Christ!

DYSART (*sternly*): Go on.

ALAN (*to* DYSART): I can't.

DYSART: Of course you can. You're doing wonderfully.

ALAN (*to* DYSART): No, please. *Don't make me!*

DYSART (*firm*): Don't think: just answer. You were happy at that second, weren't you? When you realised about your dad. How lots of people have secrets, not just you?

ALAN (*to* DYSART): Yes.

DYSART: You felt sort of free, didn't you? I mean, free to do anything?

ALAN (*to* DYSART, *looking at* JILL): Yes!

DYSART: What was she doing?

ALAN (*to* DYSART): Holding my hand.

DYSART: And that was good?

ALAN (*to* DYSART): Oh, yes!

DYSART: Remember what you thought. *As if it's happening to you now. This very moment* . . . What's in your head?

ALAN (*to* DYSART): Her eyes. *She's* the one with eyes! . . . I keep looking at them, because I really want –

DYSART: To look at her breasts?

ALAN (*to* DYSART): Yes.

DYSART: Like in the film.

ALAN (*to* DYSART): Yes . . . Then she starts to scratch my hand.

JILL: You're really very nice, you know that?

ALAN (*to* DYSART): Moving her nails on the back. Her face so warm. Her eyes.

DYSART: You want her very much?

ALAN (*to* DYSART): Yes . . .

JILL: I love your eyes.

(*She kisses him.*)

(*Whispering.*) Let's go!

ALAN: Where?

JILL: I know a place. It's right near here.

ALAN: Where?

JILL: Surprise! . . . Come on!

(*She darts away round the circle, across the stage and up the left side.*)

Come *on!*

ALAN (*to* DYSART): She runs ahead. I follow. And then — and then — !

(*He halts.*)

DYSART: What?

ALAN (*to* DYSART): I see what she means.

DYSART: What? . . . Where are you? . . . Where has she taken you?

ALAN (*to* JILL): *The Stables?*

JILL: Of course!

SCENE 32

CHORUS *makes a warning hum.*
The horse-actors enter, and ceremonially put on their masks — first raising them high above their heads. NUGGET *stands in the central tunnel.*

ALAN (*recoiling*): No!

JILL: Where else? They're perfect!

ALAN: No!

(*He turns his head from her.*)

JILL: Or do you want to go home now and face your dad?

ALAN: No!

JILL: Then come on!

(*He edges nervously past the horse standing at the left, which turns its neck and even moves a challenging step after him.*)

ALAN: Why not your place?

JILL: I can't. Mother doesn't like me bringing back boys. I told you. . . . Anyway, the Barn's better.

ALAN: No!

JILL: All that straw. It's cosy.

ALAN: No.

JILL: *Why not?*

ALAN: Them!

JILL: Dalton will be in bed . . . What's the matter? . . . Don't you want to?

ALAN (*aching to*): Yes!

JILL: So?

ALAN (*desperate*): *Them!* . . . *Them!* . . .

JILL: Who?

ALAN (*low*): Horses.

JILL: *Horses?* . . . You're really dotty, aren't you? . . . What do you mean?

(*He starts shaking.*)

Oh, you're freezing . . . Let's get under the straw. You'll be warm there.

ALAN (*pulling away*): No!

JILL: What on earth's the matter with you? . . .

(*Silence. He won't look at her.*)

Look, if the sight of horses offends you, my lord, we can just shut the door. You won't have to see them. All right?

DYSART: What door is that? In the barn?

ALAN (*to* DYSART): Yes.

DYSART: So what do you do? You go in?

ALAN (*to* DYSART): Yes.

SCENE 33

A rich light falls.
Furtively ALAN *enters the square from the top end, and* JILL *follows. The horses on the circle retire out of sight on either side.* NUGGET *retreats up the tunnel and stands where he can just be glimpsed in the dimness.*

DYSART: Into the Temple? The Holy of Holies?

ALAN (*to* DYSART: *desperate*): What else can I do? . . . I can't say! I can't tell her. . . . (*To* JILL.) Shut it tight.

JILL: All right . . . You're crazy!

ALAN: Lock it.

JILL: Lock?

ALAN: Yes.

JILL: It's just an old door. What's the matter with you? They're in their boxes. They can't get out . . . Are you all right?

ALAN: Why?

JILL: You look weird.

ALAN: *Lock it!*

JILL: Ssssh! D'you want to wake up Dalton? . . . Stay there, idiot.

(*She mimes locking a heavy door, upstage.*)

DYSART: Describe the barn, please.

ALAN (*walking round it: to* DYSART): Large room. Straw everywhere. Some tools . . . (*as if picking it up off the rail where he left it in Act 1*) A hoof pick! . . .

(*He "drops" it hastily, and dashes away from the spot.*)

DYSART: Go on.
ALAN (*to* DYSART): At the end this big door. Behind it —
DYSART: Horses.
ALAN (*to* DYSART): Yes.
DYSART: How many?
ALAN (*to* DYSART): Six.
DYSART: Jill closes the door so you can't see them?
ALAN (*to* DYSART): Yes.
DYSART: And then? . . . What happens now? . . . Come on, Alan. Show me.
JILL: See, it's all shut. There's just us . . . Let's sit down. Come on.

(*They sit together on the same bench, left.*)

Hallo.
ALAN (*quickly*): Hallo.

(*She kisses him lightly. He responds. Suddenly a faint trampling of hooves, off-stage, makes him jump up.*)

JILL: What is it?

(*He turns his head upstage, listening.*)

Relax. There's no one there. Come here.

(*She touches his hand. He turns to her again.*)

You're very gentle. I love that . . .
ALAN: So are you . . . I mean . . .

(*He kisses her spontaneously. The hooves trample again, harder. He breaks away from her abruptly towards the upstage corner.*)

JILL (*rising*): What is it?
ALAN: Nothing!

(*She moves towards him. He turns and moves past her. He is clearly distressed. She contemplates him for a moment.*)

JILL (*gently*): Take your sweater off.
ALAN: What?
JILL: I will, if you will.

(*He stares at her. A pause.*

She lifts her sweater over head: he watches — then unzips his. They each remove their shoes, their socks, and their jeans. Then they look at each other diagonally across the square, in which the light is gently increasing.)

ALAN: You're . . . You're very . . .
JILL: So are you. . . . (*Pause.*) Come here.

(*He goes to her. She comes to him. They meet in the middle, and hold each other, and embrace.*)

ALAN (*to* DYSART): She put her mouth in mine. It was lovely! *Oh, it was lovely!*

(*They burst into giggles. He lays her gently on the floor in the centre of the square, and bends over her eagerly. Suddenly the noise of Equus fills the place. Hooves smash on wood. Alan straightens up, rigid. He stares straight ahead of him over the prone body of the girl.*)

DYSART: Yes, what happened then, Alan?
ALAN (*to* DYSART: *brutally*): I put it in her!
DYSART: Yes?
ALAN (*to* DYSART): I put it in her.
DYSART: You did?
ALAN (*to* DYSART): Yes!
DYSART: Was it easy?
ALAN (*to* DYSART): Yes.
DYSART: Describe it.
ALAN (*to* DYSART): I told you.
DYSART: More exactly.
ALAN (*to* DYSART): I put it in her!
DYSART: Did you?
ALAN (*to* DYSART): All the way!
DYSART: Did you, Alan?
ALAN (*to* DYSART): All the way. I shoved it. I put it in her all the way.
DYSART: Did you?
ALAN (*to* DYSART): Yes!
DYSART: Did you?
ALAN (*to* DYSART): Yes! . . . Yes!
DYSART: Give me the TRUTH! . . . Did you? . . . Honestly?
ALAN (*to* DYSART): Fuck off!

(*He collapses, lying upstage on his face.* JILL *lies on her back motionless, her head downstage, her arms extended behind her. A pause.*)

DYSART (*gently*): What was it? You

couldn't? Though you wanted to very much?

ALAN (*to* DYSART): I couldn't . . . see her.

DYSART: What do you mean?

ALAN (*to* DYSART): Only Him. Every time I kissed her — *He* was in the way.

DYSART: Who?

(ALAN *turns on his back.*)

ALAN (*to* DYSART): You *know* who! . . . When I touched her, I felt *Him.* Under me . . . His side, waiting for my hand . . . His flanks . . . I refused him. I looked. I looked right at her . . . and I couldn't do it. When I shut my eyes, I saw him at once. The streaks on his belly . . . (*With more desperation.*) I couldn't feel *her* flesh at all! I wanted the foam off his neck. His sweaty hide. Not flesh. *Hide! Horse-hide!* . . . Then I couldn't even kiss her.

(JILL *sits up.*)

JILL: What is it?

ALAN (*dodging her hand*): No!

(*He scrambles up and crouches in the corner against the rails, like a little beast in a cage.*)

JILL: Alan!

ALAN: Stop it!

(JILL *gets up.*)

JILL: It's all right . . . It's all right . . . Don't worry about it. It often happens — honest. . . . There's nothing wrong. I don't mind, you know . . . I don't at all.

(*He dashes past her downstage.*)

Alan, look at me . . . Alan? . . . Alan!

(*He collapses again by the rail.*)

ALAN: Get out! . . .

JILL: What?

ALAN (*soft*): Out!

JILL: There's nothing wrong: believe me! It's very common.

ALAN: *Get out!*

(*He snatches up the invisible pick.*)

GET OUT!

JILL: Put that down!

ALAN: Leave me alone!

JILL: Put that down, Alan. It's very dangerous. Go on, please — drop it.

(*He "drops" it, and turns from her.*)

ALAN: You ever tell anyone. Just you tell . . .

JILL: Who do you think I am? . . . I'm your friend — Alan . . .

(*She goes towards him.*)

Listen: you don't have to do anything. Try to realize that. Nothing at all. Why don't we just lie here together in the straw. And talk.

ALAN (*low*): Please . . .

JILL: Just talk.

ALAN: *Please!*

JILL: All right, I'm going . . . Let me put my clothes on first.

(*She dresses, hastily.*)

ALAN: You tell anyone! . . . Just tell and see. . . .

JILL: Oh, *stop it!* . . . I wish you could believe me. It's not in the least important.

(*Pause.*)

Anyway, I won't say anything. You know that. You know I won't. . . .

(*Pause. He stands with his back to her.*)

Goodnight, then, Alan. . . . I wish — I really wish —

(*He turns on her, hissing. His face is distorted — possessed. In horrified alarm she turns — fumbles the door open — leaves the barn — shuts the door hard behind her, and dashes up the tunnel out of sight, past the barely visible figure of* NUGGET.)

SCENE 34

ALAN *stands alone, and naked.*

A faint humming and drumming. The boy looks about him in growing terror.

DYSART: What?

ALAN (*to* DYSART): He was there. Through the door. The door was shut, but he was there! . . . He'd seen everything. I could hear him. He was laughing.

DYSART: Laughing?

ALAN (*to* DYSART): Mocking! . . . *Mocking!* . . .

(*Standing downstage he stares up towards the*

tunnel. *A great silence weighs on the square.*)

(*To the silence: terrified.*) Friend . . . Equus the Kind . . . The Merciful! . . . *Forgive me!* . . .

(*Silence.*)

It wasn't me. Not really me. Me! . . . Forgive me! . . . Take me back again! Please! . . . PLEASE!

(*He kneels on the downstage lip of the square, still facing the door, huddling in fear.*)

I'll never do it again. I swear . . . I swear! . . .

(*Silence.*)

(*In a moan.*) Please! ! ! . . .

DYSART: And He? What does He say?

ALAN (*to* DYSART: *whispering*): "Mine! . . . You're mine! . . . I am yours and you are mine!" . . . Then I see his eyes. They are rolling!

(NUGGET *begins to advance slowly, with relentless hooves, down the central tunnel.*)

"I see you. I see you. Always! Everywhere! Forever!"

DYSART: Kiss anyone and I will see?

ALAN (*to* DYSART): Yes!

DYSART: Lie with anyone and I will see?

ALAN (*to* DYSART): Yes!

DYSART: And you will fail! Forever and ever you will *fail!* You will see ME — and you will FAIL!

(*The boy turns round, hugging himself in pain. From the sides two more horses converge with* NUGGET *on the rails. Their hooves stamp angrily. The Equus noise is heard more terribly.*)

The Lord thy God is a Jealous God. He sees you. He sees you forever and ever, Alan. He sees you! . . . *He sees you!*

ALAN (*in terror*): Eyes! . . . White eyes — never closed! Eyes like flames — coming — coming! . . . God seest! God seest! . . . NO! . . .

(*Pause. He steadies himself. The stage begins to blacken.*)

(*Quieter.*) No more. No more, Equus.

(*He gets up. He goes to the bench. He takes up the invisible pick. He moves slowly upstage towards* NUGGET, *concealing the weapon behind his naked back, in the growing darkness. He stretches out his hand and fondles* NUGGET's *mask.*)

(*Gently.*) Equus . . . Noble Equus . . . Faithful and True . . . Godslave . . . Thou — God — Seest — NOTHING!

(*He stabs out* NUGGET's *eyes. The horse stamps in agony. A great screaming begins to fill the theatre, growing ever louder.* ALAN *dashes at the other two horses and blinds them too, stabbing over the rails. Their metal hooves join in the stamping.*

Relentlessly, as this happens, three more horses appear in cones of light: not naturalistic animals like the first three, but dreadful creatures out of nightmare. Their eyes flare — their nostrils flare — their mouths flare. They are archetypal images — judging, punishing, pitiless. They do not halt at the rail, but invade the square. As they trample at him, the boy leaps desperately at them, jumping high and naked in the dark, slashing at their heads with arms upraised.

The screams increase. The other horses follow into the square. The whole place is filled with cannoning, blinded horses — and the boy dodging among them, avoiding their slashing hooves as best he can. Finally they plunge off into darkness and away out of sight. The noise dies abruptly, and all we hear is ALAN *yelling in hysteria as he collapses on the ground — stabbing at his own eyes with the invisible pick.*)

ALAN: Find me! . . . Find me! . . . Find me! . . . KILL ME! . . . KILL ME! . . .

SCENE 35

The light changes quickly back to brightness. DYSART *enters swiftly, hurls a blanket on the left bench, and rushes over to* ALAN. *The boy is having convulsions on the floor.* DYSART *grabs his hands, forces them from his eyes, scoops him up in his arms and carries him over to the bench.* ALAN *hurls his arms round* DYSART *and clings to him, gasping and kicking his legs in dreadful frenzy.*

DYSART *lays him down and presses his head back on the bench. He keeps talking — urgently talking — soothing the agony as he can.*

DYSART: Here . . . Here . . . Ssssh . . . Ssssh . . . Calm now . . . Lie back. *Just lie back!* Now breathe in deep. Very deep. In . . . Out . . . In . . . Out . . . That's it. . . . In. *Out . . . In . . . Out . . .*

(The boy's breath is drawn into his body with a harsh rasping sound, which slowly grows less. DYSART *puts the blanket over him.)*

Keep it going . . . That's a good boy . . . Very good boy . . . It's all over now, Alan. It's all over. He'll go away now. You'll never see him again, I promise. You'll have no more bad dreams. No more awful nights. Think of that! . . . You are going to be well. I'm going to make you well, I promise you. . . . You'll be here for a while, but I'll be here too, so it won't be so bad. Just trust me . . .

(He stands upright. The boy lies still.)

Sleep now. Have a good long sleep. You've earned it. . . . Sleep. Just sleep. . . . I'm going to make you well.

(He steps backwards into the centre of the square. The light brightens some more. A pause.)

DYSART: I'm lying to you, Alan. He won't really go that easily. Just clop away from you like a nice old nag. Oh, no! When Equus leaves — if he leaves at all — it will be with your intestines in his teeth. And I don't stock replacements. . . . If you knew anything, you'd get up this minute and run from me fast as you could.

*(*HESTHER *speaks from her place.)*

HESTHER: The boy's in pain, Martin.
DYSART: Yes.
HESTHER: And you can take it away.
DYSART: Yes.
HESTHER: Then that has to be enough for you, surely? . . . In the end!
DYSART *(crying out)*: *All right! I'll take it away!* He'll be delivered from madness. *What then?* He'll feel himself acceptable! *What then?* Do you think feelings like his can be simply re-attached, like plasters? Stuck on to other objects we select? *Look at him! . . .* My desire might be to make this boy an ardent husband — a caring citizen — a worshipper of abstract and unifying God. My achievement, however, is more likely to make a ghost! . . . Let me tell you exactly what I'm going to do to him!

(He steps out of the square and walks round the upstage end of it, storming at the audience.)

I'll heal the rash on his body. I'll erase the welts cut into his mind by flying manes. When that's done, I'll set him on a nice mini-scooter and send him puttering off into the Normal world where animals are treated *properly*: made extinct, or put into servitude, or tethered all their lives in dim light, just to feed it! I'll give him the good Normal world where we're tethered beside them — blinking our nights away in a nonstop drench of cathode-ray over our shrivelling heads! I'll take away his Field of Ha Ha, and give him Normal places for his ecstasy — multi-lane highways driven through the guts of cities, extinguishing Place altogether, *even the idea of Place!* He'll trot on his metal pony tamely through the concrete evening — and one thing I promise you: he will never touch hide again! With any luck his private parts will come to feel as plastic to him as the products of the factory to which he will almost certainly be sent. Who knows? He may even come to find sex funny. Smirky funny. Bit of grunt funny. Trampled and furtive and entirely in control. Hopefully, he'll feel nothing at his fork but Approved Flesh. *I doubt, however, with much passion! . . .* Passion, you see, can be destroyed by a doctor. It cannot be created.

(He addresses ALAN *directly, in farewell.)*

You won't gallop any more, Alan. Horses will be quite safe. You'll save your pennies every week, till you can change that scooter in for a car, and put the odd fifty P on the gee-gees, quite forgetting that they were ever anything more to you than bearers of little profits and little losses. You will, however, be without pain. More or less completely without pain.

(Pause.

He speaks directly to the theatre, standing by the motionless body of ALAN STRANG, *under the blanket.*)

And now for me it never stops: that voice of Equus out of the cave — "Why Me? . . . Why Me? . . . Account for Me!" . . . All right — I surrender! I say it . . . In an ultimate sense I cannot know what I do in this place — yet I do ultimate things. Essentially I cannot know what I do — yet I do essential things. Irreversib!e, terminal things. I stand in the dark with a pick in my hand, striking at heads!

(*He moves away from* ALAN, *back to the downstage bench, and finally sits.*)

I need — more desperately than my children need me — a way of seeing in the dark. What way is this? . . . *What dark is this?* . . . I cannot call it ordained of God: I can't get that far. I will however pay it so much homage. There is now, in my mouth, this sharp chain. And it never comes out.

(*A long pause.*
DYSART *sits staring.*)

BLACKOUT

The first play in this group of tragedies, and the most ancient, is Sophocles' *Oedipus the King* (about 430 B.C.). It is a commonplace of dramatic criticism that *Oedipus* is a sort of detective story in which the detective, Oedipus, searches for the criminal and discovers that he himself is the object of his search. Part of the greatness of the play surely resides in the fact that Oedipus, in his relentless search for the truth, strips away all comforting illusions, pursuing his quest even when it becomes evident that he himself may be the culprit. Oedipus' triumph, and, in part, ours as we watch him, is that he is determined to know the truth at whatever cost.

In some ways, Peter Shaffer's *Equus*, too, is a sort of detective story. We are told at the start of the play that Alan Strang has blinded six horses. As the play progresses, we learn, through the psychiatrist's careful analytic or detective work, why Alan blinded the horses. The analyst uses the devices of a detective: for example, he invites himself to the boy's home to see what he can learn, and he does so on a Sunday: "If there's any tension over religion, it should be evident on a Sabbath evening." And bit by bit the full story of the crime is revealed. In Scene 6 we are told that Alan screams something that sounds like "Ek," but not until Scene 14 is this puzzle explained, when Alan's father mentions that he heard the boy say, "Equus my only begotten son." Similarly, we first hear about Jill, very casually, in Scene 12, but not until much later do we understand the part she played in Alan's life.

The stage-set itself — "tiers of seats in the fashion of a dissecting theatre" surrounding the place of action — contributes to this sense that we are watching a detective find his way, like a surgeon, to the hidden disease or crime. Two other implications of the set are also significant: the tiers surround a square that "resembles a railed boxing ring," and it is here that the two chief characters, Alan Strang and Dr. Martin Dysart, slug it out; the set perhaps also suggests a sort of courtroom, with Alan as both the witness and the criminal at the bar. The whole set, the square embraced by tiers on which spectators sit, is itself a sort of entire theater with actors and audience, but those of us who are spectators in the auditorium are linked to the action by means of our fellow spectators who, like the audience in a Greek amphitheater, sit in the tiers. We are onlookers, but insofar as we are aware of the spectators in the tiers we are looking at people like ourselves, and all of us are looking at a boy who had "always been such a gentle boy," and who had seemed, to the owner of the stable, an ideal stable-hand. We are watching, then, the uncovering of the deepest feelings that reside in what seems — or had seemed — to be a fairly ordinary boy.

But of course Alan is not a fairly ordinary boy; he had only seemed to be one. Although it is risky enough even for experts to try to psychoanalyze real people, and it is usually foolish to try to psychoanalyze characters in a play, it seems fairly clear that Alan is schizoid. That is, he has markedly withdrawn from reality. As the play progresses, we come to see that Alan, like the classic schizophrenic — at least as understood by R. D. Laing in *The Politics of Experience* (1967) — allows his outer self to live in the normal world (Alan lives a humdrum life at home and in the electrical supply store) but preserves an inner self that is radically contemptuous of the normal world and that sometimes suddenly shows itself in some violent, unsocial action. The inner life of such a person is more "real" than the outer, daily bodily life, and so Alan can insist to his god Equus, after the abortive sexual episode with Jill, "It wasn't me. Not really me." This is not mere weaseling; for the schizophrenic, there is a sharp separation between the real, inner "me" and the body that goes through a daily hateful routine.

In his prefatory material Shaffer tells us that the play had its origins in a real occurrence, but it is clear, too, that the play is also indebted to a Freudian interpretation of reality, and it may not be a coincidence that horses figure in one of Freud's most interesting analyses, the case of Little Hans: Hans feared that he would be bitten by a horse, and it seems fairly clear that the horse symbolized Hans's father, a potential castrator. We can compare Hans's father to Alan's father, Frank Strang, who deprives his child of various pleasures and who, when he pulled the child Alan off a horse, caused the boy to fall. This is not, of course, to suggest that the play is a dramatization of the case of Little Hans, or of any specific case, for Shaffer tells us that although he began with a real episode he had recently heard of, he freely changed it as he worked on his play. For Alan, the horse is not (as it was for Hans) simply frightening: it is, among other things, an escape from the father and the dull world he represents ("Come on, Trojan — bear me away"). "All that power going any way you wanted," and "Then suddenly I was on the ground where Dad pulled me. I could have bashed him." Moreover, the horse is the god Alan worships. This worship is filled with echoes from the Bible, especially with suggestions of Christ. Equus, "born in the straw," is "in chains" for "the sins of the world"; when Alan takes Nugget out of the stable, he gives the horse a lump of sugar which is "His last supper"; when the horse eats the sugar he takes upon himself Alan's "sins," and Alan says, "Into my hands he commends himself," echoing Jesus' words in Luke 23:46, "Father, into thy hands I commend my spirit." And Alan, fascinated by Nugget's eyes, believes Nugget sees everything, because Alan's mother had said, "God sees you, Alan. God's got eyes everywhere."

It is interesting to note that in the early drafts of the play both parents were religiously obsessed, but Shaffer reduced the mother's obsession and eliminated the father's, lest the audience find the boy too obvious or neat a case. As we shall see, the boy is not supposed to be understood as the sick manifestation of sick parents. The play seeks to be much more than a dramatization of schizoid behavior, and that is why it concerns us. It claims, finally, not to present one strange case but to offer a vision of life. (Similarly, if Sophocles' *Oedipus the King* were merely a dramatization of a man who killed his father and married his mother — if it were simply a dramatization of a curious episode rooted in the Oedipus complex — rather than a dramatization of what can be taken as a story of a hero, it would scarcely be of interest to more than a few psychiatrists.)

Any comments of what a play is "about" must, of course, be imprecise, for a play consists of thousands of details that inevitably make any summary and brief interpretation a distortion. Still, we can say that the play dramatizes not a curious case history but the tragic conflict between the world of passion and mystery and the world of numbness and sociability. We have seen glimpses of some such conflict in other tragedies: Oedipus' passionate desire to find out the truth about his origins, versus Iocasta's sensible suggestion that it is best to let sleeping dogs lie; or King Lear's madness on the heath ("I abjure all roofs"), versus his wicked daughters' seemingly reasonable view that old men should not try to hang on to the power they cannot effectively wield. The paradox in this play is that Dysart, the apparently rational psychiatrist who is charged with restoring Alan to the normal world, envies Alan's irrationality. It is Dysart's fate to be married to a dentist, a thoroughly sensible Scottish woman who cannot share his interest in the world of ancient art and ritual:

> I pass her a picture of the sacred acrobats of Crete leaping through the horns of running bulls — and she'll say: "Och, Martin, what an *absurred* thing to be doing! The Highland Games, now there's a *norrmal sport!*" Or she'll observe, just after I've told her a story from the Iliad: "You know, when you come to think of it, Agamemnon and that lot were nothing but a bunch of ruffians from the Gorbals, only with fancy names!" You get the picture. She's turned into a Shrink.

But what of Dysart himself? Is he an Alan who has somehow bridged the gulf and managed to live a socially useful life? First of all, as he knows, he has none of Alan's passion. His trips to Greece are not "wild returns . . . to the womb of civilization":

> Three weeks a year in the Peleponnese, every bed booked in advance, every meal paid for by vouchers, cautious jaunts in hired Fiats, suitcase crammed with Kao-Pectate! Such a fantastic surrender to the primitive. And I use that word endlessly: "primitive." "Oh, the primitive world," I say. "What instinctual truths were lost with it!" . . . I sit looking at pages of centaurs trampling the soil of Argos — and outside my window he is trying to *become one*, in a Hampshire field!

Dysart's awareness of his own lack of deep feeling and of separation from mystery makes him envy Alan, particularly Alan's pain. "His pain. His own. He made it." It is a curious fact that as we look at the sufferings of tragic characters — Oedipus insisting on an agonizing search for the truth that culminates when he blinds himself, Lear rejecting the shelter of a daughter's roof in preference to a stormy heath — we feel that these sufferings are, in a way, their most precious possession. Lesser people are numbed by sufferings, but by taking on sufferings tragic heroes somehow fulfill themselves. They choose their way of life, and all that it entails. With Melville's Ahab they say, "Oh, now I feel my topmost greatness in my topmost grief." Some such awareness causes Dysart to say, "That boy has known a passion more ferocious than I have felt in any second of my life. And let me tell you something: I envy it." He has been critical of his way, and he goes on to dissect his own failure:

> The finicky, critical husband looking through his art books on mythical Greece. What worship has *he* ever known? Real worship! Without worship you shrink, it's as brutal as that . . . I shrank my own life.

If Alan's tragedy is that he has chosen a life radically different from the normal world's, and he must suffer for it, Dysart's is that he chose the normal world, and he suffers — though less intensely — from the knowledge that he has made the wrong choice. Even at the start of the play we heard suggestions to this effect. Dysart tells us that he is

> all reined up in old language and old assumptions, straining to jump clean-hoofed on to a whole new track of being I only suspect is there. I can't see it, because my educated, average head is being held at the wrong angle. I can't jump because the bit forbids it, and my own basic force — my horsepower, if you like — is too little. The only thing I know for sure is this: a horse's head is finally unknowable to me. Yet I handle children's heads — which I must presume to be more complicated, at least in the area of my chief concern. . . . In a way, it has nothing to do with this boy. The doubts have been there for years, piling up steadily in this dreary place. It's only the extremity of this case that's made them active. I know that. The *extremity* is the point.

Tragic heroes thrive on "extremity," situations in which all of the normal responses, all of the world's good sense, prove to be inadequate, or at least are found to be inadequate by the passionate individual who cannot let well enough alone, who cannot go along with the way of the world. We can think of Oedipus' determination to learn of his parentage, or Lear's determination to do more than merely subsist. As Arthur Miller puts it on page 306, the tragic hero "is ready to lay down his life, if need be, to secure one thing — his sense of personal dignity."

Dysart clearly sees himself as one who does go the way of the world, as one who is unwilling, or unable, to lay down his life in order to achieve his personal dignity. His job is to make people normal, to make healthy the sick, but he has come to feel that he is the "priest" of the "murderous God of Health." On the first night after he meets Alan he dreams that he sacrifices children to the "normal," but he cannot bring himself to sacrifice himself to his new insight. On the other hand, Alan, superficially a most unlikely tragic hero, rides with the god Equus against the world of the normal, against "The Hosts of Hoover. The Hosts of Philco. . . . The House of Remington and all its tribe." It is Dysart's job to reconcile Alan to the normal world that Dysart scorns and yet participates in. It is, in short, Dysart's sickening job to deprive Alan of the worship of Equus. "Can you think of anything worse one can do to anybody than to take away their worship?" Or to take away the pain by which a worshipper knows he has preserved himself from the deadly claims of a normal, socialized world? Dysart may be able to cure Alan of his worship of Equus, but only at the cost of robbing Alan of his most precious possession. "If you knew anything, you'd get up this minute and run from me as fast as you could. . . . My desire might be to make this boy an ardent husband — a caring citizen — a worshipper of abstract and unifying God. My achievement, however, is more likely to make a ghost." If we have read *Oedipus* and *Lear*, we are familiar with a vision that shows greatness finding itself in a painful sacrifice of self. And this sacrifice somehow purifies or strengthens the society that survives it. In *Equus*, Shaffer suggests that the sacrifice of the deeply feeling hero brings not new strength or health to society but only death, or death in life, for it represents only the triumph of the normal.

The normal, reasonable, social world has always been opposed to the world of tragic heroes and tragic poets. Plato, in *The Republic*, in a passage called "The Myth of Er," tells how the tragic king Agamemnon chose to be reincarnated as an eagle, thereby implying that the passionate, tragic figure is at heart really less than a human being, not more than one. And in the same book Plato bans the tragic poets from his ideal city because they feed the passions instead of starving them as rational men wish. *The Republic* is no less great a vision of man than any tragic play, but it is a very different vision, and — like a tragic play — it cannot tell the whole truth.

A few words must be said about the nudity in Scene 33 because it has provoked much comment. Surely, however, one thing it does not provoke is any erotic feeling. It is not strictly necessary, since in an earlier scene Alan simply mimes taking off his clothes, but it is entirely justifiable theatrically. In a way, it is foreshadowed in Scene 23, when Dysart explains to Alan's mother that the boy is "at a most delicate stage of treatment! He's totally exposed." And so in Scene 33, when Alan, reliving the sexual episode with Jill, collapses under the stress of his betrayal and failure, it is not only literally appropriate but also symbolically appropriate for him to be utterly naked, utterly vulnerable. Of course Shakespeare was content, when Lear tears at his clothes, to keep Lear minimally attired, and O'Neill similarly did not strip the Emperor Jones of every shred of clothing. But, as Brecht says (see p. 573), much tragic drama is a sort of striptease in which an individual's "innermost being is . . . driven into the open," and Shaffer has only made explicit and theatrical what is implicit. If the device has a fault, it is not that it is obscene but that it may embarrass an audience.

The Poetics

Aristotle

Translated by L. J. Potts

It is no exaggeration to say that the history of tragic criticism is a series of footnotes to Aristotle. In a fragmentary treatise usually called the *Poetics*, Aristotle (384–322 B.C.) raises almost all the points that have subsequently been argued, such as the nature of the hero, the emotional effect on the spectator, the coherence of the plot. Whether or not he gave the right answers, it has seemed for more than two thousand years that he asked the right questions.

[ART IS IMITATION]

Let us talk of the art of poetry as a whole, and its different species with the particular force of each of them; how the fables must be put together if the poetry is to be well formed; also what are its elements and their different qualities; and all other matters pertaining to the subject.

To begin in the proper order, at the beginning. The making of epics and of tragedies, and also comedy, and the art of the dithyramb, and most flute and lyre art, all have this in common, that they are imitations. But they differ from one another in three respects: the different kinds of medium in which they imitate, the different objects they imitate, and the different manner in which they imitate (when it does differ).... When the imitators imitate the doings of people, the people in the imitation must be either high or low; the characters almost always follow this line exclusively, for all men differ in character according to their degree of goodness or badness. They must therefore be either above our norm, or below it, or normal; as, in painting, Polygnōtus depicted superior, Pauson inferior, and Dionysius normal, types. It is clear that each variant of imitation

Reprinted from *Aristotle on the Art of Fiction* by L. J. Potts by permission of Cambridge University Press. © 1953 by Cambridge University Press.

that I have mentioned will have these differences, and as the object imitated varies in this way so the works will differ. Even in the ballet, and in flute and lyre music, these dissimilarities can occur; and in the art that uses prose, or verse without music.... This is the difference that marks tragedy out from comedy; comedy is inclined to imitate persons below the level of our world, tragedy persons above it.

[ORIGINS OF POETRY]

There seem to be two causes that gave rise to poetry in general, and they are natural. The impulse to imitate is inherent in man from his childhood; he is distinguished among the animals by being the most imitative of them, and he takes the first steps of his education by imitating. Everyone's enjoyment of imitation is also inborn. What happens with works of art demonstrates this: though a thing itself is disagreeable to look at, we enjoy contemplating the most accurate representations of it — for instance, figures of the most despicable animals, or of human corpses. The reason for this lies in another fact: learning is a great pleasure, not only to philosophers but likewise to everyone else, however limited his gift for it may be. He enjoys looking at these representations, because in the act of studying them he is learning — identifying the object by an inference (for instance, recognizing who is the original of a portrait); since, if he happens not to have already seen the object depicted, it will not be the imitation as such that is giving him pleasure, but the finish of the workmanship, or the colouring, or some such other cause.

And just as imitation is natural to us, so also are music and rhythm (metres, clearly, are constituent parts of rhythms). Thus, from spontaneous beginnings, mankind developed poetry by a series of mostly minute changes out of these improvisations.

[THE ELEMENTS OF TRAGEDY]

Let us now discuss tragedy, having first picked up from what has been said the definition of its essence that has so far emerged. Tragedy, then, is an imitation of an action of high importance, complete and of some amplitude; in language enhanced by distinct and varying beauties; acted not narrated; by means of pity and fear effecting its purgation of these emotions. By the beauties enhancing the language I mean rhythm and melody; by "distinct and varying" I mean that some are produced by metre alone, and others at another time by melody.

Now since the imitating is done by actors, it would follow of necessity that one element in a tragedy must be the *Mise en scène*. Others are Melody and Language, for these are the media in which the imitating is done. By Language, I mean the component parts of the verse, whereas Melody has an entirely sensuous effect. Again, since the object imitated is an action, and doings are done by persons, whose individuality will be determined by their Character and their Thought (for these are the factors we have in mind when we define the quality of their doings), it follows that there are two natural causes of these doings, Thought and Character; and these causes determine the good or ill fortune of everyone. But the Fable is the imitation of the action; and by the Fable I mean the whole structure of the incidents. By Character I mean the factor that enables us to define the particular quality of the people involved in the doings; and Thought is shown in everything they say when they are demonstrating a fact or disclosing an opinion. There are therefore necessarily six elements in every tragedy, which give it its quality; and they are the Fable, Character, Language, Thought, the *Mise en scène*, and Melody. Two of these are the media in which the imitating is done, one is the manner of imitation, and three are its objects; there is

no other element besides these. Numerous poets have turned these essential components to account; all of them are always present — the *Mise en scene*, Character, the Fable, Language, Melody, and Thought.

The chief of these is the plotting of the incidents; for tragedy is an imitation not of men but of doings, life, happiness; unhappiness is located in doings, and our end is a certain kind of doing, not a personal quality; it is their characters that give men their quality, but their doings that make them happy or the opposite. So it is not the purpose of the actors to imitate character, but they include character as a factor in the doings. Thus it is the incidents (that is to say the Fable) that are the end for which tragedy exists; and the end is more important than anything else. Also, without an action there could not be a tragedy, but without Character there could. (In fact, the tragedies of most of the moderns are non-moral, and there are many non-moral poets of all periods; this also applies to the paintings of Zeuxis, if he is compared with Polygnōtus, for whereas Polygnōtus is a good portrayer of character the painting of Zeuxis leaves it out.) Again, if any one strings together moral speeches with the language and thought well worked out, he will be doing what is the business of tragedy; but it will be done much better by a tragedy that handles these elements more weakly, but has a fable with the incidents connected by a plot. Further, the chief means by which tragedy moves us, Irony of events and Disclosure, are elements in the Fable. A pointer in the same direction is that beginners in the art of poetry are able to get the language and characterization right before they can plot their incidents, and so were almost all the earliest poets.

So the source and as it were soul of tragedy is the Fable; and Character comes next. For, to instance a parallel from the art of painting, the most beautiful colours splashed on anyhow would not be as pleasing as a recognizable picture in black and white. Tragedy is an imitation of an action, and it is chiefly for this reason that it imitates the persons involved.

Third comes Thought: that is, the ability to say what circumstances allow and what is appropriate to them. It is the part played by social morality and rhetoric in making the dialogue: the old poets made their characters talk like men of the world, whereas our contemporaries make them talk like public speakers. Character is what shows a man's disposition — the kind of things he chooses or rejects when his choice is not obvious. Accordingly those speeches where the speaker shows no preferences or aversions whatever are non-moral. Thought, on the other hand, is shown in demonstrating a matter of fact or disclosing a significant opinion.

Fourth comes the Language. By Language I mean, as has already been said, words used semantically. It has the same force in verse as in prose.

Of the remaining elements, Melody is the chief of the enhancing beauties. The *Mise en scène* can excite emotion, but it is the crudest element and least akin to the art of poetry; for the force of tragedy exists even without stage and actors; besides, the fitting out of a *Mise en scène* belongs more to the wardrobe-master's art than to the poet's.

[THE TRAGIC FABLE]

So much for analysis. Now let us discuss in what sort of way the incidents should be plotted, since that is the first and chief consideration in tragedy. Our data are that tragedy is an imitation of a whole and complete action of some amplitude (a thing can be whole and yet quite lacking in amplitude). Now a whole is that which has a beginning, a middle, and an end. A beginning is that which does not itself necessarily follow anything else, but which leads naturally to another event or development; an end is the opposite, that which itself naturally (either of necessity or most commonly) follows something else, but nothing else comes after it; and a middle is that which itself follows something else and is followed by another thing. So, well-plotted fables must not begin or end casually, but must follow the pattern here described.

But, besides this, a picture, or any other composite object, if it is to be beautiful, must not only have its parts properly arranged, but be of an appropriate size; for beauty depends on size and structure. Accordingly, a minute picture cannot be beautiful (for when our vision has almost lost its sense of time it becomes confused); nor can an immense one (for we cannot take it all in together, and so our vision loses its unity and wholeness) — imagine a picture a thousand miles long! So, just as there is a proper size for bodies and pictures (a size that can be well surveyed), there is also a proper amplitude for fables (what can be kept well in one's mind). The length of the performance on the stage has nothing to do with art; if a hundred tragedies had to be produced, the length of the production would be settled by the clock, as the story goes that another kind of performance once was. But as to amplitude, the invariable rule dictated by the nature of the action is the fuller the more beautiful so long as the outline remains clear; and for a simple rule of size, the number of happenings that will make a chain of probability (or necessity) to change a given situation from misfortune to good fortune or from good fortune to misfortune is the minimum.

[UNITY]

Unity in a fable does not mean, as some think, that it has one man for its subject. To any one man many things happen — an infinite number — and some of them do not make any sort of unity; and in the same way one man has many doings which cannot be made into a unit of action. . . . Accordingly, just as in the other imitative arts the object of each imitation is a unit, so, since the fable is an imitation of an action, that action must be a complete unit, and the events of which it is made up must be so plotted that if any of these elements is moved or removed the whole is altered and upset. For when a thing can be included or not included without making any noticeable difference, that thing is no part of the whole.

[PROBABILITY]

From what has been said it is also clear that it is not the poet's business to tell what has happened, but the kind of things that would happen — what is possible according to probability or necessity. The difference between the historian and the poet is not the difference between writing in verse or prose; the work of Herodotus could be put into verse, and it would be just as much a history in verse as it is in prose. The difference is that the one tells what has happened, and the other the kind of things that would happen. It follows therefore that poetry is more philosophical and of higher value than history; for poetry unifies more, whereas history aggregates. To unify is to make a man of a certain description say or do the things that suit him, probably or necessarily, in the circumstances (this is the point of the descriptive proper names in poetry); what Alcibiades did or what happened to him is an aggregation. In comedy this has now become clear. They first plot the fable on a base of probabilities, and then find imaginary names for the people — unlike the lampooners, whose work was an aggregation of personalities. But in tragedy they keep to the names of real people. This is because possibility depends on conviction; if a thing has not happened we are not yet convinced that it is possible, but if it has happened it is clearly possible, for it would not have happened if it were impossible. Even tragedies, however, sometimes have all their persons fictitious except for one or two known names; and sometimes they have not a single known name, as in the *Anthos* of Agathon, in which both the events and the names are equally fictitious, without in the least reducing the delight it gives. It is not, therefore, requisite at all costs to keep to the traditional fables from which our tragedies draw their subject-matter. It would be absurd to insist on that, since even the known legends are known only to a few, and yet the delight is shared by every one. . . .

[SIMPLE AND COMPLEX FABLES]

The action imitated must contain incidents that evoke fear and pity, besides being a complete action; but this effect is accentuated when these incidents occur logically as well as unexpectedly, which will be more sensational than if they happen arbitrarily, by chance. Even when events are accidental the sensation is greater if they appear to have a purpose, as when the statue of Mitys at Argos killed the man who had caused his death, by falling on him at a public entertainment. Such things appear not to have happened blindly. Inevitably, therefore, plots of this sort are finer.

Some fables are simple, others complex: for the obvious reason that the original actions imitated by the fables are the one or the other. By a simple action I mean one that leads to the catastrophe in the way we have laid down, directly and singly, without Irony of events or Disclosure.

An action is complex when the catastrophe involves Disclosure, or Irony, or both. But these complications should develop out of the very structure of the fable, so that they fit what has gone before, either necessarily or probably. To happen after something is by no means the same as to happen because of it.

[IRONY]

Irony is a reversal in the course of events, of the kind specified, and, as I say, in accordance with probability or necessity. Thus in the *Oedipus* the arrival of the messenger, which was expected to cheer Oedipus up by releasing him from his fear about his mother, did the opposite by showing him who he was; and in the *Lynceus* [Abas], who was awaiting sentence of death, was acquitted, whereas his prosecutor Dănaüs was killed, and all this arose out of what had happened previously.

A Disclosure, as the term indicates, is a change from ignorance to knowledge; if the people are marked out for good fortune it leads to affection, if for misfortune, to enmity. Disclosure produces its finest effect when it is connected with Irony, as the disclosure in the *Oedipus* is. There are indeed other sorts of Disclosure: the process I have described can even apply to inanimate objects of no significance, and mistakes about what a man has done or not done can be cleared up. But the sort I have specified is more a part of the fable and of the action than any other sort; for this coupling of Irony and Disclosure will carry with it pity or fear, which we have assumed to be the nature of the doings tragedy imitates; and further, such doings will constitute good or ill fortune. Assuming then that it is a disclosure of the identity of persons, it may be of one person only, to the other, when the former knows who the latter is; or sometimes both have to be disclosed — for instance, the sending of the letter led Orestes to the discovery of Iphigeneia, and there had to be another disclosure to make him known to her.

This then is the subject-matter of two elements in the Fable, Irony and Disclosure. A third element is the Crisis of feeling. Irony and Disclosure have been defined; the Crisis of feeling is a harmful or painful experience, such as deaths in public, violent pain, physical injuries, and everything of that sort.

[THE TRAGIC PATTERN]

Following the proper order, the next subject to discuss after this would be: What one should aim at and beware of in plotting fables; that is to say, What will produce the tragic effect. Since, then, tragedy, to be at its finest, requires a complex, not a simple, structure, and its structure should also imitate fearful and pitiful events (for that is the peculiarity of this sort of imitation), it is clear: first, that decent people must not be shown passing from good fortune to misfortune (for that is not fearful or pitiful but disgusting); again, vicious people must not be shown passing from misfortune to good fortune (for that is the most untragic situation possible — it has none of the requisites, it is neither humane, nor pitiful, nor fearful); nor again should an utterly evil man fall from good fortune into misfortune (for though a plot of that kind would be humane, it would not induce pity or fear — pity is induced by undeserved misfortune, and fear by the misfortunes of normal people, so that this situation will be neither pitiful nor fearful). So we are left with the man between these extremes: that is to say, the kind of man who neither is distinguished for excellence and virtue, nor comes to grief on account of baseness and vice, but on account of some error; a man of great reputation and prosperity, like Oedipus and Thyestes and conspicuous people of such families as theirs. So, to be well informed, a fable must be single rather than (as some say) double — there must be no change from misfortune to good fortune, but only the opposite, from good fortune to misfortune; the cause must not be vice, but a great error; and the man must be either of the type specified or better, rather than worse. This is borne out by the practice of poets; at first they picked a fable at random and made an inventory of its contents, but now the finest tragedies are plotted, and concern a few families — for example, the tragedies about Alcmeon, Oedipus, Orestes, Mĕlĕāger, Thyestes, Tĕlĕphus, and any others whose lives were attended by terrible experiences or doings.

This is the plot that will produce the technically finest tragedy. Those critics are therefore wrong who censure Euripides on this very ground — because he does this in his tragedies, and many of them end in misfortune; for it is, as I have said, the right thing to do. This is clearly demonstrated on the stage in the competitions, where such plays, if they succeed, are the most tragic, and Euripides, even if he is inefficient in every other respect, still shows himself the most tragic of our poets. The next best plot, which is said by some people to be the best, is the tragedy with a double plot, like the *Odyssey*, ending in one way for the better people and in the opposite way for the worse. But it is the weakness of theatrical performances that gives priority to this kind; when poets write what the audience would like to happen, they are in leading strings. This is not the pleasure proper to tragedy, but rather to comedy, where the greatest enemies in the fable, say Orestes and Aegisthus, make friends and go off at the end, and nobody is killed by anybody.

[THE TRAGIC EMOTIONS]

The pity and fear can be brought about by the *Mise en scène*; but they can also come from the mere plotting of the incidents, which is preferable, and better poetry. For, without seeing anything, the fable ought to have been so plotted that if one heard the bare facts, the chain of circumstances would make one shudder and pity. That would happen to anyone who heard the fable of the *Oedipus*. To produce this effect by the *Mise en scène* is less artistic and puts one at the mercy of the technician; and those who use it not to frighten but merely to startle have lost touch with tragedy altogether. We should not try to get all sorts of pleasure from tragedy, but the particular tragic pleasure. And clearly, since this pleasure coming from pity and fear has to be produced by imitation, it is by his handling of the incidents that the poet must create it.

Let us, then, take next the kind of circumstances that seem terrible or lamentable. Now, doings of that kind must be between friends, or enemies, or neither. If an enemy injures an enemy, there is no pity either beforehand or at the time, except on account of the bare fact; nor is there if they are neutral; but when sufferings are engendered among the affections — for example, if murder is done or planned, or some similar outrage is committed, by brother on brother, or son on father, or mother on son, or son on mother — that is the thing to aim at.

Though it is not permissible to ruin the traditional fables — I mean, such as the killing of Clytemnestra by Orestes, or Erĭphyle by Alcmeon — the poet should use his own invention to refine on what has been handed down to him. Let me explain more clearly what I mean by "refine." The action may take place, as the old poets used to make it, with the knowledge and understanding of the participants; this was how Euripides made Medea kill her children. Or they may do it, but in ignorance of the horror of the deed, and then afterwards discover the tie of affection, like the Oedipus of Sophocles; his act was outside the play, but there are examples where it is inside the tragedy itself — Alcmeon in the play by Astydămas, or Tĕlĕgōnus in *The Wounded Odysseus*. Besides these, there is a third possibility: when a man is about to do some fatal act in ignorance, but is enlightened before he does it. These are the only possible alternatives. One must either act or not act, and either know or not know. Of these alternatives, to know, and to be about to act, and then not to act, is thoroughly bad — it is disgusting without being tragic, for there is no emotional crisis; accordingly poets only rarely create such situations, as in the *Antigone*, when Haemon fails to kill Creon. Next in order is to act; and if the deed is done in ignorance and its nature is disclosed afterwards, so much the better — there is no bad taste in it, and the revelation is overpowering. But the last is best; I mean, like Měrŏpe in the *Cresphontes*, intending to kill her son, but recognizing him and not killing him; and the brother and sister in the *Iphigeneia*; and in the *Helle*, the son recognizing his mother just as he was going to betray her. — This is the reason for what was mentioned earlier: that the subject-matter of our tragedies is drawn from a few families. In their search for matter they discovered this recipe in the fables, not by cunning but by luck. So they are driven to have recourse to those families where such emotional crises have occurred. . . .

[CHARACTER]

And in the characterization, as in the plotting of the incidents, the aim should always be either necessity or probability: so that they say or do such things as it is necessary or probable that they would, being what they are; and that for this to follow that is either necessary or probable. . . . As for extravagant incidents, there should be none in the story, or if there are they should be kept outside the tragedy, as is the one in the *Oedipus* of Sophocles.

Since tragedy is an imitation of people above the normal, we must be like good portrait-painters, who follow the original model closely, but refine on it; in the same way the poet, in imitating people whose character is choleric or phlegmatic, and so forth, must keep them as they are and at the same time make them attractive. So Homer made Achilles noble, as well as a pattern of obstinacy. . . .

[CHORUS]

Treat the chorus as though it were one of the actors; it should be an organic part of the play and reinforce it, not as it is in Euripides, but as in Sophocles. In their successors the songs belong no more to the fable than to that of any other tragedy. This has led to the insertion of borrowed lyrics, an innovation for which Agathon was responsible.

Tragedy and the Common Man

Arthur Miller

Arthur Miller's "Tragedy and the Common Man" was written while his *Death of a Salesman* was running on Broadway. Implicitly a defense of his play, the essay's assertions about the nature of the tragic hero have implications for other plays about middle-class figures and even for earlier tragedies with heroes of high rank.

In this age few tragedies are written. It has often been held that the lack is due to a paucity of heroes among us, or else that modern man has had the blood drawn out of his organs of belief by the skepticism of science, and the heroic attack on life cannot feed on an attitude of reserve and circumspection. For one reason or another, we are often held to be below tragedy — or tragedy above us. The inevitable conclusion is, of course, that the tragic mode is archaic, fit only for the very highly placed, the kings or the kingly, and where this admission is not made in so many words it is most often implied.

I believe that the common man is as apt a subject for tragedy in its highest sense as kings were. On the face of it this ought to be obvious in the light of modern psychiatry, which bases its analysis upon classific formulations, such as the Oedipus and Orestes complexes, for instance, which were enacted by royal beings, but which apply to everyone in similar emotional situations.

More simply, when the question of tragedy in art is not at issue, we never hesitate to attribute to the well-placed and the exalted the very same mental processes as the lowly. And finally, if the exaltation of tragic action were truly a property of the high-bred character alone, it is inconceivable that the mass of mankind should

Reprinted by permission of International Creative Management. Copyright © 1949, 1977 by Arthur Miller.

cherish tragedy above all other forms, let alone be capable of understanding it.

As a general rule, to which there may be exceptions unknown to me, I think the tragic feeling is evoked in us when we are in the presence of a character who is ready to lay down his life, if need be, to secure one thing — his sense of personal dignity. From Orestes to Hamlet, Medea to Macbeth, the underlying struggle is that of the individual attempting to gain his "rightful" position in his society.

Sometimes he is one who has been displaced from it, sometimes one who seeks to attain it for the first time, but the fateful wound from which the inevitable events spiral is the wound of indignity, and its dominant force is indignation. Tragedy, then, is the consequence of a man's total compulsion to evaluate himself justly.

In the sense of having been initiated by the hero himself, the tale always reveals what has been called his "tragic flaw," a failing that is not peculiar to grand or elevated characters. Nor is it necessarily a weakness. The flaw, or crack in the character, is really nothing — and need be nothing — but his inherent unwillingness to remain passive in the face of what he conceives to be a challenge to his dignity, his image of his rightful status. Only the passive, only those who accept their lot without active retaliation, are "flawless." Most of us are in that category.

But there are among us today, as there always have been, those who act against the scheme of things that degrades them, and in the process of action, everything we have accepted out of fear or insensitivity or ignorance is shaken before us and examined, and from this total onslaught by an individual against the seemingly stable cosmos surrounding us — from this total examination of the "unchangeable" environment — comes the terror and the fear that is classically associated with tragedy.

More important, from this total questioning of what has been previously unquestioned, we learn. And such a process is not beyond the common man. In revolutions around the world, these past thirty years, he has demonstrated again and again this inner dynamic of all tragedy.

Insistence upon the rank of the tragic hero, or the so-called nobility of his character, is really but a clinging to the outward forms of tragedy. If rank or nobility of character was indispensable, then it would follow that the problems of those with rank were the particular problems of tragedy. But surely the right of one monarch to capture the domain from another no longer raises our passions, nor are our concepts of justice what they were to the mind of an Elizabethan king.

The quality in such plays that does shake us, however, derives from the underlying fear of being displaced, the disaster inherent in being torn away from our chosen image of what and who we are in this world. Among us today this fear is as strong, and perhaps stronger, than it ever was. In fact, it is the common man who knows this fear best.

Now, if it is true that tragedy is the consequence of a man's total compulsion to evaluate himself justly, his destruction in the attempt posits a wrong or an evil in his environment. And this is precisely the morality of tragedy and its lesson. The discovery of the moral law, which is what the enlightenment of tragedy consists of, is not the discovery of some abstract or metaphysical quantity.

The tragic right is a condition of life, a condition in which the human personality is able to flower and realize itself. The wrong is the condition which suppresses man, perverts the flowing out of his love and creative instinct. Tragedy enlightens — and it must, in that it points the heroic finger at the enemy of man's freedom. The thrust for freedom is the quality in tragedy which exalts. The revolutionary questioning of the stable environment is what terrifies. In no way is the common man debarred from such thoughts or such actions.

Seen in this light, our lack of tragedy may be partially accounted for by the turn which modern literature has taken toward the purely psychiatric view of life, or the purely sociological. If all our miseries, our indignities, are born and bred within our minds, then all action, let alone the heroic action, is obviously impossible.

And if society alone is responsible for the cramping of our lives, then the protagonist must needs be so pure and faultless as to force us to deny his validity as a character. From neither of these views can tragedy derive, simply because neither represents a balanced concept of life. Above all else, tragedy requires the finest appreciation by the writer of cause and effect.

No tragedy can therefore come about when its author fears to question absolutely everything, when he regards any institution, habit or custom as being either everlasting, immutable or inevitable. In the tragic view the need of man to wholly realize himself is the only fixed star, and whatever it is that hedges his nature and lowers it is ripe for attack and examination. Which is not to say that tragedy must preach revolution.

The Greeks could probe the very heavenly origin of their ways and return to confirm the rightness of laws. And Job could face God in anger, demanding his right, and end in submission. But for a moment everything is in suspension, nothing is accepted, and in this stretching and tearing apart of the cosmos, in the very action of so doing, the character gains "size," the tragic stature which is spuriously attached to the royal or the high born in our minds. The commonest of men may take on that stature to the extent of his willingness to throw all he has into the contest, the battle to secure his rightful place in his world.

There is a misconception of tragedy with which I have been struck in review after review, and in many conversations with writers and readers alike. It is the idea that tragedy is of necessity allied to pessimism. Even the dictionary says nothing more about the word than that it means a story with a sad or unhappy ending. This impression is so firmly fixed that I almost hesitate to claim that in truth tragedy implies more optimism in its author than does comedy, and that its final result ought to be the reinforcement of the onlooker's brightest opinions of the human animal.

For, if it is true to say that in essence the tragic hero is intent upon claiming his whole due as a personality, and if this struggle must be total and without reservation, then it automatically demonstrates the indestructible will of man to achieve his humanity.

The possibility of victory must be there in tragedy. Where pathos rules, where pathos is finally derived, a character has fought a battle he could not possibly have won. The pathetic is achieved when the protagonist is, by virtue of his witlessness, his insensitivity, or the very air he gives off, incapable of grappling with a much superior force.

Pathos truly is the mode for the pessimist.

But tragedy requires a nicer balance between what is possible and what is impossible. And it is curious, although edifying, that the plays we revere, century after century, are the tragedies. In them, and in them alone, lies the belief — optimistic, if you will — in the perfectibility of man.

It is time, I think, that we who are without kings, took up this bright thread of our history and followed it to the only place it can possibly lead in our time — the heart and spirit of the average man.

COMEDY

LYSISTRATA

Aristophanes

English version by Dudley Fitts

Nothing of much interest is known about Aristophanes (c. 450 B.C.–c. 385 B.C.). An Athenian, he competed for about forty years in the annual festivals of comic drama to which three playwrights each contributed one play. His first play was produced in 427 B.C., his last extant play in 388 B.C., but he is known to have written two comedies after this date. Of the forty or so plays he wrote, eleven survive. *Lysistrata* (accent on the second syllable) was produced in 411 B.C.

PERSONS REPRESENTED

LYSISTRATA
KALONIKE
MYRRHINE
LAMPITO
CHORUS
COMMISSIONER
KINESIAS
SPARTAN HERALD
SPARTAN AMBASSADOR
A SENTRY

Until the *éxodos*, the CHORUS is divided into two hemichori: the first, of Old Men; the second, of Old Women. Each of these has its KORYPHAIOS [i.e., leader]. In the *éxodos*, the hemichori return as Athenians and Spartans.

The supernumeraries include the BABY SON of Kinesias; STRATYL-LIS, a member of the hemichorus of Old Women; various individual speakers, both Spartan and Athenian.

Scene: Athens. First, a public square; later, beneath the walls of the Akropolis; later, a courtyard within the Akropolis.

Patrick Hines in the Phoenix Theater production of *Lysistrata* in New York, 1959. (Photograph: Joseph Abeles Studio.)

PROLOGUE

[*Athens; a public square; early morning;* LYSISTRATA *alone.*]

LYSISTRATA:
If someone had invited them to a festival —
of Bacchos, say; or to Pan's shrine, or to
    Aphrodite's°[1]
over at Kolias —, you couldn't get through
    the streets,
what with the drums and the dancing. But
    now,
not a woman in sight!

5   Except — oh, yes!

[*Enter* KALONIKE.]

Here's one of my neighbors, at last. Good
morning, Kalonike.
    KALONIKE: Good morning, Lysistrata.
                        Darling,
don't frown so! You'll ruin your face!
    LYSISTRATA: Never mind my face.
Kalonike,
the way we women behave! Really, I don't
10   blame the men
for what they say about us.
    KALONIKE: No; I imagine they're right.
    LYSISTRATA:
For example: I call a meeting
to think out a most important matter — and
    what happens?
The women all stay in bed!
    KALONIKE: Oh, they'll be along.
It's hard to get away, you know: a husband, a
15   cook,

Lysistrata by Aristophanes: New English Version by Dudley Fitts, copyright 1954 by Harcourt Brace Jovanovich, Inc. and reprinted with their permission. *Caution:* All rights, including professional, amateur, motion picture, recitation, lecturing, public reading, radio broadcasting, and television are strictly reserved. Inquiries on all rights should be addressed to Harcourt Brace Jovanovich, Inc., 757 Third Avenue, New York, N.Y. 10017.

[1] The degree sign (°) indicates a footnote, which is keyed to the text by the line number. Text references are printed in **boldface** type; the annotation follows in lightface type.
2 **Bacchos, Pan, Aphrodite:** The first two are gods associated with wine; Aphrodite is the goddess of love.

a child . . . Home life can be *so* demanding!
    LYSISTRATA:
What I have in mind is even more demanding.
    KALONIKE:
Tell me: what is it?
    LYSISTRATA: It's big.
    KALONIKE: Goodness! *How* big?
    LYSISTRATA:
Big enough for all of us.
    KALONIKE: But we're not all here!
    LYSISTRATA:
We would be, if *that's* what was up!
                    No, Kalonike, 20
this is something I've been turning over for
    nights,
long sleepless nights.
    KALONIKE:
          It must be getting worn down, then,
if you've spent so much time on it.
    LYSISTRATA: Worn down or not,
it comes to this: Only we women can save
    Greece!
    KALONIKE:
Only we women? Poor Greece!
    LYSISTRATA: Just the same, 25
it's up to us. First, we must liquidate
the Peloponnesians —
    KALONIKE: Fun, fun!
    LYSISTRATA: — and then the Boiotians.°
    KALONIKE:
Oh! But not those heavenly eels!
    LYSISTRATA: You needn't worry.
I'm not talking about eels. — But here's the
    point:
If we can get the women from those places — 30
all those Boiotians and Peloponnesians —
to join us women here, why, we can save
all Greece!
    KALONIKE: But dearest Lysistrata!
How can women do a thing so austere, so
political? We belong at home. Our only
    armor's 35
our perfumes, our saffron dresses and
our pretty little shoes!
    LYSISTRATA: Exactly. Those
transparent dresses, the saffron, the

27 **Boiotia:** A country north of Attika, noted for the crudity of its inhabitants and the excellence of its seafood.

perfume, those pretty shoes —
KALONIKE: Oh?
LYSISTRATA: Not a single man would lift
his spear —
KALONIKE:
40   I'll scnd my dress to the dyer's tomorrow!
LYSISTRATA:
— or grab a shield —
KALONIKE: The sweetest little negligée —
LYSISTRATA:
— or haul out his sword.
KALONIKE: I know where I can buy
the dreamiest sandals!
LYSISTRATA:
                        Well, so you see. Now, shouldn't
the women have come?
KALONIKE: Come? They should have *flown*!
LYSISTRATA:
Athenians are always late.
45   But imagine!
There's no one here from the South Shore, or
        from Salamis.
KALONIKE:
Things are hard over in Salamis, I swear.
They have to get going at dawn.
LYSISTRATA: And nobody from Acharnai.
I thought they'd be here hours ago.
KALONIKE: Well, you'll get
50   that awful Theagenes woman: she'll be
a sheet or so in the wind.
                                But look!
Someone at last! Can you see who they are?

[*Enter* MYRRHINE *and other women.*]

LYSISTRATA:
They're from Anagyros.
KALONIKE: They certainly are.
You'd know them anywhere, by the scent.
MYRRHINE:
Sorry to be late, Lysistrata.
55   Oh come,
don't scowl so. Say something!
LYSISTRATA: My dear Myrrhine,
what is there to say? After all,
you've been pretty casual about the whole
        thing.
MYRRHINE: Couldn't find
my girdle in the dark, that's all.
                                But what *is*
"the whole thing"?
60   KALONIKE: No, we've got to wait
for those Boiotians and Peloponnesians.
LYSISTRATA:
That's more like it. — But, look!

Here's Lampito!

[*Enter* LAMPITO *with women from Sparta.*]

LYSISTRATA: Darling Lampito,
how pretty you are today! What a nice color!
Goodness, you look as though you could
        strangle a bull!   65
LAMPITO:
Ah think Ah could! It's the work-out
in the gym every day; and, of co'se that dance
        of ahs
where y' kick yo' own tail.
KALONIKE: What an adorable figure!
LAMPITO:
Lawdy, when y' touch me lahk that,
Ah feel lahk a heifer at the altar!
LYSISTRATA: And this young lady?   70
Where is she from?
LAMPITO: Boiotia. Social-Register type.
LYSISTRATA:
Ah. "Boiotia of the fertile plain."
KALONIKE: And if you look,
you'll find the fertile plain has just been
        mowed.
LYSISTRATA:
And this lady?
LAMPITO: Hagh, wahd, handsome. She
        comes from Korinth.
KALONIKE:
High and wide's the word for it.
LAMPITO: Which one of you   75
called this heah meeting, and why?
LYSISTRATA: I did.
LAMPITO: Well, then, tell us:
What's up?
MYRRHINE: Yes, darling, what *is* on your
        mind, after all?
LYSISTRATA:
I'll tell you. — But first, one little question.
MYRRHINE: Well?
LYSISTRATA:
It's your husbands. Fathers of your children.
        Doesn't it bother you
that they're always off with the Army? I'll
        stake my life,   80
not one of you has a man in the house this
        minute!
KALONIKE:
Mine's been in Thrace the last five months,
        keeping an eye
on that General.
MYRRHINE: Mine's been in Pylos for seven.
LAMPITO: And mahn,
whenever he gets a *dis*charge, he goes raht back

85 with that li'l ole shield of his, and enlists again!
LYSISTRATA:
And not the ghost of a lover to be found!
From the very day the war began —
                              those Milesians!
I could skin them alive!
                    — I've not seen so much, even,
as one of those leather consolation prizes. —
But there! What's important is: If I've found
90   a way
to end the war, are you with me?
    MYRRHINE: I should *say* so!
Even if I have to pawn my best dress and
drink up the proceeds.
    KALONIKE: Me, too! Even if they split me
right up the middle, like a flounder.
    LAMPITO: Ah'm shorely with you.
95 Ah'd crawl up Taygetos° on mah knees
if that'd bring peace.
    LYSISTRATA: All right, then; here it is:
Women! Sisters!
If we really want our men to make peace,
we must be ready to give up —
    MYRRHINE: Give up what?
Quick, tell us!
    LYSISTRATA:
                    But *will* you?
100   MYRRHINE: We will, even if it kills us.
    LYSISTRATA:
Then we must give up going to bed with our
        men.
    [*Long silence.*]
Oh? So now you're sorry? Won't look at me?
Doubtful? Pale? All teary-eyed?
                        But come: be frank with me.
Will you do it, or not? Well? Will you do it?
    MYRRHINE: I couldn't. No.
Let the war go on.
105   KALONIKE: Nor I. Let the war go on.
    LYSISTRATA:
You, you little flounder,
ready to be split up the middle?
    KALONIKE: Lysistrata, no!
I'd walk through fire for you — you *know* I
        would! — but don't
ask us to give up *that!* Why, there's nothing
        like it!
    LYSISTRATA:
And you?
    BOIOTIAN:
110   No. I must say *I'd* rather walk through fire.

95 **Taygetos:** A mountain range.

LYSISTRATA:
What an utterly perverted sex we women are!
No wonder poets write tragedies about us.
There's only one thing we can think of.
                        But you from Sparta:
if you stand by me, we may win yet! Will you?
It means so much!
    LAMPITO: Ah sweah, it means *too* much!   115
By the Two Goddesses, it does! Asking a girl
to sleep — Heaven knows how long! — in a
        great big bed
with nobody there but herself! But Ah'll stay
        with you!
Peace comes first!
    LYSISTRATA: Spoken like a true Spartan!
    KALONIKE:
But if —
        oh dear!
                — if we give up what you tell us to,   120
will there *be* any peace?
    LYSISTRATA:
                    Why, mercy, of course there will!
We'll just sit snug in our very thinnest gowns,
perfumed and powdered from top to bottom,
        and those men
simply won't stand still! And when we say No,
they'll go out of their minds! And there's your
        peace.   125
You can take my word for it.
    LAMPITO: Ah seem to remember
that Colonel Menelaos threw his sword away
when he saw Helen's breast all bare.
    KALONIKE: But, goodness me!
What if they just get up and leave us?
    LYSISTRATA: In that case
we'll have to fall back on ourselves, I suppose.   130
But they won't.
    KALONIKE:
                I must say that's not much help. But
what if they drag us into the bedroom?
    LYSISTRATA: Hang on to the door.
    KALONIKE:
What if they slap us?
    LYSISTRATA: If they do, you'd better give in.
But be sulky about it. Do I have to teach you
        how?
You know there's no fun for men when they
        have to force you.   135
There are millions of ways of getting them to
        see reason.
Don't you worry: a man
doesn't like it unless the girl co-operates.
    KALONIKE:
I suppose so. Oh, all right. We'll go along.

LAMPITO:
Ah imagine us Spahtans can arrange a peace.
140   But you
Athenians! Why, you're just war-mongerers!
LYSISTRATA: Leave that to me.
I know how to make them listen.
LAMPITO: Ah don't see how.
After all, they've got their boats; and there's
      lots of money
piled up in the Akropolis.°
LYSISTRATA: The Akropolis? Darling,
145 we're taking over the Akropolis today!
That's the older women's job. All the rest of us
are going to the Citadel to sacrifice — you
      understand me?
And once there, we're in for good!
LAMPITO: Whee! Up the rebels!
Ah can see you're a good strat*eeg*ist.
LYSISTRATA: Well, then, Lampito,
150 what we have to do now is take a solemn oath.
LAMPITO:
Say it. We'll sweah.
LYSISTRATA: This is it.
— But where's our Inner Guard?
                  — Look, Guard: you see this shield?
Put it down here. Now bring me the victim's
      entrails.
KALONIKE:
But the oath?
LYSISTRATA:
            You remember how in Aischylos' *Seven*
they killed a sheep and swore on a shield?
155   Well, then?
KALONIKE:
But I don't see how you can swear for peace
      on a shield.
LYSISTRATA:
What else do you suggest?
KALONIKE: Why not a white horse?
We could swear by that.
LYSISTRATA:
            And where will you get a white horse?
KALONIKE:
I never thought of that. W*hat* can we *do*?
LYSISTRATA: I have it!
Let's set this big black wine-bowl on the
160   ground
and pour in a gallon or so of Thasian, and
      swear

144 **Akropolis:** At the beginning of the war,
Perikles stored emergency funds in the Akropolis,
the citadel sacred to Athene.

not to add one drop of water.
LAMPITO: Ah lahk *that* oath!
LYSISTRATA:
Bring the bowl and the wine-jug.
KALONIKE: Oh, what a simply *huge* one!
LYSISTRATA:
Set it down. Girls, place your hands on the
      gift-offering.

O Goddess of Persuasion! And thou, O
      Loving-cup: 165
Look upon this our sacrifice, and
be gracious!

KALONIKE:
See the blood spill out. How red and pretty
      it is!
LAMPITO:
And Ah must say it smells good.
MYRRHINE: Let me swear first!
KALONIKE:
No, by Aphrodite, we'll match for it!   170
LYSISTRATA:
Lampito: all of you women: come, touch the
      bowl,
and repeat after me — remember, this is an
      oath — :
I WILL HAVE NOTHING TO DO WITH
      MY HUSBAND OR MY LOVER
KALONIKE:
I will have nothing to do with my husband or
      my lover
LYSISTRATA:
THOUGH HE COME TO ME IN PITI-
      ABLE CONDITION   175
KALONIKE:
Though he come to me in pitiable condition
(Oh Lysistrata! This is killing me!)
LYSISTRATA:
IN MY HOUSE I WILL BE UNTOUCH-
      ABLE
KALONIKE:
In my house I will be untouchable
LYSISTRATA:
IN MY THINNEST SAFFRON SILK   180
KALONIKE:
In my thinnest saffron silk
LYSISTRATA:
AND MAKE HIM LONG FOR ME.
KALONIKE:
And make him long for me.
LYSISTRATA:
I WILL NOT GIVE MYSELF
KALONIKE:
I will not give myself   185

LYSISTRATA:
AND IF HE CONSTRAINS ME
KALONIKE:
And if he constrains me
LYSISTRATA:
I WILL BE COLD AS ICE AND NEVER
   MOVE
KALONIKE:
I will be cold as ice and never move
LYSISTRATA:
I WILL NOT LIFT MY SLIPPERS
190   TOWARD THE CEILING
KALONIKE:
I will not lift my slippers toward the ceiling
LYSISTRATA:
OR CROUCH ON ALL FOURS LIKE THE
   LIONESS IN THE CARVING
KALONIKE:
Or crouch on all fours like the lioness in the
   carving
LYSISTRATA:
AND IF I KEEP THIS OATH LET ME
   DRINK FROM THIS BOWL
KALONIKE:
And if I keep this oath let me drink from this
195   *bowl*
LYSISTRATA:
IF NOT, LET MY OWN BOWL BE
   FILLED WITH WATER.
KALONIKE:
If not, let my own bowl be filled with water.
LYSISTRATA:
You have all sworn?
MYRRHINE: We have.
LYSISTRATA: Then thus
I sacrifice the victim.

   [*Drinks largely.*]

KALONIKE: Save some for us!
200 Here's to you, darling, and to you, and to you!
                      [*Loud cries off-stage.*]
LAMPITO:
What's all *that* whoozy-goozy?
   LYSISTRATA: Just what I told you.
The older women have taken the Akropolis.
Now you, Lampito,
rush back to Sparta. We'll take care of things
   here. Leave
these girls here for hostages.
205   The rest of you,
up to the Citadel: and mind you push in the
   bolts.
KALONIKE:
But the men? Won't they be after us?

LYSISTRATA: Just you leave
the men to me. There's not fire enough in the
   world,
or threats either, to make me open these doors
except on my own terms.
KALONIKE: I hope not, by Aphrodite!   210
After all,
we've got a reputation for bitchiness to live
   up to.

                                      [*Exeunt.*]

PARODOS:
CHORAL EPISODE

[*The hillside just under the Akropolis. Enter*
CHORUS OF OLD MEN *with burning torches*
and braziers; much puffing and coughing.]

KORYPHAIOS(man):
Forward march, Drakes, old friend: never you
   mind
that damn big log banging hell down on your
   back.
CHORUS(men):
                          [STROPHE 1]
There's this to be said for longevity:
You see things you thought that you'd never
   see.
   Look, Strymodoros, who would have thought
   it?   5
   We've caught it —
              the New Femininity!
The wives of our bosom, our board, our bed —
Now, by the gods, they've gone ahead
And taken the Citadel (Heaven knows why!),
Profanèd the sacred statuar-y,   10
              And barred the doors,
              The subversive whores!
KORYPHAIOS(m):
Shake a leg there, Philurgos, man: the
   Akropolis or bust!
Put the kindling around here. We'll build one
   almighty big
bonfire for the whole bunch of bitches, every
   last one;   15
and the first we fry will be old Lykon's woman.
CHORUS(m):
                          [ANTISTROPHE 1]
They're not going to give me the old horse-
   laugh!
No, by Demeter, they won't pull this off!
   Think of Kleomenes: even he

20 Didn't go free
           till he brought me his stuff.
A good man he was, all stinking and shaggy,
Bare as an eel except for the bag he
Covered his rear with. God, what a mess!
25 Never a bath in six years, I'd guess.
                              Pure Sparta, man!
                              He also ran.

KORYPHAIOS(m):
That was a siege, friends! Seventeen ranks
     strong
we slept at the Gate. And shall we not do as
     much
against these women, whom God and
     Euripides hate?
If we don't, I'll turn in my medals from
30   Marathon.
CHORUS(m):

                                        [STROPHE 2]
Onward and upward! A little push,
     And we're there.
Ouch, my shoulders! I could wish
     For a pair
35 Of good strong oxen. Keep your eye
     On the fire there, it mustn't die.
                    Akh! Akh!
     The smoke would make a cadaver cough!

Holy Herakles, a hot spark   [ANTISTROPHE 2]
40   Bit my eye!
Damn this hellfire, damn this work!
     So say I.
Onward and upward just the same.
(Laches, remember the Goddess: for shame!)
45   Akh! Akh!
     The smoke would make a cadaver cough!
KORYPHAIOS(m):
At last (and let us give suitable thanks to God
for his infinite mercies) I have managed to
     bring
my personal flame to the common goal. It
     breathes, it lives.
Now, gentlemen, let us consider. Shall we
50   insert
the torch, say, into the brazier, and thus
     extract
a kindling brand? And shall we then, do you
     think,
push on to the gate like valiant sheep? On the
     whole, yes.
But I would have you consider this, too: if
     they —
55 I refer to the women — should refuse to open,
what then? Do we set the doors afire

and smoke them out? At ease, men. Meditate.
Akh, the smoke! Woof! What we really need
is the loan of a general or two from the Samos
     Command.
At least we've got this lumber off our backs.   60
That's something. And now let's look to our
     fire.

O Pot, brave Brazier, touch my torch with
     flame!
Victory, Goddess, I invoke thy name!
Strike down these paradigms of female pride,
And we shall hang our trophies up inside.   65

[Enter CHORUS OF OLD WOMEN on the walls
of the Akropolis, carrying jars of water.]

KORYPHAIOS(woman):
Smoke, girls, smoke! There's smoke all over
     the place!
Probably fire, too. Hurry, girls! Fire! Fire!
CHORUS(women):
     Nikodike, run!   [STROPHE 1]
     Or Kalyke's done
     To a turn, and poor Kritylla's   70
     Smoked like a ham.
               Damn
     These old men! Are we too late?
     I nearly died down at the place
     Where we fill our jars:
          Slaves pushing and jostling —   75
          Such a hustling
     I never saw in all my days.

     But here's water at last. [ANTISTROPHE 1]
     Haste, sisters, haste!
     Slosh it on them, slosh it down,   80
     The silly old wrecks!
               Sex
     Almighty! What they want's
     A hot bath? Good. Send one down.
     Athena of Athens town,
          Trito-born!° Helm of Gold!   85
          Cripple the old
     Firemen! Help us help them drown!

[The OLD MEN capture a woman,
STRATYLLIS.]

STRATYLLIS:
Let me go! Let me go!
KORYPHAIOS(w):   You walking corpses,

85 Trito-born: i.e., Athene, said to be born near
Lake Tritonis, in Libya.

have you no shame?

KORYPHAIOS^(m):

90   I wouldn't have believed it!
An army of women in the Akropolis!

KORYPHAIOS^(w):

So we scare you, do we? Grandpa, you've seen
only our pickets yet!

KORYPHAIOS^(m):   Hey, Phaidrias!
Help me with the necks of these jabbering
    hens!

KORYPHAIOS^(w):

Down with your pots, girls! We'll need both
    hands
if these antiques attack us.

95   KORYPHAIOS^(m):   Want your face kicked in?

KORYPHAIOS^(w):

Want your balls chewed off?

KORYPHAIOS^(m):   Look out! I've got a stick!

KORYPHAIOS^(w):

You lay a half-inch of your stick on Stratyllis,
and you'll never stick again!

KORYPHAIOS^(m):

Fall apart!

KORYPHAIOS^(w):

                    I'll spit up your guts!

KORYPHAIOS^(m):   Euripides!° Master!
How well you knew women!

100   KORYPHAIOS^(w):   Listen to him, Rhodippe,
up with the pots!

KORYPHAIOS^(m):

                    Demolition of God,
what good are your pots?

KORYPHAIOS^(w):

                    You refugee from the tomb,
what good is your fire?

KORYPHAIOS^(m):

                    Good enough to make a pyre
to barbecue you!

KORYPHAIOS^(w):

                    We'll squizzle your kindling!

KORYPHAIOS^(m):

You think so?

KORYPHAIOS^(w):

105   Yah! Just hang around a while!

KORYPHAIOS^(m):

Want a touch of my torch?

KORYPHAIOS^(w):   It needs a good soaping.

KORYPHAIOS^(m):

How about you?

KORYPHAIOS^(w):

                    Soap for a senile bridegroom!

99 **Euripides**: A tragic dramatist.

KORYPHAIOS^(m):

Senile? Hold your trap!

KORYPHAIOS^(w):   Just *you* try to hold it!

KORYPHAIOS^(m):

The yammer of women!

KORYPHAIOS^(w):   Oh is that so?
You're not in the jury room now, you know.   110

KORYPHAIOS^(m):

Gentlemen, I beg you, burn off that woman's
    hair!

KORYPHAIOS^(w):

Let it come down!

[*They empty their pots on the men.*]

KORYPHAIOS^(m):

What a way to drown!

KORYPHAIOS^(w):   Hot, hey?

KORYPHAIOS^(m):   Say,
enough!

KORYPHAIOS^(w):

    Dandruff
needs watering. I'll make you   115
nice and fresh.

KORYPHAIOS^(m):

                    For God's sake, you,
hold off!

SCENE I

[*Enter a* COMMISSIONER *accompanied by
four constables.*]

COMMISSIONER:

These degenerate women! What a racket of
    little drums,
what a yapping for Adonis on every house-top!
It's like the time in the Assembly when I was
    listening
to a speech — out of order, as usual — by that
    fool
Demostratos,° all about troops for Sicily,°   5
that kind of nonsense —
                    and there was his wife
trotting around in circles howling
Alas for Adonis!° —
                    and Demostratos insisting

5 **Demostratos**: Athenian orator and jingoist
politician; **Sicily**: A reference to the Sicilian Expedition (416 B.C.), in which Athens was
decisively defeated.
8 **Adonis**: Fertility god.

we must draft every last Zakynthian that can
    walk —
10 and his wife up there on the roof,
drunk as an owl, yowling
Oh weep for Adonis! —
            and that damned ox Demostratos
mooing away through the rumpus. That's what
    we get
for putting up with this wretched woman-
    business!
    KORYPHAIOS(m):
Sir, you haven't heard the half of it. They
15   laughed at us!
Insulted us! They took pitchers of water
and nearly drowned us! We're still wringing
    out our clothes,
for all the world like unhousebroken brats.
    COMMISSIONER:
Serves you right, by Poseidon!
20 Whose fault is it if these women-folk of ours
get out of hand? We coddle them,
we teach them to be wasteful and loose. You'll
    see a husband
go into a jeweler's. "Look," he'll say,
"jeweler," he'll say, "you remember that gold
    choker
you made for my wife? Well, she went to a
25   dance last night
and broke the clasp. Now, I've got to go to
    Salamis,
and can't be bothered. Run over to my house
    tonight,
will you, and see if you can put it together for
    her."
Or another one
goes to a cobbler — a good strong workman,
30   too,
with an awl that was never meant for child's
    play. "Here,"
he'll tell him, "one of my wife's shoes is
    pinching
her little toe. Could you come up about noon
and stretch it out for her?"
                Well, what do you expect?
35 Look at me, for example, I'm a Public Officer,
and it's one of my duties to pay off the sailors.
And where's the money? Up there in the
    Akropolis!
And those blasted women slam the door in my
    face!
But what are we waiting for?
                — Look here, constable,
40 stop sniffing around for a tavern, and get us

some crowbars. We'll force their gates! As a
    matter of fact,
I'll do a little forcing myself.

[*Enter* LYSISTRATA, *above, with* MYRRHINE,
KALONIKE, *and the* BOIOTIAN.]

    LYSISTRATA: No need of forcing.
Here I am, of my own accord. And all this talk
about locked doors —! We don't need locked
    doors,
but just the least bit of common sense.   45
    COMMISSIONER:
Is that so, ma'am!
                — Where's my constable?
                        — Constable,
arrest that woman, and tie her hands behind
    her.
    LYSISTRATA:
If he touches me, I swear by Artemis
there'll be one scamp dropped from the public
    pay-roll tomorrow!
    COMMISSIONER:
Well, constable? You're not afraid, I suppose?
    Grab her,   50
two of you, around the middle!
    KALONIKE: No, by Pandrosos!
Lay a hand on her, and I'll jump on you so
    hard
your guts will come out the back door!
    COMMISSIONER: That's what *you* think!
Where's the sergeant? — Here, you: tie up that
    trollop first,
the one with the pretty talk!
    MYRRHINE: By the Moon-Goddess,   55
just try! They'll have to scoop you up with a
    spoon!
    COMMISSIONER:
Another one!
                Officer, seize that woman!
                                I swear
I'll put an end to this riot!
    BOIOTIAN: By the Taurian,
one inch closer, you'll be one screaming bald-
    head!
    COMMISSIONER:
Lord, what a mess! And my constables seem
    ineffective.   60
But — women get the best of us? By God, no!
                        — Skythians!
Close ranks and forward march!
    LYSISTRATA: "Forward," indeed!
By the Two Goddesses, what's the sense in
    that?

They're up against four companies of women
armed from top to bottom.

65   COMMISSIONER: Forward, my Skythians!
    LYSISTRATA:
Forward, yourselves, dear comrades!
You grainlettucebeanseedmarket girls!
You garlicandonionbreadbakery girls!
Give it to 'em! Knock 'em down! Scratch 'em!
Tell 'em what you think of 'em!

[*General mêlée; the Skythians yield.*]

70   — Ah, that's enough!
Sound a retreat: good soldiers don't rob the
    dead.
    COMMISSIONER:
A nice day *this* has been for the police!
    LYSISTRATA:
Well, there you are. — Did you really think we
    women
would be driven like slaves? Maybe now you'll
    admit
that a woman knows something about spirit.

75   COMMISSIONER: Spirit enough,
especially spirits in bottles! Dear Lord Apollo!
    KORYPHAIOS[m]:
Your Honor, there's no use talking to them.
    Words
mean nothing whatever to wild animals like
    these.
Think of the sousing they gave us! and the
    water

80 was not, I believe, of the purest.
    KORYPHAIOS[w]:
You shouldn't have come after us. And if you
    try it again,
you'll be one eye short! — Although, as a
    matter of fact,
what I like best is just to stay at home and
    read,
like a sweet little bride: never hurting a soul,
    no,
never going out. But if you *must* shake hor-

85   nets' nests,
look out for the hornets.
    CHORUS[m]:

                [STROPHE 1]
Of all the beasts that God hath wrought
    What monster's worse than woman?
Who shall encompass with his thought

90   Their guile unending? No man.

They've seized the Heights, the Rock, the
    Shrine —
But to what end? I wot not.

Sure there's some clue to their design!
    Have you the key? I thought not.
    KORYPHAIOS[m]:
We might question them, I suppose. But I
    warn you, sir,   95
don't believe anything you hear! It would be
    un-Athenian
not to get to the bottom of this plot.
    COMMISSIONER: Very well.
My first question is this: Why, so help you
    God,
did you bar the gates of the Akropolis?
    LYSISTRATA: Why?
To keep the money, of course. No money, no
    war.   100
    COMMISSIONER:
You think that money's the cause of war?
    LYSISTRATA: I do.
Money brought about that Peisandros°
    business
and all the other attacks on the State. Well
    and good!
They'll not get another cent here!
    COMMISSIONER: And what will you do?
    LYSISTRATA:
What a question! From now on, we intend   105
to control the Treasury.
    COMMISSIONER: Control the Treasury!
    LYSISTRATA:
Why not? Does that seem strange? After all,
we control our household budgets.
    COMMISSIONER: But that's different!
    LYSISTRATA:
"Different"? What do you mean?
    COMMISSIONER: I mean simply this:
it's the Treasury that pays for National
    Defense.   110
    LYSISTRATA:
Unnecessary. We propose to abolish war.
    COMMISSIONER:
Good God. — And National Security?
    LYSISTRATA: Leave that to us.
    COMMISSIONER:
You?
    LYSISTRATA:
    Us.
    COMMISSIONER:
    We're done for, then!
    LYSISTRATA: Never mind.
We women will save you in spite of yourselves.

---

102 **Peisandros**: A plotter against the Athenian
democracy.

COMMISSIONER: What nonsense!
LYSISTRATA:
115   If you like. But you must accept it, like it or
         not.
COMMISSIONER:
Why, this is downright subversion!
LYSISTRATA: Maybe it is.
But we're going to save you, Judge.
         COMMISSIONER: I don't *want* to be saved.
LYSISTRATA:
Tut. The death-wish. All the more reason.
         COMMISSIONER: But the idea
of women bothering themselves about peace
         and war!
LYSISTRATA:
Will you listen to me?
120   COMMISSIONER: Yes. But be brief, or I'll —
LYSISTRATA:
This is no time for stupid threats.
         COMMISSIONER: By the gods,
I can't stand any more!
         AN OLD WOMAN: Can't stand? Well, well.
COMMISSIONER:
That's enough out of you, you old buzzard!
Now, Lysistrata: tell me what you're thinking.
LYSISTRATA:
Glad to.
125   Ever since this war began
We women have been watching you men,
         agreeing with you,
keeping our thoughts to ourselves. That
         doesn't mean
we were happy: we weren't, for we saw how
         things were going;
but we'd listen to you at dinner
arguing this way and that.
130   — Oh you, and your big
Top Secrets! —
                 And then we'd grin like little patriots
(though goodness knows we didn't feel like
         grinning) and ask you:
"Dear, did the Armistice come up in Assembly
         today?"
And you'd say, "None of your business! Pipe
         down!," you'd say.
And so we would.
135   AN OLD WOMAN: I wouldn't have, by God!
COMMISSIONER:
You'd have taken a beating, then!
                                  — Go on.

LYSISTRATA:
Well, we'd be quiet. But then, you know, all
         at once

you men would think up something worse
         than ever.
Even *I* could see it was fatal. And, "Darling,"
         I'd say,
"have you gone completely mad?" And my
         husband would look at me   140
and say, "Wife, you've got your weaving to
         attend to.
Mind your tongue, if you don't want a slap.
         'War's
a man's affair!' "°
COMMISSIONER:
                 Good words, and well pronounced.
LYSISTRATA:
You're a fool if you think so.
                         It was hard enough
to put up with all this banquet-hall strategy.   145
But then we'd hear you out in the public
         square:
"Nobody left for the draft-quota here in
         Athens?"
you'd say; and, "No," someone else would say,
         "not a man!"
And so we women decided to rescue Greece.
You might as well listen to us now: you'll
         have to, later.   150
COMMISSIONER:
You rescue Greece? Absurd.
LYSISTRATA: You're the absurd one.
COMMISSIONER:
You expect me to take orders from a woman?
                                  I'd die first!
LYSISTRATA:
Heavens, if that's what's bothering you, take
         my veil,
here, and wrap it around your poor head.
         KALONIKE: Yes,
and you can have my market-basket, too.   155
Go home, tighten your girdle, do the washing,
         mind
your beans! "War's
a woman's affair!"
KORYPHAIOS⁽ʷ⁾:
                 Ground pitchers! Close ranks!
CHORUS⁽ʷ⁾:
                                  [ANTISTROPHE]
         This is a dance that I know well,
              My knees shall never yield.   160
         Wobble and creak I may, but still
              I'll keep the well-fought field.

---

143 **War's a man's affair:** Quoted from Homer's
Iliad, VI, 492, Hector to his wife Andromache.

Valor and grace march on before,
Love prods us from behind.
165 Our slogan is EXCELSIOR,
Our watchword SAVE MANKIND.
KORYPHAIOS⁽ʷ⁾:
Women, remember your grandmothers! Remember
that little old mother of yours, what a stinger
she was!
On, on, never slacken. There's a strong wind
astern!
LYSISTRATA:
170 O Eros of delight! O Aphrodite! Kyprian!
If ever desire has drenched our breasts or
dreamed
in our thighs, let it work so now on the men
of Hellas
that they shall tail us through the land, slaves,
slaves
to Woman, Breaker of Armies!
COMMISSIONER: And if we do?
LYSISTRATA:
Well, for one thing, we shan't have to watch
175 you
going to market, a spear in one hand, and
heaven knows
what in the other.
KALONIKE: Nicely said, by Aphrodite!
LYSISTRATA:
As things stand now, you're neither men nor
women.
Armor clanking with kitchen pans and pots —
180 you sound like a pack of Korybantes!
COMMISSIONER:
A man must do what a man must do.
LYSISTRATA: So I'm told.
But to see a General, complete with Gorgon-
shield,
jingling along the dock to buy a couple of
herrings!
KALONIKE:
I saw a Captain the other day — lovely fellow
he was,
nice curly hair — sitting on his horse; and —
185 can you believe it? —
he'd just bought some soup, and was pouring
it into his helmet!
And there was a soldier from Thrace
swishing his lance like something out of
Euripides,
and the poor fruit-store woman got so scared
that she ran away and let him have his figs
190 free!

COMMISSIONER:
All this is beside the point.
                    Will you be so kind
as to tell me how you mean to save Greece?
LYSISTRATA: Of course.
Nothing could be simpler.
COMMISSIONER: I assure you, I'm all ears.
LYSISTRATA:
Do you know anything about weaving?
Say the yarn gets tangled: we thread it   195
this way and that through the skein, up and
down,
until it's free. And it's like that with war.
We'll send our envoys
up and down, this way and that, all over Greece,
until it's finished.
COMMISSIONER: Yarn? Thread? Skein?   200
Are you out of your mind? I tell you,
war is a serious business.
LYSISTRATA: So serious
that I'd like to go on talking about weaving.
COMMISSIONER:
All right. Go ahead.
LYSISTRATA: The first thing we have to do
is to wash our yarn, get the dirt out of it.   205
You see? Isn't there too much dirt here in
Athens?
You must wash those men away.
                    Then our spoiled wool —
that's like your job-hunters, out for a life
of no work and big pay. Back to the basket,
citizens or not, allies or not,   210
or friendly immigrants.
                    And your colonies?
Hanks of wool lost in various places. Pull them
together, weave them into one great whole,
and our voters are clothed for ever.
COMMISSIONER: It would take a woman
to reduce state questions to a matter of carding
and weaving.   215
LYSISTRATA:
You fool! Who were the mothers whose sons
sailed off
to fight for Athens in Sicily?
COMMISSIONER: Enough!
I beg you, do not call back those memories.
LYSISTRATA: And then,
instead of the love that every woman needs,
we have only our single beds, where we can
dream   220
of our husbands off with the Army.
                    Bad enough for wives!
But what about our girls, getting older every
day,

and older, and no kisses?
COMMISSIONER: Men get older, too.
LYSISTRATA:
Not in the same sense.
                          A soldier's discharged,
and he may be bald and toothless, yet he'll
225   find
a pretty young thing to go to bed with.
                              But a woman!
Her beauty is gone with the first grey hair.
She can spend her time
consulting the oracles and the fortune-tellers,
230   but they'll never send her a husband.
       COMMISSIONER:
Still, if a man can rise to the occasion —
       LYSISTRATA:
Rise? Rise, yourself!

   [Furiously.]

Go invest in a coffin!
                   You've money enough.
                           I'll bake you
a cake for the Underworld.
                       And here's your funeral
wreath!

   [She pours water upon him.]

   MYRRHINE:
        And here's another!

   [More water.]

   KALONIKE:
235   And here's
my contribution!

   [More water.]

LYSISTRATA: What are you waiting for?
All aboard Styx Ferry!
                 Charon's° calling for you!
It's sailing-time: don't disrupt the schedule!
       COMMISSIONER:
The insolence of women! And to me!
240   No, by God, I'll go back to town and show
the rest of the Commission what might hap-
        pen to them.
                    [Exit COMMISSIONER.]
       LYSISTRATA:
Really, I suppose we should have laid out his
        corpse
on the doorstep, in the usual way.
                        But never mind.

   237 Charon: God who ferried the souls of the
newly dead across the Styx to Hades.

We'll give him the rites of the dead tomorrow
   morning.
        [Exit LYSISTRATA with MYRRHINE and
                                KALONIKE.]

PARABASIS: CHORAL EPISODE

KORYPHAIOS(m):
                                    [ODE 1]
Sons of Liberty, awake! The day of glory is at
   hand.
   CHORUS(m):
I smell tyranny afoot, I smell it rising from
   the land.
I scent a trace of Hippias,° I sniff upon the
   breeze
A dismal Spartan hogo that suggests King
   Kleisthenes.°
Strip, strip for action, brothers!   5
Our wives, aunts, sisters, mothers
Have sold us out: the streets are full of godless
   female rages.
Shall we stand by and let our women confis-
   cate our wages?
   KORYPHAIOS(m):
                              [EPIRRHEMA 1]
Gentlemen, it's a disgrace to Athens, a disgrace
to all that Athens stands for, if we allow these
   grandmas   10
to jabber about spears and shields and making
   friends
with the Spartans. What's a Spartan? Give me
   a wild wolf
any day. No. They want the Tyranny back, I
   suppose.
Are we going to take that? No. Let us look like
the innocent serpent, but be the flower under
   it,   15
as the poet sings. And just to begin with,
I propose to poke a number of teeth
down the gullet of that harridan over there.
   KORYPHAIOS(w):
                                [ANTODE 1]
Oh, is that so? When you get home, your own
   mammá won't know you!
   CHORUS(w):
Who do you think we are, you senile bravos?
   Well, I'll show you.   20

   3 Hippias: An Athenian tyrant (d. 490 B.C.).
   4 Kleisthenes: An ambisexual Athenian.

I bore the sacred vessels in my eighth year,
    and at ten
I was pounding out the barley for Athena
    Goddess; then
    They made me Little Bear
    At the Braunonian Fair;
I'd held the Holy Basket by the time I was of
25   age,
The Blessed Dry Figs had adorned my plump
    décolletage.

KORYPHAIOS⁽ʷ⁾:

[ANTEPIRRHEMA 1]
A "disgrace to Athens," am I, just at the
    moment
I'm giving Athens the best advice she ever had?
Don't I pay taxes to the State? Yes, I pay
    them
30 in baby boys. And what do you contribute,
    you impotent horrors? Nothing but waste: all
    our Treasury,° dating back to the Persian
        Wars,
    gone! rifled! And not a penny out of your
        pockets!
Well, then? Can you cough up an answer to
    that?
Look out for your own gullet, or you'll get a
35   crack
from this old brogan that'll make your teeth
    see stars!

CHORUS⁽ᵐ⁾:

Oh insolence!   [ODE 2]
Am I unmanned?
Incontinence!
40   Shall my scarred hand
Strike never a blow
To curb this flow-
ing female curse?

Leipsydrion!°
45   Shall I betray
The laurels won
On that great day?
Come, shake a leg,
Shed old age, beg
50   The years reverse!

32 **Treasury**: Money originally contributed by
Athens and her allies, intended to finance an extension of the sea-war against Persia. Since the
failure of the Sicilian Expedition, the contributions
of the allies had fallen off; and the fund itself was
now being raided by Athenian politicians.
44 **Leipsydrion**: A place where patriots had
gallantly fought.

KORYPHAIOS⁽ᵐ⁾:

[EPIRRHEMA 2]
Give them an inch, and we're done for! We'll
    have them
launching boats next and planning naval
    strategy,
sailing down on us like so many Artemisias.
Or maybe they have ideas about the cavalry.
That's fair enough, women are certainly good   55
in the saddle. Just look at Mikon's paintings,
all those Amazons wrestling with all those
    men!
On the whole, a straitjacket's their best uni-
    form.

CHORUS⁽ʷ⁾:

Tangle with me,   [ANTODE 2]
And you'll get cramps.   60
Ferocity
's no use now, Gramps!
By the Two,
I'll get through
To you wrecks yet!   65

I'll scramble your eggs,
I'll burn your beans,
With my two legs.
You'll see such scenes
As never yet   70
Your two eyes met.
A curse? You bet!

KORYPHAIOS⁽ʷ⁾:

[ANTEPIRRHEMA 2]
If Lampito stands by me, and that delicious
    Theban girl,
Ismenia — what good are *you*? You and your
    seven
Resolutions! Resolutions? Rationing Boiotian
    eels   75
and making our girls go without them at
    Hekate's Feast!
That was statesmanship! And we'll have to put
    up with it
and all the rest of your decrepit legislation
until some patriot — God give him strength! —
grabs you by the neck and kicks you off the
    Rock.
    80

SCENE II

[*Re-enter* LYSISTRATA *and her lieutenants.*]

KORYPHAIOS⁽ʷ⁾ [*Tragic tone*]:
Great Queen, fair Architect of our emprise,

Why lookst thou on us with foreboding eyes?
LYSISTRATA:
The behavior of these idiotic women!
There's something about the female temperament
that I can't bear!
5   KORYPHAIOS^(w):
                              What in the world do you mean?
LYSISTRATA:
Exactly what I say.
     KORYPHAIOS^(w):
                         What dreadful thing has happened?
Come, tell us: we're all your friends.
          LYSISTRATA: It isn't easy
to say it; yet, God knows, we can't hush it up.
     KORYPHAIOS^(w):
Well, then? Out with it!
          LYSISTRATA: To put it bluntly,
we're dying to get laid.
10   KORYPHAIOS^(w):   Almighty God!
     LYSISTRATA:
Why bring God into it? — No, it's just as I
     say.
I can't manage them any longer: they've gone
     man-crazy,
they're all trying to get out.
                              Why, look:
one of them was sneaking out the back door
15   over there by Pan's cave; another
was sliding down the walls with rope and
     tackle;
another was climbing aboard a sparrow, ready
     to take off
for the nearest brothel — I dragged *her* back
     by the hair!
They're all finding some reason to leave.
                              Look there!
There goes another one.
20   — Just a minute, you!
Where are you off to so fast?
          FIRST WOMAN: I've got to get home.
I've a lot of Milesian wool, and the worms are
     spoiling it.
     LYSISTRATA:
Oh bother you and your worms! Get back inside!
     FIRST WOMAN:
I'll be back right away, I swear I will.
25   I just want to get it stretched out on my bed.
          LYSISTRATA:
You'll do no such thing. You'll stay right here.
          FIRST WOMAN: And my wool?
You want it ruined?
          LYSISTRATA: Yes, for all I care.

SECOND WOMAN:
Oh dear! My lovely new flax from Amorgos —
I left it at home, all uncarded!
     LYSISTRATA: Another one!   30
And all she wants is someone to card her flax.
Get back in there!
     SECOND WOMAN:
                    But I swear by the Moon-Goddess,
the minute I get it done, I'll be back!
     LYSISTRATA: I say No.
If you, why not all the other women as well?
     THIRD WOMAN:
O Lady Eileithyia!° Radiant goddess! Thou
intercessor for women in childbirth! Stay, I
     pray thee,   35
oh stay this parturition. Shall I pollute
a sacred spot?
     LYSISTRATA:
                    And what's the matter with *you?*
     THIRD WOMAN:
I'm having a baby — any minute now.
     LYSISTRATA:
But you weren't pregnant yesterday.
     THIRD WOMAN: Well, I am today.
Let me go home for a midwife, Lysistrata: 40
there's not much time.
     LYSISTRATA: I never heard such nonsense.
What's that bulging under your cloak?
     THIRD WOMAN: A little baby boy.
     LYSISTRATA:
It certainly isn't. But it's something hollow,
like a basin or — Why, it's the helmet of
     Athena!
And you said you were having a baby.
     THIRD WOMAN: Well, I am! So there!   45
     LYSISTRATA:
Then why the helmet?
     THIRD WOMAN: I was afraid that my pains
might begin here in the Akropolis; and I
     wanted
to drop my chick into it, just as the dear
     doves do.
     LYSISTRATA:
Lies! Evasions! — But at least one thing's clear:
you can't leave the place before your puri-
     fication.   50
     THIRD WOMAN:
But I can't stay here in the Akropolis! Last
     night I dreamed
of the Snake.
     FIRST WOMAN:
And those horrible owls, the noise they make!

34 Eileithyia: Goddess of childbirth.

I can't get a bit of sleep; I'm just about dead.

LYSISTRATA:

You useless girls, that's enough: Let's have no
    more lying.

Of course you want your men. But don't you
55   imagine

that they want you just as much? I'll give you
    my word,

their nights must be pretty hard.

                                    Just stick it out!

A little patience, that's all, and our battle's
    won.

I have heard an Oracle. Should you like to
    hear it?

FIRST WOMAN:

An Oracle? Yes, tell us!

60   LYSISTRATA: Here is what it says:

WHEN   SWALLOWS   SHALL   THE
    HOOPOE SHUN

AND SPURN HIS HOT DESIRE,

ZEUS WILL PERFECT WHAT THEY'VE
    BEGUN

AND SET THE LOWER HIGHER.

FIRST WOMAN:

65 Does that mean we'll be on top?

LYSISTRATA:

BUT IF THE SWALLOWS SHALL FALL
    OUT

AND TAKE THE HOOPOE'S BAIT,

A CURSE MUST MARK THEIR HOUR
    OF DOUBT,

INFAMY SEAL THEIR FATE.

THIRD WOMAN:

I swear, *that* Oracle's all too clear.

70   FIRST WOMAN: Oh the dear gods!

LYSISTRATA:

Let's not be downhearted, girls. Back to our
    places!

The god has spoken. How can we possibly
    fail him?

[*Exit* LYSISTRATA *with the dissident women.*]

CHORAL EPISODE

CHORUS(m):

                                    [STROPHE]

I know a little story that I learned way back
    in school

Goes like this:

Once upon a time there was a young man —
    and no fool —

Named Melanion; and his

One aversi-on was marriage. He loathed the
    very thought.   5

So he ran off to the hills, and in a special grot

Raised a dog, and spent his days

Hunting rabbits. And it says

That he never never never did come home.

It might be called a refuge *from* the womb.   10

All right,

        all right,

                all right!

We're as bright as young Melanion, and we
    hate the very sight

Of you women!

A MAN:

How about a kiss, old lady?

A WOMAN:

Here's an onion for your eye!   15

A MAN:

A kick in the guts, then?

A WOMAN:

Try, old bristle-tail, just try!

A MAN:

Yet they say Myronides

On hands and knees

Looked just as shaggy fore and aft as I!   20

CHORUS(w):   [ANTISTROPHE]

Well, *I* know a little story, and it's just as
    good as yours.

Goes like this:

Once there was a man named Timon — a
    rough diamond, of course,

And that whiskery face of his

Looked like murder in the shrubbery. By God,
    he was a son   25

Of the Furies, let me tell you! And what did
    he do but run

From the world and all its ways,

Cursing mankind! And it says

That his choicest execrations as of then

Were leveled almost wholly at *old* men.   30

All right,

        all right,

                all right!

But there's one thing about Timon: he could
    always stand the sight

Of us women.

A WOMAN:

How about a crack in the jaw, Pop?

A MAN:

I can take it, Ma — no fear!   35

A WOMAN:

How about a kick in the face?

A MAN:

You'd reveal your old caboose?

A WOMAN:
What I'd show,
I'll have you know,
40 Is an instrument you're too far gone to use.

SCENE III

[*Re-enter* LYSISTRATA.]

LYSISTRATA:
Oh, quick, girls, quick! Come here!
   A WOMAN: What is it?
   LYSISTRATA: A man.
A man simply bulging with love.
                  O Kyprian Queen,°
O Paphian, O Kythereian! Hear us and aid us!
   A WOMAN:
Where is this enemy?
   LYSISTRATA:
                Over there, by Demeter's shrine.
   A WOMAN:
5 Damned if he isn't. But who *is* he?
   MYRRHINE: My husband.
Kinesias.
   LYSISTRATA:
          Oh then, get busy! Tease him! Under-
mine him!
Wreck him! Give him everything — kissing,
tickling, nudging,
whatever you generally torture him with — :
give him everything
except what we swore on the wine we would
not give.
   MYRRHINE:
Trust me.
   LYSISTRATA:
10   I do. But I'll help you get him started.
The rest of you women, stay back.

[*Enter* KINESIAS.]

KINESIAS: Oh God! Oh my God!
I'm stiff from lack of exercise. All I can do to
stand up.
   LYSISTRATA:
Halt! Who are you, approaching our lines?
   KINESIAS: Me? I.
   LYSISTRATA:
A man?
   KINESIAS:
       You have eyes, haven't you?
   LYSISTRATA: Go away.

2 **Kyprian Queen:** Aphrodite, goddess of love.

KINESIAS:
Who says so?
   LYSISTRATA:
          Officer of the Day.
   KINESIAS: Officer, I beg you, 15
by all the gods at once, bring Myrrhine out.
   LYSISTRATA:
Myrrhine? And who, my good sir, are you?
   KINESIAS:
Kinesias. Last name's Pennison. Her husband.
   LYSISTRATA:
Oh, of course. I beg your pardon. We're glad
to see you.
We've heard so much about you. Dearest
Myrrhine 20
is always talking about Kinesias — never nibbles
an egg
or an apple without saying
"Here's to Kinesias!"
   KINESIAS: Do you really mean it?
   LYSISTRATA: I do.
When we're discussing men, she always says
"Well, after all, there's nobody like Kinesias!" 25
   KINESIAS:
Good God. — Well, then, please send her
down here.
   LYSISTRATA:
And what do *I* get out of it?
   KINESIAS: A standing promise.
   LYSISTRATA:
I'll take it up with her.
                  [*Exit* LYSISTRATA.]
   KINESIAS: But be quick about it!
Lord, what's life without a wife? Can't eat.
Can't sleep.
Every time I go home, the place is so
empty, so 30
insufferably sad. Love's killing me, Oh,
hurry!

[*Enter* MANES, *a slave, with* KINESIAS' *baby;
the voice of* MYRRHINE *is heard off-stage.*]

MYRRHINE:
   But of course I love him! Adore him —
But no,
he hates love. No. I won't go down.

[*Enter* MYRRHINE, *above.*]

KINESIAS: Myrrhine!
Darlingest Myrrhinette! Come down quick!
   MYRRHINE:
Certainly not.
   KINESIAS: Not? But why, Myrrhine? 35

MYRRHINE:
Why? You don't need me.
KINESIAS:
                    Need you? My God, *look* at me!
MYRRHINE:
So long!

[*Turns to go.*]

KINESIAS:
          Myrrhine, Myrrhine, Myrrhine!
If not for my sake, for our child!

[*Pinches* BABY.]

                    — All right, you: pipe up!
BABY:
Mummie! Mummie! Mummie!
KINESIAS: You hear that?
40 Pitiful, I call it. Six days now
with never a bath; no food; enough to break
     your heart!
MYRRHINE:
My darlingest child! What a father *you*
     acquired!
KINESIAS:
At least come down for his sake.
MYRRHINE: I suppose I must.
Oh, this mother business!

                              [*Exit.*]

KINESIAS: How pretty she is! And younger!
The harder she treats me, the more bothered
     I get.

[MYRRHINE *enters, below.*]

45 MYRRHINE:
               Dearest child,
you're as sweet as your father's horrid. Give me
     a kiss.
KINESIAS:
Now don't you see how wrong it was to get
     involved
in this scheming League of women? It's bad
for us both.
MYRRHINE:
               Keep your hands to yourself!
KINESIAS: But our house
going to rack and ruin?
MYRRHINE: I don't care.
50 KINESIAS: And your knitting
all torn to pieces by the chickens? Don't you
     care?
MYRRHINE:
Not at all.
KINESIAS:
               And our debt to Aphrodite?

Oh, *won't* you come back?
MYRRHINE:
                    No. — At least, not until you men
make a treaty and stop this war.
KINESIAS: Why, I suppose
that might be arranged.
MYRRHINE: Oh? Well, I suppose   55
I might come down then. But meanwhile,
I've sworn not to.
KINESIAS:
                    Don't worry. — Now let's have fun.
MYRRHINE:
No! Stop it! I said no!
                    — Although, of course,
I *do* love you.
KINESIAS:
                    I know you do. Darling Myrrhine:
come, shall we?
MYRRHINE: Are you out of your mind? In
     front of the child?   60
KINESIAS:
Take him home, Manes.

               [*Exit* MANES *with* BABY.]
                    There. He's gone.
                              Come on!
There's nothing to stop us now.
MYRRHINE: You devil! But where?
KINESIAS:
In Pan's cave. What could be snugger than
     that?
MYRRHINE:
But my purification before I go back to the
     Citadel?
KINESIAS:
Wash in the Klepsydra.°
MYRRHINE: And my oath?
KINESIAS: Leave the oath to me.   65
After all, I'm the man.
MYRRHINE: Well . . . if you say so.
                    I'll go find a bed.
KINESIAS:
Oh, bother a bed! The ground's good enough
     for me.
MYRRHINE:
No. You're a bad man, but you deserve some-
     thing better than dirt.
                              [*Exit* MYRRHINE.]
KINESIAS:
What a love she is! And how thoughtful!

___

65 **Klepsydra**: A sacred spring beneath the walls
of the Akropolis. Kinesias' suggestion has overtones
of blasphemy.

[*Re-enter* MYRRHINE.]

MYRRHINE: Here's your bed.
Now let me get my clothes off.
70   But, good horrors!
We haven't a mattress.
        KINESIAS: Oh, forget the mattress!
        MYRRHINE: No.
Just lying on blankets? Too sordid.
        KINESIAS: Give me a kiss.
        MYRRHINE:
Just a second.
                            [*Exit* MYRRHINE.]
        KINESIAS: I swear, I'll explode!

[*Re-enter* MYRRHINE.]

MYRRHINE: Here's your mattress.
I'll just take my dress off.
                            But look —
where's our pillow?
        KINESIAS: I don't *need* a pillow!
75   MYRRHINE: Well, *I* do.
                            [*Exit* MYRRHINE.]
        KINESIAS:
I don't suppose even Herakles
would stand for this!

[*Re-enter* MYRRHINE.]

MYRRHINE: There we are. Ups-a-daisy!
        KINESIAS:
So we are. Well, come to bed.
        MYRRHINE: But I wonder:
is everything ready now?
        KINESIAS:
                    I can swear to that. Come, darling!
        MYRRHINE:
Just getting out of my girdle.
                            But remember, now,
80   what you promised about the treaty.
        KINESIAS: Yes, yes, yes!
        MYRRHINE:
But no coverlet!
        KINESIAS: Damn it, I'll be
your coverlet!
        MYRRHINE:
                    Be right back.
                            [*Exit* MYRRHINE.]
        KINESIAS: This girl and her coverlets
will be the death of me.

[*Re-enter* MYRRHINE.]

MYRRHINE: Here we are. Up you go!

KINESIAS:
Up? I've been up for ages.
        MYRRHINE: Some perfume?   85
KINESIAS:
No, by Apollo!
        MYRRHINE: Yes, by Aphrodite!
I don't care whether you want it or not.
                            [*Exit* MYRRHINE.]
        KINESIAS:
For love's sake, hurry!

[*Re-enter* MYRRHINE.]

MYRRHINE:
Here, in your hand. Rub it right in.
        KINESIAS: Never cared for perfume.
And this is particularly strong. Still, here goes.   90
        MYRRHINE:
What a nitwit I am! I brought you the
        Rhodian bottle.
        KINESIAS:
Forget it.
        MYRRHINE:
                No trouble at all. You just wait here.
                            [*Exit* MYRRHINE.]
        KINESIAS:
God damn the man who invented perfume!

[*Re-enter* MYRRHINE.]

MYRRHINE:
At last! The right bottle!
        KINESIAS: I've got the rightest
bottle of all, and it's right here waiting for you.   95
Darling, forget everything else. Do come to
        bed.
        MYRRHINE:
Just let me get my shoes off.
                            — And, by the way,
you'll vote for the treaty?
        KINESIAS: I'll think about it.
                            [MYRRHINE *runs away*.]·
There! That's done it! The damned woman,
she gets me all bothered, she half kills me,   100
and off she runs! What'll I do? Where
can I get laid?
                    — And you, little prodding pal,
who's going to take care of *you?* No, you and I
had better get down to old Foxdog's Nursing
        Clinic.
        CHORUS[m]:
Alas for the woes of man, alas   105
        Specifically for you.
She's brought you to a pretty pass:
        What are you going to do?

110 Split, heart! Sag, flesh! Proud spirit, crack!
Myrrhine's got you on your back.
KINESIAS:
The agony, the protraction!
KORYPHAIOS(m):   Friend,
What woman's worth a damn?
They bitch us all, world without end.
KINESIAS:
Yet they're so damned sweet, man!
KORYPHAIOS(m):
115 Calamitous, that's what I say.
You should have learned that much today.
CHORUS(m):
O blessed Zeus, roll womankind.
Up into one great ball;
Blast them aloft on a high wind,
120   And once there, let them fall.
Down, down they'll come, the pretty dears,
And split themselves on our thick spears.

[*Exit* KINESIAS.]

SCENE IV

[*Enter a* SPARTAN HERALD.]

HERALD:
Gentlemen, Ah beg you will be so kind
as to direct me to the Central Committee.
Ah have a communication.

[*Re-enter* COMMISSIONER.]

COMMISSIONER: Are you a man,
or a fertility symbol?
HERALD:
        Ah refuse to answer that question!
Ah'm a certified herald from Spahta, and Ah've
5   come
to talk about an ahmistice.
COMMISSIONER: Then why
that spear under your cloak?
HERALD: Ah have no speah!
COMMISSIONER:
You don't walk naturally, with your tunic
poked out so. You have a tumor, maybe,
or a hernia?
HERALD: You lost yo' mahnd, man?
10 COMMISSIONER: Well,
something's up, I can see that. And I don't
    like it.
HERALD:
Colonel, Ah resent this.
COMMISSIONER: So I see. But what *is* it?
HERALD: A staff

with a message from Spahta.
COMMISSIONER:
        Oh. I know about those staffs.
Well, then, man, speak out: How are things
    in Sparta?
HERALD:
Hahd, Colonel, hahd! We're at a standstill. 15
Cain't seem to think of anything but women.
COMMISSIONER:
How curious! Tell me, do you Spartans think
that maybe Pan's to blame?
HERALD:
Pan? No. Lampito and her little naked friends.
They won't let a man come nigh them.   20
COMMISSIONER:
How are you handling it?
HERALD: Losing our mahnds,
if y' want to know, and walking around
        hunched over
lahk men carrying candles in a gale.
The women have swohn they'll have nothing
        to do with us
until we get a treaty.
COMMISSIONER: Yes. I know.   25
It's a general uprising, sir, in all parts of
        Greece.
But as for the answer —
                Sir: go back to Sparta
and have them send us your Armistice
        Commission.
I'll arrange things in Athens.
                And I may say
that my standing is good enough to make them
        listen.   30
HERALD:
A man after mah own haht! Seh, Ah thank
    you.
                [*Exit* HERALD.]

CHORAL EPISODE

CHORUS(m):
                        [STROPHE]
Oh these women! Where will you find
A slavering beast that's more unkind?
    Where a hotter fire?
Give me a panther, any day.
He's not so merciless as they,   5
    And panthers don't conspire.
CHORUS(w):
                    [ANTISTROPHE]
We may be hard, you silly old ass,

But who brought you to this stupid pass?
You're the ones to blame.
10 Fighting with us, your oldest friends,
Simply to serve your selfish ends —
Really, you have no shame!
KORYPHAIOS^(m):
No, I'm through with women for ever.
KORYPHAIOS^(w):   If you say so.
Still, you might put some clothes on. You look
   too absurd
15 standing around naked. Come, get into this
   cloak.
KORYPHAIOS^(m):
Thank you; you're right. I merely took it off
because I was in such a temper.
KORYPHAIOS^(w):   That's much better.
Now you resemble a man again.
                    Why have you been so horrid?
And look: there's some sort of insect in your
   eye.
Shall I take it out?
KORYPHAIOS^(m):
20   An insect, is it? So that's
what's been bothering me. Lord, yes: take it
   out!
KORYPHAIOS^(w):
You might be more polite.
                    — But, heavens!
What an enormous mosquito!
KORYPHAIOS^(m):   You've saved my life.
That mosquito was drilling an artesian well
in my left eye.
KORYPHAIOS^(w):
25   Let me wipe
those tears away. — And now: one little kiss?
KORYPHAIOS^(m):
No, no kisses.
KORYPHAIOS^(w):
                    You're so difficult.
KORYPHAIOS^(m):
You impossible women! How you do get
   around us!
The poet was right: Can't live with you, or
   without you.
30 But let's be friends.
And to celebrate, you might join us in an Ode.
CHORUS^(m and w):
          Let it never be said   [STROPHE 1]
          That my tongue is malicious:
          Both by word and by deed
I would set an example that's noble and
35   gracious.
          We've had sorrow and care
          Till we're sick of the tune.

Is there anyone here
Who would like a small loan?
          My purse is crammed,   40
          As you'll soon find;
And you needn't pay me back if the Peace gets
   signed.

I've invited to lunch   [STROPHE 2]
Some Karystian rips —
An esurient bunch,   45
But I've ordered a menu to water their lips.
          I can still make soup
          And slaughter a pig.
          You're all coming, I hope?
          But a bath first, I beg!   50
          Walk right up
          As though you owned the place,
And you'll get the front door slammed to in
   your face.

SCENE V

[*Enter* SPARTAN AMBASSADOR, *with en-
tourage.*]

KORYPHAIOS^(m):
The Commission has arrived from Sparta.
                    How oddly
they're walking!
                    Gentlemen, welcome to Athens!
How is life in Lakonia?
AMBASSADOR: Need we discuss that?
Simply use your eyes.
CHORUS^(m):   The poor man's right:
                    What a sight!
AMBASSADOR: Words fail me.   5
But come, gentlemen, call in your Commis-
   sioners,
and let's get down to a Peace.
CHORAGOS^(m):
                    The state we're in! Can't bear
a stitch below the waist. It's a kind of pelvic
paralysis.
COMMISSIONER:
                    Won't somebody call Lysistrata? —
Gentlemen,
we're no better off than you.
AMBASSADOR: So I see.   10
A SPARTAN:
Seh, do y'all feel a certain strain
early in the morning?

AN ATHENIAN:
I do, sir. It's worse than a strain.
A few more days, and there's nothing for us
but Kleisthenes,
that broken blossom.

CHORAGOS (m):
But you'd better get dressed again.
You know these people going around Athens
with chisels,
looking for statues of Hermes.°

ATHENIAN: Sir, you are right.

SPARTAN:
He certainly is! Ah'll put mah own clothes
back on.

[*Enter* ATHENIAN COMMISSIONERS.]

COMMISSIONER:
Gentlemen from Sparta, welcome. This is a
sorry business.

SPARTAN [*To one of his own group*]:
Colonel, we got dressed just in time. Ah sweah,
if they'd seen us the way we were, there'd have
been a new wah
between the states.

COMMISSIONER:
Shall we call the meeting to order?
Now, Lakonians,
what's your proposal?

AMBASSADOR:
We propose to consider peace.

COMMISSIONER:
Good. That's on our minds, too.
— Summon Lysistrata.
We'll never get anywhere without her.

AMBASSADOR: Lysistrata?
Summon Lysis-*any*body! Only, summon!

KORYPHAIOS (m): No need to summon:
here she is, herself.

[*Enter* LYSISTRATA.]

COMMISSIONER: Lysistrata! Lion of women!
This is your hour to be
hard and yielding, outspoken and shy, austere
and
gentle. You see here
the best brains of Hellas (confused, I admit,
by your devious charming) met as one man

16 **statues of Hermes:** The statues were the
Hermai, stone posts set up in various parts of
Athens. Just before the sailing of the Sicilian
Expedition, a group of anonymous vandals
mutilated these statues with chisels. This was con-
sidered an unhappy augury.

to turn the future over to you.

LYSISTRATA: That's fair enough,
unless you men take it into your heads
to turn to each other instead of to us. But I'd
know
soon enough if you did.
— Where is Reconciliation?
Go, some of you: bring her here.
[*Exeunt two women.*]
And now, women,
lead the Spartan delegates to me: not roughly
or insultingly, as our men handle them, but
gently,
politely, as ladies should. Take them by the
hand,
or by anything else if they won't give you their
hands.

[*The* SPARTANS *are escorted over.*]

There. — The Athenians next, by any convenient handle.

[*The* ATHENIANS *are escorted.*]

Stand there, please. — Now, all of you, listen
to me.

[*During the following speech the two
women re-enter, carrying an enormous statue
of a naked girl; this is* RECONCILIATION.]

I'm only a woman, I know; but I've a mind,
and, I think, not a bad one: I owe it to my
father
and to listening to the local politicians.
So much for that.
Now, gentlemen,
since I have you here, I intend to give you a
scolding.
We are all Greeks.
Must I remind you of Thermopylai,° of
Olympia,
of Delphoi? names deep in all our hearts?
Are they not a common heritage?
Yet you men
go raiding through the country from both
sides,
Greek killing Greek, storming down Greek
cities —
and all the time the Barbarian across the sea

50 **Thermopylai:** A narrow pass where, in 480
B.C., an army of 300 Spartans held out for three
days against a vastly superior Persian force.

is waiting for his chance!
                    — That's my first point.
AN ATHENIAN:
Lord! I can hardly contain myself.
LYSISTRATA: As for you Spartans:
Was it so long ago that Perikleides°
came here to beg our help? I can see him still,
his grey face, his sombre gown. And what did
60   he want?
An army from Athens. All Messene
was hot at your heels, and the sea-god splitting
    your land.
Well, Kimon and his men,
four thousand strong, marched out and saved
    all Sparta.
And what thanks do we get? You come back
65   to murder us.
AN ATHENIAN:
They're aggressors, Lysistrata!
A SPARTAN: Ah admit it.
When Ah look at those laigs, Ah sweah Ah'll
    aggress mahself!
LYSISTRATA:
And you, Athenians: do you think you're
    blameless?
Remember that bad time when we were
    helpless,
70   and an army came from Sparta,
and that was the end of the Thessalian
    menace,
the end of Hippias and his allies.
                    And that was Sparta,
and only Sparta; but for Sparta, we'd be
cringing slaves today, not free Athenians.

[From this point, the male responses are less
to LYSISTRATA than to the statue.]

A SPARTAN:
A well shaped speech.
75   AN ATHENIAN: Certainly it has its points.
LYSISTRATA:
Why are we fighting each other? With all this
    history
of favors given and taken, what stands in the
    way
of making peace?
AMBASSADOR: Spahta is ready, ma'am,
so long as we get that place back.
LYSISTRATA: What place, man?

58 **Perikleides**: A Spartan ambassador to Athens,
who successfully urged Athenians to aid Sparta in
putting down a rebellion.

AMBASSADOR:
Ah refer to Pylos.
COMMISSIONER:
                    Not a chance, by God!   80
LYSISTRATA:
Give it to them, friend.
COMMISSIONER:
But — what shall we have to bargain with?
LYSISTRATA:
Demand something in exchange.
COMMISSIONER: Good idea. — Well, then:
Cockeville first, and the Happy Hills, and the
    country
between the Legs of Megara.
AMBASSADOR: Mah government objects.
LYSISTRATA:
Over-ruled. Why fuss about a pair of legs?   85

[General assent. The statue is removed.]

AN ATHENIAN:
I want to get out of these clothes and start
    my plowing.
A SPARTAN:
Ah'll fertilize mahn first, by the Heavenly
    Twins!
LYSISTRATA:
And so you shall,
once you've made peace. If you are serious,
go, both of you, and talk with your allies.   90
COMMISSIONER:
Too much talk already. No, we'll stand
    together.
we've only one end in view. All that we
    want
is our women; and I speak for our allies.
AMBASSADOR:
Mah government concurs.
AN ATHENIAN: So does Karystos.
LYSISTRATA:
Good. — But before you come inside   95
to join your wives at supper, you must perform
the usual lustration. Then we'll open
our baskets for you, and all that we have is
    yours.
But you must promise upright good behavior
from this day on. Then each man home with
    his woman!   100
AN ATHENIAN:
Let's get it over with.
A SPARTAN: Lead on. Ah follow.
AN ATHENIAN:
Quick as a cat can wink!
                    [Exeunt all but the CHORUSES.]

CHORUS^(w).:

Embroideries and   [ANTISTROPHE 1]
Twinkling ornaments and
105   Pretty dresses — I hand
Them all over to you, and with never a qualm.
They'll be nice for your daughters
On festival days
When the girls bring the Goddess
110   The ritual prize.
Come in, one and all:
Take what you will.
I've nothing here so tightly corked that you
can't make it spill.

[ANTISTROPHE 2]
You may search my house,
115   But you'll not find
The least thing of use,
Unless your two eyes are keener than mine.
Your numberless brats
Are half starved? and your slaves?
120   Courage, grandpa! I've lots
Of grain left, and big loaves.
I'll fill your guts,
I'll go the whole hog;
But if you come too close to me, remember:
'ware the dog!

[*Exeunt* CHORUSES.]

EXODOS

[A DRUNKEN CITIZEN *enters, approaches the
gate, and is halted by a sentry.*]

CITIZEN:
Open. The. Door.
SENTRY: Now, friend, just shove along!
— So you want to sit down. If it weren't such
an old joke,
I'd tickle your tail with this torch. Just the
sort of gag
this audience appreciates.
CITIZEN: I. Stay. Right. Here.
SENTRY:
Get away from there, or I'll scalp you! The
5   gentlemen from Sparta
are just coming back from dinner.
[*Exit* CITIZEN; *the general company re-
enters; the two* CHORUSES *now represent*
SPARTANS *and* ATHENIANS.]
A SPARTAN: Ah must say,
Ah never tasted better grub.
AN ATHENIAN: And those Lakonians!

They're gentlemen, by the Lord! Just goes to
show,
a drink to the wise is sufficient.
COMMISSIONER: And why not?
A sober man's an ass.   10
Men of Athens, mark my words: the only
efficient
Ambassador's a drunk Ambassador. Is that
clear?
Look: we go to Sparta,
and when we get there we're dead sober. The
result?
Everyone cackling at everyone else. They make
speeches;   15
and even if we understand, we get it all wrong
when we file our reports in Athens. But
today — !
Everybody's happy. Couldn't tell the difference
between *Drink to Me Only* and
The Star-Spangled Athens.
What's a few lies,   20
washed down in good strong drink?

[*Re-enter the* DRUNKEN CITIZEN.]

SENTRY: God almighty,
he's back again!
CITIZEN: I. Resume. My. Place.
A SPARTAN [*To an* ATHENIAN]:
Ah beg yo', seh,
take yo' instrument in yo' hand and play
for us.
Ah'm told   25
yo' understand the intricacies of the floot?
Ah'd lahk to execute a song and dance
in honor of Athens,
and, of cohse, of Spahta.
CITIZEN:
Toot. On. Your. Flute.

[*The following song is a solo — an aria —
accompanied by the flute. The* CHORUS OF
SPARTANS *begins a slow dance.*]

A SPARTAN:
O Memory,   30
Let the Muse speak once more
In my young voice. Sing glory.
Sing Artemision's shore,
Where Athens fluttered the Persians. *Alalai*,
Sing glory, that great   35
Victory! Sing also
Our Leonidas and his men,
Those wild boars, sweat and blood
Down in a red drench. Then, then

40 The barbarians broke, though they had stood
Numberless as the sands before!

O Artemis,°
Virgin Goddess, whose darts
Flash in our forests: approve
45 This pact of peace and join our hearts,
From this day on, in love.
Huntress, descend!

LYSISTRATA:
All that will come in time.
                              But now, Lakonians,
take home your wives. Athenians, take yours.
Each man be kind to his woman; and you,
50   women,
be equally kind. Never again, pray God,
shall we lose our way in such madness.

KORYPHAIOS (Athenian):   And now
let's dance our joy.

[*From this point the dance becomes general.*]

CHORUS (Athenian):
Dance, you Graces
                          Artemis, dance
Dance, Phoibos,° Lord of dancing
                                        Dance,
55 In a scurry of Maenads, Lord Dionysos°
                          Dance, Zeus Thunderer
                  Dance, Lady Hera°
Queen of the sky
                  Dance, dance, all you gods

42 **Artemis:** Goddess of virginity, of the hunt, and of childbirth.
55 **Phoibos:** God of the sun.
56 **Maenads, Lord Dionysos:** The maenads were ecstatic women in the train of Dionysos, god of wine.
57 **Hera:** Wife of Zeus.

Dance witness everlasting of our pact
Evohí Evohé   60
Dance for the dearest
                          the Bringer of Peace
Deathless Aphrodite!

COMMISSIONER:
Now let us have another song from Sparta.

CHORUS (Spartan):
From Taygetos, from Taygetos,
      Lakonian Muse, come down.   65
Sing to the Lord Apollo
      Who rules Amyklai Town.

Sing Athena of the House of Brass!°
Sing Leda's Twins,° that chivalry
      Resplendent on the shore   70
Of our Eurotas; sing the girls
      That dance along before:

Sparkling in dust their gleaming feet,
      Their hair a Bacchant fire,
And Leda's daughter, thyrsos° raised,   75
      Leads their triumphant choir.

CHORUSES (S and A):
Evohé!
      Evohaí!
            Evohé!
                  We pass
      Dancing
            dancing
                  to greet
Athena of the House of Brass.

68 **Athena of the House of Brass:** A temple standing on the Akropolis of Sparta.
69 **Leda's Twins:** Leda, raped by Zeus, bore quadruplets: two daughters, Helen and Klytaimnestra, and two sons, Kastor and Polydeukes.
75 **thyrsos:** A staff twined with ivy, carried by Dionysos and his followers.

Of the hundreds of ancient Greek comedies that were written, only eleven by Aristophanes and four by Menander (c. 342 B.C.–299 B.C.) are extant, and three of Menander's four survive only in long fragments. Aristophanes seems to have written about forty plays, Menander more than twice as many. Hundreds of other men wrote comedies in ancient Greece, but they are mere names, or names attached to brief fragments. This means that when we talk about Greek comedy we are really talking about a fraction of Aristophanes' work, and an even smaller fraction of Menander's.

Greek comedy is customarily divided into three kinds: Old Comedy (486 B.C., when comedy was first given official recognition at the festival called the City Dionysia, to 404 B.C., the end of the Peloponnesian War, when Athens was humbled and freedom of speech was curtailed); Middle Comedy (404 B.C. to 336 B.C., the accession of Alexander, when Athens was no longer free); and New Comedy (336 B.C. to c. 250 B.C., the approximate date of the last fragments). Of Old Comedy, there are Aristophanes' plays; of Middle Comedy, there is *Plutus*, one of Aristophanes' last plays; of New Comedy, there are Menander's fragments and his recently discovered *Dyskolos* (*The Disagreeable Man*).

Old Comedy is a curious combination of obscenity, farce, political allegory, satire, and lyricism. Puns, literary allusions, phallic jokes, political jibes, etc. periodically give way to joyful song; Aristophanes seems to have been something of a combination of Joyce, Swift, and Shelley. Other comparisons may be helpful. Perhaps we can say that in their loosely connected episodes and in their rapid shifts from lyricism and fantasy to mockery the plays are something like a Marx Brothers movie (Harpo's musical episodes juxtaposed with Groucho's irreverent wisecracks and outrageous ogling), though the plays are more explicitly political; and they are something like the rock musical, *Hair*, which combined lyricism and politics with sex.

Normally Aristophanes' plays have the following structure:

1. *Prologos*, prologue or exposition. Someone has a bright idea, and sets it forth either in monologue or dialogue. In *Lysistrata*, the prologue consists of lines 1–212, in which Lysistrata persuades the women to refrain from sex with their husbands and thus compel their husbands to give up the war.

2. *Parodos*, entrance of the chorus. The twenty-four or so members of the chorus express their opinion of the idea. (The *koryphaios* or leader of the chorus perhaps sang some lines by himself.) *Lysistrata* is somewhat unusual in having two half-choruses or *hemichori*, one of Old Men and another of Old Women, each with its own leader. Probably each half-chorus had twelve members.

3. *Epeisodion*, episode or scene. In the first scene of *Lysistrata* the women defeat the Commissioner. (A scene in this position, that is, before the *parabasis*, is sometimes called the *agon* or debate.)

4. *Parabasis*, usually an elaborate composition in which the leader of the chorus ordinarily sheds his dramatic character and addresses the audience on the poet's behalf, the other actors having briefly retired. The *parabasis* in *Lysistrata* is unusual; it is much shorter than those in Aristophanes' earlier plays, and the chorus does not speak directly for the playwright.

5. *Epeisodia*, episodes or scenes, sometimes briefly separated by choral songs. These episodes have to do with the working out of the original bright idea. In *Lysistrata* the first scene of this group (labeled Scene II because we have already had one scene before the *parabasis*) shows the women seeking to desert the cause, the second shows Myrrhine — loyal to the idea — tormenting her husband Kinesias, the third shows the Athenian Commissioner discomfited by an erection, and the fourth shows the Spartan ambassadors similarly discomfited.

6. *Exodos* or final scene, customarily of reconciliation and rejoicing. There is often talk of a wedding and a feast. In this play a Spartan sings in praise not only of Sparta but also of Athens, and the chorus praises the deities worshipped in both states.

Perhaps all Old Comedy was rather like this, but it should be remembered that even Aristophanes' eleven plays do not all follow the pattern exactly. *Lysistrata*, for example, is unusual in having two hemichori and in having the chorus retain its identity during the parabasis. But *Lysistrata* (the accent is on the second syllable, and the name in effect means "Disbander-of-the-Army") is typical in its political concern, in its fantasy, in its bawdry, and in its revelry. It touches on serious, destructive themes, but it is joyous and extravagant, ending with a newly unified society. These points require some explanation.

First, Aristophanes' political concern. *Lysistrata* is the last of Aristophanes' three plays opposing the Peloponnesian War (the earlier two are *Acharnians* and *Peace*). This drawn-out war (431–404 B.C.), named for a peninsula forming the southern part of Greece, was fought between Athens (with some allies) and a confederacy headed by Sparta. Though enemies at the time of the play, in 478 B.C. Athens and Sparta and other communities had become allied in order to defeat a common enemy, the Persians, but once the Persian threat was destroyed, Athens deprived most of its allies of their autonomy and, in effect, Athens ruled an empire. Moreover, Athens tried to extend its empire. The war ultimately cost Athens its overseas empire and its leadership on the mainland. In 413 B.C. Athens had suffered an especially disastrous naval defeat; it had made something of a recovery by the time of *Lysistrata* (performed 411 B.C.), but the cost in manpower and money was enormous. Yet Athens persisted in its dream of conquest and of colonizing. To counter this fantastic idea Aristophanes holds up another fantastic idea: the women will end the war by a sex strike. Actually, this is not one fantastic idea but two, for the idea of a sex strike is not more fantastic (for Athenians of the fifth century B.C.) than the idea of women playing a role — not to speak of a decisive role — in national affairs. Lysistrata, reporting her husband's view, is reporting the view of every Athenian: "War's a man's affair." (He was quoting from Homer's *Iliad*, so the point was beyond dispute.) And so there is something wild in her suggestion that the women can save the Greek cities (her hope goes beyond Athens, to Sparta and the other combatants), and in her comparison of the state to a ball of tangled yarn:

> COMMISSIONER:
> All this is beside the point.
>   Will you be so kind
> as to tell me how you mean to save Greece?
>   LYSISTRATA:
>   Of course.
>
> Nothing could be simpler.

COMMISSIONER:
                    I assure you, I'm all ears.
    LYSISTRATA:
Do you know anything about weaving?
Say the yarn gets tangled: we thread it
this way and that through the skein, up and down,
until it's free. And it's like that with war.
We'll send our envoys
up and down, this way and that, all over Greece,
until it's finished.
    COMMISSIONER:
                    Yarn? Thread? Skein?
Are you out of your mind? I tell you,
war is a serious business.
    LYSISTRATA:
                    So serious
that I'd like to go on talking about weaving.
    COMMISSIONER:
All right. Go ahead.
    LYSISTRATA:
                    The first thing we have to do
is to wash our yarn, get the dirt out of it.
You see? Isn't there too much dirt here in Athens?
You must wash those men away.
                    Then our spoiled wool —
that's like your job-hunters, out for a life
of no work and big pay. Back to the basket,
citizens or not, allies or not,
or friendly immigrants.
                    And your colonies?
Hanks of wool lost in various places. Pull them
together, weave them into one great whole,
and our voters are clothed for ever.

To the Commissioner, this is utterly fantastic:

COMMISSIONER:
                    It would take a woman
    to reduce state questions to a matter of carding and weaving.

   Such is the male view, and so these fantastic women, in order to exert influence, must resort to another fantastic idea, the sex strike, and here we encounter Aristophanes' famous bawdry. In fact the play's reputation for bawdry is grossly exaggerated. Until recently, when pornography was hard to get, Lysistrata — because it was literature — provided one of the few available texts that talked of erections and of female delight in sex, and Aubrey Beardsley's illustrations (1896) doubtless helped to establish the book's reputation as a sexual stimulus. But it is really pretty tame stuff compared to what is now readily available, and the play, for all its sexual jokes, is not really about sex but about peace, harmony, union. Union between husbands and wives, between all in Athens, and between Athens and the other Greek-speaking communities. Almost the last lines of the play are:

But now, Lakonians,
take home your wives. Athenians, take yours.
Each man be kind to his woman; and you, women,
be equally kind. Never again, pray God,
shall we lose our way in such madness.

Sex, of course, has brought about this union, for only when Athenian and Spartan men are both afflicted by the power of sex, and thus share a single overriding concern, are they able to compromise on the less important political differences that have divided them. And so, as we think about the play, the heroine is, finally, not so much the fantastic Lysistrata (she is also very much a male Athenian's idea of a woman: "To put it bluntly," she says, "we're dying to get laid"); the real heroine of the play is a rather shadowy figure, a statue of a nude female called Reconciliation, because reconciliation, not sex, is really what the play is about.

During the years of the Vietnam War, one often saw a bumper-sticker, "Make love, not war." The two activities are not mutually incompatible, but we get the idea; Aristophanes, some twenty-five centuries earlier, got the idea too. He saw in sexual union a symbol of a power so great that it subdues even conquest-mad armies. One might say that sex in this play deflects men from divisive self-assertiveness and (may we say?) brings them to their senses. Restored to their senses, they can perceive the mutual good.

One final point: the whole play, of course, not only is utterly improbable but also is utterly impossible: the women complain that they are sex-starved because the men are away at the war, but we soon find that the women will remedy this situation by withholding sex from the men — who, we thought, were away at the war. How can one withhold sex from men who are supposedly not present? But Old Comedy never worried about such consistency.

A few words should be said about Middle Comedy and New Comedy. Middle Comedy is a convenient label to apply to the lost plays that must have marked the transition from Old Comedy to New Comedy, that is, to the surviving work of Menander. In New Comedy, written when Athens' political greatness was gone, and when political invective was impossible, the chorus has dwindled to musicians and dancers who perform intermittently, characters tend to be types (the young lover, the crabby old father, etc.), and the plot is regularly a young man's wooing of a maid. Fortune seems unfair and unpredictable, but in the end the virtuous are rewarded. The personal satire and obscenity of Old Comedy are gone, and in their place is a respectably conducted tale showing how, after humorous difficulties, the young man achieves his goal. The plot steadily moves toward the happy ending, which is far more integral than the more or less elusive allegoric (or metaphoric) union at the end of *Lysistrata*. It was New Comedy that influenced Rome (which could scarcely have imitated the political satire of Old Comedy), and through Rome modern Europe. Shakespeare, for example, whose comedies have been described as obstacle races to the altar, was a descendant of Menander though he knew nothing of Menander's work first-hand.

A MIDSUMMER NIGHT'S DREAM

William Shakespeare

Edited by Wolfgang Clemens

William Shakespeare (1564–1616) was born in Stratford, England, of middle-class parents. Nothing of interest is known about his early years, but by 1590 he was acting and writing plays in London. He early worked in all three Elizabethan dramatic genres — tragedy, comedy, and history. *Romeo and Juliet*, for example, was written about 1595, the year of *Richard II*, and in the following year he wrote *A Midsummer Night's Dream*. Other major comedies are *The Merchant of Venice* (1596–1597), *As You Like It* (1599–1600), and *Twelfth Night* (1599–1600). His last major works, *The Winter's Tale* (1610–1611) and *The Tempest* (1611), are usually called "romances"; these plays have happy endings but they seem more meditative and less joyful than the earlier comedies.

[DRAMATIS PERSONAE

THESEUS, *Duke of Athens*
EGEUS, *father to Hermia*
LYSANDER } *in love with Hermia*
DEMETRIUS }
PHILOSTRATE, *Master of the Revels to Theseus*
PETER QUINCE, *a carpenter;* PROLOGUE *in the play*
SNUG, *a joiner;* LION *in the play*
NICK BOTTOM, *a weaver;* PYRAMUS *in the play*
FRANCIS FLUTE, *a bellows mender;* THISBY *in the play*
TOM SNOUT, *a tinker;* WALL *in the play*
ROBIN STARVELING, *a tailor;* MOONSHINE *in the play*
HIPPOLYTA, *Queen of the Amazons, betrothed to Theseus*

HERMIA, *daughter to Egeus, in love with Lysander*
HELENA, *in love with Demetrius*
OBERON, *King of the Fairies*
TITANIA, *Queen of the Fairies*
PUCK, *or Robin Goodfellow*
PEASEBLOSSOM }
COBWEB }
MOTH } *fairies*
MUSTARDSEED }
Other FAIRIES *attending their King and Queen*
ATTENDANTS *on Theseus and Hippolyta*

Scene: Athens, and a wood near it]

A scene from the Royal Shakespeare Theatre production of *A Midsummer Night's Dream*, directed by Peter Brook, 1970. (Photograph: David Farrell.)

469

[ACT I]

[SCENE I. *The palace of* THESEUS.]

Enter THESEUS, HIPPOLYTA, [PHILOSTRATE,] *with others.*

THESEUS.
Now, fair Hippolyta, our nuptial hour
Draws on apace. Four happy days bring in
Another moon; but, O, methinks, how slow
This old moon wanes! She lingers°1 my desires,
5   Like to a stepdame, or a dowager,
Long withering out a young man's revenue.°
HIPPOLYTA:
Four days will quickly steep themselves in night,
Four nights will quickly dream away the time;
And then the moon, like to a silver bow
10 New-bent in heaven, shall behold the night
Of our solemnities.
THESEUS: Go, Philostrate,
Stir up the Athenian youth to merriments,
Awake the pert° and nimble spirit of mirth,
Turn melancholy forth to funerals;
15 The pale companion° is not for our pomp.°
                        [*Exit* PHILOSTRATE.]
Hippolyta, I wooed thee with my sword,°
And won thy love, doing thee injuries;
But I will wed thee in another key,
With pomp, with triumph, and with reveling.

(*Enter* EGEUS *and his daughter* HERMIA, *and* LYSANDER, *and* DEMETRIUS.)

EGEUS:
20 Happy be Theseus, our renownèd Duke!
THESEUS:
Thanks, good Egeus.° What's the news with thee?

From *A Midsummer Night's Dream* by William Shakespeare, edited by Wolfgang Clemens. Copyright © 1963 Wolfgang Clemens. Copyright © 1963 by Sylvan Barnet. Reprinted by arrangement with The New American Library, Inc., New York, N.Y.
1 The degree sign (°) indicates a footnote, which is keyed to the text by line number. Text references are printed in **bold face** type; the annotation follows in roman type.
I.i. 4 **lingers** makes to linger, delays   6 **Long withering out a young man's revenue** diminishing the young man's money (because she must be supported by him)   13 **pert** lively   15 **companion** fellow (contemptuous)   15 **pomp** festive procession   16 **I wooed thee with my sword** (Theseus had captured Hippolyta when he conquered the Amazons)   21 **Egeus** (pronounced "E-gé-us")

EGEUS:
Full of vexation come I, with complaint
Against my child, my daughter Hermia.
Stand forth, Demetrius. My noble lord,
This man hath my consent to marry her.   25
Stand forth, Lysander. And, my gracious Duke
This man hath bewitched the bosom of my child.
Thou, thou, Lysander, thou hast given her rhymes,
And interchanged love tokens with my child.
Thou hast by moonlight at her window sung,   30
With feigning voice, verses of feigning love,
And stol'n the impression of her fantasy°
With bracelets of thy hair, rings, gauds, conceits,
Knacks,° trifles, nosegays, sweetmeats, messengers
Of strong prevailment in unhardened youth.   35
With cunning hast thou filched my daughter's heart,
Turned her obedience, which is due to me,
To stubborn harshness. And, my gracious Duke,
Be it so she will not here before your Grace
Consent to marry with Demetrius,   40
I beg the ancient privilege of Athens:
As she is mine, I may dispose of her,
Which shall be either to this gentleman
Or to her death, according to our law
Immediately° provided in that case.   45
THESEUS:
What say you, Hermia? Be advised, fair maid.
To you your father should be as a god,
One that composed your beauties; yea, and one
To whom you are but as a form in wax
By him imprinted and within his power   50
To leave the figure or disfigure it.
Demetrius is a worthy gentleman.
HERMIA:
So is Lysander.
THESEUS: In himself he is;
But in this kind, wanting your father's voice,° 55
The other must be held the worthier.

32 **stol'n the impression of her fantasy** fraudulently impressed your image upon her imagination   33–34 **gauds, conceits, Knacks** trinkets, cleverly devised tokens, knickknacks   45 **Immediately** expressly   54 **But in . . . father's voice** but in this particular respect, lacking your father's approval

HERMIA:
I would my father looked but with my eyes.
THESEUS:
Rather your eyes must with his judgment look.
HERMIA:
I do entreat your Grace to pardon me.
I know not by what power I am made bold,
60   Nor how it may concern my modesty,
In such a presence here to plead my thoughts;
But I beseech your Grace that I may know
The worst that may befall me in this case,
If I refuse to wed Demetrius.
THESEUS:
65   Either to die the death, or to abjure
Forever the society of men.
Therefore, fair Hermia, question your desires;
Know of° your youth, examine well your
     blood,°
Whether, if you yield not to your father's
     choice,
70   You can endure the livery of a nun,
For aye to be in shady cloister mewed,°
To live a barren sister all your life,
Chanting faint hymns to the cold fruitless
     moon.°
Thrice-blessèd they that master so their blood,
75   To undergo such maiden pilgrimage;
But earthlier happy is the rose distilled,°
Than that which, withering on the virgin
     thorn,
Grows, lives, and dies in single blessedness.
HERMIA:
So will I grow, so live, so die, my lord,
80   Ere I will yield my virgin patent° up
Unto his lordship, whose unwished yoke
My soul consents not to give sovereignty.
THESEUS:
Take time to pause; and, by the next new
     moon —
The sealing day betwixt my love and me,
85   For everlasting bond of fellowship —
Upon that day either prepare to die
For disobedience to your father's will,
Or else to wed Demetrius, as he would,
Or on Diana's altar to protest
90   For aye austerity and single life.
DEMETRIUS:
Relent, sweet Hermia: and, Lysander, yield
Thy crazèd title° to my certain right.

LYSANDER:
You have her father's love, Demetrius;
Let me have Hermia's: do you marry him.
EGEUS:
Scornful Lysander! True, he hath my love,   95
And what is mine my love shall render him.
And she is mine, and all my right of her
I do estate unto° Demetrius.
LYSANDER:
I am, my lord, as well derived as he,
As well possessed,° my love is more than his;   100
My fortunes every way as fairly ranked
(If not with vantage°) as Demetrius';
And, which is more than all these boasts can
     be,
I am beloved of beauteous Hermia.
Why should not I then prosecute my right?   105
Demetrius, I'll avouch it to his head,°
Made love to Nedar's daughter, Helena,
And won her soul; and she, sweet lady, dotes,
Devoutly dotes, dotes in idolatry,
Upon this spotted° and inconstant man.   110
THESEUS:
I must confess that I have heard so much,
And with Demetrius thought to have spoken
     thereof;
But, being overfull of self-affairs,
My mind did lose it. But, Demetrius, come;
And come, Egeus. You shall go with me;   115
I have some private schooling for you both.
For you, fair Hermia, look you arm yourself
To fit your fancies to your father's will,
Or else the law of Athens yields you up —
Which by no means we may extenuate —   120
To death, or to a vow of single life.
Come, my Hippolyta. What cheer, my love?
Demetrius and Egeus, go along.
I must employ you in some business
Against° our nuptial, and confer with you   125
Of something nearly° that concerns yourselves.
EGEUS:
With duty and desire we follow you
     (*Exeunt [all but* LYSANDER *and* HERMIA].)
LYSANDER:
How now, my love! Why is your cheek so
     pale?
How chance° the roses there do fade so fast?
HERMIA:
Belike° for want of rain, which I could well   130

---

68 **Know of** ascertain from   68 **blood** passions   71
mewed caged   73 **moon** i.e., Diana, goddess of
chastity   76 **distilled** made into perfumes   80
patent privilege   92 **crazèd title** flawed claim

98 **estate unto** settle upon   100 **As well possessed**
as rich   102 **If not with vantage** if not better   106
to his head in his teeth   110 **spotted** i.e., morally
stained   125 **Against** in preparation for   126
nearly closely   129 **How chance** how does it come
that   130 **Belike** perhaps

Beteem° them from the tempest of my eyes.
LYSANDER:
Ay me! For aught that I could ever read,
Could ever hear by tale or history,
The course of true love never did run smooth;
135 But, either it was different in blood —
HERMIA:
O cross! Too high to be enthralled to low!
LYSANDER:
Or else misgraffèd° in respect of years —
HERMIA:
O spite! Too old to be engaged to young!
LYSANDER:
Or else it stood upon the choice of friends —
HERMIA:
140 O hell! To choose love by another's eyes!
LYSANDER:
Or, if there were a sympathy in choice,
War, death, or sickness did lay siege to it,
Making it momentany° as a sound,
Swift as a shadow, short as any dream,
145 Brief as the lightning in the collied° night,
That, in a spleen,° unfolds both heaven and
     earth,
And ere a man hath power to say "Behold!"
The jaws of darkness do devour it up:
So quick bright things come to confusion.
HERMIA:
150 If then true lovers have been ever crossed,
It stands as an edict in destiny:
Then let us teach our trial patience,°
Because it is a customary cross,
As due to love as thoughts and dreams and
     sighs,
155 Wishes and tears, poor Fancy's° followers.
LYSANDER:
A good persuasion.° Therefore, hear me,
     Hermia.
I have a widow aunt, a dowager
Of great revenue, and she hath no child.
From Athens is her house remote seven
     leagues,
160 And she respects me as her only son.
There, gentle Hermia, may I marry thee,
And to that place the sharp Athenian law
Cannot pursue us. If thou lovest me, then,
Steal forth thy father's house tomorrow night;

And in the wood, a league without the town,   165
Where I did meet thee once with Helena,
To do observance to a morn of May,
There will I stay for thee.
HERMIA: My good Lysander!
I swear to thee, by Cupid's strongest bow,
By his best arrow with the golden head,°   170
By the simplicity of Venus' doves,
By that which knitteth souls and prospers
     loves,
And by that fire which burned the Carthage
     queen,°
When the false Troyan under sail was seen,
By all the vows that ever men have broke,   175
In number more than ever women spoke,
In that same place thou hast appointed me,
Tomorrow truly will I meet with thee.
LYSANDER:
Keep promise, love. Look, here comes Helena.

(*Enter* HELENA.)

HERMIA:
God speed fair Helena! Whither away?   180
HELENA:
Call you me fair? That fair again unsay.
Demetrius loves your fair.° O happy fair!
Your eyes are lodestars,° and your tongue's
     sweet air°
More tunable than lark to shepherd's ear,
When wheat is green, when hawthorn buds
     appear.   185
Sickness is catching. O, were favor° so,
Yours would I catch, fair Hermia, ere I go;
My ear should catch your voice, my eye your
     eye,
My tongue should catch your tongue's sweet
     melody.
Were the world mine, Demetrius being
     bated,°   190
The rest I'd give to be to you translated.°
O, teach me how you look, and with what art
You sway the motion of Demetrius' heart!
HERMIA:
I frown upon him, yet he loves me still.
HELENA:
O that your frowns would teach my smiles
     such skill!   195

---

131 **Beteem** bring forth 137 **misgraffèd** ill matched, misgrafted 143 **momentany** momentary, passing 145 **collied** blackened 146 **spleen** flash 152 **teach our trial patience** i.e., teach ourselves to be patient 155 **Fancy's** Love's 156 **persuasion** principle

170 **arrow with the golden head** (Cupid's gold-headed arrows caused love, the leaden ones dislike) 173 **Carthage queen** Dido (who burned herself on a funeral pyre when the Trojan Aeneas left her) 182 **fair** beauty 183 **lodestars** guiding stars 183 **air** music 186 **favor** looks 190 **bated** excepted 191 **translated** transformed

HERMIA:
I give him curses, yet he gives me love.
    HELENA:
O that my prayers could such affection move!
    HERMIA:
The more I hate, the more he follows me.
    HELENA:
The more I love, the more he hateth me.
    HERMIA:
200 His folly, Helena, is no fault of mine.
    HELENA:
None, but your beauty: would that fault were
    mine!
    HERMIA:
Take comfort. He no more shall see my face;
Lysander and myself will fly this place.
Before the time I did Lysander see,
205 Seemed Athens as a paradise to me.
O, then, what graces in my love do dwell,
That he hath turned a heaven unto a hell!
    LYSANDER:
Helen, to you our minds we will unfold.
Tomorrow night, when Phoebe° doth behold
210 Her silver visage in the wat'ry glass,
Decking with liquid pearl the bladed grass,
A time that lovers' flights doth still° conceal,
Through Athens' gates have we devised to
    steal.
    HERMIA:
And in the wood, where often you and I
215 Upon faint primrose beds were wont to lie,
Emptying our bosoms of their counsel sweet,
There my Lysander and myself shall meet,
And thence from Athens turn away our eyes,
To seek new friends and stranger companies.°
220 Farewell, sweet playfellow. Pray thou for us;
And good luck grant thee thy Demetrius!
Keep word, Lysander. We must starve our
    sight
From lovers' food till tomorrow deep mid-
    night.
    LYSANDER:
I will, my Hermia.   (Exit HERMIA.)
            Helena, adieu.
225 As you on him, Demetrius dote on you!
                    (Exit LYSANDER.)
    HELENA:
How happy some o'er other some° can be!
Through Athens I am thought as fair as she.

---

209 **Phoebe** the moon   212 **still** always   219
stranger companies the company of strangers   226
some o'er other some some in comparison with
others

But what of that? Demetrius thinks not so;
He will not know what all but he do know.
And as he errs, doting on Hermia's eyes,   230
So I, admiring of his qualities.
Things base and vile, holding no quantity,°
Love can transpose to form and dignity.
Love looks not with the eyes, but with the
    mind,
And therefore is winged Cupid painted blind.   235
Nor hath Love's mind of any judgment taste;
Wings, and no eyes, figure° unheedy haste:
And therefore is Love said to be a child,
Because in choice he is so oft beguiled.
As waggish boys in game themselves forswear,   240
So the boy Love is perjured everywhere.
For ere Demetrius looked on Hermia's eyne,°
He hailed down oaths that he was only mine;
And when this hail some heat from Hermia
    felt,
So he dissolved, and show'rs of oaths did melt.   245
I will go tell him of fair Hermia's flight.
Then to the wood will he tomorrow night
Pursue her; and for this intelligence°
If I have thanks, it is a dear expense:°
But herein mean I to enrich my pain,   250
To have his sight thither and back again.
                              (Exit.)

[SCENE II. QUINCE'S house.]

Enter QUINCE the Carpenter, and SNUG the
Joiner, and BOTTOM the Weaver, and FLUTE
the Bellows Mender, and SNOUT the Tinker,
and STARVELING the Tailor.°

QUINCE: Is all our company here?
BOTTOM: You were best to call them generally,° man by man, according to the scrip.
QUINCE: Here is the scroll of every man's
name, which is thought fit, through all Athens,   5
to play in our interlude° before the Duke and
the Duchess, on his wedding day at night.

---

232 **holding no quantity** having no proportion
(therefore unattractive)   237 **figure** symbolize
242 **eyne** eyes   248 **intelligence** piece of news
249 **dear expense** (1) expense gladly incurred (2)
heavy cost (in Demetrius' opinion)   I.ii.s.d. (the
names of the clowns suggest their trades. *Bottom*
skein on which the yarn is wound; *Quince* quines,
blocks of wood used for building; *Snug* close-fitting;
Flute suggesting fluted bellows [for church organs];
Snout spout of a kettle; *Starveling* an allusion to
the proverbial thinness of tailors)   3 **generally**
(Bottom means "individually")   6 **interlude** dramatic entertainment

BOTTOM: First, good Peter Quince, say what the play treats on; then read the names of the
10 actors; and so grow to a point.

QUINCE: Marry,° our play is, "The most lamentable comedy, and most cruel death of Pyramus and Thisby."

BOTTOM: A very good piece of work, I as-
15 sure you, and a merry. Now, good Peter Quince, call forth your actors by the scroll. Masters, spread yourselves.

QUINCE: Answer as I call you. Nick Bottom, the weaver.

20 BOTTOM: Ready. Name what part I am for, and proceed.

QUINCE: You, Nick Bottom, are set down for Pyramus.

BOTTOM: What is Pyramus? A lover, or a
25 tyrant?

QUINCE: A lover that kills himself, most gallant, for love.

BOTTOM: That will ask some tears in the true performing of it: if I do it, let the audi-
30 ence look to their eyes. I will move storms, I will condole° in some measure. To the rest: yet my chief humor° is for a tyrant. I could play Ercles° rarely, or a part to tear a cat in, to make all split.

35   The raging rocks
        And shivering shocks
        Shall break the locks
            Of prison gates;
        And Phibbus' car°
40   Shall shine from far,
        And make and mar
            The foolish Fates.

This was lofty! Now name the rest of the players. This is Ercles' vein, a tyrant's vein. A
45 lover is more condoling.

QUINCE: Francis Flute, the bellows mender.

FLUTE: Here, Peter Quince.

QUINCE: Flute, you must take Thisby on you.

50 FLUTE: What is Thisby? A wand'ring knight?

QUINCE: It is the lady that Pyramus must love.

FLUTE: Nay, faith, let not me play a woman. I have a beard coming.
55

QUINCE: That's all one.° You shall play it in a mask, and you may speak as small° as you will.

BOTTOM: An° I may hide my face, let me play Thisby too, I'll speak in a monstrous
60 little voice, "Thisne, Thisne!" "Ah Pyramus, my lover dear! Thy Thisby dear, and lady dear!"

QUINCE: No, no; you must play Pyramus: and, Flute, you Thisby.
65

BOTTOM: Well, proceed.

QUINCE: Robin Starveling, the tailor.

STARVELING: Here, Peter Quince.

QUINCE: Robin Starveling, you must play Thisby's mother. Tom Snout, the tinker.
70

SNOUT: Here, Peter Quince.

QUINCE: You, Pyramus' father: myself, Thisby's father: Snug, the joiner; you, the lion's part. And I hope here is a play fitted.

SNUG: Have you the lion's part written?
75 Pray you, if it be, give it me, for I am slow of study.

QUINCE: You may do it extempore, for it is nothing but roaring.

BOTTOM: Let me play the lion too. I will
80 roar that° I will do any man's heart good to hear me. I will roar, that I will make the Duke say, "Let him roar again, let him roar again."

QUINCE: An you should do it too terribly, you would fright the Duchess and the ladies,
85 that they would shriek; and that were enough to hang us all.

ALL: That would hang us, every mother's son.

BOTTOM: I grant you, friends, if you should
90 fright the ladies out of their wits, they would have no more discretion but to hang us: but I will aggravate° my voice so that I will roar you as gently as any sucking dove; I will roar you an 'twere° any nightingale.
95

QUINCE: You can play no part but Pyramus; for Pyramus is a sweet-faced man; a proper° man as one shall see in a summer's day; a most lovely, gentlemanlike man: therefore you must needs play Pyramus.
100

BOTTOM: Well, I will undertake it. What beard were I best to play it in?

11 Marry (an interjection, originally an oath, "By the Virgin Mary") 31 condole lament 32 humor disposition 33 Ercles Hercules (a part notorious for ranting) 39 Phibbus' car (mispronunciation for "Phoebus' car," or chariot, i.e., the sun)

56 That's all one it makes no difference 57 small softly 59 An if 81 that so that 93 aggravate (Bottom means "moderate") 95 an 'twere as if it were 97 proper handsome

QUINCE: Why, what you will.

BOTTOM: I will discharge it in either your
105 straw-color beard, your orange-tawny beard,
your purple-in-grain° beard, or your French-
crown-color° beard, your perfit° yellow.

QUINCE: Some of your French crowns° have
no hair at all, and then you will play bare-
110 faced.° But, masters, here are your parts; and
I am to entreat you, request you, and desire
you, to con° them by tomorrow night; and
meet me in the palace wood, a mile without
the town, by moonlight. There will we re-
115 hearse, for if we meet in the city, we shall be
dogged with company, and our devices°
known. In the meantime I will draw a bill of
properties,° such as our play wants. I pray you,
fail me not.

120 BOTTOM: We will meet; and there we may
rehearse most obscenely° and courageously.
Take pains; be perfit: adieu.

QUINCE: At the Duke's Oak we meet.

BOTTOM: Enough; hold or cut bowstrings.°

(*Exeunt.*)

[ACT II

SCENE I. *A wood near Athens.*]

Enter a FAIRY *at one door, and* ROBIN GOOD-
FELLOW [PUCK] *at another.*

PUCK:

How now, spirit! Whither wander you?

FAIRY:

Over hill, over dale,
    Thorough bush, thorough brier,
Over park, over pale,°
5   Thorough flood, thorough fire,
I do wander everywhere,
Swifter than the moon's sphere;°
And I serve the Fairy Queen,

To dew her orbs° upon the green.
The cowslips tall her pensioners° be: 10
In their gold coats spots you see;
Those be rubies, fairy favors,°
In those freckles live their savors.°
I must go seek some dewdrops here,
And hang a pearl in every cowslip's ear.   15
Farewell, thou lob° of spirits; I'll be gone.
Our Queen and all her elves come here anon.

PUCK:

The King doth keep his revels here tonight.
Take heed the Queen come not within his
    sight.
For Oberon is passing fell and wrath,°   20
Because that she as her attendant hath
A lovely boy, stolen from an Indian king;
She never had so sweet a changeling.°
And jealous Oberon would have the child
Knight of his train, to trace° the forests wild.   25
But she perforce withholds the lovèd boy,
Crowns him with flowers, and makes him all
    her joy.
And now they never meet in grove or green,
By fountain clear, or spangled starlight sheen,°
But they do square,° that all their elves for
    fear   30
Creep into acorn cups and hide them there.

FAIRY:

Either I mistake your shape and making quite,
Or else you are that shrewd and knavish sprite
Called Robin Goodfellow. Are not you he
That frights the maidens of the villagery,°   35
Skim milk, and sometimes labor in the quern,°
And bootless° make the breathless housewife
    churn,
And sometime make the drink to bear no
    barm,°
Mislead night wanderers, laughing at their
    harm?
Those that Hobgoblin call you, and sweet
    Puck,   40

106 **purple-in-grain** dyed with a fast purple 106–
107 **French-crown-color** color of French gold coin
107 **perfit** perfect 108 **crowns** (1) gold coins (2)
heads bald from the French disease (syphilis) 109–
110 **barefaced** (1) bald (2) brazen 112 **con**
study 116 **devices** plans 117–118 **bill of properties** list of stage furnishings 121 **obscenely** (Bottom means "seemly") 124 **hold or cut bowstrings**
i.e., keep your word or give it up (?)
II.i.4 **pale** enclosed land, park 7 **moon's sphere**
(according to the Ptolemaic system the moon was
fixed in a hollow sphere that surrounded and re-
volved about the earth)

9 **orbs** fairy rings, i.e., circles of darker grass 10
pensioners bodyguards (referring to Elizabeth I's
bodyguard of fifty splendid young noblemen) 12
favors gifts 13 **savors** perfumes 16 **lob** lubber,
clumsy fellow 20 **passing fell and wrath** very
fierce and angry 23 **changeling** (usually a child
left behind by fairies in exchange for one stolen,
but here applied to the stolen child) 25 **trace**
traverse 29 **starlight sheen** brightly shining starlight 30 **square** clash, quarrel 35 **villagery** villag-
ers 36 **quern** hand mill for grinding grain 37
bootless in vain 38 **barm** yeast, froth

You do their work, and they shall have good
   luck.
Are not you he?
    PUCK: Thou speakest aright;
I am that merry wanderer of the night.
I jest to Oberon, and make him smile,
45 When I a fat and bean-fed horse beguile,
Neighing in likeness of a filly foal:
And sometime lurk I in a gossip's° bowl,
In very likeness of a roasted crab;°
And when she drinks, against her lips I bob
50 And on her withered dewlap° pour the ale.
The wisest aunt, telling the saddest° tale,
Sometime for three-foot stool mistaketh me;
Then slip I from her bum, down topples she,
And "tailor"° cries, and falls into a cough;
And then the whole quire° hold their hips
55   and laugh,
And waxen° in their mirth, and neeze,° and
   swear
A merrier hour was never wasted° there.
But, room, fairy! Here comes Oberon.
    FAIRY:
And here my mistress. Would that he were
   gone!

(*Enter* [OBERON,] *the King of Fairies, at one
door, with his train; and* [TITANIA,] *the
Queen, at another, with hers.*)

    OBERON:
60 Ill met by moonlight, proud Titania.
    TITANIA:
What, jealous Oberon! Fairy, skip hence.
I have forsworn his bed and company.
    OBERON:
Tarry, rash wanton;° am not I thy lord?
    TITANIA:
Then I must be thy lady: but I know
65 When thou hast stolen away from fairy land
And in the shape of Corin° sat all day,
Playing on pipes of corn,° and versing love
To amorous Phillida. Why art thou here,
Come from the farthest steep of India?

But that, forsooth, the bouncing° Amazon,   70
Your buskined° mistress and your warrior love,
To Theseus must be wedded, and you come
To give their bed joy and prosperity.
    OBERON:
How canst thou thus for shame, Titania,
Glance at my credit with Hippolyta,   75
Knowing I know thy love to Theseus?
Didst not thou lead him through the glimmer-
   ing night
From Perigenia, whom he ravishèd?
And make him with fair Aegles break his faith,
With Ariadne and Antiopa?°   80
    TITANIA:
These are the forgeries of jealousy:
And never, since the middle summer's spring,°
Met we on hill, in dale, forest, or mead,
By pavèd° fountain or by rushy brook,
Or in the beachèd margent° of the sea,   85
To dance our ringlets to the whistling wind,
But with thy brawls thou hast disturbed our
   sport.
Therefore the winds, piping to us in vain,
As in revenge, have sucked up from the sea
Contagious° fogs; which, falling in the land,   90
Hath every pelting° river made so proud,
That they have overborne their continents.°
The ox hath therefore stretched his yoke in
   vain,
The plowman lost his sweat, and the green
   corn
Hath rotted ere his youth attained a beard;   95
The fold stands empty in the drownèd field,
And crows are fatted with the murrion flock;°
The nine men's morris° is filled up with mud;
And the quaint mazes° in the wanton green,°
For lack of tread, are undistinguishable.   100
The human mortals want their winter here;
No night is now with hymn or carol blest.

---

47 **gossip's** old woman's 48 **crab** crab apple 50 **dewlap** fold of skin on the throat 51 **saddest** most serious 54 **tailor** (suggesting the posture of a tailor squatting; or a term of abuse: Middle English *tail-lard*, "thief") 55 **quire** company, choir 56 **waxen** increase 56 **neeze** sneeze 57 **wasted** passed 63 **rash wanton** hasty willful creature 66 **Corin** (like *Phillida*, line 68, a traditional name for a lover in pastoral poetry) 67 **pipes of corn** musical instruments made of grain stalks

70 **bouncing** swaggering 71 **buskined** wearing a hunter's boot (buskin) 78–80 **Perigenia, Aegles, Ariadne, Antiopa** (girls Theseus loved and deserted) 82 **middle summer's spring** beginning of midsummer 84 **pavèd** i.e., with pebbly bottom 85 **margent** margin, shore 90 **contagious** generating pestilence 91 **pelting** petty 92 **continents** containers (i.e., banks) 94 **corn** grain 97 **murrion flock** flock dead of cattle disease (murrain) 98 **nine men's morris** square cut in the turf (for a game in which each player has nine counters or "men") 99 **quaint mazes** intricate meandering paths on the grass (kept fresh by running along them) 99 **wanton green** grass growing without check

Therefore the moon, the governess of floods,
Pale in her anger, washes all the air,
105 That rheumatic diseases do abound.
And thorough this distemperature° we see
The seasons alter: hoary-headed frosts
Fall in the fresh lap of the crimson rose,
And on old Hiems'° thin and icy crown
110 An odorous chaplet° of sweet summer buds
Is, as in mockery, set. The spring, the summer,
The childing° autumn, angry winter, change
Their wonted liveries;° and the mazèd° world,
By their increase, now knows not which is
    which.
115 And this same progeny of evils comes
From our debate,° from our dissension;
We are their parents and original.
    OBERON:
Do you amend it, then; it lies in you:
Why should Titania cross her Oberon?
120 I do but beg a little changeling boy,
To be my henchman.°
    TITANIA: Set your heart at rest.
The fairy land buys not° the child of me.
His mother was a vot'ress° of my order,
And, in the spicèd Indian air, by night,
125 Full often hath she gossiped by my side,
And sat with me on Neptune's yellow sands,
Marking th' embarkèd traders on the flood;
When we have laughed to see the sails
    conceive
And grow big-bellied with the wanton wind;
Which she, with pretty and with swimming
130   gait
Following — her womb then rich with my
    young squire —
Would imitate, and sail upon the land,
To fetch me trifles, and return again,
As from a voyage, rich with merchandise.
135 But she, being mortal, of that boy did die;
And for her sake do I rear up her boy,
And for her sake I will not part with him.
    OBERON:
How long within this wood intend you stay?
    TITANIA:
Perchance till after Theseus' wedding day.
140 If you will patiently dance in our round,°

And see our moonlight revels, go with us.
If not, shun me, and I will spare° your haunts.
    OBERON:
Give me that boy, and I will go with thee.
    TITANIA:
Not for thy fairy kingdom. Fairies, away!
We shall chide downright, if I longer stay.   145
        (Exeunt [TITANIA with her train].)
    OBERON:
Well, go thy way. Thou shalt not from this
    grove
Till I torment thee for this injury.
My gentle Puck, come hither. Thou remem-
    b'rest
Since° once I sat upon a promontory,
And heard a mermaid, on a dolphin's back,   150
Uttering such dulcet and harmonious breath,
That the rude sea grew civil° at her song,
And certain stars shot madly from their
    spheres,
To hear the sea maid's music.
    PUCK: I remember.
    OBERON:
That very time I saw, but thou couldst not,   155
Flying between the cold moon and the earth,
Cupid all armed. A certain aim he took
At a fair vestal° thronèd by the west,
And loosed his love shaft smartly from his
    bow,
As it should° pierce a hundred thousand
    hearts.   160
But I might° see young Cupid's fiery shaft
Quenched in the chaste beams of the wat'ry
    moon,
And the imperial vot'ress passèd on,
In maiden meditation, fancy-free.°
Yet marked I where the bolt of Cupid fell.   165
It fell upon a little western flower,
Before milk-white, now purple with love's
    wound,
And maidens call it love-in-idleness.°
Fetch me that flow'r; the herb I showed thee
    once:
The juice of it on sleeping eyelids laid   170
Will make or man or woman° madly dote

---

106 **distemperature** disturbance in nature 109 **old Hiems'** the winter's 110 **chaplet** wreath 112 **childing** breeding, fruitful 113 **wonted liveries** accustomed apparel 113 **mazèd** bewildered 116 **debate** quarrel 121 **henchman** page 122 **The fairy land buys not** i.e., even your whole domain could not buy 123 **vot'ress** woman who has taken a vow 140 **round** circular dance

142 **spare** keep away from 149 **Since** when 152 **civil** well behaved 158 **vestal** virgin (possibly an allusion to Elizabeth, the Virgin Queen) 160 **As it should** as if it would 161 **might** could 164 **fancy-free** free from the power of love 168 **love-in-idleness** pansy 171 **or man or woman** either man or woman

Upon the next live creature that it sees.
Fetch me this herb, and be thou here again
Ere the leviathan° can swim a league.
    PUCK:
175 I'll put a girdle round about the earth
In forty minutes.   [*Exit.*]
    OBERON: Having once this juice,
I'll watch Titania when she is asleep,
And drop the liquor of it in her eyes.
The next thing then she waking looks upon,
180 Be it on lion, bear, or wolf, or bull,
On meddling monkey, or on busy° ape,
She shall pursue it with the soul of love.
And ere I take this charm from off her sight,
As I can take it with another herb,
185 I'll make her render up her page to me.
But who comes here? I am invisible,
And I will overhear their conference.

    (*Enter* DEMETRIUS, HELENA *following him.*)

    DEMETRIUS:
I love thee not, therefore pursue me not.
Where is Lysander and fair Hermia?
190 The one I'll slay, the other slayeth me.
Thou told'st me they were stol'n unto this
    wood;
And here am I, and wood° within this wood,
Because I cannot meet my Hermia.
Hence, get thee gone, and follow me no more!
    HELENA:
195 You draw me, you hardhearted adamant;°
But yet you draw not iron, for my heart
Is true as steel. Leave you your power to draw,
And I shall have no power to follow you.
    DEMETRIUS:
Do I entice you? Do I speak you fair?°
200 Or, rather, do I not in plainest truth
Tell you, I do not nor I cannot love you?
    HELENA:
And even for that do I love you the more.
I am your spaniel; and, Demetrius,
The more you beat me, I will fawn on you.
Use me but as your spaniel, spurn me, strike
205   me,
Neglect me, lose me; only give me leave,
Unworthy as I am, to follow you.
What worser place can I beg in your love —
And yet a place of high respect with me —

Than to be usèd as you use your dog?   210
    DEMETRIUS:
Tempt not too much the hatred of my spirit,
For I am sick when I do look on thee.
    HELENA:
And I am sick when I look not on you.
    DEMETRIUS:
You do impeach° your modesty too much,
To leave the city, and commit yourself   215
Into the hands of one that loves you not,
To trust the opportunity of night
And the ill counsel of a desert° place
With the rich worth of your virginity.
    HELENA:
Your virtue is my privilege.° For that   220
It is not night when I do see your face,
Therefore I think I am not in the night;
Nor doth this wood lack worlds of company,
For you in my respect° are all the world.
Then how can it be said I am alone   225
When all the world is here to look on me?
    DEMETRIUS:
I'll run from thee and hide me in the brakes,°
And leave thee to the mercy of wild beasts.
    HELENA:
The wildest hath not such a heart as you.
Run when you will, the story shall be changed: 230
Apollo flies, and Daphne° holds the chase;
The dove pursues the griffin;° the mild hind°
Makes speed to catch the tiger; bootless speed,
When cowardice pursues, and valor flies.
    DEMETRIUS:
I will not stay° thy questions. Let me go!   235
Or, if thou follow me, do not believe
But I shall do thee mischief in the wood.
    HELENA:
Ay, in the temple, in the town, the field,
You do me mischief. Fie, Demetrius!
Your wrongs do set a scandal on my sex.   240
We cannot fight for love, as men may do;
We should be wooed, and were not made to
    woo.
                [*Exit* DEMETRIUS.]
I'll follow thee, and make a heaven of hell,
To die upon° the hand I love so well.   [*Exit.*]

---

174 **leviathan** sea monster, whale 181 **busy** meddlesome 192 **wood** out of my mind (with perhaps an additional pun on "wooed") 195 **adamant** (1) very hard gem (2) loadstone, magnet 199 **speak you fair** speak kindly to you

214 **impeach** expose to reproach 218 **desert** deserted, uninhabited 220 **Your virtue is my privilege** your inherent power is my warrant 224 **in my respect** in my opinion 227 **brakes** thickets 231 **Daphne** a nymph who fled from Apollo (at her prayer she was changed into a laurel tree) 232 **griffin** fabulous monster with an eagle's head and a lion's body 232 **hind** doe 235 **stay** wait for 244 **To die upon** dying by

OBERON:
Fare thee well, nymph: ere he do leave this
245   grove,
Thou shalt fly him, and he shall seek thy love.

(*Enter* PUCK.)

Hast thou the flower there? Welcome,
      wanderer.
PUCK:
Ay, there it is.
OBERON: I pray thee, give it me.
I know a bank where the wild thyme blows,
250 Where oxlips and the nodding violet grows,
Quite overcanopied with luscious woodbine,
With sweet musk roses, and with eglantine.
There sleeps Titania sometime of the night,
Lulled in these flowers with dances and delight;
And there the snake throws° her enameled
255   skin,
Weed° wide enough to wrap a fairy in.
And with the juice of this I'll streak her eyes,
And make her full of hateful fantasies.
Take thou some of it, and seek through this
      grove.
260 A sweet Athenian lady is in love
With a disdainful youth. Anoint his eyes;
But do it when the next thing he espies
May be the lady. Thou shalt know the man
By the Athenian garments he hath on.
265 Effect it with some care that he may prove
More fond on her° than she upon her love:
And look thou meet me ere the first cock crow.
PUCK:
Fear not, my lord, your servant shall do so.
                                        (*Exeunt.*)

[SCENE II. *Another part of the wood.*]

Enter TITANIA, *Queen of Fairies, with her
train.*

TITANIA:
Come, now a roundel° and a fairy song;
Then, for the third part of a minute, hence;
Some to kill cankers in the musk-rose buds,
Some war with reremice° for their leathern
      wings
5 To make my small elves coats, and some keep
      back

The clamorous owl, that nightly hoots and
      wonders
At our quaint° spirits. Sing me now asleep.
Then to your offices, and let me rest.

(FAIRIES *sing.*)

1ST FAIRY:
You spotted snakes with double tongue,
      Thorny hedgehogs, be not seen;   10
Newts and blindworms,° do no wrong,
      Come not near our Fairy Queen.

CHORUS:
      Philomele,° with melody
      Sing in our sweet lullaby;
Lulla, lulla, lullaby, lulla, lulla, lullaby: 15
      Never harm
      Nor spell nor charm,
      Come our lovely lady nigh;
So, good night, with lullaby.

1ST FAIRY:
Weaving spiders, come not here;   20
      Hence, you long-legged spinners, hence!
Beetles black, approach not near;
      Worm nor snail, do no offense.

CHORUS:
      Philomele, with melody, &c.

2ND FAIRY:
Hence, away! Now all is well.   25
One aloof stand sentinel.
            [*Exeunt* FAIRIES. TITANIA *sleeps.*]

(*Enter* OBERON [*and squeezes the flower on*
TITANIA's *eyelids*].)

OBERON:
What thou seest when thou dost wake,
Do it for thy truelove take;
Love and languish for his sake.
Be it ounce,° or cat, or bear,   30
Pard,° or boar with bristled hair,
In thy eye that shall appear
When thou wak'st, it is thy dear.
Wake when some vile thing is near.   [*Exit.*]

(*Enter* LYSANDER *and* HERMIA.)
LYSANDER:
Fair love, you faint with wand'ring in the
      wood;   35
And to speak troth,° I have forgot our way.

255 **throws** casts off   256 **Weed** garment   266
fond on her foolishly in love with her
II.ii.1 **roundel** dance in a ring   4 **reremice** bats

7 **quaint** dainty   11 **blindworms** small snakes   13
Philomele nightingale   30 **ounce** lynx   31 **Pard**
leopard   36 **troth** truth

We'll rest us, Hermia, if you think it good,
And tarry for the comfort of the day.
HERMIA:
Be't so, Lysander. Find you out a bed;
40 For I upon this bank will rest my head.
LYSANDER:
One turf shall serve as pillow for us both,
One heart, one bed, two bosoms, and one
    troth.
HERMIA:
Nay, good Lysander. For my sake, my dear,
Lie further off yet, do not lie so near.
LYSANDER:
45 O, take the sense,° sweet, of my innocence!
Love takes the meaning° in love's conference.
I mean, that my heart unto yours is knit,
So that but one heart we can make of it:
Two bosoms interchainèd with an oath;
50 So then two bosoms and a single troth.°
Then by your side no bed-room me deny,
For lying so, Hermia, I do not lie.°
HERMIA:
Lysander riddles very prettily.
Now much beshrew° my manners and my
    pride,
55 If Hermia meant to say Lysander lied.
But, gentle friend, for love and courtesy
Lie further off, in human modesty.
Such separation as may well be said
Becomes a virtuous bachelor and a maid,
So far be distant; and, good night, sweet
60   friend.
Thy love ne'er alter till thy sweet life end!
LYSANDER:
Amen, amen, to that fair prayer, say I,
And then end life when I end loyalty!
Here is my bed. Sleep give thee all his rest!
HERMIA:
With half that wish the wisher's eyes be
65   pressed!   [They sleep.]

(Enter PUCK.)

PUCK:
  Through the forest have I gone,
  But Athenian found I none,
  On whose eyes I might approve°
  This flower's force in stirring love.

Night and silence. — Who is here?   70
Weeds° of Athens he doth wear:
This is he, my master said,
Despisèd the Athenian maid;
And here the maiden, sleeping sound,
On the dank and dirty ground.   75
Pretty soul! She durst not lie
Near this lack-love, this kill-courtesy.
Churl,° upon thy eyes I throw
All the power this charm doth owe.°
When thou wak'st, let love forbid   80
Sleep his seat on thy eyelid.
So awake when I am gone,
  For I must now to Oberon.   (Exit.)

(Enter DEMETRIUS and HELENA, running.)

HELENA:
Stay, though thou kill me, sweet Demetrius.
DEMETRIUS:
I charge thee, hence, and do not haunt me
    thus.   85
HELENA:
O, wilt thou darkling° leave me? Do not so.
DEMETRIUS:
Stay, on thy peril! I alone will go.   [Exit.]
HELENA:
O, I am out of breath in this fond° chase!
The more my prayer, the lesser is my grace.
Happy is Hermia, wheresoe'er she lies,   90
For she hath blessèd and attractive eyes.
How came her eyes so bright? Not with salt
    tears.
If so, my eyes are oft'ner washed than hers.
No, no, I am as ugly as a bear,
For beasts that meet me run away for fear. 95
Therefore no marvel though Demetrius
Do, as a monster, fly my presence thus.
What wicked and dissembling glass of mine
Made me compare with Hermia's sphery
    eyne?°
But who is here? Lysander! On the ground! 100
Dead? Or asleep? I see no blood, no wound.
Lysander, if you live, good sir, awake.
  LYSANDER [awaking]:
And run through fire I will for thy sweet sake.
Transparent° Helena! Nature shows art,
That through thy bosom makes me see thy
    heart.   105
Where is Demetrius? O, how fit a word

45 take the sense understand the true meaning   46
Love takes the meaning lovers understand the true
meaning of what they say to each other   50 troth
faithful love   52 lie be untrue   54 beshrew curse
(but commonly, as here, in a light sense)   68
approve try

71 Weeds garments   78 Churl boorish fellow   79
owe possess   86 darkling in the dark   88 fond
(1) doting (2) foolish   99 sphery eyne starry eyes
104 Transparent bright

Is that vile name to perish on my sword!
HELENA:
Do not say so, Lysander, say not so.
What though he love your Hermia? Lord,
    what though?
110 Yet Hermia still loves you. Then be content.
    LYSANDER:
Content with Hermia! No; I do repent
The tedious minutes I with her have spent.
Not Hermia but Helena I love:
Who will not change a raven for a dove?
115 The will° of man is by his reason swayed
And reason says you are the worthier maid.
Things growing are not ripe until their season:
So I, being young, till now ripe not° to reason.
And touching now the point of human skill,°
120 Reason becomes the marshal to my will,
And leads me to your eyes, where I o'erlook
Love's stories, written in love's richest book.
    HELENA:
Wherefore was I to this keen mockery born?
When at your hands did I deserve this scorn?
125 Is't not enough, is't not enough, young man,
That I did never, no, nor never can,
Deserve a sweet look from Demetrius' eye,
But you must flout° my insufficiency?
Good troth,° you do me wrong, good sooth,
    you do,
130 In such disdainful manner me to woo.
But fare you well. Perforce I must confess
I thought you lord of more true gentleness.°
O, that a lady, of one man refused,
Should of another therefore be abused!
                        (Exit.)
    LYSANDER:
135 She sees not Hermia. Hermia, sleep thou there,
And never mayst thou come Lysander near!
For as a surfeit of the sweetest things
The deepest loathing to the stomach brings,
Or as the heresies that men do leave
140 Are hated most of those they did deceive,
So thou, my surfeit and my heresy,
Of all be hated, but the most of me!
And, all my powers, address° your love and
    might
To honor Helen and to be her knight!
                        (Exit.)

HERMIA [awaking]:
Help me, Lysander, help me! Do thy best   145
To pluck this crawling serpent from my breast!
Ay me, for pity! What a dream was here!
Lysander, look how I do quake with fear.
Methought a serpent eat° my heart away,
And you sat smiling at his cruel prey.°   150
Lysander! What, removed? Lysander! Lord!
What, out of hearing? Gone? No sound, no
    word?
Alack, where are you? Speak, an if° you hear;
Speak, of° all loves! I swoon almost with fear.
No? Then I well perceive you are not nigh.   155
Either death or you I'll find immediately.
                        (Exit.)

[ACT III

SCENE I. *The wood.* TITANIA *lying asleep.*]

Enter the clowns: [QUINCE, SNUG, BOTTOM,
FLUTE, SNOUT, *and* STARVELING].

BOTTOM: Are we all met?
QUINCE: Pat,° pat; and here's a marvail's°
convenient place for our rehearsal. This green
plot shall be our stage, this hawthorn brake°
our tiring house,° and we will do it in action   5
as we will do it before the Duke.
BOTTOM: Peter Quince?
QUINCE: What sayest thou, bully° Bottom?
BOTTOM: There are things in this comedy of
Pyramus and Thisby that will never please.   10
First, Pyramus must draw a sword to kill himself; which the ladies cannot abide. How
answer you that?
SNOUT: By'r lakin,° a parlous° fear.
STARVELING: I believe we must leave the   15
killing out, when all is done.
BOTTOM: Not a whit. I have a device to
make all well. Write me a prologue, and let
the prologue seem to say, we will do no
harm with our swords, and that Pyramus is   20
not killed indeed; and, for the more better
assurance, tell them that I Pyramus am not
Pyramus, but Bottom the weaver. This will
put them out of fear.

---

115 **will** desire 118 **ripe not** have not ripened
119 **touching now . . . human skill** now reaching
the fulness of human reason 128 **flout** jeer at
129 **Good troth** indeed (an expletive, like "good
sooth") 132 **gentleness** noble character 143
address apply

149 **eat** ate (pronounced "et") 150 **prey** act of
preying 153 **an if** if 154 **of** for the sake of
III.i.2 **Pat** exactly, on the dot 2 **marvail's** (Quince
means "marvelous") 4 **brake** thicket 5 **tiring
house** attiring house, dressing room 8 **bully** good
fellow 14 **By'r lakin** by our lady (ladykin = little
lady) 14 **parlous** perilous, terrible

25 QUINCE: Well, we will have such a prologue, and it shall be written in eight and six.°

BOTTOM: No, make it two more; let it be written in eight and eight.

SNOUT: Will not the ladies be afeared of the
30 lion?

STARVELING: I fear it, I promise you.

BOTTOM: Masters, you ought to consider with yourselves. To bring in — God shield us! — a lion among ladies, is a most dreadful thing.
35 For there is not a more fearful wild fowl than your lion living; and we ought to look to't.

SNOUT: Therefore another prologue must tell he is not a lion.

BOTTOM: Nay, you must name his name,
40 and half his face must be seen through the lion's neck, and he himself must speak through, saying thus, or to the same defect — "Ladies" — or, "Fair ladies — I would wish you" — or, "I would request you" — or, "I would en-
45 treat you — not to fear, not to tremble: my life for yours. If you think I come hither as a lion, it were pity of my life.° No, I am no such thing. I am a man as other men are." And there indeed let him name his name, and tell
50 them plainly, he is Snug the joiner.

QUINCE: Well, it shall be so. But there is two hard things; that is, to bring the moonlight into a chamber; for, you know, Pyramus and Thisby meet by moonlight.
55 SNOUT: Doth the moon shine that night we play our play?

BOTTOM: A calendar, a calendar! Look in the almanac; find out moonshine, find out moonshine.
60 QUINCE: Yes, it doth shine that night.

BOTTOM: Why, then may you leave a casement of the great chamber window, where we play, open, and the moon may shine in at the casement.
65 QUINCE: Ay; or else one must come in with a bush of thorns° and a lantern, and say he comes to disfigure,° or to present, the person of Moonshine. Then, there is another thing: we must have a wall in the great chamber; for
70 Pyramus and Thisby, says the story, did talk through the chink of a wall.

SNOUT: You can never bring in a wall. What say you, Bottom?

BOTTOM: Some man or other must present Wall: and let him have some plaster, or some
75 loam, or some roughcast° about him, to signify Wall; and let him hold his fingers thus, and through that cranny shall Pyramus and Thisby whisper.

QUINCE: If that may be, then all is well.
80 Come, sit down, every mother's son, and rehearse your parts. Pyramus, you begin. When you have spoken your speech, enter into that brake; and so everyone according to his cue.

(Enter Robin [PUCK].)

PUCK:
What hempen homespuns° have we swag-
85 g'ring here,
So near the cradle of the Fairy Queen?
What, a play toward!° I'll be an auditor;
An actor too perhaps, if I see cause.

QUINCE: Speak, Pyramus. Thisby, stand forth.
90 PYRAMUS [BOTTOM]:
Thisby, the flowers of odious savors sweet —

QUINCE: Odors, odors.

PYRAMUS:
— odors savors sweet:
So hath thy breath, my dearest Thisby dear.
But hark, a voice! Stay thou but here awhile,
95 And by and by° I will to thee appear.

(Exit.)

PUCK:
A stranger Pyramus than e'er played here!

[*Exit.*]

THISBY [FLUTE]: Must I speak now?

QUINCE: Ay, marry, must you. For you must understand he goes but to see a noise that he
100 heard, and is to come again.

THISBY:
Most radiant Pyramus, most lily-white of hue,
   Of color like the red rose on triumphant brier,
Most brisky juvenal,° and eke° most lovely Jew,
   As true as truest horse, that yet would never tire,
105 I'll meet thee, Pyramus, at Ninny's° tomb.

---

26 **in eight and six** in alternate lines of eight and six syllables (ballad stanza) 47 **pity of my life** a bad thing for me 66 **bush of thorns** (legend held that the man in the moon had been placed there for gathering firewood on Sunday) 67 **disfigure** (Bottom means "figure," "represent")

76 **roughcast** lime mixed with gravel to plaster outside walls 85 **hempen homespuns** coarse fellows (clad in homespun cloth of hemp) 87 **toward in** preparation 96 **by and by** shortly 104 **juvenal** youth 104 **eke** also 106 **Ninny's** (blunder for "Ninus'"; Ninus was the legendary founder of Nineveh)

QUINCE: "Ninus' tomb," man. Why, you must not speak that yet. That you answer to Pyramus. You speak all your part at once, cues and all. Pyramus enter. Your cue is past; it is "never tire."

THISBY:
O — as true as truest horse, that yet would never tire.

[Re-enter PUCK, and BOTTOM with an ass's head.]

PYRAMUS:
If I were fair, Thisby, I were only thine.

QUINCE: O monstrous! O strange! We are haunted. Pray, masters! Fly, masters! Help!

[Exeunt all the clowns but BOTTOM.]

PUCK:
I'll follow you, I'll lead you about a round,°
    Through bog, through bush, through brake, through brier.
Sometime a horse I'll be, sometime a hound,
    A hog, a headless bear, sometime a fire;
And neigh, and bark, and grunt, and roar, and burn,
Like horse, hound, hog, bear, fire, at every turn.   (Exit.)

BOTTOM: Why do they run away? This is a knavery of them to make me afeard.

(Enter SNOUT.)

SNOUT: O Bottom, thou art changed! What do I see on thee?

BOTTOM: What do you see? You see an ass head of your own, do you?   [Exit SNOUT.]

(Enter QUINCE.)

QUINCE: Bless thee, Bottom! Bless thee! Thou art translated.°   (Exit.)

BOTTOM: I see their knavery. This is to make an ass of me; to fright me, if they could. But I will not stir from this place, do what they can. I will walk up and down here, and will sing, that they shall hear I am not afraid.   [Sings.]
    The woosel° cock so black of hue,
        With orange-tawny bill,
    The throstle with his note so true,
        The wren with little quill° —

TITANIA [awaking]:
What angel wakes me from my flow'ry bed?

BOTTOM [sings]:
    The finch, the sparrow, and the lark,   140
        The plain-song cuckoo° gray,
    Whose note full many a man doth mark,
        And dares not answer nay —
for, indeed, who would set his wit° to so foolish a bird? Who would give a bird the lie,°   145
though he cry "cuckoo" never so?°

TITANIA:
I pray thee, gentle mortal, sing again:
Mine ear is much enamored of thy note;
So is mine eye enthrallèd to thy shape;
And thy fair virtue's force perforce doth move me   150
On the first view to say, to swear, I love thee.

BOTTOM: Methinks, mistress, you should have little reason for that. And yet, to say the truth, reason and love keep little company together nowadays; the more the pity, that   155
some honest neighbors will not make them friends. Nay, I can gleek° upon occasion.

TITANIA:
Thou art as wise as thou art beautiful.

BOTTOM: Not so, neither; but if I had wit enough to get out of this wood, I have enough   160
to serve mine own turn.

TITANIA:
Out of this wood do not desire to go.
Thou shalt remain here, whether thou wilt or no.
I am a spirit of no common rate.°
The summer still doth tend° upon my state;   165
And I do love thee. Therefore, go with me.
I'll give thee fairies to attend on thee,
And they shall fetch thee jewels from the deep,
And sing, while thou on pressèd flowers dost sleep:
And I will purge thy mortal grossness so,   170
That thou shalt like an airy spirit go.
Peaseblossom! Cobweb! Moth!° And Mustardseed!

(Enter four Fairies [PEASEBLOSSOM, COBWEB, MOTH, and MUSTARDSEED].)

116 about a round roundabout   129 translated transformed   135 woosel ouzel, blackbird   138 quill (literally, "reed pipe"; here, "piping voice")

141 the plain-song cuckoo the cuckoo, who sings a simple song   144 set his wit use his intelligence to answer   145 give a bird the lie contradict a bird (the cuckoo's song supposedly tells a man he is a cuckold)   146 never so ever so often   157 gleek make a satirical jest   164 rate rank   165 still doth tend always waits upon   172 Moth (pronounced "mote," and probably a speck rather than an insect is denoted)

PEASEBLOSSOM:
Ready.
COBWEB:
   And I.
MOTH: And I.
MUSTARDSEED: And I.
ALL: Where shall we go.
TITANIA:
Be kind and courteous to this gentleman;
175 Hop in his walks, and gambol in his eyes;
Feed him with apricocks and dewberries,°
With purple grapes, green figs, and mulberries;
The honey bags steal from the humblebees,°
And for night tapers crop their waxen thighs,
180 And light them at the fiery glowworm's eyes,
To have my love to bed and to arise;
And pluck the wings from painted butterflies,
To fan the moonbeams from his sleeping eyes.
Nod to him, elves, and do him courtesies.
PEASEBLOSSOM:
Hail, mortal!
COBWEB: Hail!
MOTH: Hail!
185 MUSTARDSEED: Hail!
BOTTOM: I cry your worships mercy,°
heartily: I beseech your worship's name.
COBWEB:
Cobweb.
BOTTOM: I shall desire you of more acquain-
190 tance,° good Master Cobweb: if I cut my
finger,° I shall make bold with you. Your
name, honest gentleman?
PEASEBLOSSOM:
Peaseblossom.
BOTTOM: I pray you, commend me to
195 Mistress Squash,° your mother, and to Master
Peascod, your father. Good Master Pease-
blossom. I shall desire you of more acquaintance too. Your name, I beseech you, sir?
MUSTARDSEED:
Mustardseed.
200 BOTTOM: Good Master Mustardseed, I know
your patience well. That same cowardly, giant-
like ox-beef hath devoured° many a gentleman
of your house. I promise you your kindred hath

176 **apricocks and dewberries** apricots and black-
berries 178 **humblebees** bumblebees 186 **l cry
your worships mercy** I beg pardon of your honors
189–190 **I shall desire you of more acquaintance**
I shall want to be better acquainted with you
190–191 **if I cut my finger** (cobweb was used for
stanching blood) 195 **Squash** unripe pea pod
202 **devoured** (because beef is often eaten with
mustard)

made my eyes water ere now. I desire you of
more acquaintance, good Master Mustardseed. 205
TITANIA:
Come, wait upon him; lead him to my bower.
The moon methinks looks with a wat'ry eye;
And when she weeps, weeps every little flower,
Lamenting some enforcèd° chastity.
Tie up my lover's tongue, bring him silently. 210
  (*Exit* [TITANIA *with* BOTTOM *and* FAIRIES].)

[SCENE II. *Another part of the wood.*]

Enter [OBERON,] *King of Fairies, and Robin
Goodfellow* [PUCK].

OBERON:
I wonder if Titania be awaked;
Then, what it was that next came in her eye,
Which she must dote on in extremity.°
Here comes my messenger. How now, mad
   spirit!
What night-rule° now about this haunted
   grove? 5
PUCK:
My mistress with a monster is in love.
Near to her close° and consecrated bower,
While she was in her dull and sleeping hour,
A crew of patches,° rude mechanicals,°
That work for bread upon Athenian stalls, 10
Were met together to rehearse a play,
Intended for great Theseus' nuptial day.
The shallowest thickskin of that barren sort,°
Who Pyramus presented in their sport,
Forsook his scene, and entered in a brake. 15
When I did him at this advantage take,
An ass's nole° I fixèd on his head.
Anon° his Thisby must be answerèd,
And forth my mimic comes. When they him
   spy,
As wild geese that the creeping fowler eye, 20
Or russet-pated choughs, many in sort,°
Rising and cawing at the gun's report,
Sever themselves and madly sweep the sky,
So, at his sight, away his fellows fly;
And, at our stamp, here o'er and o'er one falls; 25
He murder cries, and help from Athens calls.

209 **enforcèd** violated
III.ii.3 **in extremity** to the extreme 5 **night-rule**
happenings during the night 7 **close** private,
secret 9 **patches** fools, clowns 9 **rude mechanicals** uneducated workingmen 13 **barren sort** stupid
group 17 **nole** "noodle," head 18 **Anon** presently
21 **russet-pated . . . in sort** gray-headed jackdaws,
many in a flock

Their sense thus weak, lost with their fears
    thus strong,
Made senseless things begin to do them wrong;
For briers and thorns at their apparel snatch;
Some sleeves, some hats, from yielders all
30   things catch.
I led them on in this distracted fear,
And left sweet Pyramus translated there:
When in that moment, so it came to pass,
Titania waked, and straightway loved an ass.
    OBERON:
35 This falls out better than I could devise.
But hast thou yet latched° the Athenian's eyes
With the love juice, as I did bid thee do?
    PUCK:
I took him sleeping — that is finished too —
And the Athenian woman by his side;
That, when he waked, of force° she must be
40   eyed.

(*Enter* DEMETRIUS *and* HERMIA.)

    OBERON:
Stand close:° this is the same Athenian.
    PUCK:
This is the woman, but not this the man.
    DEMETRIUS:
O, why rebuke you him that loves you so?
Lay breath so bitter on your bitter foe.
    HERMIA:
45 Now I but chide; but I should use thee worse,
For thou, I fear, hast given me cause to curse.
If thou hast slain Lysander in his sleep,
Being o'er shoes in blood, plunge in the deep,
And kill me too.
50 The sun was not so true unto the day
As he to me. Would he have stolen away
From sleeping Hermia? I'll believe as soon
This whole° earth may be bored, and that the
    moon
May through the center creep, and so displease
55 Her brother's° noontide with th' Antipodes.
It cannot be but thou hast murd'red him.
So should a murderer look, so dead,° so grim.
    DEMETRIUS:
So should the murdered look; and so should I,
Pierced through the heart with your stern
    cruelty.
60 Yet you, the murderer, look as bright, as clear,

As yonder Venus in her glimmering sphere.
    HERMIA:
What's this to my Lysander? Where is he?
Ah, good Demetrius, wilt thou give him me?
    DEMETRIUS:
I had rather give his carcass to my hounds.
    HERMIA:
Out, dog! Out, cur! Thou driv'st me past the
    bounds   65
Of maiden's patience. Hast thou slain him,
    then?
Henceforth be never numb'red among men!
O, once tell true! Tell true, even for my sake!
Durst thou have looked upon him being
    awake?
And hast thou killed him sleeping? O brave
    touch!°   70
Could not a worm, an adder, do so much?
An adder did it; for with doubler tongue
Than thine, thou serpent, never adder stung.
    DEMETRIUS:
You spend your passion on a misprised mood:°
I am not guilty of Lysander's blood;   75
Nor is he dead, for aught that I can tell.
    HERMIA:
I pray thee, tell me then that he is well.
    DEMETRIUS:
An if I could, what should I get therefore?°
    HERMIA:
A privilege, never to see me more.
And from thy hated presence part I so.   80
See me no more, whether he be dead or no.
        (*Exit.*)
    DEMETRIUS:
There is no following her in this fierce vein.
Here therefore for a while I will remain.
So sorrow's heaviness doth heavier grow
For debt that bankrout sleep doth sorrow
    owe;°   85
Which now in some slight measure it will pay,
If for his tender° here I make some stay.

        (*Lie down [and sleep].*)

    OBERON:
What hast thou done? Thou hast mistaken
    quite,
And laid the love juice on some truelove's
    sight.
Of thy misprision° must perforce ensue   90

---

36 **latched** fastened (or possibly "moistened") 40
of force by necessity 41 **close** concealed 53
whole solid 55 **Her brother's** i.e., the sun's 57
dead deadly pale   70 **brave touch** splendid exploit (ironic) 74 **misprised mood** mistaken anger 78 **therefore** in return 85 **For debt . . . sorrow owe** because of the debt that bankrupt sleep owes to sorrow 87 **tender** offer 90 **misprision** mistake

Some true love turned, and not a false turned
    true.
PUCK:
Then fate o'errules, that, one man holding
    troth,
A million fail, confounding oath on oath.°
OBERON:
About the wood go swifter than the wind,
95 And Helena of Athens look thou find.
All fancy-sick° she is and pale of cheer,°
With sighs of love, that costs the fresh blood
    dear:
By some illusion see thou bring her here.
I'll charm his eyes against she do appear.°
PUCK:
100 I go, I go; look how I go,
Swifter than arrow from the Tartar's bow.
                                    [Exit.]
OBERON:
        Flower of this purple dye,
        Hit with Cupid's archery,
        Sink in apple of his eye.
105   When his love he doth espy,
        Let her shine as gloriously
        As the Venus of the sky.
        When thou wak'st, if she be by,
        Beg of her for remedy.

(Enter PUCK.)

PUCK:
110   Captain of our fairy band,
        Helena is here at hand;
        And the youth, mistook by me,
        Pleading for a lover's fee.
        Shall we their fond pageant° see?
115   Lord, what fools these mortals be!
OBERON:
        Stand aside. The noise they make
        Will cause Demetrius to awake.
PUCK:
        Then will two at once woo one;
        That must needs be sport alone;°
120   And those things do best please me
        That befall prepost'rously.

(Enter LYSANDER and HELENA.)

LYSANDER:

Why should you think that I should woo in
    scorn?
Scorn and derision never come in tears:
Look, when I vow, I weep; and vows so born,
    In their nativity all truth appears.   125
How can these things in me seem scorn to you,
Bearing the badge of faith,° to prove them
    true?
HELENA:
You do advance° your cunning more and
    more.
When truth kills truth, O devilish-holy fray!
These vows are Hermia's: will you give her
    o'er?   130
    Weigh oath with oath, and you will nothing
    weigh.
Your vows to her and me, put in two scales,
Will even weigh; and both as light as tales.
LYSANDER:
I had no judgment when to her I swore.
HELENA:
Nor none, in my mind, now you give her o'er.   135
LYSANDER:
Demetrius loves her, and he loves not you.
DEMETRIUS [awaking]:
O Helen, goddess, nymph, perfect, divine!
To what, my love, shall I compare thine eyne?
Crystal is muddy. O, how ripe in show°
Thy lips, those kissing cherries, tempting grow! 140
That pure congealèd white, high Taurus'°
    snow,
Fanned with the eastern wind, turns to a crow
When thou hold'st up thy hand: O, let me
    kiss
This princess of pure white, this seal of bliss!
HELENA:
O spite! O hell! I see you all are bent   145
To set against me for your merriment:
If you were civil° and knew courtesy,
You would not do me thus much injury.
Can you not hate me, as I know you do,
But you must join in souls to mock me too?   150
If you were men, as men you are in show,
You would not use a gentle° lady so;
To vow, and swear, and superpraise my parts,°
When I am sure you hate me with your hearts.
You both are rivals, and love Hermia;   155

---

93 **confounding oath on oath** breaking oath after
oath 96 **fancy-sick** love-sick 96 **cheer** face 99
against she do appear in preparation for her appearance 114 **fond pageant** foolish exhibition 119
alone unique, supreme

127 **badge of faith** (Lysander means his tears)
128 **advance** exhibit, display 139 **show** appearance
141 **Taurus'** of the Taurus Mountains (in Turkey)
147 **civil** civilized 152 **gentle** well-born 153 **parts**
qualities

And now both rivals to mock Helena:
A trim° exploit, a manly enterprise,
To conjure tears up in a poor maid's eyes
With your derision! None of noble sort
160 Would so offend a virgin, and extort°
A poor soul's patience, all to make you sport.
　　LYSANDER:
You are unkind, Demetrius. Be not so;
For you love Hermia; this you know I know.
And here, with all good will, with all my heart,
165 In Hermia's love I yield you up my part;
And yours of Helena to me bequeath,
Whom I do love, and will do till my death.
　　HELENA:
Never did mockers waste more idle° breath.
　　DEMETRIUS:
Lysander, keep thy Hermia; I will none.
170 If e'er I loved her, all that love is gone.
My heart to her but as guestwise sojourned,
And now to Helen is it home returned,
There to remain.
　　LYSANDER:　　Helen, it is not so.
　　DEMETRIUS:
Disparage not the faith thou dost not know,
175 Lest, to thy peril, thou aby it dear.°
Look, where thy love comes; yonder is thy
　　dear.

(*Enter* HERMIA.)

　　HERMIA:
Dark night, that from the eye his° function
　　takes,
The ear more quick of apprehension makes;
Wherein it doth impair the seeing sense,
180 It pays the hearing double recompense.
Thou art not by mine eye, Lysander, found;
Mine ear, I thank it, brought me to thy sound.
But why unkindly didst thou leave me so?
　　LYSANDER:
Why should he stay, whom love doth press to
　　go?
　　HERMIA:
185 What love could press Lysander from my side?
　　LYSANDER:
Lysander's love, that would not let him bide,
Fair Helena, who more engilds the night
Than all yon fiery oes° and eyes of light.
Why seek'st thou me? Could not this make
　　thee know,

The hate I bare thee made me leave thee so?　190
　　HERMIA:
You speak not as you think: it cannot be.
　　HELENA:
Lo, she is one of this confederacy!
Now I perceive they have conjoined all three
To fashion this false sport, in spite of me.
Injurious° Hermia! Most ungrateful maid!　195
Have you conspired, have you with these con-
　　trived
To bait° me with this foul derision?
Is all the counsel that we two have shared,
The sister's vows, the hours that we have
　　spent,
When we have chid the hasty-footed time　200
For parting us — O, is all forgot?
All school days friendship, childhood inno-
　　cence?
We, Hermia, like two artificial° gods,
Have with our needles created both one flower,
Both on one sampler,° sitting on one cushion,　205
Both warbling of one song, both in one key;
As if our hands, our sides, voices, and minds,
Had been incorporate.° So we grew together,
Like to a double cherry, seeming parted,
But yet an union in partition;　　　　　　210
Two lovely berries molded on one stem;
So, with two seeming bodies, but one heart;
Two of the first, like coats in heraldry,
Due but to one, and crownèd with one crest.°
And will you rent° our ancient love asunder,　215
To join with men in scorning your poor
　　friend?
It is not friendly, 'tis not maidenly.
Our sex, as well as I, may chide you for it,
Though I alone do feel the injury.
　　HERMIA:
I am amazèd at your passionate words.　　220
I scorn you not. It seems that you scorn me.
　　HELENA:
Have you not set Lysander, as in scorn,
To follow me and praise my eyes and face?
And made your other love, Demetrius
(Who even but now did spurn me with his
　　foot),　　　　　　　　　　　　　　225

157 **trim** splendid (ironical)　160 **extort** wear out
by torturing　168 **idle** vain, futile　175 **aby it dear**
pay dearly for it　177 **his** its (the eye's)　188 **oes**
orbs

195 **Injurious** insulting　196–197 **contrived To bait**
plotted to assail　203 **artificial** skilled in art　205
sampler work of embroidery　208 **incorporate** one
body　213–214 **Two of . . . one crest** (Helena
apparently envisages a shield on which the coat of
arms appears twice but which has a single crest;
Helena and Hermia have two bodies but a single
heart)　215 **rent** rend, tear

To call me goddess, nymph, divine and rare,
Precious, celestial? Wherefore speaks he this
To her he hates? And wherefore doth Lysander
Deny your love,° so rich within his soul,
230 And tender me (forsooth) affection,
But by your setting on, by your consent?
What though I be not so in grace° as you,
So hung upon with love, so fortunate,
But miserable most, to love unloved?
235 This you should pity rather than despise.

HERMIA:
I understand not what you mean by this.

HELENA:
Ay, do! Persever,° counterfeit sad° looks,
Make mouths° upon me when I turn my back;
Wink each at other; hold the sweet jest up.
240 This sport, well carried, shall be chronicled.
If you have any pity, grace, or manners,
You would not make me such an argument.°
But fare ye well. 'Tis partly my own fault,
Which death or absence soon shall remedy.

LYSANDER:
245 Stay, gentle Helena; hear my excuse:
My love, my life, my soul, fair Helena!

HELENA:
O excellent!

HERMIA:
Sweet, do not scorn her so.

DEMETRIUS:
If she cannot entreat,° I can compel.

LYSANDER:
Thou canst compel no more than she entreat.
Thy threats have no more strength than her
250 weak prayers.
Helen, I love thee; by my life, I do!
I swear by that which I will lose for thee,
To prove him false that says I love thee not.

DEMETRIUS:
I say I love thee more than he can do.

LYSANDER:
255 If thou say so, withdraw and prove it too.

DEMETRIUS:
Quick, come!

HERMIA: Lysander, whereto tends all this?

LYSANDER:
Away, you Ethiope!°

DEMETRIUS: No, no; he'll

Seem to break loose; take on as° you would
follow,
But yet come not: you are a tame man, go!

LYSANDER:
Hang off, thou cat, thou burr! Vile thing, let
loose,   260
Or I will shake thee from me like a serpent!

HERMIA:
Why are you grown so rude! What change is
this,
Sweet love?

LYSANDER:
          Thy love! Out, tawny Tartar, out!
Out, loathèd med'cine! O hated potion, hence!

HERMIA:
Do you not jest?

HELENA: Yes, sooth;° and so do you.   265

LYSANDER:
Demetrius, I will keep my word° with thee.

DEMETRIUS:
I would I had your bond, for I perceive
A weak bond holds you. I'll not trust your
word.

LYSANDER:
What, should I hurt her, strike her, kill her
dead?
Although I hate her, I'll not harm her so.   270

HERMIA:
What, can you do me greater harm than hate?
Hate me! Wherefore? O me! What news, my
love!
Am not I Hermia? Are not you Lysander?
I am as fair now as I was erewhile.°
Since night° you loved me; yet since night you
left me.   275
Why, then you left me — O, the gods forbid! —
In earnest, shall I say?

LYSANDER: Ay, by my life!
And never did desire to see thee more.
Therefore be out of hope, of question, of
doubt;
Be certain, nothing truer. 'Tis no jest   280
That I do hate thee, and love Helena.

HERMIA:
O me! You juggler! You canker blossom!°
You thief of love! What, have you come by
night

229 your love his love for you   232 in grace in favor   237 persever persevere (but accented on second syllable)   237 sad grave   238 Make mouths make mocking faces   242 argument subject (of scorn)   248 entreat prevail by entreating   257 Ethiope blackamoor (brunette)

258 take on as make a fuss as if   265 sooth truly   266 my word my promise to fight with you   274 erewhile a little while ago   275 Since night since the beginning of this night   282 canker blossom dog rose (or possibly worm that cankers the blossom)

And stol'n my love's heart from him?

HELENA: Fine, i' faith!

285 Have you no modesty, no maiden shame,
No touch of bashfulness? What, will you tear
Impatient answers from my gentle tongue?
Fie, fie! You counterfeit, you puppet, you!

HERMIA:

Puppet? Why so? Ay, that way goes the game.
290 Now I perceive that she hath made compare°
Between our statures; she hath urged her
    height,
And with her personage, her tall personage,
Her height, forsooth, she hath prevailed with
    him.
And are you grown so high in his esteem,
295 Because I am so dwarfish and so low?
How low am I, thou painted maypole? Speak!
How low am I? I am not yet so low
But that my nails can reach unto thine eyes.

HELENA:

I pray you, though you mock me, gentlemen,
300 Let her not hurt me, I was never curst;°
I have no gift at all in shrewishness;
I am a right maid° for my cowardice.
Let her not strike me. You perhaps may think,
Because she is something lower than myself,
That I can match her.

305 HERMIA: Lower! Hark, again!

HELENA:

Good Hermia, do not be so bitter with me.
I evermore did love you, Hermia,
Did ever keep your counsels, never wronged
    you;
Save that, in love unto Demetrius,
310 I told him of your stealth unto this wood.
He followed you; for love I followed him.
But he hath chid me hence, and threatened
    me
To strike me, spurn me, nay, to kill me too.
And now, so you will let me quiet go,
315 To Athens will I bear my folly back,
And follow you no further. Let me go.
You see how simple and how fond° I am.

HERMIA:

Why, get you gone. Who is't that hinders
    you?

HELENA:

A foolish heart, that I leave here behind.

HERMIA:

What, with Lysander?

HELENA: With Demetrius.   320

LYSANDER:

Be not afraid. She shall not harm thee,
    Helena.

DEMETRIUS:

No, sir, she shall not, though you take her
    part.

HELENA:

O, when she's angry, she is keen and shrewd!°
She was a vixen when she went to school;
And though she be but little, she is fierce.   325

HERMIA:

"Little" again! Nothing but "low" and
    "little"!
Why will you suffer her to flout me thus?
Let me come to her.

LYSANDER: Get you gone, you dwarf;
You minimus,° of hind'ring knotgrass° made;
You bead, you acorn!

DEMETRIUS: You are too officious   330
In her behalf that scorns your services.
Let her alone. Speak not of Helena;
Take not her part; for, if thou dost intend°
Never so little show of love to her,
Thou shalt aby° it.

LYSANDER: Now she holds me not.   335
Now follow, if thou dar'st, to try whose right,
Of thine or mine, is most in Helena.

DEMETRIUS:

Follow! Nay, I'll go with thee, cheek by jowl.
        [*Exeunt* LYSANDER *and* DEMETRIUS.]

HERMIA:

You, mistress, all this coil is 'long of you:°
Nay, go not back.

HELENA: I will not trust you, I,   340
Nor longer stay in your curst company.
Your hands than mine are quicker for a fray,
My legs are longer though, to run away.

HERMIA:

I am amazed,° and know not what to say.
        Exeunt [HELENA *and* HERMIA].

OBERON:

This is thy negligence. Still thou mistak'st,   345
Or else committ'st thy knaveries willfully.

PUCK:

Believe me, king of shadows, I mistook.
Did not you tell me I should know the man

290 **compare** comparison 300 **curst** quarrelsome
302 **right maid** true young woman 317 **fond** foolish

323 **keen and shrewd** sharp-tongued and shrewish
329 **minimus** smallest thing 329 **knotgrass** (a
weed that allegedly stunted one's growth) 333
intend give sign, direct (or possibly "pretend")
335 **aby** pay for 339 **all this coil is 'long of you**
all this turmoil is brought about by you 344
amazed in confusion

By the Athenian garments he had on?
350 And so far blameless proves my enterprise,
That I have 'nointed an Athenian's eyes;
And so far am I glad it so did sort,°
As this their jangling I esteem a sport.
    OBERON:
Thou see'st these lovers seek a place to fight.
355 Hie therefore, Robin, overcast the night.
The starry welkin° cover thou anon
With drooping fog, as black as Acheron;°
And lead these testy° rivals so astray,
As° one come not within another's way.
360 Like to Lysander sometime frame thy tongue,
Then stir Demetrius up with bitter wrong;°
And sometime rail thou like Demetrius.
And from each other look thou lead them
    thus,
Till o'er their brows death-counterfeiting sleep
365 With leaden legs and batty° wings doth creep.
Then crush this herb into Lysander's eye,
Whose liquor hath this virtuous° property,
To take from thence all error with his might,
And make his eyeballs roll with wonted sight.
370 When they next wake, all this derision°
Shall seem a dream and fruitless vision,
And back to Athens shall the lovers wend,
With league whose date° till death shall never
    end.
Whiles I in this affair do thee employ,
375 I'll to my queen and beg her Indian boy;
And then I will her charmèd eye release
From monster's view, and all things shall be
    peace.
    PUCK:
My fairy lord, this must be done with haste,
For night's swift dragons cut the clouds full
    fast,
380 And yonder shines Aurora's harbinger;°
At whose approach, ghosts, wand'ring here and
    there,
Troop home to churchyards: damnèd spirits
    all,
That in crossways and floods have burial,
Already to their wormy beds are gone.
For fear lest day should look their shames
385   upon,

They willfully themselves exile from light,
And must for aye consort with black-browed
    night.
    OBERON:
But we are spirits of another sort.
I with the Morning's love° have oft made
    sport;
And, like a forester, the groves may tread, 390
Even till the eastern gate, all fiery-red,
Opening on Neptune with fair blessèd beams,
Turns into yellow gold his salt green streams.
But, notwithstanding, haste; make no delay.
We may effect this business yet ere day. 395
                [Exit.]
    PUCK:
    Up and down, up and down,
    I will lead them up and down:
    I am feared in field and town:
    Goblin,° lead them up and down.
    Here comes one. 400

(Enter LYSANDER.)

    LYSANDER:
Where art thou, proud Demetrius? Speak thou
    now.
    PUCK:
Here, villain; drawn° and ready. Where art
    thou?
    LYSANDER:
I will be with thee straight.
    PUCK: Follow me, then,
To plainer° ground.
              [Exit LYSANDER.]

(Enter DEMETRIUS.)

    DEMETRIUS: Lysander! Speak again!
Thou runaway, thou coward, art thou fled? 405
Speak! In some bush? Where dost thou hide
    thy head?
    PUCK:
Thou coward, art thou bragging to the stars,
Telling the bushes that thou look'st for wars,
And wilt not come? Come, recreant! Come,
    thou child!
I'll whip thee with a rod. He is defiled 410
That draws a sword on thee.
    DEMETRIUS: Yea, art thou there?

---

352 **sort** turn out   356 **welkin** sky   357 **Acheron** one of the rivers of the underworld   358 **testy** excited, angry   359 **As** that   361 **wrong** insult   365 **batty** bat-like   367 **virtuous** potent   370 **derision** i.e., ludicrous delusion   373 **With league whose date** in union whose term   380 **Aurora's harbinger** dawn's herald (i.e., the morning star)

389 **the Morning's love** Aurora (or possibly her lover Cephalus)   399 **Goblin** Hobgoblin (one of Puck's names)   402 **drawn** with drawn sword   404 **plainer** more level

PUCK:
Follow my voice. We'll try no manhood° here.
(*Exeunt.*)

[*Enter* LYSANDER.]

LYSANDER:
He goes before me and still dares me on:
When I come where he calls, then he is gone.
415 The villain is much lighter-heeled than I.
I followed fast, but faster he did fly,
That fallen am I in dark uneven way,
And here will rest me. [*Lies down.*] Come,
    thou gentle day!
For if but once thou show me thy gray light,
420 I'll find Demetrius, and revenge this spite.
[*Sleeps.*]

([*Enter*] *Robin* [PUCK] *and* DEMETRIUS.)

PUCK:
Ho, ho, ho! Coward, why com'st thou not?
DEMETRIUS:
Abide me,° if thou dar'st; for well I wot°
Thou runn'st before me, shifting every place,
And dar'st not stand, nor look me in the face.
Where art thou now?
425 PUCK: Come hither. I am here.
DEMETRIUS:
Nay, then, thou mock'st me. Thou shalt buy
    this dear,°
If ever I thy face by daylight see.
Now, go thy way. Faintness constraineth me
To measure out my length on this cold bed.
430 By day's approach look to be visited.°
[*Lies down and sleeps.*]

(*Enter* HELENA.)

HELENA:
O weary night, O long and tedious night,
Abate° thy hours! Shine comforts from the
    east,
That I may back to Athens by daylight,
From these that my poor company detest:
And sleep, that sometimes shuts up sorrow's
435   eye,
Steal me awhile from mine own company.
(*Sleep.*)
PUCK:
    Yet but three? Come one more.

Two of both kinds makes up four.
  Here she comes, curst° and sad:
  Cupid is a knavish lad,   440
  Thus to make poor females mad.

[*Enter* HERMIA.]

HERMIA:
Never so weary, never so in woe;
  Bedabbled with the dew and torn with
    briers,
I can no further crawl, no further go;
  My legs can keep no pace with my desires.   445
Here will I rest me till the break of day.
Heavens shield Lysander, if they mean a fray!
[*Lies down and sleeps.*]
PUCK:
  On the ground
  Sleep sound:
  I'll apply   450
  To your eye,
Gentle lover, remedy.

[*Squeezing the juice on* LYSANDER's *eye.*]

  When thou wak'st,
  Thou tak'st
  True delight   455
  In the sight
Of thy former lady's eye:
And the country proverb known,
That every man should take his own,
In your waking shall be shown.   460
  Jack shall have Jill;
  Nought shall go ill;
The man shall have his mare again, and all
  shall be well.
[*Exit.*]

[ACT IV

SCENE I. *The wood.* LYSANDER, DEMETRIUS,
HELENA, *and* HERMIA, *lying asleep.*]

Enter [TITANIA,] *Queen of Fairies, and* [BOT-
TOM *the*] *Clown, and* FAIRIES; *and* [OBERON,]
the King, behind them.

TITANIA:
Come, sit thee down upon this flow'ry bed,
  While I thy amiable cheeks do coy,°

---

412 **try no manhood** have no test of valor   422
Abide me wait for me   422 **wot** know   426 **buy
this dear** pay dearly for this   430 **look to be visited**
be sure to be sought out   432 **Abate** make shorter

439 **curst** cross
IV.i.2 **While I . . . do coy** while I caress your
lovely cheeks

And stick musk roses in thy sleek smooth head,
And kiss thy fair large ears, my gentle joy.

5 BOTTOM: Where's Peaseblossom?

PEASEBLOSSOM:
Ready.

BOTTOM: Scratch my head, Peaseblossom.
Where's Mounsieur Cobweb?

COBWEB:
Ready.

10 BOTTOM: Mounsieur Cobweb, good mounsieur, get you your weapons in your hand, and
kill me a red-hipped humblebee on the top of
a thistle; and, good mounsieur, bring me the
honey bag. Do not fret yourself too much in
15 the action, mounsieur; and, good mounsieur,
have a care the honey bag break not; I would
be loath to have you overflown with a honey
bag, signior. Where's Mounsieur Mustardseed?

MUSTARDSEED:
Ready.

20 BOTTOM: Give me your neaf,° Mounsieur
Mustardseed. Pray you, leave your curtsy,°
good mounsieur.

MUSTARDSEED:
What's your will?

BOTTOM: Nothing, good mounsieur, but to
25 help Cavalery° Cobweb to scratch. I must to
the barber's, mounsieur; for methinks I am
marvail's° hairy about the face; and I am such
a tender ass, if my hair do but tickle me, I
must scratch.

TITANIA:
What, wilt thou hear some music, my sweet
30 love?

BOTTOM: I have a reasonable good ear in
music. Let's have the tongs and the bones.°

TITANIA:
Or say, sweet love, what thou desirest to eat.

BOTTOM: Truly, a peck of provender. I
35 could munch your good dry oats. Methinks I
have a great desire to a bottle° of hay. Good
hay, sweet hay, hath no fellow.°

TITANIA:
I have a venturous fairy that shall seek
The squirrel's hoard, and fetch thee new nuts.

40 BOTTOM: I had rather have a handful or two

of dried peas. But, I pray you, let none of your
people stir me: I have an exposition of° sleep
come upon me.

TITANIA:
Sleep thou, and I will wind thee in my arms.
Fairies, be gone, and be all ways° away. 45
        [Exeunt FAIRIES.]
So doth the woodbine the sweet honeysuckle
Gently entwist; the female ivy° so
Enrings the barky fingers of the elm.
O, how I love thee! How I dote on thee!
        [They sleep.]

(Enter Robin Goodfellow [PUCK].)

OBERON [advancing]:
Welcome, Good Robin. See'st thou this sweet
   sight? 50
Her dotage now I do begin to pity:
For, meeting her of late behind the wood,
Seeking sweet favors° for this hateful fool,
I did upbraid her, and fall out with her.
For she his hairy temples then had rounded 55
With coronet of fresh and fragrant flowers;
And that same dew, which sometime° on the
   buds
Was wont° to swell, like round and orient°
   pearls,
Stood now within the pretty flouriets'° eyes,
Like tears, that did their own disgrace bewail. 60
When I had at my pleasure taunted her,
And she in mild terms begged my patience,
I then did ask of her her changeling child;
Which straight she gave me, and her fairy sent
To bear him to my bower in fairy land. 65
And now I have the boy, I will undo
This hateful imperfection of her eyes:
And, gentle Puck, take this transformèd scalp
From off the head of this Athenian swain,
That, he awaking when the other° do, 70
May all to Athens back again repair,
And think no more of this night's accidents,°
But as the fierce vexation of a dream.
But first I will release the Fairy Queen.
    Be as thou wast wont to be; 75
    See as thou wast wont to see.
    Dian's bud o'er Cupid's flower
    Hath such force and blessèd power.

20 **neaf** fist, hand 21 **leave your curtsy** i.e., stop
bowing, leave your hat on (a curtsy was any gesture
of respect) 25 **Cavalery** i.e., Cavalier 27 **marvail's** (Bottom means "marvelous") 32 **the tongs
and the bones** rustic music, made by tongs struck
with metal and by bone clappers held between the
fingers 36 **bottle** bundle 37 **fellow** equal

42 **exposition of** (Bottom means "disposition for")
45 **all ways** in every direction 47 **female ivy**
(called female because it clings to the elm and is
supported by it) 53 **favors** love tokens (probably
flowers) 57 **sometime** formerly 58 **Was wont**
used to 58 **orient** lustrous 59 **flouriets'** flowerets'
70 **other** others 72 **accidents** happenings

Now, my Titania, wake you, my sweet Queen:

TITANIA:

80 My Oberon, what visions have I seen!
Methought I was enamored of an ass.

OBERON:

There lies your love.

TITANIA: How came these things to pass?
O, how mine eyes do loathe his visage now!

OBERON:

Silence awhile. Robin, take off this head.
85 Titania, music call; and strike more dead
Than common sleep of all these five the sense.

TITANIA:

Music, ho, music! Such as charmeth sleep!

PUCK:

Now, when thou wak'st, with thine own fool's
    eyes peep.

OBERON:

Sound, music! [*Music.*] Come, my Queen, take
    hands with me,
And rock the ground whereon these sleepers
90   be. [*Dance.*]
Now thou and I are new in amity,
And will tomorrow midnight solemnly°
Dance in Duke Theseus' house triumphantly,°
And bless it to all fair prosperity.
95 There shall the pairs of faithful lovers be
Wedded, with Theseus, all in jollity.

PUCK:

Fairy King, attend, and mark:
I do hear the morning lark.

ODERON:

Then, my Queen, in silence sad,°
100 Trip we after night's shade.
We the globe can compass soon,
Swifter than the wand'ring moon.

TITANIA:

Come, my lord; and in our flight,
Tell me how it came this night,
105 That I sleeping here was found
With these mortals on the ground.
                 (*Exeunt.*)

(*Wind horn. Enter* THESEUS, *and all his
train;* [HIPPOLYTA, EGEUS].)

THESEUS:

Go, one of you, find out the forester,
For now our observation° is performed;
And since we have the vaward° of the day,

My love shall hear the music of my hounds. 110
Uncouple in the western valley; let them go.
Dispatch, I say, and find the forester.
            [*Exit an* ATTENDANT.]
We will, fair Queen, up to the mountain's top,
And mark the musical confusion
Of hounds and echo in conjunction. 115

HIPPOLYTA:

I was with Hercules and Cadmus once,
When in a wood of Crete they bayed° the
    bear
With hounds of Sparta. Never did I hear
Such gallant chiding; for, besides the groves,
The skies, the fountains, every region near 120
Seemed all one mutual cry. I never heard
So musical a discord, such sweet thunder.

THESEUS:

My hounds are bred out of the Spartan kind,
So flewed, so sanded;° and their heads are
    hung
With ears that sweep away the morning dew; 125
Crook-kneed, and dew-lapped like Thessalian
    bulls;
Slow in pursuit, but matched in mouth like
    bells,
Each under each.° A cry° more tunable
Was never holloed to, nor cheered with horn,
In Crete, in Sparta, nor in Thessaly. 130
Judge when you hear. But, soft!° What
    nymphs are these?

EGEUS:

My lord, this is my daughter here asleep;
And this, Lysander; this Demetrius is;
This Helena, old Nedar's Helena:
I wonder of their being here together. 135

THESEUS:

No doubt they rose up early to observe
The rite of May; and, hearing our intent,
Came here in grace of our solemnity.°
But speak, Egeus. Is not this the day
That Hermia should give answer of her choice? 140

EGEUS:

It is, my lord.

THESEUS:

Go, bid the huntsmen wake them with their
    horns.

92 **solemnly** ceremoniously 93 **triumphantly** in festive procession 99 **sad** serious, solemn 108 **observation** observance, i.e., of the rite of May (cf. I.i.167) 109 **vaward** vanguard, i.e., morning

117 **bayed** brought to bay 124 **So flewed, so sanded** i.e., like Spartan hounds, with hanging cheeks and of sandy color 128 **Each under each** of different tone (like the chime of bells) 128 **cry** pack of hounds 131 **soft** stop 138 **in grace of our solemnity** in honor of our festival

(Shout within. They all start up. Wind horns.)

Good morrow, friends. Saint Valentine is past:
Begin these wood birds but to couple now?°
LYSANDER:
Pardon, my lord.
145   THESEUS: I pray you all, stand up.
I know you two are rival enemies.
How comes this gentle concord in the world,
That hatred is so far from jealousy,°
To sleep by hate, and fear no enmity?
LYSANDER:
150 My lord, I shall reply amazedly,°
Half sleep, half waking: but as yet, I swear,
I cannot truly say how I came here.
But, as I think — for truly would I speak,
And now I do bethink me, so it is —
155 I came with Hermia hither. Our intent
Was to be gone from Athens, where we might,
Without° the peril of the Athenian law —
EGEUS:
Enough, enough, my lord; you have enough.
I beg the law, the law, upon his head.
They would have stol'n away; they would,
160   Demetrius,
Thereby to have defeated° you and me,
You of your wife and me of my consent,
Of my consent that she should be your wife.
DEMETRIUS:
My lord, fair Helen told me of their stealth,°
165 Of this their purpose hither to this wood,
And I in fury hither followed them,
Fair Helena in fancy° following me.
But, my good lord, I wot not by what power —
But by some power it is — my love to Hermia,
170 Melted as the snow, seems to me now
As the remembrance of an idle gaud,°
Which in my childhood I did dote upon;
And all the faith, the virtue° of my heart,
The object and the pleasure of mine eye,
175 Is only Helena. To her, my lord,
Was I betrothed ere I saw Hermia:
But, like a sickness,° did I loathe this food;
But, as in health, come to my natural taste,
Now I do wish it, love it, long for it,

And will for evermore be true to it.   180
THESEUS:
Fair lovers, you are fortunately met.
Of this discourse we more will hear anon.
Egeus, I will overbear your will,
For in the temple, by and by,° with us
These couples shall eternally be knit;   185
And, for the morning now is something worn,°
Our purposed hunting shall be set aside.
Away with us to Athens! Three and three,
We'll hold a feast in great solemnity.
Come, Hippolyta.   190
      [Exeunt THESEUS, HIPPOLYTA, EGEUS, *and train.]*
DEMETRIUS:
These things seem small and undistinguishable,
Like far-off mountains turnèd into clouds.
HERMIA:
Methinks I see these things with parted eye,°
When everything seems double.
HELENA: So methinks:
And I have found Demetrius like a jewel,   195
Mine own, and not mine own.
DEMETRIUS: Are you sure
That we are awake? It seems to me
That yet we sleep, we dream. Do not you think
The Duke was here, and bid us follow him?
HERMIA:
Yea, and my father.
HELENA: And Hippolyta.   200
LYSANDER:
And he did bid us follow to the temple.
DEMETRIUS:
Why, then, we are awake. Let's follow him,
And by the way let us recount our dreams.
      [Exeunt.]
BOTTOM *[awaking]*: When my cue comes,
call me, and I will answer. My next is, "Most   205
fair Pyramus." Heigh-ho! Peter Quince? Flute,
the bellows mender? Snout, the tinker? Starveling? God's my life,° stol'n hence, and left me
asleep? I have had a most rare vision. I have
had a dream, past the wit of man to say what   210
dream it was. Man is but an ass, if he go
about° to expound this dream. Methought I
was — there is no man can tell what. Methought I was — and methought I had — but
man is but a patched° fool if he will offer to   215

144 **Begin these . . . couple now** (it was supposed
that birds began to mate on February 14, St. Valentine's Day)   148 **jealousy** suspicion   150 **amazedly**
confusedly   157 **Without** outside of   161 **defeated**
deprived by fraud   164 **stealth** stealthy flight   167
in fancy in love, doting   171 **idle gaud** worthless
trinket   173 **virtue** power   177 **like a sickness** like
one who is sick

184 **by and by** shortly   186 **something worn** somewhat spent   193 **with parted eye** i.e., with the
eyes out of focus   208 **God's my life** an oath (possibly from "God bless my life")   211–212 **go
about** endeavor   215 **patched** (referring to the
patchwork dress of jesters)

say what methought I had. The eye of man hath not heard, the ear of man hath not seen, man's hand is not able to taste, his tongue to conceive, nor his heart to report, what my 220 dream was. I will get Peter Quince to write a ballet° of this dream. It shall be called "Bottom's Dream," because it hath no bottom; and I will sing it in the latter end of a play, before the Duke. Peradventure to make it the 225 more gracious, I shall sing it at her death.°

[*Exit.*]

[SCENE II. *Athens.* QUINCE's *house.*]

Enter QUINCE, FLUTE,° *Thisby and the rabble* [SNOUT, STARVELING].

QUINCE: Have you sent to Bottom's house? Is he come home yet?

STARVELING: He cannot be heard of. Out of doubt he is transported.°

5 FLUTE: If he come not, then the play is marred. It goes not forward, doth it?

QUINCE: It is not possible. You have not a man in all Athens able to discharge° Pyramus but he.

10 FLUTE: No, he hath simply the best wit of any handicraft man in Athens.

QUINCE: Yea, and the best person too; and he is a very paramour for a sweet voice.

FLUTE: You must say "paragon." A para-15 mour is, God bless us, a thing of nought.°

(*Enter* SNUG *the Joiner.*)

SNUG: Masters, the Duke is coming from the temple, and there is two or three lords and ladies more married. If our sport had gone forward, we had all been made men.°

20 FLUTE: O sweet bully Bottom! Thus hath he lost sixpence a day° during his life. He could not have scaped sixpence a day. An the Duke had not given him sixpence a day for playing Pyramus, I'll be hanged. He would 25 have deserved it. Sixpence a day in Pyramus, or nothing.

(*Enter* BOTTOM.)

BOTTOM: Where are these lads? Where are these hearts?

QUINCE: Bottom! O most courageous° day! O most happy hour! 30

BOTTOM: Masters, I am to discourse wonders: but ask me not what; for if I tell you, I am not true Athenian. I will tell you everything, right as it fell out.

QUINCE: Let us hear, sweet Bottom. 35

BOTTOM: Not a word of me.° All that I will tell you is, that the Duke hath dined. Get your apparel together, good strings to your beards, new ribbons to your pumps; meet presently° at the palace; every man look o'er his part; for 40 the short and the long is, our play is preferred.° In any case, let Thisby have clean linen; and let not him that plays the lion pare his nails, for they shall hang out for the lion's claws. And, most dear actors, eat no onions nor 45 garlic, for we are to utter sweet breath,° and I do not doubt but to hear them say it is a sweet comedy. No more words. Away! Go, away!

[*Exeunt.*]

[ACT V

SCENE I. *Athens. The palace of* THESEUS.]

Enter THESEUS, HIPPOLYTA, *and* PHILO-STRATE, [LORDS, *and* ATTENDANTS].

HIPPOLYTA:
'Tis strange, my Theseus, that these lovers speak of.

THESEUS:
More strange than true. I never may believe
These antique° fables, nor these fairy toys.°
Lovers and madmen have such seething brains,
Such shaping fantasies,° that apprehend 5
More than cool reason ever comprehends.
The lunatic, the lover and the poet
Are of imagination all compact.°
One sees more devils than vast hell can hold,
That is the madman. The lover, all as frantic, 10
Sees Helen's beauty in a brow of Egypt.°

221 **ballet** ballad 225 **her death** i.e., Thisby's death in the play
IV.ii.s.d. **Flute** (Shakespeare seems to have forgotten that Flute and Thisby are the same person) 4 **transported** carried off (by the fairies) 8 **discharge** play 15 **a thing of nought** a wicked thing 19 **made men** men whose fortunes are made 21 **sixpence a day** (a pension)

29 **courageous** brave, splendid 36 **of me** from me 39 **presently** immediately 41–42 **preferred** put forward, recommended 46 **breath** (1) exhalation (2) words
V.i.3 **antique** (1) ancient (2) grotesque (antic) 3 **fairy toys** trifles about fairies 5 **fantasies** imagination 8 **compact** composed 11 **brow of Egypt** face of a gypsy

The poet's eye, in a fine frenzy rolling,
Doth glance from heaven to earth, from earth
    to heaven;
And as imagination bodies forth
15 The forms of things unknown, the poet's pen
Turns them to shapes, and gives to airy
    nothing
A local habitation and a name.
Such tricks hath strong imagination,
That, if it would but apprehend some joy,
20 It comprehends some bringer of that joy;°
Or in the night, imagining some fear,°
How easy is a bush supposed a bear!

HIPPOLYTA:
But all the story of the night told over,
And all their minds transfigured so together,
25 More witnesseth than fancy's images,
And grows to something of great constancy;°
But, howsoever, strange and admirable.°

(*Enter Lovers:* LYSANDER, DEMETRIUS,
HERMIA *and* HELENA.)

THESEUS:
Here come the lovers, full of joy and mirth.
Joy, gentle friends! Joy and fresh days of love
Accompany your hearts!
30 LYSANDER: More than to us
Wait in your royal walks, your board, your bed!
THESEUS:
Come now, what masques,° what dances
    shall we have,
To wear away this long age of three hours
Between our aftersupper° and bedtime?
35 Where is our usual manager of mirth?
What revels are in hand? Is there no play,
To ease the anguish of a torturing hour?
Call Philostrate.
PHILOSTRATE: Here, mighty Theseus.
THESEUS:
Say, what abridgment° have you for this
    evening?
What masque? What music? How shall we
40   beguile
The lazy time, if not with some delight?

PHILOSTRATE:
There is a brief° how many sports are ripe:°
Make choice of which your Highness will see
    first. [*Giving a paper.*]
THESEUS:
"The battle with the Centaurs, to be sung
By an Athenian eunuch to the harp."   45
We'll none of that. That have I told my love,
In glory of my kinsman Hercules.
"The riot of the tipsy Bacchanals,
Tearing the Thracian singer° in their rage."
That is an old device;° and it was played   50
When I from Thebes came last a conqueror.
"The thrice three Muses mourning for the
    death
Of Learning, late deceased in beggary."
That is some satire, keen and critical,
Not sorting with° a nuptial ceremony.   55
"A tedious brief scene of young Pyramus
And his love Thisby; very tragical mirth."
Merry and tragical? Tedious and brief?
That is, hot ice and wondrous strange snow.
How shall we find the concord of this discord?   60
PHILOSTRATE:
A play there is, my lord, some ten words long,
Which is as brief as I have known a play;
But by ten words, my lord, it is too long,
Which makes it tedious. For in all the play
There is not one word apt, one player fitted.   65
And tragical, my noble lord, it is,
For Pyramus therein doth kill himself.
Which, when I saw rehearsed, I must confess,
Made mine eyes water; but more merry tears
The passion° of loud laughter never shed.   70
THESEUS:
What are they that do play it?
PHILOSTRATE:
Hard-handed men, that work in Athens here,
Which never labored in their minds till now;
And now have toiled their unbreathed°
    memories
With this same play, against° your nuptial.   75
THESEUS:
And we will hear it.
PHILOSTRATE: No, my noble lord;
It is not for you. I have heard it over,
And it is nothing, nothing in the world;
Unless you can find sport in their intents,

---

20 **It comprehends . . . that joy** it includes an
imagined bringer of the joy   21 **fear** object of fear
26 **constancy** consistency (and reality)   27 **admirable** wonderful   32 **masques** courtly entertainments
with masked dancers   34 **aftersupper** refreshment
served after early supper   39 **abridgment** entertainment (to abridge or shorten the time)

42 **brief** written list   42 **ripe** ready to be presented
49 **Thracian singer** Orpheus   50 **device** show   55
sorting with suited to   70 **passion** strong emotion
74 **unbreathed** unexercised   75 **against** in preparation for

80 Extremely stretched and conned with cruel
     pain,
To do you service.
     THESEUS: I will hear that play;
For never anything can be amiss,
When simpleness and duty tender it.
Go, bring them in: and take your places,
     ladies.   [*Exit* PHILOSTRATE.]
     HIPPOLYTA:
85 I love not to see wretchedness o'ercharged,°
And duty in his service perishing.
     THESEUS:
Why, gentle sweet, you shall see no such
     thing.
     HIPPOLYTA:
He says they can do nothing in this kind.°
     THESEUS:
The kinder we, to give them thanks for
     nothing.
90 Our sport shall be to take what they mistake:
And what poor duty cannot do, noble respect
Takes it in might,° not merit.
Where I have come, great clerks° have
     purposèd
To greet me with premeditated welcomes;
95 Where I have seen them shiver and look pale,
Make periods in the midst of sentences,
Throttle their practiced accent in their fears,
And, in conclusion, dumbly have broke off,
Not paying me a welcome. Trust me, sweet,
100 Out of this silence yet I picked a welcome;
And in the modesty of fearful duty
I read as much as from the rattling tongue
Of saucy and audacious eloquence.
Love, therefore, and tongue-tied simplicity
105 In least speak most, to my capacity.°

     [*Enter* PHILOSTRATE.]

     PHILOSTRATE:
·So please your Grace, the Prologue is ad-
     dressed.°
     THESEUS:
Let him approach.   [*Flourish trumpets.*]

     (*Enter the* PROLOGUE [QUINCE].)

     PROLOGUE:
If we offend, it is with our good will.

That you should think, we come not to
     offend,
But with good will. To show our simple skill,   110
     That is the true beginning of our end.°
Consider, then, we come but in despite.
     We do not come, as minding to content
     you,
Our true intent is. All for your delight,
     We are not here. That you should here
     repent you,   115
The actors are at hand; and, by their show,°
You shall know all, that you are like to know.
     THESEUS: This fellow doth not stand upon
points.°
     LYSANDER: He hath rid his prologue like a   120
rough colt; he knows not the stop.° A good
moral, my lord: it is not enough to speak, but
to speak true.
     HIPPOLYTA: Indeed he hath played on this
prologue like a child on a recorder;° a sound,   125
but not in government.°
     THESEUS: His speech was like a tangled
chain; nothing impaired, but all disordered.
Who is next?

     (*Enter* PYRAMUS *and* THISBY *and* WALL *and*
MOONSHINE *and* LION [*as in dumbshow*].)

     PROLOGUE:
Gentles, perchance you wonder at this show;   130
     But wonder on, till truth make all things
     plain.
This man is Pyramus, if you would know;
     This beauteous lady Thisby is certain.
This man, with lime and roughcast, doth
     present
Wall, that vile Wall which did these lovers
     sunder;   135
And through Wall's chink, poor souls, they are
     content
     To whisper. At the which let no man
     wonder.
This man, with lantern, dog, and bush of
     thorn,
     Presenteth Moonshine; for, if you will know,

---

85 **wretchedness o'ercharged** lowly people overbur-
dened   88 **in this kind** in this kind of thing (i.e.,
acting)   92 **Takes it in might** considers the ability
and the effort made   93 **clerks** scholars   105 **to my
capacity** according to my understanding   106 **addressed** ready

111 **end** aim   116 **show** (probably referring to a
kind of pantomime — "dumb show" — that was to
follow, in which the action of the play was acted
without words while the Prologue gave his account)
119 **stand upon points** (1) care about punctuation
(2) worry about niceties   121 **stop** (1) technical
term for the checking of a horse (2) mark of punctuation   125 **recorder** flutelike instrument   126
government control

140 By moonshine did these lovers think no scorn
　　To meet at Ninus' tomb, there, there to woo.
This grisly beast, which Lion hight° by name,
The trusty Thisby, coming first by night,
Did scare away, or rather did affright;
145 And, as she fled, her mantle she did fall,°
　　Which Lion vile with bloody mouth did
　　　stain.
Anon comes Pyramus, sweet youth and tall,°
　　And finds his trusty Thisby's mantle slain:
Whereat, with blade, with bloody blameful
　　blade,
　　He bravely broached° his boiling bloody
150 　breast;
And Thisby, tarrying in mulberry shade,
　　His dagger drew, and died. For all the rest,
Let Lion, Moonshine, Wall, and lovers twain
　　At large° discourse, while here they do
　　remain.
155 THESEUS: I wonder if the lion be to speak.
DEMETRIUS: No wonder, my lord. One lion
may, when many asses do.
　　　　(Exit LION, THISBY and MOONSHINE.)
　　WALL:
In this same interlude it doth befall
That I, one Snout by name, present a wall;
160 And such a wall, as I would have you think,
That had in it a crannied hole or chink,
Through which the lovers, Pyramus and
　　Thisby,
Did whisper often very secretly.
This loam, this roughcast, and this stone, doth
　　show
165 That I am that same wall; the truth is so;
And this the cranny is, right and sinister,°
Through which the fearful lovers are to
　　whisper.
THESEUS: Would you desire lime and hair to
speak better?
170 DEMETRIUS: It is the wittiest partition° that
ever I heard discourse, my lord.
THESEUS: Pyramus draws near the wall.
Silence!
　　PYRAMUS:
O grim-looked night! O night with hue so
　　black!
175 O night, which ever art when day is not!

O night, O night! Alack, alack, alack,
　　I fear my Thisby's promise is forgot!
And thou, O wall, O sweet, O lovely wall,
That stand'st between her father's ground and
　　mine!
Thou wall, O wall, O sweet and lovely wall, 180
Show me thy chink, to blink through with
　　mine eyne!

[Wall holds up his fingers.]

Thanks, courteous wall. Jove shield thee well
　　for this!
But what see I? No Thisby do I see.
O wicked wall, through whom I see no bliss!
　　Cursed be thy stones for thus deceiving me! 185
THESEUS: The wall, methinks, being sen-
sible,° should curse again.°
PYRAMUS: No, in truth, sir, he should not.
"Deceiving me" is Thisby's cue. She is to enter
now, and I am to spy her through the wall. 190
You shall see it will fall pat° as I told you.
Yonder she comes.

　　(Enter THISBY.)

　　THISBY:
O wall, full often hast thou heard my moans,
　　For parting my fair Pyramus and me!
My cherry lips have often kissed thy stones, 195
　　Thy stones with lime and hair knit up in
　　thee.
　　PYRAMUS:
I see a voice: now will I to the chink,
To spy an I can hear my Thisby's face.
Thisby!
　　THISBY:
My love thou art, my love I think. 200
　　PYRAMUS:
Think what thou wilt, I am thy lover's grace;°
And, like Limander,° am I trusty still.
　　THISBY:
And I like Helen,° till the Fates me kill.
　　PYRAMUS:
Not Shafalus to Procrus° was so true.
　　THISBY:
As Shafalus to Procrus, I to you. 205
　　PYRAMUS:
O kiss me through the hole of this vile wall!

142 hight is called　145 fall let fall　147 tall brave
150 bravely broached gallantly stabbed　154 At
large at length　166 right and sinister i.e., running
right and left, horizontal　170 wittiest partition
most intelligent wall (with a pun on "partition," a
section of a book or of an oration)

186–187 sensible conscious　187 again in return
191 pat exactly　201 thy lover's grace thy gracious
lover　202 Limander (Bottom means Leander, but
blends him with Alexander)　203 Helen (Hero,
beloved of Leander, is probably meant)　204
Shafalus to Procrus (Cephalus and Procris are
meant, legendary lovers)

THISBY:
I kiss the wall's hole, not your lips at all.

PYRAMUS:
Wilt thou at Ninny's tomb meet me straightway?

THISBY:
'Tide life, 'tide death,° I come without delay.
[Exeunt PYRAMUS and THISBY.]

WALL:
210 Thus have I, Wall, my part dischargèd so;
And, being done, this wall away doth go.
[Exit.]

THESEUS: Now is the moon used° between
the two neighbors.

DEMETRIUS: No remedy, my lord, when
215 walls are so willful to hear without warning.°

HIPPOLYTA: This is the silliest stuff that
ever I heard.

THESEUS: The best in this kind° are but
shadows; and the worst are no worse, if im-
220 agination amend them.

HIPPOLYTA: It must be your imagination
then, and not theirs.

THESEUS: If we imagine no worse of them
than they of themselves, they may pass for ex-
225 cellent men. Here come two noble beasts in,
a man and a lion.

(Enter LION and MOONSHINE.)

LION:
You, ladies, you, whose gentle hearts do fear
The smallest monstrous mouse that creeps on
floor,
May now perchance both quake and tremble
here,
230 When lion rough in wildest rage doth roar.
Then know that I, as Snug the joiner, am
A lion fell,° nor else no lion's dam;
For, if I should as lion come in strife
Into this place, 'twere pity on my life.°
235 THESEUS: A very gentle° beast, and of a
good conscience.

DEMETRIUS: The very best at a beast, my
lord, that e'er I saw.

LYSANDER: This lion is a very fox for his
valor.   240

THESEUS: True; and a goose for his discretion.

DEMETRIUS: Not so, my lord; for his valor
cannot carry° his discretion, and the fox carries the goose.   245

THESEUS: His discretion, I am sure, cannot
carry his valor; for the goose carries not the
fox. It is well. Leave it to his discretion, and
let us listen to the moon.

MOONSHINE:
This lanthorn° doth the hornèd moon present —   250

DEMETRIUS: He should have worn the horns
on his head.°

THESEUS: He is no crescent, and his horns
are invisible within the circumference.

MOONSHINE:
This lanthorn doth the hornèd moon present;   255
Myself the man i' th' moon do seem to be.

THESEUS: This is the greatest error of all the
rest. The man should be put into the lanthorn.
How is it else the man i' th' moon?

DEMETRIUS: He dares not come there for   260
the candle; for, you see, it is already in snuff.°

HIPPOLYTA: I am aweary of this moon.
Would he would change!

THESEUS: It appears, by his small light of discretion, that he is in the wane; but yet, in   265
courtesy, in all reason, we must stay the time.

LYSANDER: Proceed, Moon.

MOONSHINE: All that I have to say is to tell
you that the lanthorn is the moon; I, the man
i' th' moon; this thorn bush, my thorn bush;   270
and this dog, my dog.

DEMETRIUS: Why, all these should be in the
lanthorn; for all these are in the moon. But,
silence! Here comes Thisby.

(Enter THISBY.)

THISBY:
This is old Ninny's tomb. Where is my love?   275

LION: Oh — [The LION roars. THISBY runs
off.]

209 'Tide life, 'tide death come (betide) life or
death   211 moon used (the quartos read thus, the
Folio reads *morall downe*. Among suggested emen-
dations are "mural down," and "moon to see")
214–215 when walls . . . without warning i.e.,
when walls are so eager to listen without warning
the parents (?)   218 in this kind of this sort, i.e.,
plays (or players?)   232 lion fell fierce lion (perhaps with a pun on *fell* = "skin")   234 pity on
my life a dangerous thing for me   235 gentle
gentlemanly, courteous

244 carry carry away   249 lanthorn (so spelled,
and perhaps pronounced "lant-horn," because lan-
terns were commonly made of horn)   251–252
horns on his head (cuckolds were said to have
horns)   261 in snuff (1) in need of snuffing (2)
resentful

DEMETRIUS: Well roared, Lion.

THESEUS: Well run, Thisby.

HIPPOLYTA: Well shone, Moon. Truly, the
280 moon shines with a good grace.

[*The* LION *shakes* THISBY's *mantle, and exit.*]

THESEUS: Well moused,° Lion.

DEMETRIUS: And then came Pyramus.

LYSANDER: And so the lion vanished.

(*Enter* PYRAMUS.)

PYRAMUS:

Sweet Moon, I thank thee for thy sunny
   beams;
285 I thank thee, Moon, for shining now so bright;
For, by thy gracious, golden, glittering gleams,
   I trust to take of truest Thisby sight.
      But stay, O spite!°
      But mark, poor knight,
290   What dreadful dole° is here!
      Eyes, do you see?
      How can it be?
   O dainty duck! O dear!
      Thy mantle good,
295   What, stained with blood!
   Approach, ye Furies fell!°
      O Fates, come, come,
      Cut thread and thrum;°
   Quail,° crush, conclude, and quell!°

300 THESEUS: This passion, and the death of a
dear friend, would go near to make a man look
sad.

HIPPOLYTA: Beshrew° my heart, but I pity
the man.

PYRAMUS:

305 O wherefore, Nature, didst thou lions frame?
   Since lion vile hath here deflow'red my
      dear:
Which is — no, no — which was the fairest
      dame
   That lived, that loved, that liked, that
      looked with cheer.°
      Come, tears, confound;
310   Out, sword, and wound
   The pap of Pyramus;
      Ay, that left pap,
      Where heart doth hop.
                                  [*Stabs himself.*]

Thus die I, thus, thus, thus.
   Now am I dead,   315
   Now am I fled;
My soul is in the sky.
   Tongue, lose thy light;
   Moon, take thy flight.
                        [*Exit* MOONSHINE.]
   Now die, die, die, die, die.   [*Dies.*]   320

DEMETRIUS: No die, but an ace,° for him;
for he is but one.

LYSANDER: Less than an ace, man; for he is
dead, he is nothing.

THESEUS: With the help of a surgeon he   325
might yet recover, and yet prove an ass.

HIPPOLYTA: How chance° Moonshine is
gone before Thisby comes back and finds her
lover?

THESEUS: She will find him by starlight.   330
Here she comes; and her passion° ends the
play.

[*Enter* THISBY.]

HIPPOLYTA: Methinks she should not use a
long one for such a Pyramus. I hope she will
be brief.   335

DEMETRIUS: A mote will turn the balance,
which Pyramus, which Thisby, is the better;
he for a man, God warr'nt us; she for a
woman, God bless us!

LYSANDER: She hath spied him already with   340
those sweet eyes.

DEMETRIUS: And thus she means,° videlicet:

THISBY:

   Asleep, my love?
      What, dead, my dove?
   O Pyramus, arise!   345
      Speak, speak. Quite dumb?
      Dead, dead? A tomb
   Must cover thy sweet eyes.
      These lily lips,
      This cherry nose,   350
   These yellow cowslip cheeks,
      Are gone, are gone.
      Lovers, make moan.
   His eyes were green as leeks.
      O Sisters Three,°   355
      Come, come to me,
   With hands as pale as milk;
      Lay them in gore,

---

281 **moused** shaken (like a mouse)   288 **spite**
vexation   290 **dole** sorrowful thing   296 **fell** fierce
298 **thread and thrum** i.e., everything (*thrum* =
the end of the warp thread)   299 **Quail** destroy
299 **quell** kill   303 **Beshrew** curse (but a mild
word)   308 **cheer** countenance

321 **No die, but an ace** not a die (singular of
"dice"), but a one-spot on a die   327 **How chance**
how does it come that   331 **passion** passionate
speech   342 **means** laments   355 **Sisters Three**
i.e., the three Fates

360 Since you have shore°
With shears his thread of silk.
Tongue, not a word.
Come, trusty sword,
Come, blade, my breast imbrue!°

[*Stabs herself.*]

And, farewell, friends.
365 Thus Thisby ends.
Adieu, adieu, adieu.   [*Dies.*]

THESEUS: Moonshine and Lion are left to bury the dead.

DEMETRIUS: Ay, and Wall too.

370 BOTTOM [*starting up*]: No, I assure you; the wall is down that parted their fathers. Will it please you to see the epilogue, or to hear a Bergomask dance° between two of our company?

375 THESEUS: No epilogue, I pray you; for your play needs no excuse. Never excuse, for when the players are all dead, there need none to be blamed. Marry, if he that writ it had played Pyramus and hanged himself in Thisby's gar-
380 ter, it would have been a fine tragedy: and so it is, truly; and very notably discharged. But, come, your Bergomask. Let your epilogue alone.

[*A dance.*]

The iron tongue of midnight hath told°
twelve.
385 Lovers, to bed; 'tis almost fairy time.
I fear we shall outsleep the coming morn,
As much as we this night have overwatched.
This palpable-gross° play hath well beguiled
The heavy gait of night. Sweet friends, to bed.
390 A fortnight hold we this solemnity,
In nightly revels and new jollity.   (*Exeunt.*)

(*Enter* PUCK [*with a broom*].)

PUCK:
Now the hungry lion roars,
   And the wolf behowls the moon;
Whilst the heavy plowman snores,
395   All with weary task fordone.°
Now the wasted° brands do glow,
   Whilst the screech owl, screeching loud,
Puts the wretch that lies in woe
   In remembrance of a shroud.

400 Now it is the time of night,
   That the graves, all gaping wide,
Every one lets forth his sprite,
   In the churchway paths to glide:
And we fairies, that do run
405   By the triple Hecate's team,°
From the presence of the sun,
   Following darkness like a dream,
Now are frolic.° Not a mouse
Shall disturb this hallowed house:
410 I am sent, with broom, before,
To sweep the dust behind the door.°

(*Enter King and Queen of Fairies with all their train.*)

OBERON:
Through the house give glimmering light,
   By the dead and drowsy fire:
Every elf and fairy sprite
415   Hop as light as bird from brier;
And this ditty, after me,
Sing, and dance it trippingly.

TITANIA:
First, rehearse your song by rote,
To each word a warbling note:
Hand in hand, with fairy grace,
420 Will we sing, and bless this place.

[*Song and dance.*]

OBERON:
Now, until the break of day,
Through this house each fairy stray.
To the best bride-bed will we,
Which by us shall blessèd be;
425
And the issue there create°
Ever shall be fortunate.
So shall all the couples three
Ever true in loving be;
And the blots of Nature's hand
430 Shall not in their issue stand.
Never mole, harelip, nor scar.
Nor mark prodigious,° such as are
Despisèd in nativity.
Shall upon their children be.
435

405 **triple Hecate's team** i.e., because she had three names: Phoebe in Heaven, Diana on Earth, Hecate in Hades. (Like her chariot — drawn by black horses or dragons — the elves were abroad only at night; but III.ii.388–391 says differently) 408 **frolic** frolicsome 411 **behind the door** i.e., from behind the door (Puck traditionally helped with household chores) 426 **create** created 433 **mark prodigious** ominous birthmark

359 **shore** shorn 363 **imbrue** stain with blood 373 **Bergomask dance** rustic dance 384 **told** counted, tolled 388 **palpable-gross** obviously grotesque 395 **fordone** worn out 396 **wasted** used-up

With this field-dew consecrate,
Every fairy take his gait,°
And each several° chamber bless,
Through this palace, with sweet peace,
440 And the owner of it blest
Ever shall in safety rest.
Trip away; make no stay;
Meet me all by break of day.

Exeunt [all but PUCK].

PUCK:
If we shadows have offended,
445 Think but this, and all is mended:
That you have but slumb'red here,
While these visions did appear.
And this weak and idle° theme,

No more yielding but° a dream,
Gentles, do not reprehend: 450
If you pardon, we will mend.
And, as I am an honest Puck,
If we have unearnèd luck
Now to scape the serpent's tongue,°
We will make amends ere long;   455
Else the Puck a liar call:
So, good night unto you all.
Give me your hands,° if we be friends,
And Robin shall restore amends.°   [*Exit.*]

FINIS

437 **take his gait** proceed   438 **several** individual
448 **idle** foolish

449 **No more yielding but** yielding no more than
454 **to scape the serpent's tongue** i.e., to escape
hisses from the audience   458 **Give me your hands**
applaud   459 **restore amends** make amends

Speaking broadly, there are in the Renaissance two comic traditions,
which may be called "critical comedy" (or "bitter comedy") and "romantic
comedy" (or "sweet comedy"). The former claims, in Hamlet's words, that
the "purpose of playing . . . is to hold, as 'twere, the mirror up to nature; to
show virtue her own feature, scorn her own image, and the very age and body
of the time his form and pressure." Because it aims to hold a mirror up to
the audience, its dramatis personae are usually urban citizens — jealous husbands, foolish merchants, and the like. These are ultimately punished, at
times merely by exposure, at times by imprisonment or fines or some such
thing. The second kind of comedy, romantic comedy, seeks less to correct
than to delight with scenes of pleasant behavior. It does not hold a mirror
to the audience; rather, it leads the audience into an elegant dream world
where charming gentlefolk live in a timeless existence. Thomas Heywood, a
playwright contemporary with Shakespeare, briefly set forth the characteristics
of both traditions in *An Apology for Actors* (1612). A comedy, he said,

> is pleasantly contrived with merry accidents, and intermixed with apt
> and witty jests. . . . And what then is the subject of this harmless
> mirth? Either in the shape of a clown to show others their slovenly
> behavior, that they may reform that simplicity in themselves, which
> others make their sport, . . . or to refresh such weary spirits as are tired
> with labors or study, to moderate the cares and heaviness of the mind,
> that they may return to their trades and faculties with more zeal and
> earnestness, after some small soft and pleasant retirement.

When we think of *A Midsummer Night's Dream*, we think not of critical comedy that seeks to reform "slovenly behavior" but of romantic comedy
that offers "harmless mirth," "sport," and the refreshing of "such weary
spirits as are tired with labors or study." Yet even *A Midsummer Night's
Dream* has its touches of critical comedy, its elements that, in Heywood's

words, "may reform" by holding up a mirror to unsocial behavior. There is some satire — a little satire of the crabby father, Egeus, and rather more of the young lovers and of the well-meaning rustics who bumblingly stage a play in an effort to please their duke (and to win pensions), but mostly the play is pervaded by genial spirits and a humane vision that make it moral without moralizing. The first book on Shakespeare's morality, Elizabeth Griffith's *The Morality of Shakespeare's Dramas* (1775), rather impatiently dismissed *A Midsummer Night's Dream*: "I shall not trouble my readers with the Fable of this piece, as I can see no general moral that can be deducted from the Argument."

For one thing, all of the people — including the fairies — in *A Midsummer Night's Dream* are basically decent creatures. Egeus is at first irascible, but at the end of the play we hear no more of his insistence that his daughter marry the young man of his choice; Theseus had engaged in youthful indiscretions, but that was long ago and in another country, and now he is the very model of a benevolent ruler; the fairy king and queen bicker, but at the end they are reconciled and they bless the bridal beds of the newlyweds. The rustics, though inept actors and sometimes too impressed by their own theatrical abilities, are men of good intentions. And if in the last act the young aristocratic lovers are a little too confident of their superiority to the rustic actors, we nevertheless feel that they are fundamentally decent; after all, their comments on the performance are more or less in tune with our own.

If *A Midsummer Night's Dream*, then, employs satire only sparingly, what does it do, and what is it about? Perhaps we can get somewhere near to an answer by briefly looking at some of the interrelationships of the stories that make up the intricate plot. There is the story of Theseus and Hippolyta, who will be married in four days; the story of the four young lovers; the story of Bottom and his fellow craftsmen, who are rehearsing a play; and the story of the quarreling fairies. All these stories are related, and eventually come together: the lovers marry on the same day as Theseus and Hippolyta; the craftsmen perform their play at the wedding; the fairies come to witness the wedding and bless it. One of the play's themes, of course, is love, as shown in the contrasts between the stately love of Theseus and Hippolyta, the changeable romantic love of the four young Athenians, the love of Pyramus. and Thisby in the play that the craftsmen are rehearsing, the quarrel between the fairy king and queen, and even Titania's infatuation with Bottom. All these stories play against one another, sometimes very subtly, and sometimes explicitly, as when Lysander, having shifted his affection from Hermia to Helena, says, "Reason says you are the worthier maid" (II.ii. 116), and Bottom in the next scene accepts Titania's love, saying, "Reason and love keep little company together nowadays" (III.i.154–55). The nature of reason is also implicitly discussed in the play, in the numerous references to "fantasy" and "fancy," or imagination. There is scarcely a scene that does not touch on the matter of the power of the imagination. In the opening scene, for example, Egeus says that Lysander has corrupted Hermia's fantasy (I.i.32), and Duke Theseus tells Hermia that she must perceive her suitors as her father perceives them. The most famous of these references is Theseus' speech on "the lunatic, the lover, and the poet" (V.1.7). In addition to setting the time and place, the images help to define the nature of fantasy: there is an emphasis on night and moonlight during the period of confusion, and then references to the "morning lark," "day," and so on, when Theseus (the spokesman for reason) enters the woods and the lovers are properly paired (IV.i.98 ff.). The last scene reintroduces night, and the lovers have moved from the dark wood back to the civilized world of Athens, and the night will bring them to bed. The plot of *A Midsummer Night's Dream*, then, juxtaposes speech against speech, image against image, and scene against scene, telling not simply a story but a story that "grows to something of great constancy, . . . strange and admirable." *

* This last paragraph of commentary, beginning on the previous page, is from *The Complete Signet Classic Shakespeare*, edited by Sylvan Barnet. Copyright © 1972 by Harcourt Brace Jovanovich. Reprinted by permission.

Le Misantrope.

THE MISANTHROPE

Molière

English version by Richard Wilbur

Jean Baptiste Poquelin (1622–1673), who took the name Molière, was born into a prosperous middle-class family. For a while he studied law and philosophy, but by 1643 he was acting. He became the head of a theatrical company which had its initial difficulties and later, thanks largely to Molière's comedies, its great successes. In 1662 he married Armande Béjart. The marriage apparently was unhappy, but the capricious and flirtatious Armande proved to be an accomplished actress. Molière continued to act, with great success in comedy, until his death. In one of those improbable things that happen in real life but that are too strange for art, Molière died of a hemorrhage that he suffered while playing the title role in his comedy *The Hypochondriac*. The early plays are highly farcical; among the later and greater plays are *The Highbrow Ladies* (1659), *Tartuffe* (1664), *Don Juan* (1665), *The Misanthrope* (1666), and *The Miser* (1668).

CHARACTERS

ALCESTE, *in love with Célimène*
PHILINTE, *Alceste's friend*
ORONTE, *in love with Célimène*
CÉLIMÈNE, *Alceste's beloved*
ÉLIANTE, *Célimène's cousin*
ARSINOÉ, *a friend of Célimène's*
ACASTE } *Marquesses*
CLITANDRE
BASQUE, *Célimène's servant*
A GUARD *of the Marshalsea*
DUBOIS, *Alceste's valet*

The Scene throughout is in Célimène's house at Paris.

Frontispiece of *Le Misanthrope, Comedie,* Paris, Jean Ribov, 1662. (Photograph: Courtesy of The Houghton Library, Harvard University.)

507

ACT I

SCENE I. [PHILINTE, ALCESTE.]

PHILINTE:
Now, what's got into you?
ALCESTE (*seated*):   Kindly leave me alone.
PHILINTE:
Come, come, what is it? This lugubrious
  tone . . .
ALCESTE:
Leave me, I said; you spoil my solitude.
PHILINTE:
Oh, listen to me, now, and don't be rude.
ALCESTE:
I choose to be rude, Sir, and to be hard of
5   hearing.
PHILINTE:
These ugly moods of yours are not endearing;
Friends though we are, I really must insist . . .
ALCESTE (*abruptly rising*):
Friends? Friends, you say? Well, cross me off
  your list.

Molière's *The Misanthrope*, translated by Richard
Wilbur. Copyright © 1954, 1955, by Richard
Wilbur. Reprinted by permission of Harcourt Brace
Jovanovich, Inc.
  Caution: Professionals and amateurs are hereby warned that this translation, being fully protected
under the copyright laws of the United States of
America, the British Empire, including the Dominion
of Canada, and all other countries which are signa-
tories to the Universal Copyright Convention and
the International Copyright Union, is subject to
royalty. All rights, including professional, amateur,
motion picture, recitation, lecturing, public reading,
radio broadcasting, and television, are strictly reserved. Particular emphasis is laid on the question
of readings, permission for which must be secured
from the author's agent in writing. Inquiries on professional rights (except for amateur rights) should
be addressed to Mr. Gilbert Parker, Curtis Brown,
Ltd., 575 Madison Avenue, New York, N.Y. 10022;
inquiries on translation rights should be addressed to
Harcourt Brace Jovanovich, Inc., 757 Third Avenue,
New York, N.Y. 10017. The amateur acting rights
are controlled exclusively by the Dramatists Play
Service, Inc., 440 Park Avenue South, New York,
N.Y. 10016. No amateur performance of the play
may be given without obtaining in advance the written permission of the Dramatists Play Service, Inc.,
and paying the requisite fee.

I've been your friend till now, as you well
  know;
But after what I saw a moment ago   10
I tell you flatly that our ways must part.
I wish no place in a dishonest heart.
PHILINTE:
Why, what have I done, Alceste? Is this quite
  just?
ALCESTE:
My God, you ought to die of self-disgust.
I call your conduct inexcusable, Sir,   15
And every man of honor will concur.
I see you almost hug a man to death,
Exclaim for joy until you're out of breath,
And supplement these loving demonstrations
With endless offers, vows, and protestations; 20
Then when I ask you "Who was that?" I find
That you can barely bring his name to mind!
Once the man's back is turned, you cease to
  love him,
And speak with absolute indifference of him!
By God, I say it's base and scandalous   25
To falsify the heart's affections thus;
If I caught myself behaving in such a way,
I'd hang myself for shame, without delay.
PHILINTE:
It hardly seems a hanging matter to me;
I hope that you will take it graciously   30
If I extend myself a slight reprieve,
And live a little longer, by your leave.
ALCESTE:
How dare you joke about a crime so grave?
PHILINTE:
What crime? How else are people to behave?
ALCESTE:
I'd have them be sincere, and never part   35
With any word that isn't from the heart.
PHILINTE:
When someone greets us with a show of
  pleasure,
It's but polite to give him equal measure,
Return his love the best that we know how,
And trade him offer for offer, vow for vow.   40
ALCESTE:
No, no, this formula you'd have me follow,
However fashionable, is false and hollow,
And I despise the frenzied operations
Of all these barterers of protestations,
These lavishers of meaningless embraces,   45
These utterers of obliging commonplaces,

Who court and flatter everyone on earth
And praise the fool no less than the man of
    worth.
Should you rejoice that someone fondles you,
50   Offers his love and service, swears to be true,
And fills your ears with praises of your name,
When to the first damned fop he'll say the
    same?
No, no: no self-respecting heart would dream
Of prizing so promiscuous an esteem;
55   However high the praise, there's nothing worse
Than sharing honors with the universe.
Esteem is founded on comparison:
To honor all men is to honor none.
Since you embrace this indiscriminate vice,
60   Your friendship comes at far too cheap a price:
I spurn the easy tribute of a heart
Which will not set the worthy man apart:
I choose, Sir, to be chosen; and in fine,
The friend of mankind is no friend of mine.
    PHILINTE:
65   But in polite society, custom decrees
That we show certain outward courtesies. . . .
    ALCESTE:
Ah, no! we should condemn with all our force
Such false and artificial intercourse.
Let men behave like men; let them display
70   Their inmost hearts in everything they say;
Let the heart speak, and let our sentiments
Not mask themselves in silly compliments.
    PHILINTE:
In certain cases it would be uncouth
And most absurd to speak the naked truth;
75   With all respect for your exalted notions,
It's often best to veil one's true emotions.
Wouldn't the social fabric come undone
If we were wholly frank with everyone?
Suppose you met with someone you couldn't
    bear;
80   Would you inform him of it then and there?
    ALCESTE:
Yes.
    PHILINTE:
      Then you'd tell old Emilie it's pathetic
The way she daubs her features with cosmetic
And plays the gay coquette at sixty-four?
    ALCESTE:
I would.
    PHILINTE:
      And you'd call Dorilas a bore,
85   And tell him every ear at court is lame
From hearing him brag about his noble name?
    ALCESTE:
Precisely.

    PHILINTE:
    Ah, you're joking.
    ALCESTE: *Au contraire:*
In this regard there's none I'd choose to spare.
All are corrupt; there's nothing to be seen
In court or town but aggravates my spleen.   90
I fall into deep gloom and melancholy
When I survey the scene of human folly,
Finding on every hand base flattery,
Injustice, fraud, self-interest, treachery. . . .
Ah, it's too much; mankind has grown so base,   95
I mean to break with the whole human race.
    PHILINTE:
This philosophic rage is a bit extreme;
You've no idea how comical you seem;
Indeed, we're like those brothers in the play
Called *School for Husbands,* one of whom was
    prey . . .   100
    ALCESTE:
Enough, now! None of your stupid similes.
    PHILINTE:
Then let's have no more tirades, if you please.
The world won't change, whatever you say or
    do;
And since plain speaking means so much to
    you,
I'll tell you plainly that by being frank   105
You've earned the reputation of a crank,
And that you're thought ridiculous when you
    rage
And rant against the manners of the age.
    ALCESTE:
So much the better; just what I wish to hear.
No news could be more grateful to my ear.   110
All men are so detestable in my eyes,
I should be sorry if they thought me wise.
    PHILINTE:
Your hatred's very sweeping, is it not?
    ALCESTE:
Quite right: I hate the whole degraded lot.
    PHILINTE:
Must all poor human creatures be embraced,   115
Without distinction, by your vast distaste?
Even in these bad times, there are surely a
    few . . .
    ALCESTE:
No, I include all men in one dim view:
Some men I hate for being rogues: the others
I hate because they treat the rogues like
    brothers,   120
And, lacking a virtuous scorn for what is vile,
Receive the villain with a complaisant smile.
Notice how tolerant people choose to be
Toward that bold rascal who's at law with me.

125 His social polish can't conceal his nature;
One sees at once that he's a treacherous
creature;
No one could possibly be taken in
By those soft speeches and that sugary grin.
The whole world knows the shady means by
which
130 The low-brow's grown so powerful and rich,
And risen to a rank so bright and high
That virtue can but blush, and merit sigh.
Whenever his name comes up in conversation,
None will defend his wretched reputation;
Call him knave, liar, scoundrel, and all the
135 rest,
Each head will nod, and no one will protest.
And yet his smirk is seen in every house,
He's greeted everywhere with smiles and bows,
And when there's any honor that can be got
140 By pulling strings, he'll get it, like as not.
My God! It chills my heart to see the ways
Men come to terms with evil nowadays;
Sometimes, I swear, I'm moved to flee and
find
Some desert land unfouled by humankind.
            PHILINTE:
145 Come, let's forget the follies of the times
And pardon mankind for its petty crimes;
Let's have an end of rantings and of railings,
And show some leniency toward human fail-
ings.
This world requires a pliant rectitude;
150 Too stern a virtue makes one stiff and rude;
Good sense views all extremes with detesta-
tion,
And bids us to be noble in moderation.
The rigid virtues of the ancient days
Are not for us; they jar with all our ways
155 And ask of us too lofty a perfection.
Wise men accept their times without objec-
tion,
And there's no greater folly, if you ask me,
Than trying to reform society.
Like you, I see each day a hundred and one
160 Unhandsome deeds that might be better done,
But still, for all the faults that meet my view,
I'm never known to storm and rave like you.
I take men as they are, or let them be,
And teach my soul to bear their frailty;
And whether in court or town, whatever the
165 scene,
My phlegm's as philosophic as your spleen.
            ALCESTE:
This phlegm which you so eloquently com-
mend,

Does nothing ever rile it up, my friend?
Suppose some man you trust should treacher-
ously
Conspire to rob you of your property,   170
And do his best to wreck your reputation?
Wouldn't you feel a certain indignation?
            PHILINTE:
Why, no. These faults of which you so com-
plain
Are part of human nature, I maintain,
And it's no more a matter for disgust   175
That men are knavish, selfish and unjust,
Than that the vulture dines upon the dead,
And wolves are furious, and apes ill-bred.
            ALCESTE:
Shall I see myself betrayed, robbed, torn to
bits,
And not . . . Oh, let's be still and rest our wits.   180
Enough of reasoning, now. I've had my fill.
            PHILINTE:
Indeed, you would do well, Sir, to be still.
Rage less at your opponent, and give some
thought
To how you'll win this lawsuit that he's
brought.
            ALCESTE:
I assure you I'll do nothing of the sort.   185
            PHILINTE:
Then who will plead your case before the
court?
            ALCESTE:
Reason and right and justice will plead for me.
            PHILINTE:
Oh, Lord. What judges do you plan to see?
            ALCESTE:
Why, none. The justice of my cause is clear.
            PHILINTE:
Of course, man; but there's politics to fear. . . .   190
            ALCESTE:
No, I refuse to lift a hand. That's flat.
I'm either right, or wrong.
            PHILINTE: Don't count on that.
            ALCESTE:
No, I'll do nothing.
            PHILINTE: Your enemy's influence
Is great, you know . . .
            ALCESTE: That makes no difference.
            PHILINTE:
It will; you'll see.
            ALCESTE: Must honor bow to guile?   195
If so, I shall be proud to lose the trial.
            PHILINTE:
Oh, really . . .
            ALCESTE: I'll discover by this case

Whether or not men are sufficiently base
And impudent and villainous and perverse
200 To do me wrong before the universe.
    PHILINTE:
What a man!
    ALCESTE:
              Oh, I could wish, whatever the cost,
Just for the beauty of it, that my trial were
    lost.
    PHILINTE:
If people heard you talking so, Alceste,
They'd split their sides. Your name would be a
    jest.
    ALCESTE:
So much the worse for jesters.
205   PHILINTE: May I enquire
Whether this rectitude you so admire,
And these hard virtues you're enamored of
Are qualities of the lady whom you love?
It much surprises me that you, who seem
210 To view mankind with furious disesteem,
Have yet found something to enchant your
    eyes
Amidst a species which you so despise.
And what is more amazing, I'm afraid,
Is the most curious choice your heart has
    made.
215 The honest Éliante is fond of you,
Arsinoé, the prude, admires you too;
And yet your spirit's been perversely led
To choose the flighty Célimène instead,
Whose brittle malice and coquettish ways
220 So typify the manners of our days.
How is it that the traits you most abhor
Are bearable in this lady you adore?
Are you so blind with love that you can't find
    them?
Or do you contrive, in her case, not to mind
    them?
    ALCESTE:
225 My love for that young widow's not the kind
That can't perceive defects; no, I'm not blind.
I see her faults, despite my ardent love,
And all I see I fervently reprove.
And yet I'm weak; for all her falsity,
230 That woman knows the art of pleasing me,
And though I never cease complaining of her,
I swear I cannot manage not to love her.
Her charm outweighs her faults; I can but aim
To cleanse her spirit in my love's pure flame.
    PHILINTE:
235 That's no small task; I wish you all success.
You think then that she loves you?
    ALCESTE: Heavens, yes!

I wouldn't love her did she not love me.
    PHILINTE:
Well, if her taste for you is plain to see,
Why do these rivals cause you such despair?
    ALCESTE:
True love, Sir, is possessive, and cannot bear   240
To share with all the world. I'm here today
To tell her she must send that mob away.
    PHILINTE:
If I were you, and had your choice to make,
Éliante, her cousin, would be the one I'd
    take;
That honest heart, which cares for you alone,   245
Would harmonize far better with your own.
    ALCESTE:
True, true: each day my reason tells me so;
But reason doesn't rule in love, you know.
    PHILINTE:
I fear some bitter sorrow is in store;
This love . . .

SCENE II. [ORONTE, ALCESTE, PHILINTE.]

ORONTE (to ALCESTE):
           The servants told me at the door
That Éliante and Célimène were out,
But when I heard, dear Sir, that you were
    about,
I came to say, without exaggeration,
That I hold you in the vastest admiration,   5
And that it's always been my dearest desire
To be the friend of one I so admire.
I hope to see my love of merit requited,
And you and I in friendship's bond united.
I'm sure you won't refuse — if I may be
    frank —   10
A friend of my devotedness — and rank.

(*During this speech of* ORONTE'S ALCESTE *is
abstracted, and seems unaware that he is
being spoken to. He only breaks off his
reverie when* ORONTE *says:*)

It was for you, if you please, that my words
    were intended.
    ALCESTE:
For me, Sir?
    ORONTE:
           Yes, for you. You're not offended?
    ALCESTE:
By no means. But this much surprises me. . . .
The honor comes most unexpectedly. . . .   15
    ORONTE:
My high regard should not astonish you;
The whole world feels the same. It is your due.

ALCESTE:
Sir . . .
ORONTE:
     Why, in all the State there isn't one
Can match your merits; they shine, Sir, like
    the sun.
ALCESTE:
Sir . . .
ORONTE:
20   You are higher in my estimation
Than all that's most illustrious in the nation.
ALCESTE:
Sir . . .
ORONTE:
     If I lie, may heaven strike me dead!
To show you that I mean what I have said,
Permit me, Sir, to embrace you most sincerely,
And swear that I will prize our friendship
25   dearly.
Give me your hand. And now, Sir, if you
    choose,
We'll make our vows.
ALCESTE: Sir . . .
ORONTE: What! You refuse?
ALCESTE:
Sir, it's a very great honor you extend:
But friendship is a sacred thing, my friend;
30 It would be profanation to bestow
The name of friend on one you hardly know.
All parts are better played when well-rehearsed;
Let's put off friendship, and get acquainted
    first.
We may discover it would be unwise
35 To try to make our natures harmonize.
ORONTE:
By heaven! You're sagacious to the core;
This speech has made me admire you even
    more.
Let time, then, bring us closer day by day;
Meanwhile, I shall be yours in every way.
40 If, for example, there should be anything
You wish at court, I'll mention it to the King.
I have his ear, of course; it's quite well known
That I am much in favor with the throne.
In short, I am your servant. And now, dear
    friend,
45 Since you have such fine judgment, I intend
To please you, if I can, with a small sonnet
I wrote not long ago. Please comment on it,
And tell me whether I ought to publish it.
ALCESTE:
You must excuse me, Sir; I'm hardly fit
To judge such matters.
ORONTE: Why not?

ALCESTE: I am, I fear, 50
Inclined to be unfashionably sincere.
ORONTE:
Just what I ask; I'd take no satisfaction
In anything but your sincere reaction.
I beg you not to dream of being kind.
ALCESTE:
Since you desire it, Sir, I'll speak my mind. 55
ORONTE:
Sonnet. It's a sonnet. . . . *Hope* . . . The poem's
    addressed
To a lady who wakened hopes within my
    breast.
Hope . . . this is not the pompous sort of thing,
Just modest little verses, with a tender ring.
ALCESTE:
Well, we shall see.
ORONTE: *Hope* . . . I'm anxious to hear 60
Whether the style seems properly smooth and
    clear,
And whether the choice of words is good or
    bad.
ALCESTE:
We'll see, we'll see.
ORONTE: Perhaps I ought to add
That it took me only a quarter-hour to write it.
ALCESTE:
The time's irrelevant, Sir: kindly recite it. 65
ORONTE (*reading*):
   Hope comforts us awhile, 'tis true,
   Lulling our cares with careless laughter,
   And yet such joy is full of rue,
   My Phyllis, if nothing follows after.
PHILINTE:
I'm charmed by this already; the style's de-
    lightful. 70
ALCESTE (*sotto voce, to* PHILINTE):
How can you say that? Why, the thing is
    frightful.
ORONTE:
   Your fair face smiled on me awhile,
   But was it kindness so to enchant me?
   'Twould have been fairer not to smile,
   If hope was all you meant to grant me. 75
PHILINTE:
What a clever thought! How handsomely you
    phrase it!
ALCESTE (*sotto voce, to* PHILINTE):
You know the thing is trash. How dare you
    praise it?
ORONTE:
   If it's to be my passion's fate
   Thus everlastingly to wait,
   Then death will come to set me free: 80

For death is fairer than the fair;
Phyllis, to hope is to despair
When one must hope eternally.

PHILINTE:
The close is exquisite — full of feeling and grace.

ALCESTE (*sotto voce, aside*):
85   Oh, blast the close; you'd better close your face
Before you send your lying soul to hell.

PHILINTE:
I can't remember a poem I've liked so well.

ALCESTE (*sotto voce, aside*):
Good Lord!

ORONTE (*to* PHILINTE):
                I fear you're flattering me a bit.

PHILINTE:
Oh, no!

ALCESTE (*sotto voce, aside*):
              What else d'you call it, you hypocrite?

ORONTE (*to* ALCESTE):
But you, Sir, keep your promise now: don't shrink
90   From telling me sincerely what you think.

ALCESTE:
Sir, these are delicate matters; we all desire
To be told that we've the true poetic fire.
But once, to one whose name I shall not mention,
95   I said, regarding some verse of his invention,
That gentlemen should rigorously control
That itch to write which often afflicts the soul;
That one should curb the heady inclination
To publicize one's little avocation;
100 And that in showing off one's works of art
One often plays a very clownish part.

ORONTE:
Are you suggesting in a devious way
That I ought not . . .

ALCESTE: Oh, that I do not say.
Further, I told him that no fault is worse
105 Than that of writing frigid, lifeless verse,
And that the merest whisper of such a shame
Suffices to destroy a man's good name.

ORONTE:
D'you mean to say my sonnet's dull and trite?

ALCESTE:
I don't say that. But I went on to cite
110 Numerous cases of once-respected men
Who came to grief by taking up the pen.

ORONTE:
And am I like them? Do I write so poorly?

ALCESTE:
I don't say that. But I told this person, "Surely

You're under no necessity to compose;
Why you should wish to publish, heaven knows.   115
There's no excuse for printing tedious rot
Unless one writes for bread, as you do not.
Resist temptation, then, I beg of you;
Conceal your pastimes from the public view;
And don't give up, on any provocation,   120
Your present high and courtly reputation,
To purchase at a greedy printer's shop
The name of silly author and scribbling fop."
These were the points I tried to make him see.

ORONTE:
I sense that they are also aimed at me;   125
But now — about my sonnet — I'd like to be told . . .

ALCESTE:
Frankly, that sonnet should be pigeonholed.
You've chosen the worst models to imitate.
The style's unnatural. Let me illustrate:
For example, *Your fair face smiled on me awhile*,   130
Followed by, *'Twould have been fairer not to smile!*
Or this: *such joy is full of rue;*
Or this: *For death is fairer than the fair;*
Or, *Phyllis, to hope is to despair*
When one must hope eternally!   135
This artificial style, that's all the fashion,
Has neither taste, nor honesty, nor passion;
It's nothing but a sort of wordy play,
And nature never spoke in such a way.
What, in this shallow age, is not debased?   140
Our fathers, though less refined, had better taste;
I'd barter all that men admire today
For one old love song I shall try to say:
     If the King had given me for my own
     Paris, his citadel,   145
     And I for that must leave alone
     Her whom I love so well,
     I'd say then to the Crown,
     Take back your glittering town;
     My darling is more fair, I swear,   150
     My darling is more fair.
The rhyme's not rich, the style is rough and old,
But don't you see that it's the purest gold
Beside the tinsel nonsense now preferred,
And that there's passion in its every word?   155
     If the King had given me for my own
     Paris, his citadel,
     And I for that must leave alone
     Her whom I love so well,

160
    I'd say then to the Crown,
    Take back your glittering town;
    My darling is more fair, I swear,
    My darling is more fair.
There speaks a loving heart. (*To* PHILINTE.)
    You're laughing, eh?
165 Laugh on, my precious wit. Whatever you say,
I hold that song's worth all the bibelots
That people hail today with ah's and oh's.
    ORONTE:
And I maintain my sonnet's very good.
    ALCESTE:
It's not at all surprising that you should.
You have your reasons; permit me to have
170   mine
For thinking that you cannot write a line.
    ORONTE:
Others have praised my sonnet to the skies.
    ALCESTE:
I lack their art of telling pleasant lies.
    ORONTE:
You seem to think you've got no end of wit.
    ALCESTE:
175 To praise your verse, I'd need still more of it.
    ORONTE:
I'm not in need of your approval, Sir.
    ALCESTE:
That's good; you couldn't have it if you were.
    ORONTE:
Come now, I'll lend you the subject of my
    sonnet;
I'd like to see you try to improve upon it.
    ALCESTE:
I might, by chance, write something just as
180   shoddy;
But then I wouldn't show it to everybody.
    ORONTE:
You're most opinionated and conceited.
    ALCESTE:
Go find your flatterers, and be better treated.
    ORONTE:
Look here, my little fellow, pray watch your
    tone.
    ALCESTE:
My great big fellow, you'd better watch your
185   own.
    PHILINTE (*stepping between them*):
Oh, please, please, gentlemen! This will never
    do.
    ORONTE:
The fault is mine, and I leave the field to you.
I am your servant, Sir, in every way.
    ALCESTE:
And I, Sir, am your most abject valet.

SCENE III. [PHILINTE, ALCESTE.]

    PHILINTE:
Well, as you see, sincerity in excess
Can get you into a very pretty mess;
Oronte was hungry for appreciation. . . .
    ALCESTE:
Don't speak to me.
    PHILINTE: What?
    ALCESTE: No more conversation.
    PHILINTE:
Really, now . . .
    ALCESTE: Leave me alone.
    PHILINTE: If I . . .
    ALCESTE: Out of my sight!   5
    PHILINTE:
But what . . .
    ALCESTE: I won't listen.
    PHILINTE: But . . .
    ALCESTE: Silence!
    PHILINTE: Now, is it polite . . .
    ALCESTE:
By heaven, I've had enough. Don't follow me.
    PHILINTE:
Ah, you're just joking. I'll keep you company.

ACT II

SCENE I. [ALCESTE, CÉLIMÈNE.]

    ALCESTE:
Shall I speak plainly, Madam? I confess
Your conduct gives me infinite distress,
And my resentment's grown too hot to
    smother.
Soon, I foresee, we'll break with one another.
If I said otherwise, I should deceive you;   5
Sooner or later, I shall be forced to leave you,
And if I swore that we shall never part,
I should misread the omens of my heart.
    CÉLIMÈNE:
You kindly saw me home, it would appear,
So as to pour invectives in my ear.   10
    ALCESTE:
I've no desire to quarrel. But I deplore
Your inability to shut the door
On all these suitors who beset you so.
There's what annoys me, if you care to know.
    CÉLIMÈNE:
Is it my fault that all these men pursue me?   15
Am I to blame if they're attracted to me?
And when they gently beg an audience,

Ought I to take a stick and drive them hence?
ALCESTE:
Madam, there's no necessity for a stick;
20 A less responsive heart would do the trick.
Of your attractiveness I don't complain;
But those your charms attract, you then detain
By a most melting and receptive manner,
And so enlist their hearts beneath your banner.
25 It's the agreeable hopes which you excite
That keep these lovers round you day and
      night;
Were they less liberally smiled upon,
That sighing troop would very soon be gone.
But tell me, Madam, why it is that lately
30 This man Clitandre interests you so greatly?
Because of what high merits do you deem
Him worthy of the honor of your esteem?
Is it that your admiring glances linger
On the splendidly long nail of his little finger?
35 Or do you share the general deep respect
For the blond wig he chooses to affect?
Are you in love with his embroidered hose?
Do you adore his ribbons and his bows?
Or is it that this paragon bewitches
Your tasteful eye with his vast German
40   breeches?
Perhaps his giggle, or his falsetto voice,
Makes him the latest gallant of your choice?
CÉLIMÈNE:
You're much mistaken to resent him so.
Why I put up with him you surely know:
45 My lawsuit's very shortly to be tried,
And I must have his influence on my side.
ALCESTE:
Then lose your lawsuit, Madam, or let it drop;
Don't torture me by humoring such a fop.
CÉLIMÈNE:
You're jealous of the whole world, Sir.
ALCESTE: That's true,
50 Since the whole world is well-received by you.
CÉLIMÈNE:
That my good nature is so unconfined
Should serve to pacify your jealous mind;
Were I to smile on one, and scorn the rest,
Then you might have some cause to be
      distressed.
ALCESTE:
55 Well, if I mustn't be jealous, tell me, then,
Just how I'm better treated than other men.
CÉLIMÈNE:
You know you have my love. Will that not
      do?
ALCESTE:
What proof have I that what you say is true?

CÉLIMÈNE:
I would expect, Sir, that my having said it
Might give the statement a sufficient credit.   60
ALCESTE:
But how can I be sure that you don't tell
The selfsame thing to other men as well?
CÉLIMÈNE:
What a gallant speech! How flattering to me!
What a sweet creature you make me out to be!
Well then, to save you from the pangs of
      doubt,   65
All that I've said I hereby cancel out;
Now, none but yourself shall make a monkey
      of you:
Are you content?
ALCESTE:
              Why, why am I doomed to love you?
I swear that I shall bless the blissful hour
When this poor heart's no longer in your
      power!   70
I make no secret of it: I've done my best
To exorcise this passion from my breast;
But thus far all in vain; it will not go;
It's for my sins that I must love you so.
CÉLIMÈNE:
Your love for me is matchless, Sir; that's clear. 75
ALCESTE:
Indeed, in all the world it has no peer;
Words can't describe the nature of my passion,
And no man ever loved in such a fashion.
CÉLIMÈNE:
Yes, it's a brand-new fashion, I agree:
You show your love by castigating me,   80
And all your speeches are enraged and rude.
I've never been so furiously wooed.
ALCESTE:
Yet you could calm that fury, if you chose.
Come, shall we bring our quarrels to a close?
Let's speak with open hearts, then, and
      begin . . .   85

SCENE II. [CÉLIMÈNE, ALCESTE, BASQUE.]

CÉLIMÈNE:
What is it?
BASQUE: Acaste is here.
CÉLIMÈNE: Well, send him in.

SCENE III. [CÉLIMÈNE, ALCESTE.]

ALCESTE:
What! Shall we never be alone at all?
You're always ready to receive a call,
And you can't bear, for ten ticks of the clock,

Not to keep open house for all who knock.
CÉLIMÈNE:
5 I couldn't refuse him: he'd be most put out.
ALCESTE:
Surely that's not worth worrying about.
CÉLIMÈNE:
Acaste would never forgive me if he guessed
That I consider him a dreadful pest.
ALCESTE:
If he's a pest, why bother with him then?
CÉLIMÈNE:
10 Heavens! One can't antagonize such men;
Why, they're the chartered gossips of the court,
And have a say in things of every sort.
One must receive them, and be full of charm;
They're no great help, but they can do you
harm,
15 And though your influence be ever so great,
They're hardly the best people to alienate.
ALCESTE:
I see, dear lady, that you could make a case
For putting up with the whole human race;
These friendships that you calculate so
nicely . . .

SCENE IV. [ALCESTE, CÉLIMÈNE, BASQUE.]

BASQUE:
Madam, Clitandre is here as well.
ALCESTE: Precisely.
CÉLIMÈNE:
Where are you going?
ALCESTE: Elsewhere.
CÉLIMÈNE: Stay.
ALCESTE: No, no.
CÉLIMÈNE:
Stay, Sir.
ALCESTE:
        I can't.
CÉLIMÈNE: I wish it.
ALCESTE: No, I must go.
I beg you, Madam, not to press the matter;
5 You know I have no taste for idle chatter.
CÉLIMÈNE:
Stay. I command you.
ALCESTE: No, I cannot stay.
CÉLIMÈNE:
Very well; you have my leave to go away.

SCENE V. [ÉLIANTE, PHILINTE, ACASTE,
CLITANDRE, ALCESTE, CÉLIMÈNE, BASQUE.]

ÉLIANTE (to CÉLIMÈNE):
The Marquesses have kindly come to call.
Were they announced?

CÉLIMÈNE:
                Yes. Basque, bring chairs for all.
(BASQUE provides the chairs, and exits.)
(To ALCESTE.) You haven't gone?
ALCESTE: No; and I shan't depart
Till you decide who's foremost in your heart.
CÉLIMÈNE:
Oh, hush.
ALCESTE:
        It's time to choose; take them, or me. 5
CÉLIMÈNE:
You're mad.
ALCESTE:
            I'm not, as you shall shortly see.
CÉLIMÈNE:
Oh?
ALCESTE:
    You'll decide.
CÉLIMÈNE: You're joking now, dear friend.
ALCESTE:
No, no; you'll choose; my patience is at an
end.
CLITANDRE:
Madam, I come from court, where poor
Cléonte
Behaved like a perfect fool, as is his wont. 10
Has he no friend to counsel him, I wonder,
And teach him less unerringly to blunder?
CÉLIMÈNE:
It's true, the man's a most accomplished
dunce;
His gauche behavior charms the eye at once;
And every time one sees him, on my word, 15
His manner's grown a trifle more absurd.
ACASTE:
Speaking of dunces, I've just now conversed
With old Damon, who's one of the very worst;
I stood a lifetime in the broiling sun
Before his dreary monologue was done. 20
CÉLIMÈNE:
Oh, he's a wondrous talker, and has the power
To tell you nothing hour after hour:
If, by mistake, he ever came to the point,
The shock would put his jawbone out of
joint.
ÉLIANTE (to PHILINTE):
The conversation takes its usual turn, 25
And all our dear friends' ears will shortly burn.
CLITANDRE:
Timante's a character, Madam.
CÉLIMÈNE: Isn't he, though?
A man of mystery from top to toe,
Who moves about in a romantic mist
On secret missions which do not exist. 30

His talk is full of eyebrows and grimaces;
How tired one gets of his momentous faces;
He's always whispering something confidential
Which turns out to be quite inconsequential;
35 Nothing's too slight for him to mystify;
He even whispers when he says "good-by."
    ACASTE:
Tell us about Géralde.
    CÉLIMÈNE: That tiresome ass.
He mixes only with the titled class,
And fawns on dukes and princes, and is bored
40 With anyone who's not at least a lord.
The man's obsessed with rank, and his dis-
    courses
Are all of hounds and carriages and horses;
He uses Christian names with all the great,
And the word Milord, with him, is out of date.
    CLITANDRE:
45 He's very taken with Bélise, I hear.
    CÉLIMÈNE:
She is the dreariest company, poor dear.
Whenever she comes to call, I grope about
To find some topic which will draw her out,
But, owing to her dry and faint replies,
50 The conversation wilts, and droops, and dies.
In vain one hopes to animate her face
By mentioning the ultimate commonplace;
But sun or shower, even hail or frost
Are matters she can instantly exhaust.
55 Meanwhile her visit, painful though it is,
Drags on and on through mute eternities,
And though you ask the time, and yawn, and
    yawn,
She sits there like a stone and won't be gone.
    ACASTE:
Now for Adraste.
    CÉLIMÈNE: Oh, that conceited elf
60 Has a gigantic passion for himself;
He rails against the court, and cannot bear it
That none will recognize his hidden merit;
All honors given to others give offense
To his imaginary excellence.
    CLITANDRE:
65 What about young Cléon? His house, they say,
Is full of the best society, night and day.
    CÉLIMÈNE:
His cook has made him popular, not he:
It's Cléon's table that people come to see.
    ÉLIANTE:
He gives a splendid dinner, you must admit.
    CÉLIMÈNE:
70 But must he serve himself along with it?
For my taste, he's a most insipid dish
Whose presence sours the wine and spoils the
    fish.

    PHILINTE:
Damis, his uncle, is admired no end.
What's your opinion, Madam?
    CÉLIMÈNE: Why, he's my friend.
    PHILINTE:
He seems a decent fellow, and rather clever.   75
    CÉLIMÈNE:
He works too hard at cleverness, however.
I hate to see him sweat and struggle so
To fill his conversation with bons mots.
Since he's decided to become a wit
His taste's so pure that nothing pleases it;   80
He scolds at all the latest books and plays,
Thinking that wit must never stoop to praise,
That finding fault's a sign of intellect,
That all appreciation is abject,
And that by damning everything in sight   85
One shows oneself in a distinguished light.
He's scornful even of our conversations:
Their trivial nature sorely tries his patience;
He folds his arms, and stands above the battle,
And listens sadly to our childish prattle.   90
    ACASTE:
Wonderful, Madam! You've hit him off pre-
    cisely.
    CLITANDRE:
No one can sketch a character so nicely.
    ALCESTE:
How bravely, Sirs, you cut and thrust at all
These absent fools, till one by one they fall:
But let one come in sight, and you'll at once   95
Embrace the man you lately called a dunce,
Telling him in a tone sincere and fervent
How proud you are to be his humble servant.
    CLITANDRE:
Why pick on us? Madame's been speaking,
    Sir.
And you should quarrel, if you must, with her. 100
    ALCESTE:
No, no, by God, the fault is yours, because
You lead her on with laughter and applause,
And make her think that she's the more de-
    lightful
The more her talk is scandalous and spiteful.
Oh, she would stoop to malice far, far less   105
If no such claque approved her cleverness.
It's flatterers like you whose foolish praise
Nourishes all the vices of these days.
    PHILINTE:
But why protest when someone ridicules
Those you'd condemn, yourself, as knaves or
    fools?   110
    CÉLIMÈNE:
Why, Sir? Because he loves to make a fuss.
You don't expect him to agree with us,

When there's an opportunity to express
His heaven-sent spirit of contrariness?
115 What other people think, he can't abide;
Whatever they say, he's on the other side;
He lives in deadly terror of agreeing;
'Twould make him seem an ordinary being.
Indeed, he's so in love with contradiction,
He'll turn against his most profound convic-
120   tion
And with a furious eloquence deplore it,
If only someone else is speaking for it.
    ALCESTE:
Go on, dear lady, mock me as you please;
You have your audience in ecstasies.
    PHILINTE:
125 But what she says is true: you have a way
Of bridling at whatever people say;
Whether they praise or blame, your angry
      spirit
Is equally unsatisfied to hear it.
    ALCESTE:
Men, Sir, are always wrong, and that's the
      reason
130 That righteous anger's never out of season;
All that I hear in all their conversation
Is flattering praise or reckless condemnation.
    CÉLIMÈNE:
But . . .
    ALCESTE:
            No, no, Madam, I am forced to state
That you have pleasures which I deprecate,
And that these others, here, are much to
135   blame
For nourishing the faults which are your
      shame.
    CLITANDRE:
I shan't defend myself, Sir; but I vow
I'd thought this lady faultless until now.
    ACASTE:
I see her charms and graces, which are many;
140 But as for faults, I've never noticed any.
    ALCESTE:
I see them, Sir; and rather than ignore them,
I strenuously criticize her for them.
The more one loves, the more one should
      object
To every blemish, every least defect.
145 Were I this lady, I would soon get rid
Of lovers who approved of all I did,
And by their slack indulgence and applause
Endorsed my follies and excused my flaws.
    CÉLIMÈNE:
If all hearts beat according to your measure,
The dawn of love would be the end of plea-
150   sure;

And love would find its perfect consummation
In ecstasies of rage and reprobation.
    ÉLIANTE:
Love, as a rule, affects men otherwise,
And lovers rarely love to criticize.
They see their lady as a charming blur,   155
And find all things commendable in her.
If she has any blemish, fault, or shame,
They will redeem it by a pleasing name.
The pale-faced lady's lily-white, perforce;
The swarthy one's a sweet brunette, of course; 160
The spindly lady has a slender grace;
The fat one has a most majestic pace;
The plain one, with her dress in disarray,
They classify as *beauté négligée*;
The hulking one's a goddess in their eyes,   165
The dwarf, a concentrate of Paradise;
The haughty lady has a noble mind;
The mean one's witty, and the dull one's
      kind;
The chatterbox has liveliness and verve,
The mute one has a virtuous reserve.   170
So lovers manage, in their passion's cause,
To love their ladies even for their flaws.
    ALCESTE:
But I still say . . .
    CÉLIMÈNE: I think it would be nice
To stroll around the gallery once or twice.
What! You're not going, Sirs?
    CLITANDRE *and* ACASTE: No, Madam, no. 175
    ALCESTE:
You seem to be in terror lest they go.
Do what you will, Sirs; leave, or linger on,
But I shan't go till after you are gone.
    ACASTE:
I'm free to linger, unless I should perceive
Madame is tired, and wishes me to leave.   180
    CLITANDRE:
And as for me, I needn't go today
Until the hour of the King's *coucher*.
    CÉLIMÈNE (*to* ALCESTE):
You're joking, surely?
    ALCESTE: Not in the least; we'll see
Whether you'd rather part with them, or me.

    SCENE VI. [ALCESTE, CÉLIMÈNE, ÉLIANTE,
    ACASTE, PHILINTE, CLITANDRE, BASQUE.]

    BASQUE (*to* ALCESTE):
Sir, there's a fellow here who bids me state
That he must see you, and that it can't wait.
    ALCESTE:
Tell him that I have no such pressing affairs.

BASQUE:
It's a long tailcoat that this fellow wears,
With gold all over.
CÉLIMÈNE (*to* ALCESTE):
                You'd best go down and see.
Or — have him enter.

SCENE VII. [ALCESTE, CÉLIMÈNE, ÉLIANTE,
ACASTE, PHILINTE, CLITANDRE, GUARD.]

ALCESTE (*confronting the* GUARD):
             Well, what do you want with me?
Come in, Sir.
GUARD: I've a word, Sir, for your ear.
ALCESTE:
Speak it aloud, Sir; I shall strive to hear.
GUARD:
The Marshals have instructed me to say
You must report to them without delay.
ALCESTE:
Who? Me, Sir?
GUARD: Yes, Sir; you.
ALCESTE: But what do they want?
PHILINTE (*to* ALCESTE):
To scotch your silly quarrel with Oronte.
CÉLIMÈNE (*to* PHILINTE):
What quarrel?
PHILINTE: Oronte and he have fallen out
Over some verse he spoke his mind about;
The Marshals wish to arbitrate the matter.
ALCESTE:
Never shall I equivocate or flatter!
PHILINTE:
You'd best obey their summons; come, let's go.
ALCESTE:
How can they mend our quarrel, I'd like to
    know?
Am I to make a cowardly retraction,
And praise those jingles to his satisfaction?
I'll not recant; I've judged that sonnet rightly.
It's bad.
PHILINTE:
        But you might say so more politely. . . .
ALCESTE:
I'll not back down; his verses make me sick.
PHILINTE:
If only you could be more politic!
But come, let's go.
ALCESTE: I'll go, but I won't unsay
A single word.
PHILINTE: Well, let's be on our way.
ALCESTE:
Till I am ordered by my lord the King
To praise that poem, I shall say the thing

Is scandalous, by God, and that the poet
Ought to be hanged for having the nerve to
    show it.

(*To* CLITANDRE *and* ACASTE, *who are laughing.*)

By heaven, Sirs, I really didn't know
That I was being humorous.
CÉLIMÈNE: Go, Sir, go;
Settle your business.
ALCESTE: I shall, and when I'm through,
I shall return to settle things with you.

ACT III

SCENE I. [CLITANDRE, ACASTE.]

CLITANDRE:
Dear Marquess, how contented you appear;
All things delight you, nothing mars your
    cheer.
Can you, in perfect honesty, declare
That you've a right to be so debonair?
ACASTE:
By Jove, when I survey myself, I find
No cause whatever for distress of mind.
I'm young and rich; I can in modesty
Lay claim to an exalted pedigree;
And owing to my name and my condition
I shall not want for honors and position.
Then as to courage, that most precious trait,
I seem to have it, as was proved of late
Upon the field of honor, where my bearing,
They say, was very cool and rather daring.
I've wit, of course; and taste in such perfection
That I can judge without the least reflection,
And at the theater, which is my delight,
Can make or break a play on opening night,
And lead the crowd in hisses or bravos,
And generally be known as one who knows.
I'm clever, handsome, gracefully polite;
My waist is small, my teeth are strong and
    white;
As for my dress, the world's astonished eyes
Assure me that I bear away the prize.
I find myself in favor everywhere,
Honored by men, and worshiped by the fair;
And since these things are so, it seems to me
I'm justified in my complacency.
CLITANDRE:
Well, if so many ladies hold you dear,
Why do you press a hopeless courtship here?

ACASTE:
Hopeless, you say? I'm not the sort of fool
That likes his ladies difficult and cool.
Men who are awkward, shy, and peasantish
May pine for heartless beauties, if they wish,
35   Grovel before them, bear their cruelties,
Woo them with tears and sighs and bended
   knees,
And hope by dogged faithfulness to gain
What their poor merits never could obtain.
For men like me, however, it makes no sense
40   To love on trust, and foot the whole expense.
Whatever any lady's merits be,
I think, thank God, that I'm as choice as she;
That if my heart is kind enough to burn
For her, she owes me something in return;
45   And that in any proper love affair
The partners must invest an equal share.
      CLITANDRE:
You think, then, that our hostess favors you?
      ACASTE:
I've reason to believe that that is true.
      CLITANDRE:
How did you come to such a mad conclusion?
You're blind, dear fellow. This is sheer delu-
50   sion.
      ACASTE:
All right, then: I'm deluded and I'm blind.
      CLITANDRE:
Whatever put the notion in your mind?
      ACASTE:
Delusion.
      CLITANDRE:
            What persuades you that you're right?
      ACASTE:
I'm blind.
      CLITANDRE:
            But have you any proofs to cite?
      ACASTE:
I tell you I'm deluded.
55   CLITANDRE: Have you, then,
Received some secret pledge from Célimène?
      ACASTE:
Oh, no: she scorns me.
      CLITANDRE: Tell me the truth, I beg.
      ACASTE:
She just can't bear me.
      CLITANDRE: Ah, don't pull my leg.
Tell me what hope she's given you, I pray.
      ACASTE:
60   I'm hopeless, and it's you who win the day.
She hates me thoroughly, and I'm so vexed
I mean to hang myself on Tuesday next.

CLITANDRE:
Dear Marquess, let us have an armistice
And make a treaty. What do you say to this?
If ever one of us can plainly prove   65
That Célimène encourages his love,
The other must abandon hope, and yield,
And leave him in possession of the field.
      ACASTE:
Now, there's a bargain that appeals to me;
With all my heart, dear Marquess, I agree.   70
But hush.

SCENE II. [CÉLIMÈNE, ACASTE, CLITANDRE.]

CÉLIMÈNE:
      Still here?
CLITANDRE: 'Twas love that stayed our feet.
CÉLIMÈNE:
I think I heard a carriage in the street.
Whose is it? D'you know?

SCENE III. [CÉLIMÈNE, ACASTE, CLITANDRE,
            BASQUE.]

BASQUE: Arsinoé is here,
Madame.
CÉLIMÈNE:
      Arsinoé, you say? Oh, dear.
BASQUE:
Éliante is entertaining her below.
CÉLIMÈNE:
What brings the creature here, I'd like to
   know?
      ACASTE:
They say she's dreadfully prudish, but in fact   5
I think her piety . . .
      CÉLIMÈNE: It's all an act.
At heart she's worldly, and her poor success
In snaring men explains her prudishness.
It breaks her heart to see the beaux and
   gallants
Engrossed by other women's charms and tal-
   ents,   10
And so she's always in a jealous rage
Against the faulty standards of the age.
She lets the world believe that she's a prude
To justify her loveless solitude,
And strives to put a brand of moral shame   15
On all the graces that she cannot claim.
But still she'd love a lover; and Alceste
Appears to be the one she'd love the best.

His visits here are poison to her pride;
She seems to think I've lured him from her
20   side;
And everywhere, at court or in the town,
The spiteful, envious woman runs me down.
In short, she's just as stupid as can be,
Vicious and arrogant in the last degree,
25   And . . .

SCENE IV. [ARSINOÉ, CÉLIMÈNE, CLITANDRE,
ACASTE.]

CÉLIMÈNE:
     Ah! What happy chance has brought
you here?
I've thought about you ever so much, my dear.
ARSINOÉ:
I've come to tell you something you should
     know.
CÉLIMÈNE:
How good of you to think of doing so!

(CLITANDRE *and* ACASTE *go out, laughing.*)

SCENE V. [ARSINOÉ, CÉLIMÈNE.]

ARSINOÉ:
It's just as well those gentlemen didn't tarry.
CÉLIMÈNE:
Shall we sit down?
ARSINOÉ   That won't be necessary.
Madam, the flame of friendship ought to burn
Brightest in matters of the most concern;
And as there's nothing which concerns us
5   more
Than honor, I have hastened to your door
To bring you, as your friend, some informa-
     tion
About the status of your reputation.
I visited, last night, some virtuous folk,
And, quite by chance, it was of you they
10   spoke;
There was, I fear, no tendency to praise
Your light behavior and your dashing ways.
The quantity of gentlemen you see
And your by now notorious coquetry
15   Were both so vehemently criticized
By everyone, that I was much surprised.
Of course, I needn't tell you where I stood;
I came to your defense as best I could,
Assured them you were harmless, and declared
20   Your soul was absolutely unimpaired.

But there are some things, you must realize,
One can't excuse, however hard one tries,
And I was forced at last into conceding
That your behavior, Madam, is misleading,
That it makes a bad impression, giving rise   25
To ugly gossip and obscene surmise,
And that if you were more *overtly* good,
You wouldn't be so much misunderstood.
Not that I think you've been unchaste — no!
     no!
The saints preserve me from a thought so low!   30
But mere good conscience never did suffice:
One must avoid the outward show of vice.
Madam, you're too intelligent, I'm sure,
To think my motives anything but pure
In offering you this counsel — which I do   35
Out of a zealous interest in you.
CÉLIMÈNE:
Madam, I haven't taken you amiss;
I'm very much obliged to you for this;
And I'll at once discharge the obligation
By telling you about *your* reputation.   40
You've been so friendly as to let me know
What certain people say of me, and so
I mean to follow your benign example
By offering you a somewhat similar sample.
The other day, I went to an affair   45
And found some most distinguished people
     there
Discussing piety, both false and true.
The conversation soon came round to you.
Alas! Your prudery and bustling zeal
Appeared to have a very slight appeal.   50
Your affectation of a grave demeanor,
Your endless talk of virtue and of honor,
The aptitude of your suspicious mind
For finding sin where there is none to find,
Your towering self-esteem, that pitying face   55
With which you contemplate the human race,
Your sermonizings and your sharp aspersions
On people's pure and innocent diversions —
All these were mentioned, Madam, and, in fact,
Were roundly and concertedly attacked.   60
"What good," they said, "are all these outward
     shows,
When everything belies her pious pose?
She prays incessantly; but then, they say,
She beats her maids and cheats them of their
     pay;
She shows her zeal in every holy place,   65
But still she's vain enough to paint her face;
She holds that naked statues are immoral,
But with a naked *man* she'd have no quarrel."

Of course, I said to everybody there
70 That they were being viciously unfair;
But still they were disposed to criticize you,
And all agreed that someone should advise you
To leave the morals of the world alone,
And worry rather more about your own.
They felt that one's self-knowledge should be
75   great
Before one thinks of setting others straight;
That one should learn the art of living well
Before one threatens other men with hell,
And that the Church is best equipped, no
       doubt,
80 To guide our souls and root our vices out.
Madam, you're too intelligent, I'm sure,
To think my motives anything but pure
In offering you this counsel — which I do
Out of a zealous interest in you.
       ARSINOÉ:
85 I dared not hope for gratitude, but I
Did not expect so acid a reply;
I judge, since you've been so extremely tart,
That my good counsel pierced you to the
       heart.
       CÉLIMÈNE:
Far from it, Madam. Indeed, it seems to me
90 We ought to trade advice more frequently.
One's vision of oneself is so defective
That it would be an excellent corrective.
If you are willing, Madam, let's arrange
Shortly to have another frank exchange
95 In which we'll tell each other, *entre nous*,
What you've heard tell of me, and I of you.
       ARSINOÉ:
Oh, people never censure you, my dear;
It's me they criticize. Or so I hear.
       CÉLIMÈNE:
Madam, I think we either blame or praise
100 According to our taste and length of days.
There is a time of life for coquetry,
And there's a season, too, for prudery.
When all one's charms are gone, it is, I'm
       sure,
Good strategy to be devout and pure:
105 It makes one seem a little less forsaken.
Some day, perhaps, I'll take the road you've
       taken:
Time brings all things. But I have time
       aplenty,
And see no cause to be a prude at twenty.
       ARSINOÉ:
You give your age in such a gloating tone
110 That one would think I was an ancient crone;
We're not so far apart, in sober truth,

That you can mock me with a boast of youth!
Madam, you baffle me. I wish I knew
What moves you to provoke me as you do.
       CÉLIMÈNE:
For my part, Madam, I should like to know   115
Why you abuse me everywhere you go.
Is it my fault, dear lady, that your hand
Is not, alas, in very great demand?
If men admire me, if they pay me court
And daily make me offers of the sort   120
You'd dearly love to have them make to you,
How can I help it? What would you have me
       do?
If what you want is lovers, please feel free
To take as many as you can from me.
       ARSINOÉ:
Oh, come. D'you think the world is losing
       sleep   125
Over the flock of lovers which you keep,
Or that we find it difficult to guess
What price you pay for their devotedness?
Surely you don't expect us to suppose
Mere merit could attract so many beaux?   130
It's not your virtue that they're dazzled by;
Nor is it virtuous love for which they sigh.
You're fooling no one, Madam; the world's not
       blind;
There's many a lady heaven has designed
To call men's noblest, tenderest feelings out, 135
Who has no lovers dogging her about;
From which it's plain that lovers nowadays
Must be acquired in bold and shameless ways,
And only pay one court for such reward
As modesty and virtue can't afford.   140
Then don't be quite so puffed up, if you
       please,
About your tawdry little victories;
Try, if you can, to be a shade less vain,
And treat the world with somewhat less dis-
       dain.
If one were envious of your amours,   145
One soon could have a following like yours;
Lovers are no great trouble to collect
If one prefers them to one's self-respect.
       CÉLIMÈNE:
Collect them then, my dear; I'd love to see
You demonstrate that charming theory;   150
Who knows, you might . . .
       ARSINOÉ: Now, Madam, that will do;
It's time to end this trying interview.
My coach is late in coming to your door,
Or I'd have taken leave of you before.
       CÉLIMÈNE:
Oh, please don't feel that you must rush away; 155

I'd be delighted, Madam, if you'd stay.
However, lest my conversation bore you,
Let me provide some better company for you;
This gentleman, who comes most apropos,
160 Will please you more than I could do, I know.

SCENE VI. [ALCESTE, CÉLIMÈNE, ARSINOÉ.]

CÉLIMÈNE:

Alceste, I have a little note to write
Which simply must go out before tonight;
Please entertain *Madame*; I'm sure that she
Will overlook my incivility.

SCENE VII. [ALCESTE, ARSINOÉ.]

ARSINOÉ:

Well, Sir, our hostess graciously contrives
For us to chat until my coach arrives;
And I shall be forever in her debt
For granting me this little tête-à-tête.
5 We women very rightly give our hearts
To men of noble character and parts,
And your especial merits, dear Alceste,
Have roused the deepest sympathy in my
     breast.
Oh, how I wish they had sufficient sense
10 At court, to recognize your excellence!
They wrong you greatly, Sir. How it must hurt
     you
Never to be rewarded for your virtue!

ALCESTE:

Why, Madam, what cause have I to feel
     aggrieved?
What great and brilliant thing have I
     achieved?
15 What service have I rendered to the King
That I should look to him for anything?

ARSINOÉ:

Not everyone who's honored by the State
Has done great services. A man must wait
Till time and fortune offer him the chance.
20 Your merit, Sir, is obvious at a glance,
And . . .

ALCESTE:

          Ah, forget my merit; I am not neglected.
The court, I think, can hardly be expected
To mine men's souls for merit, and unearth
Our hidden virtues and our secret worth.

ARSINOÉ:

Some virtues, though, are far too bright to
25   hide;
Yours are acknowledged, Sir, on every side.

Indeed, I've heard you warmly praised of late
By persons of considerable weight.

ALCESTE:

This fawning age has praise for everyone,
And all distinctions, Madam, are undone.   30
All things have equal honor nowadays,
And no one should be gratified by praise.
To be admired, one only need exist,
And every lackey's on the honors list.

ARSINOÉ:

I only wish, Sir, that you had your eye   35
On some position at court, however high;
You'd only have to hint at such a notion
For me to set the proper wheels in motion;
I've certain friendships I'd be glad to use
To get you any office you might choose.   40

ALCESTE:

Madam, I fear that any such ambition
Is wholly foreign to my disposition.
The soul God gave me isn't of the sort
That prospers in the weather of a court.
It's all too obvious that I don't possess   45
The virtues necessary for success.
My one great talent is for speaking plain;
I've never learned to flatter or to feign;
And anyone so stupidly sincere
Had best not seek a courtier's career.   50
Outside the court, I know, one must dispense
With honors, privilege, and influence;
But still one gains the right, foregoing these,
Not to be tortured by the wish to please.
One needn't live in dread of snubs and slights, 55
Nor praise the verse that every idiot writes,
Nor humor silly Marquesses, nor bestow
Politic sighs on Madam So-and-So.

ARSINOÉ:

Forget the court, then; let the matter rest.
But I've another cause to be distressed   60
About your present situation, Sir.
It's to your love affair that I refer.
She whom you love, and who pretends to love
     you,
Is, I regret to say, unworthy of you.

ALCESTE:

Why, Madam? Can you seriously intend   65
To make so grave a charge against your friend?

ARSINOÉ:

Alas, I must. I've stood aside too long
And let that lady do you grievous wrong;
But now my debt to conscience shall be paid:
I tell you that your love has been betrayed.   70

ALCESTE:

I thank you, Madam; you're extremely kind.
Such words are soothing to a lover's mind.

ARSINOÉ:

Yes, though she *is* my friend, I say again
You're very much too good for Célimène.
75 She's wantonly misled you from the start.

ALCESTE:

You may be right; who knows another's heart?
But ask yourself if it's the part of charity
To shake my soul with doubts of her sincerity.

ARSINOÉ:

Well, if you'd rather be a dupe than doubt
her,
80 That's your affair. I'll say no more about her.

ALCESTE:

Madam, you know that doubt and vague
suspicion
Are painful to a man in my position;
It's most unkind to worry me this way
Unless you've some real proof of what you say.

ARSINOÉ:

85 Sir, say no more: all doubts shall be removed,
And all that I've been saying shall be proved.
You've only to escort me home, and there
We'll look into the heart of this affair.
I've ocular evidence which will persuade you
Beyond a doubt, that Célimène's betrayed
90 you.
Then, if you're saddened by that revelation,
Perhaps I can provide some consolation.

ACT IV

Scene i. [ÉLIANTE, PHILINTE.]

PHILINTE:

Madam, he acted like a stubborn child;
I thought they never would be reconciled;
In vain we reasoned, threatened, and appealed;
He stood his ground and simply would not
yield.
5 The Marshals, I feel sure, have never heard
An argument so splendidly absurd.
"No, gentlemen," said he, "I'll not retract.
His verse is bad: extremely bad, in fact.
Surely it does the man no harm to know it.
10 Does it disgrace him, not to be a poet?
A gentleman may be respected still,
Whether he writes a sonnet well or ill.
That I dislike his verse should not offend him;
In all that touches honor, I commend him;
15 He's noble, brave, and virtuous — but I fear
He can't in truth be called a sonneteer.

I'll gladly praise his wardrobe; I'll endorse
His dancing, or the way he sits a horse;
But, gentlemen, I cannot praise his rhyme.
In fact, it ought to be a capital crime 20
For anyone so sadly unendowed
To write a sonnet, and read the thing aloud."
At length he fell into a gentler mood
And, striking a concessive attitude,
He paid Oronte the following courtesies: 25
"Sir, I regret that I'm so hard to please,
And I'm profoundly sorry that your lyric
Failed to provoke me to a panegyric."
After these curious words, the two embraced,
And then the hearing was adjourned — in
haste. 30

ÉLIANTE:

His conduct has been very singular lately;
Still, I confess that I respect him greatly.
The honesty in which he takes such pride
Has — to my mind — it's noble, heroic side.
In this false age, such candor seems outra-
geous; 35
But I could wish that it were more contagious.

PHILINTE:

What most intrigues me in our friend Alceste
Is the grand passion that rages in his breast.
The sullen humors he's compounded of
Should not, I think, dispose his heart to love; 40
But since they do, it puzzles me still more
That he should choose your cousin to adore.

ÉLIANTE:

It does, indeed, belie the theory
That love is born of gentle sympathy,
And that the tender passion must be based 45
On sweet accords of temper and of taste.

PHILINTE:

Does she return his love, do you suppose?

ÉLIANTE:

Ah, that's a difficult question, Sir. Who knows?
How can we judge the truth of her devotion?
Her heart's a stranger to its own emotion. 50
Sometimes it thinks it loves, when no love's
there;
At other times it loves quite unaware.

PHILINTE:

I rather think Alceste is in for more
Distress and sorrow than he's bargained for;
Were he of my mind, Madam, his affection 55
Would turn in quite a different direction,
And we would see him more responsive to
The kind regard which he receives from you.

ÉLIANTE:

Sir, I believe in frankness, and I'm inclined,

60 In matters of the heart, to speak my mind.
I don't oppose his love for her; indeed,
I hope with all my heart that he'll succeed,
And were it in my power, I'd rejoice
In giving him the lady of his choice.
65 But if, as happens frequently enough
In love affairs, he meets with a rebuff —
If Célimène should grant some rival's suit —
I'd gladly play the role of substitute;
Nor would his tender speeches please me less
Because they'd once been made without suc-
70   cess.

PHILINTE:
Well, Madam, as for me, I don't oppose
Your hopes in this affair; and heaven knows
That in my conversations with the man
I plead your cause as often as I can.
75 But if those two should marry, and so remove
All chance that he will offer you his love,
Then I'll declare my own, and hope to see
Your gracious favor pass from him to me.
In short, should you be cheated of Alceste,
80 I'd be most happy to be second best.

ÉLIANTE:
Philinte, you're teasing.

PHILINTE: Ah, Madam, never fear;
No words of mine were ever so sincere,
And I shall live in fretful expectation
Till I can make a fuller declaration.

SCENE II. [ALCESTE, ÉLIANTE, PHILINTE.]

ALCESTE:
Avenge me, Madam! I must have satisfaction,
Or this great wrong will drive me to distrac-
    tion!

ÉLIANTE:
Why, what's the matter? What's upset you so?

ALCESTE:
Madam, I've had a mortal, mortal blow.
5 If Chaos repossessed the universe,
I swear I'd not be shaken any worse.
I'm ruined....I can say no more....My
    soul ...

ÉLIANTE:
Do try, Sir, to regain your self-control.

ALCESTE:
Just heaven! Why were so much beauty and
    grace
10 Bestowed on one so vicious and so base?

ÉLIANTE:
Once more, Sir, tell us....

ALCESTE: My world has gone to wrack;

I'm — I'm betrayed; she's stabbed me in the
    back:
Yes, Célimène (who would have thought it of
    her?)
Is false to me, and has another lover.

ÉLIANTE:
Are you quite certain? Can you prove these
    things?   15

PHILINTE:
Lovers are prey to wild imaginings
And jealous fancies. No doubt there's some
    mistake....

ALCESTE:
Mind your own business, Sir, for heaven's sake.
(To ÉLIANTE.) Madam, I have the proof that
    you demand
Here in my pocket, penned by her own hand.   20
Yes, all the shameful evidence one could want
Lies in this letter written to Oronte —
Oronte! whom I felt sure she couldn't love,
And hardly bothered to be jealous of.

PHILINTE:
Still, in a letter, appearances may deceive;   25
This may not be so bad as you believe.

ALCESTE:
Once more I beg you, Sir, to let me be;
Tend to your own affairs; leave mine to me.

ÉLIANTE:
Compose yourself; this anguish that you
    feel ...

ALCESTE:
Is something, Madam, you alone can heal.   30
My outraged heart, beside itself with grief,
Appeals to you for comfort and relief.
Avenge me on your cousin, whose unjust
And faithless nature has deceived my trust;
Avenge a crime your pure soul must detest.   35

ÉLIANTE:
But how, Sir?

ALCESTE:
                Madam, this heart within my breast
Is yours; pray take it; redeem my heart from
    her,
And so avenge me on my torturer.
Let her be punished by the fond emotion,
The ardent love, the bottomless devotion,   40
The faithful worship which this heart of mine
Will offer up to yours as to a shrine.

ÉLIANTE:
You have my sympathy, Sir, in all you suffer;
Nor do I scorn the noble heart you offer;
But I suspect you'll soon be mollified,   45
And this desire for vengeance will subside.

When some belovèd hand has done us wrong
We thirst for retribution — but not for long;
However dark the deed that she's committed,
50 A lovely culprit's very soon acquitted.
Nothing's so stormy as an injured lover,
And yet no storm so quickly passes over.
    ALCESTE:
No, Madam, no — this is no lovers' spat;
I'll not forgive her; it's gone too far for that;
55 My mind's made up; I'll kill myself before
I waste my hopes upon her any more.
Ah, here she is. My wrath intensifies.
I shall confront her with her tricks and lies,
And crush her utterly, and bring you then
60 A heart no longer slave to Célimène.

SCENE III. [CÉLIMÈNE, ALCESTE.]

    ALCESTE (*aside*):
Sweet heaven, help me to control my passion.
    CÉLIMÈNE (*aside*):
Oh, Lord. (*To* ALCESTE.) Why stand there
    staring in that fashion?
And what d'you mean by those dramatic sighs,
And that malignant glitter in your eyes?
    ALCESTE:
I mean that sins which cause the blood to
5   freeze
Look innocent beside your treacheries;
That nothing Hell's or Heaven's wrath could
    do
Ever produced so bad a thing as you.
    CÉLIMÈNE:
Your compliments were always sweet and
    pretty.
    ALCESTE:
10 Madam, it's not the moment to be witty.
No, blush and hang your head; you've ample
    reason,
Since I've the fullest evidence of your treason.
Ah, this is what my sad heart prophesied;
Now all my anxious fears are verified;
15 My dark suspicion and my gloomy doubt
Divined the truth, and now the truth is out.
For all your trickery, I was not deceived;
It was my bitter stars that I believed.
But don't imagine that you'll go scot-free;
20 You shan't misuse me with impunity.
I know that love's irrational and blind;
I know the heart's not subject to the mind,
And can't be reasoned into beating faster;
I know each soul is free to choose its master;
25 Therefore had you but spoken from the heart,

Rejecting my attention from the start,
I'd have no grievance, or at any rate
I could complain of nothing but my fate.
Ah, but so falsely to encourage me —
That was a treason and a treachery   30
For which you cannot suffer too severely,
And you shall pay for that behavior dearly.
Yes, now I have no pity, not a shred;
My temper's out of hand; I've lost my head;
Shocked by the knowledge of your double-deal-
    ings,   35
My reason can't restrain my savage feelings;
A righteous wrath deprives me of my senses,
And I won't answer for the consequences.
    CÉLIMÈNE:
What does this outburst mean? Will you
    please explain?
Have you, by any chance, gone quite insane?   40
    ALCESTE:
Yes, yes, I went insane the day I fell
A victim to your black and fatal spell,
Thinking to meet with some sincerity
Among the treacherous charms that beckoned
    me.
    CÉLIMÈNE:
Pooh. Of what treachery can you complain?   45
    ALCESTE:
How sly you are, how cleverly you feign!
But you'll not victimize me any more.
Look: here's a document you've seen before.
This evidence, which I acquired today,
Leaves you, I think, without a thing to say.   50
    CÉLIMÈNE:
Is this what sent you into such a fit?
    ALCESTE:
You should be blushing at the sight of it.
    CÉLIMÈNE:
Ought I to blush? I truly don't see why.
    ALCESTE:
Ah, now you're being bold as well as sly;
Since there's no signature, perhaps you'll
    claim . . .   55
    CÉLIMÈNE:
I wrote it, whether or not it bears my name.
    ALCESTE:
And you can view with equanimity
This proof of your disloyalty to me!
    CÉLIMÈNE:
Oh, don't be so outrageous and extreme.
    ALCESTE:
You take this matter lightly, it would seem.   60
Was it no wrong to me, no shame to you,
That you should send Oronte this billet-doux?

CÉLIMÈNE:
Oronte! Who said it was for him?

ALCESTE: Why, those
Who brought me this example of your prose.
But what's the difference? If you wrote the
65   letter
To someone else, it pleases me no better.
My grievance and your guilt remain the same.

CÉLIMÈNE:
But need you rage, and need I blush for
     shame,
If this was written to a *woman* friend?

ALCESTE:
70 Ah! Most ingenious. I'm impressed no end;
And after that incredible evasion
Your guilt is clear. I need no more persuasion.
How dare you try so clumsy a deception?
D'you think I'm wholly wanting in perception?
75 Come, come, let's see how brazenly you'll try
To bolster up so palpable a lie:
Kindly construe this ardent closing section
As nothing more than sisterly affection!
Here, let me read it. Tell me, if you dare to,
That this is for a woman . . .

CÉLIMÈNE: I don't care to.
80 What right have you to badger and berate me,
And so highhandedly interrogate me?

ALCESTE:
Now, don't be angry; all I ask of you
Is that you justify a phrase or two . . .

CÉLIMÈNE:
85 No, I shall not. I utterly refuse,
And you may take those phrases as you choose.

ALCESTE:
Just show me how this letter could be meant
For a woman's eyes, and I shall be content.

CÉLIMÈNE:
No, no, it's for Oronte; you're perfectly right.
90 I welcome his attentions with delight,
I prize his character and his intellect,
And everything is just as you suspect.
Come, do your worst now; give your rage free
     rein;
But kindly cease to bicker and complain.

ALCESTE (*aside*):
95 Good God! Could anything be more inhuman?
Was ever a heart so mangled by a woman?
When I complain of how she has betrayed me,
She bridles, and commences to upbraid me!
She tries my tortured patience to the limit;
100 She won't deny her guilt; she glories in it!
And yet my heart's too faint and cowardly
To break these chains of passion, and be free,

To scorn her as it should, and rise above
This unrewarded, mad, and bitter love.
(*To* CÉLIMÈNE.) Ah, traitress, in how confident
     a fashion   105
You take advantage of my helpless passion,
And use my weakness for your faithless charms
To make me once again throw down my arms!
But do at least deny this black transgression;
Take back that mocking and perverse confes-
     sion;   110
Defend this letter and your innocence,
And I, poor fool, will aid in your defense.
Pretend, pretend, that you are just and true,
And I shall make myself believe in you.

CÉLIMÈNE:
Oh, stop it. Don't be such a jealous dunce,   115
Or I shall leave off loving you at once.
Just why should I *pretend*? What could impel
     me
To stoop so low as that? And kindly tell me
Why, if I loved another, I shouldn't merely
Inform you of it, simply and sincerely!   120
I've told you where you stand, and that admis-
     sion
Should altogether clear me of suspicion;
After so generous a guarantee,
What right have you to harbor doubts of me?
Since women are (from natural reticence)   125
Reluctant to declare their sentiments,
And since the honor of our sex requires
That we conceal our amorous desires,
Ought any man for whom such laws are
     broken
To question what the oracle has spoken?   130
Should he not rather feel an obligation
To trust that most obliging declaration?
Enough, now. Your suspicions quite disgust
     me;
Why should I love a man who doesn't trust
     me?
I cannot understand why I continue,   135
Fool that I am, to take an interest in you.
I ought to choose a man less prone to doubt,
And give you something to be vexed about.

ALCESTE:
Ah, what a poor enchanted fool I am;
These gentle words, no doubt, were all a sham,   140
But destiny requires me to entrust
My happiness to you, and so I must.
I'll love you to the bitter end, and see
How false and treacherous you dare to be.

CÉLIMÈNE:
No, you don't really love me as you ought.   145

ALCESTE:
I love you more than can be said or thought;
Indeed, I wish you were in such distress
That I might show my deep devotedness.
Yes, I could wish that you were wretchedly
    poor,
150 Unloved, uncherished, utterly obscure;
That fate had set you down upon the earth
Without possessions, rank, or gentle birth;
Then, by the offer of my heart, I might
Repair the great injustice of your plight;
155 I'd raise you from the dust, and proudly prove
The purity and vastness of my love.
    CÉLIMÈNE:
This is a strange benevolence indeed!
God grant that I may never be in need. . . .
Ah, here's Monsieur Dubois, in quaint dis-
    guise.

SCENE IV. [CÉLIMÈNE, ALCESTE, DUBOIS.]

ALCESTE:
Well, why this costume? Why those fright-
    ened eyes?
What ails you?
    DUBOIS:
            Well, Sir, things are most mysterious.
    ALCESTE:
What do you mean?
    DUBOIS: I fear they're very serious.
    ALCESTE:
What?
    DUBOIS:
        Shall I speak more loudly?
    ALCESTE: Yes; speak out.
    DUBOIS:
Isn't there someone here, Sir?
5   ALCESTE: Speak, you lout!
Stop wasting time.
    DUBOIS: Sir, we must slip away.
    ALCESTE:
How's that?
    DUBOIS: We must decamp without delay.
    ALCESTE:
Explain yourself.
    DUBOIS: I tell you we must fly.
    ALCESTE:
What for?
    DUBOIS:
            We mustn't pause to say good-by.
    ALCESTE:
Now what d'you mean by all of this, you
10   clown?

DUBOIS:
I mean, Sir, that we've got to leave this town.
    ALCESTE:
I'll tear you limb from limb and joint from
    joint
If you don't come more quickly to the point.
    DUBOIS:
Well, Sir, today a man in a black suit,
Who wore a black and ugly scowl to boot,   15
Left us a document scrawled in such a hand
As even Satan couldn't understand.
It bears upon your lawsuit, I don't doubt;
But all hell's devils couldn't make it out.
    ALCESTE:
Well, well, go on. What then? I fail to see   20
How this event obliges us to flee.
    DUBOIS:
Well, Sir, an hour later, hardly more,
A gentleman who's often called before
Came looking for you in an anxious way.
Not finding you, he asked me to convey   25
(Knowing I could be trusted with the same)
The following message. . . . Now, what was his
    name?
    ALCESTE:
Forget his name, you idiot. What did he say?
    DUBOIS:
Well, it was one of your friends, Sir, anyway.
He warned you to begone, and he suggested   30
That if you stay, you may well be arrested.
    ALCESTE:
What? Nothing more specific? Think, man,
    think!
    DUBOIS:
No, Sir. He had me bring him pen and ink,
And dashed you off a letter which, I'm sure,
Will render things distinctly less obscure.   35
    ALCESTE:
Well — let me have it!
    CÉLIMÈNE: What is this all about?
    ALCESTE:
God knows; but I have hopes of finding out.
How long am I to wait, you blitherer?
    DUBOIS (after a protracted search for the
        letter):
I must have left it on your table, Sir.
    ALCESTE:
I ought to . . .
    CÉLIMÈNE:
            No, no, keep your self-control;   40
Go find out what's behind his rigmarole.
    ALCESTE:
It seems that fate, no matter what I do,

Has sworn that I may not converse with you;
But, Madam, pray permit your faithful lover
45 To try once more before the day is over.

ACT V

SCENE I. [ALCESTE, PHILINTE.]

ALCESTE:
No, it's too much. My mind's made up, I tell
    you.
PHILINTE:
Why should this blow, however hard, compel
    you . . .
ALCESTE:
No, no, don't waste your breath in argument;
Nothing you say will alter my intent;
5 This age is vile, and I've made up my mind
To have no further commerce with mankind.
Did not truth, honor, decency, and the laws
Oppose my enemy and approve my cause?
My claims were justified in all men's sight;
10 I put my trust in equity and right;
Yet, to my horror and the world's disgrace,
Justice is mocked, and I have lost my case!
A scoundrel whose dishonesty is notorious
Emerges from another lie victorious!
15 Honor and right condone his brazen fraud,
While rectitude and decency applaud!
Before his smirking face, the truth stands
    charmed,
And virtue conquered, and the law disarmed!
His crime is sanctioned by a court decree!
20 And not content with what he's done to me,
The dog now seeks to ruin me by stating
That I composed a book now circulating,
A book so wholly criminal and vicious
That even to speak its title is seditious!
25 Meanwhile Oronte, my rival, lends his credit
To the same libelous tale, and helps to spread
    it!
Oronte! a man of honor and of rank,
With whom I've been entirely fair and frank;
Who sought me out and forced me, willy-nilly,
30 To judge some verse I found extremely silly;
And who, because I properly refused
To flatter him, or see the truth abused,
Abets my enemy in a rotten slander!
There's the reward of honesty and candor!
35 The man will hate me to the end of time
For failing to commend his wretched rhyme!

And not this man alone, but all humanity
Do what they do from interest and vanity;
They prate of honor, truth, and righteousness,
But lie, betray, and swindle nonetheless. 40
Come then: man's villainy is too much to
    bear;
Let's leave this jungle and this jackal's lair.
Yes! treacherous and savage race of men,
You shall not look upon my face again.
    PHILINTE:
Oh, don't rush into exile prematurely; 45
Things aren't as dreadful as you make them,
    surely.
It's rather obvious, since you're still at large,
That people don't believe your enemy's charge.
Indeed, his tale's so patently untrue
That it may do more harm to him than you. 50
    ALCESTE:
Nothing could do that scoundrel any harm:
His frank corruption is his greatest charm,
And, far from hurting him, a further shame
Would only serve to magnify his name.
    PHILINTE:
In any case, his bald prevarication 55
Has done no injury to your reputation,
And you may feel secure in that regard.
As for your lawsuit, it should not be hard
To have the case reopened, and contest
This judgment . . .
    ALCESTE: No, no, let the verdict rest. 60
Whatever cruel penalty it may bring,
I wouldn't have it changed for anything.
It shows the times' injustice with such clarity
That I shall pass it down to our posterity
As a great proof and signal demonstration 65
Of the black wickedness of this generation.
It may cost twenty thousand francs; but I
Shall pay their twenty thousand, and gain
    thereby
The right to storm and rage at human evil,
And send the race of mankind to the devil. 70
    PHILINTE:
Listen to me . . .
    ALCESTE:
              Why? What can you possibly say?
Don't argue, Sir; your labor's thrown away.
Do you propose to offer lame excuses
For men's behavior and the times' abuses?
    PHILINTE:
No, all you say I'll readily concede: 75
This is a low, conniving age indeed;
Nothing but trickery prospers nowadays,
And people ought to mend their shabby ways.

Yes, man's a beastly creature; but must we then
80 Abandon the society of men?
Here in the world, each human frailty
Provides occasion for philosophy,
And that is virtue's noblest exercise;
If honesty shone forth from all men's eyes,
85 If every heart were frank and kind and just.
What could our virtues do but gather dust
(Since their employment is to help us bear
The villainies of men without despair)?
A heart well-armed with virtue can endure. . . .

ALCESTE:

90 Sir, you're a matchless reasoner, to be sure;
Your words are fine and full of cogency;
But don't waste time and eloquence on me.
My reason bids me go, for my own good.
My tongue won't lie and flatter as it should;
God knows what frankness it might next
95   commit,
And what I'd suffer on account of it.
Pray let me wait for Célimène's return
In peace and quiet. I shall shortly learn,
By her response to what I have in view,
100 Whether her love for me is feigned or true.

PHILINTE:

Till then, let's visit Éliante upstairs.

ALCESTE:

No, I am too weighed down with somber cares.
Go to her, do; and leave me with my gloom
Here in the darkened corner of this room.

PHILINTE:

105 Why, that's no sort of company, my friend;
I'll see if Éliante will not descend.

SCENE II. [CÉLIMÈNE, ORONTE, ALCESTE.]

ORONTE:

Yes, Madam, if you wish me to remain
Your true and ardent lover, you must deign
To give me some more positive assurance.
All this suspense is quite beyond endurance.
5 If your heart shares the sweet desires of mine,
Show me as much by some convincing sign;
And here's the sign I urgently suggest:
That you no longer tolerate Alceste,
But sacrifice him to my love, and sever
10 All your relations with the man forever.

CÉLIMÈNE:

Why do you suddenly dislike him so?
You praised him to the skies not long ago.

ORONTE:

Madam, that's not the point. I'm here to find
Which way your tender feelings are inclined.

Choose, if you please, between Alceste and me,   15
And I shall stay or go accordingly.

ALCESTE (emerging from the corner):

Yes, Madam, choose; this gentleman's demand
Is wholly just, and I support his stand.
I too am true and ardent; I too am here
To ask you that you make your feelings clear.   20
No more delays, now; no equivocation;
The time has come to make your declaration.

ORONTE:

Sir, I've no wish in any way to be
An obstacle to your felicity.

ALCESTE:

Sir, I've no wish to share her heart with you;   25
That may sound jealous, but at least it's true.

ORONTE:

If, weighing us, she leans in your direction . . .

ALCESTE:

If she regards you with the least affection . . .

ORONTE:

I swear I'll yield her to you there and then.

ALCESTE:

I swear I'll never see her face again.   30

ORONTE:

Now, Madam, tell us what we've come to hear.

ALCESTE:

Madam, speak openly and have no fear.

ORONTE:

Just say which one is to remain your lover.

ALCESTE:

Just name one name, and it will all be over.

ORONTE:

What! Is it possible that you're undecided?   35

ALCESTE:

What! Can your feelings possibly be divided?

CÉLIMÈNE:

Enough: this inquisition's gone too far:
How utterly unreasonable you are!
Not that I couldn't make the choice with ease;
My heart has no conflicting sympathies;   40
I know full well which one of you I favor,
And you'd not see me hesitate or waver.
But how can you expect me to reveal
So cruelly and bluntly what I feel?
I think it altogether too unpleasant   45
To choose between two men when both are present;
One's heart has means more subtle and more kind
Of letting its affections be divined,
Nor need one be uncharitably plain
To let a lover know he loves in vain.   50

ORONTE:

No, no, speak plainly; I for one can stand it.
I beg you to be frank.

ALCESTE: And I demand it.
The simple truth is what I wish to know,
And there's no need for softening the blow.
55 You've made an art of pleasing everyone,
But now your days of coquetry are done:
You have no choice now, Madam, but to choose,
For I'll know what to think if you refuse;
I'll take your silence for a clear admission
60 That I'm entitled to my worst suspicion.
    ORONTE:
I thank you for this ultimatum, Sir,
And I may say I heartily concur.
    CÉLIMÈNE:
Really, this foolishness is very wearing:
Must you be so unjust and overbearing?
65 Haven't I told you why I must demur?
Ah, here's Éliante; I'll put the case to her.

SCENE III. [ÉLIANTE, PHILINTE, CÉLIMÈNE, ORONTE, ALCESTE.]

    CÉLIMÈNE:
Cousin, I'm being persecuted here
By these two persons, who, it would appear,
Will not be satisfied till I confess
Which one I love the more, and which the less,
5 And tell the latter to his face that he
Is henceforth banished from my company.
Tell me, has ever such a thing been done?
    ÉLIANTE:
You'd best not turn to me; I'm not the one
To back you in a matter of this kind:
10 I'm all for those who frankly speak their mind.
    ORONTE:
Madam, you'll search in vain for a defender.
    ALCESTE:
You're beaten, Madam, and may as well surrender.
    ORONTE:
Speak, speak, you must; and end this awful
    strain.
    ALCESTE:
Or don't, and your position will be plain.
    ORONTE:
15 A single word will close this painful scene.
    ALCESTE:
But if you're silent, I'll know what you mean.

SCENE IV. [ARSINOÉ, CÉLIMÈNE, ÉLIANTE, ALCESTE, PHILINTE, ACASTE, CLITANDRE, ORONTE.]

ACASTE (to CÉLIMÈNE):
Madam, with all due deference, we two
Have come to pick a little bone with you.
    CLITANDRE (to ORONTE and ALCESTE):
I'm glad you're present, Sirs, as you'll soon
    learn,
Our business here is also your concern.
    ARSINOÉ (to CÉLIMÈNE):
Madam, I visit you so soon again   5
Only because of these two gentlemen,
Who came to me indignant and aggrieved
About a crime too base to be believed.
Knowing your virtue, having such confidence
    in it,
I couldn't think you guilty for a minute,   10
In spite of all their telling evidence;
And, rising above our little difference,
I've hastened here in friendship's name to see
You clear yourself of this great calumny.
    ACASTE:
Yes, Madam, let us see with what composure   15
You'll manage to respond to this disclosure.
You lately sent Clitandre this tender note.
    CLITANDRE:
And this one, for Acaste, you also wrote.
    ACASTE (to ORONTE and ALCESTE):
You'll recognize this writing, Sirs, I think;
The lady is so free with pen and ink   20
That you must know it all too well, I fear.
But listen: this is something you should hear.

"How absurd you are to condemn my light-
heartedness in society, and to accuse me of
being happiest in the company of others.   25
Nothing could be more unjust; and if you do
not come to me instantly and beg pardon for
saying such a thing, I shall never forgive you as
long as I live. Our big bumbling friend the
Viscount . . ."   30

What a shame that he's not here.

"Our big bumbling friend the Viscount,
whose name stands first in your complaint, is
hardly a man to my taste; and ever since the
day I watched him spend three-quarters of an   35
hour spitting into a well, so as to make circles
in the water, I have been unable to think
highly of him. As for the little Marquess . . ."

In all modesty, gentlemen, that is I.

"As for the little Marquess, who sat squeez-   40
ing my hand for such a long while yesterday, I
find him in all respects the most trifling
creature alive; and the only things of value
about him are his cape and his sword. As for
the man with the green ribbons . . ."   45

(To ALCESTE.) It's your turn now, Sir.

"As for the man with the green ribbons, he amuses me now and then with his bluntness and his bearish ill-humor; but there are many
50 times indeed when I think him the greatest bore in the world. And as for the sonneteer . . ."

(*To* ORONTE.) Here's your helping.

"And as for the sonneteer, who has taken it
55 into his head to be witty, and insists on being an author in the teeth of opinion, I simply cannot be bothered to listen to him, and his prose wearies me quite as much as his poetry. Be assured that I am not always so well-enter-
60 tained as you suppose; that I long for your company, more than I dare to say, at all these entertainments to which people drag me; and that the presence of those one loves is the true and perfect seasoning to all one's pleasures."

65 CLITANDRE: And now for me.

"Clitandre, whom you mention, and who so pesters me with his saccharine speeches, is the last man on earth for whom I could feel any affection. He is quite mad to suppose that I
70 love him, and so are you, to doubt that you are loved. Do come to your senses; exchange your suppositions for his; and visit me as often as possible, to help me bear the annoyance of his unwelcome attentions."

75 It's sweet character that these letters show,
And what to call it, Madam, you well know.
Enough. We're off to make the world acquainted
With this sublime self-portrait that you've painted.
ACASTE:
Madam, I'll make you no farewell oration;
80 No, you're not worthy of my indignation.
Far choicer hearts than yours, as you'll discover,
Would like this little Marquess for a lover.

SCENE V. [CÉLIMÈNE, ÉLIANTE, ARSINOÉ, ALCESTE, ORONTE, PHILINTE.]

ORONTE:
So! After all those loving letters you wrote,
You turn on me like this, and cut my throat!
And your dissembling, faithless heart, I find,
Has pledged itself by turns to all mankind!
5 How blind I've been! But now I clearly see;
I thank you, Madam, for enlightening me.
My heart is mine once more, and I'm content;

The loss of it shall be your punishment.
(*To* ALCESTE.) Sir, she is yours; I'll seek no more to stand
Between your wishes and this lady's hand.   10

SCENE VI. [CÉLIMÈNE, ÉLIANTE, ARSINOÉ, ALCESTE, PHILINTE.]

ARSINOÉ (*to* CÉLIMÈNE):
Madam, I'm forced to speak. I'm far too stirred
To keep my counsel, after what I've heard.
I'm shocked and staggered by your want of morals.
It's not my way to mix in others' quarrels;
But really, when this fine and noble spirit,   5
This man of honor and surpassing merit,
Laid down the offering of his heart before you,
How *could* you . . .
ALCESTE:
            Madam, permit me, I implore you,
To represent myself in this debate.
Don't bother, please, to be my advocate.   10
My heart, in any case, could not afford
To give your services their due reward;
And if I chose, for consolation's sake,
Some other lady, 'twould not be you I'd take.
ARSINOÉ:
What makes you think you could, Sir? And how dare you   15
Imply that I've been trying to ensnare you?
If you can for a moment entertain
Such flattering fancies, you're extremely vain.
I'm not so interested as you suppose
In Célimène's discarded gigolos.   20
Get rid of that absurd illusion, do.
Women like me are not for such as you.
Stay with this creature, to whom you're so attached;
I've never seen two people better matched.

SCENE VII. [CÉLIMÈNE, ÉLIANTE, ALCESTE, PHILINTE.]

ALCESTE (*to* CÉLIMÈNE):
Well, I've been still throughout this exposé,
Till everyone but me has said his say.
Come, have I shown sufficient self-restraint?
And may I now . . .
CÉLIMÈNE: Yes, make your just complaint.
Reproach me freely, call me what you will;   5
You've every right to say I've used you ill.
I've wronged you, I confess it; and in my shame

I'll make no effort to escape the blame.
The anger of those others I could despise;
10 My guilt toward you I sadly recognize.
Your wrath is wholly justified, I fear;
I know how culpable I must appear,
I know all things bespeak my treachery,
And that, in short, you've grounds for hating
  me.
Do so; I give you leave.
15 ALCESTE: Ah, traitress — how,
How should I cease to love you, even now?
Though mind and will were passionately bent
On hating you, my heart would not consent.
(*To* ÉLIANTE *and* PHILINTE.) Be witness to my
  madness, both of you;
20 See what infatuation drives one to;
But wait; my folly's only just begun,
And I shall prove to you before I'm done
How strange the human heart is, and how far
From rational we sorry creatures are.
(*To* CÉLIMÈNE.) Woman, I'm willing to for-
25   get your shame,
And clothe your treacheries in a sweeter name;
I'll call them youthful errors, instead of crimes,
And lay the blame on these corrupting times.
My one condition is that you agree
30 To share my chosen fate, and fly with me
To that wild, trackless, solitary place
In which I shall forget the human race.
Only by such a course can you atone
For those atrocious letters; by that alone
35 Can you remove my present horror of you,
And make it possible for me to love you.
    CÉLIMÈNE:
What! I renounce the world at my young age,
And die of boredom in some hermitage?
    ALCESTE:
Ah, if you really loved me as you ought,
You wouldn't give the world a moment's
40   thought;
Must you have me, and all the world beside?
    CÉLIMÈNE:
Alas, at twenty one is terrified
Of solitude. I fear I lack the force
And depth of soul to take so stern a course.
45 But if my hand in marriage will content you,

Why, there's a plan which I might well
  consent to,
And . . .
    ALCESTE:
          No, I detest you now. I could excuse
Everything else, but since you thus refuse
To love me wholly, as a wife should do,
And see the world in me, as I in you,   50
Go! I reject your hand, and disenthrall
My heart from your enchantments, once for
  all.

SCENE VIII. [ÉLIANTE, ALCESTE, PHILINTE.]

    ALCESTE (*to* ÉLIANTE):
Madam, your virtuous beauty has no peer;
Of all this world you only are sincere;
I've long esteemed you highly, as you know;
Permit me ever to esteem you so,
And if I do not now request your hand,   5
Forgive me, Madam, and try to understand.
I feel unworthy of it; I sense that fate
Does not intend me for the married state,
That I should do you wrong by offering you
My shattered heart's unhappy residue,   10
And that in short . . .
    ÉLIANTE: Your argument's well taken:
Nor need you fear that I shall feel forsaken.
Were I to offer him this hand of mine,
Your friend Philinte, I think, would not
  decline.
    PHILINTE:
Ah, Madam, that's my heart's most cherished
  goal,   15
For which I'd gladly give my life and soul.
    ALCESTE (*to* ÉLIANTE *and* PHILINTE):
May you be true to all you now profess,
And so deserve unending happiness.
Meanwhile, betrayed and wronged in every-
  thing,
I'll flee this bitter world where vice is king, 20
And seek some spot unpeopled and apart
Where I'll be free to have an honest heart.
    PHILINTE:
Come, Madam, let's do everything we can
To change the mind of this unhappy man.

The introduction to this volume (pp. 9–10) makes the rather obvious point that in both tragedy and comedy we have characters who are motivated by some ideal, and that (for example) the tragic hero who hunts out the polluted man in Thebes or who kills his wife because he thinks she is unfaithful is neither more nor less impassioned than the comic lover who writes sonnets to his mistress' eyebrow. Whether the passion is noble or comic depends not on its depth, or its persistence, but on its context, and especially on its object.

The passion for honesty that drives Molière's misanthrope, Alceste, is said by the equable Éliante to have "its noble, heroic side," and her view has found wide acceptance among audiences and readers. Alceste is sometimes seen as a tragic figure caught in a comic world, and the play is sometimes said to be a sort of tragic comedy. Alceste demands honesty, and he fulminates against flattery and other forms of insincerity that apparently compose the entire life of the other figures. Surrounded by trimmers and gossips and worse, he alone (if we except the gentle Éliante) seems to hold to a noble ideal. The only other ideal given much prominence is Philinte's, a code of such easy tolerance that it is at times almost indistinguishable from mere passive acceptance of everything.

What case can be made that Alceste is comic, not tragic? A few points suggest themselves. First, this champion of honesty is in love (or thinks he is) with a coquette. What can be more comic than the apostle of plain-dealing being himself in the power of the irrational, especially when this power deposits him at the feet of Célimène, a woman who employs all the devices that in others infuriate him? Second, his demand for honesty is indiscriminate; he is as offended at trivial courtesies as at the law's injustice. Philinte "ought to die of self-disgust" for his "crime" of effusively greeting a casual acquaintance whose name he cannot even recall. So disproportionate is Alceste's passion that when he pops onstage in IV.ii, saying to Éliante, "Avenge me, Madam," he is funny, though the words in themselves are scarcely amusing. It is worth comparing a few other lines in this scene with some roughly similar lines in *Othello*. Alceste (still talking to Éliante about Célimène's letter to a rival suitor) says, "My world has gone to wrack" ("Ah! tout est ruiné!"). When, early in the play, Brabantio had cautioned Othello that Desdemona might deceive him, Othello had said, "My life upon her faith," and, in the middle of the play "Perdition catch my soul / But I do love thee! And when I love thee not, / Chaos is come again." Later, poisoned by Iago's insinuations, he believes Desdemona is faithless, and chaos comes again as he calls her a devil, banishes her from his sight, and finally suffocates her. But Othello is "the noble Moor," whose nobility is demonstrated early in the play by his language and his actions. And Desdemona, "the divine Desdemona," "the grace of heaven," and "the sweetest innocent / That e'er did lift up eye," demonstrates her worth in every line and deed. On the other hand, Alceste, lacking all sense of proportion, is at the outset surly and evidently funny. In the very first scene his tirade against Philinte's "loving demonstrations" offered to one who is almost a stranger evokes Philinte's good-natured

> It hardly seems a hanging matter to me;
> I hope that you will take it graciously
> If I extend myself a slight reprieve,
> And live a little longer, by your leave;

but this droll reply acerbates Alceste:

> How dare you joke about a crime so grave?

Alceste is thus laughably introduced; his passion is comic because it is disproportionate — and also because it leads to no action; Othello is heroically introduced (after an initial scene in which he is slandered), and his passion is tragic because it is frightening and pitiable, especially because it leads him to murder an innocent woman who, as he has said, is the center of his being.

Alceste's remark about joking provides a thread that may be followed usefully. He cannot take a joke. Whenever he is laughed at, he becomes indignant, but indignation (when motivated by a desire to protect the self from criticism) itself evokes further laughter because of the gap between the indignant man's presentation of himself and his real worth. Comedy does not allow people to strike attitudes. The man who protests that his argument *is* valid, dammit, or that he *has* a sense of humor, or that his opponent is a fool, is likely to evoke laughter by his monolithic insistence on his merit. When Philinte laughs at the old poem Alceste quotes, Alceste resorts to bitter irony, and when told that his frankness has made him ridiculous, he irritably replies:

> So much the better; just what I wish to hear.
> No news could be more grateful to my ear.
> All men are so detestable in my eyes.
> I should be sorry if they thought me otherwise.

He hopes that he will lose his lawsuit, just to prove that the world *is* as bad as he thinks it is. (An odd psychological state, resembling Master Ford's in Shakespeare's *Merry Wives of Windsor*, whose "God be praised for my jealousy" reveals the comic figure's infatuation with his abnormality.) And when Alceste is told that his hope that he will lose his lawsuit would reduce all hearers to laughter and would make his name a jest, he ill-humoredly replies, "So much the worse for jesters." When his persistent refusal to praise a trivial poem moves two auditors to laughter, he again employs frigid irony, and concludes the scene ominously:

> By heaven, Sirs, I really didn't know
> That I was being humorous.
>   CÉLIMÈNE: Go, Sir; go;
> Settle your business.
>   ALCESTE: I shall, and when I'm through,
> I shall return to settle things with you.

Alceste, unable to laugh at the folly of others, cannot, of course, tolerate laughter at himself. When Philinte puts into practice the frankness Alceste stormily advocates, Alceste's response is the indignation we have been commenting on. A sense of humor (as distinct from derisive laughter) involves the ability to laugh at what one values, and among the things one values is the self. Children can laugh at surprises and at the distress of other children, but they cannot laugh at themselves because they cannot see themselves in perspective, at a distance, as it were. The mature man can laugh at (for example) mimicry of himself, but the child or the immature adult will, like Alceste, sulk or fly into a rage.

In *The Misanthrope* it is entirely possible that Molière is in some degree mimicking himself. In 1662 Molière at forty married Armande Béjart, a woman less than half his age. The marriage seems to have been unhappy, apparently because his wife enjoyed attracting the attentions of other men. Some critics, pressing this point, assume that if the play is autobiographical, Alceste must be expressing Molière's point of view, and therefore he cannot be a comic figure. If anything, the autobiographic origin shows only that Molière had (which no one has doubted) a sense of humor. He could laugh at himself. Alceste's courtship of Célimène may in some degree represent Molière's unhappy marriage to a flirtatious and unappreciative woman, but the point is that Molière apparently could stand back and laugh at his own exasperation, which Alceste cannot do. (Molière subtitled the play "The Atrabilious Man in Love"; one cannot hear Alceste speaking thus of himself.) Alceste can only, rather childishly, try to maintain his way, and demand that his special merit be noted and rewarded:

> However high the praise, there's nothing worse
> Than sharing honors with the universe.
> Esteem is founded on comparison:
> To honor all men is to honor none.
> Since you embrace this indiscriminate vice,
> Your friendship comes at far too cheap a price;
> I spurn the easy tribute of a heart
> Which will not set the worthy man apart:
> I choose, Sir, to be chosen; and in fine,
> The friend of mankind is no friend of mine.

Once or twice, when he confesses that his love for Célimène is irrational, he seems to have some perspective, but mostly the scenes of Alceste as lover serve to reveal again and again his consuming egotism. His love is so great, he tells Célimène, that he wishes she were in some peril so that he could prove his love by saving her. Célimène aptly replies that Alceste's is "a strange benevolence indeed."

The argument thus far has tried to make the point that Alceste is funny — funny because (among other things) his anger is indiscriminate and disproportionate, because he is a sort of philosopher and yet is in love, and because his *idée fixe*, frankness, when turned against him, exasperates him. But when we return to Éliante's reference to his "noble, heroic side," and we recall his passion for honesty and his passionate desire to be himself, and when we see the hollowness all about him, the comic figure begins to take on a tragic aspect; and when at the end he departs from the stage unrepentant and bitter, banishing himself from the company of men, we feel that the usual comic plot too has taken on a tragic aspect. But this is hardly to say that Alceste is tragic and *The Misanthrope* a tragedy. One cannot, for example, imagine Alceste committing suicide. He is not an Othello.

MAJOR BARBARA

Bernard Shaw

Bernard Shaw (1856–1950) was born in Dublin of Anglo-Irish stock. His father drank too much, his mother — something of an Ibsenite "new woman" — went to London to make her way as singer and voice teacher. Shaw worked in a Dublin real estate office for a while (he did not attend a college or university), and then followed his mother to London, where he wrote critical reviews, and five novels (1879–1883) before turning playwright. His first play, begun with William Archer (playwright and translator of Ibsen), was abandoned in 1885, and then entirely revised by Shaw into *Widowers' Houses* (1892). He had already shown, in a critical study entitled *The Quintessence of Ibsenism* (1891), that he regarded the stage as a pulpit and soap box; before the nineteenth century was over, he wrote nine more plays, in order (he said) to espouse socialism effectively. *Major Barbara* (1905) is his comic masterpiece, but at least a dozen of his plays have established themselves in the repertoire, including one tragedy, *Saint Joan* (1924).

Undershaft (Brewster Mason) visits Lady Britomart (Elizabeth Spriggs) to meet Sara (Lisa Harrow) and Barbara (Judi Dench) in the Royal Shakespeare Company production of *Major Barbara* directed by Clifford Williams and designed by Ralph Koltai, Aldwych, 1970. (Photograph: Patrick Eagar.)

ACT I

It is after dinner in January 1906, in the library in LADY BRITOMART UNDERSHAFT'S *house in Wilton Crescent. A large and comfortable settee is in the middle of the room, upholstered in dark leather. A person sitting on it (it is vacant at present) would have, on his right,* LADY BRITOMART'S *writing table, with the lady herself busy at it; a smaller writing table behind him on his left; the door behind him on* LADY BRITOMART'S *side; and a window with a window seat directly on his left. Near the window is an armchair.*

LADY BRITOMART *is a woman of fifty or thereabouts, well dressed and yet careless of her dress, well bred and quite reckless of her breeding, well mannered and yet appallingly outspoken and indifferent to the opinion of her interlocutors, amiable and yet peremptory, arbitrary, and high-tempered to the last bearable degree, and withal a very typical managing matron of the upper class, treated as a naughty child until she grew into a scolding mother, and finally settling down with plenty of practical ability and worldly experience, limited in the oddest way with domestic and class limitations, conceiving the universe exactly as if it were a large house in Wilton Crescent, though handling her corner of it very effectively on that assumption, and being quite enlightened and liberal as to the books in the library, the pictures on the walls, and the music in the portfolios, and the articles in the papers.*

Her son, STEPHEN, *comes in. He's a gravely correct young man under 25, taking himself very seriously, but still in some awe of his mother, from childish habit and bachelor shyness rather than from any weakness of character.*

STEPHEN: Whats the matter?

LADY BRITOMART: Presently, Stephen.

(STEPHEN *submissively walks to the settee*

Major Barbara by George Bernard Shaw. Copyright 1907, 1913, 1930, 1941, George Bernard Shaw. Copyright 1957, The Public Trustee as Executor of the Estate of George Bernard Shaw. Copyright © 1971, The Trustees of the British Museum, The Governors and Guardians of The National Gallery of Ireland and Royal Academy of Dramatic Art. Reprinted by permission of Dodd, Mead & Company, Inc., and The Society of Authors for the Estate of George Bernard Shaw.

and sits down. He takes up a Liberal weekly called The Speaker.)

LADY BRITOMART: Dont begin to read, Stephen. I shall require all your attention.

STEPHEN: It was only while I was waiting —

LADY BRITOMART: Dont make excuses, Stephen. (*He puts down The Speaker.*) Now! (*She finishes her writing; rises; and comes to the settee.*) I have not kept you waiting very long, I think.

STEPHEN: Not at all, mother.

LADY BRITOMART: Bring me my cushion. (*He takes the cushion from the chair at the desk and arranges it for her as she sits down on the settee.*) Sit down. (*He sits down and fingers his tie nervously.*) Don't fiddle with your tie, Stephen: there is nothing the matter with it.

STEPHEN: I beg your pardon. (*He fiddles with his watch chain instead.*)

LADY BRITOMART: Now are you attending to me, Stephen?

STEPHEN: Of course, mother.

LADY BRITOMART: No: it's not of course. I want something much more than your everyday matter-of-course attention. I am going to speak to you very seriously, Stephen. I wish you would let that chain alone.

STEPHEN (*hastily relinquishing the chain*): Have I done anything to annoy you, mother? If so, it was quite unintentional.

LADY BRITOMART (*astonished*): Nonsense! (*With some remorse.*) My poor boy, did you think I was angry with you?

STEPHEN: What is it, then, mother? You are making me very uneasy.

LADY BRITOMART (*squaring herself at him rather aggressively*): Stephen: may I ask how soon you intend to realize that you are a grown-up man, and that I am only a woman?

STEPHEN (*amazed*): Only a —

LADY BRITOMART: Dont repeat my words, please: it is a most aggravating habit. You must learn to face life seriously, Stephen. I really cannot bear the whole burden of our family affairs any longer. You must advise me: you must assume the responsibility.

STEPHEN: I!

LADY BRITOMART: Yes, you, of course. You

were 24 last June. Youve been at Harrow and Cambridge. Youve been to India and Japan. You must know a lot of things, now; unless you have wasted your time most scandalously. Well, advise me.

STEPHEN (*much perplexed*): You know I have never interfered in the household —

LADY BRITOMART: No: I should think not. I dont want you to order the dinner.

STEPHEN: I mean in our family affairs.

LADY BRITOMART: Well, you must interfere now; for they are getting quite beyond me.

STEPHEN (*troubled*): I have thought sometimes that perhaps I ought; but really, mother, I know so little about them; and what I do know is so painful! it is so impossible to mention some things to you — (*He stops, ashamed.*)

LADY BRITOMART: I suppose you mean your father.

STEPHEN (*almost inaudibly*): Yes.

LADY BRITOMART: My dear: we cant go on all our lives not mentioning him. Of course you were quite right not to open the subject until I asked you to; but you are old enough now to be taken into my confidence, and to help me to deal with him about the girls.

STEPHEN: But the girls are all right. They are engaged.

LADY BRITOMART (*complacently*): Yes: I have made a very good match for Sarah. Charles Lomax will be a millionaire at 35. But that is ten years ahead and in the meantime his trustees cannot under the terms of his father's will allow him more than £800 a year.

STEPHEN: But the will says also that if he increases his income by his own exertions, they may double the increase.

LADY BRITOMART: Charles Lomax's exertions are much more likely to decrease his income than to increase it. Sarah will have to find at least another £800 a year for the next ten years; and even then they will be as poor as church mice. And what about Barbara? I thought Barbara was going to make the most brilliant career of all of you. And what does she do? Joins the Salvation Army; discharges her maid; lives on a pound a week; and walks in one evening with a professor of Greek whom she has picked up in the street, and who pretends to be a Salvationist, and actually plays the big drum for her in public because he has fallen head over ears in love with her.

STEPHEN: I was certainly rather taken aback when I heard they were engaged. Cusins is a very nice fellow, certainly: nobody would ever guess that he was born in Australia; but —

LADY BRITOMART: Oh, Adolphus Cusins will make a very good husband. After all, nobody can say a word against Greek: it stamps a man at once as an educated gentleman. And my family, thank Heaven, is not a pig-headed Tory one. We are Whigs, and believe in liberty. Let snobbish people say what they please: Barbara shall marry, not the man they like, but the man I like.

STEPHEN: Of course I was thinking only of his income. However, he is not likely to be extravagant.

LADY BRITOMART: Dont be too sure of that, Stephen. I know your quiet, simple, refined, poetic people like Adolphus: quite content with the best of everything! They cost more than your extravagant people, who are always as mean as they are second rate. No: Barbara will need at least £2000 a year. You see it means two additional households. Besides, my dear, you must marry soon. I dont approve of the present fashion of philandering bachelors and late marriages; and I am trying to arrange something for you.

STEPHEN: It's very good of you, mother; but perhaps I had better arrange that for myself.

LADY BRITOMART: Nonsense! you are much too young to begin matchmaking: you would be taken in by some pretty little nobody. Of course I dont mean that you are not to be consulted: you know that as well as I do. (STEPHEN *closes his lips and is silent.*) Now dont sulk, Stephen.

STEPHEN: I am not sulking, mother. What has all this got to do with — with — my father?

LADY BRITOMART: My dear Stephen: where is the money to come from? It is easy enough for you and the other children to live on my income as long as we are in the same house; but I cant keep four families in four separate houses. You know how poor my father is: he has barely seven thousand a year now; and really, if he were not the Earl of Stevenage, he would have to give up society. He can do nothing for us. He says, naturally enough, that it is absurd that he should be asked to provide for the children of a man who is rolling in money. You see, Stephen, your father must be fabulously wealthy, because there is always a war going on somewhere.

STEPHEN: You need not remind me of that, mother. I have hardly ever opened a newspaper in my life without seeing our name in it. The Undershaft torpedo! The Undershaft quick firers! The Undershaft ten inch! the Undershaft disappearing rampart gun! the Undershaft submarine! and now the Undershaft aerial battleship! At Harrow they called me the Woolwich Infant. At Cambridge it was the same. A little brute at King's who was always trying to get up revivals, spoilt my Bible — your first birthday present to me — by writing under my name, 'Son and heir to Undershaft and Lazarus, Death and Destruction Dealers: address Christendom and Judea.' But that was not so bad as the way I was kowtowed to everywhere because my father was making millions by selling cannons.

LADY BRITOMART: It is not only the cannons, but the war loans that Lazarus arranges under cover of giving credit for the cannons. You know, Stephen, it's perfectly scandalous. Those two men, Andrew Undershaft and Lazarus, positively have Europe under their thumbs. That is why your father is able to behave as he does. He is above the law. Do you think Bismarck or Gladstone or Disraeli could have openly defied every social and moral obligation all their lives as your father has? They simply wouldnt have dared. I asked Gladstone to take it up. I asked The Times to take it up. I asked the Lord Chamberlain to take it up. But it was just like asking them to declare war on the Sultan. They wouldnt. They said they couldnt touch him. I believe they were afraid.

STEPHEN: What could they do? He does not actually break the law.

LADY BRITOMART: Not break the law! He is always breaking the law. He broke the law when he was born: his parents were not married.

STEPHEN: Mother! Is that true?

LADY BRITOMART: Of course it's true: that was why we separated.

STEPHEN: He married without letting you know this!

LADY BRITOMART (rather taken aback by this inference): Oh no. To do Andrew justice, that was not the sort of thing he did. Besides, you know the Undershaft motto: Unashamed. Everybody knew.

STEPHEN: But you said that was why you separated.

LADY BRITOMART: Yes, because he was not content with being a foundling himself: he wanted to disinherit you for another foundling. That was what I couldnt stand.

STEPHEN (ashamed): Do you mean for — for — for —

LADY BRITOMART: Dont stammer, Stephen. Speak distinctly.

STEPHEN: But this is so frightful to me, mother. To have to speak to you about such things!

LADY BRITOMART: It's not pleasant for me, either, especially if you are still so childish that you must make it worse by a display of embarrassment. It is only in the middle classes, Stephen, that people get into a state of dumb helpless horror when they find that there are wicked people in the world. In our class, we have to decide what is to be done with wicked people; and nothing should disturb our self-possession. Now ask your question properly.

STEPHEN: Mother: have you no consideration for me? For Heaven's sake either treat me as a child, as you always do, and tell me nothing at all; or tell me everything and let me take it as best I can.

LADY BRITOMART: Treat you as a child! What do you mean? It is most unkind and ungrateful of you to say such a thing. You know I have never treated any of you as children. I have always made you my companions and friends, and allowed you perfect freedom to do and say whatever you liked, so long as you liked what I could approve of.

STEPHEN (desperately): I daresay we have been the very imperfect children of a very perfect mother; but I do beg you to let me alone for once, and tell me about this horrible business of my father wanting to set me aside for another son.

LADY BRITOMART (amazed): Another son! I never said anything of the kind. I never dreamt of such a thing. This is what comes of interrupting me.

STEPHEN: But you said —

LADY BRITOMART (cutting him short): Now be a good boy, Stephen, and listen to me patiently. The Undershafts are descended from a foundling in the parish of St Andrew Undershaft in the city. That was long ago, in the reign of James the First. Well this foundling was adopted by an armorer and gun-maker. In the course of time the foundling succeeded to the business; and from some notion of gratitude, or some vow or something, he adopted another foundling, and left the business to him. And that foundling did the same. Ever since that, the cannon business has always been left to an adopted foundling named Andrew Undershaft.

STEPHEN: But did they never marry? Were there no legitimate sons?

LADY BRITOMART: Oh yes: they married just as your father did; and they were rich enough to buy land for their own children and leave them well provided for. But they always adopted and trained some foundling to succeed them in the business; and of course they always quarrelled with their wives furiously over it. Your father was adopted in that way; and he pretends to consider himself bound to keep up the tradition and adopt somebody to leave the business to. Of course I was not going to stand that. There may have been some reason for it when the Undershafts could only marry women in their own class, whose sons were not fit to govern great estates. But there could be no excuse for passing over my son.

STEPHEN (dubiously): I am afraid I should make a poor hand of managing a cannon foundry.

LADY BRITOMART: Nonsense! you could easily get a manager and pay him a salary.

STEPHEN: My father evidently had no great opinion of my capacity.

LADY BRITOMART: Stuff, child! you were only a baby: it had nothing to do with your capacity. Andrew did it on principle, just as he did every perverse and wicked thing on principle. When my father remonstrated, Andrew actually told him to his face that history tells us of only two successful institutions: one the Undershaft firm, and the other the Roman Empire under the Antonines. That was because the Antonine emperors all adopted their successors. Such rubbish! The Stevenages are as good as the Antonines, I hope; and you are a Stevenage. But that was Andrew all over. There you have the man! Always clever and unanswerable when he was defending nonsense and wickedness: always awkward and sullen when he had to behave sensibly and decently!

STEPHEN: Then it was on my account that your home life was broken up, mother. I am sorry.

LADY BRITOMART: Well, dear, there were other differences. I really cannot bear an immoral man. I am not a Pharisee, I hope; and I should not have minded his merely doing wrong things: we are none of us perfect. But your father didnt exactly do wrong things: he said them and thought them: that was what was so dreadful. He really had a sort of religion of wrongness. Just as one doesnt mind men practising immorality so long as they own that they are in the wrong by preaching morality; so I couldn't forgive Andrew for preaching immorality while he practised morality. You would all have grown up without principles, without any knowledge of right and wrong, if he had been in the house. You know, my dear, your father was a very attractive man in some ways. Children did not dislike him; and he took advantage of it to put the wickedest ideas into their heads, and make them quite unmanageable. I did not dislike him myself: very far from it; but nothing can bridge over moral disagreement.

STEPHEN: All this simply bewilders me, mother. People may differ about matters of opinion, or even about religion; but how can they differ about right and wrong? Right is right; and wrong is wrong; and if a man cannot distinguish them properly, he is either a fool or a rascal: thats all.

LADY BRITOMART (touched): Thats my own boy (she pats his cheek)! Your father never could answer that: he used to laugh and get out of it under cover of some affectionate nonsense. And now that you understand the situation, what do you advise me to do?

STEPHEN: Well, what can you do?

LADY BRITOMART: I must get the money somehow.

STEPHEN: We cannot take money from him. I had rather go and live in some cheap place like Bedford Square or even Hampstead than take a farthing of his money.

LADY BRITOMART: But after all, Stephen, our present income comes from Andrew.

STEPHEN (shocked): I never knew that.

LADY BRITOMART: Well, you surely didnt suppose your grandfather had anything to give me. The Stevenages could not do everything for you. We gave you social position. Andrew had to contribute something. He had a very good bargain, I think.

STEPHEN (bitterly): We are utterly dependent on him and his cannons, then?

LADY BRITOMART: Certainly not: the money is settled. But he provided it. So you see it is not a question of taking money from him or not: it is simply a question of how much. I don't want any more for myself.

STEPHEN: Nor do I.

LADY BRITOMART: But Sarah does; and Barbara does. That is, Charles Lomax and Adolphus Cusins will cost them more. So I must put my pride in my pocket and ask for it, I suppose. That is your advice, Stephen, is it not?

STEPHEN: No.

LADY BRITOMART (*sharply*): Stephen!

STEPHEN: Of course if you are determined —

LADY BRITOMART: I am not determined: I ask your advice; and I am waiting for it. I will not have all the responsibility thrown on my shoulders.

STEPHEN (*obstinately*): I would die sooner than ask him for another penny.

LADY BRITOMART (*resignedly*): You mean that *I* must ask him. Very well, Stephen: it shall be as you wish. You will be glad to know that your grandfather concurs. But he thinks I ought to ask Andrew to come here and see the girls. After all, he must have some natural affection for them.

STEPHEN: Ask him here!!!

LADY BRITOMART: Do not repeat my words, Stephen. Where else can I ask him?

STEPHEN: I never expected you to ask him at all.

LADY BRITOMART: Now dont tease, Stephen. Come! you see that it is necessary that he should pay us a visit, dont you?

STEPHEN (*reluctantly*): I suppose so, if the girls cannot do without his money.

LADY BRITOMART: Thank you, Stephen: I knew you would give me the right advice when it was properly explained to you. I have asked your father to come this evening. (STEPHEN *bounds from his seat.*) Dont jump, Stephen: it fidgets me.

STEPHEN (*in utter consternation*): Do you mean to say that my father is coming here tonight — that he may be here at any moment?

LADY BRITOMART (*looking at her watch*): I said nine. (*He gasps. She rises.*) Ring the bell, please. (STEPHEN *goes to the smaller writing table; presses a button on it; and sits at it with his elbows on the table and his head in his hands, outwitted and overwhelmed.*) It is ten minutes to nine yet; and I have to prepare the girls. I asked Charles Lomax and Adolphus to dinner on purpose that they might be here.

Andrew had better see them in case he should cherish any delusions as to their being capable of supporting their wives. (*The butler enters:* LADY BRITOMART *goes behind the settee to speak to him.*) Morrison: go up to the drawing room and tell everybody to come down here at once. (MORRISON *withdraws.* LADY BRITOMART *turns to* STEPHEN.) Now remember, Stephen: I shall need all your countenance and authority. (*He rises and tries to recover some vestige of these attributes.*) Give me a chair, dear. (*He pushes a chair forward from the wall to where she stands, near the smaller writing table. She sits down; and he goes to the armchair, into which he throws himself.*) I dont know how Barbara will take it. Ever since they made her a major in the Salvation Army she has developed a propensity to have her own way and order people about which quite cows me sometimes. It's not ladylike: I'm sure I dont know where she picked it up. Anyhow, Barbara shant bully me; but still it's just as well that your father should be here before she has time to refuse to meet him or make a fuss. Dont look nervous, Stephen: it will only encourage Barbara to make difficulties. *I* am nervous enough, goodness knows; but I dont shew it.

(SARAH *and* BARBARA *come in with their respective young men,* CHARLES LOMAX *and* ADOLPHUS CUSINS. SARAH *is slender, bored, and mundane.* BARBARA *is robuster, jollier, much more energetic.* SARAH *is fashionably dressed:* BARBARA *is in Salvation Army uniform.* LOMAX, *a young man about town, is like many other young men about town. He is afflicted with a frivolous sense of humor which plunges him at the most inopportune moments into paroxysms of imperfectly suppressed laughter.* CUSINS *is a spectacled student, slight, thin haired, and sweet voiced, with a more complex form of* LOMAX'S *complaint. His sense of humor is intellectual and subtle, and is complicated by an appalling temper. The lifelong struggle of a benevolent temperament and a high conscience against impulses of inhuman ridicule and fierce impatience has set up a chronic strain which has visibly wrecked his constitution. He is a most implacable, determined, tenacious, intolerant person who by mere force of character presents himself as — and indeed actually is — considerate, gentle, ex-*

planatory, even mild and apologetic, capable possibly of murder, but not of cruelty or coarseness. By the operation of some instinct which is not merciful enough to blind him with the illusions of love, he is obstinately bent on marrying BARBARA. LOMAX *likes* SARAH *and thinks it will be rather a lark to marry her. Consequently he has not attempted to resist* LADY BRITOMART'S *arrangements to that end.*

All four look as if they had been having a good deal of fun in the drawing room. The girls enter first, leaving the swains outside. SARAH *comes to the settee.* BARBARA *comes in after her and stops at the door.)*

BARBARA: Are Cholly and Dolly to come in?

LADY BRITOMART (*forcibly*): Barbara: I will not have Charles called Cholly: the vulgarity of it positively makes me ill.

BARBARA: It's all right, mother: Cholly is quite correct nowadays. Are they to come in?

LADY BRITOMART: Yes, if they will behave themselves.

BARBARA (*through the door*): Come in, Dolly; and behave yourself.

(BARBARA *comes to her mother's writing table.* CUSINS *enters smiling, and wanders towards* LADY BRITOMART.)

SARAH (*calling*): Come in, Cholly. (LOMAX *enters, controlling his features very imperfectly, and places himself vaguely between* SARAH *and* BARBARA.)

LADY BRITOMART (*peremptorily*): Sit down, all of you. (*They sit.* CUSINS *crosses to the window and seats himself there.* LOMAX *takes a chair.* BARBARA *sits at the writing table and* SARAH *on the settee.*) I dont in the least know what you are laughing at, Adolphus. I am surprised at you, though I expected nothing better from Charles Lomax.

CUSINS (*in a remarkably gentle voice*): Barbara has been trying to teach me the West Ham Salvation March.

LADY BRITOMART: I see nothing to laugh at in that; nor should you if you are really converted.

CUSINS (*sweetly*): You were not present. It was really funny, I believe.

LOMAX: Ripping.

LADY BRITOMART: Be quiet, Charles. Now listen to me, children. Your father is coming here this evening.

(*General stupefaction.* LOMAX, SARAH, *and* BARBARA *rise:* SARAH *scared, and* BARBARA *amused and expectant.*)

LOMAX (*remonstrating*): Oh I say!

LADY BRITOMART: You are not called on to say anything, Charles.

SARAH: Are you serious, mother?

LADY BRITOMART: Of course I am serious. It is on your account, Sarah, and also on Charles's. (*Silence.* SARAH *sits, with a shrug.* CHARLES *looks painfully unworthy.*) I hope you are not going to object, Barbara.

BARBARA: I! why should I? My father has a soul to be saved like anybody else. He's quite welcome as far as I am concerned. (*She sits on the table, and softly whistles 'Onward, Christian Soldiers.'*)

LOMAX (*still remonstrant*): But really, dont you know! Oh I say!

LADY BRITOMART (*frigidly*): What do you wish to convey, Charles?

LOMAX: Well, you must admit that this is a bit thick.

LADY BRITOMART (*turning with ominous suavity to* CUSINS): Adolphus: you are a professor of Greek. Can you translate Charles Lomax's remarks into reputable English for us?

CUSINS (*cautiously*): If I may say so, Lady Brit, I think Charles has rather happily expressed what we all feel. Homer, speaking of Autolycus, uses the same phrase. πυκινὸν δόμον ἐλθεῖν means a bit thick.

LOMAX (*handsomely*): Not that I mind, you know, if Sarah dont. (*He sits.*)

LADY BRITOMART (*crushingly*): Thank you. Have I your permission, Adolphus, to invite my own husband to my own house?

CUSINS (*gallantly*): You have my unhesitating support in everything you do.

LADY BRITOMART: Tush! Sarah: have you nothing to say?

SARAH: Do you mean that he is coming regularly to live here?

LADY BRITOMART: Certainly not. The spare room is ready for him if he likes to stay for a day or two and see a little more of you; but there are limits.

SARAH: Well, he cant eat us, I suppose. *I* dont mind.

LOMAX (*chuckling*): I wonder how the old man will take it.

LADY BRITOMART: Much as the old woman will, no doubt, Charles.

LOMAX (*abashed*): I didnt mean — at least —

LADY BRITOMART: You didnt think, Charles. You never do; and the result is, you never mean anything. And now please attend to me, children. Your father will be quite a stranger to us.

LOMAX: I suppose he hasnt seen Sarah since she was a little kid.

LADY BRITOMART: Not since she was a little kid, Charles, as you express it with that elegance of diction and refinement of thought that seem never to desert you. Accordingly — er — (*Impatiently.*) Now I have forgotten what I was going to say. That comes of your provoking me to be sarcastic, Charles. Adolphus: will you kindly tell me where I was.

CUSINS (*sweetly*): You were saying that as Mr Undershaft has not seen his children since they were babies, he will form his opinion of the way you have brought them up from their behavior tonight, and that therefore you wish us all to be particularly careful to conduct ourselves well, especially Charles.

LADY BRITOMART (*with emphatic approval*): Precisely.

LOMAX: Look here, Dolly: Lady Brit didnt say that.

LADY BRITOMART (*vehemently*): I did, Charles. Adolphus's recollection is perfectly correct. It is most important that you should be good; and I do beg you for once not to pair off into opposite corners and giggle and whisper while I am speaking to your father.

BARBARA: All right, mother. We'll do you credit. (*She comes off the table, and sits in her chair with ladylike elegance.*)

LADY BRITOMART: Remember, Charles, that Sarah will want to feel proud of you instead of ashamed of you.

LOMAX: Oh I say! theres nothing to be exactly proud of, dont you know.

LADY BRITOMART: Well, try and look as if there was.

(*MORRISON, pale and dismayed, breaks into the room in unconcealed disorder.*)

MORRISON: Might I speak a word to you, my lady?

LADY BRITOMART: Nonsense! Shew him up.

MORRISON: Yes, my lady. (*He goes.*)

LOMAX: Does Morrison know who it is?

LADY BRITOMART: Of course. Morrison has always been with us.

LOMAX: It must be a regular corker for him, dont you know.

LADY BRITOMART: Is this a moment to get on my nerves, Charles, with your outrageous expressions?

LOMAX: But this is something out of the ordinary, really —

MORRISON (*at the door*): The — er — Mr Undershaft. (*He retreats in confusion.*)

(ANDREW UNDERSHAFT *comes in. All rise.* LADY BRITOMART *meets him in the middle of the room behind the settee.*

ANDREW *is, on the surface, a stoutish, easygoing elderly man, with kindly patient manners, and an engaging simplicity of character. But he has a watchful, deliberate, waiting, listening face, and formidable reserves of power, both bodily and mental, in his capacious chest and long head. His gentleness is partly that of a strong man who has learnt by experience that his natural grip hurts ordinary people unless he handles them very carefully, and partly the mellowness of age and success. He is also a little shy in his present very delicate situation.*)

LADY BRITOMART: Good evening, Andrew.

UNDERSHAFT: How d'ye do, my dear.

LADY BRITOMART: You look a good deal older.

UNDERSHAFT (*apologetically*): I am somewhat older. (*Taking her hand with a touch of courtship.*) Time has stood still with you.

LADY BRITOMART (*throwing away his hand*): Rubbish! This is your family.

UNDERSHAFT (*surprised*): Is it so large? I am sorry to say my memory is failing very badly in some things. (*He offers his hand with paternal kindness to* LOMAX.)

LOMAX (*jerkily shaking his hand*): Ahdedoo.

UNDERSHAFT: I can see you are my eldest. I am very glad to meet you again, my boy.

LOMAX (*remonstrating*): No, but look here dont you know — (*Overcome.*) Oh I say!

LADY BRITOMART (*recovering from momentary speechlessness*): Andrew: do you mean to say that you dont remember how many children you have?

UNDERSHAFT: Well, I am afraid I —. They have grown so much — er. Am I making any ridiculous mistake? I may as well confess: I recollect only one son. But so many things have happened since, of course — er —

LADY BRITOMART (*decisively*): Andrew: you

are talking nonsense. Of course you have only one son.

UNDERSHAFT: Perhaps you will be good enough to introduce me, my dear.

LADY BRITOMART: That is Charles Lomax, who is engaged to Sarah.

UNDERSHAFT: My dear sir, I beg your pardon.

LOMAX: Notatall. Delighted, I assure you.

LADY BRITOMART: This is Stephen.

UNDERSHAFT (bowing): Happy to make your acquaintance, Mr Stephen. Then (going to CUSINS) you must be my son. (Taking CUSINS' hands in his.) How are you, my young friend? (To LADY BRITOMART.) He is very like you, my love.

CUSINS: You flatter me, Mr Undershaft. My name is Cusins: engaged to Barbara. (Very explicitly.) That is Major Barbara Undershaft, of the Salvation Army. That is Sarah, your second daughter. This is Stephen Undershaft, your son.

UNDERSHAFT: My dear Stephen, I beg your pardon.

STEPHEN: Not at all.

UNDERSHAFT: Mr Cusins: I am much indebted to you for explaining so precisely. (Turning to SARAH.) Barbara, my dear —

SARAH (prompting him): Sarah.

UNDERSHAFT: Sarah, of course. (They shake hands. He goes over to BARBARA.) Barbara — I am right this time, I hope?

BARBARA: Quite right. (They shake hands.)

LADY BRITOMART (resuming command): Sit down, all of you. Sit down, Andrew. (She comes forward and sits on the settee. CUSINS also brings his chair forward on her left. BARBARA and STEPHEN resume their seats. LOMAX gives his chair to SARAH and goes for another.)

UNDERSHAFT: Thank you, my love.

LOMAX (conversationally, as he brings a chair forward between the writing table and the settee, and offers it to UNDERSHAFT): Takes you some time to find out exactly where you are, dont it?

UNDERSHAFT (accepting the chair, but remaining standing): That is not what embarrasses me, Mr Lomax. My difficulty is that if I play the part of a father, I shall produce the effect of an intrusive stranger; and if I play the part of a discreet stranger, I may appear a callous father.

LADY BRITOMART: There is no need for you to play any part at all, Andrew. You had much better be sincere and natural.

UNDERSHAFT (submissively): Yes, my dear: I daresay that will be best. (He sits down comfortably.) Well, here I am. Now what can I do for you all?

LADY BRITOMART: You need not do anything, Andrew. You are one of the family. You can sit with us and enjoy yourself.

(A painfully conscious pause. BARBARA makes a face at LOMAX, whose too long suppressed mirth immediately explodes in agonized neighings.)

LADY BRITOMART (outraged): Charles Lomax: if you can behave yourself, behave yourself. If not, leave the room.

LOMAX: I'm awfully sorry, Lady Brit; but really you know, upon my soul! (He sits on the settee between LADY BRITOMART and UNDERSHAFT, quite overcome.)

BARBARA: Why dont you laugh if you want to, Cholly? It's good for your inside.

LADY BRITOMART: Barbara: you have had the education of a lady. Please let your father see that; and dont talk like a street girl.

UNDERSHAFT: Never mind me, my dear. As you know, I am not a gentleman; and I was never educated.

LOMAX (encouragingly): Nobody'd know it, I assure you. You look all right, you know.

CUSINS: Let me advise you to study Greek, Mr Undershaft. Greek scholars are privileged men. Few of them know Greek; and none of them know anything else; but their position is unchallengeable. Other languages are the qualifications of waiters and commercial travellers: Greek is to a man of position what the hallmark is to silver.

BARBARA: Dolly: dont be insincere. Cholly: fetch your concertina and play something for us.

LOMAX (jumps up eagerly, but checks himself to remark doubtfully to UNDERSHAFT): Perhaps that sort of thing isnt in your line, eh?

UNDERSHAFT: I am particularly fond of music.

LOMAX (delighted): Are you? Then I'll get it. (He goes upstairs for the instrument.)

UNDERSHAFT: Do you play, Barbara?

BARBARA: Only the tambourine. But Cholly's teaching me the concertina.

UNDERSHAFT: Is Cholly also a member of the Salvation Army?

BARBARA: No: he says it's bad form to be a dissenter. But I dont despair of Cholly. I made him come yesterday to a meeting at the dock gates, and take the collection in his hat.

UNDERSHAFT (*looks whimsically at his wife*): !!

LADY BRITOMART: It is not my doing, Andrew. Barbara is old enough to take her own way. She has no father to advise her.

BARBARA: Oh yes she has. There are no orphans in the Salvation Army.

UNDERSHAFT: Your father there has a great many children and plenty of experience, eh?

BARBARA (*looking at him with quick interest and nodding*): Just so. How did you come to understand that? (LOMAX *is heard at the door trying the concertina.*)

LADY BRITOMART: Come in, Charles. Play us something at once.

LOMAX: Righto! (*He sits down in his former place, and preludes.*)

UNDERSHAFT: One moment, Mr Lomax. I am rather interested in the Salvation Army. Its motto might be my own: Blood and Fire.

LOMAX (*shocked*): But not your sort of blood and fire, you know.

UNDERSHAFT: My sort of blood cleanses: my sort of fire purifies.

BARBARA: So do ours. Come down tomorrow to my shelter — the West Ham shelter — and see what we're doing. We're going to march to a great meeting in the Assembly Hall at Mile End. Come and see the shelter and then march with us: it will do you a lot of good. Can you play anything?

UNDERSHAFT: In my youth I earned pennies, and even shillings occasionally, in the streets and in public house parlors by my natural talent for stepdancing. Later on, I became a member of the Undershaft orchestral society, and performed passably on the tenor trombone.

LOMAX (*scandalized — putting down the concertina*): Oh I say!

BARBARA: Many a sinner has played himself into heaven on the trombone, thanks to the Army.

LOMAX (*to* BARBARA, *still rather shocked*): Yes; but what about the cannon business, dont you know? (*To* UNDERSHAFT.) Getting into heaven is not exactly in your line, is it?

LADY BRITOMART: Charles!!!

LOMAX: Well; but it stands to reason, dont it? The cannon business may be necessary and all that: we cant get on without cannons; but it isnt right, you know. On the other hand, there may be a certain amount of tosh about the Salvation Army — I belong to the Established Church myself — but still you cant deny that it's religion; and you cant go against religion, can you? At least unless youre downright immoral, dont you know.

UNDERSHAFT: You hardly appreciate my position, Mr Lomax —

LOMAX (*hastily*): I'm not saying anything against you personally —

UNDERSHAFT: Quite so, quite so. But consider for a moment. Here I am, a profiteer in mutilation and murder. I find myself in a specially amiable humor just now because, this morning, down at the foundry, we blew twenty-seven dummy soldiers into fragments with a gun which formerly destroyed only thirteen.

LOMAX (*leniently*): Well, the more destructive war becomes, the sooner it will be abolished, eh?

UNDERSHAFT: Not at all. The more destructive war becomes the more fascinating we find it. No, Mr Lomax: I am obliged to you for making the usual excuse for my trade; but I am not ashamed of it. I am not one of those men who keep their morals and their business in watertight compartments. All the spare money my trade rivals spend on hospitals, cathedrals, and other receptacles for conscience money, I devote to experiments and researches in improved methods of destroying life and property. I have always done so; and I always shall. Therefore your Christmas card moralities of peace on earth and goodwill among men are of no use to me. Your Christianity, which enjoins you to resist not evil, and to turn the other check, would make me a bankrupt. My morality — my religion — must have a place for cannons and torpedoes in it.

STEPHEN (*coldly — almost sullenly*): You speak as if there were half a dozen moralities and religions to choose from, instead of one true morality and one true religion.

UNDERSHAFT: For me there is only one true morality; but it might not fit you, as you do not manufacture aerial battleships. There is only one true morality for every man; but every man has not the same true morality.

LOMAX (*overtaxed*): Would you mind saying that again? I didnt quite follow it.

CUSINS: It's quite simple. As Euripides says, one man's meat is another man's poison morally as well as physically.

UNDERSHAFT: Precisely.

LOMAX: Oh, that! Yes, yes, yes. True. True.

STEPHEN: In other words, some men are honest and some are scoundrels.

BARBARA: Bosh! There are no scoundrels.

UNDERSHAFT: Indeed? Are there any good men?

BARBARA: No. Not one. There are neither good men nor scoundrels: there are just children of one Father; and the sooner they stop calling one another names the better. You neednt talk to me: I know them. Ive had scores of them through my hands: scoundrels, criminals, infidels, philanthropists, missionaries, county councillors, all sorts. Theyre all just the same sort of sinner; and theres the same salvation ready for them all.

UNDERSHAFT: May I ask have you ever saved a maker of cannons?

BARBARA: No. Will you let me try?

UNDERSHAFT: Well, I will make a bargain with you. If I go to see you tomorrow in your Salvation Shelter, will you come the day after to see me in my cannon works?

BARBARA: Take care. It may end in your giving up the cannons for the sake of the Salvation Army.

UNDERSHAFT: Are you sure it will not end in your giving up the Salvation Army for the sake of the cannons?

BARBARA: I will take my chance of that.

UNDERSHAFT: And I will take my chance of the other. (*They shake hands on it.*) Where is your shelter?

BARBARA: In West Ham. At the sign of the cross. Ask anybody in Canning Town. Where are your works?

UNDERSHAFT: In Perivale St Andrews. At the sign of the sword. Ask anybody in Europe.

LOMAX: Hadnt I better play something?

BARBARA: Yes. Give us Onward, Christian Soldiers.

LOMAX: Well, thats rather a strong order to begin with, dont you know. Suppose I sing Thourt passing hence, my brother. It's much the same tune.

BARBARA: It's too melancholy. You get saved, Cholly; and youll pass hence, my brother, without making such a fuss about it.

LADY BRITOMART: Really, Barbara, you go on as if religion were a pleasant subject. Do have some sense of propriety.

UNDERSHAFT: I do not find it an unpleasant subject, my dear. It is the only one that capable people really care for.

LADY BRITOMART (*looking at her watch*): Well, if you are determined to have it, I insist on having it in a proper and respectable way. Charles: ring for prayers.

(*General amazement.* STEPHEN *rises in dismay.*)

LOMAX (*rising*): Oh I say!

UNDERSHAFT (*rising*): I am afraid I must be going.

LADY BRITOMART: You cannot go now, Andrew: it would be most improper. Sit down. What will the servants think?

UNDERSHAFT: My dear: I have conscientious scruples. May I suggest a compromise? If Barbara will conduct a little service in the drawing room, with Mr Lomax as organist, I will attend it willingly. I will even take part, if a trombone can be procured.

LADY BRITOMART: Dont mock, Andrew.

UNDERSHAFT (*shocked — to* BARBARA): You dont think I am mocking, my love, I hope.

BARBARA: No, of course not; and it wouldnt matter if you were: half the Army came to their first meeting for a lark. (*Rising.*) Come along. (*She throws her arm round her father and sweeps him out, calling to the others from the threshold.*) Come, Dolly. Come, Cholly.

(CUSINS *rises.*)

LADY BRITOMART: I will not be disobeyed by everybody. Adolphus: sit down. (*He does not.*) Charles: you may go. You are not fit for prayers: you cannot keep your countenance.

LOMAX: Oh I say! (*He goes out.*)

LADY BRITOMART (*continuing*): But you, Adolphus, can behave yourself if you choose to. I insist on your staying.

CUSINS: My dear Lady Brit: there are things in the family prayer book that I couldnt bear to hear you say.

LADY BRITOMART: What things, pray?

CUSINS: Well, you would have to say before all the servants that we have done things we ought not to have done, and left undone things we ought to have done, and that there is no health in us. I cannot bear to hear you doing yourself such an injustice, and Barbara such an injustice. As for myself, I flatly deny it: I have done my best. I shouldnt dare to marry Barbara — I couldnt look you in the face — if it were true. So I must go to the drawing room.

LADY BRITOMART (*offended*): Well, go. (*He starts for the door.*) And remember this, Adolphus (*he turns to listen*): I have a very strong suspicion that you went to the Salvation Army to worship Barbara and nothing else. And I quite appreciate the very clever way in which you systematically humbug me. I have found you out. Take care Barbara doesnt. Thats all.

CUSINS (*with unruffled sweetness*): Dont tell on me. (*He steals out.*)

LADY BRITOMART: Sarah: if you want to go, go. Anything's better than to sit there as if you wished you were a thousand miles away.

SARAH (*languidly*): Very well, mamma. (*She goes.*)

(LADY BRITOMART, *with a sudden flounce, gives way to a little gust of tears.*)

STEPHEN (*going to her*): Mother: whats the matter?

LADY BRITOMART (*swishing away her tears with her handkerchief*): Nothing. Foolishness. You can go with him, too, if you like, and leave me with the servants.

STEPHEN: Oh, you mustnt think that, mother. I — I dont like him.

LADY BRITOMART: The others do. That is the injustice of a woman's lot. A woman has to bring up her children; and that means to restrain them, to deny them things they want, to set them tasks, to punish them when they do wrong, to do all the unpleasant things. And then the father, who has nothing to do but pet them and spoil them, comes in when all her work is done and steals their affection from her.

STEPHEN: He has not stolen our affection from you. It is only curiosity.

LADY BRITOMART (*violently*): I wont be consoled, Stephen. There is nothing the matter with me. (*She rises and goes towards the door.*)

STEPHEN: Where are you going, mother?

LADY BRITOMART: To the drawing room, of course. (*She goes out. Onward, Christian Soldiers, on the concertina, with tambourine accompaniment, is heard when the door opens.*) Are you coming, Stephen?

STEPHEN: No. Certainly not. (*She goes. He sits down on the settee, with compressed lips and an expression of strong dislike.*)

ACT II

The yard of the West Ham shelter of the Salvation Army is a cold place on a January morning. The building itself, an old warehouse, is newly whitewashed. Its gabled end projects into the yard in the middle, with a door on the ground floor, and another in the loft above it without any balcony or ladder, but with a pulley rigged over it for hoisting sacks. Those who come from this central gable end into the yard have the gateway leading to the street on their left, with a stone horse-trough just beyond it, and, on the right, a penthouse shielding a table from the weather. There are forms at the table; and on them are seated a man and a woman, both much down on their luck, finishing a meal of bread (one thick slice each, with margarine and golden syrup) and diluted milk.

The man, a workman out of employment, is young, agile, a talker, a poser, sharp enough to be capable of anything in reason except honesty or altruistic considerations of any kind. The woman is a commonplace old bundle of poverty and hard-worn humanity. She looks sixty and probably is forty-five. If they were rich people, gloved and muffed and well wrapped up in furs and overcoats, they would be numbed and miserable; for it is a grindingly cold raw January day; and a glance at the background of grimy warehouses and leaden sky visible over the whitewashed walls of the yard would drive any idle rich person straight to the Mediterranean. But these two, being no more troubled with visions of the Mediterranean than of the moon, and being compelled to keep more of their clothes in the pawnshop, and less on their persons, in winter than in summer, are not depressed by the cold: rather are they stung into vivacity, to which their meal has just now given an almost jolly turn. The man takes a pull at his mug, and then gets up and moves about the yard with his hands deep in his pockets, occasionally breaking into a stepdance.

THE WOMAN: Feel better arter your meal, sir?

THE MAN: No. Call that a meal! Good enough for you, praps; but wot is it to me, an intelligent workin man.

THE WOMAN: Workin man! Wot are you?

THE MAN: Painter.

THE WOMAN (*sceptically*): Yus, I dessay.

THE MAN: Yus, you dessay! I know. Every loafer that cant do nothink calls isself a painter. Well, I'm a real painter: grainer, finisher, thirty-eight bob a week when I can get it.

THE WOMAN: Then why dont you go and get it?

THE MAN: I'll tell you why. Fust: I'm intelligent — fffff! it's rotten cold here (*he dances a step or two*) — yes: intelligent beyond the station o life into which it has pleased the capitalists to call me; and they dont like a man that sees through em. Second, an intelligent bein needs a doo share of appiness; so I drink somethink cruel when I get the chawnce. Third, I stand by my class and do as little as I can so's to leave arf the job for me fellow workers. Fourth, I'm fly enough to know wots inside the law and wots outside it; and inside it I do as the capitalists do: pinch wot I can lay me ands on. In a proper state of society I am sober, industrious and honest: in Rome, so to speak, I do as the Romans do. Wots the consequence? When trade is bad — and it's rotten bad just now — and the employers az to sack arf their men, they generally start on me.

THE WOMAN: Whats your name?

THE MAN: Price. Bronterre O'Brien Price. Usually called Snobby Price, for short.

THE WOMAN: Snobby's a carpenter, aint it? You said you was a painter.

PRICE: Not that kind of snob, but the genteel sort. I'm too uppish, owing to my intelligence, and my father being a Chartist and a reading, thinking man: a stationer, too. I'm none of your common hewers of wood and drawers of water; and dont you forget it. (*He returns to his seat at the table, and takes up his mug.*) Wots your name?

THE WOMAN: Rummy Mitchens, sir.

PRICE (*quaffing the remains of his milk to her*): Your elth, Miss Mitchens.

RUMMY (*correcting him*): Missis Mitchens.

PRICE: Wot! Oh Rummy, Rummy! Respectable married woman, Rummy, gittin rescued by the Salvation Army by pretendin to be a bad un. Same old game!

RUMMY: What am I to do? I cant starve. Them Salvation lasses is dear good girls; but the better you are, the worse they likes to think you were before they rescued you. Why shouldnt they av a bit o credit, poor loves? theyre worn to rags by their work. And where would they get the money to rescue us if we was to let on we're no worse than other people? You know what ladies and gentlemen are.

PRICE: Thievin swine! Wish I ad their job, Rummy, all the same. Wot does Rummy stand for? Pet name praps?

RUMMY: Short for Romola.

PRICE: For wot!?

RUMMY: Romola. It was out of a new book. Somebody me mother wanted me to grow up like.

PRICE: We're companions in misfortune, Rummy. Both on us got names that nobody cawnt pronounce. Consequently I'm Snobby and youre Rummy because Bill and Sally wasnt good enough for our parents. Such is life!

RUMMY: Who saved you, Mr Price? Was it Major Barbara?

PRICE: No: I come here on my own. I'm going to be Bronterre O'Brien Price, the converted painter. I know wot they like. I'll tell em how I blasphemed and gambled and wopped my poor old mother —

RUMMY (*shocked*): Used you to beat your mother?

PRICE: Not likely. She used to beat me. No matter: you come and listen to the converted painter, and youll hear how she was a pious woman that taught me me prayers at er knee, an how I used to come home drunk and drag her out o bed be er snow white airs, an lam into er with the poker.

RUMMY: Thats whats so unfair to us women. Your confessions is just as big lies as ours: you dont tell what you really done no more than us; but you men can tell your lies right out at the meetins and be made much of for it; while the sort o confessions we az to make az to be wispered to one lady at a time. It ain't right, spite of all their piety.

PRICE: Right! Do you spose the Army'd be allowed if it went and did right? Not much. It combs our air and makes us good little blokes to be robbed and put upon. But I'll play the game as good as any of em. I'll see somebody struck by lightnin, or hear a voice sayin 'Snobby Price: where will you spend eternity?' I'll av a time of it, I tell you.

RUMMY: You wont be let drink, though.

PRICE: I'll take it out in gorspellin, then. I dont want to drink if I can get fun enough any other way.

(JENNY HILL, *a pale, overwrought, pretty Salvation lass of 18, comes in through the yard gate, leading* PETER SHIRLEY, *a half hardened, half worn-out elderly man, weak with hunger.*)

JENNY (*supporting him*): Come! pluck up. I'll get you something to eat. Youll be all right then.

PRICE (*rising and hurrying officiously to take the old man off* JENNY's *hands*): Poor old man! Cheer up, brother: youll find rest and peace and appiness ere. Hurry up with the food, miss: e's fair done. (JENNY *hurries into the shelter.*) Ere, buck up, daddy! she's fetchin y'a thick slice o breadn treacle, an a mug o skyblue. (*He seats him at the corner of the table.*)

RUMMY (*gaily*): Keep up your old art! Never say die!

SHIRLEY: I'm not an old man. I'm only 46. I'm as good as ever I was. The grey patch come in my hair before I was thirty. All it wants is three pennorth o hair dye: am I to be turned on the streets to starve for it? Holy God! Ive worked ten to twelve hours a day since I was thirteen, and paid my way all through; and now am I to be thrown into the gutter and my job given to a young man that can do it no better than me because Ive black hair that goes white at the first change?

PRICE (*cheerfully*): No good jawrin about it. Youre ony a jumped-up, jerked-off, orspittle-turned-out incurable of an ole workin man: who cares about you? Eh? Make the thievin swine give you a meal: theyve stole many a one from you. Get a bit o your own back. (JENNY *returns with the usual meal.*) There you are, brother. Awsk a blessin an tuck that into you.

SHIRLEY (*looking at it ravenously but not touching it, and crying like a child*): I never took anything before.

JENNY (*petting him*): Come, come! the Lord sends it to you: he wasnt above taking bread from his friends; and why should you be? Besides, when we find you a job you can pay us for it if you like.

SHIRLEY (*eagerly*): Yes, yes: thats true. I can pay you back: it's only a loan. (*Shivering.*) Oh Lord! oh Lord! (*He turns to the table and attacks the meal ravenously.*)

JENNY: Well, Rummy, are you more comfortable now?

RUMMY: God bless you, lovely! youve fed my body and saved my soul, havnt you? (JENNY, *touched, kisses her.*) Sit down and rest a bit: you must be ready to drop.

JENNY: Ive been going hard since morning. But theres more work than we can do. I mustnt stop.

RUMMY: Try a prayer for just two minutes. Youll work all the better after.

JENNY (*her eyes lighting up*): Oh isnt it wonderful how a few minutes prayer revives you! I was quite lightheaded at twelve o'clock, I was so tired; but Major Barbara just sent me to pray for five minutes; and I was able to go on as if I had only just begun. (*To* PRICE.) Did you have a piece of bread?

PRICE (*with unction*): Yes, miss; but Ive got the piece that I value more; and thats the peace that passeth hall hannerstennin.

RUMMY (*fervently*): Glory Hallelujah!

(BILL WALKER, *a rough customer of about 25, appears at the yard gate and looks malevolently at* JENNY.)

JENNY: That makes me so happy. When you say that, I feel wicked for loitering here. I must get to work again.

(*She is hurrying to the shelter, when the new-comer moves quickly up to the door and intercepts her. His manner is so threatening that she retreats as he comes at her truculently, driving her down the yard.*)

BILL: Aw knaow you. Youre the one that took awy maw girl. Youre the one that set er agen me. Well, I'm gowin to ev er aht. Not that Aw care a carse for er or you: see? Bat Aw'll let er knaow; and Aw'll let you knaow. Aw'm gowing to give her a doin thatll teach er to cat awy from me. Nah in wiv you and tell er to cam aht afore Aw cam in and kick er aht. Tell er Bill Walker wants er. She'll knaow wot thet means; and if she keeps me witin itll be worse. You stop to jawr beck at me; and Aw'll stawt on you: d'ye eah? Theres your wy. In you gow. (*He takes her by the arm and slings her towards the door of the shelter. She falls on her hand and knee.* RUMMY *helps her up again.*)

PRICE (*rising, and venturing irresolutely towards* BILL): Easy there, mate. She aint doin you no arm.

BILL: Oo are you callin mite? (*Standing*

over him threateningly.) Youre gowing to stend ap for er, aw yer? Put ap your ends.

RUMMY (*running indignantly to him to scold him*): Oh, you great brute — (*He instantly swings his left hand back against her face. She screams and reels back to the trough, where she sits down, covering her bruised face with her hands and rocking herself and moaning with pain.*)

JENNY (*going to her*): Oh, God forgive you! How could you strike an old woman like that?

BILL (*seizing her by the hair so violently that she also screams, and tearing her away from the old woman*): You Gawd forgimme again an Aw'll Gawd forgive you one on the jawr thetll stop you pryin for a week. (*Holding her and turning fiercely on* PRICE.) Ev you ennything to sy agen it?

PRICE (*intimidated*): No, matey: she aint anything to do with me.

BILL: Good job for you! Aw'd pat two meals into you and fawt you with one finger arter, you stawved cur. (*To* JENNY.) Nah are you gowin to fetch aht Mog Ebbijem; or em Aw to knock your fice off you and fetch her meself?

JENNY (*writhing in his grasp*): Oh please someone go in and tell Major Barbara — (*She screams again as he wrenches her head down; and* PRICE *and* RUMMY *flee into the shelter.*)

BILL: You want to gow in and tell your Mijor of me, do you?

JENNY: Oh please dont drag my hair. Let me go.

BILL: Do you or downt you? (*She stifles a scream.*) Yus or nao?

JENNY: God give me strength —

BILL (*striking her with his fist in the face*): Gow an shaow her thet, and tell her if she wants one lawk it to cam and interfere with me. (JENNY, *crying with pain, goes into the shed. He goes to the form and addresses the old man.*) Eah: finish your mess; an git aht o maw wy.

SHIRLEY (*springing up and facing him fiercely, with the mug in his hand*): You take a liberty with me, and I'll smash you over the face with the mug and cut your eye out. Aint you satisfied — young whelps like you — with takin the bread out o the mouths of your elders that have brought you up and slaved for you, but you must come shovin and cheekin and bullyin in here, where the bread o charity is sickenin in our stummicks?

BILL (*contemptuously, but backing a little*):

Wot good are you, you aold palsy mag? Wot good are you?

SHIRLEY: As good as you and better. I'll do a day's work agen you or any fat young soaker of your age. Go and take my job at Horrockses, where I worked for ten year. They want young men there: they cant afford to keep men over forty-five. Theyre very sorry — give you a character and happy to help you to get anything suited to your years — sure a steady man wont be long out of a job. Well, let em try you. Theyll find the differ. What do you know? Not as much as how to beeyave yourself — laying your dirty fist across the mouth of a respectable woman!

BILL: Downt provowk me to ly it acrost yours: d'ye eah?

SHIRLEY (*with blighting contempt*): Yes: you like an old man to hit, dont you, when youve finished with the women. I aint seen you hit a young one yet.

BILL (*stung*): You loy, you aold soupkitchener, you. There was a yang menn eah. Did Aw offer to itt him or did Aw not?

SHIRLEY: Was he starvin or was he not? Was he a man or only a crosseyed thief an a loafer? Would you hit my son-in-law's brother?

BILL: Oo's ee?

SHIRLEY: Todger Fairmile o Balls Pond. Him that won £20 off the Japanese wrastler at the music hall by standin out 17 minutes 4 seconds agen him.

BILL (*sullenly*): Aw'm nao music awl wrastler. Ken he box?

SHIRLEY: Yes: an you cant.

BILL: Wot! Aw cawnt, cawnt Aw? Wots thet you sy (*threatening him*)?

SHIRLEY (*not budging an inch*): Will you box Todger Fairmile if I put him on to you? Say the word.

BILL (*subsiding with a slouch*): Aw'll stend ap to enny menn alawy, if he was ten Todger Fairmawls. But Aw dont set ap to be a perfeshnal.

SHIRLEY (*looking down on him with unfathomable disdain*): You box! Slap an old woman with the back o your hand! You hadnt even the sense to hit her where a magistrate couldnt see the mark of it, you silly young lump of conceit and ignorance. Hit a girl in the jaw and ony make her cry! If Todger Fairmile'd done it, she wouldnt a got up inside o ten minutes, no more than you would if he got on to you. Yah! I'd set about you myself if I had a week's feedin in me instead o two months' starvation. (*He turns his back on him and sits down moodily at the table.*)

BILL (*following him and stooping over him to drive the taunt in*): You loy! youve the bread and treacle in you that you cam eah to beg.

SHIRLEY (*bursting into tears*): Oh God! it's true: I'm only an old pauper on the scrap heap. (*Furiously.*) But youll come to it yourself; and then youll know. Youll come to it sooner than a teetotaller like me, fillin yourself with gin at this hour o the mornin!

BILL: Aw'm nao gin drinker, you oald lawr; bat wen Aw want to give my girl a bloomin good awdin Aw lawk to ev a bit o devil in me: see? An eah Aw emm, talkin to a rotten aold blawter like you sted o givin her wot for. (*Working himself into a rage.*) Aw'm gowin in there to fetch her aht. (*He makes vengefully for the shelter door.*)

SHIRLEY: Youre going to the station on a stretcher, more likely; and theyll take the gin and the devil out of you there when they get you inside. You mind what youre about: the major here is the Earl o Stevenage's granddaughter.

BILL (*checked*): Garn!

SHIRLEY: Youll see.

BILL (*his resolution oozing*): Well, Aw aint dan nathin to er.

SHIRLEY: Spose she said you did! who'd believe you?

BILL (*very uneasy, skulking back to the corner of the penthouse*): Gawd! theres no jastice in this cantry. To think wot them people can do! Aw'm as good as er.

SHIRLEY: Tell her so. It's just what a fool like you would do.

(BARBARA, *brisk and businesslike, comes from the shelter with a note book, and addresses herself to* SHIRLEY. BILL, *cowed, sits down in the corner of a form, and turns his back on them.*)

BARBARA: Good morning.

SHIRLEY (*standing up and taking off his hat*): Good morning, miss.

BARBARA: Sit down: make yourself at home. (*He hesitates; but she puts a friendly hand on his shoulder and makes him obey.*) Now then! since youve made friends with us, we want to know all about you. Names and addresses and trades.

SHIRLEY: Peter Shirley. Fitter. Chucked out two months ago because I was too old.

BARBARA (*not at all surprised*): Youd pass still. Why didnt you dye your hair?

SHIRLEY: I did. Me age come out at a coroner's inquest on me daughter.

BARBARA: Steady?

SHIRLEY: Teetotaller. Never out of a job before. Good worker. And sent to the knackers like an old horse!

BARBARA: No matter: if you did your part God will do his.

SHIRLEY (*suddenly stubborn*): My religion's no concern of anybody but myself.

BARBARA (*guessing*): I know. Secularist?

SHIRLEY (*hotly*): Did I offer to deny it?

BARBARA: Why should you? My own father's a Secularist, I think. Our Father — yours and mine — fulfills himself in many ways; and I daresay he knew what he was about when he made a Secularist of you. So buck up, Peter! we can always find a job for a steady man like you. (SHIRLEY, *disarmed and a little bewildered, touches his hat. She turns from him to* BILL.) Whats your name?

BILL (*insolently*): Wots thet to you?

BARBARA (*calmly making a note*): Afraid to give his name. Any trade?

BILL: Oo's afride to give is nime? (*Doggedly, with a sense of heroically defying the House of Lords in the person of Lord Stevenage.*) If you want to bring a chawge agen me, bring it. (*She waits, unruffled.*) Moy nime's Bill Walker.

BARBARA (*as if the name were familiar: trying to remember how*): Bill Walker? (*Recollecting.*) Oh, I know: youre the man that Jenny Hill was praying for inside just now. (*She enters his name in her note book.*)

BILL: Oo's Jenny Ill? And wot call as she to pry for me?

BARBARA: I dont know. Perhaps it was you that cut her lip.

BILL (*defiantly*): Yus, it was me that cat her lip. Aw aint afride o you.

BARBARA: How could you be, since youre not afraid of God? Youre a brave man, Mr Walker. It takes some pluck to do our work here; but none of us dare lift our hand against a girl like that, for fear of her father in heaven.

BILL (*sullenly*): I want nan o your kentin jawr. I spowse you think Aw cam eah to beg from you, like this demmiged lot eah. Not me. Aw downt want your bread and scripe and ketlep. Aw dont blieve in your Gawd, no more than you do yourself.

BARBARA (*sunnily apologetic and ladylike, as*

on a new footing with him): Oh, I beg your pardon for putting your name down, Mr Walker. I didnt understand. I'll strike it out.

BILL (*taking this as a slight, and deeply wounded by it*): Eah! you let maw nime alown. Aint it good enaff to be in your book?

BARBARA (*considering*): Well, you see, theres no use putting down your name unless I can do something for you, is there? Whats your trade?

BILL (*still smarting*): Thets nao concern o yours.

BARBARA: Just so. (*Very businesslike.*) I'll put you down as (*writing*) the man who — struck — poor little Jenny Hill — in the mouth.

BILL (*rising threateningly*): See eah. Awve ed enaff o this.

BARBARA (*quite sunny and fearless*): What did you come to us for?

BILL: Aw cam for maw gel, see? Aw cam to tike her aht o this and to brike er jawr for er.

BARBARA (*complacently*): You see I was right about your trade. (BILL, *on the point of retorting furiously, finds himself, to his great shame and terror, in danger of crying instead. He sits down again suddenly.*) Whats her name?

BILL (*dogged*): Er nime's Mog Ebbijem: thets wot her nime is.

BARBARA: Mog Habbijam! Oh, she's gone to Canning Town, to our barracks there.

BILL (*fortified by his resentment of Mog's perfidy*): Is she? (*Vindictively.*) Then Aw'm gowing to Kennintahn arter her. (*He crosses to the gate; hesitates; finally comes back at* BARBARA.) Are you loyin to me to git shat o me?

BARBARA: I dont want to get shut of you. I want to keep you here and save your soul. Youd better stay: youre going to have a bad time today, Bill.

BILL: Oo's gowing to give it to me? You, preps?

BARBARA: Someone you dont believe in. But youll be glad afterwards.

BILL (*slinking off*): Aw'll gow to Kennintahn to be aht o reach o your tangue. (*Suddenly turning on her with intense malice.*) And if Aw downt fawnd Mog there, Aw'll cam beck and do two years for you, selp me Gawd if Aw downt!

BARBARA (*a shade kindlier, if possible*): It's no use, Bill. She's got another bloke.

BILL: Wot!

BARBARA: One of her own converts. He fell in love with her when he saw her with her soul saved, and her face clean, and her hair washed.

BILL (*surprised*): Wottud she wash it for, the carroty slat? It's red.

BARBARA: It's quite lovely now, because she wears a new look in her eyes with it. It's a pity youre too late. The new bloke has put your nose out of joint, Bill.

BILL: Aw'll put his nowse aht o joint for him. Not that Aw care a carse for er, mawnd thet. But Aw'll teach her to drop me as if Aw was dirt. And Aw'll teach him to meddle with maw judy. Wots iz bleedin nime?

BARBARA: Sergeant Todger Fairmile.

SHIRLEY (*rising with grim joy*): I'll go with him, miss. I want to see them two meet. I'll take him to the infirmary when it's over.

BILL (*to* SHIRLEY, *with undissembled misgiving*): Is thet im you was speakin on?

SHIRLEY: Thats him.

BILL: Im that wrastled in the music awl?

SHIRLEY: The competitions at the National Sportin Club was worth nigh a hundred a year to him. He's gev em up now for religion; so he's a bit fresh for want of the exercise he was accustomed to. He'll be glad to see you. Come along.

BILL: Wots is wight?

SHIRLEY: Thirteen four. (BILL's *last hope expires.*)

BARBARA: Go and talk to him, Bill. He'll convert you.

SHIRLEY: He'll convert your head into a mashed potato.

BILL (*sullenly*): Aw aint afride of im. Aw aint afride of ennybody. Bat e can lick me. She's dan me. (*He sits down moodily on the edge of the horse trough.*)

SHIRLEY: You aint going. I thought not. (*He resumes his seat.*)

BARBARA (*calling*): Jenny!

JENNY (*appearing at the shelter door with a plaster on the corner of her mouth*): Yes, Major.

BARBARA: Send Rummy Mitchens out to clear away here.

JENNY: I think she's afraid.

BARBARA (*her resemblance to her mother flashing out for a moment*): Nonsense! she must do as she's told.

JENNY (*calling into the shelter*): Rummy: the Major says you must come.

(JENNY *comes to* BARBARA, *purposely keeping on the side next* BILL, *lest he should suppose that she shrank from him or bore malice.*)

BARBARA: Poor little Jenny! Are you tired? (*Looking at the wounded cheek.*) Does it hurt?

JENNY: No: it's all right now. It was nothing.

BARBARA (*critically*): It was as hard as he could hit, I expect. Poor Bill! You dont feel angry with him, do you?

JENNY: Oh no, no, no: indeed I dont, Major, bless his poor heart!

(BARBARA *kisses her; and she runs away merrily into the shelter.* BILL *writhes with an agonizing return of his new and alarming symptoms, but says nothing.* RUMMY MITCH-ENS *comes from the shelter.*)

BARBARA (*going to meet* RUMMY): Now Rummy, bustle. Take in those mugs and plates to be washed; and throw the crumbs about for the birds.

RUMMY *takes the three plates and mugs; but* SHIRLEY *takes back his mug from her, as there is still some milk left in it.*)

RUMMY: There aint any crumbs. This aint a time to waste good bread on birds.

PRICE (*appearing at the shelter door*): Gentleman come to see the shelter, Major. Says he's your father.

BARBARA: All right. Coming. (SNOBBY *goes back into the shelter, followed by* BARBARA.)

RUMMY (*stealing across to* BILL *and addressing him in a subdued voice, but with intense conviction*): I'd av the lor of you, you flat eared pignosed potwalloper, if she'd let me. Youre no gentleman, to hit a lady in the face. (BILL, *with greater things moving in him, takes no notice.*)

SHIRLEY (*following her*): Here! in with you and dont get yourself into more trouble by talking.

RUMMY (*with hauteur*): I aint ad the pleasure o being hintroduced to you, as I can remember. (*She goes into the shelter with the plates.*)

SHIRLEY: Thats the —

BILL (*savagely*): Downt you talk to me, d'ye eah? You lea me alown, or Aw'll do you a mischief. Aw'm not dirt under your feet, ennywy.

SHIRLEY (*calmly*): Dont you be afeerd. You

aint such prime company that you need expect to be sought after. (*He is about to go into the shelter when* BARBARA *comes out, with* UNDERSHAFT *on her right.*)

BARBARA: Oh, there you are, Mr Shirley! (*Between them.*) This is my father: I told you he was a Secularist, didn't I? Perhaps youll be able to comfort one another.

UNDERSHAFT (*startled*): A Secularist! Not the least in the world: on the contrary, a confirmed mystic.

BARBARA: Sorry, I'm sure. By the way, papa, what is your religion? in case I have to introduce you again.

UNDERSHAFT: My religion? Well, my dear, I am a Millionaire. That is my religion.

BARBARA: Then I'm afraid you and Mr Shirley wont be able to comfort one another after all. Youre not a Millionaire, are you, Peter?

SHIRLEY: No; and proud of it.

UNDERSHAFT (*gravely*): Poverty, my friend, is not a thing to be proud of.

SHIRLEY (*angrily*): Who made your millions for you? Me and my like. Whats kep us poor? Keepin you rich. I wouldnt have your conscience, not for all your income.

UNDERSHAFT: I wouldnt have your income, not for all your conscience, Mr Shirley. (*He goes to the penthouse and sits down on a form.*)

BARBARA (*stopping* SHIRLEY *adroitly as he is about to retort*): You wouldnt think he was my father, would you, Peter? Will you go into the shelter and lend the lasses a hand for a while: we're worked off our feet.

SHIRLEY (*bitterly*): Yes: I'm in their debt for a meal, aint I?

BARBARA: Oh, not because youre in their debt, but for love of them, Peter, for love of them. (*He cannot understand, and is rather scandalized.*) There! dont stare at me. In with you; and give that conscience of yours a holiday. (*Bustling him into the shelter.*)

SHIRLEY (*as he goes in*): Ah! it's a pity you never was trained to use your reason, miss. Youd have been a very taking lecturer on Secularism.

(BARBARA *turns to her father.*)

UNDERSHAFT: Never mind me, my dear. Go about your work; and let me watch it for a while.

BARBARA: All right.

UNDERSHAFT: For instance, whats the matter with that outpatient over there?

BARBARA (*looking at* BILL, *whose attitude has never changed, and whose expression of brooding wrath has deepened*): Oh, we shall cure him in no time. Just watch. (*She goes over to* BILL *and waits. He glances up at her and casts his eyes down again, uneasy, but grimmer than ever.*) It would be nice to just stamp on Mog Habbijam's face, wouldnt it, Bill?

BILL (*starting up from the trough in consternation*): It's a loy: Aw never said so. (*She shakes her head.*) Oo taold you wot was in moy mawnd?

BARBARA: Only your new friend.

BILL: Wot new friend?

BARBARA: The devil, Bill. When he gets round people they get miserable, just like you.

BILL (*with a heartbreaking attempt at devil-may-care cheerfulness*): Aw aint miserable. (*He sits down again, and stretches his legs in an attempt to seem indifferent.*)

BARBARA: Well, if youre happy, why dont you look happy, as we do?

BILL (*his legs curling back in spite of him*): Aw'm eppy enaff, Aw tell you. Woy cawnt you lea me alown? Wot ev I dan to you? Aw aint smashed your fice, ev Aw?

BARBARA (*softly: wooing his soul*): It's not me thats getting at you, Bill.

BILL: Oo else is it?

BARBARA: Somebody that doesnt intend you to smash women's faces, I suppose. Somebody or something that wants to make a man of you.

BILL (*blustering*): Mike a menn o me! Aint Aw a menn? eh? Oo sez Aw'm not a menn?

BARBARA: Theres a man in you somewhere, I suppose. But why did he let you hit poor little Jenny Hill? That wasnt very manly of him, was it?

BILL (*tormented*): Ev dan wiv it, Aw tell you. Chack it. Aw'm sick o your Jenny Ill and er silly little fice.

BARBARA: Then why do you keep thinking about it? Why does it keep coming up against you in your mind? Youre not getting converted, are you?

BILL (*with conviction*): Not ME. Not lawkly.

BARBARA: Thats right, Bill. Hold out against it. Put out your strength. Dont lets get you cheap. Todger Fairmile said he wrestled for three nights against his salvation harder than he ever wrestled with the Jap at the music hall. He gave in to the Jap. when his arm was going to break. But he didnt give in to his salvation until his heart was going to break. Perhaps youll escape that. You havnt any heart, have you?

BILL: Wot d'ye mean? Woy aint Aw got a awt the sime as ennybody else?

BARBARA: A man with a heart wouldnt have bashed poor little Jenny's face, would he?

BILL (*almost crying*): Ow, will you lea me alown? Ev Aw ever offered to meddle with you, that you cam neggin and provowkin me lawk this? (*He writhes convulsively from his eyes to his toes.*)

BARBARA (*with a steady soothing hand on his arm and a gentle voice that never lets him go*): It's your soul thats hurting you, Bill, and not me. Weve been through it all ourselves. Come with us, Bill. (*He looks wildly round.*) To brave manhood on earth and eternal glory in heaven. (*He is on the point of breaking down.*) Come. (*A drum is heard in the shelter; and* BILL, *with a gasp, escapes from the spell as* BARBARA *turns quickly.* ADOLPHUS *enters from the shelter with a big drum.*) Oh! there you are, Dolly. Let me introduce a new friend of mine, Mr Bill Walker. This is my bloke, Bill: Mr Cusins. (CUSINS *salutes with his drumstick.*)

BILL: Gowin to merry im?

BARBARA: Yes.

BILL (*fervently*): Gawd elp im! Gaw-aw-aw-awd elp im!

BARBARA: Why? Do you think he wont be happy with me?

BILL: Awve aony ed to stend it for a mawnin: e'll ev to stend it for a lawftawm.

CUSINS: That is a frightful reflection, Mr Walker. But I cant tear myself away from her.

BILL: Well, Aw ken. (*To* BARBARA.) Eah! do you knaow where Aw'm gowin to, and wot Aw'm gowin to do?

BARBARA: Yes: youre going to heaven; and youre coming back here before the week's out to tell me so.

BILL: You loy. Aw'm gowin to Kennintahn, to spit in Todger Fairmawl's eye. Aw beshed Jenny Ill's fice; an nar Aw'll git me aown fice beshed and cam beck and shaow it to er. Ee'll itt me ardern Aw itt her. Thatll mike us square. (*To* ADOLPHUS.) Is thet fair or is it not? Youre a genlmn: you oughter knaow.

BARBARA: Two black eyes wont make one white one, Bill.

BILL: Aw didnt awst you. Cawnt you never keep your mahth shat? Oy awst the genlmn.

CUSINS (*reflectively*): Yes: I think youre right, Mr Walker. Yes: I should do it. It's curious: it's exactly what an ancient Greek would have done.

BARBARA: But what good will it do?

CUSINS: Well, it will give Mr Fairmile some exercise; and it will satisfy Mr Walker's soul.

BILL: Rot! there aint nao such a thing as a saoul. Ah kin you tell wevver Awve a saoul or not? You never seen it.

BARBARA: Ive seen it hurting you when you went against it.

BILL (*with compressed aggravation*): If you was maw gel and took the word aht o me mahth lawk thet, Aw'd give you sathink youd feel urtin, Aw would. (*To* ADOLPHUS.) You tike maw tip, mite. Stop er jawr; or youll doy afoah your tawm (*With intense expression.*) Wore aht: thets wot youll be: wore aht. (*He goes away through the gate.*)

CUSINS (*looking after him*): I wonder!

BARBARA: Dolly! (*indignant, in her mother's manner*).

CUSINS: Yes, my dear, it's very wearing to be in love with you. If it lasts, I quite think I shall die young.

BARBARA: Should you mind?

CUSINS: Not at all. (*He is suddenly softened, and kisses her over the drum, evidently not for the first time, as people cannot kiss over a big drum without practice.* UNDERSHAFT *coughs.*)

BARBARA: It's all right, papa, weve not forgotten you. Dolly: explain the place to papa: I havnt time. (*She goes busily into the shelter.*)

(UNDERSHAFT *and* ADOLPHUS *now have the yard to themselves.* UNDERSHAFT, *seated on a form, and still keenly attentive, looks hard at* ADOLPHUS. ADOLPHUS *looks hard at him.*)

UNDERSHAFT: I fancy you guess something of what is in my mind, Mr Cusins. (CUSINS *flourishes his drumsticks as if in the act of beating a lively rataplan, but makes no sound.*) Exactly so. But suppose Barbara finds you out!

CUSINS: You know, I do not admit that I am imposing on Barbara. I am quite genuinely interested in the views of the Salvation Army. The fact is, I am a sort of collector of religions; and the curious thing is that I find I can believe them all. By the way, have you any religion?

UNDERSHAFT: Yes.

CUSINS: Anything out of the common?

UNDERSHAFT: Only that there are two things necessary to Salvation.

CUSINS (*disappointed, but polite*): Ah, the Church Catechism. Charles Lomax also belongs to the Established Church.

UNDERSHAFT: The two things are —

CUSINS: Baptism and —

UNDERSHAFT: No. Money and gunpowder.

CUSINS (*surprised, but interested*): That is the general opinion of our governing classes. The novelty is in hearing any man confess it.

UNDERSHAFT: Just so.

CUSINS: Excuse me: is there any place in your religion for honor, justice, truth, love, mercy and so forth?

UNDERSHAFT: Yes: they are the graces and luxuries of a rich, strong, and safe life.

CUSINS: Suppose one is forced to choose between them and money or gunpowder?

UNDERSHAFT: Choose money and gunpowder; for without enough of both you cannot afford the others.

CUSINS: That is your religion?

UNDERSHAFT: Yes.

(*The cadence of this reply makes a full close in the conversation,* CUSINS *twists his face dubiously and contemplates* UNDERSHAFT. UNDERSHAFT *contemplates him.*)

CUSINS: Barbara wont stand that. You will have to choose between your religion and Barbara.

UNDERSHAFT: So will you, my friend. She will find out that that drum of yours is hollow.

CUSINS: Father Undershaft: you are mistaken: I am a sincere Salvationist. You do not understand the Salvation Army. It is the army of joy, of love, of courage: it has banished the fear and remorse and despair of the old hell-ridden evangelical sects: it marches to fight the devil with trumpet and drum, with music and dancing, with banner and palm, as becomes a sally from heaven by its happy garrison. It picks the waster out of the public house and makes a man of him: it finds a worm wriggling in a back kitchen, and lo! a woman! Men and women of rank too, sons and daughters of the Highest. It takes the poor professor of Greek, the most artificial and self-suppressed of human creatures, from his meal of roots, and lets loose the rhapsodist in him; reveals the true worship of Dionysos to him; sends him down the public street drumming dithyrambs. (*He plays a thundering flourish on the drum.*)

UNDERSHAFT: You will alarm the shelter.

CUSINS: Oh, they are accustomed to these sudden ecstasies. However, if the drum worries you — (*He pockets the drumsticks; unhooks the drum; and stands it on the ground opposite the gateway.*)

UNDERSHAFT: Thank you.

CUSINS: You remember what Euripides says about your money and gunpowder?

UNDERSHAFT: No.

CUSINS (*declaiming*):

One and another
In money and guns may outpass his brother;
And men in their millions float and flow
And seethe with a million hopes as leaven;
And they win their will; or they miss their will;
And their hopes are dead or are pined for still;
    But who'er can know
    As the long days go
That to live is happy, has found his heaven.

My translation: what do you think of it?

UNDERSHAFT: I think, my friend, that if you wish to know, as the long days go, that to live is happy, you must first acquire money enough for a decent life, and power enough to be your own master.

CUSINS: You are damnably discouraging. (*He resumes his declamation.*)

    Is it so hard a thing to see
    That the spirit of God — whate'er it be —
The law that abides and changes not, ages long,
The Eternal and Nature-born: these things be strong?
What else is Wisdom? What of Man's endeavor,
Or God's high grace so lovely and so great?
To stand from fear set free? to breathe and wait?
To hold a hand uplifted over Fate?
And shall not Barbara be loved for ever?

UNDERSHAFT: Euripides mentions Barbara, does he?

CUSINS: It is a fair translation. The word means Loveliness.

UNDERSHAFT: May I ask — as Barbara's father — how much a year she is to be loved for ever on?

CUSINS: As for Barbara's father, that is more your affair than mine. I can feed her by teaching Greek: that is about all.

UNDERSHAFT: Do you consider it a good match for her?

CUSINS (*with polite obstinacy*): Mr Undershaft: I am in many ways a weak, timid, ineffectual person; and my health is far from satisfactory. But whenever I feel that I must have anything, I get it, sooner or later. I feel that way about Barbara. I dont like marriage: I feel intensely afraid of it; and I dont know what I shall do with Barbara or what she will do with me. But I feel that I and nobody else must marry her. Please regard that as settled. — Not that I wish to be artibrary; but why should I waste your time in discussing what is inevitable?

UNDERSHAFT: You mean that you will stick at nothing: not even the conversion of the Salvation Army to the worship of Dionysos.

CUSINS: The business of the Salvation Army is to save, not to wrangle about the name of the pathfinder. Dionysos or another: what does it matter?

UNDERSHAFT (*rising and approaching him*): Professor Cusins: you are a young man after my own heart.

CUSINS: Mr Undershaft: you are, as far as I am able to gather, a most infernal old rascal; but you appeal very strongly to my sense of ironic humor.

(UNDERSHAFT *mutely offers his hand. They shake.*)

UNDERSHAFT (*suddenly concentrating himself*): And now to business.

CUSINS: Pardon me. We are discussing religion. Why go back to such an uninteresting and unimportant subject as business?

UNDERSHAFT: Religion is our business at present, because it is through religion alone that we can win Barbara.

CUSINS: Have you, too, fallen in love with Barbara?

UNDERSHAFT: Yes, with a father's love.

CUSINS: A father's love for a grown-up daughter is the most dangerous of all infatuations. I apologize for mentioning my own pale, coy, mistrustful fancy in the same breath with it.

UNDERSHAFT: Keep to the point. We have to win her; and we are neither of us Methodists.

CUSINS: That doesnt matter. The power Barbara wields here — the power that wields Barbara herself — is not Calvinism, not Presbyterianism, not Methodism —

UNDERSHAFT: Not Greek Paganism either, eh?

CUSINS: I admit that. Barbara is quite original in her religion.

UNDERSHAFT (*triumphantly*): Aha! Barbara Undershaft would be. Her inspiration comes from within herself.

CUSINS: How do you suppose it got there?

UNDERSHAFT (*in towering excitement*): It is the Undershaft inheritance. I shall hand on my torch to my daughter. She shall make my converts and preach my gospel —

CUSINS: What! Money and gunpowder!

UNDERSHAFT: Yes, money and gunpowder. Freedom and power. Command of life and command of death.

CUSINS (*urbanely: trying to bring him down to earth*): This is extremely interesting, Mr Undershaft. Of course you know that you are mad.

UNDERSHAFT (*with redoubled force*): And you?

CUSINS: Oh, mad as a hatter. You are welcome to my secret since I have discovered yours. But I am astonished. Can a madman make cannons?

UNDERSHAFT: Would anyone else than a madman make them? And now (*with surging energy*) question for question. Can a sane man translate Euripides?

CUSINS: No.

UNDERSHAFT (*seizing him by the shoulder*): Can a sane woman make a man of a waster or a woman of a worm?

CUSINS (*reeling before the storm*): Father Colossus — Mammoth Millionaire —

UNDERSHAFT (*pressing him*): Are there two mad people or three in this Salvation shelter today?

CUSINS: You mean Barbara is as mad as we are?

UNDERSHAFT (*pushing him lightly off and resuming his equanimity suddenly and completely*): Pooh, Professor! let us call things by their proper names. I am a millionaire; you are a poet: Barbara is a savior of souls. What have we three to do with the common mob of slaves and idolators? (*He sits down again with a shrug of contempt for the mob.*)

CUSINS: Take care! Barbara is in love with the common people. So am I. Have you never felt the romance of that love?

UNDERSHAFT (*cold and sardonic*): Have you ever been in love with Poverty, like St Francis? Have you ever been in love with Dirt, like St Simeon! Have you ever been in love with disease and suffering, like our nurses and philanthropists? Such passions are not virtues, but the most unnatural of all the vices. This love of the common people may please an earl's granddaughter and a university professor; but I have been a common man and a poor man; and it has no romance for me. Leave it to the poor to pretend that poverty is a blessing: leave it to the coward to make a religion of his cowardice by preaching humility: we know better than that. We three must stand together above the common people: how else can we help their children to climb up beside us? Barbara must belong to us, not to the Salvation Army.

CUSINS: Well, I can only say that if you think you will get her away from the Salvation Army by talking to her as you have been talking to me, you don't know Barbara.

UNDERSHAFT: My friend: I never ask for what I can buy.

CUSINS (*in a white fury*): Do I understand you to imply that you can buy Barbara?

UNDERSHAFT: No; but I can buy the Salvation Army.

CUSINS: Quite impossible.

UNDERSHAFT: You shall see. All religious organizations exist by selling themselves to the rich.

CUSINS: Not the Army. That is the Church of the poor.

UNDERSHAFT: All the more reason for buying it.

CUSINS: I don't think you quite know what the Army does for the poor.

UNDERSHAFT: Oh yes I do. It draws their teeth: that is enough for me as a man of business.

CUSINS: Nonsense! It makes them sober —

UNDERSHAFT: I prefer sober workmen. The profits are larger.

CUSINS: — honest —

UNDERSHAFT: Honest workmen are the most economical.

CUSINS: — attached to their homes —

UNDERSHAFT: So much the better: they will put up with anything sooner than change their shop.

CUSINS: — happy —

UNDERSHAFT: An invaluable safeguard against revolution.

CUSINS: — unselfish —

UNDERSHAFT: Indifferent to their own interests, which suits me exactly.

CUSINS: — with their thoughts on heavenly things —

UNDERSHAFT (*rising*): And not on Trade Unionism nor Socialism. Excellent.

CUSINS (*revolted*): You really are an infernal old rascal.

UNDERSHAFT (*indicating* PETER SHIRLEY, *who has just come from the shelter and strolled dejectedly down the yard between them*): And this is an honest man!

SHIRLEY: Yes; and what av I got by it? (*He passes on bitterly and sits on the form, in the corner of the penthouse.*)

(SNOBBY PRICE, *beaming sactimoniously, and* JENNY HILL, *with a tambourine full of coppers, come from the shelter and go to the drum, on which* JENNY *begins to count the money.*)

UNDERSHAFT (*replying to* SHIRLEY): Oh, your employers must have got a good deal by it from first to last. (*He sits on the table, with one foot on the side form.* CUSINS, *overwhelmed, sits down on the same form nearer the shelter.* BARBARA *comes from the shelter to the middle of the yard. She is excited and a little overwrought.*)

BARBARA: We've just had a splendid experience meeting at the other gate in Cripps's lane. I've hardly ever seen them so much moved as they were by your confession, Mr Price.

PRICE: I could almost be glad of my past wickedness if I could believe that it would elp to keep hathers stright.

BARBARA: So it will, Snobby. How much, Jenny?

JENNY: Four and tenpence, Major.

BARBARA: Oh Snobby, if you had given your poor mother just one more kick, we should have got the whole five shillings!

PRICE: If she heard you say that, miss, she'd be sorry I didnt. But I'm glad. Oh what a joy it will be to her when she hears I'm saved!

UNDERSHAFT: Shall I contribute the odd twopence, Barbara? The millionaire's mite, eh? (*He takes a couple of pennies from his pocket.*)

BARBARA: How did you make that twopence?

UNDERSHAFT: As usual. By selling cannons, torpedoes, submarines, and my new patent Grand Duke hand grenade.

BARBARA: Put it back in your pocket. You cant buy your salvation here for twopence: you must work it out.

UNDERSHAFT: Is twopence not enough? I can afford a little more, if you press me.

BARBARA: Two million millions would not be enough. There is bad blood on your hands; and nothing but good blood can cleanse them. Money is no use. Take it away. (*She turns to* CUSINS.) Dolly: you must write another letter for me to the papers. (*He makes a wry face.*) Yes: I know you dont like it; but it must be done. The starvation this winter is beating us: everybody is unemployed. The General says we must close this shelter if we cant get more money. I force the collections at the meetings until I am ashamed: dont I, Snobby?

PRICE: It's a fair treat to see you work it, miss. The way you got them up from three-and-six to four-and-ten with that hymn, penny by penny and verse by verse, was a caution. Not a Cheap Jack on Mile End Waste could touch you at it.

BARBARA: Yes; but I wish we could do without it. I am getting at last to think more of the collection than of the people's souls. And what are those hatfuls of pence and halfpence? We want thousands! tens of thousands! hundreds of thousands! I want to convert people, not to be always begging for the Army in a way I'd die sooner than beg for myself.

UNDERSHAFT (*in profound irony*): Genuine unselfishness is capable of anything, my dear.

BARBARA (*unsuspectingly, as she turns away to take the money from the drum and put it in a cash bag she carries*): Yes, isnt it? (UNDERSHAFT *looks sardonically at* CUSINS.)

CUSINS (*aside to* UNDERSHAFT): Mephistopheles! Machiavelli!

BARBARA (*tears coming into her eyes as she ties the bag and pockets it*): How are we to feed them? I cant talk religion to a man with bodily hunger in his eyes. (*Almost breaking down.*) It's frightful.

JENNY (*running to her*): Major, dear —

BARBARA (*rebounding*): No: dont comfort

me. It will be all right. We shall get the money.

UNDERSHAFT: How?

JENNY: By praying for it, of course. Mrs Baines says she prayed for it last night; and she has never prayed for it in vain: never once. (*She goes to the gate and looks out into the street.*)

BARBARA (*who has dried her eyes and regained her composure*): By the way, dad, Mrs Baines has come to march with us to our big meeting this afternoon; and she is very anxious to meet you, for some reason or other. Perhaps she'll convert you.

UNDERSHAFT: I shall be delighted, my dear.

JENNY (*at the gate: excitedly*): Major! Major! heres that man back again.

BARBARA: What man?

JENNY: The man that hit me. Oh, I hope he's coming back to join us.

(BILL WALKER, *with frost on his jacket, comes through the gate, his hands deep in his pockets and his chin sunk between his shoulders, like a cleaned-out gambler. He halts between* BARBARA *and the drum.*)

BARBARA: Hullo, Bill! Back already!

BILL (*nagging at her*): Bin talkin ever sence, ev you?

BARBARA: Pretty nearly. Well, has Todger paid you out for poor Jenny's jaw?

BILL: Nao e aint.

BARBARA: I thought your jacket looked a bit snowy.

BILL: Sao it is snaowy. You want to knaow where the snaow cam from, downt you?

BARBARA: Yes.

BILL: Well, it cam from orf the grahnd in Pawkinses Corner in Kennintahn. It got rabbed orf be maw shaoulders: see?

BARBARA: Pity you didnt rub some off with your knees, Bill! That would have done you a lot of good.

BILL (*with sour mirthless humor*): Aw was sivin another menn's knees at the tawm. E was kneelin on moy ed, e was.

JENNY: Who was kneeling on your head?

BILL: Todger was. E was pryin for me: pryin camfortable wiv me as a cawpet. Sow was Mog. Sao was the aol bloomin meetin. Mog she sez 'Ow Lawd brike is stabborn sperrit; bat downt urt is dear art.' Thet was wot she said. 'Downt urt is dear art'! An er blowk — thirteen stun

four! — kneelin wiv all is wight on me. Fanny, aint it?

JENNY: Oh no. We're so sorry, Mr Walker.

BARBABA (*enjoying it frankly*): Nonsense! of course it's funny. Served you right, Bill! You must have done something to him first.

BILL (*doggedly*): Aw did wot Aw said Aw'd do. Aw spit in is eye. E looks ap at the skoy and sez, 'Ow that Aw should be fahnd worthy to be spit upon for the gospel's sike!' e sez; an Mog sez 'Glaory Alelloolier!'; an then e called me Braddher, an dahned me as if Aw was a kid and e was me mather worshin me a Setterda nawt. Aw ednt jast nao shaow wiv im at all. Arf the street pryed; an the tather arf larfed fit to split theirselves. (*To* BARBARA.) There! are you settisfawd nah?

BARBARA (*her eyes dancing*): Wish I'd been there, Bill.

BILL: Yus: youd a got in a hextra bit o talk on me, wouldnt you?

JENNY: I'm so sorry, Mr Walker.

BILL (*fiercely*): Downt you gow being sorry for me: youve no call. Listen cah. Aw browk your jawr.

JENNY: No, it didn't hurt me: indeed it didnt, except for a moment. It was only that I was frightened.

BILL: Aw downt want to be forgive be you, or be ennybody. Wot Aw did Aw'll py for. Aw trawd to gat me aown jawr browk to settisfaw you —

JENNY (*distressed*): Oh no —

BILL (*impatiently*): Tell y' Aw did: cawnt you listen to wots bein taold you? All Aw got be it was bein mide a sawt of in the pablic street for me pines. Well, if Aw cawnt settisfaw you one way, Aw ken anather. Listen cah! Aw ed two quid sived agen the frost; an Awve a pahnd of it left. A mite o mawn last week ed words with the judy e's gowing to merry. E give er wot-for; an e's bin fawnd fifteen bob. E ed a rawt to itt er cause they was gowin to be merrid; but Aw ednt nao rawt to itt you! sao put anather fawv bob on an call it a pahnd's worth. (*He produces a sovereign.*) Eahs the manney. Tike it; and lets ev no more o your forgivin an pryin and your Mijor jawrin me. Let wot Aw dan be dan an pide for; and let there be an end of it.

JENNY: Oh, I couldnt take it, Mr Walker. But if you would give a shilling or two to poor Rummy Mitchens! you really did hurt her; and she's old.

BILL (*contemptuously*): Not lawkly. Aw'd give her anather as soon as look at er. Let her ev the lawr o me as she threatened! She aint forgiven me: not mach. Wot Aw dan to er is not on me mawnd — wot she (*indicating BARBARA*) mawt call on me conscience — no more than stickin a pig. It's this Christian gime o yours that Aw wownt ev plyed agen me: this bloomin forgivin an neggin an jawrin that mikes a menn thet sore that iz lawf's a burdn to im. Aw wownt ev it, Aw tell you; sao tike your mannev and stop thraowin your silly beshed fice hap agen me.

JENNY: Major: may I take a little of it for the Army?

BARBARA: No: the Army is not to be bought. We want your soul, Bill; and we'll take nothing less.

BILL (*bitterly*): Aw knaow. Me an maw few shillins is not good enaff for you. Youre a earl's grendorter, you are. Nathink less than a andered pahnd for you.

UNDERSHAFT: Come Barbara! you could do a great deal of good with a hundred pounds. If you will set this gentleman's mind at ease by taking his pound, I will give the other ninety-nine.

(BILL, *dazed by such opulence, instinctively touches his cap.*)

BARBARA: Oh, youre too extravagant, papa. Bill offers twenty pieces of silver. All you need offer is the other ten. That will make the standard price to buy anybody who's for sale. I'm not; and the Army's not. (*To BILL.*) Youll never have another quiet moment, Bill, until you come round to us. You cant stand out against your salvation.

BILL (*sullenly*): Aw cawnt stend aht agen music awl wrastlers and awtful tangued women. Awve offered to py. Aw can do no more. Tike it or leave it. There it is. (*He throws the sovereign on the drum, and sits down on the horse-trough. The coin fascinates SNOBBY PRICE, who takes an early opportunity of dropping his cap on it.*)

(MRS BAINES *comes from the shelter. She is dressed as a Salvation Army Commissioner. She is an earnest looking woman of about 40, with a caressing, urgent voice, and an appealing manner.*)

BARBARA: This is my father, Mrs Baines. (UNDERSHAFT *comes from the table, taking his hat off with marked civility*). Try what you can do with him. He wont listen to me, because he remembers what a fool I was when I was a baby. (*She leaves them together and chats with* JENNY.)

MRS BAINES: Have you been shewn over the shelter, Mr Undershaft? You know the work we're doing, of course.

UNDERSHAFT (*very civilly*): The whole nation knows it, Mrs Baines.

MRS BAINES: No, sir: the whole nation does not know it, or we should not be crippled as we are for want of money to carry our work through the length and breadth of the land. Let me tell you that there would have been rioting this winter in London but for us.

UNDERSHAFT: You really think so?

MRS BAINES: I know it. I remember 1886, when you rich gentlemen hardened your hearts against the cry of the poor. They broke the windows of your clubs in Pall Mall.

UNDERSHAFT (*gleaming with approval of their method*): And the Mansion House Fund went up next day from thirty thousand pounds to seventy-nine thousand! I remember quite well.

MRS BAINES: Well, wont you help me to get at the people? They wont break windows then. Come here, Price. Let me shew you to this gentleman. (*Price comes to be inspected.*) Do you remember the window breaking?

PRICE: My ole father thought it was the revolution, maam.

MRS BAINES: Would you break windows now?

PRICE: Oh no, maam. The windows of caven av bin opened to me. I know now that the rich man is a sinner like myself.

RUMMY (*appearing above at the loft door*): Snobby Price!

SNOBBY: Wot is it?

RUMMY: Your mother's askin for you at the other gate in Cripps's Lane. She's heard about your confession. (*Price turns pale.*)

MRS BAINES: Go, Mr Price; and pray with her.

JENNY: You can go through the shelter, Snobby.

PRICE (*to* MRS BAINES): I couldnt face her now, maam, with all the weight of my sins fresh on me. Tell her she'll find her son at ome, waitin for her in prayer. (*He skulks off through the gate, incidentally stealing the sovereign on his way out by picking up his cap from the drum.*)

MRS BAINES (*with swimming eyes*): You see how we take the anger and the bitterness against you out of their hearts, Mr Undershaft.

UNDERSHAFT: It is certainly most convenient and gratifying to all large employers of labor, Mrs Baines.

MRS BAINES: Barbara: Jenny: I have good news: most wonderful news. (JENNY *runs to her.*) My prayers have been answered. I told you they would, Jenny, didnt I?

JENNY: Yes, yes.

BARBARA (*moving nearer to the drum*): Have we got money enough to keep the shelter open?

MRS BAINES: I hope we shall have enough to keep all the shelters open. Lord Saxmundham has promised us five thousand pounds —

BARBARA: Hooray!

JENNY: Glory!

MRS BAINES: — if —

BARBARA: 'If!' If what?

MRS BAINES: — if five other gentlemen will give a thousand each to make it up to ten thousand.

BARBARA: Who is Lord Saxmundham? I never heard of him.

UNDERSHAFT (*who has pricked up his ears at the peer's name, and is now watching* BARBARA *curiously*): A new creation, my dear. You have heard of Sir Horace Bodger?

BARBARA: Bodger! Do you mean the distiller? Bodger's whiskey!

UNDERSHAFT: That is the man. He is one of the greatest of our public benefactors. He restored the cathedral at Hakington. They made him a baronet for that. He gave half a million to the funds of his party: they made him a baron for that.

SHIRLEY: What will they give him for the five thousand?

UNDERSHAFT: There is nothing left to give him. So the five thousand, I should think, is to save his soul.

MRS BAINES: Heaven grant it may! O Mr Undershaft, you have some very rich friends. Cant you help us towards the other five thousand? We are going to hold a great meeting this afternoon at the Assembly Hall in the Mile End Road. If I could only announce that one gentleman had come forward to support Lord Saxmundham, others would follow. Dont you know somebody? couldnt you? wouldn't you? (*her eyes fill with tears*) oh,

think of those poor people, Mr Undershaft: think of how much it means to them, and how little to a great man like you.

UNDERSHAFT (*sardonically gallant*): Mrs Baines: you are irresistible. I cant disappoint you; and I cant deny myself the satisfaction of making Bodger pay up. You shall have your five thousand pounds.

MRS BAINES: Thank God!

UNDERSHAFT: You dont thank me?

MRS BAINES: Oh sir, dont try to be cynical: dont be ashamed of being a good man. The Lord will bless you abundantly; and our prayers will be like a strong fortification round you all the days of your life. (*With a touch of caution.*) You will let me have the cheque to shew at the meeting, wont you? Jenny: go in and fetch a pen and ink. (JENNY *runs to the shelter door.*)

UNDERSHAFT: Do not disturb Miss Hill: I have a fountain pen (JENNY *halts. He sits at the table and writes the cheque.* CUSINS *rises to make room for him. They all watch him silently.*)

BILL (*cynically, aside to* BARBARA, *his voice and accent horribly debased*): Wot prawce selvytion nah?

BARBARA: Stop. (UNDERSHAFT *stops writing: they all turn to her in surprise.*) Mrs Baines: are you really going to take this money?

MRS BAINES (*astonished*): Why not, dear?

BARBARA: Why not! Do you know what my father is? Have you forgotten that Lord Saxmundham is Bodger the whisky man? Do you remember how we implored the County Council to stop him from writing Bodger's Whisky in letters of fire against the sky; so that the poor drink-ruined creatures on the Embankment could not wake up from their snatches of sleep without being reminded of their deadly thirst by that wicked sky sign? Do you know that the worst thing I have had to fight here is not the devil, but Bodger, Bodger, Bodger, with his whisky, his distilleries, and his tied houses? Are you going to make our shelter another tied house for him, and ask me to keep it?

BILL: Rotten dranken whisky it is too.

MRS BAINES: Dear Barbara: Lord Saxmundham has a soul to be saved like any of us. If heaven has found the way to make a good use of his money, are we to set ourselves up against the answer to our prayers?

BARBARA: I know he has a soul to be saved. Let him come down here; and I'll do my best to help him to his salvation. But he wants to send his cheque down to buy us, and go on being as wicked as ever.

UNDERSHAFT (*with a reasonableness which* CUSINS *alone perceives to be ironical*): My dear Barbara: alcohol is a very necessary article. It heals the sick —

BARBARA: It does nothing of the sort.

UNDERSHAFT: Well, it assists the doctor: that is perhaps a less questionable way of putting it. It makes life bearable to millions of people who could not endure their existence if they were quite sober. It enables Parliament to do things at eleven at night that no sane person would do at eleven in the morning. Is it Bodger's fault that this inestimable gift is deplorably abused by less than one per cent of the poor? (*He turns again to the table; signs the cheque; and crosses it.*)

MRS BAINES: Barbara: will there be less drinking or more if all those poor souls we are saving come tomorrow and find the doors of our shelters shut in their faces? Lord Saxmundham gives us the money to stop drinking — to take his own business from him.

CUSINS (*impishly*): Pure self-sacrifice on Bodger's part, clearly! Bless dear Bodger! (BARBARA *almost breaks down as* ADOLPHUS, *too, fails her.*)

UNDERSHAFT (*tearing the cheque and pocketing the book as he rises and goes past* CUSINS *to* MRS BAINES): I also, Mrs Baines, may claim a little disinterestedness. Think of my business! think of the widows and orphans! the men and lads torn to pieces with shrapnel and poisoned with lyddite! (MRS BAINES *shrinks; but he goes on remorselessly*) the oceans of blood, not one drop of which is shed in a really just cause! the ravaged crops! the peaceful peasants forced, women and men, to till their fields under the fire of opposing armies on pain of starvation! the bad blood of the fierce little cowards at home who egg on others to fight for the gratification of their national vanity! All this makes money for me: I am never richer, never busier than when the papers are full of it. Well, it is your work to preach peace on earth and good will to men. (MRS BAINES's *face lights up again.*) Every convert you make is a vote against war. (*Her lips move in prayer.*) Yet I give you this money to help you to

hasten my own commercial ruin. (*He gives her the cheque.*)

CUSINS (*mounting the form in an ecstasy of mischief*): The millennium will be inaugurated by the unselfishness of Undershaft and Bodger. Oh be joyful! (*He takes the drumsticks from his pocket and flourishes them.*)

MRS BAINES (*taking the cheque*): The longer I live the more proof I see that there is an Infinite Goodness that turns everything to the work of salvation sooner or later. Who would have thought that any good could have come out of war and drink? And yet their profits are brought today to the feet of salvation to do its blessed work. (*She is affected to tears.*)

JENNY (*running to* MRS BAINES *and throwing her arms around her*): Oh dear! how blessed, how glorious it all is!

CUSINS (*in a convulsion of irony*): Let us seize this unspeakable moment. Let us march to the great meeting at once. Excuse me just an instant. (*He rushes into the shelter.* JENNY *takes her tambourine from the drum head.*)

MRS BAINES: Mr Undershaft: have you ever seen a thousand people fall on their knees with one impulse and pray? Come with us to the meeting. Barbara shall tell them that the Army is saved, and saved through you.

CUSINS (*returning impetuously from the shelter with a flag and a trombone, and coming between* MRS BAINES *and* UNDERSHAFT): You shall carry the flag down the first street, Mrs Baines (*he gives her the flag*). Mr Undershaft is a gifted trombonist: he shall intone an Olympian diapason to the West Ham Salvation March. (*Aside to* UNDERSHAFT, *as he forces the trombone on him.*) Blow, Machiavelli, blow.

UNDERSHAFT (*aside to him, as he takes the trombone*): The trumpet in Zion! (CUSINS *rushes to the drum, which he takes up and puts on.* UNDERSHAFT *continues, aloud.*) I will do my best. I could vamp a bass if I knew the tune.

CUSINS: It is a wedding chorus from one of Donizetti's operas; but we have converted it. We convert everything to good here, including Bodger. You remember the chorus. 'For thee immense rejoicing — immenso giubilo — immenso giubilo.' (*With drum obbligato.*) Rum tum ti tum tum, tum tum ti ta —

BARBARA: Dolly: you are breaking my heart.

CUSINS: What is a broken heart more or less here? Dionysos Undershaft has descended. I am possessed.

MRS BAINES: Come, Barbara: I must have my dear Major to carry the flag with me.

JENNY: Yes, yes, Major darling.

CUSINS (*snatches the tambourine out of* JENNY's *hand and mutely offers it to* BARBARA).

BARBARA (*coming forward a little as she puts the offer behind her with a shudder, whilst* CUSINS *recklessly tosses the tambourine back to* JENNY *and goes to the gate*): I cant come.

JENNY: Not come!

MRS BAINES (*with tears in her eyes*): Barbara: do you think I am wrong to take the money?

BARBARA (*impulsively going to her and kissing her*): No, no: God help you, dear, you must: you are saving the Army. Go; and may you have a great meeting!

JENNY: But arnt you coming?

BARBARA: No. (*She begins taking off the silver S brooch from her collar.*)

MRS BAINES: Barbara: what are you doing?

JENNY: Why are you taking your badge off? You cant be going to leave us, Major.

BARBARA (*quietly*): Father: come here.

UNDERSHAFT (*coming to her*): My dear! (*Seeing that she is going to pin the badge on his collar, he retreats to the penthouse in some alarm.*)

BARBARA (*following him*): Dont be frightened. (*She pins the badge on and steps back towards the table, shewing him to the others.*) There! It's not much for £5000, is it?

MRS BAINES: Barbara: if you wont come and pray with us, promise me you will pray for us.

BARBARA: I cant pray now. Perhaps I shall never pray again.

MRS BAINES: Barbara!

JENNY: Major!

BARBARA (*almost delirious*): I cant bear any more. Quick march!

CUSINS (*calling to the procession in the street outside*): Off we go. Play up, there! Immenso giubilo. (*He gives the time with his drum; and the band strikes up the march, which rapidly becomes more distant as the procession moves briskly away.*)

MRS BAINES: I must go, dear. Youre overworked: you will be all right tomorrow. We'll never lose you. Now Jenny: step out with the old flag. Blood and Fire! (*She marches out through the gate with her flag.*)

JENNY: Glory Hallelujah! (*flourishing her tambourine and marching*).

UNDERSHAFT (*to* CUSINS, *as he marches out past him easing the slide of his trombone*): 'My ducats and my daughter'!

CUSINS (*following him out*): Money and gunpowder!

BARBARA: Drunkenness and Murder! My God: why hast thou forsaken me?

(*She sinks on the form with her face buried in her hands. The march passes away into silence.* BILL WALKER *steals across to her.*)

BILL (*taunting*): Wot prawce selvytion nah?

SHIRLEY: Dont you hit her when she's down.

BILL: She itt me wen aw wiz dahn. Waw shouldnt Aw git a bit o me aown beck?

BARBARA (*raising her head*): I didnt take your money, Bill.

(*She crosses the yard to the gate and turns her back on the two men to hide her face from them.*)

BILL (*sneering after her*): Naow, it warnt enaff for you. (*Turning to the drum, he misses the money.*) Ellow! If you aint took it sammun else ez. Weres it gorn? Bly me if Jenny Ill didnt tike it arter all!

RUMMY (*screaming at him from the loft*): You lie, you dirty blackguard! Snobby Price pinched it off the drum when he took up his cap. I was up here all the time an see im do it.

BILL: Wot! Stowl maw manney! Waw didnt you call thief on him, you silly aold macker you?

RUMMY: To serve you aht for ittin me acrost the ficc. It's cost y'pahnd, that az. (*Raising a pæan of squalid triumph.*) I done you. I'm even with you. Uve ad it aht o y — (BILL *snatches up* SHIRLEY's *mug and hurls it at her. She slams the loft door and vanishes. The mug smashes against the door and falls in fragments.*)

BILL (*beginning to chuckle*): Tell us, aol menn, wot o'clock this mawnin was it wen im as they call Snobby Prawce was sived?

BARBARA (*turning to him more composedly, and with unspoiled sweetness*): About half past twelve, Bill. And he pinched your pound at a quarter to two. I know. Well, you cant afford to lose it. I'll send it to you.

BILL (*his voice and accent suddenly improv-*

ing): Not if Aw wiz to stawve for it. Aw aint to be bought.

SHIRLEY: Aint you? Youd sell yourself to the devil for a pint o'beer; only there aint no devil to make the offer.

BILL (*unashamed*): Sao Aw would, mite, and often cv, cheerful. But she cawnt baw me. (*Approaching* BARBARA.) You wanted maw saoul, did you? Well, you aint got it.

BARBARA: I nearly got it, Bill. But weve sold it back to you for ten thousand pounds.

SHIRLEY: And dear at the money!

BARBARA: No, Peter: it was worth more than money.

BILL (*salvationproof*): It's nao good: you cawnt get rahnd me nah. Aw downt blieve in it; and Awve seen tody that Aw was rawt. (*Going.*) Sao long, aol soupkitchener! Ta, ta, Mijor Earl's Grendorter! (*Turning at the gate.*) Wot prawce selvytion nah? 'Snobby Prawce! Ha! ha!

BARBARA (*offering her hand*): Goodbye, Bill.

BILL (*taken aback, half plucks his cap off; then shoves it on again defiantly*): Git aht. (BARBARA *drops her hand, discouraged. He has a twinge of remorse.*) But thets aw rawt, you knaow. Nathink pasnl. Naow mellice. Sao long, Judy. (*He goes.*)

BARBARA: No malice. So long, Bill.

SHIRLEY (*shaking his head*): You make too much of him, miss, in your innocence.

BARBARA (*going to him*): Peter: I'm like you now. Cleaned out, and lost my job.

SHIRLEY: Youve youth an hope. Thats two better than me.

BARBARA: I'll get you a job, Peter. Thats hope for you: the youth will have to be enough for me. (*She counts her money.*) I have just enough left for two teas at Lockharts, a Rowton doss for you, and my tram and bus home. (*He frowns and rises with offended pride. She takes his arm.*) Dont be proud, Peter: it's sharing between friends. And promise me youll talk to me and not let me cry. (*She draws him towards the gate.*)

SHIRLEY: Well, I'm not accustomed to talk to the like of you —

BARBARA (*urgently*): Yes, yes: you must talk to me. Tell me about Tom Paine's books and Bradlaugh's lectures. Come along.

SHIRLEY: Ah, if you would only read Tom Paine in the proper spirit, miss! (*They go out through the gate together.*)

ACT III

Next day after lunch LADY BRITOMART *is writing in the library in Wilton Crescent.* SARAH *is reading in the armchair near the window.* BARBARA, *in ordinary fashionable dress, pale and brooding, is on the settee.* CHARLES LOMAX *enters. He starts on seeing* BARBARA *fashionably attired and in low spirits.*

LOMAX: Youve left off your uniform!

(BARBARA *says nothing; but an expression of pain passes over her face.*)

LADY BRITOMART (*warning him in low tones to be careful*): Charles!

LOMAX (*much concerned, coming behind the settee and bending sympathetically over* BARBARA): I'm awfully sorry, Barbara. You know I helped you all I could with the concertina and so forth. (*Momentously.*) Still, I have never shut my eyes to the fact that there is a certain amount of tosh about the Salvation Army. Now the claims of the Church of England —

LADY BRITOMART: Thats enough, Charles. Speak of something suited to your mental capacity.

LOMAX: But surely the Church of England is suited to all our capacities.

BARBARA (*pressing his hand*): Thank you for your sympathy, Cholly. Now go and spoon with Sarah.

LOMAX (*dragging a chair from the writing table and seating himself affectionately by* SARAH's *side*): How is my ownest today?

SARAH: I wish you wouldnt tell Cholly to do things, Barbara. He always comes straight and does them. Cholly: we're going to the works this afternoon.

LOMAX: What works?

SARAH: The cannon works.

LOMAX: What? your governor's shop!

SARAH: Yes.

LOMAX: Oh I say!

(CUSINS *enters in poor condition. He also starts visibly when he sees* BARBARA *without her uniform.*)

BARBARA: I expected you this morning, Dolly. Didnt you guess that?

CUSINS (*sitting down beside her*): I'm sorry. I have only just breakfasted.

SARAH: But weve just finished lunch.

BARBARA: Have you had one of your bad nights?

CUSINS: No: I had rather a good night: in fact, one of the most remarkable nights I have ever passed.

BARBARA: The meeting?

CUSINS: No: after the meeting.

LADY BRITOMART: You should have gone to bed after the meeting. What were you doing?

CUSINS: *Drinking*.

LADY BRITOMART.	Adolphus!
SARAH.	Dolly!
BARBARA.	Dolly!
LOMAX.	Oh I say!

LADY BRITOMART: What were you drinking, may I ask?

CUSINS: A most devilish kind of Spanish burgundy, warranted free from added alcohol: a Temperance burgundy in fact. Its richness in natural alcohol made any addition superfluous.

BARBARA: Are you joking, Dolly?

CUSINS (*patiently*): No. I have been making a night of it with the nominal head of this household: that is all.

LADY BRITOMART: Andrew made you drunk!

CUSINS: No: he only provided the wine. I think it was Dionysos who made me drunk. (*To* BARBARA.) I told you I was possessed.

LADY BRITOMART: Youre not sober yet. Go home to bed at once.

CUSINS: I have never before ventured to reproach you, Lady Brit; but how could you marry the Prince of Darkness?

LADY BRITOMART: It was much more excusable to marry him than to get drunk with him. That is a new accomplishment of Andrew's, by the way. He usent to drink.

CUSINS: He doesnt now. He only sat there and completed the wreck of my moral basis, the rout of my convictions, the purchase of my soul. He cares for you, Barbara. That is what makes him so dangerous to me.

BARBARA: That has nothing to do with it, Dolly. There are larger loves and diviner dreams than the fireside ones. You know that, dont you?

CUSINS: Yes: that is our understanding. I know it. I hold to it. Unless he can win me on that holier ground he may amuse me for a while; but he can get no deeper hold, strong as he is.

BARBARA: Keep to that; and the end will be right. Now tell me what happened at the meeting?

CUSINS: It was an amazing meeting. Mrs Baines almost died of emotion. Jenny Hill simply gibbered with hysteria. The Prince of Darkness played his trombone like a madman: its brazen roarings were like the laughter of the damned. 117 conversions took place then and there. They prayed with the most touching sincerity and gratitude for Bodger, and for the anonymous donor of the £5000. Your father would not let his name be given.

LOMAX: That was rather fine of the old man, you know. Most chaps would have wanted the advertisement.

CUSINS: He said all the charitable institutions would be down on him like kites on a battle-field if he gave his name.

LADY BRITOMART: Thats Andrew all over. He never does a proper thing without giving an improper reason for it.

CUSINS: He convinced me that I have all my life been doing improper things for proper reasons.

LADY BRITOMART: Adolphus: now that Barbara has left the Salvation Army, you had better leave it too. I will not have you playing that drum in the streets.

CUSINS: Your orders are already obeyed, Lady Brit.

BARBARA: Dolly: were you ever really in earnest about it? Would you have joined if you had never seen me?

CUSINS (*disingenuously*): Well — er — well, possibly, as a collector of religious —

LOMAX (*cunningly*): Not as a drummer, though, you know. You are a very clearheaded brainy chap, Dolly; and it must have been apparent to you that there is a certain amount of tosh about —

LADY BRITOMART: Charles: if you must drivel, drivel like a grown-up man and not like a schoolboy.

LOMAX (*out of countenance*): Well, drivel is drivel, dont you know, whatever a man's age.

LADY BRITOMART: In good society in England, Charles, men drivel at all ages by repeating silly formulas with an air of wisdom. Schoolboys make their own formulas out of slang, like you. When they reach your age, and get political private secretaryships and things of that sort, they drop slang and get their formulas out of The Spectator or The Times. You had better confine yourself to The Times. You will find that there.is a certain amount of tosh about The Times; but at least its language is reputable.

LOMAX (*overwhelmed*): You are so awfully strong-minded, Lady Brit —

LADY BRITOMART: Rubbish! (MORRISON *comes in.*) What is it?

MORRISON: If you please, my lady, Mr Undershaft has just drove up to the door.

LADY BRITOMART: Well, let him in. (MORRISON *hesitates.*) Whats the matter with you?

MORRISON: Shall I announce him, my lady; or is he at home here, so to speak, my lady?

LADY BRITOMART: Announce him.

MORRISON: Thank you, my lady. You wont mind my asking, I hope. The occasion is in a manner of speaking new to me.

LADY BRITOMART: Quite right. Go and let him in.

MORRISON: Thank you, my lady. (*He withdraws.*)

LADY BRITOMART: Children: go and get ready. (SARAH *and* BARBARA *go upstairs for their out-of-door wraps.*) Charles: go and tell Stephen to come down here in five minutes: you will find him in the drawing room. (CHARLES *goes.*) Adolphus: tell them to send round the carriage in about fifteen minutes. (ADOLPHUS *goes.*)

MORRISON (*at the door*): Mr Undershaft.

(UNDERSHAFT ·*comes in.* MORRISON *goes out.*)

UNDERSHAFT: Alone! How fortunate!

LADY BRITOMART (*rising*): Dont be sentimental, Andrew. Sit down. (*She sits on the settee: he sits beside her, on her left. She comes to the point before he has time to breathe.*) Sarah must have £800 a year until Charles Lomax comes into his property. Barbara will need more, and need it permanently, because Adolphus hasnt any property.

UNDERSHAFT (*resignedly*): Yes, my dear: I will see to it. Anything else? for yourself, for instance?

LADY BRITOMART: I want to talk to you about Stephen.

UNDERSHAFT (*rather wearily*): Dont, my dear. Stephen doesnt interest me.

LADY BRITOMART: He does interest me. He is our son.

UNDERSHAFT: Do you really think so? He has induced us to bring him into the world; but he chose his parents very incongruously, I think. I see nothing of myself in him, and less of you.

LADY BRITOMART: Andrew: Stephen is an excellent son, and a most steady, capable, highminded young man. You are simply trying to find an excuse for disinheriting him.

UNDERSHAFT: My dear Biddy: the Undershaft tradition disinherits him. It would be dishonest of me to leave the cannon foundry to my son.

LADY BRITOMART: It would be most unnatural and improper of you to leave it to anyone else, Andrew. Do you suppose this wicked and immoral tradition can be kept up for ever? Do you pretend that Stephen could not carry on the foundry just as well as all the other sons of the big business houses?

UNDERSHAFT: Yes: he could learn the office routine without understanding the business, like all the other sons; and the firm would go on by its own momentum until the real Undershaft — probably an Italian or a German — would invent a new method and cut him out.

LADY BRITOMART: There is nothing that any Italian or German could do that Stephen could not do. And Stephen at least has breeding.

UNDERSHAFT: The son of a foundling! Nonsense!

LADY BRITOMART: My son, Andrew! And even you may have good blood in your veins for all you know.

UNDERSHAFT: True. Probably I have. That is another argument in favor of a foundling.

LADY BRITOMART: Andrew: dont be aggravating. And dont be wicked. At present you are both.

UNDERSHAFT: This conversation is part of the Undershaft tradition, Biddy. Every Undershaft's wife has treated him to it ever since the house was founded. It is mere waste of breath. If the tradition be ever broken it will be for an abler man than Stephen.

LADY BRITOMART (*pouting*): Then go away.

UNDERSHAFT (*deprecatory*): Go away!

LADY BRITOMART: Yes: Go away. If you will do nothing for Stephen, you are not wanted here. Go to your foundling, whoever he is; and look after him.

UNDERSHAFT: The fact is, Biddy —

LADY BRITOMART: Dont call me Biddy. I dont call you Andy.

UNDERSHAFT: I will not call my wife Britomart: it is not good sense. Seriously, my love, the Undershaft tradition has landed me in a difficulty. I am getting on in years; and my partner Lazarus has at last made a stand and insisted that the succession must be settled once way or the other; and of course he is quite right. You see, I havent found a fit successor yet.

LADY BRITOMART (obstinately): There is Stephen.

UNDERSHAFT: Thats just it: all the foundlings I can find are exactly like Stephen.

LADY BRITOMART: Andrew!

UNDERSHAFT: I want a man with no relations and no schooling: that is, a man who would be out of the running altogether if he were not a strong man. And I cant find him. Every blessed foundling nowadays is snapped up in his infancy by Barnardo homes, or School Board officers, or Boards of Guardians; and if he shews the least ability he is fastened on by schoolmasters; trained to win scholarships like a racehorse; crammed with secondhand ideas; drilled and disciplined in docility and what they call good taste; and lamed for life so that he is fit for nothing but teaching. If you want to keep the foundry in the family, you had better find an eligible foundling and marry him to Barbara.

LADY BRITOMART: Ah! Barbara! Your pet! You would sacrifice Stephen to Barbara.

UNDERSHAFT: Cheerfully. And you, my dear, would boil Barbara to make soup for Stephen.

LADY BRITOMART: Andrew: this is not a question of our likings and dislikings: it is a question of duty. It is your duty to make Stephen your successor.

UNDERSHAFT: Just as much as it is your duty to submit to your husband. Come, Biddy! these tricks of the governing class are of no use with me. I am one of the governing class myself; and it is waste of time giving tracts to a missionary. I have the power in this matter; and I am not to be humbugged into using it for your purposes.

LADY BRITOMART: Andrew: you can talk my head off; but you cant change wrong into right. And your tie is all on one side. Put it straight.

UNDERSHAFT (disconcerted): It wont stay unless it's pinned (he fumbles at it with childish grimaces) —

(STEPHEN comes in.)

STEPHEN (at the door): I beg your pardon (about to retire).

LADY BRITOMART: No: come in, Stephen. (STEPHEN comes forward to his mother's writing table.)

UNDERSHAFT (not very cordially): Good afternoon.

STEPHEN (coldly): Good afternoon.

UNDERSHAFT (to LADY BRITOMART): He knows all about the tradition, I suppose?

LADY BRITOMART: Yes. (To STEPHEN.) It is what I told you last night, Stephen.

UNDERSHAFT (sulkily): I understand you want to come into the cannon business.

STEPHEN: I go into the trade! Certainly not.

UNDERSHAFT (opening his eyes, greatly eased in mind and manner): Oh! in that case —

LADY BRITOMART: Cannons are not trade, Stephen. They are enterprise.

STEPHEN: I have no intention of becoming a man of business in any sense. I have no capacity for business and no taste for it. I intend to devote myself to politics.

UNDERSHAFT (rising): My dear boy: this is an immense relief to me. And I trust it may prove an equally good thing for the country. I was afraid you would consider yourself disparaged and slighted. (He moves towards STEPHEN as if to shake hands with him.)

LADY BRITOMART (rising and interposing): Stephen: I cannot allow you to throw away an enormous property like this.

STEPHEN (stiffly): Mother: there must be an end of treating me as a child, if you please. (LADY BRITOMART recoils, deeply wounded by his tone.) Until last night I did not take your attitude seriously, because I did not think you meant it seriously. But I find now that you left me in the dark as to matters which you should have explained to me years ago. I am extremely hurt and offended. Any further discussion of my intentions had better take place with my father, as between one man and another.

LADY BRITOMART: Stephen! (She sits down again, her eyes filling with tears.)

UNDERSHAFT (with grave compassion): You see, my dear, it is only the big men who can be treated as children.

STEPHEN: I am sorry, mother, that you have forced me —

UNDERSHAFT (*stopping him*): Yes, yes, yes, yes: thats all right, Stephen. She wont interfere with you any more: your independence is achieved: you have won your latchkey. Dont rub it in; and above all, dont apologize. (*He resumes his seat.*) Now what about your future, as between one man and another — I beg your pardon, Biddy: as between two men and a woman.

LADY BRITOMART (*who has pulled herself together strongly*): I quite understand, Stephen. By all means go your own way if you feel strong enough. (STEPHEN *sits down magisterially in the chair at the writing table with an air of affirming his majority.*)

UNDERSHAFT: It is settled that you do not ask for the succession to the cannon business.

STEPHEN: I hope it is settled that I repudiate the cannon business.

UNDERSHAFT: Come, come! dont be so devilishly sulky: it's boyish. Freedom should be generous. Besides, I owe you a fair start in life in exchange for disinheriting you. You cant become prime minister all at once. Havnt you a turn for something? What about literature, art, and so forth?

STEPHEN: I have nothing of the artist about me, either in faculty or character, thank Heaven!

UNDERSHAFT: A philosopher, perhaps? Eh?

STEPHEN: I make no such ridiculous pretension.

UNDERSHAFT: Just so. Well, there is the army, the navy, the Church, the Bar. The Bar requires some ability. What about the Bar?

STEPHEN: I have not studied law. And I am afraid I have not the necessary push — I believe that is the name barristers give to their vulgarity — for success in pleading.

UNDERSHAFT: Rather a difficult case, Stephen. Hardly anything left but the stage, is there? (STEPHEN *makes an impatient movement.*) Well, come! is there anything you know or care for?

STEPHEN (*rising and looking at him steadily*): I know the difference between right and wrong.

UNDERSHAFT (*hugely tickled*): You dont say so! What! no capacity for business, no knowledge of law, no sympathy with art, no pretension to philosophy; only a simple knowledge of

the secret that has puzzled all the philosophers, baffled all the lawyers, muddled all the men of business, and ruined most of the artists: the secret of right and wrong. Why, man, youre a genius, a master of masters, a god! At twentyfour, too!

STEPHEN (*keeping his temper with difficulty*): You are pleased to be facetious. I pretend to nothing more than any honorable English gentleman claims as his birthright (*he sits down angrily*).

UNDERSHAFT: Oh, thats everybody's birthright. Look at poor little Jenny Hill, the Salvation lassie! she would think you were laughing at her if you asked her to stand up in the street and teach grammar or geography or mathematics or even drawing room dancing; but it never occurs to her to doubt that she can teach morals and religion. You are all alike, you respectable people. You cant tell me the bursting strain of a ten-inch gun, which is a very simple matter; but you all think you can tell me the bursting strain of a man under temptation. You darent handle high explosives; but youre all ready to handle honesty and truth and justice and the whole duty of man, and kill one another at that game. What a country! What a world!

LADY BRITOMART (*uneasily*): What do you think he had better do, Andrew?

UNDERSHAFT: Oh, just what he wants to do. He knows nothing and he thinks he knows everything. That points clearly to a political career. Get him a private secretaryship to someone who can get him an Under Secretaryship; and then leave him alone. He will find his natural and proper place in the end on the Treasury Bench.

STEPHEN (*springing up again*): I am sorry, sir, that you force me to forget the respect due to you as my father. I am an Englishman and I will not hear the Government of my country insulted. (*He thrusts his hands in his pockets, and walks angrily across to the window.*)

UNDERSHAFT (*with a touch of brutality*): The government of your country! I am the government of your country: I, and Lazarus. Do you suppose that you and half a dozen amateurs like you, sitting in a row in that foolish gabble shop, can govern Undershaft and Lazarus? No, my friend: you will do what pays us. You will make war when it suits us, and keep peace when it doesnt. You will find out that trade requires certain measures when we have decided on those measures. When I want anything to keep my dividends up, you will discover that my want is a national need. When other people want something to keep my dividends down, you will call out the police and military. And in return you shall have the support and applause of my newspapers, and the delight of imagining that you are a great statesman. Government of your country! Be off with you, my boy, and play with your caucuses and leading articles and historical parties and great leaders and burning questions and the rest of your toys. I am going back to my counting-house to pay the piper and call the tune.

STEPHEN (*actually smiling, and putting his hand on his father's shoulder with indulgent patronage*): Really, my dear father, it is impossible to be angry with you. You dont know how absurd all this sounds to me. You are very properly proud of having been industrious enough to make money; and it is greatly to your credit that you have made so much of it. But it has kept you in circles where you are valued for your money and deferred to for it, instead of in the doubtless very old-fashioned and behind-the-times public school and university where I formed my habits of mind. It is natural for you to think that money governs England; but you must allow me to think I know better.

UNDERSHAFT: And what does govern England, pray?

STEPHEN: Character, father, character.

UNDERSHAFT: Whose character? Yours or mine?

STEPHEN: Neither yours nor mine, father, but the best elements in the English national character.

UNDERSHAFT: Stephen: Ive found your profession for you. Youre a born journalist. I'll start you with a high-toned weekly review. There!

(*Before* STEPHEN *can reply* SARAH, BARBARA, LOMAX, *and* CUSINS *come in ready for walking.* BARBARA *crosses the room to the window and looks out.* CUSINS *drifts amiably to the armchair.* LOMAX *remains near the door, whilst* SARAH *comes to her mother.*

STEPHEN *goes to the smaller writing table and busies himself with his letters.*)

SARAH: Go and get ready, mamma: the carriage is waiting. (LADY BRITOMART *leaves the room.*)

UNDERSHAFT (*to* SARAH): Good day, my dear. Good afternoon, Mr Lomax.

LOMAX (*vaguely*): Ahdedoo.

UNDERSHAFT (*to* CUSINS): Quite well after last night, Euripides, eh?

CUSINS: As well as can be expected.

UNDERSHAFT: Thats right. (*To* BARBARA.) So you are coming to see my death and devastation factory, Barbara?

BARBARA (*at the window*): You came yesterday to see my salvation factory. I promised you a return visit.

LOMAX (*coming forward between* SARAH *and* UNDERSHAFT): Youll find it awfully interesting. Ive been through the Woolwich Arsenal; and it gives you a ripping feeling of security, you know, to think of the lot of beggars we could kill if it came to fighting. (*To* UNDERSHAFT, *with sudden solemnity.*) Still, it must be rather an awful reflection for you, from the religious point of view as it were. Youre getting on, you know, and all that.

SARAH: You dont mind Cholly's imbecility, papa, do you?

LOMAX (*much taken aback*): Oh I say!

UNDERSHAFT: Mr Lomax looks at the matter in a very proper spirit, my dear.

LOMAX: Just so. Thats all I meant, I assure you.

SARAH: Are you coming, Stephen?

STEPHEN: Well, I am rather busy — er — (*Magnanimously.*) Oh well, yes: I'll come. That is, if there is room for me.

UNDERSHAFT: I can take two with me in a little motor I am experimenting with for field use. You wont mind its being rather unfashionable. It's not painted yet; but it's bullet proof.

LOMAX (*appalled at the prospect of confronting Wilton Crescent in an unpainted motor*): Oh I say!

SARAH: The carriage for me, thank you. Barbara doesnt mind what she's seen in.

LOMAX: I say, Dolly, old chap: do you really mind the car being a guy? Because of course if you do I'll go in it. Still —

CUSINS: I prefer it.

LOMAX: Thanks awfully, old man. Come, my ownest. (*He hurries out to secure his seat in the carriage.* SARAH *follows him.*)

CUSINS (*moodily walking across to* LADY BRITOMART's *writing table*): Why are we two coming to this Works Department of Hell? that is what I ask myself.

BARBARA: I have always thought of it as a sort of pit where lost creatures with blackened faces stirred up smoky fires and were driven and tormented by my father? Is it like that, dad?

UNDERSHAFT (scandalized): My dear! It is a spotlessly clean and beautiful hillside town.

CUSINS: With a Methodist chapel? Oh do say theres a Methodist chapel.

UNDERSHAFT: There are two: a Primitive one and a sophisticated one. There is even an Ethical Society; but it is not much patronized, as my men are all strongly religious. In the High Explosives Sheds they object to the presence of Agnostics as unsafe.

CUSINS: And yet they dont object to you!

BARBARA: Do they obey all your orders?

UNDERSHAFT: I never give them any orders. When I speak to one of them it is 'Well, Jones, is the baby doing well? and has Mrs Jones made a good recovery?' 'Nicely, thank you, sir.' And thats all.

CUSINS: But Jones has to be kept in order. How do you maintain discipline among your men?

UNDERSHAFT: I dont. They do. You see, the one thing Jones wont stand is any rebellion from the man under him, or any assertion of social equality between the wife of the man with 4 shillings a week less than himself, and Mrs Jones! Of course they all rebel against me, theoretically. Practically, every man of them keeps the man just below him in his place. I never meddle with them. I never bully them. I dont even bully Lazarus. I say that certain things are to be done; but I dont order anybody to do them. I dont say, mind you, that there is no ordering about and snubbing and even bullying. The men snub the boys and order them about; the carmen snub the sweepers; the artisans snub the unskilled laborers; the foremen drive and bully both the laborers and artisans; the assistant engineers find fault with the foremen; the chief engineers drop on the assistants; the departmental managers worry the chiefs; and the clerks have tall hats and hymnbooks and keep up the social tone by refusing to associate on equal terms with anybody. The result is a colossal profit, which comes to me.

CUSINS (revolted): You really are a — well, what I was saying yesterday.

BARBARA: What was he saying yesterday?

UNDERSHAFT: Never mind, my dear. He thinks I have made you unhappy. Have I?

BARBARA: Do you think I can be happy in this vulgar silly dress? I! who have worn the uniform. Do you understand what you have done to me? Yesterday I had a man's soul in my hand. I set him in the way of life with his face to salvation. But when we took your money he turned back to drunkenness and derision. (With intense conviction.) I will never forgive you that. If I had a child, and you destroyed its body with your explosives — if you murdered Dolly with your horrible guns — I could forgive you if my forgiveness would open the gates of heaven to you. But to take a human soul from me, and turn it into the soul of a wolf! that is worse than any murder.

UNDERSHAFT: Does my daughter despair so easily? Can you strike a man to the heart and leave no mark on him?

BARBARA (her face lighting up): Oh, you are right: he can never be lost now: where was my faith?

CUSINS: Oh, clever clever devil!

BARBARA: You may be a devil; but God speaks through you sometimes. (She takes her father's hands and kisses them.) You have given me back my happiness: I feel it deep down now, though my spirit is troubled.

UNDERSHAFT: You have learnt something. That always feels at first as if you had lost something.

BARBARA: Well, take me to the factory of death; and let me learn something more. There must be some truth or other behind all this frightful irony. Come, Dolly. (She goes out.)

CUSINS: My guardian angel! (To UNDERSHAFT.) Avaunt! (He follows BARBARA.)

STEPHEN (quietly, at the writing table): You must not mind Cusins, father. He is a very amiable good fellow; but he is a Greek scholar and naturally a little eccentric.

UNDERSHAFT: Ah, quite so. Thank you, Stephen. Thank you. (He goes out.)

(STEPHEN smiles patronizingly; buttons his coat responsibly; and crosses the room to the door. LADY BRITOMART, dressed for out-of-doors, opens it before he reaches it. She looks round for others; looks at STEPHEN; and turns to go without a word.)

STEPHEN (embarrassed): Mother —

LADY BRITOMART: Dont be apologetic, Stephen. And dont forget that you have outgrown your mother. (*She goes out.*)

(*Perivale St Andrews lies between two Middlesex hills, half climbing the northern one. It is an almost smokeless town of white walls, roofs of narrow green slates or red tiles, tall trees, domes, campaniles, and slender chimney shafts, beautifully situated and beautiful in itself. The best view of it is obtained from the crest of a slope about half a mile to the east, where the high explosives are dealt with. The foundry lies hidden in the depths between, the tops of its chimneys sprouting like huge skittles into the middle distance. Across the crest runs an emplacement of concrete, with a firestep, and a parapet which suggests a fortification, because there is a huge cannon of the obsolete Woolwich Infant pattern peering across it at the town. The cannon is mounted on an experimental gun carriage: possibly the original model of the Undershaft disappearing rampart gun alluded to by STEPHEN. The firestep, being a convenient place to sit, is furnished here and there with straw disc cushions; and at one place there is the additional luxury of a fur rug.*)

BARBARA *is standing on the firestep, looking over the parapet towards the town. On her right is the cannon; on her left the end of a shed raised on piles, with a ladder of three or four steps up to the door, which opens outwards and has a little wooden landing at the threshold, with a fire bucket in the corner of the landing. Several dummy soldiers more or less mutilated, with straw protruding from their gashes, have been shoved out of the way under the landing. A few others are nearly upright against the shed; and one has fallen forward and lies, like a grotesque corpse, on the emplacement. The parapet stops short of the shed, leaving a gap which is the beginning of the path down the hill through the foundry to the town. The rug is on the firestep near this gap. Down on the emplacement behind the cannon is a trolley carrying a huge conical bombshell with a red band painted on it. Further to the right is the door of an office, which, like the sheds, is of the lightest possible construction.*

CUSINS *arrives by the path from the town.*)

BARBARA: Well?

CUSINS: Not a ray of hope. Everything perfect! wonderful! real! It only needs a cathedral to be a heavenly city instead of a hellish one.

BARBARA: Have you found out whether they have done anything for old Peter Shirley?

CUSINS: They have found him a job as gatekeeper and timekeeper. He's frightfully miserable. He calls the time-keeping brainwork, and says he isnt used to it; and his gate lodge is so splendid that he's ashamed to use the rooms, and skulks in the scullery.

BARBARA: Poor Peter!

(STEPHEN *arrives from the town. He carries a fieldglass.*)

STEPHEN (*enthusiastically*): Have you two seen the place? Why did you leave us?

CUSINS: I wanted to see everything I was not intended to see; and Barbara wanted to make the men talk.

STEPHEN: Have you found anything discreditable?

CUSINS: No. They call him Dandy Andy and are proud of his being a cunning old rascal; but it's all horribly, frightfully, immorally, unanswerably perfect.

(SARAH *arrives.*)

SARAH: Heavens! what a place! (*She crosses to the trolley.*) Did you see the nursing home!? (*She sits down on the shell.*)

STEPHEN: Did you see the libraries and schools!?

SARAH: Did you see the ball room and the banqueting chamber in the Town Hall!?

STEPHEN: Have you gone into the insurance fund, the pension fund, the building society, the various applications of cooperation!?

(UNDERSHAFT *comes from the office, with a sheaf of telegrams in his hand.*)

UNDERSHAFT: Well, have you seen everything? I'm sorry I was called away. (*Indicating the telegrams.*) Good news from Manchuria.

STEPHEN: Another Japanese victory?

UNDERSHAFT: Oh, I don't know. Which side wins does not concern us here. No: the good news is that the aerial battleship is a tremendous success. At the first trial it has wiped out a fort with three hundred soldiers in it.

CUSINS (*from the platform*): Dummy soldiers?

UNDERSHAFT (*striding across to* STEPHEN *and kicking the prostrate dummy brutally out of his way*): No: the real thing.

(CUSINS *and* BARBARA *exchange glances. Then* CUSINS *sits on the step and buries his face in his hands.* BARBARA *gravely lays her hand on his shoulder. He looks up at her in whimsical desperation.*)

UNDERSHAFT: Well, Stephen, what do you think of the place?

STEPHEN: Oh, magnificent. A perfect triumph of modern industry. Frankly, my dear father, I have been a fool: I had no idea of what it all meant: of the wonderful forethought, the power of organization, the administrative capacity, the financial genius, the colossal capital it represents. I have been repeating to myself as I came through your streets 'Peace hath her victories no less renowned than War.' I have only one misgiving about it all.

UNDERSHAFT: Out with it.

STEPHEN: Well, I cannot help thinking that all this provision for every want of your workmen may sap their independence and weaken their sense of responsibility. And greatly as we enjoyed our tea at that splendid restaurant — how they gave us all that luxury and cake and jam and cream for threepence I really cannot imagine! — still you must remember that restaurants break up home life. Look at the continent, for instance! Are you sure so much pampering is really good for the men's characters?

UNDERSHAFT: Well you see, my dear boy, when you are organizing civilization you have to make up your mind whether trouble and anxiety are good things or not. If you decide that they are, then, I take it, you simply dont organize civilization; and there you are, with trouble and anxiety enough to make us all angels! But if you decide the other way, you may as well go through with it. However, Stephen, our characters are safe here. A sufficient dose of anxiety is always provided by the fact that we may be blown to smithereens at any moment.

SARAH: By the way, papa, where do you make the explosives?

UNDERSHAFT: In separate little sheds, like that one. When one of them blows up, it costs very little; and only the people quite close to it are killed.

(STEPHEN, *who is quite close to it, looks at it rather scaredly, and moves away quickly to the cannon. At the same moment the door of the shed is thrown abruptly open; and a foreman in overalls and list slippers comes out on the little landing and holds the door for* LOMAX, *who appears in the doorway.*)

LOMAX (*with studied coolness*): My good fellow: you neednt get into a state of nerves. Nothing's going to happen to you; and I suppose it wouldnt be the end of the world if anything did. A little bit of British pluck is what you want, old chap. (*He descends and strolls across to* SARAH.)

UNDERSHAFT (*to the foreman*): Anything wrong, Bilton?

BILTON (*with ironic calm*): Gentleman walked into the high explosives shed and lit a cigaret, sir: thats all.

UNDERSHAFT: Ah, quite so. (*Going over to* LOMAX.) Do you happen to remember what you did with the match?

LOMAX: Oh come! I'm not a fool. I took jolly good care to blow it out before I chucked it away.

BILTON: The top of it was red hot inside, sir.

LOMAX: Well, suppose it was! I didnt chuck it into any of your messes.

UNDERSHAFT: Think no more of it, Mr Lomax. By the way, would you mind lending me your matches.

LOMAX (*offering his box*): Certainly.

UNDERSHAFT: Thanks. (*He pockets the matches.*)

LOMAX (*lecturing to the company generally*): You know, these high explosives dont go off like gunpowder, except when theyre in a gun. When theyre spread loose, you can put a match to them without the least risk: they just burn quietly like a bit of paper. (*Warming to the scientific interest of the subject.*) Did you know that, Undershaft? Have you ever tried?

UNDERSHAFT: Not on a large scale, Mr Lomax. Bilton will give you a sample of gun cotton when you are leaving if you ask him. You can experiment with it at home. (BILTON *looks puzzled.*)

SARAH: Bilton will do nothing of the sort, papa. I suppose it's your business to blow up the Russians and Japs; but you might really stop short of blowing up poor Cholly. (BILTON *gives it up and retires into the shed.*)

LOMAX: My ownest, there is no danger. (*He sits beside her on the shell.*)

(LADY BRITOMART *arrives from the town with a bouquet.*)

LADY BRITOMART (*impetuously*): Andrew: you shouldnt have let me see this place.

UNDERSHAFT: Why, my dear?

LADY BRITOMART: Never mind why: you shouldnt have: thats all. To think of all that (*indicating the town*) being yours! and that you have kept it to yourself all these years!

UNDERSHAFT: It does not belong to me. I belong to it. It is the Undershaft inheritance.

LADY BRITOMART: It is not. Your ridiculous cannons and that noisy banging foundry may be the Undershaft inheritance; but all that plate and linen, all that furniture and those houses and orchards and gardens belong to us. They belong to me: they are not a man's business. I wont give them up. You must be out of your senses to throw them all away; and if you persist in such folly, I will call in a doctor.

UNDERSHAFT (*stooping to smell the bouquet*): Where did you get the flowers, my dear?

LADY BRITOMART: Your men presented them to me in your William Morris Labor Church.

CUSINS: Oh! It needed only that. A Labor Church! (*He mounts the firestep distractedly, and leans with his elbows on the parapet, turning his back to them.*)

LADY BRITOMART: Yes, with Morris's words in mosaic letters ten feet high round the dome. NO MAN IS GOOD ENOUGH TO BE ANOTHER MAN'S MASTER. The cynicism of it!

UNDERSHAFT: It shocked the men at first, I am afraid. But now they take no more notice of it than of the ten commandments in church.

LADY BRITOMART: Andrew: you are trying to put me off the subject of the inheritance by profane jokes. Well, you shant. I dont ask it any longer for Stephen: he has inherited far too much of your perversity to be fit for it. But Barbara has rights as well as Stephen. Why should not Adolphus succeed to the inheritance? I could manage the town for him; and he can look after the cannons, if they are really necessary.

UNDERSHAFT: I should ask nothing better if Adolphus were a foundling. He is exactly the sort of new blood that is wanted in English business. But he's not a foundling; and theres an end of it. (*He makes for the office door.*)

CUSINS (*turning to them*): Not quite. (*They all turn and stare at him.*) I think — Mind! I am not committing myself in any way as to my future course — but I think the foundling difficulty can be got over. (*He jumps down to the emplacement.*)

UNDERSHAFT (*coming back to him*): What do you mean?

CUSINS: Well, I have something to say which is in the nature of a confession.

SARAH:
LADY BRITOMART:
BARBARA:
STEPHEN: } Confession!

LOMAX: Oh I say!

CUSINS: Yes, a confession. Listen, all. Until I met Barbara I thought myself in the main an honorable, truthful man, because I wanted the approval of my conscience more than I wanted anything else. But the moment I saw Barbara, I wanted her far more than the approval of my conscience.

LADY BRITOMART: Adolphus!

CUSINS: It is true. You accused me yourself, Lady Brit, of joining the Army to worship Barbara; and so I did. She bought my soul like a flower at a street corner; but she bought it for herself.

UNDERSHAFT: What! Not for Dionysos or another?

CUSINS: Dionysos and all the others are in herself. I adored what was divine in her, and was therefore a true worshipper. But I was romantic about her too. I thought she was a woman of the people, and that a marriage with a professor of Greek would be far beyond the wildest social ambitions of her rank.

LADY BRITOMART: Adolphus!!

LOMAX: Oh I say!!!

CUSINS: When I learnt the horrible truth —

LADY BRITOMART: What do you mean by the horrible truth, pray?

CUSINS: That she was enormously rich; that her grandfather was an earl; that her father was the Prince of Darkness —

UNDERSHAFT: Chut!

CUSINS: — and that I was only an adventurer trying to catch a rich wife, then I stooped to deceive her about my birth.

BARBARA (*rising*): Dolly!

LADY BRITOMART: Your birth! Now Adolphus, dont dare to make up a wicked story for the sake of these wretched cannons. Remember: I have seen photographs of your parents; and the Agent General for South Western Australia knows them personally and has assured me that they are most respectable married people.

CUSINS: So they are in Australia; but here they are outcasts. Their marriage is legal in Australia, but not in England. My mother is my father's deceased wife's sister; and in this island I am consequently a foundling. (*Sensation.*)

BARBARA: Silly! (*She climbs to the cannon, and leans, listening, in the angle it makes with the parapet.*)

CUSINS: Is the subterfuge good enough, Machiavelli?

UNDERSHAFT (*thoughtfully*): Biddy: this may be a way out of the difficulty.

LADY BRITOMART: Stuff! A man cant make cannons any the better for being his own cousin instead of his proper self. (*She sits down on the rug with a bounce that expresses her downright contempt for their casuistry.*)

UNDERSHAFT (*to* CUSINS): You are an educated man. That is against the tradition.

CUSINS: Once in ten thousand times it happens that the schoolboy is a born master of what they try to teach him. Greek has not destroyed my mind: it has nourished it. Besides, I did not learn it at an English public school.

UNDERSHAFT: Hm! Well, I cannot afford to be too particular: you have cornered the foundling market. Let it pass. You are eligible, Euripides: you are eligible.

BARBARA: Dolly: yesterday morning, when Stephen told us all about the tradition, you became very silent; and you have been strange and excited ever since. Were you thinking of your birth then?

CUSINS: When the finger of Destiny suddenly points at a man in the middle of his breakfast, it makes him thoughtful.

UNDERSHAFT: Aha! You have had your eye on the business, my young friend, have you?

CUSINS: Take care! There is an abyss of moral horror between me and your accursed aerial battleships.

UNDERSHAFT: Never mind the abyss for the present. Let us settle the practical details and leave your final decision open. You know that you will have to change your name. Do you object to that?

CUSINS: Would any man named Adolphus — any man called Dolly! — object to be called something else?

UNDERSHAFT: Good. Now, as to money! I propose to treat you handsomely from the beginning. You shall start at a thousand a year.

CUSINS (*with sudden heat, his spectacles twinkling with mischief*): A thousand! You dare offer a miserable thousand to the son-in-law of a millionaire! No, by Heavens, Machiavelli! you shall not cheat me. You cannot do without me; and I can do without you. I must have two thousand five hundred a year for two years. At the end of that time, if I am a failure, I go. But if I am a success, and stay on, you must give me the other five thousand.

UNDERSHAFT: What other five thousand?

CUSINS: To make the two years up to five thousand a year. The two thousand five hundred is only half pay in case I should turn out a failure. The third year I must have ten per cent on the profits.

UNDERSHAFT (*taken aback*): Ten per cent! Why, man, do you know what my profits are?

CUSINS: Enormous, I hope: otherwise I shall require twenty-five per cent.

UNDERSHAFT: But, Mr Cusins, this is a serious matter of business. You are not bringing any capital into the concern.

CUSINS: What! no capital! Is my mastery of Greek no capital? Is my access to the subtlest thought, the loftiest poetry yet attained by humanity, no capital? My character! my intellect! my life! my career! what Barbara calls my soul! are these no capital? Say another word; and I double my salary.

UNDERSHAFT: Be reasonable —

CUSINS (*peremptorily*): Mr Undershaft: you have my terms. Take them or leave them.

UNDERSHAFT (*recovering himself*): Very well. I note your terms; and I offer you half.

CUSINS (*disgusted*): Half!

UNDERSHAFT (*firmly*): Half.

CUSINS: You call yourself a gentleman; and you offer me half!!

UNDERSHAFT: I do not call myself a gentleman; but I offer you half.

CUSINS: This to your future partner! your successor! your son-in-law!

BARBARA: You are selling your own soul,

Dolly, not mine. Leave me out of the bargain, please.

UNDERSHAFT: Come! I will go a step further for Barbara's sake. I will give you three fifths; but that is my last word.

CUSINS: Done!

LOMAX: Done in the eye! Why, *I* get only eight hundred, you know.

CUSINS: By the way, Mac, I am a classical scholar, not an arithmetical one. Is three fifths more than half or less?

UNDERSHAFT: More, of course.

CUSINS: I would have taken two hundred and fifty. How you can succeed in business when you are willing to pay all that money to a University don who is obviously not worth a junior clerk's wages! — well! What will Lazarus say?

UNDERSHAFT: Lazarus is a gentle romantic Jew who cares for nothing but string quartets and stalls at fashionable theatres. He will be blamed for your rapacity in money matters, poor fellow! as he has hitherto been blamed for mine. You are a shark of the first order, Euripides. So much the better for the firm!

BARBARA: Is the bargain closed, Dolly? Does your soul belong to him now?

CUSINS: No: the price is settled: that is all. The real tug of war is still to come. What about the moral question?

LADY BRITOMART: There is no moral question in the matter at all, Adolphus. You must simply sell cannons and weapons to people whose cause is right and just, and refuse them to foreigners and criminals.

UNDERSHAFT (*determined*): No: None of that. You must keep the true faith of an Armorer, or you dont come in here.

CUSINS: What on earth is the true faith of an Armorer?

UNDERSHAFT: To give arms to all men who offer an honest price for them, without respect of persons or principles: to aristocrat and republican, to Nihilist and Tsar, to Capitalist and Socialist, to Protestant and Catholic, to burglar and policeman, to black man, white man and yellow man, to all sorts and conditions, all nationalities, all faiths, all follies, all causes and all crimes. The first Undershaft wrote up in his shop IF GOD GAVE THE HAND, LET NOT MAN WITHHOLD THE SWORD. The second wrote up ALL HAVE THE RIGHT TO FIGHT: NONE HAVE THE RIGHT TO JUDGE. The third wrote up TO MAN THE WEAPON: TO HEAVEN THE VICTORY. The fourth had no literary turn; so he did not write up anything; but he sold cannons to Napoleon under the nose of George the Third. The fifth wrote up PEACE SHALL NOT PREVAIL SAVE WITH A SWORD IN HER HAND. The sixth, my master, was the best of all. He wrote up NOTHING IS EVER DONE IN THIS WORLD UNTIL MEN ARE PREPARED TO KILL ONE ANOTHER IF IT IS NOT DONE. After that, there was nothing left for the seventh to say. So he wrote up, simply, UNASHAMED.

CUSINS: My good Machiavelli, I shall certainly write something up on the wall; only, as I shall write it in Greek, you wont be able to read it. But as to your Armorer's faith, if I take my neck out of the noose of my own morality I am not going to put it into the noose of yours. I shall sell cannons to whom I please and refuse them to whom I please. So there!

UNDERSHAFT: From the moment when you become Andrew Undershaft, you will never do as you please again. Dont come here lusting for power, young man.

CUSINS: If power were my aim I should not come here for it. You have no power.

UNDERSHAFT: None of my own, certainly.

CUSINS: I have more power than you, more will. You do not drive this place: it drives you. And what drives the place?

UNDERSHAFT (*enigmatically*): A will of which I am a part.

BARBARA (*startled*): Father! Do you know what you are saying; or are you laying a snare for my soul?

CUSINS: Dont listen to his metaphysics, Barbara. The place is driven by the most rascally part of society, the money hunters, the pleasure hunters, the military promotion hunters; and he is their slave.

UNDERSHAFT: Not necessarily. Remember the Armorer's Faith. I will take an order from a good man as cheerfully as from a bad one. If you good people prefer preaching and shirking to buying my weapons and fighting the rascals, dont blame me. I can make cannons: I cannot make courage and conviction. Bah! you tire me, Euripides, with your morality mongering. Ask Barbara: she understands. (*He suddenly reaches up and takes* BARBARA's *hands, looking powerfully into her eyes.*) Tell him, my love, what power really means.

BARBARA (*hypnotized*): Before I joined the

Salvation Army, I was in my own power; and the consequence was that I never knew what to do with myself. When I joined it, I had not time enough for all the things I had to do.

UNDERSHAFT (*approvingly*): Just so. And why was that, do you suppose?

BARBARA: Yesterday I should have said, because I was in the power of God. (*She resumes her self-possession, withdrawing her hands from his with a power equal to his own.*) But you came and shewed me that I was in the power of Bodger and Undershaft. Today I feel — oh! how can I put it into words? Sarah: do you remember the earthquake at Cannes, when we were little children? — how little the surprise of the first shock mattered compared to the dread and horror of waiting for the second? That is how I feel in this place today. I stood on the rock I thought eternal; and without a word of warning it reeled and crumbled under me. I was safe with an infinite wisdom watching me, an army marching to Salvation with me; and in a moment, at a stroke of your pen in a cheque book, I stood alone; and the heavens were empty. That was the first shock of the earthquake: I am waiting for the second.

UNDERSHAFT: Come, come, my daughter! dont make too much of your tinpot tragedy. What do we do here when we spend years of work and thought and thousands of pounds of solid cash on a new gun or an aerial battleship that turns out just a hairsbreadth wrong after all? Scrap it. Scrap it without wasting another hour or another pound on it. Well, you have made for yourself something that you call a morality or a religion or what not. It doesn't fit the facts. Well, scrap it. Scrap it and get one that does fit. That is what is wrong with the world at present. It scraps its obsolete steam engines and dynamos; but it wont scrap its old prejudices and its old moralities and its old religions and its old political constitutions. Whats the result? In machinery it does very well; but in morals and religion and politics it is working at a loss that brings it nearer bankruptcy every year. Dont persist in that folly. If your old religion broke down yesterday, get a newer and a better one for tomorrow.

BARBARA: Oh how gladly I would take a better one to my soul! But you offer me a worse one. (*Turning on him with sudden vehe-*

mence.) Justify yourself: shew me some light through the darkness of this dreadful place, with its beautifully clean workshops, and respectable workmen, and model homes.

UNDERSHAFT: Cleanliness and respectability do not need justification, Barbara: they justify themselves. I see no darkness here, no dreadfulness. In your Salvation shelter I saw poverty, misery, cold and hunger. You gave them bread and treacle and dreams of heaven. I give from thirty shillings a week to twelve thousand a year. They find their own dreams; but I look after the drainage.

BARBARA: And their souls?

UNDERSHAFT: I save their souls just as I saved yours.

BARBARA (*revolted*): You saved my soul! What do you mean?

UNDERSHAFT: I fed you and clothed you and housed you. I took care that you should have money enough to live handsomely — more than enough; so that you could be wasteful, careless, generous. That saved your soul from the seven deadly sins.

BARBARA (*bewildered*): The seven deadly sins!

UNDERSHAFT: Yes, the deadly seven. (*Counting on his fingers.*) Food, clothing, firing, rent, taxes, respectability and children. Nothing can lift those seven millstones from Man's neck but money; and the spirit cannot soar until the millstones are lifted. I lifted them from your spirit. I enabled Barbara to become Major Barbara; and I saved her from the crime of poverty.

CUSINS: Do you call poverty a crime?

UNDERSHAFT: The worst of crimes. All the other crimes are virtues beside it: all the other dishonors are chivalry itself by comparison. Poverty blights whole cities; spreads horrible pestilences; strikes dead the very souls of all who come within sight, sound, or smell of it. What you call crime is nothing: a murder here and a theft there, a blow now and a curse then: what do they matter? they are only the accidents and illnesses of life: there are not fifty genuine professional criminals in London. But there are millions of poor people, abject people, dirty people, ill fed, ill clothed people. They poison us morally and physically: they kill the happiness of society: they force us to do away with our own liberties and to organize unnatural cruelties for fear they should rise against us and drag us down into their abyss. Only fools fear crime: we all fear poverty. Pah! (*turning on* BARBARA) you talk of your half-saved ruffian in West Ham: you accuse me of dragging his soul back to perdition. Well, bring him to me here; and I will drag his soul back again to salvation for you. Not by words and dreams; but by thirtyeight shillings a week, a sound house in a handsome street, and a permanent job. In three weeks he will have a fancy waistcoat; in three months a tall hat and a chapel sitting; before the end of the year he will shake hands with a duchess at a Primrose League meeting, and join the Conservative Party.

BARBARA: And will he be the better for that?

UNDERSHAFT: You know he will. Dont be a hypocrite, Barbara. He will be better fed, better housed, better clothed, better behaved; and his children will be pounds heavier and bigger. That will be better than an American cloth mattress in a shelter, chopping firewood, eating bread and treacle, and being forced to kneel down from time to time to thank heaven for it: knee drill, I think you call it. It is cheap work converting starving men with a Bible in one hand and a slice of bread in the other. I will undertake to convert West Ham to Mahometanism on the same terms. Try your hand on my men: their souls are hungry because their bodies are full.

BARBARA: And leave the east end to starve?

UNDERSHAFT (*his energetic tone dropping into one of bitter and brooding remembrance*): I was an east ender. I moralized and starved until one day I swore that I would be a full-fed free man at all costs; that nothing should stop me except a bullet, neither reason nor morals nor the lives of other men. I said 'Thou shalt starve ere I starve'; and with that word I became free and great. I was a dangerous man until I had my will: now I am a useful, beneficent, kindly person. That is the history of most self-made millionaires, I fancy. When it is the history of every Englishman we shall have an England worth living in.

LADY BRITOMART: Stop making speeches, Andrew. This is not the place for them.

UNDERSHAFT (*punctured*): My dear: I have no other means of conveying my ideas.

LADY BRITOMART: Your ideas are nonsense. You got on because you were selfish and unscrupulous.

UNDERSHAFT: Not at all. I had the strongest scruples about poverty and starvation. Your moralists are quite unscrupulous about both: they make virtues of them. I had rather be a thief than a pauper. I had rather be a murderer than a slave. I dont want to be either; but if you force the alternative on me, then, by Heaven, I'll choose the braver and more moral one. I hate poverty and slavery worse than any other crimes whatsoever. And let me tell you this. Poverty and slavery have stood up for centuries to your sermons and leading articles: they will not stand up to my machine guns. Dont preach at them: dont reason with them. Kill them.

BARBARA: Killing. Is that your remedy for everything?

UNDERSHAFT: It is the final test of conviction, the only lever strong enough to overturn a social system, the only way of saying Must. Let six hundred and seventy fools loose in the streets; and three policemen can scatter them. But huddle them together in a certain house in Westminster; and let them go through certain ceremonies and call themselves certain names until at last they get the courage to kill; and your six hundred and seventy fools become a government. Your pious mob fills up ballot papers and imagines it is governing its masters; but the ballot paper that really governs is the paper that has a bullet wrapped up in it.

CUSINS: That is perhaps why, like most intelligent people, I never vote.

UNDERSHAFT: Vote! Bah! When you vote, you only change the names of the cabinet. When you shoot, you pull down governments, inaugurate new epochs, abolish old orders and set up new. Is that historically true, Mr Learned Man, or is it not?

CUSINS: It is historically true. I loathe having to admit it. I repudiate your sentiments. I abhor your nature. I defy you in every possible way. Still, it is true. But it ought not to be true.

UNDERSHAFT: Ought! ought! ought! ought! ought! Are you going to spend your life saying ought, like the rest of our moralists? Turn your oughts into shalls, man. Come and make explosives with me. Whatever can blow men up can blow society up. The history of the world is the history of those who had courage enough to embrace this truth. Have you the courage to embrace it, Barbara?

LADY BRITOMART: Barbara: I positively forbid you to listen to your father's abominable wickedness. And you, Adolphus, ought to know better than to go about saying that wrong things are true. What does it matter whether they are true if they are wrong?

UNDERSHAFT: What does it matter whether they are wrong if they are true?

LADY BRITOMART (*rising*): Children: come home instantly. Andrew: I am exceedingly sorry I allowed you to call on us. You are wickeder than ever. Come at once.

BARBARA (*shaking her head*): It's no use running away from wicked people, mamma.

LADY BRITOMART: It is every use. It shews your disapprobation of them.

BARBARA: It does not save them.

LADY BRITOMART: I can see that you are going to disobey me. Sarah: are you coming home or are you not?

SARAH: I daresay it's very wicked of papa to make cannons; but I dont think I shall cut him on that account.

LOMAX (*pouring oil on the troubled waters*): The fact is, you know, there is a certain amount of tosh about this notion of wickedness. It doesnt work. You must look at facts. Not that I would say a word in favor of anything wrong; but then, you see, all sorts of chaps are always doing all sorts of things; and we have to fit them in somehow, dont you know. What I mean is that you cant go cutting everybody; and thats about what it comes to. (*Their rapt attention to his eloquence makes him nervous.*) Perhaps I dont make myself clear.

LADY BRITOMART: You are lucidity itself, Charles. Because Andrew is successful and has plenty of money to give to Sarah, you will flatter him and encourage him in his wickedness.

LOMAX (*unruffled*): Well, where the carcase is, there will the eagles be gathered, dont you know. (*To* UNDERSHAFT.) Eh? What?

UNDERSHAFT: Precisely. By the way, may I call you Charles?

LOMAX: Delighted. Cholly is the usual ticket.

UNDERSHAFT (*to* LADY BRITOMART): Biddy —

LADY BRITOMART (*violently*): Dont dare call me Biddy. Charles Lomax: you are a fool. Adolphus Cusins: you are a Jesuit. Stephen: you are a prig. Barbara: you are a lunatic. Andrew: you are a vulgar tradesman. Now you all know my opinion; and my conscience is clear, at all events. (*She sits down with a vehemence that the rug fortunately softens.*)

UNDERSHAFT: My dear: you are the incarnation of morality. (*She snorts.*) Your conscience is clear and your duty done when you have called everybody names. Come, Euripides! It is getting late; and we all want to go home. Make up your mind.

CUSINS: Understand this, you old demon —

LADY BRITOMART: Adolphus!

UNDERSHAFT: Let him alone, Biddy. Proceed, Euripides.

CUSINS: You have me in a horrible dilemma. I want Barbara.

UNDERSHAFT: Like all young men, you greatly exaggerate the difference between one young woman and another.

BARBARA: Quite true, Dolly.

CUSINS: I also want to avoid being a rascal.

UNDERSHAFT (*with biting contempt*): You lust for personal righteousness, for self-approval, for what you call a good conscience, for what Barbara calls salvation, for what I call patronizing people who are not so lucky as yourself.

CUSINS: I do not: all the poet in me recoils from being a good man. But there are things in me that I must reckon with. Pity —

UNDERSHAFT: Pity! The scavenger of misery.

CUSINS: Well, love.

UNDERSHAFT: I know. You love the needy and the outcast: you love the oppressed races, the negro, the Indian ryot, the underdog everywhere. Do you love the Japanese? Do you love the English?

CUSINS: No. Every true Englishman detests the English. We are the wickedest nation on earth; and our success is a moral horror.

UNDERSHAFT: That is what comes of your gospel of love, is it?

CUSINS: May I not love even my father-in-law?

UNDERSHAFT: Who wants your love, man? By what right do you take the liberty of offering it to me? I will have your due heed and respect, or I will kill you. But your love! Damn your impertinence!

CUSINS (*grinning*): I may not be able to control my affections, Mac.

UNDERSHAFT: You are fencing, Euripides. You are weakening: your grip is slipping. Come! try your last weapon. Pity and love have broken in your hand: forgiveness is still left.

CUSINS: No: forgiveness is a beggar's refuge. I am with you there: we must pay our debts.

UNDERSHAFT: Well said. Come! you will suit me. Remember the words of Plato.

CUSINS (starting): Plato! You dare quote Plato to me!

UNDERSHAFT: Plato says, my friend, that society cannot be saved until either the Professors of Greek take to making gunpowder, or else the makers of gunpowder become Professors of Greek.

CUSINS: Oh, tempter, cunning tempter!

UNDERSHAFT: Come! choose, man, choose.

CUSINS: But perhaps Barbara will not marry me if I make the wrong choice.

BARBARA: Perhaps not.

CUSINS (desperately perplexed): You hear!

BARBARA: Father: do you love nobody?

UNDERSHAFT: I love my best friend.

LADY BRITOMART: And who is that, pray?

UNDERSHAFT: My bravest enemy. That is the man who keeps me up to the mark.

CUSINS: You know, the creature is really a sort of poet in his way. Suppose he is a great man, after all!

UNDERSHAFT: Suppose you stop talking and make up your mind, my young friend.

CUSINS: But you are driving me against my nature. I hate war.

UNDERSHAFT: Hatred is the coward's revenge for being intimidated. Dare you make war on war? Here are the means: my friend Mr Lomax is sitting on them.

LOMAX (springing up): Oh I say! You dont mean that this thing is loaded, do you? My ownest: come off it.

SARAH (sitting placidly on the shell): If I am to be blown up, the more thoroughly it is done the better. Dont fuss, Cholly.

LOMAX (to UNDERSHAFT, strongly remonstrant): Your own daughter, you know!

UNDERSHAFT: So I see. (To CUSINS.) Well, my friend, may we expect you here at six tomorrow morning?

CUSINS (firmly): Not on any account. I will see the whole establishment blown up with its own dynamite before I will get up at five. My hours are healthy, rational hours: eleven to five.

UNDERSHAFT: Come when you please: before a week you will come at six and stay until I turn you out for the sake of your health. (Calling.) Bilton! (He turns to LADY BRITOMART, who rises.) My dear: let us leave these two young people to themselves for a moment. (BILTON comes from the shed.) I am going to take you through the gun cotton shed.

BILTON (barring the way): You cant take anything explosive in here, sir.

LADY BRITOMART: What do you mean? Are you alluding to me?

BILTON (unmoved): No, maam. Mr Undershaft has the other gentleman's matches in his pocket.

LADY BRITOMART (abruptly): Oh! I beg your pardon. (She goes into the shed.)

UNDERSHAFT: Quite right, Bilton, quite right: here you are. (He gives BILTON the box of matches.) Come, Stephen. Come, Charles. Bring Sarah. (He passes into the shed.)

(BILTON opens the box and deliberately drops the matches into the fire-bucket.)

LOMAX: Oh! I say. (BILTON stolidly hands him the empty box.) Infernal nonsense! Pure scientific ignorance! (He goes in.)

SARAH: Am I all right, Bilton?

BILTON: Youll have to put on list slippers, miss: thats all. Weve got em inside. (She goes in.)

STEPHEN (very seriously to CUSINS): Dolly, old fellow, think. Think before you decide. Do you feel that you are a sufficiently practical man? It is a huge undertaking, an enormous responsibility. All this mass of business will be Greek to you.

CUSINS: Oh, I think it will be much less difficult than Greek.

STEPHEN: Well, I just want to say this before I leave you to yourselves. Dont let anything I have said about right and wrong prejudice you against this great chance in life. I have satisfied myself that the business is one of the highest character and a credit to our country. (Emotionally.) I am very proud of my father. I — (Unable to proceed, he presses CUSINS' hand and goes hastily into the shed, followed by BILTON.)

(BARBARA and CUSINS, left alone together, look at one another silently.)

CUSINS: Barbara: I am going to accept this offer.

BARBARA: I thought you would.

CUSINS: You understand, dont you, that I had to decide without consulting you. If I had thrown the burden of the choice on you, you would sooner or later have despised me for it.

BARBARA: Yes: I did not want you to sell your soul for me any more than for this inheritance.

CUSINS: It is not the sale of my soul that troubles me: I have sold it too often to care about that. I have sold it for a professorship. I have sold it for an income. I have sold it to escape being imprisoned for refusing to pay taxes for hangmen's ropes and unjust wars and things that I abhor. What is all human conduct but the daily and hourly sale of our souls for trifles? What I am now selling it for is neither money nor position nor comfort, but for reality and for power.

BARBARA: You know that you will have no power, and that he has none.

CUSINS: I know. It is not for myself alone. I want to make power for the world.

BARBARA: I want to make power for the world too; but it must be spiritual power.

CUSINS: I think all power is spiritual: these cannons will not go off by themselves. I have tried to make spiritual power by teaching Greek. But the world can never be really touched by a dead language and a dead civilization. The people must have power; and the people cannot have Greek. Now the power that is made here can be wielded by all men.

BARBARA: Power to burn women's houses down and kill their sons and tear their husbands to pieces.

CUSINS: You cannot have power for good without having power for evil too. Even mother's milk nourishes murderers as well as heroes. This power which only tears men's bodies to pieces has never been so horribly abused as the intellectual power, the imaginative power, the poetic, religious power that can enslave men's souls. As a teacher of Greek I gave the intellectual man weapons against the common man. I now want to give the common man weapons against the intellectual man. I love the common people. I want to arm them against the lawyers, the doctors, the priests, the literary men, the professors, the artists, and the politicians, who, once in authority, are more disastrous and tyrannical than all the fools, rascals, and impostors. I want a power simple enough for common men to use, yet strong enough to force the intellectual oligarchy to use its genius for the general good.

BARBARA: Is there no higher power than that (pointing to the shell)?

CUSINS: Yes; but that power can destroy the higher powers just as a tiger can destroy a man: therefore Man must master that power first. I admitted this when the Turks and Greeks were last at war. My best pupil went out to fight for Hellas. My parting gift to him was not a copy of Plato's Republic, but a revolver and a hundred Undershaft cartridges. The blood of every Turk he shot — if he shot any — is on my head as well as on Undershaft's. That act committed me to this place for ever. Your father's challenge has beaten me. Dare I make war on war? I must. I will. And now, is it all over between us?

BARBARA (touched by his evident dread of her answer): Silly baby Dolly! How could it be!

CUSINS (overjoyed): Then you — you — you — Oh for my drum! (He flourishes imaginary drumsticks.)

BARBARA (angered by his levity): Take care, Dolly, take care. Oh, if only I could get away from you and from father and from it all! if I could have the wings of a dove and fly away to heaven!

CUSINS: And leave me!

BARBARA: Yes, you, and all the other naughty mischievous children of men. But I cant. I was happy in the Salvation Army for a moment. I escaped from the world into a paradise of enthusiasm and prayer and soul saving; but the moment our money ran short, it all came back to Bodger: it was he who saved our people: he, and the Prince of Darkness, my papa. Undershaft and Bodger: their hands stretch everywhere: when we feed a starving fellow creature, it is with their bread, because there is no other bread; when we tend the sick, it is in the hospitals they endow; if we turn from the churches they build, we must kneel on the stones of the streets they pave. As long as that lasts, there is no getting away from them. Turning our backs on Bodger and Undershaft is turning our backs on life.

CUSINS: I thought you were determined to turn your back on the wicked side of life.

BARBARA: There is no wicked side: life is all one. And I never wanted to shirk my share in whatever evil must be endured, whether it be sin or suffering. I wish I could cure you of middle-class ideas, Dolly.

CUSINS (gasping): Middle cl — ! A snub! A social snub to me! from the daughter of a foundling!

BARBARA: That is why I have no class, Dolly: I come straight out of the heart of the whole people. If I were middle-class I should turn my back on my father's business; and we should both live in an artistic drawing room, with you reading the reviews in one corner, and I in the other at the piano, playing Schumann: both very superior persons, and neither of us a bit of use. Sooner than that, I would sweep out the guncotton shed, or be one of Bodger's barmaids. Do you know what would have happened if you had refused papa's offer?

CUSINS: I wonder!

BARBARA: I should have given you up and married the man who accepted it. After all, my dear old mother has more sense than any of you. I felt like her when I saw this place — felt that I must have it — that never, never, never could I let it go; only she thought it was the houses and the kitchen ranges and the linen and china, when it was really all the human souls to be saved: not weak souls in starved bodies, sobbing with gratitude for a scrap of bread and treacle, but fullfed, quarrelsome, snobbish, uppish creatures, all standing on their little rights and dignities, and thinking that my father ought to be greatly obliged to them for making so much money for him — and so he ought. That is where salvation is really wanted. My father shall never throw it in my teeth again that my converts were bribed with bread. (*She is transfigured.*) I have got rid of the bribe of bread. I have got rid of the bribe of heaven. Let God's work be done for its own sake: the work he had to create us to do because it cannot be done except by living men and women. When I die, let him be in my debt, not I in his; and let me forgive him as becomes a woman of my rank.

CUSINS: Then the way of life lies through the factory of death?

BARBARA: Yes, through the raising of hell to heaven and of man to God, through the unveiling of an eternal light in the Valley of The Shadow. (*Seizing him with both hands.*)

Oh, did you think my courage would never come back? did you believe that I was a deserter? that I, who have stood in the streets, and taken my people to my heart, and talked of the holiest and greatest things with them, could ever turn back and chatter foolishly to fashionable people about nothing in a drawing room? Never, never, never, never: Major Barbara will die with the colors. Oh! and I have my dear little Dolly boy still; and he has found me my place and my work. Glory Hallelujah! (*She kisses him.*)

CUSINS: My dearest: consider my delicate health. I cannot stand as much happiness as you can.

BARBARA: Yes: it is not easy work being in love with me, is it? But it's good for you. (*She runs to the shed, and calls, childlike.*) Mamma! Mamma! (BILTON *comes out of the shed, followed by* UNDERSHAFT.) I want Mamma.

UNDERSHAFT: She is taking off her list slippers, dear. (*He passes on to* CUSINS.) Well? What does she say?

CUSINS: She has gone right up into the skies.

LADY BRITOMART (*coming from the shed and stopping on the steps, obstructing* SARAH, *who follows with* LOMAX. BARBARA *clutches like a baby at her mother's skirt*): Barbara: when will you learn to be independent and to act and think for yourself? I know as well as possible what that cry of 'Mamma, Mamma,' means. Always running to me!

SARAH (*touching* LADY BRITOMART'S *ribs with her finger tips and imitating a bicycle horn*): Pip! pip!

LADY BRITOMART (*highly indignant*): How dare you say Pip! pip! to me, Sarah? You are both very naughty children. What do you want, Barbara?

BARBARA: I want a house in the village to live in with Dolly. (*Dragging at the skirt.*) Come and tell me which one to take.

UNDERSHAFT (*to* CUSINS): Six o'clock tomorrow morning, Euripides.

THE END

One of the earliest English remarks about comedy, Sir Philip Sidney's written about 1580, runs thus:

> Comedy is an imitation of the common errors of our life, which he representeth in the most ridiculous and scornful sort that may be; so that it is impossible that any beholder can be content to be such a one.

Sidney is indebted to Italian commentators, who in turn are indebted to Roman commentators, and behind them are the Greeks, notably Aristotle. Along the way, of course, there are lots of variations, but the basic ideas may fairly be said to constitute the "classical" theory of comedy:

1. The characters are ignoble
2. Their actions arouse derision (rather than, say, terror or pity)
3. The spectators, if they have resembled the dramatis personae, leave the theater morally improved after seeing the absurdity of such behavior.

The "classical" theory, often stated before Sidney, has since been restated at least as often. Almost every comic dramatist who has commented on his work has offered it as his justification. Shaw, in a preface to his *Complete Plays*, put it thus:

> If I make you laugh at yourself, remember that my business as a classic writer of comedies is "to chasten morals with ridicule"; and if I sometimes make you feel like a fool, remember that I have by the same action cured your folly, just as the dentist cures your toothache by pulling out your tooth. And I never do it without giving you plenty of laughing gas.

To begin with the laughing gas in *Major Barbara*: the first act suggests that the play is a drawing-room comedy, full of aristocratic people bouncing elegant lines off each other. (Lady Brit, of course, affects innocence, but she is accomplished at getting what she wants.) Sample:

> I am not a Pharisee, I hope; and I should not have minded his merely doing wrong things: we are none of us perfect. But your father didnt exactly do wrong things: he said them and thought them: that was what was so dreadful. He really had a sort of religion of wrongness. Just as one doesnt mind men practising immorality so long as they own that they are in the wrong by preaching morality; so I couldnt forgive Andrew for preaching immorality while he practised morality.

Another sample:

> CUSINS: Let me advise you to study Greek, Mr. Undershaft. Greek scholars are privileged men. Few of them know Greek; and none of them know anything else; but their position is unchallengeable. Other languages are the qualifications of waiters and commercial travellers: Greek is to a man of position what the hallmark is to silver.

If Shaw had been content to write a comedy in the classical tradition, he would have contrived a plot which would probably have involved an unsuitable wooer of Barbara, maybe a rich old aristocrat, maybe a parvenu, maybe a fortune hunter, who would finally be unmasked and then displaced by an appropriately young and charming and socially acceptable bridegroom. But Shaw turned to comedy as a propagandist. He had been deeply impressed by Ibsen's plays, and he saw in the drama an opportunity to preach his economic ideas to a wider audience than is normally reached by the pamphleteer. For Shaw, the heart of Ibsen's plays lies in such a "discussion" as the one in *A Doll's House*, where Nora explains to her husband that things are all wrong in their apparently happy marriage. (The interested reader is advised to look at Shaw's *The Quintessence of Ibsenism*, especially the next to the last chapter, "The Technical Novelty," which insists that post-Ibsen plays must replace the old formula of exposition-situation-unraveling with "exposition, situation, and discussion; and the discussion is the test of the playwright.... The serious playwright recognizes not only the main test of his highest powers, but also the real center of his play's interest.")

What Shaw does, then, is introduce massive discussions into a comedy that at first seems to be doing little more than spoofing Lady Brit and holding her son Stephen up to rather obvious ridicule. Stephen is not merely an ass; he is made to serve as a sort of straightman for Undershaft, who expounds at length unconventional ideas about munitions, sin, power, and poverty. These ideas require discussion because Shaw, unlike most comic writers, is not content with the traditional views. Comic playwrights usually criticize eccentric behavior, and at least implicitly suggest that there is a reasonable norm, known to all men of sense, from which fools depart. But because Shaw believed that society's norm is itself foolish, he devotes much of his play to expounding a new creed. Shaw reverses the old joke about the entire platoon being out of step except Johnny; for Shaw, the deviant, Johnny, *is* in step, and the rest of the platoon is laughably out of step. During the central part of *Major Barbara*, then, Undershaft, the eccentric, is for Shaw the least laughable character. Even Barbara, the heroine, is exposed as a fool, though with great tenderness, and is forced to shed her conventional illusions. So great is the tenderness that as we see her world collapse, she seems almost a tragic figure:

> I stood on the rock I thought eternal; and without a word of warning it reeled and crumbled under me.

But Undershaft dispels the tragedy, harshly but necessarily, with, "Come, come, my daughter! dont make too much of your little tinpot tragedy.... Dont persist in that folly. If your old religion broke down yesterday, get a newer and a better one for tomorrow."

Enough has been said to give some idea of the novelty of Shaw's comic practice, however conventional his theory. But one should note, too, that in one important way his practice is conventional: his plays have the stock quack doctors, pompous statesmen, dragonlike matrons, and young lovers of traditional comedy. And in *Major Barbara* he even uses the ancient motif of the foundling who proves to be a suitable husband for the heroine.

Something more, however, must be said of Undershaft. Having allowed Undershaft to triumph over Barbara, Shaw does not stop; very late in the play Undershaft himself is threatened with the loss of *his* illusions when Barbara and Adolphus Cusins will make their presence felt in the munitions factory. The play ends with the usual marriage, joy, and promise of a newly organized society; in its suggestion, however, that this new society is not a return to a sensible world that was lost before the play began (think, for example, of the end of *As You Like It*, where the duke is restored to his realm), but rather is the beginning of a totally new sort of world, it marks a departure from comic practice. Maybe that is why the end of the play has seemed to most audiences the least amusing part.

THE MATCHMAKER

Thornton Wilder

Thornton Wilder (1897–1975) was born in Madison, Wisconsin, the son of an editor and publisher. When his father was appointed consul general in Hong Kong, Wilder accompanied him, but he returned to the United States for some of his high school years and for college. He attended Oberlin, was graduated from Yale (1918), did further study in Rome, and received a Master's degree from Princeton in 1926. *The Bridge of San Luis Rey* (1928), a novel, brought him a Pulitzer Prize and fame; two of his plays, *Our Town* (1938) and *The Skin of Our Teeth* (1942), also won Pulitzer Prizes. *The Matchmaker* (1954), which has been turned into a musical comedy, *Hello Dolly* (1964), is a revision of his *The Merchant of Yonkers*, which is an adaptation of an Austrian play that itself was adapted from an English play.

CHARACTERS

HORACE VANDERGELDER, *a merchant of Yonkers, New York*

CORNELIUS HACKL
BARNABY TUCKER } *clerks in his store*
MALACHI STACK

AMBROSE KEMPER, *an artist*
JOE SCANLON, *a barber*
RUDOLPH } *waiters*
AUGUST

A CABMAN
MRS. DOLLY LEVI } *friends of Vander-*
MISS FLORA VAN HUYSEN } *gelder's late wife*
MRS. IRENE MOLLOY, *a milliner*
MINNIE FAY, *her assistant*
ERMENGARDE, *Vandergelder's niece*
GERTRUDE, *Vandergelder's housekeeper*
Miss Van Huysen's COOK

Time: The early 80's.

Act I. Vandergelder's house in Yonkers, New York.
Act II. Mrs. Molloy's hat shop, New York.
Act III. The Harmonia Gardens Restaurant on the Battery, New York.
Act IV. Miss Van Huysen's house, New York.

Act III of the Royal Court Theatre production of *The Matchmaker*, directed by Tyrone Guthrie, Liverpool, 1954. (Photograph: Harvard Theatre Collection.)

ACT I

Living room of MR. VANDERGELDER'S *house, over his hay, feed and provision store in Yonkers, fifteen miles north of New York City. Articles from the store have overflowed into this room; it has not been cleaned for a long time and is in some disorder, but it is not sordid or gloomy.*

There are three entrances. One at the center back leads into the principal rooms of the house. One on the back right (all the directions are from the point of view of the actors) opens on steps which descend to the street door. One on the left leads to ERMENGARDE'S *room.*

In the center of the room is a trap door; below it is a ladder descending to the store below.

Behind the trap door and to the left of it is a tall accountant's desk; to the left of it is an old-fashioned stove with a stovepipe going up into the ceiling. Before the desk is a tall stool. On the right of the stage is a table with some chairs about it.

MR. VANDERGELDER'S *Gladstone bag, packed for a journey, is beside the desk.*

It is early morning.

This play is based upon a comedy by Johann Nestroy, *Einen Jux will er sich machen* (Vienna, 1842), which was in turn based upon an English original, *A Day Well Spent* (London, 1835) by John Oxenford.

The Matchmaker from *Three Plays* by Thornton Wilder. Copyright © 1955, 1957 by Thornton Wilder. Copyright 1939 by Thornton Wilder, an earlier version under the title of "The Merchant of Yonkers." Reprinted by permission of Harper & Row, Publishers, Inc. *Caution: The Long Christmas Dinner and Other Plays in One Act is the sole property of the author and is fully protected by copyright. The plays herein may not be acted by professionals or amateurs without formal permission and the payment of a royalty. All rights, including professional, amateur, stock, radio and television, broadcasting, motion picture, recitation, lecturing, public reading, and the rights of translation into foreign languages are reserved. All professional inquiries and all requests for amateur rights should be addressed to Samuel French, 25 West 45 Street, New York, New York.*

*(*VANDERGELDER, *sixty, choleric, vain and sly, wears a soiled dressing gown. He is seated with a towel about his neck, in a chair beside the desk, being shaved by* JOE SCANLON. VANDERGELDER *is smoking a cigar and holding a hand mirror.* AMBROSE KEMPER *is angrily striding about the room.)*

VANDERGELDER *(loudly)*: I tell you for the hundredth time you will never marry my niece.

AMBROSE *(thirty; dressed as an "artist")*: And I tell you for the thousandth time that I will marry your niece; and right soon, too.

VANDERGELDER: Never!

AMBROSE: Your niece is of age, Mr. Vandergelder. Your niece has consented to marry me. This is a free country, Mr. Vandergelder — not a private kingdom of your own.

VANDERGELDER: There are no free countries for fools, Mr. Kemper. Thank you for the honor of your visit — good morning.

JOE *(fifty; lanky; mass of gray hair falling into his eyes)*: Mr. Vandergelder, will you please sit still one minute? If I cut your throat it'll be practically unintentional.

VANDERGELDER: Ermengarde is not for you, nor for anybody else who can't support her.

AMBROSE: I tell you I can support her. I make a very good living.

VANDERGELDER: No, sir! A living is made, Mr. Kemper, by selling something that everybody needs at least once a year. Yes, sir! And a million is made by producing something that everybody needs every day. You artists produce something that nobody needs at any time. You may sell a picture once in a while, but you'll make no living. Joe, go over there and stamp three times. I want to talk to Cornelius. *(Joe crosses to trap door and stamps three times.)*

AMBROSE: Not only can I support her now, but I have considerable expectations.

VANDERGELDER: *Expectations!* We merchants don't do business with them. I don't keep accounts with people who promise somehow to pay something someday, and I don't allow my niece to marry such people.

AMBROSE: Very well, from now on you might as well know that I regard any way we can find to get married is right and fair. Ermengarde is of age, and there's no law . . . (VANDERGELDER *rises and crosses toward* AMBROSE. JOE SCANLON *follows him complainingly and tries to find a chance to cut his hair even while he is standing.*)

VANDERGELDER: Law? Let me tell you something, Mr. Kemper: most of the people in the world are fools. The law is there to prevent crime; we men of sense are there to prevent foolishness. It's I, and not the law, that will prevent Ermengarde from marrying you, and I've taken some steps already. I've sent her away to get this nonsense out of her head.

AMBROSE: Ermengarde's . . . not here?

VANDERGELDER: She's gone — east, west, north, south. I thank you for the honor of your visit. (*Enter* GERTRUDE — *eighty; deaf; half blind; and very pleased with herself.*)

GERTRUDE: Everything's ready, Mr. Vandergelder. Ermengarde and I have just finished packing the trunk.

VANDERGELDER: Hold your tongue! (JOE *is shaving* VANDERGELDER'*s throat, so he can only wave his hands vainly.*)

GERTRUDE: Yes, Mr. Vandergelder, Ermengarde's ready to leave. Her trunk's all marked. Care Miss Van Huysen, 8 Jackson Street, New York.

VANDERGELDER (*breaking away from* JOE): Hell and damnation! Didn't I tell you it was a secret?

AMBROSE (*picks up hat and coat — kisses* GERTRUDE): Care Miss Van Huysen, 8 Jackson Street, New York. Thank you very much. Good morning, Mr. Vandergelder. (*Exit* AMBROSE, *to the street.*)

VANDERGELDER: It won't help you, Mr. Kemper — (*To* GERTRUDE.) Deaf! And blind! At least you can do me the favor of being dumb!

GERTRUDE: Chk — chk! Such a temper! Lord save us! (CORNELIUS *puts his head up through the trap door. He is thirty-three; mock-deferential — he wears a green apron and is in his shirt-sleeves.*)

CORNELIUS: Yes, Mr. Vandergelder?

VANDERGELDER: Go in and get my niece's trunk and carry it over to the station. Wait! Gertrude, has Mrs. Levi arrived yet? (CORNELIUS *comes up the trap door, steps into the room and closes the trap door behind him.*)

GERTRUDE: Don't shout. I can hear perfectly well. Everything's clearly marked.

(*Exit left.*)

VANDERGELDER: Have the buggy brought round to the front of the store in half an hour.

CORNELIUS: Yes, Mr. Vandergelder.

VANDERGELDER: This morning I'm joining my lodge parade and this afternoon I'm going to New York. Before I go, I have something important to say to you and Barnaby. Good news. Fact is — I'm going to promote you. How old are you?

CORNELIUS: Thirty-three, Mr. Vandergelder.

VANDERGELDER: What?

CORNELIUS: Thirty-three.

VANDERGELDER: That all? That's a foolish age to be at. I thought you were forty.

CORNELIUS: Thirty-three.

VANDERGELDER: A man's not worth a cent until he's forty. We just pay 'em wages to make mistakes — don't we, Joe?

JOE: You almost lost an ear on it, Mr. Vandergelder.

VANDERGELDER: I was thinking of promoting you to chief clerk.

CORNELIUS: What am I now, Mr. Vandergelder?

VANDERGELDER: You're an impertinent fool, that's what you are. Now, if you behave yourself, I'll promote you from impertinent fool to chief clerk, with a raise in your wages. And Barnaby may be promoted from idiot apprentice to incompetent clerk.

CORNELIUS: Thank you, Mr. Vandergelder.

VANDERGELDER: However, I want to see you again before I go. Go in and get my niece's trunk.

CORNELIUS: Yes, Mr. Vandergelder.

(*Exit* CORNELIUS, *left.*)

VANDERGELDER: Joe — the world's getting crazier every minute. Like my father used to say: the horses'll be taking over the world soon.

JOE (*presenting mirror*): I did what I could, Mr. Vandergelder, what with you flying in and out of the chair. (*He wipes the last of the soap from* VANDERGELDER'*s face.*)

VANDERGELDER: Fine, fine, Joe, you do a fine job, the same fine job you've done me for twenty years. Joe . . . I've got special reasons for looking my best today . . . isn't there something a little extry you could do, something a little special? I'll pay you right up to fifty cents — see what I mean? Do some of those things you do to the young fellas. Touch me up; smarten me up a bit.

JOE: All I know is fifteen cents' worth, like usual, Mr. Vandergelder; and that includes everything that's decent to do to a man.

VANDERGELDER: Now hold your horses, Joe — all I meant was . . .

JOE: I've shaved you for twenty years and you never asked me no such question before.

VANDERGELDER: Hold your horses, I say, Joe! I'm going to tell you a secret. But I don't want you telling it to that riffraff down to the barbershop what I'm going to tell you now. All I ask of you is a little extry because I'm thinking of getting married again; and this very afternoon I'm going to New York to call on my intended, a very refined lady.

JOE: Your gettin' married is none of my business, Mr. Vandergelder. I done everything to you I know, and the charge is fifteen cents like it always was, and . . . (CORNELIUS *crosses, left to right, and exit, carrying a trunk on his shoulder.* ERMENGARDE *and* GERTRUDE *enter from left.*) I don't dye no hair, not even for fifty cents I don't!

VANDERGELDER: Joe Scanlon, get out!

JOE: And lastly, it looks to me like you're pretty rash to judge which is fools and which isn't fools, Mr. Vandergelder. People that's et onions is bad judges of who's et onions and who ain't. Good morning, ladies; good morning, Mr. Vandergelder. (*Exit* JOE.)

VANDERGELDER: Well, what do you want?

ERMENGARDE (*twenty-four; pretty, sentimental*): Uncle! You said you wanted to talk to us.

VANDERGELDER: Oh yes. Gertrude, go and get my parade regalia — the uniform for my lodge parade.

GERTRUDE: What? Oh yes. Lord have mercy! (*Exit* GERTRUDE, *back center.*)

VANDERGELDER: I had a talk with that artist of yours. He's a fool. (ERMENGARDE *starts to cry.*) Weeping! weeping! You can go down and weep for a while in New York where it won't be noticed. (*He sits on desk chair, puts tie round neck and calls her over to tie it for him.*) Ermengarde! I told him that when you were old enough to marry you'd marry someone who could support you. I've done you a good turn. You'll come and thank me when you're fifty.

ERMENGARDE: But Uncle, I love him!

VANDERGELDER: I tell you you don't.

ERMENGARDE: But I *do!*

VANDERGELDER: And I tell you you don't. Leave those things to me.

ERMENGARDE: If I don't marry Ambrose I know I'll die.

VANDERGELDER: What of?

ERMENGARDE: A broken heart.

VANDERGELDER: Never heard of it. Mrs. Levi is coming in a moment to take you to New York. You are going to stay two or three weeks with Miss Van Huysen, an old friend of your mother's. (GERTRUDE *re-enters with coat, sash and sword. Enter from the street, right,* MALACHI STACK.) You're not to receive any letters except from me. I'm coming to New York myself today and I'll call on you tomorrow. (*To* MALACHI.) Who are you?

MALACHI (*fifty; sardonic; apparently innocent smile; pretense of humility*): Malachi Stack, your honor. I heard you wanted an apprentice in the hay, feed, provision and hardware business.

VANDERGELDER: An apprentice at your age?

MALACHI: Yes, your honor; I bring a lot of experience to it.

VANDERGELDER: Have you any letters of recommendation?

MALACHI (*extending a sheaf of soiled papers*): Yes, indeed, your honor! First-class recommendation.

VANDERGELDER: Ermengarde! Are you ready to start?

ERMENGARDE: Yes.

VANDERGELDER: Well, go and get ready some more. Ermengarde! Let me know the minute Mrs. Levi gets here.

ERMENGARDE: Yes, Uncle Horace. (ERMENGARDE *and* GERTRUDE *exit.* VANDERGELDER *examines the letters, putting them down one by one.*)

VANDERGELDER: I don't want an able seaman. Nor a typesetter. And I don't want a hospital cook.

MALACHI: No, your honor, but it's all experience. Excuse me! (*Selects a letter.*) This one is from your former partner, Joshua Van Tuyl, in Albany. (*He puts letters from table back into pocket.*)

VANDERGELDER: ". . . for the most part honest and reliable . . . occasionally willing and diligent." There seems to be a certain amount of hesitation about these recommendations.

MALACHI: Businessmen aren't writers, your honor. There's only one businessman in a thousand that can write a good letter of recommendation, your honor. Mr. Van Tuyl sends his best wishes and wants to know if you can use me in the provision and hardware business.

VANDERGELDER: Not so fast, not so fast! What's this "your honor" you use so much?

MALACHI: Mr. Van Tuyl says you're President of the Hudson River Provision Dealers' Recreational, Musical and Burial Society.

VANDERGELDER: I am; but there's no "your honor" that goes with it. Why did you come to Yonkers?

MALACHI: I heard that you'd had an apprentice that was a good-for-nothing, and that you were at your wit's end for another.

VANDERGELDER: Wit's end, wit's end! There's no dearth of good-for-nothing apprentices.

MALACHI: That's right, Mr. Vandergelder. It's employers there's a dearth of. Seems like you hear of a new one dying every day.

VANDERGELDER: What's that? Hold your tongue. I see you've been a barber, and a valet too. Why have you changed your place so often?

MALACHI: Changed my place, Mr. Vandergelder? When a man's interested in experience . . .

VANDERGELDER: Do you drink?

MALACHI: No, thanks. I've just had breakfast.

VANDERGELDER: I didn't ask you whether — Idiot! I asked you if you were a drunkard.

MALACHI: No, sir! No! Why, looking at it from all sides I don't even like liquor.

VANDERGELDER: Well, if you keep on looking at it from all sides, out you go. Remember that. Here. (*Gives him remaining letters.*) With all your faults, I'm going to give you a try.

MALACHI: You'll never regret it, Mr. Vandergelder. You'll never regret it.

VANDERGELDER: Now today I want to use you in New York. I judge you know your way around New York?

MALACHI: Do I know New York? Mr. Vandergelder, I know every hole and corner in New York.

VANDERGELDER: Here's a dollar. A train leaves in a minute. Take that bag to the Central Hotel on Water Street, have them save me a room. Wait for me. I'll be there about four o'clock.

MALACHI: Yes, Mr. Vandergelder. (*Picks up the bag, starts out, then comes back.*) Oh, but first, I'd like to meet the other clerks I'm to work with.

VANDERGELDER: You haven't time. Hurry now. The station's across the street.

MALACHI: Yes, sir. (*Away — then back once more.*) You'll see, sir, you'll never regret it. . . .

VANDERGELDER: I regret it already. Go on. Off with you. (*Exit* MALACHI, *right. The following speech is addressed to the audience. During it* MR. VANDERGELDER *takes off his dressing gown, puts on his scarlet sash, his sword and his bright-colored coat. He is already wearing light blue trousers with a red stripe down the sides.*)

VANDERGELDER: Ninety-nine per cent of the people in the world are fools and the rest of us are in great danger of contagion. But I wasn't always free of foolishness as I am now. I was once young, which was foolish; I fell in love; and for a while I was poor, which was more foolish than all the other things put together. Then my wife died, which was foolish of her; I grew older, which was sensible of me; then I became a rich man, which is as sensible as it is rare. Since you see I'm a man of sense, I guess you were surprised to hear that I'm planning to get married again. Well, I've two reasons for it. In the first place, I like my house run with order, comfort and economy. That's a woman's work; but even a woman can't do it well if she's merely being paid for it. In order to run a house well, a woman must have the feeling that she owns it. Marriage is a bribe to make a housekeeper think she's a householder. Did you ever watch an ant carry a burden twice its size? What excitement! What patience! What will! Well, that's what I think of when I see a woman running a house. What giant passions in those little bodies — what quarrels with the butcher for the best cut — what fury at discovering a moth in a cupboard! Believe me! — if women could harness their natures to something bigger than a house and a baby carriage — tck! tck! — they'd change the world. And the second reason, ladies and gentlemen? Well, I see by your faces you've guessed it already. There's nothing like mixing with women to bring out all the foolishness in a man of sense. And that's a risk I'm willing to take. I've just turned sixty, and I've just laid side by side the last dollar of my first half million. So if I should lose my head a little, I still have enough money to buy it back. After many years' caution and hard work, I have earned a right to a little risk and adventure, and I'm thinking of getting married. Yes, like all you other fools, I'm willing to risk a little security for a certain amount of adventure. Think it over. (*Exit back center.* AMBROSE *enters from the street, crosses left, and whistles softly.* ERMENGARDE *enters from left.*)

ERMENGARDE: Ambrose! If my uncle saw you!

AMBROSE: Sh! Get your hat.

ERMENGARDE: My hat!

AMBROSE: Quick! Your trunk's at the station. Now quick! We're running away.

ERMENGARDE: Running away!

AMBROSE: Sh!

ERMENGARDE: Where?

AMBROSE: To New York. To get married.

ERMENGARDE: Oh, Ambrose, I can't do that. Ambrose dear — it wouldn't be proper!

AMBROSE: Listen. I'm taking you to my friend's house. His wife will take care of you.

ERMENGARDE: But, Ambrose, a girl can't go on a train with a man. I can see you don't know anything about girls.

AMBROSE: But I'm telling you we're going to get married!

ERMENGARDE: Married! But what would *Uncle* say?

AMBROSE: We don't care what Uncle'd say — we're eloping.

ERMENGARDE: Ambrose Kemper! How can you use such an awful word!

AMBROSE: Ermengarde, you have the soul of a field mouse.

ERMENGARDE (*crying*): Ambrose, why do you say such cruel things to me? (*Enter* MRS. LEVI, *from the street, right. She stands listening.*)

AMBROSE: For the last time I beg you — get your hat and coat. The train leaves in a few minutes. Ermengarde, we'll get married tomorrow. . . .

ERMENGARDE: Oh, Ambrose! I see you don't understand anything about weddings. Ambrose, don't you *respect* me? . . .

MRS. LEVI (*uncertain age; mass of sandy hair; impoverished elegance; large, shrewd but generous nature, an assumption of worldly cynicism conceals a tireless amused enjoyment of life. She carries a handbag and a small brown paper bag*): Good morning, darling girl — how are you? (*They kiss.*)

ERMENGARDE: Oh, good morning, Mrs. Levi.

MRS. LEVI: And who is this gentleman who is so devoted to you?

ERMENGARDE: This is Mr. Kemper, Mrs. Levi. Ambrose, this is . . . Mrs. Levi . . . she's an old friend. . . .

MRS. LEVI: Mrs. Levi, born Gallagher. Very happy to meet you, Mr. Kemper.

AMBROSE: Good morning, Mrs. Levi.

MRS. LEVI: Mr. Kemper, *the artist!* Delighted! Mr. Kemper, may I say something very frankly?

AMBROSE: Yes, Mrs. Levi.

MRS. LEVI: This thing you were planning to do is a very great mistake.

ERMENGARDE: Oh, Mrs. Levi, please explain to Ambrose — of *course!* I want to marry him, but to *elope!* . . . How . . .

MRS. LEVI: Now, my dear girl, you go in and keep one eye on your uncle. I wish to talk to Mr. Kemper for a moment. You give us a warning when you hear your Uncle Horace coming. . . .

ERMENGARDE: Ye-es, Mrs. Levi. (*Exit* ERMENGARDE, *back center.*)

MRS. LEVI: Mr. Kemper, I was this dear girl's mother's oldest friend. Believe me, I am on your side. I hope you two will be married very soon, and I think I can be of real service to you. Mr. Kemper, I always go right to the point.

AMBROSE: What is the point, Mrs. Levi?

MRS. LEVI: Mr. Vandergelder is a very rich man, Mr. Kemper, and Ermengarde is his only relative.

AMBROSE: But I am not interested in Mr. Vandergelder's money. I have enough to support a wife and family.

MRS. LEVI: Enough? How much is enough when one is thinking about children and the future? The future is the most expensive luxury in the world, Mr. Kemper.

AMBROSE: Mrs. Levi, what is the point?

MRS. LEVI: Believe me, Mr. Vandergelder wishes to get rid of Ermengarde, and if you follow my suggestions he will even permit her to marry you. You see, Mr. Vandergelder is planning to get married himself.

AMBROSE: What? That monster!

MRS. LEVI: Mr. Kemper!

AMBROSE: Married! To you, Mrs. Levi?

MRS. LEVI (*taken aback*): Oh, no, no . . . NO! I am merely arranging it. I am helping him find a suitable bride.

AMBROSE: For Mr. Vandergelder there are no suitable brides.

MRS. LEVI: I think we can safely say that Mr. Vandergelder will be married to someone by the end of next week.

AMBROSE: What are you suggesting, Mrs. Levi?

MRS. LEVI: I am taking Ermengarde to New York on the next train. I shall not take her to Miss Van Huysen's, as is planned; I shall take her to my house. I wish you to call for her at my house at five thirty. Here is my card.

AMBROSE: "Mrs. Dolly Gallagher Levi. Varicose veins reduced."

MRS. LEVI (*trying to take back card*): I beg your pardon . . .

AMBROSE (*holding card*): I beg *your* pardon. "Consultations free."

MRS. LEVI: I meant to give you my other card. Here.

AMBROSE: "Mrs. Dolly Gallagher Levi. Aurora Hosiery. Instruction in the guitar and mandolin." You do all these things, Mrs. Levi?

MRS. LEVI: Two and two make four, Mr. Kemper — always did. So you will come to my house at five thirty. At about six I shall take you both with me to the Harmonia Gardens Restaurant on the Battery; Mr. Vandergelder will be there and everything will be arranged.

AMBROSE: How?

MRS. LEVI: Oh, I don't know. One thing will lead to another.

AMBROSE: How do I know that I can trust you, Mrs. Levi? You could easily make our situation worse.

MRS. LEVI: Mr. Kemper, your situation could not possibly be worse.

AMBROSE: I wish I knew what you get out of this, Mrs. Levi.

MRS. LEVI: That is a very proper question. I get two things: profit and pleasure.

AMBROSE: How?

MRS. LEVI: Mr. Kemper, I am a woman who arranges things. At present I am arranging Mr. Vandergelder's domestic affairs. Out of it I get — shall we call it: little pickings? I need little pickings, Mr. Kemper, and especially just now, when I haven't got my train fare back to New York. You see: I am frank with you.

AMBROSE: That's your profit, Mrs. Levi; but where do you get your pleasure?

MRS. LEVI: My pleasure? Mr. Kemper, when you artists paint a hillside or a river you change everything a little, you make thousands of little changes, don't you? Nature is never completely satisfactory and must be corrected. Well, I'm like you artists. Life as it is is never quite interesting enough for me — I'm bored, Mr. Kemper, with life as it is — and so I do things. I put my hand in here, and I put my hand in there, and I watch and I listen — and often I'm very much amused.

AMBROSE (*rises*): Not in my affairs, Mrs. Levi.

MRS. LEVI: Wait, I haven't finished. There's another thing. I'm very interested in this household here — in Mr. Vandergelder and all that idle, frozen money of his. I don't like the thought of it lying in great piles, useless, motionless, in the bank, Mr. Kemper. Money should circulate like rain water. It should be flowing down among the people, through dressmakers and restaurants and cabmen, setting up a little business here, and furnishing a good time there. Do you see what I mean?

AMBROSE: Yes, I do.

MRS. LEVI: New York should be a very happy city, Mr. Kemper, but it isn't. My late husband came from Vienna; now there's a city that understands this. I want New York to be more like Vienna and less like a collection of nervous and tired ants. And if you and Ermengarde get a good deal of Mr. Vandergelder's money, I want you to see that it starts flowing in and around a lot of people's lives. And for that reason I want you to come with me to the Harmonia Gardens Restaurant tonight. (*Enter* ERMENGARDE.)

ERMENGARDE: Mrs. Levi, Uncle Horace is coming.

MRS. LEVI: Mr. Kemper, I think you'd better be going. . . . (AMBROSE *crosses to trap door and disappears down the ladder, closing trap as he goes.*) Darling girl, Mr. Kemper and I have had a very good talk. You'll see: Mr. Vandergelder and I will be dancing at your wedding very soon — (*Enter* VANDERGELDER *at back. He has now added a splendid plumed hat to his costume and is carrying a standard or small flag bearing the initials of his lodge.*) Oh, Mr. Vandergelder, how handsome you look! You take my breath away. Yes, my dear girl, I'll see you soon. (*Exit* ERMENGARDE *back center.*) Oh, Mr. Vandergelder, I wish Irene Molloy could see you now. But then! I don't know what's come over you lately. You seem to be growing younger every day.

VANDERGELDER: Allowing for exaggeration, Mrs. Levi. If a man eats careful there's no reason why he should look old.

MRS. LEVI: You never said a truer word.

VANDERGELDER: I'll never see fifty-five again.

MRS. LEVI: Fifty-five! Why, I can see at a glance that you're the sort that will be stamping about at a hundred — and eating five meals a day, like my Uncle Harry. At fifty-five my Uncle Harry was a mere boy. I'm a judge of hands, Mr. Vandergelder — show me your hand. (*Looks at it.*) Lord in heaven! What a life line!

VANDERGELDER: Where?

MRS. LEVI: From *here* to *here*. It runs right off your hand. I don't know where it goes. They'll have to hit you on the head with a mallet. They'll have to stifle you with a sofa pillow. You'll bury us all! However, to return to our business — Mr. Vandergelder, I suppose you've changed your mind again. I suppose you've given up all idea of getting married.

VANDERGELDER (*complacently*): Not at all, Mrs. Levi. I have news for you.

MRS. LEVI: News?

VANDERGELDER: Mrs. Levi, I've practically decided to ask Mrs. Molloy to be my wife.

MRS. LEVI (*taken aback*): You have?

VANDERGELDER: Yes, I have.

MRS. LEVI: Oh, you have! Well, I guess that's just about the best news I ever heard. So there's nothing more for me to do but wish you every happiness under the sun and say goodbye. (*Crosses as if to leave.*)

VANDERGELDER (*stopping her*): Well — Mrs. Levi — Surely I thought —

MRS. LEVI: Well, I did have a little suggestion to make — but I won't. You're going to marry Irene Molloy, and that closes the matter.

VANDERGELDER: What suggestion was that, Mrs. Levi?

MRS. LEVI: Well — I *had* found *another* girl for you.

VANDERGELDER: Another?

MRS. LEVI: The most wonderful girl, the ideal wife.

VANDERGELDER: Another, eh? What's her name?

MRS. LEVI: Her name?

VANDERGELDER: Yes!

MRS. LEVI (*groping for it*): Err . . . er . . . her *name?* — Ernestina — Simple. *Miss* Ernestina Simple. But now of course all that's too late. After all, you're engaged — you're practically engaged to marry Irene Molloy.

VANDERGELDER: Oh, I ain't engaged to Mrs. Molloy!

MRS. LEVI: Nonsense! You can't break poor Irene's heart now and change to another girl. . . . When a man at your time of life calls four times on an attractive widow like that — and sends her a pot of geraniums — that's practically an engagement!

VANDERGELDER: That ain't an engagement!

MRS. LEVI: And yet — ! If only you were free! I've found this treasure of a girl. Every moment I felt like a traitor to Irene Molloy — but let me tell you: I couldn't help it. I told this girl all about you, just as though you were a free man. Isn't that dreadful? The fact is: she has fallen in love with you already.

VANDERGELDER: Ernestina?

MRS. LEVI: Ernestina Simple.

VANDERGELDER: Ernestina Simple.

MRS. LEVI: Of course she's a very different idea from Mrs. Molloy, Ernestina is. Like her name — simple, domestic, practical.

VANDERGELDER: Can she cook?

MRS. LEVI: Cook, Mr. Vandergelder? I've had two meals from her hands, and — as I live — I don't know what I've done that God should reward me with such meals.

MRS. LEVI (*continues*): Her duck! Her steak!

VANDERGELDER: Eh! Eh! In this house we don't eat duck and steak every day, Mrs. Levi.

MRS. LEVI: But didn't I tell you? — that's the wonderful part about it. Her duck — what was it? Pigeon! I'm alive to tell you. I don't know how she does it. It's a secret that's come down in her family. The greatest chefs would give their right hands to know it. And the steaks? Shoulder of beef — four cents a pound. Dogs wouldn't eat. But when Ernestina passes her hands over it — !!

VANDERGELDER: Allowing for exaggeration, Mrs. Levi.

MRS. LEVI: No exaggeration. I'm the best cook in the world myself, and I *know* what's good.

VANDERGELDER: Hm. How old is she, Mrs. Levi?

MRS. LEVI: Nineteen, well — say twenty.

VANDERGELDER: Twenty, Mrs. Levi? Girls of twenty are apt to favor young fellows of their own age.

MRS. LEVI: But you don't listen to me. And you don't know the girl. Mr. Vandergelder, she has a positive horror of flighty, brainless young men. A fine head of gray hair, she says, is worth twenty shined up with goose grease. No, sir. "I like a man that's *settled*" — in so many words she said it.

VANDERGELDER: That's . . . that's not usual, Mrs. Levi.

MRS. LEVI: Usual? I'm not wearing myself to the bone hunting up *usual* girls to interest you, Mr. Vandergelder. Usual, indeed. Listen to me. Do you know the sort of pictures she has on her wall? Is it any of these young Romeos and Lochinvars? No — it's Moses on the Mountain — that's what she's got. If you want to make her happy, you give her a picture of Methuselah surrounded by his grandchildren. That's my advice to you.

VANDERGELDER: I hope . . . hm . . . that she

has some means, Mrs. Levi. I have a large household to run.

MRS. LEVI: Ernestina? She'll bring you five thousand dollars a year.

VANDERGELDER: Eh! Eh!

MRS. LEVI: Listen to me, Mr. Vandergelder. You're a man of sense, I hope. A man that can reckon. In the first place, she's an orphan. She's been brought up with a great saving of food. What does she eat herself? Apples and lettuce. It's what she's been used to eat and what she likes best. She saves you two thousand a year right there. Secondly, she makes her own clothes — out of old tablecloths and window curtains. And she's the best-dressed woman in Brooklyn this minute. She saves you a thousand dollars right there. Thirdly, her health is of iron —

VANDERGELDER: But, Mrs. Levi, that's not money in the pocket.

MRS. LEVI: We're talking about marriage, aren't we, Mr. Vandergelder? The money she saves while she's in Brooklyn is none of your affair — but if she were your wife that would be *money*. Yes, sir, that's money.

VANDERGELDER: What's her family?

MRS. LEVI: Her father — God be good to him! He was the best — what am I trying to say? — the best undertaker in Brooklyn, respected, esteemed. He knew all the best people — knew them well, even before they died. So — well, that's the way it is. (*Lowering her voice, intimately.*) Now let me tell you a little more of her appearance. Can you hear me: as I say, a beautiful girl, beautiful, I've seen her go down the street — you know what I mean? — the young men get dizzy. They have to lean against lampposts. And she? Modest, eyes on the ground — I'm not going to tell you any more.... Couldn't you come to New York today?

VANDERGELDER: I was thinking of coming to New York this afternoon....

MRS. LEVI: You were? Well now, I wonder if something could be arranged — oh, she's so eager to see you! Let me see ...

VANDERGELDER: Could I ... Mrs. Levi, could I give you a little dinner, maybe?

MRS. LEVI: Really, come to think of it, I don't see where I could get the time. I'm so busy over that wretched lawsuit of mine. Yes. If I win it, I don't mind telling you, I'll be what's called a very rich woman. I'll own half of Long Island, that's a fact. But just now I'm at my wit's end for a little help, just enough money to finish it off. My wit's end! (*She looks in her handbag.*

In order not to hear this, VANDERGELDER *has a series of coughs, sneezes and minor convulsions.*) But perhaps I could arrange a little dinner; I'll see. Yes, for that lawsuit all I need is fifty dollars, and Staten Island's as good as mine. I've been trotting all over New York for you, trying to find you a suitable wife.

VANDERGELDER: Fifty dollars! !

MRS. LEVI: Two whole months I've been ...

VANDERGELDER: Fifty dollars, Mrs. Levi ... is no joke. (*Producing purse.*) I don't know where money's gone to these days. It's in hiding.... There's twenty ... well, there's twenty-five. I can't spare no more, not now I can't.

MRS. LEVI: Well, this will help — will help somewhat. Now let me tell you what we'll do. I'll bring Ernestina to that restaurant on the Battery. You know it: the Harmonia Gardens. It's good, but it's not flashy. Now, Mr. Vandergelder, I think it'd be nice if just this once you'd order a real nice dinner. I guess you can afford it.

VANDERGELDER: Well, just this once.

MRS. LEVI: A chicken wouldn't hurt.

VANDERGELDER: Chicken! ! — Well, just this once.

MRS. LEVI: And a little wine.

VANDERGELDER: Wine? Well, just this once.

MRS. LEVI: Now about Mrs. Molloy — what do you think? Shall we call that subject closed?

VANDERGELDER: No, not at all, Mrs. Levi, I want to have dinner with Miss ... with Miss ...

MRS. LEVI: Simple.

VANDERGELDER: With Miss Simple; but first I want to make another call on Mrs. Molloy.

MRS. LEVI: Dear, dear, dear! And Miss Simple? What races you make me run! Very well; I'll meet you on one of those benches in front of Mrs. Molloy's hat store at four thirty, as usual. (*Trap door rises, and* CORNELIUS' *head appears.*)

CORNELIUS: The buggy's here, ready for the parade, Mr. Vandergelder.

VANDERGELDER: Call Barnaby. I want to talk to both of you.

CORNELIUS: Yes, Mr. Vandergelder. (*Exit* CORNELIUS *down trap door. Leaves trap open.*)

MRS. LEVI: Now do put your thoughts in order, Mr. Vandergelder. I can't keep upsetting and disturbing the finest women in New York City unless you mean business.

VANDERGELDER: Oh, I mean business all right!

MRS. LEVI: I hope so. Because, you know, you're playing a very dangerous game.

VANDERGELDER: Dangerous? — Dangerous, Mrs. Levi?

MRS. LEVI: Of course, it's dangerous — and there's a name for it! You're tampering with these women's affections, aren't you? And the only way you can save yourself now is to be married to *someone* by the end of next week. So think that over! (*Exit center back. Enter* CORNELIUS *and* BARNABY, *by the trap door.*)

VANDERGELDER: This morning I'm joining my lodge parade, and this afternoon I'm going to New York. When I come back, there are going to be some changes in the house here. I'll tell you what the change is, but I don't want you discussing it amongst yourselves: you're going to have a mistress.

BARNABY (*seventeen; round-faced, wide-eyed innocence; wearing a green apron*): I'm too young, Mr. Vandergelder! !

VANDERGELDER: Not yours! Death and damnation! Not yours, idiot — *mine!* (*Then realizing*) Hey! Hold your tongue until you're spoken to! I'm thinking of getting married.

CORNELIUS (*crosses, hand outstretched*): Many congratulations, Mr. Vandergelder, and my compliments to the lady.

VANDERGELDER: That's none of your business. Now go back to the store. (*The boys start down the ladder,* BARNABY *first.*) Have you got any questions you want to ask before I go?

CORNELIUS: Mr. Vandergelder — er — Mr. Vandergelder, does the chief clerk get one evening off every week?

VANDERGELDER: So that's the way you begin being chief clerk, is it? When I was your age I got up at five; I didn't close the shop until ten at night, and then I put in a good hour at the account books. The world's going to pieces. You elegant ladies lie in bed until six and at nine o'clock at night you rush to close the door so fast the line of customers bark their noses. No, sir — you'll attend to the store as usual, and on Friday and Saturday nights you'll remain open until ten — now hear what I say! This is the first time I've been away from the store overnight. When I come back I want to hear that you've run the place perfectly in my absence. If I hear of any foolishness, I'll discharge you. An evening free! Do you suppose that *I* had evenings free? (*At the top of his complacency.*) If I'd had evenings free I wouldn't be what I am now! (*He marches out, right.*)

BARNABY (*watching him go*): The horses nearly ran away when they saw him. What's the matter, Cornelius?

CORNELIUS (*sits in dejected thought*). Chief clerk! Promoted from chief clerk to chief clerk.

BARNABY: Don't you like it?

CORNELIUS: Chief clerk! — and if I'm good, in ten years I'll be promoted to chief clerk again. Thirty-three years old and I still don't get an evening free? When am I going to begin to live?

BARNABY: Well — ah . . . you can begin to live on Sundays, Cornelius.

CORNELIUS: That's not living. Twice to church, and old Wolf-trap's eyes on the back of my head the whole time. And as for holidays! What did we do last Christmas? All those canned tomatoes went bad and exploded. We had to clean up the mess all afternoon. Was that living?

BARNABY (*holding his nose at the memory of the bad smell*): No ! ! !

CORNELIUS (*rising with sudden resolution*): Barnaby, how much money have you got — where you can get at it?

BARNABY: Oh — three dollars. Why, Cornelius?

CORNELIUS: You and I are going to New York.

BARNABY: Cornelius! ! ! We can't! Close the store?

CORNELIUS: Some more rotten-tomato cans are going to explode.

BARNABY: Holy cabooses! How do you know?

CORNELIUS: I know they're rotten. All you have to do is to light a match under them. They'll make such a smell that customers can't come into the place for twenty-four hours. That'll get us an evening free. We're going to New York too, Barnaby, we're going to live! I'm going to have enough adventures to last me until I'm *partner.* So go and get your Sunday clothes on.

BARNABY: Wha-a-a-t?

CORNELIUS: Yes, I mean it. We're going to have a good meal; and we're going to be in danger; and we're going to get almost arrested; and we're going to spend all our money.

BARNABY: Holy cabooses! !

CORNELIUS: And one more thing: we're not coming back to Yonkers until we've kissed a girl.

BARNABY: Kissed a girl! Cornelius, you can't do that. You don't know any girls.

CORNELIUS: I'm thirty-three. I've got to begin sometime.

BARNABY: I'm only seventeen, Cornelius. It isn't so urgent for me.

CORNELIUS: Don't start backing down now — if the worst comes to the worst and we get discharged from here we can always join the Army.

BARNABY: Uh — did I hear you say that you'd be old Wolf-trap's partner?

CORNELIUS: How can I help it? He's growing old. If you go to bed at nine and open the store at six, you get promoted upward whether you like it or not.

BARNABY: My! Partner.

CORNELIUS: Oh, there's no way of getting away from it. You and I will be Vandergelders.

BARNABY: I? Oh, no — I may rise a little, but I'll never be a Vandergelder.

CORNELIUS: Listen — everybody thinks when he gets rich he'll be a different kind of rich person from the rich people he sees around him, later on he finds out there's only one kind of rich person, and he's it.

BARNABY: Oh, but I'll —

CORNELIUS: No. The best of all would be a person who has all the good things a poor person has, and all the good meals a rich person has, but that's never been known. No, you and I are going to be Vandergelders; all the more reason, then, for us to try and get some living and some adventure into us now — will you come, Barnaby?

BARNABY (in a struggle with his fears, a whirlwind of words): But Wolf-trap — KRR-pt, Gertrude-KRR-pt — (With a sudden cry of agreement.) Yes, Cornelius! (Enter MRS. LEVI, ERMENGARDE and GERTRUDE from back center. The boys start down the ladder, CORNELIUS last.)

MRS. LEVI: Mr. Hackl, is the trunk waiting at the station?

CORNELIUS: Yes, Mrs. Levi. (Closes the trap door.)

MRS. LEVI: Take a last look, Ermengarde.

ERMENGARDE: What?

MRS. LEVI: Take a last look at your girlhood home, dear. I remember when I left my home. I gave a whinny like a young colt, and off I went. (ERMENGARDE and GERTRUDE exit.)

ERMENGARDE (as they go): Oh, Gertrude, do you think I ought to get married this way? A young girl has to be so careful! (MRS. LEVI is alone. She addresses the audience.)

MRS. LEVI: You know, I think I'm going to have this room with blue wallpaper, — yes, in blue! (Hurries out after the others. BARNABY comes up trap door, looks off right, then lies on floor, gazing down through the trap door.)

BARNABY: All clear up here, Cornelius! Cornelius — hold the candle steady a minute — the bottom row's all right — but try the top now . . . they're swelled up like they are ready to bust! (BANG.) Holy CABOOSES! (BANG, BANG.) Cornelius! I can smell it up here! (Rises and dances about, holding his nose.)

CORNELIUS (rushing up the trap door): Get into your Sunday clothes, Barnaby. We're going to New York! (As they run out . . . there is a big explosion. A shower of tomato cans comes up from below, as —

THE CURTAIN FALLS)

ACT II

MRS. MOLLOY's hat shop, New York City.

There are two entrances. One door at the extreme right of the back wall, to MRS. MOLLOY's workroom; one at the back left corner, to the street. The whole left wall is taken up with the show windows, filled with hats. It is separated from the shop by a low brass rail, hung with net; during the act both MRS. MOLLOY and BARNABY stoop under the rail and go into the shop window. By the street door stands a large cheval glass. In the middle of the back wall is a large wardrobe or clothes cupboard, filled with ladies' coats, large enough for CORNELIUS to hide in. At the left, beginning at the back wall, between the wardrobe and the workroom door, a long counter extends toward the audience, almost to the footlights. In the center of the room is a large round table with a low-hanging red cloth. There are a small gilt chair by the wardrobe and two chairs in front of the counter. Over the street door and the workroom door are bells which ring when the doors are opened.

As the curtain rises, MRS. MOLLOY is in the window, standing on a box, reaching up to put hats on the stand. MINNIE FAY is sewing by the counter. MRS. MOLLOY has a pair of felt overshoes, to be removed later.

MRS. MOLLOY: Minnie, you're a fool. Of course I shall marry Horace Vandergelder.

MINNIE: Oh, Mrs. Molloy! I didn't ask you.

I wouldn't dream of asking you such a personal question.

MRS. MOLLOY: Well, it's what you meant, isn't it? And there's your answer. I shall certainly marry Horace Vandergelder if he asks me. (*Crawls under window rail, into the room, singing loudly.*)

MINNIE: I know it's none of my business . . .

MRS. MOLLOY: Speak up, Minnie, I can't hear you.

MINNIE: . . . but do you . . . do you . . . ?

MRS. MOLLOY (*having crossed the room, is busy at the counter*): Minnie, you're a fool. Say it: Do I love him? Of course, I don't love him. But I have two good reasons for marrying him just the same. Minnie, put something on that hat. It's not ugly enough. (*Throws hat over counter.*)

MINNIE (*catching and taking hat to table*): Not ugly enough!

MRS. MOLLOY: I couldn't sell it. Put a . . . put a sponge on it.

MINNIE: Why, Mrs. Molloy, you're in such a *mood* today.

MRS. MOLLOY: In the first place I shall marry Mr. Vandergelder to get away from the millinery business. I've hated it from the first day I had anything to do with it. Minnie, I hate hats. (*Sings loudly again.*)

MINNIE: Why, what's the matter with the millinery business?

MRS. MOLLOY (*crossing to window with two hats*): I can no longer stand being suspected of being a wicked woman, while I have nothing to show for it. I can't stand it. (*She crawls under rail into window.*)

MINNIE: Why, no one would dream of suspecting you —

MRS. MOLLOY (*on her knees, she looks over the rail*): Minnie, you're a fool. All millineresses are suspected of being wicked women. Why, half the time all those women come into the shop merely to look at me.

MINNIE: Oh!

MRS. MOLLOY: They enjoy the suspicion. But they aren't certain. If they were *certain* I was a wicked woman, they wouldn't put foot in this place again. Do I go to restaurants? No, it would be bad for business. Do I go to balls, or theatres, or operas? No, it would be bad for business. The only men I ever meet are feather merchants. (*Crawls out of window, but gazes intently into the street.*) What are those two young men doing out there on that park bench?

Take my word for it, Minnie, either I marry Horace Vandergelder, or I break out of this place like a fire engine. I'll go to every theatre and ball and opera in New York City. (*Returns to counter, singing again.*)

MINNIE: But Mr. Vandergelder's not . . .

MRS. MOLLOY: Speak up, Minnie, I can't hear you.

MINNIE: . . . I don't think he's attractive.

MRS. MOLLOY: But what I think he is — and it's very important — I think he'd make a good fighter.

MINNIE: Mrs. Molloy!

MRS. MOLLOY: Take my word for it, Minnie: the best part of married life is the fights. The rest is merely so-so.

MINNIE (*fingers in ears*): I won't listen.

MRS. MOLLOY: Peter Molloy — God rest him! — was a fine arguing man. I pity the woman whose husband slams the door and walks out of the house at the beginning of an argument. Peter Molloy would stand up and fight for hours on end. He'd even throw things, Minnie, and there's no pleasure to equal that. When I felt tired I'd start a good bloodwarming fight and it'd take ten years off my age; now Horace Vandergelder would put up a good fight; I know it. I've a mind to marry him.

MINNIE: I think they're just awful, the things you're saying today.

MRS. MOLLOY: Well, I'm enjoying them myself, too.

MINNIE (*at the window*): Mrs. Molloy, those two men out in the street —

MRS. MOLLOY: What?

MINNIE: Those men. It looks as if they meant to come in here.

MRS. MOLLOY: Well now, it's time some men came into this place. I give you the younger one, Minnie.

MINNIE: Aren't you terrible! (MRS. MOLLOY *sits on center table, while* MINNIE *takes off her felt overshoes.*)

MRS. MOLLOY: Wait till I get my hands on that older one! Mark my words, Minnie, we'll get an adventure out of this yet. Adventure, adventure! Why does everybody have adventures except me, Minnie? Because I have no spirit, I have no gumption. Minnie, they're coming in here. Let's go into the workroom and make them wait for us for a minute.

MINNIE: Oh, but Mrs. Molloy . . . my work! . . .

MRS. MOLLOY (*running to workroom*): Hurry

up, be quick now, Minnie! (*They go out to workroom.* BARNABY *and* CORNELIUS *run in from street, leaving front door open. They are dressed in the stiff discomfort of their Sunday clothes.* CORNELIUS *wears a bowler hat,* BARNABY *a straw hat too large for him.*)

BARNABY: No one's here.

CORNELIUS: Some women were here a minute ago. I saw them. (*They jump back to the street door and peer down the street.*) That's Wolf-trap all right! (*Coming back.*) Well, we've got to hide here until he passes by.

BARNABY: He's sitting down on that bench. It may be quite a while.

CORNELIUS: When these women come in, we'll have to make conversation until he's gone away. We'll pretend we're buying a hat. How much money have you got now?

BARNABY (*counting his money*): Forty cents for the train — seventy cents for dinner — twenty cents to see the whale — and a dollar I lost — I have seventy cents.

CORNELIUS: And I have a dollar seventy-five. I wish I knew how much hats cost!

BARNABY: Is this an adventure, Cornelius?

CORNELIUS: No, but it may be.

BARNABY: I think it is. There we wander around New York all day and nothing happens; and then we come to the quietest street in the whole city and suddenly Mr. Vandergelder turns the corner. (*Going to door.*) I think that's an adventure. I think . . . Cornelius! That Mrs. Levi is there now. She's sitting down on the bench with him.

CORNELIUS: What do you know about that! We know only one person in all New York City, and there she is!

BARNABY: Even if our adventure came along now I'd be too tired to enjoy it. Cornelius, why isn't this an adventure?

CORNELIUS: Don't be asking that. When you're in an adventure, you'll know it all right.

BARNABY: Maybe I wouldn't. Cornelius, let's arrange a signal for you to give me when an adventure's really going on. For instance, Cornelius, you say . . . uh . . . uh . . . *pudding*; you say *pudding* to me as if it's an adventure we're in.

CORNELIUS: I wonder where the lady who runs this store is? What's her name again?

BARNABY: Mrs. Molloy, hats for ladies.

CORNELIUS: Oh yes. I must think over what I'm going to say when she comes in. (*To counter.*) "Good afternoon, Mrs. Molloy, wonder-ful weather we're having. We've been looking everywhere for some beautiful hats."

BARNABY: That's fine, Cornelius!

CORNELIUS: "Good afternoon, Mrs. Molloy; wonderful weather . . ." We'll make her think we're very rich. (*One hand in trouser pocket, the other on back of chair.*) "Good afternoon, Mrs. Molloy . . ." You keep one eye on the door the whole time. "We've been looking everywhere for . . ." (*Enter* MRS. MOLLOY *from the workroom.*)

MRS. MOLLOY (*behind the counter*): Oh, I'm sorry. Have I kept you waiting? Good afternoon, gentlemen.

CORNELIUS (*hat off*): Here, Cornelius Hackl.

BARNABY (*hat off*): Here, Barnaby Tucker.

MRS. MOLLOY: I'm very happy to meet you. Perhaps I can help you. Won't you sit down?

CORNELIUS: Thank you, we will. (*The boys place their hats on the table, then sit down at the counter facing* MRS. MOLLOY.) You see, Mrs. Molloy, we're looking for hats. We've looked everywhere. Do you know what we heard? Go to Mrs. Molloy's, they said. So we came here. Only place we *could* go . . .

MRS. MOLLOY: Well, now, that's *very* complimentary.

CORNELIUS: . . . and we were right. Everybody was right.

MRS. MOLLOY: You wish to choose some hats for a friend?

CORNELIUS: Yes, exactly. (*Kicks* BARNABY.)

BARNABY: Yes, exactly.

CORNELIUS: We were thinking of five or six, weren't we, Barnaby?

BARNABY: Er — five.

CORNELIUS: You see, Mrs. Molloy, money's no object with us. None at all.

MRS. MOLLOY: Why, Mr. Hackl . . .

CORNELIUS (*rises and goes toward street door*): . . . I beg your pardon, what an interesting street! Something happening every minute. Passers-by, and . . . (BARNABY *runs to join him.*)

MRS. MOLLOY: You're from out of town, Mr. Hackl?

CORNELIUS (*coming back*): Yes, ma'am — Barnaby, just keep your eye on the street, will you? You won't see that in Yonkers every day. (BARNABY *remains kneeling at street door.*)

BARNABY: Oh yes, I will.

CORNELIUS: Not all of it.

MRS. MOLLOY: Now this friend of yours — couldn't she come in with you someday and choose her hats herself?

CORNELIUS (*sits at counter*): No. Oh, no. It's a surprise for her.

MRS. MOLLOY: Indeed? That may be a little difficult, Mr. Hackl. It's not entirely customary. — Your friend's very interested in the street, Mr. Hackl.

CORNELIUS: Oh yes. Yes. He has reason to be.

MRS. MOLLOY: You said you were from out of town?

CORNELIUS: Yes, we're from Yonkers.

MRS. MOLLOY: Yonkers?

CORNELIUS: Yonkers . . . yes, Yonkers. (*He gazes rapt into her eyes.*) You should know Yonkers, Mrs. Molloy. Hudson River; Palisades; drives; some say it's the most beautiful town in the world; that's what they say.

MR. MOLLOY: Is that so!

CORNELIUS (*rises*): Mrs. Molloy, if you ever had a Sunday free, I'd . . . we'd like to show you Yonkers. Y'know, it's very historic, too.

MRS. MOLLOY: That's very kind of you. Well, perhaps . . . now about those hats. (*Takes two hats from under counter, and crosses to back center of the room.*)

CORNELIUS (*following*): Is there . . . Have you a . . . Maybe Mr. Molloy would like to see Yonkers too?

MRS. MOLLOY: Oh, I'm a widow, Mr. Hackl.

CORNELIUS (*joyfully*): You are! (*With sudden gravity.*) Oh, that's too bad. Mr. Molloy would have enjoyed Yonkers.

MRS. MOLLOY: Very likely. Now about these hats. Is your friend dark or light?

CORNELIUS: Don't think about that for a minute. Any hat you'd like would be perfectly all right with her.

MRS. MOLLOY: Really! (*She puts one on.*) Do you like this one?

CORNELIUS (*in awe-struck admiration*): Barnaby! (*In sudden anger.*) Barnaby! Look! (*Barnaby turns; unimpressed, he laughs vaguely, and turns to door again.*) Mrs. Molloy, that's the most beautiful hat I ever saw. (*Barnaby now crawls under the rail into the window.*)

MRS. MOLLOY: Your friend is acting very strangely, Mr. Hackl.

CORNELIUS: Barnaby, stop acting strangely. When the street's quiet and empty, come back and talk to us. What was I saying? Oh yes: Mrs. Molloy, you should know Yonkers.

MRS. MOLLOY (*hat off*): The fact is, I have a friend in Yonkers. Perhaps you know him. It's always so foolish to ask in cases like that, isn't it? (*They both laugh over this with increasing congeniality.* MRS. MOLLOY *goes to counter with hats from table.* CORNELIUS *follows.*) It's a Mr. Vandergelder.

CORNELIUS (*stops abruptly*): What was that you said?

MRS. MOLLOY: Then you do know him?

CORNELIUS: Horace Vandergelder?

MRS. MOLLOY: Yes, that's right.

CORNELIUS: Know him! (*Look to* BARNABY.) Why, no. No!

BARNABY: No! No!

CORNELIUS (*starting to glide about the room, in search of a hiding place*): I beg your pardon, Mrs. Molloy — what an attractive shop you have! (*Smiling fixedly at her he moves to the workshop door.*) And where does this door lead to? (*Opens it, and is alarmed by the bell which rings above it.*)

MRS. MOLLOY: Why, Mr. Hackl, that's my workroom.

CORNELIUS: Everything here is so interesting. (*Looks under counter.*) Every corner. Every door, Mrs. Molloy. Barnaby, notice the interesting doors and cupboards. (*He opens the cupboard door.*) Deeply interesting. Coats for ladies. (*Laughs.*) Barnaby, make a note of the table. Precious piece of furniture, with a low-hanging cloth, I see. (*Stretches his leg under table.*)

MRS. MOLLOY (*taking a hat from box left of wardrobe*): Perhaps your friend might like some of this new Italian straw. Mr. Vandergelder's a substantial man and very well liked, they tell me.

CORNELIUS: A lovely man, Mrs. Molloy.

MRS. MOLLOY: Oh yes — charming, charming!

CORNELIUS (*smiling sweetly*): Has only one fault, as far as I know; he's hard as nails; but apart from that, as you say, a charming nature, ma'am.

MRS. MOLLOY: And a large circle of friends — ?

CORNELIUS: Yes, indeed, yes indeed — five or six.

BARNABY: Five!

CORNELIUS: He comes and calls on you here from time to time, I suppose.

MRS. MOLLOY (*turns from mirror where she has been putting a hat on*): This summer we'll be wearing ribbons down our back. Yes, as a matter of fact I am expecting a call from him this afternoon. (*Hat off.*)

BARNABY: I think . . . Cornelius! I think . . . !!

MRS. MOLLOY: Now to show you some more hats —

BARNABY: Look out! (*He takes a flying leap over the rail and flings himself under the table.*)

CORNELIUS: Begging your pardon, Mrs. Molloy. (*He jumps into the cupboard.*)

MRS. MOLLOY: Gentlemen! Mr. Hackl! Come right out of there this minute!

CORNELIUS (*sticking his head out of the wardrobe door*): Help us just this once, Mrs. Molloy! We'll explain later!

MRS. MOLLOY: Mr. Hackl!

BARNABY: We're as innocent as can be, Mrs. Molloy.

MRS. MOLLOY: But really! Gentlemen! I can't have this! *What are you doing?*

BARNABY: Cornelius! Cornelius! Pudding?

CORNELIUS (*a shout*): Pudding! (*They disappear. Enter from the street* MRS. LEVI, *followed by* MR. VANDERGELDER. VANDERGELDER *is dressed in a too-bright checked suit, and wears a green derby — or bowler — hat. He is carrying a large ornate box of chocolates in one hand, and a cane in the other.*)

MRS. LEVI: Irene, my darling child, how *are* you? Heaven be good to us, how well you look! (*They kiss.*)

MRS. MOLLOY: But what a surprise! And Mr. Vandergelder in New York — what a pleasure!

VANDERGELDER (*swaying back and forth on his heels complacently*): Good afternoon, Mrs. Molloy. (*They shake hands.* MRS. MOLLOY *brings chair from counter for him. He sits at left of table.*)

MRS. LEVI: Yes, Mr. Vandergelder's in New York. Yonkers lies up there — *decimated* today. Irene, we thought we'd pay you a very short call. Now you'll tell us if it's inconvenient, won't you?

MRS. MOLLOY (*placing a chair for* MRS. LEVI *at right of table*): Inconvenient, Dolly! The idea! Why, it's sweet of you to come. (*She notices the boys' hats on the table — sticks a spray of flowers into crown of* CORNELIUS' *bowler and winds a piece of chiffon round* BARNABY'S *panama.*)

VANDERGELDER: We waited outside a moment.

MRS. LEVI: Mr. Vandergelder thought he saw two customers coming in — two men.

MRS. MOLLOY: Men! Men, Mr. Vandergelder? Why, what will you be saying next?

MRS. LEVI: Then we'll sit down for a minute or two. . . .

MRS. MOLLOY (*wishing to get them out of the shop into the workroom*): Before you sit down — (*She pushes them both.*) Before you sit down, there's something I want to show you. I want to show Mr. Vandergelder my workroom, too.

MRS. LEVI: I've seen the workroom a hundred times. I'll stay right here and try on some of these hats.

MRS. MOLLOY: No, Dolly, you come too. I have something for you. Come along, everybody. (*Exit* MRS. LEVI *to workroom.*) Mr. Vandergelder, I want your advice. You don't know how helpless a woman in business is. Oh, I feel I need advice every minute from a fine business head like yours. (*Exit* VANDERGELDER *to workroom.* MRS. MOLLOY *shouts this line and then slams the workroom door.*) Now I shut the door!! (*Exit* MRS. MOLLOY. CORNELIUS *puts his head out of the wardrobe door and gradually comes out into the room, leaving door open.*)

CORNELIUS: Hsst!

BARNABY (*pokes his head out from under the table*): Maybe she wants us to go, Cornelius?

CORNELIUS: Certainly I won't go. Mrs. Molloy would think we were just thoughtless fellows. No, all I want is to stretch a minute.

BARNABY: What are you going to do when he's gone, Cornelius? Are we just going to run away?

CORNELIUS: Well . . . I don't know yet. I like Mrs. Molloy a lot. I wouldn't like her to think badly of me. I think I'll buy a hat. We can walk home to Yonkers, even if it takes us all night. I wonder how much hats cost. Barnaby, give me all the money you've got. (*As he leans over to take the money, he sneezes. Both return to their hiding places in alarm; then emerge again.*) My, all those perfumes in that cupboard tickle my nose! But I like it in there . . . it's a woman's world, and very different.

BARNABY: I like it where I am, too; only I'd like it better if I had a pillow.

CORNELIUS (*taking coat from wardrobe*): Here, take one of these coats. I'll roll it up for you so it won't get mussed. Ladies don't like to have their coats mussed.

BARNABY: That's fine. Now I can just lie here and hear Mr. Vandergelder talk. (CORNELIUS goes slowly above table towards cheval mirror, repeating MRS. MOLLOY's line dreamily.)

CORNELIUS: "This summer we'll be wearing ribbons down our back...."

BARNABY: Can I take off my shoes, Cornelius? (CORNELIUS does not reply. He comes to the footlights and addresses the audience, in completely simple naïve sincerity:)

CORNELIUS: Isn't the world full of wonderful things. There we sit cooped up in Yonkers for years and years and all the time wonderful people like Mrs. Molloy are walking around in New York and we don't know them at all. I don't know whether — from where you're sitting — you can see — well, for instance, the way (he points to the edge of his right eye) her eye and forehead and cheek come together, up here. Can you? And the kind of fireworks that shoot out of her eyes all the time. I tell you right now: a fine woman is the greatest work of God. You can talk all you like about Niagara Falls and the Pyramids; they aren't in it at all. Of course, up there at Yonkers they came into the store all the time, and bought this and that, and I said, "Yes, ma'am," and "That'll be seventy-five cents, ma'am"; and I watched them. But today I've talked to one, equal to equal, equal to equal, and to the finest one that ever existed, in my opinion. They're so different from men! Everything that they say and do is so different that you feel like laughing all the time. (He laughs.) Golly, they're different from men. And they're awfully mysterious, too. You never can be really sure what's going on in their heads. They have a kind of wall around them all the time — of pride and a sort of play-acting: I bet you could know a woman a hundred years without ever being really sure whether she liked you or not. This minute I'm in danger. I'm in danger of losing my job and my future and everything that people think is important; but I don't care. Even if I have to dig ditches for the rest of my life, I'll be a ditch digger who once had a wonderful day.

Barnaby!

BARNABY: Oh, you woke me up!

CORNELIUS (kneels): Barnaby, we can't go back to Yonkers yet and you know why.

BARNABY: Why not?

CORNELIUS: We've had a good meal. We've had an adventure. We've been in danger of getting arrested. There's only one more thing we've got to do before we go back to be successes in Yonkers.

BARNABY: Cornelius! You're never going to kiss Mrs. Molloy!

CORNELIUS: Maybe.

BARNABY: But she'll scream.

CORNELIUS: Barnaby, you don't know anything at all. You might as well know right now that everybody except us goes through life kissing right and left all the time.

BARNABY (pauses for reflection: humbly): Well, thanks for telling me, Cornelius. I often wondered. (Enter MRS. LEVI from workroom.)

MRS. LEVI: Just a minute, Irene. I must find my handkerchief. (CORNELIUS, caught by the arrival of MRS. LEVI, drops to his hands and knees, and starts very slowly to crawl back to the wardrobe, as though the slowness rendered him invisible. MRS. LEVI, leaning over the counter, watches him. From the cupboard he puts his head out of it and looks pleadingly at her.) Why, Mr. Hackl, I thought you were up in Yonkers.

CORNELIUS: I almost always am, Mrs. Levi. Oh, Mrs. Levi, don't tell Mr. Vandergelder! I'll explain everything later.

BARNABY (puts head out): We're terribly innocent, Mrs. Levi.

MRS. LEVI: Why, who's that?

BARNABY: Barnaby Tucker — just paying a call.

MRS. LEVI (looking under counter and even shaking out her skirts): Well, who else is here?

CORNELIUS: Just the two of us, Mrs. Levi, that's all.

MRS. LEVI: Old friends of Mrs. Molloy's, is that it?

CORNELIUS: We never knew her before a few minutes ago, but we like her a lot — don't we, Barnaby? In fact, I think she's ... I think she's the finest person in the world. I'm ready to tell that to anybody.

MRS. LEVI: And does she think you're the finest person in the world?

CORNELIUS: Oh, no. I don't suppose she even notices that I'm alive.

MRS. LEVI: Well, I think she must notice that you're alive in that cupboard, Mr. Hackl. Well, if I were you, I'd get back into it right away. Somebody could be coming in any minute. (CORNELIUS disappears. She sits unconcernedly in chair right. Enter MRS. MOLLOY.)

MRS. MOLLOY (leaving door open and looking

about in concealed alarm): Can I help you, Dolly?

MRS. LEVI: No, no, no. I was just blowing my nose. (*Enter* VANDERGELDER *from workroom.*)

VANDERGELDER: Mrs. Molloy, I've got some advice to give you about your business. (MRS. MOLLOY *comes to the center of the room and puts* BARNABY's *hat on floor in window, then* CORNELIUS' *hat on the counter.*)

MRS. LEVI: Oh, advice from Mr. Vandergelder! The whole city should hear this.

VANDERGELDER (*standing in the workroom door, pompously*): In the first place, the aim of business is to make profit.

MRS. MOLLOY: Is that so?

MRS. LEVI: I never heard it put so clearly before. Did you hear it?

VANDERGELDER (*crossing the room to the left*): You pay those girls of yours too much. You pay them as much as men. Girls like that enjoy their work. Wages, Mrs. Molloy, are paid to make people do work they don't want to do.

MRS. LEVI: Mr. Vandergelder thinks so ably. And that's exactly the way his business is run up in Yonkers.

VANDERGELDER (*patting her hand*): Mrs. Molloy, I'd like for you to come up to Yonkers.

MRS. MOLLOY: That would be very nice. (*He hands her the box of chocolates.*) Oh, thank you. As a matter of fact, I know someone from Yonkers, someone else.

VANDERGELDER (*hangs hat on the cheval mirror*): Oh? Who's that? (MRS. MOLLOY *puts chocolates on table and brings gilt chair forward and sits center at table facing the audience.*)

MRS. MOLLOY: Someone quite well-to-do, I believe, though a little free and easy in his behavior. Mr. Vandergelder, do you know Mr. Cornelius Hackl in Yonkers?

VANDERGELDER: I know him like I know my own boot. He's my head clerk.

MRS. MOLLOY: Is that so?

VANDERGELDER: He's been in my store for ten years.

MRS. MOLLOY: Well, I never!

VANDERGELDER: Where would you have known him? (MRS. MOLLOY *is in silent confusion. She looks for help to* MRS. LEVI, *seated at right end of table.*)

MRS. LEVI (*groping for means to help* MRS. MOLLOY): Err . . . blah . . . err . . . bl . . . er . . . Oh, just one of those chance meetings, I suppose.

MRS. MOLLOY: Yes, oh yes! One of those chance meetings.

VANDERGELDER: What? Chance meetings? Cornelius Hackl has no right to chance meetings. Where was it?

MRS. MOLLOY: Really, Mr. Vandergelder, it's very unlike you to question me in such a way. I think Mr. Hackl is better known than you think he is.

VANDERGELDER: Nonsense.

MRS. MOLLOY: He's in New York often, and he's very well liked.

MRS. LEVI (*having found her idea, with decision*): Well, the truth might as well come out now as later. Mr. Vandergelder, Irene is quite right. Your head clerk is often in New York. Goes everywhere; has an army of friends. Everybody knows Cornelius Hackl.

VANDERGELDER (*laughs blandly and sits in chair at left of table*): He never comes to New York. He works all day in my store and at nine o'clock at night he goes to sleep in the bran room.

MRS. LEVI: So you think. But it's not true.

VANDERGELDER: Dolly Gallagher, you're crazy.

MRS. LEVI: Listen to me. You keep your nose so deep in your account books you don't know what goes on. Yes, by day, Cornelius Hackl is your faithful trusted clerk — that's true; but by night! Well, he leads a double life, that's all! He's here at the opera; at the great restaurants; in all the fashionable homes . . . why, he's at the Harmonia Gardens Restaurant three nights a week. The fact is, he's the wittiest, gayest, naughtiest, most delightful man in New York. Well, he's just *the* famous Cornelius Hackl!

VANDERGELDER (*sure of himself*): It ain't the same man. If I ever thought Cornelius Hackl came to New York, I'd discharge him.

MRS. LEVI: Who took the horses out of Jenny Lind's carriage and pulled her through the streets?

MRS. MOLLOY: Who?

MRS. LEVI: Cornelius Hackl! Who dressed up as a waiter at the Fifth Avenue Hotel the other night and took an oyster and dropped it right down Mrs. . . . (*Rises.*) No, it's too wicked to tell you!

MRS. MOLLOY: Oh yes, Dolly, tell it! Go on!

MRS. LEVI: No. But it *was* Cornelius Hackl.

VANDERGELDER (*loud*): It ain't the same man. Where'd he get the money?

MRS. LEVI: But he's very rich.

VANDERGELDER (*rises*): Rich! I keep his money in my own safe. He has a hundred and forty-six dollars and thirty-five cents.

MRS. LEVI: Oh, Mr. Vandergelder, you're killing me! Do come to your senses. He's one of *the* Hackls. (MRS. MOLLOY *sits at chair right of table where* MRS. LEVI *has been sitting.*)

VANDERGELDER: *The* Hackls?

MRS. LEVI: They built the Raritan Canal.

VANDERGELDER: Then why should he work in my store?

MRS. LEVI: Well, I'll tell you. (*Sits at the center of the table, facing the audience.*)

VANDERGELDER (*striding about*): I don't want to hear! I've got a headache! I'm going home. *It ain't the same man!!* He sleeps in my bran room. You can't get away from facts. I just made him my chief clerk.

MRS. LEVI: If you had any sense you'd make him partner. (*Rises, crosses to* MRS. MOLLOY.) Now Irene, I can see you were as taken with him as everybody else is.

MRS. MOLLOY: Why, I only met him once, very hastily.

MRS. LEVI: Yes, but I can see that you were taken with him. Now don't you be thinking of marrying him!

MRS. MOLLOY (*her hands on her cheeks*): Dolly! What are you saying! Oh!

MRS. LEVI: Maybe it'd be fine. But think it over carefully. He breaks hearts like hickory nuts.

VANDERGELDER: Who?

MRS. LEVI: Cornelius Hackl!

VANDERGELDER: Mrs. Molloy, how often has he called on you?

MRS. MOLLOY: Oh, I'm telling the truth. I've only seen him once in my life. Dolly Levi's been exaggerating so, I don't know where to look! (*Enter* MINNIE *from workroom and crosses to window.*)

MINNIE: Excuse me, Mrs. Molloy. I must get together that order for Mrs. Parkinson.

MRS. MOLLOY: Yes, we must get that off before closing.

MINNIE: I want to send it off by the errand girl. (*Having taken a hat from the window.*) Oh, I almost forgot the coat. (*She starts for the wardrobe.*)

MRS. MOLLOY (*running to the wardrobe to prevent her*): Oh, oh! I'll do that, Minnie! (*But she is too late.* MINNIE *opens the right-hand cupboard door and falls back in terror, and screams:*)

MINNIE: Oh, Mrs. Molloy! Help! There's a man! (MRS. MOLLOY *with the following speech pushes her back to the workroom door.* MINNIE *walks with one arm pointing at the cupboard. At the end of each of* MRS. MOLLOY'S *sentences she repeats — at the same pitch and degree — the words:*) There's a man!

MRS. MOLLOY (*slamming cupboard door*): Minnie, you imagined it. You're tired, dear. You go back in the workroom and lie down. Minnie, you're a fool; hold your tongue!

MINNIE: There's a man! (*Exit* MINNIE *to workroom.* MRS. MOLLOY *returns to the front of the stage.* VANDERGELDER *raises his stick threateningly.*)

VANDERGELDER: If there's a man there, we'll get him out. Whoever you are, come out of there! (*Strikes table with his stick.*)

MRS. LEVI (*goes masterfully to the cupboard — sweeps her umbrella around among the coats and closes each door as she does so*): Nonsense! There's no man there. See! Miss Fay's nerves have been playing tricks on her. Come now, let's sit down again. What were you saying, Mr. Vandergelder? (*They sit,* MRS. MOLLOY *right,* MRS. LEVI *center,* VANDERGELDER *left. A sneeze is heard from the cupboard. They all rise, look towards cupboard, then sit again.*) Well now . . . (*Another tremendous sneeze. With a gesture that says,*) "I can do no more: God bless you!" (*They all rise.* MRS. MOLLOY *stands with her back to the cupboard.*)

MRS. MOLLOY (*to* VANDERGELDER): Yes, there is a man in there. I'll explain it all to you another time. Thank you very much for coming to see me. Good afternoon, Dolly. Good afternoon, Mr. Vandergelder.

VANDERGELDER: You're protecting a man in there!

MRS. MOLLOY (*with back to cupboard*): There's a very simple explanation, but for the present, good afternoon. (*Barnaby now sneezes twice, lifting the table each time.* VANDERGELDER, *right of table, jerks off the tablecloth.* BARNABY *pulls cloth under table and rolls himself up in it.* MRS. MOLLOY *picks up the box of chocolates, which has rolled on the floor.*)

MRS. LEVI: Lord, the whole room's *crawling* with men! I'll never get over it.

VANDERGELDER: The world is going to pieces! I can't believe my own eyes!

MRS. LEVI: Come, Mr. Vandergelder. Ernestina Simple is waiting for us.

VANDERGELDER (*finds his hat and puts it on*): Mrs. Molloy, I shan't trouble you again, and *vice versa*. (MRS. MOLLOY *is standing transfixed in front of cupboard, clasping the box of chocolates.* VANDERGELDER *snatches the box from her and goes out.*)

MRS. LEVI (*crosses to her*): Irene, when I think of all the interesting things you have in this room! (*Kisses her.*) Make the most of it, dear. (*Raps cupboard.*) Good-by! (*Raps on table with umbrella.*) Good-by! (*Exit* MRS. LEVI. MRS. MOLLOY *opens door of cupboard.* CORNELIUS *steps out.*)

MRS. MOLLOY: So that was one of your practical jokes, Mr. Hackl?

CORNELIUS: No, no, Mrs. Molloy!

MRS. MOLLOY: Come out from under that, Barnaby Tucker, you troublemaker! (*She snatches the cloth and spreads it back on table.* MINNIE *enters.*) There's nothing to be afraid of, Minnie, I know all about these gentlemen.

CORNELIUS: Mrs. Molloy, we realize that what happened here —

MRS. MOLLOY: You think because you're rich you can make up for all the harm you do, is that it?

CORNELIUS: No, no!

BARNABY (*on the floor putting shoes on*): No, no!

MRS. MOLLOY: Minnie, this is the famous Cornelius Hackl who goes round New York tying people into knots; and that's Barnaby Tucker, another troublemaker.

BARNABY: How d'you do?

MRS. MOLLOY: Minnie, choose yourself any hat and coat in the store. We're going out to dinner. If this Mr. Hackl is so rich and gay and charming, he's going to be rich and gay and charming to us. He dines three nights a week at the Harmonia Gardens Restaurant, does he? Well, he's taking us there now.

MINNIE: Mrs. Molloy, are you sure it's safe?

MRS. MOLLOY: Minnie, hold your tongue. We're in a position to put these men into jail if they so much as squeak.

CORNELIUS: Jail, Mrs. Molloy?

MRS. MOLLOY: Jail, Mr. Hackl. Officer Cogarty does everything I tell him to do. Minnie, you and I have been respectable for years; now we're in disgrace, we might as well make the most of it. Come into the workroom with me; I know some ways we can perk up our appearances. Gentlemen, we'll be back in a minute.

CORNELIUS: Uh — Mrs. Molloy, I hear there's an awfully good restaurant at the railway station.

MRS. MOLLOY (*high indignation*): Railway station? Railway station? Certainly not! No, sir! You're going to give us a good dinner in the heart of the fashionable world. Go on in, Minnie! Don't you boys forget that you've made us lose our reputations, and now the fashionable world's the only place we can eat. (MRS. MOLLOY *exits to workroom.*)

BARNABY: She's angry at us, Cornelius. Maybe we'd better run away now.

CORNELIUS: No, I'm going to go through with this if it kills me. Barnaby, for a woman like that a man could consent to go back to Yonkers and be a success.

BARNABY: All I know is no woman's going to make a success out of me.

CORNELIUS: Jail or no jail, we're going to take those ladies out to dinner. So grit your teeth. (*Enter* MRS. MOLLOY *and* MINNIE *from workroom dressed for the street.*)

MRS. MOLLOY: Gentlemen, the cabs are at the corner, so forward march! (*She takes a hat — which will be* BARNABY'S *at the end of Act III — and gives it to* MINNIE.)

CORNELIUS: Yes, ma'am. (BARNABY *stands shaking his empty pockets warningly.*) Oh, Mrs. Molloy . . . is it far to the restaurant? Couldn't we walk?

MRS. MOLLOY (*pauses a moment, then*): Minnie, take off your things. We're not going.

OTHERS: Mrs. Molloy!

MRS. MOLLOY: Mr. Hackl, I don't go anywhere I'm not wanted. Good night. I'm not very happy to have met you. (*She crosses the stage as though going to the workroom door.*)

OTHERS: Mrs. Molloy!

MRS. MOLLOY: I suppose you think we're not fashionable enough for you? Well, I won't be a burden to you. Good night, Mr. Tucker. (*The others follow her behind counter:* CORNELIUS, BARNABY, *then* MINNIE.)

CORNELIUS: We want you to come with us more than anything in the world, Mrs. Molloy. (MRS. MOLLOY *turns and pushes the three back. They are now near the center of the stage, to the right of the table,* MRS. MOLLOY *facing the audience.*)

MRS. MOLLOY: No, you don't! Look at you! Look at the pair of them, Minnie! Scowling, both of them!

CORNELIUS: Please, Mrs. Molloy!

MRS. MOLLOY: Then smile. (*To* BARNABY) Go on, smile! No, that's not enough. Minnie, you come with me and we'll get our own supper.

CORNELIUS: Smile, Barnaby, you lout!

BARNABY: My face can't smile any stronger than that.

MRS. MOLLOY: Then do something! Show some interest. Do something lively: sing!

CORNELIUS: I can't sing, really I can't.

MRS. MOLLOY: We're wasting our time, Minnie. They don't want us.

CORNELIUS: Barnaby, what can you sing? Mrs. Molloy, all we know are sad songs.

MRS. MOLLOY: That doesn't matter. If you want us to go out with you, you've got to sing something. (*All this has been very rapid; the boys turn up to counter, put their heads together, confer and abruptly turn, stand stiffly and sing "Tenting tonight; tenting tonight; tenting on the old camp ground." The four of them now repeat the refrain, softly harmonizing. At the end of the song, after a pause,* MRS. MOLLOY, *moved, says:*)

MRS. MOLLOY: We'll come! (*The boys shout joyfully.*) You boys go ahead. (CORNELIUS *gets his hat from counter; as he puts it on he discovers the flowers on it.* BARNABY *gets his hat from window. They go out whistling. Minnie turns and puts her hat on at the mirror.*) Minnie, get the front door key — I'll lock the workroom. (MRS. MOLLOY *goes to workroom.* MINNIE *takes key from hook left of wardrobe and goes to* MRS. MOLLOY, *at the workroom door. She turns her around.*)

MINNIE: Why, Mrs. Molloy, you're crying! (MRS. MOLLOY *flings her arms round Minnie.*)

MRS. MOLLOY: Oh, Minnie, the world is full of wonderful things. Watch me, dear, and tell me if my petticoat's showing. (*She crosses to door, followed by* MINNIE, *as —*

THE CURTAIN FALLS)

ACT III

Veranda at the Harmonia Gardens Restaurant on the Battery, New York.

This room is informal and rustic. The main restaurant is indicated to be off stage back right.

There are three entrances: swinging double doors at the center of the back wall leading to the kitchen; one on the right wall (perhaps up a few steps and flanked by potted palms) to the street; one on the left wall to the staircase leading to the rooms above.

On the stage are two tables, left and right, each with four chairs. It is now afternoon and they are not yet set for dinner.

Against the back wall is a large folding screen. Also against the back wall are hat and coat racks.

As the curtain rises, VANDERGELDER *is standing, giving orders to* RUDOLPH, *a waiter.* MALACHI STACK *sits at table left.*

VANDERGELDER: Now, hear what I say. I don't want you to make any mistakes. I want a table for three.

RUDOLPH (*tall "snob" waiter, alternating between cold superiority and rage. German accent*): For three.

VANDERGELDER: There'll be two ladies and myself.

MALACHI: It's a bad combination, Mr. Vandergelder. You'll regret it.

VANDERGELDER: And I want a chicken.

MALACHI: A chicken! You'll regret it.

VANDERGELDER: Hold your tongue. Write it down: chicken.

RUDOLPH: Yes, sir. Chicken Esterhazy? Chicken cacciatore? Chicken à la crème — ?

VANDERGELDER (*exploding*): A chicken! A chicken like everybody else has. And with the chicken I want a bottle of wine.

RUDOLPH: Moselle? Chablis? Vouvray?

MALACHI: He doesn't understand you, Mr. Vandergelder. You'd better speak louder.

VANDERGELDER (*spelling*): W-I-N-E.

RUDOLPH: Wine.

VANDERGELDER: Wine! And I want this table removed. We'll eat at that table alone. (*Exit* RUDOLPH *through service door at back.*)

MALACHI: There are some people coming in here now, Mr. Vandergelder. (VANDERGELDER *goes to back right to look at the newcomers.*)

VANDERGELDER: What! Thunder and damnation! It's my niece Ermengarde! What's she doing here?! — Wait till I get my hands on her.

MALACHI (*running up to him*): Mr. Vandergelder! You must keep your temper!

VANDERGELDER: And there's that rascal artist with her. Why, it's a plot. I'll throw them in jail.

MALACHI: Mr. Vandergelder! They're old enough to come to New York. You can't throw people into jail for coming to New York.

VANDERGELDER: And there's Mrs. Levi! What's she doing with them? It's a plot. It's a conspiracy! What's she saying to the cabman? Go up and hear what she's saying.

MALACHI (*listening at entrance, right*): She's telling the cabman to wait, Mr. Vandergelder. She's telling the young people to come in and have a good dinner, Mr. Vandergelder.

VANDERGELDER: I'll put an end to this.

MALACHI: Now, Mr. Vandergelder, if you lose your temper, you'll make matters worse. Mr. Vandergelder, come here and take my advice.

VANDERGELDER: Stop pulling my coat. What's your advice?

MALACHI: Hide, Mr. Vandergelder. Hide behind this screen, and listen to what they're saying.

VANDERGELDER (*being pulled behind the screen*): Stop pulling at me. (*They hide behind the screen as* MRS. LEVI, ERMENGARDE *and* AMBROSE *enter from the right.* AMBROSE *is carrying* ERMENGARDE'S *luggage.*)

ERMENGARDE: But I don't want to eat in a restaurant. It's not proper.

MRS. LEVI: Now, Ermengarde, dear, there's nothing wicked about eating in a restaurant. There's nothing wicked, even, about being in New York. Clergymen just make those things up to fill out their sermons.

ERMENGARDE: Oh, I wish I were in Yonkers, where *nothing* ever happens!

MRS. LEVI: Ermengarde, you're hungry. That's what's troubling you.

ERMENGARDE: Anyway, after dinner you must promise to take me to Aunt Flora's. She's been waiting for me all day and she must be half dead of fright.

MRS. LEVI: All right but of course, you know at Miss Van Huysen's you'll be back in your uncle's hands.

AMBROSE (*hands raised to heaven*): I can't stand it.

MRS. LEVI (*to* AMBROSE): Just keep telling yourself how pretty she is. Pretty girls have very little opportunity to improve their other advantages.

AMBROSE: Listen, Ermengarde! You don't want to go back to your uncle. Stop and think! That old man with one foot in the grave!

MRS. LEVI: And the other three in the cashbox.

AMBROSE: Smelling of oats —

MRS. LEVI: And axle grease.

MALACHI: That's not true. It's only partly true.

VANDERGELDER (*loudly*): Hold your tongue! I'm going to teach them a lesson.

MALACHI (*whisper*): Keep your temper, Mr. Vandergelder. Listen to what they say.

MRS. LEVI (*hears this; throws a quick glance toward the screen; her whole manner changes*): Oh, dear, what was I saying? The Lord be praised, how glad I am that I found you two dreadful children just as you were about to break poor dear Mr. Vandergelder's heart.

AMBROSE: He's got no heart to break!

MRS. LEVI (*vainly signaling*): Mr. Vandergelder's a much kinder man than you think.

AMBROSE: Kinder? He's a wolf.

MRS. LEVI: Remember that he leads a very lonely life. Now you're going to have dinner upstairs. There are some private rooms up there, — just meant for shy timid girls like Ermengarde. Come with me. (*She pushes the young people out left,* AMBROSE *carrying the luggage.*)

VANDERGELDER (*coming forward*): I'll show them! (*He sits at table right.*)

MALACHI: Everybody should eavesdrop once in a while, I always say. There's nothing like eavesdropping to show you that the world outside your head is different from the world inside your head.

VANDERGELDER (*producing a pencil and paper*): I want to write a note. Go and call that cabman in here. I want to talk to him.

MALACHI: No one asks advice of a cabman, Mr. Vandergelder. They see so much of life that they have no ideas left.

VANDERGELDER: Do as I tell you.

MALACHI: Yes, sir. Advice of a cabman! (*Exit right.* VANDERGELDER *writes his letter.*)

VANDERGELDER: "My dear Miss Van Huysen" (*To audience.*) Everybody's dear in a letter. It's enough to make you give up writing 'em. "My dear Miss Van Huysen. This is Ermengarde and that rascal Ambrose Kemper. They are trying to run away. Keep them in your house until I come." (MALACHI *returns with an enormous* CABMAN *in a high hat and a long coat. He carries a whip.*)

CABMAN (*entering*): What's he want?

VANDERGELDER: I want to talk to you.

CABMAN: I'm engaged. I'm waiting for my parties.

VANDERGELDER (*folding letter and writing address*): I know you are. Do you want to earn five dollars?

CABMAN: Eh?

VANDERGELDER: I asked you, do you want to earn five dollars?

CABMAN: I don't know. I never tried.

VANDERGELDER: When those parties of yours come downstairs, I want you to drive them to this address. Never mind what they say, drive them to this address. Ring the bell: give this letter to the lady of the house: see that they get in the door and keep them there.

CABMAN: I can't make people go into a house if they don't want to.

VANDERGELDER (*producing purse*): Can you for ten dollars?

CABMAN: Even for ten dollars, I can't do it alone.

VANDERGELDER: This fellow here will help you.

MALACHI (*sitting at table left*): Now I'm pushing people into houses.

VANDERGELDER: There's the address: Miss Flora Van Huysen, 8 Jackson Street.

CABMAN: Even if I get them in the door I can't be sure they'll stay there.

VANDERGELDER: For fifteen dollars you can.

MALACHI: Murder begins at twenty-five.

VANDERGELDER: Hold your tongue! (*To* CABMAN.) The lady of the house will help you. All you have to do is to sit in the front hall and see that the man doesn't run off with the girl. I'll be at Miss Van Huysen's in an hour or two and I'll pay you then.

CABMAN: If they call the police, I can't do anything.

VANDERGELDER: It's perfectly honest business. Perfectly honest.

MALACHI: Every man's the best judge of his own honesty.

VANDERGELDER: The young lady is my niece. (*The* CABMAN *laughs, skeptically.*) The young lady is my niece!! (*The* CABMAN *looks at* MALACHI *and shrugs.*) She's trying to run away with a good-for-nothing and we're preventing it.

CABMAN: Oh, I know them, sir. They'll win in the end. Rivers don't run uphill.

MALACHI: What did I tell you, Mr. Vandergelder? Advice of a cabman.

VANDERGELDER (*hits table with his stick*): Stack! I'll be back in half an hour. See that the

table's set for three. See that nobody else eats here. Then go and join the cabman on the box.

MALACHI: Yes, sir. (*Exit* VANDERGELDER *right.*)

CABMAN: Who's your friend?

MALACHI: Friend!! That's not a friend; that's an employer I'm trying out for a few days.

CABMAN: You won't like him.

MALACHI: I can see you're in business for yourself because you talk about liking employers. No one's ever liked an employer since business began.

CABMAN: AW — !

MALACHI: No, sir. I suppose you think *your* horse likes you?

CABMAN: My old Clementine? She'd give her right feet for me.

MALACHI: That's what all employers think. You imagine it. The streets of New York are full of cab horses winking at one another. Let's go in the kitchen and get some whiskey. I can't push people into houses when I'm sober. No, I've had about fifty employers in my life, but this is the most employer of them all. He talks to everybody as though he were paying them.

CABMAN: I had an employer once. He watched me from eight in the morning until six at night — just sat there and watched me. Oh, dear! Even my mother didn't think I was as interesting as that. (CABMAN *exits through service door.*)

MALACHI (*following him off*): Yes, being employed is like being loved: you know that somebody's thinking about you the whole time. (*Exits. Enter right,* MRS. MOLLOY, MINNIE, BARNABY *and* CORNELIUS.)

MRS. MOLLOY: See! Here's the place I meant! Isn't it fine? Minnie, take off your things; we'll be here for hours.

CORNELIUS (*stopping at door*): Mrs. Molloy, are you sure you'll like it here? I think I feel a draught.

MRS. MOLLOY: Indeed, I do like it. We're going to have a fine dinner right in this room; it's private, and it's elegant. Now we're all going to forget our troubles and call each other by our first names. Cornelius! Call the waiter.

CORNELIUS: Wait — wait — I can't make a sound. I must have caught a cold on that ride. Wai — No! It won't come.

MRS. MOLLOY: I don't believe you. Barnaby, you call him.

BARNABY (*boldly*): Waiter! Waiter! (COR-NELIUS *threatens him.* BARNABY *runs left.*)

MINNIE: I never thought I'd be in such a place in my whole life. Mrs. Molloy, is this what they call a "café"?

MRS. MOLLOY (*sits at table left, facing audience*): Yes, this is a café. Sit down, Minnie. Cornelius, Mrs. Levi gave us to understand that every waiter in New York knew you.

CORNELIUS: They will. (BARNABY *sits at chair left;* MINNIE *in chair back to audience. Enter* RUDOLPH *from service door.*)

RUDOLPH: Good evening, ladies and gentlemen.

CORNELIUS (*shaking his hand*): How are you, Fritz? How are you, my friend?

RUDOLPH: I am Rudolph.

CORNELIUS: Of course. Rudolph, of course. Well, Rudolph, these ladies want a little something to eat — you know what I mean? Just if you can find the time — we know how busy you are.

MRS. MOLLOY: Cornelius, there's no need to be so familiar with the waiter. (*Takes menu from* RUDOLPH.)

CORNELIUS: Oh, yes, there is.

MRS. MOLLOY (*passing menu across*): Minnie, what do you want to eat?

MINNIE: Just anything, Irene.

MRS. MOLLOY: No, speak up, Minnie. What do you want?

MINNIE: No, really, I have no appetite at all. (*Swings round in her chair and studies the menu, horrified at the prices.*) Oh . . . Oh . . . I'd like some sardines on toast and a glass of milk.

CORNELIUS (*takes menu from her*): Great grindstones! What a sensible girl. Barnaby, shake Minnie's hand. She's the most sensible girl in the world. Rudolph, bring us gentlemen two glasses of beer, a loaf of bread and some cheese.

MRS. MOLLOY (*takes menu*): I never heard such nonsense. Cornelius, we've come here for a good dinner and a good time. Minnie, have you ever eaten pheasant?

MINNIE: Pheasant? No-o-o-o!

MRS. MOLLOY: Rudolph, have you any pheasant?

RUDOLPH: Yes, ma'am. Just in from New Jersey today.

MRS. MOLLOY: Even the pheasants are leaving New Jersey. (*She laughs loudly, pushing* CORNELIUS, *then* RUDOLPH; *not from menu.*)

Now, Rudolph, write this down: mock turtle soup; pheasant; mashed chestnuts; green salad; and some nice red wine. (RUDOLPH *repeats each item after her.*)

CORNELIUS (*losing all his fears, boldly*): All right, Barnaby, you watch me. (*He reads from the bill of fare.*) Rudolph, write this down: Neapolitan ice cream; hothouse peaches; champagne . . .

ALL: Champagne! (BARNABY *spins round in his chair.*)

CORNELIUS (*holds up a finger*): . . . and a German band. Have you got a German band?

MRS. MOLLOY: No, Cornelius, I won't let you be extravagant. Champagne, but no band. Now, Rudolph, be quick about this. We're hungry. (*Exit* RUDOLPH *to kitchen.* MRS. MOLLOY *crosses to right.*) Minnie, come upstairs. I have an idea about your hair. I think it'd be nice in two wee horns —

MINNIE (*hurrying after her, turns and looks at the boys*): Oh! Horns! (*They go out right. There is a long pause.* CORNELIUS *sits staring after them.*)

BARNABY: Cornelius, in the Army, you have to peel potatoes all the time.

CORNELIUS (*not turning*): Oh, that doesn't matter. By the time we get out of jail we can move right over to the Old Men's Home. (*Another waiter,* AUGUST, *enters from service door bearing a bottle of champagne in cooler, and five glasses.* MRS. MOLLOY *re-enters right, followed by* MINNIE, *and stops* AUGUST.)

MRS. MOLLOY: Waiter! What's that? What's that you have?

AUGUST (*young waiter; baby face; is continually bursting into tears*): It's some champagne, ma'am.

MRS. MOLLOY: Cornelius; it's our champagne. (*All gather round* AUGUST.)

AUGUST: No, no. It's for His Honor the Mayor of New York and he's very impatient.

MRS. MOLLOY: Shame on him! The Mayor of New York has more important things to be impatient about. Cornelius, open it. (CORNELIUS *takes the bottle, opens it and fills the glasses.*)

AUGUST: Ma'am, he'll kill me.

MRS. MOLLOY: Well, have a glass first and die happy.

AUGUST (*sits at table right, weeping*): He'll kill me. (RUDOLPH *lays the cloth on the table, left.*)

MRS. MOLLOY: I go to a public restaurant for

the first time in ten years and all the waiters burst into tears. There, take that and stop crying, love. (*She takes a glass to* AUGUST *and pats his head, then comes back.*) Barnaby, make a toast!

BARNABY (*center of the group, with naïve sincerity*): I? . . . uh . . . To all the ladies in the world . . . may I get to know more of them . . . and . . . may I get to know them better. (*There is a hushed pause.*)

CORNELIUS (*softly*): To the ladies!

MRS. MOLLOY: That's *very* sweet and *very* refined. Minnie, for that I'm going to give Barnaby a kiss.

MINNIE: Oh!

MRS. MOLLOY: Hold your tongue, Minnie. I'm old enough to be his mother, and — (*indicating a height three feet from the floor*) a dear wee mother I would have been too. Barnaby, this is for you from all the ladies in the world. (*She kisses him.* BARNABY *is at first silent and dazed, then:*)

BARNABY: Now I can go back to Yonkers, Cornelius. Pudding. Pudding! Pudding! (*He spins round and falls on his knees.*)

MRS. MOLLOY: Look at Barnaby. He's not strong enough for a kiss. His head can't stand it. (*Exit* AUGUST, *right service door, with tray and cooler. The sound of "Les Patineurs" waltz comes from off left.* CORNELIUS *sits in chair facing audience, top of table.* MINNIE *at left.* BARNABY *at right and* MRS. MOLLOY *back to audience.*) Minnie, I'm enjoying myself. To think that this goes on in hundreds of places every night, while I sit at home darning my stockings. (MRS. MOLLOY *rises and dances, alone, slowly about the stage.*) Cornelius, dance with me.

CORNELIUS (*rises*): Irene, the Hackls don't dance. We're Presbyterian.

MRS. MOLLOY: Minnie, you dance with me. (MINNIE *joins her.* CORNELIUS *sits again.*)

MINNIE: Lovely music.

MRS. MOLLOY: Why, Minnie, you dance beautifully.

MINNIE: We girls dance in the workroom when you're not looking, Irene.

MRS. MOLLOY: You thought I'd be angry! Oh dear, no one in the world understands anyone else in the world. (*The girls separate.* MINNIE *dances off to her place at the table.* MRS. MOLLOY *sits thoughtfully at table right. The music fades away.*) Cornelius! Jenny Lind and all those other ladies — do you see them all the time?

CORNELIUS (*rises and joins her at table right*): Irene, I've put them right out of my head. I'm interested in . . . (RUDOLPH *has entered by the service door. He now flings a tablecloth between them on table.*)

MRS. MOLLOY: Rudolph, what are you doing?

RUDOLPH: A table's been reserved here. Special orders.

MRS. MOLLOY: Stop right where you are. That party can eat inside. This veranda's ours.

RUDOLPH: I'm very sorry. This veranda is open to anybody who wants it. Ah, there comes the man who brought the order. (*Enter* MALACHI *from the kitchen, drunk.*)

MRS. MOLLOY (*to* MALACHI): Take your table away from here. We got here first, Cornelius, throw him out.

MALACHI: Ma'am, my employer reserved this room at four o'clock this afternoon. You can go and eat in the restaurant. My employer said it was very important that he have a table alone.

MRS. MOLLOY: No, sir. We got here first and we're going to stay here — alone, too. (MINNIE *and* BARNABY *come forward.*)

RUDOLPH: Ladies and gentlemen!

MRS. MOLLOY: Shut up, you! (*To* MALACHI.) You're an impertinent, idiotic kill-joy.

MALACHI (*very pleased*): That's an insult!

MRS. MOLLOY: All the facts about you are insults. (*To* CORNELIUS.) Cornelius, do something. Knock it over! The table.

CORNELIUS: Knock it over. (*After a shocked struggle with himself* CORNELIUS *calmly overturns the table.* AUGUST *rights the table and picks up cutlery, weeping copiously.*)

RUDOLPH (*in cold fury*): I'm sorry, but this room can't be reserved for anyone. If you want to eat alone, you must go upstairs. I'm sorry, but that's the rule.

MRS. MOLLOY: We're having a nice dinner alone and we're going to stay here. Cornelius, knock it over. (CORNELIUS *overturns the table again. The girls squeal with pleasure. The waiter* AUGUST *again scrambles for the silver.*)

MALACHI: Wait till you see my employer!

RUDOLPH (*bringing screen down*): Ladies and gentlemen! I'll tell you what we'll do. There's a big screen here. We'll put the screen up between the tables. August, come and help me.

MRS. MOLLOY: I won't eat behind a screen. I won't. Minnie, make a noise. We're not animals in a menagerie. Cornelius, no screen. Minnie, there's a fight. I feel ten years younger. No screen! No screen! (*During the struggle with the screen all talk at once.*)

MALACHI (*loud and clear and pointing to entrance at right*): Now you'll learn something. There comes my employer now, getting out of that cab.

CORNELIUS (*coming to him, taking off his coat*): Where? I'll knock him down too. (BARNABY *has gone up to right entrance. He turns and shouts clearly:*)

BARNABY: Cornelius, it's Wolf-trap. Yes, it is!

CORNELIUS: Wolf-trap! Listen, everybody. I think the screen's a good idea. Have you got any more screens, Rudolph? We could use three or four. (*He pulls the screen forward again.*)

MRS. MOLLOY: Quiet down, Cornelius, and stop changing your mind. Hurry up, Rudolph, we're ready for the soup. (*During the following scene* RUDOLPH *serves the meal at the table left, as unobtrusively as possible. The stage is now divided in half. The quartet's table is at the left. Enter* VANDERGELDER *from the right. Now wears overcoat and carries the box of chocolates.*)

VANDERGELDER: Stack! What's the meaning of this? I told you I wanted a table alone. What's that? (VANDERGELDER *hits the screen twice with his stick.* MRS. MOLLOY *hits back twice with a spoon. The four young people sit:* BARNABY *facing audience;* MRS. MOLLOY *right,* MINNIE *left, and* CORNELIUS *back to audience.*)

MALACHI: Mr. Vandergelder, I did what I could. Mr. Vandergelder, you wouldn't believe what wild savages the people of New York are. There's a woman over there, Mr. Vandergelder — civilization hasn't touched her.

VANDERGELDER: Everything's wrong. You can't even manage a thing like that. Help me off with my coat. Don't kill me. Don't kill me. (*During the struggle with the overcoat* MR. VANDERGELDER's *purse flies out of his pocket and falls by the screen.* VANDERGELDER *goes to the coat tree and hangs his coat up.*)

MRS. MOLLOY: Speak up! I can't hear you.

CORNELIUS: My voice again. Barnaby, how's your throat? Can you speak?

BARNABY: Can't make a sound.

MRS. MOLLOY: Oh, all right. Bring your heads together, and we'll whisper.

VANDERGELDER: Who are those people over there?

MALACHI: Some city sparks and their girls, Mr. Vandergelder. What goes on in big cities, Mr. Vandergelder — best not think of it.

VANDERGELDER: Has that couple come down from upstairs yet? I hope they haven't gone off without your seeing them.

MALACHI: No, sir. Myself and the cabman have kept our eyes on everything.

VANDERGELDER (*sits at right of table, profile to the audience*): I'll sit here and wait for my guests. You go out to the cab.

MALACHI: Yes, sir. (VANDERGELDER *unfurls newspaper and starts to read.* MALACHI *sees the purse on the floor and picks it up.*) Eh, what's that? A purse. Did you drop something, Mr. Vandergelder?

VANDERGELDER: No. Don't bother me any more. Do as I tell you.

MALACHI (*stooping over. Coming center*): A purse. That fellow over there must have let it fall during the misunderstanding about the screen. No, I won't look inside. Twenty-dollar bills, dozens of them. I'll go over and give it to him. (*Starts toward* CORNELIUS, *then turns and says to audience:*) You're surprised? You're surprised to see me getting rid of this money so quickly, eh? I'll explain it to you. There was a time in my life when my chief interest was picking up money that didn't belong to me. The law is there to protect property, but — sure, the law doesn't care whether a property owner deserves his property or not, and the law has to be corrected. There are several thousands of people in this country engaged in correcting the law. For a while, I too was engaged in the redistribution of superfluities. A man works all his life and leaves a million to his widow. She sits in hotels and eats great meals and plays cards all afternoon and evening, with ten diamonds on her fingers. Call in the robbers! Call in the robbers! Or a man leaves it to his son who stands leaning against bars all night boring a bartender. Call in the robbers! Stealing's a weakness. There are some people who say you shouldn't have any weaknesses at all — no vices. But if a man has no vices, he's in great danger of making vices out of his virtues, and there's a spectacle. We've all seen them: men who were monsters of philanthropy and women who were dragons of purity. We've seen people who told the truth, though the Heavens fall, — and the Heavens fell. No, no — nurse one vice in your bosom. Give it the attention it deserves and let your virtues spring up modestly around it. Then you'll have the miser who's no liar; and the drunkard who's the benefactor of a whole city. Well, after I'd had that weakness of stealing for a while, I found another: I took to whisky — whisky took to me. And then I discovered an important rule that I'm going to pass on to you: Never support two weaknesses at the same time. It's your combination sinners — your lecherous liars and your miserly drunkards — who dishonor the vices and bring them into bad repute. So now you see why I want to get rid of this money: I want to keep my mind free to do the credit to whiskey that it deserves. And my last word to you, ladies and gentlemen, is this: one vice at a time. (*Goes over to* CORNELIUS.) Can I speak to you for a minute?

CORNELIUS (*rises*): You certainly can. We all want to apologize to you about that screen — that little misunderstanding. (*They all rise, with exclamations of apology.*) What's your name, sir?

MALACHI: Stack, sir. Malachi Stack. If the ladies will excuse you, I'd like to speak to you for a minute. (*Draws* CORNELIUS *down to front of stage.*) Listen, boy, have you lost . . . ? Come here . . . (*Leads him further down, out of* VANDERGELDER's *hearing.*) Have you lost something?

CORNELIUS: Mr. Stack, in this one day I've lost everything I own.

MALACHI: There it is. (*Gives him purse.*) Don't mention it.

CORNELIUS: Why, Mr. Stack . . . you know what it is? It's a miracle. (*Looks toward the ceiling.*)

MALACHI: Don't mention it.

CORNELIUS: Barnaby, come here a minute. I want you to shake hands with Mr. Stack. (BARNABY, *napkin tucked into his collar, joins them.*) Mr. Stack's just found the purse I lost, Barnaby. You know — the purse full of money.

BARNABY (*shaking his hand vigorously*): You're a wonderful man, Mr. Stack.

MALACHI: Oh, it's nothing — nothing.

CORNELIUS: I'm certainly glad I went to church all these years. You're a good person to know, Mr. Stack. In a way. Mr. Stack, where do you work?

MALACHI: Well, I've just begun. I work for a Mr. Vandergelder in Yonkers. (CORNELIUS *is thunderstruck. He glances at* BARNABY *and turns to* MALACHI *with awe. All three are swaying slightly, back and forth.*)

CORNELIUS: You do? It's a miracle. (*He points to the ceiling.*) Mr. Stack, I know you don't need it — but can I give you something for . . . for the good work?

MALACHI (*putting out his hand*): Don't mention it. It's nothing. (*Starts to go left.*)

CORNELIUS: Take that. (*Hands him a note.*)

MALACHI (*taking note*): Don't mention it.

CORNELIUS: And that. (*Another note.*)

MALACHI (*takes it and moves away*): I'd better be going.

CORNELIUS: Oh, here. And that.

MALACHI (*hands third note back*): No . . . I might get to like them. (*Exit left.* CORNELIUS *bounds exultantly back to table.*)

CORNELIUS: Irene, I feel a lot better about everything. Irene, I feel so well that I'm going to tell the truth.

MRS. MOLLOY: I'd forgotten that, Minnie. Men get drunk so differently from women. All right, what is the truth?

CORNELIUS: If I tell the truth, will you let me . . . will you let me put my arm around your waist? (MINNIE *screams and flings her napkin over her face.*)

MRS. MOLLOY: Hold your tongue, Minnie. All right, you can put your arm around my waist just to show it can be done in a gentlemanly way; but I might as well warn you: a corset is a corset.

CORNELIUS (*his arm around her; softly*): You're a wonderful person, Mrs. Molloy.

MRS. MOLLOY: Thank you. (*She removes his hand from around her waist.*) All right, now that's enough. What is the truth?

CORNELIUS: Irene, I'm not as rich as Mrs. Levi said I was.

MRS. MOLLOY: Not rich!

CORNELIUS: I almost never came to New York. And I'm not like she said I was, — bad. And I think you ought to know that at this very minute Mr. Vandergelder's sitting on the other side of that screen.

MRS. MOLLOY: What! Well, he's not going to spoil any party of mine. So *that's* why we have been whispering? Let's forget all about Mr. Vandergelder and have some more wine. (*They start to sing softly:* "The Sidewalks of New York." *Enter* MRS. LEVI, *from the street, in an elaborate dress.* VANDERGELDER *rises.*)

MRS. LEVI: Good evening, Mr. Vandergelder.

VANDERGELDER: Where's — where's Miss Simple?

MRS. LEVI: Mr. Vandergelder, I'll never trust a woman again as long as I live.

VANDERGELDER: Well? What is it?

MRS. LEVI: She ran away this afternoon and got married!

VANDERGELDER: She did?

MRS. LEVI: Married, Mr. Vandergelder, to a young boy of fifty.

VANDERGELDER: She did?

MRS. LEVI: Oh, I'm as disappointed as you are. I-can't-eat-a-thing-what-have-you-ordered?

VANDERGELDER: I ordered what you told me to, a chicken. (*Enter* AUGUST. *He goes to* VANDERGELDER'*s table.*)

MRS. LEVI: I don't think I could face a chicken. Oh, waiter. How do you do? What's your name?

AUGUST: August, ma'am.

MRS. LEVI: August, this is Mr. Vandergelder of Yonkers — Yonkers' most influential citizen, in fact. I want you to see that he's served with the best you have and served promptly. And there'll only be the two of us. (MRS. LEVI *gives one set of cutlery to* AUGUST. VANDERGELDER *puts chocolate box under table.*) Mr. Vandergelder's been through some trying experiences today — what with men hidden all over Mrs. Molloy's store — like Indians in ambush.

VANDERGELDER (*between his teeth*): Mrs. Levi, you don't have to tell him everything about me. (*The quartet commences singing again very softly.*)

MRS. LEVI: Mr. Vandergelder, if you're thinking about getting married, you might as well learn right now you have to let women be women. Now, August, we want excellent service.

AUGUST: Yes, ma'am. (*Exits to kitchen.*)

VANDERGELDER: You've managed things very badly. When I plan a thing it takes place. (MRS. LEVI *rises.*) Where are you going?

MRS. LEVI: Oh, I'd just like to see who's on the other side of that screen. (MRS. LEVI *crosses to the other side of the stage and sees the quartet. They are frightened and fall silent.*)

CORNELIUS (*rising*): Good evening, Mrs. Levi. (MRS. LEVI *takes no notice, but, taking up the refrain where they left off, returns to her place at the table right.*)

VANDERGELDER: Well, who was it?

MRS. LEVI: Oh, just some city sparks entertaining their girls, I guess.

VANDERGELDER: Always wanting to know everything; always curious about everything; always putting your nose into other people's affairs. Anybody who lived with you would get as nervous as a cat.

MRS. LEVI: What? What's that you're saying.

VANDERGELDER: I said anybody who lived with you would —

MRS. LEVI: Horace Vandergelder, get that idea right out of your head this minute. I'm surprised that you even mentioned such a thing. Understand once and for all that I have no intention of marrying you.

VANDERGELDER: I didn't mean that.

MRS. LEVI: You've been hinting around at such a thing for some time, but from now on put such ideas right out of your head.

VANDERGELDER: Stop talking that way. That's not what I meant at all.

MRS. LEVI: I hope not. I should hope not. Horace Vandergelder, you go your way. (*Points a finger.*) and I'll go mine. (*Points in same direction.*) I'm not some Irene Molloy, whose head can be turned by a pot of geraniums. Why, the idea of you even suggesting such a thing.

VANDERGELDER: Mrs. Levi, you misunderstood me.

MRS. LEVI: I certainly hope I did. If I had any intention of marrying again it would be to a far more pleasure-loving man than you. Why I'd marry Cornelius Hackl before I'd marry you. (CORNELIUS *raises his head in alarm. The others stop eating and listen.*) However, we won't discuss it any more. (*Enter* AUGUST *with a tray.*) Here's August with our food. I'll serve it, August.

AUGUST: Yes, ma'am. (*Exit* AUGUST.)

MRS. LEVI: Here's some white meat for you, and some giblets, very tender and very good for you. No, as I said before, you go your way and I'll go mine. — Start right in on the wine. I think you'll feel better at once. However, since you brought the matter up, there's one more thing I think I ought to say.

VANDERGELDER (*rising in rage*): I didn't bring the matter up at all.

MRS. LEVI: We'll have forgotten all about it in a moment, but — sit down, sit down, we'll close the matter forever in just a moment, but there's one more thing I ought to say. (VANDERGELDER *sits down.*) It's true, I'm a woman who likes to know everything that's going on; who likes to manage things, you're perfectly right about that. But I wouldn't like to manage anything as disorderly as your household, as out of control, as untidy. You'll have to do that yourself, God helping you.

VANDERGELDER: It's not out of control.

MRS. LEVI: Very well, let's not say another

word about it. Take some more of that squash, it's good. No, Horace, a complaining, quarrelsome, friendless soul like you is no sort of companion for me. You go your way (*Peppers her own plate.*) and I'll go mine. (*Peppers his plate.*)

VANDERGELDER: Stop saying that.

MRS. LEVI: I won't say another word.

VANDERGELDER: Besides . . . I'm not those things you said I am.

MRS. LEVI: What? — Well, I guess you're friendless, aren't you? Ermengarde told me this morning you'd even quarreled with your barber — a man who's held a razor to your throat for twenty years! Seems to me that's sinking pretty low.

VANDERGELDER: Well, . . . but . . . my clerks, they . . .

MRS. LEVI: They like you? Cornelius Hackl and that Barnaby? Behind your back they call you Wolf-trap. (*Quietly the quartet at the other table have moved up to the screens — bringing chairs for* MRS. MOLLOY *and* MINNIE. *Wine glasses in hand, they overhear this conversation.*)

VANDERGELDER (*blanching*): They don't.

MRS. LEVI: No, Horace. It looks to me as though I were the last person in the world that liked you, and even I'm just so-so. No, for the rest of my life I intend to have a good time. You'll be able to find some housekeeper who can prepare you three meals for a dollar a day — it can be done, you know, if you like cold baked beans. You'll spend your last days listening at keyholes, for fear someone's cheating you. Take some more of that.

VANDERGELDER: Dolly, you're a damned exasperating woman.

MRS. LEVI: There! You see? That's the difference between us. I'd be nagging you all day to get some spirit into you. You could be a perfectly charming, witty, amiable man, if you wanted to.

VANDERGELDER (*rising, bellowing*): I don't want to be charming.

MRS. LEVI: But you are. Look at you now. You can't hide it.

VANDERGELDER (*sits*): Listen at keyholes! Dolly, you have no right to say such things to me.

MRS. LEVI: At your age you ought to enjoy hearing the honest truth.

VANDERGELDER: My age! My age! You're always talking about my age.

MRS. LEVI: I don't know what your age is, but I do know that up at Yonkers with bad food and bad temper you'll double it in six months. Let's talk of something else; but before we leave the subject there's one more thing I *am* going to say.

VANDERGELDER: Don't!

MRS. LEVI: Sometimes, just sometimes, I think I'd be tempted to marry you out of sheer pity; and if the confusion in your house gets any worse I may *have* to.

VANDERGELDER: I haven't asked you to marry me.

MRS. LEVI: Well, *please don't*.

VANDERGELDER: And my house is not in confusion.

MRS. LEVI: What? With your niece upstairs in the restaurant right now?

VANDERGELDER: I've fixed that better than you know.

MRS. LEVI: And your clerks skipping around New York behind your back?

VANDERGELDER: They're in Yonkers where they always are.

MRS. LEVI: Nonsense!

VANDERGELDER: What do you mean, nonsense?

MRS. LEVI: Cornelius Hackl's the other side of that screen this very minute.

VANDERGELDER: It ain't the same man!

MRS. LEVI: All right. Go on. Push it, knock it down. Go and see.

VANDERGELDER (*goes to screen, pauses in doubt, then returns to his chair again*): I don't believe it.

MRS. LEVI: All right. All right. Eat your chicken. Of course, Horace, if your affairs went from bad to worse and you became actually miserable, I might feel that it was my duty to come up to Yonkers and be of some assistance to you. After all, I was your wife's oldest friend.

VANDERGELDER: I don't know how you ever got any such notion. Now understand, once and for all, I have *no intention of marrying anybody*. Now, I'm tired and I don't want to talk. (CORNELIUS *crosses to extreme left,* MRS. MOLLOY *following him.*)

MRS. LEVI: I won't say another word, either.

CORNELIUS: Irene, I think we'd better go. You take this money and pay the bill. Oh, don't worry, it's not mine.

MRS. MOLLOY: No, no, I'll tell you what we'll do. You boys put on our coats and veils, and if he comes stamping over here, he'll think you're girls.

CORNELIUS: What! Those things!

MRS. MOLLOY: Yes. Come on. (*She and* MINNIE *take the clothes from the stand.*)

VANDERGELDER (*rises*): I've got a headache. I've had a bad day. I'm going to Flora Van Huysen's, and then I'm going back to my hotel. (*Reaches for his purse.*) So, here's the money to pay for the dinner. (*Searching another pocket.*) Here's the money to pay for the ... (*Going through all his pockets.*) Here's the money ... I've lost my purse!!

MRS. LEVI: Impossible! I can't imagine you without your purse.

VANDERGELDER: It's been stolen. (*Searching overcoat.*) Or I left it in the cab. What am I going to do? I'm new at the hotel; they don't know me. I've never been here before ... Stop eating the chicken, I can't pay for it!

MRS. LEVI (*laughing gaily*): Horace, I'll be able to find some money. Sit down and calm yourself.

VANDERGELDER: Dolly Gallagher, I gave you twenty-five dollars this morning.

MRS. LEVI: I haven't a cent. I gave it to my lawyer. We can borrow it from Ambrose Kemper, upstairs.

VANDERGELDER: I wouldn't take it.

MRS. LEVI: Cornelius Hackl will lend it to us.

VANDERGELDER: He's in Yonkers. — Waiter! (CORNELIUS *comes forward dressed in* MRS. MOLLOY's *coat, thrown over his shoulder like a cape.* MRS. LEVI *is enjoying herself immensely.* VANDERGELDER *again goes to back wall to examine the pockets of his overcoat.*)

MRS. MOLLOY: Cornelius, is that Mr. Vandergelder's purse?

CORNELIUS: I didn't know it myself. I thought it was money just wandering around loose that didn't belong to anybody.

MRS. MOLLOY: Goodness! That's what politicians think!

VANDERGELDER: Waiter! (*A band off left starts playing a polka.* BARNABY *comes forward dressed in* MINNIE's *hat, coat and veil.*)

MINNIE: Irene, doesn't Barnaby make a lovely girl? He just ought to stay that way. (MRS. LEVI *and* VANDERGELDER *move their table upstage while searching for the purse.*)

MRS. MOLLOY: Why should we have our evening spoiled? Cornelius, I can teach you to dance in a few minutes. Oh, he won't recognize you.

MINNIE: Barnaby, it's the easiest thing in the world. (*They move their table up against the back wall.*)

MRS. LEVI: Horace, you danced with me at your wedding and you danced with me at mine. Do you remember?

VANDERGELDER: No. Yes.

MRS. LEVI: Horace, you were a good dancer then. Don't confess to me that you're too old to dance.

VANDERGELDER: I'm not too old. I just don't want to dance.

MRS. LEVI: Listen to that music. Horace, do you remember the dances in the firehouse at Yonkers on Saturday nights? You gave me a fan. Come, come on! (VANDERGELDER *and* MRS. LEVI *start to dance.* CORNELIUS, *dancing with* MRS. MOLLOY, *bumps into* VANDERGELDER, *back to back.* VANDERGELDER, *turning, fails at first to recognize him, then does and roars:*)

VANDERGELDER: You're discharged! Not a word! You're fired! Where's that idiot, Barnaby Tucker? He's fired too. (*The four young people, laughing, start rushing out the door to the street.* VANDERGELDER, *pointing at* MRS. MOLLOY, *shouts:*) You're discharged!

MRS. MOLLOY (*pointing at him*): You're discharged! (*Exit.*)

VANDERGELDER: You're discharged! (*Enter from left,* AMBROSE *and* ERMENGARDE. *To* ERMENGARDE.) I'll lock you up for the rest of your life, young lady.

ERMENGARDE: Uncle! (*She faints in* AMBROSE's *arms.*)

VANDERGELDER (*to* AMBROSE): I'll have you arrested. Get out of my sight. I never want to see you again.

AMBROSE (*carrying* ERMENGARDE *across to exit right*): You can't do anything to me, Mr. Vandergelder. (*Exit* AMBROSE *and* ERMENGARDE.)

MRS. LEVI (*who has been laughing heartily, follows the distraught* VANDERGELDER *about the stage as he continues to hunt for his purse*): Well, there's your life, Mr. Vandergelder! Without niece — without clerks — without bride — and without your purse. *Will you marry me now?*

VANDERGELDER: No! (*To get away from her, he dashes into the kitchen.* MRS. LEVI, *still laughing, exclaims to the audience:*)

MRS. LEVI: Damn!! (*And rushes off right.*

THE CURTAIN FALLS)

ACT IV

MISS FLORA VAN HUYSEN's *house.*

This is a prosperous spinster's living room and is filled with knickknacks, all in bright colors, and hung with family portraits, bird cages, shawls, etc.

There is only one entrance — a large double door in the center of the back wall. Beyond it one sees the hall which leads left to the street door and right to the kitchen and the rest of the house. On the left are big windows hung with lace curtains on heavy draperies. Front left is MISS VAN HUYSEN's *sofa, covered with bright-colored cushions, and behind it a table. On the right is another smaller sofa.* MISS VAN HUYSEN *is lying on the sofa. The cook is at the window, left.* MISS VAN HUYSEN, *fifty, florid, stout and sentimental, is sniffing at smelling salts.* COOK *(enormous) holds a china mixing bowl.*

COOK: No, ma'am. I could swear I heard a cab drawing up to the door.

MISS VAN H.: You imagined it. Imagination. Everything in life . . . like that . . . disappointment . . . illusion. Our plans . . . our hopes . . . what becomes of them? Nothing. The story of my life. *(She sings for a moment.)*

COOK: Pray God nothing's happened to the dear girl. Is it a long journey from Yonkers?

MISS VAN H.: No; but long enough for a thousand things to happen.

COOK: Well, we've been waiting all day. Don't you think we ought to call the police about it?

MISS VAN H.: The police! If it's God's will, the police can't prevent it. Oh, in three days, in a week, in a year, we'll know what's happened. . . . And if anything *has* happened to Ermengarde, it'll be a lesson to *him* — that's what it'll be.

COOK: To who?

MISS VAN H.: To that cruel uncle of hers, of course, — to Horace Vandergelder, and to everyone else who tries to separate young lovers. Young lovers have enough to contend with as it is. Who should know that better than I? No one. The story of my life. *(Sings for a moment, then.)* There! Now I hear a cab. Quick!

COOK: No. No, ma'am. I don't see anything.

MISS VAN H.: There! What did I tell you? Everything's imagination — illusion.

COOK: But surely, if they'd changed their plans Mr. Vandergelder would have sent you a message.

MISS VAN H.: Oh, I know what's the matter. That poor child probably thought she was coming to another prison — to another tyrant. If she'd known that I was her friend, and a friend of all young lovers, she'd be here by now. Oh, yes, she would. Her life shall not be crossed with obstacles and disappointments as . . . Cook, a minute ago my smelling salts were on this table. Now they've completely disappeared.

COOK: Why, there they are, ma'am, right there in your hand.

MISS VAN H.: Goodness! How did they get there? I won't inquire. Stranger things have happened!

COOK: I suppose Mr. Vandergelder was sending her down with someone?

MISS VAN H.: Two can go astray as easily as . . . *(She sneezes.)*

COOK: God bless you! *(Runs to window.)* Now, here's a carriage stopping. *(The doorbell rings.)*

MISS VAN H.: Well, open the door, Cook. *(COOK exits.)* It's probably some mistake. *(Sneezes again.)* God bless you! *(Sounds of altercation off in hall.)* It almost sounds as though I heard voices.

CORNELIUS *(off)*: I don't want to come in. This is a free country, I tell you.

CABMAN *(off)*: Forward march!

MALACHI *(off)*: In you go. We have orders.

CORNELIUS *(off)*: You can't make a person go where he doesn't want to go. *(Enter* MALACHI, *followed by* COOK. *The* CABMAN *bundles* BARNABY *and* CORNELIUS *into the room, but they fight their way back into the hall.* CORNELIUS *has lost* MRS. MOLLOY's *coat, but* BARNABY *is wearing* MINNIE's *clothes.)*

MALACHI: Begging your pardon, ma'am, are you Miss Van Huysen?

MISS VAN H.: Yes, I am, unfortunately. What's all this noise about?

MALACHI: There are two people here that Mr. Vandergelder said must be brought to this house and kept here until he comes. And here's his letter to you.

MISS VAN H.: No one has any right to tell me whom I'm to keep in my house if they don't want to stay.

MALACHI: You're right, ma'am. Everybody's always talking about people breaking into houses, ma'am; but there are more people in the world who want to break out of houses, that's what I always say. — Bring them in, Joe. (*Enter* CORNELIUS *and* BARNABY *being pushed by the* CABMAN.)

CORNELIUS: This young lady and I have no business here. We jumped into a cab and asked to be driven to the station and these men brought us to the house and forced us to come inside. There's been a mistake.

CABMAN: Is your name Miss Van Huysen?

MISS VAN H.: Everybody's asking me if my name's Miss Van Huysen. I think that's a matter I can decide for myself. Now will you all be quiet while I read this letter? . . . "This is Ermengarde and that rascal Ambrose Kemper . . ." Now I know who you two are, anyway. "They are trying to run away . . ." Story of my life. "Keep them in your house until I come." Mr. Kemper, you have nothing to fear. (*To* CABMAN.) Who are you?

CABMAN: I'm Joe. I stay here until the old man comes. He owes me fifteen dollars.

MALACHI: That's right, Miss Van Huysen, we must stay here to see they don't escape.

MISS VAN H. (*to* BARNABY): My dear child, take off your things. We'll all have some coffee. (*To* MALACHI *and* CABMAN.) You two go out and wait in the hall. I'll send coffee out to you. Cook, take them. (COOK *pushes* MALACHI *and* CABMAN *into the hall.*)

CORNELIUS: Ma'am, we're not the people you're expecting, and there's no reason . . .

MISS VAN H.: Mr. Kemper, I'm not the tyrant you think I am. . . . You don't have to be afraid of me. . . . I know you're trying to run away with this innocent girl. . . . All my life I have suffered from the interference of others. You shall not suffer as I did. So put yourself entirely in my hands. (*She lifts* BARNABY's *veil.*) Ermengarde! (*Kisses him on both cheeks.*) Where's your luggage?

BARNABY: It's — uh — uh — it's . . .

CORNELIUS: Oh, I'll find it in the morning. It's been mislaid.

MISS VAN H.: Mislaid! How like life! Well, Ermengarde; you shall put on some of my clothes.

BARNABY: Oh, I know I wouldn't be happy, really.

MISS VAN H.: She's a shy little thing, isn't she? Timid little darling! . . . Cook! Put some gingerbread in the oven and get the coffee ready . . .

COOK: Yes, ma'am. (*Exits to kitchen.*)

MISS VAN H.: . . . while I go and draw a good hot bath for Ermengarde.

CORNELIUS: Oh, oh — Miss Van Huysen . . .

MISS VAN H.: Believe me, Ermengarde, your troubles are at an end. You two will be married tomorrow. (*To* BARNABY.) My dear, you look just like I did at your age, and your sufferings have been as mine. While you're bathing, I'll come and tell you the story of my life.

BARNABY: Oh, I don't want to take a bath. I always catch cold.

MISS VAN H.: No, dear, you won't catch cold. I'll slap you all over. I'll be back in a minute. (*Exit.*)

CORNELIUS (*looking out of window*): Barnaby, do you think we could jump down from this window?

BARNABY: Yes — we'd kill ourselves.

CORNELIUS: We'll just have to stay here and watch for something to happen. Barnaby, the situation's desperate.

BARNABY: It began getting desperate about half-past four and it's been getting worse ever since. Now I have to take a bath and get slapped all over. (*Enter* MISS VAN HUYSEN *from kitchen.*)

MISS VAN H.: Ermengarde, you've still got those wet things on. Your bath's nearly ready. Mr. Kemper, you come into the kitchen and put your feet in the oven. (*The doorbell rings. Enter* COOK.) What's that? It's the doorbell. I expect it's your uncle.

COOK: There's the doorbell. (*At window.*) It's *another* man and a girl in a cab!

MISS VAN H.: Well, go and let them in, Cook. Now, come with me, you two. Come, Ermengarde. (*Exit* COOK. MISS VAN HUYSEN *drags* CORNELIUS *and the protesting* BARNABY *off into the kitchen.*)

COOK (*off*): No, that's impossible. Come in, anyway. (*Enter* ERMENGARDE, *followed by* AMBROSE, *carrying the two pieces of luggage.*) There's some mistake. I'll tell Miss Van Huysen, but there's some mistake.

ERMENGARDE: But, I tell you, I *am* Mr. Vandergelder's niece; I'm Ermengarde.

COOK: Beg your pardon, Miss, but you *can't* be Miss Ermengarde.

ERMENGARDE: But — but — here I *am*. And that's my baggage.

COOK: Well, I'll tell Miss Van Huysen who you *think* you are, but she won't like it. (*Exits.*)

AMBROSE: You'll be all right now, Ermengarde. I'd better go before she sees me.

ERMENGARDE: Oh, no. You must stay. I feel so strange here.

AMBROSE: I know, but Mr. Vandergelder will be here in a minute. . . .

ERMENGARDE: Ambrose, you can't go. You can't leave me in this crazy house with those drunken men in the hall. Ambrose . . . Ambrose, let's say you're someone else that my uncle sent down to take care of me. Let's say you're — you're Cornelius Hackl!

AMBROSE: Who's Cornelius Hackl?

ERMENGARDE: You know. He's chief clerk in Uncle's store.

AMBROSE: I don't want to be Cornelius Hackl. No, no, Ermengarde, come away with me now, I'll take you to my friend's house. Or I'll take you to Mrs. Levi's house.

ERMENGARDE: Why, it was Mrs. Levi who threw us right at Uncle Horace's face. Oh, I wish I were back in Yonkers where nothing ever happens. (*Enter* MISS VAN HUYSEN.)

MISS VAN H.: What's all this I hear? Who do you say you are?

ERMENGARDE: Aunt Flora . . . don't you remember me? I'm Ermengarde.

MISS VAN H.: And you're Mr. Vandergelder's niece?

ERMENGARDE: Yes, I am.

MISS VAN H.: Well, that's very strange indeed, because he has just sent me another niece named Ermengarde. She came with a letter, from him, explaining everything. Have you got a letter from him?

ERMENGARDE: No . . .

MISS VAN H.: Really! — And who is this?

ERMENGARDE: This is Cornelius Hackl, Aunt Flora.

MISS VAN H.: Never heard of him.

ERMENGARDE: He's chief clerk in Uncle's store.

MISS VAN H.: Never heard of him. The other Ermengarde came with the man she's in love with, and that *proves* it. She came with Mr. Ambrose Kemper.

AMBROSE (*shouts*): Ambrose Kemper!

MISS VAN H.: Yes, Mr. Hackl, and Mr. Ambrose Kemper is in the kitchen there now *with his feet in the oven.* (ERMENGARDE *starts to cry.* MISS VAN HUYSEN *takes her to the sofa. They both sit.*) Dear child, what is your trouble?

ERMENGARDE: Oh, dear. I don't know what to do.

MISS VAN H. (*in a low voice*): Are you in love with this man?

ERMENGARDE: Yes, I am.

MISS VAN H.: I could see it — and are people trying to separate you?

ERMENGARDE: Yes, they are.

MISS VAN H.: I could see it — who? Horace Vandergelder?

ERMENGARDE: Yes.

MISS VAN H.: That's enough for me. I'll put a stop to Horace Vandergelder's goings on. (MISS VAN HUYSEN *draws* AMBROSE *down to sit on her other side.*) Mr. Hackl, think of me as your friend. Come in the kitchen and get warm. . . . (*She rises and starts to go out.*) We can decide later who everybody is. My dear, would you like a good hot bath?

ERMENGARDE: Yes, I would.

MISS VAN H.: Well, when Ermengarde comes out you can go in. (*Enter* CORNELIUS *from the kitchen.*)

CORNELIUS: Oh, Miss Van Huysen . . .

ERMENGARDE: Why, Mr. Hack — !!

CORNELIUS (*sliding up to her, urgently*): Not yet! I'll explain. I'll explain everything.

MISS VAN H.: Mr. Kemper! — Mr. Kemper! This is Mr. Cornelius Hackl. (*To* AMBROSE.) Mr. Hackl, this is Mr. Ambrose Kemper. (*Pause, while the men glare at one another.*) Perhaps you two know one another?

AMBROSE: No!

CORNELIUS: No, we don't.

AMBROSE (*hotly*): Miss Van Huysen, I know that man is not Ambrose Kemper.

CORNELIUS (*ditto*): And he's not Cornelius Hackl.

MISS VAN H.: My dear young men, what does it matter what your names are? The important thing is that you are you. (*To* AMBROSE.) You are alive and breathing, aren't you, Mr. Hackl? (*Pinches* AMBROSE's *left arm.*)

AMBROSE: Ouch, Miss Van Huysen.

MISS VAN H.: This dear child imagines she is Horace Vandergelder's niece Ermengarde.

ERMENGARDE: But I —

MISS VAN H.: The important thing is that you're all in love. Everything else is illusion. (*She pinches* CORNELIUS' *arm.*)

CORNELIUS: Ouch! Miss Van Huysen!

MISS VAN H. (*comes down and addresses the audience*): Everybody keeps asking me if I'm Miss Van Huys . . . (*She seems suddenly to be stricken with doubt as to who she is; her face shows bewildered alarm. She pinches herself on the upper arm and is abruptly and happily relieved.*) Now, you two gentlemen sit down and have a nice chat while this dear child has a good hot bath. (*The doorbell rings.* ERMENGARDE *exits,* MISS VAN HUYSEN *about to follow her, but stops. Enter* COOK.)

COOK: There's the doorbell again.

MISS VAN H.: Well, answer it. (*She and* ERMENGARDE *exit to kitchen.*)

COOK (*at window, very happy about all these guests*): It's a cab and three ladies. I never saw such a night. (*Exit to front door.*)

MISS VAN H.: Gentlemen, you can rest easy. I'll see that Mr. Vandergelder lets his nieces marry you both. (*Enter* MRS. LEVI.)

MRS. LEVI: Flora, how are you?

MISS VAN H.: Dolly Gallagher! What brings you here?

MRS. LEVI: Great Heavens, Flora, what are those two drunken men doing in your hall?

MISS VAN H.: I don't know. Horace Vandergelder sent them to me.

MRS. LEVI: Well, I've brought you two girls in much the same condition. Otherwise they're the finest girls in the world. (*She goes up to the door and leads in* MRS. MOLLOY. MINNIE *follows.*) I want you to meet Irene Molloy and Minnie Fay.

MISS VAN H.: Delighted to know you.

MRS. LEVI: Oh, I see you two gentlemen are here, too. Mr. Hackl, I was about to look for you (*pointing about the room*) *somewhere* here.

CORNELIUS: No, Mrs. Levi. I'm ready to face anything now.

MRS. LEVI: Mr. Vandergelder will be here in a minute. He's downstairs trying to pay for a cab without any money.

MRS. MOLLOY (*holding* VANDERGELDER's *purse*): Oh, I'll help him.

MRS. LEVI: Yes, will you, dear? You had to pay the restaurant bills. You must have hundreds of dollars there it seems.

MRS. MOLLOY: This is his own purse he lost. I can't give it back to him without seeming . . .

MRS. LEVI: I'll give it back to him. — There, you help him with this now. (*She gives* MRS. MOLLOY *a bill and puts the purse airily under her arm.*)

VANDERGELDER (*off*): Will somebody please pay for this cab? (MRS. MOLLOY *exits to front door.*)

MRS. MOLLOY (*off stage*): I'll take care of that, Mr. Vandergelder. (*As* MR. VANDERGELDER *enters,* MALACHI *and the* CABMAN *follow*

him in. VANDERGELDER *carries overcoat, stick and box of chocolates.*)

CABMAN: Fifteen dollars, Mr. Vandergelder.

MALACHI: Hello, Mr. Vandergelder.

VANDERGELDER (*to* MALACHI): You're discharged! (*To* CABMAN.) You too! (MALACHI *and* CABMAN *go out and wait in the hall.*) So I've caught up with you at last! (*To* AMBROSE.) I never want to see you again! (*To* CORNELIUS.) You're discharged! Get out of the house, both of you. (*He strikes sofa with his stick; a second after,* MISS VAN HUYSEN *strikes him on the shoulder with a folded newspaper or magazine.*)

MISS VAN H. (*forcefully*): Now then you. Stop ordering people out of my house. You can shout and carry on in Yonkers, but when you're in my house you'll behave yourself.

VANDERGELDER: They're both dishonest scoundrels.

MISS VAN H.: Take your hat off. Gentlemen, you stay right where you are.

CORNELIUS: Mr. Vandergelder, I can explain —

MISS VAN H.: There aren't going to be any explanations. Horace, stop scowling at Mr. Kemper and forgive him.

VANDERGELDER: That's not Kemper, that's a dishonest rogue named Cornelius Hackl.

MISS VAN H.: You're crazy. (*Points to* AMBROSE.) That's Cornelius Hackl.

VANDERGELDER: I guess I know my own chief clerk.

MISS VAN H.: I don't care what their names are. You shake hands with them both, or out you go.

VANDERGELDER: Shake hands with those dogs and scoundrels!

MRS. LEVI: Mr. Vandergelder, you've had a hard day. You don't want to go out in the rain now. Just for form's sake, you shake hands with them. You can start quarreling with them tomorrow.

VANDERGELDER (*gives* CORNELIUS *one finger to shake*): There! Don't regard that as a handshake. (*He turns to* AMBROSE, *who mockingly offers him one finger.*) Hey! I never want to see you again. (MRS. MOLLOY *enters from front door.*)

MRS. MOLLOY: Miss Van Huysen.

MISS VAN H.: Yes, dear?

MRS. MOLLOY: Do I smell coffee?

MISS VAN H.: Yes, dear.

MRS. MOLLOY: Can I have some, good and black?

MISS VAN H.: Come along, everybody. We'll all go into the kitchen and have some coffee. (*As they all go:*) Horace, you'll be interested to know there are two Ermengardes in there. . . .

VANDERGELDER: Two!! (*Last to go is* MINNIE, *who revolves about the room dreamily waltzing, a finger on her forehead.* MRS. LEVI *has been standing at one side. She now comes forward, in thoughtful mood.* MINNIE *continues her waltz round the left sofa and out to the kitchen.* MRS. LEVI, *left alone, comes to the front, addressing an imaginary* EPHRAIM.)

MRS. LEVI: Ephraim Levi, I'm going to get married again. Ephraim, I'm marrying Horace Vandergelder for his money. I'm going to send his money out doing all the things you taught me. Oh, it won't be a marriage in the sense that we had one — but I shall certainly make him happy, and Ephraim — I'm tired. I'm tired of living from hand to mouth, and I'm asking your permission, Ephraim — will you give me away? (*Now addressing the audience, she holds up the purse.*) Money! Money! — it's like the sun we walk under; it can kill or cure. — Mr. Vandergelder's money! Vandergelder's never tired of saying most of the people in the world are fools, and in a way he's right, isn't he? Himself, Irene, Cornelius, myself! But there comes a moment in everybody's life when he must decide whether he'll live among human beings or not — a fool among fools or a fool alone.

As for me, I've decided to live among them.

I wasn't always so. After my husband's death I retired into myself. Yes, in the evenings, I'd put out the cat, and I'd lock the door, and I'd make myself a little rum toddy; and before I went to bed I'd say a little prayer, thanking God that I was independent — that no one else's life was mixed up with mine. And when ten o'clock sounded from Trinity Church tower, I fell off to sleep and I was a perfectly contented woman. And one night, after two years of this, an oak leaf fell out of my Bible. I had placed it there on the day my husband asked me to marry him; a perfectly good oak leaf — but without color and without life. And suddenly I realized that for a long time I had not shed one tear; nor had I been filled with the wonderful hope that something or other would turn out well. I saw that I was like that

oak leaf, and on that night I decided to rejoin the human race.

Yes, we're all fools and we're all in danger of destroying the world with our folly. But the surest way to keep us out of harm is to give us the four or five human pleasures that are our right in the world, — and that takes a little money!

The difference between a little money and no money at all is enormous — and can shatter the world. And the difference between a little money and an enormous amount of money is very slight — and that, also, can shatter the world.

Money, I've always felt, money — pardon my expression — is like manure; it's not worth a thing unless it's spread about encouraging young things to grow.

Anyway, — that's the opinion of the second Mrs. Vandergelder. (VANDERGELDER *enters with two cups of coffee. With his back, he closes both doors.*)

VANDERGELDER: Miss Van Huysen asked me to bring you this.

MRS. LEVI: Thank you both. Sit down and rest yourself. What's been going on in the kitchen?

VANDERGELDER: A lot of foolishness. Everybody falling in love with everybody. I forgave 'em; Ermengarde and that artist.

MRS. LEVI: I knew you would.

VANDERGELDER: I made Cornelius Hackl my partner.

MRS. LEVI: You won't regret it.

VANDERGELDER: Dolly, you said some mighty unpleasant things to me in the restaurant tonight . . . all that about my house . . . and everything.

MRS. LEVI: Let's not say another word about it.

VANDERGELDER: Dolly, you have a lot of faults —

MRS. LEVI: Oh, I know what you mean.

VANDERGELDER: You're bossy, scheming, inquisitive . . .

MRS. LEVI: Go on.

VANDERGELDER: But you're a wonderful woman. Dolly, marry me.

MRS. LEVI: Horace! (*Rises.*) Stop right there.

VANDERGELDER: I know I've been a fool about Mrs. Molloy, and that other woman.

But, Dolly, forgive me and marry me. (*He goes on his knees.*)

MRS. LEVI: Horace, I don't dare. No. I don't dare.

VANDERGELDER: What do you mean?

MRS. LEVI: You know as well as I do that you're the first citizen of Yonkers. Naturally, you'd expect your wife to keep open house, to have scores of friends in and out all the time. Any wife of yours should be used to that kind of thing.

VANDERGELDER (*after a brief struggle with himself*): Dolly, you can live any way you like.

MRS. LEVI: Horace, you can't deny it, your wife would have to be a *somebody*. Answer me: am I a somebody?

VANDERGELDER: You are . . . you are. Wonderful woman.

MRS. LEVI: Oh, you're partial. (*She crosses, giving a big wink at the audience, and sits on sofa right.* VANDERGELDER *follows her on his knees.*) Horace, it won't be enough for you to load your wife with money and jewels; to insist that she be a benefactress to half the town. (*He rises and, still struggling with himself, coughs so as not to hear this.*) No, she must be a somebody. Do you really think I have it in me to be a credit to you?

VANDERGELDER: Dolly, everybody knows that you could do anything you wanted to do.

MRS. LEVI: I'll try. With your help, I'll try — and by the way, I found your purse. (*Holds it up.*)

VANDERGELDER: Where did you —! Wonderful woman!

MRS. LEVI: It just walked into my hand. I don't know how I do it. Sometimes I frighten myself. Horace, take it. Money walks out of my hands, too.

VANDERGELDER: Keep it. Keep it.

MRS. LEVI: Horace! (*Half laughing, half weeping, and with an air of real affection for him.*) I never thought . . . I'd ever . . . hear you say a thing like that! (BARNABY *dashes in from the kitchen in great excitement. He has discarded* MINNIE's *clothes.*)

BARNABY: Oh! Excuse me. I didn't know anybody was here.

VANDERGELDER (*bellowing*): Didn't know anybody was here. Idiot!

MRS. LEVI (*putting her hand on* VANDERGELDER's *arm; amiably*): Come in Barnaby. Come in. (VANDERGELDER *looks at her a minute; then says, imitating her tone.*)

VANDERGELDER: Come in, Barnaby. Come in.

BARNABY: Cornelius is going to marry Mrs. Molloy!!

MRS. LEVI: Isn't that fine! Horace! . . . (MRS. LEVI *rises, and indicates that he has an announcement to make.*)

VANDERGELDER: Barnaby, go in and tell the rest of them that Mrs. Levi has consented —

MRS. LEVI: *Finally* consented!

VANDERGELDER: Finally consented to become my wife.

BARNABY: Holy cabooses. (*Dashes back to the doorway.*) Hey! Listen, everybody! Wolftrap — I mean — Mr. Vandergelder is going to marry Mrs. Levi. (MISS VAN HUYSEN *enters followed by all the people in this act. She is now carrying the box of chocolates.*)

MISS VAN H.: Dolly, that's the best news I ever heard. (*She addresses the audience.*) There isn't any more coffee; there isn't any more gingerbread; but there are three couples in my house and they're all going to get married. And do you know, one of those Ermengardes wasn't a dear little girl at all — she was a boy! Well, that's what life is: disappointment, illusion.

MRS. LEVI (*to audience*): There isn't any more coffee; there isn't any more gingerbread, and there isn't any more play — but there is one more thing we have to do. . . . Barnaby, come here. (*She whispers to him, pointing to the audience. Then she says to the audience:*) I think the youngest person here ought to tell us what the moral of the play is. (BARNABY *is reluctantly pushed forward to the footlights.*)

BARNABY: Oh, I think it's about . . . I think it's about adventure. The test of an adventure is that when you're in the middle of it, you say to yourself, "Oh, now I've got myself into an awful mess; I wish I were sitting quietly at home." And the sign that something's wrong with you is when you sit quietly at home wishing you were out having lots of adventure. What we would like for you is that you have just the right amount of sitting quietly at home and just the right amount of — adventure! So that now we all want to thank you for coming tonight, and we all hope that in your lives you have just the right amount of — adventure!

(THE CURTAIN FALLS)

Just beneath the title of his play, Wilder put "A Farce in Four Acts." When we think of the low esteem in which farce is held, it is almost pedantic to mention that *The Matchmaker* is a slight revision of an earlier play by Wilder, *The Merchant of Yonkers* (1938), which in turn is derived from an Austrian play, Johann Nestroy's *Einen Jux will er sich machen* (*Out for a Good Time*, 1842), which itself is an adaptation of an English comedy, John Oxenford's *A Day Well Spent; or, Three Adventures* (1835). A long lineage for a play in what is thought to be a humble genre.

A few words about farce may be useful. It is generally considered a kind of comedy that depends more heavily on physical action than on wit, or, to put it somewhat differently, on plot rather than on subtlety of character. But no good playwright scorns plot, and subtlety of character is not a *sine qua non* of good comedy. Perhaps what identifies farce is amusing overt desperation. In a way, all drama — comedy and tragedy — deals with desperate people: Othello falls into a fit; Hedda fires pistols; Major Barbara is (for a while) heartbroken; even Undershaft meets his match in Cusins, who at one point is said to be "desperately perplexed." But the desperation is usually intermittent, and rarely unsettles the dramatis personae in comedy, where pressures are most often released in the civilized form of banter, and where all but a few crabby fathers or foolish wooers usually preserve good manners. In farce the desperation bursts to the surface, and characters are driven about the stage, hiding under tables, inventing grotesque lies, and leaping into outlandish disguises. (In one of his films Charlie Chaplin escapes his ardent pursuers by standing rigid, a shade on his head, disguising himself as a floor lamp.)

And this is the sort of thing we get in *The Matchmaker*. Wilder contrives — or, rather, adapts — a plot that reveals engaging desperation all around. Cornelius Hackl, Horace Vandergelder's clerk, wants to spend a day in New York, to have a good dinner, to be in danger, to almost get arrested, and to kiss a girl (he is thirty-three); Mrs. Irene Molloy wants to escape the monotonous life of a widowed milliner ("I can no longer stand being suspected of being a wicked woman, while I have nothing to show for it. I can't stand it."), and Dolly Levi wants a husband and the fun that distributing his money will bring. Even Horace Vandergelder, despite his grumblings and his sermons, despite his dreary "caution and hard work," wants "a little risk and adventure." Wilder gives us four acts in which people are taxed to their uttermost, and respond in entertaining zany ways. Small sample: Horace Vandergelder, about to marry, is informing his junior clerk of his plans:

> VANDERGELDER: ... When I come back, there are going to be some changes in the house here. I'll tell you what the change is, but I don't want you discussing it amongst yourselves: you're going to have a mistress.
> BARNABY (*seventeen; round-faced, wide-eyed innocence; wearing a green apron*): I'm too young, Mr. Vandergelder!!

What does it add up to? We can, of course, hunt through a play and find some scraps of a message. There are, for instance, a few lines that glance at the underpaid working class: Vandergelder says to Mrs. Molloy, "You pay those girls of yours too much. You pay them as much as men. Girls like that enjoy their work. Wages, Mrs. Molloy, are paid to make people do work they don't want to do." Malachi's suggestion that thieves are engaged in the useful task of redistributing wealth might fit here too, but we hardly take seriously these criticisms of bourgeois morality. They may appeal briefly to our anarchic impulses, but we laugh at them rather than think hard about them. There is, of course, the larger, more pervasive theme, which Wilder summarized thus: "My play is about the aspirations of the young (and not only of the young) for a fuller, freer participation in life." Any number of speeches could be cited as evidence, but perhaps the most explicit is one of Dolly's: "And suddenly I realized that for a long time I had not shed one tear; nor had I been filled with the wonderful hope that something or other would turn out well. . . . and on that night I decided to rejoin the human race. . . . Money, I've always felt, money — pardon my expression — is like manure; it's not worth a thing unless it's spread about encouraging young things to grow."

Yet the play's value is surely not entirely dependent upon such speeches, or upon its theme. For one thing, the theme is that of almost all comedy, and we can scarcely value Wilder for presenting a stock theme. In an interview (printed in *Writers at Work*, ed. Malcolm Cowley) Wilder remarked that the didactic content of a literary work probably has two origins. It is there because it gave the author his initial impetus, but it tends to disappear. It "starts the motor. Or let us say: many of the things we eat are cooked over a gas stove, but there is no taste of gas in the food." It gives the author a sense that he is doing something respectable, and, Wilder added, it also gives the audience something that audiences normally expect. But the didactic content is, paradoxically, a sugar coating, both for author and for audience. Shaw had said that the heart of his plays was a message, and he found the audience would accept the message only when it was sugar-coated with an amusing plot. But for Wilder the heart of a play is its presentation of "the pure event," "experience for experience's sake — rather than for moral improvement's sake." Those who want a moral will find it in *The Matchmaker*; those who want an experience, an adventure (as Cornelius Hackl and Horace Vandergelder do) will find it there too.

The Comic Rhythm

Susanne K. Langer

> In Boswell's *Life of Doctor Johnson* we hear of a man who intended to be a philosopher but who failed because "cheerfulness was always breaking in." Susanne K. Langer is a philosopher, but she does not see cheerfulness as an enemy. She sees in comedy a dramatization of the basic biological patterns of persistence and growth, "human vitality holding its own in the world amid the surprises of unplanned coincidence."

The pure sense of life is the underlying feeling of comedy, developed in countless different ways. To give a general phenomenon one name is not to make all its manifestations one thing, but only to bring them conceptually under one head. Art does not generalize and classify; art sets forth the individuality of forms which discourse, being essentially general, has to suppress. The sense of life is always new, infinitely complex, therefore infinitely variable in its possible expressions. This sense, or "enjoyment" as Alexander would call it,[1] is the realization in direct feeling of what sets organic nature apart from inorganic: self-preservation, self-restoration, functional tendency, purpose. Life is teleological, the rest of nature is, apparently, mechanical; to maintain the pattern of vitality in a non-living universe is the most elementary instinctual purpose. An organism tends to keep its equilibrium amid the bombardment of aimless forces that beset it, to regain equilibrium when it has been disturbed, and to pursue a sequence of actions dictated by the need of keeping all its interdependent parts constantly renewed, their structure intact. Only organisms have needs; lifeless objects whirl or slide or tumble about, are shattered and scattered, stuck together, piled up, without showing any impulse to return to some pre-eminent condition and function. But living things strive to persist in a particular chemical balance, to maintain a particular temperature, to repeat particular functions, and to develop along particular lines, achieving a growth that seems to be preformed in their earliest, rudimentary, protoplasmic structure.

That is the basic biological pattern which all living things share: the round of conditioned and conditioning organic processes that produces the life rhythm. When this rhythm is disturbed, all activities in the total complex are modified by the break; the organism as a whole is out of balance. But, within a wide range of conditions, it struggles to retrieve its original dynamic form by overcoming and removing the obstacle, or if this proves impossible, it develops a slight variation of its typical form and activity and carries on life with a new balance of functions — in other words, it adapts itself to the situation. A tree, for instance, that is bereft of the sunshine it needs by the encroachment of other trees, tends to grow tall and thin until it can spread its own branches in the light. A fish that has most of its tail bitten off partly overcomes the disturbance of its locomotion patterns by growing new tissue, replacing some of the tail, and partly adapts to its new condition by modifying the normal uses of its fins, swimming effectively without trying to correct the list of its whole body in the water, as it did at first.

Reprinted by permission of Charles Scribner's Sons from *Feeling and Form* by Susanne K. Langer. Copyright 1953 by Charles Scribner's Sons.

[1] S. Alexander, *Space, Time and Deity*. See Vol. I, p. 12.

But the impulse to survive is not spent only in defense and accommodation; it appears also in the varying power of organisms to seize on opportunities. Consider how chimney swifts, which used to nest in crevasses among rocks, have exploited the products of human architecture, and how unfailingly mice find the warmth and other delights of our kitchens. All creatures live by opportunities, in a world fraught with disasters. That is the biological pattern in most general terms. . . .

Mankind has its rhythm of animal existence, too — the strain of maintaining a vital balance amid the alien and impartial chances of the world, complicated and heightened by passional desires. The pure sense of life springs from that basic rhythm, and varies from the composed well-being of sleep to the intensity of spasm, rage, or ecstasy. But the process of living is incomparably more complex for human beings than for even the highest animals; man's world is, above all, intricate and puzzling. The powers of language and imagination have set it utterly apart from that of other creatures. In human society an individual is not, like a member of a herd or a hive, exposed only to others that visibly or tangibly surround him, but is consciously bound to people who are absent, perhaps far away, at the moment. Even the dead may still play into his life. His awareness of events is far greater than the scope of his physical perceptions. Symbolic construction has made this vastly involved and extended world; and mental adroitness is his chief asset for exploiting it. The pattern of his vital feeling, therefore, reflects his deep emotional relation to those symbolic structures that are his realities, and his instinctual life modified in almost every way by thought — a brainy opportunism in face of an essentially dreadful universe.

This human life-feeling is the essence of comedy. It is at once religious and ribald, knowing and defiant, social and freakishly individual. The illusion of life which the comic poet creates is the oncoming future fraught with dangers and opportunities, that is, with physical or social events occurring by chance and building up the coincidences with which individuals cope according to their lights. This ineluctable future — ineluctable because its countless factors are beyond human knowledge and control — is Fortune. Destiny in the guise of Fortune is the fabric of comedy; it is developed by comic action, which is the upset and recovery of the protagonist's equilibrium, his contest with the world and his triumph by wit, luck, personal power, or even humorous, or ironical, or philosophical acceptance of mischance. Whatever the theme — serious and lyrical as in *The Tempest*, coarse slapstick as in the *Schwänke* of Hans Sachs, or clever and polite social satire — the immediate sense of life is the underlying feeling of comedy, and dictates its rhythmically structured unity, that is to say its organic form.

Comedy is an art form that arises naturally wherever people are gathered to celebrate life, in spring festivals, triumphs, birthdays, weddings, or initiations. For it expresses the elementary strains and resolutions of animate nature, the animal drives that persist even in human nature, the delight man takes in his special mental gifts that make him the lord of creation; it is an image of human vitality holding its own in the world amid the surprises of unplanned coincidence. The most obvious occasions for the performance of comedies are thanks or challenges to fortune. What justifies the term "Comedy" is not that the ancient ritual procession, the Comus, honoring the god of that name, was the source of this great art form — for comedy has arisen in many parts of the world, where the Greek god with his particular worship was unknown — but that the Comus was a fertility rite, and the god it celebrated a fertility god, a symbol of perpetual rebirth, eternal life. . . .

Because comedy abstracts, and reincarnates for our perception, the motion and rhythm of living, it enhances our vital feeling, much as the presentation of space in painting enhances our awareness of visual space. The virtual life on the stage is not diffuse and only half felt, as actual life usually is: virtual life, always moving visibly into the future, is intensified, speeded up, exaggerated; the exhibition of vitality rises to a breaking point, to mirth and laughter. We laugh in the theater at small incidents and drolleries which would hardly rate a chuckle offstage. It is not for such psychological reasons that we go there to be amused, nor are we bound by rules of politeness to hide our hilarity, but these trifles at which we laugh are really funnier *where they occur* than they would be elsewhere; they are employed in the play, not merely brought in casually. They occur where the tension of dialogue or other action reaches a high point. As thought breaks into speech — as the wave breaks into form — vitality breaks into humor.

Humor is the brilliance of drama, a sudden heightening of the vital rhythm. A good comedy, therefore, builds up to every laugh; a performance that has been filled up with jokes at the indiscretion of the comedian or of his writer may draw a long series of laughs, yet leave the spectator without any clear impression of a very funny play. The laughs, moreover, are likely to be of a peculiar sameness, almost perfunctory, the formal recognition of a timely "gag."

The amoral character of the comic protagonist goes through the whole range of what may be called the comedy of laughter. Even the most civilized products of this art — plays that George Meredith would honor with the name of "comedy," because they provoke "thoughtful laughter" — do not present moral distinctions and issues, but only the ways of wisdom and of folly. Aristophanes, Menander, Molière — practically the only authors this most exacting of critics admitted as truly comic poets — are not moralists, yet they do not flout or deprecate morality; they have, literally, "no use" for moral principles — that is, they do not use them. Meredith, like practically all his contemporaries, labored under the belief that poetry must teach society lessons, and that comedy was valuable for what it revealed concerning the social order.[2] He tried hard to hold its exposé of foibles and vindication of common sense to an ethical standard, yet in his very efforts to jus-

[2] His well-known little work is called *An Essay on Comedy, and the Uses of the Comic Spirit*. These uses are entirely non-artistic. Praising the virtues of "good sense" (which is whatever has survival value in the eyes of society), he says: "The French have a school of stately comedy to which they can fly for renovation whenever they have fallen away from it; and their having such a school is the main reason why, as John Stuart Mill pointed out, they know men and women more accurately than we do." And a few pages later: "The *Femmes Savantes* is a capital instance of the uses of comedy in teaching the world to understand what ails it. The French had felt the burden of this new nonsense [the fad of academic learning, new after the fad of excessive nicety and precision in speech, that had marked the *Précieuses*]; but they had to see the comedy several times before they were consoled in their suffering by seeing the cause of it exposed."

tify its amoral personages he only admitted their amoral nature, and their simple relish for life, as when he said: "The heroines of comedy are like women of the world, not necessarily heartless from being clear-sighted.... Comedy is an exhibition of their battle with men, and that of men with them...."

There it is, in a nutshell: the contest of men and women — the most universal contest, humanized, in fact civilized, yet still the primitive joyful challenge, the self-preservation and self-assertion whose progress is the comic rhythm....

The same impulse that drove people, even in prehistoric times, to enact fertility rites and celebrate all phases of their biological existence, sustains their eternal interest in comedy. It is in the nature of comedy to be erotic, risqué, and sensuous if not sensual, impious, and even wicked. This assures it a spontaneous emotional interest, yet a dangerous one: for it is easy and tempting to command an audience by direct stimulation of feeling and fantasy, not by artistic power. But where the formulation of feeling is really achieved, it probably reflects the whole development of mankind and man's world, for feeling is the intaglio image of reality. The sense of precariousness that is the typical tension of light comedy was undoubtedly developed in the eternal struggle with chance that every farmer knows only too well — with weather, blights, beasts, birds and beetles. The embarrassments, perplexities and mounting panic which characterize that favorite genre, comedy of manners, may still reflect the toils of ritual and taboo that complicated the caveman's existence. Even the element of aggressiveness in comic action serves to develop a fundamental trait of the comic rhythm — the deep cruelty of it, as all life feeds on life. There is no biological truth that feeling does not reflect, and that good comedy, therefore, will not be prone to reveal.

But the fact that the rhythm of comedy is the basic rhythm of life does not mean that biological existence is the "deeper meaning" of all its themes, and that to understand the play is to interpret all the characters as symbols and the story as a parable, a disguised rite of spring or fertility magic, performed four hundred and fifty times on Broadway. The stock characters are probably symbolic both in origin and in appeal. There are such independently symbolic factors, or residues of them, in all the arts,[3] but their value for art lies in the degree to which

[3] E.g., the symbolization of the zodiac in some sacred architecture, of our bodily orientation in the picture plane, or of walking measure, a primitive measure of actual time, in music. But a study of such non-artistic symbolic functions would require a monograph.

their significance can be "swallowed" by the single symbol, the art work. Not the derivation of personages and situations, but of the rhythm of "felt life" that the poet puts upon them, seems to me to be of artistic importance: the essential comic feeling, which is the sentient aspect of organic unity, growth, and self-preservation.

Some Prefatory Words on Comedy

Louis Kronenberger

Louis Kronenberger (1904–80) was born in Cincinnati and graduated from the University of Cincinnati before moving to New York in the 1920s, where he became a free-lance literary critic and essayist. From 1938 to 1961 he was the drama critic for *Time* magazine. In the essay we reprint, from the preface to *The Thread of Laughter* (a book on English stage comedy), Kronenberger argues that, although comedy appeals to the malice in us by exposing human frailty, comedy is not malevolent but, on the contrary, offers a sort of purgation or catharsis of our malice, and it is even kindly in that it brings us to a tolerant recognition that we are all "fellow-fools and sinners." But the dependence of comedy on social relationships means that much comedy soon becomes dated, because the foibles or even the sins of one age are not those of another.

Comedy appeals to the laughter, which is in part at least the malice, in us; for comedy is concerned with human imperfection, with people's failure to measure up either to the world's or to their own conception of excellence. All tragedy is idealistic and says in effect, "The pity of it" — that owing to this fault of circumstance or that flaw of character, a man who is essentially good does evil, a man who is essentially great is toppled from the heights. But all comedy tends to be skeptical and says in effect, "The absurdity of it" — that in spite of his fine talk or noble resolutions, a man is the mere creature of pettiness and vanity and folly. Tragedy is always lamenting the Achilles tendon, the destructive flaw in man; but comedy, in a sense, is always looking for it. Not cheaply, out of malevolence or cynicism; but rather because even at his greatest, man offers some touch of the fatuous and small, just as a murderer, even at his cleverest, usually makes some fatal slip. In tragedy men aspire to more than they can achieve; in comedy, they pretend to more.

The difference, again, between the two is the very question of difference. A great tragic hero — an Oedipus or Lear — strikes us as tre-

mendously far removed from common humanity. But comedy, stripping off the war-paint and the feathers, the college degrees or the military medals, shows how very like at bottom the hero is to everybody else. Tragedy cannot flourish without giving its characters a kind of aura of poetry, or idealism, or doom; comedy scarcely functions till the aura has been dispelled. And as it thrives on a revelation of the true rather than the trumped-up motive, as it is in one way sustained by imposture, so in another it is sustained by incongruity. Here is the celebrated philosopher cursing the universe because he has mislaid a book. Here are all those who, like King Canute, would bid the clock go backward or the waves stand still. Here is not only the cheat, but the victim who but for his own dishonest desires could never be cheated.

Comedy, in brief, is criticism. If through laughing at others we purge ourselves of certain spiteful and ungenerous instincts — as through tragedy we achieve a higher and more publicized catharsis — that is not quite the whole of it. Comedy need not be hostile to idealism; it need only show how far human beings fall short of the ideal. The higher comedy mounts, the airier and more brilliant its forms, the more are we aware of man's capacity for being foolish or self-deluded or complacent; in the very highest comedy, such as the finale of Mozart's *Marriage of Figaro*, we are in a very paradise of self-deceptions and misunderstand-

From *The Thread of Laughter: Chapters on English Stage Comedy from Jonson to Maugham*, by Louis Kronenberger. Copyright 1952 by Louis Kronenberger. Reprinted by permission of Alfred A. Knopf, Inc.

ings and cross-purposes. At the heart of high comedy there is always a strain of melancholy, as round the edges there is all gaiety and ebullience and glitter; and Schiller was perhaps right in regarding high comedy as the greatest of all literary forms.

Comedy is criticism, then, because it exposes human beings for what they are in contrast to what they profess to be. How much idealism, it asks, shall we find entirely free from self-love? How much beneficence is born of guilt, how much affection is produced by flattery? At its most severe, doubtless, comedy is not just skeptical but cynical; and asks many of the same questions, returning many of the same answers, as that prince — or at any rate duke — of cynics, La Rochefoucauld. "Pride," La Rochefoucauld remarked, "does not wish to owe, and vanity does not wish to pay." Or again: "To establish oneself in the world, one does all one can to seem established there." Of these and many similar maxims, a play or story might easily be written; from each much cold and worldly comedy, or harsh and worldly farce, might be contrived. But comedy need not be so harsh, and seldom is: though it can be harsher still, can be — as in Ben Jonson — gloating and sardonic. But always it is the enemy, not of virtue or idealism, but of hypocrisy and pretense; and what it does in literature is very much, I suppose, what experience does for most of us in life: it knocks the bloom off the peach, the gilt off the gingerbread.

But though the comic spirit is, in Meredith's phrase, "humanely malign," it is also kindly and even companionable, in the sense that it brings men together as fellow-fools and sinners, and is not only criticism but understanding. Comedy is always jarring us with the evidence that we are no better than other people, and always comforting us with the knowledge that most other people are no better than we are. It makes us more critical but it leaves us more tolerant; and to that extent it performs a very notable social function. Its whole character, indeed — quite aside from that point — is rather social than individual.

The social basis rests in the very subject-matter of comedy — in all that has to do with one's life as part of a group; with one's wish to charm or persuade or deceive or dazzle others. Thus no exhibitionist can exist in solitude, no hypocrite or poseur can work without an audience. There are indeed so many social situations that engender comedy that many of them are notably hackneyed. There are all kinds of classic family jokes — the mother-in-law joke preeminently; but equally the rich-uncle theme, or the country cousin, or the visiting relative who forgets to leave, or the one that proffers advice, or the one that prophesies disaster. Right in the home there is the precocious brat or the moping adolescent; there are countless varieties of comic servants; and there is finally the question, though it perhaps belongs in a different category, of who heads the family — the husband or the wife.

The idea of husband and wife more likely belongs with the social aspects of sex, with the War Between the Sexes as it is fought out in the drawing room. As a purely sexual conflict, this war would not be social; but by the same token it would not be comedy. The question whether man really makes the decisions — including the decision to marry — or is merely permitted to think he does, is, whatever the answer, thoroughly social in nature. Or there is the business of how men and women perform in society for one another's benefit: being the fearless protector or the clinging vine, the woman who always understands or the man who is never understood. We have social comedy again when we pit one nationality as well as one sex against another, when the American puritan is ensnared by a continental siren, or when the suitor is German and humorless, and the besought one is French and amused. There is still another social aspect when we add a third person to the situation, a mistress as well as a wife, or a lover as well as a husband; or — for the situation need not be illicit, it need only be triangular — when the wife's old beau or the husband's old flame reappears on the scene. Or there is the man who does not know which of two sisters, or two heiresses, or two widows to marry; or the girl which of a half dozen suitors.

Comedy, indeed, must gain admittance into any part of the world — including prisons and sickrooms and funerals — where people are thrown together. Any institution involving hierarchies and rivalries — for example, a university — is a perfect hotbed of it. There will be everybody's relation to the President or the President's wife; or the President's relation to the President's wife; or to his trustees; all the struggles for precedence and the problems of protocol; the progressives on the faculty and the die-hards; the wives who can't help looking dowdy, the wives who suppose they look chic. For obviously any institution, whether a college or a department store, an artist colony or a country club, provides a cross-section of social types and traits, and brings us face to face with a hundred things out of which comedy is distilled: ambition and pride, arrogance and obsequiousness; a too-slavish following or a too-emphatic flouting of convention; all the stratagems men use in order to outwit or get their way. . . .

And this brings up the point that though Comedy has its permanent subject-matter and even its body of laws, it is liable, like everything else, to changes in fashion and taste, to differences of sensibility. One generation's pleasure is the next generation's embarrassment: much that the Victorians shuddered at merely makes us laugh, much that they laughed at might well make us shudder. One always reacts — and quite fortunately — from the vantage-point of one's own age; and it is probably a mistake, and certainly a waste of breath, to be arrogant or snobbish or moral about what amuses or does not amuse one: we may fancy we are less callous than our grandfathers and only be less callous about different things. The cuckold was clearly, in Restoration comedy, a figure to hoot at. Simply for being cuckolded we do not today find a man so comic, or even comic at all: though the moment we add an extra element to his role, such as his elation over cuckolding others, he becomes a comic figure for us. To what extent sex itself is a comic theme must naturally vary with the morality of a particular age: there are times when it seems shocking for a man ever to have a mistress; there are times when it seems even more shocking for a man never to have one. Right in the same age, what is considered virtue by the parson may be termed repression by the psychiatrist; and in such an age, which is usually one of moral transition, we may well find conflicting comedy values. The pendulum-swing of taste always makes it hard for people to know what they really like: if they are in revolt against gentility, they are likely to confuse what is funny with what is merely bold or obscene; if they are converts to gentility, they will be too much outraged by the indecent to inquire whether it is funny. There is nothing at which the Comic Spirit must smile more than our fickle and inconstant notions as to what constitutes comedy. We need not always look back to Shakespeare's drearier clowns as an instance of how tastes change: sometimes we need only attend a revival of what convulsed us ten years before.

TRAGICOMEDY

THE CHERRY ORCHARD

Anton Chekhov

Translated by Stark Young

Anton Chekhov (1860–1904) received his medical degree from the University of Moscow in 1884, but he had already published some stories. His belief that his medical training assisted him in writing about people caused some people to find him cold, but on the whole the evidence suggests that he was a genial, energetic young man with considerable faith in reason and (as befitted a doctor) in science, and with very little faith in religion and in heroics. His major plays are *The Seagull* (1896), *Uncle Vanya* (1899), *Three Sisters* (1901), and, finally, *The Cherry Orchard* (1903), written during his last illness.

CHARACTERS

RANEVSKAYA, LYUBOFF ANDREEVNA, *a landowner*
ANYA, *her daughter, seventeen years old*
VARYA, *her adopted daughter, twenty-four years old*
GAYEFF, LEONID ANDREEVICH, *brother of Ranevskaya*
LOPAHIN, YERMOLAY ALEXEEVICH, *a merchant*
TROFIMOFF, PYOTR SERGEEVICH, *a student*
SEMYONOFF-PISHTCHIK, BORIS BORISOVICH, *a landowner*
CHARLOTTA IVANOVNA, *a governess*
EPIHODOFF, SEMYON PANTELEEVICH, *a clerk*
DUNYASHA, *a maid*
FIERS, *a valet, an old man of eighty-seven*
YASHA, *a young valet*
A PASSERBY *or* STRANGER
THE STATIONMASTER
A POST-OFFICE CLERK
VISITORS, SERVANTS

Scene: The action takes place on the estate of L. A. RANEVSKAYA.

Act I of the original production of *The Cherry Orchard* in 1904. (Photograph reproduced from J. L. Styan, *Chekhov in Performance.* Copyright 1971 by Cambridge University Press.)

ACT I

A room that is still called the nursery. One of the doors leads into ANYA's *room. Dawn, the sun will soon be rising. It is May, the cherry trees are in blossom but in the orchard it is cold, with a morning frost. The windows in the room are closed. Enter* DUNYASHA *with a candle and* LOPAHIN *with a book in his hand.*

LOPAHIN: The train got in, thank God! What time is it?

DUNYASHA: It's nearly two. (*Blows out her candle.*) It's already daylight.

LOPAHIN: But how late was the train? Two hours at least. (*Yawning and stretching.*) I'm a fine one, I am, look what a fool thing I did! I drove here on purpose just to meet them at the station, and then all of a sudden I'd overslept myself! Fell asleep in my chair. How provoking! — You could have waked me up.

DUNYASHA: I thought you had gone. (*Listening.*) Listen, I think they are coming now.

LOPAHIN (*listening*): No — No, there's the luggage and one thing and another. (*A pause.*) Lyuboff Andreevna has been living abroad five years. I don't know what she is like now — She is a good woman. An easy-going, simple woman. I remember when I was a boy about fifteen, my father, who is at rest — in those days he ran a shop here in the village — hit me in the face with his fist, my nose was bleeding — We'd come to the yard together for something or other, and he was a little drunk. Lyuboff Andreevna, I can see her now, still so young, so slim, led me to the washbasin here in this very room, in the nursery. "Don't cry," she says, "little peasant, it will be well in time for your wedding" — (*A pause.*) Yes, little peasant — My father was a peasant truly, and here I am in a white waistcoat and yellow shoes. Like a pig rooting in a pastry shop — I've got this rich, lots of money, but if you really stop and think of it, I'm just a peasant — (*Turning the pages of a book.*) Here I was

Reprinted by permission of Flora Roberts, Inc. Copyright 1939, 1941, 1947, 1950 by Stark Young. Copyright © 1956 by Stark Young. *Caution:* Professionals and amateurs are hereby warned that this play, being fully protected under the copyright laws of the United States of America, the British Commonwealth, including Canada, and all other countries of the Copyright Union, is subject to a royalty. All rights, including professional, amateur, motion pictures, recitation, public reading, radio broadcasting, television, and the rights of translation into foreign languages are strictly reserved. In its present form the play is dedicated to the reading public only.

reading a book and didn't get a thing out of it. Reading and went to sleep. (*A pause.*)

DUNYASHA: And all night long the dogs were not asleep, they know their masters are coming.

LOPAHIN: What is it, Dunyasha, you're so —

DUNYASHA: My hands are shaking. I'm going to faint.

LOPAHIN: You're just so delicate, Dunyasha. And all dressed up like a lady, and your hair all done up! Mustn't do that. Must know your place.

(*Enter* EPIHODOFF, *with a bouquet: he wears a jacket and highly polished boots with a loud squeak. As he enters he drops the bouquet.*)

EPIHODOFF (*picking up the bouquet*): Look, the gardener sent these, he says to put them in the dining room. (*Giving the bouquet to* DUNYASHA.)

LOPAHIN: And bring me some kvass.

DUNYASHA: Yes, sir. (*Goes out.*)

EPIHODOFF: There is a morning frost now, three degrees of frost (*sighing*) and the cherries all in bloom. I cannot approve of our climate — I cannot. Our climate can never quite rise to the occasion. Listen, Yermolay Alexeevich, allow me to subtend, I bought myself, day before yesterday, some boots and they, I venture to assure you, squeak so that it is impossible. What could I grease them with?

LOPAHIN: Go on. You annoy me.

EPIHODOFF: Every day some misfortune happens to me. But I don't complain, I am used to it and I even smile.

(DUNYASHA *enters, serves* LOPAHIN *the kvass.*)

EPIHODOFF: I'm going. (*Stumbling over a chair and upsetting it.*) There (*as if triumphant*), there, you see, pardon the expression, a circumstance like that, among others — It is simply quite remarkable. (*Goes out.*)

DUNYASHA: And I must tell you, Yermolay Alexcevich, that Epihodoff has proposed to me.

LOPAHIN: Ah!

DUNYASHA: I don't know really what to — He is a quiet man but sometimes when he starts talking, you can't understand a thing he means. It's all very nice, and full of feeling, but just doesn't make any sense. I sort of like him. He loves me madly. He's a man that's unfortunate, every day there's something or other. They tease him around here, call him twenty-two misfortunes —

LOPAHIN (*cocking his ear*): Listen, I think they are coming —

DUNYASHA: They are coming! But what's the matter with me — I'm cold all over.

LOPAHIN: They're really coming. Let's go meet them. Will she recognize me? It's five years we haven't seen each other.

DUNYASHA (*excitedly*): I'm going to faint this very minute. Ah, I'm going to faint!

(*Two carriages can be heard driving up to the house.* LOPAHIN *and* DUNYASHA *hurry out. The stage is empty. In the adjoining rooms a noise begins.* FIERS *hurries across the stage, leaning on a stick; he has been to meet* LYUBOFF ANDREEVNA, *and wears an old-fashioned livery and a high hat; he mutters something to himself, but you cannot understand a word of it. The noise offstage gets louder and louder. A voice: "Look! Let's go through here —"* LYUBOFF ANDREEVNA, ANYA *and* CHARLOTTA IVANOVNA, *with a little dog on a chain, all of them dressed for traveling,* VARYA, *in a coat and kerchief,* GAYEFF, SEMYONOFF-PISHTCHIK, LOPAHIN, DUNYASHA, *with a bundle and an umbrella,* SERVANTS *with pieces of luggage — all pass through the room.*)

ANYA: Let's go through here. Mama, do you remember what room this is?

LYUBOFF ANDREEVNA (*happily, through her tears*): The nursery!

VARYA: How cold it is, my hands are stiff. (*To* LYUBOFF ANDREEVNA.) Your rooms, the white one and the violet, are just the same as ever, Mama.

LYUBOFF ANDREEVNA: The nursery, my dear beautiful room — I slept here when I was little — (*Crying.*) And now I am like a child — (*Kisses her brother and* VARYA, *then her brother again.*) And Varya is just the same as ever, looks like a nun. And I knew Dunyasha — (*Kisses* DUNYASHA.)

GAYEFF: The train was two hours late. How's that? How's that for good management?

CHARLOTTA (*to* PISHTCHIK): My dog he eats nuts too.

PISHTCHIK (*astonished*): Think of that!

(*Everybody goes out except* ANYA *and* DUNYASHA.)

DUNYASHA: We waited so long — (*Taking off* ANYA's *coat and hat.*)

ANYA: I didn't sleep all four nights on the way. And now I feel so chilly.

DUNYASHA: It was Lent when you left, there was some snow then, there was frost, and now? My darling (*laughing and kissing her*), I waited so long for you, my joy, my life — I'm telling you now, I can't keep from it another minute.

ANYA (*wearily*): There we go again —

DUNYASHA: The clerk Epihodoff, proposed to me after Holy Week.

ANYA: You're always talking about the same thing — (*Arranging her hair.*) I've lost all my hairpins — (*She is tired to the point of staggering.*)

DUNYASHA: I just don't know what to think. He loves me, loves me so!

ANYA (*looks in through her door, tenderly*): My room, my windows, it's just as if I had never been away. I'm home! Tomorrow morning I'll get up, I'll run into the orchard — Oh, if I only could go to sleep! I haven't slept all the way, I was tormented by anxiety.

DUNYASHA: Day before yesterday, Pyotr Sergeevich arrived.

ANYA (*joyfully*): Petya!

DUNYASHA: He's asleep in the bathhouse, he lives there. I am afraid, he says, of being in the way. (*Taking her watch from her pocket and looking at it.*) Somebody ought to wake him up. It's only that Varvara Mikhailovna told us not to. Don't you wake him up, she said.

VARYA (*enter* VARYA *with a bunch of keys at her belt*): Dunyasha, coffee, quick — Mama is asking for coffee.

DUNYASHA: This minute. (*Goes out.*)

VARYA: Well, thank goodness, you've come back. You are home again. (*Caressingly.*) My darling is back! My precious is back!

ANYA: I've had such a time.

VARYA: I can imagine!

ANYA: I left during Holy Week, it was cold then. Charlotta talked all the way and did her tricks. Why did you fasten Charlotta on to me — ?

VARYA: But you couldn't have traveled alone, darling; not at seventeen!

ANYA: We arrived in Paris, it was cold there

and snowing. I speak terrible French. Mama lived on the fifth floor; I went to see her; there were some French people in her room, ladies, an old priest with his prayer book, and the place was full of tobacco smoke — very dreary. Suddenly I began to feel sorry for Mama, so sorry, I drew her to me, held her close and couldn't let her go. Then Mama kept hugging me, crying — yes —

VARYA (*tearfully*): Don't — oh, don't —

ANYA: Her villa near Menton she had already sold, she had nothing left, nothing. And I didn't have a kopeck left. It was all we could do to get here. And Mama doesn't understand! We sit down to dinner at a station and she orders, insists on the most expensive things and gives the waiters rouble tips. Charlotta does the same. Yasha too demands his share; it's simply dreadful. Mama has her butler, Yasha, we've brought him here —

VARYA: I saw the wretch.

ANYA: Well, how are things? Has the interest on the mortgage been paid?

VARYA: How could we?

ANYA: Oh, my God, my God — !

VARYA: In August the estate is to be sold —

ANYA: My God — !

LOPAHIN (*looking in through the door and mooing like a cow*): Moo-o-o — (*Goes away.*)

VARYA (*tearfully*): I'd land him one like that — (*Shaking her fist.*)

ANYA (*embracing* VARYA *gently*): Varya, has he proposed? (VARYA *shakes her head.*) But he loves you — Why don't you have it out with him, what are you waiting for?

VARYA: I don't think anything will come of it for us. He is very busy, he hasn't any time for me — And doesn't notice me. God knows, it's painful for me to see him — Everybody talks about our marriage, everybody congratulates us, and the truth is, there's nothing to it — it's all like a dream — (*In a different tone.*) You have a brooch looks like a bee.

ANYA (*sadly*): Mama bought it. (*Going toward her room, speaking gaily, like a child.*) And in Paris I went up in a balloon!

VARYA: My darling is back! My precious is back! (DUNYASHA *has returned with the coffee pot and is making coffee.* VARYA *is standing by the door.*) Darling, I'm busy all day long with the house and I go around thinking things. If only you could be married to a rich man, I'd be more at peace too, I would go all by myself

to a hermitage — then to Kiev — to Moscow, and I'd keep going like that from one holy place to another — I would go on and on. Heavenly!

ANYA: The birds are singing in the orchard. What time is it now?

VARYA: It must be after two. It's time you were asleep, darling. (*Going into* ANYA's *room.*) Heavenly!

YASHA (YASHA *enters with a lap robe and a traveling bag. Crossing the stage airily*): May I go through here?

DUNYASHA: We'd hardly recognize you, Yasha; you've changed so abroad!

YASHA: Hm — And who are you?

DUNYASHA: When you left here, I was like that — (*Her hand so high from the floor.*) I'm Dunyasha, Fyodor Kozoyedoff's daughter. You don't remember!

YASHA: Hm — You little peach! (*Looking around before he embraces her; she shrieks and drops a saucer;* YASHA *hurries out.*)

VARYA (*at the door, in a vexed tone*): And what's going on here?

DUNYASHA (*tearfully*): I broke a saucer —

VARYA: That's good luck.

ANYA (*emerging from her room*): We ought to tell Mama beforehand: Petya is here —

VARYA: I told them not to wake him up.

ANYA (*pensively*): Six years ago our father died, a month later our brother Grisha was drowned in the river, such a pretty little boy, just seven. Mama couldn't bear it, she went away, went away without ever looking back — (*Shuddering.*) How I understand her, if she only knew I did. (*A pause.*) And Petya Trofimoff was Grisha's tutor, he might remind —

FIERS (*enter* FIERS; *he is in a jacket and white waistcoat. Going to the coffee urn, busy with it*): The mistress will have her breakfast here — (*Putting on white gloves.*) Is the coffee ready? (*To* DUNYASHA, *sternly.*) You! What about the cream?

DUNYASHA: Oh, my God — (*Hurrying out.*)

FIERS (*busy at the coffee urn*): Oh, you good-for-nothing — ! (*Muttering to himself.*) Come back from Paris — And the master used to go to Paris by coach — (*Laughing.*)

VARYA: Fiers, what are you — ?

FIERS: At your service. (*Joyfully.*) My mistress is back! It's what I've been waiting for! Now I'm ready to die — (*Crying for joy.*)

(LYUBOFF ANDREEVNA, GAYEFF *and* SEMYO-
NOFF-PISHTCHIK *enter;* SEMYONOFF-PISHTCHIK
is in a podyovka of fine cloth and sharovary.
GAYEFF *enters; he makes gestures with his
hands and body as if he were playing billiards.*)

LYUBOFF ANDREEVNA: How is it? Let me
remember — Yellow into the corner! Duplicate
in the middle!

GAYEFF: I cut into the corner. Sister, you
and I slept here in this very room once, and
now I am fifty-one years old, strange as that
may seem —

LOPAHIN: Yes, time passes.

GAYEFF: What?

LOPAHIN: Time, I say, passes.

GAYEFF: And it smells like patchouli here.

ANYA: I'm going to bed. Good night, Mama.
(*Kissing her mother.*)

LYUBOFF ANDREEVNA: My sweet little child.
(*Kissing her hands.*) You're glad you are home?
I still can't get myself together.

ANYA: Good-by, Uncle.

GAYEFF (*kissing her face and hands*): God
be with you. How like your mother you are!
(*To his sister.*) Lyuba, at her age you were
exactly like her.

(ANYA *shakes hands with* LOPAHIN *and*
PISHTCHIK, *goes out and closes the door
behind her.*)

LYUBOFF ANDREEVNA: She's very tired.

PISHTCHIK: It is a long trip, I imagine.

VARYA (*to* LOPAHIN *and* PISHTCHIK): Well,
then, sirs? It's going on three o'clock, time for
gentlemen to be going.

LYUBOFF ANDREEVNA (*laughing*): The same
old Varya. (*Drawing her to her and kissing
her.*) There, I'll drink my coffee, then we'll all
go. (FIERS *puts a small cushion under her
feet.*) Thank you, my dear. I am used to
coffee. Drink it day and night. Thank you, my
dear old soul. (*Kissing* FIERS.)

VARYA: I'll go see if all the things have
come. (*Goes out.*)

LYUBOFF ANDREEVNA: Is it really me sitting
here? (*Laughing.*) I'd like to jump around and
wave my arms. (*Covering her face with her
hands.*) But I may be dreaming! God knows I
love my country, love it deeply, I couldn't look
out of the car window, I just kept crying.
(*Tearfully.*) However, I must drink my coffee.

Thank you, Fiers, thank you, my dear old
friend. I'm so glad you're still alive.

FIERS: Day before yesterday.

GAYEFF: He doesn't hear well.

LOPAHIN: And I must leave right now. It's
nearly five o'clock in the morning, for Kharkov. What a nuisance! I wanted to look at
you — talk — You are as beautiful as ever.

PISHTCHIK (*breathing heavily*): Even more
beautiful — In your Paris clothes — It's a feast
for the eyes —

LOPAHIN: Your brother, Leonid Andreevich
here, says I'm a boor, a peasant money grubber, but that's all the same to me, absolutely.
Let him say it. All I wish is you'd trust me as
you used to, and your wonderful, touching eyes
would look at me as they did. Merciful God!
My father was a serf; belonged to your grandfather and your father; but you, your own self,
you did so much for me once that I've
forgotten all that and love you like my own
kin — more than my kin.

LYUBOFF ANDREEVNA: I can't sit still — I
can't. (*Jumping up and walking about in great
excitement.*) I'll never live through this happiness — Laugh at me, I'm silly — My own little
bookcase — ! (*Kissing the bookcase.*) My little
table!

GAYEFF: And in your absence the nurse here
died.

LYUBOFF ANDREEVNA (*sitting down and
drinking coffee*): Yes, may she rest in Heaven!
They wrote me.

GAYEFF: And Anastasy died. Cross-eyed Pe-
trushka left me and lives in town now at the
police officer's. (*Taking out of his pocket a
box of hard candy and sucking a piece.*)

PISHTCHIK: My daughter, Dashenka — sends
you her greetings —

LOPAHIN: I want to tell you something very
pleasant, cheerful. (*Glancing at his watch.*)
I'm going right away. There's no time for
talking. Well, I'll make it two or three words.
As you know, your cherry orchard is to be sold
for your debts; the auction is set for August
twenty-second, but don't you worry, my dear,
you just sleep in peace, there's a way out of it.
Here's my plan. Please listen to me. Your
estate is only thirteen miles from town.
They've run the railroad by it. Now if the
cherry orchard and the land along the river
were cut up into building lots and leased for
summer cottages, you'd have at the very lowest

twenty-five thousand roubles per year income.

GAYEFF: Excuse me, what rot!

LYUBOFF ANDREEVNA: I don't quite understand you, Yermolay Alexeevich.

LOPAHIN: At the very least you will get from the summer residents twenty-five roubles per year for a two-and-a-half acre lot and if you post a notice right off, I'll bet you anything that by autumn you won't have a single patch of land free, everything will be taken. In a word, my congratulations, you are saved. The location is wonderful, the river's so deep. Except, of course, it all needs to be tidied up, cleared — For instance, let's say, tear all the old buildings down and this house, which is no good any more, and cut down the old cherry orchard —

LYUBOFF ANDREEVNA: Cut down? My dear, forgive me, you don't understand at all. If there's one thing in the whole province that's interesting — not to say remarkable — it's our cherry orchard.

LOPAHIN: The only remarkable thing about this cherry orchard is that it's very big. There's a crop of cherries once every two years and even that's hard to get rid of. Nobody buys them.

GAYEFF: This orchard is even mentioned in the encyclopedia.

LOPAHIN (glancing at his watch): If we don't cook up something and don't get somewhere, the cherry orchard and the entire estate will be sold at auction on the twenty-second of August. Do get it settled then! I swear there is no other way out. Not a one!

FIERS: There was a time, forty-fifty years ago when the cherries were dried, soaked, pickled, cooked into jam and it used to be —

GAYEFF: Keep quiet, Fiers.

FIERS: And it used to be that the dried cherries were shipped by the wagon-load to Moscow and to Kharkov. And the money there was! And the dried cherries were soft then, juicy, sweet, fragrant — They had a way of treating them then —

LYUBOFF ANDREEVNA: And where is that way now?

FIERS: They have forgotten it. Nobody remembers it.

PISHTCHIK (to LYUBOFF ANDREEVNA): What's happening in Paris? How is everything? Did you eat frogs?

LYUBOFF ANDREEVNA: I ate crocodiles.

PISHTCHIK: Think of it — !

LOPAHIN: Up to now in the country there have been only the gentry and the peasants, but now in summer the villa people too are coming in. All the towns, even the least big ones, are surrounded with cottages. In about twenty years very likely the summer resident will multiply enormously. He merely drinks tea on the porch now, but it might well happen that on this two-and-a-half acre lot of his, he'll go in for farming, and then your cherry orchard would be happy, rich, splendid —

GAYEFF (getting hot): What rot!

(Enter VARYA and YASHA.)

VARYA: Here, Mama. Two telegrams for you. (Choosing a key and opening the old bookcase noisily.) Here they are.

LYUBOFF ANDREEVNA: From Paris (Tearing up the telegrams without reading them.) Paris, that's all over —

GAYEFF: Do you know how old this bookcase is, Lyuba? A week ago I pulled out the bottom drawer and looked, and there the figures were burned on it. The bookcase was made exactly a hundred years ago. How's that? Eh? You might celebrate its jubilee. It's an inanimate object, but all the same, be that as it may, it's a bookcase.

PISHTCHIK (in astonishment): A hundred years — ! Think of it — !

GAYEFF: Yes — quite something — (Shaking the bookcase.) Dear, honored bookcase! I saluted your existence, which for more than a hundred years has been directed toward the clear ideals of goodness and justice; your silent appeal to fruitful endeavor has not flagged in all the course of a hundred years, sustaining (tearfully) through the generations of our family, our courage and our faith in a better future and nurturing in us ideals of goodness and of a social consciousness.

(A pause.)

LOPAHIN: Yes.

LYUBOFF ANDREEVNA: You're the same as ever, Lenya.

GAYEFF (slightly embarrassed): Carom to the right into the corner pocket. I cut into the side pocket!

LOPAHIN (glancing at his watch): Well, it's time for me to go.

YASHA (handing medicine to LYUBOFF ANDREEVNA): Perhaps you'll take the pills now —

PISHTCHIK: You should never take medicaments, dear madam — They do neither harm nor good — Hand them here, dearest lady. (*He takes the pillbox, shakes the pills out into his palm, blows on them, puts them in his mouth and washes them down with kvass.*) There! Now!

LYUBOFF ANDREEVNA (*startled*): Why, you've lost your mind!

PISHTCHIK: I took all the pills.

LOPAHIN: Such a glutton!

(*Everyone laughs.*)

FIERS: The gentleman stayed with us during Holy Week, he ate half a bucket of pickles — (*Muttering.*)

LYUBOFF ANDREEVNA: What is he muttering about?

VARYA: He's been muttering like that for three years. We're used to it.

YASHA: In his dotage.

(CHARLOTTA IVANOVNA *in a white dress — she is very thin, her corset laced very tight — with a lorgnette at her belt, crosses the stage.*)

LOPAHIN: Excuse me, Charlotta Ivanovna, I haven't had a chance yet to welcome you. (*Trying to kiss her hand.*)

CHARLOTTA (*drawing her hand away*): If I let you kiss my hand, 'twould be my elbow next, then my shoulder —

LOPAHIN: No luck for me today. (*Everyone laughs.*) Charlotta Ivanovna, show us a trick!

CHARLOTTA: No. I want to go to bed. (*Exit.*)

LOPAHIN: In three weeks we shall see each other. (*Kissing* LYUBOFF ANDREEVNA'S *hand.*) Till then, good-by. It's time. (*To* GAYEFF.) See you soon. (*Kissing* PISHTCHIK.) See you soon. (*Shaking* VARYA'S *hand, then* FIERS' *and* YASHA'S.) I don't feel like going. (*To* LYUBOFF ANDREEVNA.) If you think it over and make up your mind about the summer cottages, let me know and I'll arrange a loan of something like fifty thousand roubles. Think it over seriously.

VARYA (*angrily*): Do go on, anyhow, will you!

LOPAHIN: I'm going, I'm going — (*Exit.*)

GAYEFF: Boor. However, pardon — Varya is going to marry him, it's Varya's little fiancé.

VARYA: Don't talk too much, Uncle.

LYUBOFF ANDREEVNA: Well, Varya, I should be very glad. He's a good man.

PISHTCHIK: A man, one must say truthfully — A most worthy — And my Dashenka — says also that — she says all sorts of things — (*Snoring but immediately waking up.*) Nevertheless, dearest lady, oblige me — With a loan of two hundred and forty roubles — Tomorrow the interest on my mortgage has got to be paid —

VARYA (*startled*): There's not any money, none at all.

LYUBOFF ANDREEVNA: Really, I haven't got anything.

PISHTCHIK: I'll find it, somehow. (*Laughing.*) I never give up hope. There, I think to myself, all is lost, I am ruined and lo and behold — a railroad is put through my land and — they paid me. And then, just watch, something else will turn up — if not today, then tomorrow — Dashenka will win two hundred thousand — She has a ticket.

LYUBOFF ANDREEVNA: We've finished the coffee, now we can go to bed.

FIERS (*brushing* GAYEFF'S *clothes, reprovingly*): You put on the wrong trousers again. What am I going to do with you!

VARYA (*softly*): Anya is asleep. (*Opening the window softly.*) Already the sun's rising — it's not cold. Look, Mama! What beautiful trees! My Lord, what air! The starlings are singing!

GAYEFF (*opening another window*): The orchard is all white. You haven't forgotten, Lyuba? That long lane there runs straight — as a strap stretched out. It glistens on moonlight nights. Do you remember? You haven't forgotten it?

LYUBOFF ANDREEVNA (*looking out of the window on to the orchard*): Oh, my childhood, my innocence! I slept in this nursery and looked out on the orchard from here, every morning happiness awoke with me, it was just as it is now, then, nothing has changed. (*Laughing with joy.*) All, all white! Oh, my orchard! After a dark, rainy autumn and cold winter, you are young again and full of happiness. The heavenly angels have not deserted you — If I only could lift the weight from my breast, from my shoulders, if I could only forget my past!

GAYEFF: Yes, and the orchard will be sold for debt, strange as that may seem.

LYUBOFF ANDREEVNA: Look, our dear mother is walking through the orchard — In a white dress! (*Laughing happily.*) It's she.

GAYEFF: Where?

VARYA: God be with you, Mama!

LYUBOFF ANDREEVNA: There's not anybody, it only seemed so. To the right, as you turn to the summerhouse, a little white tree is leaning there, looks like a woman — (*Enter* TROFIMOFF, *in a student's uniform, well worn, and glasses.*) What a wonderful orchard! The white masses of blossoms, the sky all blue.

TROFIMOFF: Lyuboff Andreevna! (*She looks around at him.*) I will just greet you and go immediately. (*Kissing her hand warmly.*) I was told to wait until morning, but I hadn't the patience —

(LYUBOFF ANDREEVNA *looks at him puzzled.*)

VARYA (*tearfully*): This is Petya Trofimoff —

TROFIMOFF: Petya Trofimoff, the former tutor of your Grisha — Have I really changed so?

(LYUBOFF ANDREEVNA *embraces him; and crying quietly.*)

GAYEFF (*embarrassed*): There, there, Lyuba.

VARYA (*crying*): I told you, Petya, to wait till tomorrow.

LYUBOFF ANDREEVNA: My Grisha — My boy — Grisha — Son —

VARYA: What can we do, Mama? It's God's will.

TROFIMOFF (*in a low voice, tearfully*): There, there —

LYUBOFF ANDREEVNA (*weeping softly*): My boy was lost, drowned — Why? Why, my friend? (*More quietly.*) Anya is asleep there, and I am talking so loud — Making so much noise — But why, Petya? Why have you lost your looks? Why do you look so much older?

TROFIMOFF: A peasant woman on the train called me a mangy-looking gentleman.

LYUBOFF ANDREEVNA: You were a mere boy then, a charming young student, and now your hair's not very thick any more and you wear glasses. Are you really a student still? (*Going to the door.*)

TROFIMOFF: Very likely I'll be a perennial student.

LYUBOFF ANDREEVNA (*kissing her brother, then* VARYA): Well, go to bed — You've grown older too, Leonid.

PISHTCHIK (*following her*): So that's it, we are going to bed now. Oh, my gout! I'm staying here — I'd like, Lyuboff Andreevna, my soul, tomorrow morning — Two hundred and forty roubles —

GAYEFF: He's still at it.

PISHTCHIK: Two hundred and forty roubles — To pay interest on the mortgage.

LYUBOFF ANDREEVNA: I haven't any money, my dove.

PISHTCHIK: I'll pay it back, my dear — It's a trifling sum —

LYUBOFF ANDREEVNA: Oh, very well, Leonid will give — You give it to him, Leonid.

GAYEFF: Oh, certainly, I'll give it to him. Hold out your pockets.

LYUBOFF ANDREEVNA: What can we do, give it, he needs it — He'll pay it back.

(LYUBOFF ANDREEVNA, TROFIMOFF, PISHTCHIK *and* FIERS *go out.* GAYEFF, VARYA *and* YASHA *remain.*)

GAYEFF: My sister hasn't yet lost her habit of throwing money away. (*To* YASHA.) Get away, my good fellow, you smell like hens.

YASHA (*with a grin*): And you are just the same as you used to be, Leonid Andreevich.

GAYEFF: What? (*To* VARYA.) What did he say?

VARYA (*to* YASHA): Your mother has come from the village, she's been sitting in the servants' hall every since yesterday, she wants to see you —

YASHA: The devil take her!

VARYA: Ach, shameless creature!

YASHA: A lot I need her! She might have come tomorrow. (*Goes out.*)

VARYA: Mama is just the same as she was, she hasn't changed at all. If she could, she'd give away everything she has.

GAYEFF: Yes — If many remedies are prescribed for an illness, you may know the illness is incurable. I keep thinking, I rack my brains, I have many remedies, a great many, and that means, really, I haven't any at all. It would be fine to inherit a fortune from somebody, it would be fine to marry off our Anya to a very rich man, it would be fine to go to Yaroslavl and try our luck with our old aunt, the Countess. Auntie is very, very rich.

VARYA (*crying*): If God would only help us!

GAYEFF: Don't bawl! Auntie is very rich but she doesn't like us. To begin with, Sister married a lawyer, not a nobleman — (ANYA *appears at the door.*) Married not a nobleman and behaved herself, you could say, not very virtuously. She is good, kind, nice, I love her very much, but no matter how much you allow for the extenuating circumstances, you must admit she's a depraved woman. You feel it in her slightest movement.

VARYA (*whispering*): Anya is standing in the door there.

GAYEFF: What? (*A pause.*) It's amazing, something got in my right eye. I am beginning to see poorly. And on Thursday, when I was in the District Court —

(ANYA *enters.*)

VARYA: But why aren't you asleep, Anya?

ANYA: I don't feel like sleeping. I can't.

GAYEFF: My little girl — (*Kissing* ANYA's *face and hands.*) My child — (*Tearfully.*) You are not my niece, you are my angel, you are everything to me. Believe me, believe —

ANYA: I believe you, Uncle. Everybody loves you, respects you — But dear Uncle, you must keep quiet, just keep quiet — What were you saying, just now, about my mother, about your own sister? What did you say that for?

GAYEFF: Yes, yes — (*Putting her hand up over his face.*) Really, it's terrible! My God! Oh, God, save me! And today I made a speech to the bookcase — So silly! And it was only when I finished it that I could see it was silly.

VARYA: It's true, Uncle, you ought to keep quiet. Just keep quiet. That's all.

ANYA: If you kept quiet, you'd have more peace.

GAYEFF: I'll keep quiet. (*Kissing* ANYA's *and* VARYA's *hands.*) I'll keep quiet. Only this, it's about business. On Thursday I was in the District Court; well, a few of us gathered around and a conversation began about this and that, about lots of things; apparently it will be possible to arrange a loan on a promissory note to pay the bank the interest due.

VARYA: If the Lord would only help us!

GAYEFF: Tuesday I shall go and talk it over again. (*To* VARYA.) Don't bawl! (*To* ANYA.) Your mother will talk to Lopahin; of course, he won't refuse her ... And as soon as you rest up, you will go to Yaroslavl to your great-aunt, the Countess. There, that's how we will move from three directions, and the business is in the bag. We'll pay the interest. I am convinced of that — (*Putting a hard candy in his mouth.*) On my honor I'll swear, by anything you like, that the estate shall not be sold! (*Excitedly.*) By my happiness, I swear! Here's my hand, call me a worthless, dishonorable man, if I allow it to come up for auction! With all my soul I swear it!

ANYA (*a quieter mood returns to her; she is happy*): How good you are, Uncle, how clever! (*Embracing her uncle.*) I feel easy now! I feel easy! I'm happy!

FIERS (FIERS *enters, reproachfully*): Leonid Andreevich, have you no fear of God? When are you going to bed?

GAYEFF: Right away, right away. You may go, Fiers. For this once I'll undress myself. Well, children, beddy bye — More details tomorrow, and now, go to bed. (*Kissing* ANYA *and* VARYA.) I am a man of the eighties — It is a period that's not admired, but I can say, nevertheless, that I've suffered no little for my convictions in the course of my life. It is not for nothing that the peasant loves me. One must know the peasant! One must know from what —

ANYA: Again, Uncle!

VARYA: You, Uncle dear, keep quiet.

FIERS (*angrily*): Leonid Andreevich!

GAYEFF: I'm coming, I'm coming — Go to bed. A double bank into the side pocket! A clean shot — (*Goes out,* FIERS *hobbling after him.*)

ANYA: I feel easy now. I don't feel like going to Yaroslavl; I don't like Great-aunt; but still I feel easy. Thanks to Uncle. (*Sits down.*)

VARYA: I must get to sleep. I'm going. And there was unpleasantness here during your absence. In the old servants' quarters, as you know, live only the old servants: Yephemushka, Polya, Yevstignay, well, and Karp. They began to let every sort of creature spend the night with them — I didn't say anything. But then I hear they've spread the rumor that I'd given orders to feed them nothing but beans. Out of stinginess, you see — And all that from Yevstignay — Very well, I think to myself. If that's the way it is, I think to myself, then you just wait. I call in Yevstignay — (*Yawning.*) He comes — How is it, I say, that you, Yevstignay — You're such a fool — (*Glancing at* ANYA.) Anitchka — (*A pause.*) Asleep! (*Takes* ANYA *by her arm.*) Let's go to bed — Come on! — (*Leading her.*) My little darling fell asleep! Come on — (*They* go. *Far away beyond the orchard a shepherd is playing on a pipe.* TROFIMOFF *walks across the stage and, seeing* VARYA *and* ANYA, *stops.*) Shh — She is asleep — asleep — Let's go, dear.

ANYA (*softly, half dreaming*): I'm so tired — All the bells! — Uncle — dear — And Mama and Uncle — Varya.

VARYA: Come on, my dear, come on. (*They go into* ANYA's *room.*)

TROFIMOFF (*tenderly*): My little sun! My spring!

ACT II

A field. An old chapel, long abandoned, with crooked walls, near it a well, big stones that apparently were once tombstones, and an old bench. A road to the estate of GAYEFF *can be seen. On one side poplars rise, casting their shadows, the cherry orchard begins there. In the distance a row of telegraph poles; and far, far away, faintly traced on the horizon, is a large town, visible only in the clearest weather. The sun will soon be down.* CHARLOTTA, YASHA *and* DUNYASHA *are sitting on the bench;* EPIHODOFF *is standing near and playing the guitar; everyone sits lost in thought.* CHARLOTTA *wears an old peak cap (fourrage); she has taken a rifle from off her shoulders and is adjusting the buckle on the strap.*

CHARLOTTA (*pensively*): I have no proper passport, I don't know how old I am — it always seems to me I'm very young. When I was a little girl, my father and mother traveled from fair to fair and gave performances, very good ones. And I did *salto mortale* and different tricks. And when Papa and Mama died, a German lady took me to live with her and began teaching me. Good. I grew up. And became a governess. But where I came from and who I am I don't know — Who my parents were, perhaps they weren't even married — I don't know. (*Taking a cucumber out of her pocket and beginning to eat it.*) I don't know a thing. (*A pause.*) I'd like so much to talk but there's not anybody. I haven't anybody.

EPIHODOFF (*playing the guitar and singing*): "What care I for the noisy world, what care I

for friends and foes." — How pleasant it is to play the mandolin!

DUNYASHA: That's a guitar, not a mandolin. (*Looking into a little mirror and powdering her face.*)

EPIHODOFF: For a madman who is in love this is a mandolin — (*Singing.*) "If only my heart were warm with the fire of requited love."

(YASHA *sings with him.*)

CHARLOTTA: How dreadfully these people sing — Phooey! Like jackals.

DUNYASHA (*to* YASHA): All the same what happiness to have been abroad.

YASHA: Yes, of course. I cannot disagree with you. (*Yawning and then lighting a cigar.*)

EPIHODOFF: That's easily understood. Abroad everything long since attained its complete development.

YASHA: That's obvious.

EPIHODOFF: I am a cultured man. I read all kinds of remarkable books, but the trouble is I cannot discover my own inclinations, whether to live or to shoot myself, but nevertheless, I always carry a revolver on me. Here it is — (*Showing a revolver.*)

CHARLOTTA: That's done. Now I am going. (*Slinging the rifle over her shoulder.*) You are a very clever man, Epihodoff, and a very terrible one; the women must love you madly. Brrrr-r-r-r! (*Going.*) These clever people are all so silly, I haven't anybody to talk with. I'm always alone, alone, I have nobody and — Who I am, why I am, is unknown — (*Goes out without hurrying.*)

EPIHODOFF: Strictly speaking, not touching on other subjects, I must state about myself, in passing, that fate treats me mercilessly, as a storm does a small ship. If, let us suppose, I am mistaken, then why, to mention one instance, do I wake up this morning, look and there on my chest is a spider of terrific size — There, like that. (*Showing the size with both hands.*) And also I take some kvass to drink and in it I find something in the highest degree indecent, such as a cockroach. (*A pause.*) Have you read Buckle? (*A pause.*) I desire to trouble you, Avdotya Feodorovna, with a couple of words.

DUNYASHA: Speak.

EPIHODOFF: I have a desire to speak with you alone — (*Sighing.*)

DUNYASHA (*embarrassed*): Very well — But bring me my cape first — by the cupboard — It's rather damp here —

EPIHODOFF: Very well — I'll fetch it — Now I know what I should do with my revolver — (*Takes the guitar and goes out playing.*)

YASHA: Twenty-two misfortunes! Between us he's a stupid man, it must be said. (*Yawning.*)

DUNYASHA: God forbid he should shoot himself. (*A pause.*) I've grown so uneasy, I'm always fretting. I was only a girl when I was taken into the master's house, and now I've lost the habit of simple living — and here are my hands white, white as a lady's. I've become so delicate, fragile, ladylike, afraid of everything — Frightfully so. And, Yasha, if you deceive me, I don't know what will happen to my nerves.

YASHA (*kissing her*): You little cucumber! Of course every girl must behave properly. What I dislike above everything is for a girl to conduct herself badly.

DUNYASHA: I have come to love you passionately, you are educated, you can discuss anything. (*A pause.*)

YASHA (*yawning*): Yes, sir — To my mind it is like this: If a girl loves someone, it means she is immoral. (*A pause.*) It is pleasant to smoke a cigar in the clear air — (*Listening.*) They are coming here — It is the ladies and gentlemen —

(DUNYASHA *impulsively embraces him.*)

YASHA: Go to the house, as though you had been to bathe in the river, go by this path, otherwise, they might meet you and suspect me of making a rendezvous with you. That I cannot tolerate.

DUNYASHA (*with a little cough*): Your cigar has given me the headache. (*Goes out.*)

(YASHA *remains, sitting near the chapel.* LYUBOFF ANDREEVNA, GAYEFF *and* LOPAHIN *enter.*)

LOPAHIN: We must decide definitely, time doesn't wait. Why, the matter's quite simple. Are you willing to lease your land for summer cottages or are you not? Answer in one word, yes or no? Just one word!

LYUBOFF ANDREEVNA: Who is it smokes those disgusting cigars out here — ? (*Sitting down.*)

GAYEFF: The railroad running so near is a great convenience. (*Sitting down.*) We made a trip to town and lunched there — Yellow in the side pocket! Perhaps I should go in the house first and play one game —

LYUBOFF ANDREEVNA: You'll have time.

LOPAHIN: Just one word! (*Imploringly.*) Do give me your answer!

GAYEFF (*yawning*): What?

LYUBOFF ANDREEVNA (*looking in her purse*): Yesterday there was lots of money in it. Today there's very little. My poor Varya! For the sake of economy she feeds everybody milk soup, and in the kitchen the old people get nothing but beans, and here I spend money — senselessly — (*Dropping her purse and scattering gold coins.*) There they go scattering! (*She is vexed.*)

YASHA: Allow me, I'll pick them up in a second. (*Picking up the coins.*)

LYUBOFF ANDREEVNA: If you will, Yasha. And why did I go in town for lunch — ? Your restaurant with its music is trashy, the tablecloths smell of soap — Why drink so much, Lyonya? Why eat so much? Why talk so much? Today in the restaurant you were talking a lot again, and all of it beside the point. About the seventies, about the decadents. And to whom? Talking to waiters about the decadents!

LOPAHIN: Yes.

GAYEFF (*waving his hand*): I am incorrigible, that's evident — (*To* YASHA, *irritably.*) What is it? — You are forever swirling around in front of us!

YASHA (*laughing*): I cannot hear your voice without laughing.

GAYEFF (*to his sister*): Either I or he —

LYUBOFF ANDREEVNA: Go away, Yasha. Go on —

YASHA (*giving* LYUBOFF ANDREEVNA *her purse*): I am going right away. (*Barely suppressing his laughter.*) This minute. (*Goes out.*)

LOPAHIN: The rich Deriganoff intends to buy your estate. They say he is coming personally to the auction.

LYUBOFF ANDREEVNA: And where did you hear that?

LOPAHIN: In town they are saying it.

GAYEFF: Our Yaroslavl aunt promised to send us something, but when and how much she will send, nobody knows —

LOPAHIN: How much will she send? A hundred thousand? Two hundred?

LYUBOFF ANDREEVNA: Well — maybe ten, fifteen thousand — we'd be thankful for that.

LOPAHIN: Excuse me, but such light-minded people as you are, such odd, unbusinesslike people, I never saw. You are told in plain Russian that your estate is being sold up and you just don't seem to take it in.

LYUBOFF ANDREEVNA: But what are we to do? Tell us what?

LOPAHIN: I tell you every day. Every day I tell you the same thing. Both the cherry orchard and the land have got to be leased for summer cottages, it has to be done right now, quick — The auction is right under your noses. Do understand! Once you finally decide that there are to be summer cottages, you will get all the money you want, and then you'll be saved.

LYUBOFF ANDREEVNA: Summer cottages and summer residents — it is so trivial, excuse me.

GAYEFF: I absolutely agree with you.

LOPAHIN: I'll either burst out crying, or scream, or faint. I can't bear it! You are torturing me! (*To* GAYEFF.) You're a perfect old woman!

GAYEFF: What?

LOPAHIN: A perfect old woman! (*About to go.*)

LYUBOFF ANDREEVNA (*alarmed*): No, don't go, stay, my lamb, I beg you. Perhaps we will think of something!

LOPAHIN: What is there to think about?

LYUBOFF ANDREEVNA: Don't go, I beg you. With you here it is more cheerful anyhow — (*A pause.*) I keep waiting for something, as if the house were about to tumble down on our heads.

GAYEFF (*deep in thought*): Double into the corner pocket — Bank into the side pocket —

LYUBOFF ANDREEVNA: We have sinned so much —

LOPAHIN: What sins have you — ?

GAYEFF (*puts a hard candy into his mouth*): They say I've eaten my fortune up in hard candies — (*Laughing.*)

LYUBOFF ANDREEVNA: Oh, my sins — I've always thrown money around like mad, recklessly, and I married a man who accumulated nothing but debts. My husband died from champagne — he drank fearfully — and to my misfortune I fell in love with another man. I lived with him, and just at that time — it was my first punishment — a blow over the head:

right here in the river my boy was drowned and I went abroad — went away for good, never to return, never to see this river again — I shut my eyes, ran away, beside myself, and he after me — mercilessly, brutally. I bought a villa near Menton, because he fell ill there, and for three years I knew no rest day or night, the sick man exhausted me, my soul dried up. And last year when the villa was sold for debts, I went to Paris and there he robbed me of everything, threw me over, took up with another woman; I tried to poison myself — so stupid, so shameful — And suddenly I was seized with longing for Russia, for my own country, for my little girl — (*Wiping away her tears.*) Lord, Lord, have mercy, forgive me my sins! Don't punish me any more! (*Getting a telegram out of her pocket.*) I got this today from Paris, he asks forgiveness, begs me to return — (*Tears up the telegram.*) That sounds like music somewhere. (*Listening.*)

GAYEFF: It is our famous Jewish orchestra. You remember, four violins, a flute and double bass.

LYUBOFF ANDREEVNA: Does it still exist? We ought to get hold of it sometime and give a party.

LOPAHIN (*listening*): Can't hear it — (*Singing softly.*) "And for money the Germans will frenchify a Russian." (*Laughing.*) What a play I saw yesterday at the theatre, very funny!

LYUBOFF ANDREEVNA: And most likely there was nothing funny about it. You shouldn't look at plays, but look oftener at yourselves. How gray all your lives are, what a lot of idle things you say!

LOPAHIN: That's true. It must be said frankly this life of ours is idiotic — (*A pause.*) My father was a peasant, an idiot, he understood nothing, he taught me nothing, he just beat me in his drunken fits and always with a stick. At bottom I am just as big a dolt and idiot as he was. I wasn't taught anything, my handwriting is vile, I write like a pig — I am ashamed for people to see it.

LYUBOFF ANDREEVNA: You ought to get married, my friend.

LOPAHIN: Yes — That's true.

LYUBOFF ANDREEVNA: To our Varya, perhaps. She is a good girl.

LOPAHIN: Yes.

LYUBOFF ANDREEVNA: She comes from simple people, and she works all day long, but the main thing is she loves you. And you, too, have liked her a long time.

LOPAHIN: Why not? I am not against it — She's a good girl. (*A pause.*)

GAYEFF: They are offering me a position in a bank. Six thousand a year — Have you heard that?

LYUBOFF ANDREEVNA: Not you! You stay where you are —

FIERS (FIERS *enters, bringing an overcoat. To* GAYEFF): Pray, Sir, put this on, it's damp.

GAYEFF (*putting on the overcoat*): You're a pest, old man.

FIERS: That's all right — This morning you went off without letting me know. (*Looking him over.*)

LYUBOFF ANDREEVNA: How old you've grown, Fiers!

FIERS: At your service.

LOPAHIN: She says you've grown very old!

FIERS: I've lived a long time. They were planning to marry me off before your papa was born. (*Laughing.*) And at the time the serfs were freed I was already the head footman. I didn't want to be freed then, I stayed with the masters — (*A pause.*) And I remember, everybody was happy, but what they were happy about they didn't know themselves.

LOPAHIN: In the old days it was fine. At least they flogged.

FIERS (*not hearing*): But, of course. The peasants stuck to the masters, the masters stuck to the peasants, and now everything is all smashed up, you can't tell about anything.

GAYEFF: Keep still, Fiers. Tomorrow I must go to town. They have promised to introduce me to a certain general who might make us a loan.

LOPAHIN: Nothing will come of it. And you can rest assured you won't pay the interest.

LYUBOFF ANDREEVNA: He's just raving on. There aren't any such generals.

(TROFIMOFF, ANYA *and* VARYA *enter.*)

GAYEFF: Here they come.

ANYA: There is Mama sitting there.

LYUBOFF ANDREEVNA (*tenderly*): Come, come — My darlings — (*Embracing* ANYA *and* VARYA.) If you only knew how I love you both! Come sit by me — there — like that.

(*Everybody sits down.*)

LOPAHIN: Our perennial student is always strolling with the young ladies.

TROFIMOFF: It's none of your business.

LOPAHIN: He will soon be fifty and he's still a student.

TROFIMOFF: Stop your stupid jokes.

LOPAHIN: But why are you so peevish, you queer duck?

TROFIMOFF: Don't you pester me.

LOPAHIN (*laughing*): Permit me to ask you, what do you make of me?

TROFIMOFF: Yermolay Alexeevich, I make this of you: you are a rich man, you'll soon be a millionaire. Just as it is in the metabolism of nature, a wild beast is needed to eat up everything that comes his way; so you, too, are needed.

(*Everyone laughs.*)

VARYA: Petya, you'd better tell us about the planets.

LYUBOFF ANDREEVNA: No, let's go on with yesterday's conversation.

TROFIMOFF: What was it about?

GAYEFF: About the proud man.

TROFIMOFF: We talked a long time yesterday, but didn't get anywhere. In a proud man, in your sense of the word, there is something mystical. Maybe you are right, from your standpoint, but if we are to discuss it in simple terms, without whimsy, then what pride can there be, is there any sense in it, if man physiologically is poorly constructed, if in the great majority he is crude, unintelligent, profoundly miserable. One must stop admiring oneself. One must only work.

GAYEFF: All the same, you will die.

TROFIMOFF: Who knows? And what does it mean — you will die? Man may have a hundred senses, and when he dies only the five that are known to us may perish, and the remaining ninety-five go on living.

LYUBOFF ANDREEVNA: How clever you are, Petya!

LOPAHIN (*ironically*): Terribly!

TROFIMOFF: Humanity goes forward, perfecting its powers. Everything that's unattainable now will some day become familiar, understandable; it is only that one must work and must help with all one's might those who seek the truth. With us in Russia so far only a very few work. The great majority of the intelligentsia that I know are looking for nothing, doing nothing, and as yet have no capacity for work. They call themselves intelligentsia, are free and easy with the servants, treat the peasants like animals, educate themselves poorly, read nothing seriously, do absolutely nothing; about science they just talk and about art they understand very little. Every one of them is serious, all have stern faces; they all talk of nothing but important things, philosophize, and all the time everybody can see that the workmen eat abominably, sleep without any pillows, thirty or forty to a room, and everywhere there are bedbugs, stench, dampness, moral uncleanness — And apparently with us, all the fine talk is only to divert the attention of ourselves and of others. Show me where we have the day nurseries they are always talking so much about, where are the reading rooms? They only write of these in novels, for the truth is there are not any at all. There is only filth, vulgarity, orientalism — I am afraid of very serious faces and dislike them. I'm afraid of serious conversations. Rather than that let's just keep still.

LOPAHIN: You know I get up before five o'clock in the morning and work from morning till night. Well, I always have money, my own and other people's, on hand, and I see what the people around me are. One has only to start doing something to find out how few honest and decent people there are. At times when I can't go to sleep, I think: Lord, thou gavest us immense forests, unbounded fields and the widest horizons, and living in the midst of them we should indeed be giants —

LYUBOFF ANDREEVNA: You feel the need for giants — They are good only in fairy tales, anywhere else they only frighten us.

(*At the back of the stage* EPIHODOFF *passes by, playing the guitar.*)

LYUBOFF ANDREEVNA (*lost in thought*): Epihodoff is coming —

ANYA (*lost in thought*): Epihodoff is coming.

GAYEFF: The sun has set, ladies and gentlemen.

TROFIMOFF: Yes.

GAYEFF (*not loud and as if he were declaiming*): Oh, Nature, wonderful, you gleam with eternal radiance, beautiful and indifferent, you, whom we call Mother, combine in yourself both life and death, you give life and you take it away.

VARYA (*beseechingly*): Uncle!

ANYA: Uncle, you're doing it again!

TROFIMOFF: You'd better bank the yellow into the side pocket.

GAYEFF: I'll be quiet, quiet.

(*All sit absorbed in their thoughts. There is only the silence.* FIERS *is heard muttering to himself softly. Suddenly a distant sound is heard, as if from the sky, like the sound of a snapped string, dying away, mournful.*)

LYUBOFF ANDREEVNA: What's that?

LOPAHIN: I don't know. Somewhere far off in a mine shaft a bucket fell. But somewhere very far off.

GAYEFF: And it may be some bird — like a heron.

TROFIMOFF: Or an owl —

LYUBOFF ANDREEVNA (*shivering*): It's unpleasant, somehow. (*A pause.*)

FIERS: Before the disaster it was like that. The owl hooted and the samovar hummed without stopping, both.

GAYEFF: Before what disaster?

FIERS: Before the emancipation. (*A pause.*)

LYUBOFF ANDREEVNA: You know, my friends, let's go. Twilight is falling. (*To* ANYA.) You have tears in your eyes — What is it, my dear little girl? (*Embracing her.*)

ANYA: It's just that, Mama. It's nothing.

TROFIMOFF: Somebody is coming.

(*A* STRANGER *appears in a shabby white cap, and an overcoat; he is a little drunk.*)

THE STRANGER: Allow me to ask you, can I go straight through here to the station?

GAYEFF: You can. Go by that road.

THE STRANGER: I am heartily grateful to you. (*Coughing.*) The weather is splendid — (*Declaiming.*) Brother of mine, suffering brother — Go out to the Volga, whose moans — (*To* VARYA.) Mademoiselle, grant a hungry Russian man some thirty kopecks —

(VARYA *is frightened and gives a shriek.*)

LOPAHIN (*angrily*): There's a limit to everything.

LYUBOFF ANDREEVNA (*flustered*): Take this — Here's this for you — (*Searching in her purse.*) No silver — It's all the same, here's a gold piece for you —

THE STRANGER: I am heartily grateful to you. (*Goes out. Laughter.*)

VARYA (*frightened*): I'm going — I'm going — Oh, Mama, you poor little Mama! There's nothing in the house for people to eat, and you gave him a gold piece.

LYUBOFF ANDREEVNA: What is to be done with me, so silly? I shall give you all I have in the house. Yermolay Alexeevich, you will lend me some this once more! —

LOPAHIN: Agreed.

LYUBOFF ANDREEVNA: Let's go, ladies and gentlemen, it's time. And here, Varya, we have definitely made a match for you, I congratulate you.

VARYA (*through her tears*): Mama, that's not something to joke about.

LOPAHIN: Achmelia, get thee to a nunnery.

GAYEFF: And my hands are trembling; it is a long time since I have played billiards.

LOPAHIN: Achmelia, oh nymph, in thine orisons be all my sins remember'd —

LYUBOFF ANDREEVNA: Let's go, my dear friends, it will soon be suppertime.

VARYA: He frightened me. My heart is thumping so!

LOPAHIN: I remind you, ladies and gentlemen: August twenty-second the cherry orchard will be auctioned off. Think about that! — Think! —

(*All go out except* TROFIMOFF *and* ANYA.)

ANYA (*laughing*): My thanks to the stranger, he frightened Varya, now we are alone.

TROFIMOFF: Varya is afraid we might begin to love each other and all day long she won't leave us to ourselves. With her narrow mind she cannot understand that we are above love. To sidestep the petty and illusory, which prevent our being free and happy, that is the aim and meaning of our life. Forward! We march on irresistibly toward the bright star that burns there in the distance. Forward! Do not fall behind, friends!

ANYA (*extending her arms upward*): How well you talk! (*A pause.*) It's wonderful here today!

TROFIMOFF: Yes, the weather is marvelous.

ANYA: What have you done to me, Petya, why don't I love the cherry orchard any longer the way I used to? I loved it so tenderly, it seemed to me there was not a better place on earth than our orchard.

TROFIMOFF: All Russia is our orchard. The earth is immense and beautiful, and on it are many wonderful places. (*A pause.*) Just think, Anya: your grandfather, great-grandfather and all your ancestors were slave owners, in possession of living souls, and can you doubt that from every cherry in the orchard, from every leaf, from every trunk, human beings are looking at you, can it be that you don't hear their voices? To possess living souls, well, that depraved all of you who lived before and who are living now, so that your mother and you, and your uncle no longer notice that you live by debt, at somebody else's expense, at the expense of those very people whom you wouldn't let past your front door — We are at least two hundred years behind the times, we have as yet absolutely nothing, we have no definite attitude toward the past, we only philosophize, complain of our sadness or drink vodka. Why, it is quite clear that to begin to live in the present we must first atone for our past, must be done with it; and we can atone for it only through suffering, only through uncommon, incessant labor. Understand that, Anya.

ANYA: The house we live in ceased to be ours long ago, and I'll go away, I give you my word.

TROFIMOFF: If you have the household keys, throw them in the well and go away. Be free as the wind.

ANYA (*transported*): How well you said that!

TROFIMOFF: Believe me, Anya, believe me! I am not thirty yet, I am young, I am still a student, but I have already borne so much! Every winter I am hungry, sick, anxious, poor as a beggar, and — where has destiny not chased me, where haven't I been! And yet, my soul has always, every minute, day and night, been full of inexplicable premonitions. I have a premonition of happiness, Anya, I see it already —

ANYA (*pensively*): The moon is rising.

(EPIHODOFF *is heard playing on the guitar, always the same sad song. The moon rises. Somewhere near the poplars* VARYA *is looking for* ANYA *and calling:* "Anya! Where are you?")

TROFIMOFF: Yes, the moon is rising. (*A pause.*) Here is happiness, here it comes, comes always nearer and nearer, I hear its footsteps now. And if we shall not see it, shall not come to know it, what does that matter? Others will see it!

VARYA (*off*): Anya! Where are you?

TROFIMOFF: Again, that Varya! (*Angrily.*) It's scandalous!

ANYA: Well, let's go to the river. It's lovely there.

TROFIMOFF: Let's go. (*They go out.*)

VARYA (*off*): Anya! Anya!

ACT III

The drawing room, separated by an arch from the ballroom. A chandelier is lighted. A Jewish orchestra is playing — the same that was mentioned in Act II. Evening. In the ballroom they are dancing grand rond. *The voice of* SEMYONOFF-PISHTCHIK: *"Promenade à une paire!" They enter the drawing room; in the first couple are* PISHTCHIK *and* CHARLOTTA IVANOVNA; *in the second,* TROFIMOFF *and* LYUBOFF ANDREEVNA; *in the third,* ANYA *with the* POST-OFFICE CLERK; *in the fourth,* VARYA *with the* STATION-MASTER et cetera — VARYA *is crying softly and wipes away her tears while she is dancing.* DUNYASHA *is in the last couple through the drawing room.* PISHTCHIK *shouts: "Grand rond, balancez!" and "Les Cavaliers à genoux et remerciez vos dames!"*

FIERS *in a frock coat goes by with seltzer water on a tray.* PISHTCHIK *and* TROFIMOFF *come into the drawing room.*

PISHTCHIK: I am full-blooded, I have had two strokes already, and dancing is hard for me, but as they say, if you are in a pack of dogs, you may bark and bark, but you must still wag your tail. At that, I have the health of a horse. My dear father — he was a great joker — may he dwell in Heaven — used to talk as if our ancient line, the Semyonoff-Pishtchiks, were descended from the very horse that Caligula made a Senator — (*Sitting down.*) But here's my trouble: I haven't any money. A hungry dog believes in nothing but meat — (*Snoring but waking at once.*) And the same way with me — I can't talk about anything but money.

TROFIMOFF: Well, to tell you the truth, there is something of a horse about your figure.

PISHTCHIK: Well — a horse is a fine animal — You can sell a horse —

(*The sound of playing billiards comes from the next room.* VARYA *appears under the arch to the ballroom.*)

TROFIMOFF (*teasing*): Madam Lopahin! Madam Lopahin!

VARYA (*angrily*): A mangy-looking gentleman!

TROFIMOFF: Yes, I am a mangy-looking gentleman, and proud of it!

VARYA (*in bitter thought*): Here we have gone and hired musicians and what are we going to pay them with? (*Goes out.*)

TROFIMOFF (*to* PISHTCHIK): If the energy you have wasted in the course of your life trying to find money to pay the interest had gone into something else, you could very likely have turned the world upside down before you were done with it.

PISHTCHIK: Nietzsche — the philosopher — the greatest — the most celebrated — a man of tremendous mind — says in his works that one may make counterfeit money.

TROFIMOFF: And have you read Nietzsche?

PISHTCHIK: Well — Dashenka told me. And I'm in such a state now that I could make counterfeit money myself — Day after tomorrow three hundred and ten roubles must be paid — one hundred and thirty I've on hand — (*Feeling in his pockets, alarmed.*) The money is gone! I have lost the money! (*Tearfully.*) Where is the money? (*Joyfully.*) Here it is, inside the lining — I was in quite a sweat —

(LYUBOFF ANDREEVNA *and* CHARLOTTA IVANOVNA *come in.*)

LYUBOFF ANDREEVNA (*humming lazginka, a Georgian dance*): Why does Leonid take so long? What's he doing in town? (*To* DUNYASHA.) Dunyasha, offer the musicians some tea —

TROFIMOFF: In all probability the auction did not take place.

LYUBOFF ANDREEVNA: And the musicians came at an unfortunate moment and we planned the ball at an unfortunate moment — Well, it doesn't matter. (*Sitting down and singing softly.*)

CHARLOTTA (*gives* PISHTCHIK *a deck of cards*): Here is a deck of cards for you, think of some one card.

PISHTCHIK: I have thought of one.

CHARLOTTA: Now, shuffle the deck. Very good. Hand it here; oh, my dear Monsieur Pishtchik. *Ein, zwei, drei!* Now look for it, it's in your coat pocket —

PISHTCHIK (*getting a card out of his coat pocket*): The Eight of Spades, that's absolutely right! (*Amazed.*) Fancy that!

CHARLOTTA (*holding a deck of cards in her palm; to* TROFIMOFF): Tell me quick now, which card is on top?

TROFIMOFF: What is it? Well — the Queen of Spades.

CHARLOTTA: Right! (*To* PISHTCHIK.) Well? Which card's on top?

PISHTCHIK: The Ace of Hearts.

CHARLOTTA: Right! (*Strikes the deck against her palm; the deck of cards disappears.*) And what beautiful weather we are having today!

(*A mysterious feminine voice answers her, as if from under the floor:* "Oh, yes. The weather is splendid, madame." "You are so nice, you're my ideal —" *The voice:* "Madame, you too please me greatly.")

THE STATIONMASTER (*applauding*): Madam Ventriloquist, bravo!

PISHTCHIK (*amazed*): Fancy that! Most charming Charlotta Ivanovna — I am simply in love with you.

CHARLOTTA: In love? (*Shrugging her shoulders.*) Is it possible that you can love? *Guter Mensch aber schlechter Musikant.*

TROFIMOFF (*slapping* PISHTCHIK *on the shoulder*): You horse, you —

CHARLOTTA: I beg your attention, one more trick. (*Taking a lap robe from the chair.*) Here is a very fine lap robe — I want to sell it — (*Shaking it out.*) Wouldn't somebody like to buy it?

PISHTCHIK (*amazed*): Fancy that!

CHARLOTTA: *Ein, zwei, drei!*

(*She quickly raises the lowered robe, behind it stands* ANYA, *who curtseys, runs to her mother, embraces her and runs back into the ballroom amid the general delight.*)

LYUBOFF ANDREEVNA (*applauding*): Bravo, bravo — !

CHARLOTTA: Now again! *Ein, zwei, drei!*

(*Lifting the robe: behind it stands* VARYA, *she bows.*)

PISHTCHIK (*amazed*): Fancy that!

CHARLOTTA: That's all. (*Throwing the robe at* PISHTCHIK, *curtseying and running into the ballroom.*)

PISHTCHIK (*hurrying after her*): You little rascal — What a girl! What a girl! (*Goes out.*)

LYUBOFF ANDREEVNA: And Leonid is not here yet. What he's doing in town so long, I don't understand! Everything is finished there, either the estate is sold by now, or the auction didn't take place. Why keep it from us so long?

VARYA (*trying to comfort her*): Uncle has bought it, I am sure of that.

TROFIMOFF (*mockingly*): Yes.

VARYA: Great-aunt sent him power of attorney to buy it in her name and transfer the debt. She did this for Anya. And I feel certain, God willing, that Uncle will buy it.

LYUBOFF ANDREEVNA: Our Yaroslavl great-aunt has sent fifteen thousand to buy the estate in her name — She doesn't trust us, but that wouldn't be enough to pay the interest even — (*Covering her face with her hands.*) Today my fate will be decided, my fate —

TROFIMOFF (*teasing* VARYA): Madam Lopahin!

VARYA (*angrily*): Perennial student! You have already been expelled from the University twice.

LYUBOFF ANDREEVNA: But why are you angry, Varya? He teases you about Lopahin, what of it? Marry Lopahin if you want to, he is a good man, interesting. If you don't want to, don't marry him; darling, nobody is making you do it.

VARYA: I look at this matter seriously, Mama, one must speak straight out. He's a good man, I like him.

LYUBOFF ANDREEVNA: Then marry him. What there is to wait for I don't understand!

VARYA: But I can't propose to him myself, Mama. It's two years now; everyone has been talking to me about him, everyone talks, and he either remains silent or jokes. I understand. He's getting rich, he's busy with his own affairs, and has no time for me. If there were money, ever so little, even a hundred roubles, I would drop everything, and go far away. I'd go to a nunnery.

TROFIMOFF: How saintly!

VARYA (*to* TROFIMOFF): A student should be intelligent! (*In a low voice, tearfully.*) How homely you have grown, Petya, how old you've got. (*To* LYUBOFF ANDREEVNA, *no longer* crying.) It is just that I can't live without working, Mama. I must be doing something every minute.

YASHA (YASHA *enters. Barely restraining his laughter*): Epihodoff has broken a billiard cue! — (*Goes out.*)

VARYA: But why is Epihodoff here? Who allowed him to play billiards? I don't understand these people — (*Goes out.*)

LYUBOFF ANDREEVNA: Don't tease her, Petya; you can see she has troubles enough without that.

TROFIMOFF: She is just too zealous. Sticking her nose into things that are none of her business. All summer she gave us no peace, neither me nor Anya; she was afraid a romance would spring up between us. What business is that of hers? And besides I haven't shown any signs of it. I am so remote from triviality. We are above love!

LYUBOFF ANDREEVNA: Well, then, I must be beneath love. (*Very anxiously.*) Why isn't Leonid here? Just to tell us whether the estate is sold or not? Calamity seems to me so incredible that I don't know what to think, I'm lost — I could scream this minute — I could do something insane. Save me, Petya. Say something, do say. . . .

TROFIMOFF: Whether the estate is sold today or is not sold — is it not the same? There is no turning back, the path is all grown over. Calm yourself, my dear, all that was over long ago. One mustn't deceive oneself, one must for once at least in one's life look truth straight in the eye.

LYUBOFF ANDREEVNA: What truth? You see where the truth is and where the untruth is, but as for me, it's as if I had lost my sight, I see nothing. You boldly decide all important questions, but tell me, my dear boy, isn't that because you are young and haven't had time yet to suffer through any one of your problems? You look boldly ahead, and isn't that because you don't see and don't expect anything terrible, since life is still hidden from your young eyes? You are braver, more honest, more profound than we are, but stop and think, be magnanimous, have a little mercy on me, just a little. Why, I was born here. My father and mother lived here and my grandfather. I love this house, I can't imagine my life without the cherry orchard and if it is very necessary to sell it, then sell me along with the orchard — (*Embracing* TROFIMOFF *and kissing him on the forehead.*) Why, my son was

drowned here — (*Crying.*) Have mercy on me, good, kind man.

TROFIMOFF: You know I sympathize with you from the bottom of my heart.

LYUBOFF ANDREEVNA: But that should be said differently, differently — (*Taking out her handkerchief; a telegram falls on the floor.*) My heart is heavy today, you can't imagine how heavy. It is too noisy for me here, my soul trembles at every sound, I tremble all over and yet I can't go off to myself, when I am alone the silence frightens me. Don't blame me, Petya — I love you as one of my own. I should gladly have given you Anya's hand, I assure you, only, my dear, you must study and finish your course. You do nothing. Fate simply flings you about from place to place, and that's so strange — Isn't that so? Yes? And you must do something about your beard, to make it grow somehow — (*Laughing.*) You look funny!

TROFIMOFF (*picking up the telegram*): I do not desire to be beautiful.

LYUBOFF ANDREEVNA: This telegram is from Paris. I get one every day. Yesterday and today too. That wild man has fallen ill again, something is wrong again with him — He asks forgiveness, begs me to come, and really I ought to make a trip to Paris and stay awhile near him. Your face looks stern, Petya, but what is there to do, my dear, what am I to do, he is ill, he is alone, unhappy and who will look after him there, who will keep him from doing the wrong thing, who will give him his medicine on time? And what is there to hide or keep still about? I love him, that's plain. I love him, love him — It's a stone about my neck, I'm sinking to the bottom with it, but I love that stone and live without it I cannot. (*Pressing* TROFIMOFF'S *hand.*) Don't think harshly of me, Petya, don't say anything to me, don't —

TROFIMOFF (*tearfully*): Forgive my frankness, for God's sake! Why, he picked your bones.

LYUBOFF ANDREEVNA: No, no, no, you must not talk like that. (*Stopping her ears.*)

TROFIMOFF: But he is a scoundrel, only you, you are the only one that doesn't know it. He is a petty scoundrel, a nonentity —

LYUBOFF ANDREEVNA (*angry but controlling herself*): You are twenty-six years old or twenty-seven, but you are still a schoolboy in the second grade!

TROFIMOFF: Very well!

LYUBOFF ANDREEVNA: You should be a man

— at your age you should understand people who love. And you yourself should love someone — you should fall in love! (*Angrily.*) Yes, yes! And there is no purity in you; you are simply smug, a ridiculous crank, a freak —

TROFIMOFF (*horrified*): What is she saying!

LYUBOFF ANDREEVNA: "I am above love!" You are not above love, Petya, you are, as our Fiers would say, just a good-for-nothing. Imagine, at your age, not having a mistress — !

TROFIMOFF (*horrified*): This is terrible! What is she saying! (*Goes quickly into the ballroom, clutching his head.*) This is horrible — I can't bear it, I am going — (*Goes out but immediately returns.*) All is over between us. (*Goes out into the hall.*)

LYUBOFF ANDREEVNA (*shouting after him*): Petya, wait! You funny creature, I was joking! Petya! (*In the hall you hear someone running up the stairs and suddenly falling back down with a crash. You hear ANYA and VARYA scream but immediately you hear laughter.*) What's that?

ANYA (ANYA *runs in. Laughing*): Petya fell down the stairs! (*Runs out.*)

LYUBOFF ANDREEVNA: What a funny boy that Petya is — ! (*The STATIONMASTER stops in the center of the ballroom and begins to recite "The Sinner" by A. Tolstoi. They listen to him but he has recited only a few lines when the strains of a waltz are heard from the hall and the recitation is broken off. They all dance.* TROFIMOFF, ANYA, VARYA *and* LYUBOFF ANDREEVNA *come in from the hall.*) But, Petya — but, dear soul — I beg your forgiveness — Let's go dance. (*She dances with* TROFIMOFF. ANYA *and* VARYA *dance.* FIERS *enters, leaving his stick by the side door.* YASHA *also comes into the drawing room and watches the dancers.*)

YASHA: What is it, Grandpa?

FIERS: I don't feel very well. In the old days there were generals, barons, admirals dancing at our parties, and now we send for the post-office clerk and the stationmaster, and even they are none too anxious to come. Somehow I've grown feeble. The old master, the grandfather, treated everybody with sealing-wax for all sicknesses. I take sealing-wax every day, have done so for twenty-odd years or more; it may be due to that that I'm alive.

YASHA: You are tiresome, Grandpa. (*Yawning.*) Why don't you go off and die?

FIERS: Aw, you — good-for-nothing! — (*Muttering.*)

(TROFIMOFF *and* LYUBOFF ANDREEVNA *dance in the ballroom and then in the drawing room.*)

LYUBOFF ANDREEVNA: *Merci.* I'll sit down awhile — (*Sitting down.*) I'm tired.

ANYA (ANYA *enters. Agitated*): And just now in the kitchen some man was saying that the cherry orchard had been sold today.

LYUBOFF ANDREEVNA: Sold to whom?

ANYA: He didn't say who to. He's gone.

(*Dancing with* TROFIMOFF, *they pass into the ballroom.*)

YASHA: It was some old man babbling there. A stranger.

FIERS: And Leonid Andreevich is still not here, he has not arrived. The overcoat he has on is light, midseason — let's hope he won't catch cold. Ach, these young things!

LYUBOFF ANDREEVNA: I shall die this minute. Go, Yasha, find out who it was sold to.

YASHA: But he's been gone a long time, the old fellow. (*Laughing.*)

LYUBOFF ANDREEVNA (*with some annoyance*): Well, what are you laughing at? What are you so amused at?

YASHA: Epihodoff is just too funny. An empty-headed man. Twenty-two misfortunes!

LYUBOFF ANDREEVNA: Fiers, if the estate is sold, where will you go?

FIERS: Wherever you say, there I'll go.

LYUBOFF ANDREEVNA: Why do you look like that? Aren't you well? You know you ought to go to bed —

FIERS: Yes — (*With a sneer.*) I go to bed and without me who's going to serve, who'll take care of things? I'm the only one in the whole house.

YASHA (*to* LYUBOFF ANDREEVNA): Lyuboff Andreevna, let me ask a favor of you, do be so kind! If you ever go back to Paris, take me with you, please do! It's impossible for me to stay here. (*Looking around him, and speaking in a low voice.*) Why talk about it? You can see for yourself it's an uncivilized country, an immoral people and not only that, there's the boredom of it. The food they give us in that kitchen is abominable and there's that Fiers, too, walking about and muttering all kinds of words that are out of place. Take me with you, be so kind!

PISHTCHIK (*enters*): Allow me to ask you — for a little waltz, most beautiful lady — (LYUBOFF ANDREEVNA *goes with him.*) Charming lady, I must borrow a hundred and eighty roubles from you — will borrow — (*dancing*) a hundred and eighty roubles — (*They pass into the ballroom.*)

YASHA (*singing low*): "Wilt thou know the unrest in my soul!"

(*In the ballroom a figure in a gray top hat and checked trousers waves both hands and jumps about; there are shouts of "Bravo, Charlotta Ivanovna!"*)

DUNYASHA (*stopping to powder her face*): The young lady orders me to dance — there are a lot of gentlemen and very few ladies — but dancing makes my head swim and my heart thump. Fiers Nikolaevich, the post-office clerk said something to me just now that took my breath away.

(*The music plays more softly.*)

FIERS: What did he say to you?
DUNYASHA: You are like a flower, he says.
YASHA (*yawning*): What ignorance — ! (*Goes out.*)
DUNYASHA: Like a flower — I am such a sensitive girl, I love tender words awfully.
FIERS: You'll be getting your head turned.

(EPIHODOFF *enters.*)

EPIHODOFF: Avdotya Feodorovna, you don't want to see me — It's as if I were some sort of insect. (*Sighing.*) Ach, life!
DUNYASHA: What do you want?
EPIHODOFF: Undoubtedly you may be right. (*Sighing.*) But of course, if one considers it from a given point of view, then you, I will allow myself so to express it, forgive my frankness, absolutely led me into a state of mind. I know my fate, every day some misfortune happens to me, but I have long since become accustomed to that, and so I look on my misfortunes with a smile. You gave me your word and, although I —
DUNYASHA: I beg you, we'll talk later on, but leave me now in peace. I'm in a dream now. (*Playing with her fan.*)
EPIHODOFF: I have a something wrong happens every day — I will allow myself so to express it — I just smile, I even laugh.
VARYA (*enters from the ballroom*): You are not gone yet, Semyon? What a really disrespectful man you are! (*To* DUNYASHA.) Get out of here, Dunyasha. (*To* EPIHODOFF.) You either play billiards and break a cue or you walk about the drawing room like a guest.

EPIHODOFF: Allow me to tell you, you cannot make any demands on me.
VARYA: I'm not making any demands on you, I'm talking to you. All you know is to walk from place to place but not do any work. We keep a clerk, but what for, nobody knows.
EPIHODOFF (*offended*): Whether I work, whether I walk, whether I eat, or whether I play billiards are matters to be discussed only by people of understanding and my seniors.
VARYA: You dare to say that to me! (*Flying into a temper.*) You dare? So I don't understand anything? Get out of here! This minute!
EPIHODOFF (*alarmed*): I beg you to express yourself in a delicate manner.
VARYA (*beside herself*): This very minute, get out of here! Get out! (*He goes to the door; she follows him.*) Twenty-two misfortunes! Don't you dare breathe in here! Don't let me set eyes on you! (EPIHODOFF *has gone out, but his voice comes from outside the door: "I shall complain about you."*) Ah, you are coming back? (*Grabbing the stick that* FIERS *put by the door.*) Come on, come — come on, I'll show you — Ah, you are coming? You are coming? Take that then — !

(*She swings the stick, at the very moment when* LOPAHIN *is coming in.*)

LOPAHIN: Most humbly, I thank you.
VARYA (*angrily and ironically*): I beg your pardon!
LOPAHIN: It's nothing at all. I humbly thank you for the pleasant treat.
VARYA: It isn't worth your thanks. (*Moving away, then looking back and asking gently.*) I haven't hurt you?
LOPAHIN: No, it's nothing. There's a great bump coming though.

(*Voices in the ballroom: "Lopahin has come back." "Yermolay Alexeevich!"*)

PISTCHIK (*enters*): See what we see, hear what we hear — ! (*He and* LOPAHIN *kiss one another.*) You smell slightly of cognac, my dear, my good old chap. And we are amusing ourselves here too.
LYUBOFF ANDREEVNA (*enters*): Is that you, Yermolay Alexeevich? Why were you so long? Where is Leonid?
LOPAHIN: Leonid Andreevich got back when I did, he's coming.
LYUBOFF ANDREEVNA (*agitated*): Well, what? Was there an auction? Do speak!
LOPAHIN (*embarrassed, afraid of showing the*

joy he feels): The auction was over by four o'clock — We were late for the train, had to wait till half-past nine. (*Sighing heavily.*) Ugh, my head's swimming a bit!

(GAYEFF *enters; with his right hand he carries his purchases, with his left he wipes away his tears.*)

LYUBOFF ANDREEVNA: Lyona, what? Lyona, eh? (*Impatiently, with tears in her eyes.*) Quick, for God's sake —

GAYEFF (*not answering her, merely waving his hand; to* FIERS, *crying*): Here, take it — There are anchovies, some Kertch herrings — I haven't eaten anything all day — What I have suffered! (*The door into the billiard room is open; you hear the balls clicking and* YASHA's *voice: "Seven and eighteen!"* GAYEFF's *expression changes, he is no longer crying.*) I'm terribly tired. You help me change, Fiers. (*Goes to his room through the ballroom,* FIERS *behind him.*)

PISHTCHIK: What happened at the auction? Go on, tell us!

LYUBOFF ANDREEVNA: Is the cherry orchard sold?

LOPAHIN: It's sold.

LYUBOFF ANDREEVNA: Who bought it?

LOPAHIN: I bought it. (*A pause.* LYUBOFF ANDREEVNA *is overcome. She would have fallen had she not been standing near the chair and table.* VARYA *takes the keys from her belt, throws them on the floor in the middle of the drawing room and goes out.*) I bought it. Kindly wait a moment, ladies and gentlemen, everything is muddled up in my head, I can't speak — (*Laughing.*) We arrived at the auction, Deriganoff was already there. Leonid Andreevich had only fifteen thousand and Deriganoff right off bids thirty over and above indebtedness. I see how things are, I match him with forty thousand. He forty-five. I fifty-five. That is to say he raises it by fives, I by tens — So it ended. Over and above the indebtedness, I bid up to ninety thousand, it was knocked down to me. The cherry orchard is mine now. Mine! (*Guffawing.*) My God, Lord, the cherry orchard is mine! Tell me I'm drunk, out of my head, that I'm imagining all this — (*Stamps his feet.*) Don't laugh at me! If only my father and grandfather could rise from their graves and see this whole business, see how their Yermolay, beaten, half-illiterate Yermolay, who used to run around barefoot in winter, how that very Yermolay has bought an estate that nothing in the world can beat. I bought the estate where grandfather and father were slaves, where you wouldn't even let me in the kitchen. I am asleep, it's only some dream of mine, it only seems so to me — That's nothing but the fruit of your imagination, covered with the darkness of the unknown — (*Picking up the keys, with a gentle smile.*) She threw down the keys, wants to show she is not mistress any more — (*Jingling the keys.*) Well, it's all the same. (*The orchestra is heard tuning up.*) Hey, musicians, play, I want to hear you! Come on, everybody, and see how Yermolay Lopahin will swing the ax in the cherry orchard, how the trees will fall to the ground! We are going to build villas and our grandsons and great-grandsons will see a new life here — Music, play! (*The music is playing.* LYUBOFF ANDREEVNA *has sunk into a chair, crying bitterly.* LOPAHIN *reproachfully.*) Why, then, didn't you listen to me? My poor dear, it can't be undone now. (*With tears.*) Oh, if this could all be over soon, if somehow our awkward, unhappy life would be changed!

PISHTCHIK (*taking him by the arm, in a low voice*): She is crying. Come on in the ballroom, let her be by herself — Come on — (*Taking him by the arm and leading him into the ballroom.*)

LOPAHIN: What's the matter? Music, there, play up! (*Sarcastically.*) Everything is to be as I want it! Here comes the new squire, the owner of the cherry orchard. (*Quite accidentally, he bumps into the little table, and very nearly upsets the candelabra.*) I can pay for everything!

(*Goes out with* PISHTCHIK. *There is nobody left either in the ballroom or the drawing room but* LYUBOFF ANDREEVNA, *who sits all huddled up and crying bitterly. The music plays softly.* ANYA *and* TROFIMOFF *enter hurriedly.* ANYA *comes up to her mother and kneels in front of her.* TROFIMOFF *remains at the ballroom door.*)

ANYA: Mama — ! Mama, you are crying? My dear, kind, good Mama, my beautiful, I love you — I bless you. The cherry orchard is sold, it's not ours any more, that's true, true; but don't cry, Mama, you've your life still left you, you've your good, pure heart ahead of you — Come with me, come on, darling, away from here, come on — We will plant a new orchard, finer than this one, you'll see it, you'll understand; and joy, quiet, deep joy will sink into your heart, like the sun at evening, and you'll smile, Mama! Come, darling, come on!

ACT IV

The same setting as in Act I. There are neither curtains on the windows nor are there any pictures on the walls. Only a little furniture remains piled up in one corner as if for sale. A sense of emptiness is felt. Near the outer door, at the rear of the stage, is a pile of suitcases, traveling bags, and so on. The door on the left is open, and through it VARYA's *and* ANYA's *voices are heard.* LOPAHIN *is standing waiting.* YASHA *is holding a tray with glasses of champagne. In the hall* EPIHODOFF *is tying up a box, offstage at the rear there is a hum. It is the peasants who have come to say good-by.* GAYEFF's *voice: "Thanks, brothers, thank you."*

YASHA: The simple folk have come to say good-by. I am of the opinion, Yermolay Alexeevich, that the people are kind enough but don't understand anything.

(The hum subsides. LYUBOFF ANDREEVNA *enters through the hall with* GAYEFF; *she is not crying, but is pale, her face quivers, she is not able to speak.)*

GAYEFF: You gave them your purse, Lyuba. Mustn't do that! Mustn't do that

LYUBOFF ANDREEVNA: I couldn't help it! I couldn't help it!

(Both go out.)

LOPAHIN *(calling through the door after them)*: Please, I humbly beg you! A little glass at parting. I didn't think to bring some from town, and at the station I found just one bottle. Please! *(A pause.)* Well, then, ladies and gentlemen! You don't want it? *(Moving away from the door.)* If I'd known that, I wouldn't have bought it. Well, then I won't drink any either. *(*YASHA *carefully sets the tray down on a chair.)* At least, you have some, Yasha.

YASHA: To those who are departing! Pleasant days to those who stay behind! *(Drinking.)* This champagne is not the real stuff, I can assure you.

LOPAHIN: Eight roubles a bottle. *(A pause.)* It's devilish cold in here.

YASHA: They didn't heat up today, we are leaving anyway. *(Laughing.)*

LOPAHIN: What are you laughing about?

YASHA: For joy.

LOPAHIN: Outside it's October, but it's sunny and still, like summer. Good for building. *(Looking at his watch, then through the door.)* Ladies and gentlemen, bear in mind we have forty-six minutes in all till train time! Which means you have to go to the station in twenty minutes. Hurry up a little.

TROFIMOFF *(in an overcoat, entering from outside)*: Seems to me it is time to go. The carriages are ready. The devil knows where my rubbers are. They've disappeared. *(In the door.)* Anya, my rubbers are not here! I can't find them.

LOPAHIN: And I have to go to Harkoff. I'm going on the same train with you. I'm going to live in Harkoff all winter. I've been dilly-dallying along with you, I'm tired of doing nothing. I can't be without work, look, I don't know what to do with my hands here, see, they are dangling somehow, as if they didn't belong to me.

TROFIMOFF: We are leaving right away, and you'll set about your useful labors again.

LOPAHIN: Here, drink a glass.

TROFIMOFF: I shan't.

LOPAHIN: It's to Moscow now?

TROFIMOFF: Yes. I'll see them off to town, and tomorrow to Moscow.

LOPAHIN: Yes — Maybe the professors are not giving their lectures. I imagine they are waiting till you arrive.

TROFIMOFF: That's none of your business.

LOPAHIN: How many years is it you've been studying at the University?

TROFIMOFF: Think of something newer. This is old and flat. *(Looking for his rubbers.)* You know, perhaps, we shall not see each other again; therefore, permit me to give you one piece of advice at parting! Don't wave your arms! Cure yourself of that habit — of arm waving. And also of building summer cottages, figuring that the summer residents will in time become individual landowners; figuring like that is arm waving too — Just the same, however, I like you. You have delicate soft fingers like an artist, you have a delicate soft heart —

LOPAHIN *(embracing him)*: Good-by, my

dear boy. Thanks for everything. If you need it, take some money from me for the trip.

TROFIMOFF: Why should I? There's no need for it.

LOPAHIN: But you haven't any!

TROFIMOFF: I have. Thank you. I got some for a translation. Here it is in my pocket. (*Anxiously.*) But my rubbers are gone.

VARYA (*from another room*): Take your nasty things! (*Throws a pair of rubbers on to the stage.*)

TROFIMOFF: But what are you angry about, Varya? Hm — Why, these are not my rubbers.

LOPAHIN: In the spring I planted twenty-seven hundred acres of poppies and now I've made forty thousand clear. And when my poppies were in bloom, what a picture it was! So look, as I say, I've made forty thousand, which means I'm offering you a loan because I can afford to. Why turn up your nose? I'm a peasant — I speak straight out.

TROFIMOFF: Your father was a peasant, mine — an apothecary — and from that absolutely nothing follows. (LOPAHIN *takes out his wallet.*) Leave it alone, leave it alone — If you gave me two hundred thousand even, I wouldn't take it. I am a free man. And everything that you all value so highly and dearly, both rich man and beggars, has not the slightest power over me, it's like a mere feather floating in the air. I can get along without you, I can pass you by, I am strong and proud. Humanity is moving toward the loftiest truth, toward the loftiest happiness that is possible on earth and I am in the front ranks.

LOPAHIN: Will you get there?

TROFIMOFF: I'll get there. (*A pause.*) I'll get there, or I'll show the others the way to get there.

(*In the distance is heard the sound of an ax on a tree.*)

LOPAHIN: Well, good-by, my dear boy. It's time to go. We turn up our noses at one another, but life keeps on passing. When I work a long time without stopping, my thoughts are clearer, and it seems as if I, too, know what I exist for, and, brother, how many people are there in Russia who exist, nobody knows for what? Well, all the same, it's not that that keeps things circulating. Leonid Andreevich, they say, has accepted a position — he'll be in a bank, six thousand a year —

the only thing is he won't stay there, he's very lazy —

ANYA (*in the doorway*): Mama begs of you until she's gone, not to cut down the orchard.

TROFIMOFF: Honestly, haven't you enough tact to — (*Goes out through the hall.*)

LOPAHIN: Right away, right away — What people, really! (*Goes out after him.*)

ANYA: Has Fiers been sent to the hospital?

YASHA: I told them to this morning. They must have sent him.

ANYA (*to* EPIHODOFF, *who is passing through the room*): Semyon Panteleevich, please inquire whether or not they have taken Fiers to the hospital.

YASHA (*huffily*): This morning, I told Igor. Why ask ten times over!

EPIHODOFF: The venerable Fiers, according to my conclusive opinion, is not worth mending, he ought to join his forefathers. And I can only envy him. (*Putting a suitcase on a hatbox and crushing it.*) Well, there you are, of course. I knew it. (*Goes out.*)

YASHA (*mockingly*): Twenty-two misfortunes —

VARYA (*on the other side of the door*): Have they taken Fiers to the hospital?

ANYA: They have.

VARYA: Then why didn't they take the letter to the doctor?

ANYA: We must send it on after *them* — (*Goes out.*)

VARYA (*from the next room*): Where is Yasha? Tell him his mother has come, she wants to say good-by to him.

YASHA (*waving his hand*): They merely try my patience.

(DUNYASHA *has been busying herself with the luggage; now when* YASHA *is left alone, she goes up to him.*)

DUNYASHA: If you'd only look at me once, Yasha. You are going away — leaving me — (*Crying and throwing herself on his neck.*)

YASHA: Why are you crying? (*Drinking champagne.*) In six days I'll be in Paris again. Tomorrow we will board the express train and dash off out of sight; somehow, I can't believe it. *Vive la France!* It doesn't suit me here — I can't live here — Can't help that. I've seen enough ignorance — enough for me. (*Drinking champagne.*) Why do you cry? Behave yourself properly, then you won't be crying.

DUNYASHA (*powdering her face, looking into*

a small mirror): Send me a letter from Paris. I loved you, Yasha, you know, loved you so! I am a tender creature, Yasha!

YASHA: They are coming here. (*Bustling about near the suitcases, humming low.*)

(LYUBOFF ANDREEVNA, GAYEFF, ANYA *and* CHARLOTTA IVANOVNA *enter.*)

GAYEFF: We should be going. There is very little time left. (*Looking at* YASHA.) Who is it smells like herring!

LYUBOFF ANDREEVNA: In about ten minutes let's be in the carriage — (*Glancing around the room.*) Good-by, dear house, old Grandfather. Winter will pass, spring will be here, but you won't be here any longer, they'll tear you down. How much these walls have seen! (*Kissing her daughter warmly.*) My treasure, you are beaming, your eyes are dancing like two diamonds. Are you happy? Very?

ANYA: Very! It's the beginning of a new life, Mama!

GAYEFF (*gaily*): Yes, indeed, everything is fine now. Before the sale of the cherry orchard, we all were troubled, distressed, and then when the question was settled definitely, irrevocably, we all calmed down and were even cheerful — I'm a bank official. I am a financier now — Yellow ball into the side pocket, anyway, Lyuba, you look better, no doubt about that.

LYUBOFF ANDREEVNA: Yes. My nerves are better, that's true. (*They hand her her hat and coat.*) I sleep well. Carry out my things, Yasha. It's time. (*To* ANYA.) My little girl, we shall see each other again soon — I am going to Paris, I shall live there on the money your Yaroslavl great-aunt sent for the purchase of the estate — long live Great-aunt! But that money won't last long.

ANYA: Mama, you'll come back soon, soon — Isn't that so? I'll prepare myself, pass the examination at high school, and then I'll work, I will help you. We'll read all sorts of books together. Mama, isn't that so? (*Kissing her mother's hands.*) We'll read in the autumn evenings, read lots of books, and a new, wonderful world will open up before us — (*Daydreaming.*) Mama, do come —

LYUBOFF ANDREEVNA: I'll come, my precious. (*Embracing her daughter.*)

(LOPAHIN *enters with* CHARLOTTA *who is softly humming a song.*)

GAYEFF: Lucky Charlotta: she's singing!

CHARLOTTA (*taking a bundle that looks like a baby wrapped up*): My baby, bye, bye — (A *baby's cry is heard: Ooah, ooah — ! Hush, my darling, my dear little boy. (Ooah, ooah — !*) I am so sorry for you! (*Throwing the bundle back.*) Will you please find me a position? I cannot go on like this.

LOPAHIN: We will find something, Charlotta Ivanovna, don't worry.

GAYEFF: Everybody is dropping us, Varya is going away. — All of a sudden we are not needed.

CHARLOTTA: I have no place in town to live. I must go away. (*Humming.*) It's all the same —

(PISHTCHIK *enters.*)

LOPAHIN: The freak of nature — !

PISHTCHIK (*out of breath*): Ugh, let me catch my breath — I'm exhausted — My honored friends — Give me some water —

GAYEFF: After money, I suppose? This humble servant will flee from sin! (*Goes out.*)

PISHTCHIK: It's a long time since I was here — Most beautiful lady — (*To* LOPAHIN.) You here — ? Glad to see you — a man of the greatest intellect — Here — Take it — (*Giving* LOPAHIN *some money.*) Four hundred roubles — That leaves eight hundred and forty I still owe you —

LOPAHIN (*with astonishment, shrugging his shoulders*): I must be dreaming. But where did you get it?

PISHTCHIK: Wait — I'm hot — Most extraordinary event. Some Englishmen came and found on my land some kind of white clay — (*To* LYUBOFF ANDREEVNA.) And four hundred for you — Beautiful lady — Wonderful lady — (*Handing over the money.*) The rest later. (*Taking a drink of water.*) Just now a young man was saying on the train that some great philosopher recommends jumping off roofs — "Jump!" he says, and "therein lies the whole problem." (*With astonishment.*) You don't say! Water!

LOPAHIN: And what Englishmen were they?

PISHTCHIK: I leased them the parcel of land with the clay for twenty-four years — And now, excuse me, I haven't time — I must run along — I'm going to Znoykoff's — To Kardamonoff's — I owe everybody — (*Drinking.*) I wish you well — I'll drop in on Thursday —

LYUBOFF ANDREEVNA: We are moving to

town right away, and tomorrow I'm going abroad —

PISHTCHIK: What? (*Alarmed.*) Why to town? That's why I see furniture — Suitcases — Well, no matter — (*Tearfully.*) No matter — Men of the greatest minds — those Englishmen — No matter — Good luck! God will help you — No matter — Everything in this world comes to an end — (*Kissing* LYUBOFF ANDREEVNA's *hand.*) And should the report reach you that my end has come, think of that well-known horse and say: "There was once on earth a so and so — Semyonoff Pishtchik — The kingdom of Heaven be his." Most remarkable weather — yes — (*Going out greatly disconcerted, but immediately returning and speaking from the door.*) Dashenka sends her greetings! (*Goes out.*)

LYUBOFF ANDREEVNA: And now we can go. I am leaving with two worries. First, that Fiers is sick. (*Glancing at her watch.*) We still have five minutes —

ANYA: Mama, Fiers has already been sent to the hospital. Yasha sent him off this morning.

LYUBOFF ANDREEVNA: My second worry — is Varya. She is used to getting up early and working, and now without any work she is like a fish out of water. She has grown thin, pale and cries all the time, poor thing — (*A pause.*) You know this, Yermolay Alexeevich: I dreamed — of marrying her to you. And there was every sign of your getting married.(*Whispering to* ANYA, *who beckons to* CHARLOTTA; *both go out.*) She loves you, you are fond of her, and I don't know, don't know why it is you seem to avoid each other — I don't understand it!

LOPAHIN: I don't understand it either, I must confess. It's all strange somehow — If there's still time, I am ready right now even — Let's finish it up — and *basta,* but without you I feel I won't propose.

LYUBOFF ANDREEVNA: But that's excellent. Surely it takes only a minute. I'll call her at once.

LOPAHIN: And to fit the occasion there's the champagne. (*Looking at the glasses.*) Empty, somebody has already drunk them. (YASHA *coughs.*) That's what's called lapping it up —

LYUBOFF ANDREEVNA (*vivaciously*): Splendid! We'll go out — Yasha, *allez!* I'll call her — (*Through the door.*) Varya, drop everything and come here. Come on! (*Goes out with* YASHA.)

LOPAHIN (*looking at his watch*): Yes —

(*A pause. Behind the door you hear smothered laughter, whispering, finally* VARYA *enters.*)

VARYA (*looking at the luggage a long time*): That's strange, I just can't find it —

LOPAHIN: What are you looking for?

VARYA: I packed it myself and don't remember where. (*A pause.*)

LOPAHIN: Where do you expect to go now, Varvara Mikhailovna?

VARYA: I? To Regulin's. I agreed to go there to look after the house — As a sort of housekeeper.

LOPAHIN: That's in Yashnevo? It's nigh on to seventy miles. (*A pause.*) And here ends life in this house —

VARYA (*examining the luggage*): But where is it? Either I put it in the trunk, perhaps — Yes, life in this house is ended — it won't be any more—

LOPAHIN: And I am going to Harkoff now — By the next train. I've a lot to do. And I am leaving Epihodoff — on the ground here — I've hired him.

VARYA: Well!

LOPAHIN: Last year at this time it had already been snowing, if you remember, and now it's quiet, it's sunny. It's only that it's cold, about three degrees of frost.

VARYA: I haven't noticed. (*A pause.*) And besides our thermometer is broken — (*A pause. A voice from the yard through the door.*) Yermolay Alexeevich —

LOPAHIN (*as if he had been expecting this call for a long time*): This minute! (*Goes out quickly.*)

(VARYA, *sitting on the floor, putting her head on a bundle of clothes, sobs quietly. The door opens,* LYUBOFF ANDREEVNA *enters cautiously.*)

VARYA (*she is not crying any longer, and has wiped her eyes*): Yes, it's time, Mama. I can get to Regulin's today, if we are just not too late for the train — (*Through the door.*) Anya, put your things on! (ANYA, *then* GAYEFF *and* CHARLOTTA IVANOVNA *enter.* GAYEFF *has on a warm overcoat, with a hood. The servants gather, also the drivers.* EPIHODOFF *busies himself with the luggage.*) Now we can be on our way.

ANYA (*joyfully*): On our way!

GAYEFF: My friends, my dear, kind friends! Leaving this house forever, can I remain silent, can I restrain myself from expressing, as we say, farewell, those feelings that fill now my whole being —

ANYA (*beseechingly*): Uncle!

VARYA: Dear Uncle, don't!

GAYEFF (*dejectedly*): Bank the yellow into the side pocket — I am silent —

(TROFIMOFF *and then* LOPAHIN *enter.*)

TROFIMOFF: Well, ladies and gentlemen, it's time to go!

LOPAHIN: Epihodoff, my coat!

LYUBOFF ANDREEVNA: I'll sit here just a minute more. It's as if I had never seen before what the walls in this house are like, what kind of ceilings, and now I look at them greedily, with such tender love —

GAYEFF: I remember when I was six years old, on Trinity Day, I sat in this window and watched my father going to Church —

LYUBOFF ANDREEVNA: Are all the things taken out?

LOPAHIN: Everything, I think. (*Putting on his overcoat. To* EPIHODOFF.) Epihodoff, you see that everything is in order.

EPIHODOFF (*talking in a hoarse voice*): Don't worry, Yermolay Alexeevich!

LOPAHIN: Why is your voice like that?

EPIHODOFF: Just drank some water, swallowed something.

YASHA (*with contempt*): The ignorance —

LYUBOFF ANDREEVNA: We are going and there won't be a soul left here —

LOPAHIN: Till spring.

VARYA (*she pulls an umbrella out from a bundle, it looks as if she were going to hit someone;* LOPAHIN *pretends to be frightened*): What do you, what do you — I never thought of it.

TROFIMOFF: Ladies and gentlemen, let's get in the carriages — It's time! The train is coming any minute.

VARYA: Petya, here they are, your rubbers, by the suitcase. (*Tearfully.*) And how dirty yours are, how old — !

TROFIMOFF (*putting on the rubbers*): Let's go, ladies and gentlemen!

GAYEFF (*greatly embarrassed, afraid he will cry*): The train — The station — Cross into the side, combination off the white into the corner —

LYUBOFF ANDREEVNA: Let's go!

LOPAHIN: Everybody here? Nobody there? (*Locking the side door on the left.*) Things are stored here, it must be locked up, let's go!

ANYA: Good-by, house! Good-by, the old life!

TROFIMOFF: Long live the new life!

(*Goes out with* ANYA. VARYA *casts a glance around the room and, without hurrying, goes out.* YASHA *and* CHARLOTTA, *with her dog, go out.*)

LOPAHIN: And so, till spring. Out, ladies and gentlemen — Till we meet. (*Goes out.*)

(LYUBOFF ANDREEVNA *and* GAYEFF *are left alone. As if they had been waiting for this, they throw themselves on one another's necks sobbing, but smothering their sobs as if afraid of being heard.*)

GAYEFF (*in despair*): Oh, Sister, Sister —

LYUBOFF ANDREEVNA: Oh, my dear, my lovely, beautiful orchard! My life, my youth, my happiness, good-by!

ANYA (ANYA's *voice, gaily, appealingly*): Mama — !

TROFIMOFF (TROFIMOFF's *voice, gaily, excitedly*): Aaooch!

LYUBOFF ANDREEVNA: For the last time, just to look at the walls, at the window — My dear mother used to love to walk around in this room —

GAYEFF: Oh, Sister, Sister — !

ANYA (ANYA's *voice*): Mama — !

TROFIMOFF (TROFIMOFF's *voice*): Aaooch — !

LYUBOFF ANDREEVNA: We are coming! (*They go out.*)

(*The stage is empty. You hear the keys locking all the doors, then the carriages drive off. It grows quiet. In the silence you hear the dull thud of an ax on a tree, a lonely, mournful sound. Footsteps are heard. From the door on the right* FIERS *appears. He is dressed as usual, in a jacket and a white waistcoat, slippers on his feet. He is sick.*)

FIERS (*going to the door and trying the knob*): Locked. They've gone. (*Sitting down on the sofa.*) They forgot about me — No matter — I'll sit here awhile — And Leonid Andreevich, for sure, didn't put on his fur coat, he went off with his top coat — (*Sighing anxiously.*) And I didn't see to it — The young saplings! (*He mutters something that cannot be understood.*) Life has gone by, as if I hadn't lived at all — (*Lying down.*) I'll lie down awhile — You haven't got any strength, nothing is left, nothing — Ach, you — good-for-nothing — (*He lies still.*)

(*There is a far-off sound as if out of the sky, the sound of a snapped string, dying away, sad. A stillness falls, and there is only the thud of an ax on a tree, far away in the orchard.*)

At the end of *The Cherry Orchard*, the old servant Fiers, forgotten by the family he has long served, wanders onto the stage, locked within the house that is no longer theirs. Is he comic, in his mutterings, in his old maidish frettings about Leonid Andreevich's inadequate coat, and in his implicit realization that although he is concerned about the aristocrats the aristocrats are unconcerned about him? Or is he tragic, dying in isolation? Or neither? The comedy is scarcely uproarious; if there is humor in his realization that his life has been trivial, this humor is surely tinged with melancholy. And the "tragic" reading is also ambiguous: first, the text does not say that he dies; second, if it can be assumed that he dies, the death of an ill eighty-seven-year-old man can scarcely seem untimely; and third, Fiers does not seem particularly concerned about dying.

If this play ends with a death, then, it is not the sort of death that Byron had in mind when he said, "All tragedies are finished by a death, / All comedies are ended by a marriage." We are in the dramatic world that Shaw spoke of when he said that "the curtain no longer comes down on a hero slain or married: it comes down when the audience has seen enough of the life presented to it, . . . and must either leave the theatre or miss its last train." Chekhov insisted that *The Cherry Orchard* was a comedy, but what sort of comedy? In the latter part of the last act there is almost a proposal of marriage, but, typically, it never gets made. For two years everyone has joked about the anticipated marriage between Lopahin and Varya, but when these two are thrust together they are overcome by embarrassment, and the interview is dissipated in small talk. Not that (of course) a comedy must end with a marriage; marriage is only the conventional way of indicating a happy union, or reunion, that symbolizes the triumph of life. But in this play we *begin* with a reunion — the family is reunited in the ancestral home — and we end with a separation, the inhabitants scattering when the home is sold.

Another way of getting at *The Cherry Orchard* is to notice that in this play, although there are innumerable references to Time between the first speech, when Lopahin says "The train got in, thank God! What time is it?" and the last act, where there is much talk about catching the outbound train, Time does not function as it usually functions either in tragedy or in comedy. In tragedy we usually feel, If there had only been more time. . . . For example, in *Romeo and Juliet* Friar Laurence writes a letter to Romeo, explaining that Juliet will take a potion that will put her in a temporary, death-like trance, but the letter is delayed, Romeo mistakenly hears that Juliet is dead, and he kills himself. A few moments after his suicide Juliet revives. Had Friar

Laurence's message arrived on schedule, or had Romeo not been so quick to commit suicide, no great harm would have been done. In *King Lear*, Edmund repents that he has ordered a soldier to kill Cordelia, and a messenger hurries out to change the order, but he is too late.

If in tragedy we usually feel the pressure of time, in comedy there is usually a sense of leisure. Things are difficult now, but in the course of time they will work themselves out. Sooner or later people will realize that the strange goings-on are due to the existence of identical twins; sooner or later the stubborn parents will realize that they cannot forever stand in the way of young lovers; sooner or later the money will turn up and all will be well. In the world of comedy, one is always safe in relying on time. In *The Cherry Orchard*, Lopahin insists, correctly enough, that the family must act *now* if it is to save the orchard: "We must decide definitely, time won't wait." There is ample time to act on Lopahin's suggestion that the orchard be leased for summer houses, and the play covers a period from May to October, but the plan is not acted on because to the aristocrats any sort of selling is unthinkable, and although one Pishtchik is in the course of time miraculously redeemed from financial ruin by some Englishmen who discover and buy "some kind of white clay" on *his* land, time brings Mme. Ranevskaya and her brother Gayeff no such good fortune. So far as the main happenings in the play are concerned, time neither presses nor preserves; it only passes.

During the passage of time in this play, the orchard is lost (tragic?) and the characters reveal themselves to be funny (comic?). The loss of the orchard is itself a happening of an uncertain kind. It stands, partly, for the end of an old way of life. But if that way once included intelligent and gracious aristocrats, it also included slavery, and in any case it now is embodied in the irresponsible heirs we see on the stage, Mme. Ranevskaya and her brother Gayeff, along with their deaf and near-senile servant Fiers. For Gayeff the orchard is important chiefly because it lends prestige, since it is mentioned in the encyclopedia. Mme. Ranevskaya sees more to it. For her it is "all white" and it is "young again and full of happiness"; we are momentarily touched by her vision, but there is yet another way of seeing the orchard: for Trofimoff, a student who envisions a new society as an orchard for all men, the ancestral cherry orchard is haunted by the serfs of the bad old days. Moreover, although the orchard is much talked about, it seems to have decayed to a trivial ornament. Long ago its crop was regularly harvested, pickled, and sold, thus providing food and income, but now "nobody remembers" the pickling formula and nobody buys the crop. There seems to be some truth to Lopahin's assertion that "the only remarkable thing about this cherry orchard is that it's very big," and although one must point out that this remark is made by a despised merchant, Lopahin is neither a fool nor the "money grubber" that Gayeff thinks he is. Lopahin delights in nature put to use. He made "forty thousand clear" from poppies, "And when my poppies were in bloom, what a picture it was!" His enthusiasm for the flowers is undercut for us only a little, if at all, by the fact that they were of use to him and to others.

Lopahin's serious concern, whether for his poppies or for the future of the cherry orchard, contrasts interestingly with Mme. Ranevskaya's and with Gayeff's sporadic passion for the orchard. Mme. Ranevskaya says, "I can't imagine my life without the cherry orchard," and she doubtless means what she says, but that her words have not much relation to reality is indicated by her meaningless addition, "If it is very necessary to sell it, then sell me along with the orchard." After the orchard has been sold, Gayeff confesses, "everything is fine now. Before the sale of the cherry orchard, we all were troubled, distressed, and then when the question was settled definitely, irrevocably, we all calmed down and were even cheerful — I'm a bank official. . . . Lyuba, you look better, no doubt about that." His sister agrees: "Yes. My nerves are better, that's true. . . . I sleep well. Carry out my things, Yasha. It's time." She returns to her lover in Paris, Gayeff goes off to a job in the bank, and though we can imagine that the orchard will continue to be an occasional topic of conversation, we cannot imagine that the loss has in any way changed them. The play ends, but things will go on in the same way; neither a tragic nor a comic action has been completed.

The characters no less than the action are tragicomic. Their longings would touch the heart if only these people did not so quickly digress or engage in little actions that call their depth into doubt. Charlotta laments that she has no proper passport and that her deceased parents may not have been married: "Where I came from and who I am I don't know." And then, having touched on the mighty subject of one's identity, the subject that is the stuff of tragedy in which heroes endure the worst in order to know who they are, she begins to eat a cucumber, and somehow that simple and entirely necessary act diminishes her dignity — though it does not totally dissipate our glimpse of her alienation. In the same scene, when Epihodoff confesses that although he reads "all kinds of remarkable books" he "cannot discover [his] own inclinations," we hear another echo of the tragic hero's quest for self-knowledge, but we also hear an echo from the world of comedy, say of the pedant who guides his life by a textbook. Epihodoff, perhaps like a tragic hero, is particularly concerned with whether to live or to shoot himself, but this racking doubt is diminished by his prompt explanation that since he may someday decide on suicide, he always carries a revolver, which he proceeds to show to his listeners. Almost all of the characters bare their souls, but their slightly addled minds and their hungry bodies expose them to a gentle satirical treatment so that they evoke a curious amused pathos. One can, for example, sympathize with Mme. Ranevskaya's despair — but one cannot forget that she is scatterbrained and that domestic duties and local pieties occupy her mind only occasionally and that her disreputable lover in Paris means as much as the orchard she thinks she cannot live without. And when Gayeff says, "On my honor I'll swear, by anything you like, that the estate shall not be sold," we know that he has very little honor and even less ability to focus on the problem (mostly he takes refuge in thoughts about billiards, and somehow his habit of eating candy does not enhance his status in our eyes) and that the estate will be sold.

Finally, something must be said about the ambiguous treatment of the future. We know, from his correspondence, that Chekhov looked forward to a new and happier society. Russia, like much of the rest of Europe, was ceasing to be an agrarian society, but if the death throes were evident, one could not be so confident about the birth pangs. Something of the presence of two worlds is hinted at in the stage direction at the beginning of the second act, where we see the estate with its orchard, and also "in the distance a row of telegraph poles; and far, far away, faintly traced on the horizon, is a large town." The telegraph poles and the town silently represent the new industrial society, but Trofimoff the student speaks at length of the glorious possibilities of the future, and his speeches were sufficiently close to the bone for the censor to delete two passages sharply critical of the present. But we cannot take Trofimoff's speeches quite at face value. He is a student, but he is almost thirty and still has not received his degree. His speeches in Act II are moving, especially those on the need to work rather than to talk if the future is to be better than the past, but we cannot quite rid ourselves of the suspicion that Trofimoff talks rather than works. Certainly he is contemptuous of the merchant Lopahin, who delights in work. And, worse, Trofimoff frets too much about his overshoes, thinks he is "above love," and is so confounded by Mme. Ranevskaya's remark, "Imagine, at your age, not having a mistress," that he falls down a flight of stairs. None of these personal failings invalidates his noble view of the future; certainly none of them turns this view into a comic pipedream, and yet all of these things, along with a certain nostalgia that we feel for the past, do suffuse even his noblest statements about the future with a delicate irony that puts them, along with the much praised but totally neglected cherry orchard, firmly in the tragicomic world. One understands why Chekhov called the play a comedy, and one understands why Stanislavsky (who directed the first production and played the part of Gayeff) told Chekhov, "It is definitely not a comedy . . . but a tragedy." Perhaps neither of the men fully wanted to see the resonant ambiguities in the play.

SIX CHARACTERS IN SEARCH OF AN AUTHOR

A Comedy in the Making

Luigi Pirandello

English version by Edward Storer

Luigi Pirandello (1867–1936) was born in Sicily, the son of the owner of a profitable sulfur mine. Pirandello studied at Rome and then at Bonn, where in 1891 he received a doctorate for a thesis on Sicilian dialect. Back in Rome he wrote poetry, fiction, and literary criticism, and taught Italian at a teachers college. Troubles came thick: his family, and his wife's, suffered financial setbacks, and his wife became intermittently insane. But from 1917 onward he had great success in the theater with many of his forty or so plays. Among the best-known plays are *Right You Are (If You Think You Are)* (1917), *Six Characters in Search of an Author* (1921), and *Henry IV* (1922). In 1934 Pirandello was awarded the Nobel Prize. Curiously, this philosophic skeptic was a supporter of Italian fascism, and he gave his Nobel medal to be melted down for Mussolini's Abyssinian campaign.

CHARACTERS OF THE COMEDY IN THE MAKING

THE FATHER	THE SON	MADAME PACE
THE MOTHER	THE BOY	(THE BOY *and* THE CHILD
THE STEP-DAUGHTER	THE CHILD	*do not speak*)

ACTORS OF THE COMPANY

THE MANAGER	L'INGENUE	MACHINIST
LEADING LADY	JUVENILE LEAD	MANAGER'S SECRETARY
LEADING MAN	OTHER ACTORS AND ACTRESSES	DOOR-KEEPER
SECOND LADY	PROPERTY MAN	SCENE-SHIFTERS
LEAD	PROMPTER	

Daytime. The Stage of a Theatre.
    N. B.   The Comedy is without acts or scenes. The performance is interrupted once, without the curtain being lowered, when the manager and the chief characters withdraw to arrange the scenario. A second interruption of the action takes place when, by mistake, the stage hands let the curtain down.

A scene from *Six Characters in Search of an Author*. (Photograph: The Bettmann Archive.)

ACT I

The spectators will find the curtain raised and the stage as it usually is during the day time. It will be half dark, and empty, so that from the beginning the public may have the impression of an impromptu performance.

Prompter's box and a small table and chair for the manager.

Two other small tables and several chairs scattered about as during rehearsals.

The ACTORS *and* ACTRESSES *of the company enter from the back of the stage: first one, then another, then two together; nine or ten in all. They are about to rehearse a Pirandello play: Mixing It Up.[1] Some of the company move off towards their dressing rooms. The* PROMPTER, *who has the "book" under his arm, is waiting for the manager in order to begin the rehearsal.*

The ACTORS *and* ACTRESSES, *some standing, some sitting, chat and smoke. One perhaps reads a paper; another cons his part.*

Finally, the MANAGER *enters and goes to the table prepared for him. His* SECRETARY *brings him his mail, through which he glances. The* PROMPTER *takes his seat, turns on a light, and opens the "book."*

THE MANAGER (*throwing a letter down on the table*): I can't see. (*To* PROPERTY MAN.) Let's have a little light, please!

PROPERTY MAN: Yes sir, yes, at once. (*A light comes down on to the stage.*)

THE MANAGER (*clapping his hands*): Come along! Come along! Second act of "Mixing It Up." (*Sits down.*)

(*The* ACTORS *and* ACTRESSES *go from the front of the stage to the wings, all except the three who are to begin the rehearsal.*)

THE PROMPTER (*reading the "book"*): "Leo Gala's house. A curious room serving as dining-room and study."

From *Naked Masks: Five Plays by Luigi Pirandello* edited by Eric Bentley. Copyright © 1922, 1952 by E. P. Dutton, renewal 1950 by Fausto Stefano & Lietta Pirandello. Reprinted by permission of the publisher, E. P. Dutton.

THE MANAGER (*to* PROPERTY MAN): Fix up the old red room.

PROPERTY MAN (*noting it down*): Red set, All right!

THE PROMPTER (*continuing to read from the "book"*): "Table already laid and writing desk with books and papers. Book-shelves. Exit rear to Leo's bedroom. Exit left to kitchen. Principal exit to right."

THE MANAGER (*energetically*): Well, you understand: The principal exit over there; here, the kitchen. (*Turning to actor who is to play the part of* SOCRATES.) You make your entrances and exits here. (*To* PROPERTY MAN.) The baize doors at the rear, and curtains.

PROPERTY MAN (*noting it down*): Right!

PROMPTER (*reading as before*): "When the curtain rises, Leo Gala, dressed in cook's cap and apron, is busy beating an egg in a cup. Philip, also dressed as a cook, is beating another egg. Guido Venanzi is seated and listening."

LEADING MAN (*to* MANAGER): Excuse me, but must I absolutely wear a cook's cap?

THE MANAGER (*annoyed*): I imagine so. It says so there anyway. (*Pointing to the "book."*)

LEADING MAN: But it's ridiculous!

THE MANAGER (*jumping up in a rage*): Ridiculous? Ridiculous? Is it my fault if France won't send us any more good comedies, and we are reduced to putting on Pirandello's works, where nobody understands anything, and where the author plays the fool with us all? (*The* ACTORS *grin. The* MANAGER *goes to* LEADING MAN *and shouts.*) Yes sir, you put on the cook's cap and beat eggs. Do you suppose that with all this egg-beating business you are on an ordinary stage? Get that out of your head. You represent the shell of the eggs you are beating! (*Laughter and comments among the* ACTORS.) Silence! and listen to my explanation, please! (*To* LEADING MAN.) "The empty form of reason without the fullness of instinct, which is blind." — You stand for reason, your wife is instinct. It's a mixing up of the parts, according to which you who act your own part become the puppet of yourself. Do you understand?

LEADING MAN: I'm hanged if I do.

THE MANAGER: Neither do I. But let's get on with it. It's sure to be a glorious failure anyway. (*Confidentially.*) But I say, please face three-quarters. Otherwise, what with the abstruseness of the dialogue, and the public that won't be able to hear you, the whole thing will go to hell. Come on! come on!

PROMPTER: Pardon sir, may I get into my box? There's a bit of a draught.

THE MANAGER: Yes, yes, of course!

(*At this point, the* DOOR-KEEPER *has entered from the stage door and advances towards the manager's table, taking off his braided cap. During this manoeuvre, the* SIX CHARACTERS *enter, and stop by the door at back of stage, so that when the* DOOR-KEEPER *is about to announce their coming to the* MANAGER, *they are already on the stage. A tenuous light surrounds them, almost as if irradiated by them — the faint breath of their fantastic reality.*

This light will disappear when they come forward towards the actors. They preserve, however, something of the dream lightness in which they seem almost suspended; but this does not detract from the essential reality of their forms and expressions.

He who is known as THE FATHER *is a man of about 50: hair, reddish in colour, thin at the temples; he is not bald, however; thick moustaches, falling over his still fresh mouth, which often opens in an empty and uncertain smile. He is fattish, pale; with an especially wide forehead. He has blue, oval-shaped eyes, very clear and piercing. Wears light trousers and a dark jacket. He is alternatively mellifluous and violent in his manner.*

THE MOTHER *seems crushed and terrified as if by an intolerable weight of shame and abasement. She is dressed in modest black and wears a thick widow's veil of crêpe. When she lifts this, she reveals a wax-like face. She always keeps her eyes downcast.*

THE STEP-DAUGHTER *is dashing, almost impudent, beautiful. She wears mourning too, but with great elegance. She shows contempt for the timid half-frightened manner of the wretched* BOY [14 *years old, and also dressed in black*]; *on the other hand, she displays a lively tenderness for her little sister,* THE CHILD [*about four*], *who is dressed in white, with a black silk sash at the waist.*

THE SON [22] *is tall, severe in his attitude of contempt for* THE FATHER, *supercilious and indifferent to* THE MOTHER. *He looks as if he had come on the stage against his will.*)

DOOR-KEEPER (*cap in hand*): Excuse me, sir . . .

THE MANAGER (*rudely*): Eh? What is it?

DOOR-KEEPER (*timidly*): These people are asking for you, sir.

THE MANAGER (*furious*): I am rehearsing, and you know perfectly well no one's allowed to come in during rehearsals! (*Turning to the* CHARACTERS.) Who are you, please? What do you want?

THE FATHER (*coming forward a little, followed by the others who seem embarrassed*): As a matter of fact . . . we have come here in search of an author . . .

THE MANAGER (*half angry, half amazed*): An author? What author?

THE FATHER: Any author, sir.

THE MANAGER: But there's no author here. We are not rehearsing a new piece.

THE STEP-DAUGHTER (*vivaciously*): So much the better, so much the better! We can be your new piece.

AN ACTOR (*coming forward from the others*): Oh, do you hear that?

THE FATHER (*to* STEP-DAUGHTER): Yes, but if the author isn't here . . . (*to* MANAGER) unless you would be willing . . .

THE MANAGER: You are trying to be funny.

THE FATHER: No, for Heaven's sake, what are you saying? We bring you a drama, sir.

THE STEP-DAUGHTER: We may be your fortune.

THE MANAGER: Will you oblige me by going away? We haven't time to waste with mad people.

THE FATHER (*mellifluously*): Oh sir, you know well that life is full of infinite absurdities, which, strangely enough, do not even need to appear plausible, since they are true.

THE MANAGER: What the devil is he talking about?

THE FATHER: I say that to reverse the ordinary process may well be considered a madness: that is, to create credible situations, in order that they may appear true. But permit me to observe that if this be madness, it is the sole *raison d'être* of your profession, gentlemen. (*The* ACTORS *look hurt and perplexed.*)

THE MANAGER (*getting up and looking at him*): So our profession seems to you one worthy of madmen then?

THE FATHER: Well, to make seem true that which isn't true . . . without any need . . . for a joke as it were . . . Isn't that your mission, gentlemen: to give life to fantastic characters on the stage?

THE MANAGER (*interpreting the rising anger of the* COMPANY): But I would beg you to believe, my dear sir, that the profession of the comedian is a noble one. If today, as things go, the playwrights give us stupid comedies to play and puppets to represent instead of men, remember we are proud to have given life to immortal works here on these very boards! (*The* ACTORS, *satisfied, applaud their* MANAGER.)

THE FATHER (*interrupting furiously*): Exactly, perfectly, to living beings more alive than those who breathe and wear clothes: beings less real perhaps, but truer! I agree with you entirely. (*The* ACTORS *look at one another in amazement.*)

THE MANAGER: But what do you mean? Before, you said . . .

THE FATHER: No, excuse me, I meant it for you, sir, who were crying out that you had no time to lose with madmen, while no one better than yourself knows that nature uses the instrument of human fantasy in order to pursue her high creative purpose.

THE MANAGER: Very well, -- but where does all this take us?

THE FATHER: Nowhere! It is merely to show you that one is born to life in many forms, in many shapes, as tree, or as stone, as water, as butterfly, or as woman. So one may also be born a character in a play.

THE MANAGER (*with feigned comic dismay*): So you and these other friends of yours have been born characters?

THE FATHER: Exactly, and alive as you see! (MANAGER *and* ACTORS *burst out laughing.*)

THE FATHER (*hurt*): I am sorry you laugh, because we carry in us a drama, as you can guess from this woman here veiled in black.

THE MANAGER (*losing patience at last and almost indignant*): Oh, chuck it! Get away please! Clear out of here! (*To* PROPERTY MAN.) For Heaven's sake, turn them out!

THE FATHER (*resisting*): No, no, look here, we . . .

THE MANAGER (*roaring*): We come here to work, you know.

LEADING ACTOR: One cannot let oneself be made such a fool of.

THE FATHER (*determined, coming forward*): I marvel at your incredulity, gentlemen. Are you not accustomed to see the characters created by an author spring to life in yourselves and face each other? Just because there is no "book" (*pointing to the* PROMPTER'S *box*) which contains us, you refuse to believe . . .

THE STEP-DAUGHTER (*advances towards* MANAGER, *smiling and coquettish*): Believe me, we are really six most interesting characters, sir; side-tracked however.

THE FATHER: Yes, that is the word! (*To* MANAGER *all at once.*) In the sense, that is, that the author who created us alive no longer wished, or was no longer able, materially to put us into a work of art. And this was a real crime, sir; because he who has had the luck to be born a character can laugh even at death. He cannot die. The man, the writer, the instrument of the creation will die, but his creation does not die. And to live for ever, it does not need to have extraordinary gifts or to be able to work wonders. Who was Sancho Panza? Who was Don Abbondio? Yet they live eternally because — live germs as they were — they had the fortune to find a fecundating matrix, a fantasy which could raise and nourish them: make them live for ever!

THE MANAGER: That is quite all right. But what do you want here, all of you?

THE FATHER: We want to live.

THE MANAGER (*ironically*): For Eternity?

THE FATHER: No, sir, only for a moment . . . in you.

AN ACTOR: Just listen to him!

LEADING LADY: They want to live, in us . . . !

JUVENILE LEAD (*pointing to the* STEP-DAUGHTER): I've no objection, as far as that one is concerned!

THE FATHER: Look here! look here! The comedy has to be made. (*To the* MANAGER.) But if you and your actors are willing, we can soon concert it among ourselves.

THE MANAGER (*annoyed*): But what do you want to concert? We don't go in for concerts here. Here we play dramas and comedies!

THE FATHER: Exactly! That is just why we have come to you.

THE MANAGER: And where is the "book"?

THE FATHER: It is in us! (*The* ACTORS *laugh.*) The drama is in us, and we are the drama. We are impatient to play it. Our inner passion drives us on to this.

THE STEP-DAUGHTER (*disdainful, alluring, treacherous, full of impudence*): My passion, sir! Ah, if you only knew! My passion for him! (*Points to the* FATHER *and makes a pretence of embracing him. Then she breaks out into a loud laugh.*)

THE FATHER (*angrily*): Behave yourself! And please don't laugh in that fashion.

THE STEP-DAUGHTER: With your permission, gentlemen, I, who am a two months' orphan, will show you how I can dance and sing. (*Sings and then dances* Prenez garde à Tchou-Tchin-Tchou.)

Les chinois sont un peuple malin,
De Shangaî à Pékin,
Ils ont mis des écriteaux partout:
Prenez garde à Tchou-Tchin-Tchou.

ACTORS AND ACTRESSES: Bravo! Well done! Tip-top!

THE MANAGER: Silence! This isn't a café concert, you know! (*Turning to the* FATHER *in consternation.*) Is she mad?

THE FATHER: Mad? No, she's worse than mad.

THE STEP-DAUGHTER (*to* MANAGER): Worse? Worse? Listen! Stage this drama for us at once! Then you will see that at a certain moment I . . . when this little darling here . . . (*Takes the* CHILD *by the hand and leads her to the* MANAGER.) Isn't she a dear? (*Takes her up and kisses her.*) Darling! Darling! (*Puts her down again and adds feelingly.*) Well, when God suddenly takes this dear little child away from that poor mother there; and this imbecile here (*seizing hold of the* BOY *roughly and pushing him forward*) does the stupidest things, like the fool he is, you will see me run away. Yes, gentlemen, I shall be off. But the moment hasn't arrived yet. After what has taken place between him and me (*indicates the* FATHER *with a horrible wink*) I can't remain any longer in this society, to have to witness the anguish of this mother here for that fool . . . (*Indicates the* SON.) Look at him! Look at him! See how indifferent, how frigid he is, because he is the legitimate son.

He despises me, despises him (*pointing to the* BOY), despises this baby here; because . . . we are bastards. (*Goes to the* MOTHER *and embraces her.*) And he doesn't want to recognize her as his mother — she who is the common mother of us all. He looks down upon her as if she were only the mother of us three bastards. Wretch! (*She says all this very rapidly, excitedly. At the word "bastards" she raises her voice, and almost spits out the final "Wretch!"*)

THE MOTHER (*to the* MANAGER, *in anguish*): In the name of these two little children, I beg you . . . (*She grows faint and is about to fall.*) Oh God!

THE FATHER (*coming forward to support her as do some of the* ACTORS): Quick, a chair, a chair for this poor widow!

THE ACTORS: Is it true? Has she really fainted?

THE MANAGER: Quick, a chair! Here!

(*One of the* ACTORS *brings a chair, the* OTHERS *proffer assistance. The* MOTHER *tries to prevent the* FATHER *from lifting the veil which covers her face.*)

THE FATHER: Look at her! Look at her!

THE MOTHER: No, no; stop it please!

THE FATHER (*raising her veil*): Let them see you!

THE MOTHER (*rising and covering her face with her hands, in desperation*): I beg you, sir, to prevent this man from carrying out his plan which is loathsome to me.

THE MANAGER (*dumbfounded*): I don't understand at all. What is the situation? Is this lady your wife? (*To the* FATHER).

THE FATHER: Yes, gentlemen: my wife!

THE MANAGER: But how can she be a widow if you are alive? (*The* ACTORS *find relief for their astonishment in a loud laugh.*)

THE FATHER: Don't laugh! Don't laugh like that, for Heaven's sake. Her drama lies just here in this: she has had a lover, a man who ought to be here.

THE MOTHER (*with a cry*): No! No!

THE STEP-DAUGHTER: Fortunately for her, he is dead. Two months ago as I said. We are in mourning, as you see.

THE FATHER: He isn't here you see, not because he is dead. He isn't here — look at her a moment and you will understand — because her drama isn't a drama of the love of two men for whom she was incapable of feeling anything except possibly a little gratitude — gratitude not for me but for the other. She isn't a woman, she is a mother, and her drama — powerful sir, I assure you — lies, as a matter of fact, all in these four children she has had by two men.

THE MOTHER: I had them? Have you got the courage to say that I wanted them? (*To the* COMPANY.) It was his doing. It was he who gave me that other man, who forced me to go away with him.

THE STEP-DAUGHTER: It isn't true.

THE MOTHER (*startled*): Not true, isn't it?

THE STEP-DAUGHTER: No, it isn't true, it just isn't true.

THE MOTHER: And what can you know about it?

THE STEP-DAUGHTER: It isn't true. Don't believe it. (*To* MANAGER.) Do you know why she says so? For that fellow there. (*Indicates the* SON.) She tortures herself, destroys herself on account of the neglect of that son there; and she wants him to believe that if she abandoned him when he was only two years old, it was because he (*indicates the* FATHER) made her do so.

THE MOTHER (*vigorously*): He forced me to it, and I call God to witness it. (*To the* MANAGER.) Ask him (*indicates* HUSBAND) if it isn't true. Let him speak. You (*to* DAUGHTER) are not in a position to know anything about it.

THE STEP-DAUGHTER: I know you lived in peace and happiness with my father while he lived. Can you deny it?

THE MOTHER: No, I don't deny it . . .

THE STEP-DAUGHTER: He was always full of affection and kindness for you. (*To the* BOY, *angrily*.) It's true, isn't it? Tell them! Why don't you speak, you little fool?

THE MOTHER: Leave the poor boy alone. Why do you want to make me appear ungrateful, daughter? I don't want to offend your father. I have answered him that I didn't abandon my house and my son through any fault of mine, nor from any wilful passion.

THE FATHER: It is true. It was my doing.

LEADING MAN (*to the* COMPANY): What a spectacle!

LEADING LADY: We are the audience this time.

JUVENILE LEAD: For once, in a way.

THE MANAGER (*beginning to get really interested*): Let's hear them out. Listen!

THE SON: Oh yes, you're going to hear a fine bit now. He will talk to you of the Demon of Experiment.

THE FATHER: You are a cynical imbecile. I've told you so already a hundred times. (*To the* MANAGER.) He tries to make fun of me on account of this expression which I have found to excuse myself with.

THE SON (*with disgust*): Yes, phrases! phrases!

THE FATHER: Phrases! Isn't everyone consoled when faced with a trouble or fact he doesn't understand, by a word, some simple word, which tells us nothing and yet calms us?

THE STEP-DAUGHTER: Even in the case of remorse. In fact, especially then.

THE FATHER: Remorse? No, that isn't true. I've done more than use words to quieten the remorse in me.

THE STEP-DAUGHTER: Yes, there was a bit of money too. Yes, yes, a bit of money. There were the hundred lire he was about to offer me in payment, gentlemen . . . (*Sensation of horror among the* ACTORS.)

THE SON (*to the* STEP-DAUGHTER): This is vile.

THE STEP-DAUGHTER: Vile? There they were in a pale blue envelope on a little mahogany table in the back of Madame Pace's shop. You know Madame Pace — one of those ladies who attract poor girls of good family into their ateliers, under the pretext of their selling *robes et manteaux*.

THE SON: And he thinks he has bought the right to tyrannize over us all with those hundred lire he was going to pay; but which, fortunately — note this, gentlemen — he had no chance of paying.

THE STEP-DAUGHTER: It was a near thing, though, you know! (*Laughs ironically*.)

THE MOTHER (*protesting*): Shame, my daughter, shame!

THE STEP-DAUGHTER: Shame indeed! This is my revenge! I am dying to live that scene . . . The room . . . I see it . . . Here is the window with the mantles exposed, there the divan, the looking-glass, a screen, there in front of the window the little mahogany table with the blue envelope containing one hundred lire. I see it. I see it. I could take hold of it . . . But you, gentlemen, you ought to turn your backs now: I am almost nude, you know. But I don't blush: I leave that to him. (*Indicating* FATHER.)

THE MANAGER: I don't understand this at all.

THE FATHER: Naturally enough. I would ask you, sir, to exercise your authority a little here, and let me speak before you believe all she is trying to blame me with. Let me explain.

THE STEP-DAUGHTER: Ah yes, explain it in your own way.

THE FATHER: But don't you see that the whole trouble lies here. In words, words. Each one of us has within him a whole world of things, each man of us his own special world. And how can we ever come to an understanding if I put in the words I utter the sense and value of things as I see them; while you who listen to me must inevitably translate them according to the conception of things each one of you has within himself. We think we understand each other, but we never really do. Look here! This woman (*indicating the* MOTHER) takes all my pity for her as a specially ferocious form of cruelty.

THE MOTHER: But you drove me away.

THE FATHER: Do you hear her? I drove her away! She believes I really sent her away.

THE MOTHER: You know how to talk, and I don't; but, believe me, sir (*to* MANAGER), after he had married me . . . who knows why? . . . I was a poor insignificant woman . . .

THE FATHER: But, good Heavens! it was just for your humility that I married you. I loved this simplicity in you. (*He stops when he sees she makes signs to contradict him, opens his arms wide in sign of desperation, seeing how hopeless it is to make himself understood.*) You see she denies it. Her mental deafness, believe me, is phenomenal, the limit: (*touches his forehead*) deaf, deaf, mentally deaf! She has plenty of feeling. Oh yes, a good heart for the children; but the brain — deaf, to the point of desperation — !

THE STEP-DAUGHTER: Yes, but ask him how his intelligence has helped us.

THE FATHER: If we could see all the evil that may spring from good, what should we do? (*At this point the* LEADING LADY, *who is biting her lips with rage at seeing the* LEADING MAN *flirting with the* STEP-DAUGHTER, *comes forward and says to the* MANAGER.)

LEADING LADY: Excuse me, but are we going to rehearse today?

MANAGER: Of course, of course; but let's hear them out.

JUVENILE LEAD: This is something quite new.

L'INGENUE: Most interesting!

LEADING LADY: Yes, for the people who like that kind of thing. (*Casts a glance at* LEADING MAN.)

THE MANAGER (*to* FATHER): You must please explain yourself quite clearly. (*Sits down.*)

THE FATHER: Very well then: listen! I had in my service a poor man, a clerk, a secretary of mine, full of devotion, who became friends with her. (*Indicating the* MOTHER.) They understood one another, were kindred souls in fact, without, however, the least suspicion of any evil existing. They were incapable even of thinking of it.

THE STEP-DAUGHTER: So he thought of it — for them!

THE FATHER: That's not true. I meant to do good to them — and to myself, I confess, at the same time. Things had come to the point that I could not say a word to either of them without their making a mute appeal, one to the other, with their eyes. I could see them silently asking each other how I was to be kept in countenance, how I was to be kept quiet. And this, believe me, was just about enough of itself to keep me in a constant rage, to exasperate me beyond measure.

THE MANAGER: And why didn't you send him away then — this secretary of yours?

THE FATHER: Precisely what I did, sir. And then I had to watch this poor woman drifting forlornly about the house like an animal without a master, like an animal one has taken in out of pity.

THE MOTHER: Ah yes . . . !

THE FATHER (*suddenly turning to the* MOTHER): It's true about the son anyway, isn't it?

THE MOTHER: He took my son away from me first of all.

THE FATHER: But not from cruelty. I did it so that he should grow up healthy and strong by living in the country.

THE STEP-DAUGHTER (*pointing to him ironically*): As one can see.

THE FATHER (*quickly*): Is it my fault if he

has grown up like this? I sent him to a wet nurse in the country, a peasant, as *she* did not seem to me strong enough, though she is of humble origin. That was, anyway, the reason I married her. Unpleasant all this may be, but how can it be helped? My mistake possibly, but there we are! All my life I have had these confounded aspirations towards a certain moral sanity. (*At this point the* STEP-DAUGHTER *bursts into a noisy laugh.*) Oh, stop it! Stop it! I can't stand it.

THE MANAGER: Yes, please stop it, for Heaven's sake.

THE STEP-DAUGHTER: But imagine moral sanity from him, if you please — the client of certain ateliers like that of Madame Pace!

THE FATHER: Fool! That is the proof that I am a man! This seeming contradiction, gentlemen, is the strongest proof that I stand here a live man before you. Why, it is just for this very incongruity in my nature that I have had to suffer what I have. I could not live by the side of that woman (*indicating the* MOTHER) any longer; but not so much for the boredom she inspired me with as for the pity I felt for her.

THE MOTHER: And so he turned me out — .

THE FATHER: — well provided for! Yes, I sent her to that man, gentlemen . . . to let her go free of me.

THE MOTHER: And to free himself.

THE FATHER: Yes, I admit it. It was also a liberation for me. But great evil has come of it. I meant well when I did it; and I did it more for her sake than mine. I swear it. (*Crosses his arms on his chest; then turns suddenly to the* MOTHER.) Did I ever lose sight of you until that other man carried you off to another town, like the angry fool he was? And on account of my pure interest in you . . . my pure interest, I repeat, that had no base motive in it . . . I watched with the tenderest concern the new family that grew up around her. She can bear witness to this. (*Points to the* STEP-DAUGHTER.)

THE STEP-DAUGHTER: Oh yes, that's true enough. When I was a kiddie, so so high, you know, with plaits over my shoulders and knickers longer than my skirts, I used to see him waiting outside the school for me to come out. He came to see how I was growing up.

THE FATHER: This is infamous, shameful!

THE STEP-DAUGHTER: No. Why?

THE FATHER: Infamous! infamous! (*Then excitedly to* MANAGER, *explaining.*) After she (*indicating* MOTHER) went away, my house seemed suddenly empty. She was my incubus, but she filled my house. I was like a dazed fly alone in the empty rooms. This boy here (*indicating the* SON) was educated away from home, and when he came back, he seemed to me to be no more mine. With no mother to stand between him and me, he grew up entirely for himself, on his own, apart, with no tie of intellect or affection binding him to me. And then — strange but true — I was driven, by curiosity at first and then by some tender sentiment, towards her family, which had come into being through my will. The thought of her began gradually to fill up the emptiness I felt all around me. I wanted to know if she were happy in living out the simple daily duties of life. I wanted to think of her as fortunate and happy because far away from the complicated torments of my spirit. And so, to have proof of this, I used to watch that child coming out of school.

THE STEP-DAUGHTER: Yes, yes. True. He used to follow me in the street and smiled at me, waved his hand, like this. I would look at him with interest, wondering who he might be. I told my mother, who guessed at once. (*The* MOTHER *agrees with a nod.*) Then she didn't want to send me to school for some days; and when I finally went back, there he was again — looking so ridiculous — with a paper parcel in his hands. He came close to me, caressed me, and drew out a fine straw hat from the parcel, with a bouquet of flowers — all for me!

THE MANAGER: A bit discursive this, you know!

THE SON (*contemptuously*): Literature! Literature!

THE FATHER: Literature indeed! This is life, this is passion!

THE MANAGER: It may be, but it won't act.

THE FATHER: I agree. This is only the part leading up. I don't suggest this should be staged. She (*pointing to the* STEP-DAUGHTER), as you see, is no longer the flapper with plaits down her back — .

THE STEP-DAUGHTER: — and the knickers showing below the skirt!

THE FATHER: The drama is coming now, sir; something new, complex, most interesting.

THE STEP-DAUGHTER: As soon as my father died . . .

THE FATHER: — there was absolute misery for them. They came back here, unknown to me. Through her stupidity! (*Pointing to the* MOTHER.) It is true she can barely write her own name; but she could anyhow have got her daughter to write to me that they were in need . . .

THE MOTHER: And how was I to divine all this sentiment in him?

THE FATHER: That is exactly your mistake, never to have guessed any of my sentiments.

THE MOTHER: After so many years apart, and all that had happened . . .

THE FATHER: Was it my fault if that fellow carried you away? It happened quite suddenly; for after he had obtained some job or other, I could find no trace of them; and so, not unnaturally, my interest in them dwindled. But the drama culminated unforeseen and violent on their return, when I was impelled by my miserable flesh that still lives . . . Ah! what misery, what wretchedness is that of the man who is alone and disdains debasing *liaisons!* Not old enough to do without women, and not young enough to go and look for one without shame. Misery? It's worse than misery; it's a horror; for no woman can any longer give him love; and when a man feels this . . . One ought to do without, you say? Yes, yes, I know. Each of us when he appears before his fellows is clothed in a certain dignity. But every man knows what unconfessable things pass within the secrecy of his own heart. One gives way to the temptation, only to rise from it again, afterwards, with a great eagerness to re-establish one's dignity, as if it were a tombstone to place on the grave of one's shame, and a monument to hide and sign the memory of our weaknesses. Everybody's in the same case. Some folks haven't the courage to say certain things, that's all!

THE STEP-DAUGHTER: All appear to have the courage to do them though.

THE FATHER: Yes, but in secret. Therefore, you want more courage to say these things. Let a man but speak these things out, and folks at once label him a cynic. But it isn't true. He is like all the others, better indeed, because he isn't afraid to reveal with the light of the intelligence the red shame of human bestiality on which most men close their eyes so as not to see it.

Woman — for example, look at her case! She turns tantalizing inviting glances on you. You seize her. No sooner does she feel herself in your grasp than she closes her eyes. It is the sign of her mission, the sign by which she says to man: "Blind yourself, for I am blind."

THE STEP-DAUGHTER: Sometimes she can close them no more: when she no longer feels the need of hiding her shame to herself, but dry-eyed and dispassionately, sees only that of the man who has blinded himself without love. Oh, all these intellectual complications make me sick, disgust me — all this philosophy that uncovers the beast in man, and then seeks to save him, excuse him . . . I can't stand it, sir. When a man seeks to "simplify" life bestially, throwing aside every relic of humanity, every chaste aspiration, every pure feeling, all sense of ideality, duty, modesty, shame . . . then nothing is more revolting and nauseous than a certain kind of remorse — crocodiles' tears, that's what it is.

THE MANAGER: Let's come to the point. This is only discussion.

THE FATHER: Very good, sir! But a fact is like a sack which won't stand up when it is empty. In order that it may stand up, one has to put into it the reason and sentiment which have caused it to exist. I couldn't possibly know that after the death of that man, they had decided to return here, that they were in misery, and that she (*pointing to the* MOTHER) had gone to work as a modiste, and at a shop of the type of that of Madame Pace.

THE STEP-DAUGHTER: A real high-class modiste, you must know, gentlemen. In appearance, she works for the leaders of the best society; but she arranges matters so that these elegant ladies serve her purpose . . . without prejudice to other ladies who are . . . well . . . only so so.

THE MOTHER: You will believe me, gentlemen, that it never entered my mind that the old hag offered me work because she had her eye on my daughter.

THE STEP-DAUGHTER: Poor mamma! Do you know, sir, what that woman did when I brought her back the work my mother had finished? She would point out to me that I had torn one of my frocks, and she would give it back to my mother to mend. It was I who paid for it, always I; while this poor creature here believed she was sacrificing herself for me and these two children here, sitting up at night sewing Madame Pace's robes.

THE MANAGER: And one day you met there . . .

THE STEP-DAUGHTER: Him, him. Yes sir, an old client. There's a scene for you to play! Superb!

THE FATHER: She, the Mother arrived just then . . .

THE STEP-DAUGHTER (*treacherously*): Almost in time!

THE FATHER (*crying out*): No, in time! in time! Fortunately I recognized her . . . in time. And I took them back home with me to my house. You can imagine now her position and mine; she, as you see her; and I who cannot look her in the face.

THE STEP-DAUGHTER: Absurd! How can I possibly be expected — after that — to be a modest young miss, a fit person to go with his confounded aspirations for "a solid moral sanity"?

THE FATHER: For the drama lies all in this — in the conscience that I have, that each one of us has. We believe this conscience to be a single thing, but it is many-sided. There is one for this person, and another for that. Diverse consciences. So we have this illusion of being one person for all, of having a personality that is unique in all our acts. But it isn't true. We perceive this when, tragically perhaps, in something we do, we are as it were, suspended, caught up in the air on a kind of hook. Then we perceive that all of us was not in that act, and that it would be an atrocious injustice to judge us by that action alone, as if all our existence were summed up in that one deed. Now do you understand the perfidy of this girl? She surprised me in a place, where she ought not to have known me, just as I could not exist for her; and she now seeks to attach to me a reality such as I could never suppose I should have to assume for her in a shameful and fleeting moment of my life. I feel this above all else. And the drama, you will see, acquires a tremendous value from this point. Then there is the position of the others . . . his . . . (*Indicating the* SON.)

THE SON (*shrugging his shoulders scornfully*): Leave me alone! I don't come into this.

THE FATHER: What? You don't come into this?

THE SON: I've got nothing to do with it, and don't want to have; because you know well enough I wasn't made to be mixed up in all this with the rest of you.

THE STEP-DAUGHTER: We are only vulgar folk! He is the fine gentleman. You may have noticed, Mr. Manager, that I fix him now and again with a look of scorn while he lowers his eyes — for he knows the evil he has done me.

THE SON (*scarcely looking at her*): I?

THE STEP-DAUGHTER: You! you! I owe my life on the streets to you. Did you or did you not deny us, with your behaviour, I won't say the intimacy of home, but even that mere hospitality which makes guests feel at their ease? We were intruders who had come to disturb the kingdom of your legitimacy. I should like to have you witness, Mr. Manager, certain scenes between him and me. He says I have tyrannized over everyone. But it was just his behaviour which made me insist on the reason for which I had come into the house, — this reason he calls "vile" — into his house, with my mother who is his mother too. And I came as mistress of the house.

THE SON: It's easy for them to put me always in the wrong. But imagine, gentlemen, the position of a son, whose fate it is to see arrive one day at his home a young woman of impudent bearing, a young woman who inquires for his father, with whom who knows what business she has. This young man has then to witness her return bolder than ever, accompanied by that child there. He is obliged to watch her treat his father in an equivocal and confidential manner. She asks money of him in a way that lets one suppose he must give it her, *must*, do you understand, because he has every obligation to do so.

THE FATHER: But I have, as a matter of fact, this obligation. I owe it to your mother.

THE SON: How should I know? When had I ever seen or heard of her? One day there arrive with her (*indicating* STEP-DAUGHTER) that lad and this baby here. I am told: "This is *your* mother too, you know." I divine from her manner (*indicating* STEP-DAUGHTER *again*) why it is they have come home. I had rather not say what I feel and think about it. I shouldn't even care to confess to myself. No action can therefore be hoped for from me in this affair. Believe me, Mr. Manager, I am an "unrealized" character, dramatically speaking; and I find myself not at all at ease in their company. Leave me out of it, I beg you.

THE FATHER: What? It is just because you are so that . . .

THE SON: How do you know what I am like? When did you ever bother your head about me?

THE FATHER: I admit it. I admit it. But isn't that a situation in itself? This aloofness of yours which is so cruel to me and to your mother, who returns home and sees you almost for the first time grown up, who doesn't recognize you but knows you are her son . . . (*Pointing out the* MOTHER *to the* MANAGER.) See, she's crying!

THE STEP-DAUGHTER (*angrily, stamping her foot*): Like a fool!

THE FATHER (*indicating* STEP-DAUGHTER): She can't stand him you know. (*Then referring again to the* SON.) He says he doesn't come into the affair, whereas he is really the hinge of the whole action. Look at that lad who is always clinging to his mother, frightened and humiliated. It is on account of this fellow here. Possibly his situation is the most painful of all. He feels himself a stranger more than the others. The poor little chap feels mortified, humiliated at being brought into a home out of charity as it were. (*In confidence.*) He is the image of his father. Hardly talks at all. Humble and quiet.

THE MANAGER: Oh, we'll cut him out. You've no notion what a nuisance boys are on the stage . . .

THE FATHER: He disappears soon, you know. And the baby too. She is the first to vanish from the scene. The drama consists finally in this: when that mother re-enters my house, her family born outside of it, and shall we say superimposed on the original, ends with the death of the little girl, the tragedy of the boy and the flight of the elder daughter. It cannot go on, because it is foreign to its surroundings. So after much torment, we three remain: I, the mother, that son. Then, owing to the disappearance of that extraneous family, we too find ourselves strange to one another. We find we are living in an atmosphere of mortal desolation which is the revenge, as he (*indicating* SON) scornfully said of the Demon of Experiment, that unfortunately hides in me. Thus, sir, you see when faith is lacking, it becomes impossible to create certain states of happiness, for we lack the necessary humility. Vaingloriously, we try to substitute ourselves for this faith, creating thus for the rest of the world a reality which we believe after their fashion, while, actually, it doesn't exist. For each one of us has his own reality to be respected before God, even when it is harmful to one's very self.

THE MANAGER: There is something in what you say. I assure you all this interests me very much. I begin to think there's the stuff for a drama in all this, and not a bad drama either.

THE STEP-DAUGHTER (*coming forward*): When you've got a character like me.

THE FATHER (*shutting her up, all excited to learn the decision of the* MANAGER): You be quiet!

THE MANAGER (*reflecting, heedless of interruption*): It's new . . . hem . . . yes . . .

THE FATHER: Absolutely new!

THE MANAGER: You've got a nerve though, I must say, to come here and fling it at me like this . . .

THE FATHER: You will understand, sir, born as we are for the stage . . .

THE MANAGER: Are you amateur actors then?

THE FATHER: No. I say born for the stage, because . . .

THE MANAGER: Oh, nonsense. You're an old hand, you know.

THE FATHER: No sir, no. We act that role for which we have been cast, that role which we are given in life. And in my own case, passion itself, as usually happens, becomes a trifle theatrical when it is exalted.

THE MANAGER: Well, well, that will do. But you see, without an author . . . I could give you the address of an author if you like . . .

THE FATHER: No, no. Look here! You must be the author.

THE MANAGER: I? What are you talking about?

THE FATHER: Yes, you, you! Why not?

THE MANAGER: Because I have never been an author: that's why.

THE FATHER: Then why not turn author now? Everybody does it. You don't want any special qualities. Your task is made much easier by the fact that we are all here alive before you . . .

THE MANAGER: It won't do.

THE FATHER: What? When you see us live our drama . . .

THE MANAGER: Yes, that's all right. But you want someone to write it.

THE FATHER: No, no. Someone to take it down, possibly, while we play it, scene by scene! It will be enough to sketch it out at first, and then try it over.

THE MANAGER: Well . . . I am almost tempted. It's a bit of an idea. One might have a shot at it.

THE FATHER: Of course. You'll see what scenes will come out of it. I can give you one, at once . . .

THE MANAGER: By Jove, it tempts me. I'd like to have a go at it. Let's try it out. Come with me to my office. (*Turning to the* AC-TORS.) You are at liberty for a bit, but don't step out of the theatre for long. In a quarter of an hour, twenty minutes, all back here again! (*To the* FATHER.) We'll see what can be done. Who knows if we don't get something really extraordinary out of it?

THE FATHER: There's no doubt about it. They (*indicating the* CHARACTERS) had better come with us too, hadn't they?

THE MANAGER: Yes, yes. Come on! come on! (*Moves away and then turning to the* AC-TORS.) *Be punctual, please!* (MANAGER *and the* SIX CHARACTERS *cross the stage and go off. The other* ACTORS *remain, looking at one another in astonishment.*)

LEADING MAN: Is he serious? What the devil does he want to do?

JUVENILE LEAD: This is rank madness.

THIRD ACTOR: Does he expect to knock up a drama in five minutes?

JUVENILE LEAD: Like the improvisers!

LEADING LADY: If he thinks I'm going to take part in a joke like this . . .

JUVENILE LEAD: I'm out of it anyway.

FOURTH ACTOR: I should like to know who they are. (*Alludes to* CHARACTERS.)

THIRD ACTOR: What do you suppose? Madmen or rascals!

JUVENILE LEAD: And he takes them seriously!

L'INGENUE: Vanity! He fancies himself as an author now.

LEADING MAN: It's absolutely unheard of. If the stage has come to this . . . well I'm . . .

FIFTH ACTOR: It's rather a joke.

THIRD ACTOR: Well, we'll see what's going to happen next.

(*Thus talking, the* ACTORS *leave the stage; some going out by the little door at the back; others retiring to their dressing-rooms. The curtain remains up. The action of the play is suspended for twenty minutes.*)

ACT II

The stage call-bells ring to warn the company that the play is about to begin again.

The STEP-DAUGHTER *comes out of the* MANAGER's *office along with the* CHILD *and the* BOY. *As she comes out of the office, she cries:* —

Nonsense! nonsense! Do it yourselves! I'm not going to mix myself up in this mess. (*Turning to the* CHILD *and coming quickly with her on to the stage.*) Come on, Rosetta, let's run!

(*The* BOY *follows them slowly, remaining a little behind and seeming perplexed.*)

THE STEP-DAUGHTER (*stops, bends over the* CHILD *and takes the latter's face between her hands*): My little darling! You're frightened, aren't you? You don't know where we are, do you? (*Pretending to reply to a question of the* CHILD.) What is the stage? It's a place, baby, you know, where people play at being serious, a place where they act comedies. We've got to act a comedy now, dead serious, you know; and you're in it also, little one. (*Embraces her, pressing the little head to her breast, and rocking the* CHILD *for a moment.*) Oh darling, darling, what a horrid comedy you've got to play! What a wretched part they've found for you! A garden . . . a fountain . . . look . . . just suppose, kiddie, it's here. Where, you say? Why, right here in the middle. It's all pretence you know. That's the trouble, my pet: it's all make-believe here. It's better to imagine it though, because if they fix it up for you, it'll only be painted cardboard, painted cardboard for the rockery, the water, the plants . . . Ah, but I think a baby like this one would sooner have a make-believe fountain than a real one, so she could play with it. What a joke it'll be for the others! But for you, alas! not quite such a joke: you who are real, baby dear, and really play by a real fountain that is big and green and beautiful, with ever so many bamboos around it that are reflected in the water, and a whole lot of little ducks swimming about . . . No, Rosetta, no, your mother doesn't bother about you on account of that wretch of a son there. I'm in the devil of a temper, and as for that lad . . . (*Seizes* BOY *by the arm to force him to take* one of his hands out of his pockets.) What have you got there? What are you hiding? (Pulls his hand out of his pocket, looks into it and catches the glint of a revolver.) Ah! where did you get this? (The BOY, very pale in the face, looks at her, but does not answer). Idiot! If I'd been in your place, instead of killing myself, I'd have shot one of those two, or both of them: father and son.

(The FATHER enters from the office, all excited from his work. The MANAGER follows him.)

THE FATHER: Come on, come on dear! Come here for a minute! We've arranged everything. It's all fixed up.

THE MANAGER (also excited): If you please, young lady, there are one or two points to settle still. Will you come along?

THE STEP-DAUGHTER (following him towards the office): Ouff! what's the good, if you've arranged everything.

(The FATHER, MANAGER and STEP-DAUGHTER go back into the office again [off] for a moment. At the same time, the SON, followed by the MOTHER, comes out.)

THE SON (looking at the three entering office): Oh this is fine, fine! And to think I can't even get away!

(The MOTHER attempts to look at him, but lowers her eyes immediately when he turns away from her. She then sits down. The BOY and the CHILD approach her. She casts a glance again at the SON, and speaks with humble tones, trying to draw him into conversation.)

THE MOTHER: And isn't my punishment the worst of all? (Then seeing from the SON's manner that he will not bother himself about her.) My God! Why are you so cruel? Isn't it enough for one person to support all this torment? Must you then insist on others seeing it also?

THE SON (half to himself, meaning the MOTHER to hear, however): And they want to put it on the stage! If there was at least a reason for it! He thinks he has got at the meaning of it all. Just as if each one of us in every circumstance of life couldn't find his own explanation of it! (Pauses.) He complains he was discovered in a place where he ought not

to have been seen, in a moment of his life which ought to have remained hidden and kept out of the reach of that convention which he has to maintain for other people. And what about my case? Haven't I had to reveal what no son ought ever to reveal: how father and mother live and are man and wife for themselves quite apart from that idea of father and mother which we give them? When this idea is revealed, our life is then linked at one point only to that man and that woman; and as such it should shame them, shouldn't it?

(The MOTHER hides her face in her hands. From the dressing-rooms and the little door at the back of the stage the ACTORS and STAGE MANAGER return, followed by the PROPERTY MAN, and the PROMPTER. At the same moment, the MANAGER comes out of his office, accompanied by the FATHER and the STEP-DAUGHTER.)

THE MANAGER: Come on, come on, ladies and gentlemen! Heh! you there, machinist!

MACHINIST: Yes sir?

THE MANAGER: Fix up the white parlor with the floral decorations. Two wings and a drop with a door will do. Hurry up!

(The MACHINIST runs off at once to prepare the scene, and arranges it while the MANAGER talks with the STAGE MANAGER, the PROPERTY MAN, and the PROMPTER on matters of detail.)

THE MANAGER (to PROPERTY MAN): Just have a look, and see if there isn't a sofa or divan in the wardrobe . . .

PROPERTY MAN: There's the green one.

THE STEP-DAUGHTER: No no! Green won't do. It was yellow, ornamented with flowers — very large! and most comfortable!

PROPERTY MAN: There isn't one like that.

THE MANAGER: It doesn't matter. Use the one we've got.

THE STEP-DAUGHTER: Doesn't matter? It's most important!

THE MANAGER: We're only trying it now. Please don't interfere. (To PROPERTY MAN.) See if we've got a shop window — long and narrowish.

THE STEP-DAUGHTER: And the little table! The little mahogany table for the pale blue envelope!

PROPERTY MAN (*to* MANAGER): There's that little gilt one.

THE MANAGER: That'll do fine.

THE FATHER: A mirror.

THE STEP-DAUGHTER: And the screen! We must have a screen. Otherwise how can I manage?

PROPERTY MAN: That's all right, Miss. We've got any amount of them.

THE MANAGER (*to the* STEP-DAUGHTER): We want some clothes pegs too, don't we?

THE STEP-DAUGHTER: Yes, several, several!

THE MANAGER: See how many we've got and bring them all.

PROPERTY MAN: All right!

(*The* PROPERTY MAN *hurries off to obey his orders. While he is putting the things in their places, the* MANAGER *talks to the* PROMPTER *and then with the* CHARACTERS *and the* ACTORS.)

THE MANAGER (*to* PROMPTER): Take your seat. Look here: this is the outline of the scenes, act by act. (*Hands him some sheets of paper.*) And now I'm going to ask you to do something out of the ordinary.

PROMPTER: Take it down in shorthand?

THE MANAGER (*pleasantly surprised*): Exactly! Can you do shorthand?

PROMPTER: Yes, a little.

THE MANAGER: Good! (*Turning to a* STAGE HAND.) Go and get some paper from my office, plenty, as much as you can find.

(*The* STAGE HAND *goes off, and soon returns with a handful of paper which he gives to the* PROMPTER.)

THE MANAGER (*to* PROMPTER): You follow the scenes as we play them, and try and get the points down, at any rate the most important ones. (*Then addressing the* ACTORS.) Clear the stage, ladies and gentlemen! Come over here (*pointing to the left*) and listen attentively.

LEADING LADY: But, excuse me, we . . .

THE MANAGER (*guessing her thought*): Don't worry! You won't have to improvise.

LEADING MAN: What have we to do then?

THE MANAGER: Nothing. For the moment you just watch and listen. Everybody will get his part written out afterwards. At present we're going to try the thing as best we can. They're going to act now.

THE FATHER (*as if fallen from the clouds into the confusion of the stage*): We? What do you mean, if you please, by a rehearsal?

THE MANAGER: A rehearsal for them. (*Points to the* ACTORS.)

THE FATHER: But since we are the characters . . .

THE MANAGER: All right: "characters" then, if you insist on calling yourselves such. But here, my dear sir, the characters don't act. Here the actors do the acting. The characters are there, in the "book" (*pointing towards* PROMPTER's *box*) — when there is a "book"!

THE FATHER: I won't contradict you; but excuse me, the actors aren't the characters. They want to be, they pretend to be, don't they? Now if these gentlemen here are fortunate enough to have us alive before them . . .

THE MANAGER: Oh this is grand! You want to come before the public yourselves then?

THE FATHER: As we are . . .

THE MANAGER: I can assure you it would be a magnificent spectacle!

LEADING MAN: What's the use of us here anyway then?

THE MANAGER: You're not going to pretend that you can act? It makes me laugh! (*The* ACTORS *laugh.*) There, you see, they are laughing at the notion. But, by the way, I must cast the parts. That won't be difficult. They cast themselves. (*To the* SECOND LADY LEAD.) You play the Mother. (*To the* FATHER.) We must find her a name.

THE FATHER: Amalia, sir.

THE MANAGER: But that is the real name of your wife. We don't want to call her by her real name.

THE FATHER: Why ever not, if it is her name? . . . Still, perhaps, if that lady must . . . (*Makes a slight motion of the hand to indicate the* SECOND LADY LEAD.) I see this woman here (*means the* MOTHER) as Amalia. But do as you like. (*Gets more and more confused.*) I don't know what to say to you. Already, I begin to hear my own words ring false, as if they had another sound . . .

THE MANAGER: Don't you worry about it. It'll be our job to find the right tones. And as for her name, if you want her Amalia, Amalia it shall be; and if you don't like it, we'll find another! For the moment though, we'll call the characters in this way: (*To* JUVENILE LEAD.) You are the Son. (*To the* LEADING

LADY.) You naturally are the Step-Daughter . . .

THE STEP-DAUGHTER (*excitedly*): What? what? I, that woman there? (*Bursts out laughing.*)

THE MANAGER (*angry*): What is there to laugh at?

LEADING LADY (*indignant*): Nobody has ever dared to laugh at me. I insist on being treated with respect; otherwise I go away.

THE STEP-DAUGHTER: No, no, excuse me . . . I am not laughing at you . . .

THE MANAGER (*to* STEP-DAUGHTER): You ought to feel honored to be played by . . .

LEADING LADY (*at once, contemptuously*): "That woman there" . . .

THE STEP-DAUGHTER: But I wasn't speaking of you, you know. I was speaking of myself — whom I can't see at all in you! That is all. I don't know . . . but . . . you . . . aren't in the least like me . . .

THE FATHER: True. Here's the point. Look here, sir, our temperaments, our souls . . .

THE MANAGER: Temperament, soul, be hanged! Do you suppose the spirit of the piece is in you? Nothing of the kind!

THE FATHER: What, haven't we our own temperaments, our own souls?

THE MANAGER: Not at all. Your soul or whatever you like to call it takes shape here. The actors give body and form to it, voice and gesture. And my actors — I may tell you — have given expression to much more lofty material than this little drama of yours, which may or may not hold up on the stage. But if it does, the merit of it, believe me, will be due to my actors.

THE FATHER: I don't dare contradict you, sir; but believe me, it is a terrible suffering for us who are as we are, with these bodies of ours, these features to see . . .

THE MANAGER (*cutting him short and out of patience*): Good heavens! The make-up will remedy all that, man, the make-up . . .

THE FATHER: Maybe. But the voice, the gestures . . .

THE MANAGER: Now, look here! On the stage, you as yourself, cannot exist. The actor here acts you, and that's an end to it!

THE FATHER: I understand. And now I think I see why our author who conceived us as we are, all alive, didn't want to put us on the stage after all. I haven't the least desire to offend your actors. Far from it! But when I think that

I am to be acted by . . . I don't know by whom . . .

LEADING MAN (*on his dignity*): By me, if you've no objection!

THE FATHER (*humbly, mellifluously*): Honored, I assure you, sir. (*Bows.*) Still, I must say that try as this gentleman may, with all his good will and wonderful art, to absorb me into himself . . .

LEADING MAN: Oh chuck it! "Wonderful art!" Withdraw that, please!

THE FATHER: The performance he will give, even doing his best with make-up to look like me . . .

LEADING MAN: It will certainly be a bit difficult! (*The* ACTORS *laugh.*)

THE FATHER: Exactly! It will be difficult to act me as I really am. The effect will be rather — apart from the make-up — according as to how he supposes I am, as he senses me — if he does sense me — and not as I inside of myself feel myself to be. It seems to me then that account should be taken of this by everyone whose duty it may become to criticize us . . .

THE MANAGER: Heavens! The man's starting to think about the critics now! Let them say what they like. It's up to us to put on the play if we can. (*Looking around.*) Come on! come on! Is the stage set? (*To the* ACTORS *and* CHARACTERS.) Stand back — stand back! Let me see, and don't let's lose any more time! (*To the* STEP-DAUGHTER.) Is it all right as it is now?

THE STEP-DAUGHTER: Well, to tell the truth, I don't recognize the scene.

THE MANAGER: My dear lady, you can't possibly suppose that we can construct that shop of Madame Pace piece by piece here? (*To the* FATHER.) You said a white room with flowered wall paper, didn't you?

THE FATHER: Yes.

THE MANAGER: Well then. We've got the furniture right more or less. Bring that little table a bit further forward. (*The* STAGE HANDS *obey the order. To* PROPERTY MAN.) You go and find an envelope, if possible, a pale blue one; and give it to that gentleman. (*Indicates* FATHER.)

PROPERTY MAN: An ordinary envelope?

MANAGER AND FATHER: Yes, yes, an ordinary envelope.

PROPERTY MAN: At once, sir. (*Exit.*)

THE MANAGER: Ready, everyone! First scene

— the Young Lady. (*The* LEADING LADY *comes forward.*) No, no, you must wait. I meant her (*Indicating the* STEP-DAUGHTER.) You just watch —

THE STEP-DAUGHTER (*adding at once*): How I shall play it, how I shall live it! . . .

LEADING LADY (*offended*): I shall live it also, you may be sure, as soon as I begin!

THE MANAGER (*with his hands to his head*): Ladies and gentlemen, if you please! No more useless discussions! Scene I: the Young Lady with Madame Pace: Oh! (*Looks around as if lost.*) And this Madame Pace, where is she?

THE FATHER: She isn't with us, sir.

THE MANAGER: Then what the devil's to be done?

THE FATHER: But she is alive too.

THE MANAGER: Yes, but where is she?

THE FATHER: One minute. Let me speak! (*Turning to the* ACTRESSES.) If these ladies would be so good as to give me their hats for a moment . . .

THE ACTRESSES (*half surprised, half laughing, in chorus*): What?
Why?
Our hats?
What does he say?

THE MANAGER: What are you going to do with the ladies' hats? (*The* ACTORS *laugh.*)

THE FATHER: Oh nothing. I just want to put them on these pegs for a moment. And one of the ladies will be so kind as to take off her mantle . . .

THE ACTORS: Oh, what d'you think of that?
Only the mantle?
He must be mad.

SOME ACTRESSES: But why?
Mantles as well?

THE FATHER: To hang them up here for a moment. Please be so kind, will you?

THE ACTRESSES (*taking off their hats, one or two also their cloaks, and going to hang them on the racks*): After all, why not?
There you are!
This is really funny.
We've got to put them on show.

THE FATHER: Exactly; just like that, on show.

THE MANAGER: May we know why?

THE FATHER: I'll tell you. Who knows if, by arranging the stage for her, she does not come here herself, attracted by the very articles of her trade? (*Inviting the* ACTORS *to look towards the exit at back of stage.*) Look! Look!

(*The door at the back of stage opens and* MADAME PACE *enters and takes a few steps forward. She is a fat, oldish woman with puffy oxygenated hair. She is rouged and powdered, dressed with a comical elegance in black silk. Round her waist is a long silver chain from which hangs a pair of scissors. The* STEP-DAUGHTER *runs over to her at once amid the stupor of the actors.*)

THE STEP-DAUGHTER (*turning towards her*): There she is! There she is!

THE FATHER (*radiant*): It's she! I said so, didn't I? There she is!

THE MANAGER (*conquering his surprise, and then becoming indignant*): What sort of a trick is this?

LEADING MAN (*almost at the same time*): What's going to happen next?

JUVENILE LEAD: Where does *she* come from?

L'INGENUE: They've been holding her in reserve, I guess.

LEADING LADY: A vulgar trick!

THE FATHER (*dominating the protests*): Excuse me, all of you! Why are you so anxious to destroy in the name of a vulgar, commonplace sense of truth, this reality which comes to birth attracted and formed by the magic of the stage itself, which has indeed more right to live here than you, since it is much truer than you — if you don't mind my saying so? Which is the actress among you who is to play Madame Pace? Well, here is Madame Pace herself. And you will allow, I fancy, that the actress who acts her will be less true than this woman here, who is herself in person. You see my daughter recognized her and went over to her at once. Now you're going to witness the scene!

(*But the scene between the* STEP-DAUGHTER *and* MADAME PACE *has already begun despite the protest of the actors and the reply of the* FATHER. *It has begun quietly, naturally, in a manner impossible for the stage. So when the actors, called to attention by the* FATHER, *turn round and see* MADAME PACE, *who has placed one hand under the* STEP-DAUGHTER'S *chin to raise her head, they observe her at first with great attention, but hearing her speak in an unintelligible manner their interest begins to wane.*)

THE MANAGER: Well? well?

LEADING MAN: What does she say?

LEADING LADY: One can't hear a word.

JUVENILE LEAD: Louder! Louder please!

THE STEP-DAUGHTER (*leaving* MADAME PACE, *who smiles a Sphinx-like smile, and advancing towards the actors*): Louder? Louder? What are you talking about? These aren't matters which can be shouted at the top of one's voice. If I have spoken them out loud, it was to shame him and have my revenge. (*Indicates* FATHER.) But for Madame it's quite a different matter.

THE MANAGER: Indeed? indeed? But here, you know, people have got to make themselves heard, my dear. Even we who are on the stage can't hear you. What will it be when the public's in the theatre? And anyway, you can very well speak up now among yourselves, since we shan't be present to listen to you as we are now. You've got to pretend to be alone in a room at the back of a shop where no one can hear you.

(*The* STEP-DAUGHTER *coquettishly and with a touch of malice makes a sign of disagreement two or three times with her finger.*)

THE MANAGER: What do you mean by no?

THE STEP-DAUGHTER (*sotto voce, mysteriously*): There's someone who will hear us if she (*indicating* MADAME PACE) speaks out loud.

THE MANAGER (*in consternation*)· What? Have you got someone else to spring on us now? (*The* ACTORS *burst out laughing.*)

THE FATHER: No, no sir. She is alluding to me. I've got to be here — there behind that door, in waiting; and Madame Pace knows it. In fact, if you will allow me, I'll go there at once, so I can be quite ready. (*Moves away.*)

THE MANAGER (*stopping him*): No! Wait! wait! We must observe the conventions of the theatre. Before you are ready . . .

THE STEP-DAUGHTER (*interrupting him*): No, get on with it at once! I'm just dying, I tell you, to act this scene. If he's ready, I'm more than ready.

THE MANAGER (*shouting*): But, my dear young lady, first of all, we must have the scene between you and this lady . . . (*Indicates* MADAME PACE.) Do you understand? . . .

THE STEP-DAUGHTER: Good Heavens! She's been telling me what you know already: that mamma's work is badly done again, that the material's ruined; and that if I want her to continue to help us in our misery I must be patient . . .

MADAME PACE (*coming forward with an air of great importance*): Yes indeed, sir, I no wanta take advantage of her, I no wanta be hard . . .

(*Note:* MADAME PACE *is supposed to talk in a jargon half Italian, half English.*)

THE MANAGER (*alarmed*): What? What? She talks like that? (*The* ACTORS *burst out laughing again.*)

THE STEP-DAUGHTER (*also laughing*): Yes yes, that's the way she talks, half English, half Italian! Most comical it is!

MADAME PACE: Itta seem not verra polite gentlemen laugha atta me eef I trya best speaka English.

THE MANAGER: *Diamine!* Of course! Of course! Let her talk like that! Just what we want. Talk just like that, Madame, if you please! The effect will be certain. Exactly what was wanted to put a little comic relief into the crudity of the situation. Of course she talks like that! Magnificent!

THE STEP-DAUGHTER: Magnificent? Certainly! When certain suggestions are made to one in language of that kind, the effect is certain, since it seems almost a joke. One feels inclined to laugh when one hears her talk about an "old signore" "who wanta talka nicely with you." Nice old signore, eh, Madame?

MADAME PACE: Not so old my dear, not so old! And even if you no lika him, he won't make any scandal!

THE MOTHER (*jumping up amid the amazement and consternation of the actors who had not been noticing her. They move to restrain her*): You old devil! You murderess!

THE STEP-DAUGHTER (*running over to calm her* MOTHER): Calm yourself, Mother, calm yourself! Please don't . . .

THE FATHER (*going to her also at the same time*): Calm yourself! Don't get excited! Sit down now!

THE MOTHER: Well then, take that woman away out of my sight!

THE STEP-DAUGHTER (*to* MANAGER): It is impossible for my mother to remain here.

THE FATHER (*to* MANAGER): They can't be here together. And for this reason, you see: that woman there was not with us when we came . . . If they are on together, the whole thing is given away inevitably, as you see.

THE MANAGER: It doesn't matter. This is only a first rough sketch — just to get an idea of the various points of the scene, even confusedly . . . (*Turning to the* MOTHER *and leading her to her chair.*) Come along, my dear lady, sit down now, and let's get on with the scene . . .

(*Meanwhile, the* STEP-DAUGHTER, *coming forward again, turns to* MADAME PACE.)

THE STEP-DAUGHTER: Come on, Madame, come on!

MADAME PACE (*offended*): No, no, *grazie*. I not do anything witha your mother present.

THE STEP-DAUGHTER: Nonsense! Introduce this "old signore" who wants to talk nicely to me. (*Addressing the* COMPANY *imperiously.*) We've got to do this scene one way or another, haven't we? Come on! (*To* MADAME PACE.) You can go!

MADAME PACE: Ah yes! I go'way! I go'way! Certainly! (*Exits furious.*)

THE STEP-DAUGHTER (*to the* FATHER): Now you make your entry. No, you needn't go over here. Come here. Let's suppose you've already come in. Like that, yes! I'm here with bowed head, modest like. Come on! Out with your voice! Say "Good morning, Miss" in that peculiar tone, that special tone . . .

THE MANAGER: Excuse me, but are you the Manager, or am I? (*To the* FATHER, *who looks undecided and perplexed.*) Get on with it, man! Go down there to the back of the stage. You needn't go off. Then come right forward here.

(*The* FATHER *does as he is told, looking troubled and perplexed at first. But as soon as he begins to move, the reality of the action affects him, and he begins to smile and to be more natural. The* ACTORS *watch intently.*)

THE MANAGER (*sotto voce, quickly to the* PROMPTER *in his box*): Ready! ready? Get ready to write now.

THE FATHER (*coming forward and speaking in a different tone*): Good afternoon, Miss!

THE STEP-DAUGHTER (*head bowed down slightly, with restrained disgust*): Good afternoon!

THE FATHER (*looks under her hat which partly covers her face. Perceiving she is very young, he makes an exclamation, partly of surprise, partly of fear lest he compromise himself in a risky adventure*): Ah . . . but . . . ah . . . I say . . . this is not the first time that you have come here, is it?

THE STEP-DAUGHTER (*modestly*): No sir.

THE FATHER: You've been here before, eh? (*Then seeing her nod agreement.*) More than once? (*Waits for her to answer, looks under her hat, smiles, and then says.*) Well then, there's no need to be so shy, is there? May I take off your hat?

THE STEP-DAUGHTER (*anticipating him and with veiled disgust*): No sir . . . I'll do it myself. (*Takes it off quickly.*)

(*The* MOTHER, *who watches the progress of the scene with the* SON *and the other two children who cling to her, is on thorns; and follows with varying expressions of sorrow, indignation, anxiety, and horror the words and actions of the other two. From time to time she hides her face in her hands and sobs.*)

THE MOTHER: Oh, my God, my God!

THE FATHER (*playing his part with a touch of gallantry*): Give it to me! I'll put it down. (*Takes hat from her hands.*) But a dear little head like yours ought to have a smarter hat. Come and help me choose one from the stock, won't you?

L'INGENUE (*interrupting*): I say . . . those are our hats you know.

THE MANAGER (*furious*): Silence! silence! Don't try and be funny, if you please . . . We're playing the scene now, I'd have you notice. (*To the* STEP-DAUGHTER.) Begin again, please!

THE STEP-DAUGHTER (*continuing*): No thank you, sir.

THE FATHER: Oh, come now. Don't talk like that. You must take it. I shall be upset if you don't. There are some lovely little hats here; and then — Madame will be pleased. She expects it, anyway, you know.

THE STEP-DAUGHTER: No, no! I couldn't wear it!

THE FATHER: Oh, you're thinking about what they'd say at home if they saw you come in with a new hat? My dear girl, there's always a way round these little matters, you know.

THE STEP-DAUGHTER (*all keyed up*): No, it's not that. I couldn't wear it because I am . . . as you see . . . you might have noticed . . . (*Showing her black dress.*)

THE FATHER: . . . in mourning! Of course: I beg your pardon: I'm frightfully sorry . . .

THE STEP-DAUGHTER (*forcing herself to conquer her indignation and nausea*): Stop! Stop! It's I who must thank you. There's no need for you to feel mortified or specially sorry. Don't think any more of what I've said. (*Tries to smile.*) I must forget that I am dressed so . . .

THE MANAGER (*interrupting and turning to the* PROMPTER): Stop a minute! Stop! Don't write that down. Cut out that last bit. (*Then to the* FATHER *and* STEP-DAUGHTER.) Fine! it's going fine! (*To the* FATHER *only.*) And now you can go on as we arranged. (*To the* ACTORS.) Pretty good that scene, where he offers her the hat, eh?

THE STEP-DAUGHTER: The best's coming now. Why can't we go on?

THE MANAGER: Have a little patience! (*To the* ACTORS.) Of course, it must be treated rather lightly.

LEADING MAN: Still, with a bit of go in it!

LEADING LADY: Of course! It's easy enough! (*To* LEADING MAN.) Shall you and I try it now?

LEADING MAN: Why, yes! I'll prepare my entrance. (*Exit in order to make his entrance.*)

THE MANAGER (*to* LEADING LADY): See here! The scene between you and Madame Pace is finished. I'll have it written out properly after. You remain here . . . oh, where are you going?

LEADING LADY: One minute. I want to put my hat on again. (*Goes over to hat-rack and puts her hat on her head.*)

THE MANAGER: Good! You stay here with your head bowed down a bit.

THE STEP-DAUGHTER: But she isn't dressed in black.

LEADING LADY: But I shall be, and much more effectively than you.

THE MANAGER (*to* STEP-DAUGHTER): Be quiet please, and watch! You'll be able to learn something. (*Clapping his hands.*) Come on! come on! Entrance, please!

(*The door at rear of stage opens, and the* LEADING MAN *enters with the lively manner of an old gallant. The rendering of the scene by the* ACTORS *from the very first words is seen to be quite a different thing, though it has not in any way the air of a parody. Naturally, the* STEP-DAUGHTER *and the* FATHER, *not being able to recognize themselves in the* LEADING LADY *and the* LEADING MAN, *who deliver their words in different tones and with a different psychology, express, sometimes with smiles, sometimes with gestures, the impression they receive.*)

LEADING MAN: Good afternoon, Miss . . .

THE FATHER (*at once unable to contain himself*): No! no!

(*The* STEP-DAUGHTER, *noticing the way the* LEADING MAN *enters, bursts out laughing.*)

THE MANAGER (*furious*): Silence! And you please just stop that laughing. If we go on like this, we shall never finish.

THE STEP-DAUGHTER: Forgive me, sir, but it's natural enough. This lady (*indicating* LEADING LADY) stands there still; but if she is supposed to be me, I can assure you that if I heard anyone say "Good afternoon" in that manner and in that tone, I should burst out laughing as I did.

THE FATHER: Yes, yes, the manner, the tone . . .

THE MANAGER: Nonsense! Rubbish! Stand aside and let me see the action.

LEADING MAN: If I've got to represent an old fellow who's coming into a house of an equivocal character . . .

THE MANAGER: Don't listen to them, for Heaven's sake! Do it again! It goes fine. (*Waiting for the* ACTORS *to begin again.*) Well?

LEADING MAN: Good afternoon, Miss.

LEADING LADY: Good afternoon.

LEADING MAN (*imitating the gesture of the* FATHER *when he looked under the hat, and then expressing quite clearly first satisfaction and then fear*): Ah, but . . . I say . . . this is not the first time that you have come here, is it?

THE MANAGER: Good, but not quite so heavily. Like this. (*Acts himself.*) "This isn't the first time that you have come here" . . . (*To* LEADING LADY.) And you say: "No, sir."

LEADING LADY: No, sir.

LEADING MAN: You've been here before, more than once.

THE MANAGER: No, no, stop! Let her nod "yes" first. "You've been here before, eh?" (*The* LEADING LADY *lifts up her head slightly and closes her eyes as though in disgust. Then she inclines her head twice.*)

THE STEP-DAUGHTER (*unable to contain herself*): Oh my God! (*Puts a hand to her mouth to prevent herself from laughing.*)

THE MANAGER (*turning round*): What's the matter?

THE STEP-DAUGHTER: Nothing, nothing!

THE MANAGER (*to* LEADING MAN): Go on!

LEADING MAN: You've been here before, eh? Well then, there's no need to be so shy, is there? May I take off your hat?

(*The* LEADING MAN *says this last speech in such a tone and with such gestures that the* STEP-DAUGHTER, *though she has her hand to her mouth, cannot keep from laughing.*)

LEADING LADY (*indignant*): I'm not going to stop here to be made a fool of by that woman there.

LEADING MAN: Neither am I! I'm through with it!

THE MANAGER (*shouting to* STEP-DAUGHTER): Silence! for once and all, I tell you!

THE STEP-DAUGHTER: Forgive me! forgive me!

THE MANAGER: You haven't any manners: that's what it is! You go too far.

THE FATHER (*endeavouring to intervene*): Yes, it's true, but excuse her . . .

THE MANAGER: Excuse what? It's absolutely disgusting.

THE FATHER: Yes, sir, but believe me, it has such a strange effect when . . .

THE MANAGER: Strange? Why strange? Where is it strange?

THE FATHER: No, sir; I admire your actors — this gentleman here, this lady; but they are certainly not us!

THE MANAGER: I should hope not. Evidently they cannot be you, if they are actors.

THE FATHER: Just so: actors! Both of them act our parts exceedingly well. But, believe me, it produces quite a different effect on us. They want to be us, but they aren't, all the same.

THE MANAGER: What is it then anyway?

THE FATHER: Something that is . . . that is theirs — and no longer ours . . .

THE MANAGER: But naturally, inevitably. I've told you so already.

THE FATHER: Yes, I understand . . . I understand . . .

THE MANAGER: Well then, let's have no more of it! (*Turning to the* ACTORS.) We'll have the rehearsals by ourselves, afterwards, in the ordinary way. I never could stand rehearsing with the author present. He's never satisfied! (*Turning to* FATHER *and* STEP-DAUGHTER.) Come on! Let's get on with it again; and try and see if you can't keep from laughing.

THE STEP-DAUGHTER: Oh, I shan't laugh any more. There's a nice little bit coming for me now: you'll see.

THE MANAGER: Well then: when she says "Don't think any more of what I've said. I must forget, etc.," you (*addressing the* FATHER) come in sharp with "I understand, I understand"; and then you ask her . . .

THE STEP-DAUGHTER (*interrupting*): What?

THE MANAGER: Why she is in mourning.

THE STEP-DAUGHTER: Not at all! See here: when I told him that it was useless for me to be thinking about my wearing mourning, do you know how he answered me? "Ah well," he said, "then let's take off this little frock."

THE MANAGER: Great! Just what we want, to make a riot in the theatre!

THE STEP-DAUGHTER: But it's the truth!

THE MANAGER: What does that matter? Acting is our business here. Truth up to a certain point, but no further.

THE STEP-DAUGHTER: What do you want to do then?

THE MANAGER: You'll see, you'll see! Leave it to me.

THE STEP-DAUGHTER: No sir! What you want to do is to piece together a little romantic sentimental scene out of my disgust, out of all the reasons, each more cruel and viler than the other, why I am what I am. He is to ask me why I'm in mourning; and I'm to answer with tears in my eyes, that it is just two months since papa died. No sir, no! He's got to say to me; as he did say: "Well, let's take off this little dress at once." And I; with my two months' mourning in my heart, went there behind that screen, and with these fingers tingling with shame . . .

THE MANAGER (*running his hands through his hair*): For Heaven's sake! What are you saying?

THE STEP-DAUGHTER (*crying out excitedly*): The truth! The truth!

THE MANAGER: It may be. I don't deny it, and I can understand all your horror; but you must surely see that you can't have this kind of thing on the stage. It won't go.

THE STEP-DAUGHTER: Not possible, eh? Very well! I'm much obliged to you — but I'm off!

THE MANAGER: Now be reasonable! Don't lose your temper!

THE STEP-DAUGHTER: I won't stop here! I won't! I can see you've fixed it all up with him in your office. All this talk about what is possible for the stage . . . I understand! He wants to get at his complicated "cerebral drama," to have his famous remorses and torments acted; but I want to act my part, *my part!*

THE MANAGER (*annoyed, shaking his shoulders*): Ah! Just *your* part! But, if you will pardon me, there are other parts than yours: His (*indicating the* FATHER) and hers (*indicating the* MOTHER)! On the stage you can't have a character becoming too prominent and overshadowing all the others. The thing is to pack them all into a neat little framework and then act what is actable. I am aware of the fact that everyone has his own interior life which he wants very much to put forward. But the difficulty lies in this fact: to set out just so much as is necessary for the stage, taking the other characters into consideration, and at the same time hint at the unrevealed interior life of each. I am willing to admit, my dear young lady, that from your point of view it would be a fine idea if each character could tell the public all his troubles in a nice monologue or a regular one hour lecture. (*Good humoredly.*) You must restrain yourself, my dear, and in your own interest, too; because this fury of yours, this exaggerated disgust you show, may make a bad impression, you know. After you have confessed to me that there were others before him at Madame Pace's and more than once . . .

THE STEP-DAUGHTER (*bowing her head, impressed*): It's true. But remember those others mean him for me all the same.

THE MANAGER (*not understanding*): What? The others? What do you mean?

THE STEP-DAUGHTER: For one who has gone wrong, sir, he who was responsible for the first fault is responsible for all that follow. He is responsible for my faults, was, even before I was born. Look at him, and see if it isn't true!

THE MANAGER: Well, well! And does the weight of so much responsibility seem nothing to you? Give him a chance to act it, to get it over!

THE STEP-DAUGHTER: How? How can he act all his "noble remorses," all his "moral torments," if you want to spare him the horror of being discovered one day — after he had asked her what he did ask her — in the arms of her, that already fallen woman, that child, sir, that child he used to watch come out of school? (*She is moved.*)

(*The* MOTHER *at this point is overcome with emotion, and breaks out into a fit of crying. All are touched. A long pause.*)

THE STEP-DAUGHTER (*as soon as the* MOTHER *becomes a little quieter, adds resolutely and gravely*): At present, we are unknown to the public. Tomorrow, you will act us as you wish, treating us in your own manner. But do you really want to see drama, do you want to see it flash out as it really did?

THE MANAGER: Of course! That's just what I do want, so I can use as much of it as is possible.

THE STEP-DAUGHTER: Well then, ask that Mother there to leave us.

THE MOTHER (*changing her low plaint into a sharp cry*): No! No! Don't permit it, sir, don't permit it!

THE MANAGER: But it's only to try it.

THE MOTHER: I can't bear it. I can't.

THE MANAGER: But since it has happened already . . . I don't understand!

THE MOTHER: It's taking place now. It happens all the time. My torment isn't a pretended one. I live and feel every minute of my torture. Those two children there — have you heard them speak? They can't speak any more. They cling to me to keep up my torment actual and vivid for me. But for themselves, they do not exist, they aren't any more. And she (*indicating the* STEP-DAUGHTER) has run away, she has left me, and is lost. If I now see her here before me, it is only to renew for me the tortures I have suffered for her too.

THE FATHER: The eternal moment! She (*indicating the* STEP-DAUGHTER) is here to catch me, fix me, and hold me eternally in the stocks for that one fleeting and shameful moment of my life. She can't give it up! And you sir, cannot either fairly spare me it.

THE MANAGER: I never said I didn't want to act it. It will form, as a matter of fact, the nucleus of the whole first act right up to her surprise. (*Indicates the* MOTHER.)

THE FATHER: Just so! This is my punishment: the passion in all of us that must culminate in her final cry.

THE STEP-DAUGHTER: I can hear it still in my ears. It's driven me mad, that cry! — You can put me on as you like; it doesn't matter. Fully dressed, if you like — provided I have at least the arm bare; because, standing like this (*she goes close to the* FATHER *and leans her head on his breast*) with my head so, and my arms round his neck, I saw a vein pulsing in my arm here; and then, as if that live vein had awakened disgust in me, I closed my eyes like this, and let my head sink on his breast. (*Turning to the* MOTHER.) Cry out mother! Cry out! (*Buries head in* FATHER's *breast, and with her shoulders raised as if to prevent her hearing the cry, adds in tones of intense emotion.*) Cry out as you did then!

THE MOTHER (*coming forward to separate them*): No! My daughter, my daughter! (*And after having pulled her away from him.*) You brute! you brute! She is my daughter! Don't you see she's my daughter?

THE MANAGER (*walking backwards towards footlights*): Fine! fine! Damned good! And then, of course — curtain!

THE FATHER (*going towards him excitedly*): Yes, of course, because that's the way it really happened.

THE MANAGER (*convinced and pleased*): Oh, yes, no doubt about it. Curtain here, curtain!

(*At the reiterated cry of the* MANAGER, *the* MACHINIST *lets the curtain down, leaving the* MANAGER *and the* FATHER *in front of it before the footlights.*)

THE MANAGER: The darned idiot! I said "curtain" to show the act should end there, and he goes and lets it down in earnest. (*To the* FATHER, *while he pulls the curtain back to go on to the stage again.*) Yes, yes, it's all right. Effect certain! That's the right ending. I'll guarantee the first act at any rate.

ACT III

When the curtain goes up again, it is seen that the stage hands have shifted the bit of scenery used in the last part, and have rigged up instead at the back of the stage a drop, with some trees, and one or two wings. A portion of a fountain basin is visible. The MOTHER *is sitting on the right with the two children by her side. The* SON *is on the same side, but away from the others. He seems bored, angry, and full of shame. The* FATHER *and the* STEP-DAUGHTER *are also seated towards the right front. On the other side (left) are the* ACTORS, *much in the positions they occupied before the curtain was lowered. Only the* MANAGER *is standing up in the middle of the stage, with his hand closed over his mouth in the act of meditating.*

THE MANAGER (*shaking his shoulders after a brief pause*): Ah yes: the second act! Leave it to me, leave it all to me as we arranged, and you'll see! It'll go fine!

THE STEP-DAUGHTER: Our entry into his house (*indicates* FATHER) in spite of him . . . (*Indicates the* SON.)

THE MANAGER (*out of patience*): Leave it to me, I tell you!

THE STEP-DAUGHTER: Do let it be clear, at any rate, that it is in spite of my wishes.

THE MOTHER (*from her corner, shaking her head*): For all the good that's come of it . . .

THE STEP-DAUGHTER (*turning towards her quickly*): It doesn't matter. The more harm done us, the more remorse for him.

THE MANAGER (*impatiently*): I understand! Good Heavens! I understand! I'm taking it into account.

THE MOTHER (*supplicatingly*): I beg you, sir, to let it appear quite plain that for conscience' sake I did try in every way . . .

THE STEP-DAUGHTER (*interrupting indignantly and continuing for the* MOTHER): . . . to pacify me, to dissuade me from spiting him. (*To* MANAGER.) Do as she wants: satisfy her, because it is true! I enjoy it immensely. Anyhow, as you can see, the meeker she is, the more she tries to get at his heart, the more distant and aloof does he become.

THE MANAGER: Are we going to begin this second act or not?

THE STEP-DAUGHTER: I'm not going to talk

any more now. But I must tell you this: you can't have the whole action take place in the garden, as you suggest. It isn't possible!

THE MANAGER: Why not?

THE STEP-DAUGHTER: Because he (*indicates the* SON *again*) is always shut up alone in his room. And then there's all the part of that poor dazed-looking boy there which takes place indoors.

THE MANAGER: Maybe! On the other hand, you will understand — we can't change scenes three or four times in one act.

THE LEADING MAN: They used to once.

THE MANAGER: Yes, when the public was up to the level of that child there.

THE LEADING LADY: It makes the illusion easier.

THE FATHER (*irritated*): The illusion! For Heaven's sake, don't say illusion. Please don't use that word, which is particularly painful for us.

THE MANAGER (*astounded*): And why, if you please?

THE FATHER: It's painful, cruel, really cruel; and you ought to understand that.

THE MANAGER: But why? What ought we to say then? The illusion, I tell you, sir, which we've got to create for the audience . . .

THE LEADING MAN: With our acting.

THE MANAGER: The illusion of a reality.

THE FATHER: I understand; but you, perhaps, do not understand us. Forgive me! You see . . . here for you and your actors, the thing is only — and rightly so . . . a kind of game . . .

THE LEADING LADY (*interrupting indignantly*): A game! We're not children here, if you please! We are serious actors.

THE FATHER: I don't deny it. What I mean is the game, or play, of your art, which has to give, as the gentleman says, a perfect illusion of reality.

THE MANAGER: Precisely — !

THE FATHER: Now, if you consider the fact that we (*indicates himself and the other five* CHARACTERS), as we are, have no other reality outside of this illusion . . .

THE MANAGER (*astonished, looking at his* ACTORS, *who are also amazed*): And what does that mean?

THE FATHER (*after watching them for a moment with a wan smile*): As I say, sir, that which is a game of art for you is our sole reality. (*Brief pause. He goes a step or two*

nearer the MANAGER *and adds.*) But not only for us, you know, by the way. Just you think it over well. (*Looks him in the eyes.*) Can you tell me who you are?

THE MANAGER (*perplexed, half smiling*): What? Who am I? I am myself.

THE FATHER: And if I were to tell you that this isn't true, because you and I . . . ?

THE MANAGER: I should say you were mad — ! (*The* ACTORS *laugh.*)

THE FATHER: You're quite right to laugh: because we are all making believe here. (*To* MANAGER.) And you can therefore object that it's only for a joke that the gentleman there (*indicates the* LEADING MAN), who naturally is himself, has to be me, who am on the contrary myself — this thing you see here. You see I've caught you in a trap! (*The* ACTORS *laugh.*)

THE MANAGER (*annoyed*): But we've had all this over once before. Do you want to begin again?

THE FATHER: No, no! That wasn't my meaning! In fact, I should like to request you to abandon this game of art (*looking at the* LEADING LADY *as if anticipating her*) which you are accustomed to play here with your actors, and to ask you seriously once again: who are you?

THE MANAGER (*astonished and irritated, turning to his* ACTORS): If this fellow here hasn't got a nerve! A man who calls himself a character comes and asks me who I am!

THE FATHER (*with dignity, but not offended*): A character, sir, may always ask a man who he is. Because a character has really a life of his own, marked with his especial characteristics; for which reason he is always "somebody." But a man — I'm not speaking of you now — may very well be "nobody."

THE MANAGER: Yes, but you are asking these questions of me, the boss, the manager! Do you understand?

THE FATHER: But only in order to know if you, as you really are now, see yourself as you once were with all the illusions that were yours then, with all the things both inside and outside of you as they seemed to you — as they were then indeed for you. Well, sir, if you think of all those illusions that mean nothing to you now, of all those things which don't even *seem* to you to exist any more, while once they *were* for you, don't you feel that — I won't say these boards — but the very earth under your feet is sinking away from you when you reflect that in the same way this *you* as you feel it today — all this present reality of yours — is fated to seem a mere illusion to you tomorrow?

THE MANAGER (*without having understood much, but astonished by the specious argument*): Well, well! And where does all this take us anyway?

THE FATHER: Oh, nowhere! It's only to show you that if we (*indicating the* CHARACTERS) have no other reality beyond the illusion, you too must not count overmuch on your reality as you feel it today, since, like that of yesterday, it may prove an illusion for you tomorrow.

THE MANAGER (*determining to make fun of him*): Ah, excellent! Then you'll be saying next that you, with this comedy of yours that you brought here to act, are truer and more real than I am.

THE FATHER (*with the greatest seriousness*). But of course; without doubt!

THE MANAGER: Ah, really?

THE FATHER: Why, I thought you'd understand that from the beginning.

THE MANAGER: More real than I?

THE FATHER: If your reality can change from one day to another . . .

THE MANAGER: But everyone knows it can change. It is always changing, the same as anyone else's.

THE FATHER (*with a cry*): No, sir, not ours! Look here! That is the very difference! Our reality doesn't change: it can't change! It can't be other than what it is, because it is already fixed for ever. It's terrible. Ours is an immutable reality which should make you shudder when you approach us if you are really conscious of the fact that your reality is a mere transitory and fleeting illusion, taking this form today and that tomorrow, according to the conditions, according to your will, your sentiments, which in turn are controlled by an intellect that shows them to you today in one manner and tomorrow . . . who knows how? . . . Illusions of reality represented in this fatuous comedy of life that never ends, nor can ever end! Because if tomorrow it were to end . . . then why, all would be finished.

THE MANAGER: Oh for God's sake, will you *at least* finish with this philosophizing and let us try and shape this comedy which you yourself have brought me here? You argue and philosophize a bit too much, my dear sir. You know you seem to me almost, almost . . . (*Stops and looks him over from head to foot.*) Ah, by the way, I think you introduced yourself to me as a — what shall . . . we say — a "character," created by an author who did not afterward care to make a drama of his own creations.

THE FATHER: It is the simple truth, sir.

THE MANAGER: Nonsense! Cut that out, please! None of us believes it, because it isn't a thing, as you must recognize yourself, which one can believe seriously. If you want to know, it seems to me you are trying to imitate the manner of a certain author whom I heartily detest — I warn you — although I have unfortunately bound myself to put on one of his works. As a matter of fact, I was just starting to rehearse it, when you arrived. (*Turning to the* ACTORS.) And this is what we've gained — out of the frying-pan into the fire!

THE FATHER: I don't know to what author you may be alluding, but believe me I feel what I think; and I seem to be philosophizing only for those who do not think what they feel, because they blind themselves with their own sentiment. I know that for many people this self-blinding seems much more "human"; but the contrary is really true. For man never reasons so much and becomes so introspective as when he suffers; since he is anxious to get at the cause of his sufferings, to learn who has produced them, and whether it is just or unjust that he should have to bear them. On the other hand, when he is happy, he takes his happiness as it comes and doesn't analyze it, just as if happiness were his right. The animals suffer without reasoning about their sufferings. But take the case of a man who suffers and begins to reason about it. Oh no! it can't be allowed! Let him suffer like an animal, and then — ah yet, he is "human"!

THE MANAGER: Look here! Look here! You're off again, philosophizing worse than ever.

THE FATHER: Because I suffer, sir! I'm not philosophizing: I'm crying aloud the reason of my sufferings.

THE MANAGER (*makes brusque movement as he is taken with a new idea*): I should like to know if anyone has ever heard of a character who gets right out of his part and perorates and speechifies as you do. Have you ever heard of a case? I haven't.

THE FATHER: You have never met such a

case, sir, because authors, as a rule, hide the labour of their creations. When the characters are really alive before their author, the latter does nothing but follow them in their action, in their words, in the situations which they suggest to him; and he has to will them the way they will themselves — for there's trouble if he doesn't. When a character is born, he acquires at once such an independence, even of his own author, that he can be imagined by everybody even in many other situations where the author never dreamed of placing him; and so he acquires for himself a meaning which the author never thought of giving him.

THE MANAGER: Yes, yes, I know this.

THE FATHER: What is there then to marvel at in us? Imagine such a misfortune for characters as I have described to you: to be born of an author's fantasy, and be denied life by him; and then answer me if these characters left alive, and yet without life, weren't right in doing what they did do and are doing now, after they have attempted everything in their power to persuade him to give them their stage life. We've all tried him in turn, I, she (*indicating the* STEP-DAUGHTER) *and she* (*indicating the* MOTHER).

THE STEP-DAUGHTER: It's true. I too have sought to tempt him, many, many times, when he has been sitting at his writing table, feeling a bit melancholy, at the twilight hour. He would sit in his armchair too lazy to switch on the light, and all the shadows that crept into his room were full of our presence coming to tempt him. (*As if she saw herself still there by the writing table, and was annoyed by the presence of the* ACTORS.) Oh, if you would only go away, go away and leave us alone — mother here with that son of hers — I with that child — that boy there always alone — and then I with him (*just hints at the* FATHER) — and then I alone, alone . . . in those shadows! (*Makes a sudden movement as if in the vision she has of herself illuminating those shadows she wanted to seize hold of herself.*) Ah! my life! my life! Oh, what scenes we proposed to him — and I tempted him more than any of the others!

THE FATHER: Maybe. But perhaps it was your fault that he refused to give us life: because you were too insistent, too troublesome.

THE STEP-DAUGHTER: Nonsense! Didn't he make me so himself? (*Goes close to the* MANAGER *to tell him as if in confidence.*) In my opinion he abandoned us in a fit of depression, of disgust for the ordinary theatre as the public knows it and likes it.

THE SON: Exactly what it was, sir; exactly that!

THE FATHER: Not at all! Don't believe it for a minute. Listen to me! You'll be doing quite right to modify, as you suggest, the excesses both of this girl here, who wants to do too much, and of this young man, who won't do anything at all.

THE SON: No, nothing!

THE MANAGER: You too get over the mark occasionally, my dear sir, if I may say so.

THE FATHER: I? When? Where?

THE MANAGER: Always! Continuously! Then there's this insistence of yours in trying to make us believe you are a character. And then too, you must really argue and philosophize less, you know, much less.

THE FATHER: Well, if you want to take away from me the possibility of representing the torment of my spirit which never gives me peace, you will be suppressing me: that's all. Every true man, sir, who is a little above the level of the beasts and plants does not live for the sake of living, without knowing how to live; but he lives so as to give a meaning and a value of his own to life. For me this is *everything*. I cannot give up this, just to represent a mere fact as she (*indicating the* STEP-DAUGHTER) wants. It's all very well for her, since her "vendetta" lies in the "fact." I'm not going to do it. It destroys my *raison d'être*.

THE MANAGER: Your *raison d'être!* Oh, we're going ahead fine! First she starts off, and then you jump in. At this rate, we'll never finish.

THE FATHER: Now, don't be offended! Have it your own way — provided, however, that within the limits of the parts you assign us each one's sacrifice isn't too great.

THE MANAGER: You've got to understand that you can't go on arguing at your own pleasure. Drama is action, sir, action and not confounded philosophy.

THE FATHER: All right. I'll do just as much arguing and philosophizing as everybody does when he is considering his own torments.

THE MANAGER: If the drama permits! But for Heaven's sake, man, let's get along and come to the scene.

THE STEP-DAUGHTER: It seems to me we've got too much action with our coming into his house. (*Indicating* FATHER.) You said, before, you couldn't change the scene every five minutes.

THE MANAGER: Of course not. What we've got to do is to combine and group up all the facts in one simultaneous, close-knit action. We can't have it as you want, with your little brother wandering like a ghost from room to room, hiding behind doors and meditating a project which — what did you say it did to him?

THE STEP-DAUGHTER: Consumes him, sir, wastes him away!

THE MANAGER: Well, it may be. And then at the same time, you want the little girl there to be playing in the garden . . . one in the house, and the other in the garden: isn't that it?

THE STEP-DAUGHTER: Yes, in the sun, in the sun! That is my only pleasure: to see her happy and careless in the garden after the misery and squalor of the horrible room where we all four slept together. And I had to sleep with her — I, do you understand? — with my vile contaminated body next to hers; with her folding me fast in her loving little arms. In the garden, whenever she spied me, she would run to take me by the hand. She didn't care for the big flowers, only the little ones; and she loved to show me them and pet me.

THE MANAGER: Well then, we'll have it in the garden. Everything shall happen in the garden; and we'll group the other scenes there. (*Calls a* STAGE HAND.) Here, a back-cloth with trees and something to do as a fountain basin. (*Turning round to look at the back of the stage.*) Ah, you've fixed it up. Good! (*To* STEP-DAUGHTER.) This is just to give an idea, of course. The Boy, instead of hiding behind the doors, will wander about here in the garden, hiding behind the trees. But it's going to be rather difficult to find a child to do that scene with you where she shows you the flowers. (*Turning to the* BOY.) Come forward a little, will you please? Let's try it now! Come along! come along! (*Then seeing him come shyly forward, full of fear and looking lost.*) It's a nice business, this lad here. What's the matter with him? We'll have to give him a word or two to say. (*Goes close to him, puts a hand on his shoulders, and leads him behind one of the trees.*) Come on! come on! Let me see you a little! Hide here . . . yes, like that. Try and show your head just a little as if you

were looking for someone . . . (*Goes back to observe the effect, when the* BOY *at once goes through the action.*) Excellent! fine! (*Turning to* STEP-DAUGHTER.) Suppose the little girl there were to surprise him as he looks round, and run over to him, so we could give him a word or two to say?

THE STEP-DAUGHTER: It's useless to hope he will speak, as long as that fellow there is here . . . (*Indicates the* SON.) You must send him away first.

THE SON (*jumping up*): Delighted! Delighted! I don't ask for anything better. (*Begins to move away.*)

THE MANAGER (*at once stopping him*): No! No! Where are you going? Wait a bit!

(*The* MOTHER *gets up alarmed and terrified at the thought that he is really about to go away. Instinctively she lifts her arms to prevent him, without, however, leaving her seat.*)

THE SON (*to* MANAGER *who stops him*): I've got nothing to do with this affair. Let me go please! Let me go!

THE MANAGER: What do you mean by saying you've got nothing to do with this?

THE STEP-DAUGHTER (*calmly, with irony*): Don't bother to stop him: he won't go away.

THE FATHER: He has to act the terrible scene in the garden with his mother.

THE SON (*suddenly resolute and with dignity*): I shall act nothing at all. I've said so from the very beginning. (*To the* MANAGER.) Let me go!

THE STEP-DAUGHTER (*going over to the* MANAGER): Allow me? (*Puts down the* MANAGER's *arm which is restraining the* SON.) Well, go away then, if you want to! (*The* SON *looks at her with contempt and hatred. She laughs and says.*) You see, he can't, he can't go away! He is obliged to stay here, indissolubly bound to the chain. If I, who fly off when that happens which has to happen, because I can't bear him — if I am still here and support that face and expression of his, you can well imagine that he is unable to move. He has to remain here, has to stop with that nice father of his, and that mother whose only son he is. (*Turning to the* MOTHER.) Come on, mother, come along! (*Turning to* MANAGER *to indicate her.*) You see, she was getting up to keep him back. (*To the* MOTHER, *beckoning her with her hand.*) Come on! come on! (*Then to*

MANAGER.) You can imagine how little she wants to show these actors of yours what she really feels; but so eager is she to get near him that . . . There, you see? She is willing to act her part. (*And in fact, the* MOTHER *approaches him; and as soon as the* STEP-DAUGHTER *has finished speaking, opens her arms to signify that she consents.*)

THE SON (*suddenly*): No! no! If I can't go away, then I'll stop here; but I repeat: I act nothing!

THE FATHER (*to* MANAGER *excitedly*): You can force him, sir.

THE SON: Nobody can force me.

THE FATHER: I can.

THE STEP-DAUGHTER: Wait a minute, wait . . . First of all, the baby has to go to the fountain . . . (*Runs to take the* CHILD *and leads her to the fountain.*)

THE MANAGER: Yes, yes of course; that's it. Both at the same time.

(*The second* LADY LEAD *and the* JUVENILE LEAD *at this point separate themselves from the group of* ACTORS. *One watches the* MOTHER *attentively; the other moves about studying the movements and manner of the* SON *whom he will have to act.*)

THE SON (*to* MANAGER): What do you mean by both at the same time? It isn't right. There was no scene between me and her. (*Indicates the* MOTHER.) Ask her how it was!

THE MOTHER: Yes, it's true. I had come into his room . . .

THE SON: Into my room, do you understand? Nothing to do with the garden.

THE MANAGER: It doesn't matter. Haven't I told you we've got to group the action?

THE SON (*observing the* JUVENILE LEAD *studying him*): What do you want?

THE JUVENILE LEAD: Nothing! I was just looking at you.

THE SON (*turning towards the second* LADY LEAD): Ah! she's at it too: to re-act her part! (*Indicating the* MOTHER.)

THE MANAGER: Exactly! And it seems to me that you ought to be grateful to them for their interest.

THE SON: Yes, but haven't you yet perceived that it isn't possible to live in front of a mirror which not only freezes us with the image of ourselves, but throws our likeness back at us with a horrible grimace?

THE FATHER. That is true, absolutely true. You must see that.

THE MANAGER (*to second* LADY LEAD *and* JUVENILE LEAD): He's right! Move away from them!

THE SON: Do as you like. I'm out of this!

THE MANAGER: Be quiet, you, will you? And let me hear your mother! (*To* MOTHER.) You were saying you had entered . . .

THE MOTHER: Yes, into his room, because I couldn't stand it any longer. I went to empty my heart to him of all the anguish that tortures me . . . But as soon as he saw me come in . . .

THE SON: Nothing happened! There was no scene. I went away, that's all! I don't care for scenes!

THE MOTHER: It's true, true. That's how it was.

THE MANAGER: Well now, we've got to do this bit between you and him. It's indispensable.

THE MOTHER: I'm ready . . . when you are ready. If you could only find a chance for me to tell him what I feel here in my heart.

THE FATHER (*going to* SON *in a great rage*): You'll do this for your mother, for your mother, do you understand?

THE SON (*quite determined*): I do nothing!

THE FATHER (*taking hold of him and shaking him*): For God's sake, do as I tell you! Don't you hear your mother asking you for a favor? Haven't you even got the guts to be a son?

THE SON (*taking hold of the* FATHER): No! No! And for God's sake stop it, or else . . . (*General agitation. The* MOTHER, *frightened, tries to separate them.*)

THE MOTHER (*pleading*): Please! please!

THE FATHER (*not leaving hold of the* SON): You've got to obey, do you hear?

THE SON (*almost crying from rage*): What does it mean, this madness you've got? (*They separate.*) Have you no decency, that you insist on showing everyone our shame? I won't do it! I won't! And I stand for the will of our author in this. He didn't want to put us on the stage, after all!

THE MANAGER: Man alive! You came here . . .

THE SON (*indicating* FATHER): He did! I didn't!

THE MANAGER: Aren't you here now?

THE SON: It was his wish, and he dragged us

along with him. He's told you not only the things that did happen, but also things that have never happened at all.

THE MANAGER: Well, tell me then what did happen. You went out of your room without saying a word?

THE SON: Without a word, so as to avoid a scene!

THE MANAGER: And then what did you do?

THE SON: Nothing . . . walking in the garden . . . (*Hesitates for a moment with expression of gloom.*)

THE MANAGER (*coming closer to him, interested by his extraordinary reserve*): Well, well . . . walking in the garden . . .

THE SON (*exasperated*): Why on earth do you insist? It's horrible! (*The* MOTHER *trembles, sobs, and looks towards the fountain.*)

THE MANAGER (*slowly observing the glance and turning towards the* SON *with increasing apprehension*): The baby?

THE SON: There in the fountain . . .

THE FATHER (*pointing with tender pity to the* MOTHER): She was following him at the moment . . .

THE MANAGER (*to the* SON *anxiously*): And then you . . .

THE SON: I ran over to her; I was jumping in to drag her out when I saw something that froze my blood . . . the boy standing stock still, with eyes like a madman's, watching his little drowned sister, in the fountain! (*The* STEP-DAUGHTER *bends over the fountain to hide the* CHILD. *She sobs.*) Then . . . (*A revolver shot rings out behind the trees where the* BOY *is hidden.*)

THE MOTHER (*with a cry of terror runs over in that direction together with several of the* ACTORS *amid general confusion*): My son! My son! (*Then amid the cries and exclamations one hears her voice.*) Help! Help!

THE MANAGER (*pushing the* ACTORS *aside while they lift up the* BOY *and carry him off*): Is he really wounded?

SOME ACTORS: He's dead! dead!

OTHER ACTORS: No, no, it's only make believe, it's only pretence!

THE FATHER (*with a terrible cry*): Pretence? Reality, sir, reality!

THE MANAGER: Pretence? Reality? To hell with it all! Never in my life has such a thing happened to me. I've lost a whole day over these people, a whole day!

CURTAIN.

In an essay on *Six Characters in Search of an Author*, published several years after the play, Pirandello wryly noted that he had the "misfortune" to be a philosophical writer. Such a writer, he explained, is not content to present characters and stories for the pleasure of presenting them, but is moved by a "profound spiritual need." Something should be said, then, of Pirandello's philosophy, which can be found not only in the plays and in his essay on *Six Characters*, but also in an essay of 1908 entitled "Umorismo" ("Humor"). Reality is fluid, and beyond the grasp of reason. But man *has* reason, and he cannot tolerate a fluid, irrational world, so he sets up reasonable — but false — categories. He creates laws, codes of ethics, religions, and other "communal lies," but in certain dreadful moments he may become aware that these creations are distortions of reality.

In *Six Characters*, take as an example this speech by the Father:

Each of us when he appears before his fellows is clothed in a certain dignity. But every man knows what unconfessable things pass within the secrecy of his own heart. One gives way to the temptation, only to rise from it again, afterwards, with a great eagerness to re-establish one's dignity, as if it were a tombstone to place on the grave of one's shame, and a monument to hide and sign the memory of our weaknesses. Everybody's in the same case. Some folks haven't the courage to say certain things, that's all!

Now, such an attack on the apparent dignity of man is not unprecedented. *King Lear*, for example, offers an even more terrifying indictment of man's hypocrisy, penetrating the fair outside to the "mischief" that breeds about the heart. But Lear's remarks are the remarks of an overwrought speaker, and though we cannot dismiss his insights, we do not take them as the whole truth. Lear forces on us the awareness of the vast discrepancy between appearance and reality, but (1) we do not doubt that there *is* a reality, and (2) the play itself offers evidence that reality is not exactly what the tragic hero, at the height of his agony, perceives it to be. We remember, for example, Cordelia in *King Lear*, and we know that goodness and love are not mere illusions.

Pirandello went beyond suggesting that dignity is an illusion; he suggested that the idea of any sort of coherent personality is an illusion, and that all experience is illusory. Men have, of course, for centuries touched on the idea that what we call reality may be only illusion. One thinks, for example, of Plato, and of Shakespeare's numerous references to the world as a stage. Near the end of *Macbeth*, for example, the protagonist says:

> Life's but a walking shadow, a poor player
> That struts and frets his hour upon the stage
> And then is heard no more. It is a tale
> Told by an idiot, full of sound and fury
> Signifying nothing.

But such a passage is the remark of a particular character, not of Shakespeare. It is not Shakespeare but Macbeth who — finding that he cannot enjoy the crown for which he has given up his humanity and his soul — says that life signifies nothing. To the viewer of *Macbeth*, the significance is fairly clear: the violence that Macbeth does to others he unknowingly does also to himself, and this man who acts as though the lives of others have no significance comes to find his own life lacking any. In short, though Macbeth finds no significance in life, the play clearly implies one. Or take the end of *A Midsummer Night's Dream*, when Puck, in the epilogue, says:

> If we shadows have offended,
> Think but this, and all is mended:
> That you have but slumb'red here,
> While these visions did appear.
> And this weak and idle theme,
> No more yielding but a dream.

Shakespeare is graciously suggesting that his "weak and idle" play yields no more than a dream — but, first, we recognize these words for the modest untruth that they are, and, second, we know that the play itself refutes them, since in this play the several dreams in fact are not "weak and idle" (that is, foolish) but accurate indications of what happens. Macbeth and Puck, then, are not Shakespeare's spokesmen — but Pirandello's Father in *Six Characters* is indeed Pirandello's spokesman when he explains to the superficial Manager that the Manager's "reality is a mere transitory and fleeting illusion, taking this form today and that tomorrow, according to the conditions, according to your will, your sentiments, which in turn are controlled by an intellect that shows them to you today in one manner and tomorrow . . . who knows how?" After all, the Father explains, each day we see things differently; we dismiss as illusions what we earlier took for reality, and we will later dismiss as illusions what we at this moment take for reality:

> Well, sir, if you think of all those illusions that mean nothing to you now, of all those things which don't even *seem* to you to exist any more, while once they *were* for you, don't you feel that — I won't say these boards — but the very earth under your feet is sinking away from you when you reflect that in the same way this *you* as you feel it today — all this present reality of yours — is fated to seem a mere illusion to you tomorrow?

In effect Pirandello is saying that both external reality and personality are fluid, incoherent, elusive, and, for all practical purposes, unreal.

This extreme relativism had been introduced earlier in the play, especially in the Father's speech on conscience, which rejects the concept of personality, of a dominant ego:

> We believe this conscience to be a single thing, but it is many-sided. There is one for this person, and another for that. Diverse consciences. So we have this illusion of being one person for all, of having a personality that is unique in all our acts. But it isn't true. We perceive this when, tragically perhaps, in something we do, we are as it were, suspended, caught up in the air on a kind of hook. Then we perceive that all of us was not in that act, and that it would be an atrocious injustice to judge us by that action alone, as if all our existence were summed up in that one deed.

And the Father is not Pirandello's only spokesman. For example, the churlish Son scoffs at the Father but makes a similar point: "He [the Father] thinks he has got at the meaning of it all. Just as if each one of us in every circumstance of life couldn't find his own explanation of it!"

We have said that Pirandello suggested it was his "misfortune" to be a philosophical writer, and we have tried to sketch the philosophy underlying the play. But *Six Characters* is a play rather than a philosophic treatise, and we should not neglect Pirandello's vivid characterizations and his energetic conflicts. He memorably embodies in his play his vision of characters struggling to express themselves and to achieve reality even though they have no faith in reality. When the Manager impatiently explains to the Father, "Drama is action, sir, action and not confounded philosophy," Pirandello is making a little joke at the expense of those who are impatient with ideas in drama, but he has throughout taken care to embody his philosophy in the theatrical action of a tragicomedy. The serious concerns of the characters seem absurd to the Actors, and the Actors' efforts to impersonate the Characters seem ludicrous to the Characters. The tragic aspects of the play are obvious — for example, the drowning of the little Child, the suicide of the Boy, the emotional paralysis of the Son. Some of the comic aspects are equally obvious — especially the satire on the theater, and the occasional deflation of the Father (he has "aspirations towards a certain moral sanity," but he visits a brothel). But the struggle of the deeply-feeling Characters against the shallow Actors can only be characterized as tragicomic. That the chief spokesman for the Characters, the Father, argues against the concept of personality yet desperately seeks to achieve a full reality in a play to be performed by Actors whom he regards as less real than himself, is perhaps the tragicomic paradox at the heart of the play.

WILD STRAWBERRIES

Ingmar Bergman

Translated by Lars Malmström and David Kushner

Ingmar Bergman, born in 1918, in Uppsala, Sweden, the son of a Lutheran clergyman, has said that for him "religious problems are continuously alive." Although he began his professional career as a stage actor and playwright, and he continued to be active in the theater until 1966 when he resigned as head of the Royal Dramatic Theater, his international fame is as a writer and director of films. His first screenplay, *Torment* (1944), established him as a writer of screenplays; the next year he directed his first film, *Crisis*. Among other major films in an extremely prolific career are *Smiles of a Summer Night* (1955), *The Seventh Seal* (1956), *Wild Strawberries* (1957), *The Silence* (1963), and *Persona* (1966).

CAST

PROFESSOR ISAK BORG	ISAK'S WIFE	CHARLOTTA
SARA	HER LOVER	ANGELICA
MARIANNE	AUNT	MRS. AKERMAN
EVALD	ALMAN	ANNA
AGDA	AKERMAN	THE TWINS
ANDERS	UNCLE ARON	HAGBART
VIKTOR	SIGFRID	BENJAMIN
ISAK'S MOTHER	SIGBRITT	PROMOTER
MRS. ALMAN		

Note: There are no cast listings for TIGER and JAKOB because the scene in which these characters appear (see pp. 724–725) did not appear in the finished film.

Top: Still photograph from *Wild Strawberries*, illustrating pages 727–728. (Reprinted from *Four Screenplays of Ingmar Bergman*, courtesy of Simon and Schuster, Inc.) *Bottom:* Still photograph from the filmscript of *Wild Strawberries*, illustrating Victor Sjöström as Professor Borg on page 728. (Photograph reproduced by permission of the publishers, Lorrimer Publishing, London.)

[At the age of seventy-six, I feel that I'm much too old to lie to myself. But, of course, I can't be too sure. My complacent attitude towards my own truthfulness could be dishonesty in disguise, although I don't quite know what I might want to hide. Nevertheless, if for some reason I would have to evaluate myself, I am sure that I would do so without shame or concern for my reputation. But if I should be asked to express an opinion about someone else, I would be considerably more cautious. There is the greatest danger in passing such judgment. In all probability one is guilty of errors, exaggerations, even tremendous lies. Rather than commit such follies, I remain silent.

As a result, I have of my own free will withdrawn almost completely from society, because one's relationship with other people consists mainly of discussing and evaluating one's neighbour's conduct. Therefore I have found myself rather alone in my old age. This is not a regret but a statement of fact. All I ask of life is to be left alone and to have the opportunity to devote myself to the few things which continue to interest me, however superficial they may be. For example, I derive pleasure from keeping up with the steady progress made in my profession (I once taught bacteriology), I find relaxation in a game of golf, and now and then I read some memoirs or a good detective story.

My life has been filled with work, and for that I am grateful. It began with a struggle for daily bread and developed into the continuous pursuit of a beloved science. I have a son living in Lund who is a physician and has been married for many years. He has no children. My MOTHER is still living and quite active despite her advanced age (she is ninety-six). She lives in the vicinity of Huskvarna. We seldom see each other.

My nine sisters and brothers are dead, but they left a number of children and grandchildren. I have very little contact with my relatives. My wife Karin died many years

ago. Our marriage was quite unhappy. I am fortunate in having a good housekeeper.

That is all I have to say about myself. Perhaps I ought to add that I am an old pedant, and at times quite trying, both to myself and to the people who have to be around me. I detest emotional outbursts, women's tears and the crying of children. On the whole, I find loud noises and sudden startling occurrences most disconcerting.

Later I will come back to the reason for writing this story, which is, as nearly as I can make it, a true account of the events, dreams and thoughts which befell me on a certain day.][1]

In the early morning of Saturday, the first of June, I had a strange and very unpleasant dream. I dreamed that I was taking my usual morning stroll through the streets. It was quite early and no human being was in sight. This was a bit surprising to me. I also noted that there were no vehicles parked along the kerbs. The city seemed strangely deserted, as if it were a holiday morning in the middle of summer.

The sun was shining brightly and made sharp black shadows, but it gave off no warmth. Even though I walked on the sunny side, I felt chilly.

The stillness was also remarkable. I usually stroll along a broad, tree-lined boulevard, and even before sunrise the sparrows and crows are as a rule extremely noisy. Besides, there is always the perpetual roar from the centre of the city. But this morning nothing was heard, the silence was absolute, and my footsteps echoed almost anxiously against the walls of the buildings. I began to wonder what had happened.

Just at that moment I passed the shop of a watchmaker-optometrist, whose sign had always been a large clock that gave the exact time. Under this clock hung a picture of a pair of giant eyeglasses with staring eyes. On my morning walks I had always smiled to myself at this slightly grotesque detail in the street scene.

To my amazement, the hands of the clock had disappeared. The dial was blank, and

Wild Strawberries from Four Screen Plays of Ingmar Bergman by Ingmar Bergman. Copyright © 1960 by Ingmar Bergman. Reprinted by permission of Simon & Schuster, a Division of Gulf & Western Corporation.

[1] In the film, the scene in square brackets appears before the credits against shots of Isak in the library.

below it someone had smashed both of the eyes so that they looked like watery, infected sores.

Instinctively I pulled out my own watch to check the time, but I found that my old reliable gold timepiece had also lost its hands. I held it to my ear to find out if it was still ticking. Then I heard my heart beat. It was pounding very fast and irregularly. I was overwhelmed by an inexplicable feeling of frenzy.

I put my watch away and leaned for a few moments against the wall of a building until the feeling had passed. My heart calmed down and I decided to return home.

To my joy, I saw that someone was standing on the street corner. His back was towards me. I rushed up to him and touched his arm. He turned quickly and to my horror I found that the man had no face under his soft felt hat.

I pulled my hand back and in the same moment the entire figure collapsed as if it were made of dust or frail splinters. On the sidewalk lay a pile of clothes. The person himself had disappeared without a trace. I looked around in bewilderment and realized that I must have lost my way. I was in a part of the city where I had never been before.

I stood on an open square surrounded by high, ugly apartment buildings. From this narrow square, streets spread out in all directions. Everyone was dead; there was not a sign of a living soul.

High above me the sun shone completely white, and light forced its way down between the houses as if it were the blade of a razor-sharp knife. I was so cold that my entire body shivered.

Finally I found the strength to move again and chose one of the narrow streets at random. I walked as quickly as my pounding heart allowed, yet the street seemed to be endless.

Then I heard the tolling of bells and suddenly I was standing on another open square near an unattractive little church of red brick. There was no graveyard next to it and the church was surrounded on all sides by grey-walled buildings.

Not far from the church a funeral procession was wending its way slowly through the streets, led by an ancient hearse and followed by some old-fashioned hired carriages. These were pulled by pairs of meagre-looking horses, weighed down under enormous black shabracks. I stopped and uncovered my head. It was an intense relief to see living creatures, hear the sound of horses trotting and church bells ringing. Then everything happened very quickly and so frighteningly that even as I write this I still feel a definite uneasiness.

The hearse was just about to turn in front of the church gate when suddenly it began to sway and rock like a ship in a storm. I saw that one of the wheels had come loose and was rolling towards me with a loud clatter. I had to throw myself to one side to avoid being hit. It struck the church wall right behind me and splintered into pieces.

The other carriages stopped at a distance but no one got out or came to help. The huge hearse swayed and teetered on its three wheels. Suddenly the coffin was thrown out and fell into the street. As if relieved, the hearse straightened and rolled on towards a side street, followed by the other carriages.

The tolling of the church bells had stopped and I stood alone with the overturned, partly smashed coffin. Gripped by a fearful curiosity, I approached. A hand stuck out from the pile of splintered boards. When I leaned forward, the dead hand clutched my arm and pulled me down towards the casket with enormous force. I struggled helplessly against it as the corpse slowly rose from the coffin. It was a man dressed in a frock coat.

To my horror, I saw that the corpse was myself. I tried to free my arm, but he held it in a powerful grip. All this time he stared at me without emotion and seemed to be smiling scornfully.

In this moment of senseless horror, I awakened and sat up in my bed. It was three in the morning and the sun was already reflecting from the rooftops opposite my window. I closed my eyes and I muttered words of reality against my dream — against all the evil and frightening dreams which have haunted me these last few years.

ISAK: My name is Isak Borg. I am still alive. I am seventy-six years old.[2] I really feel quite well.

(When I had muttered these words I felt calmer, drank a glass of water, and lay down to ponder on the day which was ahead of me. I knew immediately what I should do. I got

---

[2] In the film, Isak is seventy-eight.

*out of bed, pulled open the curtains, found
the weather radiant, and breathed in the fine
morning air. Then I put on my robe and
went through the apartment (where the
clocks were striking three) to the room of my
old housekeeper. When I opened the door
she sat up immediately, wide awake.)*

AGDA: Are you ill, Professor?

ISAK: Listen, Miss Agda, will you please prepare some breakfast? I'm taking the car.

AGDA: You're taking the car, Professor?

ISAK: Yes, I'll drive down to Lund with my
own two hands. I've never believed in aero-
planes.

AGDA: Dear Professor! Go back to sleep and
I'll bring you coffee at nine o'clock and then
we'll start at ten, as was decided.

ISAK: Very well then, I'll go without eating.

AGDA: And who's going to pack the frock
coat?

ISAK: I'll do that myself.

AGDA: And what will become of me?

ISAK: Miss Agda, you can go with me in the
car or take the aeroplane — that's up to you.

AGDA: For an entire year I've been looking
forward to being present at the ceremony when
you become a Jubilee Doctor, and everything
was perfectly organised. Now you come and tell
me that you're going to drive down instead of
going by plane.

ISAK: The presentation is not until five
o'clock, and if I leave at once I'll have fourteen
hours in which to get there.

AGDA: Everything will be ruined that way.
Your son will be waiting at Malmö airport.
What will he say?

ISAK: You can make some explanation, Miss
Agda.

AGDA: If you take the car, I won't be with
you at the ceremony.

ISAK: Now listen, Miss Agda.

AGDA: You can take the car and drive there
and destroy the most solemn day of my life . . .

ISAK: We are not married, Miss Agda.

AGDA: I thank God every night that we're
not. For seventy-four years I have acted according to my own principles, and they won't fail
me today.

ISAK: Is that your last word on this matter,
Miss Agda?

AGDA: That is my last word. But I'll be saying
a lot to myself about mean old gentlemen who
think only of themselves and never about the

feelings of others who have served them faith-
fully for forty years.

ISAK: I really don't know how I've been able
to stand your immense hunger for power all
these years.

AGDA: Just tell me and it can be ended tomorrow.

ISAK: Anyway, I'm going to drive, and you
may do whatever the hell you want to. I'm a
grown man and I don't have to put up with
your bossiness.

*(Our last words, I must admit, were spoken
rather loudly, partly because of MISS AGDA's
unruly temper and partly because I had gone
to the bathroom, where I shaved and completed my morning toilet. When I came out
of the bathroom, I found to my surprise that
MISS AGDA was busy packing my frock coat
and other necessities. She seemed to have
come to her senses and I tried a friendly pat
on her back to make her understand that I
had forgiven her.)*

ISAK: There is no one who can pack like you.

AGDA: Is that so.

ISAK: Old sourpuss.

*(I was very angry that she didn't answer.
True, my last words weren't very well chosen,
but MISS AGDA has a way of being cross which
would try the patience of a saint.)*

AGDA: Should I boil a couple of eggs to go
with the coffee, sir?

ISAK: Yes, thank you, that's very kind of you,
Miss Agda. Thank you, dear Miss Agda.

*(Without noticing my efforts to be nice in
spite of everything, the old lady disappeared
into the kitchen.)*

ISAK: Jubilee Doctor! Damn stupidity. The
faculty could just as well make me jubilee idiot.
I'm going to buy something for the old sourpuss to sweeten her up a little. I hate people
who are slow to forget. I can't even hurt a fly;
how could I ever hurt Miss Agda?

(Then she appeared in the doorway.)

AGDA: Do you want toast?

ISAK: No, thank you for everything. Don't
trouble yourself over me.

AGDA: Why are *you* sour?

*(I didn't have time to answer before the door
closed in my face. I dressed and went into
the dining-room, where my breakfast was*

waiting. The morning sun threw a bright stripe across the dining-room table. MISS AGDA *puttered about quietly with a coffee pot and poured steaming coffee into my personal cup.*)

ISAK: Won't you have a cup too?

AGDA: No, thanks.

(MISS AGDA *went over to water the flowers in the window and turned her back to me quite naturally but in a very definite way. Then the door of a nearby room opened and my daughter-in-law,* MARIANNE, *entered. She was still wearing pyjamas and was smoking a cigarette.*)

ISAK: May I ask why my esteemed daughter-in-law is out of bed at this hour of the morning?

MARIANNE: It's a little difficult to sleep when you and Miss Agda are shouting at each other loud enough to shake the walls.

ISAK: Surely no one here has been shouting.

AGDA: Of course not, no one here has been shouting.

MARIANNE: You're going by car to Lund.

ISAK: Yes, I think so.

MARIANNE: May I go with you?

ISAK: What? You want to go home?

MARIANNE: Yes, I want to go home.

ISAK: Home to Evald?

MARIANNE: That's it. You don't have to ask my reasons. If I could afford it, I would take the train.

ISAK: Of course you can go with me.

MARIANNE: I'll be ready in about ten minutes.

(MARIANNE *put out her cigarette in an ash tray on the table, went into her room and closed the door.* AGDA *brought another cup but said nothing. We were both surprised but had to remain silent about* MARIANNE's *sudden decision to go home to my son* EVALD. *Nevertheless, I felt obliged to shake my head.*)

AGDA: Good Lord!

([*Shortly after half past three, I drove my car out of the garage.* MARIANNE *came out through the front gate dressed in slacks and a short jacket (she is a stately young woman): I looked up towards the window to see if* AGDA *was standing there. She was. I waved to her but she did not wave back. Angrily I got*

into the car, slammed the door and started the engine.][3] *Silently we left the quiet, sleeping city.* MARIANNE *was about to light a cigarette.*)

ISAK: Please don't smoke.

MARIANNE: Of course.

ISAK: I can't stand cigarette smoke.

MARIANNE: I forgot.

ISAK: Besides, cigarette smoking is both expensive and unhealthy. There should be a law against women smoking.

MARIANNE: The weather is nice.

ISAK: Yes, but oppressive. I have a feeling that we'll have a storm.

MARIANNE: So do I.

ISAK: Now take the cigar. Cigars are an expression of the fundamental idea of smoking. A stimulant and a relaxation. A manly vice.

MARIANNE: And what vices may a woman have?

ISAK: Crying, bearing children, and gossiping about the neighbours.

MARIANNE: How old are you really, Father Isak?

ISAK: Why do you want to know?

MARIANNE: No real reason. Why?

ISAK: I know why you asked.

MARIANNE: Oh.

ISAK: Don't pretend. You don't like me and you never have.

MARIANNE: I know you only as a father-in-law.

ISAK: Why are you going home again?

MARIANNE: An impulse. That's all.

ISAK: Evald happens to be my son.

MARIANNE: Yes, I'm sure he is.

ISAK: So, it may not be so strange that I ask you.

MARIANNE: This is something which really does not concern you.

ISAK: Do you want to hear my opinion?

(*She provoked me with her unshakable calm and remoteness. Besides, I was very curious and a little worried.*)

ISAK: Evald and I are very much alike. We have our principles.

MARIANNE: You don't have to tell me.

ISAK: This *loan* for example. Evald got a loan from me with which to complete his studies. He was to have paid it back when he became a

3 The scene in square brackets does not appear in the finished film.

lecturer at the university. It became a matter of honour for him to pay it back at the rate of five thousand per year. Although I realise that it's difficult for him, a bargain is a bargain.

MARIANNE: For us it means that we can never have a holiday together and that your son works himself to death.

ISAK: You have an income of your own.

MARIANNE: . . . Especially when you're stinking rich and have no need for the money.

ISAK: A bargain is a bargain, my dear Marianne. And I know that Evald understands and respects me.

MARIANNE: That may be true, but he also hates you.

(*Her calm, almost matter-of-fact tone startled me. I tried to look into her eyes, but she stared straight ahead and her face remained expressionless.*)

ISAK: Evald and I have never coddled each other.

MARIANNE: I believe you.

ISAK: I'm sorry that you dislike me, because I rather like you.

MARIANNE: That's nice.

ISAK: Tell me, what do you really have against me?

MARIANNE: Do you want me to be frank?

ISAK: Please.

MARIANNE: You are an old egotist, Father. You are completely inconsiderate and you have never listened to anyone but yourself. All this is well hidden behind your mask of old-fashioned charm and your friendliness. But you are hard as nails, even though everyone depicts you as a great humanitarian. We who have seen you at close range, we know what you really are. You can't fool us. For instance, do you remember when I came to you a month ago? I had some idiotic idea that you would help Evald and me. So I asked to stay with you for a few weeks. Do you remember what you said?

ISAK: I told you that you were most cordially welcome.

MARIANNE: This is what you really said, but I'm sure you've forgotten: Don't try to pull me into your marital problems because I don't give a damn about them, and everyone has his own troubles.

ISAK: Did I say that?

MARIANNE: You said more than that.

ISAK: That was the worst, I hope.

MARIANNE: This is what you said, word for

word: I have no respect for suffering of the soul, so don't come to me and complain. But if you need spiritual masturbation, I can make an appointment for you with some good quack, or perhaps with a minister, it's so popular these days.

ISAK: Did I say that?

MARIANNE: You have rather inflexible opinions, Father. It would be terrible to have to depend on you in any way.

ISAK: Is that so. Now, if I am honest, I must say that I've enjoyed having you around the house.

MARIANNE: Like a cat.

ISAK: Like a cat, or a human being, it's the same thing. You are a fine young woman and I'm sorry that you dislike me.

MARIANNE: I don't dislike you.

ISAK: Oh.

MARIANNE: I feel sorry for you.

(*I could hardly keep from laughing at her odd tone of voice and lack of logic. She herself laughed, by the way, and it cleared the air a bit.*)

ISAK: I really would like to tell you about a dream I had this morning.

MARIANNE: I'm not very interested in dreams.

ISAK: No, perhaps not.

(*We drove for a while in silence. The sun stood high in the sky and the road was brilliantly white. Suddenly I had an impulse. I slowed down and swung the car into a small side road on the left, leading down to the sea. It was a twisting, forest road, bordered by piles of newly cut timber which smelled strongly in the heat of the sun.* MARIANNE *looked up, a bit surprised, but remained silent. I parked the car in a curve of the road.*)

ISAK: Come, I'll show you something.

(*She sighed quietly and followed me down the little hill to the gate. Now we could see the large yellow house set among the birch trees, with its terrace facing the bay. The house slept behind closed doors and drawn blinds.*)

ISAK: Every summer for the first twenty years of my life we lived out here. There were ten of us children. Yes, you probably know that.

MARIANNE: What a ridiculous old house.

ISAK: It is an antique.

MARIANNE: Do people live here now?

ISAK: Not this summer.

MARIANNE: I'll go down to the water and take a dip if you don't mind. We have lots of time.

ISAK: I'll go over to the wild strawberry patch for a moment.

(*I suddenly found that I was speaking without a listener.* MARIANNE *was lazily making her way down to the beach.*)

ISAK: The old strawberry patch . . .

(*I went towards the house and immediately found the spot, but it seemed to be much smaller and less impressive than I had remembered. There were still many wild strawberries, however. I sat down next to an old apple tree that stood alone and ate the berries, one by one. I may very well have become a little sentimental. Perhaps I was a little tired and somewhat melancholy. It's not unlikely that I began to think about one thing or another that was associated with my childhood haunts.*

I had a strange feeling of solemnity, as if this were a day of decision. (It was not the only time that day that I was to feel that way.) The quietness of the summer morning. The calm bay. The birds' brilliant concert in the foliage. The old sleeping house. The aromatic apple tree which leaned slightly, supporting my back. The wild strawberries.

I don't know how it happened, but the day's clear reality flowed into dreamlike images. I don't even know if it was a dream, or memories which arose with the force of real events. I do not know how it began either, but I think it was when I heard the playing of a piano.

Astonished, I turned my head and looked at the house, a short distance up the hill. It had been transformed in a strange way. The façade, which only a few moments ago was so blind and shut, was now alive and the sun glittered on the open windows. White curtains swayed in the warm summer breeze. The gaudy awnings were rolled halfway down; smoke came from the chimney. The old summer-house seemed to be bursting with life. You could hear the music of the piano (it was something by Waldteufel), happy voices echoing through the open windows, laughter, footsteps, the cries of chil-

dren, the squeaking of the pump. Someone started to sing up there on the second floor. It was a strong, almost Italian bel-canto tenor. In spite of all this, not a human being was in sight. For a few moments the scene still had a feeling of unreality, like a mirage which could instantly evaporate and be lost in silence.

Suddenly I saw her. When I turned round after looking at the strangely transformed house I discovered her where she was kneeling in her sun-yellow cotton dress, picking wild strawberries. I recognized her immediately and I became excited. She was so close to me that I could touch her, but my lingering feeling of the evanescence of the situation prevented me from making her notice my presence. (I was amused. Mental image or dream or whatever this was, she looked just as I remembered her: a girl in a yellow summer dress, freckled and tanned and glowing with light-hearted young womanhood.)

I sat for a few minutes and silently looked at her. Finally I couldn't help calling out her name, rather quietly but nevertheless quite audibly. She didn't react. I tried once more, a little louder.)

ISAK: Sara . . . It's me, your cousin Isak . . . I've become a little old, of course, and do not quite look as I used to. But you haven't changed the slightest bit. Little cousin, can't you hear me?

(*She didn't hear me, but eagerly continued to pick the wild strawberries, putting them into a small straw basket. I understood then that one cannot easily converse with one's memories. This discovery did not make me particularly sad. I decided to keep quiet and hoped that this unusual and pleasant situation would last as long as possible.*

Then, a boy came strolling down the hill. He was already growing a small moustache despite the fact that he couldn't have been more than eighteen or nineteen years old. He was dressed in a shirt and trousers and wore his student's cap pushed way back on his head. He stepped right behind SARA, *took off his glasses and wiped them with a large white handkerchief. (I recognised him as my brother* SIGFRID, *one year older than myself. We shared many happy moments and troubles. He died, by the way, relatively young, of pyelitis. He was a lecturer in Slavic languages at Uppsala University.*)

SIGFRID: Good morning, sweet cousin. What are you doing?

SARA: Can't you see that I'm picking wild strawberries, stupid?

SIGFRID: And who shall be favoured with these tasty berries, plucked in the morning watch by a dulcet young maiden?

SARA: Oh you! Don't you know that Uncle Aron's birthday is today? I forgot to prepare a present for him. So, he gets a basket of wild strawberries. That's good enough, isn't it?

SIGFRID: I'll help you.

SARA: You know, Charlotta and Sigbritt have sewn a sampler for him and Angelica has baked a cake and Anna has painted a really pretty picture and Kristina and Birgitta have written a song which they'll sing.

SIGFRID: That's best of all, because Uncle Aron is stone deaf.

SARA: He will be very happy and you are stupid.

SIGFRID: And the nape of your neck is deuced pretty.

(SIGFRID *quickly bent over the girl and rather gallantly kissed her on her downy neck.* SARA *became rather annoyed.*)

SARA: You know that you're not allowed to do that.

SIGFRID: Who said so?

SARA: I said so. Besides, you are a particularly unbearable little snot who thinks he's something.

SIGFRID: I'm your cousin, and you're sweet on me.

SARA: On you!

SIGFRID: Come here and I'll kiss you on the mouth.

SARA: If you don't keep away I'll tell Isak that you try to kiss me all the time.

SIGFRID: Little Isak. I can beat him easily with one hand tied behind my back.

SARA: Isak and I are secretly engaged. You know that very well.

SIGFRID: Yes, your engagement is so secret that the whole house knows about it.

SARA: Could I help it if the twins ran around and blabbered everything?

SIGFRID: Then when are you going to get married? When are you going to get married? When are you going to get married?

SARA: I'll tell you one thing, of your four brothers I can't decide which is the least vain. But I think it's Isak. In any case, he's the kindest. And you are the most awful, the most unbearable, the most stupid, the most idiotic, the most ridiculous, the most cocky — I can't think of enough names to call you.

SIGFRID: Admit that you're a little sweet on me.

SARA: Besides, you smoke smelly cigars.

SIGFRID: That's a man's smell, isn't it?

SARA: Besides, the twins, who know *everything*, say that you've done *rather* nasty things with the oldest Berglund girl. And she's not a *really nice* girl, the twins say. And I believe them.

SIGFRID: If you only knew how pretty you are when you blush like that. Now you must kiss me. I can't stand it any more. I'm completely in love with you, now that I think about it.

SARA: Oh, that's only talk. The twins say that you're crazy about girls. Is it really true?

(*Suddenly he kissed her hard and rather skilfully. She was carried away by this game and returned his kiss with a certain fierceness. But then she was conscious-stricken and threw herself down on the ground, knocking over the basket of wild strawberries. She was very angry and began crying with excitement.*)

SIGFRID: Don't scream. Someone might come.

SARA: Look at the wild strawberries, all spilled. And what will Isak say? He is so kind and really loves me. Oh, how sorry I am, oh, what you've done to me. You've turned me into a bad woman, at least *nearly*. Go away. I don't want to see you any more, at least not before breakfast. I have to hurry. Help me pick up the strawberries. And look, I've got a spot on my dress.

(*Then the gong suddenly sounded, announcing that breakfast was being served. The sound seemed to bring forth many human beings not far from where I stood, an astonished onlooker.*

The flag with the Swedish-Norwegian Union emblem went up and instantly stiffened against the light summer clouds, big brother HAGBART, *dressed in his cadet uniform, handled the ropes expertly. From the bath-house one could hear wild laughter, and through the louvered door tumbled two red-headed girls about thirteen years old, as identical as two wild strawberries. They laughed so hard they could hardly walk, and they whispered things to each other that were apparently both very secret and quite amusing.* SIGBRITT, *tall and lanky, with thick hair in heavy rolls across her forehead, came out carrying the baby's bassinet and placed it in the shadow of the arbour.* CHARLOTTA *(the diligent, self-sacrificing sister who carried the responsibilities of the household on her round shoulders) rushed out on the veranda and shouted to* SARA *and* SIGFRID *to hurry. Seventeen-year-old* BENJAMIN *dived out of some bushes, his pimply face red from the sun, and looked around with an annoyed expression.*[4] *In his hand he held a thick, open book.* ANGELICA *(the beauty of the family) came skipping out of the woods, joined the twins, and was immediately made part of some hilarious secret. Finally, fifteen-year-old* ANNA *came running out of the house, asked* HAGBART *about something, then raised her voice and started to shout for* ISAK. *I arose, surprised and worried, unable to answer her cry.)*

TWINS (*in unison*): I think that Isak is out fishing with Father and they probably can't hear the gong. And Father said, by the way, that we shouldn't wait to eat. That's what Father said, I definitely remember.

(Oh, yes, FATHER *and I were out fishing together. I felt a secret and completely inexplicable happiness at this message, and I stood for a long while wondering what I should do in this new old world which I was suddenly given the opportunity to visit.*

The rest of the family had entered the house and something was being discussed quite loudly inside. Only SIGBRITT'S *little child remained on the terrace, sleeping in the shadows of the tall lilac bushes. Curiosity overwhelmed me. I went slowly up the slope towards the house and soon found myself in the long, dark corridor which was connected with the foyer by glass doors. From there I had a good view into the large,* sunlit dining-room with its white table already set for breakfast, the light furniture, the wallpaper, the figurines, the palms, the airy summer curtains, the scoured white wooden floor with its broad planks and blue rag rugs, the pictures and the sampler, the large, crownlike chandelier.*

There they were now, my nine brothers and sisters, my AUNT *and* UNCLE ARON. *The only ones missing were* FATHER, MOTHER *and I.*

Everyone was standing behind his chair, with lowered head, and hands clenched together. AUNT *recited the prayer 'In Jesus's name to the table we go, Bless You for the food You bestow.' After which the whole troop sat down with much chatter and scraping of chairs. My aunt (a stately woman in her best years, endowed with a powerful sense of authority and a resonant voice) demanded silence.)*

AUNT: Benjamin will immediately go and wash his hands. How long is it going to take you to learn cleanliness?

BENJAMIN: I *have* washed my hands.

AUNT: Sigbritt, pass the porridge to Angelica and give the twins their portions. Your fingernails are coal-black. Pass me the bread, Hagbart. Who taught you to spread so much butter on the bread? Can you do that at the military academy? Charlotta, the salt-cellar is stopped up. How often have I told you that it shouldn't be left out in the open, because the salt gets humid.

BENJAMIN: I *have* washed my hands, but I have paint under my nails.

UNCLE ARON: Who has picked wild strawberries for me?

SARA: I have. (*Louder.*) I have.

AUNT: You have to speak up, my child. You know that Uncle Aron is a bit hard of hearing.

SARA (*thunderously*): I have!

ARON: Oh my, you remembered Uncle Aron's birthday. That was really very kind of you.

HAGBART: Couldn't Uncle Aron have a little drink for breakfast in honour of the day?

AUNT: A drink at breakfast when Father isn't home is completely out of the question.

TWINS (*in unison*): Uncle Aron has already had three drinks. I know. I know. We saw him at eight o'clock when we went down to the bath-house.

---

[4] In the film, Benjamin is seen jumping down from a tree.

AUNT: The twins should hold their tongues and eat. Besides, you haven't made your beds and as punishment you'll have to dry the dinner silverware. Benjamin must not bite his nails. Don't sit and jump on the chair, Anna. You aren't a child any more.

ANNA: I want to give Uncle Aron my picture, please, Auntie. Can't we give him our presents now, right away?

AUNT: Where is your picture?

ANNA: Here under the table.

AUNT: You'll have to wait until we've eaten.

SIGFRID: It's a very advanced work of art, I'd say. It's a picture of Tristan and Isolde, but you can't tell for sure which one is Tristan.

SARA: Oh, he always spoils things, the little fop! Now he's making Anna unhappy. See if she doesn't start to cry.

ANNA: Not at all. I can overlook Sigfrid's faults.

TWINS (*together*): By the way, what were Sara and Sigfrid up to in the wild strawberry patch this morning? We saw everything from the bath-house.

SIGBRITT: Calm down now, children!

CHARLOTTA: Someone should put gags on the twins.

AUNT: Twins, keep still or leave the table.

BENJAMIN: Doesn't a person have freedom of expression, eh?

SIGFRID: Shut up, you snotnoses.

ANGELICA: Sara is blushing, Sara is blushing, Sara is blushing.

TWINS: Sigfrid is blushing, too. Ha-ha! Sigfrid and Sara! Sigfrid and Sara! Sigfrid and Sara!

AUNT (*thunderously*): Quiet! We'll have quiet at the table!

ARON: What did you say? Of course we shall be happy.

(*The* TWINS *snigger in the silence.* SARA *throws the porridge spoon at her tormentors.*)

CHARLOTTA: But, Sara!

SARA: They're just lying! They're liars!

(SARA *rose from the table so violently that her chair turned over. She stood hesitantly for a moment, her face red and tears splashing down her cheeks. Then she ran away furiously, throwing herself at the door and out into the hall.*

She opened the glass door and disap-

peared out on the porch, where I could hear her sobbing violently. Gentle CHARLOTTA *came out of the dining-room and went past me on her way to console* SARA.

I could hear their voices from the darkness of the foyer and I came closer stealthily. SARA *sat on a red stool (which* GRANDMOTHER *once used, when she wanted to take off her rubber boots) while* CHARLOTTA *stood in front of her, patting her gently on the head. The miserable girl pressed her tear-stained face against* CHARLOTTA's *skirt over and over again. The tinted light from the stained-glass windows of the outer door painted the whole picture in a strange way.*)

SARA: Isak is so refined. He is so enormously refined and moral and sensitive and he wants us to read poetry together and he talks about the after-life and wants to play duets on the piano and he likes to kiss only in the dark and he talks about sinfulness. I think he is extremely intellectual and morally aloof and I feel so worthless, and I *am* so worthless, you can't deny that. But sometimes I get the feeling that I'm much older than Isak, do you know what I mean? And then I think he's a child even if we are the same age, and then Sigfrid is so fresh and exciting and I want to go home. I don't want to be here all summer, to be a laughing stock for the twins and the rest of you — no, I don't want that.

CHARLOTTA: I'll talk to Sigfrid, I will! If he doesn't leave you alone, I'll see to it that he gets a few more chores to do. Father will arrange that without any trouble. He also thinks Sigfrid is nasty and needs a little work to keep him out of mischief.

SARA: Poor little Isak, he is so kind to me. Oh, how unfair everything is.

CHARLOTTA: Everything will work out for the best, you'll see. Listen, now they're singing for Uncle Aron.

SARA: Isn't it crazy to write a song for a deaf man! That's typical of the twins.

(*Then two girlish voices sang a song that could be heard throughout the house.* CHARLOTTA *placed her arm around* SARA's *shoulders and* SARA *blew her nose quite loudly.*

Both girls returned to the dining-room, where the mood had become very lively.[5]

---

[5] In the film, the girls do not return to the dining-room.

Uncle ARON *had arisen, his round perspiring face lit like a lantern, and he had tears in his eyes. He held a sheet of music before him while the twins stood nearby and sang with all their might. When they had finished everyone applauded, and Uncle* ARON *kissed them on the forehead and wiped his face with a napkin. My* AUNT *rose from the table and proposed a quadruple cheer. Everyone got up and hurrahed. Suddenly* ANNA *shouted and pointed out the window. Everyone turned to look.)*

ANNA: Look, here comes Father.

AUNT: Well, finally! Sigbritt, take out the porridge bowl and have it warmed. Charlotta, you bring up more milk from the cellar.

(The women fussed around, but SARA *ran out of the house, down the slope, and disappeared behind the small arbour which stood on the edge of the birch-tree pasture. I followed her with curiosity, but lost her. Suddenly I stood alone at the wild strawberry patch. A feeling of emptiness and sadness came over me. I was awakened by a girl's voice asking me something. I looked up.*

In front of me stood a young lady in shorts and a boy's checked shirt. She was very tanned and her blonde hair was tangled and bleached by the sun and the sea. She sucked on an unlit pipe, wore wooden sandals on her feet and dark glasses on her nose.)

SARA: Is this your shack?

ISAK: No, it isn't.

SARA: It's a good thing you're the truthful type. My old man owns the whole peninsula . . . including the shack.

ISAK: I lived here once. Two hundred years ago.

SARA Uh huh. Is that your jalopy standing up at the gate?

ISAK: It's my jalopy, yes.

SARA: Looks like an antique.

ISAK: It *is* an antique, just like its owner.

SARA: You've got a sense of humour about yourself, too. That's fantastic. Where are you heading, by the way? In which direction, I mean.

ISAK: I'm going to Lund.

SARA: What a fantastic coincidence. I'm on my way to Italy.

ISAK: I'd feel very honoured if you came along.

SARA: My name is Sara. Silly name, isn't it?

ISAK: My name is Isak. Rather silly too.

SARA: Weren't they married?

ISAK: Unfortunately not. It was Abraham and Sara.

SARA: Shall we take off?

ISAK: I have another lady with me. Here she comes. This is Sara, and this is Marianne. We'll have company to Lund. Sara is going to Italy but she has agreed to travel part of the way with us.

SARA: Now you're being ironic again, but it suits you.

(We began walking towards the car. MAR-IANNE *and I exchanged amused glances, the first contact between us. When we came to the car, two young men with round blond crew-cut heads popped up.[6] They were also wearing checked shirts, shorts, wooden sandals and sunglasses. Each carried a rucksack.)*

SARA: Hey, fellows. I've got a lift nearly all the way to Italy. This is Anders, and this one with the glasses is Viktor, called Vicke . . . and this is Father Isak.

VIKTOR: Hello.

ISAK: Hello.

ANDERS: How do you do, sir.

ISAK: Hello.

SARA: That cookie you're staring at so hard, her name is Marianne.

MARIANNE: Hello.

BOYS (*together*): Hello.

SARA: It's a pretty big car.

ISAK: Just jump in. There's room for everybody. We can put the baggage in the boot, if you don't mind.

(We packed things away, and then we all got into the car. I drove carefully, leaving my childhood world behind. SARA *took off her sunglasses and laughed. She was very much like her namesake of the past.)*

SARA: Of course I have to tell Isak that Anders and I are going steady. We are crazy about each other. Viktor is with us as a chaperon. That was decided by the old man. Viktor is also in love with me and is watching Anders like a madman. This was a brilliant idea of my old man. I'll probably have to seduce Viktor

---

[6] In the film, one of the young men has dark hair.

to get him out of the way. I'd better tell Isak that I'm a virgin. That's why I can talk so brazenly.

(*I looked at her through the rear-view mirror. She was sitting comfortably with her legs on the backs of the folding seats.* ANDERS *had a proprietary arm around her shoulders and looked rather angry, for which I could hardly blame him.* VIKTOR, *on the other hand, seemed completely disinterested and stared fixedly at the nape of* MARIANNE'S *neck — and whatever else he could glimpse of her figure.*)

SARA: I smoke a pipe. Viktor says it's healthier. He's crazy about everything that's healthy.

(*No one answered, or considered any comment necessary. We continued our trip in a silence which was by no means unpleasant, just a little shy. The weather had become quite warm, almost oppressive, and we had opened all the windows. The road was broad and straight. I was in a spirited mood. The day had been full of stimulating surprises.*)

ISAK: I had a first love whose name was Sara.
SARA: She was like me, of course.
ISAK: As a matter of fact, she was rather like you.
SARA: What happened to her?
ISAK: She married my brother Sigfrid and had six children. Now she's seventy-five years old and a rather beautiful little old lady.
SARA: I can't imagine anything worse than getting old. Oh, excuse me. I think I said something stupid.

(*Her tone was so sincerely repentant that everyone burst into laughter. And then it happened.*
We were on a broad, blind right curve. I kept hard to the left and at that moment a little black car came speeding straight towards us. I had time to see MARIANNE *brace her right hand against the windshield and I heard* SARA *scream. Then I slammed on the brakes with all my strength. Our big car skidded to the left and went off the road into a pasture. The black car disappeared with a squeal, rolled over and fell into a deep ditch to the right of the road. Startled, we stared at one another; we had escaped without a scratch. Some thick black tyre tracks and several big marks on the road*

surface were the only signs of the other car. A short distance away, a couple of rotating wheels stuck up from the ditch.
All of us began running towards it and then stopped in astonishment. The overturned car's radio sang a morning hymn. Two people crawled out of the ditch, a man and a woman, in the midst of a violent quarrel which was on the verge of coming to blows. When they saw us watching they immediately stopped and the man limped towards me.)

ALMAN: How are you? There's nothing for me to say. The blame is completely ours. We have no excuses. It was my wife who was driving. Are you all right? Everyone safe and sound? Thank God for that.

(*He mumbled nervously, took off his glasses and put them on again, and looked at us with frightened glances.*)

ALMAN: The would-be murderers should introduce themselves. Alman is my name. I'm an engineer at the Stockholm electric power plant. Back there is my wife, Berit. She used to be an actress, and it was that fact we were discussing when . . . when . . . when . . .

(*He interrupted himself with an artificial laugh and waved at his wife. When she remained motionless, he took a few limping steps towards her.*)

ISAK: How is your leg?
ALMAN: It's not from this. I've been crippled for years. Unfortunately it's not only my leg that's crippled, according to my wife. Come here now, Berit, and make your apologies.

(*The woman mustered her courage. She moved jerkily in spite of her rotund body.*)

BERIT: Please, pretty please forgive me, as children say. It was my fault, everything. I was just going to hit my husband when that curve appeared. One thing is obvious: God punishes some people immediately — or what do you think, Sten? You're a Catholic.
ISAK: Perhaps we should take a look at your car and see if we can't put it right side up again.
ALMAN: Please don't trouble yourself over us. I beg of you.
BERIT: Shut up now, Sten darling. Some people do have completely unselfish intentions, even if you don't believe it.

ALMAN: My wife is a little nervous, I think. But we've had a shock. That's the word. A shock.

(*He laughed once more and tore off his glasses and put them on again. The young men had already jumped down into the ditch and were trying to lift the little car.* MARIANNE *ran back to our car and backed it down the road. With the help of a rope which I always carry in the boot, we succeeded in getting the other car on an even keel.* MR. ALMAN *suddenly cheered up, threw off his jacket and rolled up his shirt sleeves. Then he put his shoulder alongside* SARA, VIKTOR *and* ANDERS *and began to push.*)

BERIT: Now watch the engineer closely, see how he matches his strength with the young boys, how he tenses his feeble muscles to impress the pretty girl. Sten darling, watch out that you don't have a haemorrhage.

ALMAN: My wife loves to embarrass me in front of strangers. I let her — it's psychotherapy.

(*We towed and shoved and pushed and suddenly the little car was standing on the road. By then, of course, its radio had gone dead.* ALMAN *sat down behind the wheel of the dented car and got the motor started. The car had gone a few feet when one of the front wheels rolled off abruptly and slid far down into the ravine.*)

BERIT: A true picture of our marriage.

(ALMAN *stood hesitantly on the gleaming white road, perspiring nervously.* MARIANNE, *who had stayed out of the whole scene, was still sitting behind the wheel of our car. The youngsters sat down at the edge of the road. All of us were a little upset.*)

ISAK: I can't see any other way out. The lady and the gentleman must ride with us to the nearest petrol station. There you can telephone for help.

ALMAN: Don't trouble yourself over us. We'll have a refreshing walk. Won't we, Berit?

BERIT: With his leg. Dear Lord, that would be a scream.

ALMAN: In her delightful way my wife has just said thank you for both of us.

(*Silently we climbed into the car, which was suddenly completely filled.* (MARIANNE *drove; I sat beside her.* MR. *and* MRS.

ALMAN *were on the folding seats. The three youngsters occupied the back seat.*) ALMAN *whistled some popular tune softly but soon fell silent. No one had any particular desire to converse.* MARIANNE *drove very calmly and carefully.*

Suddenly BERIT ALMAN *started to cry. Her husband carefully put his arm around her shoulders, but she drew away and pulled out a handkerchief, which she began tearing with her fingernails.*)

ALMAN: I can never tell if my wife is really crying or putting on an act. Dammit, I think these are real tears. Well, that's the way it is when you see death staring you in the face.

BERIT: Can't you shut up?

ALMAN: My wife has unusual powers of the imagination. For two years she made me believe that she had cancer and pestered all our friends with all kinds of imaginary symptoms, despite the fact that the doctors couldn't find anything the matter. She was so convincing that we believed her more than the doctors. That's pretty clever, admit it. It's such stuff that saints are made of! Look, now she's crying about a death scare. It's a pity we don't have a movie camera around. Lights! Action! Camera! It's a 'take,' as they say in the film world.

MARIANNE: It's understandable that you're upset, Mr. Alman, but how about leaving your wife alone for a little while?

ALMAN: A woman's tears are meant for women. Don't criticize a woman's tears — they're holy. You are beautiful, dear Miss whatever your name is. But Berit here is beginning to get a little shabby. That's why you can afford to defend her.

MARIANNE: Allow me to feel compassion for your wife for different reasons.

ALMAN: Very sarcastic! Still, you don't seem to be at all hysterical. But Berit is a genius at hysterics. Do you know what that means from my point of view?

MARIANNE: You're a Catholic, aren't you? That's what your wife said.

ALMAN: Quite right. That is my way of enduring. I ridicule my wife and she ridicules me. She has her hysterics and I have my Catholicism. But we need each other's company. It's only out of pure selfishness that we haven't murdered each other by now.[7]

---

[7] In the film, after Alman's speech, we see Isak looking out of the window of the car.

(BERIT *turned towards her husband and slapped his face. He dropped his glasses, which he had fortunately just taken off. His large nose swelled and began to bleed. His froglike mouth twitched spasmodically as if he were on the verge of tears, but he immediately got control of himself, pulled out a handkerchief and pressed it to his nose, blinked his eyes and laughed.* VIKTOR *leaned forward, picked up the glasses and slowly handed them to him.*)

ALMAN: Right on the beat. It's called syncopation, isn't it? Ha-ha! Isn't it comic? If I had a stop watch, I could have timed the explosion on the nose.

BERIT (*screams*): Shut up! Shut up! Shut up!

(MARIANNE *turned pale. She applied the brakes and slowly stopped the car.*)

MARIANNE: Maybe this is the terrible truth and maybe it's just what's called letting off steam. But we have three children in the car and for their sake may I ask the lady and the gentleman to get out immediately. There is a house back there; maybe they have a telephone. The walk won't be too strenuous.

(*All of us were silent after* MARIANNE'S *speech. Without another word,* STEN ALMAN *stepped out of the car. His face was ashen grey and his nose was still bleeding. His wife looked at us and suddenly made a heroic attempt to say something sincere.*)

BERIT: Forgive us if you can.

(*Then* BERIT *got out and stood by her husband, who had turned his back on us. He had pulled out a comb and a pocket mirror and was straightening the hair on his white scalp. His wife took his bloody handkerchief and blew her nose. Then she touched his elbow, but he was suddenly very tired and hung his head. They sat down close to each other by the road. They looked like two scolded schoolchildren sitting in a corner.*

MARIANNE *started the car, and we quickly drove away from this strange marriage.*

The petrol station between Gränna and Huskvarna lies on a hill with a wide view over a very beautiful, richly foliaged landscape. We stopped to fill up the tank and decided to have lunch at a hotel some kilometers farther south.

It was with mixed feelings that I saw this region again. First, because I began my medical practice here (incidentally, it lasted for fifteen years; I succeeded the local doctor). Second, because my old MOTHER *lives near here in a large house. She is ninety-six now and is generally considered a miracle of health and vitality, although her ability to move around has diminished considerably during the last few years.*

The petrol-station owner was a big, blond man with a broad face, abnormally large hands and long arms.)

AKERMAN: Ah ha! So the doctor is out driving. Shall it be a full tank? Well, well, so it is, and those are children and grandchildren, I know. Have you got the key to the petrol tank, Doctor?

ISAK: Hello, Henrik. You recognise me.

AKERMAN: Recognise! Doctor, you were there when I was born. And then you delivered all my brothers. And fixed our cuts and scratches and took care of us, as you did of everybody while you were a doctor around here.

ISAK: And things are going well for you?

AKERMAN: Couldn't be better! I'm married, you know, and I have heirs. (*Shouts.*) Eva!

(EVA *came out of the petrol-station. She was a young woman, gypsy-like, with long, thick hair and a generous smile. She was in an advanced stage of pregnancy.*)

AKERMAN: Here you see Dr. Borg himself in person. This is the man that Ma and Pa and the whole district still talk about. The world's best doctor.

(*I looked at* MARIANNE *who was standing to the side. She applauded somewhat sarcastically and bowed. The three youngsters were in the midst of a lively dispute and pointing in different directions.* EVA *stepped up and shook my hand.*)

AKERMAN: I suggest that we name our new baby for the doctor. Isak Akerman is a good name for a prime minister.

EVA: But what if it's a girl?

AKERMAN: Eva and I only make boys. Do you want oil and water too?

ISAK: Yes, thank you. And your father is well, in spite of his bad back?

AKERMAN: Well, it's getting a bit hard for the old man, you know, but the old lady is a little bombshell.

(The last was said in greatest confidence as we bent over the dip stick to see if we needed more oil. We did.)

AKERMAN: And now you'll be visiting *your* mother, eh, Doctor?

ISAK: I suppose so.

AKERMAN: She's a remarkable lady, your mother, although she must be at least ninety-five.

ISAK: Ninety-six.

AKERMAN: Well, well, how about that.

ISAK: How much is all this?

AKERMAN: Eva and I want it to be on the house.

ISAK: No, I can't allow that.

AKERMAN: Don't insult us, Doctor! We can do things in the grand manner, too, even if we live here in little Gränna.

ISAK: There isn't the slightest reason you should pay for my petrol. I appreciate your kindness, but . . .

AKERMAN: One remembers things, you know. One doesn't forget one's gratitude, and there are some things that can never be paid back.

(AKERMAN became a little serious and I a little sentimental. We looked at each other quite moved. EVA stepped up and stood beside her husband. She squinted in the sun and beamed like a big strawberry in her red dress.)

EVA *(like an echo)*: No, we don't forget. We don't forget.

AKERMAN: Just ask anybody in town or in the hills around here, and they remember the doctor and know what the doctor did for them.

(I looked around, but MARIANNE had disappeared. No, she had got into the car. The youngsters were still busy with their discussion.)

ISAK: Perhaps I should have remained here.

AKERMAN: I don't understand.

ISAK: What? What did you say, Henrik?

AKERMAN: You said that you should have stayed here, Doctor.

ISAK: Did I say that? Yes, perhaps. Thank you anyway. Send me word and I may come to be godfather for the new Akerman. You know where to reach me.

(I shook hands with them and we parted. MARIANNE called the youngsters and we continued our trip to the inn.)

Our lunch was a success. We had a large table on the open terrace and enjoyed a most magnificent view across Lake Vättern. The head waiter, one of my former patients, did everything to satisfy our slightest wish.

I became very lively, I must admit, and told the youngsters about my years as a country doctor. I told them humorous anecdotes which had a great deal of human interest. These were a great success (I don't think they laughed just out of politeness) and I had wine with the food (which was excellent) and cognac with my coffee.

ANDERS *suddenly rose and began to recite with both feeling and talent.)*

ANDERS: 'Oh, when such beauty shows itself in each facet of creation, then how beautiful must be the eternal source of this emanation!'

(None of us thought of laughing at him. He sat down immediately and emptied his coffee cup in embarrassment. SARA was the one who broke the silence.)

SARA: Anders will become a minister and Viktor a doctor.

VIKTOR: We swore that we wouldn't discuss God or science on the entire trip. I consider Anders' lyrical outburst as a breach of our agreement.

SARA: Oh, it was beautiful!

VIKTOR: Besides, I can't understand how a modern man can become a minister. Anders isn't a complete idiot.

ANDERS: Let me tell you, your rationalism is incomprehensible nonsense. And you aren't an idiot either.

VIKTOR: In my opinion the modern —

ANDERS: In my opinion —

VIKTOR: In my opinion a modern man looks his insignificance straight in the eye and believes in himself and his biological death. Everything else is nonsense.

ANDERS: And in my opinion modern man exists only in your imagination. Because man looks at his death with horror and can't bear his own insignificance.

VIKTOR: All right. Religion for the people. Opium for the aching limb. If that's what you want.

SARA: Aren't they fantastically sweet? I always agree with the one who's spoken last. Isn't this all extremely interesting?

VIKTOR *(angry)*: When you were a child

you believed in Santa Claus. Now you believe in God.

ANDERS: And you have always suffered from an astonishing lack of imagination.

VIKTOR: What do you think about it, Professor?

ISAK: Dear boys, you would receive my opinion with ironic indulgence, whatever I happened to say. That's why I'm keeping quiet.

SARA: Then think how very unlucky they are.

ISAK: No, Sara. They are very, very lucky.

(MARIANNE *laughed and lit my cigar. I leaned back in my chair and squinted at the light filtering down between the table umbrellas. The boys looked surprised as I began to recite.*)

ISAK: 'Where is the friend I seek everywhere? Dawn is the time of loneliness and care. When twilight comes, when twilight comes . . .' What comes after that, Anders?

MARIANNE: 'When twilight comes I am still yearning.'

ANDERS: 'Though my heart is burning, burning. I see His trace of glory . . .'

SARA: You're religious, aren't you, Professor?

ISAK: 'I see His trace of glory and power, In an ear of grain and the fragrance of flower . . .'

MARIANNE: 'In every sign and breath of air. His love is there. His voice whispers in the summer breeze . . .'

(*Silence.*)

VIKTOR: As a love poem, it isn't too bad.

SARA: Now I've become very solemn. I can become quite solemn for no reason at all.

(*I rose from the table.*)

ISAK: I want to pay a visit to my mother, who happens to live nearby. You can remain here and enjoy yourselves for a while. I'll be back soon.

MARIANNE: May I come with you?

ISAK: Of course. Goodbye for now, young friends.

(*I was in a good mood and felt very happy.* MARIANNE *suddenly took my arm and walked beside me. In passing, I patted her hand.*

The house was surrounded by an ancient, parklike garden and protected from onlookers by a wall as tall as a man. Inside, everything was quiet and somewhat unreal. The sky had clouded over, and the grey light sharpened the contours of the landscape so that it looked like a skillfully painted set in an old theatre.

In a little round drawing-room filled with storm-grey light and graced by light, delicate furniture, an old nurse in uniform sat embroidering. On the carpet next to her chair a fat white poodle lay looking at us with sleepy, lidded eyes. When the nurse saw us she immediately arose, smiling politely, to greet us and shake our hands. She introduced herself as SISTER ELISABET. *I asked her quietly how my mother was and if it was convenient for us to visit her.* SISTER ELISABET *answered that* MRS. BORG *was quite well and would be happy with our visit because she was usually rather lonely. I pointed out that it was unfortunate that my visits were rather infrequent, because of the difficult journey, and* SISTER ELISABET *said that she understood. After this hushed introduction, the Sister asked us to wait for a few minutes and disappeared into a nearby room.* MARIANNE *became a little nervous with all the solemnity and pulled out a cigarette from a crushed pack and was just about to light it.*)

ISAK: Please don't smoke. Mother hates the smell of tobacco and her senses are as sharp as those of an animal in the woods.

(*At the same moment,* SISTER ELISABET *returned and told us that we were welcome.*

The room was rather small and oddly irregular, but it had a lofty ceiling. On the walls hung many beautiful and expensive paintings. Heavy draperies covered the doors. In a corner stood a tall porcelain stove with a fire burning. At the room's only window stood an incongruous desk which did not harmonize with the other pieces of furniture. My MOTHER *was sitting in a big chair. She was dressed entirely in black and wore a small lace cap on her head. She was busy entering figures in a large blue ledger. When she recognised me, she immediately rose from her seat (although with some difficulty) and walked towards us with many small steps; she seemed to be shoving one foot in front of the other without her soles ever leaving the floor. She smiled cordially and stretched forth both her hands. I grasped them and then kissed her with a son's reverence.*)

MOTHER: I just sent a telegram to tell you that I was thinking about you today. Today is your big day. And then you come here!

ISAK: Well, I had a moment of inspiration, Mother!

MOTHER: Is that your wife standing back there, Isak? You will ask her to leave the room immediately. I refuse to talk with her. She has hurt us too much.

ISAK: Mother, darling, this is not Karin. This is Evald's wife, my daughter-in-law, Marianne!

MOTHER: Well, then, she can come here and greet me.

MARIANNE: How do you do, Mrs. Borg. (*Curtsies.*)

MOTHER: I've seen you in a photograph. Evald showed it to me. He was extremely proud of your beauty. By the way, why are you travelling this way?

MARIANNE: I've been in Stockholm, visiting.

MOTHER: Why aren't you home with Evald and taking care of your child?

MARIANNE: Evald and I don't have any children.

MOTHER: Isn't it strange with young people nowadays? I bore ten children. Will someone please bring me that large box standing over there.

(*She pointed at a brown cardboard box on a chair.* MARIANNE *picked it up and placed it on the desk in front of the old lady. Both of us helped lift the lid.*)

MOTHER: My mother lived in this house before me. And you children often visited here. Do you remember, Isak?

ISAK: I remember quite well.

MOTHER: In this box are some of your toys. I've tried to think which of you owned what.

(MOTHER *looked bewilderedly into the big box, as if she expected to find all her children there among the toys and things. Then she shook her head and looked up at* MARIANNE.)

MOTHER: Ten children, and all of them dead except Isak. Twenty grandchildren. None of them visits me except Evald, once a year. It's quite all right — I don't complain — but I have fifteen great-grandchildren whom I've never seen. I send letters and presents for fifty-three birthdays and anniversaries every year. I get kind thank-you notes, but no one visits me except by accident or when someone needs a loan. I am tiresome, of course.

ISAK: Don't look at it that way, Mother dear!

MOTHER: And then I have another fault. I don't die. The inheritance doesn't materialise according to the nice, neat schedules made up by smart young people.

(*She laughed sarcastically and shook her head. Then she pulled a doll out of the box. It was an old doll, with fine gold hair and a porcelain face (a little scratched) and a beautiful lace gown.*)

MOTHER: This doll's name is Goldcrown and it belonged to Sigbritt. She got it when she was eight years old. I sewed the dress myself. She never liked it much, so Charlotta took it over and cared for it. I remember it clearly.

(*She dropped the doll and picked up a little box of bright-coloured tin soldiers and poked in it with a small, sharp finger.*)

MOTHER: Hagbart's tin soldiers. I never liked his war games. He was shot while hunting moose. We never understood each other.

(*This she said in a matter-of-fact tone, completely without sentimentality. She threw the tin soldiers into the box and fished out a photograph.*)

MOTHER: Can you see who this is? This is Sigfrid when he was three years old and you when you were two, and here is Father and me. Good Lord, how one looked in those days. It was taken in 1883.

ISAK: May I see that picture?

MOTHER (*uninterested*): Yes, of course, you can have it. It's only trash. Here is a colouring book. Maybe it belonged to the twins, or perhaps to Anna or Angelica. I really don't know because all of them have put their names in the book. And then it says: 'I am Anna's best friend.' But Anna has written: 'I love Angelica.' and Kristina has scribbled: 'Most of all in the whole world I love Father best.' And Birgitta has added: 'I am going to marry Father.' Isn't that amusing? I laughed when I read it.

(MARIANNE *took the book from her and turned the pages. It was partly scribbled on and partly painted with great vitality and strong colours. The light in the small room grew dimmer as the sky darkened outside. In the distance the thunder was already rumbling in the sky.* MOTHER *picked up a toy locomotive and looked at it closely.*)

MOTHER: I think that this is Benjamin's locomotive because he was always so amused by trains and circuses and such things. I suppose that's why he became an actor. We quarrelled often about it because I wanted him to have an honest profession. And I was right. He didn't make it. I told him that several times. He didn't believe me, but I was right. It doesn't pay much to talk. Isn't it cold in here? The fire doesn't really warm.

ISAK: No, it isn't particularly cold.

(*She turned her head towards the darkened skies outside. The trees stood heavy, as if waiting.*)

MOTHER: I've always felt chilly as long as I can remember. What does that mean? You're a doctor? Mostly in the stomach. Here.

ISAK: You have low blood pressure.

MOTHER: Do you want me to ask Sister Elisabet to make some tea for us so we can sit down and talk for a while? Wouldn't that be . . .

ISAK: No, Mother, thank you. We don't want to trouble you any more. We've just had lunch and we're rather in a hurry.

MOTHER: Look here for a moment. Sigbritt's eldest boy will be fifty. I'm thinking of giving him my father's old gold watch. Can I give it to him, even though the hands have loosened? It is so difficult to find presents for those who have everything. But the watch is beautiful and it can probably be repaired.

(*She looked anxiously, appealingly, from* MARIANNE *to me and back to* MARIANNE. *She had opened the lid of the old gold watch and the blank dial stared at me. I suddenly remembered my early-morning dream: the blank clock face and my own watch which lacked hands, the hearse and my dead self.*)

MOTHER: I remember when Sigbritt's boy had just been born and lay there in his basket in the lilac arbour at the summerhouse. Now he will be fifty years old. And little cousin Sara, who always went around carrying him, cradling him, and who married Sigfrid, that no-good. Now you have to go so that you'll have time for all the things you must do. I'm very grateful for your visit and I hope we'll see each other sometime. Give my best regards to Evald. Goodbye.

(*She offered me her cheek and I bent down*

and kissed it. It was very cold but unbelievably soft and full of sharp little lines. MARIANNE *curtsied and my mother answered her gesture with an abstract smile.* SISTER ELISABET *opened the door as if she had been listening to us. In a few minutes we were out in the grey daylight, which hurt our eyes with its piercing sharpness.*

Once again MARIANNE *took my arm, and when she did so I was filled with gratitude towards this quiet, independent girl with her naked, observant face.*

When we reached the inn the youngsters were no longer there. The waitress told us that the young lady was waiting at the car. The head waiter stood nearby bowing and looking as if he had just had another of his old ulcer-attacks.

Sure enough, SARA *was leaning against the car looking as though she were ready to cry.*)

MARIANNE: Where are Anders and Viktor?

(SARA *pointed without answering. Down on the slope the boys stood glaring at each other with furious expressions on their faces. Every so often one of them would utter some terrible expletive at the other.*)

SARA: When you left they were talking away about the existence of God. Finally they got so angry that they began shouting at each other. Then Anders grabbed Viktor's arm and tried to twist it off, and Viktor said that was a pretty lousy argument for the existence of God. Then I said that I thought they could skip God and pay some attention to me for a while instead, and then they said that I could stop babbling because I didn't understand that it was a debate of principles, and then I said that whether there was a God or not, they were real wet blankets. Then I left and they ran down the hill to settle things because each of them insisted that the other had hurt his innermost feelings. So now they're going to slug it out.

(MARIANNE *put on a very wise countenance and started off to calm down the two debaters. I stepped into the car.* SARA *looked at the departing* MARIANNE *with envy.*)

SARA: Well, which one of the boys do *you* like the most?

ISAK: Which do you like best?

SARA: I don't know. Anders will become a minister. But he is rather masculine and warm, you know. But a minister's wife! But Viktor's funny in another way. Viktor will go far, you know.

ISAK: What do you mean by that?

SARA (*tired*): A doctor earns more money. And it's old-fashioned to be a minister. But he has nice legs. And a strong neck. But how *can* one believe in God!

(SARA *sighed and we sank into our own thoughts.*

MARIANNE *came up the hill bringing with her the two fighting cocks, barely reconciled. She sat down behind the wheel and we continued our trip.*

The sun shone white on the blue-black clouds which towered above the dark, gleaming surface of Lake Vättern. The breeze coming from the open side windows did not cool us any longer, and in the south summer lightning cut across the sky with thin, jagged scratches. Because of the approaching storm, and all the good food and wine, I became rather sleepy. I silently blessed my luck in having MARIANNE *beside me as a reliable chauffeur.*

ANDERS *and* VIKTOR *sat in sullen silence.* SARA *yawned again and again and blinked her eyes.*

I fell asleep, but during my nap I was pursued by dreams and images which seemed extremely real and were very humiliating to me.

I record these in the order in which they occurred, without the slightest intention of commenting on their possible meaning. I have never been particularly enthusiastic about the psychoanalytical theory of dreams as the fulfillment of desires in a negative or positive direction. Yet I cannot deny that in these dreams there was something like a warning, which bore into my consciousness and embedded itself there with relentless determination. I have found that during the last few years I glide rather easily into a twilight world of memories and dreams which are highly personal. I've often wondered if this is a sign of increasing senility. Sometimes I've also asked myself if it is a harbinger of approaching death.[8]

[8] In the film, as the dream sequence begins the following shots are seen:

Dissolve to the dark sky with large birds circling, wheeling and shrieking. Dissolve to more large birds flying among the tree tops. Dissolve to a basket of wild strawberries spilled on the grass.

Again I found myself at the wild strawberry patch of my childhood, but I was not alone. SARA *was there, and this time she turned her face towards mine and looked at me for a long time. I knew that I sat there looking old, ugly and ridiculous. A Professor Emeritus who was going to be made a Jubilee Doctor. The saddest thing about it was that although* SARA *spoke to me in a grieved and penetrating tone, I couldn't answer her except in stammered, one-syllable words. This, of course, increased the pain of my dream.*

Between us stood a little woven basket filled with strawberries; around us lay a strange, motionless twilight, heavy with dull expectations. SARA *leaned towards me and spoke in such a low voice that I had difficulty grasping her words.*)

SARA: Have you looked at yourself in the mirror, Isak? You haven't. Then I'll show you how you look.

(*She picked up a mirror that lay hidden under the small strawberry basket and showed me my face, which looked old and ugly in the sinking twilight. I carefully pushed away the looking glass and I could see that* SARA *had tears in her eyes.*)

SARA: You are a worried old man who will die soon, but I have my whole life before me . . . Oh, now you're offended.

ISAK: No, I'm not offended.

SARA: Yes, you are offended because you can't bear to hear the truth. And the truth is that I've been too considerate. One can easily be unintentionally cruel that way.

ISAK: I understand.

SARA: No, you don't understand. We don't speak the same language. Look at yourself in the mirror again. No, don't look away.

ISAK: I see.

SARA: Now listen. I'm about to marry your brother Sigfrid. He and I love each other, and it's all like a game. Look at your face now. Try to smile! All right, now you're smiling.

ISAK: It hurts.

SARA: You, a Professor Emeritus, ought to know why it hurts. But you don't. Because in spite of all your knowledge you don't really know anything.

(*She threw away the mirror and it shattered. The wind began to blow through the trees, and from somewhere the crying of a child could be heard. She arose immediately, drying her tears.*)

SARA: I have to go. I promised to look after Sigbritt's little boy.

ISAK: Don't leave me.

SARA: What did you say?

ISAK: Don't leave me.

SARA: You stammer so much that I can't hear your words. Besides, they don't really matter.

(*I saw her run up to the arbour. The old house was draped in the grey twilight. She lifted the crying child and cradled it in her arms. The sky turned black above the sea and large birds circled overhead, screeching towards the house, which suddenly seemed ugly and poor. There was something fateful and threatening in this twilight, in the crying of the child, in the shrieking of the black birds.* SARA *cradled the baby and her voice, half singing, was very distant and sorrowful.*)

SARA: My poor little one, you shall sleep quietly now. Don't be afraid of the wind. Don't be afraid of the birds, the jackdaws and the sea gulls. Don't be afraid of the waves from the sea. I'm with you. I'm holding you tight. Don't be afraid, little one. Soon it will be another day. No one can hurt you; I am with you; I'm holding you.

(*But her voice was sorrowful and tears ran down her cheeks without end. The child became silent, as if it were listening, and I wanted to scream until my lungs were bloody.*

Now I saw that a door had opened in the house and someone was standing there shouting for SARA. *It was my brother* SIGFRID.

She ran towards him, gave him the child, and they both disappeared into the house and closed the door.

Suddenly I noticed that the wind had died and the birds had flown away. All the windows in the house shone festively. Over the horizon stood a jagged moon, and music from a piano penetrated the stillness of the strawberry patch.

I went closer and pressed my face against the brightly lit dining-room window. An elegantly laid table stood before me and SARA *sat behind the piano, playing. She was wearing an expensive but old-fashioned dress and her hair was piled on top of her head, which* made her face look womanly and mature. Then SIGFRID entered the room and they both sat down immediately at the table. They laughed and joked and celebrated some kind of event. The moon rose higher in the heavens and the scene inside became obscure. I rapped on the window so that they would hear me and let me in. But they did not notice me; they were too preoccupied with each other.

On the window sill lay many splinters of glass, and in my eager attempt to get their attention I accidentally cut my hand.

Turning away, I was blinded by the moonlight, which threw itself against me with an almost physical force.

I heard a voice calling my name, and then I saw that the door had been opened. Someone was standing in the doorway and I recognised MR. ALMAN. *He bowed politely though stiffly and invited me inside.*

He led me down a short corridor and unlocked a narrow door. We entered a large windowless room with benches arranged like an amphitheatre. There sat about ten youngsters, amongst whom I immediately recognised SARA, ANDERS *and* VIKTOR. *On one of the low walls hung a large blackboard, and on a work table in the centre of the room stood a microscope.*

I realised that this was the hall where I used to hold my polyclinical lectures and examinations. ALMAN *sat down and asked me to take a seat at the short end of the table. For a few moments he studied some papers in a dossier. The audience remained completely still.*)

ALMAN: Do you have your examination book with you?

ISAK: Yes, of course. Here it is.

ALMAN: Thank you.

(*I handed him the examination book and he flipped through it distractedly. Then he leaned forward and looked at me for a long time. After that he gestured towards the microscope.*)

ALMAN: Will you please identify the bacteriological specimen in the microscope. Take your time.

(*I arose, stepped up to the instrument and adjusted it. But whatever I did, I couldn't find any specimen. The only thing I saw was my own eye, which stared back at me in an absurd enlargement.*)

ISAK: There must be something wrong with the microscope.

(ALMAN *bent over and peered into it. Then he regarded me seriously and shook his head.*)

ALMAN: There is nothing wrong with the microscope.

ISAK: I can't see anything.

(*I sank down on the chair and wetted my lips. No one moved or said anything.*)

ALMAN: Will you please read this text.

(*He pointed to the blackboard which hung behind him. Something was printed on it in large crooked letters. I made a great effort to interpret what was written:* INKE TAN MA-GROV STAK FARSIN LOS KRET FAJNE KASERTE MJOTRON PRESETE.)

ALMAN: What does it mean?

ISAK: I don't know.

ALMAN: Oh, really?

ISAK: I'm a doctor, not a linguist.

ALMAN: Then let me tell you, Professor Borg, that on the blackboard is written the first duty of a doctor. Do you happen to know what this is?

ISAK: Yes, if you let me think for a moment.

ALMAN: Take your time.

ISAK: A doctor's first duty . . . a doctor's first duty . . . a doctor's . . . Oh, I've forgotten.

(*A cold sweat broke out on my forehead, but I still looked* ALMAN *straight in the eye. He leaned towards me and spoke in a calm, polite tone.*)

ALMAN: A doctor's first duty *is to ask forgiveness.*

ISAK: Of course, now I remember!

(*Relieved, I laughed but immediately became silent.* ALMAN *looked wearily at his papers and smothered a yawn.*)

ALMAN: Moreover, you are guilty of guilt.

ISAK: Guilty of guilt?

ALMAN: I have noted that you don't understand the accusation.

ISAK: Is it serious?

ALMAN: Unfortunately, Professor.

(*Next to me stood a table with a water de-*canter. *I poured a glass, but spilled a lot of it on the table and the tray.*)

ISAK: I have a bad heart. I'm an old man, Mr. Alman, and I must be treated with consideration. That's only right.

ALMAN: There is nothing concerning your heart in my papers. Perhaps you wish to end the examination?

ISAK: No, no, for heaven's sake, no!

(ALMAN *arose and lit a small lamp which hung from a cord in the ceiling. Under the lamp (very brightly lit) sat a woman wrapped in a hospital robe and wearing wooden sandals on her feet.*)

ALMAN: Will you please make an anamnesis and diagnosis of this patient.

ISAK: But the patient is dead.

(*At that moment the woman arose and began laughing as if she had just heard a great joke.* ALMAN *leaned across the table and wrote something in my examination book.*)

ISAK: What are you writing in my book?

ALMAN: My conclusion.

ISAK: And that is . . .

ALMAN: That you're incompetent.

ISAK: Incompetent.

ALMAN: Furthermore, Professor Borg, you are accused of some smaller but nonetheless serious offences. (ISAK *remains silent.*) Indifference, selfishness, lack of consideration.

ISAK: No.

ALMAN: These accusations have been made by your wife. Do you want to be confronted by her?

ISAK: But my wife has been dead for many years.

ALMAN: Do you think I'm joking? Will you please come with me voluntarily. You have no choice in any case. Come!

(ALMAN *placed the examination book in his pocket, made a sign for me to follow him, opened the door and led me into a forest.*

The trunks of the trees stood close together. Twilight had almost passed. Dead trees were strewn on the ground and the earth was covered with decaying leaves. Our feet sank into this soft carpet with every step, and mud oozed up around them. From behind the foliage the moon shone steadily, like an inflamed eye, and it was as warm as inside a hothouse. ALMAN *turned around.*)

ALMAN: Watch out, Professor Borg. You'll find many snakes here.

(*Suddenly I saw a small, gleaming body which twisted around and disappeared in one of* ALMAN'*s wet footsteps. I stepped swiftly aside but nearly trod on a large grey creature which pulled away. Wherever I looked, snakes seemed to well forth from the swampy, porous ground. Finally we arrived at a clearing in the forest, but we halted at the very edge. The moon shone in our eyes and we hid among the shadows of the trees. The clearing stretched out before us. It was overgrown with twisted roots. At one end a black cliff fell away into a body of water. On the sides, the trees stood lofty and lifeless, as if burdened by each other's enormous shadows. Then a giggling laugh was heard and I discovered a woman standing near the hill. She was dressed in a long black gown and her face was averted from us. She made movements with her hands, as if to ward off someone. She laughed continually and excitedly. A man stood half hidden, leaning against a tree trunk. His face, which I glimpsed, was large and flat, but his eyebrows were quite bushy and his forehead protruded over his eyes. He made gestures with his hand and said some unintelligible words, which made the woman laugh uncontrollably. Suddenly she became serious, and a harassed, discontented expression appeared on her face. She bent over and picked up a small purse. The man stretched out his hand and jokingly began to pull the pins out of her skilfully pompadoured hair. She pretended to be very angry and flailed the air around her furiously. This amused the man, who continued his game. When she finally walked away he followed and took hold of her shoulders. Petrified, she stopped and turned her pale, embittered face towards her pursuer. He muttered something and stretched out his other hand towards her breast. She moved away, but couldn't free herself. When she saw that she was caught, she began to twist and squirm as if the man's grip on her shoulders hurt intensely. The man continued to mutter incoherent words, as if to an animal. Suddenly she freed herself and ran with bent knees and a shuffling step in a semicircle. The man remained standing, waiting and breathless. He perspired heavily and wiped his face over and over again with the* back of his hand. The woman stopped as if exhausted and regarded the man, wide-eyed and gaping. She was also out of breath. Then she began running again but pretended to trip and fell on her hands and knees. Her large rump swayed like a black balloon over the ground. She lowered her face between her arms and began crying, rocking and swaying. The man knelt at her side, took a firm grasp of her hair, pulled her face upward, backward and forced her to open her eyes. He panted with effort the whole time. She teetered and nearly fell to the side, but the man straddled her and leaned over her heavily. Suddenly she was completely still, with closed eyes and a swollen, pale face. Then she collapsed, rolled over, and received the man between her open knees.)

ALMAN: Many men forget a woman who has been dead for thirty years. Some preserve a sweet, fading picture, but *you* can always recall this scene in your memory. Strange, isn't it? Tuesday, May 1, 1917, you stood here and heard and saw exactly what that woman and that man said and did.

(*The woman sat up and smoothed her gown over her short, thick thighs. Her face was blank and almost distorted in its puffy slackness. The man had got up and was wandering around aimlessly with his hands hanging at his sides.*)

WOMAN: Now I will go home and tell this to Isak and I know exactly what he'll say: Poor little girl, how I pity you. As if he were God himself. And then I'll cry and say: Do you really feel pity for me? And he'll say: I feel infinitely sorry for you. And then I'll cry some more and ask him if he can forgive me. And then he'll say: You shouldn't ask forgiveness from me. I have nothing to forgive. But he doesn't mean a word of it, because he's completely cold. And then he'll suddenly be very tender and I'll yell at him that he's not really sane and that such hypocritical nobility is sickening. And then he'll say that he'll bring me a sedative and that he understands everything. And then I'll say that it's his fault that I am the way I am, and then he'll look very sad and will say that he is to blame. But he doesn't care about anything because he's completely cold.

(*She arose with effort and shook out her hair and began combing it and pinning it up in the same careful way that it was before. The man sat down on a stone a little further away. He smoked quietly. I couldn't see his gaze below the protruding eyebrows, but his voice was calm and scornful.)*

MAN: You're insane, the way you're carrying on.

(The woman laughed and went into the forest.

I turned around. ALMAN *had a strange, wry smile on his face. We stood quietly for a few moments.)*

ISAK: Where is she?

ALMAN: You know. She is gone. Everyone is gone. Can't you hear how quiet it is? Everything has been dissected, Professor Borg. A surgical masterpiece. There is no pain, no bleeding, no quivering.

ISAK: It is rather quiet.

ALMAN: A perfect achievement of its kind, Professor.

ISAK: And what is the penalty?

ALMAN: Penalty? I don't know. The usual one, I suppose.

ISAK: The usual one?

ALMAN: Of course. Loneliness.

ISAK: Loneliness?

ALMAN: Exactly. *Loneliness.*

ISAK: Is there no grace?

ALMAN: Don't ask me. I don't know anything about such things.

(Before I had time to answer, ALMAN *had disappeared, and I stood alone in the complete stillness of the moonlight and the forest. [Then I heard a voice quite close to me.)*

SARA: Didn't you have to go with them to get your father?

(The girl stretched out her hand, but when she saw my face she immediately withdrew it.)

ISAK: Sara . . . It wasn't always like this. If only you had stayed with me. If only you could have had a little patience.

(The girl did not seem to hear what I was saying but began to look restless.)

SARA: Hurry up.

(I followed her as well as I could, but she moved so much more easily and faster than I.)

ISAK: I can't run, don't you understand?

SARA: But hurry up.

ISAK: I can't see you any more.

SARA: But here I am.

ISAK: Wait for me.

(She materialised for a moment and then she was gone. The moon disappeared into darkness and I wanted to cry with wild, childish sorrow, but I could not.][9]

At that moment, I awoke. The car stood still and the storm was over, but it was still drizzling slightly. We were in the neighbourhood of the Strömsnäs Foundry, where the road wanders between rich forests on one side and river rapids on the other. Everything was completely silent. The three children had left the car and MARIANNE *sat quietly smoking a cigarette and blowing the smoke through the open window. Gusts of strong and pleasant odours came from the wet forest.)*

ISAK: What is this?

MARIANNE: The children wanted to get out for a moment and stretch their legs. They are over there.

(She made a gesture towards a clearing near the river. All three were busy picking flowers.)

ISAK: But it's still raining.

MARIANNE: I told them about the ceremony today, and they insisted on paying homage to you.

ISAK *(sighs)*: Good Lord.

MARIANNE: Did you sleep well?

ISAK: Yes, but I dreamed. Can you imagine — the last few months I've had the most peculiar dreams. It's really odd.

MARIANNE: What's odd?

ISAK: It's as if I'm trying to say something to myself which I don't want to hear when I'm awake.

MARIANNE: And what would that be?

ISAK: That I'm dead, although I live.

(MARIANNE reacted violently. Her gaze blackened and she took a deep breath. Throwing her cigarette out the window, she turned towards me.)

---

9 The scene in square brackets does not appear in the print of the film distributed in England.

MARIANNE: Do you know that you and Evald are very much alike?

ISAK: You told me that.

MARIANNE: Do you know that Evald has said the very same thing?

ISAK: About me? Yes, I can believe that.

MARIANNE: No, about himself.

ISAK: But he's only thirty-eight years old.

MARIANNE: May I tell you everything, or would it bore you?

ISAK: I'd be grateful if you would tell me.

MARIANNE: It was a few months ago. I wanted to talk to Evald and we took the car and went down to the sea. It was raining, just like now. Evald sat where you are sitting and I drove. . . .

EVALD: Can't you stop the windshield wipers?

MARIANNE: Then we won't be able to see the ocean.

EVALD: They're working so hard it makes me nervous.

MARIANNE (*shuts them off*): Very well.

(*They sit in silence for a few minutes, looking at the rain, which streams down the windshield quietly. The sea merges with the clouds in an infinite greyness.* EVALD *strokes his long, bony face and looks expectantly at his wife. He talks jokingly, calmly.*)

EVALD: So now you have me trapped. What did you want to say? Something unpleasant, of course.

MARIANNE: I wish I didn't have to tell you about it.

EVALD: I understand. You've found someone else.

MARIANNE: Now don't be childish.

EVALD (*mimicking her*): Now don't be childish. What do you expect me to think? You come and say in a funereal voice that you want to talk to me. We take the car and go down to the sea. It rains and it's hard for you to begin. Good Lord, Marianne, let's have it. This is an excellent moment for the most intimate confidence. But for heaven's sake, don't keep me dangling.

MARIANNE: Now I feel like laughing. What do you really think I'm going to say? That I've murdered someone, or embezzled the faculty funds? I'm pregnant, Evald.

EVALD: Oh, is that so.

MARIANNE: That's the way it is. And seeing how careless we've been recently, there isn't much to be surprised about, is there?

EVALD: And you're sure?

MARIANNE: The report on the test came yesterday.

EVALD: Oh. Oh, yes. So that was the secret.

MARIANNE: Another thing I want to tell you. I shall have this child.

EVALD: That seems to be clear.

MARIANNE: Yes, it is!

MARIANNE (*voice over*): We sat quietly for a long time, and I felt the hatred growing big and thick between us. Evald looked out through the wet window, whistled soundlessly and looked as if he were cold. Somewhere in my stomach I was shivering so hard that I could barely sit upright. Then he opened the door and got out of the car and marched through the rain down to the beach. He stopped under a big tree and stood there for a long while. Finally I also stepped out and went to him. His face and hair were wet and the rain fell down his cheeks to the sides of his mouth.

EVALD (*calmly*): You know that I don't want to have any children. You also know that you'll have to choose between me and the child.

MARIANNE (*looks at him*): Poor Evald.

EVALD: Please don't 'poor' me. I'm of sound mind and I've made my position absolutely clear. It's absurd to live in this world, but it's even more ridiculous to populate it with new victims and it's most absurd of all to believe that they will have it any better than us.

MARIANNE: That is only an excuse.

EVALD: Call it whatever you want. Personally I was an unwelcome child in a marriage which was a nice imitation of hell. Is the old man really sure that I'm his son? Indifference, fear, infidelity and guilt feelings — those were my nurses.

MARIANNE: All this is very touching, but it doesn't excuse the fact that you're behaving like a child.

EVALD: I have to be at the hospital at three o'clock and have neither the time nor the desire to talk any more.

MARIANNE: You're a coward!

EVALD: Yes, that's right. This life disgusts me and I don't think that I need a responsibility which will force me to exist another day longer than I want to. You know all that, and you know that I'm serious and that this isn't some kind of hysteria, as you once thought.

MARIANNE (*voice over*): We went towards

the car, he in front and I following. I had begun to cry. I don't know why. But the tears couldn't be seen in the rain. We sat in the car, thoroughly wet and cold, but the hatred throbbed in us so painfully that we didn't feel cold. I started the car and turned it towards the road. Evald sat fiddling with the radio. His face was completely calm and closed.

MARIANNE: I know that you're wrong.

EVALD: There is nothing which can be called right or wrong. One functions according to one's needs; you can read that in an elementary-school textbook.

MARIANNE: And what do we need?

EVALD: You have a damned need to live, to exist and create life.

MARIANNE: And how about you?

EVALD: My need is to be dead. Absolutely, totally dead.

(*I've tried to relate* MARIANNE's *story as carefully as possible. My reaction to it was very mixed. But my strongest feeling was a certain sympathy towards her for this sudden confidence, and when* MARIANNE *fell silent she looked so hesitant that I felt obliged to say something even though I wasn't very sure of my own voice.*)

ISAK: If you want to smoke a cigarette, you may.

MARIANNE: Thank you.

ISAK: Why have you told me all this?

(MARIANNE *didn't answer at once. She took her time lighting a cigarette and puffed a few times. I looked at her, but she turned her head away and pretended to look at the three youngsters, who had picked up some kind of soft drink which they shared in great amity.*)

MARIANNE: When I saw you together with your mother, I was gripped by a strange fear.

ISAK: I don't understand.

MARIANNE: I thought, here is his mother. A very ancient woman, completely ice-cold, in some ways more frightening than death itself. And here is her son, and there are light-years of distance between them. And he himself says that he is a living death. And Evald is on the verge of becoming just as lonely and cold — and dead. And then I thought that there is only coldness and death, and death and loneliness, all the way. Somewhere it must end.

ISAK: But you are going back to Evald.

MARIANNE: Yes, to tell him that I can't

agree to his condition. I want my child; no one can take it from me. Not even the person I love more than anyone else.

(*She turned her pale, tearless face towards me, and her gaze was black, accusing, desperate. I suddenly felt shaken in a way which I had never experienced before.*)

ISAK: Can I help you?

MARIANNE: No one can help me. We are too old, Isak. It has gone too far.

ISAK: What happened after your talk in the car?

MARIANNE: Nothing. I left him the very next day.

ISAK: Haven't you heard from him?

MARIANNE: No. No, Evald is rather like you.

(*She shook her head and bent forward as if to protect her face. I felt cold; it had become quite chilly after the rain.*)

MARIANNE: Those two wretched people whom I made leave the car — what was their name again?

ISAK: I was just thinking about Alman and his wife. It reminded me of my own marriage.

MARIANNE: I don't want Evald and I to become like . . .

ISAK: Poor Evald grew up in all that.

MARIANNE: But we love each other.

(*Her last words were a low outburst. She stopped herself immediately and moved her hands towards her face, then stopped again. We sat quietly for a few moments.*)

ISAK: We must get on. Signal to the children.

(MARIANNE *nodded, started the motor and blew the horn.* SARA *came laughing through the wet grass, closely followed by her two cavaliers. She handed me a large bouquet of wild flowers wrapped in wet newspapers. All three of them had friendly, mocking eyes.* SARA *cleared her throat solemnly.*)

SARA: We heard that you are celebrating this day. Now we want to pay our respects to you with these simple flowers and to tell you that we are *very* impressed that you are so old and that you've been a doctor for fifty years. And we know, of course, that you are a *wise* and *venerable* old man. One who regards us youngsters with *lenience* and gentle irony. One who knows *all* about life and who has learned all the prescriptions by heart.

(*She gave me the flowers with a little mock curtsy and kissed my cheek. The boys bowed and laughed, embarrassed. I couldn't answer. I only thanked them very briefly and rather bluntly. The children probably thought that I had been hurt by their joke.*

After a few more hours' travel, we reached Lund. When we finally stopped at EVALD's *house, a small rotund woman ran out and approached us quickly. To my surprise and pleasure I discovered that it was* MISS AGDA.)

AGDA: So you did come. Evald and I had just given up hope. It's relaxing and convenient to drive, isn't it? Now, Professor, you'll have to put on your frock coat immediately. Hello, Marianne. I've prepared Evald for your arrival.

ISAK: So, Miss Agda, you came after all.

AGDA: I considered it my duty. But the fun is gone. There's nothing you can say that will make me feel different. Who are these young people? Are they going to the ceremony too?

MARIANNE: These are good friends of ours, and if there is any food in the kitchen, invite them in.

AGDA: And why shouldn't there be? I've had a lot of things to arrange here, believe me.

(EVALD *met us in the foyer. He was already dressed in evening clothes and seemed nervous. Everything was extremely confused, but* MISS AGDA *was a pillar of strength in the maelstrom. Without raising her voice, and dressed in her best dress (especially made for the occasion), she sent the children, the married couple, servants and an old professor in different directions. Within ten minutes, everything was in order.*

Just before that, EVALD, MARIANNE *and I had a chance to say hello. I wouldn't want to give the impression that our reunion was marked by overwhelming cordiality. This has never been the case in our family.*)

EVALD: Hello, Father. Welcome.

ISAK: Hello, Evald. Thank you. As you can see, I brought Marianne with me.

EVALD: Hello, Marianne.

MARIANNE: Can I take my things upstairs?

EVALD: Do you want to stay in the guest room as usual, Father?

ISAK: Thank you, that would be just fine.

EVALD: Let me take your suitcase. It's rather heavy.

ISAK: Thank you, I'll take it myself.

EVALD: Did you have a nice trip?

MARIANNE: Yes, thanks it's been pleasant.

EVALD: Who were those youngsters you had with you?

MARIANNE: Don't know. They're going to Italy.

EVALD: They looked rather nice.

ISAK: They are really very nice.

(*We had come to the second floor.* EVALD *politely opened the door to the guest room and I entered.* AGDA *came after us as if she were rolling on ball bearings, forced her way in and took the suitcase, putting it on a chair.*)

AGDA: I bought new shoelaces, and I took the liberty of bringing the white waistcoat to your evening dress if you should want to go to the banquet after the ceremony. And you forgot your razor blades, Professor.

(*She unpacked, murmuring sounds of worried concern. I didn't listen. Instead I listened to the conversation between* MARIANNE *and* EVALD *outside the half-closed door. Their voices were formal and faultlessly polite.*)

MARIANNE: No, I'll go tomorrow, so don't worry.

EVALD: Do you intend to stay in a hotel?

MARIANNE (*gay*): Why? We can share a bedroom for another night, if you have no objection. Help me to unpack.

EVALD: It was really nice to see you. And unexpected.

MARIANNE: I feel the same way. Are we going to the dinner afterwards, or what do you want to do?

EVALD: I'll just call Stenberg and tell him that I'm bringing a lady. He arranges such things.

(*The door was closed, so I couldn't hear any more of the conversation. I had sat down on the bed to take off my shoes.* MISS AGDA *helped me, but she wasn't very gracious.*

[*Oddly enough, there were three Jubilee Doctors that year. The dean's office had thoughtfully placed us three old men in a special room while the procession was arranged out in the large vestibule of the university hall. I happened to know one of the other two who were going to be honoured. He was an old schoolmate, the former Bishop* JAKOB HOVELIUS. *We greeted each other cordially and embraced. The third old man seemed rather atrophied and declined all conversation. It turned out that he was the former Professor of Roman Law,* CARL-ADAM TIGER *(a great fighter in his time and a man who, according to his students, really lived up to his name).)*

ISAK: How comforting it is to meet another old corpse. How are you nowadays, my dear Jakob?

JAKOB: I enjoy my leisure. But don't ask me if I do it *cum dignitate.*

ISAK: Do you know the third man to be honoured?

JAKOB: Of course. It's Carl-Adam Tiger, Professor of Roman Law.

ISAK: The Tiger! Good Lord!

JAKOB: He has three interests left in life. A thirty-year-old injustice, a goldfish, and his bowels.

ISAK: Do you think that we are like that?

JAKOB: What's your opinion? As Schopenhauer says somewhere, 'Dreams are a kind of lunacy and lunacy a kind of dream.' But life is also supposed to be a kind of dream, isn't it? Draw your own conclusion.

ISAK: Do you remember how in our youth we fought with each other on what we called the metaphysical questions?

JAKOB: How could I forget?

ISAK: And what do you believe now?

JAKOB: I'll tell you, I've ceased thinking about all that. One of these days, knowledge will be achieved.

ISAK: My, how surprised you'll be.

JAKOB: And you. But one has a right to be curious.

TIGER: Gentlemen, do you think I'd have time to make a small secret visit before the great farce begins?

ISAK: I don't know, Professor Tiger.

TIGER (*sighs*): *In dubio non est agendum.* When in doubt, don't, as the old Romans used to say. I'll stay here.][10]

(*THE FESTIVITIES*

What should I describe? Trumpet fanfares, bells ringing, field-cannon salutes, masses of people, the giant procession from the univer-

[10] The scene in square brackets does not appear in the finished film.

sity to the cathedral, the white-dressed garland girls, royalty, old age, wisdom, beautiful music, stately Latin sentences which echoed off the huge vaults. The students and their girls, women in bright, magnificent dresses, this strange rite with its heavy symbolism but as meaningless as a passing dream. Then I saw SARA *with her two boys among the onlookers outside the cathedral. They waved to me and suddenly looked childishly happy and full of expectations. Among the lecturers was* EVALD, *tall and serious, disinterested and absent. Inside the church, I saw* MARIANNE *in her white dress and next to her sat* MISS AGDA, *pale and with her lips pressed tightly together. The ceremonial lecture was dull (as usual). The whole thing went on endlessly (as usual) and the garland girls had to go out and relieve themselves in the little silver pot in the sacristy. But we adults unfortunately had to stay where we were. As you know, culture provides us with these moments of refined torture.* PROFESSOR TIGER *looked as if he were dying, my friend the* BISHOP *fell asleep, and more than one of those present seemed ready to faint. Even our behinds, which have withstood long academic services, lectures, dusty dissertations and dull dinners, started to become numb and ache in silent protest.*

I surprised myself by returning to the happenings of the day, and it was then that I decided to recollect and write down everything that had happened. I was beginning to see a remarkable causality in this chain of unexpected, entangled events. At the same time, I couldn't escape recalling the BISHOP's *words: 'Dreams are a kind of lunacy and lunacy a kind of dream, but life is also supposed to be a dream, isn't it . . .'*

After the ceremony there was a banquet, but I really felt too tired to go. I took a cab home and found MISS AGDA *in my room busy making my bed the way I like (very high under my head and folded neatly at my feet). A heating pad was already connected and my sleeping pills stood on the table. Almost at once,* MISS AGDA *began helping me with my shoes and evening dress, and I felt a great warmth towards this extraordinary, faithful, thoughtful old woman. I would really have liked to become friends with her again, and I repented the morning's thoughtless utterances (which, I noticed, she had by no means forgotten).)*

ISAK: Did you enjoy the ceremony?

AGDA: Yes, thank you.

ISAK: Are you tired, Miss Agda?

AGDA: I won't deny it.

ISAK: Take one of my sleeping pills.

AGDA: No, thanks.

ISAK: Oh, Miss Agda, I'm sorry for this morning.

AGDA: Are you sick, Professor?

ISAK: No. Why?

AGDA: I don't know, but that sounds alarming.

ISAK: Oh really, is it so unusual for me to ask forgiveness?

AGDA: Do you want the water decanter on the table?

ISAK: No, thanks.

(*We pottered about for a while, silently.*)

AGDA: Thanks anyway.

ISAK: Oh, Miss Agda.

AGDA: What do you want, Professor?

ISAK: Don't you think that we who have known each other for two generations could drop formality and say '*du*' to each other?

AGDA: No, I don't really think so.

ISAK: Why not, if I may ask?

AGDA: Have you brushed your teeth, Professor?

ISAK: Yes, thanks.

AGDA: Now, I'll tell you. I beg to be excused from all intimacies. It's all right the way it is between us now.

ISAK: But, dear Miss Agda, we are old now.

AGDA: Speak for yourself, Professor. A woman has to think of her reputation, and what would people say if the two of us suddenly started to say '*du*' to each other?

ISAK: Yes, what would people say?

AGDA: They would ridicule us.

ISAK: Do you always act correctly?

AGDA: Nearly always. At our age one ought to know how to behave. Isn't that so, Professor?

ISAK: Good night, Miss Agda.

AGDA: Good night, Professor. I will leave the door ajar. And you know where I am if you should want something. Good night, Professor.

ISAK: Good night, Miss Agda.

(*I was just going to lie down in bed (I had been sitting on the edge in my old robe) when I heard singing and music from the garden. I thought I recognised the voices and walked over to the window and lifted the* blinds. *Down there under the trees I recognised my three companions from the trip. They sang to their heart's delight, and* ANDERS *accompanied them on his guitar.*)

SARA: Hey, Father Isak! You were fantastic when you marched in the procession. We were real proud that we knew you. Now we're going on.

ANDERS: We got a lift all the way to Hamburg.

VIKTOR: With a fifty-year-old deaconess. Anders is already sweet on the old girl.

ANDERS: Stop babbling!

VIKTOR: We came to say goodbye.

ISAK: Goodbye, and thank you for your company.

SARA: Goodbye, Father Isak. Do you know that it is really you I love, today, tomorrow and forever?

ISAK: I'll remember that.

VIKTOR: Goodbye, Professor.

ISAK: Goodbye, Viktor.

ANDERS: Goodbye, Professor. Now we have to run.

ISAK: Let me hear from you sometime.

(*Those last words I said to myself, and rather quietly. The children waved to me and were swallowed up by the summer night. I heard their laughter, and then they were gone.*

At the same moment, I heard voices out in the foyer. It was EVALD *and* MARIANNE. *They whispered out of consideration to me and I heard the rustle of* MARIANNE's *evening gown. I called to* EVALD. *He entered the room, but stopped at the door.*)

ISAK: Are you home already?

EVALD: Marianne had to change shoes. Her heel broke.

ISAK: So you are going to the dance?

EVALD: Yes, I suppose so.

ISAK: A-ha.

EVALD: How are you otherwise?

ISAK: Fine, thanks.

EVALD: How's the heart holding up?

ISAK: Excellently.

EVALD: Good night, and sleep well.

(*He turned and went through the door. I asked him to come back. He looked very surprised. I felt surprised myself, and confused. I didn't really know what to say.*)

ISAK: Sit down a moment.

EVALD: Is it something special?

(*He sat obediently on the chair near the bed. His starched shirt rustled and his hands hung a little tiredly across his knees. I realised that my son was becoming middle-aged.*)

ISAK: May I ask you what's going to happen between you and Marianne? (EVALD *shakes his head.*) Forgive my asking.
EVALD: I know nothing.
ISAK: It's not my business, but . . .
EVALD: What?
ISAK: But shouldn't . . .
EVALD: I have asked her to remain with me.
ISAK: And how will it . . . I mean . . .
EVALD: I can't be without her.
ISAK: You mean you can't live alone.
EVALD: I can't be without *her*. That's what I mean.
ISAK: I understand.
EVALD: It will be as she wants.
ISAK: And if she wants . . . I mean, does she want?
EVALD: She says that she'll think it over. I don't really know.
ISAK: Regarding that loan you had from me . . .
EVALD: Don't worry, you'll get your money.
ISAK: I didn't mean that.
EVALD: You'll get your money all right.

(EVALD *rose and nodded to me. Just then* MARIANNE *appeared in the door. She had on a very simple but extraordinarily beautiful white dress.*)

MARIANNE: How are you, Father Isak?
ISAK: Fine, thanks. Very well.
MARIANNE: I broke a heel, so we had to come home to change. Can I wear these shoes instead?
ISAK: They look fine.

(MARIANNE *came up to me. She smelled good and rustled in a sweet, womanly way. She leaned over me.*)

ISAK: Thanks for your company on the trip.
MARIANNE: Thank *you*.
ISAK: I like you, Marianne.
MARIANNE: I like you too, Father Isak.

(*She kissed me lightly on the cheek and disappeared. They exchanged a few words outside the door. I heard their steps on the stairs and then the door slamming in the foyer. I* heard my heart and my old watch. I heard the tower clock strike eleven, with the light tones designating the four quarter hours and the heavier sounds marking the hour.

Now it began to rain, not very hard, but quietly and evenly. A lulling sound. The street lamp swung on its cord and threw shadows on the light-coloured window blinds.

Whenever I am restless or sad, I usually try to recall memories from my childhood, to calm down. This is the way it was that night too, and I wandered back to the summerhouse and the wild strawberry patch and everything I had dreamed or remembered or experienced during this long day.[11]

I sat under the tree by the wild strawberry patch and it was a warm, sunny day with soft summer skies and a mild breeze coming through the birches. Down at the dock, my sisters and brothers were romping with UNCLE ARON. My AUNT went by, together with SARA: They were laden with large baskets. Everyone laughed and shouted to each other and applauded when the red sail went up the mast of the old yacht (an ancient relic from the days of my parents' childhood; a mad impulse of our grandfather, the Admiral). SARA turned around and when she caught sight of me she put down her baskets and ran towards me.*)

SARA: Isak, darling, there are no wild strawberries left. Aunt wants you to search for your father. We will sail around the peninsula and pick you up on the other side.
ISAK: I have already searched for him, but I can't find either Father or Mother.
SARA: Your mother was supposed to go with him.
ISAK: Yes, but I can't find them.
SARA: I will help you.

(*She took me by the hand and suddenly we found ourselves at a narrow sound with deep, dark water. The sun shone brightly on the opposite side, which rose softly into a meadow. Down at the beach on the other side of the dark water a gentleman sat, dressed in*

---

[11] In the film, at the beginning of the dream sequence, the camera dissolves from Isak asleep to the family coming out of the summerhouse and the scene of the family down by the dock appears a little later during the conversation between Isak and Sara.

white with his hat on the back of his head and an old pipe in his mouth. He had a soft, blond beard and pince-nex. He had taken off his shoes and stockings and between his hands he held a long slender bamboo pole. A red float lay motionless on the shimmering water.

Farther up the bank sat my MOTHER. *She wore a bright summer dress and a big hat which shaded her face. She was reading a book.* SARA *dropped my hand and pointed to my parents. Then she was gone. I looked for a long time at the pair on the other side of the water. I tried to shout to them but not a word came from my mouth. Then my* FA-THER *raised his head and caught sight of*

me. He lifted his hand and waved, laughing. My MOTHER *looked up from her book. She also laughed and nodded.*

Then I saw the old yacht with its red sail. It cruised so smoothly in the mild breeze. In the prow stood UNCLE ARON, *singing some sentimental song, and I saw my brothers and sisters and* AUNT *and* SARA, *who lifted up* SIGBRITT's *little boy. I shouted to them, but they didn't hear me.*

I dreamed that I stood by the water and shouted towards the bay, but the warm summer breeze carried away my cries and they did not reach their destination. Yet I wasn't sorry about that; I felt, on the contrary, rather lighthearted.)

It is sometimes argued that although film can be violent, serious, and sad, it is inherently anti-tragic. If tragedy is chiefly concerned with man asserting himself and exhausting himself in some painfully constricting "boundary situation" (Hamlet called upon to revenge his father's death, King Lear forced to recognize his own lack of self-knowledge) and if comedy is chiefly concerned with man living most fully by getting along with his fellows in this not-too-bad world, the camera (it has been argued) is better suited to comedy because as it records trees, skies, rivers, crowds, even cups of hot coffee and people going to bed or getting out of bed, it gives us a sense of the abundance and vitality of life, of rich diversity and of ongoingness rather than of pressure and exhaustion and finality. There is probably a good deal to this view; in any case, although in Bergman's film *Wild Strawberries* we have a story about the movement toward death, it is wonderfully suffused with a sense of the continuing vitality or richness of ordinary life.

The gist of Bergman's story has clear affinities with tragic stories: a man, near to death, finds that he has made a mistake. Dr. Isak Borg at the start thinks that he withdrew from society for highly civilized reasons: when we express opinions about people, he says, we are likely to be "guilty of errors, exaggerations, even tremendous lies," and "rather than commit such follies, I remain silent. As a result, I have of my own free will withdrawn almost completely from society." (Here he is a true heir to those materialistic ideas of the late nineteenth century, such as Darwinism and Marxism, that substituted scientific certainties for religious and metaphysical certainties but soon left thoughtful men without confidence in anything, even in the distinction between the tragic and the comic, as the Theater of the Absurd demonstrates.) All that Dr. Borg asks of life "is to be left alone," to be allowed to continue his scientific studies, to play golf, and to read an occasional detective story. To keep life at a distance he developed, therefore, a somewhat courtly manner but life has a way of breaking in, and now, old, he finds he is troubled with dreams. The film begins with a dream of shattered eyeglasses, a watch without hands, a faceless man who turns out to be bodiless too, and a hearse carrying Dr. Borg's corpse. As he later puts it, his dreams tell him "that I'm dead, although I live." Moreover as the story progresses we learn that both his ninety-six-year-old mother and his thirty-eight-year-old son (who knows that he was an unwanted child) are also living a death-in-life.

But this dark story is transfused with something of the stuff of comedy. First, there is the doctor's moderately genial ironic attitude toward himself and others; even at the start, although he is mistaken about the reasons for his withdrawal, he nevertheless looks at himself with a sort of entertaining irony. Second, there are a good many scenes that are funny: the doctor and his house-keeper bicker as though they are a married couple, two children compose a song as a birthday present for a deaf uncle, an incipient divinity student argues with an incipient scientist about the existence of God and is reduced to twist-ing his rival's arm ("Viktor said that was a pretty lousy argument for the exist-ence of God"). Third, we are continually reminded, as comedy reminds us and as tragedy does not, of the business of pushing on through daily life: people smoke and eat (in tragedy does anyone eat except at a great banquet?) and even go to the bathroom: just before the bestowal of honorary degrees on three distinguished old men, one of them is said to have only three interests in life, "a thirty-year-old injustice, a goldfish, and his bowels," and this honorable old man at this ceremonious moment is anxious to get to the bathroom; "the gar-land girls had to go out and relieve themselves in the little silver pot in the sacristy. But we adults unfortunately had to stay where we were." Fourth, and most important, the story moves not only toward the doctor's self-recognition or anagnorisis, but toward his reunion with society, or with life.

This reunion is largely brought about through two women, his daughter-in-law Marianne and a young girl named Sara whom they meet by chance, and also through the doctor's memories of a young girl (also named Sara) to whom he was engaged but who did not marry him because even in his youth his seriousness and his refinement had something deathly in them. Through these women, and the two young men who accompany Sara, the ice around the doctor's heart begins to melt. For example, at the beginning of the film, talk-ing about a loan he had made to his son and which his son finds difficult to repay, the doctor matter-of-factly says, "A bargain is a bargain," but near the end of the story he is moved to alter the bargain — though his son interrupts him and his thoughts must go unspoken. (It is in tragedy that a bargain is a bargain, that actions have remorseless consequences; in comedy bad bargains have a way of dissolving, and in *Wild Strawberries* Borg's own bad bargain with life, so to speak, is dissolved, and he is given a second chance.)

This movement from death to life, from isolation to union — even though, of course, the life of a seventy-eight-year-old man will end relatively soon — is marked by such symbolic details as the transition from the faceless clock of his initial dream to the ticking watch and the striking clock near the end, and by such actions as his attempt to ease his son's debt and — comically — by his attempt to establish a more intimate relationship with his old housekeeper (but she firmly rejects his suggestion that now that forty years have passed, perhaps they can use the *du* [equivalent to the French *tu*] form of address). It is most effectively conveyed, however (putting aside the wonderful photography), through the gentle laughter that periodically recurs through the story. Laughter, of course, can be hostile, the derisive laughter we engage in when we feel superior. And in *Wild Strawberries* there are occasional artificial laughs, bitter laughs, and nervous laughs. But most of the laughter is social, shared by all concerned. Even its first occurrence is of this sort. Early, when the doctor says that he has enjoyed having Marianne around, she replies, somewhat bitterly, "like a cat"; he laughs, she joins in the laughter, and "it cleared the air a bit." This cleansing power of shared laughter, in *Wild Strawberries* usually stimulated by women or young people, manifests itself again and again. Amused by Sara and her two boyfriends, "Marianne and I exchanged amused glances, the first contact between us"; a little later "everyone burst into laughter"; later, moved by the generosity and affection of an old acquaintance, the doctor tells "humorous anecdotes which had a great deal of human interest. These were a great success (I don't think they laughed just out of politeness)." (We can note here that Dr. Borg is still reserved, still judging himself and others, but he is now far more humane, far more social.) Later, "Marianne laughed and lit my cigar," and this leads them to recite a poem together — another step in the doctor's union with society, a step made even more clear by the contrast provided by his mother's house, which is "protected from onlookers by a wall as tall as a man." Later, the last thing he hears from the three young people who have helped him to find a new self through contact with others is their laughter. Finally (to cut short what could be a long list) at the end of the film, when he has a vision of his father accompanied by his mother, fishing in a river, his father waves to him and laughs, and so does his mother. His last words are, "I felt . . . rather lighthearted."

This final vision, so different from the initial dream of the hearse and the clock without hands, is implicitly a vision of man in contact with the mysterious sources of life (man and woman on an idyllic riverbank, the man's fishing rod gracefully rising to the heavens) and is explicitly a vision of Dr. Borg's happy reunion with the past; the meanings join, to affirm that the past lives again in the present, and that the present itself — the life of Dr. Borg specifically — is not an isolated or dead moment but something vitally united with a vast world of people and things.

HAPPY DAYS

Samuel Beckett

Samuel Beckett (b. 1906) was born in Dublin of middle-class Protestant parents. He was educated at Trinity College, Dublin, where he took his degree in modern languages, graduating in 1927. He went to Paris the next year where he met James Joyce, a fellow Irishman, and translated parts of *Finnegans Wake* into French. He stayed in France until 1930 when he returned to Dublin to take up a lectureship in French at Trinity College. He soon decided against teaching and began a number of years of wandering, living in London, traveling about Germany and France, and then settling in Paris in 1937. During World War II, after narrowly escaping capture by the Gestapo for his work in the French Resistance, he fled to Roussillon in southwestern France, where he remained until the end of the war, when he returned to Paris. In 1961, the year he was writing *Happy Days*, he married a French woman, Suzanne Deschevaux-Dumesnil. In 1969 he was awarded the Nobel Prize for Literature though he refused to go to Stockholm for the ceremonies. Always a reclusive figure, he still lives in Paris with his wife. His best-known works include the novels *Molloy* (1951), *Malone Dies* (1951), and *The Unnamable* (1953); short stories, *More Pricks Than Kicks* (1934); plays, *Waiting for Godot* (first published in French as *En attendant Godot* in 1952 but translated by Beckett into English and published in 1954), *Endgame* (1957), and *Happy Days* (1961). Numerous shorter works, including scripts for radio and television, and even for a movie entitled *Film*, starring Buster Keaton, complete what John Updike has called "a single holy book."

CHARACTERS

WINNIE, *a woman about fifty*
WILLIE, *a man about sixty*

Peggy Ashcroft in the National Theatre Production of *Happy Days*, directed by Sir Peter Hall, 1975. (Photograph: Zoë Dominic F.R.P.S.)

ACT I

Expanse of scorched grass rising centre to low mound. Gentle slopes down to front and either side of stage. Back an abrupter fall to stage level. Maximum of simplicity and symmetry.

Blazing light.

Very pompier trompe-l'oeil* backcloth to represent unbroken plain and sky receding to meet in far distance.

Imbedded up to above her waist in exact centre of mound, WINNIE. *About fifty, well preserved, blond for preference, plump, arms and shoulders bare, low bodice, big bosom, pearl necklet. She is discovered sleeping, her arms on the ground before her, her head on her arms. Beside her on ground to her left a capacious black bag, shopping variety, and to her right a collapsible collapsed parasol, beak of handle emerging from sheath.*

To her right and rear, lying asleep on ground, hidden by mound, WILLIE.

Long pause. A bell rings piercingly, say ten seconds, stops. She does not move. Pause. Bell more piercingly, say five seconds. She wakes. Bell stops. She raises her head, gazes front. Long pause. She straightens up, lays her hands flat on ground, throws back her head and gazes at zenith. Long pause.

WINNIE (*gazing at zenith*): Another heavenly day. (*Pause. Head back level, eyes front, pause. She clasps hands to breast, closes eyes. Lips move in inaudible prayer, say ten seconds. Lips still. Hands remain clasped. Low.*) For Jesus Christ sake Amen. (*Eyes open, hands unclasp, return to mound. Pause. She clasps hands to breast again, closes eyes, lips move again in inaudible addendum, say five seconds. Low.*) World without end Amen. (*Eyes open, hands unclasp, return to mound. Pause.*) Begin, Winnie. (*Pause.*) Begin your day, Winnie. (*Pause. She turns to bag, rummages in it without moving it from its place, brings out toothbrush, rummages again, brings out flat tube of toothpaste, turns back front, unscrews cap of tube, lays cap on ground, squeezes with*

Reprinted by permission of Grove Press, Inc. Copyright © 1961 by Grove Press, Inc.
   * Ordinary illusionistic.

difficulty small blob of paste on brush, holds tube in one hand and brushes teeth with other. She turns modestly aside and back to her right to spit out behind mound. In this position her eyes rest on WILLIE. *She spits out. She cranes a little further back and down. Loud.*) Hoo-oo! (*Pause. Louder.*) Hoo-oo! (*Pause. Tender smile as she turns back front, lays down brush.*) Poor Willie — (*examines tube, smile off*) — running out — (*looks for cap*) — ah well — (*finds cap*) — can't be helped — (*screws on cap*) — just one of those old things — (*lays down tube*) — another of those old things — (*turns towards bag*) — just can't be cured — (*rummages in bag*) — cannot be cured — (*brings out small mirror, turns back front*) — ah yes — (*inspects teeth in mirror*) — poor dear Willie — (*testing upper front teeth with thumb, indistinctly*) — good Lord! — (*pulling back upper lip to inspect gums, do.*) — good God! — (*pulling back corner of mouth, mouth open, do.*) — ah well — (*other corner, do.*) — no worse — (*abandons inspection, normal speech*) — no better, no worse — (*lays down mirror*) — no change — (*wipes fingers on grass*) — no pain — (*looks for toothbrush*) — hardly any — (*takes up toothbrush*) — great thing that — (*examines handle of brush*) — nothing like it — (*examines handle, reads*) — pure . . . what? — (*pause*) — what? — (*lays down brush*) — ah yes — (*turns towards bag*) — poor Willie — (*rummages in bag*) — no zest — (*rummages*) — for anything — (*brings out spectacles in case*) — no interest — (*turns back front*) — in life — (*takes spectacles from case*) — poor dear Willie — (*lays down case*) — sleep for ever — (*opens spectacles*) — marvellous gift — (*puts on spectacles*) — nothing to touch it — (*looks for toothbrush*) — in my opinion — (*takes up toothbrush*) — always said so — (*examines handle of brush*) — wish I had it — (*examines handle, reads*) — genuine . . . pure . . . what? — (*lays down brush*) — blind next — (*takes off spectacles*) — ah well — (*lays down spectacles*) — seen enough — (*feels in bodice for handkerchief*) — I suppose — (*takes out folded handkerchief*) — by now — (*shakes out handkerchief*) — what are those wonderful lines — (*wipes one eye*) — woe woe is me — (*wipes the other*) — to see what I see — (*looks for* spectacles) — ah yes — (*takes up spectacles*) — wouldn't miss it — (*starts polishing spectacles, breathing on lenses*) — or would I? — (*polishes*) — holy light — (*polishes*) — bob up out of dark — (*polishes*) — blaze of hellish light. (*Stops polishing, raises face to sky, pause, head back level, resumes polishing, stops polishing, cranes back to her right and down.*) Hoo-oo! (*Pause. Tender smile as she turns back front and resumes polishing. Smile off.*) Marvellous gift — (*stops polishing, lays down spectacles*) — wish I had it — (*folds handkerchief*) — ah well — (*puts handkerchief back in bodice*) — can't complain — (*looks for spectacles*) — no no — (*takes up spectacles*) — mustn't complain — (*holds up spectacles, looks through lens*) — so much to be thankful for — (*looks through other lens*) — no pain — (*puts on spectacles*) — hardly any — (*looks for toothbrush*) — wonderful thing that — (*takes up toothbrush*) — nothing like it — (*examines handle of brush*) — slight headache sometimes — (*examines handle, reads*) — guaranteed ... genuine ... pure ... what? — (*looks closer*) — genuine pure ... — (*takes handkerchief from bodice*) — ah yes — (*shakes out handkerchief*) — occasional mild migraine — (*starts wiping handle of brush*) — it comes — (*wipes*) — then goes — (*wiping mechanically*) — ah yes — (*wiping*) — many mercies — (*wiping*) — great mercies — (*stops wiping, fixed lost gaze, brokenly*) — prayers perhaps not for naught — (*pause, do.*) - first thing — (*pause, do.*) — last thing — (*head down, resumes wiping, stops wiping, head up, calmed, wipes eyes, folds handkerchief, puts it back in bodice, examines handle of brush, reads*) — fully guaranteed ... genuine pure ... — (*looks closer*) — genuine pure ... (*Takes off spectacles, lays them and brush down, gazes before her.*) Old things. (*Pause.*) Old eyes. (*Long pause.*) On, Winnie. (*She casts about her, sees parasol, considers it at length, takes it up and develops from sheath a handle of surprising length. Holding butt of parasol in right hand she cranes back and down to her right to hang over* WILLIE.) Hoo-oo! (*Pause.*) Willie! (*Pause.*) Wonderful gift. (*She strikes down at him with beak of parasol.*) Wish I had it. (*She strikes again. The parasol slips from her grasp and falls behind mound. It is immediately restored to her by* WILLIE's *invisible hand.*) Thank you, dear. (*She transfers parasol to left hand, turns back front and examines right palm.*) Damp. (*Returns parasol to right hand, examines left palm.*) Ah well, no worse. (*Head up, cheerfully.*) No better, no worse, no change. (*Pause. Do.*) No pain. (*Cranes back to look down at* WILLIE, *holding parasol by butt as before.*) Don't go off on me again now dear will you please, I may need you. (*Pause.*) No hurry, no hurry, just don't curl up on me again. (*Turns back front, lays down parasol, examines palms together, wipes them on grass.*) Perhaps a shade off colour just the same. (*Turns to bag, rummages in it, brings out revolver, holds it up, kisses it rapidly, puts it back, rummages, brings out almost empty bottle of red medicine, turns back front, looks for spectacles, puts them on, reads label.*) Loss of spirits ... lack of keenness ... want of appetite ... infants ... children ... adults ... six level ... tablespoonfuls   daily — (*head   up, smile*) — the old style! — (*smile off, head down, reads*) — daily ... before and after ... meals ... instantaneous ... (*looks closer*) ... improvement. (*Takes off spectacles, lays them down, holds up bottle at arm's length to see level, unscrews cap, swigs it off head well back, tosses cap and bottle away in* WILLIE's *direction. Sound of breaking glass.*) Ah that's better! (*Turns to bag, rummages in it, brings out lipstick, turns back front, examines lipstick.*) Running out. (*Looks for spectacles.*) Ah well. (*Puts on spectacles, looks for mirror.*) Musn't complain. (*Takes up mirror, starts doing lips.*) What is that wonderful line? (*Lips.*) Oh fleeting joys — (*lips*) — oh something lasting woe. (*Lips. She is interrupted by disturbance from* WILLIE. *He is sitting up. She lowers lipstick and mirror and cranes back and down to look at him. Pause. Top back of* WILLIE's *bald head, trickling blood, rises to view above slope, comes to rest.* WINNIE *pushes up her spectacles. Pause. His hand appears with handkerchief, spreads it on skull, disappears. Pause. The hand appears with boater, club ribbon, settles it on head, rakish angle, disappears. Pause.* WINNIE *cranes a little further back and down.*) Slip on your drawers, dear, before you get singed. (*Pause.*) No? (*Pause.*) Oh I see, you still have some of that stuff left. (*Pause.*) Work it well in, dear. (*Pause.*) Now the other. (*Pause. She turns back front, gazes before her. Happy expression.*) Oh this is going to be another happy day! (*Pause. Happy expression off. She pulls down spectacles and resumes lips.* WILLIE *opens newspaper, hands invisible. Tops of yellow sheets appear on either side of his head.* WIN-

NIE *finishes lips, inspects them in mirror held a little further away.*) Ensign crimson. (WILLIE *turns page.* WINNIE *lays down lipstick and mirror, turns towards bag.*) Pale flag.

(WILLIE *turns page.* WINNIE *rummages in bag, brings out small ornate brimless hat with crumpled feather, turns back front, straightens hat, smooths feather, raises it towards head, arrests gesture as* WILLIE *reads.*)

WILLIE: His Grace and Most Reverend Father in God Dr. Carolus Hunter dead in tub.

(*Pause.*)

WINNIE (*gazing front, hat in hand, tone of fervent reminiscence*): Charlie Hunter! (*Pause.*) I close my eyes — (*she takes off spectacles and does so, hat in one hand, spectacles in other,* WILLIE *turns page*) — and am sitting on his knees again, in the back garden at Borough Green, under the horse-beech. (*Pause. She opens eyes, puts on spectacles, fiddles with hat.*) Oh the happy memories!

(*Pause. She raises hat towards head, arrests gesture as* WILLIE *reads.*)

WILLIE: Opening for smart youth.

(*Pause. She raises hat towards head, arrests gesture, takes off spectacles, gazes front, hat in one hand, spectacles in other.*)

WINNIE: My first ball! (*Long pause.*) My second ball! (*Long pause. Closes eyes.*) My first kiss! (*Pause.* WILLIE *turns page.* WINNIE *opens eyes.*) A Mr. Johnson, or Johnston, or perhaps I should say John*stone*. Very bushy moustache, very tawny. (*Reverently.*) Almost ginger! (*Pause.*) Within a toolshed, though whose I cannot conceive. We had no toolshed and he most certainly had no toolshed. (*Closes eyes.*) I see the piles of pots. (*Pause.*) The tangles of bast. (*Pause.*) The shadows deepening among the rafters.

(*Pause. She opens eyes, puts on spectacles, raises hat towards head, arrests gesture as* WILLIE *reads.*)

WILLIE: Wanted bright boy.

(*Pause.* WINNIE *puts on hat hurriedly, looks for mirror.* WILLIE *turns page.* WINNIE *takes up mirror, inspects hat, lays down mirror, turns towards bag. Paper disappears.* WINNIE *rummages in bag, brings out magnifying-glass, turns back front, looks for toothbrush. Paper reappears, folded, and begins to fan* WILLIE's *face, hand invisible.* WINNIE *takes up toothbrush and examines handle through glass.*

WINNIE: Fully guaranteed . . . (WILLIE *stops fanning*) . . . genuine pure . . . (*Pause.* WILLIE *resumes fanning.* WINNIE *looks closer, reads.*) Fully guaranteed . . . (WILLIE *stops fanning*) . . . genuine pure . . . (*Pause.* WILLIE *resumes fanning.* WINNIE *lays down glass and brush, takes handkerchief from bodice, takes off and polishes spectacles, puts on spectacles, looks for glass, takes up and polishes glass, lays down glass, looks for brush, takes up brush and wipes handle, lays down brush, puts handkerchief back in bodice, looks for glass, takes up glass, looks for brush, takes up brush and examines handle through glass.*) Fully guaranteed . . . (WILLIE *stops fanning*) . . . genuine pure . . . (*pause,* WILLIE *resumes fanning*) . . . hog's (WILLIE *stops fanning, pause*) . . . setae. (*Pause.* WINNIE *lays down glass and brush, paper disappears,* WINNIE *takes off spectacles, lays them down, gazes front.*) Hog's setae. (*Pause.*) That is what I find so wonderful, that not a day goes by — (*smile*) — to speak in the old style — (*smile off*) — hardly a day, without some addition to one's knowledge however trifling, the addition I mean, provided one takes the pains. (WILLIE's *hand reappears with a postcard which he examines close to eyes.*) And if for some strange reason no further pains are possible, why then just close the eyes — (*she does so*) — and wait for the day to come — (*opens eyes*) — the happy day to come when flesh melts at so many degrees and the night of the moon has so many hundred hours. (*Pause.*) That is what I find so comforting when I lose heart and envy the brute beast. (*Turning towards* WILLIE.) I hope you are taking in — (*She sees postcard, bends lower.*) What is that you have there, Willie, may I see? (*She reaches down with hand and* WILLIE *hands her card. The hairy forearm appears above slope, raised in gesture of giving, the hand open to take back, and remains in this position till card is returned.* WINNIE *turns back front and examines card.*) Heavens what are they up to! (*She looks for spectacles, puts them on and examines card.*) No but this is just genuine pure filth! (*Examines card.*) Make any nice-minded person want to vomit! (*Impatience of* WILLIE's *fingers. She looks for glass, takes it up and examines card through glass. Long pause.*) What does that creature in the background think he's doing? (*Looks closer.*) Oh no really! (*Impatience of fingers. Last long look. She lays down glass, takes edge of card between right forefinger and thumb, averts head, takes nose between left forefinger and thumb.*) Pah! (*Drops card.*) Take it away! (WILLIE's *arm disappears. His hand reappears immediately, holding card.* WINNIE *takes off spectacles, lays them down, gazes before her. During what follows* WILLIE *continues to relish card, varying angles and distance from his eyes.*) Hog's setae. (*Puzzled expression.*) What exactly is a hog? (*Pause. Do.*) A sow of course I know, but a hog . . . (*Puzzled expression off.*) Oh well what does it matter, that is what I always say, it will come back, that is what I find so wonderful, all comes back. (*Pause.*) All? (*Pause.*) No, not all. (*Smile.*) No no. (*Smile off.*) Not quite. (*Pause.*) A part. (*Pause.*) Floats up, one fine day, out of the blue. (*Pause.*) That is what I find so wonderful. (*Pause. She turns towards bag. Hand and card disappear. She makes to rummage in bag, arrests gesture.*) No. (*She turns back front. Smile.*) No no. (*Smile off.*) Gently Winnie. (*She gazes front.* WILLIE's *hand reappears, takes off hat, disappears with hat.*) What then? (*Hand reappears, takes handkerchief from skull, disappears with handkerchief. Sharply, as to one not paying attention.*) Winnie! (WILLIE *bows head out of sight.*) What *is* the alternative? (*Pause.*) What *is* the al — (WILLIE *blows nose loud and long, head and hands invisible. She turns to look at him. Pause. Head reappears. Pause. Hand reappears with handkerchief, spreads it on skull, disappears. Pause. Hand reappears with boater, settles it on head, rakish angle, disappears. Pause.*) Would I had let you sleep on. (*She turns back front. Intermittent plucking at grass, head up and down, to animate following.*) Ah yes, if only I could bear to be alone, I mean prattle away with not a soul to hear. (*Pause.*) Not that I flatter myself you hear much, no Willie, God forbid. (*Pause.*) Days perhaps when you hear nothing. (*Pause.*) But days too when you answer. (*Pause.*) So that I may say at all times, even when you do not answer and perhaps hear nothing, something of this is being heard, I am not merely talking to myself, that is in the wilderness, a thing I could never

bear to do — for any length of time. (*Pause.*) That is what enables me to go on, go on talking that is. (*Pause.*) Whereas if you were to die — (*smile*) — to speak in the old style — (*smile off*) — or go away and leave me, then what would I do, what *could* I do, all day long, I mean between the bell for waking and the bell for sleep? (*Pause.*) Simply gaze before me with compressed lips. (*Long pause while she does so. No more plucking.*) Not another word as long as I drew breath, nothing to break the silence of this place. (*Pause.*) Save possibly, now and then, every now and then, a sigh into my looking-glass. (*Pause.*) Or a brief . . . gale of laughter, should I happen to see the old joke again. (*Pause. Smile appears, broadens and seems about to culminate in laugh when suddenly replaced by expression of anxiety.*) My hair! (*Pause.*) Did I brush and comb my hair? (*Pause.*) I may have done. (*Pause.*) Normally I do. (*Pause.*) There is so little one *can* do. (*Pause.*) One does it all. (*Pause.*) All one can. (*Pause.*) Tis only human. (*Pause.*) Human nature. (*She begins to inspect mound, looks up.*) Human weakness. (*She resumes inspection of mound, looks up.*) Natural weakness. (*She resumes inspection of mound.*) I see no comb. (*Inspects.*) Nor any hairbrush. (*Looks up. Puzzled expression. She turns to bag, rummages in it.*) The comb is here. (*Back front. Puzzled expression. Back to bag. Rummages.*) The brush is here. (*Back front. Puzzled expression.*) Perhaps I put them back, after use. (*Pause. Do.*) But normally I do not put things back, after use, no, I leave them lying about and put them back all together, at the end of the day. (*Smile.*) To speak in the old style. (*Pause.*) The sweet old style. (*Smile off.*) And yet . . . I seem . . . to remember . . . (*Suddenly careless.*) Oh well, what does it matter, that is what I always say, I shall simply brush and comb them later on, purely and simply, I have the whole — (*Pause. Puzzled.*) Them? (*Pause.*) Or it? (*Pause.*) Brush and comb it? (*Pause.*) Sounds improper somehow. (*Pause. Turning a little towards* WILLIE.) What would you say, Willie? (*Pause. Turning a little further.*) What would you say, Willie, speaking of your hair, them or it? (*Pause.*) The hair on your head, I mean. (*Pause. Turning a little further.*) The hair on your head, Willie, what would you say speaking of the hair on your head, them or it?

(*Long pause.*)

WILLIE: It.

WINNIE (*turning back front, joyful*): Oh you are going to talk to me today, this is going to be a happy day! (*Pause. Joy off.*) Another happy day. (*Pause.*) Ah well, where was I, my hair, yes, later on, I shall be thankful for it later on. (*Pause.*) I have my — (*raises hands to hat*) — yes, on, my hat on — (*lowers hands*) — I cannot take it off now. (*Pause.*) To think there are times one cannot take off one's hat, not if one's life were at stake. Times one cannot put it on, times one cannot take it off. (*Pause.*) How often I have said, Put on your hat now, Winnie, there is nothing else for it, take off your hat now, Winnie, like a good girl, it will do you good, and did not. (*Pause.*) Could not. (*Pause. She raises hand, frees a strand of hair from under hat, draws it towards eye, squints at it, lets it go, hand down.*) Golden you called it, that day, when the last guest was gone — (*hand up in gesture of raising a glass*) — to your golden . . . may it never (*voice breaks*) . . . may it never . . . (*Hand down. Head down. Pause. Low.*) That day. (*Pause. Do.*) What day? (*Pause. Head up. Normal voice.*) What now? (*Pause.*) Words fail, there are times when even they fail. (*Turning a little towards* WILLIE.) Is that not so, Willie? (*Pause. Turning a little further.*) Is not that so, Willie, that even words fail, at times? (*Pause. Back front.*) What is one to do then, until they come again? Brush and comb the hair, if it has not been done, or if there is some doubt, trim the nails if they are in need of trimming, these things tide one over. (*Pause.*) That is what I mean. (*Pause.*) That is all I mean. (*Pause.*) That is what I find so wonderful, that not a day goes by — (*smile*) — to speak in the old style — (*smile off*) — without some blessing — (WILLIE *collapses behind slope, his head disappears,* WINNIE *turns towards event*) — in disguise. (*She cranes back and down.*) Go back into your hole now, Willie, you've exposed yourself enough. (*Pause.*) Do as I say, Willie, don't lie sprawling there in this hellish sun, go back into your hole. (*Pause.*) Go on now, Willie. (WILLIE *invisible starts crawling left towards hole.*) That's the man. (*She follows his progress with her eyes.*) Not head first, stupid, how are you going to turn? (*Pause.*) That's it . . . right round . . . now . . . back in. (*Pause.*) Oh I know it is not easy, dear, crawling backwards, but it is rewarding in the end. (*Pause.*) You have left your vaseline behind.

(*She watches as he crawls back for vaseline.*) The lid! (*She watches as he crawls back towards hole. Irritated.*) Not head first, I tell you! (*Pause.*) More to the right. (*Pause.*) The *right*, I said. (*Pause. Irritated.*) Keep your tail down, can't you! (*Pause.*) Now. (*Pause.*) There! (*All these directions loud. Now in her normal voice, still turned towards him.*) Can you hear me? (*Pause.*) I beseech you, Willie, just yes or no, can you hear me, just yes or nothing.

(*Pause.*)

WILLIE: Yes.

WINNIE (*turning front, same voice*): And now?

WILLIE (*irritated*): Yes.

WINNIE (*less loud*): And now?

WILLIE (*more irritated*): Yes.

WINNIE (*still less loud*): And now? (*A little louder.*) And now?

WILLIE (*violently*): Yes!

WINNIE (*same voice*): Fear no more the heat o' the sun. (*Pause.*) Did you hear that?

WILLIE (*irritated*): Yes.

WINNIE (*same voice*): What? (*Pause.*) What?

WILLIE (*more irritated*): Fear no more.

(*Pause.*)

WINNIE (*same voice*): No more what? (*Pause.*) Fear no more what?

WILLIE (*violently*): Fear no more!

WINNIE (*normal voice, gabbled*): Bless you Willie I do appreciate your goodness I know what an effort it costs you, now you may relax I shall not trouble you again unless I am obliged to, by that I mean unless I come to the end of my own resources which is most unlikely, just to know that in theory you can hear me even though in fact you don't is all I need, just to feel you there within earshot and conceivably on the qui vive is all I ask, not to say anything I would not wish you to hear or liable to cause you pain, not to be just babbling away on trust as it is were not knowing and something gnawing at me. (*Pause for breath.*) Doubt. (*Places index and second finger on heart area, moves them about, brings them to rest.*) Here. (*Moves them slightly.*) Abouts. (*Hand away.*) Oh no doubt the time will come when before I can utter a word I must make sure you heard the one that went before and then no doubt another come another time when I must learn to talk to myself a thing I could never bear to do such wilderness. (*Pause.*) Or gaze before me with compressed lips. (*She does so.*) All day long. (*Gaze and lips again.*) No. (*Smile.*) No no. (*Smile off.*) There is of course the bag. (*Turns towards it.*) There will always be the bag. (*Back front.*) Yes, I suppose so. (*Pause.*) Even when you are gone, Willie. (*She turns a little towards him.*) You *are* going, Willie, aren't you? (*Pause. Louder.*) You *will* be going soon, Willie, won't you? (*Pause. Louder.*) Willie! (*Pause. She cranes back and down to look at him.*) So you have taken off your straw, that is wise. (*Pause.*) You do look snug, I must say, with your chin on your hands and the old blue eyes like saucers in the shadows. (*Pause.*) Can you see me from there I wonder, I still wonder. (*Pause.*) No? (*Back front.*) Oh I know it does not follow when two are gathered together — (*faltering*) — in this way — (*normal*) — that because one sees the other the other sees the one, life has taught me that . . . too. (*Pause.*) Yes, life I suppose, there is no other word. (*She turns a little towards him.*) Could you see me, Willie, do you think, from where you are, if you were to raise your eyes in my direction? (*Turns a little further.*) Lift up your eyes to me, Willie, and tell me can you see me, do that for me, I'll lean back as far as I can. (*Does so. Pause.*) No? (*Pause.*) Well never mind. (*Turns back painfully front.*) The earth is very tight today, can it be I have put on flesh, I trust not. (*Pause. Absently, eyes lowered.*) The great heat possibly. (*Starts to pat and stroke ground.*) All things expanding, some more than others. (*Pause. Patting and stroking.*) Some less. (*Pause. Do.*) Oh I can well imagine what is passing through your mind, it is not enough to have to listen to the woman, now I must look at her as well. (*Pause. Do.*) Well it is very understandable. (*Pause. Do.*) Most understandable. (*Pause. Do.*) One does not appear to be asking a great deal, indeed at times it would seem hardly possible — (*voice breaks, falls to a murmur*) — to ask less — of a fellow-creature — to put it mildly — whereas actually — when you think about it — look into your heart — see the other — what he needs — peace — to be left in peace — then perhaps the moon — all this time — asking for the moon. (*Pause. Stroking hand suddenly still. Lively.*) Oh I say, what have we here? (*Bending head to ground, incredulous.*) Looks like life of some kind! (*Looks for spectacles, puts

them on, bends closer. Pause.*) An emmet! (*Recoils. Shrill.*) Willie, an emmet, a live emmet! (*Seizes magnifying-glass, bends to ground again, inspects through glass.*) Where's it gone? (*Inspects.*) Ah! (*Follows its progress through grass.*) Has like a little white ball in its arms. (*Follows progress. Hand still. Pause.*) It's gone in. (*Continues a moment to gaze at spot through glass, then slowly straightens up, lays down glass, takes off spectacles and gazes before her, spectacles in hand. Finally.*) Like a little white ball.

(*Long pause. Gesture to lay down spectacles.*)

WILLIE: Eggs.
WINNIE (*arresting gesture*): What?

(*Pause.*)

WILLIE: Eggs. (*Pause. Gesture to lay down glasses.*) Formication.
WINNIE (*arresting gesture*): What?

(*Pause.*)

WILLIE: Formication.

(*Pause. She lays down spectacles, gazes before her. Finally.*)

WINNIE (*murmur*): God. (*Pause.* WILLIE *laughs quietly. After a moment she joins in. They laugh quietly together.* WILLIE *stops. She laughs on a moment alone.* WILLIE *joins in. They laugh together. She stops.* WILLIE *laughs on a moment alone. He stops. Pause. Normal voice.*) Ah well what a joy in any case to hear you laugh again, Willie, I was convinced I never would, you never would. (*Pause.*) I suppose some people might think us a trifle irreverent, but I doubt it. (*Pause.*) How can one better magnify the Almighty than by sniggering with him at his little jokes, particularly the poorer ones? (*Pause.*) I think you would back me up there, Willie. (*Pause.*) Or were we perhaps diverted by two quite different things? (*Pause.*) Oh well, what does it matter, that is what I always say, so long as one . . . you know . . . what is that wonderful line . . . laughing wild . . . something something laughing wild amid severest woe. (*Pause.*) And now? (*Long pause.*) Was I lovable once, Willie? (*Pause.*) Was I ever lovable? (*Pause.*) Do not misunderstand my question, I am not asking you if you loved me, we know all about that,

I am asking you if you found me lovable —
at one stage. (*Pause.*) No? (*Pause.*) You
can't? (*Pause.*) Well I admit it is a teaser.
And you have done more than your bit already, for the time being, just lie back now
and relax, I shall not trouble you again unless
I am compelled to, just to know you are there
within hearing and conceivably on the semi-
alert is ... er ... paradise enow. (*Pause.*) The
day is now well advanced. (*Smile.*) To speak
in the old style. (*Smile off.*) And yet it is
perhaps a little soon for my song. (*Pause.*) To
sing too soon is a great mistake, I find. (*Turning towards bag.*) There is of course the bag.
(*Looking at bag.*) The bag. (*Back front.*)
Could I enumerate its contents? (*Pause.*) No.
(*Pause.*) Could I, if some kind person were to
come along and ask, What all have you got in
that big black bag, Winnie? give an exhaustive
answer? (*Pause.*) No. (*Pause.*) The depths in
particular, who knows what treasures. (*Pause.*)
What comforts. (*Turns to look at bag.*) Yes,
there is the bag. (*Back front.*) But something
tells me, Do not overdo the bag, Winnie, make
use of it of course, let it help you ... along,
when stuck, by all means, but cast your mind
forward, something tells me, cast your mind
forward, Winnie, to the time when words
must fail — (*she closes eyes, pause, opens eyes*)
— and do not overdo the bag. (*Pause. She
turns to look at bag.*) Perhaps just one quick
dip. (*She turns back front, closes eyes, throws
out left arm, plunges hand in bag and brings
out revolver. Disgusted.*) You again! (*She
opens eyes, brings revolver front and contemplates it. She weighs it in her palm.*) You'd
think the weight of this thing would bring it
down among the ... last rounds. But no. It
doesn't. Ever uppermost, like Browning.
(*Pause.*) Brownie ... (*Turning a little towards
WILLIE.*) Remember Brownie, Willie? (*Pause.*)
Remember how you used to keep on at me
to take it away from you? Take it away, Winnie, take it away, before I put myself out of
my misery. (*Back front. Derisive.*) Your misery! (*To revolver.*) Oh I suppose it's a comfort to know you're there, but I'm tired of
you. (*Pause.*) I'll leave you out, that's what
I'll do. (*She lays revolver on ground to her
right.*) There, that's your home from this day
out. (*Smile.*) The old style! (*Smile off.*) And
now? (*Long pause.*) Is gravity what it was,
Willie, I fancy not. (*Pause.*) Yes, the feeling
more and more that if I were not held — (*ges-

ture*) — in this way, I would simply float up
into the blue. (*Pause.*) And that perhaps some
day the earth will yield and let me go, the pull
is so great, yes, crack all round me and let me
out. (*Pause.*) Don't you ever have that feeling,
Willie, of being sucked up? (*Pause.*) Don't
you have to cling on sometimes, Willie?
(*Pause. She turns a little towards him.*) Willie.

(*Pause.*)

WILLIE: *Sucked* up?
WINNIE: Yes love, up into the blue, like gossamer. (*Pause.*) No? (*Pause.*) You don't?
(*Pause.*) Ah well, natural laws, natural laws, I
suppose it's like everything else, it all depends
on the creature you happen to be. All I can
say is for my part is that for me they are not
what they were when I was young and ... foolish and ... (*faltering, head down*) ... beautiful ... possibly ... lovely ... in a way ... to
look at. (*Pause. Head up.*) Forgive me, Willie, sorrow keeps breaking in. (*Normal voice.*)
Ah well what a joy in any case to know you
are there, as usual, and perhaps awake, and
perhaps taking all this in, some of all this,
what a happy day for me ... it will have been.
(*Pause.*) So far. (*Pause.*) What a blessing
nothing grows, imagine if all this stuff were
to start growing. (*Pause.*) Imagine. (*Pause.*)
Ah yes, great mercies. (*Long pause.*) I can say
no more. (*Pause.*) For the moment. (*Pause.
Turns to look at bag. Back front. Smile.*) No
no. (*Smile off. Looks at parasol.*) I suppose I
might — (*takes up parasol*) — yes, I suppose I
might ... hoist this thing now. (*Begins to un-
furl it. Following punctuated by mechanical
difficulties overcome.*) One keeps putting off —
putting up — for fear of putting up — too soon
— and the day goes by — quite by — without
one's having put up — at all. (*Parasol now
fully open. Turned to her right she twirls it
idly this way and that.*) Ah yes, so little to say,
so little to do, and the fear so great, certain
days, of finding oneself ... left, with hours still
to run, before the bell for sleep, and nothing
more to say, nothing more to do, that the days
go by, certain days go by, quite by, the bell
goes, and little or nothing said, little or nothing
done. (*Raising parasol.*) That is the danger.
(*Turning front.*) To be guarded against. (*She
gazes front, holding up parasol with right
hand. Maximum pause.*) I used to perspire
freely. (*Pause.*) Now hardly at all. (*Pause.*)

The heat is much greater. (*Pause.*) The per-spiration much less. (*Pause.*) That is what I find so wonderful. (*Pause.*) The way man adapts himself. (*Pause.*) To changing condi-tions. (*She transfers parasol to left hand. Long pause.*) Holding up wearies the arm. (*Pause.*) Not if one is going along. (*Pause.*) Only if one is at rest. (*Pause.*) That is a curious ob-servation. (*Pause.*) I hope you heard that, Wil-lie, I should be grieved to think you had not heard that. (*She takes parasol in both hands. Long pause.*) I am weary, holding it up, and I cannot put it down. (*Pause.*) I am worse off with it up than with it down, and I cannot put it down. (*Pause.*) Reason says, Put it down, Winnie, it is not helping you, put the thing down and get on with something else. (*Pause.*) I cannot. (*Pause.*) I cannot move. (*Pause.*) No, something must happen, in the world, take place, some change, I cannot, if I am to move again. (*Pause.*) Willie. (*Mildly.*) Help. (*Pause.*) No? (*Pause.*) Bid me put this thing down, Willie, I would obey you instantly, as I have always done, honoured and obeyed. (*Pause.*) Please, Willie. (*Mildly.*) For pity's sake. (*Pause.*) No? (*Pause.*) You can't? (*Pause.*) Well I don't blame you, no, it would ill become me, who cannot move, to blame my Willie because he cannot speak. (*Pause.*) For-tunately I am in tongue again. (*Pause.*) That is what I find so wonderful, my two lamps, when one goes out the other burns brighter. (*Pause.*) Oh yes, great mercies. (*Maximum pause. The parasol goes on fire. Smoke, flames if feasible. She sniffs, looks up, throws parasol to her right behind mound, cranes back to watch it burning. Pause.*) Ah earth you old extinguisher. (*Back front.*) I presume this has occurred before, though I cannot recall it. (*Pause.*) Can you, Willie? (*Turns a little to-wards him.*) Can you recall this having oc-curred before? (*Pause. Cranes back to look at him.*) Do you know what has occurred, Willie? (*Pause.*) Have you gone off on me again? (*Pause.*) I do not ask if you are alive to all that is going on, I merely ask if you have not gone off on me again. (*Pause.*) Your eyes ap-pear to be closed, but that has no particular sig-nificance we know. (*Pause.*) Raise a finger, dear, will you please, if you are not quite sense-less. (*Pause.*) Do that for me, Willie please, just the little finger, if you are still conscious. (*Pause. Joyful.*) Oh all five, you are a darling today, now I may continue with an easy mind.

(*Back front.*) Yes, what ever occurred that did not occur before and yet . . . I wonder, yes, I confess I wonder. (*Pause.*) With the sun blaz-ing so much fiercer down, and hourly fiercer, is it not natural things should go on fire never known to do so, in this way I mean, spon-taneous like. (*Pause.*) Shall I myself not melt perhaps in the end, or burn, oh I do not mean necessarily burst into flames, no, just little by little be charred to a black cinder, all this — (*ample gesture of arms*) — visible flesh. (*Pause.*) On the other hand, did I ever know a temperate time? (*Pause.*) No. (*Pause.*) I speak of temperate times and torrid times, they are empty words. (*Pause.*) I speak of when I was not yet caught — in this way — and had my legs and had the use of my legs, and could seek out a shady place, like you, when I was tired of the sun, or a sunny place when I was tired of the shade, like you, and they are all empty words. (*Pause.*) It is no hotter today than yesterday, it will be no hotter tomorrow than today, how could it, and so on back into the far past, forward into the far future. (*Pause.*) And should one day the earth cover my breasts, then I shall never have seen my breasts, no one ever seen my breasts. (*Pause.*) I hope you caught something of that, Willie, I should be sorry to think you had caught nothing of all that, it is not every day I rise to such heights. (*Pause.*) Yes, something seems to have occurred, something has seemed to occur, and nothing has occurred, nothing at all, you are quite right, Willie. (*Pause.*) The sunshade will be there again tomorrow, beside me on this mound, to help me through the day. (*Pause. She takes up mirror.*) I take up this little glass, I shiver it on a stone — (*does so*) — I throw it away — (*does so far behind her*) — it will be in the bag again tomorrow, without a scratch, to help me through the day. (*Pause.*) No, one can do nothing. (*Pause.*) That is what I find so wonderful, the way things . . . (*voice breaks, head down*) . . . things . . . so wonder-ful. (*Long pause, head down. Finally turns, still bowed, to bag, brings out unidentifiable odds and ends, stuffs them back, fumbles deeper, brings out finally musical-box, winds it up, turns it on, listens for a moment holding it in both hands, huddled over it, turns back front, straightens up and listens to tune, holding box to breast with both hands. It plays the Waltz Duet "I love you so" from The Merry Widow. Gradually happy expression. She sways to the rhythm. Music stops. Pause. Brief burst of hoarse song without words — musical-box tune — from* WILLIE. *Increase of happy expression. She lays down box.*) Oh this will have been a happy day! (*She claps hands.*) Again, Willie, again! (*Claps.*) Encore, Willie, please! (*Pause. Happy expression off.*) No? You won't do that for me? (*Pause.*) Well it is very understandable, very understandable. One cannot sing just to please someone, however much one loves them, no, song must come from the heart, that is what I always say, pour out from the inmost, like a thrush. (*Pause.*) How often I have said, in evil hours, Sing now, Winnie, sing your song, there is nothing else for it, and did not. (*Pause.*) Could not. (*Pause.*) No, like the thrush, or the bird of dawning, with no thought of benefit, to oneself or anyone else. (*Pause.*) And now? (*Long pause. Low.*) Strange feeling. (*Pause. Do.*) Strange feeling that someone is looking at me. I am clear, then dim, then gone, then dim again, then clear again, and so on, back and forth, in and out of someone's eye. (*Pause. Do.*) Strange? (*Pause. Do.*) No, here all is strange. (*Pause. Normal voice.*) Something says, Stop talking now, Winnie, for a minute, don't squander all your words for the day, stop talking and do something for a change, will you? (*She raises hands and holds them open before her eyes. Apostrophic.*) Do something! (*She closes hands.*) What claws! (*She turns to bag, rummages in it, brings out finally a nailfile, turns back front and begins to file nails. Files for a time in silence, then the following punctuated by filing.*) There floats up — into my thoughts — a Mr. Shower — a Mr. and perhaps a Mrs. Shower — no — they are holding hands — his fiancée then more likely — or just some — loved one. (*Looks closer at nails.*) Very brittle today. (*Resumes filing.*) Shower — Shower — does the name mean anything — to you, Willie — evoke any reality, I mean — for you, Willie — don't answer if you don't — feel up to it — you have done more — than your bit — already — Shower — Shower. (*Inspects filed nails.*) Bit more like it. (*Raises head, gazes front.*) Keep yourself nice, Winnie, that's what I always say, come what may, keep yourself nice. (*Pause. Resumes filing.*) Yes — Shower — Shower — (*stops filing, raises head, gazes front, pause*) — or Cooker, perhaps I should say Cooker. (*Turning a little towards* WILLIE.) Cooker, Willie, does Cooker strike a chord? (*Pause. Turns a little further. Louder.*) Cooker, Willie, does Cooker ring a bell, the name Cooker? (*Pause. She cranes back to look at him. Pause.*) Oh really! (*Pause.*) Have you no handkerchief, darling? (*Pause.*) Have you no delicacy? (*Pause.*) Oh, Willie, you're not eating it! Spit it out, dear, spit it out! (*Pause. Back front.*) Ah well, I suppose it's only natural. (*Break in voice.*) Human. (*Pause. Do.*) What *is* one to do? (*Head down. Do.*) All day long. (*Pause. Do.*) Day after day. (*Pause. Head up. Smile. Calm.*) The old style! (*Smile off. Resumes nails.*) No, done him. (*Passes on to next.*) Should have put on my glasses. (*Pause.*) Too late now. (*Finishes left hand, inspects it.*) Bit more human. (*Starts right hand. Following punctuated as before.*) Well anyway — this man Shower — or Cooker — no matter — and the woman — hand in hand — in the other hands bags — kind of big brown grips — standing there gaping at me — and at last this man Shower — or Cooker — ends in er anyway — stake my life on that — What's she doing? he says — What's the idea? he says — stuck up to her diddies in the bleeding ground — coarse fellow — What does it mean? he says — What's it meant to mean? — and so on — lot more stuff like that — usual drivel — Do you hear me? he says — I do, she says, God help me — What do you mean, he says, God help you? (*Stops filing, raises head, gazes front.*) And you, she says, what's the idea of you, she says, what are you meant to mean? It is because you're still on your two flat feet, with your old ditty full of tinned muck and changes of underwear, dragging me up and down this fornicating wilderness, coarse creature, fit mate — (*with sudden violence*) — let go of my hand and drop for God's sake, she says, drop! (*Pause. Resumes filing.*) Why doesn't he dig her out? he says — referring to you, my dear — What good is she to him like that? — What good is he to her like that? — and so on — usual tosh — Good! she says, have a heart for God's sake — Dig her out, he says, dig her out, no sense in her like that — Dig her out with what? she says — I'd dig her out with my bare hands, he says — must have been man and — wife. (*Files in silence.*) Next thing they're away — hand in hand — and the bags — dim — then gone — last human kind — to stray this way. (*Finishes right hand, inspects it, lays down file, gazes front.*) Strange thing, time like this, drift up into the mind. (*Pause.*) Strange?

(*Pause.*) No, here all is strange. (*Pause.*) Thankful for it in any case. (*Voice breaks.*) Most thankful. (*Head down. Pause. Head up. Calm.*) Bow and raise the head, bow and raise, always that. (*Pause.*) And now? (*Long pause. Starts putting things back in bag, toothbrush last. This operation, interrupted by pauses as indicated, punctuates following.*) It is perhaps a little soon — to make ready — for the night — (*stops tidying, head up, smile*) — the old style! — (*smile off, resumes tidying*) — and yet I do — make ready for the night — feeling it at hand — the bell for sleep — saying to myself — Winnie — it will not be long now, Winnie — until the bell for sleep. (*Stops tidying, head up.*) Sometimes I am wrong. (*Smile.*) But not often. (*Smile off.*) Sometimes all is over, for the day, all done, all said, all ready for the night, and the day not over, far from over, the night not ready, far, far from ready. (*Smile.*) But not often. (*Smile off.*) Yes, the bell for sleep, when I feel it at hand, and so make ready for the night — (*gesture*) — in this way, sometimes I am wrong — (*smile*) — but not often. (*Smile off. Resumes tidying.*) I used to think — I say I used to think — that all these things — put back into the bag — if too soon — put back too soon — could be taken out again — if necessary — if needed — and so on — indefinitely — back into the bag — back out of the bag — until the bell — went. (*Stops tidying, head up, smile.*) But no. (*Smile broader.*) No no. (*Smile off. Resumes tidying.*) I suppose this — might seem strange — this — what shall I say — this what I have said — yes — (*she takes up revolver*) — strange — (*she turns to put revolver in bag*) — were it not — (*about to put revolver in bag she arrests gesture and turns back front*) — were it not — (*she lays down revolver to her right, stops tidying, head up*) — that all seems strange. (*Pause.*) Most strange. (*Pause.*) Never any change. (*Pause.*) And more and more strange. (*Pause. She bends to mound again, takes up last object, i.e., toothbrush, and turns to put it in bag when her attention is drawn to disturbance from* WILLIE. *She cranes back and to her right to see. Pause.*) Weary of your hole, dear? (*Pause.*) Well I can understand that. (*Pause.*) Don't forget your straw. (*Pause.*) Not the crawler you were, poor darling. (*Pause.*) No, not the crawler I gave my heart to. (*Pause.*) The hands and knees, love, try the hands and knees. (*Pause.*) The knees! The knees! (*Pause.*) What a curse, mobility! (*She follows with eyes his progress towards her behind mound, i.e., towards place he occupied at beginning of act.*) Another foot, Willie, and you're home. (*Pause as she observes last foot.*) Ah! (*Turns back front laboriously, rubs neck.*) Crick in my neck admiring you. (*Rubs neck.*) But it's worth it, well worth it. (*Turning slightly towards him.*) Do you know what I dream sometimes? (*Pause.*) What I dream sometimes, Willie. (*Pause.*) That you'll come round and live this side where I could see you. (*Pause. Back front.*) I'd be a different woman. (*Pause.*) Unrecognizable. (*Turning slightly towards him.*) Or just now and then, come round this side just every now and then and let me feast on you. (*Back front.*) But you can't, I know. (*Head down.*) I know. (*Pause. Head up.*) Well anyway — (*looks at toothbrush in her hand*) — can't be long now — (*looks at brush*) — until the bell. (*Top back of* WILLIE's *head appears above slope.* WINNIE *looks closer at brush.*) Fully guaranteed ... (*head up*) ... what's this it was? (*WILLIE's hand appears with handkerchief, spreads it on skull, disappears.*) Genuine pure ... fully guaranteed ... (*WILLIE's hand appears with boater, settles it on head, rakish angle, disappears*) ... genuine pure ... ah! hog's setae. (*Pause.*) What is a hog exactly? (*Pause. Turns slightly towards* WILLIE.) What exactly is a hog, Willie, do you know, I can't remember. (*Pause. Turning a little further, pleading.*) What *is* a hog, Willie, please!

(*Pause.*)

WILLIE: Castrated male swine. (*Happy expression appears on* WINNIE's *face.*) Reared for slaughter.

(*Happy expression increases.* WILLIE *opens newspaper, hands invisible. Tops of yellow sheets appear on either side of his head.* WINNIE *gazes before her with happy expression.*)

WINNIE: Oh this *is* a happy day! This will have been another happy day! (*Pause.*) After all. (*Pause.*) So far.

(*Pause. Happy expression off.* WILLIE *turns page. Pause. He turns another page. Pause.*)

WILLIE: Opening for smart youth.

(*Pause.* WINNIE *takes off hat, turns to put it in bag, arrests gesture, turns back front. Smile.*)

WINNIE: No. (*Smile broader.*) No no. (*Smile off. Puts on hat again, gazes front, pause.*) And now? (*Pause.*) Sing. (*Pause.*) Sing your song, Winnie. (*Pause.*) No? (*Pause.*) Then pray. (*Pause.*) Pray your prayer, Winnie.

(*Pause.* WILLIE *turns page. Pause.*)

WILLIE: Wanted bright boy.

(*Pause.* WINNIE *gazes before her.* WILLIE *turns page. Pause. Newspaper disappears. Long pause.*)

WINNIE: Pray your old prayer, Winnie.

(*Long pause.*)

CURTAIN

ACT II

SCENE *as before.*

WINNIE *imbedded up to neck, hat on head, eyes closed. Her head, which she can no longer turn, nor bow, nor raise, faces front motionless throughout act. Movements of eyes as indicated.*
    Bag and parasol as before. Revolver conspicuous to her right on mound.
    Long pause.
    Bell rings loudly. She opens eyes at once. Bell stops. She gazes front. Long pause.

WINNIE: Hail, holy light. (*Long pause. She closes her eyes. Bell rings loudly. She opens eyes at once. Bell stops. She gazes front. Long smile. Smile off. Long pause.*) Someone is looking at me still. (*Pause.*) Caring for me still. (*Pause.*) That is what I find so wonderful. (*Pause.*) Eyes on my eyes. (*Pause.*) What is that unforgettable line? (*Pause. Eyes right.*) Willie. (*Pause. Louder.*) Willie. (*Pause. Eyes front.*) May one still speak of time? (*Pause.*) Say it is a long time now, Willie, since I saw you. (*Pause.*) Since I heard you. (*Pause.*) May one? (*Pause.*) One does. (*Smile.*) The old style! (*Smile off.*) There is so little one can speak of. (*Pause.*) One speaks of it all. (*Pause.*) All one can. (*Pause.*) I used to think ... (*pause*) ... I say I used to think that

I would learn to talk alone. (*Pause.*) By that I mean to myself, the wilderness. (*Smile.*) But no. (*Smile broader.*) No no. (*Smile off.*) Ergo you are there. (*Pause.*) Oh no doubt you are dead, like the others, no doubt you have died, or gone away and left me, like the others, it doesn't matter, you are there. (*Pause. Eyes left.*) The bag too is there, the same as ever, I can see it. (*Pause. Eyes right. Louder.*) The bag is there, Willie, as good as ever, the one you gave me that day ... to go to market. (*Pause. Eyes front.*) That day. (*Pause.*) What day? (*Pause.*) I used to pray. (*Pause.*) I say I used to pray. (*Pause.*) Yes, I must confess I did. (*Smile.*) Not now. (*Smile broader.*) No no. (*Smile off. Pause.*) Then ... now ... what difficulties here, for the mind. (*Pause.*) To have been always what I am — and so changed from what I was. (*Pause.*) I am the one, I say the one, then the other. (*Pause.*) Now the one, then the other. (*Pause.*) There is so little one can say, one says it all. (*Pause.*) All one can. (*Pause.*) And no truth in it anywhere. (*Pause.*) My arms. (*Pause.*) My breasts. (*Pause.*) What arms? (*Pause.*) What breasts? (*Pause.*) Willie. (*Pause.*) What Willie? (*Sudden vehement affirmation.*) My Willie! (*Eyes right, calling.*) Willie! (*Pause. Louder.*) Willie! (*Pause. Eyes front.*) Ah well, not to know, not to know for sure, great mercy, all I ask. (*Pause.*) Ah yes ... then ... now ... beechen green ... this ... Charlie ... kisses ... this ... all that ... deep trouble for the mind. (*Pause.*) But it does not trouble mine. (*Smile.*) Not now. (*Smile broader.*) No no. (*Smile off. Long pause. She closes eyes. Bell rings loudly. She opens eyes. Pause.*) Eyes float up that seem to close in peace ... to see ... in peace. (*Pause.*) Not mine. (*Smile.*) Not now. (*Smile broader.*) No no. (*Smile off. Long pause.*) Willie. (*Pause.*) Do you think the earth has lost its atmosphere, Willie? (*Pause.*) Do you, Willie? (*Pause.*) You have no opinion? (*Pause.*) Well that is like you, you never had any opinion about anything. (*Pause.*) It's understandable. (*Pause.*) Most. (*Pause.*) The earthball. (*Pause.*) I sometimes wonder. (*Pause.*) Perhaps not quite all. (*Pause.*) There always remains something. (*Pause.*) Of everything. (*Pause.*) Some remains. (*Pause.*) If the mind were to go. (*Pause.*) It won't of course. (*Pause.*) Not quite. (*Pause.*) Not mine. (*Smile.*) Not now. (*Smile broader.*) No no. (*Smile off. Long pause.*) It might be the eternal cold. (*Pause.*) Everlasting perishing cold. (*Pause.*) Just chance, I take it, happy chance. (*Pause.*) Oh yes, great mercies, great mercies. (*Pause.*) And now? (*Long pause.*) The face. (*Pause.*) The nose. (*She squints down.*) I can see it . . . (*squinting down*) . . . the tip . . . the nostrils . . . breath of life . . . that curve you so admired . . . (*pouts*) . . . a hint of lip . . . (*pouts again*) . . . if I pout them out . . . (*sticks out tongue*) . . . the tongue of course . . . you so admired . . . if I stick it out . . . (*sticks it out again*) . . . the tip . . . (*eyes up*) . . . suspicion of brow . . . eyebrow . . . imagination possibly . . . (*eyes left*) . . . cheek . . . no . . . (*eyes right*) . . . no . . . (*distends cheeks*) . . . even if I puff them out . . . (*eyes left, distends cheeks again*) . . . no . . . no damask. (*Eyes front.*) That is all. (*Pause.*) The bag of course . . . (*eyes left*) . . . a little blurred perhaps . . . but the bag. (*Eyes front. Offhand.*) The earth of course and sky. (*Eyes right.*) The sunshade you gave me . . . that day . . . (*pause*) . . . that day . . . the lake . . . the reeds. (*Eyes front. Pause.*) What day? (*Pause.*) What reeds? (*Long pause. Eyes close. Bell rings loudly. Eyes open. Pause. Eyes right.*) Brownie of course. (*Pause.*) You remember Brownie, Willie, I can see him. (*Pause.*) Brownie is there, Willie, beside me. (*Pause. Loud.*) Brownie is there, Willie. (*Pause. Eyes front.*) That is all. (*Pause.*) What would I do without them? (*Pause.*) What would I do without them, when words fail? (*Pause.*) Gaze before me, with compressed lips. (*Long pause while she does so.*) I cannot. (*Pause.*) Ah yes, great mercies, great mercies. (*Long pause. Low.*) Sometimes I hear sounds. (*Listening expression. Normal voice.*) But not often. (*Pause.*) They are a boon, sounds are a boon, they help me . . . through the day. (*Smile.*) The old style! (*Smile off.*) Yes, those are happy days, when there are sounds. (*Pause.*) When I hear sounds. (*Pause.*) I used to think . . . (*pause*) . . . I say I used to think they were in my head. (*Smile.*) But no. (*Smile broader.*) No no. (*Smile off.*) That was just logic. (*Pause.*) Reason. (*Pause.*) I have not lost my reason. (*Pause.*) Not yet. (*Pause.*) Not all. (*Pause.*) Some remains. (*Pause.*) Sounds. (*Pause.*) Like little . . . sunderings, little falls . . . apart. (*Pause. Low.*) It's things, Willie. (*Pause. Normal voice.*) In the bag, outside the bag. (*Pause.*) Ah yes, things have their life, that is what I always say, *things* have a life. (*Pause.*) Take my looking-glass, it doesn't need

me. (*Pause.*) The bell. (*Pause.*) It hurts like a knife. (*Pause.*) A gouge. (*Pause.*) One cannot ignore it. (*Pause.*) How often . . . (*pause*) . . . I say how often I have said, Ignore it, Winnie, ignore the bell, pay no heed, just sleep and wake, sleep and wake, as you please, open and close the eyes, as you please, or in the way you find most helpful. (*Pause.*) Open and close the eyes, Winnie, open and close, always that. (*Pause.*) But no. (*Smile.*) Not now. (*Smile broader.*) No no. (*Smile off. Pause.*) What now? (*Pause.*) What now, Willie? (*Long pause.*) There is my story of course, when all else fails. (*Pause.*) A life. (*Smile.*) A long life. (*Smile off.*) Beginning in the womb, where life used to begin, Mildred has memories, she will have memories, of the womb, before she dies, the mother's womb. (*Pause.*) She is now four or five already and has recently been given a big waxen dolly. (*Pause.*) Fully clothed, complete outfit. (*Pause.*) Shoes, socks, undies, complete set, frilly frock, gloves. (*Pause.*) White mesh. (*Pause.*) A little white straw hat with a chin elastic. (*Pause.*) Pearly necklet. (*Pause.*) A little picture-book with legends in real print to go under her arm when she takes her walk. (*Pause.*) China blue eyes that open and shut. (*Pause. Narrative.*) The sun was not well up when Milly rose, descended the steep . . . (*pause*) . . . slipped on her nightgown, descended all alone the steep wooden stairs, backwards on all fours, though she had been forbidden to do so, entered the . . . (*pause*) . . . tiptoed down the silent passage, entered the nursery and began to undress Dolly. (*Pause.*) Crept under the table and began to undress Dolly. (*Pause.*) Scolding her . . . the while. (*Pause.*) Suddenly a mouse — (*Long pause.*) Gently, Winnie. (*Long pause. Calling.*) Willie! (*Pause. Louder.*) Willie! (*Pause. Mild reproach.*) I sometimes find your attitude a little strange, Willie, all this time, it is not like you to be wantonly cruel. (*Pause.*) Strange? (*Pause.*) No. (*Smile.*) Not here. (*Smile broader.*) Not now. (*Smile off.*) And yet . . . (*Suddenly anxious.*) I do hope nothing is amiss. (*Eyes right, loud.*) Is all well, dear? (*Pause. Eyes front. To herself.*) God grant he did not go in head foremost! (*Eyes right, loud.*) You're not stuck, Willie? (*Pause. Do.*) You're not jammed, Willie? (*Eyes front, distressed.*) Perhaps he is crying out for help all this time and I do not hear him! (*Pause.*) I do of course hear cries. (*Pause.*) But they are in my head surely. (*Pause.*) Is it possible that . . . (*Pause. With finality.*) No no, my head was always full of cries. (*Pause.*) Faint confused cries. (*Pause.*) They come. (*Pause.*) Then go. (*Pause.*) As on a wind. (*Pause.*) That is what I find so wonderful. (*Pause.*) They cease. (*Pause.*) Ah yes, great mercies, great mercies. (*Pause.*) The day is now well advanced. (*Smile. Smile off.*) And yet it is perhaps a little soon for my song. (*Pause.*) To sing too soon is fatal, I always find. (*Pause.*) On the other hand it is possible to leave it too late. (*Pause.*) The bell goes for sleep and one has not sung. (*Pause.*) The whole day has flown — (*smile, smile off*) — flown by, quite by, and no song of any class, kind or description. (*Pause.*) There is a problem here. (*Pause.*) One cannot sing . . . just like that, no. (*Pause.*) It bubbles up, for some unknown reason, the time is ill chosen, one chokes it back. (*Pause.*) One says, Now is the time, it is now or never, and one cannot. (*Pause.*) Simply cannot sing. (*Pause.*) Not a note. (*Pause.*) Another thing, Willie, while we are on this subject. (*Pause.*) The sadness after song. (*Pause.*) Have you run across that, Willie? (*Pause.*) In the course of your experience. (*Pause.*) No? (*Pause.*) Sadness after intimate sexual intercourse one is familiar with of course. (*Pause.*) You would concur with Aristotle there, Willie, I fancy. (*Pause.*) Yes, that one knows and is prepared to face. (*Pause.*) But after song . . . (*Pause.*) It does not last of course. (*Pause.*) That is what I find so wonderful. (*Pause.*) It wears away. (*Pause.*) What are those exquisite lines? (*Pause.*) Go forget me why should something o'er that something shadow fling . . . go forget me . . . why should sorrow . . . brightly smile . . . go forget me . . . never hear me . . . sweetly smile . . . brightly sing . . . (*Pause. With a sigh.*) One loses one's classics. (*Pause.*) Oh not all. (*Pause.*) A part. (*Pause.*) A part remains. (*Pause.*) That is what I find so wonderful, a part remains, of one's classics, to help one through the day. (*Pause.*) Oh yes, many mercies, many mercies. (*Pause.*) And now? (*Pause.*) And now, Willie? (*Long pause.*) I call to the eye of the mind . . . Mr. Shower — or Cooker. (*She closes her eyes. Bell rings loudly. She opens her eyes. Pause.*) Hand in hand, in the other hands bags. (*Pause.*) Getting on . . . in life. (*Pause.*) No longer young, not yet old. (*Pause.*) Standing there gaping at me. (*Pause.*) Can't have been a bad bosom, he says, in its day. (*Pause.*) Seen worse shoulders, he says, in my time. (*Pause.*) Does she feel her legs? he says. (*Pause.*) Is there any life in her legs? he says. (*Pause.*) Has she anything on underneath? he says. (*Pause.*) Ask her, he says, I'm shy. (*Pause.*) Ask her what? she says. (*Pause.*) Is there any life in her legs. (*Pause.*) Has she anything on underneath. (*Pause.*) Ask her yourself, she says. (*Pause. With sudden violence.*) Let go of me for Christ sake and drop! (*Pause. Do.*) Drop dead! (*Smile.*) But no. (*Smile broader.*) No no. (*Smile off.*) I watch them recede. (*Pause.*) Hand in hand — and the bags. (*Pause.*) Dim. (*Pause.*) Then gone. (*Pause.*) Last human kind — to stray this way. (*Pause.*) Up to date. (*Pause.*) And now? (*Pause. Low.*) Help. (*Pause. Do.*) Help, Willie. (*Pause. Do.*) No? (*Long pause. Narrative.*) Suddenly a mouse . . . (*Pause.*) Suddenly a mouse ran up her little thigh and Mildred, dropping Dolly in her fright, began to scream — (WINNIE *gives a sudden piercing scream*) — and screamed and screamed — (WINNIE *screams twice*) — screamed and screamed and screamed and screamed till all came running, in their night attire, papa, mamma, Bibby and . . . old Annie, to see what was the matter . . . (*pause*) . . . what on earth could possibly be the matter. (*Pause.*) Too late. (*Pause.*) Too late. (*Long pause. Just audible.*) Willie. (*Pause. Normal voice.*) Ah well, not long now, Winnie, can't be long now, until the bell for sleep. (*Pause.*) Then you may close your eyes, then you *must* close your eyes — and keep them closed. (*Pause.*) Why say that again? (*Pause.*) I used to think . . . (*pause*) . . . I say I used to think there was no difference between one fraction of a second and the next. (*Pause.*) I used to say . . . (*pause*) . . . I say I used to say, Winnie, you are changeless, there is never any difference between one fraction of a second and the next. (*Pause.*) Why bring that up again? (*Pause.*) There is so little one can bring up, one brings up all. (*Pause.*) All one can. (*Pause.*) My neck is hurting me. (*Pause. With sudden violence.*) My neck is hurting me! (*Pause.*) Ah that's better. (*With mild irritation.*) Everything within reason. (*Long pause.*) I can do no more. (*Pause.*) Say no more. (*Pause.*) But I must say more. (*Pause.*) Problem here. (*Pause.*) No, something must move, in the world, I can't any more. (*Pause.*) A zephyr. (*Pause.*) A breath. (*Pause.*) What are those immortal lines? (*Pause.*) It might be the eternal dark.

(*Pause.*) Black night without end. (*Pause.*) Just chance, I take it, happy chance. (*Pause.*) Oh yes, abounding mercies. (*Long pause.*) And now? (*Pause.*) And now, Willie? (*Long pause.*) That day. (*Pause.*) The pink fizz. (*Pause.*) The flute glasses. (*Pause.*) The last guest gone. (*Pause.*) The last bumper with the bodies nearly touching. (*Pause.*) The look. (*Long pause.*) What day? (*Long pause.*) What look? (*Long pause.*) I hear cries. (*Pause.*) Sing. (*Pause.*) Sing your old song, Winnie.

(*Long pause. Suddenly alert expression. Eyes switch right.* WILLIE's *head appears to her right round corner of mound. He is on all fours, dressed to kill — top hat, morning coat, striped trousers, etc., white gloves in hand. Very long bushy white Battle of Britain moustache. He halts, gazes front, smoothes moustache. He emerges completely from behind mound, turns to his left, halts, looks up at* WINNIE. *He advances on all fours towards centre, halts, turns head front, gazes front, strokes moustache, straightens tie, adjusts hat, advances a little further, halts, takes off hat and looks up at* WINNIE. *He is now not far from centre and within her field of vision. Unable to sustain effort of looking up he sinks head to ground.*)

WINNIE (*mondaine*): Well this is an unexpected pleasure! (*Pause.*) Reminds me of the day you came whining for my hand. (*Pause.*) I worship you, Winnie, be mine. (*He looks up.*) Life a mockery without Win. (*She goes off into a giggle.*) What a get up, you do look a sight! (*Giggles.*) Where are the flowers? (*Pause.*) That smile today. (WILLIE *sinks head.*) What's that on your neck, an anthrax? (*Pause.*) Want to watch that, Willie, before it gets a hold on you. (*Pause.*) Where were you all this time? (*Pause.*) What were you doing all this time? (*Pause.*) Changing? (*Pause.*) Did you not hear me screaming for you? (*Pause.*) Did you get stuck in your hole? (*Pause. He looks up.*) That's right, Willie, look at me. (*Pause.*) Feast your old eyes, Willie. (*Pause.*) Does anything remain? (*Pause.*) Any remains? (*Pause.*) No? (*Pause.*) I haven't been able to look after it, you know. (*He sinks his head.*) You are still recognizable, in a way. (*Pause.*) Are you thinking of coming to live this side now ... for a bit maybe? (*Pause.*) No? (*Pause.*) Just a brief call? (*Pause.*) Have

you gone deaf, Willie? (*Pause.*) Dumb? (*Pause.*) Oh I know you were never one to talk, I worship you Winnie be mine and then nothing from that day forth only titbits from Reynolds' News. (*Eyes front. Pause.*) Ah well, what matter, that's what I always say, it will have been a happy day, after all, another happy day. (*Pause.*) Not long now, Winnie. (*Pause.*) I hear cries. (*Pause.*) Do you ever hear cries, Willie? (*Pause.*) No? (*Eyes back on* WILLIE.) Willie. (*Pause.*) Look at me again, Willie. (*Pause.*) Once more, Willie. (*He looks up. Happily.*) Ah! (*Pause. Shocked.*) What ails you, Willie, I never saw such an expression! (*Pause.*) Put on your hat, dear, it's the sun, don't stand on ceremony, I won't mind. (*He drops hat and gloves and starts to crawl up mound towards her. Gleeful.*) Oh I say, this is terrific! (*He halts, clinging to mound with one hand, reaching up with the other.*) Come on, dear, put a bit of jizz into it, I'll cheer you on. (*Pause.*) Is it me you're after, Willie ... or is it something else? (*Pause.*) Do you want to touch my face ... again? (*Pause.*) Is it a kiss you're after, Willie ... or is it something else? (*Pause.*) There was a time when I could have given you a hand. (*Pause.*) And then a time before that again when I did give you a hand. (*Pause.*) You were always in dire need of a hand, Willie. (*He slithers back to foot of mound and lies with face to ground.*) Brrum! (*Pause. He rises to hands and knees, raises his face towards her.*) Have another go, Willie, I'll cheer you on. (*Pause.*) Don't look at me like that! (*Pause. Vehement.*) Don't look at me like that! (*Pause. Low.*) Have you gone off your head, Willie? (*Pause. Do.*) Out of your poor old wits, Willie?

(*Pause.*)

WILLIE (*just audible*): Win.

(*Pause.* WINNIE's *eyes front. Happy expression appears, grows.*)

WINNIE: Win! (*Pause.*) Oh this *is* a happy day, this will have been another happy day! (*Pause.*) After all. (*Pause.*) So far.

(*Pause. She hums tentatively beginning of song, then sings softly, musical-box tune.*)

    Though I say not
    What I may not
    Let you hear,

Yet the swaying
Dance is saying,
Love me dear!
Every touch of fingers
Tells me what I know,
Says for you,
It's true, it's true,
You love me so!

(*Pause. Happy expression off. She closes her
eyes. Bell rings loudly. She opens her eyes.
She smiles, gazing front. She turns her eyes,
smiling, to* WILLIE, *still on his hands and
knees looking up at her. Smile off. They
look at each other. Long pause.*)

CURTAIN

In a later section to this book, "Writing About Drama," we suggest (page 798) that you can often generate material for thought and thus for understanding by asking yourself questions, especially by asking the question "What is this doing?" Our afterwords to the plays in the book contain, in addition to background information, some critical comments, and most of these comments are the answers we arrived at after we asked ourselves that question.

For *Happy Days*, aside from the background information on the development of modern tragicomedy given in "The Nature of Drama" at the beginning of this book, especially on pages 14–19, we need perhaps only mention that Beckett wrote *Happy Days* in English, in 1960–61. (He sometimes writes his plays and novels in French, but in *Happy Days* beyond describing the backdrop as *pompier trompe-l'oeil* — "ordinary illusionistic" — French is implied only in Winnie's uncertainty whether hair is "them" or "it," for in French "hair" is plural, *les cheveux*.)

We want, then, in this Afterword, to ask questions — but we shall not provide answers. The Afterword represents some of the kind of thinking that lies behind a critical essay; we leave it to you to do the rest of the thinking that would turn these questions into developed thoughts that you might want to share with someone, perhaps in an essay.

SETTING AND PROPERTIES

1. In another of Beckett's plays, *Endgame*, two characters are in garbage cans. What would be gained or lost if Winnie were in a garbage can instead of in a mound?

2. Is there some dramatic significance or advantage to burying Winnie in a mound, rather than at ground level?

3. Why is Winnie's bag black, rather than, say, brightly colored or patterned?

4. What do you imagine is the audience's reaction when the parasol goes on fire? How does this reaction compare to Winnie's and Willie's reaction?

GESTURES AND MOVEMENTS

1. In the second act, when Winnie is buried up to the chin, gestures of course are fewer than in the first act. But what gestures or movements are there in Act II?

2. When at the end Willie crawls up the mound, and Winnie exclaims, "Don't look at me like that! Have you gone out of your head, Willie?" is

Willie expressing renewed love, or is he thinking of shooting her with the revolver? Is it relevant that Willie is said to be "dressed to kill"?

SOUND EFFECTS

1. The bell that wakes Winnie rings "piercingly." Why not, instead, a cheery cuckoo clock, or a musical sound? Winnie several times mentions "the bell for sleep," but we never hear it, even though it might easily have sounded at the end of Act I. *Should* we have heard it?

2. In the first act the bell rings twice, at the beginning. In the second act it rings several times, interrupting Winnie's monologues. Is there any meaning to this? Does it perhaps mean that time is moving faster — and what does *that* mean?

3. Why the waltz duet, "I love you so," from *The Merry Widow*, rather than some other song?

DIALOGUE

1. How does Beckett keep Winnie's talk from being dull jabbering? By what means does the dialogue hold our attention?

2. Take the first few lines, and imagine how each is spoken:

> "Another heavenly day."
> "For Jesus Christ sake Amen. . . . World without end Amen."
> "Begin, Winnie. . . . Begin your day, Winnie."

CHARACTER

1. The first director of *Happy Days*, Alan Schneider, said that Beckett originally conceived of Winnie's part as a male part, but changed his mind because pockets wouldn't work as well as a handbag. Docs the meaning of the present play depend to any degree on the fact that one character is male, the other female?

2. One critic (A. Alvarez, in *Samuel Beckett*) says that the play offers "a sour view of a cozy marriage . . . . [Beckett] finds [Winnie] and her manic defenses ludicrous at best." How profitable is this line of thinking?

STRUCTURE

It has been said of Beckett's most widely known play, *Waiting for Godot*, that in it nothing happens, twice. How appropriate is this as a summary of *Happy Days*?

MEANING

On page 742 Winnie tells how a man and a woman came by, and she reproduces their conversation:

> What's she doing? he says — What's the idea? he says — stuck up to her diddies in the bleeding ground — coarse fellow — What does it mean? he says — What's it meant to mean? — and so on — lot more stuff like that — usual drivel — Do you hear me? he says — I do, she says, God help me — What do you mean, he says, God help you? . . . And you, she says, what's the idea of you, she says, what are you meant to mean?

Is Beckett here telling us that the play has no meaning?

THE DUMB WAITER

Harold Pinter

Harold Pinter (b. 1930) was born in London, the son of a tailor. He attended the Royal Academy of Dramatic Art, and from 1949 until 1957 he acted in a touring repertory company throughout the British Isles. In 1957 he wrote his first play; later in the same year he wrote *The Dumb Waiter* — though it was not produced until 1960. Another play, *The Birthday Party*, was produced in 1958. He won critical acclaim finally with *The Caretaker* in 1960. Besides *The Homecoming* (1965), he has written radio and television scripts, and several films, most notably *The Servant* and *The Go-Between*. His as yet unproduced film adaptation of Marcel Proust's *Remembrance of Things Past* was published in 1977.

CHARACTERS

BEN
GUS

A scene from *The Dumb Waiter*. (Photograph: Joseph Abeles Studio.)

Scene: A basement room. Two beds, flat against the back wall. A serving hatch, closed, between the beds. A door to the kitchen and lavatory, left. A door to a passage, right.

BEN *is lying on a bed, left, reading a paper.* GUS *is sitting on a bed, right, tying his shoe-laces, with difficulty. Both are dressed in shirts, trousers and braces.*

Silence.

GUS *ties his laces, rises, yawns and begins to walk slowly to the door, left. He stops, looks down, and shakes his foot.*

BEN *lowers his paper and watches him.* GUS *kneels and unties his shoe-lace and slowly takes off the shoe. He looks inside it and brings out a flattened matchbox. He shakes it and examines it. Their eyes meet.* BEN *rattles his paper and reads.* GUS *puts the matchbox in his pocket and bends down to put on his shoe. He ties his lace, with difficulty.* BEN *lowers his paper and watches him.* GUS *walks to the door, left, stops, and shakes the other foot. He kneels, unties his shoe-lace, and slowly takes off the shoe. He looks inside it and brings out a flattened cigarette packet. He shakes it and examines it. Their eyes meet.* BEN *rattles his paper and reads.* GUS *puts the packet in his pocket, bends down, puts on his shoe and ties the lace.*

He wanders off, left.

BEN *slams the paper down on the bed and glares after him. He picks up the paper and lies on his back, reading.*

Silence.

A lavatory chain is pulled twice off, but the lavatory does not flush.

Silence.

GUS *re-enters, left, and halts at the door, scratching his head.* BEN *slams down the paper.*

BEN: Kaw!

(*He picks up the paper.*)

What about this? Listen to this!

(*He refers to the paper.*)

Reprinted by permission of Grove Press, Inc. Copyright © 1960 by Harold Pinter.

A man of eighty-seven wanted to cross the road. But there was a lot of traffic, see? He couldn't see how he was going to squeeze through. So he crawled under a lorry.

GUS: He what?

BEN: He crawled under a lorry. A stationary lorry.

BEN: No?

BEN: The lorry started and ran over him.

GUS: Go on!

BEN: That's what it says here.

GUS: Get away.

BEN: It's enough to make you want to puke, isn't it?

GUS: Who advised him to do a thing like that?

BEN: A man of eighty-seven crawling under a lorry!

GUS: It's unbelievable.

BEN: It's down here in black and white.

GUS: Incredible.

(*Silence.*

GUS *shakes his head and exits.* BEN *lies back and reads.*

The lavatory chain is pulled once off left, but the lavatory does not flush.

BEN *whistles at an item in the paper.*

GUS *re-enters.*)

I want to ask you something.

BEN: What are you doing out there?

GUS: Well, I was just —

BEN: What about the tea?

GUS: I'm just going to make it.

BEN: Well, go on, make it.

GUS: Yes, I will. (*He sits in a chair. Ruminatively.*) He's laid on some very nice crockery this time, I'll say that. It's sort of striped. There's a white stripe.

(BEN *reads.*)

It's very nice. I'll say that.

(BEN *turns the page.*)

You know, sort of round the cup. Round the rim. All the rest of it's black, you see. Then the saucer's black, except for right in the middle, where the cup goes, where it's white.

(BEN *reads.*)

Then the plates are the same, you see. Only they've got a black stripe — the plates — right across the middle. Yes, I'm quite taken with the crockery.

BEN (*still reading*): What do you want plates for? You're not going to eat.

GUS: I've brought a few biscuits.

BEN: Well, you'd better eat them quick.

GUS: I always bring a few biscuits. Or a pie. You know I can't drink tea without anything to eat.

BEN: Well, make the tea then, will you? Time's getting on.

(GUS *brings out the flattened cigarette packet and examines it.*)

GUS: You got any cigarettes? I think I've run out.

(*He throws the packet high up and leans forward to catch it.*)

I hope it won't be a long job, this one.

(*Aiming carefully, he flips the packet under his bed.*)

Oh, I wanted to ask you something.

BEN (*slamming his paper down*): Kaw!

GUS: What's that?

BEN: A child of eight killed a cat!

GUS: Get away.

BEN: It's a fact. What about that, eh? A child of eight killing a cat!

GUS: How did he do it?

BEN: It was a girl.

GUS: How did she do it?

BEN: She —

(*He picks up the paper and studies it.*)

It doesn't say.

GUS: Why not?

BEN: Wait a minute. It just says — Her brother, aged eleven, viewed the incident from the toolshed.

GUS: Go on!

BEN: That's bloody ridiculous.

(*Pause.*)

GUS: I bet he did it.

BEN: Who?

GUS: The brother.

BEN: I think you're right.

(*Pause.*)

(*Slamming down the paper.*) What about that, eh? A kid of eleven killing a cat and blaming it on his little sister of eight! It's enough to —

(*He breaks off in disgust and seizes the paper.* GUS *rises.*)

GUS: What time is he getting in touch?

(BEN *reads.*)

What time is he getting in touch?

BEN: What's the matter with you? It could be any time. Any time.

GUS (*moves to the foot of* BEN's *bed*): Well, I was going to ask you something.

BEN: What?

GUS: Have you noticed the time that tank takes to fill ?

BEN: What tank?

GUS: In the lavatory.

BEN: No. Does it?

GUS: Terrible.

BEN: Well, what about it?

GUS: What do you think's the matter with it?

BEN: Nothing.

GUS: Nothing?

BEN: It's got a deficient ballcock, that's all.

GUS: A deficient what?

BEN: Ballcock.

GUS: No? Really?

BEN: That's what I should say.

GUS: Go on! That didn't occur to me.

(GUS *wanders to his bed and presses the mattress.*)

I didn't have a very restful sleep today, did you? It's not much of a bed. I could have done with another blanket too. (*He catches sight of a picture on the wall.*) Hello, what's this? (*Peering at it.*) "The First Eleven." Cricketers. You seen this, Ben?

BEN (*reading*): What?

GUS: The first eleven.

BEN: What?

GUS: There's a photo here of the first eleven.

BEN: What first eleven?

GUS (*studying the photo*): It doesn't say.

BEN: What about that tea?

GUS: They all look a bit old to me.

(GUS *wanders downstage, looks out front, then all about the room.*)

I wouldn't like to live in this dump. I wouldn't mind if you had a window, you could see what it looked like outside.

BEN: What do you want a window for?

GUS: Well, I like to have a bit of a view, Ben. It whiles away the time.

(*He walks about the room.*)

I mean, you come into a place when it's still dark, you come into a room you've never seen before, you sleep all day, you do your job, and then you go away in the night again.

(*Pause.*)

I like to get a look at the scenery. You never get the chance in this job.

BEN: You get your holidays, don't you?

GUS: Only a fortnight.

BEN (*lowering the paper*): You kill me. Anyone would think you're working every day. How often do we do a job? Once a week? What are you complaining about?

GUS: Yes, but we've got to be on tap though, haven't we? You can't move out of the house in case a call comes.

BEN: You know what your trouble is?

GUS: What?

BEN: You haven't got any interests.

GUS: I've got interests.

BEN: What? Tell me one of your interests.

(*Pause.*)

GUS: I've got interests.

BEN: Look at me. What have I got?

GUS: I don't know. What?

BEN: I've got my woodwork. I've got my model boats. Have you ever seen me idle? I'm never idle. I know how to occupy my time, to its best advantage. Then when a call comes, I'm ready.

GUS: Don't you ever get a bit fed up?

BEN: Fed up? What with?

(*Silence.*

BEN *reads.* GUS *feels in the pocket of his jacket, which hangs on the bed.*)

GUS: You got any cigarettes? I've run out.

(*The lavatory flushes off left.*)

There she goes.

(GUS *sits on his bed.*)

No, I mean, I say the crockery's good. It is. It's very nice. But that's about all I can say for this place. It's worse than the last one. Remember that last place we were in? Last time, where was it? At least there was a wireless there. No, honest. He doesn't seem to bother much about our comfort these days.

BEN: When are you going to stop jabbering?

GUS: You'd get rheumatism in a place like this, if you stay long.

BEN: We're not staying long. Make the tea, will you? We'll be on the job in a minute.

(GUS *picks up a small bag by his bed and brings out a packet of tea. He examines it and looks up.*)

GUS: Eh, I've been meaning to ask you.

BEN: What the hell is it now?

GUS: Why did you stop the car this morning, in the middle of that road?

BEN (*lowering the paper*): I thought you were asleep.

GUS: I was, but I woke up when you stopped. You did stop, didn't you?

(*Pause.*)

In the middle of that road. It was still dark, don't you remember? I looked out. It was all misty. I thought perhaps you wanted to kip, but you were sitting up dead straight, like you were waiting for something.

BEN: I wasn't waiting for anything.

GUS: I must have fallen asleep again. What was all that about then? Why did you stop?

BEN (*picking up the paper*): We were too early.

GUS: Early? (*He rises.*) What do you mean? We got the call, didn't we, saying we were to start right away. We did. We shoved out on the dot. So how could we be too early?

BEN (*quietly*): Who took the call, me or you?

GUS: You.

BEN: We were too early.

GUS: Too early for what?

(*Pause.*)

You mean someone had to get out before we got in?

(*He examines the bedclothes.*)

I thought these sheets didn't look too bright. I thought they ponged a bit. I was too tired to notice when I got in this morning. Eh, that's taking a bit of a liberty, isn't it? I don't want to share my bed-sheets. I told you things were going down the drain. I mean, we've always had clean sheets laid on up till now. I've noticed it.

BEN: How do you know those sheets weren't clean?

GUS: What do you mean?

BEN: How do you know they weren't clean? You've spent the whole day in them, haven't you?

GUS: What, you mean it might be my pong? (*He sniffs sheets.*) Yes. (*He sits slowly on bed.*) It could be my pong, I suppose. It's difficult to tell. I don't really know what I pong like, that's the trouble.

BEN (*referring to the paper*): Kaw!

GUS: Eh, Ben.

BEN: Kaw!

GUS: Ben.

BEN: What?

GUS: What town are we in? I've forgotten.

BEN: I've told you. Birmingham.

GUS: Go on!

(*He looks with interest about the room.*)

That's in the Midlands. The second biggest city in Great Britain. I'd never have guessed.

(*He snaps his fingers.*)

Eh, it's Friday today, isn't it? It'll be Saturday tomorrow.

BEN: What about it?

GUS (*excited*): We could go and watch the Villa.

BEN: They're playing away.

GUS: No, are they? Caarr! What a pity.

BEN: Anyway, there's no time. We've got to get straight back.

GUS: Well, we have done in the past, haven't we? Stayed over and watched a game, haven't we? For a bit of relaxation.

BEN: Things have tightened up, mate. They've tightened up.

(GUS *chuckles to himself.*)

GUS: I saw the Villa get beat in a cup tie once. Who was it against now? White shirts. It was one-all at half-time. I'll never forget it. Their opponents won by a penalty. Talk about drama. Yes, it was a disputed penalty. Disputed. They got beat two-one, anyway, because of it. You were there yourself.

BEN: Not me.

GUS: Yes, you were there. Don't you remember that disputed penalty?

BEN: No.

GUS: He went down just inside the area. Then they said he was just acting. I didn't think the other bloke touched him myself. But the referee had the ball on the spot.

BEN: Didn't touch him! What are you talking about? He laid him out flat!

GUS: Not the Villa. The Villa don't play that sort of game.

BEN: Get out of it.

(*Pause.*)

GUS: Eh, that must have been here, in Birmingham.

BEN: What must?

GUS: The Villa. That must have been here.

BEN: They were playing away.

GUS: Because you know who the other team was? It was the Spurs. It was Tottenham Hotspur.

BEN: Well, what about it?

GUS: We've never done a job in Tottenham.

BEN: How do you know?

GUS: I'd remember Tottenham.

(BEN *turns on his bed to look at him.*)

BEN: Don't make me laugh, will you?

(BEN *turns back and reads.* GUS *yawns and speaks through his yawn.*)

GUS: When's he going to get in touch!

(*Pause.*)

Yes, I'd like to see another football match. I've always been an ardent football fan. Here, what about coming to see the Spurs tomorrow?

BEN (*tonelessly*): They're playing away.

GUS: Who are?

BEN: The Spurs.

GUS: Then they might be playing here.

BEN: Don't be silly.

GUS: If they're playing away they might be playing here. They might be playing the Villa.

BEN (*tonelessly*): But the Villa are playing away.

(*Pause. An envelope slides under the door, right,* GUS *sees it. He stands, looking at it.*)

GUS: Ben.

BEN: Away. They're all playing away.

GUS: Ben, look here.

BEN: What?
GUS: Look.

(BEN *turns his head and sees the envelope. He stands.*)

BEN: What's that?
GUS: I don't know.
BEN: Where did it come from?
GUS: Under the door.
BEN: Well, what is it?
GUS: I don't know.

(*They stare at it.*)

BEN: Pick it up.
GUS: What do you mean?
BEN: Pick it up!

(GUS *slowly moves towards it, bends and picks it up.*)

What is it?
GUS: An envelope.
BEN: Is there anything on it?
GUS: No.
BEN: Is it sealed?
GUS: Yes.
BEN: Open it.
GUS: What?
BEN: Open it!

(GUS *opens it and looks inside.*)

What's in it?

(GUS *empties twelve matches into his hand.*)

GUS: Matches.
BEN: Matches?
GUS: Yes.
BEN: Show it to me.

(GUS *passes the envelope.* BEN *examines it.*)

Nothing on it. Not a word.
GUS: That's funny, isn't it?
BEN: It came under the door?
GUS: Must have done.
BEN: Well, go on.
GUS: Go on where?
BEN: Open the door and see if you can catch anyone outside.
GUS: Who, me?
BEN: Go on!

(GUS *stares at him, puts the matches in his pocket, goes to his bed and brings a revolver*
from under the pillow. He goes to the door, opens it, looks out and shuts it.)

GUS: No one.

(*He replaces the revolver.*)

BEN: What did you see?
GUS: Nothing.
BEN: They must have been pretty quick.

(GUS *takes the matches from pocket and looks at them.*)

GUS: Well, they'll come in handy.
BEN: Yes.
GUS: Won't they?
BEN: Yes, you're always running out, aren't you?
GUS: All the time.
BEN: Well, they'll come in handy then.
GUS: Yes.
BEN: Won't they?
GUS: Yes, I could do with them. I could do with them too.
BEN: You could, eh?
GUS: Yes.
BEN: Why?
GUS: We haven't got any.
BEN: Well, you've got some now, haven't you?
GUS: I can light the kettle now.
BEN: Yes, you're always cadging matches. How many have you got there?
GUS: About a dozen.
BEN: Well, don't lose them. Red too. You don't even need a box.

(GUS *probes his ear with a match.*)

(*Slapping his hand*). Don't waste them! Go on, go and light it.
GUS: Eh?
BEN: Go and light it.
GUS: Light what?
BEN: The kettle.
GUS: You mean the gas.
BEN: Who does?
GUS: You do.
BEN (*his eyes narrowing*): What do you mean, I mean the gas?
GUS: Well, that's what you mean, don't you? The gas.
BEN (*powerfully*): If I say go and light the kettle I mean go and light the kettle.
GUS: How can you light a kettle?

BEN: It's a figure of speech! Light the kettle. It's a figure of speech!

GUS: I've never heard it.

BEN: Light the kettle! It's common usage!

GUS: I think you've got it wrong.

BEN (*menacing*): What do you mean?

GUS: They say put on the kettle.

BEN (*taut*): Who says?

(*They stare at each other, breathing hard.*)

(*Deliberately.*) I have never in all my life heard anyone say put on the kettle.

GUS: I bet my mother used to say it.

BEN: Your mother? When did you last see your mother?

GUS: I don't know, about —

BEN: Well, what are you talking about your mother for?

(*They stare.*)

Gus, I'm not trying to be unreasonable. I'm just trying to point out something to you.

GUS: Yes, but —

BEN: Who's the senior partner here, me or you?

GUS: You.

BEN: I'm only looking after your interests, Gus. You've got to learn, mate.

GUS: Yes, but I've never heard —

BEN (*vehemently*): Nobody says light the gas! What does the gas light?

GUS: What does the gas — ?

BEN (*grabbing him with two hands by the throat, at arm's length*): THE KETTLE, YOU FOOL!

(*GUS takes the hands from his throat.*)

GUS: All right, all right.

(*Pause.*)

BEN: Well, what are you waiting for?

GUS: I want to see if they light.

BEN: What?

GUS: The matches.

(*He takes out the flattened box and tries to strike.*)

No.

(*He throws the box under the bed.
BEN stares at him.
GUS raises his foot.*)

Shall I try it on here?

(*BEN stares. GUS strikes a match on his shoe. It lights.*)

Here we are.

BEN (*wearily*): Put on the bloody kettle, for Christ's sake.

(*BEN goes to his bed, but, realising what he has said, stops and half turns. They look at each other. GUS slowly exits, left. BEN slams his paper down on the bed and sits on it, head in hands.*)

GUS (*entering*): It's going.

BEN: What?

GUS: The stove.

(*GUS goes to his bed and sits.*)

I wonder who it'll be tonight.

(*Silence.*)

Eh, I've been wanting to ask you something.

BEN (*putting his legs on the bed*): Oh, for Christ's sake.

GUS: No. I was going to ask you something.

(*He rises and sits on BEN's bed.*)

BEN: What are you sitting on my bed for?

(*GUS sits.*)

What's the matter with you? You're always asking me questions. What's the matter with you?

GUS: Nothing.

BEN: You never used to ask me so many damn questions. What's come over you?

GUS: No, I was just wondering.

BEN: Stop wondering. You've got a job to do. Why don't you just do it and shut up?

GUS: That's what I was wondering about.

BEN: What?

GUS: The job.

BEN: What job?

GUS (*tentatively*): I thought perhaps you might know something.

(*BEN looks at him.*)

I thought perhaps you — I mean — have you got any idea — who it's going to be tonight?

BEN: Who what's going to be?

(*They look at each other.*)

GUS (*at length*): Who it's going to be.

(*Silence.*)

BEN: Are you feeling all right?
GUS: Sure.
BEN: Go and make the tea.
GUS: Yes, sure.

(GUS *exits, left,* BEN *looks after him. He then takes his revolver from under the pillow and checks it for ammunition.* GUS *re-enters.*)

The gas has gone out.
BEN: Well, what about it?
GUS: There's a meter.
BEN: I haven't got any money.
GUS: Nor have I.
BEN: You'll have to wait.
GUS: What for?
BEN: For Wilson.
GUS: He might not come. He might just send a message. He doesn't always come.
BEN: Well, you'll have to do without it, won't you?
GUS: Blimey.
BEN: You'll have a cup of tea afterwards. What's the matter with you?
GUS: I like to have one before.

(BEN *holds the revolver up to the light and polishes it.*)

BEN: You'd better get ready anyway.
GUS: Well, I don't know, that's a bit much, you know, for my money.

(*He picks up a packet of tea from the bed and throws it into the bag.*)

I hope he's got a shilling, anyway, if he comes. He's entitled to have. After all, it's his place, he could have seen there was enough gas for a cup of tea.
BEN: What do you mean, it's his place?
GUS: Well, isn't it?
BEN: He's probably only rented it. It doesn't have to be his place.
GUS: I know it's his place. I bet the whole house is. He's not even laying on any gas now either.

(GUS *sits on his bed.*)

It's his place all right. Look at all the other places. You go to this address, there's a key there, there's a teapot, there's never a soul in sight — (*He pauses.*) Eh, nobody ever hears a thing, have you ever thought of that? We never get any complaints, do we, too much noise or anything like that? You never see a soul, do you? — except the bloke who comes. You ever noticed that? I wonder if the walls are sound-proof. (*He touches the wall above his head.*) Can't tell. All you do is wait, eh? Half the time he doesn't even bother to put in an appearance, Wilson.
BEN: Why should he? He's a busy man.
GUS (*thoughtfully*): I find him hard to talk to, Wilson. Do you know that, Ben?
BEN: Scrub round it, will you?

(*Pause.*)

GUS: There are a number of things I want to ask him. But I can never get round to it, when I see him.

(*Pause.*)

I've been thinking about the last one.
BEN: What last one?
GUS: That girl.

(BEN *grabs the paper, which he reads.*)

(*Rising, looking down at* BEN.) How many times have you read that paper?

(BEN *slams the paper down and rises.*)

BEN (*angrily*): What do you mean?
GUS: I was just wondering how many times you'd —
BEN: What are you doing, criticising me?
GUS: No, I was just —
BEN: You'll get a swipe round your earhole if you don't watch your step.
GUS: Now look here, Ben —
BEN: I'm not looking anywhere! (*He addresses the room.*) How many times have I — ! A bloody liberty!
GUS: I didn't mean that.
BEN: You just get on with it, mate. Get on with, that's all.

(BEN *gets back on the bed.*)

GUS: I was just thinking about that girl, that's all.

(GUS *sits on his bed.*)

She wasn't much to look at, I know, but still. It was a mess though, wasn't it? What a mess. Honest, I can't remember a mess like that one. They don't seem to hold together like men, women. A looser texture, like. Didn't she spread, eh? She didn't half spread. Kaw! But I've been meaning to ask you.

(BEN *sits up and clenches his eyes.*)

Who clears up after we've gone? I'm curious about that. Who does the clearing up? Maybe they don't clear up. Maybe they just leave them there, eh? What do you think? How many jobs have we done? Blimey, I can't count them. What if they never clear anything up after we've gone.

BEN (*pityingly*): You mutt. Do you think we're the only branch of this organisation? Have a bit of common. They got departments for everything.

GUS: What cleaners and all?

BEN: You birk!

GUS: No, it was that girl made me start to think —

(*There is a loud clatter and racket in the bulge of wall between the beds, of something descending. They grab their revolvers, jump up and face the wall. The noise comes to a stop. Silence. They look at each other.* BEN *gestures sharply towards the wall.* GUS *approaches the wall slowly. He bangs it with his revolver. It is hollow.* BEN *moves to the head of his bed, his revolver cocked.* GUS *puts his revolver on his bed and pats along the bottom of the centre panel. He finds a rim. He lifts the panel. Disclosed is a serving hatch, a "dumb waiter." A wide box is held by pulleys.* GUS *peers into the box. He brings out a piece of paper.*)

BEN: What is it?

GUS: You have a look at it.

BEN: Read it.

GUS (*reading*): Two braised steak and chips. Two sago puddings. Two teas without sugar.

BEN: Let me see that. (*He takes the paper.*)

GUS (*to himself*): Two teas without sugar.

BEN: Mmnn.

GUS: What do you think of that?

BEN: Well —

(*The box goes up.* BEN *levels his revolver.*)

GUS: Give us a chance! They're in a hurry, aren't they?

(BEN *re-reads the note.* GUS *looks over his shoulder.*)

That's a bit — that's a bit funny, isn't it?

BEN (*quickly*): No. It's not funny. It probably used to be a café here, that's all. Upstairs. These places change hands very quickly.

GUS: A café?

BEN: Yes.

GUS: What, you mean this was the kitchen, down here?

BEN: Yes, they change hands overnight, these places. Go into liquidation. The people who run it, you know, they don't find it a going concern, they move out.

GUS: You mean the people who ran this place didn't find it a going concern and moved out?

BEN: Sure.

GUS: WELL, WHO'S GOT IT NOW?

(*Silence.*)

BEN: What do you mean, who's got it now?

GUS: Who's got it now? If they moved out, who moved in?

BEN: Well, that all depends —

(*The box descends with a clatter and bang.* BEN *levels his revolver.* GUS *goes to the box and brings out a piece of paper.*)

GUS (*reading*): Soup of the day. Liver and onions. Jam tart.

(*A pause.* GUS *looks at* BEN. BEN *takes the note and reads it. He walks slowly to the hatch.* GUS *follows.* BEN *looks into the hatch but not up it.* GUS *puts his hand on* BEN'S *shoulder.* BEN *throws it off.* GUS *puts his finger to his mouth. He leans on the hatch and swiftly looks up it.* BEN *flings him away in alarm.* BEN *looks at the note. He throws his revolver on the bed and speaks with decision.*)

BEN: We'd better send something up.

GUS: Eh?

BEN: We'd better send something up.

GUS: Oh! Yes. Yes. Maybe you're right.

(*They are both relieved at the decision.*)

BEN (*purposefully*): Quick! What have you got in that bag?

GUS: Not much.

(GUS *goes to the hatch and shouts up it.*)

Wait a minute!

BEN: Don't do that!

(GUS *examines the contents of the bag and brings them out, one by one.*)

GUS: Biscuits. A bar of chocolate. Half a pint of milk.
BEN: That all?
GUS: Packet of tea.
BEN: Good.
GUS: We can't send the tea. That's all the tea we've got.
BEN: Well, there's no gas. You can't do anything with it, can you?
GUS: Maybe they can send us down a bob.
BEN: What else is there?
GUS (*reaching into bag*): One Eccles cake.
BEN: One Eccles cake?
GUS: Yes.
BEN: You never told me you had an Eccles cake.
GUS: Didn't I?
BEN: Why only one? Didn't you bring one for me?
GUS: I didn't think you'd be keen.
BEN: Well, you can't send up one Eccles cake, anyway.
GUS: Why not?
BEN: Fetch one of those plates.
GUS: All right.

(GUS *goes towards the door, left, and stops.*)

Do you mean I can keep the Eccles cake then?
BEN: Keep it?
GUS: Well, they don't know we've got it, do they?
BEN: That's not the point.
GUS: Can't I keep it?
BEN: No, you can't. Get the plate.

(GUS *exits, left.* BEN *looks in the bag. He brings out a packet of crisps. Enter* GUS *with a plate.*)

(*Accusingly, holding up the crisps.*) Where did these come from?
GUS: What?
BEN: Where did these crisps come from?
GUS: Where did you find them?
BEN (*hitting him on the shoulder*): You're playing a dirty game, my lad!
GUS: I only eat those with beer!
BEN: Well, where were you going to get the beer?
GUS: I was saving them till I did.
BEN: I'll remember this. Put everything on the plate.

(*They pile everything on to the plate. The box goes up without the plate.*)

Wait a minute!

(*They stand.*)

GUS: It's gone up.
BEN: It's all your stupid fault, playing about!
GUS: What do we do now?
BEN: We'll have to wait till it comes down.

(BEN *puts the plate on the bed, puts on his shoulder holster, and starts to put on his tie.*)

You'd better get ready.

(GUS *goes to his bed, puts on his tie, and starts to fix his holster.*)

GUS: Hey, Ben.
BEN: What?
GUS: What's going on here?

(*Pause.*)

BEN: What do you mean?
GUS: How can this be a café?
BEN: It used to be a café.
GUS: Have you seen the gas stove?
BEN: What about it?
GUS: It's only got three rings.
BEN: So what?
GUS: Well, you couldn't cook much on three rings, not for a busy place like this.
BEN (*irritably*): That's why the service is slow!

(BEN *puts on his waistcoat.*)

GUS: Yes, but what happens when we're not here? What do they do then? All these menus coming down and nothing going up. It might have been going on like this for years.

(BEN *brushes his jacket.*)

What happens when we go?

(BEN *puts on his jacket.*)

They can't do much business.

(*The box descends. They turn about.* GUS *goes to the hatch and brings out a note.*)

GUS (*reading*): Macaroni Pastitsio. Ormitha Macarounada.
BEN: What was that?

GUS: Macaroni Pastitsio. Ormitha Macarounada.

BEN: Greek dishes.

GUS: No.

BEN: That's right.

GUS: That's pretty high class.

BEN: Quick before it goes up.

(GUS *puts the plate in the box.*)

GUS (*calling up the hatch*): Three McVitie and Price! One Lyons Red Label! One Smith's Crisps! One Eccles cake! One Fruit and Nut!

BEN: Cadbury's.

GUS (*up the hatch*): Cadbury's!

BEN (*handing the milk*): One bottle of milk.

GUS (*up the hatch*): One bottle of milk! Half a pint! (*He looks at the label.*) Express Dairy! (*He puts the bottle in the box.*)

(*The box goes up.*)

Just did it.

BEN: You shouldn't shout like that.

GUS: Why not?

BEN: It isn't done.

(BEN *goes to his bed.*)

Well, that should be all right, anyway, for the time being.

GUS: You think so, eh?

BEN: Get dressed, will you? It'll be any minute now.

(GUS *puts on his waistcoat.* BEN *lies down and looks up at the ceiling.*)

GUS: This is some place. No tea and no biscuits.

BEN: Eating makes you lazy, mate. You're getting lazy, you know that? You don't want to get slack on your job.

GUS: Who me?

BEN: Slack, mate, slack.

GUS: Who me? Slack?

BEN: Have you checked your gun? You haven't even checked your gun. It looks disgraceful, anyway. Why don't you ever polish it?

(GUS *rubs his revolver on the sheet.* BEN *takes out a pocket mirror and straightens his tie.*)

GUS: I wonder where the cook is. They must have had a few, to cope with that. Maybe they had a few more gas stoves. Eh! Maybe there's another kitchen along the passage.

BEN: Of course there is! Do you know what it takes to make an Ormitha Macarounada?

GUS: No, what?

BEN: An Ormitha — ! Buck your ideas up, will you?

GUS: Takes a few cooks, eh?

(GUS *puts his revolver in his holster.*)

The sooner we're out of this place the better.

(*He puts on his jacket.*)

Why doesn't he get in touch? I feel like I've been here years. (*He takes his revolver out of its holster to check the ammunition.*) We've never let him down though, have we? We've never let him down. I was thinking only the other day, Ben. We're reliable, aren't we?

(*He puts his revolver back in its holster.*)

Still, I'll be glad when it's over tonight.

(*He brushes his jacket.*)

I hope the bloke's not going to get excited tonight, or anything. I'm feeling a bit off. I've got a splitting headache.

(*Silence.*
The box descends. BEN *jumps up.*
GUS *collects the note.*)

(*Reading.*) One Bamboo Shoots, Water Chestnuts and Chicken. One Char Siu and Beansprouts.

BEN: Beansprouts?

GUS: Yes.

BEN: Blimey.

GUS: I wouldn't know where to begin.

(*He looks back at the box. The packet of tea is inside it. He picks it up.*)

They've sent back the tea.

BEN (*anxious*): What'd they do that for?

GUS: Maybe it isn't tea-time.

(*The box goes up. Silence.*)

BEN (*throwing the tea on the bed, and speaking urgently*): Look here. We'd better tell them.

GUS: Tell them what?

BEN: That we can't do it, we haven't got it.

GUS: All right then.

BEN: Lend us your pencil. We'll write a note.

(GUS, *turning for a pencil, suddenly discovers the speaking-tube, which hangs on the right wall of the hatch facing his bed.*)

GUS: What's this?
BEN: What?
GUS: This.
BEN (*examining it*): This? It's a speaking-tube.
GUS: How long has that been there?
BEN: Just the job. We should have used it before, instead of shouting up there.
GUS: Funny I never noticed it before.
BEN: Well, come on.
GUS: What do you do?
BEN: See that? That's a whistle.
GUS: What, this?
BEN: Yes, take it out. Pull it out.

(GUS *does so.*)

That's it.
GUS: What do we do now?
BEN: Blow into it.
GUS: Blow?
BEN: It whistles up there if you blow. Then they know you want to speak. Blow.

(GUS *blows. Silence.*)

GUS (*tube at mouth*): I can't hear a thing.
BEN: Now you speak! Speak into it!

(GUS *looks at* BEN, *then speaks into the tube.*)

GUS: The larder's bare!
BEN: Give me that!

(*He grabs the tube and puts it to his mouth.*)

(*Speaking with great deference.*) Good evening. I'm sorry to — bother you, but we just thought we'd better let you know that we haven't got anything left. We sent up all we had. There's no more food down here.

(*He brings the tube slowly to his ear.*)

What?

(*To mouth.*)

What?

(*To ear. He listens. To mouth.*)

No, all we had we sent up.

(*To ear. He listens. To mouth.*)

Oh, I'm very sorry to hear that.

(*To ear. He listens. To* GUS.)

The Eccles cake was stale.

(*He listens. To* GUS.)

The chocolate was melted.

(*He listens. To* GUS.)

The milk was sour.

GUS: What about the crisps?
BEN (*listening*): The biscuits were mouldy.

(*He glares at* GUS. *Tube to mouth.*)

Well, we're very sorry about that.

(*Tube to ear.*)

What?

(*To mouth.*)

What?

(*To ear.*)

Yes. Yes.

(*To mouth.*)

Yes certainly. Certainly. Right away.

(*To ear. The voice has ceased. He hangs up the tube.*)

(*Excitedly.*) Did you hear that?
GUS: What?
BEN: You know what he said? Light the kettle! Not put on the kettle! Not light the gas! But light the kettle!
GUS: How can we light the kettle?
BEN: What do you mean?
GUS: There's no gas.
BEN (*clapping hand to head*): Now what do we do?
GUS: What did he want us to light the kettle for?
BEN: For tea. He wanted a cup of tea.
GUS: *He* wanted a cup of tea! What about me? I've been wanting a cup of tea all night!
BEN (*despairingly*): What do we do now?
GUS: What are we supposed to drink?

(BEN *sits on his bed, staring.*)

What about us?

(BEN *sits.*)

I'm thirsty too. I'm starving. And he wants a cup of tea. That beats the band, that does.

(BEN *lets his head sink on to his chest.*)

I could do with a bit of sustenance myself. What about you? You look as if you could do with something too.

(GUS *sits on his bed.*)

We send him up all we've got and he's not satisfied. No, honest, it's enough to make the cat laugh. Why did you send him up all that stuff? (*Thoughtfully.*) Why did I send it up?

(*Pause.*)

Who knows what he's got upstairs? He's probably got a salad bowl. They must have something up there. They won't get much from down here. You notice they didn't ask for any salads? They've probably got a salad bowl up there. Cold meat, radishes, cucumbers. Watercress. Roll mops.

(*Pause.*)

Hardboiled eggs.

(*Pause.*)

The lot. They've probably got a crate of beer too. Probably eating my crisps with a pint of beer now. Didn't have anything to say about those crisps, did he? They do all right, don't worry about that. You don't think they're just going to sit there and wait for stuff to come up from down here, do you? That'll get them nowhere.

(*Pause.*)

They do all right.

(*Pause.*)

And he wants a cup of tea.

(*Pause.*)

That's past a joke, in my opinion.

(*He looks over at* BEN, *rises, and goes to him.*)

What's the matter with you? You don't look too bright. I feel like an Alka-Seltzer myself.

(BEN *sits up.*)

BEN (*in a low voice*): Time's getting on.
GUS: I know. I don't like doing a job on an empty stomach.
BEN (*wearily*): Be quiet a minute. Let me give you your instructions.
GUS: What for? We always do it the same way, don't we?
BEN: Let me give you your instructions.

(GUS *sighs and sits next to* BEN *on the bed. The instructions are stated and repeated automatically.*)

When we get the call, you go over and stand behind the door.
GUS: Stand behind the door.
BEN: If there's a knock on the door you don't answer it.
GUS: If there's a knock on the door I don't answer it.
BEN: But there won't be a knock on the door.
GUS: So I won't answer it.
BEN: When the bloke comes in —
GUS: When the bloke comes in —
BEN: Shut the door behind him.
GUS: Shut the door behind him.
BEN: Without divulging your presence.
GUS: Without divulging my presence.
BEN: He'll see me and come towards me.
GUS: He'll see you and come towards you.
BEN: He won't see you.
GUS (*absently*): Eh?
BEN: He won't see you.
GUS: He won't see me.
BEN: But he'll see me.
GUS: He'll see you.
BEN: He won't know you're there.
GUS: He won't know you're there.
BEN: He won't know *you're* there.
GUS: He won't know I'm there.
BEN: I take out my gun.
GUS: You take out your gun.
BEN: He stops in his tracks.
GUS: He stops in his tracks.
BEN: If he turns round —
GUS: If he turns round —
BEN: You're there.
GUS: I'm here.

(BEN *frowns and presses his forehead.*)

You've missed something out.
BEN: I know. What?

GUS: I haven't taken my gun out, according to you.

BEN: You take your gun out —

GUS: After I've closed the door.

BEN: After you've closed the door.

GUS: You've never missed that out before, you know that?

BEN: When he sees you behind him —

GUS: Me behind him —

BEN: And me in front of him —

GUS: And you in front of him —

BEN: He'll feel uncertain —

GUS: Uneasy.

BEN: He won't know what to do.

GUS: So what will he do?

BEN: He'll look at me and he'll look at you.

GUS: We won't say a word.

BEN: We'll look at him.

GUS: He won't say a word.

BEN: He'll look at us.

GUS: And we'll look at him.

BEN: Nobody says a word.

(*Pause.*)

GUS: What do we do if it's a girl?

BEN: We do the same.

GUS: Exactly the same?

BEN: Exactly.

(*Pause.*)

GUS: We don't do anything different?

BEN: We do exactly the same.

GUS: Oh.

(GUS *rises, and shivers.*)

Excuse me.

(*He exits through the door on the left.* BEN *remains sitting on the bed, still.*

The lavatory chain is pulled once off left, but the lavatory does not flush.

Silence.

GUS *re-enters and stops inside the door, deep in thought. He looks at* BEN, *then walks slowly across to his own bed. He is troubled. He stands, thinking. He turns and looks at* BEN. *He moves a few paces towards him.*)

(*Slowly in a low, tense voice.*) Why did he send us matches if he knew there was no gas?

(*Silence.*

BEN *stares in front of him.* GUS *crosses to the left side of* BEN, *to the foot of his bed, to get to his other ear.*)

BEN: Why did he send us matches if he knew there was no gas?

(BEN *looks up.*)

Why did he do that?

BEN: Who?

GUS: Who sent us those matches?

BEN: What are you talking about?

(GUS *stares down at him.*)

GUS (*thickly*): Who is it upstairs?

BEN (*nervously*): What's one thing to do with another?

GUS: Who is it, though?

BEN: What's one thing to do with another?

(BEN *fumbles for his paper on the bed.*)

GUS: I asked you a question.

BEN: Enough!

GUS (*with growing agitation*): I asked you before. Who moved in? I asked you. You said the people who had it before moved out. Well, who moved in?

BEN (*hunched*): Shut up.

GUS: I told you, didn't I?

BEN (*standing*): Shut up!

GUS (*feverishly*): I told you before who owned this place, didn't I? I told you.

(BEN *hits him viciously on the shoulder.*)

I told you who ran this place, didn't I?

(BEN *hits him viciously on the shoulder.*)

(*Violently.*) Well, what's he playing all these games for? That's what I want to know. What's he doing it for?

BEN: What games?

GUS (*passionately, advancing*): What's he doing it for? We've been through our tests, haven't we? We got right through our tests, years ago, didn't we? We took them together, don't you remember, didn't we? We've proved ourselves before now, haven't we? We've always done our job. What's he doing all this for? What's the idea? What's he playing these games for?

(*The box in the shaft comes down behind them. The noise is this time accompanied by a shrill whistle, as it falls.* GUS *rushes to the hatch and seizes the note.*)

(*Reading.*) Scampi!

(*He crumples the note, picks up the tube, takes out the whistle, blows and speaks.*)

WE'VE GOT NOTHING LEFT! NOTHING! DO YOU UNDERSTAND?

(BEN *seizes the tube and flings* GUS *away. He follows* GUS *and slaps him hard, back-handed, across the chest.*)

BEN: Stop it! You maniac!
GUS: But you heard!

BEN (*savagely*): That's enough! I'm warning you!

(*Silence.*
BEN *hangs the tube. He goes to his bed and lies down. He picks up his paper and reads.*
Silence.
The box goes up.
They turn quickly, their eyes meet. BEN *turns to his paper.*
Slowly GUS *goes back to his bed, and sits.*
Silence.
The hatch falls back into place.
They turn quickly, their eyes meet. BEN *turns back to his paper.*
Silence.
BEN *throws his paper down.*)

BEN: Kaw!

(*He picks up the paper and looks at it.*)

Listen to this!

(*Pause.*)

What about that, eh?

(*Pause.*)

Kaw!

(*Pause.*)

Have you ever heard such a thing?
GUS (*dully*): Go on!
BEN: It's true.
GUS: Get away.
BEN: It's down here in black and white.
GUS (*very low*): Is that a fact?
BEN: Can you imagine it.
GUS: It's unbelievable.
BEN: It's enough to make you want to puke, isn't it?

GUS (*almost inaudible*): Incredible.

(BEN *shakes his head. He puts the paper down and rises. He fixes the revolver in his holster.*
GUS *stands up. He goes towards the door on the left.*)

BEN: Where are you going?
GUS: I'm going to have a glass of water.

(*He exits.* BEN *brushes dust off his clothes and shoes. The whistle in the speaking-tube blows. He goes to it, takes the whistle out and puts the tube to his ear. He listens. He puts it to his mouth.*)

BEN: Yes.

(*To ear. He listens. To mouth.*)

Straight away. Right.

(*To ear. He listens. To mouth.*)

Sure we're ready.

(*To ear. He listens. To mouth.*)

Understood. Repeat. He has arrived and will be coming in straight away. The normal method to be employed. Understood.

(*To ear. He listens. To mouth.*)

Sure we're ready.

(*To ear. He listens. To mouth.*)

Right.

(*He hangs the tube up.*)

Gus!

(*He takes out a comb and combs his hair, adjusts his jacket to diminish the bulge of the revolver. The lavatory flushes off left.* BEN *goes quickly to the door, left.*)

Gus!

(*The door right opens sharply.* BEN *turns, his revolver levelled at the door.*
GUS *stumbles in.*
He is stripped of his jacket, waistcoat, tie, holster and revolver.
He stops, body stooping, his arms at his sides.
He raises his head and looks at BEN.
A long silence.
They stare at each other.)

CURTAIN

I've never started a play from any kind of abstract idea or theory and never envisaged my own characters as messengers of death, doom, heaven or the milky way or, in other words, as allegorical representations of any particular force, whatever that may mean. When a character cannot be comfortably defined or understood in terms of the familiar, the tendency is to perch him on a symbolic shelf, out of harm's way. Once there, he can be talked about but not lived with.*

Probably most or even all of the dramatists represented in this book could say the same thing: it is impossible to believe that (for example) Shakespeare began *King Lear* with "any kind of abstract idea" — in fact, he must have begun it with reading or seeing the old play *King Leir*, and felt that he could do it much better, make the characters breathe and make the story move us. And probably every dramatist in this book would be distressed if, because we could not find a character familiar, we turned the character into a tidy symbol and talked about it but did not live with it in all its unfamiliarity.

Still, when we read or see a good play we inevitably feel that it has some meaning, that it adds up to something. That's what makes any work of art different from, say, a story in a newspaper. If we read on page 1 of *The Daily Record* that a gunman killed another, we don't bother to think of the meaning; the story is in the paper simply because it happened, not because the happening has any significance. But a work of art has not only the concrete immediacy of experience — the sort of thing that newspapers and history books are full of; it has something of the distillation or significance of experience that we find (usually in a highly abstract form) in philosophy.

The meaning of a good play, however, is not usually to be found in a philosophical or preachy speech; rather, it is diffused throughout the play, from the first line to the last, or, rather, from our first view of the stage to the last. In "The Language of Drama" (pages 23–28) we call attention to the meaning of Ibsen's set in *A Doll's House*, and to the meanings of the costumes and gestures, as well as of the dialogue and even of the sound of the door slamming at the end of the play. If we were similarly analyzing *The Dumb Waiter* we would, for example, call attention to the fact that near the end of the play, when he is probably about to be murdered by his partner Ben, Gus "is stripped of his jacket, waistcoat, tie, holster, and revolver." Here, as when Nora in *A Doll's House* takes off her fancy costume, or when the mad King Lear tears off his clothing, we see the stripping away of those accoutrements that conceal humanity's essential vulnerability.

We might consider, too, the characterization in the play (What sort of people are Gus and Ben? Why is it that we learn almost nothing of their background, nothing about why they do what they do?), or we might consider the setting (What is implied by "a basement room"?), but instead we shall briefly glance at the structure of the play. The germ of the play —

*Harold Pinter, "Writing for the Theatre," in *The New British Drama*, ed. Henry Popkin (New York: Grove, 1964), pp. 575–76.

two hit-men wait to do a job — probably owes something to Ernest Heming-way's short story "The Killers," in which two hired assassins engage in flat small talk while waiting for their victim; but it owes something also to gang-ster films and suspense films. The gangster film, however, usually has a plot, with what Aristotle calls a beginning, a middle, and an end: it begins with a situation that is fairly stable, fairly understandable — for instance, a young hood joins an organization of gangsters; the film proceeds to a middle — the consequences of the beginning and the causes of the end (the middle of the gangster film may show the youngster pushing his way to the top of the mob); and it concludes with the end, which is caused by the middle and which does not seem to lead to anything further (having rubbed out the apparent opposition, the new boss is now himself rubbed out by a younger contender, or by the police, or — as in *The Godfather, Part II* — the central figure finds that his success has brought him nothing, for he cannot share it with his family). A suspense film, too, usually has an easily perceptible structure, for example, the scary hunt for the criminals, the forces of evil waiting be-hind closed doors for the good guy who pursues them, mysterious messages, and finally a resolution in which (usually) virtue is rewarded.

In *The Dumb Waiter* we get suspense and mystery (the sudden clatter of the previously unnoticed dumb waiter, the envelope with matches that is slipped under the door, the erratic flushing of the toilet, the whistling of the speaking-tube, and, of course, the mysterious orders from above), but we are not given the satisfaction of witnessing a story unfold episode by episode. Gus and Ben are waiting for their victim, and near the end of the play, when Gus goes to the toilet, Ben learns that the victim will be "coming in straight away." He levels his revolver at the door — and Gus walks in. The two stare at each other, there is "a long silence," and the play ends. Anton Chekhov, talking about the importance of foreshadowing and of inevitability in drama, said that if there is a gun on the wall in the first act, it must go off in the last act — but here no gun goes off. Has Pinter, then, merely written an hour's worth of small talk with no shape to it? Not quite. First, although at the start of the drama we see two men waiting, we do not clearly understand until about the middle that they are hired murderers waiting for their victim. And it is not until the end of the play that we learn (as the two men them-selves learn) who the victim is. Ben does not kill Gus in the play, but it seems almost certain that he will kill Gus, for Ben has been consistently presented (in contrast to Gus) as a mindless hood who unthinkingly follows the orders given to him. Or, to put it a little differently, we come to understand that Gus, by the very doubts he has expressed throughout the play, is doomed to be eradicated (the toilet flushes, just before the end) by a system that brooks no questions. The play is not mere chitchat; it progresses, in the sense that *we* come to an understanding.

Second, and more obvious as a structural pattern, at the start of the play we hear Ben recount two newspaper stories of death — one of an eighty-seven-year-old man who was killed while crawling under a lorry (i.e., a truck), and the other of an eight-year-old girl who killed a cat. The first story, then, introduces the motif of the unpredictability of death (at the end of the play, Gus, who thinks he is the killer, finds that he is the victim); the second news story, too, introduces a note of surprise, but now the surprise is tinged with the mystery of the suspense story, for Gus doubts the accuracy of the newspaper report and he conjectures that in fact the girl's eleven-year-old brother was the real killer of the cat. Whether or not Gus is right, then, the seemingly trivial dialogue at the beginning of the play is preparation for the dialogue and the action at the end of the play. Or, rather, for the silence and the inaction. We are left wondering, just as at the start we wonder which child did in fact kill the cat.

At the end of the play, then, Pinter leaves us with an ambiguity, but the play has been ambiguous from the start. If we are annoyed by the uncertainty of the resolution of the plot, we may be even more annoyed by the uncertainty of the meaning, but this is perhaps because we mistakenly expect playwrights to be philosophers who answer our largest questions. Perhaps we should recall that in *King Lear* we get no answer to Lear's agonized question, asked over the body of his beloved daughter Cordelia, "Why should a dog, a horse, a rat, have life, / And thou no breath at all?" The question is unforgettable; the answer is not forthcoming. In A *Midsummer Night's Dream* Lear's question is asked comically, when Pyramus laments the seeming death, at the jaws of a lion, of his beloved Thisby: "O wherefore, Nature, didst thou lions frame?" Not answers, but an experience of life, is what the best playwrights offer.

Comedy, Tragedy, and Tragicomedy

Cyrus Hoy

Professor Hoy's essay is chiefly not about a particular dramatic form but about a distinctive vision of the disparity between the ideal and the reality. This vision he finds in the profoundest comedies, which he argues are close to tragedies. He further pursues his argument in a book, *The Hyacinth Room*, which includes discussions of playwrights ranging from Euripides to Ionesco.

In one of the later incidents of the *Satyricon* of Petronius, the disreputable poet Eumolpus relates the story of the widow of Ephesus. It is a well-known tale; Jeremy Taylor related it, in his *Holy Dying*, in the mid-seventeenth century; and in our own time, Christopher Fry has made it the subject of a one-act play, *A Phoenix Too Frequent*. Briefly, the story goes like this: A married woman of Ephesus, famed for her virtue, determines, upon the death of her husband, to immure herself in his underground vault and end her life with his, for she finds her loss unendurable. She is accompanied by a devoted maid, and is hailed throughout the city as "the one true and brilliant example of chastity and love." The ladies spend five days in the tomb without food. At this point, the governor of the province orders some robbers to be crucified near the vault where the widow mourns. A soldier is placed on guard, to watch over the crosses, lest anyone take down a body for burial. When, the next night, he sees a light among the tombs, curiosity leads him to discover its source. Finding the lady weeping over the body of the dead man, he correctly surmises her intentions. Bringing his supper into the tomb, he sets about urging the mourner not to persist in useless grief, but she will not be dissuaded. Neither will she accept his offer of food. But the maid is framed of weaker stuff. She partakes of the soldier's food and drink, and thus refreshed,

Reprinted by permission of the author from the *Virginia Quarterly Review*.

sets about to assail her mistress's obstinacy ("What will you gain by all this, if you faint away with hunger, if you bury yourself alive, if you breathe out your undoomed soul before Fate calls for it?"). The lady's resolution is broken; she eats; and then, even as she has been persuaded to live, so is she persuaded to love. The soldier is young, handsome, and eloquent; and the maid, again, is helpful, pleading to her mistress to be gracious ("Wilt thou fight love even when love pleases thee?"). So, in Eumolpus's words, the lady and the soldier pass "not only their wedding night together, but the next and a third, of course shutting the door of the vault, so that any friend or stranger who came to the tomb would imagine that this most virtuous lady had breathed her last over her husband's body." But meanwhile, the parents of one of the crucified robbers, noting that the watch is ill-kept, come in the dark and make off with the body of their man. When the soldier discovers the loss, he is distraught; by the laws of Ephesus, his body must be fixed in the place of the stolen corpse. He explains to the lady what has happened, declaring that he will not wait for a court-martial, but will punish his own neglect with his own hand. It is now the lady's turn to urge the arguments against self-slaughter, and in doing so, she shows herself as practical as she was passionate. "Heaven forbid," she cries, "that I should look at the same moment on the dead bodies of two men whom I love. No, I would rather make a dead man useful, than send a live man to death." Whereupon she orders her husband's body to be taken out of the coffin and fixed up on the empty cross. "The soldier," says Eumolpus in conclusion, "availed himself of this far-seeing woman's device, and the people wondered the next day by what means the dead man had ascended the cross."

The sailors to whom Eumolpus tells this sophisticated tale greet it with a roar of laughter, which is altogether as it should be, for the irony of the reversal on which the story turns derives from the fine display of the incongruity of human intention and human deed which the Ephesian Widow's tergiversations afford; and incongruity is the essence of comedy. The Widow of Ephesus's high-flown intentions end in an all too human surrender, and her tale is but further testimony to the sad truth that, though the spirit be willing, the flesh is weak. Boundless is the will to do good, but the power of performance is sadly limited; the elevated purpose issues but feebly in action; and the generally inadequate standard of human conduct makes a travesty of the ideals that nourish man's illusions about himself and what he can achieve. The discrepancy between the noble intention and the ignoble deed points directly to the most glaring incongruity in the human condition: that which exists between man as he is, and man as he might be, or as he thinks he might be. "Every man," says Conrad in *The Secret Sharer*, "sets up for himself secretly" an "ideal conception of [his] own personality" to which he would be faithful if he could. The extent to which he is able to keep faith with this ideal of self will go far toward determining his personal destiny. But everything must turn, finally, on the nature of the ideal conception. Is it humanly possible to be faithful to it? If so, is it worth the effort? The questions are relevant, because there is always the possibility that the pursuit of the ideal may turn out to be a delusion and a snare. In a world in which man's purposes are infirm, his knowledge imperfect, and his highest endeavors doomed to issue, ultimately, in death, it is safe to say that any effort to keep faith with the ideal is fated to meet with no more than partial success. The spectacle of man seeking, in despite of all the odds, to fulfill an ideal of self, to live up to his own best intentions, may be a deeply moving and ennobling one; but there comes a point at which the pity that we feel for the embattled idealist gives way to amusement at one who steadfastly refuses to recognize the conditions of his all too

human frailty. Tears turn to laughter as the tragic struggle ends in a rather grotesque effort to transcend the limits of mortality. In one sense it is deeply tragic that the Widow of Ephesus is not able to remain faithful to her ideal of virtuous bereavement; and the fact that she is not might be taken as all too symptomatic of the scurvy tricks that life plays on men and women, undermining their most pious intents, thwarting their most earnest desires, making sport generally of their finest gestures in the direction of heroic virtue. This is the great irony of life: that man can envision an ideal of good, can passionately desire to achieve it, and yet fails to live up to it. The failure can occasion either tears or laughter: tears in recognition of the fact that this is the way life is; laughter at the folly of those who fail to recognize that this is the way life is. The protagonists of tragedy and comedy alike are deficient in their knowledge of human limitations, of what they can hope to achieve and what it is the better part of wisdom not to attempt. In a word, they are lacking in self-knowledge. But there is this difference: that while the tragic protagonist's lack of self-knowledge leads to destruction, the comic protagonist's lack of self-knowledge leads instead to a rude awakening in which he is made aware — often cruelly so — of the truth about himself, and is left to live with it — often a fate worse than death. This at least is true of the protagonists of the greatest comedy: plays that probe so deeply into the irony of human fate as to bring them close upon tragedy. By comic protagonists in this sense I have in mind characters such as Jonson's Volpone, Shakespeare's Angelo in *Measure for Measure*, Molière's Alceste in *Le Misanthrope*, Chekhov's Uncle Vanya, Pirandello's Henry IV. Since all these characters are found in plays that are generally regarded as inhabiting the border regions between tragedy and comedy, and since the term "comedy" generally connotes either farce or comedy of manners, it will be best to label such characters "tragicomic," reserving the adjective "comic" for the Widow of Ephesus and her kind.

She is decidedly not tragic. When her noble intentions collapse, and she goes the way of all flesh, we are not moved to pity; we merely shake our heads knowingly. But her failure to fulfill her ideal of virtue, to remain faithful to her particular conception of self, is fraught with tragic potential. This will be clear if we turn to another lady, also possessed of an ideal of virtuous bereavement, and listen as she declares her intention — not, in this case, to immolate herself on her husband's tomb — but never to re-marry upon her husband's death.

Nor earth to me give food, nor heaven light,
Sport and repose lock from me day and night,
To desperation turn my trust and hope,
An anchor's cheer in prison be my scope,
Each opposite that blanks the face of joy,
Meet what I would have well, and it destroy,
Both here and hence pursue me lasting strife,
If once a widow ever I be wife.

The speaker here is, of course, the Player Queen in *Hamlet* (III,2,214 ff.), and in the presence of her, we are but one short step from tragedy; for the Player Queen, as everyone knows, is but a thin disguise for the real Queen Gertrude. The Player King responds to his wife's grandiloquence in respectful but guarded tones:

I do believe you think what now you speak,
But what we do determine oft we break.
Purpose is but the slave to memory,
Of violent birth but poor validity,

and he continues with a succession of epigrammatic couplets, each having reference to the discrepancy between human intention and deed:

What to ourselves in passion we propose.
The passion ending, doth the purpose lose.

.   .   .

Our wills and fates do so contrary run,
That our devices still are overthrown;
Our thoughts are ours, their ends none of our own. . . .

Gertrude, viewing the scene, declares that "the lady doth protest too much," and her words have the ring of one who knows whereof she speaks. She has heard all this before, having presumably made similar protestations to the dead King Hamlet. Her ideal of self, if she can be truly said ever to have possessed one, has been shattered, and whatever the effect of this on Gertrude herself, it has precipitated the tragedy of her son.

What our argument comes to, then, is this: that in serious drama, comic or tragic, we are confronted with what is, at bottom, a single truth about the human condition. Man is possessed of an ideal of human conduct, but circumstances together with his own inherent failings conspire to make the belief that the ideal can be fulfilled a finally illusory one. But man persists in despite of all the odds, and in his persistence he may appear as nobly enduring, stubbornly unyielding, foolishly blind, or a combination of all three. The more forcibly and apparently these diverse qualities are linked in combination, the more surely sounds the note of tragicomedy.

As an example of the fully developed tragicomic protagonist, there is the figure of the already mentioned Angelo in Shakespeare's *Measure for Measure*. In the context of the play as a whole, Angelo cannot be viewed as the protagonist of *Measure for Measure*; that rôle clearly falls to the Duke Vincentio, and Angelo must be cast in the rôle of antagonist, both to the Duke and to Isabella. But in the context of the drama that goes forth within the soul of Angelo — which is all that I am concerned with here — Angelo, or the part of him which passes in public under this name, is engaged in desperate struggle with his baser self, his private devil. He is well named; and his name gives us the clue to what he aspires to be, which is nothing less than angelic. He would deny his bodily nature, with all that that implies, for in his ideal conception of himself, he sees himself as one beyond the reach of physical desire, as proof against the clamorous demands of human passion. Since the unique quality in the nature of man is precisely his duality, Angelo, in denying the sensual half of his being, is in effect denying his very humanity. In this respect, the comments made about him by the other characters in the play are instructive. The Duke, for instance, makes some penetrating observations on the character of his Deputy in I,3, when he visits the Friar's cell after his supposed departure from Vienna:

Lord Angelo is precise;
Stands at a guard with envy; scarce confesses
That his blood flows; or that his appetite
Is more to bread than stone: hence shall we see,
If power change purpose — what our seemers be.

(I,3,50 ff.)

And Lucio, the fantastic, characterizes him in similar terms for the benefit of Isabella in the following scene (I,4) — the only occasion in the play when the usually foul-mouthed courtier and the righteous Duke are in accord:

> Lord Angelo; a man whose blood
> Is very snow-broth; one who never feels
> The wanton stings and motions of the sense;
> But doth rebate and blunt his natural edge
> With profits of the mind, study and fast.
>
> (I,4,57 ff.)

But the blood, the very seat of life, which Angelo has sought to deny, will assert itself in the end. "Blood, thou art blood," says Angelo in grim if belated acceptance of a truth he has sought long to ignore; and with that, the struggle that has been waged within him ends in the capitulation of his ideal self to his basest instincts. The angel and the devil have fought, and the devil has won. "Let's write 'good Angel' on the devil's horn, / 'Tis now the devil's crest," he says in conclusion (II,4,16–17). In striving to be more than man, he has ended a good deal less. Recognizing this truth, he puts it to use in the course of his temptation of Isabella later in the same scene (II,4,134–5): "Be that you are," he urges her, "That is, a woman; if you be more, you're none." But she will not be corrupted, and Angelo turns from persuasion to threats. If he cannot be an angel, he will be a very demon of the flesh: "I have begun, / And now I give my sensual race the rein," he announces, and then proceeds to state the terms on which Isabella can redeem her brother. His fall is complete, and thereafter he has forfeited any share in the divine — the angelic — nature which man might justly claim. One of the Duke's octosyllabic couplets near the end of III,2 notes with appropriate horror the infamy that is here:

> O, what may man within him hide,
> Though angel on the outward side.

And at the beginning of V,1, when the Duke refers Isabella to Angelo for justice, she calls him by his own name: "O worthy duke, / You bid me seek redemption of the devil." When the truth has been revealed, and he stands forth in his shame, he judges himself with unsparing severity; "immediate sentence . . . and sequent death" is all the grace he begs (V,1,369–70). And he is still craving "death more willingly than mercy" (" 'Tis my deserving, and I do entreat it") in the last lines that he speaks in the

play (V,1,472–3). By then he is a strangely dignified and absurd figure: dignified for the manner in which he endures his shame, absurd in the willful blindness through which he has brought it on himself. He has been duped on every hand — by the Duke, by Isabella, by Mariana — he who has seemed to be so thoroughly in command both of himself and of events around him. His reputation for "gravity" (in which, as he admits himself in hushed tones on one occasion, he takes pride) falls from him, and he stands exposed: a singularly unsuccessful lecher, and that when he has reached years of discretion, too. Nothing less than the dignity of death could make him an object of tragic pity, and Shakespeare has denied him that, leaving him instead clutching the tatters of his unyielding pride, stubbornly reiterating his request for death as the only proper punishment for his offenses, and having it denied him. He is doomed not to get what he seeks. The incongruity that I have already stated to be of the essence of comedy is grimly apparent here in the incongruous distance that separates Angelo's pride from Angelo's shame — that separates Angelo as he is, and Angelo as he thinks he might have been, and this is surely the principal reason why *Measure for Measure* is one of Shakespeare's grimmest plays.

The grimness is intensified because Angelo's ideal of self-righteous virtue is such a false one: false both because virtue of the thoroughgoing kind that he has sought is beyond human achievement, and because it is not altogether desirable that it should be within human reach. He has shown himself lamentably ignorant in the knowledge of self, which is to say, in the knowledge of what a man is, and to what he can legitimately aspire. He has draped himself in a cloak of self-righteous virtue, and in it he cuts as ill a figure as does Malvolio in his crossgarters and yellow stockings. And the comparison does not end there, for Malvolio is but a shallower Angelo: more vain, and with even less to justify his vanity. Still, if we do not feel for Angelo the tragic pity that we accord a Hamlet or an Othello or a Lear, we do pity him nonetheless. His ideal is at once so right and so wrong: right because it is surely proper for man to aspire to virtue, wrong because it can never be proper for him to aspire to it self-righteously. It is wrong, too, in the sense that it is the wrong ideal for him. Angelo's ideal conception of self is an ascetic ideal, and in his blindness and his pride, he never sees that he is not the ascetic type. He is no more capable of asceticism than the Widow of Ephesus was of sacrificing herself to her husband's memory, or than the Player Queen — to say nothing of Queen Gertrude — was of refraining from a second marriage. He has deceived himself about human limitations generally, and his personal limitations in particular. And the final crushing irony is that the very things Angelo has sought most feverishly to avoid — the sensual, the physical, the passionate — are precisely the objects of his most secret longings. He is in the terrible position of one who is inwardly seeking the very things that his conscious will has pledged itself to avoid.

Angelo's position is terrible, but because he is a single figure, and that not the principal one, in a larger scene, we are not shown the full intensity of its terror. For that, we must turn to Greek tragedy, and to the *Bacchae* of Euripides. In the figure of Pentheus, the Theban king who opposes himself to Dionysus, we have the tragic extreme of the tragicomic Angelo, even as Malvolio is the comic extreme. Malvolio, Angelo, Pentheus: what these three very diverse characters have in common is what comedy, tragicomedy, and tragedy have in common. All three are possessed of an ideal of virtuous conduct which is more or less febrile as they are more or less tragic, but an ideal which nonetheless fails, all along the line, to square with the facts of life. In their virtuous zeal, they are dedicated to imposing their ideal of conduct upon the world that lies within their charge, be this the kingdom of Thebes, the city of Vienna, or the lower domestic regions of the Lady Olivia's house in Illyria; they are determined that, because they are virtuous, there shall be no more cakes and ale. All three are humiliated for their presumption. For Malvolio, the humiliation is an end in itself; for Angelo, it involves the shame of public exposure; for Pentheus, it is the prelude to a terrible death.

In seeking to prevent the introduction of Dionysiac rites into Thebes, Pentheus is by implication seeking to deny the existence of the Dionysiac principle in man, even as he has sought to deny its existence in himself. He would prohibit the women of Thebes from participating in the Bacchic ceremonies on Mount Cithaeron, which he is convinced are only a pretext for gatherings of lecherous men and lewd women, just as Angelo decrees that all "the houses of resort" in the suburbs of Vienna be pulled down. As guardians of the public morality, there is much to be said for both; the difficulty is that they would impose restrictions on the conduct of human life which mortal flesh is not able to endure. Seeking to realize a perhaps noble but illusory ideal of life, they are in fact enemies of life. Pompey, the part tapster, part bawd of *Measure for Measure*, says that if Angelo would enforce the laws against immorality in Vienna, he must "geld and splay all the youth in the city," which may be a sad comment on human nature, but is nonetheless true. And the case is even clearer in the *Bacchae*, where Pentheus stands forth as the open enemy of Dionysus, the god of earthly fertility. Pentheus, in his pride, like Angelo, would legislate human weakness out of existence; he would deliver mankind from the infirmities of the flesh by fiat; and he must inevitably pay the price of such presumption. The Chorus comments appropriately:

They who in pride pretend
Beyond man's limit, will lose what lay
Close to their hand and sure.
(lines 396–8)

And later in the same ode the Chorus speaks of the happiness of him who is

Watchful to keep aloof both mind and heart
From men whose pride claims more than mortals may.
(lines 427–8)

The task that Pentheus has appointed himself is impossible for any man to accomplish; it is the more so for him, being the kind of man he is. For Pentheus, like Angelo, is fatally drawn to the very pleasures of human life which he seeks most fervently to deny, both in himself and others. Again the final, crushing — here altogether tragic — irony: the Dionysiac principle against which Pentheus has vowed eternal enmity is strong in him, so strong that through its operation the king is lured to his own destruction. There comes the terrible scene in which god and king confront each other. It is the measure of Pentheus's blindness that he fails throughout the play to recognize Dionysus as the god in person (just as he has refused to acknowledge Dionysus's deity), and he persists in mistaking the figure before him as a mere Bacchic priest. Bit by bit, as he and the god converse, Pentheus betrays an all too passionate interest in the details of the Bacchic revels, and the god is quick to seize upon this. Would the king care to view the revels at first hand, he asks; and Pentheus confesses that he would. It can be arranged, says the god, but the king must disguise himself as a bacchanal, lest he be recognized as an interloper. The king, who is by now altogether under the god's sway, consents; and he appears a little later clad in woman's clothes, thyrsus in hand and fawnskin draped about him, ready to go. Thus bedizened, the grave and dignified king is led by the god through the streets of Thebes, en route to Mount Cithaeron. Having been humiliated in the eyes of his people (shades of Malvolio in his cross garters and yellow stockings) he is ready for the slaughter at the hands of the bacchae, with his mother at their head.

The principle of fertility, of life, has asserted itself and triumphed, as it always does. The enemies of life have been vanquished, even as they always are, whether the enemies of life take the form of a Pentheus, an Angelo, or one of the wretched old men — the perpetual enemy of youth and vitality — who would prevent the marriage of the young lovers, and who are eternally appearing in comedy, from Menander through Plautus and Terence to the present. Comedy notoriously ends in marriage, even as tragedy typically ends in death; and the dance with which comedy traditionally closes — even such a sophisticated piece as *The Way of the World* has one — is something of an act of faith, an affirmation that life, in spite of its follies and its miseries, is worthwhile, and worthy to be perpetuated. Comedy implies, then, an acceptance of life, which implies as well an acceptance of man, and to accept man, one must be prepared to forgive all the weakness and the treachery and the downright depravity which, in spite of man's best intentions, he is continually guilty of. To accept and to forgive, one must be, above everything else, clear-sighted about what man is, and what can be properly expected of him. Only then will one refrain from asking the impossible, of himself and of others, and being plunged into the depths of tragic despair when the impossible is not achieved. Comedy is nothing if not hardheadedly realistic about the nature of man and the nature of human life; but it can also be compassionate in its forgiveness and its acceptance of human failings, because it recognizes the existence of these. That is why the burden of com-

edy, again and again, turns on the need for man to undeceive himself about the limitations of humanity, to see life for what it is, and to make the best of it.

For a fine demonstration of this double theme of acceptance and forgiveness in the terms of sheerest comedy, it is tempting to turn to the operatic stage, and da Ponte's libretto for Mozart's *Così fan tutte*. It is an elegant, rather cynical, and yet finally compassionate performance, and it stands squarely in the tradition of great comedy. We are confronted with two pairs of lovers: the sisters Fiordiligi and Dorabella, and their respective gallants, Guglielmo and Ferrando. The gentlemen have a cynical old bachelor friend, Don Alfonso, who assures them that, if their ladies are faithful, it is only because they have not had occasion to be otherwise. The lovers, in the fullness of their simplicity, laugh him to scorn; but then to vindicate their faith and prove the folly of Don Alfonso's suspicions, they agree to put their ladies to the test that he suggests. They announce to the sisters that they have been called to the wars, and bid them a tearful farewell, amid many protestations of eternal devotion and faith on both sides. After the lovers' departure, the sisters are prostrated with grief, Dorabella viewing her condition as especially terrible:

Relentless infatuation which thrills my very soul and will not cease till I die of grief. What a wretched example of tragic love shall I give the Eumenides if I manage to live through the horrible sound of my own sighs,

she sings. But Don Alfonso promptly goes to work. The sisters have a maid, even as the Widow of Ephesus had, and Don Alfonso bribes this soubrette, named Despina, to introduce two friends into the presence of her mistresses as prospective lovers. The two new suitors are, of course, Guglielmo and Ferrando, disguised as Albanian noblemen. Despina complies, but the sisters are indignant that she should presume so much, and the lovers' proposals are scornfully rejected. They are sent away, but they return shortly, announcing that if the ladies will not be kind, they will not live; whereupon they drink a reportedly poisonous concoction, and fall to the ground. The sisters are distraught; they call a doctor who appears (it is Despina in disguise) and restores the lovers to life. The ladies are impressed at such devotion, but still faithful to their first vows at the conclusion of Act I. But in the second act, their fall is accomplished. First Dorabella gives way to the advances of Guglielmo, then Fiordiligi yields to the suit of Ferrando. When the lovers compare notes, and find that their respective mistresses have proved false, they are plunged into gloom; that "all those tears, promises, and sighs and vows" should be utterly forgotten in so short a time! They are dedicated to vengeance. But Don Alfonso takes them in hand with timely advice: women are weak, they must not be blamed; young, old, pretty or ugly, they all do it. And he makes them repeat with him: "Così fan tutte!" Meanwhile, the sisters are prepared to marry their Albanian suitors. The farce is played through to the end, until the lovers throw off their disguises and confront the ladies with their perfidy. The sisters are overcome with shame, and court their punishment in terms worthy of an Angelo: "punish my guilt with death. I see my faults too late. With that sword pierce this unworthy breast," they sing together. All turn on Don Alfonso, who has engineered the deception. He freely admits it, and justifies having done so, thus pointing the moral of the piece:

I deceived you [addressing the sisters], but it was to undeceive your lovers, who will be wiser in future. Take my advice, join hands, you are betrothed. Kiss and be friends.

To the credit of them all, they have the wit to do just this, and the opera ends with a final chorus that sums up the wisdom which it is the special province of comedy to celebrate, even as it is the common purpose of comedy, tragedy, and tragicomedy to delineate the sundry consequences that follow when that wisdom is lacking:

Happy the man who accepts life as it really is, and in all its ups and downs takes a reasonable view; who can laugh when others weep and finds peace in the midst of the world's tumult!

New Form in the Theatre

Martin Esslin

Martin Esslin was born in Hungary and brought up in Austria, but when the Nazis entered Austria he was forced to leave, and he settled in England, where he is now director of radio drama for the British Broadcasting Corporation. In the essay that we reprint, Esslin suggests that new forms in contemporary theater were necessary because dramatists offered new content. No longer believing in such traditional ideas as the psychological consistency of characters or the coherence of plot, dramatists like Beckett and Pinter could not use the traditional dramatic forms. They smashed the old forms, then, because only by creating new forms could the new vision be adequately embodied.

Form-smashers ought certainly to be encouraged. But at the same time we should know what is being smashed; and what is taking its place.

What is form? A set of rules or prescriptions handed down through habits of craftsmanship, academic teaching, or critical practice. Some of these may be wholly arbitrary, based on considerations that have been long forgotten; others are the congealed expression of philosophical assumptions, some of which may still be valid, while others are equally forgotten and have long since become obsolete or need to be re-examined. Others again are derived from fundamental realities, such as the laws of the psychology of perception; these will resist the smashers — but even they may be swept away, for even the conditions of perception change with time. Men's wits become sharper, their eyes and ears quicker in their response, chords that grated on the ears of one generation may be tolerable or even beautiful to those of a later age.

So most forms may be, and should be, smashed. What we must remember, however, is that the new forms that take their place will also, inevitably, present new and different con-

"New Form in the Theatre" from the book *Reflections: Essays on Modern Theatre* by Martin Esslin. Copyright © 1961 by Martin Esslin. It first appeared in *The Nation* in April, 1961. Reprinted by permission of Doubleday & Company, Inc.

tents. It is a fallacy to think that there is a division between *what* is said and *how* it is said; ultimately form is content and content form — it would be quite impossible to have the statement made by Picasso in *Guernica* repainted in the style of Rubens or Velazquez; and when Picasso did repaint *Las Meninas* of Velazquez in his own style in a long series of new paintings, these turned out to have an entirely different content. Equally, you could not express the subject matter of *Hamlet* in the form of Racine or Eugene O'Neill, let alone in the form of a musical. *West Side Story* may be a retelling of *Romeo and Juliet* — it certainly does not say the same thing that Shakespeare said.

To make a musical out of *Romeo and Juliet*, however, is not an act of form-smashing; it is a perfectly traditional method of taking inspiration from the theme of an older work. The form-smashers aim at breaking up the basic rules of the art form itself.

Let us take a simple example of an established aesthetic dogma smashed — and not by revolutionaries either. For decades the aesthetics of the cinema were based on the traditional proportions of the screen; the origins of these were wholly arbitrary, probably due to such accidents as the format of the first cameras, or the standard size of film made available by industry to the early film makers. Once cinema houses around the world were equipped with screens of a certain size and shape, it became extremely difficult to change the proportions of the picture projected, and the original co-incidence was elevated into a formal principle that seemed destined to assume eventually the sacred stature of an eternal aesthetic law; film theoreticians accepted it and derived their philosophies from it. If a few directors, like Abel Gance, rebelled against it in one or two films, they could not move the established principle. Yet the day came when technical developments and economic forces coincided; when the competition of television created a demand for more spectacle and larger vistas, and technical developments in the form of various wide-screen and panoramic processes were at hand. So Cinemascope and Cinerama smashed what, a bare half century after the birth of the cinema, had come to be regarded as its basic form. It now became possible to create a much wider picture within a frame of different shape — or even a picture so large that its edges lay outside the field of vision of a pair of eyes focused on the center, so that it became possible to suggest an unframed picture, like that perceived when we are looking at reality itself.

It was soon apparent that these new forms must present a different type of content. On the Cinemascope screen, montage and quick cutting, which make up the basic grammar of the language of the normal cinema, become much more difficult, simply because it takes much longer to absorb a wider picture and therefore quicker cutting would be bewildering. In Cinerama, which attempts an illusion of reality itself, quick cutting is found to give the audience a violent physical jolt and be positively uncomfortable. So, on that very large screen, the picture has to be almost as stable as in the old live theatre; the real value of the process lies in the purveying of landscape: only one type of content, the travelogue, ideally fits that particular new form.

In other words, the old form has not been smashed; it has not been superseded. The language of the cinema has been extended in one particular direction. If the new very large screen process became the only standard of cinematic art, we should have lost a valuable form of expression.

This certainly is a very humble and a very limited example. But it makes its point; the origins of an aesthetic may be arbitrary, but once the arbitrary step has been taken, it sets up its own framework of by no means arbitrary rules which are dependent on the psychological and perceptual basis of the experience involved. Thus the origins of Greek tragedy are still obscure: we do not know *why* it was originally confined to one actor and chorus, to which another actor and later — by a daring and revolutionary innovation — a third were added. It was certainly a highly arbitrary form. Yet it is from these limitations that the character — and range of expressiveness — of Greek tragedy stemmed. And it was a form perfectly adapted to the content it was designed to express. But to that content only.

It was from that very limited, and arbitrarily limited, art form that Aristotle deduced what were for centuries regarded as the immovable laws of the aesthetics of drama. At that point a tyranny of form was established. For it is a fatal fallacy when principles deduced from existing works of art *a posteriori* are elevated into *a priori* rules. For many centuries, while certain aspects changed, it was considered an eternal principle that the drama must imitate nature, that it was based on a plot with a beginning, a middle, and a solution, and on the delineation of characters that must be consistent throughout the action.

It was against this form that Beckett, Ionesco, Genet, Harold Pinter, and a host of other dramatists rebelled. Some of them have written plays that lack plot, others have created characters that lack consistency and change their personalities completely in the course of an evening — not by logical development, but arbitrarily. They have written plays that start without a formal exposition and end without a solution. In other words they have produced a theatre that, by that *a priori* definition of the theatre, is neither possible nor permissible and could certainly not be successful. Yet, undoubtedly, these authors have written for the stage and they have been successful.

This is a case where not only have some of the rules of form been revealed as arbitrary, but where, moreover, the philosophical assumptions on which the convention rested have changed. Plays with a rationally constructed plot that start from the exposition of a problem, moral, social, or philosophical, and then proceed toward a solution presuppose a world order that is rational and known to man. Characters who remain consistent throughout the development of an action presuppose that each individual has something like an immutable and eternal essence of which all his various manifestations from the cradle to the grave are temporal and more or less fortuitous modifications: in other words, that each individual has his immortal essence, his immortal soul.

For the avant garde in the theatre of today neither of these basic assumptions holds good: they see the world as essentially mysterious and unintelligible, certainly devoid of rational purpose and hence of clearly deducible rules of conduct. And these authors have also digested the findings of modern psychology, which sees human character not as an eternal essence but as the sum of physiological and psychological factors that are in constant flux. In Beckett's *Waiting for Godot*, Pozzo appears as a self-confident and overbearing man at one moment, as a blind and defeated man at another. No explanation is given for the change; there is even room to doubt that the two manifestations of personality are the same man. In Ionesco's *Rhinoceros*, men change into beasts without warning or explanation, the victims of a psychological and physiological change that is regarded as a disease. With the loss of intelligible purpose in the universe and with the disappearance of consistent character, the drama can no longer be an equation starting from a number of known constants and working toward a solution of the unknown factors according to a well-established and sure formula. We now work with a much higher number of unknown factors and the certainty that there is no easy solution.

Here, then, in contrast to the merely technical change in the example from the cinema, we are faced not so much with an *attack* on an arbitrary form as with its internal collapse. To these avant-garde authors the traditional form of the theatre no longer makes sense because it is based on implied philosophical assumptions in which they no longer believe. This is why, say, the usual Soviet play or the Victorian melodrama strikes us as unconvincing: they express systems of values that have, to us, lost their relevance. But so, to the avant garde in the contemporary theatre, have the basic, unspoken, and implied assumptions of the usual drawing-room comedy or socially relevant play, with its careful delineation of character and neat solution. To writers like Beckett, Ionesco, or Pinter, the fact that boy gets girl in the last act, or that the desirability of racial tolerance is convincingly demonstrated, is irrelevant. The boy and the girl still

face an absurd universe; no social reform will alter its mysteriousness. By tackling a small, and to these writers irrelevant, segment of the reality of the human situation, the conventional theatre presents a distorted and unreal picture.

The attack on the *form* of the traditional theatre is thus revealed as an attack on its *content*. And if a play attempts to deal with the new content in the conventional form of logical construction, consistent characterization, and coherent language, the implied assumptions behind its form will belie its apparent content. In that sense even the blackest existentialist plays of Sartre and Camus, which present a philosophy closely akin to that of the plays of Beckett and Ionesco, contradict their explicit content by the implied content that shines through their logical and traditional construction.

The identity of form and content is even clearer in the most obvious aspect of the attack the avant-garde dramatists have launched against the traditional theatre: their resolute destruction of language and discursive thought on the stage. One of the main contents of this new theatre is the demonstration of the difficulties of communication between human beings — the inadequacy of language in establishing contact. Here, too, the smashing of form expresses a changed philosophical basis: the time has passed when an identity was believed to exist between the structure of language, the structure of logic, and the structure of reality. That is the content expressed by the formal means of the dissolution of logical discourse in the avant-garde theatre.

The destruction of old rules, old forms that fitted old contents does not, however, lead to the destruction of *all* rules, *all* form. On the contrary, plays that can do without exposition, development, solution, closely observed characters, or even logical discourse, require an even stronger discipline, an even more acute and original formal sense from their authors. For, having dispensed with the traditional means of capturing their audience's attention, having jettisoned the clichés that helped them to follow what was going on, they *must* create their own *new* convention: no communication can exist without some common ground between the transmitter of a message and its recipient. That is why the loosest of all forms of communication, lyrical poetry, has the most rigid formal patterns: regular rhythms, rhyme, highly formalized groupings of lines into stanzas. That is also the reason why abstract painting is more formally patterned than illustrative pictures. In a non-discursive, lyrical theatre of concretized images, therefore, the need for form, *new* form, but form nevertheless, is *greater* than in the naturalistic theatre. All successful examples of this kind of theatre are in fact built according to the strictest formal patterns: the correspondence between Acts I and II in *Waiting for Godot* is as close as the rhyme scheme of a sonnet; the silences of Pinter's *The Homecoming* give that play the rhythmic formality of a string quartet.

The form-smashers of the contemporary theatre, therefore, are anything but frivolous iconoclasts. They are expressing fundamental changes in contemporary thought — and they are expressing them in the only way that will give them adequate expression in terms of the stage. In doing this they may not be destroying the traditional basis of the theatre, but they are certainly adding a new dimension to it, widening, in fact, the range of its content and subject matter.

The Theatre of the Absurd has opened up a new possibility for poetry on the stage. Having renounced the function of telling a story, of exploring character, of discussing ideas, of solving problems, it has been able to concentrate on the presentation of what is essentially a *sense of being,* an intuition of the tragicomic absurdity and mystery of human existence. As such the Theatre of the Absurd is an existentialist theatre which puts a direct perception of a mode of being above all abstract considerations; it is also essentially a poetic, a lyrical theatre, for the expression of intuitions of being is the field of lyrical poetry. So, paradoxically, the theatre that attacks language, and above all language that is beautiful and poetical for its own sake, is a deeply poetical theatre, only

its poetry is a poetry of situation, movement, and concrete imagery, not one of language. Plays like *Waiting for Godot* or Ionesco's *The Chairs* eminently prove this point.

So, in this field at least, the form-smashers are not form-smashers at all; rather are they explorers who penetrate into new fields and open up new vistas. Instead of destroyers of old forms they are the bringers of new contents.

This is not to say that everything that seems avant-gardist must be good. Once the basis of a new approach has been understood, the grammar of a new kind of language learned, standards of judgment will immediately become apparent. If it is recognized that the avant-garde theatre is concerned with the presentation of complex imagery, with the exploration of the human condition in terms of an intuition of the mystery, the tragedy and comic absurdity of existence, then obviously its plays will have to be judged, not by any truth of character drawing or any ingenuity of plot, which they renounce, but by the quality of their imagery, the depth of their intuition, the validity of their poetic imagination.

Just as we have learned to discriminate between good and bad abstract painting and no longer attack Picasso because he paints women with two noses when we all know that in nature they have only one, so it should be the function of drama critics to make a minimum effort to find out the terms of reference of avant-garde writing in the theatre and judge its works within those terms and standards. There may be some form-smashers in the avant-garde theatre who have nothing to say and are therefore purely negative. Any critic worth his salt should easily be able to distinguish these from the writers who smash old forms because they feel that they have become inadequate to express new contents.

And these form-smashers, certainly, ought to be encouraged.

THE SCRIPT AND THE STAGE
Peter Arnott

The dramatic author writing his play is engaged in the same one-to-one relationship as the artist with his canvas or the sculptor with his block of stone. He shapes his material as his particular genius dictates, and is responsive only to those imperatives that he decides to set himself. The production of a play, however, is a much more complex process, involving a variety of factors, and a number of professional skills, each of which may influence the way in which the work is finally presented to the public. Theater is community, and the author must resign himself to being merely one, and not necessarily the most important member, of the group.

Of whom does this group consist? In the modern theater, the production of a play normally involves, besides the author, the director and his assistants; the actors; the set and costume designer (who may not be the same person); the lighting designer; and a stage staff responsible for the mechanical execution of the project. Although these elements have always been present, in some degree, in the theater, their relative importance has changed over the centuries, and it is necessary to consider which held first place when the play was originally conceived.

THE AUTHOR

For those accustomed to think of a play primarily as a work of literature, it comes as a shock to learn that, at some of the most productive periods of the theater, the author was by no means the most important figure. In Elizabethan London, for example, the playwright was often no more than a hack, turning out material on demand as the company's needs and the public taste dictated. As well as writing his own material, he was expected to collaborate with others, to be able to work up a scenario suggested by someone else, or to write new scenes to freshen an old play. Once his work had been sold to the company, he had no further financial interest in it, and no artistic control. Several plays which enjoyed a long life in the Elizabethan public playhouse have come down to us as patchwork pieces, continually revised or added to by different hands over the years. For a long time plays, however distinguished, were not considered as literature. It was not until Ben Jonson had the effrontery to publish his dramatic with his non-dramatic works that the playwright's status began to show a change. French playwrights of the seventeenth century were the first who found themselves able to charge substantial sums for their works, and the first, tentative beginnings of the modern system of author's royalties appear at the same time.

THE ACTORS

In the modern commercial theater, actors are normally cast for each new production on an *ad hoc* basis. When the play closes they go their separate ways, and though their paths may sometimes recross, it may well be that

About the author: PETER ARNOTT was born and educated in Great Britain, where he received degrees from the University of Wales and Oxford University. Currently professor of drama and chairman of the Drama Department at Tufts University, he has written numerous books on the theater and on ancient civilizations. Arnott is also an actor, director, and the creator of the Marionette Theater of Peter Arnott, which specializes in performing Greek drama for audiences throughout the continent.
This essay is published here for the first time with permission from the author, Peter Arnott.

they never meet on the stage again. There are, of course, important exceptions to this. The national theaters of various countries — the United States still does not have one — try to retain at least the nucleus of a permanent company for a period of years. In France, once an actor has been admitted to full membership of the Comédie Française, he may remain, if he wishes, for life. Theaters with a particular aim or identity, such as the Stratford, Ontario, Shakespeare Festival, recruit a large company for a number of plays and then stage the works in repertory. What is the exception now, however, was common practice until the present century. For most of the history of the theater, actors formed themselves into companies that worked together for years, so that the members grew to know one another's work intimately. This gave dramatists of earlier periods an advantage that they rarely enjoy today. They were writing for a known group, and could tailor the roles to particular abilities and talents. Shakespeare wrote *Hamlet* and *Othello* with Richard Burbage in mind. Molière's comedies made the best of his company's physical characteristics. Congreve and Sheridan, similarly, knew who was going to play each part before they wrote them. In this kind of company, actors tended to fall into what were called "lines of business": that is, they would specialize in playing the same kind of character, whatever the play. Certain members of the King's Men would always play the fools and clowns. Sheridan had a gallery of comic types around which to build a new work. Dickens, in *Nicholas Nickleby*, gives a delightful description of a nineteenth-century touring company in which the members are identified, not by their names, but by the roles they customarily play on stage: the swaggering hero, the angry old father, the ingenue, and so forth. You will often find, therefore, that this kind of company organization induces certain sorts of dramatic formulae in playwrights. As early as Sophocles, dramatists were returning to the same types of character, and similar kinds of dramatic situation, because they could rely on actors who were able to exploit them powerfully. The modern author usually lacks this resource. He creates his characters out of the blue. It is up to the producing agency, and the casting director, to find actors capable of bringing them to life.

THE DIRECTOR   The director is the most recent member of the producing group, and still one of the most controversial. Throughout the history of the theater, obviously, someone always had to be in charge. In the Greek theater it was usually the playwright. Aeschylus played his own leading parts, and supervised his assistant actors; as well as providing the script, he was his own composer, choreographer, and designer. The medieval theater provided a *maître de jeu*, who had general responsibility for seeing that his actors knew their lines, rehearsed their moves, and stood more or less in the right places. Shakespeare's playhouse had its "bookholder," who combined the functions of prompter and stage manager. In the eighteenth and nineteenth centuries we see the emergence of the actor-manager, a paternalistic figure who played the leading roles himself and imposed some cohesion on the company — sometimes a difficult task, for many actors were individualists, intent on drawing attention to their own performance at the expense of the ensemble effect. In the late nineteenth century the growing complexity of the theater's technical resources, and dissatisfaction with certain haphazard methods of the past, combined to create the need for a master mind who would stand apart from the production, see it as a whole, and harness its various resources to a common end. This figure emerges, in the twentieth century, as the American director, the British producer, or the European *régisseur*, and there are still widely different views as to what his function should be. Some directors have established themselves as autocrats, allowing nothing to happen on the stage that has not evolved from their minds or, at least, won their considered approval. In many cases, it has been possible to identify a given directorial style as easily as a writing style. A production by Tyrone Guthrie, or by Roger Planchon, was unmistakably his, and could be no one else's. Other directors have considered their function to be to allow the actor's initiative to predominate; they merely shape and control his creative imagination, offering suggestions, not directives. As the theater is constantly in a state of flux, so the director's role is still changing. Twenty years ago, the director expected to walk into his first rehearsal with every move of the play blocked out on paper, or at least in his mind. Now, he hopes to come to the same result after long working sessions with his actors, in the course of which a number of different approaches may be tried and discarded. Particular directors and actors may achieve a long and mutually fruitful working relationship over a number of productions, each helping and inspiring the other. The same may happen between directors and playwrights. Elia Kazan has had a long partnership with Tennessee Williams, contributing materially to the final shaping of the plays. Alan Schneider has done the same for Edward Albee.

Designers too represent a fairly recent innovation in theater practice. For most eras of the past, design as we now know it did not exist. The theater provided a conventional background for its actors. Sometimes, as in the Greek and Elizabethan theaters, this was simply the permanent architectural structure of the stage building, with the audience left to imagine the settings suggested by the language of the author. Even when the theater began to develop painted, illusionistic scenery the same stock settings were used for play after play; each playhouse owned a basic collection which could be used, with minimal adaptation, for the entire repertoire. Costumes, similarly, were drawn from stock, with the actors most of the time wearing the same sorts of clothes that they, and the audience, wore for everyday usage. The role of the designer begins to emerge in the early nineteenth century, out of the same dissatisfactions that eventually created the director. There was a growing desire for greater consistency, and greater appropriateness, in the stage picture, coupled with an increased concern for historical accuracy. The first "designed" production is usually said, with some justice, to be Shakespeare's *King John* as presented on the London stage in 1823, with every character dressed in the historical period indicated by the play, and the settings inspired by authentic medieval records. Since then, of course, the designer has developed into far more than a historical researcher, though that kind of

THE DESIGNERS

study may still represent the basis of his design. He is expected, first, to lay out the playing space in a way that will be usable by actors, and at the same time say something about the play's intent; in other words, he must provide a visual metaphor of the play's action. In the same way, the costumes must be related to the dramatic intent, as seen by the director either alone or in combination with the author. Each costume must make a statement about the character who wears it, and be related to the others as part of a unified concept. The stage lighting, usually in different hands, must also contribute to the total effect, illuminating selectively and significantly the crucial moments of the action and suggesting mood and contrast.

All these things have to be kept in mind when taking a play from the printed page and translating it into stage action. As we have stated, many of the above are functions of the modern theater only. Selective stage lighting was impossible before the appearance of gas; seventeenth-century audiences would have been astonished at the suggestion that they should sit in the dark, while only the stage was lit. But even when considering the plays of the past, it is essential to consider what practical facilities were available to the playwright, and how these influenced the form in which he wrote. Plays are rarely written in a vacuum. When they are, they tend not to be good plays. Normally, an author writes with a particular kind of theater in mind, a particular acting style, a particular audience with reasonably predictable responses. The final shape of his play will be determined by all these things.

THE PLAYHOUSE   Particularly important is the shape of the playhouse at any given period, for this largely determines not what the author says, but how he says it. Was it large or small? Spectacular or intimate? Designed to provide elaborate scenic illusion, or working largely through the active complicity of the audience's imagination? Greek plays, for instance, were written for open-air theaters which were enormous by today's standards (see p. 787). They held upwards of 15,000 spectators, and the actor was dwarfed by his environment. In such a theater there was little place for subtle visual effect, or for the intricate physical business that a modern dramatist now writes into his stage directions. As a compensating factor, the acoustics of these theaters, by reason of their bowl-shaped structure, were superb. Audiences could hear every word, even at so great a remove from the action. Thus, by necessity, the dramatist worked largely in terms of language. In Greek plays, characters tell you everything: who and what they are, what they are doing and going to do, what they feel about it all. In the smaller, more intimate modern theater Greek plays often seem unnecessarily wordy because the actors now have other resources. A modern actor may show in a look what his ancient counterpart had to express in a sentence. Directors who revive Greek plays have to keep these problems of transposition in mind.

In the Elizabethan theater, as most scholars now assume, actors worked on a deep thrust stage which could carry them into the center of their audience (see p. 788). Thus, a characteristic feature of the theater building encouraged the use of the stage soliloquy. Also, Elizabethan theaters seem

Greek Theatre of Epidaurus on the Peloponnesus east of Nauplia. (Photograph: Frederick Ayer. Photo Researchers, Inc.) For additional details about the Greek Theater, see Glossary, p. 825.

Johannes de Witt, a Continental visitor to London, made a drawing of the Swan Theatre in about the year 1596. The original drawing is lost; this is Arend van Buchel's copy of it. For additional details about the Elizabethan theater, see Glossary, p. 823.

to have relied very little on illusionistic, representational scenery. They offered, instead, a neutral space defined largely by the words of the actors. Shakespeare's characters tell you where they are, if it matters; if they do not, then the precise location is unimportant. In these circumstances the theater could develop a fast-moving pattern of action in which one scene followed rapidly on the heels of another with no necessity to drop the curtain for a change of setting. Victorian actor-managers, mounting Shakespeare on their own heavily pictorial stages, found this to be a major problem, for their productions stretched out to an inordinate length as one elaborately painted set was replaced by another. Once again, the factors governing the original production have to be taken into account, even if one intends to depart from them.

Let us now trace the progress of a production through its various stages. First, it is the task of the director to consider his interpretation of the play, and how this may be realized in practical terms. He must determine what he thinks the play means, for on this everything else will hang. If the author is living and accessible, the director will almost certainly consult him. This may be a mixed blessing, for the author will usually have his private vision of the play, shaped by his own proximity to it. The director, standing apart from the work, is able to be more objective. Authors are, notoriously, fallible directors of their own work, though a number have refused to recognize this and tried to impose their will on actors and director alike. George Bernard Shaw is a case in point; his plays contain inordinately lengthy stage directions, dictating the appearance of the stage setting, the properties, costumes and movements in such explicit detail that, if followed to the letter, they would leave the director nothing to do.

INTERPRETING A PLAY FOR THE STAGE

In the case of a dead, particularly a long-dead, author the director has different problems. He must arrive at the best interpretation that he can, aided only by the second-hand resources of scholarship. This is not to denigrate the scholar. Any intelligent director will read all the editions and commentaries that he can. But it is in the matter of bringing the play to the stage that the practitioner and the scholar conspicuously part company. Scholarship has space and leisure to be expansive. It can discuss alternative explanations, point to ambiguities, and illuminate textual problems with footnotes suggesting various ways in which they may be resolved. A good scholar is more inclined to discuss a range of interpretations than to commit himself to one. The theater, on the other hand, has to be decisive. It offers no footnotes. It cannot ask the spectator to go back and reconsider. In performance, if something is not clear at first hearing, it is not clear at all. Therefore the director, for better or worse, has to commit himself to one interpretation, to one vision of the play; and, inevitably, there will be those who disagree with him. Laurence Olivier prefaced his film of *Hamlet* with the statement that this is a play about a man who could not make up his mind. An immediate response rang out from a segment of the audience: "Wrong!" It is ever thus. The theater, unfortunately, cannot offer a variety of interpretations and ask the audience to choose. It has to settle for one; and what this is will vary with the director and his times. Part of the measure of greatness of a play is the number of different interpretations it can bear without forfeiting its dramatic viability.

The initial decision, once arrived at, carries others in its train. A directorial interpretation involves matters of setting and costume, and these are usually worked out well in advance with the appropriate people. Let us take, as an example, the case of *King Lear*. The same play may assume a number of stage shapes, depending on what the director assumes its meaning and purpose to be. Does he see it, for instance, on the most rudimentary level, as a chronicle play about certain events in remote British history? (Unlikely, perhaps; but it has been done.) The name of Lear, after all, appears in early British records, and a rough date may be assigned to him. In this case we will have a *Lear* dressed in furs and skins, and set again a background of rocks and monoliths. Alternatively, does the director see the play, as some scholars have suggested, as closely related to political events of Shakespeare's own time? Does Lear's division of his kingdom give stage form to the fears of those who looked uneasily into the future of an England whose queen would die unmarried and childless? This gives another line for sets and costumes to take. Does the director envisage the work as having a particular meaning for now, for the present generation? He may therefore decide to stage it in modern dress, against settings evoking the audience's present. As noted above, "modern-dress" Shakespeare was the regular practice before the nineteenth century; it became modish again in the 1920's and 30's, and still occasionally reappears with value today, though perhaps *Lear* is not the ideal play for such treatment. Is it a cosmic drama, located in no particular time and place, but expressive only of man's constant inhumanity to man, and his subservience to forces beyond his control? Sets and costumes may display this too, by choosing forms linked to no specific style or period but creating their own theatrical logic. Thus the stage has shown us all manner of Lears. One has been Ancient British, another Elizabethan. Olivier's production suggested an almost prehistoric world without actually depicting it, a world of towering crags and swirling mists. Gielgud chose a timeless *Lear*, dressed in costumes of stylized shape and set among abstract sculptural forms. Yet another production looked to the future and set the play in a blackened, smouldering landscape, the neo-primitive world that had survived the atomic war.

The director's basic interpretation must also decide the placement and movement of his characters. It is his task to illuminate what he considers to be the underlying pattern of the play through significant action. To this end he will create a subtext, working with his actors to build up a mental background and justification for the lines they speak. In *Lear* again, the play begins with the King's announcement that he proposes to divide his kingdom, and his challenge to his daughters to proclaim their love for him. Why does he do this? Is it simply the datum, the formal beginning to the play, which neither asks nor needs explanation? In this case, the director may stage the

Engraving of Benjamin Wilson's painting of David Garrick (1717–1770) as King Lear, Act III. (Photograph: Raymond Mander and Joe Mitchenson Theatre Collection.)

John Gielgud as Lear in the Royal Shakespeare Theatre production, Stratford-upon-Avon, England, 1955. (Photograph: Royal Shakespeare Theatre.)

opening scenes almost as a prologue, quite simply and formally, a bare proclamation. Or is there a more complex human explanation? Olivier saw Lear in this scene as a man on the verge of senility, making his momentous decision almost as a whim; and he worked up to this from his first appearance on stage, having Lear stop as if to address a remark to a soldier, then changing his mind and going on. Why does Cordelia refuse to answer? Is she simply revolted by her sisters' protestations, or is there some other reason? Nahum Tate, the Restoration playwright, was so obsessed by this problem that he postulated a love affair between Cordelia and Edgar dividing her loyalty so that she was unable to answer her father as he wished; and he carried this idea to such lengths that he rewrote the play. So far may interpretation go.

A further example. What relationship exists between Lear and the Fool? Is the latter intended to be the King's conscience? His *alter ego*? A daughter-substitute? Or an objective commentator on his master's folly? Once again, whatever interpretation is decided upon can be emphasized by the relative placing of the characters and their contact, or lack of it. Gloucester is blinded. Is the director concerned with the physical violence of the act, or its symbolic performance? If the former, the deed can be portrayed most graphically on the stage. If the latter, it can be merely suggested, not shown. All these are things which must be worked out by the director with his actors, and they must ultimately agree on the meaning of what is being done. Discrepancies of interpretation show up with painful clarity in performance. An actor may sometimes disagree totally with his director's interpretation. He will usually follow it, none the less. In the long rehearsal process, the interpretation may change. Alec Guinness has recorded that he went through several interpretations of Shakespeare's *Richard II* before he found a view of the character that satisfied him as being logical and self-consistent.

Amid all these interpretations, then, where is the play? The answer must be that it is in none of them, and all of them. The play's values change as the theaters, the actors, and the audiences change. The *Lear* we see is not the *Lear* that Burbage performed, and the Elizabethan playgoers saw, though the text is the same. The Lear of Garrick (1717–1779) was totally different from that of Edmund Kean (1787–1833). In the same way, Lincoln Center bears small resemblance to the Globe Playhouse, Drury Lane, or the Lyceum. Each generation finds a new meaning in the script, illuminating it with contemporary concerns and preoccupations. It is the theater's continual task to bring about a rapprochement between the play and its successive audiences, finding a new frame of reference in which it will be meaningful. The actor, who works in the ephemeral, who sculpts, as has been said, in snow, accepts this as a condition of his art. The text remains, but its illumination changes.

THE MECHANICS OF PRODUCTION However ornate the director's conception, the commercial theater imposes strict limitations on time and cost. A Broadway production may expect a minimum of three weeks' rehearsal; the cost, regulated by strict union standards for actors and stage crew, may be upwards of $200,000 for a nonmusical play, vastly more for a musical. In university theaters, which have

The University of Minnesota production of *King Lear* in Minneapolis, 1956. (Photograph: The University of Minnesota Theatre.)

Paul Scofield as Lear in Peter Brook's production by the Royal Shakespeare Company in London, 1962. (Photograph: Angus McBean. Harvard Theatre Collection.)

tended to become more and more the home of the classics, conditions are somewhat happier. Campus productions usually work with five or six weeks of rehearsal time, uninhibited by union hours, and the budget is far smaller when salaries do not have to be paid: perhaps as little as $1,500 for a *King Lear*. Given these differences, rehearsals in both situations tend to follow the same pattern. They will begin with a general reading of the play, during which the director explains his conception; the cast may also see preliminary designs of sets and costumes, so that they know the environment in which they will be working. Early rehearsals are conducted book-in-hand, with normally only the barest indication of a set. The principal acting areas, steps and levels are marked out on the floor with tape. Any furniture that is to hand may be used; a chair may stand in for a throne, a bench for a bed. During this period cuts and changes may still be made, imposed sometimes by such commercial considerations as the length and expense of the performance, sometimes by changes in the director's conception as he absorbs what his actors bring to their parts. Gradually, the actors memorize. It is the director's hope that parts will be learnt as rapidly as possible, as only then can serious work begin. Once they have discarded their scripts, actors can relate to one another and to their surroundings. During the course of rehearsals the other production elements are added. Actors start to work with the actual props, instead of rehearsal equivalents. In a university theater, the setting begins to grow around the actors as they rehearse. Actual steps replace the lines on the floor and walls appear where there was only empty space. In the commercial theater, again because of expense, the company may never know the actual set until the last stages of rehearsal; they do most of their work in an empty hall lit by a single bulb. In either case, the last days are spent in integrating the total production. The full set appears, and actors have to adjust to its intricacies. The full lighting plot is put into action. Sound effects and music are added. The actors are introduced to their costumes, and have to master, very rapidly, the difficulties of wearing them. There is usually one technical rehearsal, during which the actors are subordinated to the other demands of the performance; they usually move from one lighting or scene cue to the next, so that the technical staff may become accustomed to the changes. Finally, full dress rehearsals, run like a full performance, with the director no longer intervening, but confining himself to notes at the end. In the commercial theater, even this may not be the end of the process. Most Broadway productions go through a series of tryouts out-of-town, before paying public audiences. Depending on the reaction, important changes may be made in the production, or even in the script itself. It is not unknown for actors to be handed new material every day. Thus the production is established; it opens; and even then, over a long commercial run, it may change, as new actors replace the original cast or as those who were with the play from the beginning make new discoveries about it and about each other. A script, once it has been published, achieves a certain permanency. A production is always changing, and no two audiences ever see exactly the same dramatic event.

WRITING ABOUT DRAMA

People write about plays in order to clarify and to account for their responses to works that interest or excite or frustrate them. In order to put words on paper you will have to take a second and a third look at what is in front of you and at what is within you. And so writing is a way of learning. The last word is never said about complex thoughts and feelings, but when we write we hope to make at least a little progress in the difficult but rewarding job of talking about our responses. We learn, and then we hope to interest our reader because we are communicating our responses to something that for one reason or another is worth talking about.

This communication is, in effect, teaching. You may think that you are writing for the teacher, but such a belief is a misconception; when you write, *you* are the teacher. An essay on a play is an attempt to help someone to see the play as you see it. If this chapter had to be boiled down to a single sentence of advice, that sentence would be: Because you are teaching, your essay should embody those qualities that you value in teachers — probably intelligence, open-mindedness, and effort; certainly a desire to offer what help one can.

Analysis is, literally, a separation into parts in order to understand. An analysis commonly considers one part and the relation of this part to the whole. For example, it may consider only the functions of the settings in *Hedda Gabler* or the Fool in *King Lear* or the music in *Death of a Salesman*.

Analysis, of course, is not a process used only in talking about literature. It is commonly applied in thinking about almost any complex matter. Jimmy Connors plays a deadly game of tennis; what makes it so good? How does his backhand contribute to his game? What does his serve do to the opponent? Because a play is usually long and complicated, in a paper written for a college course you probably do not have enough space to analyze all aspects of the play, and so you will probably choose one aspect and relate it to the whole. Of course all of the parts are related; a study of one character, for example, will have to take some account of other characters and of plot and perhaps even of setting; but, still, an analysis may legitimately devote most of its space to one part, taking account of other parts only insofar as they are relevant to the topic.

If a work is fairly long and complex, and you are writing only a few pages, almost surely you will write an analysis of some part. Unless you have an enormous amount of time for reflection and revision, you cannot write a meaningful essay of five hundred or even a thousand words on *Oedipus* or *The Cherry Orchard*. You cannot even write on "Character in *Oedipus*" or "Symbolism in *The Cherry Orchard*." And probably you won't really want to write on such topics anyway. Probably *one* character or *one* symbol has caught your interest. Trust your feelings; you are probably on to something interesting, and it will be best to think about this smaller topic for the relatively few hours that you have. A "smaller" topic need not be dull or trivial; treated properly, it may illuminate the entire work, or, to change the metaphor, it may serve as a mine shaft that gives entry to the work. "The

Dramatic Function of the Gloucester Subplot in *King Lear*," carefully thought about, will in five hundred or a thousand words tell a reader more (and will have taught its author more) than will "*King Lear* as a Tragedy." Similarly, "Imagery of Blindness in *King Lear*" is a better topic than "Imagery in *King Lear*," and "The Meanings of 'Nature' in *King Lear*" is a better topic than "The Meaning of *King Lear*."

How do you find a topic and how do you turn it into a thesis, that is, a point you want to make? An idea may hit you suddenly; as you are reading you find yourself jotting it in the margin, "Contrast with Hedda's earlier response," or "Note the change of costume," or "too heavy irony," or "ugh." Or an idea may come slowly on rereading. Perhaps you gradually become aware that *Death of a Salesman* is both a tragedy and a social drama (a play that calls attention to a problem in the organization of society), and perhaps you come to feel that Miller's emphasis on social pressures is not entirely consistent with his effort to present Willy Loman as a tragic hero. At this point, then, you have a thesis — an angle — as well as a topic.

FROM TOPIC TO THESIS Think of it this way: a topic is a subject, and a thesis is a subject with a predicate: "Imagery in *King Lear*." is a topic, but it can be turned into a thesis thus: "Imagery helps to distinguish the characters in *King Lear*." Once you can formulate a thesis, you are well on the way to writing a good paper. But note that the more precise the formulation of the thesis, the better the paper will probably be. After all, "Imagery in *King Lear* is interesting" is a thesis, but such a vague formulation gives you little to go on. Not until you can turn it into something like "Imagery in *King Lear* serves three important purposes" are you anywhere near to being able to draft your essay.

Every literary work affords its own topics for analysis, and every essayist must set forth his own thesis, but a few useful generalizations may be made. You can often find a thesis by asking one of two questions:

1. *What is this doing?* That is, why is this scene in the novel or play? Why is the Fool in *King Lear*? Why the music in *Death of a Salesman*? Why are these lines verse and those lines prose? Why is a certain action reported to us rather than represented on the stage? What is the significance of the parts of the work? (Titles are often highly significant parts of the work: Ibsen's *Hedda Gabler* and Chekhov's *The Cherry Orchard* would be slightly different if they had other titles.)

2. *Why do I have this response?* Why do I find this scene clever, or moving, or puzzling? How did the author make this character funny or dignified or pathetic? How did he communicate the idea that this character is a bore without boring me?

The first of these questions, "What is this doing?" requires that you identify yourself with the author, wondering, for example, whether this opening scene is the best possible for this story. The second question, "Why do I have this response?" requires that you trust your feelings. If you are amused or bored or puzzled or annoyed, assume that these responses are appropriate and follow them up, at least until a rereading of the play provides other responses.

Here is a short essay, written by a student. The student has told us privately that when she began work on the paper she was hoping to write on the irrationality of the fairies in *A Midsummer Night's Dream* as a sort of mirror of the irrationality of the young lovers, but when she searched the play for supporting detail she found, to her surprise, that she had to revise the thesis.

A SAMPLE ANALYSIS

Fairy Mischief and Morality

and <u>A Midsummer Night's Dream</u>

Title is informative.

If we read <u>A Midsummer Night's Dream</u> casually, or come

away from a delightful performance, we may have the vague

impression that the fairies are wild, mischievous, willful

creatures who perhaps represent the irrational qualities of

mankind. But in fact the text lends only a little support

to this view. The irrationality of mankind is really repre-

sented chiefly by the human beings in the play--we are told

in the first scene, for example, that Demetrius used to love

Helena, but now loves Hermia--and the fairies are really

largely responsible for the happy ending finally achieved.

Opening paragraph leads us into the subject.

It is, of course, easy to see why we may think of the

fairies as wild and mischievous. Titania and Oberon have

quarreled over a little Indian boy, and their quarrel had

led to fogs, floods, and other disorders in nature. More-

over, Titania accuses Oberon of infidelity, and Oberon

returns the charge:

> How canst thou thus for shame, Titania,
> Glance at my credit with Hippolyta,
> Knowing I know thy love to Theseus?
> (II.i.74-76)[1]

Short quotation provides evidence.

[1]All quotations from this play are from the text reprinted in Sylvan Barnet, Morton Berman, and William Burto,
<u>Types of Drama</u>, 3d ed. (Boston: Little, Brown, 1981).
Further references to the play will be given parenthetically, within the text of the essay.

Footnote gives source, and explains that other footnotes will not be necessary.

Titania rejects this countercharge, saying "These are the forgeries of jealousy" (II.i.81), but we are not convinced of her innocence. It would be easy to give additional examples of speeches in which the king and queen of fairyland present unflattering pictures of each other, but probably one of the strongest pieces of evidence of their alleged irrationality is the fact that Oberon causes Titania to fall in love with the asinine Bottom. We should not forget, however, that later Oberon will take pity on her: "Her dotage now I do begin to pity" (IV.i.51).

In fact, it is largely through Oberon's sense of pity-- this time for the quarreling young lovers in the forest-- that the lovers finally are successfully paired off. And we should remember, too, before we claim that the fairies are consistently quarrelsome and mischievous, that at the very end of the play Oberon and Titania join in a song and dance blessing the newlyweds and promising healthy offspring. The fairies, though quarrelsome, are fundamentally benevolent spirits.

But what of Robin Goodfellow, the Puck of this play? Is he not mischievous? One of the fairies says Robin is a "shrewd and knavish sprite" (II.i.33) who frightens maids and plays tricks on housewives; Robin admits the charge, saying "Thou speakest aright" (II.i.42), and two lines later he says "I jest to Oberon, and make him smile," and then he goes on to describe some of his practical jokes, including his fondness for neighing to tease a horse, and pulling a stool from under an old lady. But this is not quite the whole story. The fact is, despite this speech, that we do

Citation in parentheses to reduce the number of footnotes.

The main point having been set forth, essayist now turns to an apparent exception.

Essayist concedes a point, but then goes on in the rest of the paragraph to argue that the main point nevertheless still holds.

not see Robin engage in any mischievous pranks. After all,
he does not deliberately anoint the eyes of the wrong Athenian lover. Oberon tells Robin that he will recognize the
young man by his Athenian clothing, and when Puck encounters
a young man in Athenian clothing he anoints the youth's
eyes. The fault is really Oberon's, though of course Oberon
meant well when he instructed Robin:

> A sweet Athenian lady is in love
> With a disdainful youth. Anoint his eyes;
> But do it when the next thing he espies
> May be the lady.
>
> (II.i.260–263)

So Robin's error is innocent. He is speaking honestly when
he says, "Believe me, king of shadows, I mistook" (III.ii.
347). Of course he does enjoy the confusion he mistakenly
causes, but we can hardly blame him severely for that.
After all, we enjoy it too.

    The fairies, by their very nature, of course suggest
a mysterious, irrational world, but--even though, as we have
just seen, Oberon is called the "king of shadows"--they are
not to be confused with "ghosts, wand'ring here and there,"
"damnèd spirits" who "willfully themselves exile from light/
And must for aye consort with black-browed night" (III.ii.
381–387). Oberon explicitly says, after this speech, "But
we are spirits of another sort," and his speech is filled
with references not to darkness but to light: "morning,"
"eastern gate," "blessèd beams." The closer we observe them
in the play, then, the closer their behavior is to that of
normal, decent human beings. There is plenty of irrationality in the play, but it is found for the most part in the
mortals.

Concluding paragraph summarizes, but it does not merely repeat what has come before; it offers a few brief new quotations. The paragraph ends by setting the conclusion (fairies are decent) in a fresh context (it's the mortals who are irrational).

Notice that this first-rate essay, written by a student, has a thesis, and develops the thesis effectively. The title gives the reader some idea of what is coming, and the first paragraph pretty clearly sets forth the thesis. The essay next takes up the evidence that might seem to contradict the thesis — Oberon and Titania, and Robin Goodfellow — and it shows that this evidence is not decisive. All the while, then, it is moving forward, substantiating its thesis, especially by using well-chosen quotations. The last paragraph slightly restates the thesis, in light of what the essay has demonstrated.

WRITING A COMPARISON

Something should be said about an essay organized around a comparison or a contrast between, say, two characters — in one play or even in two plays. Probably the student's first thought, after making some jottings, is to discuss one half of the comparison and then go on to the second half. Instructors and textbooks usually condemn such an organization, arguing that the essay breaks into two parts and that the second part involves a good deal of repetition of categories set up in the first part. Usually they recommend that the student organize his thoughts differently, somewhat along these lines:

1. First similarity
   a. first work (or character, or characteristic)
   b. second work
2. Secondary similarity
   a. first work
   b. second work
3. First difference
   a. first work
   b. second work
4. Second difference
   a. first work
   b. second work

and so on, for as many additional differences as seem relevant. For example, if one wishes to compare King Lear with Willy Loman in *Death of a Salesman*, one may organize the material thus:

1. First similarity: each figure's lack of self-knowledge
   a. Lear
   b. Loman
2. Second similarity: the corrupt world surrounding these figures
   a. Lear's evil daughters and their associates
   b. Society's vulgar idea of success, to which Willy subscribes
3. First difference: degree to which the character attains self-knowledge
   a. Lear's recognition
   b. Willy's continuing blindness

Here is another way of organizing a comparison and contrast:

1. First point: lack of self-knowledge
   a. similarities between Lear and Willy
   b. differences between Lear and Willy
2. Second point: the corrupt world
   a. similarities between the worlds in *King Lear* and *Salesman*
   b. differences between the worlds in *King Lear* and *Salesman*
3. Third point: degree of attainment of self-knowledge
   a. similarities between Lear and Willy
   b. differences between Lear and Willy

But a comparison need not employ either of these structures. There is even the danger that an essay employing either of them may not come into focus until the essayist stands back from his seven-layer cake and announces, in his concluding paragraph, that the odd layers taste better. In one's preparatory thinking, one may want to make comparisons in pairs (Faults: Lear and Willy; Social satire: indictment of injustice in *Lear*, and of capitalism in *Salesman*; Children: Lear's daughters, Willy's sons; Comments by other characters . . .), but one must come to some conclusions about what these add up to before writing the final version. This final version should not duplicate the thought processes; rather, it should be organized so as to make the point clearly and effectively. After reflection, one may believe that although there are superficial similarities between Lear and Willy Loman, there are essential differences; then in the finished essay one probably will not wish to obscure the main point by jumping back and forth from play to play, working through a series of similarities and differences. It may be better to discuss King Lear and then to point out that, although Willy Loman resembles him in A, B, and C, Willy in D, E, and F does *not* resemble Lear. Some repetition in the second half of the essay (for example, "Willy Loman never comes to the deep self-knowledge that we see Lear achieve") will serve to bind the two halves into a meaningful whole, making clear the degree of similarity or difference. The point of the essay presumably is not to list pairs of similarities or differences, but to illuminate a work, or works, by making thoughtful comparison. Although in a long essay one cannot postpone until page 30 a discussion of the second half of the comparison, in an essay of, say, less than ten pages nothing is wrong with setting forth one half of the comparison and then, in light of it, the second half. The essay will break into two unrelated parts if the second half makes no use of the first, or if it fails to modify the first half, but not if the second half looks back to the first half and calls attention to differences that the new material reveals. A student ought to learn how to write an essay with interwoven comparisons, but he ought also to know that there is another, simpler and clearer way to write a comparison.

Because a critical essay on a play is a judicious attempt to help a reader see what is going on in a work or in a part of a work, the voice of the critic sounds, on first hearing, impartial; but good criticism includes — at least

COMMUNICATING
JUDGMENTS

implicitly — evaluation. You can say not only that the setting changes (a neutral expression) but also that "the playwright aptly shifts the setting" or "unconvincingly introduces a new character," or "effectively juxtaposes . . ." These evaluations you support with evidence. You have feelings about the work under discussion, and you reveal them, not by continually saying "I feel" and "this moves me," but by calling attention to the degree of success or failure you perceive. Nothing is wrong with occasionally using "I," and noticeable avoidances of it — passives, "this writer," "we," and the like — suggest an offensive sham modesty; but too much talk of "I" makes a writer sound like an egomaniac.

One final remark on communicating judgments: Write sincerely. Any attempt to neglect your own thoughtful responses and replace them with fabrications designed to please an instructor will surely fail. It is hard enough to find the words that clearly communicate your responses; it is almost impossible to find the words that express your hunch about what your instructor expects your responses to be. George Orwell shrewdly commented on the obvious signs of insincere writing: "When there is a gap between one's real and one's declared aims, one turns as it were instinctively to long words and exhausted idioms, like a cuttlefish squirting out ink."

ASKING
QUESTIONS
TO GET
ANSWERS

We have already suggested that you can often find a thesis by asking two questions: What is this doing? and Why do I have this response? In a moment we will suggest many additional questions, but first we want to mention that the editorial apparatus throughout this book is intended to help you to read, enjoy, and discuss drama as fully as possible. When you are sitting down to write about a play, you may want to reread some parts of this apparatus for guidance on your topic, perhaps paying special attention to the glossary's entries on *character, convention, dialogue, diction, foil, irony, motivation, plot, suspense,* and *unity.* You may also want to reread some of the earlier material in the book, especially "The Language of Drama."

Now for additional questions that may help you to find topics and to sharpen them into theses.

PLOT. Are certain developments (for example, Lear's madness) prepared for by foreshadowing? Are certain happenings or situations recurrent? If so, what significance do you attach to them? If there is a subplot, as in *King Lear,* how is it related? What is the function of a particular scene? Why do certain scenes occur when and where they do? Why are certain episodes reported rather than presented on the stage? Are there irrelevant scenes? Does the plot depend on chance? Is the resolution satisfactory?

CHARACTER. What sort of person is So-and-so? (Of course a dramatic character is not likely to be thoroughly realistic in the sense of being a copy of someone we might know, but is the character coherent, perhaps representative of some human type?) How is the character defined? How trustworthy are the characters when they characterize themselves? Others? (Consider what the character says and does, what others say about him and do to him and also consider other characters who more or less resemble the character in question, because the similarities — and the differences — may be significant.) If a character is tragic, does the tragedy proceed from a flaw, from an intellectual error, from the malice of others, from sheer chance, or from some combination of these? If comic, do we laugh with him or at him? Are the characters adequately motivated? Do the characters change as the play goes on, or do we simply know them better at the end? Is the character so meditative that we feel he is engaged less in a dialogue with others than in a dialogue with his own mind? If so, de we feel that this character is in large degree a spokesman for the author, commenting on the world not only of the play but on the outside world too?

In a typical course paper you need not and probably should not take on all aspects of a character. With a play of great complexity — for example one of Shakespeare's major plays — a short essay may do well to take an even smaller topic, such as Lear's use of prose (Why does he sometimes speak in prose, sometimes in verse, and what does it tell us about him?) or Lear's denunciation of sex (Why is the king obsessed with the idea of lechery?). Even here we will not be able merely to hunt through the play looking at Lear's prose or his remarks about sex; we will have to pay some attention to other uses of prose in *King Lear,* or to references to sex in the play, if we are to see the exact nature of the problem we have chosen to isolate.

NONVERBAL LANGUAGE. Words are not, it has been suggested in our discussion of drama (see especially pages 23–26), the only language of drama, and a student will sometimes want to explore matters of staging. What is especially difficult for most of us confronted with only a printed page, is to catch the full dramatic quality of a play — to read the words and also to have a sense of how they will sound in the context of gestures and a setting. We tend to read drama as literature rather than as dramatic literature, or theater. (When the author is Shakespeare or Shaw, we can sometimes justly examine his works as literature, although even here we may find that things that seem flat on the page come alive in the theater.) Consider the setting, for example. Is it symbolic? Drama of the nineteenth and early twentieth centuries (for example, plays of Ibsen and Chekhov) is often thought to be "realistic," but of course even a realistic playwright or stage designer selects his material. A realistic setting can say a great deal, can serve as a symbol. Here is Ibsen on nonverbal devices:

> I can do quite a lot by manipulating the prosaic details of my plays so that they become theatrical metaphors and come to mean more than what they are; I have used costume in this way, lighting, scenery, landscape, weather; I have used trivial everyday things like inky fingers and candles; and I have used living figures as symbols of spiritual forces that act upon the hero. Perhaps these things could be brought into the context of a modern realistic play to help me to portray the modern hero and the tragic conflict which I now understand so well.[1]

In the setting of *Hedda Gabler,* for example, Ibsen uses two suggestive details as more than mere background: early in the play Hedda is distressed by

[1] Quoted by John Northam, "Ibsen's Search for the Hero," in *Ibsen,* ed. Rolf Fjelde (Englewood Cliffs, N.J.: Prentice-Hall, 1965), p. 99.

the sunlight that shines through the opened French doors, a detail that we later see helps to reveal her fear of the processes of nature. More evident and more pervasive is her tendency, when she cannot cope with her present situation, to move to the inner room, at the rear of the stage, in which hangs a picture of her late father. And over and over again in Ibsen we find the realistic setting of a nineteenth-century drawing room, with its heavy draperies and its bulky furniture, helping to convey his vision of a bourgeois world that oppresses the individual who struggles to affirm other values.

Contemporary dramatists are often explicit about the symbolic qualities of the setting. Below is an example from Miller's *Death of a Salesman:*

> Before us is the Salesman's house. We are aware of towering, angular shapes behind it, surrounding it on all sides. Only the blue light of the sky falls upon the house and forestage; the surrounding area shows an angry glow of orange. As more light appears, we see a solid vault of apartment houses around the small, fragile-seeming home.

This setting is a symbol that helps to give the play its meaning. Miller's "solid vault of apartment houses" that menaces the Salesman's house helps us to see the social forces that warp the individual.

If you set out to write an essay on gestures in *King Lear*, you may come to see how rich the play is in such a symbolic gesture as kneeling or stripping off clothing, and it is similarly rich in sound effects — chiefly, of course, the storm, but also sounds of music and of fighting. Similarly, costume (as we point out on p. 24) often reveals rather than conceals. Again, even a realistic playwright such as Ibsen uses costume symbolically, as a close reading of *Hedda Gabler* will show.

STAGING AND PRODUCTION. How would you stage the first scene of a given play? What kinds of costumes should the characters wear (assuming that these are not specified by the playwright)? If you were producing the play, what scenes or speeches might you cut, and why? Prepare a television script for the first scene of a play, indicating what the viewer would see at first (for example, a group of characters talking to each other) and then, bit by bit, what the camera would focus on. (Because the television screen is small, it cannot accommodate a view of the whole stage for more than a few moments; it must focus on a few figures in proximity, or even on the face of a single speaker or on the face of a character listening to a speaker.)

REVIEW:
HOW TO
WRITE AN
EFFECTIVE
ESSAY[2]

Everyone must work out his own procedures and rituals (John C. Calhoun liked to plough his farm before writing), but the following suggestions may provide some help.

1. Read the play carefully.

2. Choose a worthwhile and compassable subject, something that interests you and is not so big that your handling of it must be superficial. As

---

[2] This section is adapted from Sylvan Barnet, *A Short Guide to Writing about Literature,* 3rd ed. (Boston: Little, Brown, 1975), pp. 33–36.

you work, shape your topic into a thesis, moving, for example, from "The Character of Willy Loman" to "The Influence of Society on Willy Loman."

3. Reread the play, jotting down notes of all relevant matters. As you read, reflect on your reading and record your reflections. If you have a feeling or an idea, jot it down; don't assume that you will remember it when you get around to writing your essay. The margins of this book are a good place for initial jottings, but many people find that in the long run it is easiest to transfer these notes to 3×5 cards, writing on one side only.

4. Sort out your cards into some kind of reasonable divisions, and reject cards irrelevant to your topic. If you have adequately formulated your thesis (let's say, "Arthur Miller suggests that society is largely responsible for Willy Loman's plight, but Miller is not entirely consistent") you ought to be able to work out a tentative organization. As you work you may discover a better way to group your notes. If so, start reorganizing. Speaking generally, it is a good idea to organize your essay from the lesser material to the greater (to avoid anticlimax) or from the simple to the complex (to ensure intelligibility). If, for example, you are discussing the roles of three characters, it may be best to build up to the one of the three that you think the most important. If you are comparing two characters, it may be best to move from the most obvious contrasts to the least obvious. (In your opening paragraph, which will probably be almost the last thing you will write, you should of course give the reader an idea of the scope of the paper, but at this stage you are organizing the material chiefly for yourself and so you need not yet worry about an introductory paragraph.) When you have arranged your notes into a meaningful sequence of packets, you have approximately divided your material into paragraphs.

5. Get it down on paper. Most essayists find it useful to jot down some sort of outline, indicating the main idea of each paragraph and, under each main idea, supporting details that give it substance. An outline — not necessarily anything highly formal with capital and lowercase letters and Roman and Arabic numerals but merely key phrases in some sort of order — will help you to overcome the paralysis called "writer's block" that commonly afflicts professionals as well as students. A page of paper with ideas in some sort of sequence, however rough, ought to encourage you that you do have something to say. And so, despite the temptation to sharpen another pencil or to put a new ribbon into the typewriter, the best thing to do at this point is to sit down and start writing. If you don't feel that you can work from note cards and a rough outline, try another method: get something down on paper, writing freely, sloppily, automatically, or whatever, but allow your ideas about what the work means to you and how it conveys its meaning — rough as your ideas may be — to begin to take visible form. If you are like most people you can't do much precise thinking until you have committed to paper at least a rough sketch of your initial ideas. Later you can push and polish your ideas into shape, perhaps even deleting all of them and starting over, but it's a lot easier to improve your ideas once you see them in front

of you than it is to do the job in your head. On paper one word leads to another; in your head one word often blocks another.

Just keep going; you may realize, as you near the end of a sentence, that you no longer believe it. O.K.; be glad that your first idea led you to a better one, and pick up your better one and keep going with it. What you are doing is, in a sense, by trial and error pushing your way not only toward clear expression but toward sharper ideas and richer responses.

6. If there is time, reread the play, looking for additional material that strengthens or weakens your main point; take account of it in your outline or draft.

7. With your outline or draft in front of you, write a more lucid version, checking your notes for fuller details, such as supporting quotations. If, as you work, you find that some of the points in your earlier jottings are no longer relevant, eliminate them; but make sure that the argument flows from one point to the next. As you write, your ideas will doubtless become clearer; some may prove to be poor ideas. (We rarely know exactly what our ideas are until we have them set down on paper. As the little girl said, replying to the suggestion that she should think before she spoke, "How do I know what I think until I say it?") Not until you have written a draft do you really have a strong sense of how good your essay may be.

8. After a suitable interval, preferably a few days, read the draft with a view toward revising it, not with a view toward congratulating yourself. A revision, after all, is a re-vision, a second (and presumably sharper) view. When you revise, you will be in the company of Picasso, who said that in painting a picture he advanced by a series of destructions. A revision — say, the substitution of a precise word for an imprecise one — is not a matter of prettifying but of thinking. As you read, correct things that disturb you (for example, awkward repetitions that bore, inflated utterances that grate), add supporting detail where the argument is undeveloped (a paragraph of only one or two sentences is usually an undeveloped paragraph), and ruthlessly delete irrelevancies however well written they may be. But remember that a deletion probably requires some adjustment in the preceding and subsequent material. Make sure that the opening paragraph gives the readers some sense of where they will be going, and that between the opening and the closing paragraphs the argument, aided by transitions (such as "furthermore," "on the other hand," "in the next scene"), runs smoothly. The details should be relevant, the organization reasonable, the argument clear. Check all quotations for accuracy. Quotations are evidence, usually intended to support your assertions, and it is not nice to alter the evidence, even unintentionally. If there is time (there almost never is), put the revision aside, reread it in a day or two, and revise it again, especially with a view toward shortening it.

9. Type or write a clean copy, following the principles concerning margins, pagination, footnotes, and so on set forth in the next section of this discussion. If you have borrowed any ideas, be sure to give credit, usually in footnotes, to your sources. Remember that plagiarism is not limited to the

unacknowledged borrowing of words; a borrowed idea, even when put into your own words, requires acknowledgment.

10. Proofread and make corrections.

Basic Manuscript Form. Much of what follows is nothing more than common sense.

REMARKS
ABOUT
MANUSCRIPT
FORM

1. Use 8½ × 11 paper of good weight. Keep as lightweight a carbon copy as you wish, or make a photocopy, but hand in a sturdy original.

2. If you typewrite, use a reasonably fresh ribbon, double-space, and type on one side of the page only. If you submit a handwritten copy, use lined paper and write on one side of the page only, in ink, on every other line. Most instructors do *not* want papers to be enclosed in any sort of binder; and most instructors want papers to be stapled in the upper left corner; do not crimp or crease corners and expect them to hold together.

3. Leave an adequate margin — an inch or an inch and a half — at top, bottom, and sides.

4. Number the pages consecutively, using Arabic numerals in the upper right-hand corner.

5. Put your name and class or course number in the upper right-hand corner of the first page. It is a good idea to put your name in the upper right corner of each page so that your essay can be easily reassembled if a page gets separated.

6. Create your own title — one that reflects your topic or thesis. For example, a paper on *Death of a Salesman* should *not* be called "*Death of a Salesman*" but might be called "Two Kinds of Irony in *Death of a Salesman.*"

7. Center the title of your essay below the top margin of the first page. Begin the first word of the title with a capital, and capitalize each subsequent word except articles, conjunctions, and prepositions, thus: The Truth of Dreams in *A Midsummer Night's Dream.*

8. Begin the essay an inch or two below the title.

9. Your extensive revisions should have been made in your drafts, but minor last-minute revisions may be made — neatly — on the finished copy. Proofreading may catch some typographical errors, and you may notice some small weaknesses. Additions should be made *above* the line, with a caret (an upside-down v) *below* the line at the appropriate place. Indicate deletions by drawing a horizontal line through the word or words you wish to delete. Delete a single letter by drawing a vertical line through it. Use a vertical line, too, to separate words that should not have been run together.

Quotation and Quotation Marks. Excerpts from the plays you are writing about are indispensable. Such quotations not only let the reader know what you are talking about, they present the material you are responding to, thus letting the reader share your responses.

Here are some mechanical matters:

1. Identify the speaker or writer of the quotation, so that the reader is not left with a sense of uncertainty. Usually this identification precedes the quoted material (for example, "Smith says . . .") in accordance with the principle of letting the reader know where he is going, but occasionally it may follow the quotation, especially if it will provide something of a pleasant surprise. For instance, in a discussion of Arthur Miller's *Death of a Salesman*, you might quote a comment that seems to belittle the play and then reveal that Miller himself was the speaker.

2. The quotation must fit grammatically into your sentence. Suppose you want to use Hedda Gabler's line (she is imagining Løvborg's return from the party), "I see him already." Do not say:

> Near the end of the second act, when Mrs. Elvsted wonders in what condition Løvborg will return, Hedda says that she "see him already."

This version is better:

> Near the end of the second act, when Mrs. Elvsted wonders in what condition Løvborg will return, Hedda says that she sees "him already."

Or, of course, you can say,

> Near the end of the second act, when Mrs. Elvsted wonders in what condition Løvborg will return, Hedda says, "I see him already."

3. The quotation must be exact. Any material that you add — even one or two words — must be in square brackets, thus:

> When Hedda says that she sees "him [that is, Løvborg] already," she has in mind something very different from what she seems to be saying.

If you wish to omit material from within a quotation, indicate the ellipsis by three spaced periods. If a sentence ends in an omission, add a closed-up period and then three spaced periods to indicate the omission. The following example is based on a quotation from the sentences immediately above this one:

> The chapter says that "if you . . . omit material from within a quotation, [you must] indicate the ellipsis. . . . If a sentence ends in an omission, add a closed-up period and then three spaced periods. . . ."

Notice that although material preceded "If you," periods are not needed to indicate the omission because "If you" began a sentence in the original. Customarily, initial and terminal omissions are indicated only when they are part of the sentence you are quoting. Even such omissions need not be indicated when the quoted material is obviously incomplete — when, for instance, it is a word or phrase. Notice, too, that although quotations must be given word for word, the initial capitalization can be adapted, as here where "If" is reduced to "if."

When a line or more of verse is omitted from a passage that is set off, the three spaced periods are printed on a separate line:

> If we shadows have offended,
> Think but this, and all is mended:
> .   .   .
> Give me your hands, if we be friends,
> And Robin shall restore amends.

4. Distinguish between short and long quotations, and treat each appropriately. Short quotations (usually defined as less than three lines of verse or five lines of prose) are enclosed within quotation marks and run into the text (rather than set off, without quotation marks). Examples:

> Near the end of *Oedipus Rex* the Chorus reminds the audience that Oedipus "solved the famous riddle," but it does not tell us what the riddle was.

> King Lear's first long speech begins authoritatively: "Meantime we shall express our darker purpose. / Give me the map there. Know that we have divided/In three our kingdom."

Notice in the first passage that although four words only are being quoted, quotation marks are used, indicating that these are Sophocles' words, not the essayist's. Notice that in the second example a slash (diagonal line, virgule) is used to indicate the end of a line of verse other than the last line quoted. The slash is, of course, not used if the poetry is set off, indented, and printed as verse, thus:

> King Lear's first long speech begins authoritatively:

> Meantime we shall express our darker purpose.
> Give me the map there. Know that we have divided
> In three our kingdom; and 'tis our fast intent
> To shake all cares and business from our age,
> Conferring them on younger strengths, while we
> Unburthened crawl toward death.

Material that is set off (usually three or more lines of verse, five or more lines of prose) is not enclosed within quotation marks. To set it off, triple-space before and after the quotation and single-space the quotation. Poetry should be centered; prose quotations should be flush with both right and left margins. (Note: Some manuals of style call for double-spacing, some for indenting prose quotations; but whichever procedure you adopt, be consistent. Be sparing in your use of long quotations.) Use quotations as evidence, not as padding. Do not bore the reader with material that can be effectively reduced either by paraphrase or by cutting. If you cut, indicate ellipses as explained above under 3.

5. Commas and periods go inside the quotation marks. (Exception: if the quotation is immediately followed by material in parentheses or in square brackets, close the quotation, then give the parenthetic or bracketed material, and then — after the closing parenthesis or bracket, put the comma

or period.) Marks of punctuation other than periods and commas (that is, semicolons, colons, and dashes) go outside. Question marks and exclamation points go inside if they are part of the quotation, outside if they are your own.

> Hedda says to Løvborg, "So you're not going?" Can we be confident of Løvborg when he replies "I'm staying here with you and Thea"?

6. Use *single* quotation marks for material contained within a quotation that itself is within quotation marks, thus:

> The editors of *Types of Drama* say, "With Puck we look at the antics in the forest, smile tolerantly, and say with a godlike perspective, 'Lord, what fools these mortals be!'"

7. Use quotation marks around titles of short works, that is, for titles of chapters in books and for essays that might not be published by themselves. Unpublished works, even book-length dissertations, are also enclosed in quotation marks. Use italics (indicated by underlining) for books, that is, for plays, periodicals, and collections of essays.

FOOTNOTES   *A Note on Footnotes.* You may wish to use a footnote, telling the reader of your paper that the passage you are quoting is found in this book on such-and-such a page. Let us assume that you have already mentioned the author and the title of the play, and have just quoted a passage. At the end of the sentence that includes the quotation, or at the end of the quotation if you are offering it as an independent sentence, following the period type or write the number 1, elevating it slightly above the line. Do not put a period after the digit. Near the bottom of the paper, indent a few spaces and type or write the number 1, elevated and without a period. Then write (giving the appropriate page number):

> [1] Reprinted in Sylvan Barnet, Morton Berman, and William Burto, *Types of Drama*, 3d ed. (Boston: Little, Brown, 1981), p. 236.

Notice that the abbreviation for *page* is p., not pg.; the abbreviation for *pages* is pp., thus: pp. 236–237. For verse plays, whose lines are numbered, the usual procedure is not to cite a page but to cite act, scene, and line numbers in parentheses after the quotation. Give the act in capital Roman numerals, the scene in small Roman numerals, and the line in Arabic numerals. Periods follow the act and the scene.

> The lunatic, the lover and the poet
> Are of imagination all compact.
> One sees more devils than vast hell can hold,
> That is the madman. The lover, all as frantic,
> Sees Helen's beauty in a brow of Egypt.
>
> (V.i.7–11)[1]

The footnote will then read:

> [1] All quotations from *A Midsummer Night's Dream* are from the text reprinted in Sylvan Barnet, Morton Berman, and William Burto, *Types of Drama*, 3d ed. (Boston: Little, Brown, 1981).

If you have not mentioned the author or title of the work quoted, you need to give that information in the note, thus:

> [1] William Shakespeare, A *Midsummer Night's Dream,* reprinted in Sylvan Barnet, Morton Berman, and William Burto, *Types of Drama,* 3d ed. (Boston: Little, Brown, 1981).

If you have mentioned the author, but not the work, the note will go thus:

> [1] A *Midsummer Night's Dream,* reprinted in Sylvan Barnet, Morton Berman, and William Burto, *Types of Drama,* 3d ed. (Boston: Little, Brown, 1981).

In short, you need not give information in the note that is already given in the main body of the essay.

In order to eliminate writing many footnotes, each one merely citing the page of a quotation, you can say, in the first footnote, after giving the bibliographical information as above, something like this:

> All further references to this work will be given parenthetically, within the text of the essay.

Thus, when you quote the next passage from the play, at the end of the sentence — just before the period — you need only insert a pair of parentheses enclosing the page number or the act, scene, and line number. Here is an example:

> At this point Lear goes out, saying, "O Fool, I shall go mad" (p. 162).

or

> At this point Lear goes out, saying, "O Fool, I shall go mad" (II.iv.287).

Notice that in the sample analysis on pp. 799–801 we used only one footnote, and then cited all of the other quotations parenthetically.

A GLOSSARY
OF DRAMATIC TERMS

Absurd, Theater of the. Drama of such writers as Eugène Ionesco and Samuel Beckett in France and Harold Pinter in England that imitates the absurdity of man's existence. "Everything, as I see it, is an aberration," Ionesco has said. Among the basic themes are man's loneliness in a world without God, man's inability to communicate, man's dehumanization at the hands of mass media, and man's impotence in the face of society and of death. Though the plays are serious, they may contain extravagantly comic scenes in depicting a reality that is absurd, illogical, senseless, a world of futility and meaningless clichés. In Ionesco's *The Chairs* (1951) an elderly couple rush about, filling a room with chairs for nonexistent visitors. Old age is a fact, but an absurdity, too, and old people are incomprehensible. At the end of *The Chairs*, an orator, who is to deliver a solemn talk about the truths of life, turns out to be deaf and dumb and merely makes unintelligible noises and gestures to the invisible crowd. Ionesco summarizes the theme of *The Chairs* (*The New York Times*, June 1, 1958): "I have tried to deal . . . with emptiness, with frustration, with this world, at once fleeting and crushing. The characters I have used are not fully conscious of their spiritual rootlessness, but they feel it instinctively and emotionally." One basis of man's inability to communicate, and one which the "Absurd" dramatists seize upon, is the corruption of language. The absurdity of trying to communicate by means of a debased language is dramatized by Ionesco in *The Bald Soprano* (1948), where the characters speak in clichés. Because the characters are incomprehensible and the happenings illogical and baffling, the spectators cannot simply sit back in ease, but are continually challenged to grasp the play's meaning. Consult M. Esslin, *The Theatre of the Absurd*.

act. A main division in drama or opera. Act divisions probably arose in Roman theory and derive ultimately from the Greek practice of separating episodes in a play by choral interludes, but Greek (and probably Roman) plays were performed without interruption, for the choral interludes were part of the plays themselves. The division of Elizabethan plays into five acts is often the work of editors rather than authors. No play of Shakespeare's was published in his lifetime with divisions into five acts. Today an act division is commonly indicated by lowering the curtain and turning up the houselights. A **scene** is a smaller unit, either: (1) a division with no change of locale or abrupt shift of time, or (2) a division consisting of an actor or a group of actors on the stage; according to the second definition, the departure or entrance of an actor changes the composition of the group and thus produces a new scene. In an entirely different sense, the scene is the locale where a work is set. The first speech in *Romeo and Juliet* informs the audience of the play's locale: "In fair Verona, where we lay our scene. . . ." Often the décor lets the spectator know where the play is set, but during the last hundred years playwrights have tended, for the convenience of readers, to write long stage directions describing the scene. Here is the beginning of the first stage direction in Shaw's *Candida*: "A fine morning in October 1894 in the north east quarter of London, a vast district miles away from the London of Mayfair and St James's, and much less narrow, squalid, fetid and airless in its slums. . . ."

action. (1) The physical movement of an actor, whether he is leaping into Ophelia's grave or speaking softly to himself. That talk is action is easily seen in the Bastard's remark (*King John*, II.i.466): "Zounds! I was never so bethumped with words / Since I first called my brother's father dad." (2) An incident in the plot, an episode. (3) Aristotle's statement that a drama is an "imitation of an action" (*praxis*) has provoked considerable controversy; recently there has been a tendency to regard this action as the motive underlying the outward deeds of the plot. Francis Fergusson says (in *The Human Image in Dramatic Literature*, p. 116), for example, that the action of *Oedipus the King* "is the quest for Laius's slayer, . . . which persists through the changing circumstances of the play." See pp. 3–5.

aesthetic distance, or **psychical distance.** The detachment between the receptor and the work of art. The concept is chiefly associated with Edward Bullough (see the essay in his *Aesthetics*, reprinted in Melvin Rader, *A Modern Book of Aesthetics*). Bullough explains that there must be some sort of psychical "distance" (gap) between our practical self (our personal needs) and the work of art. Thus, an old man who has been treated harshly by his children may be unable to divorce his personal feelings from *King Lear*.

He may be too involved with the piece as life to see it as art. But "distance" does not mean that the receptor is totally detached or objective. Rather, he is detached from his usual personal involvements, and because of this detachment he can look with a new vigorous interest — he can look with a new sort of passion born of his new personality — at the work of art as art. Persons who do not understand the need for distance between themselves and a work, Bullough explains, commonly say that they do not wish to see a tragedy because there is enough suffering in real life. But the more sophisticated spectator at a tragedy realizes that as a picture is distanced by the frame, a play is distanced (the characters may speak verse, they perform behind footlights, and their deeds cohere to make a unified harmonious pattern); the feelings it evokes in him are not the feelings evoked by a roughly similar event in real life. In the theater we feel "rapturous awe" at what in life would be depressing. See also dramatic illusion, empathy, epic drama. Consult Oscar Budel, "Contemporary Theater and Aesthetic Distance," *PMLA*, 76 (1961), 277–291.

agon (Greek: *contest*). A debate in a Greek comedy. See p. 336. In the last few decades the term has been used (e.g., by Francis Fergusson, *The Idea of a Theater*) to designate a scene of conflict in tragedy, such as the agonizing struggle between Oedipus and Teiresias.

agroikos. See character.

alazon. See character.

alienation effect. See epic drama.

allegory. Frequently an allegory is a narrative wherein abstractions (e.g., virtue, fear) are made concrete (Mr. Virtue, Giant Fear), for the purpose of effectively communicating a moral, but in essence an allegory is merely a system of equivalents. Though allegory need not personify abstractions, allegoric drama almost always does. *Everyman* (c. 1500), an allegoric morality play, includes among its dramatis personae Death, Good Deeds, Beauty, and of course, Everyman. But morality plays may also include allegoric castles (standing for strength or chastity), roses (standing for love or virtue), etc. Consult Bernard Spivack, *Shakespeare and the Allegory of Evil.*

anagnorisis, or disclosure, discovery, recognition. For Aristotle the "recognition" or "disclosure" seems to be merely a recognition of who is who, by such tokens as birthmarks, clothes, etc., but the term has been extended to include the tragic hero's recognition of himself and/or the essence of life. Thus Othello, having murdered his faithful wife, learns he was beguiled into thinking her dishonest, and finally recognizes himself as "one not easily jealous, but being wrought / Perplexed in the extreme"; and he exacts justice from himself by suicide. See pp. 6–7.

antagonist. See protagonist.

antecedent action. See plot.

anticlimax. A descent, the lines or happenings being markedly less important or less impressive than their predecessors. In melodrama, a decrease in tension may cause disappointment and loss of interest; in comedy, a sharp descent (the beautiful princess opens her mouth and sounds like a burlesque queen) may get a desirable laugh. On the desirability of a gradual decrease in tension in tragedy (i.e., a "quiet ending"), consult Max Beerbohm, "Last Acts," in *Around Theatres.*

antimasque. See masque.

arena stage. (1) In British usage, a stage with a back wall and with an audience on three sides. (2) In American usage, a playing space surrounded by spectators, theater-in-the-round. Proponents of arena staging (in the American sense) stress the intimacy afforded by having actors in the midst of the audience, but opponents suggest that at least for some plays the intimacy ought not to be very great. (See aesthetic distance.) It has been noted, too, that even in arena staging the audience normally feels set apart from the actors, for the audience is in the dark while the actors are in an illuminated playing area. Critics of arena staging cite the following difficulties: soliloquies, asides, and direct addresses are hard to deliver in such a theater; directors, aware that the back of an actor's head is not very expressive, tend to have the actors gyrate disturbingly and meaninglessly; entrances and exits are cumbersome; little use can be made of elevation and of groupings of actors.

Apollonian. See Dionysus.

arras. See Elizabethan playhouse.

aside. See soliloquy, convention.

bombast. From a word meaning "cotton stuffing"; rant, speech that is too inflated for the occasion. In Marlowe's *Tamburlaine* (c. 1587), Tamburlaine brags thus:

> Our quivering lances, shaking in the air,
> And bullets, like Jove's dreadful thunderbolts,
> Enrolled in flames and fiery smoldering mists,
> Shall threat the gods more than Cyclopian wars:
> And with our sun-bright armor as we march,
> Will chase the stars from Heaven and dim their eyes
> That stand and muse at our admirèd arms.

bomolochos. See character.

bourgeois drama. A serious play with middle-class dramatis personae. There are a few Elizabethan tragedies of middle-class life, but bourgeois drama, with its emphasis on pathos, is more or less an eighteenth-century invention. Bourgeois dramas were written in the eighteenth and nineteenth centuries, apparently in response to the middle class's desire to see itself on the stage; the bourgeois by the eighteenth century regarded himself as a suitable replacement for the nobleman of earlier tragedy. Speaking generally, the characteristics of these plays are: middle-class dramatis personae, virtue in distress, sentimentality, and an unreasonably high moral tone. Eighteenth-century critics, not sure what to do with pathetic plays on middle-class life, used the terms *drame, drame bourgeois, comédie larmoyante* (tearful comedy), *tragédie bourgeoise, bürgerliches Trauerspiel* (bourgeois tragedy) interchangeably. (Note that a *comédie larmoyante* need not end happily, nor a *tragédie bourgeoise* end sadly.) In England, George Lillo's *The London Merchant* (1731), "a tale of private woe. A London 'prentice ruined," depicted an apprentice who murdered his benefactor. Bourgeois drama in the nineteenth century became melodrama in many hands and tragedy in Ibsen's hands. Consult Fred O. Nolte, *Early Middle Class Drama*; and Eric Auerbach, *Mimesis*, Ch. 17. On Ibsen as a bourgeois dramatist, consult Eric Bentley, *The Playwright as Thinker*. See

domestic tragedy, sentimental, and pp. 230–232, 640–641.

box set. See realism.

braggart soldier. See character.

burla. See *commedia dell'arte.*

burlesque. Any imitation which, by distortion, aims to amuse. Its subject matter is sometimes said to be faults rather than vices, and its tone is neither shrill nor savage. Thus, in distinction from satire it can be defined as a comic imitation of a mannerism or a minor fault (either in style or subject matter), contrived to arouse amusement rather than indignation. In the theater, a burlesque may be a play that amusingly criticizes another play by grotesquely imitating aspects of it, as Gay's *The Beggar's Opera* (1728) mimicked serious operas. In England, a burlesque may be a musical extravaganza in which fantasy has almost entirely ousted criticism. In America, burlesque (especially popular in the late nineteenth and first half of the twentieth century) is usually a sort of vaudeville or variety show stressing bawdy humor and sex. The sexual theme is most fully revealed in the striptease, introduced about 1920. Consult V. C. Clinton-Baddeley, *The Burlesque Tradition in the English Theater after 1660*; Gypsy Rose Lee, *The G-String Murders*. See comedy, satire.

catastrophe. See plot.

catharsis. Aristotle and countless followers said that tragedy evokes pity and fear, and that it produces in the spectator a catharsis (purgation, or, some scholars hold, purification) of these emotions: it drains or perhaps refines or modifies these emotions, and thus tragedy is socially useful. (Aristotle's *Poetics* is the subject of much controversy; one cannot with security assert that Aristotle said anything, without a counter-argument being offered. For various views of catharsis, consult F. L. Lucas, *Tragedy*, and Gerald F. Else's monumental *Aristotle's Poetics*.)

character. (1) One of the dramatis personae, e.g., King Lear. (2) The personality of such a figure. Characters are sometimes divided into **flat** and **round characters.** The former have only one "side," representing a single trait (e.g., the faithful wife, the genial drunkard); the latter have many traits and are seen, as it were, from all sides, in the round. The behavior of flat characters is thoroughly predictable, that of round characters is sometimes unexpected though credible. A **stock character** is a type that recurs in many works. For example, from Greek comedy to the present there have been numerous braggart soldiers, stubborn fathers, jealous husbands. Northrop Frye finds four chief types of comic figures: (1) the *alazon,* the imposter, boaster, hypocrite; (2) the *eiron* (see irony), the man who deprecates himself and exposes the boaster; (3) the *bomolochos,* the buffoon, or more generally, the man who entertains by his mannerisms and talk; (4) the *agroikos,* the straightman who is the unwitting butt of humor. Each of these types appears in many dresses; the *alazon,* for example, is most commonly the braggart soldier (*miles gloriosus*), but he is also the pedant, the crank, or anyone who is full of ideas that have no relation to reality. (See *commedia dell'arte;* consult Northrop Frye, *Anatomy of Criticism,* pp. 171–176.) Stock characters are not limited to comedy: the proud tragic hero is a stock character, as are, for example, the cruel stepmother and the son who wishes to avenge his father. See also motivation, plot. Consult J. L. Styan, *The Elements of Drama,* Ch. 8.

chorus. In Greek drama, a group of performers who play a role, e.g., Old Men of Corinth. (The chorus leader is the *koryphaios.*) In Aeschylus' *The Suppliants* (c. 490 B.C.), perhaps the earliest extant play, the chorus consists of the heroines, but in most Greek plays the chorus consists of subsidiary figures who comment rather helplessly on what is happening to the important people. Aeschylus reduced the chorus of fifty to twelve; Sophocles increased it to fifteen, where it remained. The Greek chorus, it is often said, is a sort of middle-man between the unusual main figures and the humdrum spectators. Elizabethan dramas occasionally had a chorus of one actor who, not a participant in the story, commented on it. The Chorus (or prologue) in Shakespeare's *Henry V* urges the audience to

Think when we talk of horses that you see them

Printing their proud hoofs i' the receiving earth;
For 'tis your thoughts that now must deck our
     kings,
Carry them here and there, jumping o'er times,
Turning the accomplishment of many years
Into an hour-glass: for the which supply,
Admit me Chorus to this history:
Who prologue-like your humble patience pray,
Gently to hear, kindly to judge, our play.

A **chorus character,** or *raisonneur,* however, such as Enobarbus in *Antony and Cleopatra,* is a character who participates in the story yet seems to be the author's mouthpiece, intelligently commenting (often with irony) on the actions of the other characters. But Alfred Harbage, in *As They Liked It,* skeptically and aptly calls such a figure "The Unreliable Spokesman." The use of the chorus, in one form or another, continues into our times, for example in T. S. Eliot's *Murder in the Cathedral,* whose "Chorus of Women of Canterbury," like a Greek chorus and like the audience, "are forced to bear witness"; and in Tennessee Williams's *The Glass Menagerie,* whose Tom Wingfield tells the audience he is "the narrator of the play, and also a character in it."

climax. See plot.

closet drama. A play suited only for reading, not for acting. Most nineteenth-century English poetic dramas (e.g., Coleridge's, Shelley's, Tennyson's) fit into this category, although Byron's plays have recently been moving out of the closet. Consult Moody Prior, *The Language of Tragedy.*

comedy. Most broadly, anything amusing — a literary work or a situation — is a comedy. More specifically, comedy is (in Dr. Johnson's words) "such a dramatic representation of human life, as may excite mirth." Dramatic comedies generally depict a movement from unhappiness to happiness, from (for example) young lovers frustrated by their parents to young lovers happily married. The unhappy situation is so presented that it entertains rather than distresses the spectator; it is ridiculous and/or diverting rather than painful.

Comic drama seems related to fertility rituals; it celebrates generation, renewal, variety (laughing away any narrow-minded persons who seek to limit life's abundance), and it celebrates man's triumphs over the chances of life. Irate parents and shipwrecks cannot prevent journeys from ending with lovers meeting. For the kinds of Greek comedy (Old, Middle, and New) see pp. 336–339. For the characters in Greek comedy, see character. Consult C. Hoy, *The Hyacinth Room; Theories of Comedy*, ed. P. Lauter; L. J. Potts, *Comedy*.

comedy of humors. A term sometimes applied to plays — notably those of Ben Jonson — wherein the characters, though somewhat individualized, obviously represent types or moods (the jealous husband, the witless pedant). A humor was a bodily liquid (blood [Latin: *sanguis*], phlegm, yellow bile, black bile) thought to control one's behavior. Allegedly, a proper mixture produced a well adjusted man, but a preponderance of any one humor produced a distorted personality. The old sense of the word survives in the phrase, "He is in a bad humor"; "sanguine," "phlegmatic," and "bilious" are also modern survivals of the old psychology of humors. **Humor characters** are common in **situational comedy;** they are engineered by a clever plot into a situation that displays their absurdity: the man who craves silence is confronted with a talkative woman; the coward is confronted by the braggart.

comedy of manners, comedy of wit. See high comedy.

comic relief. Humorous episodes in tragedy, alleged to alleviate or lighten the tragic effect. Some comic scenes in tragedy, however, not only provide "relief" but enlarge the canvas of tragedy, showing us a fuller picture of life. The clown who brings Cleopatra the poisonous asp sets her tragedy against the daily world. Critics have increasingly noted that the comic scenes (such as the macabre comments of the gravediggers in *Hamlet*) often deepen rather than alleviate the tragic effect. See tragicomedy. Consult A. P. Rossiter, *Angel with Horns*, Ch. 14.

commedia dell'arte. Italian drama, more or less improvised, performed by professionals in Italy and abroad, mostly in the sixteenth century but still alive in the early eighteenth century. In contrast to the classically-inspired written drama (*commedia erudita*) performed by actors who memorized their lines, *com-*

media dell'arte (perhaps best translated as "professional drama") employed sketches of plots (*scenario;* plural: *scenarii*) specifying entrances and exits and the gist of the dialogue; in performance these *scenarii* were fleshed out with stock bits of comic stage business (*lazzi*) or larger pieces of business (*burle*) such as practical jokes. (The singulars are *lazzo* and *burla*.) Thus a *scenario* may call for the *lazzo* of anger, or the *burla* of chasing a fly, and leave it to the actor to work out the swats and the smile when at last he munches the fly. Though these plays are said to have been improvised, the stock characters, stock situations, and stock stage business make them something more — or less — than improvised. The chief characters — most of whom wore masks — are Pantalone, an elderly Venetian merchant wearing a little cap, a red jacket, loose trousers (hence our word "pants"), and slippers: his age, amours, and avarice make him ridiculous; Dottore, a Bolognese doctor wearing a black academic gown: his age and his pedantry make him ridiculous; Capitano, a soldier, ridiculous because a braggart and a coward; several servants called *zanne* (singular: *zanni*, from *Gianni*, "Johnny") including Arlecchino (later Harlequin), who in the sixteenth century wore patches that in the next century were represented by triangles or diamonds; Brighella, a rather cruel and crafty rogue; Pulcinella, noted for his resourcefulness and his disguises; Pedrolino, a naive valet who becomes the melancholy Pagliacci and Pierrot; Colombina, who later becomes Columbine and loves Harlequin. Further, there are usually four lovers, children of the two Old Men. Consult Allardyce Nicoll, *Masks, Mimes and Miracles*, and *The World of Harlequin*; and K. M. Lea, *Italian Popular Comedy*.

complication. See plot.

confidant (feminine: **confidante**). A character in whom a principal character confides, revealing his state of mind and often furthering the exposition. Horatio is Hamlet's confidant; Oenone is Phèdre's. Although Horatio and Oenone are memorable, the confidant is sometimes absurdly vapid; though the French defended the device as more plausible than the soliloquy, the confidant may be more trouble than he is worth. In *The Critic* (1779), Sheridan ridiculed it thus: "Enter Tilburina stark mad in white satin, and her confidante stark mad in white linen."

conflict. See plot.

convention. An unrealistic device that the public agrees to tolerate. Thus, a character in a drama may express his thoughts aloud and not be heard by other characters (the **aside**), or he may speak his thoughts aloud on the empty stage (the **soliloquy**). Italian characters (e.g., Desdemona and Iago) speak English, yet are understood to be speaking Italian. In motion pictures, one image fades out, another fades in, and through this convention the audience knows that there is a shift in time or place. More generally any character-type, any theme, or motif (e.g., the suspected butler) widely used in literature or drama is a convention. Consult Harry Levin, *Refractions*; M. C. Bradbrook, *Themes and Conventions of Elizabethan Tragedy*.

cosmic irony. See irony.

cothurnus. See sock and buskin.

coup de théatre. A surprise, especially a striking turn of events in the plot. Consult Alan R. Thompson, *The Anatomy of Drama*.

crisis. See plot.

Cruelty, Theater of. Antonin Artaud (1896–1948) used the term in 1933 to refer to a drama that, working rather like a plague, would shock man out of the bonds of his "logical" or "civilized" conceptions and would release the suppressed primitive or prelogical powers within him, such as criminal instincts and erotic obsessions, revealing the "cruelty" or terrible mystery of existence. This drama, relying more on gestures, shapes, music, and light than on words (Artaud was immensely impressed by Balinese drama although he did not understand Indonesian), would bypass mere realism (i.e., psychology) and would make manifest the truly real supernatural, creating in the spectator a "kind of terror" or a purifying delirium. Artaud, a poet, actor, and director, published relatively little, but his metaphysics and his emphasis on an antirealistic theater in various ways have influenced Sartre, Camus, Beckett, Ionesco, Genet (con-

sult the preface to *The Maids*) and others: language sometimes becomes gibberish, and madness and violence are presented in order to jolt the spectator out of his comfortable false view of man and of the universe — or, in less metaphysical plays, in order to reflect on the stage the cruelty of the modern world. Consult Artaud's *The Theater and Its Double*; several articles in *Tulane Drama Review*, 8 (Winter 1963); and the "Conclusion" in Jacques Guicharnaud and June Beckelman, *Modern French Theatre*.

denouement. See plot.

deus ex machina. Literally, a god out of a machine. (1) In Greek drama a god who descends by a crane-like arrangement and solves a problem in the story, thus allowing the play to end. It was much used by Euripides; Sophocles in his old age borrowed the idea and introduced Heracles at the end of *Philoctetes* to induce the title-character to go to Troy. (2) Any unexpected and improbable device (e.g., an unexpected inheritance from a long-lost uncle in Australia) used to unknot a problem and thus conclude the work.

deuteragonist. See protagonist.

dialogue. The speech exchanged between characters, or, loosely, even the speech of a single character. Dialogue is sometimes contrasted to action, but Elizabeth Bowen aptly says that dialogue is what the characters *do* to each other, and Shaw aptly says that his plays are all talk just as Beethoven's symphonies are all music. **Stichomythia** is a special form of dialogue, wherein two speakers in a verbal duel thrust and parry in alternating lines. Example:

QUEEN:
Hamlet, thou hast thy father much offended.
HAMLET:
Mother, you have my father much offended.
QUEEN:
Come, come, you answer with an idle tongue.
HAMLET:
Go, go, you question with a wicked tongue.

See action, soliloquy. Consult J. L. Styan, *The Elements of Drama*, Chs. 1–2; and Eric Bentley, *The Life of the Drama*.

diction. (1) Choice of words, wording. Dr. Johnson objected to the "knife" ("an instrument used by butchers and cooks," he said) which Lady Macbeth says she will use to murder the King. "Words too familiar, or too remote," Johnson said, "defeat the purpose of a poet." Consult Moody Prior, *The Language of Tragedy*. (2) A performer's manner or style of speaking, including pronunciation and phrasing.

Dionysus. Greek god of wine, the phallus, the surge of growth, and (to join all these) irrational impulse. It is commonly held that Greek tragedy grew from choral celebrations in his honor; in any case, from the sixth century B.C. tragedies were performed in Athens at the **Great** (or **Greater**, or **City**) **Dionysia**, a festival in Dionysus' honor. (The Dionysiac origin is interestingly rejected by H. D. F. Kitto, in *Theatre Survey*, 1 [1960], 3–17.) Friedrich Nietzsche suggested in *The Birth of Tragedy* (1872) that Greek tragedy, usually considered calm and poised, was not the product of quiet minds. If tragedy, Nietzsche said, showed light and beauty (over which the god Apollo presided), it was nevertheless also indebted to Dionysus, who represented the frenzied, buried self-assertions of the mind. That is, Greek tragedy was the product of **Dionysian** ecstatic and violent self-assertion tamed by (or fused with) the **Apollonian** sense of reason, of moderation, and of external order. "Apollonian" is often associated with classicism, and "Dionysian" with romanticism.

direct address. See soliloquy.

disclosure, discovery. See anagnorisis.

disguising. See masque.

domestic tragedy. A serious play showing the misfortunes (especially within the family) of a private citizen rather than of a man of high rank who is involved in events that shake a realm. See bourgeois drama. Consult Henry H. Adams, *English Domestic or Homiletic Tragedy 1575 to 1642*.

double plot. See plot.

drama (from Greek *dran:* to do). (1) A play, a work that tells a story by means of impersonators. (2) The whole body of work written for the theater. (3) A serious but untragic play (see drame). (4) Events containing conflict, tension, surprise ("life is full of drama"; "the first act lacks drama"). See closet drama, comedy, melodrama, tragedy. A play is written by a **dramatist;** the art of writing plays is **dramaturgy.** A person who writes plays is also a **playwright.** (Note that the last syllable is not "-write" but "-wright," denoting a maker, as a shipwright is a maker of ships.) Consult Kenneth T. Rowe, *Write That Play;* Walter Kerr, *How Not to Write a Play;* Bernard Grebanier, *Playwriting*.

drama of ideas. See *pièce à thèse*.

dramatic illusion. The state between delusion (the spectator thinks the world on the stage is real), and full awareness (the spectator never forgets he is looking at scenery and actors). In A *Midsummer Night's Dream*, Bottom fears that delusion will occur unless the audience is carefully warned: "Write me a prologue, and let the prologue seem to say we will do no harm with our swords, and that Pyramus is not killed indeed. And, for the more better assurance, tell them that I Pyramus am not Pyramus, but Bottom the Weaver. This will put them out of fear." See aesthetic distance.

George Henry Lewes (1817–1878) introduced into English dramatic criticism the term *optique du théâtre,* taken from the French actor François René Molé (1734–1802). A spectator must have this "theater view," this understanding of "scenic illusion," if he is to enjoy the theater; if he lacks it, he will complain that Hamlet ought to be speaking Danish (see convention). *Optique du théâtre* requires that we be given not reality but a symbolic representation of it. A stage miser should finger his gold differently from a real miser; a stage character must be heard, even though in real life the character he is playing might speak softly.

Staging that aims at delusion or a high degree of illusion is **representational staging.** Here the stage-characters eat real food on stage, speak with their backs to the audience, etc. (See naturalism, realism.) When David Belasco staged *The Governor's Lady* in 1912, he was representational, placing on the stage an exact duplicate of a particular (Child's) restaurant. On the other hand, **presentational staging** is antirealistic; in Thornton Wilder's *Our Town* (1938), a drugstore counter, for example, consisted of a board across the backs of two chairs. The staging in musical comedies, ballets, and puppet shows is, of course, presentational. Presentational staging is sometimes called **theatrical staging. Theatricalism,** by its unreality, continually reminds us that we are in the theater, not in the street. On theatricalism, see style. A derogatory way of saying a work is theatrical is to say it is **stagy.**

drame. A solemn but untragic play, especially an eighteenth-century play that, quietly glorifying the bourgeois virtues, preaches and appeals to the audience's emotions. See bourgeois drama. Consult Alan R. Thompson, *The Anatomy of Drama,* which classifies most naturalistic and realistic plays (e.g., Ibsen's and Chekhov's) as *drames.*

eiron. See character.

Elizabethan playhouse. The first permanent structure built in England for plays was The Theatre, built outside the city limits of London in 1576 by James Burbage. It soon had several competitors, but little is known about any of these playhouses. The contract for one, The Fortune (built in 1600), survives; it tells us that the three-storied building was square, 80 feet on the outside, 55 feet on the inside. The stage was 43 feet broad and 27½ feet deep. It has been calculated that about 800 people (the **groundlings**) could stand around the three sides of the stage on the ground that was called the **yard,** and another 1500 could be seated in the three galleries. The other chief pieces of evidence concerning the physical nature of the theater are (1) the "De Witt drawing," which is really a copy of a sketch made by a visitor (c. 1596) to The Swan, and (2) bits of evidence that can be gleaned from the plays themselves, such as "Enter a Fairy at one door, and Robin Goodfellow at another." Conclusions vary and scholarly tempers run high; the following statements are not indisputable. Most theaters were polygonal or round structures (Shakespeare calls the theater a "wooden O") with three galleries; the yard was open to the sky. From one side a raised stage (or open **platform**) jutted into the middle. A sort of wooden canopy (the **heavens,** or the **shadow**) projected over the stage and in some theaters rested on two pillars; these pillars could conveniently serve as a hiding place for an actor supposed to be unseen by the other characters. At the rear of the stage there sometimes was a curtained alcove or booth, which when uncurtained might represent a room or a cave. The curtain is often called an **arras,** and it was probably behind this curtain that Polonius hid, only to be stabbed. At the rear of the stage (flanking the curtained space?) there were perhaps also two or three doors, through which entrances and exits were made. Probably the **tiring house** ("attiring house," i.e., dressing room) was behind the rear of the stage. Above the alcove or booth was **an area** that could be used for an **upper stage** (for example, in scenes of people standing on a city's walls); flanking the upper stage were windows, one of which may have served Juliet for her misnamed balcony scene. Some scholars argue that in a yet higher place were musicians, and at the very top — called the **top** — was an opening from which an actor could look; in *Henry VI, Part I,* Joan of Arc appears "on the top, thrusting out a torch burning." Most of the acting was done on the main stage (the platform), but the "inner stage," "upper stage," "windows," and "top" must have been useful occasionally (if they existed). The **cellar** (beneath the stage) was used, for example for the voice of the ghost in *Hamlet,* and for Ophelia's grave. Though some scenery was used, the absence of a front curtain precluded many elaborate scenic effects (much, however, could be done by carrying banners) and encouraged continuous action. The stage that was a battlefield could in an instant, by the introduction of a throne, become a room in a palace. Two readable books are A. M. Nagler, *Shakespeare's Stage,* and C. Walter Hodges, *The Globe Restored.* Nagler (Ch. 12) also gives information about a second kind of Elizabethan theater — basically a platform at one end of a hall — that catered to a courtly group. Interesting specialized items on playhouses are in *Shakespeare Survey,* 1 and 12, ed. Allardyce Nicoll.

empathy. The projection of one's feelings into a perceived object. The Germans call it *Einfühlung* — "a feeling into." Vernon Lee, one of the formulators of the idea, claimed that when we say "the mountain rises" we do so not because the mountain rises (it doesn't) but because we have often raised our eyes, head, and total muscular structure to look at mountains or other tall objects. In perceiving a mountain, we merge (unawares) its image with the previously accumulated idea of rising. We are said to empathize with a character if we flinch at a blow directed at him, or if we feel bowed with his grief; if, in short, we *experience* as well as *see* his behavior. Empathy is often distinguished from **sympathy:** we empathize if we feel *with* the character; we sympathize if we feel *for* the character. See aesthetic distance. Consult Vernon Lee's essay in *A Modern Book of Aesthetics,* ed. Melvin Rader; Herbert S. Langfeld, *The Aesthetic Attitude.*

epic drama. Bertolt Brecht (1898–1956) labeled "aristotelian" most drama before his own. He held that it aimed at enthralling the spectators by building up to a climax, thus arousing and then purging their emotions. In contrast, Brecht said, epic drama (he borrowed the phrase from Erwin Piscator) aims at arousing the audience's detached thought; it teaches, keeping the spectators alert by preventing any emotional involvement. The epic drama (probably so-called because it resembles the epic in its abundance of loosely connected scenes and its tendency to deal with a society rather than merely with a few individuals) achieves this estrangement or **alienation effect** (German: *Verfremdungseffekt*) by many means: the epic play (e.g., Brecht's *The Good Woman of Setzuan,* or his *Mother Courage*) commonly consists of a series of loosely connected scenes rather than a tightly organized plot with a climax; the settings are not realistic but merely suggest the locale, and they are often changed in full view of the audience, preventing any entrancing illusion (a night scene may be done on an illuminated stage, again to prevent the audience from emotionally entering into the play); the actor may address the audience directly, sometimes in song, and he aims not at becoming the character but at presenting him, or, to put it differently, at making a comment on him, as we might do when we put aside a cigarette and say, "He said to me, '. . . .'"; loudspeakers, films, and placards may be used, and the whole is something of a lecture-demonstration, aimed not at arousing and then quieting the audience's emotions, but at making things somewhat strange to the audience so that the audience will look sharply and will think. Consult Bertolt Brecht, "A Short Organum,"

in *Playwrights on Playwriting,* ed. Toby Cole; *Brecht on Theatre,* trans. John Willett; R. Gray, *Brecht; The Tulane Drama Review,* 6 (Sept. 1961). See pp. 573–575.

epilogue. (1) An appendix (usually a concluding address) to a play; (2) the actor who recites such an appendix (e.g., Puck, at the close of Shakespeare's *A Midsummer Night's Dream*).

exposition. See plot.

expressionism. An anti-naturalistic movement chiefly associated with Germany just after World War I, but which was foreshadowed by Strindberg, notably in his trilogy, *To Damascus* (1898–1904), and in his *A Dream Play* (1902). Expressionism does not seek to present reality dispassionately imitated, but reality passionately felt. Thus, when Mr. Zero shakes his employer (in Elmer Rice's *The Adding Machine* [1923]), the office spins; when he is on trial, the walls of the courtroom veer crazily. Speaking broadly, expressionist plays (in addition to being unrealistic) usually (1) depict types or classes (Rice's Mr. Zero; the Man, the Woman, the Nameless One in Ernst Toller's *Man and Masses* [1921], (2) employ dream sequences, (3) assume that society is responsible for man's troubles. Though Arthur Miller's *Death of a Salesman* (1949) is in many ways "realistic," it also is indebted to expressionism, especially in the scenes involving Willy's memories. (Miller originally planned to call the play *The Inside of His Head.*) Note, too, the name of Miller's hero — Loman, i.e., low man. Consult John Willett, *Expressionism.*

falling action. See plot.

farce. A sort of comedy based not on clever language or subtleties of character, but on broadly humorous situations (a man mistakenly enters the ladies' locker room), is lucidly defended by Eric Bentley in his introduction to *"Let's Get a Divorce" and Other Plays,* where he suggests that farce, like dreams, shows "the disguised fulfillment of repressed wishes." Farce is usually filled with surprise, with swift physical action, and with assault. The characters are physically and intellectually insensitive, and characterization is subordinated to plot. See also Bentley's *The Life of the Drama*. **Slapstick** (named for an implement made of two slats which resound when

————

ïïie iïoïil (i.e., tne raçaae) oï tne *skene* (or perhaps a temporary screen) and sometimes the playing-area in front of it seem to have been called the **proskenion.** Though the *skene's* façade perhaps suggested the front of a palace, there were further efforts at indicating locale: Sophocles is said to have invented scene-painting (a painted cloth or screen in front of the *skene?*), and there are allusions to **periaktoi,** upright prisms bearing a different decoration on each side. Apparently when a

new locality in the same town was to be indicated, the *periaktos* at the right was turned, when an entirely new locality was to be indicated, both *periaktoi* were turned. Other machines were the **eccyclema,** a platform that was rolled out of the *skene* to indicate a scene indoors, and the **mechane,** a crane from which a god could descend or by means of which a character could soar through the air. (See *deus ex machina.*)

Plays were put on chiefly during two holidays, the **Lenaea** (Feast of the Wine-press) in January, and the **Great** (or **Greater,** or **City**) **Dionysia** in March or April. The Lenaea was chiefly associated with comedy, the Great Dionysia with tragedy. At the latter, on each of three mornings a tragic dramatist presented three tragedies and one satyr-play. The expense was born by a **choregus,** a rich citizen ordered by the state to assume the financial burden. See comedy, satyr-play, tragedy.

The **Hellenistic theater** (i.e., theaters of, say, the third and second centuries B.C. erected in towns to which Greek culture had been spread by Alexander's conquests) seems to have been much like the Greek theater, though now the *proskenion* is apparently more highly decorated, having pillars a few feet in front of it and being fitted with painted panels called *pinakes.* And the *skene,* now of stone rather than of wood, may have had projections at the sides (*paraskenia*) and an upper story (*episkenion*). The playing-area on this upper level is the *logeion.* Consult Margarete Bieber, *The History of the Greek and Roman Theater.*

hamartia. This Greek word is variously translated as "tragic flaw" or "error" or "shortcoming" or "weakness," and in many plays it *is* a flaw or even a vice such as **hybris** (also **hubris**) — Greek for overweening pride, arrogance, excessive confidence. But in other plays it is merely a misstep, such as a choice that turns out badly. Indeed, the tragic hero may be undone by his virtue — his courage, for example, when others are not merely prudent but cowardly. See pp. 5–8. On *hamartia* and *hybris* see Richmond Lattimore, *Story Patterns in Greek Tragedy.*

happening. A kind of theatrical activity popular in the early 1960's, named for Allan Kaprow's *18 Happenings in 6 Parts* (1959). Instead of a conventional theater there is simply a place (art gallery, backyard), instead of actors who play roles there are participants, instead of a plot there are discontinuous actions or happenings. Sample: a man asks if Howard Saretta is in the audience; when there is no answer he sits down among the spectators, and someone else gets up, skips rope, washes his face, and then breaks a pair of eyeglasses. Often there is some violence directed against people (participants and audience) and against objects (here, against eyeglasses). Consult *Happenings*, ed. Michael Kirby; Susan Sontag, *Against Interpretation*; and A. Kaprow, *Art News* (May 1961).

Hellenistic theater. See Greek theater.

high comedy. Intellectual rather than physical, it requires the close attention of a sophisticated audience, flourishing (says George Meredith in his *Essay on Comedy* [1877]) in a "society of cultivated men and women . . . wherein ideas are current, and the perceptions quick." Etherege, Wycherley, Congreve, and other playwrights of the decades following the Restoration of Charles II to the throne of England (1660) wrote **Restoration comedy**, high comedy of a particular sort, often called **comedy of manners** or **comedy of wit.** Their plays abound in witty **repartee** (what Dr. Johnson called "gay remarks and unexpected answers"), and often strike modern audiences as cynical. Restoration comedy has no precise terminal date, but can be said to end about 1700, with the development of sentimental comedy, plays of venerable parents and middle-class dutiful sons who love pure young things. Example: Richard Steele's *The Conscious Lovers* (1722). Consult Thomas H. Fujimura, *The Restoration Comedy of Wit*; Louis Kronenberger, *The Thread of Laughter*; Norman N. Holland, *The First Modern Comedies*.

humor character. See comedy of humors.

hubris. See *hamartia.*

hybris. See *hamartia.*

imitation (Greek: *mimesis*). Not a pejorative term in much criticism, for it often implies a "making" or "re-creating" or "re-presenting" of a form in a substance not natural to it. Thus Michelangelo reproduced or imitated the form of Moses, in stone. For Aristotle, tragedy is the imitation (i.e., representation, re-creation) by means of words, gesture, music, and scenery, of an important action.

irony. Irony is of several sorts. **Socratic irony,** named for Socrates, who commonly feigned more ignorance than he possessed, denotes understatement. The *eiron* (see character) is the cunning fellow who plays the underdog. **Dramatic irony,** or **Sophoclean irony,** or **tragic irony** refers to a condition of affairs which is the tragic reverse of what the participants think. Thus, it is ironic that Macbeth kills Duncan, thinking he will achieve happiness; he later finds he loses all that makes life worth living. Oedipus accuses the blind prophet of corruption, but by the end of the play Oedipus learns (as the audience knew at the outset) that he himself is corrupt, that he has been mentally blind (ignorant) and that the prophet has had vision (knowledge). Oedipus meant what he said, but his words have proved to be ironic. (Aristotle's word for reversal is *peripeteia.*) We have dramatic irony, it can be said, when a speech or action is more fully understood by the spectators than by the characters. This sort of irony, based on misunderstanding, or partial knowledge, is common in tragedy, but comedy too has its misunderstandings; comic speeches or actions are ironic if they bring about the opposite of what is intended. More generally, the contrast implied in "irony" need be neither tragic nor comic; it is "ironic" that the strong man is overthrown by the weak man and that the liar unknowingly tells the truth.

irony of fate (a phrase which H. W. Fowler's *Modern English Usage* aptly says is hackneyed), or **cosmic irony,** denotes the view that God, or fate, or some sort of supernatural figure, is amused to manipulate human beings as a puppeteer manipulates his puppets. Thus, by an irony of fate the messenger delivers the prisoner's pardon an instant too late. Consult Garnett G. Sedgewick, *Of Irony*; Alan R. Thompson, *The Dry Mock*.

koryphaios. See chorus.

kothurnus. See sock and buskin.

lazzo. See *commedia dell' arte.*

Lenaea. See Greek theater.

liturgical drama. A play that is part of the church service or liturgy. In the tenth century the churchmen put on a playlet of a few lines as part of the Easter liturgy. The text is based on Mark 16:1–7: clerics dressed as the Three Marys approach the "tomb" of Christ (the altar) and are asked by a cleric, disguised as an angel, whom they seek. When they reply that they seek Christ, he tells them that Christ has risen and shows them the empty "tomb." The performers were all male, and the dialogue (in Latin) was chanted or sung; probably the gestures were stylized.

low comedy. See farce.

masque, mask, disguising. An entertainment (apparently derived from an ancient ritual) in the Renaissance court, wherein noblemen performed a dignified playlet, usually allegorical and mythological. The masque was lavishly produced, but its basic structure was generally simple: the masquers (costumed and masked noble performers) enter, supposedly having come from afar, they dance with the ladies of the court, and then they depart. Because the masquers are of the same rank as the ladies, and because performers and audience join in a dance, the masque is very close to the masked ball, Ben Jonson (1572–1637) popularized what he called the **antimasque** (a grotesque dance of monsters or clowns), performed by professionals representing chaos, who are dispelled by the courtly performers. ("Anti," from "antic," meaning "a grotesque caper" or "a fool," is sometimes written "ante" because the antimasque precedes the masque.) Consult Enid Welsford, *The Court Masque;* E. K. Chambers, *The Mediaeval Stage* and *The Elizabethan Stage.*

melodrama. Originally, in Renaissance Italy, an opera; later, a drama with occasional songs, or with music (*melos* is Greek for "song") expressing a character's thoughts, much as in films today. In the early nineteenth century plays with musical accompaniment became so stereotyped that the word acquired a second (and now dominant) meaning: a play wherein characters clearly virtuous or vicious are pitted against each other in sensational situations filled with suspense, until justice triumphs.

The situations, not the characters, are exciting. The exotic horror (castles with dungeons) dominant in early nineteenth-century melodramas was often replaced later in the century by local horror (the cruel landlord), but whether exotic or local, melodrama is improbable, and virtue — unsullied by any touch of guilt — triumphs over unlikely circumstances. Melodrama is sometimes said to be tragedy with character left out (i.e., it contains serious happenings), but by virtue of its happy ending and its one-sided characters it can better be described as comedy with good-humor left out. Some critics use "melodrama" without any pejorative connotation to describe such serious, often sensational, plays as Emlyn Williams's *Night Must Fall* (1935), Robert Ardrey's *Thunder Rock* (1939), and Arthur Miller's *All My Sons.* Consult Robert B. Heilman, *Tragedy and Melodrama.*

miracle play. A medieval play on a Biblical episode or a saint's life. Consult Arnold Williams, *The Drama of Medieval England.*

morality play. A late medieval development, popular well into the sixteenth century, allegorically dramatizing some aspect of the moral life, including such characters as Everyman, Good Deeds, and Avarice. It usually showed the conflict between good and evil, or the way in which the Christian faces death. Consult Arnold Williams, *The Drama of Medieval England;* Bernard Spivack, *Shakespeare and the Allegory of Evil.*

motivation. Grounds in character and situation that make behavior plausible. Such grounds are not always present, even in great drama: when Othello asks why Iago "hath thus ensnared my soul," Iago replies, "Demand me nothing: what you know, you know." See character. Consult J. I. M. Stewart, *Character and Motive in Shakespeare.*

naturalism. Sometimes defined, like realism, as the portrayal of "a scientifically accurate, detached picture of life, including everything and selecting nothing." The spectator looking through the peephole of the proscenium, as a scientist looks through the eyepiece of a microscope, is to feel he is witnessing life rather than a symbolic representation of life. More commonly, however, "naturalism" alludes neither to a panoramic view nor to the detailed presentation of a narrow **slice of life** (French: *tranche de vie*), but to a particular attitude held by some writers since the middle of the nineteenth century. Though claiming to be dispassionate observers, they were influenced by evolutionary thought, and regarded man not as possessed of a soul and of free will, but as a creature determined by his heredity and environment. The movement in drama can be said to begin with the Goncourt Brothers' unsuccessful *Henriette Maréchal* (1865), but it is usual to say that the opening gun in the battle for naturalism was fired in Emile Zola's dramatization (1873) of his novel, *Thérèse Raquin*. Thérèse and her lover drown her husband, but are then so guilt-ridden that they poison themselves. In his preface Zola urged that the theater be brought "into closer relation with the great movement toward truth and experimental science which has since the last century been on the increase. . . . I have chosen characters who were completely dominated by their nerves and blood." In Paris, André Antoine opened his Théâtre Libre in 1887, devoting it mostly to plays showing the power of instincts and the influence of heredity and environment. These plays were staged as untheatrically as possible; for example, the actors turned their backs to the audience. In Germany, Otto Brahm opened the Freie Bühne in 1889, and in England J. T. Grein opened the Independent Theatre in 1891, both with Ibsen's *Ghosts* (1881), a play showing the destruction of a young man by inherited syphilis. Ibsen's greatness does not allow him to be pinned down by the label "naturalist," but he can be said to be naturalistic (among other things) by virtue of his serious interest in the effects of heredity and environment. Other dramatists who wrote naturalistic plays include August Strindberg (e.g., his *Miss Julie* [1888]) and Gerhart Hauptmann (early in his career, say, through *The Weavers* [1892]), and Eugene O'Neill (again, the early plays such as *The Rope* [1918] and *Diff'rent* [1920]). Note, however, that the major naturalistic writers usually are more than naturalistic; Strindberg's *Miss Julie*, for example, has a preface that talks about the influence of heredity and environment, and it deals with sordid aspects of reality, but it also has symbolic overtones, notably in Julie's and Jean's dreams. Consult Mordecai Gorelik, *New Theatres for Old; TDR: The Drama Review*, 13 (Winter 1968); and (for Strindberg, O'Neill, and the sources of their ideas) Oscar Cargill, *Intellectual America*.

nuntius. See Senecan tragedy.

obligatory scene. See *scène à faire*.

pathos. The quality that evokes pity. The pathetic is often distinguished from the tragic; in the former, the suffering is experienced by the passive and the innocent (especially women and children), while in the latter it is experienced by persons who act, struggle, and are in some measure responsible for their sufferings. Discussing Aeschylus' *The Suppliants*, H. D. F. Kitto says in *Greek Tragedy* (2nd ed.): "The Suppliants are not only pathetic, as the victims of outrage, but also tragic, as the victims of their own misconceptions." See **bourgeois drama**, and the afterword to Arthur Miller's *Death of a Salesman*, pp. 358–360.

peripeteia (anglicized to **peripety**, meaning **reversal**). The reversal occurs when an action produces the opposite of what was intended or expected, and it is therefore a kind of irony. In *Julius Caesar*, Brutus kills Caesar in order to free Rome from tyranny, but the deed introduces tyranny into Rome. (See irony, plot.)

pièce à thèse. A play with a thesis, a play in which the dramatist argues a point. Commonly the thesis is not about, say, the benevolence of God, but about the merits or defects of some social institution; a play dealing with a social institution may also be called a **problem play** or a **drama of ideas**. Some critics distinguish between the terms, saying that a problem play merely poses a social problem, as Galsworthy does in *Strife* (1909), while a thesis play propounds a solution. Shaw says that "The material of the dramatist is always some conflict of human feeling with circumstances"; when the circumstances are "human institutions" (e.g., divorce laws, penal codes) rather than unchanging facts of life (e.g., death), and the audience is forced to meditate on the value of the institutions, we have a problem play. Shaw's essay, "The Play of Ideas," is in *Shaw on Theatre*, ed. E. J. West. Consult also Walter Kerr, *How Not to Write a Play*, Ch. 5.

pièce bien faite, or **well-made play.** A play, with much suspense and with little depth of characterization, that relies on a cleverly constructed plot, first developing a situation, then building the crisis to a climax, and then resolving the business. The type, which perhaps can be described as melodrama with the fisticuffs left out, is chiefly associated with Victorien Sardou (1831–1908), but Sardou was indebted to Eugène Scribe (1791–1861). Shaw called their plays clockwork mice, and Sardoodledom, but the influence of Sardou on Shaw's hero, Ibsen, is undeniable. See plot, and consult Walter Kerr, *How Not to Write a Play,* Ch. 10; Eric Bentley, "Homage to Scribe," *What Is Theatre?*; C. E. Montague, *Dramatic Values,* pp. 63–74; *Camille and Other Plays,* ed. Stephen S. Stanton.

plot and **character.** The plot is sometimes the "story," the "narrative," but usually it is the happenings *as the author arranges them.* In *Hamlet,* for example, the story involves the poisoning of Hamlet's father, but Shakespeare omits this scene from his plot. Aristotle, in Chapter 6 of the *Poetics,* calls plot "the whole structure of the incidents," and he speaks of plot as the "soul of tragedy," thus making it more important than character. By character he means the personalities of the figures in the story. Menander (a Greek comic dramatist) is said to have told a friend that he had finished a comedy, though he had not yet written a line of dialogue; the anecdote implies that Menander had completed his idea of *what happens* (action) and in *what order* (plot), and he would find it easy then to write the lines of the characters necessary to this plot. The separation, however, between plot and character is misleading, for the two usually interplay. Although it is true that there may be much plot and little character (as in a thriller), in most great plays there is such a fusion between what is done and the personality of the doer that we feel the truth of Henry James's questions: "What is character but the determination of incident? What is incident but the illustration of character?" (See also character.)

Most plots entail a **conflict,** wherein the protagonist is somehow opposed. If he is opposed chiefly by another person rather than by a force such as Fate or God or by an aspect of himself, the opposing figure is the antagonist. The German critic, Gustav Freytag, in *Technique of the Drama* (1863), held that a play dramatizes "the rushing forth of will power from the depths of man's soul toward the external world," and "the coming into being of a deed and its consequences on the human soul." The five-act play, he said, commonly arranged such an action into a **pyramidal structure,** consisting of a **rising action,** a **climax,** and a **falling action.** The rising action begins with the **exposition,** in which is given essential information, especially about the **antecedent action** (what has occurred before this piece of action begins). The two gossiping servants who tell each other that after a year away in Paris the young master is coming home today with his new wife are giving the audience the exposition. The exposition in Shakespeare's *The Tempest* is almost ruthlessly direct: Prospero tells his naive daughter "I should inform thee farther," and for about one hundred and fifty lines he proceeds to tell her why she is on an almost uninhabited island. The action rises through a **complication** (the protagonist is opposed) to a high point or **crisis** or **climax** (a moment at which tension is high, and which is a decisive turning point). The falling action goes through a **reversal** (if a tragedy, the protagonist loses power), and then into a **catastrophe,** also called a **denouement** (unknotting) or resolution. (Aristotle's word for the reversal is *peripeteia,* anglicized to **peripety,** and, translated as "irony of events," would in a comedy be a change from bad fortune to good, and the catastrophe would thus be happy.) The denouement frequently involves what Aristotle called an *anagnorisis* (**recognition, disclosure, discovery**). This recognition may be as simple as the identification of a long-lost brother by a birth mark, or it may involve a character's recognition of his own true condition. Shakespeare sometimes used a pyramidal structure, placing his climax neatly in the middle of what seems to us to be the third of five acts. In *Julius Caesar,* Brutus rises in the first half of the play, reaching his height in III.i, with the death of Caesar; but later in this scene he gives Marc Antony permission to speak at Caesar's funeral and thus sets in motion his own fall, which occupies the second half of the play. In *Macbeth,* the protagonist attains his height in III.i. ("Thou hast it now: King"), but he soon perceives that he is going downhill:

I am in blood
Stepped in so far that, should I wade no more,
Returning were as tedious as go o'er.

Some works have a **double plot,** that is, two plots, usually with some sort of relation. For example, the **subplot** or **underplot** (the secondary narrative) might be a grotesque version of the serious main plot. In Shakespeare's *The Tempest*, the main plot and subplot both deal with usurpation. In *King Lear*, the main plot concerns Lear's relation to his daughters, while the parallel subplot concerns Gloucester's relation to his sons. For another aspect of the subplot, see comic relief; consult William Empson, *Some Versions of Pastoral*, Ch. 2. On plotting see *pièce bien faite* and *scène à faire*.

poetic justice. A term coined by Thomas Rymer in 1678, denoting the reward of the virtuous and the punishment of the vicious. Aristotle had said or implied that the tragic hero is undone partly by some sort of personal flaw — i.e., he is at least partly responsible for the suffering he later encounters. (See *hamartia*, and pp. 5–8.) "Poetic justice," with its idea that all characters reap the harvest of their just deserts, is a hardening of Aristotle's suggestion. Consult M. A. Quinlan, *Poetic Justice in the Drama*.

problem play. See *pièce à thèse*.

prologue. (1) A preface or introduction. For the Greeks the *prologos* was the first scene, which gave the exposition. Elizabethan prologues commonly summarize the plot, as the Chorus does in the prologue to *Romeo and Juliet*, but in the English theater of the late seventeenth century, the prologue was almost an independent verse essay spoken before the play began. Consult Autrey N. Wiley, *Rare Prologues and Epilogues 1642–1700*. (2) The actor who speaks a piece of the sort described above.

proscenium stage, or **picture-frame stage.** A playing-area framed in the front, and thus separated from the audience. This frame is the **proscenium arch** or the **proscenium**; the empty space it contains, sometimes filled with a curtain, is the **proscenium opening.** Basically a **proscenium theater** has two rooms, one for the audience and another (with a hole in the mutual wall) for the performers. Such a theater is at least as old as the early seventeenth century, when the Farnese Theater was built in Parma. Consult Allardyce Nicoll, *The Development of the Theatre*.

protagonist. The chief figure in a play. In Greek the word means literally the "first contender," i.e., the chief actor (*protos:* first). The second role was given to the **deuteragonist,** the third to the **tritagonist.** The protagonist is commonly opposed by the **antagonist,** played by the deuteragonist. For the relationship between the protagonist and the antagonist, see plot.

psychical distance. See aesthetic distance.

pyramidal structure. See plot.

raisonneur. See chorus character.

rising action. See plot.

realism. The reproduction of life, especially as it appears to the eye and ear; the illusion of nature. Usually it deals with ordinary men in ordinary situations, moving in scenery that closely imitates reality. In England, T. W. Robertson (1829–1871) insisted, for example, that doorknobs not be painted on the doors but be three-dimensional. Wings and a backcloth (i.e., projecting flats at the sides and a painted cloth at the rear) were increasingly replaced by the box set (a room with the front wall missing, containing real furniture) for interior scene . Gas lighting, introduced to the stage about 1820, soon became capable of producing effects of sunlight, moonlight, etc. The dialogue, as well as the sets, came closer to what the senses perceive. Realistic plays (in prose, of course) avoided soliloquies, asides, and declamation. The great playwrights of the movement are Ibsen and Chekhov. As Mary McCarthy says of American realistic drama (*On the Contrary*), "realism is a depreciation of the real," for in "its resolve to tell the whole truth" it tends to deflate, to reveal human littleness. (It doesn't believe in exceptional, heroic people; when it treats the upper classes, it usually tends toward satire.) The oppressive box set of realistic plays, Miss McCarthy points out, "is the box or 'coffin' of average middle-class life opened at one end to reveal the corpse within." That realism shades into naturalism is clear; that in Ibsen it shades into symbolism is less obvious but is well demonstrated by John Northam, *Ibsen's Dramatic Method*. A simple example of Ibsen's symbolism: in *Hedda Gabler*, Hedda's hair is "not particularly ample," but Thea's is "unusually rich and wavy," suggesting Hedda's barrenness and Thea's fertility. Consult Mordecai Gorelik, *New Theatres for Old*; A. Nicholas Vardac, *Stage to Screen*, Chs. 4, 9; Ernest B. Watson, *Sheridan to Robertson*. In selective realism, some of the scenery (e.g., a window and a door) closely reproduces reality, but some (e.g., a framework *suggesting* a roof) does not.

recognition. See *anagnorisis.*

repartee. See high comedy.

Restoration comedy. See high comedy.

revenge play. See Senecan tragedy.

reversal. See *peripeteia.*

Roman theater. A permanent theater was not built at Rome until the first century B.C. The plays of Plautus (254?–184 B.C.) and Terence (190?–159? B.C.) were performed on temporary stages erected in the Circus Maximus and the Forum during holidays. In the permanent Roman theater, the enormous audience (40,000 or more) sat in a semicircle around a level space that was a vestige of what had been called the "orchestra" ("dancing place") of the Greek theater. Behind this vestige was the stage, running through what would have been the diameter of the circle. The long, slightly elevated stage was backed by a façade (painted to resemble two or three houses) with several doors through which actors made some of their exits and entrances, the others being made at the ends of the stage. Behind the façade was the dressing-room. The Roman theater, unlike the Greek and Hellenistic theaters, was a self-enclosed structure, built on level ground, not against a hillside. Consult Margarete Bieber, *The History of the Greek and Roman Theater.*

satire. A work ridiculing aspects of human behavior and seeking to arouse in the audience contempt for its object. Satirists almost always justify their attacks by claiming that satire is therapeutic. Shaw says, in the preface to his *Complete Plays*, "If I make you laugh at yourself, remember that my business as a classic writer of comedies is to 'chasten morals with ridicule'; and if I sometimes make you feel like a fool, remember that I have by the same action cured your folly." Satire, however, is sometimes distinguished from comedy on the grounds that satire aims to correct by ridiculing, while comedy aims simply to evoke amusement. Among notable satires are the plays of Aristophanes; Gay's *The Beggar's Opera* (1728); Brecht's *The Threepenny Opera* (1928); Kaufman, Ryskind, and Gershwin's *Of Thee I Sing* (1931) — though Kaufman himself has defined satire as "that which closes on Saturday night." See burlesque, comedy. Consult Dane F. Smith, *Plays about the Theatre in England from "The Rehearsal" in 1671 to the Licensing Act in 1737*; Northrop Frye, *Anatomy of Criticism.*

satyr-play. A piece in which there is a chorus of lewd satyrs (creatures half-man, the other half either horse or goat). The Greek tragic playwright of the fifth century B.C. presented three tragedies and a satyr-play for the dramatic festival. Apparently the satyr-play often burlesqued a hero, showing him in a ludicrous situation. Only one complete satyr-play (Euripides' *The Cyclops*) is extant; it travesties the legend of Odysseus' encounter with Polyphemus. Consult Philip W. Harsh, *A Handbook of Classical Drama.*

scene. See act.

scenery. The carpentry and painted cloths (and projected images) used on a stage. Scenery may be used to conceal parts of the stage, to decorate, to imitate or suggest locales, to establish time or to evoke mood. For comments on early scenery, see Greek theater and Elizabethan playhouse. The Elizabethan public theater did not use much scenery. In *Twelfth Night*, when Viola asks "What country, friends, is this?" she is told "This is Illyria, lady" and the audience knows all that carpenters and painters can tell them. But even before Shakespeare's birth, Renaissance Italians had placed buildings, probably of lath and cloth, at the right and left of the stage. Behind the buildings, which were three-dimensional and were embellished with moldings. projected flat pieces cut and painted to look like other buildings at a distance, and behind these flat pieces were yet other flats, still smaller. On the symbolic use of scenery, see pp. 23–24.

scenario. See *commedia dell'arte.*

scène à faire, or (in William Archer's translation of Francisque Sarcey's term) **obligatory scene.** "An obligatory scene [Archer says] is one which the audience (more or less clearly and consciously) foresees and desires, and the absence of which it may with reason resent." For example, a familiar legend may make a scene obligatory, or a dramatist may cause the audience to expect a certain scene. In *Hamlet* the play-within-the-play (III.ɪɪ) has been called such a scene: Hamlet has doubted the ghost, and we must see the ghost's words verified. Consult William Archer, *Play-making.*

selective realism. See realism.

Senecan tragedy. Any of the serious plays by the Roman author Seneca (4 B.C.–65 A.D.), or imitations of them. Of the ten extant Roman tragedies, nine are attributed to Seneca, and these were probably written not for the stage but for private readings. The heroes seem to us to be almost madmen, but perhaps they are to be regarded sympathetically as people overwhelmed by passion. Seneca's influence on the Elizabethan dramatists was considerable; the **revenge play,** with its ghosts and its deranged hero who seeks vengeance, doubtless would have been different had Seneca not existed. Among the signs of Seneca's influence are: ghosts, revenge, deeds of horror (e.g., children stewed and served to their parents), occasional stoical speeches but a predominance of passionate speeches, use of stichomythia (see dialogue), a *nuntius* (messenger) who recites in a heightened style an off-stage happening (e.g., the wounded soldier in *Macbeth,* I.ɪ). But, of course, not every use of any of these characteristics is necessarily attributable to Seneca's influence. And there are differences: e.g., the horrors in Seneca are narrated, but in *King Lear* Gloucester is blinded on the stage. Consult F. L. Lucas, *Seneca and Elizabethan Tragedy;* Madeleine Doran, *Endeavors of Art;*

Willard Farnham, *The Medieval Heritage of Elizabethan Tragedy;* Howard Baker, *Induction to Tragedy,* minimizes Seneca's influence.

sensibility. See sentimental.

sentimental. Generally a pejorative word in criticism, indicating a superabundance of tender emotion, a disproportionate amount of sentiment (feeling). It is sentimental to be intensely distressed because one has stepped on a flower. A character, say Hamlet, may display deep emotions, but they are sentimental only if they are in excess of what the situation warrants. More specifically, "sentimental" writing refers to writing wherein evil is facilely conquered, denied, overlooked, or bathed in a glow of forgiving tenderness. In the eighteenth century the ability to respond emotionally (usually tearfully) to acts of benevolence or malevolence was called **sensibility.** In its **sentimental drama** there is at the expense of reason an emphasis on tearful situations; man's benevolent emotions are overestimated, for he is assumed to be innately good, and villains reform, usually in bursts of repenting tears. There is little wit, the characters are usually of the middle class, and they demonstrate their virtue by weeping at the sight of distress. In his "Comparison between Sentimental and Laughing Comedy" (1772), Oliver Goldsmith attacked sentimental comedy, saying that in it:

> the virtues of private life are exhibited, rather than the vices exposed; and the distresses rather than the faults of mankind make our interest in the piece. . . . Almost all the characters are good, . . . and though they want humor, have abundance of sentiment and feeling. If they happen to have faults or foibles, the spectator is taught, not only to pardon, but to applaud them, in consideration of the goodness of their hearts; so that folly, instead of being ridiculed, is commended, and the comedy aims at touching our passions, without the power of being truly pathetic.

See bourgeois drama. Consult Ernest Bernbaum, *The Drama of Sensibility;* Arthur Sherbo, *English Sentimental Drama.*

slapstick. See farce.

situational comedy. See comedy of humors.

slice of life. See naturalism.

sock and **buskin.** Performers of Latin comedy wore a light slipper or sandal called the *soccus.* The sock is either this piece of footwear or comedy itself. The high boot worn by Greek tragic actors was the *cothurnus* or *kothurnus.* In Hellenistic times it acquired a very thick sole, giving the performer the height appropriate to a great man. In English this footgear (or tragic drama in general) is called the buskin, apparently from Old French *broissequin,* from Middle Dutch *brosekin,* a small leather boot. Consult Margarete Bieber, *The History of the Greek and Roman Theater.*

Socratic irony. See irony.

Sophoclean irony. See irony.

soliloquy. A speech wherein a character utters his thoughts aloud while alone. An **aside** is a speech wherein a character expresses his thoughts in words audible to the spectators but supposedly unheard by the other stage characters present. Both were important conventions in Elizabethan drama and, later, in melodrama, but the late nineteenth century sought so vigorously to present on the stage the illusion of real life that both techniques were banished. They have, however, been revived in the twentieth century, e.g., in Eugene O'Neill's *Strange Interlude,* where the asides represent the characters' thoughts and unspoken desires. In **direct address,** a character turns from the world on the stage and speaks directly to the audience, telling it, for instance, to watch closely. Consult Una Ellis-Fermor, *The Frontiers of Drama,* Ch. 6; George E. Duckworth, *The Nature of Roman Comedy;* Max Beerbohm, "Soliloquies in Drama," *Around Theatres.* The soliloquy, the aside, and direct address are all monologues, but more often a **monologue** is either a long speech delivered by one character, which may be heard but not interrupted by others in his presence, or a performance by a single actor.

sound effect. An imitative noise, usually produced by simple machinery. Though a sound effect may be a mere imitation of nature, it may also be a richly symbolic suggestion. Chekhov's *The Cherry Orchard* (1904) concludes: "There is a far-off sound as if out of the sky, the sound of a snapped string, dying away, sad. A stillness falls, and there is only the thud of an ax on a tree, far away in the orchard." Consult Frank Napier, *Noises Off.*

spectacle. The last of Aristotle's six elements of drama, spectacle denotes what appeals to the eye, e.g., costume and scenery. Greek drama was splendidly costumed and made some use of scenery. Aeschylus especially seems to have contrived moments that caught the eye, such as Agamemnon's entrance in a chariot. The Elizabethan stage, though sparse in scenery, apparently was architecturally impressive, and doubtless military scenes were embellished with waving banners. In the Restoration, spectacle sometimes got the upper hand. Alexander Pope complained:

> The play stands still; damn action and discourse,
> Back fly the scenes, and enter foot and horse;
> Pageants on pageants, in long order drawn,
> Peers, heralds, bishops, ermine, gold, and lawn.

In the nineteenth century the development of gas light and then electric light made possible elaborate sunrises and twilights, and at the end of the century (especially in Russia) there was an emphasis on ensemble acting which gave a tableau-effect. Pictorial effects in late-nineteenth-century productions of Shakespeare were often achieved at the cost of Shakespeare's lines. At the very end of the century William Poel rejected spectacle and helped establish a trend to stage Shakespeare in what was thought to be an Elizabethan manner: an uncluttered stage, allowing the action to proceed rapidly. Consult James Laver, *Drama;* A. Nicholas Vardac, *Stage to Screen,* Chs. 3–4.

stage business. Minor physical action — including posture and facial expression — by a performer. Business ranges from headscratching to an addition Henry Irving made to *The Merchant of Venice,* II.vi: in Shakespeare's scene, Jessica and Lorenzo elope and the scene ends quietly; Irving added business in which Shylock entered, and knocked on the door of his empty house while the curtain fell. His successors amplified this business; Shylock entered the house, cried out, and reappeared, etc. Consult Arthur C. Sprague, *Shakespeare and the Actors.*

stichomythia. See dialogue.

stock character. See character.

style. The mode of expression. Newman, talking of the writer's style, called it "a thinking out into language." This idea of "a thinking out" (but not into language) is applicable also to the style of the scene designer, the costume designer, etc. Kenneth Tynan in *Curtains* defines good style as "a happy consonance of manner with matter, of means with end, of tools with job." To **stylize** a play commonly means to present it with a noticeable artful manner rather than to present it realistically, though in fact realism itself is a style. A **stylized production** usually is presentational or anti-illusionistic rather than representational (see dramatic illusion). Consult George R. Kernodle, "Style, Stylization, and Styles of Acting," *Educational Theatre Journal*, 12 (1960), 251–261.

subplot. See plot.

surprise. See suspense.

surrealism. A literary movement, especially vigorous in France in the 1920's and 1930's, that insisted that reality is grasped by the unconscious, the irrational, rather than by the conscious. The best art, it is held, is the dream. Among the forerunners were Alfred Jarry, whose *Ubu Roi* (1896) combined grotesque farce with anti-bourgeois satire, August Strindberg, whose *To Damascus* (three parts, 1898–1904) and *The Dream Play* (1902) had presented dream-like worlds, and Guillaume Apollinaire, whose *Breasts of Tiresias* (1917) was called a *"drame surréaliste"* (the first use of the word) by the author. Perhaps the chief surrealist dramatist is Jean Cocteau, notably in his *Orpheus* (1926), in which a glazier is an angel and a horse dictates prophetic words. Consult Georges E. Lemaître, *From Cubism to Surrealism in French Literature.*

suspense. Uncertainty, often characterized by anxiety. Suspense is usually a curious mixture of pain and pleasure, as Gwendolen, in Oscar Wilde's *The Importance of Being Earnest*, implies: "This suspense is terrible. I hope it will last." Most great art relies more heavily on suspense than on **surprise** (the unexpected). One can rarely sit twice through a play depending on surprise; the surprise gone, the interest is gone. Suspense is usually

achieved in part by **foreshadowing** – hints of what is to come. Dumas *fils* put it this way: "The art of the theater is the art of preparations." Coleridge, who held that Shakespeare gives us not surprise but expectation and then the satisfaction of perfect knowledge, once wrote: "As the feeling with which we startle at a shooting star, compared with that of watching the sunrise at the pre-established moment, such and so low is surprise compared with expectation." Thus, in *Hamlet*, the ghost does not pop up surprisingly, but satisfies the eager expectations that have been aroused by references to "this thing," "this dreaded sight," and "this apparition." Often, in fact, Shakespeare – like the Greek dramatists – used traditional stories; the audience presumably was not surprised by the deaths of Caesar and Brutus, and it enjoyed the suspense of anticipating them. Suspense is thus related to tragic irony. The tragic character moves closer and closer to his doom, and though he may be surprised by it, we are not; we are held by suspense. On surprise, consult David L. Grossvogel, *The Self-Conscious Stage in Modern French Drama* (reprinted in paperback as *Twentieth-Century French Drama*).

symbolism. Derived from Greek *symballein*, "to throw together," which thus suggests the essential quality of symbolism, the drawing together of two worlds; it presents the concrete material world of roses, toads, caves, stars, etc., and through them reveals an otherwise invisible world. As a noun, the original Greek word denoted half of something broken in two, and thus the word suggests not something that stands for something else, but something that is part of a larger unit.

Symbolism is often distinguished from allegory. Where the allegorist commonly invents a world (the author of *Everyman* [c. 1500] invents a figure called Everyman, who seeks aid from figures called Goods, Kindred, etc.) in order to talk about the real world, the symbolist commonly presents the phenomena of what we usually call the real world in order to reveal a "higher," eternal world of which the symbol is a part. The allegorist is free to invent any number of imaginary worlds to talk about the real world, but the symbolist feels that there is only one way by which he can present the "higher" real world he envisions. The everyday world is often considered by symbolists as a concrete but transient version of a more important realm, and the symbolist who presents, say, a rose, is (he might hold) speaking about a rose and also about the eternal beauty of womanhood in the only possible way.

In the second half of the nineteenth century there arose in France the so-called **Symbolist Movement**, but it must be emphasized that symbolism of a sort is probably as old as literature. An author's insistence on some object may cause us to regard it as more than its apparent nature. For example, the forest or greenwood in *As You Like It* suggests a benevolent nature that restores man to his best part. But on the whole Shakespeare's plays do not leave the world of sensible reality. The plays of the Symbolists do. The Symbolic writer presents a world that seems to be a dream world, a world that is not the usual world enriched, but a new world. In his preface to *The Dream Play* (1902), Strindberg says he "has tried to imitate the disconnected but seemingly logical form of the dream. Anything may happen. . . . The characters split, double, multiply, vanish, solidify, blur, clarify." A play is the expression of a "soul-state" (Stéphane Mallarmé's term) rather than an imitation of an external action. See surrealism.

The best naturalists (Ibsen, Chekhov, Strindberg, and Hauptmann) at times wrote symbolic works, but the chief Symbolic dramatists are the French (if we include the Belgian Maurice Maeterlinck) and William Butler Yeats. In Maeterlink's *The Intruder* (1890) a blind old man sees with his soul the approach of Death. In *The Blind* (1890) a group of blind men are lost in a forest; their leader was a priest, but he has died. Maeterlinck occasionally said some of his plays were for marionettes, and though his statement is sometimes held to be a mildly self-deprecating joke, in fact there is much in the plays that belongs to the realm of impassive, otherworldly dolls, not surprising in the work of a writer who said he wished to study "man . . . in the presence of eternity and mystery." Paul Claudel's *Tidings Brought to Mary* (written in 1892, revised in 1899 and 1912) was acted in 1912. Claudel, who said he had gained from Arthur Rimbaud (one of the leading Symbolists) "an almost physical impression of the supernatural," in this play envelops his medieval characters in a divine world, and dramatizes salvation. In Ireland, Yeats, who compared an artistic work to a magic talisman ("it

entangles . . . a part of the Divine essence") wrote verse plays of Irish supernatural creatures and heroes. In *On Baile's Strand* (1903), for instance, Cuchulain, the protagonist, is said to have been sired by a hawk. The bird imagery is insisted on; Cuchulain's associates are chicks and nestlings, and the Fool (who represents Cuchulain on another level) is delighted with feathers. Near the conclusion of the play, Cuchulain rushes out to fight the waves, literally doing what Hamlet spoke metaphorically of doing.

In Russia, Meyerhold in 1906 staged Ibsen's *Hedda Gabler* (1890) as symbolically as possible, turning what had been a naturalistic play into a vision suggestive of another world, something (in the words of a hostile critic) "halfway between metaphysics and ballet." (Consult Nikolai Gorchakov, *The Theater in Soviet Russia*.) For symbolism in the sense of richly suggestive images, consult Alan S. Downer, "The Life of Our Design: the Function of Imagery in the Poetic Drama," *The Hudson Review*, 2 (Summer 1949), 242–260. On the Symbolist Movement, consult William Butler Yeats, *Essays and Introductions*; Arthur Symons, *The Symbolist Movement in Literature*; *Yale French Studies*, No. 9; Eric Bentley, *The Playwright as Thinker*; John Gassner, *Form and Idea in the Modern Theatre*.

theater-in-the-round. See arena stage.

Three Unities. See unity.

total theater. The idea that the theater should not try to imitate realistically an aspect of life but should embody a synthesis of all of the expressive arts, e.g., music, movement, speech, lighting, etc. The expression "total theater" probably is derived from Richard Wagner's *Gesamtkunstwerk*, "united" or "total artwork." Consult *Total Theatre*, ed. E. T. Kirby.

tragedy. For Aristotle, tragedy was a dramatic imitation (representation) of an "action of high importance." A Greek tragedy was serious, but it did not necessarily end unhappily. Aeschylus' *Eumenides*, for example, ends on a note of solemn joy. For us a tragedy is generally a play that faces evil, depicts suffering, and ends with death or (especially in the naturalistic tragedies since the latter part of the nineteenth century) ends with the hero alive but spiritually crushed. Tragedy's essence, Alfred North Whitehead says (*Science and the Modern World*, Ch. 1), resides not in unhappiness but "in the solemnity of the remorseless working of things." H. D. F. Kitto says (*The Greeks*, Ch. 4) that Greek tragedy — and perhaps one might add the great tragedy of other countries — was in part the product of intellectualism and humanism. Intellectualism let the Greeks see that human life must be lived within a great framework of what might be called the will of the gods, or Necessity: "Actions must have their consequences; ill-judged actions must have uncomfortable results." Humanism denied the Greeks an easy view of a heavenly life, and gave them an "almost fierce joy in life, the exultation in human achievement and in human personality." The tragic note, Kitto suggests, is produced by a tension between this unalterable framework and this passionate delight in life. Consult R. Sewall, *The Vision of Tragedy*; T. R. Henn, *The Harvest of Tragedy*; H. J. Muller, *The Spirit of Tragedy*.

tragicomedy. Renaissance critical theorists, embroidering on Aristotle's *Poetics*, assumed that tragedy dealt with noble (important) figures and ended with a death; comedy dealt with trivial (laughable) figures and ended with a celebration. A tragicomedy was some sort of mixture: high characters in a play ending happily, or a mingling of deaths and feasts, or, most often (as in many American films) threats of death which are happily — and unconvincingly — evaded. John Fletcher (1579–1625), who, with his collaborator Francis Beaumont, wrote graceful dramas relying heavily on passionate outbursts and surprising turns of plot, defined a tragicomedy as a play that lacks deaths (and thus is no tragedy) but "brings some near it, which is enough to make it no comedy." One of the speakers in John Dryden's *Essay of Dramatick Poesie* (1668) says: "There is no theater in the world has anything so absurd as the English tragi-comedy; . . . here a course of mirth, there another of sadness and passion, and a third of honor and a duel: thus, in two hours and a half, we run through all the fits of Bedlam." Consult Eugene Waith, *The Pattern of Tragi-Comedy*. On what can roughly be called the bitter or ironic comedy of the nineteenth and twentieth centuries, consult K. S. Guthke, *Modern Tragicomedy*; C. Hoy, *The Hyacinth Room*; and Eric Bentley, *The Life of the Drama*.

trilogy. A unit of three works. Though Greek tragic dramatists submitted three tragedies at a time, the plays are only a trilogy if they have an internal unity. Aeschylus' *Oresteia* (458 B.C.) is the only extant complete Greek trilogy; Sophocles' three plays on the Oedipus legend — *Antigone* (c. 422 B.C.), *Oedipus the King* (c. 425), and *Oedipus at Colonus* (c. 406) are not properly a trilogy because they were written at widely separated times and do not cohere into a consistent, unified whole. A modern trilogy: O'Neill's *Mourning Becomes Electra* (1931).

tritagonist. See protagonist.

underplot. See plot.

unity. Generally means something like "coherence," "congruence"; in a unified piece the parts work together and jointly contribute to the whole. The subplot of a play may parallel the main plot, or one character may be a foil to another. In any case, unity suggests "completeness" or "pattern" resulting from a controlling intelligence. In the *Poetics*, Aristotle had said that a tragedy should have a unified action, and he had mentioned that most tragedies cover a period of twenty-four hours. Italian critics, making his comments rigid, in the late sixteenth century established the **Three Unities** of Time, Place, and Action: a play (1) must not cover more than twenty-four hours, (2) must be set in one locale only, or, at worst, in various parts of a single city, and (3) must be either entirely tragic or entirely comic, rather than a mixture of (as Sir Philip Sidney said) "hornpipes and funerals." (Consult H. B. Charlton, *Castelvetro's Theory of Poetry*.) Actually, the time covered by Greek tragedies is vague; characters come from distant places in the space of relatively few lines. For example, in *Oedipus the King*, a shepherd, who lives in the "farthest" fields from Corinth, is sent for in line 863 and arrives in line 1108. Nor is unity of place invariable in Greek tragedy; there are violations of it in, for example, Aeschylus' *The Eumenides* and Sophocles' *Ajax*.

well-made play. See *pièce bien faite*.

As educational publishers we realize it is our responsibility to try constantly to improve the textbooks we publish. In order to make TYPES OF DRAMA, THIRD EDITION a better book next time, we need to know what you, our ultimate consumer, think of what we've already done. Please help us by filling out this questionnaire and returning it to Little, Brown and Company, College English Developmental Group, 34 Beacon St., Boston, Mass. 02106.

School _____ City and State _____

Instructor's Name _____

Please give us your reaction to the selections:

	Keep	Drop	Didn't read	Read in high school
A DOLL'S HOUSE	___	___	___	___
OEDIPUS THE KING	___	___	___	___
DOCTOR FAUSTUS	___	___	___	___
THE TRAGEDY OF KING LEAR	___	___	___	___
HEDDA GABLER	___	___	___	___
THE GHOST SONATA	___	___	___	___
RIDERS TO THE SEA	___	___	___	___
DESIRE UNDER THE ELMS	___	___	___	___
DEATH OF A SALESMAN	___	___	___	___
DUTCHMAN	___	___	___	___
EQUUS	___	___	___	___
LYSISTRATA	___	___	___	___
A MIDSUMMER NIGHT'S DREAM	___	___	___	___
THE MISANTHROPE	___	___	___	___
MAJOR BARBARA	___	___	___	___
THE MATCHMAKER	___	___	___	___
THE CHERRY ORCHARD	___	___	___	___
SIX CHARACTERS IN SEARCH OF AN AUTHOR	___	___	___	___
WILD STRAWBERRIES	___	___	___	___
HAPPY DAYS	___	___	___	___
THE DUMB WAITER	___	___	___	___

1. Are there any plays or playwrights not included that you would like to see included next time? _____

_____

2. Did you find the general introduction helpful? _____ How might it have been improved? _____

3. Were the headnotes and commentaries for each play useful? _____ Did they tell you too much? _____ Too little? _____

4. Did you read "The Script and the Stage?" _____ Did you find it interesting? _____ How might it be improved? _____

5. Was the section "Writing About Drama" helpful? _____
How might it be improved? _____

6. Did you use the glossary of dramatic terms? _____
How might it be improved? _____

7. Do you like the book's appearance (cover, illustrations, layout)? _____

_____

8. Do you feel your instructor should continue to assign this book? _____
Why, or why not? _____

9. Will you keep this book? _____

10. Please add any additional comments or suggestions on how we might improve this book. _____

_____

_____

Optional: Your name _____ Date _____

Address _____

May we quote you, either in promotion for this book or in future publishing ventures?

Yes _____ No _____

THANK YOU!